Experience A New Generation of Technology: The Fully Integrated Kottak Online Learning Center

McGraw-Hill invites professors and students to explore the possibilities of enhanced technology based learning. More rich and dynamic than any previously available book-specific CD-ROM or websites, the new Kottak Online Learning Center provides resources and activities in one convenient place.

Come join us at **www.mhhe.com/kottak,** and see for yourself how you can enhance your anthropology course with chapter-by-chapter instructor support tools and student learning aids such as:

➢ **Premium Content**: Access Powerweb, using the registration code on the back of this card, for course-specific, peer-reviewed articles from the scholarly and popular press, as well as student study tools and weekly updates.

➢ **Virtual Explorations:** Step into the real world of anthropology with short, professional film clips, fascinating simulations, helpful animations, and links to World Wide Web related sites and activities.

➢ **Atlas Resources:** Explore the maps from *The Kottak Anthropology Atlas* through interactive Exercises or download them electronically.

➢ **Interactive Exercises:** Learn interactively with visuals, maps, and line drawings that explore chapter content further.

➢ **Interactive Chapter Quizzes:** Test your knowledge with multiple choice, true/false, short answer, vocabulary flashcards, and essay questions.

➢ **For Instructors:** Discover the Kottak Image Library where you can find a full bank of electronic photographs, maps, charts, and line art for presentation handouts or PowerPoint slides.

Turn Over for Website Registration Code

FOR YOUR REGISTRATION CODE TO ACCESS PREMIUM CONTENT ON THE KOTTAK WEBSITE.

SEE OTHER SIDE OF THIS CARD

ANTHROPOLOGY

THE EXPLORATION OF HUMAN DIVERSITY

Tenth Edition

Conrad Phillip Kottak

University of Michigan

Boston   Burr Ridge, IL   Dubuque, IA   Madison, WI   New York   San Francisco   St. Louis
Bangkok   Bogotá   Caracas   Kuala Lumpur   Lisbon   London   Madrid   Mexico City
Milan   Montreal   New Delhi   Santiago   Seoul   Singapore   Sydney   Taipei   Toronto

To my mother,
Mariana Kottak Roberts

 Higher Education

ANTHROPOLOGY: THE EXPLORATION OF HUMAN DIVERSITY

Published by McGraw-Hill, a business unit of The McGraw-Hill Companies, Inc. 1221 Avenue of the Americas, New York, NY, 10020. Copyright © 2004, 2002, 2000, 1997, 1994, 1991, 1987, 1982, 1978, and 1974 by The McGraw-Hill Companies, Inc. All rights reserved. No part of this publication may be reproduced or distributed in any form or by any means, or stored in a database or retrieval system, without the prior written consent of The McGraw-Hill Companies, Inc., including, but not limited to, in any network or other electronic storage or transmission, or broadcast for distance learning. Some ancillaries, including electronic and print components, may not be available to customers outside the United States.

This book is printed on acid-free paper.

2 3 4 5 6 7 8 9 0 DOW/DOW 0 9 8 7 6 5 4 3

ISBN 0–07-283705-5

Publisher: *Phillip A. Butcher*
Sponsoring editor: *Kevin Witt*
Developmental editor: *Pam Gordon*
Marketing manager: *Dan Loch*
Media producer: *Shannon Gattens*
Project Manager: *Jean R. Starr*
Production Supervisor: *Carol A. Bielski*
Designer: *Mary E. Kazak*
Media PM/Supplement producer: *Marc Mattson*
Photo research coordinator: *Alexandra Ambrose*
Photo researcher: *Barbara Salz*
Cover design: *Cassandra Chu*
Interior design: *Kay Fulton*
Typeface: *10/12 Palatino*
Compositor: *Precision Graphics*
Printer: *R. R. Donnelley/Willard*

Library of Congress Cataloging-in-Publication Data

Kottak, Conrad Phillip.
   Anthropology : the exploration of human diversity / Conrad Phillip Kottak.—10th ed.
     p. cm.
   Includes bibliographical references and indexes.
   ISBN 0-07-283705-5 (softcover : alk. paper)
   1. Anthropology. I. Title.
GN25.K67 2004
301—dc21

                               2003048769

www.mhhe.com

BRIEF CONTENTS

CONTENTS

Part One   THE DIMENSIONS OF ANTHROPOLOGY   1

Part Two   PHYSICAL ANTHROPOLOGY AND ARCHAEOLOGY   57

Part Three   CULTURAL DIVERSITY   317

Part Four   THE CHANGING WORLD   **637**

ABOUT THE AUTHOR

Conrad Phillip Kottak (A.B. Columbia College, 1963; Ph.D. Columbia University, 1966) is a Professor and Chair of the Department of Anthropology at the University of Michigan, where he has taught since 1968. In 1991 he was honored for his teaching by the university and the state of Michigan. In 1992 he received an excellence in teaching award from the College of Literature, Sciences, and the Arts of the University of Michigan. And in 1999 the American Anthropological Association (AAA) awarded Professor Kottak the AAA/Mayfield Award for Excellence in the Undergraduate Teaching of Anthropology.

Professor Kottak has done ethnographic field work in Brazil (since 1962), Madagascar (since 1966), and the United States. His general interests are in the processes by which local cultures are incorporated—and resist incorporation—into larger systems. This interest links his earlier work on ecology and state formation in Africa and Madagascar to his more recent research on global change, national and international culture, and the mass media.

The third edition of Kottak's popular case study *Assault on Paradise: Social Change in a Brazilian Village*, based on his field work in Arembepe, Bahia, Brazil, was published in 1999 by McGraw-Hill. In a research project during the 1980s, Kottak blended ethnography and survey research in studying "Television's Behavioral Effects in Brazil." That research is the basis of Kottak's book *Prime-Time Society: An Anthropological Analysis of Television and Culture* (Wadsworth 1990)—a comparative study of the nature and impact of television in Brazil and the United States.

Kottak's other books include *The Past in the Present: History, Ecology and Cultural Variation in Highland Madagascar* (1980), *Researching American Culture: A Guide for Student Anthropologists* (1982) (both University of Michigan Press), and *Madagascar: Society and History* (1986) (Carolina Academic Press). The most recent editions (tenth) of his texts *Anthropology: The Exploration of Human Diversity* (this book) and *Cultural Anthropology* are being published by McGraw-Hill in summer 2003, along with a new textbook on *Physical Anthropology and Archaeology.* He is also the author of *Mirror for Humanity: A Concise Introduction to Cultural Anthropology* (3rd ed., McGraw-Hill, 2003) and (with Kathryn A. Kozaitis) *On Being Different: Diversity and Multiculturalism in the North American Mainstream* (2nd ed., McGraw-Hill, 2003).

Conrad Kottak's articles have appeared in academic journals, including *American Anthropologist, Journal of Anthropological Research, American Ethnologist, Ethnology, Human Organization,* and *Luso-Brazilian Review.* He also has written for more popular journals, including *Transaction/SOCIETY, Natural*

History, Psychology Today, and *General Anthropology.*

In recent research projects, Kottak and his colleagues have investigated the emergence of ecological awareness in Brazil, the social context of deforestation and biodiversity conservation in Madagascar, and popular participation in economic development planning in northeastern Brazil. Since 1999 Professor Kottak has been active in the University of Michigan's Center for the Ethnography of Everyday Life, supported by the Alfred P. Sloan Foundation. In that capacity, for a research project entitled "Media, Family, and Work in a Middle-Class Midwestern Town," Kottak has investigated how middle-class families draw on various media in planning, managing, and evaluating their choices and solutions with respect to the competing demands of work and family.

Conrad Kottak appreciates comments about his books from professors and students. He can be readily reached by e-mail at the following Internet address:

ckottak@umich.edu

PREFACE

Since 1968, I've regularly taught Anthropology 101 (Introduction to Anthropology) to a class of 375 to 550 students. Constant feedback from students, teaching assistants, and my fellow instructors keeps me up to date on the interests, needs, and views of the people for whom this text is written. I continue to believe that effective textbooks are rooted in enthusiasm for and enjoyment of one's own teaching experience.

As a college student, I was drawn to anthropology by its breadth and because of what it could tell me about the human condition, present and past. Since then, I've been fortunate in spending my teaching career at a university that values and unites anthropology's four subdisciplines. I have daily contact with members of all the subfields, and as a regular teacher of the four-field introductory anthropology course, I'm happy to keep up with those subfields. I love anthropology's breadth. I believe that anthropology has compiled an impressive body of knowledge about human diversity in time and space, and I'm eager to introduce that knowledge in the pages that follow. I believe strongly in anthropology's capacity to enlighten and inform. Anthropology's subject matter is intrinsically fascinating, and its focus on diversity helps students understand and interact with their fellow human beings in an increasingly interconnected world and an increasingly diverse North America.

I decided to write this book back in 1972, when there were far fewer introductory anthropology texts than there are today. The texts back then tended to be overly encyclopedic. I found them too long and too unfocused for my course and my image of contemporary anthropology. The field of anthropology was changing rapidly. Anthropologists were writing about a "new archaeology" and a "new ethnography." Fresh fossil finds and biochemical studies were challenging our understanding of human and primate evolution. Studies of monkeys and apes in their natural settings were contradicting conclusions that were based on work in zoos. Studies of language as it actually is used in society were revolutionizing overly formal and static linguistic models. In cultural anthropology, symbolic and interpretive approaches were joining ecological and materialist ones.

Today there are new issues and approaches, such as molecular anthropology and new forms of spatial analysis. The fossil and archaeological records expand every day. Profound changes have affected the people and societies ethnographers have traditionally studied. In cultural anthropology it's increasingly difficult to know when to write in the present and when to write in the past tense. Anthropology hasn't lost its excitement. Yet many texts ignore change—except maybe with a chapter tacked on at the end—and write as though anthropology and the people it studies were the same as they were a generation ago. While any competent anthropology text must present anthropology's core, it also should demonstrate anthropology's relevance to today's world. *Anthropology: The Exploration of Human Diversity*, 10th edition, has a unique set of goals and themes.

Goals

This book has three main goals. My first goal was to offer a thorough, up-to-date, and holistic introduction to anthropology that systematically approaches the course from a four-field perspective. Anthropology is a *science*—a "systematic field of study or body of knowledge that aims, through experiment, observation, and deduction, to produce reliable explanations of phenomena, with reference to the material and physical world" (*Webster's New World Encyclopedia*, 1993, p. 937). Anthropology is a humanistic science devoted to discovering, describing, and explaining similarities and differences in time and space. In *Mirror for Man,* one of the first books I ever read in anthropology, I was impressed by Clyde Kluckhohn's (1944) description of anthropology as "the science of human similarities and differences" (p. 9). Kluckhohn's statement of the need for such a field still stands: "Anthropology provides a scientific basis for dealing with the crucial dilemma of the world today: how can peoples of different appearance, mutually unintelligible languages, and dissimilar ways of life get along peaceably together?" (p. 9).

Anthropology is a science with clear links to the humanities, as it brings a comparative and cross-cultural perspective to forms of creative expression. One might say that anthropology is among the most humanistic academic fields because of its fundamental respect for human diversity. Anthropologists routinely listen to, record, and attempt to represent voices and perspectives from a multitude of times, places, nations, and cultures. Through its four subfields, anthropology brings together biological, social, cultural, linguistic, and historical approaches. Multiple and diverse perspectives offer a fuller understanding of what it means to be human than is provided by academic fields that lack anthropology's broad vision.

My second goal was to write a book that would be good for students. This book would be user-friendly in approach and pedagogy. It would stress to students why anthropology should matter to them and how they can use anthropology to understand themselves. By discussing current events in relation to anthropology's core, it would show how anthropology affects their lives. Through the unique "Beyond the Classroom boxes" (see below), the book also would highlight the work that students just like them are doing in anthropology.

It's been my aim throughout my ten editions to write the most current, timely, and up-to-date textbook available. I try to be fair and objective in covering various and sometimes diverging approaches, but I make my own views known and write in the first person when it seems appropriate. I've heard colleagues who have used other textbooks complain that some authors seem so intent on presenting every conceivable theory about an issue—the origin of agriculture, for example—that students are bewildered by the array of possibilities. Anthropology should not be made so complicated that it is impossible for beginning students to appreciate and understand it. Thus, the textbook author, like the instructor, must be able to guide the student.

My third goal was to write a book that professors, as well as students, would appreciate. The organization of this text is intended to cover core concepts and basics while also discussing prominent current issues and interests. I sought to create a text that is readable, attractive, amply illustrated, and up to date and that features an extraordinary support package, including supplements that benefit both student and professor.

New Themes

This tenth edition has *two new themes* that mirror the three goals just discussed: "Bringing It All Together" and "Understanding Ourselves."

Bringing It All Together: Most texts give lip service to the fact that anthropology is an integrated, comparative, four-field approach to human similarities and differences. This book, however, takes a truly holistic approach through the "Bringing it All Together" essays that come after Chapters 5, 8, 11, 15, 20, and 25. These essays show how anthropology's subfields and dimensions combine to interpret and explain a common topic. The topics that are "brought together" are (1) deforestation, as a threat to biological and cultural diversity, which applied anthropologists have attempted to mitigate; (2) the matter of when *Homo sapiens* became fully human, behaviorally as well as biologically, and the kinds of cultural (archaeological) evidence we have for this emergence; (3) the biological and cultural dimensions of the peopling of Polynesia, one of the last major areas to be settled by humans; (4) issues involving unity and diversity in terms of ethnicity, "race," culture, and language in Canada; (5) archaeological, physical, linguistic, and cultural features of the Basques, including their place in Europe and Basque migration to the United States; and (6) the use of cultural and linguistic symbols in the proliferation of fast food, and the biological implications of this spread, in terms of increasing obesity.

Understanding Ourselves: It's common and proper for texts to present facts and theories prominent in the field of study, but often such material seems irrelevant to the student. In anthropology particularly, facts and theories should be presented not just to be read and remembered, but because they help us understand ourselves. "Understanding Ourselves" paragraphs, found in each chapter, answer the question "So what?" For example, we see how the unique human combination of upright bipedalism and large brain size affects the birthing, maturation, and socialization of human children. Many of these discussions "bring together" the biological and cultural dimensions of anthropology, and so the overall theme of this book may be stated as "Understanding Ourselves by Bringing It All Together through Anthropology's Unique Four-Field Approach."

Pedagogy

Working closely together, the author, editors, designer, and photo researcher have developed a format for this text that supports the goal of a readable, practical, up-to-date, and attractive book. I tried to follow through with my goal of making the book student-friendly.

Here's a summary of the pedagogical features of this tenth edition of *Anthropology: The Exploration of Human Diversity*:

1. **Part openers**—This *new* element describes what is to come in the part and how part chapters work together.

2. **Chapter-opening previews**—Succinct chapter-opening outlines and concise overviews help students focus on the chapter's critical concepts and main points.

They help students understand what they should get when they read the chapter and offer a road map of what is to come.

3. **Chapter-opening vignettes**—"In the News" vignettes open every chapter, highlighting anthropology's relevance in today's world. Most of these are *new, many from 2002*. These vignettes serve as a bridge between the world we live in and the chapter content. They show how anthropology is relevant to our world and how, specifically, the content of every chapter can be found in today's headlines. Compared with the last edition, these vignettes are tied more closely to the chapter content through a *new* feature. To provide context, each now begins with an introduction and ends with a paragraph that connects the vignette to the chapter content.

4. **In-text icons**—Compared with the last edition, marginal icons more clearly guide students to information on a particular topic that is available at the Online Learning Center (see below).

5. **Intriguing *Interesting Issues* boxes**—Coverage of current issues in anthropology, many with maps and photos, raise students' awareness of some of the more provocative aspects of anthropology today.

6. **"Beyond the Classroom" boxes**—These thematic boxes highlighting student research in anthropology enable students to read about the work their peers at other schools are doing, further illustrating the relevance of anthropology in the real world.

7. **Easy-to-use end-of-chapter reviews**—Clear, concise numbered chapter summaries facilitate chapter concept review, while end-of-chapter glossaries enable students to go over the chapter's key terms.

8. **Critical Thinking, Internet, and new Atlas exercises**—Chapter-ending exercises challenge students to use their critical thinking skills to apply what they have read about in the chapter, to explore chapter concepts in greater detail via Web research, and to explore the geographic and visual dimensions of anthropology using our *new*, unique atlas.

9. **Suggested Readings**—An up-to-date list of additional reading materials, briefly annotated, comes at the end of each chapter to help guide student research.

10. **End-of-book glossary**—This feature brings together all the key terms defined at the end of each chapter for easy access and review.

11. **A new Spanish glossary**—This feature defines key terms in Spanish to help students for whom Spanish is the primary language.

Visuals

When writing this book, I was committed to creating a text with an outstanding visual program. A wealth of illustrations, including photos with thought-provoking captions, make the chapter material clear, understandable, and inviting. Maps, figures, charts, and tables are also plentiful.

Since anthropology examines and explains human diversity across space and time, students need help to conceptualize the places and time spans discussed in the book. Where in the world do people live today, and where have they lived at various times in the past? This text has an *unusually rich map program. New,* more intuitive, orientation globes help students figure out where in the world the places under discussion are located. In addition to the book's internal maps, a *new* separate *atlas* is shrink-wrapped with every copy of the text. This atlas offers important reference maps to help students. The *new* "Interpret the World" feature, found in every chapter, ties the running text to material in the atlas. Also, *new* end-of-chapter atlas questions allow students to apply atlas content.

Content and Organization

The tenth edition of *Anthropology: The Exploration of Human Diversity,* guided by very thoughtful reviewers, covers the core and basics of all four subfields, as well as prominent current issues and approaches.

Part I ("The Dimensions of Anthropology") introduces anthropology as a four-field integrated discipline, with academic and applied dimensions, that examines human biological and cultural diversity in time and space. Anthropology is discussed as a comparative and holistic science, featuring biological, social, cultural, linguistic, humanistic, and historical approaches. Part I explores links between anthropology and other fields—natural sciences, social sciences, and the humanities. "Applying Anthropology" has been moved up in the Table of Contents (from the last chapter to the second chapter) to show students immediately the real-world relevance of anthropology. Examples of applied anthropology from the various subfields are provided. This part was designed with one of my goals (as mentioned previously) for the text in mind—introducing a holistic field consisting of four subfields and two dimensions.

Part II ("Physical Anthropology and Archaeology") begins with a chapter (Chapter 3) devoted to ethics and methods in the two subfields, including the controversy surrounding the discovery and disposition of "Kennewick Man." Part II poses and gives up-to-date answers to several key questions: When did we originate, and how did we become what we are? What role do genes, the environment, society, and culture play in human variation and diversity? What can we tell about our origins and nature from the study of our nearest relatives—nonhuman primates? When and how did the primates originate? What key features of their early adaptations are still basic to our abilities, behavior, and perceptions? How did hominids develop from our primate ancestors? When, where, and how did the first hominids emerge and expand? What about the earliest real humans? How do we explain biological diversity in our own species, *Homo Sapiens?* How does such diversity relate to the idea of race? What major transitions have taken place since the emergence of *Homo sapiens?* The origin of food production (the domestication of plants and animals) was a major change in human adaptation, with profound implications for society and culture. The spread and intensification of food production are tied to the appearance of the first towns, cities, and states, and the emergence of social stratification and major inequalities.

In Part III ("Cultural Diversity") the chapters have been *reorganized* to place related content closer together. "Political Systems" (Chapter 17) now follows, more logically, "Making a Living" (Chapter 16) rather than being separated from it by two chapters. This shift permits Chapters 18 through 20 (18, "Families, Kinship, and Descent";

19, "Marriage"; and 20, "Gender") to be presented as a more coherent unit. Part III begins with a discussion of the culture concept, and the related topic of ethnicity, in relation to race and its social construction. Culture and language are linked through learning, sharing, and reliance on symbolic thought. Throughout Part III, discussions of relevant concepts, theory, and explanations are combined with rich ethnographic examples and case studies. Part III examines how sociocultural diversity is manifest and expressed in such domains as language, economic and political systems, family and kinship, marriage, gender, religion, and the arts.

Having explored diversity in the major domains of cultural life in Part III, we examine their transformations and expressions in the modern world in Part IV ("The Changing World"). Part IV is one of the key differences between this anthropology text and others. Several important questions are addressed in Part IV: How and why did the modern world system emerge? How has world capitalism affected patterns of stratification and inequality within and among nations? What were colonialism and imperialism, and what are their legacies? How do economic development and globalization affect the peoples, societies, and communities among which anthropologists have traditionally worked? How do people actively interpret and confront the world system and the products of globalization? What factors threaten continued human diversity? How can anthropologists work to ensure the preservation of that diversity?

I also want to focus on three chapters present here but not consistently found in other anthropology texts: "Human Diversity and 'Race'" (Chapter 9), "Ethnicity" (Chapter 14), and "Gender" (Chapter 20). I believe that systematic consideration of race, ethnicity, and gender is vital in an introductory anthropology text. Anthropology's distinctive four-field approach can shed special light on these subjects. Race and gender studies are fields in which anthropology has always taken the lead. I'm convinced that anthropology's special contributions to understanding the biological, social, cultural, and linguistic dimensions of race, ethnicity, and gender should be highlighted in any introductory text. They certainly are highlighted in this one—not just in their special chapters, but throughout the text, starting in Chapter 1.

Let me also focus on this edition's two chapters (Chapters 3 and 12) on *ethics and methods*. Chapter 3—*new* to this edition—considers ethics and methods in physical anthropology and archaeology, while Chapter 12 considers ethics and methods in cultural anthropology. There is a more general discussion of ethics in Chapter 2. In the previous edition, a single chapter, "In the Field," attempted to do too much by covering ethics and field methods in cultural and archaeological anthropology. In the current edition, the discussion of methods in physical and archaeological anthropology has been separated and expanded (see Chapter 3), and a separate chapter (Chapter 12) covers methods in cultural anthropology. A unique feature of previous editions of this book has been its consideration of ethics. That coverage has been expanded significantly in this edition to confront ethical concerns in general—as well as those raised specifically by the "Kennewick Man" debate and the controversy surrounding Patrick Tierney's book *Darkness in El Dorado*.

Chapter-by-Chapter Changes

Here are specific content features and changes, chapter by chapter:

1. Chapter 1 introduces anthropology as a four-field integrated discipline, with academic and applied dimensions, that focuses on human biological and cultural diversity in time and space. Anthropology is discussed as a comparative and holistic science, with links to the natural and social sciences and the humanities. Chapter 1 now concludes with a section titled "Science, Explanation, and Hypothesis Testing."

2. In Chapter 2 ("Applying Anthropology") applied anthropology is presented as a second dimension, rather than a fifth subfield, of anthropology. Examples of applied anthropology from the various subfields are provided. There is now a major section on ethics and anthropology.

3. The focus of this *new* Chapter 3 is on ethical issues and research methods in physical anthropology and archaeology. Also discussed are research design and dating techniques. I wanted to highlight the ethical issues anthropologists increasingly confront,

such as those surrounding NAGPRA and "Kennewick Man." I also wanted to show students how anthropologists do their work and how that work is relevant in understanding ourselves.

4. Chapter 4 ("Evolution and Genetics") discusses natural selection and other evolutionary principles, along with genetics and biological adaptation, including genes and disease. I hoped to provide a gentle, yet complete, introduction to these difficult topics.

5. Chapter 5 ("The Primates") surveys primate traits, trends in primate evolution, and the major primate groups. Also included is the most recent information on endangered primates and on hunting and tool use by chimpanzees. Again, I tried to cover the basics—what's interesting and relevant about primates—while avoiding the more elaborate terminology and more detailed classifications that some other texts introduce. A *new* section on bonobos has been added.

6. A thoroughly updated Chapter 6 ("Primate Evolution") explores primate evolution, including the latest theories on how and when the primates emerged. Its photos compare fossil primates with their most similar living relatives. The discussion of Miocene apes, based on the latest research, examines several possible common ancestors for humans and the apes as well as the recent Toumai discovery in Chad.

7. Chapter 7 considers early hominids—their fossils and tool making—from *Ardipithecus* and the australopithecines to *Homo habilis*, *rudolfensis*, and *erectus*. The latest finds and interpretations are covered.

8. Based on the most recent discoveries confirming the expansion of early *Homo erectus* (sometimes known as *Homo ergaster*) out of Africa, Chapter 8 ("Modern Humans") describes recent fossil finds in Europe. This chapter also includes the latest information on the various theories for the origin of *Homo sapiens*.

9. Chapter 9 ("Human Diversity and 'Race'") surveys ways of understanding human biological diversity. This chapter, which uniquely (compared with most anthropology texts) discusses both the *biological and the social components of the race concept,* includes data from U.S. Census 2000 and a section on interracial, biracial, and multiracial identity.

10. Chapter 10 ("The First Farmers") examines the origin and implications, and the costs and benefits, of food production (the domestication of plants and animals). The seven world centers of domestication are identified and discussed, with a focus on the first farmers and herders in the Middle East and the first farmers in Mexico and adjacent areas.

11. Chapter 11 examines, and introduces theories about, the emergence of towns, cities, chiefdoms, and states. Its examples include the Middle East, India/Pakistan, China, Mesoamerica, and Peru. *New* information has been added on Mesoamerican chiefdoms. Students learn how archaeologists make inferences about ancient societies from contemporary ethnographic studies. This again illustrates the texts's overall focus on anthropology as a four-field discipline in which findings from one subfield are integral to the others.

12. Chapter 12 focuses on ethics and methods in cultural anthropology, beginning with a consideration of the controversy surround Patrick Tierney's book *Darkness in El Dorado.* Ethnography and survey research are among the methods considered.

13. Chapter 13 ("Culture") has been updated.

14. Chapter 14 ("Ethnicity") has been throroughly updated, with data from the 2000 U.S. Census. The conceptual framework of this chapter has also been revised to link it more closely to the discussion of the social construction of race in Chapter 9.

15. Chapter 15 ("Language and Communication") has been updated and revised.

16. Chapter 16 ("Making a Living") has been updated.

17. Chapter 17 ("Political Systems") has been moved next to "Making a Living" so that related content is closer together. "Political Systems" has been extensively revised and rewritten to clarify and update the positions of traditional leaders and political systems in the contemporary world.

18. Chapters 18 through 20 ("Families, Kinship, and Descent"; "Marriage"; and "Gender") have been repositioned to form a unit with related content closer together. All three chapters, especially Chapter 20, "Gender," have been revised and updated. The gender chapter has a new discussion of cross-cultural similarities and differences in specific male and female roles, rights, and responsibilities.

19. Chapter 21 ("Religion") has been updated, with a *new* section on major world religions and a revised discussion of the Taliban under "Social Control."

20. Chapters 22 through 25 have been revised and updated.

Supplements

As a full-service publisher of quality educational products, McGraw-Hill does much more than just sell textbooks: It creates and publishes an extensive array of print, video, and digital supplements for students and instructors. *Anthropology* boasts an extensive, comprehensive supplements package. Orders of new (versus used) textbooks help defray the cost of developing such supplements, which is substantial. Please consult your local McGraw-Hill representative for more information on any of the supplements.

FOR THE STUDENT

The Kottak Anthropology Atlas (by John Allen and Audrey Shalinsky)—Shrink-wrapped and free with every copy of the text, the *Kottak Anthropology Atlas* offers 26 large-scale, global, full-color anthropology-related reference maps. The atlas maps are specifically tied to the content of each chapter in the text through corresponding in-text features. These features, "Interpret the World" and "Atlas Questions," ask students to consider the relationship between the topics they are studying and the world we live in. Designed specifically to help students who struggle with a lack of knowledge of geography, the *Atlas* will give students a stronger understanding of the world we live in today as well as the world of our ancestors.

The Student's Online Learning Center (by Chris Glew and Patrick Livingood)—This free Web-based, partially password-protected student supplement features a large number of helpful tools, interactive exercises and activities, links, and useful information at www.mhhe.com/kottak. To access the password-protected areas of the site, students must purchase a new copy of the text. Designed specifically to complement the individual chapters of the text, this feature gives students access to material by text chapter.

Exciting Interactivity includes:

- Virtual Explorations—Offer students the opportunity to view short film clips from *The Films from the Humanities and Sciences* on chapter-related topics and complete critical thinking activities based on the films and to work with fascinating simulations and animations which show complex processes and phenomena.

- Interactive Exercises—Allow students to engage and work interactively with visuals, maps, and line drawings and explore chapter content.

- Internet Exercises—Offer chapter-related links to World Wide Web–related sites and activities for students to complete based on the sites.

- Atlas Exercises—Offer interactive activities based on *The Kottak Anthropology Atlas* maps.

- Interactive Globe—Offers helpful geographic support.

Useful study tools include:

- Chapter objectives, outlines, and overviews—Designed to give students signposts for understanding and recognizing key chapter content.

- PowerPoint lecture notes—Offer point-by-point lecture notes on chapter sections.

- Multiple choice, true/false, and short answer questions—Give students the opportunity to quiz themselves on chapter content with feedback indicating why an answer is correct or incorrect.

- Essay questions—Allow students to explore key chapter concepts through their own writing.

- Glossary—Illustrates key terms.

- Audio Glossary—Helps students with difficult-to-pronounce words through audio pronunciation help.

- Vocabulary flashcards—Allow students to test their mastery of key vocabulary.
- Chapter-related readings—Give students the opportunity to explore topics of interest through additional readings on chapter-related topics.

Helpful links include:

- General Web links—Offer chapter-by-chapter links for further research.
- Links to *New York Times* articles—Give students immediate access to articles on chapter-related content.
- Bringing It All Together links—Offer students links related to the "Bringing It All Together" text features.
- Information on Anthropology links—Provides useful links to anthropology information.
- Study break links—Give students fun links on related topics.

Useful Information includes:

- FAQs—Give students answers to typical chapter-related questions.
- Career opportunities—Offer students related links to useful information on careers in anthropology.
- How to Ace This Course—Offers students useful study tips for success.

PowerWeb—This resource is offered free with the purchase of a new copy of the text and is available via a link at the Student's Online Learning Center. PowerWeb helps students with online research by providing access to high-quality academic sources. PowerWeb is a password-protected site that provides students with the full text of course-specific, peer-reviewed articles from the scholarly and popular press, as well as Web links, student study tools, weekly updates, and additional resources. For further information about PowerWeb, visit www.dushkin.com/powerweb/pwwt1.mhtml.

The McGraw-Hill Anthropology Supersite—Available at http://www.mhhe.com/anthrosupersite, this comprehensive, one-stop supersite provides links to book-specific McGraw-Hill websites, anthropology Web links, student tutorials, breaking news in anthropology, and timely chapter-by-chapter updates of selected McGraw-Hill anthropology textbooks.

Reflections on Anthropology: A Four-Field Reader (by Katherine A. Dettwyler and Vaughn M. Bryant)—Designed specifically to complement and follow the organization of *Anthropology,* this reader provides many varied and exciting articles that will motivate and capture a student's interest in anthropology.

***Culture Sketches: Case Studies in Anthropology,* 3rd edition** (by Holly Peters-Golden)—This brief and inexpensive collection of ethnographic case studies offers a concise introduction to thirteen cultures and exposes students to ethnography without overwhelming them. Designed specifically to complement *Anthropology,* the text exposes students to cultures which are discussed in the text.

FOR THE INSTRUCTOR

The Instructor's Resource Binder (by Chris Glew and Patrick Livingood)—This indispensable instructor supplement features a three-ring binder with tabbed sections that allows professors to integrate McGraw-Hill–provided instructor support items with their own customized course materials. The flexible format of the binder allows professors to store all indispensable course items in one handy place. McGraw-Hill–provided items include:

- Chapter outlines—Offer comprehensive reviews of chapter material for easy reference.
- Lecture topics—Provide ideas for classroom discussion sections and lectures.
- Atlas advice—Offers ideas for how to integrate and use *Kottak Anthropology Atlas*–related chapter maps in class.
- Suggested films—Provide an annotated list of useful films for classroom use.
- A complete test bank—Offers numerous multiple choice, true/false, and essay questions.
- A guide to the visual supplements—Offers guidance for using the Lecture Launcher VHS tape and the Image Library (both described below) successfully in class and includes a directory of the VHS tape.

- A correlation guide to popular anthologies and supplements—Offers chapter-by-chapter suggestions for integrating specific, useful salable supplements with the text.

The Instructor's Resource CD-ROM (by Chris Glew and Patrick Livingood)—This easy-to-use disk provides:

- PowerPoint lecture slides—Give professors ready-made chapter-by-chapter presentation notes.
- A computerized test bank—Offers numerous multiple choice, true/false, and essay questions in an easy-to-use program that is available for both Windows and Macintosh computers.
- An electronic version of the McGraw-Hill–provided resources in the Instructor's Resource Binder—Gives professors the ability to customize these useful aids.
- Atlas maps—Provide electronic versions of all of the maps in the *Kottak Anthropology Atlas* ready to be used in any applicable teaching tool.

The Lecture Launcher VHS Tape—This supplement offers professors a dynamic way to kick off lectures or illustrate key concepts by providing short (two- to four-minute) clips pulled from full-length, *Anthropology*-related films from the *Films from the Humanities and Sciences,* each tied to a chapter in the text. The Instructor's Resource Binder offers a complete guide to the Lecture Launcher VHS Tape, including a chapter-by-chapter description of each clip, the length of each clip so that instructors can queue up the tape easily, useful suggestions for incorporating the film clips in class, and discussion questions.

The Instructor's Online Learning Center (by Chris Glew and Patrick Livingood)—This password-protected site offers access to all the student online materials plus important instructor support materials and downloadable supplements such as:

- An image library—Offers professors the opportunity to create custom-made, professional-looking presentations and handouts by providing electronic versions of many of the maps, charts, line art, and photos in the text along with additional relevant

images not included in the text. All the images are ready to be used in any applicable teaching tools, including a professor's own lecture materials and McGraw-Hill–provided PowerPoint lecture slides. The Instructor's Resource Binder offers a complete guide to the Image Library, and useful suggestions for incorporating the images into teaching materials.

- Atlas Maps—Provide electronic versions of all the maps in the *Kottak Anthropology Atlas* ready to be used in any applicable teaching tool.
- An electronic version of the McGraw-Hill–provided resources in the Instructor's Resource Binder—Gives professors the ability to customize these useful aids.
- PowerPoint lecture slides—Give professors ready-made chapter-by-chapter presentation notes.
- Links to professional resources—Provide useful links to professional anthropological sites on the World Wide Web.

Faces of Culture Video Correlation Guide—For instructors using the Faces of Culture Video Series, this guide correlates each video to the appropriate chapter in the text and recommends chapter-by-chapter uses of the video series.

PowerWeb—This resource is available via a link on the Instructor's Online Learning Center. PowerWeb helps with online research by providing access to high-quality academic sources. PowerWeb is a password-protected site that provides instructors with the full text of course-specific, peer-reviewed articles from the scholarly and popular press, as well as Web links, weekly updates, and additional resources. For further information about PowerWeb, visit www.dushkin.com/powerweb/pwwt1.mhtml.

The McGraw-Hill Anthropology Supersite—Available at http://www.mhhe.com/anthrosupersite, this comprehensive, one-stop supersite provides links to book-specific McGraw-Hill websites, anthropology Web links, instructor downloads, breaking news in anthropology, and timely chapter-by-chapter updates of selected McGraw-Hill anthropology textbooks.

PageOut: The Course Website Development Center—All online content for the text is supported by WebCT, Blackboard, eCollege.com, and other course management systems. Additionally, McGraw-Hill's PageOut service is available to get professors and their courses up and running online in a matter of hours at no cost. PageOut was designed for instructors just beginning to explore Web options. Even a novice computer user can create a course website with a template provided by McGraw-Hill (no programming knowledge necessary). To learn more about PageOut, visit www.mhhe.com/pageout.

Videotapes—A wide variety of full-length videotapes from the *Films for the Humanities and Sciences* series is available to adopters of the text.

Acknowledgments

I'm grateful to many colleagues at McGraw-Hill. I thank Pam Gordon, freelance development editor, for her excellent ideas, suggestions, guidance, timetables, and work behind the scenes involving five books, including this one. I continue to enjoy working with Phil Butcher, McGraw-Hill's editorial director for social sciences and humanities. I thank him for his unflagging support as our association has entered its second decade. I'm also delighted to be working with Kevin Witt, McGraw-Hill's sponsoring editor for anthropology.

I thank Jean Starr for her work as project manager, guiding the manuscript through production and (along with Pam Gordon) keeping everything moving on schedule. Carol Bielski, production supervisor, worked with the compositor and printer to make sure everything came out right. It's always a pleasure to work with Barbara Salz, photo researcher, with whom I've worked for more than a decade. I want to thank Patrick Livingood and Chris Glew for their work on the supplements for, and Internet features of, this book. I thank Chris especially for his hard and creative work on the last two editions. I also thank Eric Lowenkron for his copyediting, Kay Fulton and Mary Kazak for conceiving and executing the design, Cassandra Chu for the cover design, and Dan Loch, a knowledgeable, creative, and enthusiastic marketing manager. Robin Mouat and Alex Ambrose also deserve thanks as art editor and photo research coordinator, as does Kathleen Cowan, McGraw-Hill's editorial assistant for anthropology.

Thanks, too, to Shannon Gattens, media producer, for creating the OLC and VHS tape, and to Marc Mattson, supplements producer, who created all the other supplements.

I also thank Wes Hall, who has handled the literary permissions, and Marty Granahan, McGraw-Hill's permissions coordinator. For their work on the atlas, I thank Ted Knight and Ava Suntoke at Dushkin and John Allen and Audrey Shalinsky, authors of the atlas. Finally, I thank Pablo Nepomnaschy for doing the Spanish glossary.

I'm very grateful to the prepublication reviewers of the tenth edition manuscript, who include:

Jane Adams
Southern Illinois University

Timi Barone
University of Nebraska at Omaha

Paul F. Brown
Minnesota State University, Mankato

Gregory Campbell
University of Montana

Garret Cook
Baylor University

Thomas Foor
University of Montana

Sharon Gursky
Texas A&M University

David Gary Kerr
University of Montana

Paul Minnis
University of Oklahoma

Beth Ritter
University of Nebraska at Omaha

Karen Schmidt
Indiana University of Pennsylvania

Andris Skreija
University of Nebraska at Omaha

Mark Stiger
Western State College

Nancy Marie White
University of South Florida

Mary S. Willis
University of Nebraska, Lincoln

I'm also grateful to the reviewers of the seventh, eighth, and ninth editions of *Anthropology: The Exploration of Human Diversity.* Their comments also have helped me in planning the tenth edition.

Their names are as follows:

Julianna Acheson
Green Mountain College

Mohamad Al-Madani
Seattle Central Community College

Robert Bee
University of Connecticut

Daniel Boxberger
Western Washington University

Ned Breschel
Morehead State University

Peter J. Brown
Emory University

Margaret Bruchez
Blinn College

Karen Burns
University of Georgia

Richard Burns
Arkansas State University

Mary Cameron
Auburn University

Dianne Chidester
University of South Dakota

Inne Choi
California Polytechnic State University–San Luis Obispo

Jeffrey Cohen
Penn State University

Barbara Cook
California Polytechnic State University–San Luis Obispo

Norbert Dannhaeuser
Texas A&M University

Michael Davis
Truman State University

Robert Dirks
Illinois State University

Bill Donner
Kutztown University of Pennsylvania

Paul Durrenberger
Pennsylvania State University

George Esber
Miami University of Ohio

Grace Fraser
Plymouth State College

Laurie Godfrey
University of Massachusetts–Amherst

Bob Goodby
Franklin Pierce College

Tom Greaves
Bucknell University

Mark Grey
University of Northern Iowa

Homes Hogue
Mississippi State University

Alice James
Shippensburg University of Pennsylvania

Richard King
Drake University

Eric Lassiter
Ball State University

Jill Leonard
University of Illinois–Urbana–Champaign

David Lipset
University of Minnesota

Jonathan Marks
University of North Carolina–Charlotte

Barbara Miller
George Washington University

John Nass, Jr.
California University of Pennsylvania

Frank Ng
California State University–Fresno

Martin Ottenheimer
Kansas State University

Leonard Plotnicov
University of Pittburgh

Janet Pollak
William Patterson College

Howard Prince
CUNY–Borough of Manhattan Community College

Steven Rubenstein
Ohio University

Mary Scott
San Francisco State University

Brian Siegel
Furman University

Esther Skirboll
Slippery Rock University of Pennsylvania

Gregory Starrett
University of North Carolina–Charlotte

Karl Steinen
State University of West Georgia

Noelle Stout
Foothill and Skyline Colleges

Susan Trencher
George Mason University

Mark Tromans
Broward Community College

Christina Turner
Virginia Commonwealth University

Donald Tyler
University of Idaho

Daniel Varisco
Hofstra University

Albert Wahrhaftig
Sonoma State University

David Webb
Kutztown University of Pennsylvania

George Westermark
Santa Clara University

Nancy White
University of South Florida

I was delighted by the enthusiasm expressed in their comments.

Students, too, regularly share their insights about this and my other texts via e-mail and thus have contributed to this book. Anyone—student or instructor—with access to e-mail can reach me at the following address: **ckottak@umich.edu.**

As usual, my wife, Isabel Wagley Kottak, has offered me understanding and support during the preparation of this edition. I renew my dedication of this book to my mother, Mariana Kottak Roberts, for kindling my interest in the human condition, for reading and commenting on what I write, and for the insights about people and society she continues to provide.

After thirty-five years of teaching, I've benefited from the knowledge, help, and advice of so many friends, colleagues, teaching assistants, and students that I can no longer fit their names into a short preface. I hope they know who they are and accept my thanks.

I'm grateful to my many colleagues at Michigan who regularly share their insights and suggest ways of making my books better. Thanks especially to my fellow 101ers: Kelly Askew, Rachel Caspari, Tom Fricke, Stuart Kirsch, Holly Peters-Golden, Elisha Renne, and Andrew Shryock. Their questions and suggestions help me keep this book current. I especially thank Joyce Marcus for her careful reading of Chapter 11. I've tried to do justice to her extensive knowledge, comments, and suggestions. I thank Milford Wolpoff, Roberto Frisancho, John Mitani, and Rachel Caspari, who are always willing to answer my questions about biological anthropology.

Since 1968 I've regularly taught Anthropology 101 ("Introduction to Anthropology"), with the help of several teaching assistants each time. Feedback from students and teaching assistants keeps me up to date on the interests, needs, and views of the people for whom this book is written. I continue to believe that effective textbooks are based in enthusiasm and in practice—in the enjoyment of teaching. I hope this product of my experience will be helpful to others.

Conrad Phillip Kottak
Ann Arbor, Michigan
ckottak@umich.edu

WALKTHROUGH

New Comparative "Bringing It All Together" Essays

Unique thematic essays—appearing after groups of related chapters—show how anthropology's subfields combine to interpret and to explain a common topic. The essays offer a truly integrated, comparative, and holistic introduction to anthropology. Through multiple and diverse perspectives, they offer students a fuller understanding of what it means to be human.

New Unique Anthropology Atlas and In-Text Atlas Features

A separate atlas, offering important reference maps, is shrink-wrapped with every copy of the text purchased new from the publisher. Designed specifically to help students who struggle with a lack of knowledge of geography, the atlas will give students a stronger understanding of the world we live in today as well as the world of our ancestors. The "Interpret the World" feature and end-of-chapter atlas questions tie the text to the maps in the atlas.

New Relevant "Understanding Ourselves" Paragraphs

"Understanding Ourselves" paragraphs help students see why anthropology should matter to them and how anthropology is relevant to their own lives.

Now Two Chapters on Ethics and Methods

Two new chapters offer expanded coverage of the important topics of ethics and methods replacing a single chapter in the previous edition.

Helpful Chapter-Opening Previews

Succinct chapter-opening outlines and concise overviews help students focus on the chapter's critical concepts and main points.

Current Chapter-Opening Vignettes

"In the News" vignettes open each chapter and show how anthropology is relevant to our world and how specifically the content of every chapter can be found in today's headlines. New in this edition, these vignettes are tied more closely to the chapter content through introductory and concluding text, which bridges the vignette to the chapter content.

Unique "Beyond the Classroom" Boxes

"Beyond the Classroom" boxes highlight undergraduate student research in anthropology and enable students to read about the work that students just like them are doing in anthropology.

Intriguing "Interesting Issues" Boxes

"Interesting Issues" boxes feature discussions of provocative aspects of anthropology today and promote critical thinking.

New Helpful Part Openers

Part opening pages describe what is to come in the part and how part chapters work together.

Outstanding and Plentiful Visuals

The text features a wealth of photos, maps, figures, charts, and tables. Intuitive orientation globes help students figure out where in the world places under discussion are located.

Easy-to-Use End-of-Chapter Reviews and Questions

Clear summaries, end-of-chapter glossaries, and suggested readings facilitate chapter concept review and help guide student research, while "Critical Thinking Questions," "Internet Exercises," and "Atlas Questions" challenge students to test themselves and apply what they have read in the chapter.

New Useful Spanish Glossary

A unique Spanish glossary defines key terms in Spanish to help students for whom Spanish is the primary language.

New Customizable Instructor's Resource Binder

This indispensable instructor supplement features a three-ring binder with tabbed sections allowing professors to integrate McGraw-Hill provided instructor support items with their own customized course materials. The flexible format of the binder allows professors to store all essential course items in one handy place.

New Exciting Lecture Launcher VHS Videotape

This supplement offers professors a dynamic way to begin lectures or illustrate key concepts, by providing short (two to four minute) video segments taken from full length, Anthropology-related films from *Films from the Humanities and Sciences*. Each video segment is tied to a text chapter.

A New Generation of Anthropology Technology

A new, fully integrated Kottak Online Learning Center offers richer and more dynamic technology than any previously available book specific CD-ROMs or websites. The website provides professors with an Image Bank and other valuable resources, and gives students all of their book-specific, technology-based resources and activities in one convenient place. In-text icons clearly guide students to information on a particular topic that is available on the Online Learning Center. See the heavy-stock password card at the start of this book for highlights of the instructor and student resources on the Online Learning Center.

WORLD COUNTRIES

MAURITANIA

SENEGAL

GAMBIA

GUINEA-BISSAU

GUINEA

SIERRA LEONE

LIBERIA

IVORY COAST

MALI

BURKINA FASO

GHANA

BENIN

TOGO

NIGER

NIGERIA

ATLANTIC OCEAN

10°

0   150   300 Miles

0   150   300 Kilometers

10°

0°

GREENLAND (DENMARK)

80°   60°   40°   20°

Arctic

ICE

UNITED KINGD

IRELAND

ANDO

PORTUGA

MOROCC

MAURITANIA

CAPE VERDE

CENTRAL AFRICA

SÃO TOMÉ AND

EQUATORIA

CONGO

C

CA

U.S.

CANADA

60°

UNITED STATES

40°

NORTH PACIFIC OCEAN

Tropic of Cancer

20°

U.S.

MEXICO

Equator

WESTERN SAMOA

TONGA

20°

Tropic of Capricorn

NORTH ATLANTIC OCEAN

GUYANA
SURINAME
FRENCH GUIANA (FR)

COLOMBIA

VENEZUELA

ECUADOR

PERU

B R A Z I L

BOLIVIA

PARAGUAY

CHILE

A R G E N T I N A

URUGUAY

SOUTH ATLANTIC OCEAN

SOUTH PACIFIC OCEAN

Antarctic Circle

90°   80°

U.S.

70°

0   300 Miles

0   300 Kilometers

THE BAHAMAS

CUBA

MEXICO

20°

JAMAICA   HAITI

BELIZE

GUATEMALA   HONDURAS

EL SALVADOR   NICARAGUA

10°

COSTA RICA   PANAMA

COLOMBIA

DOMINICAN REPUBLIC

PUERTO RICO

ST. KITTS AND NEVIS
ANTIGUA AND BARBUDA
DOMINICA

MARTINIQUE

ST. LUCIA

ST. VINCENT AND THE GRENADINES

BARBADOS
GRENADA

TRINIDAD AND TOBAGO

VENEZUELA

CARIBBEAN SEA

Scale: 1 to 125,000,000

0   1000   2000 Miles

0   1000   2000   3000 Kilometers

Note: All world maps are Robinson projection.

Part One

The Dimensions of Anthropology

In Part 1 we'll explore the two different dimensions of anthropology. Those dimensions are academic (theoretical) and applied (practical) anthropology. Anthropology is the scientific and humanistic study of the human species. It is the academic field that most systematically explores biological and cultural diversity in time and space. Anthropologists explore every aspect of human diversity: past, present, and future; biology, society, language, and culture. Anthropology compares ways of life, and the people who lived them, from radically different times and places. Anthropologists work in varied contexts, including colleges, universities, museums, government agencies, businesses, and organizations.

The academic field of anthropology as a whole is known as "general" or "four-field" anthropology. The latter name is based on its four subfields: physical (biological), archaeological, cultural, and linguistic anthropology. Cultural anthropology examines the cultural diversity of the present and the recent past. Archaeology reconstructs behavior and social life by studying material remains. Physical anthropologists study human fossils, genetics, and bodily form and growth. They also study nonhuman primates (monkeys and apes). Linguistic anthropology considers how speech varies with social factors and over time.

Besides its four subfields, anthropology has the two dimensions mentioned above: academic and applied anthropology. Applying anthropology in the world beyond anthropology entails identifying, assessing, and solving problems that affect human beings in North America and abroad. The knowledge and methods of all four subfields, alone and in combination, are used to apply anthropology. Key aspects of anthropology, whether academic or applied, include its distinctive observation-based approach to gathering data, its comparative approach, and its focus on cultural diversity.

1

WHAT IS ANTHROPOLOGY?

Overview

Anthropology is the scientific and humanistic study of the human species. It is the exploration of human diversity in time and space. Anthropology confronts basic questions of human existence: how we originated, how we have changed, and how we are still changing.

Anthropology is holistic. Holism refers to the study of the whole of the human condition: past, present, and future; biology, society, language, and culture. Anthropology is also comparative and cross-cultural. It systematically compares data from different populations and time periods. Anthropology's four subfields are cultural, archaeological, biological, and linguistic anthropology.

Culture is a key aspect of human adaptability and success. Cultures are traditions and customs, transmitted through learning, that guide the beliefs and behavior of the people exposed to them. Cultural anthropology examines the cultural diversity of the present and the recent past. Archaeology reconstructs behavior by studying material

remains. Biological anthropologists study human fossils, genetics, and bodily growth and development. They also study nonhuman primates (monkeys and apes). Linguistic anthropology considers how speech varies with social factors and over time. Anthropology's two dimensions are academic and applied. Applied anthropology uses anthropological knowledge to identify and solve social problems.

Anthropology is related to many other fields, including the sciences and the humanities. There are links to both the natural sciences (e.g., biology) and the social sciences (e.g., sociology). Anthropologists bring their distinctive cross-cultural perspective to the study of economics, politics, psychology, art, music, literature—and society in general. As scientists, anthropologists attempt to identify and explain cultural differences and similarities and to build theory about how social and cultural systems work.

For a multimedia presentation of this Overview, see the Virtual Exploration

mhhe
●com
/kottak

Hot Asset in Corporate: Anthropology Degrees

USA TODAY NEWS BRIEF

by Del Jones

February 18, 1999

"Been on any digs lately?" Anthropologists are used to hearing that question after announcing their profession. People often confuse anthropology with archaeology, which is one—but only one—of anthropology's subfields. Many anthropologists do dig in the ground, but others dig into the intricacies of cultural diversity and everyday behavior. More and more businesses are hiring anthropologists because they like its characteristic observation of behavior in natural settings and its focus on cultural diversity. Thus, as we see in this article, Hallmark Cards has hired anthropologists to observe parties, holidays, and celebrations of ethnic groups to improve its ability to design cards for targeted audiences. Anthropologists go into people's homes to see how they actually use products. This permits better product design and more effective advertising.

Don't throw away the MBA degree yet.

But as companies go global and crave leaders for a diverse workforce, a new hot degree is emerging for aspiring executives: anthropology.

The study of man is no longer a degree for museum directors. Citicorp created a vice presidency for anthropologist Steve Barnett, who discovered early warning signs to identify people who don't pay credit card bills.

Not satisfied with consumer surveys, Hallmark is sending anthropologists into the homes of immigrants, attending holidays and birthday parties to design cards they'll want.

No survey can tell engineers what women really want in a razor, so marketing consultant Hauser Design sends anthropologists into bathrooms to watch them shave their legs.

Unlike MBAs, anthropology degrees are rare: one undergraduate degree for every 26 in business and one anthropology Ph.D. for every 235 MBAs.

Textbooks now have chapters on business applications. The University of South Florida has created a course of study for anthropologists headed for commerce.

Motorola corporate lawyer Robert Faulkner got his anthropology degree before going to law school. He says it becomes increasingly valuable.

Corporate anthropologists employ varied techniques, including ethnographic observation and focus groups, such as the one shown here, which is being videotaped through a two-way mirror in California.

"When you go into business, the only problems you'll have are people problems," was the advice given to teenager Michael Koss by his father in the early 1970s.

Koss, now 44, heeded the advice, earned an anthropology degree from Beloit College in 1976, and is today CEO of the Koss headphone manufacturer.

Katherine Burr, CEO of The Hanseatic Group, has masters in both anthropology and business from the University of New Mexico. Hanseatic was among the first money management programs to predict the Asian crisis and last year produced a total return of 315% for investors.

"My competitive edge came completely out of anthropology," she says. "The world is so unknown, changes so rapidly. Preconceptions can kill you."

Companies are starving to know how people use the Internet or why some pickups, even though they are more powerful, are perceived by consumers as less powerful, says Ken Erickson, of the Center for Ethnographic Research.

It takes trained observation, Erickson says. Observation is what anthropologists are trained to do.

SOURCE: Del Jones, "Hot Asset in Corporate: Anthropology Degrees," *USA Today,* February 18, 1999, p. B1.

Many anthropologists are educators, working in colleges, universities, and museums. Many other anthropologists, like the ones discussed in this news article, work outside of academia, for example, in business. Cultural anthropologists focus on cultural diversity and the intricacies of everyday behavior and social life. A more biologically oriented anthropologist might advise an engineering team in designing accommodations, such as spacecraft seating, that have optimal fits with human anatomy. Anthropologists study human beings wherever and whenever they find them—in the Australian outback, a Turkish café, a Mesopotamian tomb, or a North American shopping mall. Anthropology is the exploration of human diversity in time and space. Anthropology studies the whole of the human condition: past, present, and future; biology, society, language, and culture. Of particular interest is the diversity that comes through human adaptability.

Human Adaptability

Humans are among the world's most adaptable animals. In the Andes of South America, people wake up in villages 16,000 feet above sea level and then trek 1,500 feet higher to work in tin mines. Tribes in the Australian desert worship animals and discuss philosophy. People survive malaria in the tropics. Men have walked on the moon. The model of the *Starship Enterprise* in Washington's Smithsonian Institution symbolizes the desire to "seek out new life and civilizations, to boldly go where no one has gone before." Wishes to know the unknown, control the uncontrollable, and bring order to chaos find expression among all peoples. Adaptability and flexibility are basic human attributes, and human diversity is the subject matter of anthropology.

Students are often surprised by the breadth of **anthropology,** which is the study of the human species and its immediate ancestors. Anthropology is a uniquely comparative and **holistic** science. Holism refers to the study of the whole of the human condition: past, present, and future; biology, society, language, and culture. Most people think that anthropologists study fossils and nonindustrial, non-Western cultures, and many of them

do. But anthropology is much more than the study of nonindustrial peoples: It is a comparative field that examines all societies, ancient and modern, simple and complex. The other social sciences tend to focus on a single society, usually an industrial nation like the United States or Canada. Anthropology, however, offers a unique cross-cultural perspective by constantly comparing the customs of one society with those of others.

People share society—organized life in groups—with other animals, including baboons, wolves, and even ants. Culture, however, is distinctly human. **Cultures** are traditions and customs, transmitted through learning, that govern the beliefs and behavior of the people exposed to them. Children learn such a tradition by growing up in a particular society, through a process called *enculturation*. Cultural traditions include customs and opinions, developed over the generations, about proper and improper behavior. These traditions answer such questions as: How should we do things? How do we make sense of the world? How do we tell right from wrong? What is right, and what is wrong? A culture produces a degree of consistency in behavior and thought among the people who live in a particular society.

The most critical element of cultural traditions is their transmission through learning rather than through biological inheritance. Culture is not itself biological, but it rests on certain features of human biology. For more than a million years, humans have had at least some of the biological capacities on which culture depends. These abilities are to learn, to think symbolically, to use language, and to employ tools and other products in organizing their lives and adapting to their environments.

Anthropology confronts and ponders major questions of human existence as it explores human biological and cultural diversity in time and space. By examining ancient bones and tools, we unravel the mysteries of human origins. When did our ancestors separate from those remote great-aunts and great-uncles whose descendants are the apes? Where and when did *Homo sapiens* originate? How has our species changed? What are we now and where are we going? How have changes in culture and society influenced biological change? Our genus, *Homo,* has been changing for more than one million years. Humans continue to adapt and change both biologically and culturally.

Adaptation, Variation, and Change

Adaptation refers to the processes by which organisms cope with environmental forces and stresses, such as those posed by climate and *topography* or terrains, also called landforms. How do organisms change to fit their environments, such as dry climates or high mountain altitudes? Like other animals, humans use biological means of adaptation. But humans are unique in also having cultural means of adaptation. Table 1.1 summarizes the cultural and biological means that humans use to adapt to high altitudes.

Interpret the World
Atlas Map 1

Map 1 shows global topography, including mountains, hills, lowlands, and plains. Mountainous terrains pose particular challenges, those associated with high altitude and oxygen deprivation. Consider four ways (one cultural and three biological) in which humans may cope with low oxygen pressure at high altitudes. Illustrating cultural (technological) adaptation would be a pressurized airplane cabin equipped with oxygen masks. There are three ways of adapting biologically to high altitudes (the mountainous regions shows in Map 1): genetic adaptation, long-term physiological adaptation, and short-term physiological adaptation. First, native populations of high altitude areas, such as the Andes of Peru and the Himalayas of Tibet and Nepal, seem to have acquired certain genetic advantages for life at very high altitudes. The Andean tendency to develop a voluminous chest and lungs probably has a genetic basis. Second, regardless of their genes, people who grow up at a high altitude become physiologically more efficient there than genetically similar people who have grown up at sea level would be. This illustrates long-term physiological adaptation during the body's growth and development. Third, humans also have the capacity for short-term or immediate physiological adaptation. Thus, when lowlanders arrive in the highlands, they immediately increase their breathing and heart rates. Where in North America would you expect to experience such a reaction? Hyperventilation increases the oxygen in their lungs and arteries. As the pulse also increases, blood reaches their tissues more rapidly. All these varied adaptive responses—cultural and biological—achieve a single goal: maintaining an adequate supply of oxygen to the body.

As human history has unfolded, the social and cultural means of adaptation have become increasingly important. In this process, humans have devised diverse ways of coping with the range of environments they have occupied in time and space. The rate of cultural adaptation and change has accelerated, particularly during the past 10,000 years. For millions of years, hunting and gathering of nature's bounty—*foraging*—was the sole basis of human subsistence. However, it took only a few

Table 1.1   Forms of Cultural and Biological Adaptation (to High Altitude)

Form of Adaptation	Type of Adaptation	Example
Technology	Cultural	Pressurized airplane cabin with oxygen masks
Genetic adaptation (occurs over generations)	Biological	Larger "barrel chests" of native highlanders
Long-term physiological adaptation (occurs during growth and development of the individual organism)	Biological	More efficient respiratory system, to extract oxygen from "thin air"
Short-term physiological adaptation (occurs spontaneously when the individual organism enters a new environment)	Biological	Increased heart rate, hyperventilation

thousand years for **food production** (the cultivation of plants and domestication of animals), which originated some 12,000–10,000 years ago, to replace foraging in most areas.

Between 6000 and 5000 B.P. (before the present), the first civilizations arose. These were large, powerful, and complex societies, such as ancient Egypt, that conquered and governed large geographic areas. Much more recently, the spread of industrial production has profoundly affected human life. Throughout human history, major innovations have spread at the expense of earlier ones. Each economic revolution has had social and cultural repercussions. Today's global economy and communications link all contemporary people, directly or indirectly, in the modern world system. People must cope with forces generated by progressively larger systems—region, nation, and world. The study of such contemporary adaptations generates new challenges for anthropology: "The cultures of world peoples need to be constantly rediscovered as these people reinvent them in changing historical circumstances" (Marcus and Fischer 1986, p. 24).

American anthropology arose out of concern for the history and cultures of Native North Americans. Ely S. Parker, or Ha-sa-no-an-da, was a Seneca Indian who made important contributions to early anthropology. Parker also served as Commissioner of Indian Affairs for the United States.

General Anthropology

The academic discipline of anthropology, also known as **general anthropology** or "four-field" anthropology, includes four main subdisciplines or subfields. They are sociocultural, archaeological, biological, and linguistic anthropology. (From here on, the shorter term *cultural anthropology* will be used as a synonym for "sociocultural anthropology.") Of the subfields, cultural anthropology has the largest membership. Most departments of anthropology teach courses in all four subfields.

For current news about anthropology, see the OLC Internet Exercises

mhhe ● com /kottak

There are historical reasons for the inclusion of four subfields in a single discipline. American anthropology arose more than a century ago out of concern for the history and cultures of the native peoples of North America. Interest in the origins and diversity of Native Americans brought together studies of customs, social life, language, and physical traits. Anthropologists are still pondering such questions as: Where did Native Americans come from? How many waves of migration brought them to the New World? What are the linguistic, cultural, and biological links among Native Americans and between them and Asia? Another reason for anthropology's inclusion of four subfields was an interest in the relation between biology (e.g., "race") and culture. More than 50 years ago, the anthropologist Ruth Benedict realized that "In World history, those who have helped to build the same culture are not necessarily of one race, and those of the same race have not all participated in one culture. In scientific language, culture is not a function of race" (Benedict 1940, Ch 2). (Note that a unified four-field anthropology did not develop in Europe, where the subdisciplines tend to exist separately.)

There are also logical reasons for the unity of American anthropology. Each subfield considers variation in time and space (that is, in different geographic areas). Cultural and archaeological anthropologists study (among many other topics) changes in social life and customs. Archaeologists have used studies of living societies and behavior patterns to imagine what life might have been like in the past. Biological anthropologists examine evolutionary changes in physical form, for example, anatomical changes that might have been associated with the origin of tool use or language. Linguistic anthropologists may reconstruct the basics of ancient languages by studying modern ones.

The subdisciplines influence each other as anthropologists talk to each other, read books and journals, and associate in professional organizations. General anthropology explores the basics of human biology, society, and culture and considers their interrelations. Anthropologists share certain key assumptions. Perhaps the most fundamental is the idea that sound conclusions about "human nature" cannot be derived from studying a single nation or cultural tradition. A comparative, cross-cultural approach is essential.

We often hear "nature versus nurture" and "genetics versus environment" questions. Consider gender differences. To what extent do male and female capacities, attitudes, and behavior reflect biological, or cultural, variation? Are there universal emotional and intellectual contrasts between the sexes? Are females less aggressive than males? Is male dominance a human universal? By examining diverse cultures, anthropology shows that many contrasts between men and women reflect cultural training rather than biology.

CULTURAL FORCES SHAPE HUMAN BIOLOGY

Cultural forces constantly mold human biology. For example, culture is a key environmental force in determining how human bodies grow and develop. Cultural traditions promote certain activities and abilities, discourage others, and set standards of physical well-being and attractiveness. Physical activities, including sports, which are influenced by culture, help build the body. For example, North American girls are encouraged to pursue, and therefore do well in, competitive track and field, swimming, diving, and many other sports. Brazilian girls, by contrast, have not fared nearly as well in international athletic competition involving individual sports as have their American and Canadian counterparts. Why are girls encouraged to excel as athletes in some nations but discouraged from engaging in physical activities in others? Why don't Brazilian women, and Latin American women generally, do better in most athletic categories? Does it have to do with "racial" differences or cultural training?

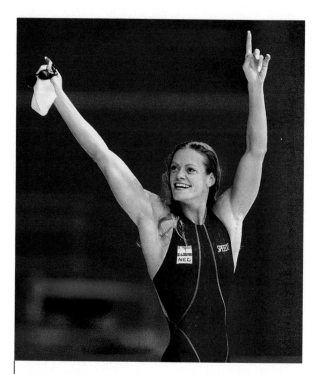

Years of swimming sculpt a distinctive physique: an enlarged upper torso, a massive neck, and powerful shoulders and back. Shown here is the Dutch swimmer Inge de Bruijn, who won multiple medals at the 2000 summer Olympics in Sydney.

Cultural standards of attractiveness and propriety influence participation and achievement in sports. Americans run or swim not just to compete but to keep trim and fit. Brazil's beauty standards accept more fat, especially in female buttocks and hips. Brazilian men have had some international success in swimming and running, but Brazil rarely sends female swimmers or runners to the Olympics. One reason Brazilian women avoid competitive swimming in particular is that sport's effects on the body. Years of swimming sculpt a distinctive physique: an enlarged upper torso, a massive neck, and powerful shoulders and back. Successful female swimmers tend to be big, strong, and bulky. The countries that produce them most consistently are the United States, Canada, Australia, Germany, the Scandinavian nations, the Netherlands, and the former Soviet Union, where this body type isn't as stigmatized as it is in Latin countries. Swimmers develop hard bodies, but Brazilian culture says that women should be soft, with big hips and buttocks, not big shoulders. Many young female swimmers in Latin America choose to abandon the sport rather than the "feminine" body ideal.

Understanding Ourselves Our parents may tell us that drinking milk and eating vegetables promote healthy growth, but they don't as readily recognize the role that culture plays in shaping our bodies. Our genetic attributes provide a foundation for our growth and development, but human biology is fairly plastic. That is, it is malleable; the environment influences how we grow. Identical twins raised from birth in radically different environments—e.g., one in the high Andes and one at sea level—will not, as adults, be physically identical. Nutrition matters in growth; so do cultural guidelines about what is proper for boys and girls to do. Culture is an environmental force that affects our development as much as do nutrition, heat, cold, and altitude. One aspect of culture is how it provides opportunities and assigns space for various activities. We get to be good at sports by practicing them. When you grew up, which was it easiest for you to engage in— baseball, golf, mountain climbing, or fencing? Think about why.

Cultural factors help explain why African Americans excel in certain sports and whites excel in others. A key factor is degree of public access to sports facilities. In our public schools, parks, sandlots, and city playgrounds, African Americans have access to baseball diamonds, basketball courts, football fields, and running tracks. However, because of restricted economic opportunities, many black families can't afford to buy hockey gear or ski equipment, take ski vacations, pay for tennis lessons, or belong to clubs with tennis courts, pools, or golf courses. In the United States, mainly white suburban boys (and, increasingly, girls) play soccer, the most popular sport in the world. In Brazil, however, soccer is the national pastime for all males—black and white, rich and poor. There is wide public access. Brazilians play soccer on the beach and in streets, squares, parks, and playgrounds. Many of Brazil's best soccer players, including the world-famous Pelé, have dark skins. When blacks have opportunities to do well in soccer, tennis, golf, or any other sport, they are physically capable of doing as well as whites.

Why does the United States have so many black football and basketball players and so few black swimmers and hockey players? The answer lies mainly in cultural factors, including variable

This Brazilian soccer team won the 2002 World Cup, defeating the German team shown on the right. What contrasts do you notice between the two teams? How do you explain them?

The 2002 German National Soccer Team.

access and opportunities. Many Brazilians practice soccer, hoping to play for money for a professional club. Similarly, American blacks are aware that certain sports have provided career opportunities for African Americans. They start developing skills in those sports in childhood. The better they do, the more likely they are to persist, and the pattern continues. Culture—specifically differential access to sports resources—has more to do with sports success than "race" does.

The Subdisciplines of Anthropology

CULTURAL ANTHROPOLOGY

Cultural anthropology is the study of human society and culture, the subfield that describes, analyzes, interprets, and explains social and cultural similarities and differences. To study and interpret cultural diversity, cultural anthropologists engage in two kinds of activity: ethnography (based on field work) and ethnology (based on cross-cultural comparison). **Ethnography** provides an account of a particular community, society, or culture. During ethnographic field work, the ethnographer gathers data that he or she organizes, describes, analyzes, and interprets to build and present that account, which may be in the form of a book, article, or film. Traditionally, ethnographers have lived in small communities (such as Arembepe, Brazil—see "Interesting Issues" on page 12) and studied local behavior, beliefs, customs, social life, economic activities, politics, and religion. What kind of experience is ethnography for the ethnographer? The box offers some clues.

For a quiz on the subdisciplines of anthropology, see the Interactive Exercise

mhhe.com/kottak

The anthropological perspective derived from ethnographic field work often differs radically from that of economics or political science. Those fields focus on national and official organizations and policies and often on elites. However, the groups that anthropologists have traditionally studied usually have been relatively poor and powerless, as are most people in the world today. Ethnographers often observe discriminatory practices directed toward such people, who experience food shortages, dietary deficiencies, and other aspects of poverty. Political scientists tend to study programs that national planners develop, while anthropologists discover how these programs work on the local level.

Cultures are not isolated. As noted by Franz Boas (1940/1966) many years ago, contact between neighboring tribes has always existed and has extended over enormous areas. "Human populations construct their cultures in interaction with one another, and not in isolation" (Wolf 1982, p.ix). Villagers increasingly participate in regional, national, and world events. Exposure to external forces comes through the mass media, migration, and modern transportation. City and nation increasingly invade local communities in the guise of tourists, development agents, government and religious officials, and political candidates. Such linkages are prominent components of regional, national, and international systems of politics, economics, and information. These larger systems increasingly affect the people and places anthropology traditionally has studied. The study of such linkages and systems is part of the subject matter of modern anthropology.

Ethnology examines, interprets, analyzes, and compares the results of ethnography—the data gathered in different societies. It uses such data to compare and contrast and to make generalizations about society and culture. Looking beyond the particular to the more general, ethnologists attempt to identify and explain cultural differences and similarities, to test hypotheses, and to build theory to enhance our understanding of how social and cultural systems work. Ethnology gets its data for comparison not just from ethnography but also from the other subfields, particularly from archaeological anthropology, which reconstructs social systems of the past. (Table 1.2 summarizes the main contrasts between ethnography and ethnology.)

ARCHAEOLOGICAL ANTHROPOLOGY

Archaeological anthropology (more simply, "archaeology") reconstructs, describes, and interprets past human behavior and cultural patterns through material remains. At sites where people live or have lived, archaeologists find artifacts, material items that humans have made or modified, such as tools, weapons, camp sites, and buildings. Plant and animal remains and ancient garbage tell stories about consumption and activi-

Table 1.2	Ethnography and Ethnology—Two Dimensions of Cultural Anthropology	
Ethnography	**Ethnology**
Requires field work to collect data	Uses data collected by a series of researchers
Often descriptive	Usually synthetic
Group/community specific	Comparative/cross-cultural

ties. Wild and domesticated grains have different characteristics, which allow archaeologists to distinguish between gathering and cultivation. Examination of animal bones reveals the ages of slaughtered animals and provides other information useful in determining whether species were wild or domesticated.

Analyzing such data, archaeologists answer several questions about ancient economies. Did the group get its meat from hunting, or did it domesticate and breed animals, killing only those of a certain age and sex? Did plant food come from wild plants or from sowing, tending, and harvesting crops? Did the residents make, trade for, or buy particular items? Were raw materials available locally? If not, where did they come from? From such information, archaeologists reconstruct patterns of production, trade, and consumption.

Archaeologists have spent much time studying potsherds, fragments of earthenware. Potsherds are more durable than many other artifacts, such as textiles and wood. The quantity of pottery fragments allows estimates of population size and density. The discovery that potters used materials that were not locally available suggests systems of trade. Similarities in manufacture and decoration at different sites may be proof of cultural connections. Groups with similar pots may be historically related. Perhaps they shared common cultural ancestors, traded with each other, or belonged to the same political system.

Many archaeologists examine paleoecology. Ecology is the study of interrelations among living things in an environment. The organisms and environment together constitute an ecosystem, a patterned arrangement of energy flows and exchanges. Human ecology studies ecosystems that include people, focusing on the ways in which human use "of nature influences and is influenced

by social organization and cultural values" (Bennett 1969, pp. 10–11). Paleoecology looks at the ecosystems of the past.

In addition to reconstructing ecological patterns, archaeologists may infer cultural transformations, for example, by observing changes in the size and type of sites and the distance between them. A city develops in a region where only towns, villages, and hamlets existed a few centuries earlier. The number of settlement levels (city, town, village, hamlet) in a society is a measure of social complexity. Buildings offer clues about political and religious features. Temples and pyramids suggest that an ancient society had an authority structure capable of marshaling the labor needed to build such monuments. The presence or absence of certain structures, like the pyramids of ancient Egypt and Mexico, reveals differences in function between settlements. For example, some towns were places where people came to attend ceremonies. Others were burial sites; still others were farming communities.

Archaeologists also reconstruct behavior patterns and life styles of the past by excavating. This involves digging through a succession of levels at a particular site. In a given area, through time, settlements may change in form and purpose, as may the connections between settlements. Excavation can document changes in economic, social, and political activities.

Although archaeologists are best known for studying prehistory, that is, the period before the invention of writing, they also study the cultures of historical and even living peoples. Studying sunken ships off the Florida coast, underwater archaeologists have been able to verify the living conditions on the vessels that brought ancestral African Americans to the New World as enslaved people. Another, even more contemporary, illustration of archaeology is a research project begun

Interesting *Issues*
Even Anthropologists Get Culture Shock

I first lived in Arembepe (Brazil) during the (North American) summer of 1962. That was between my junior and senior years at New York City's Columbia College, where I was majoring in anthropology. I went to Arembepe as a participant in a now defunct program designed to provide undergraduates with experience doing ethnography—firsthand study of an alien society's culture and social life.

Brought up in one culture, intensely curious about others, anthropologists nevertheless experience culture shock, particularly on their first field trip. Culture shock refers to the whole set of feelings about being in an alien setting, and the ensuing reactions. It is a chilly, creepy feeling of alienation, of being without some of the most ordinary, trivial (and therefore basic) cues of one's culture of origin.

As I planned my departure for Brazil in 1962, I could not know just how naked I would feel without the cloak of my own language and culture. My sojourn in Arembepe would be my first trip outside the United States. I was an urban boy who had grown up in Atlanta, Georgia, and New York City. I had little experience with rural life in my own country, none with Latin America, and I had received only minimal training in the Portuguese language.

New York City direct to Salvador, Bahia, Brazil. Just a brief stopover in Rio de Janeiro; a longer visit would be a reward at the end of field work. As our prop jet approached tropical Salvador, I couldn't believe the whiteness of the sand. "That's not snow, is it?" I remarked to a fellow field team member . . .

My first impressions of Bahia were of smells—alien odors of ripe and decaying mangoes, bananas, and passion fruit—and of swatting the ubiquitous fruit flies I had never seen before, although I had read extensively about their reproductive behavior in genetics classes. There were strange concoctions of rice, black beans, and gelatinous gobs of unidentifiable meats and floating pieces of skin. Coffee was strong and sugar crude, and every tabletop had

Figure 1.1   **Location of Arembepe, Bahia, Brazil.**

in 1973 in Tucson, Arizona. Archaeologist William Rathje has learned about contemporary life by studying modern garbage. The value of "garbology," as Rathje calls it, is that it provides "evidence of what people did, not what they think they did, what they think they should have done, or what the interviewer thinks they should have done" (Harrison, Rathje, and Hughes 1994, p. 108). What people report may contrast strongly with their real behavior as revealed by garbology. For example, containers for toothpicks and for manioc (cassava) flour to sprinkle, like Parmesan cheese, on anything one might eat. I remember oatmeal soup and a slimy stew of beef tongue in tomatoes. At one meal a disintegrating fish head, eyes still attached, but barely, stared up at me as the rest of its body floated in a bowl of bright orange palm oil . . .

I only vaguely remember my first day in Arembepe (Figure 1.1). Unlike ethnographers who have studied remote tribes in the tropical forests of interior South America or the highlands of Papua New Guinea, I did not have to hike or ride a canoe for days to arrive at my field site. Arembepe was not isolated relative to such places, only relative to every other place I had ever been . . .

I do recall what happened when we arrived. There was no formal road into the village. Entering through southern Arembepe, vehicles simply threaded their way around coconut trees, following tracks left by automobiles that had passed previously. A crowd of children had heard us coming, and they pursued our car through the village streets until we parked in front of our house, near the central square. Our first few days in Arembepe were spent with children following us everywhere. For weeks we had few moments of privacy. Children watched our every move through our living room window. Occasionally one made an incompre-

An ethnographer at work. During a 1980 visit, the author, Conrad Kottak, catches up on the news in Arembepe, a coastal community in Bahia state, northeastern Brazil, that he has been studying since 1962. How might culture shock influence one's research?

hensible remark. Usually they just stood there . . .

The sounds, sensations, sights, smells, and tastes of life in northeastern Brazil, and in Arembepe, slowly grew familiar . . . I grew accustomed to this world without Kleenex, in which globs of mucus habitually drooped from the noses of village children whenever a cold passed through Arembepe. A world where, seemingly without effort, women . . . carried 18-liter kerosene cans of water on their heads, where boys sailed kites and sported at catching houseflies in their bare hands, where

old women smoked pipes, storekeepers offered *cachaça* (common rum) at nine in the morning, and men played dominoes on lazy afternoons when there was no fishing. I was visiting a world where human life was oriented toward water—the sea, where men fished, and the lagoon, where women communally washed clothing, dishes, and their own bodies.

This description is adapted from my ethnographic study *Assault on Paradise: Social Change in a Brazilian Village*, 3rd ed. (New York: McGraw-Hill, 1999).

the garbologists discovered that the three Tucson neighborhoods that reported the lowest beer consumption actually had the highest number of discarded beer cans per household (Podolefsky and Brown 1992, p. 100)!

BIOLOGICAL, OR PHYSICAL, ANTHROPOLOGY

The subject matter of **biological,** or **physical, anthropology** is human biological diversity in time and space. The focus on biological variation

Archaeological anthropology reconstructs, describes, and interprets human behavior through material remains. In Grosse Point Park, Michigan, these high school students have made pottery using online information from an archaeological dig in Egypt.

unites five special interests within biological anthropology:

1. Human evolution as revealed by the fossil record (paleoanthropology).

2. Human genetics.

3. Human growth and development.

4. Human biological plasticity (the body's ability to change as it copes with stresses, such as heat, cold, and altitude).

5. The biology, evolution, behavior, and social life of monkeys, apes, and other nonhuman primates.

These interests link physical anthropology to other fields: biology, zoology, geology, anatomy, physiology, medicine, and public health. Osteology—the study of bones—helps paleoanthropologists, who examine skulls, teeth, and bones, to identify human ancestors and to chart changes in anatomy over time. A paleontologist is a scientist who studies fossils. A paleoanthropologist is one sort of paleontologist, one who studies the fossil

record of *human* evolution. Paleoanthropologists often collaborate with archaeologists, who study artifacts, in reconstructing biological and cultural aspects of human evolution. Fossils and tools are often found together. Different types of tools provide information about the habits, customs, and life styles of the ancestral humans who used them.

More than a century ago, Charles Darwin noticed that the variety that exists within any population permits some individuals (those with the favored, or adaptive, characteristics) to do better than others at surviving and reproducing. Genetics, which developed later, enlightens us about the causes and transmission of this variety. However, it isn't just genes that cause variety. During any individual's lifetime, the environment works along with heredity to determine biological features. For example, people with a genetic tendency to be tall will be shorter if they are poorly nourished during childhood. Thus, biological anthropology also investigates the influence of environment on the body as it grows and matures. Among the environmental factors that influence the body as it develops are nutrition, altitude, temperature, and disease, as well as

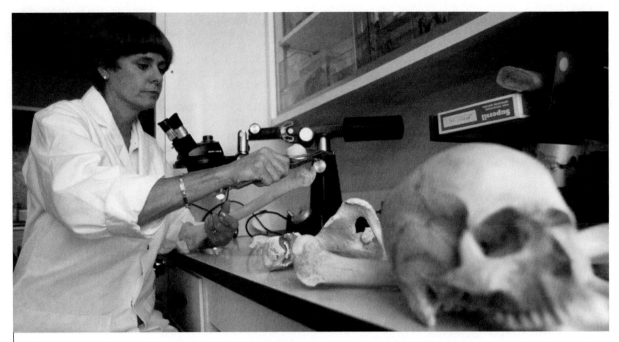

Forensic anthropologist Kathy Reichs at work. Like other forensic anthropologists, Dr. Reichs, and her mystery novel alter ego, Temperance Brennan, work with the police, medical examiners, the courts, and international organizations to identify victims of crimes, accidents, wars, and terrorism.

cultural factors, such as the standards of attractiveness we considered previously.

Biological anthropology (along with zoology) also includes primatology. The primates include our closest relatives—apes and monkeys. Primatologists study their biology, evolution, behavior, and social life, often in their natural environments. Primatology assists paleoanthropology, because primate behavior may shed light on early human behavior and human nature.

LINGUISTIC ANTHROPOLOGY

We don't know (and probably never will) when our ancestors acquired the ability to speak, although biological anthropologists have looked to the anatomy of the face and the skull to speculate about the origin of language. And primatologists have described the communication systems of monkeys and apes. We do know that well-developed, grammatically complex languages have existed for thousands of years. Linguistic anthropology offers further illustration of anthropology's interest in comparison, variation, and change. **Linguistic anthropology** studies language in its social and cultural context, across space and over time. Some linguistic anthropologists make inferences about universal features of language, linked perhaps to uniformities in the human brain. Others reconstruct ancient languages by comparing their contemporary descendants and in so doing make discoveries about history. Still others study linguistic differences to discover varied perceptions and patterns of thought in different cultures.

Historical linguistics considers variation in time, such as the changes in sounds, grammar, and vocabulary between Middle English (spoken from approximately AD 1050 to 1550) and modern English. **Sociolinguistics** investigates relationships between social and linguistic variation. No language is a homogeneous system in which everyone speaks just like everyone else. How do different speakers use a given language? How do linguistic features correlate with social factors, including class and gender differences (Tannen 1990)? One reason for variation is geography, as in regional dialects and accents. Linguistic variation also is expressed in the bilingualism of ethnic groups. Linguistic and cultural anthropologists collaborate in

Background Information

STUDENT:	Alicia Wilbur
SUPERVISING PROFESSOR:	Della Collins Cook
SCHOOL:	Indiana University
YEAR IN SCHOOL/MAJOR:	Junior and Senior/ Anthropology
FUTURE PLANS:	Ph.D. in Biological Anthropology
PROJECT TITLE:	The Utility of Hand and Foot Bones for Problems in Bioanthropology

How does this account suggest common problems of interest to more than one subfield of anthropology? Does the research have implications for cultural and applied anthropology as well as for biological and archaeological anthropology?

The large, well-preserved skeletal series from west-central Illinois, housed in the Department of Anthropology at Indiana University, has been the focus of many archaeological and bioanthropological research projects over the years. I became interested in the use of hand and foot bones to determine the stature and sex of the individuals buried in those mounds. This information is important for both archaeological and biological studies of past peoples and their cultures, but is also relevant to modern forensic and mass disaster situations. In both archaeological and modern situations, the human remains recovered may be extremely fragmentary. A single hand or foot can play an important role in identifying modern victims of crime or mass disasters.

Most equations used for estimating adult stature or determining sex from skeletal material are constructed from data on modern Europeans or modern Americans of European or African extraction. Because body proportions differ between populations, applying these equations to skeletal remains of other groups may give inaccurate results. A benefit of my study was that it was constructed on Native American remains and thus could be used for modern Native Americans' remains in forensic cases or mass disasters.

I measured femurs (the thigh bone) and hand and foot bones for 410 adult skeletons and used statistical methods to predict the sex of the individuals, with accuracies exceeding 87 percent. Stature estimation also was found to be possible with hand and foot bones, although the range given was too large to be

studying links between language and many other aspects of culture, such as how people reckon kinship and how they perceive and classify colors.

Applied Anthropology

Anthropology is not a science of the exotic carried on by quaint scholars in ivory towers. Rather, it is a holistic, comparative, biocultural field with a lot to tell the public. Anthropology's foremost professional organization, the American Anthropological Association, has formally acknowledged a public service role by recognizing that anthropology has two dimensions: (1) academic anthropology and (2) practicing or **applied anthropology.**

The latter refers to the application of anthropological data, perspectives, theory, and methods to identify, assess, and solve contemporary social problems. More and more anthropologists from the four subfields now work in such "applied" areas as public health, family planning, and economic development.

In its most general sense, applied anthropology includes any use of the knowledge and/or techniques of the four subfields to identify, assess, and solve practical problems. Because of anthropology's breadth, it has many applications. For example, the growing field of medical anthropology considers both the sociocultural and the biological contexts and implications of disease and illness. Perceptions of good and bad health, along with actual health

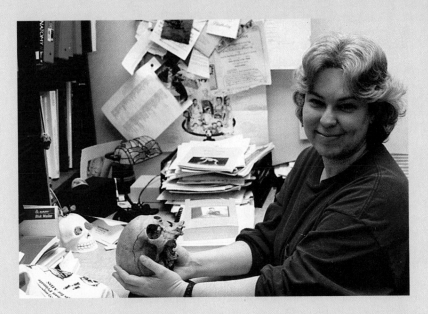

organs. Symptoms include delayed growth, mental retardation, and abnormalities of the head and face, including widely spaced eyes and an abnormally large nose. Affected individuals also may have abnormally large big toes and thumbs. There also may be breathing and swallowing difficulties.

It may yet prove possible to analyze DNA from this sample to determine if my diagnosis is correct. If so, it would be the earliest known case of this syndrome. Knowing that this individual lived to mid- to late adulthood with several physical and mental disabilities tells us something about her culture.

These types of studies on skeletal material are important for the information they give us about the past and also for their relevance to modern problems. Future research will focus on genetic and infectious diseases that beset ancient peoples as well as application of this work to modern problems.

useful in a court of law. Still, estimates resulting from these equations may be useful for delimiting a range of possible heights for preliminary identification purposes.

The project was published in the *International Journal of Osteoarchaeology* in 1998. While running statistical analyses on the hand and foot data, I noticed a discrepancy in the body proportions of one female adult. Upon carefully examining the rest of her skeleton, I discovered a suite of skeletal anomalies that suggest a rare genetic syndrome called Rubinstein-Taybi Syndrome that affects many

threats and problems, differ among cultures. Various societies and ethnic groups recognize different illnesses, symptoms, and causes and have developed different health-care systems and treatment strategies. Medical anthropologists are both biological and cultural, and both academic and applied. Applied medical anthropologists, for example, have served as cultural interpreters in public health programs, which must fit into local culture and be accepted by local people.

Other applied anthropologists work for international development agencies, such as the World Bank and USAID (the United States Agency for International Development). The job of such development anthropologists is to assess the social and cultural dimensions of economic development.

Anthropologists are experts on local cultures. Working with and drawing on the knowledge of local people, anthropologists can identify specific social conditions and needs that must be addressed and that influence the failure or success of development schemes. Planners in Washington or Paris often know little about, say, the labor necessary for crop cultivation in rural Africa. Development funds are often wasted if an anthropologist is not asked to work with the local people to identify local needs, demands, priorities, and constraints.

Projects routinely fail when planners ignore the cultural dimension of development. Problems arise from lack of attention to, and consequent lack of fit with, existing sociocultural conditions. One example is a very naive and culturally incompatible

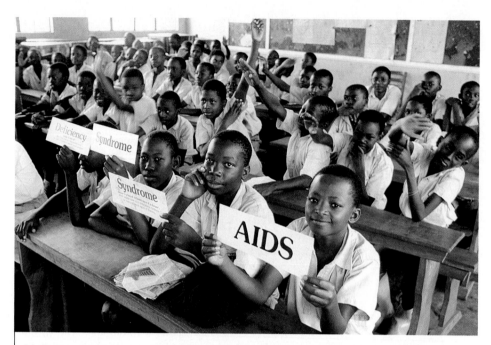

Medical anthropology studies health conditions from a cross-cultural perspective. In Uganda's Mwiri primary school, children are taught about HIV. Can you imagine a similar lesson in the primary school you attended?

project in East Africa. The major fallacy was to attempt to convert nomadic herders into farmers. The planners had absolutely no evidence that the herders, on whose land the project was to be implemented, wanted to change their economy. The herders' territory was to be used for new commercial farms, and the herders, converted into small farmers and sharecroppers. The project, whose planners included no anthropologists, totally neglected social issues. The obstacles would have been evident to any anthropologist. The herders were expected readily to give up a generations-old way of life in order to work three times harder growing rice and picking cotton. What could possibly motivate them to give up their freedom and mobility to work as sharecroppers for commercial farmers? Certainly not the meager financial return the project planners estimated for the herders—an average of $300 annually versus more than $10,000 for their new bosses, the commercial farmers.

To avoid such unrealistic projects, and to make development schemes more socially sensitive and culturally appropriate, development organizations now regularly include anthropolo-gists on planning teams. Their team colleagues may include agronomists, economists, veterinarians, geologists, engineers, and health specialists. Applied anthropologists also apply their skills in studying the human dimension of environmental degradation (e.g., deforestation, pollution). Anthropologists examine how the environment influences humans and how human activities affect the biosphere and the earth itself.

Applied anthropologists also work in North America. Garbologists help the Environmental Protection Agency, the paper industry, and packaging and trade associations. Many archaeologists now work in cultural resource management. They apply their knowledge and skills to interpret, inventory, and preserve historic resources for local, state (provincial), and federal governments. Forensic (physical) anthropologists work with the police, medical examiners, the courts, and international organizations to identify victims of crimes, accidents, wars, and terrorism. From skeletal remains they may determine age, sex, size, ethnic origin, and number of victims. Applied physical anthropologists link injury patterns to design flaws in aircraft and vehicles.

Table 1.3   The Four Subfields and Two Dimensions of Anthropology

Anthropology's Subfields (General Anthropology)	Examples of Application (Applied Anthropology)
Cultural anthropology	Development anthropology
Archaeological anthropology	Cultural resource management (CRM)
Biological or physical anthropology	Forensic anthropology
Linguistic anthropology	Study of linguistic diversity in classrooms

Ethnographers have influenced social policy by showing that strong kin ties exist in city neighborhoods whose social organization was previously considered "fragmented" or "pathological." Suggestions for improving education emerge from ethnographic studies of classrooms and surrounding communities. Linguistic anthropologists show the influence of dialect differences on classroom learning. In general, applied anthropology aims to find humane and effective ways of helping the people whom anthropologists have traditionally studied. Table 1.3 shows the four subfields and two dimensions of anthropology.

Anthropology and Other Academic Fields

As mentioned previously, one of the main differences between anthropology and the other fields that study people is holism, anthropology's unique blend of biological, social, cultural, linguistic, historical, and contemporary perspectives. Paradoxically, while distinguishing anthropology, this breadth is what also links it to many other disciplines. Techniques used to date fossils and artifacts have come to anthropology from physics, chemistry, and geology. Because plant and animal remains often are found with human bones and artifacts, anthropologists collaborate with botanists, zoologists, and paleontologists.

As a discipline that is both scientific and humanistic, anthropology has links with many other academic fields. Anthropology is a **science**—a "systematic field of study or body of knowledge that aims, through experiment, observation, and

deduction, to produce reliable explanations of phenomena, with reference to the material and physical world" (*Webster's New World Encyclopedia* 1993, p. 937). Clyde Kluckhohn (1944, p. 9) called anthropology "the science of human similarities and differences." His statement of the need for such a science still stands: "Anthropology provides a scientific basis for dealing with the crucial dilemma of the world today: how can peoples of different appearance, mutually unintelligible languages, and dissimilar ways of life get along peaceably together?" (p. 9). Anthropology has compiled an impressive body of knowledge that this textbook attempts to encapsulate.

Anthropology also has strong links to the humanities. The humanities include English, comparative literature, classics, folklore, philosophy, and the arts. These fields study languages, texts, philosophies, arts, music, performances, and other forms of creative expression. Ethnomusicology, which studies forms of musical expression on a worldwide basis, is especially closely related to anthropology. Also linked is folklore, the systematic study of tales, myths, and legends from a variety of cultures. One might well argue that anthropology is among the most humanistic of all academic fields because of its fundamental respect for human diversity. Anthropologists listen to, record, and represent voices from a multitude of nations and cultures. Anthropology values local knowledge, diverse worldviews, and alternative philosophies. Cultural anthropology and linguistic anthropology in particular bring a comparative and nonelitist perspective to forms of creative expression, including language, art, narratives, music, and dance, viewed in their social and cultural context.

CULTURAL ANTHROPOLOGY AND SOCIOLOGY

Cultural anthropology and sociology share an interest in social relations, organization, and behavior. However, important differences between these disciplines arose from the kinds of societies each traditionally studied. Initially sociologists focused on the industrial West; anthropologists, on nonindustrial societies. Different methods of data collection and analysis emerged to deal with those different kinds of societies. To study large-scale, complex nations, sociologists came to rely on questionnaires and other means of gathering masses of quantifiable data. For many years, sampling and statistical techniques have been basic to sociology, whereas statistical training has been less common in anthropology (although this is changing as anthropologists increasingly work in modern nations).

Traditional ethnographers studied small and nonliterate (without writing) populations and relied on methods appropriate to that context. "Ethnography is a research process in which the anthropologist closely observes, records, and engages in the daily life of another culture—an experience labeled as the fieldwork method—and then writes accounts of this culture, emphasizing descriptive detail" (Marcus and Fischer 1986, p. 18). One key method described in this quote is participant observation—taking part in the events one is observing, describing, and analyzing.

In many areas and topics, anthropology and sociology now are converging. As the modern world system grows, sociologists now do research in developing countries and in other places that were once mainly within the anthropological orbit. As industrialization spreads, many anthropologists now work in industrial nations, where they study diverse topics, including rural decline, inner-city life, and the role of the mass media in creating national cultural patterns.

ANTHROPOLOGY AND PSYCHOLOGY

Like sociologists, most psychologists do research in their own society. But statements about "human" psychology cannot be based solely on observations made in one society or in a single type of society. The area of cultural anthropology known as psychological anthropology studies cross-cultural variation in psychological traits. Societies instill different values by training children differently. Adult personalities reflect a culture's child-rearing practices.

Bronislaw Malinowski, an early contributor to the cross-cultural study of human psychology, is famous for his field work among the Trobriand Islanders of the South Pacific (Figure 1.2). The Trobrianders reckon kinship matrilineally. They consider themselves related to the mother and her relatives, but not to the father. The relative who disciplines the child is not the father but the mother's brother, the maternal uncle. One inherits from the uncle rather than the father. Trobrianders show a marked respect for the uncle, with whom a boy usually has a cool and distant relationship. In contrast, the Trobriand father–son relationship is friendly and affectionate.

Malinowski's work among the Trobrianders suggested modifications in Sigmund Freud's famous theory of the universality of the Oedipus complex (Malinowski 1927). According to Freud (1918/1950), boys around the age of five become sexually attracted to their mothers. The Oedipus complex is resolved, in Freud's view, when the boy overcomes his sexual jealousy of, and identifies with, his father. Freud lived in patriarchal Austria during the late 19th and early 20th centuries—a social milieu in which the father was a strong authoritarian figure. The Austrian father was the child's primary authority figure and the mother's sexual partner. In the Trobriands, the father had only the sexual role.

If, as Freud contended, the Oedipus complex always creates social distance based on jealousy toward the mother's sexual partner, this would have shown up in Trobriand society. It *did not*. Malinowski concluded that the authority structure did more to influence the father–son relationship than did sexual jealousy. Like many later anthropologists, Malinowski showed that individual psychology depends on its cultural context. Anthropologists continue to provide cross-cultural perspectives on psychoanalytic propositions (Paul 1989) as well as on issues of developmental and cognitive psychology (Shore 1996).

Understanding Ourselves How much would we know about human behavior, thought, and feeling if we studied only our own kind? What if our entire understanding of human

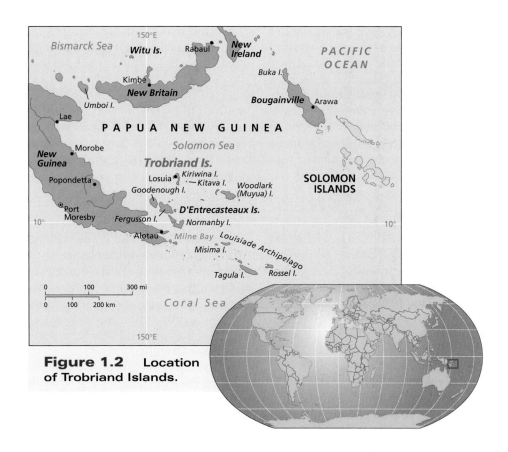

Figure 1.2 Location of Trobriand Islands.

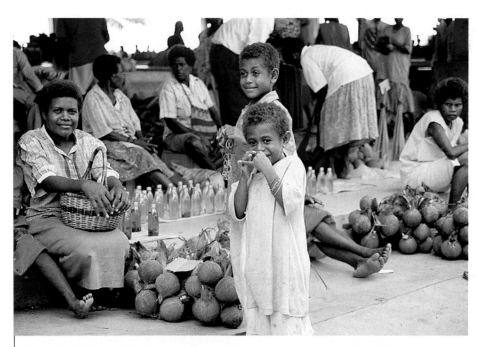

Bronislaw Malinowski is famous for his field work among the matrilineal Trobriand Islanders of the South Pacific. Does this Trobriand market scene suggest anything about the status of Trobriand women?

behavior were based on analysis of questionnaires filled out by college students in Oregon? A radical question but one that should make you think about the basis for statements about what humans are like. A primary reason why anthropology helps us understand ourselves is the cross-cultural perspective. One culture can't tell us everything we need to know about what it means to be human. Earlier we saw how cultural forces influence our physical growth. Culture also guides our emotional and cognitive growth and helps determine the kinds of personalities we have as adults. Among scholarly disciplines, anthropology stands out as the field that provides the cross-cultural test. How does television affect us? To answer that question, study not just North America in 2003 but some other place—and perhaps also some other time (such as Brazil in the 1980s; see Kottak 1990). Anthropology specializes in the study of human variation in space and time.

Science, Explanation, and Hypothesis Testing

A key feature of anthropology is its comparative, cross-cultural dimension. As was stated previously (see p. 10), *ethnology* draws on ethnographic, as well as archaeological, data to compare and contrast, and to make generalizations about, societies and cultures. As a scientific pursuit, ethnology attempts to identify and explain cultural differences and similarities, test hypotheses, and build theory to enhance our understanding of how social and cultural systems work.

In their 1996 article "Science in Anthropology," Melvin Ember and Carol R. Ember stress a key feature of science as a way of viewing the world: Science recognizes the tentativeness and uncertainty of our knowledge and understanding. Scientists strive to improve understanding by testing *hypotheses*—suggested explanations of things and events. In science, understanding means *explaining*—showing how and why the thing to be understood (the explicandum) is related to other things in some known way. Explanations rely on associations and theories. An association is an observed relationship between two or more variables. A theory is more general, suggesting or implying associations and attempting to explain them (Ember and Ember 1996).

A thing or event, for example, the freezing of water, is explained if it illustrates a general principle or association. "Water solidifies at 32 degrees" states an association between two variables: the state of the water and the air temperature. The truth of the statement is confirmed by repeated observations. In the physical sciences, such relationships are called "laws." Explanations based on such laws allow us to understand the past and predict the future.

In the social sciences, associations usually are stated probabilistically: Two or more variables *tend to be* related in a predictable way, but there are exceptions (Ember and Ember 1996). For example, in a worldwide sample of societies, the anthropologist John Whiting (1964) found a strong (but not 100 percent) association or correlation between a low-protein diet and a long postpartum sex taboo—a prohibition against sexual intercourse between husband and wife for a year or more after the birth of a child.

Laws and statistical associations explain by relating the explicandum (e.g., the postpartum sex taboo) to one or more other variables (e.g., a low-protein diet). We also want to know why such associations exist. Why do societies with low-protein diets have long postpartum sex taboos? Scientists formulate theories to explain the correlations they observe.

A **theory** is an explanatory framework that helps us understand *why* (something exists). Returning to the postpartum sex taboo, why might societies with low-protein diets develop this taboo? Whiting's theory is that the taboo is adaptive; it helps people survive and reproduce in certain environments. With too little protein in their diets, babies may develop a protein-deficiency disease called kwashiorkor. But if the mother delays her next pregnancy, her current baby, by breast-feeding longer, has a better chance to survive. Whiting suggests that parents may be unconsciously or consciously aware that having another baby too soon might jeopardize the survival of the first one. Thus, they avoid sex for more than a year after the birth of the first baby. When such abstinence becomes institutionalized, everyone is expected to respect the taboo.

A theory is an explanatory framework containing a series of statements. An association simply states an observed relationship between two or more known variables. Parts of a theory, by con-

This child's bloated body is due to protein malnutrition. This condition, known as *kwashiorkor*, comes from a West African word meaning "one-two." This refers to the practice in some societies of abruptly weaning one infant when a second one is born. With no mother's milk, the first baby may get no protein at all. What are some cultural ways of fending off kwashiorkor?

value of a theory is to promote new understanding. A theory can suggest patterns, connections, or relationships that may be confirmed by new research. Whiting's theory, for example, suggests hypotheses for future researchers to test. Because the theory proposes that the postpartum taboo is adaptive under certain conditions, one might hypothesize that certain changes would lead the taboo to disappear. By adopting birth control, for instance, families could space births without avoiding intercourse. So, too, might the taboo disappear if babies started receiving protein supplements, which would reduce the threat of kwashiorkor.

Although theories can't be proved, they can be rejected. The method of *falsification* (showing a theory to be wrong) is our main way of evaluating theories. If a theory is true, certain predictions should stand up to tests designed to disprove them. Theories that haven't been disproved are accepted (for the time being at least) because the available evidence seems to support them.

What is acceptable evidence that an explanation is probably right? Cases that have been personally selected by a researcher don't provide an acceptable test of a hypothesis or theory. (Imagine that Whiting had combed the ethnographic literature and chosen to cite only those societies that supported his theory.) Ideally, hypothesis testing should be done using a sample of cases that have been selected randomly from some statistical universe. (Whiting did this in choosing his cross-cultural sample.) The relevant variables should be measured reliably, and the strength and significance of the results should be evaluated by using legitimate statistical methods (Bernard 1994).

trast, may be difficult or impossible to observe or to know directly. With Whiting's theory, for example, it would be hard to determine whether people developed the sex taboo because they recognized that it would give babies a better chance to survive. Typically, some elements of a theory are unobservable (at least at present). In contrast, statistical associations are based entirely on observations (Ember and Ember 1996).

If an association is tested and found to recur again and again, we may consider it proved. Theories, by contrast, are unprovable. Although much evidence may support them, their truth isn't established with certainty. Many of the concepts and ideas in theories aren't directly observable or verifiable. Thus, scientists may try to explain how light behaves by postulating that it consists of "photons," which can't be observed even with the most powerful microscope. The photon is a "theoretical construct," something that can't be seen or verified directly (Ember and Ember 1996).

Why should we bother with theories if we can't prove them? According to the Embers, the main

Understanding Ourselves Science is a powerful tool for understanding ourselves. Properly, science isn't rigid or dogmatic; scientists recognize the tentativeness and uncertainty of knowledge and understanding, which they try to improve and enhance. Working to confirm laws, refine theories, and provide accurate explanations, scientists strive to be objective. Science relies on unbiased methods, such as random sampling, impartial analytic techniques, and standard statistical tests. But complete objectivity is impossible. There is always observer bias—that is, the presence of the scientist and his or her tools and methods always affects the outcome of an experiment, observation, or analysis. Through their very presence, anthropologists influence the living people and social conditions they study, as do survey researchers when they phrase questions in certain ways. Statisticians have designed techniques to measure and control for observer bias, but observer bias can't be eliminated totally. As scientists, we can only strive for objectivity and impartiality. Science, which has many limitations, certainly is not the only way we have to understand ourselves. Nevertheless, its goals of objectivity and impartiality help distinguish science from ways of knowing that are more biased, more rigid, and more dogmatic.

Summary

1. Anthropology is the holistic and comparative study of humanity. It is the systematic exploration of human biological and cultural diversity. Examining the origins of, and changes in, human biology and culture, anthropology provides explanations for similarities and differences. The four subfields of general anthropology are (socio)cultural, archaeological, biological, and linguistic. All consider variation in time and space. Each also examines adaptation—the process by which organisms cope with environmental stresses.

2. Cultural forces mold human biology, including our body types and images. Societies have particular standards of physical attractiveness. They also have specific ideas about what activities, for example, various sports, are appropriate for males and females.

3. Cultural anthropology explores the cultural diversity of the present and the recent past. Archaeology reconstructs cultural patterns, often of prehistoric populations. Biological anthropology documents diversity involving fossils, genetics, growth and development, bodily responses, and nonhuman primates. Linguistic anthropology considers diversity among languages. It also studies how speech changes in social situations and over time. Anthropology has two dimensions: academic and applied. The latter uses anthropological knowledge and methods to identify and solve social problems.

4. Concerns with biology, society, culture, and language link anthropology to many other fields—sciences and humanities. Anthropologists study art, music, and literature across cultures. But their concern is more with the creative expressions of common people than with arts designed for elites. Anthropologists examine creators and products in their social context. Sociologists traditionally study urban and industrial populations, whereas anthropologists have focused on rural, nonindustrial peoples. Psychological anthropology views human psychology in the context of social and cultural variation.

5. As scientists, anthropologists attempt to identify and explain cultural differences and similarities and to build theory about how social and cultural systems work. Scientists strive to improve understanding by testing hypotheses—suggested explanations. Explanations rely on associations and theories. An association is an observed relationship between variables. A theory is more general, suggesting or implying associations and attempting to explain them.

Key Terms

anthropology The study of the human species and its immediate ancestors.

applied anthropology The application of anthropological data, perspectives, theory, and methods to identify, assess, and solve contemporary social problems.

archaeological anthropology The study of human behavior and cultural patterns and processes through the culture's material remains.

biological anthropology The study of human biological variation in time and space; includes evolution, genetics, growth and development, and primatology.

cultural anthropology The study of human society and culture; describes, analyzes, interprets, and explains social and cultural similarities and differences.

culture Distinctly human; transmitted through learning; traditions and customs that govern behavior and beliefs.

ethnography Field work in a particular culture.

ethnology Cross-cultural comparison; the comparative study of ethnographic data, of society, and of culture.

food production Cultivation of plants and domestication (stockbreeding) of animals; first developed 10,000 to 12,000 years ago.

general anthropology The field of anthropology as a whole, consisting of cultural, archaeological, biological, and linguistic anthropology.

holistic Interested in the whole of the human condition: past, present, and future; biology, society, language, and culture.

linguistic anthropology The descriptive, comparative, and historical study of language and of linguistic similarities and differences in time, space, and society.

physical anthropology See biological anthropology.

science A systematic field of study or body of knowledge that aims, through experiment, observation, and deduction, to produce reliable explanations of phenomena, with reference to the material and physical world.

sociolinguistics Investigates relationships between social and linguistic variations.

theory An explanatory framework, containing a series of statements, that helps us understand *why* (something exists); theories suggest patterns, connections, and relationships that may be confirmed by new research.

CRITICAL THINKING QUESTIONS

For more self testing, see the self quizzes

mhhe com /kottak

1. Which do you think is more unique about anthropology: its holism or its comparative perspective? Can you think of other fields that are holistic and/or comparative?

2. Besides race and gender, what are some other areas in which anthropology's biocultural, four-field approach might shed light on current issues and debates? Would sexuality be such an area?

3. Many other disciplines are limited by their focus on powerful people and elites. How have your professors in other classes tried to justify, or compensate for, such limitations?

4. Besides the examples given in this chapter, think of some other problems or issues in the modern world to which applied anthropology might contribute.

5. What are some theories, as defined here, that you routinely use to understand the world?

Atlas Questions

Look at Map 1, "World Topography."

1. Which continent is most mountainous?

2. What are plateaus, and where are they located?

3. Which continent is least diverse in terms of terrains?

Suggested Additional Readings

Clifford, J.

1988   *The Predicament of Culture: Twentieth-Century Ethnography, Literature, and Art.* Cambridge, MA: Harvard University Press. Literary evaluation of classic and modern anthropologists and discussion of issues of ethnographic authority.

Endicott, K. M., and R. Welsch

2001   *Taking Sides: Clashing Views on Controversial Issues in Anthropology.* Guilford, CT: McGraw-Hill/Dushkin. Thirty-eight anthropologists offer opposing viewpoints on 19 polarizing issues, including ethical dilemmas.

Fagan, B. M.

2001   *People of the Earth: An Introduction to World Prehistory,* 11th ed. Upper Saddle River, NJ: Prentice-Hall. Introduction to the archaeological study of prehistoric societies, using examples from all areas.

2002   *Archeology: A Brief Introduction,* 8th ed. Upper Saddle River, NJ: Prentice-Hall. Introduction to archaeological theory, techniques, and approaches, including field survey, excavation, and analysis of materials.

Geertz, C.

1995   *After the Fact: Two Countries, Four Decades, One Anthropologist.* Cambridge, MA: Harvard University Press. A prominent cultural anthropologist reflects on his work in Morocco and Indonesia.

Harris, M.

1989   *Our Kind: Who We Are, Where We Came From, Where We Are Going.* New York: HarperCollins. Clearly written survey of the origins of humans, culture, and major sociopolitical institutions.

Marcus, G. E., and M. M. J. Fischer

1999   *Anthropology as Cultural Critique: An Experimental Moment in the Human Sciences,* 2nd ed. Chicago: University of Chicago Press. Different types of ethnographic accounts as forms of writing, a vision of modern anthropology, and a consideration of anthropologists' public and professional roles.

Nash, D.

1999   *A Little Anthropology,* 3rd ed. Upper Saddle River, NJ: Prentice-Hall. Short introduction to societies and cultures, with comments on developing nations and modern America.

Podolefsky, A., and P. J. Brown, eds.

2002   *Applying Anthropology: An Introductory Reader,* 7th ed. Boston: McGraw-Hill. Essays focusing on anthropology's relevance to contemporary life; a readable survey of the current range of activities in applied anthropology.

Wolf, E. R.

1982   *Europe and the People without History.* Berkeley: University of California Press. Influential and award-winning study of the relation between Europe and various nonindustrial populations.

INTERNET EXERCISES

1. News in Anthropology: Look at Texas A&M University's "Anthropology in the News," **http://www.tamu.edu/anthropology/news.html,** which contains links to articles relevant to anthropology.

   a. After reading the chapter in the textbook and reading some recent news articles, do you think anthropology is more or less relevant to your life?

   b. Look at the variety of topics discussed. Are the connections between the articles and anthropology clear to you? Were they clear to you before you read this chapter?

   c. Examine the first 10 articles. Which subfield of anthropology does each article relate to most closely?

   d. Browse the list of article titles. What are some of the current hot topics in the news about anthropology?

2. Careers in Anthropology: Go to the American Anthropological Association's Jobs Page (**http://aaanet.jobcontrolcenter.com/search/results/**) and Northern Kentucky's list of organizations in their area hiring anthropologists (**http://www.nku.edu/~anthro/careers.html**).

   a. What kinds of organizations are hiring anthropologists?

   b. What kinds of qualifications are these employers looking for? Do they require a graduate degree, or are they seeking people with an undergraduate degree in anthropology?

   c. What subfields are being sought by employers?

Note that these are just two job listing pages on the Web, and there are many others. If you have an interest in a field of anthropology that is not listed on these pages, use a web search engine to research what kinds of jobs are available. A good place to start is **http://www.aaanet.org/careers.htm** for more information on careers in anthropology.

See Chapter 1 at your McGraw-Hill Online Learning Center for additional review and interactive exercises.

2

APPLYING ANTHROPOLOGY?

Overview

In what ways is anthropology useful? What kind of public service role should it play? In a host of different settings anthropology is "applied" every day—used to identify and solve social problems. Applied anthropologists work for governments, agencies, and businesses. One goal of applied anthropology is to identify needs for change that local people perceive. A second goal is to work with those people to design culturally appropriate change. A third goal is to protect local people and cultural resources from harmful policies, including destructive development schemes.

An anthropologist's foremost ethical responsibility is to the people, species, and materials he or she studies. This responsibility, anthropology's "prime directive," entails respecting the well-being of humans and nonhuman primates, avoiding harm to them, and working for the conservation of the archaeological, fossil, and historical records.

Applied anthropology proceeds in all four subfields. Medical anthropology links biological and

---

Chapter Outline

The Role of the Applied Anthropologist

Ethics and Anthropology

Academic and Applied Anthropology

    Theory and Practice

Anthropology and Education

Urban Anthropology

    Urban versus Rural

Medical Anthropology

Anthropology and Business

Careers in Anthropology

---

cultural anthropology. Other domains of applied anthropology include educational, urban, and business anthropology. These domains have theoretical as well as applied dimensions. Medical anthropologists study disease and health-care systems cross-culturally. Although modern Western medicine has a scientific basis, it is also a cultural system with many elements based on custom rather than science. Educational anthropologists work in classrooms, homes, neighborhoods, and other settings relevant to education. Urban anthropologists study problems and policies involving city life and urbanization.

For business, key aspects of anthropology include ethnography and observation as ways of gathering data, cross-cultural expertise, and a focus on cultural diversity. Anthropology's comparative outlook, long-standing Third World focus, and cultural relativism offer a background for overseas work. A focus on culture and diversity is also valuable for work in North America.

Buried on a Hillside, Clues to Terror

New York Times News Brief

by Malcolm W. Browne

February 23, 1999

The news account that opened Chapter 1 described ways in which anthropology can be applied in a business context. Anthropology has many other "applications"—playing a public service role and being used to identify and solve various kinds of social problems. Applied anthropologists work for governments, agencies, and local communities, as well as for businesses. Some of anthropology's applications, while useful, can be very grim. This article describes research in Guatemala by biological and archaeological anthropologists, who also have been able to draw on the knowledge of cultural and linguistic anthropologists working in the same area. In 1982, some 376 villagers were massacred in the village of San Francisco de Nenton (Figure 2.1). Seventeen years later, scientific inquiry began to expose material evidence of that atrocity. This village's fate was common throughout Guatemala in the 1980s, as the government, with the support of the United States, sought to crush rebel guerrilla groups.

SAN FRANCISCO DE NENTON, Guatemala—On the morning of July 17, 1982, a convoy of army trucks made its way up a nearly impassable trail to this remote Mayan Indian hamlet and unloaded a company of troops . . . What happened next was a butchery that left all but four of the village's inhabitants dead and all the buildings razed . . . The rampaging troops killed all they found, shooting some villagers, blowing some up with grenades, hacking some to death, burning some or crushing them under the walls of falling buildings.

Relatives and acquaintances of the victims compiled a list of 376 villagers believed to have perished. For 17 years there had been no serious effort to check this list or details of the massacre by independent means, but finally the light of scientific inquiry has begun to expose material evidence of the atrocity . . .

But the tally of dead and missing victims of Guatemala's reign of terror is far from complete, and a band of volunteer forensic anthropologists, acting with the government's blessing, has set out to decipher a few of the massacre sites, gathering

One applied anthropology career is in forensics, as in Guatemala City's Institute for Forensic Anthropology. Identification of war victims, such as those uncovered at San Francisco de Nenton, proceeds here in 1997.

evidence from shattered bones, spent bullets and domestic objects including the pitiful remnants of children's clothing.

"We have absolutely no political objectives," said Fredy A. Peccerelli, a forensic anthropologist who heads the Foundation for Forensic Anthropology of Guatemala. "What we're attempting to do is check the accounts of witnesses and wherever possible to apply the techniques of forensic science to set the record straight. We examine massacre sites using many of the same techniques police use at crime scenes." . . .

In the San Francisco project as in dozens of other projects involving massacre sites in Guatemala, the group has had support and guidance from Dr. Clyde Collins Snow, a 71-year-old forensic anthropologist who lives in Norman, Okla. Dr. Snow, virtually a

Figure 2.1   Location of San Francisco de Nenton.

legend among forensic experts, has investigated massacres in 20 countries in Latin America, Africa, the Balkans and Asia . . .

The place where San Francisco de Nenton stood covers a cluster of picturesque hills a few miles south of the Mexican border. Adorned by an ancient Mayan pyramid, the site would make a lovely picnic ground.

But just beneath the grassy surface lies the horror the forensic team is unearthing, as it measures,

photographs, and catalogues the grim remnants before transporting them to Mr. Peccerelli's combination home and laboratory in Guatemala City. There, the bones will be X-rayed and further examined.

At one of a half-dozen burial sites discovered at San Francisco de Nenton so far, Renaldo Acevedo, a Guatemalan anthropologist, paused to look into a shallow pit where he and several colleagues had been digging . . .

A cluster of little bones covered by the faded but still colorful clothing of an adult Indian woman lay exposed.

Dr. Snow carefully dislodged one of several jawbones in the pit and held it close to his glasses. Speaking carefully in a slow Texas drawl as if addressing a tape recorder in the Oklahoma City morgue where he often works, he said:

"This is the site of a house said to have belonged to one Felipe Sylvestre. We have here a juvenile skull with several fractures, probably post-mortem. Two of the teeth are deciduous but one molar has erupted. This child was between 6 and 7 years old. Sex undetermined, but may be inferred from laboratory measurements and a statistical computer program called discriminant function analysis." . . .

A hundred yards away, working with a dental pick and toothbrush, Claudia Rivera and several other Guatemalan archeologists were excavating the village magistrate's office. So far, they had found skull parts and jaws of 11 bodies.

After a painstaking process of sorting and matching, the first batches of bones and artifacts were packed in plastic bags and cardboard cartons. The team's pickup truck doubles as a hearse, transporting the forensic treasure through the bandit-infested Guatemalan highlands to Mr. Peccerelli's laboratory in Guatemala City. There the skeletons are being laid out on tables for closer scrutiny and measurement.

"It's much the same as excavating an archeological site," Ms. Rivera said. "As the years pass, everything in a site like this decays, and it gets harder to interpret, just as ancient sites are hard to interpret. But for us this is not academic archeology. This place—how shall I say?—it has special meaning for us."

Forensic teams sometimes make as many as 200 skeletal measurements in pursuing identities. For example, slight disparities in the length of the radius and ulna arm bones can reveal a person's handedness. Another useful gauge is the degree of fusion between two adjoining pelvic bones (the pubic symphysis), which indicates an adult's age quite accurately. The ratio of an eye socket's width to its height, the distance between brow ridges, the width of nose bridges and many other facial characteristics can suggest kinships that help in tracing relatives.

In cases where relatives (and money) are available, DNA analysis is a powerful identification tool, Dr. Snow said. Even in badly decayed skeletons,

hard shells of dentine usually protect the pulp cavities of teeth, preserving the DNA inside.

SOURCE: "Buried on a Hillside, Clues to Terror," by Malcolm W. Browne, February 23, 1999, www.nytimes.com.

See the OLC Internet Exercises

/kottak

Forensic anthropology, as discussed in this article, is one form of **applied anthropology**—the application of anthropological perspectives, theory, methods, and data—in this case from all four subfields—to identify, assess, and solve social problems. As Erve Chambers (1987, p. 309) states it, applied anthropology is the "field of inquiry concerned with the relationships between anthropological knowledge and the uses of that knowledge in the world beyond anthropology." As was mentioned in Chapter 1, anthropology's foremost professional organization, the American Anthropological Association (AAA), recognizes that anthropology has two dimensions: (1) academic anthropology and (2) practicing or applied anthropology.

There are two important professional groups of applied anthropologists (also called **practicing anthropologists**). The older is the independent Society for Applied Anthropology (SfAA), founded in 1941. The second, the National Association for the Practice of Anthropology (NAPA), was established as a unit of the American Anthropological Association in 1983. (Many people belong to both groups.) Practicing anthropologists work (regularly or occasionally, full or part time) for nonacademic clients. These clients include governments, development agencies, nongovernmental organizations (NGOs), tribal and ethnic associations, interest groups, businesses, and social-service and educational agencies. Applied anthropologists work for groups that promote, manage, and assess programs aimed at influencing human social conditions. The scope of applied anthropology includes change and development abroad and social problems and policies in North America.

Applied anthropologists come from all four subfields. Biological anthropologists work in public health, nutrition, genetic counseling, substance abuse, epidemiology, aging, and mental illness. They apply their knowledge of human anatomy and physiology to the improvement of automobile

Supervised by archaeologists from India, with funding from the United Nations, these workers are cleaning and restoring the front facade of Cambodia's historic Angkor Wat temple. To decide what needs saving, and to preserve significant information about the past even when sites cannot be saved, is the work of cultural resource management (CRM).

safety standards and to the design of airplanes and spacecraft. In forensic work, biological anthropologists help the police identify skeletal remains. The account you just read shows how forensic biological and archaeological anthropologists reconstruct crimes by analyzing physical evidence.

Applied archaeology, usually called *public archaeology,* includes such activities as cultural resource management, contract archaeology, public educational programs, and historic preservation. An important role for public archaeology has been created by legislation requiring evaluation of sites threatened by dams, highways, and other construction activities. To decide what needs saving, and to preserve significant information about the past when sites cannot be saved, is the work of **cultural resource management** (CRM). CRM involves not only preserving sites but allowing their destruction if they are not significant. The "management" part of the term refers to the evaluation and decision-making process. If additional information is needed to make decisions, then survey or excavation may be done. CRM funding comes from federal, state, and local governments and from developers who must comply with preservation regulations. Cul-

tural resource managers typically work for federal, state, or county agencies. Applied cultural anthropologists sometimes work with the public archaeologists, assessing the human problems generated by the proposed change and determining how they can be reduced.

Cultural anthropologists work with social workers, businesspeople, advertising professionals, factory workers, nurses, physicians, gerontologists, mental-health professionals, school personnel, and economic development experts. Linguistic anthropology, particularly sociolinguistics, aids education. Knowledge of linguistic differences is important in an increasingly multicultural society whose populace grows up speaking many languages and dialects. Because linguistic differences may affect children's schoolwork and teachers' evaluations, many schools of education now require courses in sociolinguistics.

The Role of the Applied Anthropologist

By instilling an appreciation for human diversity, anthropology combats *ethnocentrism*—the tendency to view one's own culture as superior and to apply one's own cultural values in judging the behavior and beliefs of people raised in other cultures. This broadening, educational role affects the knowledge, values, and attitudes of people exposed to anthropology. Now we focus on the question: What contributions can anthropology make in identifying and solving problems stirred up by contemporary currents of economic, social, and cultural change?

Anthropologists have held three different positions about applying anthropology—using it to identify and solve social problems. People who hold the **ivory tower view** contend that anthropologists should avoid practical matters and concentrate on research, publication, and teaching. Those who favor what Ralph Piddington (1970) has called the **schizoid view** think that anthropologists should help carry out, but not make or criticize, policy. In this view, personal "value judgments" should be kept strictly separate from scientific investigation. The third view is **advocacy.** Its proponents assert that precisely because anthropologists are experts on human problems and social change and because they study, understand, and respect cultural values, they should make policy affecting people. In this view, proper roles for applied anthropologists include (1) identifying needs for change that local people perceive, (2) working with those people to design culturally appropriate and socially sensitive change, and (3) protecting local people from harmful policies and projects that threaten them.

I join many other anthropologists in favoring advocacy. I share the belief that no one is better qualified to propose and evaluate guidelines for society than are those who study anthropology. To be effective advocates, anthropologists must present their views clearly, thoughtfully, and forcefully to policy makers and the public. Many anthropologists do serve as social commentators and problem solvers, and as policy makers, advisers, and evaluators. We express our policy views in publications and lectures and through professional associations such as the Society for Applied Anthropology and the National Association of Practicing Anthropologists.

In this 1985 photo, Robert Goizueta (on the left), who then chaired the Board and served as CEO of the Coca-Cola Company, toasts New Coke. Despite what we read and hear frequently, "new" isn't necessarily "improved." Have you sipped any New Coke lately?

Understanding Ourselves   Is change good? American culture seems to think so. "New and improved" is a slogan we hear all the time—a lot more often than "old reliable." But new isn't always improved. People often resist change, as the Coca Cola Company (TCCC) discovered several years ago when it changed the formula of its premium soft drink and introduced "New Coke." When hordes of customers protested, TCCC brought back old, familiar, reliable Coke under the name "Coca Cola Classic," which thrives today. New Coke is history.

TCCC tried a *top-down change* (a change decided and initiated at the top of a hierarchy rather than by the communities affected by the change). The people, that is, customers, didn't ask TCCC to change its product; executives made the decision to change Coke's taste. Executives are to business decisions as policy makers are to social change programs; both stand at the top of organizations that provide goods and services to people. Smart executives and policy makers listen to people to try to determine *locally-based demand*—what the people want. What's working well (assuming it's not discriminatory or illegal) should be maintained, encouraged, and strengthened. What's

wrong, and how can it be fixed? What changes do the people—and which people—want? How can conflicting wishes and needs be accommodated? Applied anthropologists help answer these questions, which are crucial in understanding whether change is needed, and how it will work.

There was a time—the 1940s in particular—when most anthropologists focused on the application of their knowledge. During World War II, American anthropologists studied Japanese and German "culture at a distance" in an attempt to predict the behavior of the enemies of the United States. After the war, Americans did applied anthropology in the Pacific, working to gain native cooperation with American policies in various trust territories.

Modern applied anthropology differs from an earlier version that mainly served the goals of colonial regimes. Application was a central concern of early anthropology in Great Britain (in the context of colonialism) and the United States (in the context of Native American policy). Before turning to the new, we should consider some dangers of the old.

In the context of the British empire, specifically its African colonies, Malinowski (1929a) proposed that "practical anthropology" (his term for colonial applied anthropology) should focus on westernization, the diffusion of European culture into tribal societies. He contended that anthropologists should and could avoid politics by concentrating on facts and processes. However, he was actually expressing his own political views, because he questioned neither the legitimacy of colonialism nor the anthropologist's role in making it work. For instance, Malinowski saw nothing wrong with aiding colonial regimes by studying land tenure and land use, to decide how much of their land natives should keep and how much Europeans should get. Malinowski's views exemplify a historical association between anthropology, particularly in Europe, and colonialism (Maquet 1964).

Colonial anthropologists faced, as do some of their modern counterparts (Escobar 1991, 1994), problems posed by their inability to set or influence policy and the difficulty of criticizing programs in which they have participated. Anthropology's professional organizations have addressed some of these problems by establishing codes of ethics and ethics committees. Also, as Tice (1997) notes, attention to such ethical issues is paramount in the teaching of applied anthropology today.

Ethics and Anthropology

As the main organization representing the breadth of anthropology (all four subfields, academic and applied dimensions), the American Anthropological Association believes that generating and appropriately using knowledge of the peoples of the world, past and present, is a worthy goal. The production of anthropological knowledge is a dynamic process involving different and ever-evolving approaches. The mission of the AAA is to advance anthropological research and encourage the spread of anthropological knowledge through publications, teaching, public education, and application. Part of that mission is to help educate AAA members about ethical obligations and challenges (http://www.aaanet.org).

As anthropologists conduct research and engage in other professional activities, ethical issues inevitably arise. Anthropologists have typically worked abroad, outside their own society. In the context of international contacts and cultural diversity, different value systems will meet, and often compete. To guide its members in making decisions involving ethics and values, the AAA offers a Code of Ethics. The most recent Code was approved in June 1998 and updated on March 31, 1999. The Code's preamble states that anthropologists have obligations to their scholarly field, to the wider society and culture, and to the human species, other species, and the environment. This Code's aim is to offer guidelines and to promote discussion and education. Although the AAA has investigated allegations of misconduct by anthropologists, it does not adjudicate such claims. The AAA also recognizes that anthropologists belong to multiple groups—including, perhaps, a family, a community, a religion, and other organizations—each of which may have its own ethical and moral rules. Because anthropologists can find themselves in complex situations and subject to more than one ethical code, the AAA Code provides a framework, not an ironclad formula, for making decisions.

The AAA wants its members to be attentive to ethical issues, and it urges anthropology departments to include ethical training in their curricula. The AAA Code addresses several contexts in which anthropologists work. Its main points about the ethical dimensions of research may be summarized.

Anthropologists should be open and honest about all dimensions of their research projects with funding agencies, colleagues, and all parties affected by the research. These parties should be informed about the purpose(s), potential impacts, and source(s) of support for the research. Anthropologists should disseminate the results of their research in an appropriate and timely way.

Researchers should not compromise anthropological ethics in order to conduct research. They should also pay attention to proper relations between themselves as guests and the host nations and communities where they work. The AAA does not advise anthropologists to avoid taking stands on issues. Indeed, the Code states that leadership in seeking to shape actions and policies may be as ethically justifiable as inaction.

Here are some of the headings and subheadings of the Code:

A. Responsibility to people and animals

1. The primary ethical obligation of the anthropologist is to the people, species, and materials they study. This obligation takes precedence over the goal of seeking new knowledge. It can also lead to the decision not to undertake, or to discontinue, research when ethical conflicts arise. This primary ethical obligation—anthropology's "prime directive"—entails:

   Avoiding harm or wrong.

   Understanding that the production of knowledge can have positive or negative effects on the people or animals worked with or studied.

   Respecting the well-being of humans and nonhuman primates.

   Working for the long-term conservation of the archaeological, fossil, and historical records.

   Consulting actively with the affected individuals or group(s), with the goal of establishing a working relationship that will benefit all parties.

2. Researchers must do all they can to preserve the safety, dignity, and privacy of the people with whom they work. Anthropologists working with animals should not endanger their safety, psychological well-being, or survival.

3. Anthropologists should determine whether their hosts wish to remain anonymous or to receive recognition, and should try to comply with those wishes. Researchers should make clear to research participants that, despite the best efforts of the anthropologist, anonymity may be compromised or recognition fail to materialize.

4. Researchers must obtain the *informed consent* of affected parties. That is, prior to their agreement to participate, people should be told about the purpose, nature, and procedures of the research and its potential impact on them. Informed consent (agreement to take part in the research) should be obtained from anyone providing information, owning materials being studied, or otherwise having an interest that might be impacted by the research.

Margaret Mead talks with a mother and child during a revisit to the Manus of the Admiralty Islands, one of the South Pacific societies where she worked and established long-term, ongoing relationships. Mead was known for her research on the impact of cultural diversity on childhood, adolescence, and gender roles.

Informed consent does not necessarily imply or require a written or signed form.

5. Researchers who develop ongoing relationships with individuals providing information or with hosts must continue to respect the obligations of openness and informed consent.

6. Anthropologists may gain personally from their work, but they should not exploit individuals, groups, animals, or cultural or biological materials. They should recognize their debt to the communities and societies in which they work and to the people with whom they work. They should reciprocate in appropriate ways.

B. Responsibility to scholarship and science

1. Anthropologists should attempt to identify potential ethical conflicts and dilemmas when preparing proposals, and as projects proceed.

2. Anthropologists are responsible for the integrity and reputation of their field, of

scholarship, and of science. They are subject to the general moral rules of scientific and scholarly conduct. They should not deceive or knowingly misrepresent (i.e., fabricate evidence, falsify, plagiarize). They should not attempt to prevent reporting of misconduct, or obstruct the scholarly research of others.

3. Anthropologists should do all they can to preserve opportunities for future researchers to follow them to the field.

4. To the extent possible, anthropologists should disseminate their findings to the scientific and scholarly community.

5. Anthropologists should consider all reasonable requests for access to their data and materials for purposes of research. They should preserve their data for use by posterity.

C. Responsibility to the public

1. Anthropologists should strive to ensure that their findings are contextualized properly and used responsibly. Anthropologists should also consider the social and political implications of their conclusions. They should be honest about their qualifications and philosophical and political biases. They must be alert to possible harm their information might cause people with whom they work, or colleagues.

2. Anthropologists may move beyond disseminating research results to a position of advocacy. This is an individual decision, but not an ethical responsibility.

D. Ethics Pertaining to Applied Anthropology

1. The same ethical guidelines apply to all anthropological work—academic and applied. Applied anthropologists should use their results appropriately (i.e., publication, teaching, program and policy development) within a reasonable time. Applied anthropologists should be honest about their skills and intentions. They should monitor the effects of their work on everyone affected.

2. In dealings with employers, applied anthropologists should be honest about their qualifications, abilities, and goals. The applied anthropologist should review the aims and interests of the prospective employer, taking into consideration the employer's past activities and future goals. Applied anthropologists should not accept conditions contrary to professional ethics.

The full Code of Ethics, which is abbreviated and paraphrased here, is available at the AAA website (http://www.aaanet.org).

Academic and Applied Anthropology

Previously, we examined the role of applied anthropology during and immediately after World War II. Applied anthropology did not disappear during the 1950s and 1960s, but academic anthropology did most of the growing after World War II. The baby boom, which began in 1946 and peaked in 1957, fueled expansion of the American educational system and thus of academic jobs. New junior, community, and four-year colleges opened, and anthropology became a standard part of the college curriculum. During the 1950s and 1960s, most American anthropologists were college professors, although some still worked in agencies and museums.

This era of academic anthropology continued through the early 1970s. Especially during the Vietnam War, undergraduates flocked to anthropology classes to learn about other cultures. Students were especially interested in Southeast Asia, whose indigenous societies were being disrupted by war. Many anthropologists protested the superpowers' apparent disregard for non-Western lives, values, customs, and social systems.

During the 1970s, and increasingly thereafter, although most anthropologists still worked in academia, others found jobs with international organizations, government, business, hospitals, and schools. This shift toward application, though only partial, has benefited the profession. It has forced anthropologists to consider the wider social value and implications of their research.

THEORY AND PRACTICE

One of the most valuable tools in applying anthropology is the ethnographic method. Ethnographers study societies firsthand, living with and

During the Vietnam War, many anthropologists protested the superpowers' disregard for the values, customs, social systems, and lives of Third World peoples. Several anthropologists (including the author) attended this all-night Columbia University "teach-in" against the war in 1965.

gram or project always has multiple effects, some of which are unforeseen. For example, dozens of economic development projects intended to increase productivity through irrigation have worsened public health by creating waterways where diseases thrive. In an American example of unintended consequences, a program aimed at enhancing teachers' appreciation of cultural differences led to ethnic stereotyping (Kleinfeld 1975). Specifically, Native American students did not welcome teachers' frequent comments about their Indian heritage. The students felt set apart from their classmates and saw this attention to their ethnicity as patronizing and demeaning.

Anthropology and Education

Anthropology and education refers to anthropological research in classrooms, homes, and neighborhoods (see Spindler 2000). Some of the most interesting research has been done in classrooms, where anthropologists observe interactions among teachers, students, parents, and visitors. Jules Henry's classic account of the American elementary school classroom (1955) shows how students learn to conform to and compete with their peers. Anthropologists also follow students from classrooms into their homes and neighborhoods, viewing children as total cultural creatures whose enculturation and attitudes toward education belong to a context that includes family and peers.

Sociolinguists and cultural anthropologists work side by side in education research, for example, in a study of Puerto Rican seventh-graders in the urban Midwest (Hill-Burnett 1978). In classrooms, neighborhoods, and homes, anthropologists uncovered some misconceptions by teachers. For example, the teachers had mistakenly assumed that Puerto Rican parents valued education less than did non-Hispanics. However, in-depth interviews revealed that the Puerto Rican parents valued it more.

Researchers also found that certain practices were preventing Hispanics from being adequately educated. For example, the teachers' union and the board of education had agreed to teach "English as a foreign language." However, they had not provided bilingual teachers to work with Spanish-

learning from ordinary people. Ethnographers are participant-observers, taking part in the events they study in order to understand local thought and behavior. Applied anthropologists use ethnographic techniques in both foreign and domestic settings. Other "expert" participants in social-change programs may be content to converse with officials, read reports, and copy statistics. However, the applied anthropologist's likely early request is some variant of "take me to the local people." We know that people must play an active role in the changes that affect them and that "the people" have information that "the experts" lack.

Anthropological theory—the body of findings and generalizations of the subdisciplines—also guides applied anthropology. Anthropology's holistic perspective—its interest in biology, society, culture, and language—permits the evaluation of many issues that affect people. Theory aids practice, and application fuels theory. As we compare social-change policy and programs, our understanding of cause and effect increases. We add new generalizations about culture change to those discovered in traditional and ancient cultures.

Anthropology's systemic perspective recognizes that changes don't occur in a vacuum. A pro-

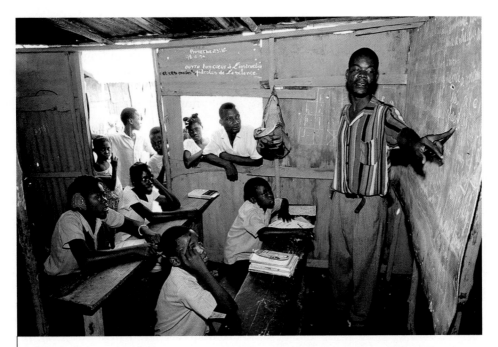

These kids get a basic education in Cite Soleil, a slum of Port-au-Prince, Haiti. What do you see here that differs from classrooms in your country? Do you think these differences would affect how you would do research in Haiti? Assume this classroom would be part of your study.

speaking students. The school started assigning all students (including non-Hispanics) with low reading scores and behavior problems to the English-as-a-foreign-language classroom.

This educational disaster brought together a teacher who spoke no Spanish, children who barely spoke English, and a group of English-speaking students with reading and behavior problems. The Spanish speakers were falling behind not just in reading but in all subjects. They could at least have kept up in the other subjects if a Spanish speaker had been teaching them science, social studies, and math until they were ready for English-language instruction in those areas.

A dramatic illustration of the relevance of applied sociolinguistics to education comes from Ann Arbor, Michigan (Figure 2.2). In 1979, the parents of several black students at the predominantly white Dr. Martin Luther King Jr. Elementary School sued the Board of Education. They claimed that their children faced linguistic discrimination in the classroom.

The children, who lived in a neighborhood housing project, spoke Black English Vernacular

See the OLC Internet Exercises

/kottak

(BEV) at home. At school, most had encountered problems with their classwork. Some had been labeled "learning-impaired" and placed in remedial reading courses. (Consider the embarrassment that children suffer and the effect on self-image of such labeling.)

The African-American parents and their attorney contended that the children had no intrinsic learning disabilities but simply did not understand everything their teachers said. Nor did their teachers always understand them. The lawyer argued that because BEV and Standard English (SE) are so similar, teachers often misinterpreted a child's correct pronunciation (in BEV) of an SE word as a reading error.

The children's attorney recruited several sociolinguists to testify on their behalf. The school board, by contrast, could not find a single qualified linguist to support its argument that there was no linguistic discrimination.

The judge ruled in favor of the children and ordered the following solution: Teachers at the King School had to attend a full-year course

In a diverse, multicultural populace, teachers should be sensitive to and knowledgeable about linguistic and cultural differences. Children need to be protected so that their ethnic or linguistic background is not used against them. That is what happens when a social variation is regarded as a learning disability.

Urban Anthropology

By 2025, the developing nations will account for 85 percent of the world's population, compared with 77 percent in 1992 (Stevens 1992). Solutions to future problems will depend increasingly on understanding non-Western cultural backgrounds. The fastest population growth rates are in the less developed countries, especially in urban areas. The world had only 16 cities with more than a million people in 1900, but there are more than 300 such cities today. By 2025, 60 percent of the global population will be urban, compared with 37 percent in 1990 (Stevens 1992). Rural migrants often move to slums, where they live in hovels without utilities and public sanitation facilities.

Interpret the World
Atlas Map 2

If current trends continue, urban population increase and the concentration of people in slums will be accompanied by rising rates of crime and water, air, and noise pollution. These problems will be most severe in the less-developed countries. Almost all (97 percent) of the projected world population increase will occur in developing countries, 34 percent in Africa alone (Lewis 1992). Map 2 in your atlas shows population growth rates worldwide; notice the very high growth rates in African countries. Although the rate of population increase is low in northern countries, such as the United States, Canada, and most European nations, global population growth will continue to affect the Northern Hemisphere, especially through international migration. There has been substantial recent migration to the United States and Canada from developing countries with high growth rates, such as India and Mexico. Can you

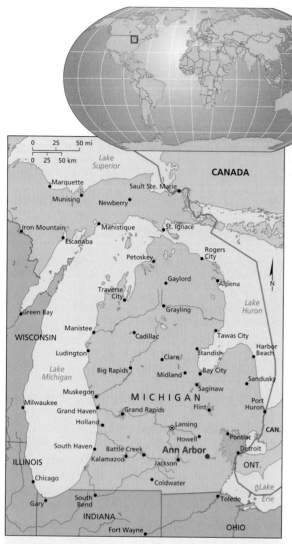

Figure 2.2 **Location of Ann Arbor, Michigan.**

designed to improve their knowledge of nonstandard dialects, particularly BEV. The judge did not advocate that the teachers learn to speak BEV or that the children do their assignments in BEV. The school's goal remained to teach the children to use SE, the standard dialect, correctly. Before this could be accomplished, however, teachers and students alike had to learn how to recognize the differences between these similar dialects. At the end of the year, most of the teachers interviewed in the local newspaper said the course had helped them.

identify other such countries (that is, those with high growth rates and significant out-migration) on Map 2?

As industrialization and urbanization spread globally, anthropologists increasingly study these processes and the social and health problems they create. Urban anthropology, which has theoretical (basic research) and applied dimensions, is the cross-cultural and ethnographic study of global urbanization and life in cities. The United States and Canada also have become popular arenas for urban anthropological research on topics such as ethnicity, poverty, class, and subcultural variations (Mullings 1987).

URBAN VERSUS RURAL

Recognizing that a city is a social context that is very different from a rural community, an early student of Third World urbanization, the anthropologist Robert Redfield, focused on contrasts between rural and urban life. He contrasted rural communities, whose social relations are on a face-to-face basis, with cities, where impersonality characterizes many aspects of life. Redfield (1941) proposed that urbanization be studied along a rural-urban continuum. He described differences in values and social relations in four sites that spanned such a continuum. In Mexico's Yucatán peninsula, Redfield compared an isolated Maya-speaking Indian community, a rural peasant village, a small provincial city, and a large capital. Several studies in Africa (Little 1971) and Asia were influenced by Redfield's view that cities are centers through which cultural innovations spread to rural and tribal areas.

In any nation, urban and rural represent different social systems. However, migrants bring rural social forms, practices, and beliefs to town. They also take back urban and national patterns when they visit, or move back permanently to, their villages of origin. Inevitably, the experiences and social units of rural areas affect adaptation to city life. Social organization based on *descent*

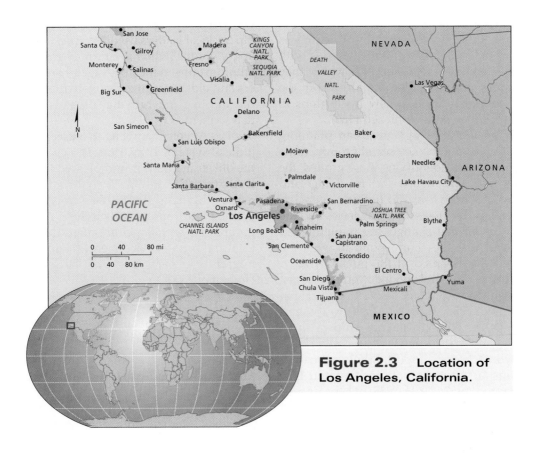

Figure 2.3 Location of Los Angeles, California.

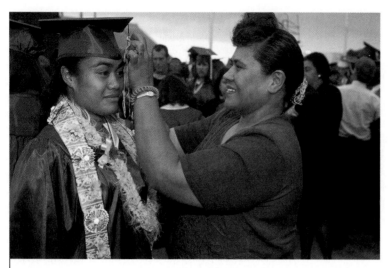

A Samoan mother adjusts the tassel of her daughter's cap as the teenager graduates from high school in Long Beach, California. California—Los Angeles specifically—has the largest Samoan immigrant community in the United States. Did your immigrant parents or grandparents settle in a city or a rural area?

The ideology of such associations is that of a gigantic kin group. The members call one another "brother" and "sister." As in an extended family, rich members help their poor relatives. When members fight among themselves, the group acts as judge. A member's improper behavior can lead to expulsion-an unhappy fate for a migrant in a large ethnically heterogeneous city.

Modern North American cities also have kin-based ethnic associations. One example comes from Los Angeles (Figure 2.3), which has the largest Samoan immigrant community (12,000 people) in the United States. Samoans in Los Angeles draw on their traditional system of *matai* (*matai* means chief; the *matai* system now refers to respect for elders) to deal with modern urban problems. One example: In 1992, a white policeman shot and killed two unarmed Samoan brothers. When a judge dismissed charges against the officer, local leaders used the *matai* system to calm angry youths (who have formed gangs, like other ethnic groups in the Los Angeles area). Clan leaders and elders organized a well-attended community meeting, in which they urged young members to be patient.

Los Angeles Samoans also used the American judicial system. They brought a civil case against the officer in question and pressed the U.S. Justice Department to initiate a civil-rights case in the matter (Mydans 1992*b*). One role for the urban applied anthropologist is to help relevant social groups deal with larger urban institutions, such as legal and social-service agencies with which recent migrants, in particular, may be unfamiliar (see Holtzman 2000).

groups—cohesive units whose members claim common ancestry—is fundamental to many rural African societies. Such organizing principles as descent provide migrants to African cities with coping mechanisms, for example, when they reside with or near extended kin already in the city. City folk also develop new institutions to meet specific urban needs (Mitchell 1966).

Applying anthropology to urban planning starts by identifying the key social groups in the urban context. After identifying those groups, the anthropologist elicits their wishes for change and helps translate those needs to funding agencies. The next step is to work with the agencies and the people to ensure that changes are implemented correctly and that they correspond to what the people said they wanted at the outset. African urban groups that an applied anthropologist would consult include ethnic associations, occupational groups, social clubs, religious groups, and burial societies. Through membership in these groups, urban Africans have wide networks of personal contacts and support. Ethnic or "tribal" associations are common both in West and East Africa (Banton 1957; Little 1965). These groups maintain links with, and provide cash support and urban lodging for, their rural relatives.

Medical Anthropology

Medical anthropology is both academic/theoretical and applied/practical. It is a field that includes both biological and sociocultural anthropologists. Medical anthropology is discussed in

See the
Virtual Exploration

mhhe
●com
/kottak

this chapter because of its many applications. Medical anthropologists examine such questions as: Which diseases affect different populations? How is illness socially constructed? How does one treat illness in effective and culturally appropriate ways?

This growing field considers the sociocultural context and implications of disease and illness (Helman 2001; Strathern and Stewart 1999). **Disease** refers to a scientifically identified health threat caused by a bacterium, virus, fungus, parasite, or other pathogen. Illness is a condition of poor health perceived or felt by an individual (Inhorn and Brown 1990). Cross-cultural research shows that perceptions of good and bad health, along with health threats and problems, are culturally constructed. Different ethnic groups and cultures recognize different illnesses, symptoms, and causes and have developed different healthcare systems and treatment strategies.

Disease also varies among cultures. Traditional and ancient foragers, because of their small numbers, mobility, and relative isolation from other groups, were not subject to most of the epidemic infectious diseases that affect agrarian and urban societies (Cohen and Armelagos 1984; Inhorn and Brown 1990). Epidemic diseases such as cholera, typhoid, and bubonic plague thrive in dense populations, and thus among farmers and city dwellers. The spread of malaria has been linked to population growth and deforestation associated with food production.

Certain diseases have spread with economic development. *Schistosomiasis* or bilharzia (liver flukes) is probably the fastest-spreading and most dangerous parasitic infection now known (Heyneman 1984). It is propagated by snails that live in ponds, lakes, and waterways, usually ones created by irrigation projects. A study done in a Nile Delta village in Egypt (Farooq 1966) illustrated the role of culture (religion) in the spread of schistosomiasis. The disease was more common among Muslims than among Christians because of an Islamic practice called *wudu,* ritual ablution (bathing) before prayer. The applied anthropology approach to reducing such diseases is to see if natives perceive a connection between the vector (e.g., snails in the water) and the disease, which can take years to develop. If they do not, such information

may be spread by enlisting active local groups and schools. With the worldwide diffusion of the electronic mass media, culturally appropriate public information campaigns have increased awareness and modified behavior that has public health consequences.

In eastern Africa, AIDS and other sexually transmitted diseases (STDs) have spread along highways, via encounters between male truckers and female prostitutes. STDs also are spread

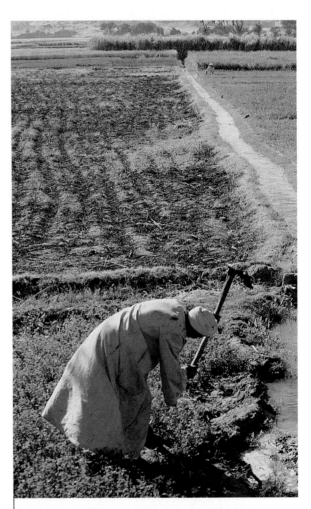

Schistosomiasis (liver flukes) is among the fastest spreading and most dangerous parasitic infections now known. It is propagated by snails that live in ponds, lakes, and waterways (often ones created by irrigation projects) such as this one in Luxor, Egypt. As an applied anthropologist, what would you do to cut the rate of infection?

through prostitution as young men from rural areas seek wage work in cities, labor camps, and mines. When the men return to their natal villages, they infect their wives (Larson 1989; Miller and Rockwell 1988). Cities are also prime sites of STD transmission in Europe, Asia, and North and South America (French 2002).

The kind and incidence of disease vary among societies, and cultures interpret and treat illness differently. Standards for sick and healthy bodies are cultural constructions that vary in time and space (Martin 1992). Still, all societies have what George Foster and Barbara Anderson (1978) call "disease-theory systems" to identify, classify, and explain illness. According to Foster and Anderson (1978), there are three basic theories about the causes of illness: personalistic, naturalistic, and emotionalistic. **Personalistic disease theories** blame illness on agents (often malicious), such as sorcerers, witches, ghosts, or ancestral spirits. **Naturalistic disease theories** explain illness in impersonal terms. One example is Western medicine or *biomedicine,* which aims to link illness to scientifically demonstrated agents that bear no personal malice toward their victims. Thus, Western medicine attributes illness to organisms (e.g., bacteria, viruses, fungi, or parasites), accidents, or toxic materials. Other naturalistic ethnomedical systems blame poor health on unbalanced body fluids. Many Latin cultures classify food, drink, and environmental conditions as "hot" or "cold." People believe their health suffers when they eat or drink hot or cold substances together or under inappropriate conditions. For example, one shouldn't drink something cold after a hot bath or eat a pineapple (a "cold" fruit) when one is menstruating (a "hot" condition).

Emotionalistic disease theories assume that emotional experiences cause illness. For example, Latin Americans may develop *susto,* or soul loss, an illness caused by anxiety or fright (Bolton 1981; Finkler 1985). Its symptoms include lethargy, vagueness, and distraction. Of course, modern psychoanalysis also focuses on the role of the emotions in physical and psychological well-being.

All societies have **health-care systems.** These consist of beliefs, customs, specialists, and techniques aimed at ensuring health and preventing, diagnosing, and curing illness. A society's illness-causation theory is important for treatment. When

illness has a personalistic cause, shamans and other magico-religious specialists may be good curers. They draw on varied techniques (occult and practical) that comprise their special expertise. A shaman may cure soul loss by enticing the spirit back into the body. Shamans may ease difficult childbirths by asking spirits to travel up the birth canal to guide the baby out (Lévi-Strauss 1967). A shaman may cure a cough by counteracting a curse or removing a substance introduced by a sorcerer.

All cultures have health-care specialists. If there is a "world's oldest profession" besides hunter and gatherer, it is curer, often a shaman. The curer's role has some universal features (Foster and Anderson 1978). Thus, curers emerge through a culturally defined process of selection (parental prodding, inheritance, visions, dream instructions) and training (apprentice shamanship, medical school). Eventually, the curer is certified by older practitioners and acquires a professional image. Patients believe in the skills of the curer, whom they consult and compensate.

Non-Western systems (traditional medicine) offer some lessons for Western medicine. For example, traditional practitioners may have more success treating certain forms of mental illness than psychotherapists do. Non-Western systems may explain mental illness by causes that are easier to identify and combat. Thus, it may be simpler to rid a body of a spirit possessor than to undo all the damage that a Freudian might attribute to an unresolved Oedipus complex.

Another reason non-Western therapy may succeed is that the mentally ill are diagnosed and treated in cohesive groups with the full support of their kin. Curing may be an intense community ritual in which the shaman heals by temporarily taking on and then rejecting the patient's illness (Lévi-Strauss 1967). In modern mental institutions, by contrast, no prior social ties link patients to each other or to doctors and nurses. Mental illness is viewed as the patient's individual burden. Psychotropic drugs are increasingly used, often effectively, to treat and control psychological disorders. However, for severe mental illness, the context of treatment may be one of isolation and alienation—separation of the afflicted person from society—rather than participation by a group in a common ritual.

What makes us sick? Maybe we can agree that germs, allergens, poor nutrition, advanced age, accidents, poisons, and environmental hazards contribute to poor health. But what about heat, cold, drafts, dryness, and humidity? What about physical activity or the lack thereof? And foods that don't go together, such as ice cream and vinegar or Coca Cola and tomato juice? How about spirits, ghosts, witches, and sorcerers?

If we're feeling sick, we often feel better once a label (diagnosis) is attached to our illness. In contemporary society, it's usually a physician who provides us with such a label—and maybe with a medicine that cures it or alleviates our suffering. In other contexts, a shaman or magico-religious specialist provides the diagnosis and treatment plan. We live in a world where alternative healthcare systems coexist, sometimes competing, sometimes complementing, one another. Never have people had access to such a wide range of choices in health care. In seeking good health and survival, it may be only natural for people to draw on alternative systems—acupuncture for one problem, chiropractic for another, medicine for a third, psychotherapy for a fourth, spiritual healing for a fifth. Think about the alternative treatment systems you may have used in the last year.

We should not lose sight, ethnocentrically, of the difference between **scientific medicine** and Western medicine per se (Lieban 1977). Despite advances in pathology, microbiology, biochemistry, surgery, diagnostic technology, and applications, many Western medical procedures have little justification in logic or fact. Overprescription of tranquilizers and drugs, unnecessary surgery, and the impersonality and inequality of the physician-patient relationship are questionable features of Western medical systems. Also, overuse of antibiotics, not just for people, but also in animal feed and antibacterial soaps, seems to be triggering an explosion of resistant microorganisms, which may pose a long-term global public health hazard.

Still, western medicine surpasses tribal treatment in many ways. Although medicines like quinine, coca, opium, ephedrine, and rauwolfia were discovered in nonindustrial societies, thousands of effective drugs are available today to treat myriad diseases. Preventive health care improved during the 20th century. Today's surgical procedures are safer and more effective than those of traditional societies.

But industrialization has spawned its own health problems. Modern stressors include noise, air, and water pollution; poor nutrition; dangerous machinery; impersonal work; isolation; poverty; homelessness; and substance abuse. Health problems in industrial nations are due as much to economic, social, political, and cultural factors as to pathogens. In modern North America, for example, poverty contributes to many illnesses. These include arthritis, heart conditions, back problems, and hearing and vision impairment. Poverty is also a factor in the differential spread of infectious diseases.

Medical anthropologists have served as cultural interpreters in public health programs, which must pay attention to native theories about the nature, causes, and treatment of illness. Successful health interventions cannot simply be forced on communities. They must fit into local cultures and be accepted by local people. When Western medicine is introduced, people usually retain many of their old methods while also accepting new ones (see Green 1987/1992). Native curers may go on treating certain conditions (like spirit possession), whereas M.D.s may deal with others. If both modern and traditional specialists are consulted and the patient is cured, the native

A traditional healer at work in Malaysia. What does this remind you of?

Background Information

STUDENT: Ann L. Bretnall

SUPERVISING PROFESSOR: David Himmelgreen

SCHOOL: University of South Florida

YEAR IN SCHOOL/MAJOR: Senior/Anthropology

FUTURE PLANS: After completion of master's in applied anthropology, work with the local social service agencies in community outreach projects

PROJECT TITLE: Establishing a Farmers Market for the Local Hispanic Community

Note how this essay links the worlds of commerce, nutrition, health, and social interaction. The comfortable and convivial atmosphere of the local farmers' market is an appropriate setting for applying anthropology—aimed at culturally appropriate education and innovation. As immigration has increased, work demands and ready access to fast foods have changed the nature of meals and diet among Latinos in the Tampa area. Ann Bretnall discusses her work organizing educational events and the participation of local community members in the farmer's market.

The Applied Anthropology program at the University of South Florida, in Tampa, gives students practical experience with community projects. The Project New Life-Good Health (Nueva Vida-Buena Salud) is one of many projects the Anthropology Department is currently working on. This project is designed to develop and implement a community-engaged nutrition and health education program targeting recently arrived Latino immigrant families. My project is to develop a church-based farmer's market for the local Hispanic community.

In recent years the Hispanic population of Hillsborough County, which includes Tampa, has significantly increased. Immigrants have arrived from Central and South America and from the Caribbean. According to U.S. Census Bureau data, the 1990 Hispanic population of Hillsborough County was 106,908, rising to 179,692 in 2000.

Project New Life-Good Health rests on two previous projects focusing on the local Hispanic community. Those projects were called "Acculturation and Nutritional Needs Assessment of Tampa" (ANNA-T) and "Promoting Adequate Nutrition" (PAN). The ANNA-T project investigated food consumption and physical activity patterns of recently arrived Latino immigrants. The research of ANNA-T helped to develop project PAN. PAN was a series of culturally tailored nutrition-education and disease-prevention seminars targeting low-income Latino families. Projects ANNA-T and PAN found there had been a significant change in diet, with a new emphasis on fast food and sodas and a reduced consumption of fresh fruits and vegetables. ANNA-T also discovered that lack of time and of social support were barriers to traditional family meals.

curer may get as much credit as or more credit than the physician.

A more personal treatment of illness that emulates the non-Western curer-patient-community relationship could probably benefit Western systems. Western medicine has tended to draw a rigid line between biological and psychological causation. Non-Western theories usually lack this sharp distinction, recognizing that poor health has intertwined physical, emotional, and social causes. The mind-body opposition is part of Western folk taxonomy, not of science.

Non-Western practitioners often treat symptoms, instead of seeking causes. Their aim—and often their result—is an immediate cure. Traditional curers often succeed with health problems that vendors, unlike the sometimes uncomfortable interactions with employees in a grocery store.

My work with the Project New Life-Good Health farmers' market involves organizing the resources necessary to implement farmers' market events. In interviews and observations, I have found genuine interest among community members and vendors. The literature I reviewed also confirms advantages to individuals involved in local farmers' markets. Efforts by community members to organize and establish the farmers' market as their own will be crucial to the success of the market as a permanent institution in their community.

To summarize, the goal of the farmers' market is to provide a venue to understand community needs, to educate, and to improve the nutrition and health of the local Hispanic community. This can be accomplished by ensuring the availability of some culturally specific foods and by introducing other healthful foods into the Hispanic diet. Our ongoing research will provide the local community with the resources to continue and manage the farmers' market as a positive and sustainable alternative within their local economy.

The goals of project New Life-Good Health are to: 1) develop a culturally appropriate nutrition-education and disease-prevention curriculum, 2) conduct a series of healthy-eating and disease-prevention seminars, and 3) develop a church-based farmers' market that includes nutrition-education and health-promotion activities for the larger community. Local farmers' markets have an open and informal setting, which provides a unique ambiance to the shopping experience. This social setting allows customers to converse easily with

western medicine classifies as psychosomatic (not a disease, therefore not an illness) and dismisses as not requiring treatment—despite the feelings of the ill patient. Non-Western medical systems tell us that patients can be treated effectively as whole beings, using any combination of methods that prove beneficial. Indeed there is a growing related field known as *holistic medicine* in contemporary North America.

Anthropology and Business

Carol Taylor (1987) discusses the value of an "anthropologist-in-residence" in a large, complex organization such as a hospital or a business. A free-ranging ethnographer can be a perceptive oddball when information and decisions usually move through a rigid hierarchy. If allowed to observe and converse freely with all types and levels of personnel, the anthropologist may acquire a unique perspective on organizational conditions and problems. For many years, anthropologists have used ethnography to study business settings (Arensberg 1987). For example, ethnographic research in an auto factory may view workers, managers, and executives as different social categories participating in a common social system. Each group has characteristic attitudes, values, and behavior patterns. These are transmitted through *microenculturation,* the process by which people learn particular roles in a limited social system. The free-ranging nature of ethnography takes the anthropologist from worker to executive. Each of these people is both an individual with a personal viewpoint and a cultural creature whose perspective is, to some extent, shared with other members of a group. Applied anthropologists have acted as "cultural brokers," translating managers' goals or workers' concerns to the other group.

Closely observing how people actually use products, anthropologists work with engineers to design products that are more user-friendly. Increasingly, anthropologists are working with high-tech companies, where they use their observational skills to study how people work, live, and use technology. Such studies can be traced to 1979, when the Xerox Palo Alto (California) Research Center (PARC) hired the anthropologist Lucy Suchman. She worked in a laboratory where researchers were trying to build artificial intelligence to help people use complicated copiers. Suchman observed and filmed people having trouble with a copying job. From her research came the realization that simplicity is more important than fancy features. That's why all Xerox copiers, no matter how complex, now include a single green copy button for when someone wants an uncomplicated copy (Weise 1999).

"[Our] graduate students keep getting snatched up by companies," says Marietta Baba (now of Michigan State University), former chair of the anthropology department at Wayne State University (WSU) in Detroit (quoted in Weise 1999). WSU trains anthropology students to observe social interactions so as to understand the underlying structures of a culture, and to apply those methods to industry. Baba estimates that about 9,000 American anthropologists work in

Professor Marietta Baba of Michigan State University is also a prominent applied anthropologist known for her studies of the automobile industry.

academia and that about 2,200 hold applied anthropology positions in industry. "But the proportions are shifting, so you're getting more and more applied ones," she says (quoted in Weise 1999). Companies hire anthropologists to gain a better understanding of their customers and to find new products and markets that engineers and marketers might never imagine. Andrea Saveri, a director at the Institute for the Future in Menlo Park, California, contends that traditional market research is limited by its question-and-answer format. "In the case of surveys, you're telling the respondent how to answer and you're not giving them any room for anything else" (quoted in Weise 1999). Saveri, who thinks ethnography is more precise and powerful than surveys, employs anthropologists to investigate the consequences of technology (Weise 1999).

For business, key features of anthropology include (1) ethnography and observation as ways of gathering data, (2) cross-cultural expertise, and (3) a focus on cultural diversity. The cross-cultural perspective enters the picture when businesses seek to know why other nations have higher (or lower) productivity than we do (Ferraro 2001). Reasons for differential productivity are cultural, social, and economic. To find them, anthropologists must focus on key features in the organization of production. Subtle but potentially important differences can emerge from workplace ethnography—close observation of workers and managers in their natural (workplace) setting.

Careers in Anthropology

Many college students find anthropology interesting and consider majoring in it. However, their parents or friends may discourage them by asking, "What kind of job are you going to get with an anthropology major?" The purpose of this section is to answer that question. The first step in answering "What do you do with an anthropology major?" is to consider the more general question "What do you do with any college major?" The answer is "Not much, without a good bit of effort, thought, and planning." A survey of graduates of the literary college of the University of Michigan showed that few had jobs that were clearly linked to their majors. Medicine, law, and many other professions require advanced degrees. Although many colleges offer bachelor's degrees in engineering, business, accounting, and social work, master's degrees are often needed to get the best jobs in those fields. Anthropologists, too, need an advanced degree, most typically a Ph.D., to find gainful employment in academic, museum, or applied anthropology.

The following discussion is aimed mainly at undergraduates who are considering an anthropology major—not at students who are considering advanced degrees in anthropology, although there are some comments for them, too. A broad college education, and even a major in anthropology, can be an excellent foundation for success in many fields. Many University of Michigan undergraduates who are planning careers in medicine, public health, or dentistry choose a joint major in anthropology and zoology. A recent survey of women executives showed that most had not majored in business but in the social sciences or humanities. Only after graduating did they study business, obtaining a master's degree in business administration. These executives felt that the breadth of their college educations had contributed to their business careers. Anthropology majors go on to medical, law, and business schools and find success in many professions that often have little explicit connection to anthropology.

Anthropology's breadth provides knowledge and an outlook on the world that are useful in many kinds of work. For example, an anthropology major combined with a master's degree in business is excellent preparation for work in international business. However, job seekers must always convince employers that they have a special and valuable "skillset."

Breadth is anthropology's hallmark. Anthropologists study people biologically, culturally, socially, and linguistically, in time and space, in developed and underdeveloped nations, in simple and complex settings. Physical anthropologists teach about human biology in time and space, including our origins and evolution. Most colleges have cultural anthropology courses that compare cultures and others that focus on particular world areas, such as Latin America, Asia, and Native North America. The knowledge of geographic areas acquired in such courses can be useful in many jobs. Anthropology's comparative outlook, its long-standing Third World focus, and its appreciation of diverse life styles combine to provide an excellent foundation for overseas employment.

Even for work in North America, the focus on culture is valuable. Every day we hear about cultural differences and about social problems whose solutions require a multicultural viewpoint—an ability to recognize and reconcile ethnic differences. Government, schools, and private firms constantly deal with people from different social classes, ethnic groups, and tribal backgrounds. Physicians, attorneys, social workers, police officers, judges, teachers, and students can all do a better job if they understand social differences in a part of the world that is one of the most ethnically diverse in history.

What if you want more than an undergraduate degree in anthropology? What if you do decide to pursue an advanced degree? Although some practicing anthropologists find jobs with only the master's degree, the more typical credential for gainful employment in anthropology is the doctorate, the Ph.D. Traditionally, most people with Ph.D.s in anthropology have expected to find employment as college teachers or in museums. Things are changing today. The American Anthropological Association has estimated that at least half of future anthropology Ph.D.s will not find work in academia. One reason for this shift is that academic jobs have become harder to get and are not clearly expanding. Another reason is that the production of Ph.D.s in anthropology has increased faster than the number of academic jobs available. A final reason is that many anthropology Ph.D.s actually prefer applied work to work in academia. Whatever the reason, there is no doubt that more and more anthropologists will be doing applied anthropology.

One place they'll be doing it is business. The cross-cultural perspective and the focus on diversity are two reasons why some North American businesses have become interested in anthropology, as we saw in the news vignette that opened Chapter 1. Also, an ethnographic focus on behavior in the daily social setting can help locate problems that plague American businesses, which tend to be overly hierarchical. Attention to the social dimension of business can only gain importance. More and more executives recognize that proper human relations are as important as economic forecasts in maximizing productivity. Contemporary applied anthropologists devise ways to deploy employees more effectively and to increase job satisfaction.

Applied anthropologists also work to help communities threatened by external systems. As highways and power-supply systems cross tribal boundaries, the "modern" world comes into conflict with historic land claims and traditions. An anthropological study is often considered necessary before permission is granted to extend a public works system across native lands.

Because construction, dams, reservoirs, and other public works may threaten archaeological sites, fields such as cultural resource management have developed. Government agencies, engineering firms, and construction companies now have jobs for people with an anthropological background because of federal legislation to protect historic and prehistoric sites.

Knowledge about the traditions and beliefs of the many social groups within a modern nation is important in planning and carrying out programs that affect those groups. Attention to social background and cultural categories helps ensure the welfare of affected ethnic groups, communities, and neighborhoods. Experience in planned social change—whether community organization in North America or economic development overseas—shows that a proper social study should be done before a project or policy is implemented. When local people want the change and it fits their lifestyle and traditions, it will be more successful, beneficial, and cost-effective. There will be not

only a more humane but a more economical solution to a real social problem.

Some agencies working overseas place particular value on anthropological training. Others seek employees with certain skills without caring much about specific academic backgrounds. Among the government agencies that hire anthropologists are USAID (the United States Agency for International Development) and USDA (the United States Department of Agriculture). These organizations hire anthropologists both full-time and as short-term consultants.

Private voluntary organizations working overseas offer other opportunities. These PVOs (a kind of NGO) include Care, Save the Children, Catholic Relief Services, Foster Parents Plan International, and Oxfam (a hunger relief organization operating out of Boston and Oxford). Some of these groups employ anthropologists full-time.

Anthropologists apply their expertise in surprisingly diverse areas. They negotiate business deals, suggest and implement organizational changes, and testify as expert witnesses. Physical anthropologist Kathy Reichs applies anthropology in her forensic work for the Office of the Chief Medical Examiner of North Carolina and for the Laboratoire de Sciences Judiciares et de Médecine Légale in Montreal, Quebec. Dr. Reichs is also a professor of anthropology at the University of North Carolina, Charlotte, a frequent expert witness in criminal trials, and the author of several mystery novels featuring the heroine Temperance Brennan—also a forensic anthropologist. Anthropologists also have worked for pharmaceutical firms interested in potential conflicts between traditional and Western medicine, and in culturally appropriate marketing of their products (e.g., Viagra) in new settings. Other anthropologists are working to help native peoples get a share of the profits when their traditional remedies, including medicinal plants, are marketed by drug companies.

People with anthropology backgrounds are doing well in many fields. Furthermore, even if the job has little or nothing to do with anthropology in a formal or obvious sense, anthropology is always useful when we work with fellow human beings. For most of us, this means every day of our lives.

SUMMARY

1. Applied anthropology uses anthropological perspectives, theory, methods, and data to identify, assess, and solve problems. Applied anthropologists have a range of employers. Examples: government agencies; development organizations; NGOs; tribal, ethnic, and interest groups; businesses; social services and educational agencies. Applied anthropologists come from all four subfields. Ethnography is one of applied anthropology's most valuable research tools. Another is the comparative, cross-cultural perspective. A systemic perspective recognizes that changes have multiple consequences, some unintended. A code of ethics guides anthropologists' research and other professional activities.

2. Anthropology and education researchers work in classrooms, homes, and other settings relevant to education. Such studies may lead to policy recommendations. Both academic and applied anthropologists study migration from rural areas to cities and across national boundaries. North America has become a popular arena for urban anthropological research on migration, ethnicity, poverty, and related topics. Although rural and urban are different social systems, there is cultural diffusion from one to the other. Rural and tribal social forms affect adjustment to the city.

3. Medical anthropology is the cross-cultural study of health problems and conditions, disease, illness, disease theories, and health-care systems. Medical anthropology includes biological and cultural anthropologists and has theoretical (academic) and applied dimensions. In a given setting, the characteristic diseases reflect diet, population density, economy, and social complexity. Native theories of illness may be personalistic, naturalistic, or emotionalistic. In applying anthropology to business, the key features are (1) ethnography and observation as ways of gathering data, (2) cross-cultural expertise, and (3) focus on cultural diversity.

4. A broad college education, including anthropology and foreign-area courses, offers excellent background for many fields. Anthropology's comparative outlook and cultural relativism provide an excellent basis for overseas employment. Even for work in North America, a focus on culture and cultural diversity is valuable. Anthropology majors attend medical, law, and business schools and succeed in many fields, some of which have little explicit connection with anthropology.

5. Experience with social-change programs, whether in North America or abroad, offers a common lesson. When local people want a change and when that change fits their life style and traditions, the change is most likely to be successful, beneficial, and cost-effective.

KEY TERMS

See the flash cards

advocacy view of applied anthropology; the belief that precisely because anthropologists are experts on human problems and social change, and because they study, understand, and respect cultural values, they should make policy affecting people.

anthropology and education Anthropological research in classrooms, homes, and neighborhoods, viewing students as total cultural creatures whose enculturation and attitudes toward education belong to a larger context that includes family, peers, and society.

applied anthropology The application of anthropological data, perspectives, theory, and methods to identify, assess, and solve contemporary social problems.

cultural resource management (CRM) The branch of applied archaeology aimed at preserving sites threatened by dams, highways, and other projects.

curer Specialized role acquired through a culturally appropriate process of selection, training, certification, and acquisition of a professional image; the curer is consulted by patients, who believe in his or her special powers, and receives some form of special consideration; a cultural universal.

disease   A scientifically identified health threat caused by a bacterium, virus, fungus, parasite, or other pathogen.

emotionalistic disease theories   Theories that assume that illness is caused by intense emotional experiences.

health-care systems   Beliefs, customs, and specialists concerned with ensuring health and preventing and curing illness; a cultural universal.

illness   A condition of poor health perceived or felt by an individual.

ivory tower view   of applied anthropology; the belief that anthropologists should avoid practical matters and concentrate on research, publication, and teaching.

medical anthropology   Unites biological and cultural anthropologists in the study of disease, health problems, health-care systems, and theories about illness in different cultures and ethnic groups.

naturalistic disease theories   Include scientific medicine; theories that explain illness in impersonal systemic terms.

personalistic disease theories   Theories that attribute illness to sorcerers, witches, ghosts, or ancestral spirits.

practicing anthropologists   Used as a synonym for applied anthropology; anthropologists who practice their profession outside of academia.

schizoid view   of applied anthropology; the belief that anthropologists should help carry out, but not make or criticize, policy, and that personal value judgments should be kept strictly separate from scientific investigation in applied anthropology.

scientific medicine   As distinguished from Western medicine, a health-care system based on scientific knowledge and procedures, encompassing such fields as pathology, microbiology, biochemistry, surgery, diagnostic technology, and applications.

For more self testing, see the self quizzes

CRITICAL THINKING QUESTIONS

mhhe
com
/kottak

1. What's your position on applied anthropology, given the three views discussed at the beginning of this chapter?
2. What else are you studying this semester? Do those fields have an applied dimension, too? Are they more or less useful than anthropology is?
3. Describe a setting in which you might use ethnography and observation to do applied anthropology. What other research methods might you also use in that setting?
4. How might ethical issues and concerns vary across anthropology's four subfields? Imagine an ethical issue that might arise for a physical anthropologist, for an archaeologist, and for a cultural anthropologist.
5. Think back to your grade school or high school classroom. Were there any social issues that might have interested an anthropologist? Were there any problems that an applied anthropologist might have been able to solve? How so?
6. What do you see as the costs and benefits of Western medicine compared with tribal medi-

cine? Are there any conditions for which you'd prefer treatment by a tribal curer than a Western curer?
7. Think of a problem in an urban setting that an applied anthropologist might be called on to solve. How do you imagine he or she would go about solving it?
8. Think of a business context you know well. How might applied anthropology help that business function better? How would the applied anthropologist gather the information to suggest improvements?

Atlas Questions

Look at Map 2, "Population Growth Rates."

1. Which continent has the highest growth rates?
2. What continents have growth rates below 1 percent per year?
3. Where does one find the highest growth rates in the western hemisphere?

SUGGESTED ADDITIONAL READINGS

Anderson, R.
1996   *Magic, Science, and Health: The Aims and Achievements of Medical Anthropology.* Fort Worth: Harcourt Brace. Up-to-date text, focusing on variation associated with race, gender, ethnicity, age, and ableness.

Bailey, E. J.
2000   *Medical Anthropology and African American Health.* Westport, CT: Bergin and Garvey. Medical issues affecting, and anthropological research involving, African Americans.

Bond, G. C., J. Kreniske, I. Susser, and J. Vincent, eds.
1997   *AIDS in Africa and the Caribbean.* Boulder, CO: Westview. This volume uses detailed ethnographic studies from Africa and the Caribbean to examine AIDS in a global and comparative context.

Brown, P. J.
1998   *Understanding and Applying Medical Anthropology.* Boston: McGraw-Hill. Medical anthropology, basic and applied.

Chambers, E.
1985   *Applied Anthropology: A Practical Guide.* Englewood Cliffs, NJ: Prentice-Hall. How to do applied anthropology, by a leader in the field.

2000   *Native Tours: The Anthropology of Travel and Tourism.* Prospect Heights, IL: Waveland. How anthropologists study the world's number one business—travel and tourism.

Eddy, E. M., and W. L. Partridge, eds.
1987   *Applied Anthropology in America,* 2nd ed. New York: Columbia University Press. Historical review of applications of anthropological knowledge in the United States.

Ferraro, G. P.
2002   *The Cultural Dimension of International Business,* 4th ed. Upper Saddle River, NJ: Prentice-Hall. How the theory and insights of cultural anthropology can influence the conduct of international business.

Gwynne, M. A.
2003   *Applied Anthropology: A Career-Oriented Approach.* Boston: Allyn and Bacon. Various applied opportunities in anthropological careers.

Helman, C.
2001   *Culture, Health, and Illness: An Introduction for Health Professionals,* 4th ed. Boston: Butterworth-Heinemann. The social context of medical practice.

Holtzman, J.
2000   *Nuer Journeys, Nuer Lives.* Boston: Allyn and Bacon. How immigrants from Sudan adapt to Minnesota's twin cities and to the American social service system.

Human Organization
    The quarterly journal of the Society for Applied Anthropology. An excellent source for articles on applied anthropology and development.

Joralemon, D.
1999   *Exploring Medical Anthropology.* Boston: Allyn and Bacon. Recent introduction to a growing field.

McDonald, J. H., ed.
2002   *The Applied Anthropology Reader.* Boston: Allyn and Bacon. Recent descriptions of case experiences and approaches.

McElroy, A., and P. K. Townsend
1996   *Medical Anthropology in Ecological Perspective,* 3rd ed. Boulder, CO: Westview. This established introduction to medical anthropology shows that field's multidisciplinary roots.

Rushing, W. A.
1995   *The AIDS Epidemic: Social Dimensions of an Infectious Disease.* Boulder, CO: Westview. The sociocultural conditions that have contributed to the spread of AIDS.

Sargent, C. F., and C. B. Brettell
1996   *Gender and Health: An International Perspective.* Upper Saddle River, NJ: Prentice-Hall. How culture affects the relation among gender, health-care organization, and health policy.

Sargent, C. F., and T. J. Johnson, eds.

1996   *Medical Anthropology: A Handbook of Theory and Method,* rev. ed. Westport, CT: Praeger Press. Articles cover theoretical perspectives, medical systems, health issues, methods in medical anthropology, and issues of policy and advocacy.

Spindler, G. D., ed.

2000   *Fifty Years of Anthropology and Education, 1950-2000: A Spindler Anthology.* Mahwah, NJ: Erlbaum Associates. Survey of the field of educational anthropology by two prominent contributors, George and Louise Spindler.

Strathern, A., and P. J. Stewart

1999   *Curing and Healing: Medical Anthropology in Global Perspective.* Durham, NC: Carolina Academic Press. Cross-cultural examples of medical anthropology.

Van Willigen, J.

2002   *Applied Anthropology: An Introduction,* 3rd ed. Westport, CT: Bergin and Garvey. Excellent review of the growth of applied anthropology and its links to general anthropology.

INTERNET EXERCISES

1. Go to the website of the CILHI **(http://www.cilhi.army.mil/)** and read about what this organization does. Go to its recent press release page **(http://www.cilhi.army.mil/recentpr.htm)** and get a sense of what some of its recent activities are.

   a. What does the CILHI do?

   b. The CILHI is one of the largest employers of forensic anthropologists in the world. How are forensic anthropologists important for its mission?

   c. Go to the profiles of some of the scientific staff **(http://www.cilhi.army.mil/scientificstaff.htm).** What kind of educational background do many of the staff members have? Where are some of the institutions they attended?

2. Go to the publication from the United States Agency for International Development (USAID) entitled "Population and the Environment: A Delicate Balance" **(http://www.usaid.gov/pop_health/pop/publications/docs/popenv.pdf).**

   a. What are some of the major environmental threats due to population growth the world faces?

   b. What can groups like USAID do in the face of these threats?

   c. What contributions does anthropology have to offer? Should organizations like USAID employ anthropologists?

   d. What is the role of applied anthropology for environmental issues?

See Chapter 2 at your McGraw-Hill Online Learning Center for additional review and interactive exercises.

Part Two

Physical Anthropology and Archaeology

In Part 2, we'll explore physical (or biological) anthropology and archaeology, two of anthropology's four subfields. Although some physical anthropologists and even archaeologists work with living people, a common interest in the past and in change—in evolution—unites physical anthropology and archaeology. Physical anthropologists and archaeologists frequently work abroad, and in teams. In Chapter 3 we'll consider some of the ethical contexts in which physical anthropologists and archaeologists operate, along with the research methods they employ. Physical anthropology and archaeology are united by their common interest in evolution, which we'll examine from a biological perspective and as a genetic process in Chapter 4.

Evolutionary principles also are illustrated by our nearest relatives—nonhuman primates, such as monkeys and apes. Chapter 5 considers traits and trends in primate anatomy, along with primate behavior and social organization. Chapter 6 examines the evolution of the primates, from their remote origins to the last common ancestor shared by humans and apes. In Chapters 7 and 8 we turn to hominid and human evolution. In Chapter 7, we'll learn about when, where, why, and how the first members of the hominid family, which includes modern humans, originated. We'll also examine (mainly in Chapter 8) the origins of physical and behavioral modernity in *Homo sapiens*. Spanning time and space, Chapter 9 considers contemporary human biological variation, its nature and causes,

while also exposing weaknesses in traditional ideas—both scientific and popular—about race and human races. The chapters in Part 2 tend to emphasize a particular subfield, such as physical anthropology in Chapters 4 through 9 and archaeology in Chapters 10 and 11. But all the chapters in Part 2 also draw on knowledge and techniques from other subfields, including cultural anthropology.

Chapters 10 and 11 focus on what archaeologists have reconstructed about the origins of food production and the state. Food production was a major innovation in human adaptation as humans began to influence, and then control, the reproduction of plants and animals. The earliest food producers, who lived in the Middle East, became the world's first farmers and herders. The changes triggered by food production, including population growth and increasing economic and social complexity, paved the way for the first states or civilizations. These were literate societies with central governments. States featured highly evolved class structures, authority systems, and patterns of exploitation unlike anything seen previously in human evolution. Archaeologists and physical anthropologists have investigated the origins and consequences of food production and state formation in both the Eastern Hemisphere (e.g., the ancient Middle East) and the Western Hemisphere (e.g., Mexico, Peru, and other parts of the Americas). Part 2 explores this panorama of origins and change—biological and cultural—across millions of years and thousands of miles.

57

3

ETHICS AND METHODS IN PHYSICAL ANTHROPOLOGY AND ARCHAEOLOGY

Overview

Because science exists in society, and in the context of law and ethics, anthropologists can't study things simply because they have potential scientific value. Anthropologists have obligations to the field of anthropology, to the wider society, and to the human species, other species, and the environment. The anthropologist's most fundamental ethical obligation is to the people, species, and materials he or she studies.

Physical anthropologists and archaeologists pursue diverse research topics, using varied methods and often working together. At an archaeological site, a physical anthropologist may complement the picture of ancient life by examining skeletons to reconstruct their physical traits, health status, and diet. Within physical anthropology, studies of nonhuman primates suggest hypotheses about behavior that humans do or do not share with our nearest relatives and with our hominid ancestors. Various methods have been used to show that humans are unusually social, compared with nonhuman primates.

Physical anthropologists also study the biology of bone—its genetics; cell structure; growth, development, and decay; and patterns of movement. Paleopathologists examine disease and injury in skeletons from archaeological sites. Molecular anthropology uses genetic analysis (of DNA sequences) to assess evolutionary relationships among ancient and contemporary populations and among species.

Archaeologists typically work in teams and across time and space. Like paleoanthropologists and paleontologists, they combine both local (excavation) and regional (systematic survey) perspectives. Sites are excavated because they are in danger of being destroyed or because they address specific research interests.

Anthropologists and paleontologists use stratigraphy and radiometric techniques to date fossils. Carbon-14 (^{14}C) dating is most effective with remains less than 40,000 years old. Potassium-argon (K/A) dating can be used for fossils older than 500,000 years.

Museums and Tribes: A Tricky Truce

NEW YORK TIMES NEWS BRIEF

by Stephen Kinzer

December 24, 2000

When bones and artifacts are discovered, who should own them? Should they belong to the owner of the land where they are found, to the discoverer, to some public entity, or to people who claim rights to that land from time immemorial? The Native American Graves Protection and Repatriation Act (NAGPRA) gives ownership of Native American physical and archaeological remains to Indians. NAGPRA requires museums to return remains and artifacts to any tribe that requests them and that can prove a "cultural affiliation" with the tribe from which they came. The 1996 discovery in Washington state of a skeleton dubbed "Kennewick Man" eventually led to a legal case between anthropologists and five Indian tribes with ancestral homelands in the area where Kennewick Man was found. The anthropologists wanted to conduct a thorough study of the 9,000-year-old fossil to see what its anatomy and DNA might tell us about the early settlement of the Western Hemisphere. The Umatilla Indians and their allies in four other Indian Nations believe they have always occupied the region where the skeleton was found. In their view, Kennewick Man was an ancestor, whom they want to rebury with dignity and without contamination from scientific testing. On August 30, 2002 U.S. Magistrate Judge John Jelderks ruled that the Kennewick remains could be subjected to scientific study.

. . . The Native American Graves Protection and Repatriation Act, was signed by President George [H. W.] Bush in November 1990 after years of discussion among scientists, museum curators and Indian groups. It seeks to reconcile two profoundly different value systems, one based on the primacy of reason and science and the other revolving around spiritual and religious values.

In the decade since the law was passed, it has had a profound effect on museums and the philosophy on which they are based. At the same time, it has had incalculable emotional and social impact on Indian tribes across the country that have recovered long-lost artifacts, many of which have enormous spiritual significance, as well as the remains of thousands of their ancestors.

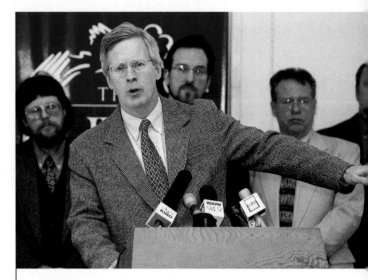

In this 1999 photo, Dr. Francis McManamon, chief archaeologist of the National Park Service and chief consulting archaeologist for the Department of the Interior, announces his readiness to launch the nondestructive scientific study of Kennewick Man.

When the law was first enacted, some Indian leaders feared that they were about to begin a period of bitter clashes with defiant museum curators. Some curators feared that their collections would be gutted as they were forced to return huge numbers of artifacts. Ten years later, however, both sides agree that their fears were exaggerated, and many say the law has actually increased understanding between tribes and museum administrators . . .

There are still some areas of conflict, especially over efforts by some tribes to recover remains that are many thousands of years old and that scientists say should be studied for vital clues about the history of human migration to the American continent. But many curators have come to agree that Indians have a right to recover their sacred artifacts and the bones of those they can legitimately claim as ancestors . . .

The 1990 law affects every museum and federal agency that owns "Native American human remains and associated funerary objects" as well as "unassociated funerary objects, sacred objects or objects of cultural patrimony." It requires each museum and agency to compile an inventory of its holdings, identify them by tribal origin and notify existing tribes of objects that appear to come from that tribe's tradition.

Under the law, museums must return all remains and artifacts to any tribe that requests them and that can prove a "cultural affiliation" with the tribe from which they came . . .

Some Indian leaders maintain that all objects from all non-European cultures in North America belong in the hands of Indians, regardless of whether those alive today can claim kinship with the cultures that produced the objects. The 1990 law, however, rejects that so-called "pan-Indian" argument. It requires that the claimant tribe prove it is a "lineal descendant" of the tribe from which the artifacts or remains came.

As a result of this provision, the law has served some tribes better than others. Southwestern tribes like the Hopi and Navajo, for example, have maintained cultural continuity over centuries and therefore have strong claims to objects in museum collections. Other tribes, including many in the Eastern United States that were decimated by successive waves of European settlement, have more trouble proving their descent from tribes that existed long ago . . .

One apparently unintended consequence of the law has been that Indian tribes have laid claim to several sets of very old human remains that have been found in the United States since the mid-1990's. Indians claim these as remains of their ancestors, since their religious tradition tells them that they were always present on the North American continent. Many scientists say that claim is dubious at best, and complain that potentially thrilling discoveries about the early peopling of the Americas may never be made if they do not have the chance to study the remains they unearth.

This issue has come into public view largely because of an intensifying legal controversy over the skeleton of a man, apparently about 9,000 years old, that was found in 1996 in Kennewick, Washington.

Five Indian tribes in the Northwest have collectively claimed Kennewick Man as an ancestor and want to rebury his remains. Scientists are protesting. They say the skeleton has features suggesting that it may be of Japanese or Polynesian origin, and that in any case no tribe or ethnic group in the world can trace its ancestry back 9,000 years. In September [2000], Interior Secretary Bruce Babbit ruled in favor of the tribes, saying he believed they were "culturally affiliated" with the Kennewick skeleton. A group of anthropologists, however, has filed a lawsuit seeking to block the reburial . . .

Despite this debate and a handful of others like it, many scientists, museum curators and tribal leaders, more than a few of whom had expected to be locked in bitter battles over ownership of valuable artifacts, say the opposite has happened . . .

"We have a collection of 800,000 objects, so in a quantitative sense the law has had a very small impact," said Rick West [director of the Smithsonian Institute's Museum of the American Indian], who is a Cheyenne Indian. "But from a qualitative standpoint I do think it has an impact, and that impact is absolutely positive.

"As institutions of culture, museums that house these materials have a vital interest in buttressing those cultures and supporting them into the future," Mr. West said. "To the extent that we believe maintenance of these cultures is important, and I think it is, museums have an obligation to support that cultural diversity . . ."

For current information on Kennewick Man see the OLC Internet Exercises

mhhe
●**com**
/kottak

Source: Excerpted from Stephen Kinzer, "Museums and Tribes: A Tricky Truce," *New York Times*, December 24, 2000, late edition, final, section 2, p. 1, column 1; www.nytimes.com.

Anthropologists could draw on various methods and theories to study and interpret Kennewick Man. Analysis of anatomy and DNA might suggest connections with similarly dated fossils in Asia or elsewhere in North or South America. (**Fossils** are remains [e.g., bones, teeth, skulls], traces, or impressions [e.g., footprints] of ancient life.) Skull form, teeth, and bones might reveal something about diet. The skeleton might be marked by evidence of fractures or disease. Anthropological theory recognizes that change, in culture and biology, is constant and ongoing. Given biological and cultural evolution, we would expect significant differences in the anatomy and artifacts of people living in the Pacific Northwest now versus people who lived 9,000 years ago. Anthropological theory and methods could be applied productively in the scientific study of Kennewick Man and similarly dated fossils found in North and South America. But science exists in society, and in the context of law and ethics. Anthropologists can't study things simply because they happen to be interesting or of value to science. Anthropologists are increasingly aware of the ethical and legal contexts in which their work proceeds. This chapter examines ethics and methods in physical anthropology and archaeology.

Ethics

Anthropologists frequently do research outside their nations of origin. As in the Guatemalan forensic anthropology study discussed in Chapter 2, physical anthropologists and archaeologists often work as members of international teams. These teams include researchers from several countries, including the *host country*—the place (e.g., Guatemala) where the research takes place. In **paleoanthropology** (a.k.a. *human paleontology*)—the study of human evolution through the fossil record—physical anthropologists and archaeologists often work together. The physical anthropologists are more interested in the bones; the archaeologists, in the artifacts. But their work may proceed jointly, as they try to infer the relation between the physical and cultural features of the remains they are examining. Much of our knowledge of early human evolution comes from Africa, where international collaboration is common.

International work exposes physical anthropologists and archaeologists to varying national and cultural procedures, value systems, and ethical and legal codes. In such contexts, the American Anthropological Association (AAA) advises anthropologists to be guided by its Code of Ethics. How do specific guidelines in the AAA Code of Ethics, which was discussed in Chapter 2, apply to physical anthropology and archaeology? To gain permission and collaboration in the host country, anthropologists need to inform officials and colleagues there about the purpose, funding, and likely results, products, and impacts of their research. They need to negotiate the matter of where the materials produced by the research will be analyzed and stored—in the host country or in the anthropologists' country—and for how long. To whom do research materials, such as bones, artifacts, and blood samples, belong? What kinds of restrictions will apply to their use?

It's crucial for anthropologists to establish and maintain proper relations between themselves as guests and the host nations, regions, and communities where they work. Remember that the anthropologist's primary ethical obliga-

Scientists designing zoo displays of primates (and other animals) need to pay special attention to ethical issues. Living conditions should be humane, ideally suggesting a natural setting. Shown here is Opening Day at the Henry Doorly Zoo in Omaha, Nebraska, whose Lied Jungle is the largest tropical rain forest exhibit in a North American zoo. What animals live in tropical forests?

tion is to the people, species, and materials he or she studies. Although nonhuman primates can't give informed consent, primatologists still must take steps to ensure that their research doesn't endanger the animals. Either government agencies or nongovernmental organizations (NGOs) may be entrusted with protecting primates. If this is the case, the anthropologist will need their permission and informed consent to conduct research.

With living humans, informed consent is a necessity—for example, in obtaining biological samples, such as blood or urine. The research subjects must be told how the samples will be collected, used, and identified, and about the potential costs and benefits to them. Informed consent is needed from anyone providing data or information, owning materials being studied, or otherwise having an interest that might be affected by the research.

The AAA Code says that anthropologists should not exploit individuals, groups, animals, or cultural or biological materials. They should recognize their debt to the people with whom they work and should reciprocate in appropriate ways. For example, it is highly appropriate for North

American anthropologists working in another country to (1) include host country colleagues in their research planning and requests for funding, (2) establish truly collaborative relationships with those colleagues and their institutions before, during, and after field work, (3) include host country colleagues in dissemination, including publication, of the research results, and (4) ensure that something is "given back" to host country colleagues. For example, research equipment and technology are allowed to remain in the host country. Or funding is provided for host country colleagues to do research, attend international meetings, or visit foreign institutions—especially those where their international collaborators work.

Physical anthropologists and archaeologists, more often than cultural anthropologists, work as members of teams. Teams include host country collaborators; typically, they also include students—graduate and undergraduate. Training students in the value of long-term collaboration is one way of preserving opportunities for future field workers to follow current researchers to the field.

Methods

There are all sorts of specialized research interests, topics, and methods within both physical anthropology and archaeology. (Given space limitations only some of them can be covered here.) Remember that physical anthropologists and archaeologists often collaborate. In the study of human evolution, the physical anthropologists focus on the fossil remains—and what they tell us about ancient human biology. The archaeologists focus on the artifacts—and what they tell us about past cultures. Often their work proceeds jointly as they try to infer the relation between the physical features and cultural features of the remains they are examining. What are some of the methods and techniques used by physical anthropologists and archaeologists?

MULTIDISCIPLINARY APPROACHES

Scientists from diverse fields, for example, soil science and **paleontology** (the study of ancient life through the fossil record), using varied techniques, collaborate with physical anthropologists and archaeologists in the study of sites where fos-

sils and/or artifacts have been found. **Palynology,** the study of ancient plants through pollen samples taken from such sites, is used to determine a site's environment at the time of occupation. Physical anthropologists and archaeologists turn to physicists and chemists for help with dating techniques. Physical anthropologists representing a subspeciality known as *bioarchaeology* may complement the picture of ancient life at a particular site by examining skeletons to reconstruct their physical traits, health status, and diet (Larson 2000). Evidence for social status may endure in hard materials—bones, jewels, buildings—through the ages. During life, bone growth and stature are influenced by diet. Genetic differences aside, taller people are often that way because they eat better than shorter people do. Differences in the stature and chemical (e.g., strontium) composition of groups of bones at a site may help distinguish privileged nobles from less fortunate commoners. To reconstruct ancient biology and ways of life, physical anthropologists, archaeologists, and their collaborators analyze the remains of humans, plants, and animals, as well as such artifacts (manufactured items) as ceramics, tiles, casts, and metals.

Physical anthropologists and archaeologists draw on low-tech as well as high-tech tools and methods. Small hand-held tools are used at excavation sites, where photos, maps, drawings, and measurements record where every find stands in relation to the site as a whole. Data are entered in field notebooks and computers.

Illustrating more sophisticated technology, sites, such a system of ancient canals, may be located and defined from the air. Aerial photos (taken from airplanes) and satellite images are forms of **remote sensing** used in site location. For example, ancient buried footpaths visible not to the naked eye but only in satellite imagery have been studied in Costa Rica by University of Colorado and National Aeronautics and Space Administration (NASA) archaeologists (Scott 2002). Up to six feet of volcanic ash, sediment, and vegetation had covered and obscured the footpaths. Images of the paths, some dating to 2,500 years ago, were first made in 1984 by a NASA aircraft using instruments that could "see" in the electromagnetic spectrum invisible to humans. In 2001 a commercial satellite took additional images of the buried footpaths, which showed up as thin red lines, reflecting the dense vegetation growing

Costa Rican footpaths as revealed from space. Footpaths up to 2,500 years old were visible in satellite imagery but not to the naked eye. The paths had been buried by volcanic ash, sediment, and vegetation. What other archeological features might be visible from space?

and sites of, say, flooding or deforestation, which can then be investigated on the ground. Anthropologists have used satellite imagery to identify, and then investigate on the ground, regions where deforestation is especially severe and where people and biodiversity, including nonhuman primates, may be at risk (Green and Sussman 1990; Kottak, Gezon, and Green 1994; Kottak 1999).

PRIMATOLOGY

Primatologists are like ethnographers in their close observation of a group of primates, in this case, nonhuman. Primate behavior has been observed in zoos (e.g., de Waal 1998) and through experimentation (e.g., Harlow 1966), but the most significant studies have been done in natural settings, among free-ranging apes, monkeys, and lemurs. You, as an anthropology student, may be given an assignment to observe primates in zoos. Try to avoid nocturnal primates, which probably will be sleeping when you visit the zoo, unless you visit the Hall of Night Animals at New York's Bronx Zoo—or a similar zoo habitat in which animals, through lighting, are fooled into switching night and day. Some primatologists have studied free-ranging nocturnal primates, such as tarsiers, owl monkeys, and the aye-aye of Madagascar. But most primates are active during the day (*diurnal*), as are humans, and are easier to study for that reason. It's also easier for humans to study terrestrial than arboreal species. In Madagascar I've raced down hills following lemurs moving rapidly through the trees. As a college student I made the mistake of studying the slow loris in New York's Central Park Zoo. That loris, a prosimian, or lemur-like animal, catches insects by staying still, then suddenly snaring bugs that land nearby. Unless there are insects in the cage, observing the slow loris (like observing the South American sloth, which is *not* a primate) is only slightly more interesting than watching an egg.

over them. The footpaths were dated on the basis of the stratigraphy (layers of geological deposits) of the Arenal volcano, which has erupted 10 times in the last 4,000 years.

Village life was established around Arenal some 4,000 years ago, and endured through the Spanish Conquest around 1500. Villagers periodically fled volcanic eruptions, returning when it was safe to resume farming of corn and beans in the nutrient-rich volcanic soil. According to team leader Payson Sheets of the University of Colorado, "they inhabited a very large region and seemed to avoid conflict, conquest and serious disease . . . They led comfortable lives, relying on an abundance of natural resources and a stable culture" (quoted in Scott 2002).

Excavation of the footpaths uncovered stone tools, pottery, and floors of ancient houses. The paths once linked a cemetery to a spring and quarries where construction stone was mined. A primary goal of a 2002 field team led by Sheets was to understand ancient activities at the cemetery, where bodies were laid to rest in stone coffins. Funerary ceramics and meal vessels, plus cooking stones, indicate that people camped, cooked, and feasted at the cemetery for long time periods (Scott 2002).

Anthropologists work with geologists, geographers, and other scientists in using satellite images to find not just ancient footpaths, roads, canals, and irrigation systems but also patterns

Since the 1950s, when primatologists began their shift from zoos to natural settings, numerous studies have been done of apes (chimps, gorillas, orangutans, and gibbons), monkeys (e.g., baboons,

This slow loris, a nocturnal primate, grasps a bug. What problems might you encounter in studying such an animal?

macaques), and lemurs (e.g., Madagascar's indrii, sifaka, and ring-tailed lemurs). *Arboreal* primates (those which spend most of their time in the trees—e.g., howler monkeys and gibbons) may be difficult to see and follow, but they typically make a lot of noise. Their communication systems, including howls and calls, can be studied and teach us about how primates communicate. Studies of primate social systems and behavior, including their mating patterns, infant care, and patterns of contact and dispersal, suggest hypotheses about behavior that humans do or do not share with our nearest relatives—and also with our hominid ancestors.

Like ethnographers, primatologists have to establish rapport (a "friendly" working relationship) with the individuals they are studying. Since language can't be used with nonhuman primates, rapport involves gradual habituation; the animals have to get used to the researcher. Animals must be identified and observed over time. Often a fledgling primatologist will join a longitudinal team that has been observing a group of monkeys or apes for years, even decades. Identification of the animals and close attention to their behavior and interactions are necessary to understand primate behavior and social organization. Particular animals may be followed for set periods of time—with each episode of behavior and interaction systematically recorded on film or in a notebook. Or the researcher can focus on certain scenes, for example, a particular tree or water source where primates congregate at particular times. Or individuals and/or places can be chosen randomly for study at particular times.

Although *Homo sapiens*, unlike most other primates, is neither a "threatened" nor an "endangered" species, many humans live in areas of poverty and overpopulation. The pressure of human activities on scarce resources, such as forested lands, creates threats for primates and animals sharing their habitat. People hunt or buy primates for food and for their assumed medicinal properties. People also clear land from, and build roads through, forested habitats where primates once thrived. Deforestation is a major threat to primates. Many cultural anthropologists work with people whose activities pose threats to primates. Working in the same areas, primatologists are experts on the precise habitat, needs, and behavior patterns of the nonhuman primates. Working together and with conservation groups and governments, cultural and physical anthropologists can apply their knowledge in devising plans to conserve forests and their animal dwellers, while also allowing people to meet their basic needs.

Interpret the World
Atlas Map 3

Map 3 in your atlas shows annual change in forest cover between 1990 and 1995. Name two countries where the forest cover has stayed the same or increased. We frequently hear about threats to Brazil's Amazon rainforest, but is Brazil one of the countries in which forests are retreating most rapidly? On what continent do you see deforestation as posing the greatest threat? Is it likely that this threat is related to high rates of population increase, as discussed in Chapter 2, and shown on Map 2 in your atlas?

ANTHROPOMETRY

Physical anthropologists use various techniques to study nutrition, growth, and development. **Anthropometry** is the measurement of human body parts and dimensions, including skeletal parts (*osteometry*). Anthropometry is done on living people as well as on skeletal remains from sites. Body mass and composition provide measures of nutritional status in living people. Body mass is calculated from height and weight. The *body mass index* (kg/m^2) is the ratio of weight in kilograms divided by height in meters squared. An adult body mass above 30 is considered at risk of overweight, while one below 18 is at risk of underweight or malnutrition. To assess body composition, subcutaneous (below the surface) fat is estimated from skin fold thickness (measured with calipers) and body circumference. These values are compared to anthropometric standards (Frisancho 1990). For a given gender and age group, values above the 85th percentile are associated with excess fat, and values below the 15th percentile are associated with leanness.

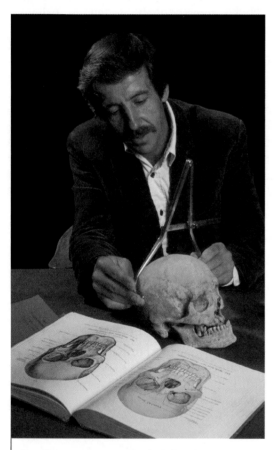

Joe Zias, a curator at Rockefeller Museum, measures an ancient skull. Anthropometry is done on skeletal remains from sites as well as on living people. Has anyone ever done anthropometry on you?

A machine called a *calorimeter* is used to measure resting metabolic rates, based on the amount of oxygen consumed and carbon dioxide produced when an individual rests for 30 minutes. The instrument calculates the body's minimum energy needs (in calories) at rest. Based on daily calories consumed, used at rest, and used in activities, scientists can determine whether conditions favor weight gain or loss. Measurement of the resting metabolic rate also reveals the extent to which weight gains or losses may reflect metabolism versus eating patterns.

Knowledge about how contemporary humans adapt (e.g., to heat and cold) and use energy (e.g., in metabolism) can be used to understand human evolution. For example, during hominid evolution brain size has increased. In contemporary humans, the brain represents just 5 percent of body weight, yet brain activity consumes 20 percent of the resting metabolic rate. During human evolution, the adaptive advantages of having a large brain must have outweighed the high cost in energy. However, increased activity would have been necessary to feed growing human bodies and brains.

Understanding Ourselves Humans are really social compared with our primate relatives. Even chimps, our closest relatives, don't cooperate nearly to the extent that we do. Apparently apes aren't wired for cooperation and altruism as we are (see "Interesting Issues," p. 68). We'll never know all the causes of human sociality, but some are based in human anatomy—from the brain to the pelvis. Consider the female pelvis, whose evolution has been guided by these facts: (1) Humans walk upright, (2) babies are born with big brains, and (3) babies have to negotiate a complicated birth canal during childbirth.

There are striking and significant contrasts between primates and humans in anatomy and in the birthing process. Nonhuman primates aren't bipedal; compared with humans, they have smaller brains, simpler birth canals, and more independent infants. As they move through the birth canal, human babies must make several turns, so that their heads and shoulders, the two body parts with the largest dimensions, are consistently aligned with the widest parts of the birth canal. Monkeys and apes don't have this problem.

Birthing assistance is almost universal in human societies. Shown here, an Uzbeki midwife uses a traditional instrument to listen to a baby's heartbeat. Locate Uzbekistan (Central Asia) in your atlas.

Unlike those of humans, primate birth canals have a constant shape.

Also, the primate infant emerges facing forward. The mother can grasp it, even pull it straight to her nipple. Human babies are born facing backward, away from the mother, and so she has trouble assisting in the birth. The presence of someone else (e.g., a midwife) to help with delivery reduces the mortality risk for human infants and their mothers.

Birthing assistance is almost universal among human societies. According to Karen Rosenberg and Wenda Trevathan (2001), our wish to have supportive, familiar people around at childbirth goes way back. On the basis of pelvic openings, and estimated infant skull sizes, of extinct hominids, Rosenberg and Trevathan (2001) conclude that such assistance may date back millions of years. Nonhuman primate mothers seek seclusion when they give birth, and act as their own midwives in the birthing process. Not so humans—social as ever. Midwives, obstetricians, baby showers—all are expressions of human sociality with deep evolutionary roots.

BONE BIOLOGY

Central to physical anthropology is **bone biology** (or skeletal biology)—the study of bone as a biological tissue, including its genetics; cell structure;

growth, development, and decay; and patterns of movement (*biomechanics*) (Katzenberg and Saunders, eds. 2000). Within bone biology, *osteology* is the study of skeletal variation and its biological and social causes. Osteologists study such variables as stature in living and ancient populations (White and Folkens 2000). The interpretation of fossil remains relies on understanding the structure and function of the skeleton. **Paleopathology** is the study of disease and injury in skeletons from archaeological sites. Some forms of cancer leave evidence in the bone. Breast cancer, for example, may spread (metastasize) skeletally, leaving holes or lesions in bones and skull. Certain infectious diseases (e.g., syphilis and tuberculosis) also mark bone, as do injuries and nutritional deficiencies (e.g., rickets, a vitamin D deficiency that deforms the bones).

In forensic anthropology, as discussed in Chapter 2, physical anthropologists work in a legal context, assisting coroners, medical examiners, and law enforcement agencies in recovering, analyzing, and identifying human remains and determining the cause of death (Nafte 2000; Prag and Neave 1997). For example, when unknown skeletal remains are found, the police and the Delaware Medical Examiner's Office call on University of Delaware physical anthropologist Karen Rosenberg to help identify the body. By examining the bones, Rosenberg can determine characteristics, such as the height, age, and sex of the person. She notes that "the police authorities always ask for the race of an unidentified person. But racial categories are, in part, culturally defined and in any case are not closed biological 'types.' Recently I identified a skeleton as possibly being Caucasian, then on subsequent examinations thought he might be African American. In actuality, when the identification was made, he turned out to be Hispanic" (Rosenberg, quoted in Moncure 1998).

MOLECULAR ANTHROPOLOGY

Molecular anthropology uses genetic analysis (of DNA sequences) to assess evolutionary links. Through molecular comparison, evolutionary

Using a novel method of scanning neural activity in people playing games, scientists have discovered that cooperation triggers pleasure in the brain. Anthropologist James Rilling and five other scientists monitored brain activity in young women playing a laboratory game called Prisoner's Dilemma. Players select greedy or cooperative strategies as they pursue financial gain. The researchers found that the choice to cooperate stimulated areas of the brain associated with pleasure and reward-seeking behavior—the same areas that respond to desserts, pictures of pretty faces, money, and cocaine (Rilling et al. 2002; Angier 2002). According to coauthor Gregory S. Berns, "In some ways, it says that we're wired to cooperate with each other" (quoted in Angier 2002).

The researchers studied 36 women age 20 to 60. Why women? Some previous studies had found male–male pairs to be more cooperative than female–female pairs, and others had found the opposite. Rilling and his colleagues didn't want to mix more cooperative and less cooperative pairs, and so they restricted their sample to one gender to control for possible differences in tendencies toward cooperation. The choice to use women rather than men was an arbitrary one.

In the experiment two women would meet each other briefly ahead of time. One was then placed in the scanner, while the other remained outside the scanning room. The two interacted by computer, playing about 20 rounds of the game. In every round, each player pressed a button to indicate whether she would "cooperate" or "defect." Her answer would be shown on-screen to the other player. Money was awarded after each round. When one player defected and the other cooperated, the defector earned $3, and the cooperator earned nothing. When both cooperated, each earned $2. If both defected, each earned $1. Mutual cooperation from start to finish was a more profitable strategy, at $40 a woman, than complete mutual defection, which yielded only $20 to each woman.

If one woman got greedy, she took the risk that the cooperative strategy might fall apart and that both players would lose money as a result. Most of the time, the women cooperated. Even occasional defections weren't always fatal to an alliance, although the woman who had been "betrayed' once might be suspicious after that. Because of occasional defections, the average per-experiment take for the participants was in the range of $30.

The scans showed that two broad areas of the brain were activated by cooperation. Both areas are rich in neurons that respond to dopamine, a brain chemical that plays a well-known role in addictive behaviors. One is the anteroventral striatum in the midbrain, just above the spinal cord. Experiments have shown that when electrodes are placed in this area, rats will repeatedly press a bar to stimulate the electrodes. They apparently receive such pleasurable feedback that they will starve to death rather than stop pressing the bar (Angier 2002).

Another brain region activated during cooperation was the orbitofrontal cortex, just above the eyes. Besides being part of the reward-processing system, this area is involved in impulse control. According to Rilling, "Every round, you're confronted with the possibility of getting an extra dollar by defecting. The choice to cooperate requires impulse control" (quoted in Angier 2002).

In some cases, the woman in the scanner played a computer and knew her partner was a machine. In other tests, women played a computer but thought it was a human. The reward circuitry of the women was considerably less responsive when they knew they were playing against a computer. The thought of a human bond, not mere monetary gain, was the source of contentment. Also, the women were asked afterward to summarize their feelings during the games. They often described feeling good when they cooperated and expressed feelings of camaraderie toward their playing partners.

Assuming the urge to cooperate is to some extent innate among humans, and is reinforced by our neural circuitry, why did it arise? Anthropologists generally assume that it took teamwork and altriusm for our ancestors to hunt large game, share food, and engage in other social activities, including raising children. A neural tendency to cooperate and to share would have conferred a survival advantage on our ancestors. Instead of "Why can't we all get along," these researchers were exploring why we get along so well.

SOURCE: Information from Angier 2002; Rilling et al. 2002; and Rilling, personal communication.

Two adult femora. The top one is normal in size and shape. The bottom one shows swelling and a ragged surface resulting from the chronic bacterial infection called osteomyelitis. These thigh bones are from the Mississippian period Hazel site in Arkansas.

related people) defined by a specific cluster of genetic traits that occur together. Native Americans have four major haplogroups, which are also linked to East Asia. Among the many sorts of questions that molecular anthropology may answer: How can DNA sequences be used to trace migration routes during the peopling of North America and the Pacific? Are there tribal-specific genetic markers among Native Americans or Pacific Islanders? Which genes influence susceptibility to which diseases? For nonhuman primates, molecular anthropologists use DNA sequences to identify parentage, and to calculate kinship and degree of inbreeding within primate colonies. We'll see later that molecular anthropologists also use "genetic clocks" to estimate divergence time (date of most recent common ancestry) among species (e.g., humans, chimps, and gorillas—5 million to 8 million years ago) and of various human groups (e.g., Neandertals and modern humans).

PALEOANTHROPOLOGY

Paleoanthropologists study early hominids through fossil remains. Typically, a team composed of scientists, students, and local workers, representing diverse backgrounds and academic fields, participates in a paleoanthropological study. Such teams may include physical anthropologists, archaeologists, paleontologists, geologists, palynologists, paleoecologists, physicists, and chemists. Their common goal is to date and reconstruct the structure, behavior, and ecology of early hominids. The geologists and paleontologists may be called in during early surveying— perhaps using remote sensing—to locate potential early hominid sites. Paleontologists help locate fossil beds containing remains of animals that can be dated and that are known to have coexisted with hominids at various time periods. Good preservation of faunal remains may suggest that hominid fossils have survived as well. Sometimes it's impossible to date the hominid fossils and artifacts found at a given site by using the most accurate and direct (radiometric) methods. In this

distance among living species, along with dates of most recent common ancestry, can be estimated. Molecular studies also have been used to assess and date the origins of modern humans and to examine their relation to extinct human groups such as the Neandertals, which thrived in Europe between 130,000 and 30,000 years ago. The scientists who successfully filed suit to examine Kennewick Man, as discussed at the beginning of this chapter, wished to compare his DNA with that of more recent and living Native Americans, and with that of Asians and Pacific Islanders, to measure evolutionary links and distances.

In 1997, ancient DNA was extracted from a Neandertal bone originally found in Germany's Neander Valley in 1856. This was the first time the DNA of a premodern human had been recovered. This DNA, from an upper arm bone (humerus), was compared with the DNA of modern humans. There were 27 differences between the Neandertal DNA and modern DNA; by contrast, samples of modern DNA show only 5 to 8 differences among the samples.

Molecular anthropologists examine relationships among ancient and contemporary populations and among species. It's well established, for example, that humans and chimpanzees have more than 98 percent of their DNA in common. Molecular anthropologists also reconstruct waves and patterns of migration and settlement. A *haplogroup* is a biological lineage (a large group of case, comparison of the faunal remains at that site with similar, but more securely dated, fauna at another site may suggest a date for those animal fossils and the hominids and artifacts associated with them.

Once potential sites have been identified, more intensive surveying begins. Archaeologists take over and search for hominid traces—bones or tools. Only hominids work rock to make tools and move rock fragments over long distances. Some early hominid sites are strewn with thousands of tools. If a site is shown to be a hominid site, much more concentrated work begins. Financial support may come from private donations and government agencies. The research project usually is headed by an archaeologist or a physical anthropologist. The field crew will continue to survey and map the area and start searching carefully for bones and artifacts eroding out of the soil. Also, they will take pollen and soil samples for ecological analysis and rock samples for use in various dating techniques. Analysis is done in laboratories, where specimens are cleaned, sorted, labeled, and identified.

Consideration of the animal habitats suggested by the site (e.g., forest, woodland, or open country) will assist the reconstruction of the paleoecological settings in which early hominids lived. Pollen samples help reveal diet. Sediments and other geological samples will suggest climatic conditions at the time of deposition. Sometimes fossils are embedded in rock, from which they must be extracted carefully. Once recovered and cleaned, fossils may be made into casts to permit wider study.

Survey and Excavation

Archaeologists and paleoanthropologists typically work in teams and across time and space. Typically, archaeologists, paleoanthropologists, and paleontologists combine both local (excavation) and regional (systematic survey) perspectives. They recognize that sites may not be discrete and isolated, but parts of larger social systems. Let's examine some of the main techniques that anthropologists use to study patterns of behavior in ancient societies, based on their material remains. Archaeologists recover remains from a series of contexts, such as pits, sites, and regions. The archaeologist also integrates data about different social units of the past, such as the household, the village, and the regional system.

SYSTEMATIC SURVEY

Archaeologists and paleoanthropologists have two basic fieldwork strategies: systematic survey and excavation. **Systematic survey** provides a regional perspective by gathering information on settlement patterns over a large area. *Settlement pattern* refers to the distribution of sites within a particular region. Regional surveys reconstruct settlement patterns by addressing several questions: Where were sites located? How big were they? What kinds of buildings did they have? How old are the sites? Ideally, a systematic survey involves walking over the entire survey area and recording the location and size of all sites. From artifacts found on the surface, the surveyor estimates when each site was occupied. A full-coverage survey isn't always possible. The ground cover may be impenetrable (e.g., thick jungle), or certain parts of the survey area may be inaccessible. Permission to survey may be denied by landowners. Surveyors may have to rely on remote sensing to help locate and map sites.

With regional data, scientists can address many questions about the prehistoric communities that lived in a given area. Archaeologists use settlement pattern information to make population estimates and to assess levels of social complexity. Among hunter-gatherers and simple farmers, there are generally low numbers of people living in small camp sites or hamlets with little variation in the architecture. Such sites are scattered fairly evenly across the landscape. With increasing social complexity, the settlement patterns become more elaborate. Population levels rise. Such social factors as trade and warfare have played a more important role in determining the location of sites (on hilltops, waterways, trade routes). In complex societies, a settlement hierarchy of sites emerges. Certain sites are larger, with greater architectural differentiation, than others. Large sites with specialized architecture (elite residences, temples, administrative buildings, meeting places) are generally interpreted as regional centers that exerted control over the smaller sites with less architectural differentiation.

See the OLC
Internet
Exercises

/kottak

EXCAVATION

Paleontologists, paleoanthropologists, and archaeologists also gather information about the past by excavating sites. During an **excavation,** scientists recover remains by digging through the cultural and natural stratigraphy—the layers of deposits that make up a site. These layers or strata are used to establish the relative time order of the materials encountered during the dig. This relative chronology is based on the principle of *superposition*: In an undisturbed sequence of strata, the oldest layer is on the bottom. Each successive layer above is younger than the one below. Thus, artifacts and fossils from lower strata are older than those recovered from higher strata in the same deposit. This relative time ordering of material remains lies at the heart of archaeological, paleoanthropological, and paleontological research.

The archaeological and fossil records are so rich, and excavation is so labor-intensive and expensive, that nobody digs a site without a good reason. Sites are excavated because they are endangered, or because they answer specific research questions. Cultural resource management (CRM), as discussed in Chapter 2, focuses on managing the preservation of archaeological sites that are threatened by modern development. Many countries require archaeological impact studies before construction can take place. If a site is at risk and the development cannot be stopped, CRM archaeologists are called in to salvage what information they can from the site. Another reason a site may be chosen for excavation is that it is well suited to answer specific research questions. For example, an archaeologist studying the origins of agriculture wouldn't want to excavate a large, fortified hilltop city with a series of buildings dating to a period well after the first appearance of farming communities. Rather, he or she would look for a small hamlet-size site located on or near good farmland and near a water source. Such a site would have evidence of an early occupation dating to the period when farming communities first appeared in that region.

Before a site is excavated, it is mapped and surface collected so that the researchers can make an informed decision about where exactly to dig. The collecting of surface materials at a given site is similar to what is done over a much larger area in a regional survey. A grid is drawn to represent and subdivide the site. Then collection units, which are equal-size sections of the grid, are marked off on the actual site. This grid enables the researchers to record the exact location of any artifact, fossil, or feature found at the site. By examining all the materials on the surface of the site, archaeologists can direct their excavations toward the areas of the site that are most likely to yield information that will address their research interests. Once an area is selected, digging begins, and the location of every artifact or feature is recorded in three dimensions.

Digging may be done according to arbitrary levels. Thus, starting from the surface, consistent amounts of soil (usually 10 or 20 centimeters) are systematically removed from the excavation unit. This technique of excavation is a quick way of digging, since everything within a certain depth is removed at once. This kind of excavation usually is done in test pits, which are used to determine how deep the deposits of a site go and to establish a rough chronology for that site.

A more labor-intensive and refined way of excavating is to dig through the stratigraphy one layer at a time. The strata, which are separated by differences in color and texture, are studied one by one. This technique provides more information about the context of the artifacts, fossils, or features because the scientist works more slowly and in meaningful layers. A given 10 centimeter level may include within it a series of successive house floors, each with artifacts. If this deposit is excavated according to arbitrary levels, all the artifacts are mixed together. But if it is excavated according to the natural stratigraphy, with each house floor excavated separately, the resulting picture is much more detailed. The procedure here is for the archaeologist to remove and bag all the artifacts from each house floor before proceeding to the level below that one.

Any excavation recovers varied material remains, such as ceramics, stone artifacts (lithics), human and animal bones, and plant remains. Such remains may be small and fragmented. To increase the likelihood that small remains will be recovered, the soil is passed through screens. To recover very small remains, such as fish bones and carbonized plant remains, archaeologists use a technique called *flotation*. Soil samples are sorted using

An archaeologist drives in another stake for a large grid at an excavation site in Teotihuacan, Mexico. Such a grid enables the researchers to record the exact location of any artifact or feature found at the site.

water and a series of very fine meshes. When the water dissolves the soil, the carbonized plant remains float to the top. The fish bones and other heavier remains sink to the bottom. Flotation requires considerable time and labor. This makes it inappropriate to use on all the soil that is excavated from a site. Flotation samples are taken from a limited number of deposits, such as house floors, trash pits, and hearths.

Kinds of Archaeology

Archaeologists pursue diverse research topics, using a wide variety of methods. Experimental archaeologists try to replicate ancient techniques and processes (e.g., tool making) under controlled conditions. Historical archaeologists use written records as guides and supplements to archaeological research. They work with remains more recent—often much more recent—than the advent of writing. Colonial archaeologists, for instance, use historical records as guides to locate and excavate postcontact sites in North and South America,

and to verify or question written accounts. Classical archaeologists usually are affiliated with university departments of classics or the history of art, rather than with anthropology departments. These classical scholars focus on the literate civilizations of the Old World, such as Greece, Rome, and Egypt. Classical archaeologists are often as (or more) interested in art—styles of architecture and sculpture—as in the social, political, and economic variables that typically interest the anthropologist. Underwater archaeology is a growing field that investigates submerged sites, most often shipwrecks. Special techniques, including remotely operated vehicles like the one shown in the movie *Titanic,* are used, but divers also do underwater survey and excavation.

In Chapter 2, cultural resource management was discussed as a form of applied (or public) anthropology, as archaeologists apply their techniques of data gathering and analysis to manage sites that are threatened by development, public works, and road building. Some CRM archaeologists are *contract archaeologists,* who typically negotiate specific contracts (rather than applying for

Scuba divers at an underwater archaeology site. Graduate degrees in underwater, or nautical, archaeology are available at East Carolina University, Florida State University, and Texas A&M University. This growing field of study investigates submerged sites, most often shipwrecks.

research grants) for their studies, which often must be done rapidly, for example, when an immediate threat to archaeological materials becomes known. Based on a membership study done for the Society of American Archaeology in 1994, Melinda Zeder (1997) found that 40 percent of the respondents worked as contract archaeologists—for firms in the private sector, state and federal agencies, and educational institutions. An equivalent 40 percent held academic positions.

Dating the Past

The archaeological record hasn't revealed every ancient society that has existed on earth; nor is the fossil record a representative sample of all the plants and animals that have ever lived. Some species and body parts are better represented than others are, for many reasons. Hard parts, such as bones and teeth, preserve better than do soft parts, such as flesh and skin. The chances of fossilization increase when remains are buried in a newly forming sediment, such as silt, gravel, or sand. Good places for bones to be buried in sediments include swamps, floodplains, river deltas, lakes, and caves. The species that inhabit such

areas have a better chance to be preserved than do animals that live in other habitats. Fossilization is also favored in areas with volcanic ash, or where rock fragments eroding from rising highlands are accumulating in valleys or lake basins. Once remains do get buried, chemical conditions must be right for fossilization to occur. If the sediment is too acidic, even bone and teeth will dissolve. The study of the processes that affect the remains of dead animals is called **taphonomy,** from the greek *taphos,* which means "tomb." Such processes include scattering by carnivores and scavengers, distortion by various forces, and the possible fossilization of the remains.

The conditions under which fossils are found also influence the fossil record. For example, fossils are more likely to be uncovered through erosion in arid areas than in wet areas. Sparse vegetation allows wind to scour the landscape and uncover fossils. The fossil record has been accumulating longer and is more extensive in Europe than in Africa because civil engineering projects and fossil hunting have been going on longer in Europe than in Africa. A world map showing where fossils have been found does not indicate the true range of ancient animals. Such a map tells us more about ancient geological activity, modern erosion, or recent human activity—such as paleontological research or road building. In considering the primate and hominid fossil records in later chapters, we'll see that different areas provide more abundant fossil evidence for different time periods. This doesn't necessarily mean that primates or hominids were not living elsewhere at the same time. What dating techniques are used to determine *when* animals that have been fossilized actually lived?

We've seen that *paleontology* is the study of ancient life through the fossil record and that *paleoanthropology* is the study of ancient humans and their immediate ancestors. These fields have established a time frame, or *chronology,* for the evolution of life. Scientists use several techniques to date fossils. These methods offer different degrees of precision and are applicable to different periods of the past.

A swamp is a good place for bones to be buried in sediments. Here a female mammoth is represented sinking into the La Brea Tarpits in Los Angeles, California. What other locales and conditions favor fossilization?

RELATIVE DATING

Chronology is established by assigning dates to geologic layers (strata) and to the material remains, such as fossils and artifacts, within them. Dating may be relative or absolute. **Relative dating** establishes a time frame in relation to other strata or materials rather than absolute dates in numbers. Many dating methods are based on the geological study of **stratigraphy,** the science that examines the ways in which earth sediments accumulate in layers known as *strata* (singular, *stratum*). As was noted previously, in an undisturbed sequence of strata, age increases with depth. Soil that erodes from a hillside into a valley covers, and is younger than, the soil deposited there previously. Stratigraphy permits relative dating. That is, the fossils in a given stratum are younger than those in the layers below and older than those in the layers above. We may not know the exact or absolute dates of the fossils, but we can place them in time relative to remains in other layers. Changing environmental forces, such as lava flows and the alternation of land and sea, cause different materials to be deposited in a given sequence of strata; this allows scientists to distinguish between the strata.

Remains of animals and plants that lived at the same time are found in the same stratum. When fossils are found within a stratigraphic sequence, scientists know their dates relative to fossils in other strata; this is relative dating. When fossils are found in a particular stratum, the associated geological features (such as frost patterning) and remains of particular plants and animals offer clues about the climate at the time of deposition.

Besides stratigraphic placement, another technique of relative dating is fluorine absorption analysis. Bones fossilizing in the same ground for the same length of time absorb the same proportion of fluorine from the local groundwater. Fluorine analysis uncovered a famous hoax involving the so-called Piltdown man, once considered an unusual and perplexing human ancestor (Winslow and Meyer 1983). The Piltdown "find," from England, turned out to be the jaw of a young orangutan attached to a *Homo sapiens* skull. Fluorine analysis showed the association to be false. The skull had much more fluorine than the jaw—impossible if they had come from the same individual and had been deposited in the same place at the same time. Someone had fabricated Piltdown man in an attempt to muddle the interpretation of the fossil record. (The attempt was partially successful—it did fool some scientists.)

ABSOLUTE DATING

The previous section reviewed relative dating based on stratigraphy and fluorine absorption analysis. Fossils also can be dated more precisely, with dates in numbers (**absolute dating**), by using several methods. For example, the ^{14}C, or carbon-14, technique is used to date organic remains. This is a *radiometric* technique (so called because it measures radioactive decay). ^{14}C is an unstable radioactive isotope of normal carbon, ^{12}C. Cosmic radiation entering the earth's atmosphere produces ^{14}C, and plants take in ^{14}C as they absorb carbon dioxide. ^{14}C moves up the food chain as animals eat plants and as predators eat other animals.

With death, the absorption of ^{14}C stops. This unstable isotope starts to break down into nitrogen (^{14}N). It takes 5,730 years for half the ^{14}C to change to nitrogen; this is the half-life of ^{14}C. After another 5,730 years only one-quarter of the original ^{14}C will remain. After yet another 5,730 years only one-eighth will be left. By measuring the proportion of ^{14}C in organic material, scientists can determine a fossil's date of death, or the date of an ancient campfire. However, because the half-life of ^{14}C is short, this dating technique is less dependable for specimens older than 40,000 years than it is for more recent remains.

For more information on radiocarbon dating, see the Virtual Exploration

mhhe
●com
/kottak

Fortunately, other radiometric dating techniques are available for earlier periods. One of the most widely used is the potassium-argon (K/A) technique. ^{40}K is a radioactive isotope of potassium that breaks down into argon-40, a gas. The half-life of ^{40}K is far longer than that of ^{14}C—1.3 *billion* years. With this method, the *older* the specimen, the more reliable the dating. Furthermore, whereas ^{14}C dating can be done only on organic remains, K/A dating can be used only for inorganic substances: rocks and minerals.

^{40}K in rocks gradually breaks down into argon-40. That gas is trapped in the rock until the rock is heated intensely (as with volcanic activity), at which point it may escape. When the rock cools, the breakdown of potassium into argon resumes. Dating is done by reheating the rock and measuring the escaping gas.

In Africa's Great Rift Valley, which runs down eastern Africa and in which early hominid fossils abound, past volcanic activity permits K/A dating.

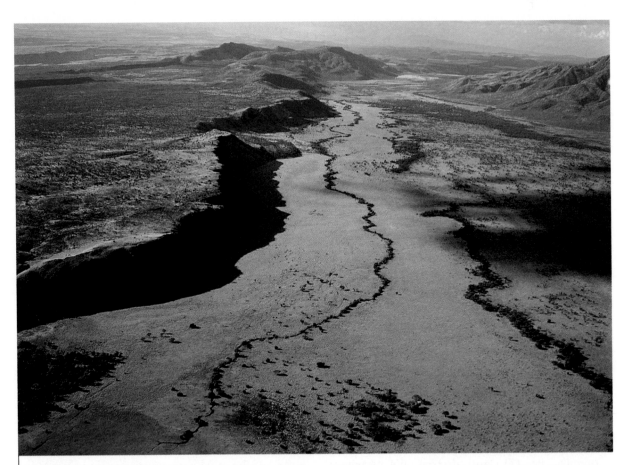

East Africa's Great Rift Valley runs through Ethiopia, Kenya (shown here), and Tanzania. What dating technique(s) can be used in this volcanic region?

Table 3.1 Absolute Dating Techniques

Technique	Abbreviation	Materials Dated	Effective Time Range
Carbon-14	^{14}C	Organic materials	Up to 40,000 years
Potassium-argon	K/A and ^{40}K	Volcanic rock	Older than 500,000 years
Uranium series	^{238}U	Minerals	Between 1,000 and 1,000,000 years
Thermoluminescence	TL	Rocks and minerals	Between 5,000 and 1,000,000 years
Electron spin resonance	ESR	Rocks and minerals	Between 1,000 and 1,000,000 years

In studies of strata containing fossils, scientists find out how much argon has accumulated in rocks since they were last heated. They then determine, using the standard ^{40}K deterioration rate, the date of that heating. Considering volcanic rocks at the top of a stratum with fossil remains, scientists establish that the fossils are *older than*, say, 1.8 million years. By dating the volcanic rocks below the fossil remains, they determine that the fossils are *younger than*, say, 2 million years. Thus, the age of the fossils and of associated material is set at between 2 million and 1.8 million years. Note that absolute dating is that in name only; it may give ranges of numbers rather than exact dates.

Many fossils were discovered before the advent of modern stratigraphy. Often we can no longer determine their original stratigraphic placement. Furthermore, fossils aren't always discovered in volcanic layers. Like ^{14}C dating, the K/A technique applies to a limited period of the fossil record. Because the half-life of ^{40}K is so long, the technique cannot be used with materials less than 500,000 years old.

Other radiometric dating techniques can be used to cross-check K/A dates, again by using minerals surrounding the fossils. One such method, *uranium series dating*, measures fission tracks produced during the decay of radioactive uranium (^{238}U) into lead. Two other radiometric techniques are especially useful for fossils that cannot be dated by ^{14}C (up to 40,000 B.P.) or ^{40}K (more than 500,000 B.P.). These methods are *thermoluminescence* (TL) and *electron spin resonance* (ESR). Both TL and ESR measure the electrons that are constantly being trapped in rocks and minerals (Shreeve 1992). Once a date is obtained for a

rock found associated with a fossil, that date also can be applied to that fossil. The time spans for which the various absolute dating techniques are applicable are summarized in Table 3.1.

MOLECULAR DATING

In 1987, in a very influential study, researchers at the University of California at Berkeley used DNA analysis to advance the idea that anatomically modern humans (AMHs) arose fairly recently (around 130,000 years ago) in Africa. Rebecca Cann, Mark Stoneking, and Allan C. Wilson (1987) analyzed genetic traits in placentas donated by 147 women whose ancestors came from various parts of the world. The researchers focused on mitochondrial DNA (mtDNA), which only the mother contributes to the fertilized egg, and thus to the child. To establish a "genetic clock," the researchers measured the variation in mtDNA in their 147 tissue samples. They cut each sample into segments to compare with the others. By estimating the number of mutations (spontaneous changes in DNA) that had taken place in each sample since its common origin with the 146 others, the researchers drew an evolutionary tree with the help of a computer. That tree started in Africa, then branched in two. One group stayed in Africa. The other one left Africa and carried its mtDNA to the rest of the world. Assuming a constant mutation rate (e.g., one mutation per 25,000 years), and counting the number of mutations in each sample, molecular anthropologists estimate the time period of the most recent common ancestor. Note that such estimates of divergence dates based on a constant mutation rate are not as widely accepted as is radiometric dating.

SUMMARY

1. Because science exists in society, and in the context of law and ethics, anthropologists can't study things simply because they happen to be interesting or of scientific value. Anthropologists have obligations to their scholarly field, to the wider society and culture (including that of the host country), and to the human species, other species, and the environment. The anthropologist's primary ethical obligation is to the people, species, and materials he or she studies.

2. Physical anthropologists and archaeologists pursue diverse research topics, using varied methods and often working together. At an archaeological site, physical anthropologists may complement the picture of ancient life by examining skeletons to reconstruct their physical traits, health status, and diet. Remote sensing may be used to locate ancient footpaths, roads, canals, and irrigation systems, which can then be investigated on the ground.

3. Studies of primates suggest hypotheses about behavior that humans do or do not share with our nearest relatives—and also with our hominid ancestors. Anthropometry, the measurement of human body parts and dimensions, is done on living people and on skeletal remains from sites. Humans are unusually social, compared with nonhuman primates. Unlike other primate babies, humans are born facing backward, away from the mother, and so she has trouble assisting in the birth. The presence of someone else (e.g., a midwife) to help with delivery reduces the mortality risk for human infants and their mothers.

4. Central to physical anthropology is bone biology—the study of bone genetics; cell structure; growth, development, and decay; and patterns of movement. Osteologists study skeletal variation and its biological and social causes. Paleopathology is the study of disease and injury in skeletons from archaeological sites. Molecular anthropology uses genetic analysis (of DNA sequences) to assess evolutionary relationships among ancient and contemporary populations and among species.

5. Archaeologists, who typically work in teams and across time and space, combine both local (excavation) and regional (systematic survey) perspectives. Archaeologists use settlement pattern information to make population estimates and to assess levels of social complexity. Sites are excavated because they are in danger of being destroyed or because they address specific research interests. There are many kinds of archaeology, such as historical, classical, and underwater archaeology.

6. The fossil record is not a representative sample of all the plants and animals that have ever lived. Hard parts, such as bones and teeth, preserve better than soft parts, such as flesh and skin, do. Anthropologists and paleontologists use stratigraphy and radiometric techniques to date fossils. Carbon-14 (^{14}C) dating is most effective with fossils less than 40,000 years old. Potassium-argon (K/A) dating can be used for fossils older than 500,000 years. ^{14}C dating is done on organic matter, whereas the K/A, ^{238}U, TL, and ESR dating techniques are used to analyze minerals that lie below and above fossils. Molecular anthropology has also been used as a dating technique, based on the assumption of a constant mutation rate.

KEY TERMS

See the flash cards

absolute dating Dating techniques that establish dates in numbers or ranges of numbers; examples include the radiometric methods of ^{14}C, K/A, ^{238}U, TL, and ESR dating.

anthropometry The measurement of human body parts and dimensions, including skeletal parts (*osteometry*).

bone biology The study of bone as a biological tissue, including its genetics; cell structure; growth, development, and decay; and patterns of movement (*biomechanics*).

excavation Digging through the layers of deposits that make up an archaeological or fossil site.

fossils Remains (e.g., bones), traces, or impressions (e.g., footprints) of ancient life.

molecular anthropology Genetic analysis, involving comparison of DNA sequences, to determine evolutionary links and distances among species and among ancient and modern populations.

paleoanthropology Study of hominid and human life through the fossil record.

paleontology Study of ancient life through the fossil record.

paleopathology Study of disease and injury in skeletons from archaeological sites.

palynology Study of ancient plants through pollen samples from archaeological or fossil sites in order to determine the site's environment at the time of occupation.

relative dating Dating technique, for example, stratigraphy, that establishes a time frame in relation to other strata or materials, rather than absolute dates in numbers.

remote sensing Use of aerial photos and satellite images to locate sites on the ground.

stratigraphy Science that examines the ways in which earth sediments are deposited in demarcated layers known as strata (singular, stratum).

systematic survey Information gathered on patterns of settlement over a large area; provides a regional perspective on the archaeological record.

taphonomy The study of the processes that affect the remains of dead animals, such as their scattering by carnivores and scavengers, their distortion by various forces, and their possible fossilization.

CRITICAL THINKING QUESTIONS

For more self testing, see the self quizzes

1. Considering anthropology's four subfields, are some more likely to use a team approach than others are? What about the equipment needs of the different subfields?

2. How might ethical issues and concerns differently affect cultural, physical, and archaeological anthropologists?

3. Name three factors that might influence an anthropologist's plans to study, or not to study, a particular topic in a particular place.

4. In practical terms, what does it mean to say that anthropologists have obligations to their scholarly field and to the wider society and culture? How might they abuse those responsibilities?

5. What three archaeological topics seem most interesting to you?

6. What three topics in physical anthropology seem most interesting to you?

7. Give two examples of how a physical anthropologist and an archaeologist might collaborate.

8. Imagine a scenario in which an archaeologist or physical anthropologist might use remote sensing.

9. What's your body mass index?

10. What are two examples of social tendencies you have that may have a deep evolutionary history?

11. Who assisted your mother in your birthing process?

12. Name two problems that might interest a bone biologist.

13. What are the strengths and limitations of relative dating? Of absolute dating?

Atlas Questions

Look at Map 3, "Annual Change in Forest Cover, 1990–1995."

1. Also consult Map 2, "Population Growth Rates." Name two countries in which deforestation is correlated with high population growth rates and two countries in which it is not.

2. On what continents do you find stable or increased forest cover? Does this surprise you given the population growth rates on those continents?

3. Is the greatest deforestation in the western hemisphere associated with the highest population growth rates?

SUGGESTED ADDITIONAL READINGS

Boaz, N. T., and A. J. Almquist
2002   *Biological Anthropology: A Synthetic Approach to Human Evolution*, 2nd ed. Upper Saddle River, NJ: Prentice-Hall. Basic text in physical anthropology; includes discussion of methods.

Katzenberg, M. A., and S. R. Saunders, eds.
2000   *Biological Anthropology of the Human Skeleton.* New York: Wiley. Analysis of skeletal and dental remains, including use of new technology.

Larsen, C. S.
2000   *Skeletons in Our Closet: Revealing Our Past through Bioarchaeology.* Princeton, NJ: Princeton University Press. How human remains from archaeological sites help us interpret lifetime events such as disease, injury, tool use, and diet.

Nafte, M.
2000   *Flesh and Bone: An Introduction to Forensic Anthropology.* Durham, NC: Carolina Academic Press. Methods and procedures, avoiding technical terminology.

Park, M. A.
2002   *Biological Anthropology*, 3rd ed. Boston: McGraw-Hill. A concise introduction, with a focus on scientific inquiry.

Prag, J., and R. Neave
1997   *Making Faces: Using Forensic and Archaeological Evidence.* College Station, TX: Texas A&M University Press. How ancient faces are reconstructed.

Renfrew, C., and P. Bahn
2000   *Archaeology: Theories, Methods, and Practice*, 3rd ed. London: Thames and Hudson. Most useful treatment of methods in archaeological anthropology.

Turnbaugh, W. A., R. Jurmain, L. Kilgore, and H. Nelson
2000   *Understanding Physical Anthropology and Archaeology.* 8th ed. Belmont, CA: Wadsworth. Introduction to these two subfields, with a discussion of methods in each.

White, T. D., and P. A. Folkens
2000   *Human Osteology*, 2nd ed. San Diego: Academic Press. Includes case studies and discussion of molecular osteology, with life-size photos of skeletal parts.

INTERNET EXERCISES

1. Dating Techniques: Go to the USGS website on Fossils, Rocks, and Time (http://pubs.usgs.gov/gip/fossils/contents.html) and read through all the sections.

   a. How do researchers use the law of superposition to date fossils?

   b. What are isotopes? How are they used by researchers to calculate numeric dates for fossils?

   c. How do relative and absolute/numeric dating techniques complement each other?

2. Go to the on-line field journal for the 2002 Warren Wilson College Field School (http://www.warren-wilson.edu/~arch/fs2002/main.html). Read the introduction and then click on Day 1. Browse through each day of the field school to get a sense of what the archaeological research was like.

   a. What are some of the investigative techniques that the archaeologists used?

   b. What were some of the significant discoveries? Why were they important?

3. Archaeological Fieldwork: Visit the Dust Cave Field School website (http://www.dustcave.ua.edu/) and read the History of Dust Cave (http://www.dustcave.ua.edu/history.htm).

   a. Watch the video prepared by CNN of the work done at Dust Cave (http://www.dustcave.ua.edu/dccnn.ram); the video is in RealPlayer format. (If you do not have a player, go to www.realplayer.com). Based on the video, is this portrayal of archaeology what you expected? Is there more to conducting field work than just digging? Was it important for the participants to be able to work as a team?

   b. Go to the "Student Research 1999" page (http://www.dustcave.ua.edu/99/stud99.htm). These are papers written by undergraduate participants at Dust Cave during the summer of 1999. Read through at least one student paper (by clicking on the photograph of that student). What did the student research? What were the conclusions? How does it contribute to the overall understanding of prehistoric life, in Dust Cave?

See Chapter 3 at your McGraw-Hill Online Learning Center for additional review and interactive exercises.

4

EVOLUTION AND GENETICS

Overview

Charles Darwin and Alfred Russel Wallace proposed that natural selection could explain the origin of species, as well as many biological differences and similarities among life forms. For natural selection to work, there needs to be (and there always is) variety within the population undergoing selection.

Darwin didn't know the precise genetic mechanisms that allowed natural selection to work. It was his contemporary Gregor Mendel who discovered that genetic traits are inherited as discrete units, now called chromosomes and genes. Mendel also discovered that hereditary traits may be inherited independently of each other, rather than as a bundle. Such traits may then reunite in new combinations. This genetic recombination supplies some of the variety on which natural selection depends.

The adaptive value of particular traits depends on the environment. If the environment changes, nature can only select from traits that are already

present in the population. If there isn't enough variety to permit adaptation to the environmental change, extinction is likely. New types don't appear just because they are needed.

Other evolutionary mechanisms work along with natural selection. Genetic drift operates most obviously in small populations, where pure chance can easily change gene frequencies. Gene flow and interbreeding keep subgroups of the same species connected genetically and thus work against speciation—the formation of new species.

There are links between genetically determined traits, such as hemoglobins in the blood, and selective forces, such as malaria. Selection through differential resistance to disease has influenced the distribution of human blood groups. Natural selection also has operated on facial features, body size and shape, and many other expressions of human biological diversity.

DNA Backs a Tribe's Tradition of Early Descent from the Jews

NEW YORK TIMES NEWS BRIEF
(BOOK REVIEW)

by Nicholas Wade

May 9, 1999

Note in this account how different lines of evidence come together to solve a problem. The Lemba of southern Africa assert remote Jewish ancestry. They retain customs believed to have survived from a distant time when they lived closer to the Jewish homeland. Yet the Lemba now live thousands of miles from that homeland, among people from whom they are physically, linguistically, and, in many ways, culturally indistinguishable. Biology, language, and culture don't go together in neat bundles. It's possible for people who look different from each other to share more genetic attributes with each other than they do with people who look much more like them. Also, people can look the same, or (in this case) share genetic traits, while speaking different languages and engaging in different cultural traditions.

The Lemba, a Bantu-speaking people of southern Africa, have a tradition that they were led out of Judea by a man named Buba. They practice circumcision, keep one day a week holy and avoid eating pork or piglike animals . . .

The . . . Lemba tradition . . . may be exactly right. A team of geneticists has found that many Lemba men carry in their male [Y] chromosome a set of DNA sequences that is distinctive of the cohanim, the Jewish priests believed to be the descendants of Aaron, [the elder brother of Moses]. This genetic signature [called the cohen genetic signature] . . . is particularly common among Lemba men who belong to the senior of their 12 groups, known as the Buba clan.

Y chromosomes are bequeathed from father to son, more or less unchanged apart from the occasional mutation. The mutations are particularly helpful for reconstructing population history because each lineage of men has its own distinctive pattern of mutations . . .

David B. Goldstein, a population geneticist at Oxford University in England, . . . tested DNA samples collected from the Lemba . . . Dr. Goldstein reported that 9 percent of Lemba men carried the cohen genetic signature, and of those who said they belonged to the Buba clan, 53 percent had the

Geneticists have discovered that Lemba men living in southern Africa have a set of DNA sequences that is distinctive of the cohanim, Jewish priests believed to be the descendants of Aaron, elder brother of Moses.

distinctive sequences. These proportions are similar to those found among the major Jewish populations.

Because the cohen genetic signature is rare or absent in all non-Jewish populations tested so far, the findings strongly support the Lemba tradition of Jewish ancestry . . .

How did a Jewish priestly male chromosome come to be found in a black, Bantu-speaking people that looks very much like its southern African neighbors? [Dr. Tudor Parfitt, director of the Center for Jewish Studies at the School of Oriental and African Studies in London,] . . . who says he believes he has found the answer, first came across the Lemba while giving a lecture in Johannesburg about Ethiopian Jews. Some people in the audience wearing yarmulkes told him they, too, were Jewish.

Dr. Parfitt visited their homes, which are in northern South Africa and Zimbabwe. Many of the Lemba, who number more than 50,000 people, are Christians, but they see no contradiction in professing Judaism, too. He learned that they had an enigmatic tradition about their origin: "We came from the north, from a place called Senna. We left Senna, we crossed Pusela, we came to Africa and there we rebuilt Senna."

Dr. Parfitt said that he was later traveling in the Hadramawt region, a former site of Jewish communities in Yemen, and mentioned the Lemba tradition of Senna to the religious leader of the holy city of Tarim. The leader was surprised to hear it because, he told Dr. Parfitt, there was a nearby village called Senna.

"So I went off to find Senna," Dr. Parfitt said. "It's very remote and had never been visited by anyone before. The local tradition is that centuries ago the valley had been very fertile, irrigated by a dam, the ruins of which are still there. And then the dam burst, they think about a thousand years ago, and the people fled."

There is a valley that leads from Senna to a port on the Yemeni coast called Sayhut. If the winds are right, a ship from Sayhut could reach southern Africa in nine days, Dr. Parfitt said. And the valley that leads from Senna to Sayhut is called the Wadi al-Masilah. Dr. Parfitt believes that Masilah may be the "Pusela" of the Lemba oral tradition . . .

Dr. Parfitt . . . said he had been excited to hear of Dr. Goldstein's genetic results confirming the Lemba tradition . . .

Dr. Parfitt said that in collecting samples from the Lemba—a swab of cells scraped from inside the cheek—he had first explained the purpose of the research to local chiefs and obtained their permission. He then told each individual what was involved, sometimes saying "your blood carries important history, the footprints of your ancestors," if he could not explain the genetics.

Being very keen to know where they came from, the Lemba lined up to give samples, Dr. Parfitt said. They were so pleased to learn the results that Dr. Parfitt was made an honorary Lemba.

Dr. Parfitt said he was particularly appreciative of the honor because Lemba tradition prohibits outside men from becoming Lembas . . . This exclusion of outside males . . . would explain why the cohen genetic signature has been preserved at high frequency among the Lemba for so many centuries.

Source: *New York Times*, May 9, 1999, late edition—final, section 1, p. 1, column 5.

When the Valley of Senna could no longer sustain its people, they fled, eventually reaching southern Africa, where, over the generations, they have assimilated both biologically and culturally. In appearance, the Lemba are indistinguishable from their African neighbors; like them, they speak a Bantu language. Biology, however, is more than meets the eye; biology extends to genetic characteristics. The Lemba retain genetic markers of a Jewish ancestry that dates back a thousand years. Genetic patterns may remain fairly stable over time, as in this case, or may change substantially. Indeed, we'll see in this chapter that genetic change is the basis of biological evolution. Although they retain both biological and cultural markers of their remote Jewish heritage, the Lemba have adapted and changed both biologically and culturally.

Compared with most other animals, humans have uniquely varied ways—cultural and biological—of evolving, of adapting to environmental stresses. Exemplifying cultural adaptation, we manipulate our artifacts and behavior in response to environmental conditions. The ancestors of the Lemba migrated after their irrigation system failed. Contemporary North Americans turn up thermostats or travel to Florida in the winter. We turn on fire hydrants, swim, or ride in air-conditioned cars from New York City to Maine to escape the summer's heat. Although such reliance on culture has increased in the course of human evolution, people haven't stopped adapting biologically. As in other species, human populations adapt genetically in response to environmental forces, and individuals react physiologically to stresses. Thus, when we work in the midday sun, sweating occurs spontaneously, cooling the skin and reducing the temperature of subsurface blood vessels.

We are ready now for a more detailed look at the principles that determine human biological adaptation, variation, and change.

Creationism and Evolution

During the 18th century, many scholars became interested in human origins, biological diversity, and our position within the classification of plants and animals. At that time, the commonly accepted explanation for the origin of species came from

According to creationism all life originated during the six days of creation described in the Bible. Catastrophism proposed that fires and floods, including the biblical deluge involving Noah's ark (depicted in this painting by the American artist Edward Hicks), destroyed certain species. How might a creationist account for differences and similarities between fossils and contemporary life forms?

ilarities and differences had been established at the time of Creation and had not changed.

Fossil discoveries during the 18th and 19th centuries raised doubts about creationism. Fossils showed that different kinds of life had once existed. If all life had originated at the same time, why weren't ancient species still around? Why weren't contemporary plants and animals found in the fossil record? A modified explanation combining creationism with **catastrophism** replaced the original doctrine. In this view, fires, floods, and other catastrophes, including the biblical flood involving Noah's ark, had destroyed ancient species. After each destructive event, God had created again, leading to contemporary species. How did the catastrophists explain certain clear similarities between fossils and modern animals? They argued that some ancient species had managed to survive in isolated areas. For example, after the biblical flood, the progeny of the animals saved on Noah's ark spread throughout the world.

The alternative to creationism and catastrophism was *transformism,* also called **evolution.** Evolutionists believed that species arose from others through a long and gradual process of transformation, or descent with modification. Charles Darwin became the best known of the evolutionists. However, he was influenced by earlier scholars, including his own grandfather. Erasmus Darwin, in a book called *Zoonomia* published in 1794, had proclaimed the common ancestry of all animal species.

Charles Darwin also was influenced by Sir Charles Lyell, the father of geology. During Darwin's famous voyage to South America aboard the *Beagle,* he read Lyell's influential book *Principles of Geology* (1837/1969), which exposed him to Lyell's principle of **uniformitarianism.** Uniformitarianism states that the present is the key to the past. Explanations for past events should be sought in the long-term action of ordinary forces that still work today. Thus, natural forces (rainfall,

Genesis, the first book of the Bible: God had created all life during six days of Creation. According to **creationism,** biological similarities and differences originated at the Creation. Characteristics of life forms were seen as immutable; they could not change. Through calculations based on genealogies in the Bible, the biblical scholars James Ussher and John Lightfoot even managed to trace the Creation to a very specific time: October 23, 4004 BC, at 9 AM.

Carolus Linnaeus (1707–1778), who accepted the biblical account of Creation, developed the first comprehensive and still influential classification, or taxonomy, of plants and animals. He grouped life forms on the basis of similarities and differences in their physical characteristics. He used traits such as the presence of a backbone to distinguish vertebrates from invertebrates and the presence of mammary glands to distinguish mammals from birds. Linnaeus viewed the differences between life forms as part of the Creator's orderly plan. Biological sim-soil deposition, earthquakes, and volcanic action) have gradually built and modified geological features such as mountain ranges. The earth's structure has been transformed gradually through natural forces operating for millions of years (see Weiner 1994).

Uniformitarianism was a necessary building block for evolutionary theory. It cast serious doubt on the belief that the world was only 6,000 years old. It would take much longer for such ordinary forces as rain and wind to produce major geological changes. The longer time span also allowed enough time for the biological changes that fossil discoveries were revealing. Darwin applied the ideas of uniformitarianism and long-term transformation through natural forces to living things. Like other evolutionists, he argued that all life forms are ultimately related. In opposition to the creationists, Darwin argued that the number of species is not immutable but has increased over time. (For more on science, evolution, and creationism, see Futuyma 1995; Gould 1999; Wilson 2002.)

Darwin offered natural selection as a principle that could explain the origin of species, biological diversity, and similarities among related life forms. His major contribution was not the theory of evolution, as most people believe, but the idea that natural selection explains evolutionary change. Natural selection wasn't Darwin's unique discovery. Working independently, the naturalist Alfred Russel Wallace had reached a similar conclusion (Shermer 2002). In a joint paper read to London's Linnaean Society in 1858, Darwin and Wallace made their discovery public. Darwin's book *On the Origin of Species* (1859/1958) offered fuller documentation but created great controversy.

For information about common misconceptions about evolution, see your OLC Internet Exercises

Natural selection is the process by which nature selects the forms most fit to survive and reproduce in a given environment. For natural selection to work on a particular population, there must be variety within that population, as there always is. Natural selection operates when there is competition for *strategic resources* (those necessary for life), such as food and space, between members of the population. Organisms whose attributes render them most fit to survive and reproduce in their environment do so in greater numbers than others do. Over the years, the less fit organisms gradually die out and the favored types survive.

The giraffe's neck can be used to illustrate how natural selection works on variety within a population. In any group of giraffes, there is always variation in neck length. When food is adequate, the animals have no problem feeding themselves with foliage. But in times when there is pressure on strategic resources, so that dietary foliage is not as abundant as usual, giraffes with longer necks have an advantage. They can feed off the higher branches. If this feeding advantage permits longer-necked giraffes to survive and reproduce even slightly more effectively than shorter-necked ones, the trait will be favored by natural selection. The giraffes with longer necks will be more likely to transmit their genetic material to future generations than will giraffes with shorter necks.

An incorrect alternative to this (Darwinian) explanation would be the inheritance of acquired characteristics. That is the idea that in each generation, individual giraffes strain their necks to reach just a bit higher. This straining somehow modifies their genetic material. Over generations of strain, the average neck gradually gets longer through the accumulation of small increments of neck length acquired during the lifetime of each generation of giraffes. This is not how evolution works. If it did work in this way, weight lifters could expect to produce especially muscular babies. Workouts that promise no gain without the pain apply to the physical development of individuals, not species. Instead, evolution works as the process of natural selection takes advantage of the variety that is already present in a population. That's how giraffes got their necks.

The process of natural selection continues as long as the relationship between the population and its environment remains the same. However, if emigration, or some change in the environment, occurs, natural selection will begin to favor types that are more likely to survive and reproduce in the new environment. This new selection will continue until an equilibrium is reached. Environmental change or migration may then occur again. Through such a gradual, branching process, involving adaptation to thousands of environments, natural selection has produced the diverse plants and animals found in the world today.

Genetics

Darwin recognized that for natural selection to operate, there must be variety in the population undergoing selection. Documenting and explaining human variation is a major concern of modern biological anthropology. Genetics, a science that emerged after Darwin, helps us understand the causes of biological variation. We now know that DNA (deoxyribonucleic acid) molecules make up genes and chromosomes, which are the basic hereditary units. Biochemical changes (mutations) in DNA provide much of the variety on which natural selection operates. (See the section on mutation on page 94.) Through sexual reproduction, recombination of the genetic traits of mother and father in each generation leads to new arrangements of the hereditary units received from each parent. Such genetic recombination also adds variety on which natural selection may operate.

Mendelian genetics studies the ways in which chromosomes transmit genes across the generations. *Biochemical genetics* examines structure, function, and changes in DNA. (Our website provides additional information on biochemical genetics.) **Population genetics** investigates natural selection and other causes of genetic variation, stability, and change in breeding populations.

MENDEL'S EXPERIMENTS

In 1856, in a monastery garden, the Austrian monk Gregor Mendel began a series of experiments that were to reveal the basic principles of genetics. Mendel studied the inheritance of seven contrasting traits in pea plants. For each trait there were only two forms. For example, plants were either tall (6 to 7 feet) or short (9 to 18 inches), with no intermediate forms. Similarly, seeds were either smooth or wrinkled, and pea color was either yellow or green.

Mendel discovered that heredity is determined by discrete particles or units. Although traits could disappear in one generation, they reemerged in their original form in later generations. For example, Mendel crossbred pure strains of tall and short plants. Their offspring were all tall. This was the first descending, or first filial, generation, designated F_1. Mendel then interbred the plants of the F_1 generation to produce a gener-

ation of grandchildren, the F_2 generation (Figure 4.1). In this generation, short plants reappeared. Among thousands of plants in the F_2 generation, there was approximately one short plant for every three tall ones.

From similar results with the other six traits, Mendel concluded that although a **dominant** form could mask the other form in *hybrid,* or mixed, individuals, the dominated trait—the **recessive**—was not destroyed; it wasn't even changed. Recessive traits would appear in unaltered form in later generations because genetic traits were inherited as discrete units.

These basic genetic units that Mendel described were factors (now called genes or alleles) located on **chromosomes.** Chromosomes are arranged in matching (homologous) pairs. Humans have 46 chromosomes, arranged in 23 pairs, one in each pair from the father and the other from the mother.

For simplicity, a chromosome may be pictured as a surface (see Figure 4.2) with several positions, to each of which we assign a lowercase letter. Each position is a **gene.** Each gene determines, wholly or partially, a particular biological trait, such as whether one's blood is A, B, or O. **Alleles** (for example, b^1 and b^2 in Figure 4.2) are biochemically different forms of a given gene. In humans, A, B, AB, and O blood types reflect different combinations of alleles of a particular gene.

In Mendel's experiments, the seven contrasting traits were determined by genes located on seven different pairs of chromosomes. The gene for height occurred in one of the seven pairs. When Mendel crossbred pure tall and pure short plants to produce his F_1 generation, each of the offspring received an allele for tallness (T) from one parent and one for shortness (t) from the other. These offspring were mixed, or **heterozygous,** with respect to height; each had two dissimilar alleles of that gene. Their parents, in contrast, had been **homozygous,** possessing two identical alleles of that gene (see Hartl and Jones 2002).

In the next generation (F_2), after the mixed plants were interbred, short plants reappeared in the ratio of one short to three talls. Knowing that shorts only produced shorts, Mendel could assume that they were genetically pure. Another fourth of the F_2 plants produced only talls. The remaining half, like the F_1 generation, were heterozygous; when interbred, they produced three talls for each short. (See Figure 4.3.)

Trait Exhibited by F₁ Hybrids	F₂ Generation (produced by crossbreeding F₁ hybrids)	
	Exhibit Dominant Trait	Exhibit Recessive Trait
Smooth seed shape	Smooth 3	Wrinkled 1
Yellow seed interior	Yellow 3	Green 1
Gray seed coat	Gray 3	White 1
Inflated pod	Inflated 3	Pinched 1
Green pod	Green 3	Yellow 1
Axial pod	Axial 3	Terminal 1
Tall stem	Tall 3	Short 1
	Offspring exhibit dominant or recessive traits in ratio of 3:1.	

Figure 4.1 **Mendel's Second Set of Experiments with Pea Plants.**

Dominant colors are shown unless otherwise indicated.

Dominance produces a distinction between **genotype,** or hereditary makeup, and *phenotype,* or expressed physical characteristics. Genotype is what you really are genetically; phenotype is what you appear as. Mendel's peas had three genotypes—TT, Tt, and tt—but only two phenotypes—tall and short. Because of dominance, the heterozygous plants were just as tall as the genetically pure tall ones. How do Mendel's discoveries apply to humans? Although some of our genetic traits follow Mendelian laws, with only two forms—dominant and recessive—other traits are determined differently. For instance, three alleles determine whether our blood type is A, B, AB, or O. People with two alleles for type O have that blood type. However, if they received a gene for either A or B from one parent and one for O from the other, they will have blood type A or B. In other words, A and B are both dominant over O. A and B are said to be *codominant.* If people inherit a gene for A from one parent and one for B from the other, they will have type AB blood, which is chemically different from the other varieties, A, B, and O.

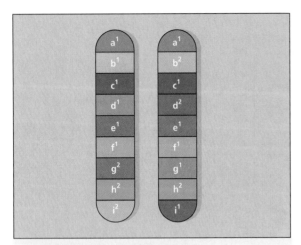

Figure 4.2   Simplified Representation of a Normal Chromosome Pair.
Letters indicate genes; superscripts indicate alleles.

	F1		F2	
	t	t	T	t
T	Tt	Tt	TT	Tt
T	Tt	Tt	tT	tt
Genotypic ratio	0:4:0		1:2:1	
Phenotypic ratio	4:0		3:1	

Figure 4.3   Punnett Squares of a Homozygous Cross and a Heterozygous Cross.
These squares show how phenotypic ratios of the F_1 and F_2 generation are generated. Colors show genotypes.

These three alleles produce four phenotypes—A, B, AB, and O—and six different genotypes—OO, AO, BO, AA, BB, and AB (Figure 4.4). There are fewer phenotypes than genotypes because O is recessive to both A and B.

INDEPENDENT ASSORTMENT AND RECOMBINATION

Through additional experiments, Mendel also formulated his law of **independent assortment.** He discovered that traits are inherited independently of one another. For example, he bred pure round yellow peas with pure wrinkled green ones. All the F_1 generation peas were round and yellow, the dominant forms. But when Mendel interbred the F_1 generation to produce the F_2, four phenotypes turned up. Round greens and wrinkled yellows had been added to the original round yellows and wrinkled greens.

The independent assortment and recombination of genetic traits provide one of the main ways by which variety is produced in any population. **Recombination** is important in biological evolution because it creates new types on which natural selection can operate.

An organism develops from a fertilized egg, or *zygote*, created by the union of two sex cells, one from each parent. The zygote grows rapidly

Figure 4.4   Determinants of Phenotypes (Blood Groups) in the ABO System.
The four phenotypes—A, B, AB, and O—are indicated in parentheses and by color.

through **mitosis,** or ordinary cell division, which continues as the organism grows. The special process by which sex cells are produced is called **meiosis.** Unlike ordinary cell division, in which two cells emerge from one, in meiosis four cells are produced from one. Each has half the genetic material of the original cell. In human meiosis, four cells, each with 23 individual chromosomes, are produced from an original cell with 23 pairs.

With fertilization of egg by sperm, the father's 23 chromosomes combine with the mother's 23 to re-create the pairs in every generation. However, the chromosomes sort independently, so that a

The chromosomes that determine sex in humans. The X chromosome (left) is clearly larger than the Y chromosome (right). What are the genotypes of males and females in terms of these chromosomes?

child's genotype is a random combination of the DNA of its four grandparents. It is conceivable that one grandparent will contribute very little to its grandchild's heredity. Independent assortment of chromosomes is a major source of variety, because the parents' genotypes can be assorted in 2^{23}, or more than 8 million, different ways.

Population Genetics

Population genetics studies stable and changing populations in which most breeding normally takes place (see Gillespie 1998; Hartl 2000). The term **gene pool** refers to all the alleles and genotypes within a breeding population—the "pool" of genetic material available. When population geneticists use the term *evolution,* they have a more specific definition in mind than the one given earlier ("descent with modification over the generations"). For geneticists, **genetic evolution** is defined as change in gene frequency, that is, in the frequency of alleles in a breeding population from generation to generation. Any factor that contributes to such a change can be considered a mechanism of genetic evolution. Those mechanisms include natural selection, mutation, random genetic drift, and gene flow (see Mayr 2001).

Mechanisms of Genetic Evolution

NATURAL SELECTION

The first mechanism of genetic evolution is natural selection, which remains the best explanation for evolution. Essential to understanding evolution through natural selection is the distinction between genotype and phenotype. Genotype refers just to hereditary factors—genes and chromosomes. Phenotype—the organism's evident biological characteristics—develops over the years as the organism is influenced by particular environmental forces. (See the photo of the identical twins on the next page. Identical twins have exactly the same genotype, but their actual biology, their phenotypes, may differ as a result of variation in the environments in which they have been raised.) Also, because of dominance, individuals with different genotypes may have identical phenotypes (like Mendel's tall pea plants). Natural selection can operate only on phenotype—on what is exposed, not on what is hidden. For example, a harmful recessive gene can't be eliminated from the gene pool if it is masked by a favored dominant.

Phenotype includes not only outward physical appearance, but also internal organs, tissues, and cells and physiological processes and systems. Many biological reactions to foods, disease, heat, cold, sunlight, and other environmental factors are not automatic, genetically programmed responses but the product of years of exposure to particular environmental stresses. Human biology is not set at birth but has considerable *plasticity.* That is, it is changeable, being affected by the environmental forces, such as diet and altitude, that we experience as we grow up (see Bogin 2001).

The environment works on the genotype to build the phenotype, and certain phenotypes do better in some environments than other phenotypes do. However, remember that favored phenotypes can be produced by different genotypes. Because natural selection works only on genes that are expressed, maladaptive recessives can be removed only when they occur in homozygous form. When a heterozygote carries a maladaptive

For an example of natural selection, see your OLC Internet Exercises

mhhe
●com
/kottak

Twin Wade on the left is bigger and taller than his brother Wyatt. How can this be if they are identical?

Selection also operates through competition for mates in a breeding population. Males may openly compete for females, or females may choose to mate with particular males because they have desirable traits. Obviously, such traits vary from species to species. Familiar examples include color in birds; male birds, such as cardinals, tend to be more brightly colored than females are. Colorful males have a selective advantage because females like them better. As, over the generations, females have opted for colorful mates, the alleles responsible for color have built up in the species. **Sexual selection,** based on differential success in mating, is the term for this process in which certain traits of one sex are selected because of advantages they confer in winning mates.

recessive, its effects are masked by the favored dominant. The process of perfecting the fit between organisms and their environment is gradual.

Directional Selection　After several generations of selection, gene frequencies will change. Adaptation through natural selection will have occurred. Once that happens, those traits that have proved to be the most **adaptive** (favored by natural selection) in that environment will be selected again and again from generation to generation. Given such *directional selection,* or long-term selection of the same trait(s), maladaptive recessive alleles will be removed from the gene pool.

Directional selection will continue as long as environmental forces stay the same. However, if the environment changes, new selective forces start working, favoring different phenotypes. This also happens when part of the population colonizes a new environment. Selection in the changed, or new, environment continues until a new equilibrium is reached. Then there is directional selection until another environmental change or migration takes place. Over millions of years, such a process of successive adaptation to a series of environments has led to biological modification and branching. The process of natural selection has led to the tremendous array of plant and animal forms found in the world today.

Selection operates *only* on traits that are present in a population. A favorable mutation *may* occur, but a population doesn't normally come up with a new genotype or phenotype just because one is needed or desirable. Many species have become extinct because they weren't sufficiently varied to adapt to environmental shifts.

There are also differences in the amount of environmental stress that organisms' genetic potential enables them to tolerate. Some species are adapted to a narrow range of environments. They are especially endangered by environmental fluctuation. Others—*Homo sapiens* among them—tolerate much more environmental variation because their genetic potential permits many adaptive possibilities. Humans can adapt rapidly to changing conditions by modifying both biological responses and learned behavior. We don't have to delay adaptation until a favorable mutation appears.

Sickle-Cell Anemia　We see that natural selection can *reduce* variety in a population through directional selection—by favoring one allele or trait over another. Selective forces also can work to *maintain* genetic variety by favoring a situation in which the frequencies of two or more alleles of a gene remain constant from generation to generation. This may be because the phenotypes they produce are neutral, equally favored, or equally opposed by selective forces. Sometimes a particular force favors (or opposes) one allele while a different but equally effective force favors (or opposes) the other allele.

One well-studied example involves two alleles, Hb^A and Hb^S, that affect the production of the beta strain (Hb) of human hemoglobin. Hemoglobin, which is located in our red blood cells, carries oxygen from our lungs to the rest of the body via the circulatory system. The allele that produces normal hemoglobin is Hb^A. Another allele, Hb^S, produces a different hemoglobin. Individuals who are homozygous for Hb^S suffer from *sickle-cell anemia*. Such anemia, in which the red blood cells are shaped like crescents or sickles, is associated with a disease that is usually fatal. This condition interferes with the blood's ability to store oxygen. It increases the heart's burden by clogging the small blood vessels.

Given the fatal disease associated with Hb^S, geneticists were surprised to discover that certain populations in Africa, India, and the Mediterranean had very high frequencies of Hb^S (Figure 4.5). In some West African populations, that frequency is around 20 percent. Researchers eventually discovered that both Hb^A and Hb^S are maintained because selective forces in certain environments favor the heterozygote over either homozygote.

Initially, scientists wondered why, if most Hb^S homozygotes died before they reached reproductive age, the harmful allele hadn't been eliminated. Why was its frequency so high? The answer turned out to lie in the heterozygote's greater fitness. Only people who were homozygous for Hb^S died from sickle-cell anemia. Heterozygotes suffered very mild anemia, if any. On the other hand, although people homozygous for Hb^A did not suffer from anemia, they were much more susceptible to *malaria*—a killer disease that continues to plague *Homo sapiens* in the tropics.

The heterozygote, with one sickle-cell allele and one normal one, was the fittest phenotype for a malarial environment. Heterozygotes have enough abnormal hemoglobin, in which malaria parasites cannot thrive, to protect against malaria. They also have enough normal hemoglobin to fend off sickle-cell anemia. The Hb^S allele has been maintained in these populations because the heterozygotes survived and reproduced in greater numbers than did people with any other phenotype.

The sickle-cell allele spread in the tropics as a result of certain economic and cultural changes—specifically, a shift from hunting and gathering to farming (Livingstone 1958). Many societies in West Africa took up a form of cultivation known as *slash and burn*. With this system, trees were cut down and burned to provide ashes for fertilizing the soil. After the land was farmed for one or two years, yields began to drop, and farmers chose another plot to slash and burn.

Slash-and-burn cultivation created breeding areas for *Anopheles* mosquitoes, which carry the malarial parasites and transmit them to people. Farming eroded and hardened the topsoil, increasing rain runoff to pools of stagnant water. The destruction of the forest promoted an increase in malarial mosquitoes, which bred more effectively in water exposed to the sun than in shaded areas. Rare in the forest, mosquitoes became common in the new environment.

Simultaneously, the new economy produced more food than the old one had. This fueled population

Figure 4.5 **Distribution of Sickle-Cell Allele and Falciparum Malaria in the Old World.**

SOURCE: Adapted from *Human Evolution: An Introduction to the New Physical Anthropology* by Joseph B. Birdsell. Copyright © 1975, 1981 by HarperCollins, Publishers, Inc. Reprinted by permission of the publisher.

Beware the *Anopheles* mosquito, vector of malaria. An adult female is shown here. What is a genetic antimalarial?

been reduced through drainage programs and insecticides. Selection against Hb^S also has occurred in the United States among Americans descended from West Africans (Diamond 1997).

MUTATION

The second mechanism of genetic evolution is mutation. Mutations, which occur spontaneously and regularly, provide new biochemical forms—variety—on which natural selection may operate. **Mutations** are changes in the DNA molecules of which genes and chromosomes are built. If a mutation occurs in a sex cell that combines with another as a fertilized egg, the new organism will carry the mutation in every cell. This may result in a biochemical difference between the mutant child and the parent. The abnormal protein associated with sickle-cell anemia is caused by just such a difference in a single allele between normal individuals and those with the disease.

Mutations occur in about 5 percent of sex cells. The rate varies from gene to gene. Many geneticists believe that most mutations are neutral, conferring neither advantage nor disadvantage. Others argue that most mutations are harmful and will be weeded out because they deviate from the types that have been selected over the generations. However, if the selective forces affecting a population change, mutations in its gene pool may acquire an adaptive advantage they lacked in the old environment.

Such chemical alterations may provide a population with entirely new phenotypes, which may offer some advantage. Variants produced through mutation can be especially significant if there is a change in selective forces. They may prove to have an advantage they lacked in the old environment. The spread of Hb^S as farming expanded offers one example.

RANDOM GENETIC DRIFT

The third mechanism of genetic evolution is **random genetic drift.** This is a change in allele frequency that results not from natural selection but from chance. Since random genetic drift is most common in small populations, it has probably been important in human evolution, because humans have lived in small groups during much of our history. In a small population, alleles are likely to be lost by chance.

growth. Villages became larger and closer together. Population density increased, providing more hosts for parasites. In this changed environment, the sickle-cell allele began to play an adaptive role.

The example of the sickle-cell allele demonstrates the relativity of evolution through natural selection: Adaptation and fitness are in relation to specific environments. Traits are not adaptive or maladaptive for all times and places. Even harmful alleles can be selected if heterozygotes have an advantage. Moreover, as the environment changes, favored phenotypes and gene frequencies can change. In malaria-free environments, normal-hemoglobin homozygotes reproduce more effectively than heterozygotes do. With no malaria, the frequency of Hb^S declines, because Hb^S homozygotes can't compete in survival and reproduction with the other types. This has happened in areas of West Africa where malaria has

For an introduction to evolution, see the Virtual Exploration

mhhe
.com
/kottak

To understand why, compare the sorting of alleles to a game involving a bag of 12 marbles, 6 red and 6 blue. In step 1, you draw six marbles from the bag. Statistically, your chances of drawing three reds and three blues are less than those of getting four of one color and two of the other. Step 2 is to fill a new bag with 12 marbles on the basis of the ratio of marbles you drew in step 1. Assume that you drew four reds and two blues: The new bag will have eight red marbles and four blue ones. Step 3 is to draw six marbles from the new bag. Your chances of drawing blues in step 3 are lower than they were in step 1, and the probability of drawing all reds increases. If you do draw all reds, the next bag (step 4) will have only red marbles.

This game is analogous to random genetic drift operating over the generations. The blue marbles were lost purely by chance. Alleles, too, can be lost by chance rather than because of any disadvantage they confer. Lost alleles can reappear in a gene pool only through mutation.

GENE FLOW

The fourth mechanism of genetic evolution is **gene flow,** the exchange of genetic material between populations of the same species. Gene flow, like mutation, works in conjunction with natural selection by providing variety on which selection can work. Gene flow may consist of direct interbreeding between formerly separated populations of the same species (e.g., Europeans, Africans, and Native Americans in the United States), or it may be indirect.

Consider the following hypothetical case (Figure 4.6). In a certain part of the world live six local populations of a certain species. P_1 is the westernmost of these populations. P_2, which interbreeds with P_1, is located 50 miles to the east. P_2 also interbreeds with P_3, located 50 miles east of P_2. Assume that each population interbreeds with, and only with, the adjacent populations. P_6 is located 250 miles from P_1 and does not directly interbreed with P_1, but it is tied to P_1 through the chain of interbreeding that ultimately links all six populations.

Assume further that some allele exists in P_1 that isn't particularly advantageous in its environment. Because of gene flow, this allele may be passed on to P_2, by it to P_3, and so on, until it eventually reaches P_6. In P_6 or along the way, the allele may encounter an environment in which it does

Dr. Heng Wang of the Deutsch Center for Special Needs Children in Middlefield, Ohio works with three siblings (in wheelchairs) at an Amish farm. These children suffer from a genetic disorder, as yet undiagnosed. Intermarriage within small groups, such as the Old Order Amish, increases the likelihood that harmful genes will be expressed in phenotype.

have a selective advantage. If this happens, it may serve, like a new mutation, as raw material on which natural selection can operate.

Alleles are spread through gene flow even when selection is not operating on the allele. In the long run, natural selection works on the variety within a population, whatever its source: mutation, drift, or gene flow. Selection and gene flow have worked together to spread the Hb^S allele in Central Africa. Frequencies of Hb^S in Africa reflect not only the intensity of malaria but also the length of time gene flow has been going on (Livingstone 1969).

Gene flow is important in the study of the origin of species. A **species** is a group of related organisms whose members can interbreed to produce offspring that can live and reproduce. A species has to

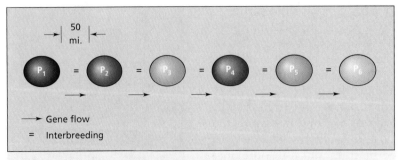

Figure 4.6   **Gene Flow between Local Populations.**
P_1–P_6 are six local populations of the same species. Each interbreeds (=) only with its neighbor(s). Although members of P_6 never interbreed with P_1, P_6 and P_1 are linked through gene flow. Genetic material that originates in P_1 eventually will reach P_6, and vice versa, as it is passed from one neighboring population to the next. Because they share genetic material in this way, P_1–P_6 remain members of the same species. In many species, local populations distributed throughout a larger territory than the 250 miles depicted here are linked through gene flow.

be able to reproduce itself through time. We know that horses and donkeys belong to different species because their offspring cannot meet the test of long-term survival. A horse and a donkey may breed to produce a mule, but mules are sterile. So are the off-spring of lions with tigers. Gene flow tends to prevent **speciation**—the formation of new species—unless subgroups of the same species are separated for a sufficient length of time.

When gene flow is interrupted, and isolated subgroups are maintained, new species may arise. Imagine that an environmental barrier arises between P_3 and P_4, so that they no longer interbreed. If over time, as a result of isolation, P_1, P_2, and P_3 become incapable of interbreeding with the other three populations, speciation will have occurred.

Human Biological Adaptation

This section considers several examples of human biological diversity that reflect adaptation to environmental stresses, such as disease, diet, and climate. There is abundant evidence for human genetic adaptation and thus for evolution (change in gene frequency) through selection working in specific environments. One example is the adaptive value of the Hb^S heterozygote and its spread in malarial environments. Adaptation and evolution go on in specific environments. There is no generally or ideally adaptive allele and no perfect phenotype. Nor can an allele be assumed to be maladaptive for all times and all places. We have seen that even Hb^S, which produces a lethal anemia, has a selective advantage in the heterozygous form in malarial environments.

Also, alleles that were once maladaptive may lose their disadvantage if the environment shifts. Color blindness (disadvantageous for hunters and forest dwellers) and a form of genetically determined diabetes are examples. Today's environment contains medical techniques that allow people with such conditions to live fairly normal lives. Formerly maladaptive alleles have thus become neutral with respect to selection. With thousands of human genes now known, new genetic traits are discovered almost every day. Such studies tend to focus on genetic abnormalities, because of their medical and treatment implications.

In June 2000 scientists announced completion of a first draft of a map of the human genome—all our genes and chromosomes—some 3 billion genetic letters in human DNA. One of the two main groups behind this discovery is the National Institutes of Health's Human Genome Project, whose website is worth a visit: **http://www.ornl.gov/hgmis/.**

Given current knowledge about genetically transmitted diseases, people with a family history of such a disease can be advised about their children's chances of being affected. Many currently incurable hereditary illnesses are destined to become neutral traits in tomorrow's medical environment. However, genetic testing raises many ethical questions. Given possible discrimination in employment and in obtaining health insurance, some members of the medical community have advised people not to be tested for genetic markers that might indicate a tendency to develop, say, Alzheimer's disease. Laws to forbid genetic discrimination are not yet fully in place. Alzheimer's is likely to become much more prevalent, and costly to treat as a public health problem, as the baby-boomer cohort ages.

Genetic discrimination isn't new. Some of its most virulent manifestations occurred in Adolph Hitler's Third Reich. More surprisingly, in 1997 it was revealed that, through the 1970s, some 60,000 people were sterilized in Sweden, and 11,000 in Finland, as part of government policies designed to weed out traits such as poor eyesight and Gypsy features (Wade 1997). This is an example of **eugenics,** a highly controversial movement aimed at genetic improvement by encouraging the reproduction of individuals with favored features and discouraging that of individuals with features deemed undesirable. Should past crimes committed in the name of eugenics prevent people from being allowed to choose benefits that genetic engineering may offer in the future? A related question: What ethical questions are raised by the cloning of human beings? Cloning can be combined with genetic enhancement—adding genes to produce desired traits. Genetic enhancement has been the main reason for cloning animals, such as Dolly the lamb, introduced in 1997 as the world's first mammal cloned from an adult donor cell.

In cloning, a cell is taken from a donor animal and inserted into an egg cell (of the same species) whose genetic material has been removed. This allows the donor's genetic material to direct the development of a new embryo, then fetus, then live animal, which will be the donor's identical twin. Successful animal cloning has made it possible to think seriously about using cloning for the genetic enhancement of human beings (Kolata 1997). Scientists could grow a person's cells in sheets in the laboratory and sprinkle those cells with genes. The cells that take up the genes could be used as donor cells to make human clones, which would contain the added genes in every cell of their bodies. With humans the first genetic enhancements would probably be genes to protect against diseases. Genes to counter AIDS and Alzheimer's disease have already been identified. Some scientists see this process as no different morally from vaccinating a child. Here are some ethical questions to consider: Who would raise human clones: scientists or families? What would be the legal status of clones? Would they be people

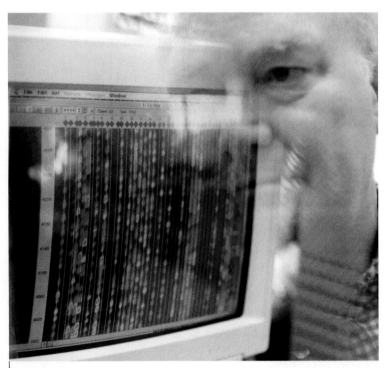

DNA specialist Craig Venter of Celera Genomics, Inc. looks at a computer monitor showing genome sequencing. On June 26, 2000 Celera announced the completion of a draft of the human genome—all our genes and chromosomes.

or products? Would they be free human beings or entities designed to satisfy wishes, whims, and medical needs of others? What do you think about the ethics of human cloning?

GENES AND DISEASE

According to the *World Health Report*, published by the World Health Organization (WHO) in Geneva, Switzerland, tropical diseases affect more than 10 percent of the world's population. Malaria, the most widespread of these diseases, afflicts between 300 million and 500 million people annually. Schistosomiasis (snail fever), a waterborne parasitic disease, affects more than 200 million. Some 120 million people have filariasis, which causes elephantiasis—lymphatic obstruction leading to the enlargement of body parts, particularly the legs and scrotum (check out the website of the World Health Organization at http://www.who.int/home/).

The malaria threat is spreading. Brazil had 560,000 cases in 1988, versus 100,000 in 1977. Worldwide, the number of malaria cases rose from 270 million in 1990 to over 400 million in 1997 (*New York Times* 1990; World Health Organization 1997). Contributing to this rise is the increasing resistance of parasites to drugs used to treat malaria. However, hundreds of millions of people are genetically resistant. Sickle-cell hemoglobin is the best known of the genetic antimalarials (Diamond 1997).

Microbes have been major selective agents for humans, particularly before the arrival of modern medicine. Some people are genetically more susceptible to certain diseases than others are, and the distribution of human blood types continues to change in response to natural selection.

After food production emerged around 10,000 years ago, infectious diseases posed a mounting risk and eventually became the foremost cause of human mortality. Food production favors infection for several reasons. Cultivation sustains larger, denser populations and a more sedentary life style than does hunting and gathering. People live closer to each other and to their own wastes, making it easier for microbes to survive and to find hosts. Domesticated animals also transmit diseases to people.

Until 1977, when the last case of smallpox was reported, smallpox had been a major threat to humans and a determinant of blood group fre-

quencies (Diamond 1990, 1997). The smallpox virus is a mutation from one of the pox viruses that plague such domesticated animals as cows, sheep, goats, horses, and pigs. Smallpox appeared in human beings after people and animals started living together. Smallpox epidemics have played important roles in world history, often killing one-fourth to one-half of the affected populations. Smallpox contributed to Sparta's defeat of Athens in 430 BC and to the decline of the Roman empire after AD 160.

The ABO blood groups have figured in human resistance to smallpox. Blood is typed according to the protein and sugar compounds on the surface of the red blood cells. Different substances (compounds) distinguish between type A and type B blood. Type A cells trigger the production of *antibodies* in B blood, so that A cells clot in B blood. The different substances work like chemical passwords; they help us distinguish our own cells from invading cells, including microbes, we ought to destroy. The surfaces of some microbes have substances similar to ABO blood group substances. We don't produce antibodies to substances similar to

AIDS is widespread in many African nations such as Rwanda—shown here—as well as in the United States, France, Thailand, Brazil, and many other countries. What would be evidence for genetic variation in susceptibility to the HIV virus?

those on our own blood cells. We can think of this as a clever evolutionary trick by the microbes to deceive their hosts, because we don't normally develop antibodies against our own biochemistry.

People with A or AB blood are more susceptible to smallpox than are people with type B or type O. Presumably this is because a substance on the smallpox virus mimics the type A substance, permitting the virus to slip by the defenses of the type A individual. By contrast, type B and type O individuals produce antibodies against smallpox because they recognize it as a foreign substance.

The relation between type A blood and susceptibility to smallpox was first suggested by the low frequencies of the A allele in areas of India and Africa where smallpox had been endemic. A comparative study done in rural India in 1965–66, during a virulent smallpox epidemic, did much to confirm this relationship. Drs. F. Vogel and M. R. Chakravartti analyzed blood samples from smallpox victims and their uninfected siblings (Diamond 1990). The researchers found 415 infected children, none ever vaccinated against smallpox. All but eight of the infected children had an uninfected (also unvaccinated) sibling.

The results of the study were clear: Susceptibility to smallpox varied with ABO type. Of the 415 infected children, 261 had the A allele; 154 lacked it. Among their 407 uninfected siblings, the ratio was reversed. Only 80 had the A allele; 327 lacked it. The researchers calculated that a type A or type AB person had a seven times greater chance of getting smallpox than did an O or B person.

In most human populations, the O allele is more common than A and B combined. A is most common in Europe; B frequencies are highest in Asia. Since smallpox was once widespread in the Old World, we might wonder why natural selection didn't eliminate the A allele entirely. The answer appears to be this: Other diseases spared the type A people and penalized those with other blood groups.

For example, type O people seem to be especially susceptible to the bubonic plague—the "Black Death" that killed a third of the population of medieval Europe. Type O people are also more likely to get cholera, which has killed as many people in India as smallpox has. On the other hand, blood group O may increase resistance to syphilis. The ravages of that venereal disease,

which may have originated in the New World, may explain the very high frequency of type O blood among the natives of Central and South America. The distribution of human blood groups appears to represent a compromise among the selective effects of many diseases.

Associations between ABO blood type and noninfectious disorders also have been noted. Type O individuals are most susceptible to duodenal and gastric ulcers. Type A individuals seem most prone to stomach and cervical cancer and ovarian tumors. However, since these noninfectious disorders tend to occur after reproduction has ended, their relevance to adaptation and evolution through natural selection is doubtful (see also Weiss 1993).

Understanding Ourselves In the weeks and months after September 11, 2001, millions of Americans started worrying about anthrax—and more generally about biological terrorism. Anthrax, we learned, is easily treated with antibiotics such as Cipro and doxycycline. But what about other diseases—ones whose cure isn't as easy and risk-free? What about smallpox, a viral disease that had been eradicated in nature? Could evildoers seize smallpox samples stored in labs and unleash an epidemic? The U.S. government started preparing for a possible smallpox attack. The plan was to increase the supply and availability of smallpox vaccine. But who would receive it? Although it is a highly effective vaccine, a smallpox inoculation has been known to kill people who otherwise would never have been exposed to the disease. Knowing what you now know about blood groups and smallpox, would you want to pay attention to an individual's ABO blood type before administering smallpox vaccine? Which recipients probably would be at greatest risk?

In the case of diseases for which there are no effective drugs, genetic resistance maintains its significance. There is probably genetic variation in susceptibility to the HIV virus, for example. We know that people exposed to HIV vary in their risk of developing AIDS and in the rate at which the disease progresses. AIDS is widespread in many African nations (and in the United States, France, and Brazil). Particularly in Africa, where treatment strategies now used in the industrial nations are not widely available, the death rate from AIDS could eventually (let us hope it does not) rival that of past epidemics of smallpox and plague. If so, AIDS could cause large shifts in human gene frequencies—again illustrating the ongoing operation of natural selection.

FACIAL FEATURES

Natural selection also affects facial features. For instance, long noses seem to be adaptive in arid areas (Brace 1964; Weiner 1954), because membranes and blood vessels inside the nose moisten the air as it is breathed in. Long noses are also adaptive in cold environments, because blood vessels warm the air as it is breathed in. This nose form distances the brain, which is sensitive to bitter cold, from raw outer air. These were adaptive biological features for humans who lived in cold climates before the invention of central heating.

The association between nose form and temperature is recognized as **Thomson's nose rule** (Thomson and Buxton 1923), which shows up statistically. In plotting the geographic distribution of nose length among human populations, the average nose does tend to be longer in areas with lower mean annual temperatures.

Other facial features also illustrate adaptation to selective forces. Among contemporary humans, average tooth size is largest among Native Australian hunters and gatherers, for whom large teeth had an adaptive advantage, given a diet based on foods with a considerable amount of sand and grit. People with small teeth—if false teeth and sand-free foods are unavailable—can't feed themselves as effectively as people with more massive dentition can (see Brace 2000).

SIZE AND BODY BUILD

Certain body builds have adaptive advantages for particular environments. The relation between body weight and temperature is summarized in **Bergmann's rule:** The smaller of two bodies similar in shape has more surface area per unit of weight. Therefore, it sheds heat more efficiently. (Heat loss occurs on the body's surface—the skin perspires.) Average body size tends to increase in cold areas and to decrease in hot ones because big bodies hold heat better than small ones do. To be

more precise, in a large sample of native populations, average adult male weight increased by 0.66 pound (0.3 kilogram) for every 1 degree Fahrenheit fall in mean annual temperature (Roberts 1953; Steegman 1975). The "pygmies" and the San, who live in hot climates and weigh only 90 pounds on the average, illustrate this relation in reverse.

Body shape differences also reflect adaptation to temperature through natural selection. The relationship between temperature and body shape in animals and birds was first recognized in 1877 by the zoologist J. A. Allen. **Allen's rule** states that the relative size of protruding body parts—ears, tails, bills, fingers, toes, limbs, and so on—increases with temperature. Among humans, slender bodies with long digits and limbs are advantageous in tropical climates. Such bodies increase body surface relative to mass and allow for more efficient heat dissipation. Among the cold-adapted Eskimos, the opposite phenotype is found. Short limbs and stocky bodies serve to conserve heat. Cold area populations tend to have larger chests and shorter arms than do people from warm areas (Roberts 1953).

This discussion of adaptive relationships between climate and body size and shape illustrates that natural selection may achieve the same effect in different ways. East African Nilotes, who live in a hot area, have tall, linear bodies with elongated extremities that increase surface area relative to mass and thus maximize heat dissipation (illustrating Allen's rule). Among the "pygmies," the reduction of body size achieves the same result (illustrating Bergmann's rule). Similarly, the large bodies of northern Europeans and the compact stockiness of the Eskimos serve the same function of heat conservation.

Interpret the World Map 4 in your atlas shows the relation between body mass index and mean annual temperature. People adapt both culturally and biologically, and some human groups haven't lived in their current habitats long enough for long-term biological adaptation to have occurred. Nevertheless, try to locate areas on the map where Bergmann's and Allen's rules are illustrated with respect to cold adaptation (big or compact bodies) and heat adaptation (small or elongated bodies).

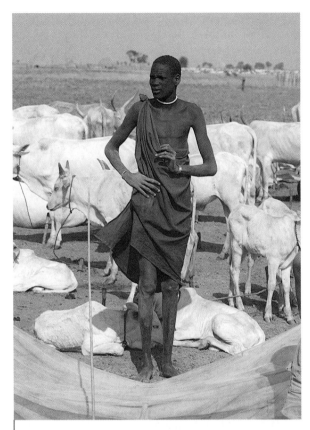

This Nilotic man, a Nuer herder from Sudan, has a tall linear body with elongated extremities (note his fingers). Such proportioning increases the surface area relative to mass and thus dissipates heat (Allen's rule). What other body form can achieve the same result?

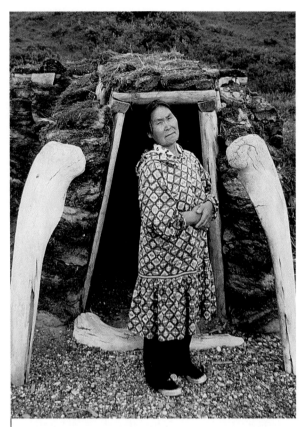

Cold weather populations tend to have relatively larger chests and shorter arms than do people from warm areas. Among the cold-adapted Inuit, such as this Alaskan woman, short limbs and stocky bodies help to conserve heat. How important is biology to cold adaptation today?

LACTOSE TOLERANCE

Many biological traits that illustrate human adaptation are not under simple genetic control. Genetic determination of such traits may be likely but unconfirmed, or several genes may interact to influence the trait in question. Sometimes there is a genetic component, but the trait also responds to stresses encountered during growth. We speak of **phenotypical adaptation** when adaptive changes occur during the individual's lifetime. Phenotypical adaptation is made possible by biological plasticity—our ability to change in response to the environments we encounter as we grow (see Frisancho 1993; Bogin 2001). Recall the discussion of physiological adaptation to high altitude in Chapter 1.

Genes and phenotypical adaptation work together to produce a biochemical difference between human groups in the ability to digest large amounts of milk—an adaptive advantage when other foods are scarce and milk is available, as it is in dairying societies. All milk, whatever its source, contains a complex sugar called *lactose*. The digestion of milk depends on an enzyme called *lactase*, which works in the small intestine. Among all mammals except humans and some of their pets, lactase production ceases after weaning, so that these animals can no longer digest milk.

Lactase production and the ability to tolerate milk vary between populations. About 90 percent of northern Europeans and their descendants are lactose tolerant; they can digest several glasses of milk with no difficulty. Similarly, about 80 percent of two African populations, the Tutsi of Rwanda and Burundi in East Africa and the Fulani of Nigeria in West Africa, produce lactase and digest milk easily. Both these groups traditionally have been herders. However, such nonherders as the Yoruba and Igbo in Nigeria, the Baganda in Uganda, the Japanese and other Asians, Eskimos, South American Indians, and many Israelis cannot digest lactose (Kretchmer 1972/1975).

However, the variable human ability to digest milk seems to be a difference of degree. Some populations can tolerate very little or no milk, but others are able to metabolize much greater quantities. Studies show that people who move from no-milk or low-milk diets to high-milk diets increase their lactose tolerance; this suggests some phenotypical adaptation. We can conclude that no simple genetic trait accounts for the ability to digest milk. Lactose tolerance appears to be one of many aspects of human biology governed both by genes and by phenotypical adaptation to environmental conditions.

Understanding Ourselves "Hey, it's all in the genes." When did you last hear a statement like that? We routinely use assumptions about genetic determination to explain, say, why tall parents have tall kids or why obesity runs in families. But how true is the statement? How much do our genes influence our bodies? The genetic causes of some of our physical traits are clear. This is true with the ABO blood group system, and with other blood factors, such as whether we are Rh positive or negative and whether we are sickle-cell carriers. But the genetic roots of other physical traits aren't so clear. A grandmother may assert that her inability to digest milk runs in her family—so they never bought milk. What would have happened if they had consumed small quantities of milk over the years? Would they gradually have become habituated to lactose? There's evidence that such habituation is possible because of the plasticity of human genotypes. Can you crease or fold your tongue by raising its sides? Some people can; some people never can; some people who never thought they could can after practice. Again, an apparent genetic limitation turns out to be more plastic.

Human biology is plastic, but only to a degree. If you're born with blood group O, you've got it for the rest of your life. The same applies to disorders due to harmful genes, such as those that cause hemophilia (transmitted on the X chromosome) and sickle-cell anemia. Still, if there's no genetic solution, there may be a cultural one. Modern medicine now treats effectively a variety of genetic disorders that once would have been much more life-threatening. Fortunately for us, plasticity through culture steps in to complement human biological plasticity.

We see that human biology changes constantly, even without genetic change. In this chapter we've considered ways in which humans adapt biologically to their environments, and the effects of such adaptation on human biological diversity. Modern biological anthropology seeks to *explain* specific aspects of human biological variation. The explanatory framework encompasses the same mechanisms—selection, mutation, drift, gene flow, and plasticity—that govern adaptation, variation, and evolution among other life forms (see Futuyma 1998; Mayr 2001).

SUMMARY

1. In the 18th century, Carolus Linnaeus developed biological taxonomy. He viewed differences and similarities among organisms as part of God's orderly plan rather than as evidence for evolution. Charles Darwin and Alfred Russel Wallace proposed that natural selection could explain the origin of species, biological diversity, and similarities among related life forms. Natural selec-

tion requires variety in the population undergoing selection.

2. Through breeding experiments with peas in 1856, Gregor Mendel discovered that genetic traits pass on as units. These are now known to be chromosomes, which occur in homologous pairs. Alleles, some dominant, some recessive, are the chemically different forms that occur at a

given genetic locus. Mendel also formulated the law of independent assortment. Each of the seven traits he studied in peas was inherited independently of all the others. Independent assortment of chromosomes and their recombination provide some of the variety needed for natural selection. But the major source of such variety is mutation, a chemical change in the DNA molecules of which genes are made.

3. Population genetics studies gene frequencies in stable and changing populations. Natural selection is the most important mechanism of evolutionary change. Others are mutation, random genetic drift, and gene flow. Given environmental change, nature selects traits already present in the population. If variety is insufficient to permit adaptation to the change, extinction is likely. New types don't appear just because they are needed.

4. One well-documented case of natural selection in contemporary human populations is that of the sickle-cell allele. In homozygous form, the sickle-cell allele, Hb^s, produces an abnormal hemoglobin. This clogs the small blood vessels, impairing the blood's capacity to store oxygen. The result is sickle-cell anemia, which is usually fatal. The distribution of Hb^s has been linked to that of malaria. Homozygotes for normal hemo-

globin are susceptible to malaria and die in great numbers. Homozygotes for the sickle-cell allele die from anemia. Heterozygotes get only mild anemia and are resistant to malaria. In a malarial environment, the heterozygote has the advantage. This explains why an apparently maladaptive allele is preserved.

5. Other mechanisms of genetic evolution complement natural selection. Random genetic drift operates most obviously in small populations, where pure chance can easily change allele frequencies. Gene flow and interbreeding keep subgroups of the same species genetically connected and thus impede speciation.

6. Differential resistance to infectious diseases has influenced the distribution of human blood groups. Natural selection also has operated on facial features and body size and shape. Phenotypical adaptation refers to adaptive changes that occur in the individual's lifetime, in response to the environment the organism encounters as it grows. Biological similarities between geographically distant populations may be due to similar but independent genetic changes, rather than to common ancestry. Or they may reflect similar physiological responses to common stresses during growth.

KEY TERMS

See the flash cards

mhhe
●com
/kottak

adaptive   Favored by natural selection in a particular environment.

allele   A biochemical variant of a particular gene.

Allen's rule   Rule stating that the relative size of protruding body parts (such as ears, tails, bills, fingers, toes, and limbs) tends to increase in warmer climates.

Bergmann's rule   Rule stating that the smaller of two bodies similar in shape has more surface area per unit of weight and can therefore dissipate heat more efficiently; hence, large bodies tend to be found in colder areas and small bodies in warmer ones.

catastrophism   View that extinct species were destroyed by fires, floods, and other catastrophes. After each destructive event, God created again, leading to contemporary species.

chromosomes   Basic genetic units, occurring in matching (homologous) pairs; lengths of DNA made up of multiple genes.

creationism   Explanation for the origin of species given in Genesis: God created the species during the original six days of Creation.

dominant   Allele that masks another allele in a heterozygote.

eugenics   Controversial movement aimed at genetic improvement by encouraging the reproduction of individuals with favored features and discouraging that of individuals with features deemed undesirable.

evolution   Belief that species arose from others through a long and gradual process of transformation, or descent with modification.

gene   Area in a chromosome pair that determines, wholly or partially, a particular biological trait, such as whether one's blood type is A, B, or O.

gene flow   Exchange of genetic material between populations of the same species through direct or indirect interbreeding.

gene pool   All the alleles and genotypes within a breeding population—the "pool" of genetic material available.

genetic evolution   Change in gene frequency within a breeding population.

genotype   An organism's hereditary makeup.

heterozygous   Having dissimilar alleles of a given gene.

homozygous   Possessing identical alleles of a particular gene.

independent assortment   Mendel's law of; chromosomes are inherited independently of one another.

meiosis   Special process by which sex cells are produced; four cells are produced from one, each with half the genetic material of the original cell.

Mendelian genetics   Studies ways in which chromosomes transmit genes across the generations.

mitosis   Ordinary cell division; DNA molecules copy themselves, creating two identical cells out of one.

mutation   Change in the DNA molecules of which genes and chromosomes are built.

natural selection   Originally formulated by Charles Darwin and Alfred Russel Wallace; the process by which nature selects the forms most fit to survive and reproduce in a given environment, such as the tropics.

phenotypical adaptation   Adaptive biological changes that occur during the individual's lifetime, made possible by biological plasticity.

population genetics   Field that studies causes of genetic variation, maintenance, and change in breeding populations.

random genetic drift   Change in gene frequency that results not from natural selection but from chance; most common in small populations.

recessive   Genetic trait masked by a dominant trait.

recombination   Following independent assortment of chromosomes, new arrangements of hereditary units produced through bisexual reproduction.

sexual selection   Based on differential success in mating, the process in which certain traits of one sex (e.g., color in male birds) are selected because of advantages they confer in winning mates.

speciation   Formation of new species; occurs when subgroups of the same species are separated for a sufficient length of time.

species   Population whose members can interbreed to produce offspring that can live and reproduce.

Thomson's nose rule   Rule stating that the average nose tends to be longer in areas with lower mean annual temperatures; based on the geographic distribution of nose length among human populations.

uniformitarianism   Belief that explanations for past events should be sought in ordinary forces that continue to work today.

CRITICAL THINKING QUESTIONS

For more self testing, see the self quizzes

mhhe
● **com**
/kottak

1. If you are (or are pretending you are) a creationist, what do you see as the most convincing evidence for evolution?

2. If you are (or are pretending you are) an evolutionist, what do you see as the least convincing evidence for evolution?

3. Which of the examples of natural selection mentioned in the book most surprised you? Can you think of examples of natural selection other than those mentioned in the book?

4. Choose five people in your classroom who illustrate a range of phenotypical diversity. Which of their features vary most evidently? How do you explain this variation? Is some of the variation due to culture rather than to biology?

5. Imagine that some of the seven traits that Mendel studied in pea plants were determined by genes on the same chromosome. How might his results have differed?

6. Give three examples of how and why identical genotypes might develop different phenotypes. (Identical twins and clones have identical genotypes.)

7. Is *Homo sapiens* more or less adaptable than other species? What makes us so adaptable? Can you think of some species that are more adaptable than we are?

8. What are two important lessons to be learned from the case of the sickle-cell allele (Hb^S)?

9. Which of the mechanisms of genetic evolution acts to prevent speciation?

10. Did anything stated in this chapter about your ABO blood type give you cause for alarm? Why?

11. How would you design the ideal body for a very cold climate? How about for a very hot one?

12. Besides those mentioned in the book, give an example of a biological trait that depends on physiological adaptation.

Atlas Questions

Look at Map 4, "Human Variations: Height and Weight."

1. Which areas have the biggest (heaviest) people? Does this illustrate Bergmann's or Allen's rule?

2. Which areas have populations with compact builds? Does this illustrate Bergmann's or Allen's rule?

3. Where are the world's smallest indigenous populations located? Which rule does this illustrate?

SUGGESTED ADDITIONAL READINGS

Bogin, B.

2001 *The Growth of Humanity.* New York: Wiley-Liss. Up-to-date perspective on human growth and development.

Cavalli-Sforza, L. L., P. Menozzi, and A. Piazza

1994 *The History and Geography of Human Genes.* Princeton, NJ: Princeton University Press. Comprehensive look at the geographic spread of human genes.

Eiseley, L.

1961 *Darwin's Century.* Garden City, NY: Doubleday, Anchor Books. Discussion of Lyell, Darwin, Wallace, and other major contributors to natural selection and transformation.

Frisancho, A. R.

1993 *Human Adaptation and Accommodation.* Ann Arbor: University of Michigan Press. Influence of the environment on phenotype, particularly during growth and development; a basic text.

Futuyma, D. J.

1995   *Science on Trial,* updated ed. Sunderland, MA: Sinauer Associates. The case of evolution versus creationism—favoring the former.

1998   *Evolutionary Biology.* Sunderland, MA: Sinauer Associates. Basic text.

Gillespie, J. H.

1998   *Population Genetics: A Concise Guide.* Baltimore: Johns Hopkins University Press. Good introduction to population genetics.

Gould, S. J.

1999   *Rock of Ages: Science and Religion in the Fullness of Life.* New York: Ballantine Books. Evolution, science, and religion by the well-known naturalist and science writer.

Hartl, D. L.

2000   *A Primer of Population Genetics,* 3rd ed. Sunderland, MA: Sinauer Associates. Short introduction to the field.

Hartl, D. L., and E. W. Jones

2002   *Essential Genetics,* 3rd ed. Sudbury, MA: Jones and Bartlett. Basic introduction to genetics.

Lewontin, R.

2000   *It Ain't Necessarily So: The Dream of the Human Genome and Other Illusions.* New York: New York Review of Books. Questions about nature, nurture, and contemporary genetic research.

Mayr, E.

2001   *What Evolution Is.* New York: Basic Books. A master scholar sums it all up.

Roberts, D. F.

1986   *Genetic Variation and Its Maintenance: With Particular Reference to Tropical Populations.* New York: Cambridge University Press. Evidence for human genetic evolution, with a focus on tropical populations.

Shermer, M.

2002   *In Darwin's Shadow: The Life and Science of Alfred Russel Wallace.* New York: Oxford University Press. The other inventor of natural selection.

Stinson, S., ed.

2000   *Human Biology: An Evolutionary and Biocultural Perspective.* New York: Wiley. Articles on physical anthropology and human biology.

Weiner, J.

1994   *The Beak of the Finch: A Story of Evolution in Our Time.* New York: Alfred A. Knopf. An excellent introduction to Darwin and to evolutionary theory.

Weiss, K. M.

1993   *Genetic Variation and Human Disease: Principles and Evolutionary Approaches.* New York: Cambridge University Press. Selection connected with human diseases.

Wilson, D. S.

2002   *Darwin's Cathedral: Evolution, Religion, and the Nature of Society.* Chicago: University of Chicago Press. Religion, sociology, and evolution.

INTERNET EXERCISES

1. Creationism: Look at the CreationWise cartoon website, **http://members.aol.com/dwr51055/humor.htm**. This site uses cartoons to express the concerns creationists have about evolution.

   a. What is the creationist version of the origin of life? What evidence do they use to support their claims? According to these cartoons, what are some of the problems that creationists have with evolution?

   b. What would be the response to these questions from a scientist who studies evolution?

2. Adaptation to Environment: Read Dennis O'Neil's page on "Adapting to Climate Extremes" (**http://anthro.palomar.edu/adapt/adapt_2.htm**).

   a. What is Bergmann's rule? What is Allen's rule?

   b. How do the !Kung and Australian Aborigines respond to cold differently from the Inuit and groups from Tierra del Fuego? Is there an adaptive reason why these groups have different responses to cold?

   c. What are the advantages of evaporative cooling? What are the disadvantages?

See Chapter 4 at your McGraw-Hill Online Learning Center for additional review and interactive exercises.

5

THE PRIMATES

Overview

Humans, apes, monkeys, and prosimians all belong to the zoological order known as primates. The apes are our closest relatives. Humans share more than 98 percent of our DNA with chimpanzees and gorillas.

Early primates, like many contemporary ones, lived in the trees. Reflecting our arboreal heritage, primates share certain anatomical features. These include grasping hands with opposable thumbs, depth and color vision, and use of the fingertip pads as the main organs of touch. With large and complex brains, humans, apes, and monkeys rely extensively on learning. Primates live in social groups and invest considerable time and energy in their offspring and kin.

Gorillas, the least arboreal apes, are vegetarians confined to equatorial Africa. Two species of chimpanzees live in the forests and woodlands of tropical Africa. All the apes and many other primate species are endangered, mainly by deforestation and human hunting. Some important developments in human evolution, such as hunting and tool making, are foreshadowed in other primates, particularly chimpanzees. It is likely that for millions of years sharing and cooperation have been basic features of human social life. Other primates show affection with their kin, but only humans have systems of kinship and marriage that permit us to maintain lifelong ties with relatives in different local groups.

Chimp Tool Sites Show Evidence of Human-like Behavior

CBC News Brief

May 26, 2002

Primatologists study nonhuman primates, such as apes, monkeys, and lemurs. The study of monkeys, and particularly of apes, our nearest zoological relatives, is of interest to anthropology mainly because their attributes and their behavior tell us something about human nature and origins. To what extent are we distinct, especially from chimpanzees, which share more than 98 percent of our DNA? What about tool making, a key ingredient in human cultural adaptation, permitting our survival and expansion? More than any other primate, chimps share the human capacity for deliberate tool manufacture, as the following news story demonstrates. As you read this account, think about how primatology and archaeology can be combined to shed light on early human behavior.

At Tai National Park (Ivory Coast), young chimps learn from their mothers how to use stone tools to crack nuts. Is this cultural behavior?

WASHINGTON—Chimpanzees in a remote West African rainforest use crude stone tools to crack open nuts, a skill which they teach to their young, researchers have found.

The chimpanzees used hammer stones to break open hard, golfball-sized nuts from panda trees.

Melissa Panger of George Washington University studies primate tool use and is a co-author of the nut cracking report, which appears in Friday's issue of the journal *Science*.

Panger said the chimps showed precise control over the force needed to break open the nuts. It takes a lot of pressure, but if too much is applied then the nuts shatter into inedible pieces, she said.

Panger's colleagues on the study were Christophe Boesch, an expert on chimpanzee behavior at the Max Planck Institute for Evolutionary Anthropology in Germany and Julio Mercader, a specialist in rainforest archaeology at the George Washington University Department of Anthropology.

The team found the nut shells and remains were concentrated in a nut cracking area called Panda 100 in Ivory Coast's Tai National Park.

The area is what archeologists call a site, and the researchers say their study is the first time archeology has been successfully applied to past chimpanzee behavior.

At the nut cracking sites, the chimps gather their nuts, put them on trees which are used as anvils, and pound the nuts with heavy stones.

Mothers showed their young how to crack the nuts, the same way humans teach their children.

The nut cracking behavior is limited to chimps living in Ivory Coast, Liberia and Guinea-Conakry, even though the nuts and stones are available to chimps in central Africa. Experts say the difference may mean it is a cultural, learned behavior.

The chimps must also select hammer stones suited to smashing nuts and carry them to where the nut trees grow — sophisticated behavior for an animal.

The unearthed materials included more than 470 stone pieces that may have flaked off when smashed against the anvils. The flakes resemble those used by early humans as knives and other tools.

"Some of the stone by-products of chimpanzee nut-cracking are similar to what we see left behind by some of our ancestors in East Africa during a period called the 'Oldowan,'" said Mercader, the lead author of the study.

Source: http://cbc.ca/stories/2002/05/23/chimp_tools020523.

Primatology is the study of nonhuman primates—fossil and living apes, monkeys, and prosimians—including their behavior and social life. Primatology is fascinating in itself, but it also helps anthropologists make inferences about the early social organization of *hominids* (members of the zoological family that includes fossil and living humans) and untangle issues of human nature and the origins of culture, such as early tool making—its nature and value. Of particular relevance to humans are two kinds of primates:

1. Those whose ecological adaptations are similar to our own: **terrestrial monkeys** and apes—that is, primates that live on the ground rather than in the trees.

2. Those that are most closely related to us: the great apes, specifically the chimpanzees and gorillas.

Our Place among Primates

Similarities between humans and apes are evident in anatomy, brain structure, genetics, and biochemistry. The physical similarities between humans and apes are recognized in zoological taxonomy—the assignment of organisms to categories (*taxa*; singular, *taxon*) according to their relationship and resemblance. Many similarities between organisms reflect their common *phylogeny*—their genetic relatedness based on common ancestry. In other words, organisms share features they have inherited from the same ancestor. Humans and apes belong to the same taxonomic superfamily, *Hominoidea* (hominoids). Monkeys are placed in two others (Ceboidea and Cercopithecoidea). This means that humans and apes are more closely related to each other than either is to monkeys.

Figure 5.1 summarizes the various levels of classification used in zoological taxonomy. Each lower-level unit belongs to the higher-level unit above it. Thus, looking toward the bottom of Figure 5.1, similar species belong to the same genus (plural, *genera*). Similar genera make up the same family, and so on through the top of Figure 5.1, where similar phyla (plural of *phylum*) are included in the same kingdom.

We see that the highest (most inclusive) taxonomic level is the *kingdom*. At that level, animals are distinguished from plants. The lowest-level taxa are species and subspecies. A *species* is a group

Compare the human and the gorilla. What similarities do you notice? What differences? Humans, gorillas, and chimps have more than 98 percent of their DNA in common.

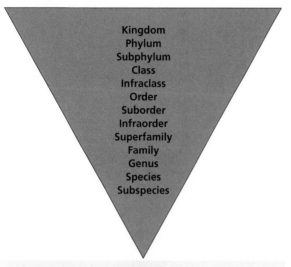

Figure 5.1   The Principal Classificatory Units of Zoological Taxonomy.   Moving down the figure, the classificatory units become more exclusive, so that "Kingdom" at the top is the most inclusive unit and "Subspecies" at the bottom is the most exclusive.

of organisms that can mate and give birth to *viable* (capable of living) and *fertile* (capable of reproducing) offspring whose own offspring are viable and fertile. *Speciation* (the formation of a new species) occurs when groups that once belonged to the same species can no longer interbreed. After a sufficiently long period of reproductive isolation, two closely related species assigned to the same genus will have evolved out of one.

At the lowest level of taxonomy, a species may have subspecies. These are its more or less, but not yet totally, isolated subgroups. Subspecies can coexist in time and space. For example, the Neandertals, who thrived between 130,000 and 30,000 years ago, often are assigned not to a separate species but merely to a different subspecies of *Homo sapiens*. Just one subspecies of *Homo sapiens* survives today.

The similarities used to assign organisms to the same taxon are called homologies, similarities they have jointly inherited from a common ancestor. Table 5.1 summarizes the place of humans in zoological taxonomy. We see in Table 5.1 that we are mammals, members of the class Mammalia. This is a major subdivision of the kingdom Animalia. Mammals share certain traits, including mammary

glands, that set them apart from other taxa, such as birds, reptiles, amphibians, and insects. Mammalian homologies indicate that all mammals share more recent common ancestry with each other than they do with any bird, reptile, or insect.

Humans are mammals that, at a lower taxonomic level, belong to the *order* Primates. Another mammalian order is Carnivora: the carnivores (dogs, cats, foxes, wolves, badgers, weasels). Rodentia (rats, mice, beavers, squirrels) form yet another mammalian order. The primates share structural and biochemical homologies that distinguish them from other mammals. These resemblances were inherited from their common early primate ancestors after those early primates became reproductively isolated from the ancestors of the other mammals.

Homologies and Analogies

Organisms should be assigned to the same taxon on the basis of homologies. The extensive biochemical homologies between apes and humans confirm our common ancestry and support our traditional joint classification as hominoids. For example, it is estimated that humans, chimpanzees, and gorillas have more than 98 percent of their DNA in common.

However, common ancestry isn't the only reason for similarities between species. Similar traits also can arise if species experience similar selective forces and adapt to them in similar ways. We call such similarities **analogies.** The process by which analogies are produced is called **convergent evolution.** For example, fish and porpoises share many analogies resulting from convergent evolution to life in the water. Like fish, porpoises, which are mammals, have fins. They are also hairless and streamlined for efficient locomotion. Analogies between birds and bats (wings, small size, light bones) illustrate convergent evolution to flying (see Angier 1998).

In theory, only homologies should be used in taxonomy. With reference to the hominoids, there is no doubt that humans, gorillas, and chimpanzees are more closely related to each other than any of the three is to orangutans, which are Asiatic apes (Ciochon 1983). Humans, chimps, and gorillas share a more recent ancestor with each other

Table 5.1 The Place of Humans (*Homo sapiens*) in Zoological Taxonomy

Homo sapiens is an Animal, Chordate, Vertebrate, Mammal, Primate, Anthropoid, Catarrhine, Hominoid, and Hominid. (Table 5.2 shows the taxonomic placement of the other primates.)

Taxon	Scientific (Latin) Name	Common (English) Name
Kingdom	Animalia	Animals
Phylum	Chordata	Chordates
Subphylum	Vertebrata	Vertebrates
Class	Mammalia	Mammals
Infraclass	Eutheria	Eutherians
Order	Primates	Primates
Suborder	Anthropoidea	Anthropoids
Infraorder	Catarrhini	Catarrhines
Superfamily	Hominoidea	Hominoids
Family	Hominidae	Hominids
Genus	*Homo*	Humans
Species	*Homo sapiens*	Recent humans
Subspecies	*Homo sapiens sapiens*	Anatomically modern humans

than they do with orangs. The *Hominidae* family is the zoological family that includes hominids—fossil and living humans. Many scientists now also place gorillas and chimps in that same family. This leaves the orangutan (genus *Pongo*) as the only member of the pongid family (Pongidae). Table 5.2 and Figure 5.2 illustrate our degree of relatedness to other primates.

Primate Tendencies

Primates are varied because they have adapted to diverse ecological niches. Some primates are active during the day; others, at night. Some eat insects; others, fruits; others, shoots, leaves, and bulk vegetation; and others, seeds or roots. Some primates live on the ground, others live in trees, and there are intermediate adaptations. However, because the earliest primates were tree dwellers, modern primates share homologies reflecting their common **arboreal** heritage.

See the Virtual Exploration

mhhe
.com
/kottak

Many trends in primate evolution are best exemplified by the anthropoids: monkeys, apes, and humans, which constitute the suborder *Anthropoidea*. The other primate suborder, Prosimii, includes lemurs, lorises, and tarsiers. These prosimians are more distant relatives of humans than are monkeys and apes. The primate trends—most developed in the anthropoids—can be summarized briefly. Together they constitute an anthropoid heritage that humans share with monkeys and apes.

1. **Grasping.** Primates have five-digited feet and hands that are suited for grasping. Certain features of hands and feet that were originally adaptive for arboreal life have been transmitted across the generations to contemporary primates. Flexible hands and feet that could encircle branches were important features in the early primates' arboreal life. Thumb opposability might have been favored by the inclusion of insects in the early primate diet. Manual dexterity makes it easier to catch insects attracted to abundant arboreal flowers and fruits. Humans and many other primates have

Table 5.2 **Primate Taxonomy**

The subdivisions of the two primate suborders: Prosimii (Prosimians) and Anthropoidea (Anthropoids). Humans (see also Table 5.1) are anthropoids who belong to the superfamily Hominoidea (the hominoids), along with the apes.

Suborder	Infraorder	Superfamily	Family	Subfamily
Prosimii (Prosimians)	Lemuriformes	Lemuroidea	Daubentoniidae (Aye-aye)	
			Indridae (Indri)	
			Lemuridae (Lemurs)	
	Lorisiformes	Lorisoidea	Lorisidae	Galaginae (Bushbabies)
				Lorisinae (Lorises)
	Tarsiiformes	Tarsioidea	Tarsiidae (Tarsiers)	
Anthropoidea (Anthropoids)	Platyrrhini	Ceboidea	Callitrichidae (Tamarins and marmosets)	
			Cebidae	Atelinae (Spider monkeys and woolly monkeys)
	Catarrhini	Cercopithecoidea	Cercopithecidae	Cercopithecinae (Macaques, guenons, and baboons)
				Colobinae (Colobines)
		Hominoidea	Hylobatidae (Gibbons and siamangs)	
			Pongidae (Orangutans)	
			Hominidae (Gorillas, chimpanzees, and humans)	

SOURCE: Adapted from R. Martin, "Classification of Primates," in S. Jones, R. Martin, and D. Pilbeam, eds., *The Cambridge Encyclopedia of Human Evolution* (Cambridge, England: Cambridge University Press, 1992), pp. 20–21.

opposable thumbs: The thumb can touch the other fingers. Some primates also have grasping feet. However, in adapting to the bipedal (two-footed) locomotion, humans eliminated most of the foot's grasping ability.

2. **Smell to Sight.** Several anatomic changes reflect the shift from smell to sight as the primates' most important means of obtaining information. Monkeys, apes, and humans have excellent *stereoscopic* (able to see in

Figure 5.2 **Primate Family Tree.** When did the common ancestors of all the Primates live?

SOURCE: From Roger Lewin, *Human Evolution: An Illustrated Introduction*, 3rd ed. (Boston: Blackwell Scientific Publications, 1993), p. 44.

depth) and color vision. The portion of the brain devoted to vision expanded, while the area concerned with smell shrank.

3. **Nose to Hand.** Sensations of touch, conveyed by *tactile* organs, also provide information. The tactile skin on a dog's or cat's nose transmits information. Cats' tactile hairs, or whiskers, also serve this function. In primates, however, the main touch organ is the hand, specifically the sensitive pads of the "fingerprint" region.

4. **Brain Complexity.** The proportion of brain tissue concerned with memory, thought, and association has increased in primates. The primate ratio of brain size to body size exceeds that of most mammals.

5. **Parental Investment.** Most primates give birth to a single offspring rather than a litter. Because of this, growing primates receive more attention and have more learning opportunities than do other mammals. Learned behavior is an important part of primate adaptation.

6. **Sociality.** Primates tend to be social animals that live with others of their species. The need for longer and more attentive care of offspring places a selective value on support by a social group.

Prosimians

The primate order has two suborders: prosimians and anthropoids. The early history of the primates is limited to prosimian-like animals known through the fossil record. (See Chapter 6.) The first anthropoids, ancestral to monkeys, apes, and humans, appeared more than 40 million years ago. Some prosimians managed to survive in Africa and Asia because they were adapted to nocturnal life. As such, they did not compete with anthropoids, which are active during the day. Prosimians (lemurs) in Madagascar had no anthropoid competitors until people colonized that island some 1,500 years ago.

In their behavior and biology, Madagascar's *lemurs*, with 33 species, show adaptations to an array of environments or ecological niches. Their diets and times of activity differ. Lemurs eat fruits, other plant foods, eggs, and insects. Some are nocturnal; others are active during the day. Some are totally arboreal; others spend some time in the trees and some on the ground. Another kind of prosimian is the *tarsier*, today confined to Indonesia, Malaysia, and the Philippines. From the fossil record, we know that 50 million years ago, several genera of tarsier-like prosimians lived in North

Primates have five-digited feet and hands, well suited for grasping. Flexible hands and feet that could encircle branches were important features in the early primates' arboreal life. In adapting to bipedal (two-footed) locomotion, hominids eliminated most of the foot's grasping ability—illustrated here by the chimpanzee.

A crown lemur. Because these prosimians were confined to Madagascar, lemurs had no anthropoid competitors until people colonized that island some 1,500 years ago. Most lemur species are now endangered by human encroachment on their forest habitat.

America and Europe, which were much warmer then than they are now (Boaz 1997). The one genus of tarsier that survived is totally nocturnal. Active at night, tarsiers don't directly compete with anthropoids, which are active during the day. Lorises are other nocturnal prosimians found in Africa and Asia.

Anthropoids

All anthropoids share resemblances that can be considered trends in primate evolution in the sense that these traits are fully developed neither in the fossils of primates that lived prior to 45 million years ago nor among contemporary prosimians.

All anthropoids have overlapping fields of vision, permitting them to see things in depth. With reduction of the snout, anthropoid eyes are placed forward in the skull and look directly ahead. The fields of vision of our eyes overlap. Depth perception, impossible without overlapping visual fields, proved adaptive in the trees. Tree-dwelling primates that could judge distance better because of depth perception survived and reproduced in greater numbers than did those that could not.

The abilities to see in depth and in color may have developed together. Both helped early anthropoids interpret their arboreal world. Superior vision made it easier to distinguish edible insects, fruits, berries, and leaves. Furthermore, having color and depth vision makes it easier to groom—to remove burrs, insects, and other small objects from other primates' hair. Grooming is one way of forming and maintaining social bonds.

Visual and tactile changes have been interrelated. Monkeys, apes, and humans have neither tactile muzzle skin nor "cat's whiskers." Instead, fingers are the main touch organs. The ends of the fingers and toes are sensitive tactile pads. Forward placement of the eyes and depth vision allow anthropoids to pick up small objects, hold them in

Background Information

STUDENT 1:	Jennifer Burns
YEAR IN SCHOOL/MAJOR:	Senior/Anthropology
FUTURE PLANS:	Field work/graduate school
STUDENT 2:	Chris Howard
YEAR IN SCHOOL/MAJOR:	Post-undergraduate/ Anthropology
FUTURE PLANS:	Graduate school
SUPERVISING PROFESSORS:	Dr. Deborah Overdorff, Dr. Beth Erhart
DEPARTMENT:	Anthropology
SCHOOL:	University of Texas at Austin
PROJECT TITLE:	A Behavioral Ecology Study of Two Lemur Species

---

Lemurs are endangered prosimians confined to the island of Madagascar. In this account, pay attention to the problems and pitfalls of primatological research. How would the logistics of studying a baboon or gorilla troop differ from the field methods described here?

Simply the word "Madagascar" conjures up brilliant images of an exotic land. Having broken off from Africa approximately 165 million years ago, this magical island mesmerizes the scientific community as 85–90 percent of its flora and fauna is endemic.

Within the heart of southeastern Madagascar, Ranomafana National Park protects 41,600 hectares of montane rain forest. The park was established at the close of the 1980s and has done a remarkable job of integrating the needs of the Malagasy people with this segment of rain forests' need for protection from further destruction. A developed infrastructure helps the park to balance local and foreign tourist groups as well as scientific research. With one main research site and two bush camp research sites, many fruitful studies are conducted over a wide variety of flora and fauna.

The aims of our project are to better understand the social dynamics and feeding ecology of two of the twelve species of lemurs living within Ranomafana National Park: the red-fronted lemur, *Eulemur fulvus rufus*, and sifaka species, *Propithecus diadema edwardsi*. For five days each week over a six-month period, behavioral and ecological data were collected on one group from each species. To aid with individual distinction and recognition, the members of each group were fitted with colored identification necklaces, with one collar of each group containing a radio transmitter. This radio-tracking device made it possible to locate the groups each morning. While these classic techniques are tremendously helpful, problems can often occur with the radio equipment. Heavy rainfall can waterlog the gear, and the rugged mountainous terrain adds strong echoes to the signal, making group location more difficult. When the radio fails, finding the groups can be nearly impossible, as they cover a tremendous area, and can easily take days, if they are found at all.

These two species are of particular interest because of their many contrasts both physically and socially. In trying to more fully define and understand the implications of terms like "dominance," "leadership," "competition," "reproductive stress," and "male versus female roles" within varying lemur species, this study hopes to not only provide new insights, but also open the door to new questions.

front of their eyes, and appraise them. Our ability to thread a needle reflects an intricate interplay of hands and eyes that took millions of years to achieve. Manual dexterity, including the opposable thumb, confers a tremendous advantage in examining and manipulating objects and is essential to a major human adaptive capacity: tool making. Among monkeys, thumb opposability is indispensable for feeding and grooming.

Another trend is increased size of the *cranium* (skull) to fit a larger brain. The brain/body size ratio is greater among anthropoids than among prosimians. Even more important, the brain's outer layer—concerned with memory, association, and integration—is relatively larger. Monkeys, apes, and humans store an array of visual images in their memories, which permits them to learn more. The ability to learn from experience and from other group members is a major reason for the success of the anthropoids compared to most other mammals.

Understanding Ourselves Think about our senses—vision, hearing, touch, smell, and taste. Where have we suffered sensory loss during our evolutionary history? Like almost all the anthropoids, humans are diurnal, active during the day. If we were night animals, we'd sense things differently. Maybe our eyes would be bigger, like those of an owl or a tarsier. Maybe we'd have biological radar systems, as bats do. Perhaps we'd develop a more acute sense of hearing or smell to penetrate the shield of the dark. As animals, humans are programmed to rise at dawn and to sleep when the sun disappears. As cultural creatures, we venture into the night with torches, lanterns, and flashlights, and we shut the dark out of our dwellings by using artificial light.

Which is most debilitating—loss of vision, hearing, or smell? Among our senses, we seem to value hearing, and above all vision, most. The anthropoids as a group are preeminently visual animals. Whole industries exist to improve our sight and hearing. But how often do you hear of a product designed to improve your ability to smell, taste, or touch things? Other animals can detect all kinds of scents and odors that help them interpret the world. Humans, by contrast, use an array of products designed *not* to improve our sense of smell, but to eliminate even the faint odors our limited olfactory apparatus permits us to smell. *Blindness* and *deafness* are common words that indicate the senses whose loss we deem most significant. The rarity of the word *anosmia*, the inability to smell, tells us something about our senses and our values. The sensory shifts that occurred in primate evolution, especially the one from smell to sight, explain something fundamental about ourselves.

Monkeys

The anthropoid suborder has two infraorders: *platyrrhines* (New World monkeys) and *catarrhines* (Old World monkeys, apes, and humans). The catarrhines (sharp-nosed) and platyrrhines (flat-nosed) take their names from Latin terms that describe the placement of the nostrils (Figure 5.3). Old World monkeys, apes, and humans are all catarrhines. Being placed in the same taxon (infraorder in this case) means that Old World monkeys, apes, and humans are more closely related to each other than to New World monkeys. In other words, one kind of monkey (Old World) is more like a human than it is like another kind of monkey (New World). The New World monkeys were reproductively isolated from the catarrhines before the latter diverged into the Old World monkeys, apes, and humans. This is why New World monkeys are assigned to a different infraorder.

All New World monkeys and many Old World monkeys are arboreal. Whether in the trees or on the ground, however, monkeys move differently from apes and humans. Their arms and legs move parallel to one another, as dogs' legs do. This contrasts with the tendency toward *orthograde posture*, the straight and upright stance of apes and humans. Unlike apes, which have longer arms than legs, and humans, who have longer legs than arms, monkeys have arms and legs of about the same length. Most monkeys also have tails, which help them maintain balance in the trees. Apes and humans lack tails. The apes' tendency toward orthograde posture is most evident when they sit down. When they move about, chimps, gorillas, and orangutans habitually use all four limbs.

NEW WORLD MONKEYS

New World monkeys live in the forests of Central and South America. There are interesting parallels between New World monkeys and some arboreal

Figure 5.3 **Nostril Structure of Catarrhines and Platyrrhines.** Above: narrow septum and "sharp nose" of a guenon, a catarrhine (Old World monkey). Below: broad septum and "flat nose" of Humboldt's woolly monkey, a platyrrhine (New World monkey). Which nose is more like your own? What does that similarity suggest?

Peanut

Figure 5.4 **The Prehensile Tail of the Spider Monkey, a New World Monkey.** Such a tail can be used to grasp a branch, or to pick up small objects, such as the peanut. Do any of the apes have grasping tails?

primates of the Old World. These analogies exhibit convergent evolution—that is, they have developed as a result of adaptation to a similar arboreal niche. Like the gibbon, a small Asiatic ape, some New World monkeys have developed a form of **brachiation**—under-the-branch swinging. Most monkeys run and jump from branch to branch, but gibbons and some New World monkeys swing through the trees, using their hands as hooks. Hand over hand, they move from branch to branch, propelled onward by the thrust of their bodies.

Unlike Old World monkeys, many New World monkeys have *prehensile*, or grasping, tails (Figure 5.4). Sometimes the prehensile tail has tactile skin, which permits it to work like a hand, for instance, in conveying food to the mouth. Old World monkeys, however, have developed their own characteristic anatomic specializations. They have rough patches of skin on the buttocks, adapted to sitting on hard rocky ground and rough branches. If the primate you see in the zoo has such patches, it's from the Old World. If it has a prehensile tail, it's a New World monkey. Among the anthropoids, there's only one nocturnal animal, a New World monkey called the night monkey or owl monkey. All other monkeys and apes, and humans, too, of course, are diurnal—active during the day.

OLD WORLD MONKEYS

The Old World monkeys have both terrestrial and arboreal species. Baboons and many macaques are terrestrial monkeys. Certain traits differentiate terrestrial and arboreal primates. Arboreal primates tend to be smaller. Smaller animals can reach a greater variety of foods in trees and shrubs, where the most abundant foods are located at the ends of branches. Low weight is adaptive for end-of-branch feeding. Arboreal monkeys are typically lithe and agile. They escape from the few predators in their environment—snakes and monkey-eating eagles—through alertness and speed. Large size, by contrast, is advantageous for terrestrial primates in dealing with their predators, which are more numerous on the ground.

Another contrast between arboreal and terrestrial primates is in sexual dimorphism—marked differences in male and female anatomy and temperament (see Fedigan 1992). Sexual dimorphism tends to be more marked in terrestrial than in arboreal species. Baboon and macaque males are larger and fiercer than are females of the same species. However, it's hard to tell, without close inspection, the sex of an arboreal monkey.

Of the terrestrial monkeys, the baboons of Africa and the (mainly Asiatic) macaques have been the subjects of many studies. Why do you think there have been more studies of terrestrial than of arboreal primates? Terrestrial monkeys have specializations in anatomy, psychology, and social behavior that enable them to cope with terrestrial life. Adult male baboons, for example, are fierce-looking animals that can weigh 100 pounds (45 kilograms). They display their long, projecting canines to intimidate predators and when confronting other baboons. Faced with a predator, a male baboon can puff up his ample mane of shoulder hair, so that the would-be aggressor perceives the baboon as larger than he actually is.

Longitudinal field research shows that, near the time of puberty, baboon and macaque males typically leave their home troop for another. Because males move in and out, females form the stable core of the terrestrial monkey troop (Cheney and Seyfarth 1990; Hinde 1983). By contrast, among

Hamadryas baboons. The male grooms the female. How does this photo illustrate sexual dimorphism?

chimpanzees and gorillas, females are more likely to emigrate and seek mates outside their natal social groups (Rodseth et al. 1991; van Schaik and van Hooff 1983; Wrangham 1980). Among terrestrial monkeys, then, the core group consists of females; among apes it is made up of males.

Apes

The Old World monkeys have their own separate superfamily (Cercopithecoidea), while humans and the apes together compose the hominoid superfamily (Hominoidea). Among the hominoids, the so-called great apes are orangutans, gorillas, and chimpanzees. Humans could be included here, too; we are sometimes called "the third African ape." The lesser (smaller) apes are the gibbons and siamangs of Southeast Asia and Indonesia.

Figure 5.5 The Limb Ratio of the Arboreal Gibbon and Terrestrial *Homo*.
How does this anatomical difference fit the modes of locomotion used by gibbons and humans?

Apes live in forests and woodlands. The light and agile gibbons, which are skilled brachiators, are completely arboreal. The heavier gorillas, chimpanzees, and adult male orangutans spend considerable time on the ground. Nevertheless, ape behavior and anatomy reveal past and present adaptation to arboreal life. For example, apes still build nests to sleep in trees. Apes have longer arms than legs, which is adaptive for brachiation (see Figure 5.5). The structure of the shoulder and clavicle (collarbone) of the apes and humans suggests that we had a brachiating ancestor. In fact, young apes still do brachiate. Adult apes tend to be too heavy to brachiate safely. Their weight is more than many branches can withstand. Gorillas and chimps now use the long arms they have inherited from their more arboreal ancestors for life on the ground. The terrestrial locomotion of chimps and gorillas is called *knuckle-walking*. In it, long arms and callused knuckles support the trunk as the apes amble around, leaning forward.

Understanding Ourselves Do you remember the "monkey bars" in your school playground and how you used them? It wasn't like a monkey. The human shoulder bone, like that of the apes, is adapted for brachiation—swinging hand over hand through the trees. Monkeys move about on four feet—whether in the trees or on the ground. Apes can stand and walk on two feet, as humans habitually do, but in the trees, and otherwise when climbing, apes and humans don't jump around as monkeys do. In climbing we extend our arms and pull up, and when we use monkey bars, we hang and move hand over hand rather than getting on top and running across, as a monkey would. Maybe the name should be changed to human bars.

A brachiator's shoulder is one clue to an arboreal heritage we share with the apes. What about nest building? Based on what we know about the habitats of early hominids, it's a good bet they took refuge in, and may even have slept in, trees. Are blankets, sheets, pillows, and mattresses the modern-day equivalent of ancestral nests made of leaves and twigs? And when we dream of falling, are we experiencing an evolutionary consciousness shared with the African apes, which build nests but occasionally wake up on the ground? Another lesson for the field primatologist—don't set up camp under a gorilla's nest.

GIBBONS

Gibbons are widespread in the forests of Southeast Asia, especially in Malaysia. Smallest of the apes, male and female gibbons have about the same

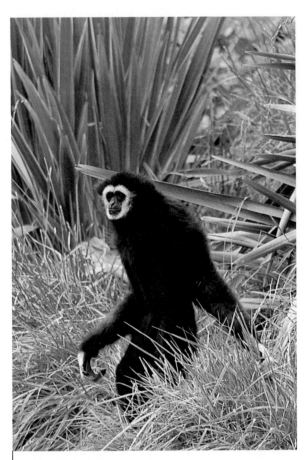

With long arms and fingers, the gibbon is the most agile of the apes. Gibbons occasionally walk upright on the ground, using their long arms as balancers. Shown here, a white-handed gibbon strolls through the forest.

average height (3 feet, or 1 meter) and weight (12 to 25 pounds, or 5 to 10 kilograms). Gibbons spend most of their time just below the forest canopy (treetops). For efficient brachiation, gibbons have long arms and fingers, with short thumbs. Slenderly built, gibbons are the most agile apes. Unlike knuckle-walkers, they use their long arms for balance when they occasionally walk erect on the ground or along a branch. Gibbons are the preeminent arboreal specialists among the apes. They subsist on a diet mainly of fruits, with occasional insects and small animals. Gibbons and siamangs, their slightly larger relatives, tend to live in *primary groups*, which are composed of a permanently bonded male and female and their preadolescent offspring. Gibbon evolutionary success is con-

firmed by their numbers and range. Hundreds of thousands of gibbons span a wide area of Southeast Asia.

ORANGUTANS

There are two existing species of orangutan, Asiatic apes that belong to the genus *Pongo*. The range of the orangutan once extended into China, but contemporary orangs are confined to two Indonesian islands. Sexual dimorphism is marked, with the adult male weighing more than twice as much as the female. The orangutan male, like his human counterpart, is intermediate in size between chimps and gorillas. Some orang males exceed 200 pounds (90 kilograms). With only half the gorilla's bulk, male orangs can be more arboreal, although they typically climb, rather than swing through, the trees. The smaller size of females and young permits them to make fuller use of the trees. Orangutans have a varied diet of fruit, bark, leaves, and insects. Because orangutans live in jungles and feed in trees, they are especially difficult to study. However, field reports about orangutans in their natural setting (MacKinnon 1974) have clarified their behavior and social organization. Orangs tend to be solitary animals. Their tightest social units consist of females and preadolescent young. Males forage alone.

GORILLAS

With just one species, *Gorilla gorilla*, there are three subspecies of gorillas. The western lowland gorilla is the animal you normally see in zoos. This, the smallest subspecies of gorilla, lives mainly in forests in the Central African Republic, Congo, Cameroon, Gabon, Equatorial Guinea, and Nigeria. The eastern lowland gorilla, of which there are only four in captivity, is slightly larger and lives in eastern Congo. There are no mountain gorillas, the third subspecies, in captivity, and it's estimated that no more than 650 of these animals survive in the wild. These are the largest gorillas with the longest hair (to keep them warm in their mountainous habitat). They are also the rarest gorillas, which Dian Fossey and other scientists have studied in Rwanda, Uganda, and eastern Congo.

Full-grown male gorillas may weigh 400 pounds (180 kilograms) and stand six feet tall (183 centimeters). Like most terrestrial primates, gorillas show marked sexual dimorphism. The average adult female weighs half as much as the male. Gorillas spend little time in the trees. It's particularly cumbersome for an adult male to move his bulk about in a tree. When gorillas sleep in trees, they build nests, which are usually no more than 10 feet (3 meters) off the ground. By contrast, the nests of chimps and female orangs may be 100 feet (30 meters) above the ground.

Most of the gorilla's day is spent feeding. Gorillas move through jungle undergrowth eating ground plants, leaves, bark, fruits, and other vegetation. Like most primates, gorillas live in social groups. The troop is a common unit of primate social organization, consisting of multiple males and females and their offspring. Although troops with up to 30 gorillas have been observed, most gorillas live in groups of from 10 to 20. Gorilla troops tend to have fairly stable memberships, with little shifting between troops (Fossey 1983). Each troop has a silver-back male, so designated because of the strip of white hair that extends down his back. This is the physical sign of full maturity among the male gorillas. The silverback is usually the only breeding male in the troop, which is why gorilla troops are sometimes called "one-male groups." However, a few younger, subordinate males may also adhere to such a one-male group (Harcourt et al. 1981; Schaller 1963).

For a quiz on primate types, see the Interactive Exercises

mhhe com /kottak

CHIMPANZEES

Chimpanzees belong to the genus *Pan*, which has two species: *Pan troglodytes* (the common chimpanzee) and *Pan paniscus* (the bonobo or "pygmy" chimpanzee) (de Waal 1997; Susman 1987). Like humans, chimps are closely related to the gorilla, although there are some obvious differences. Like gorillas, chimps live in tropical Africa, but they range over a larger area and more varied environments than gorillas do (Figure 5.6). The common chimp, *Pan troglodytes*, lives in western central Africa (Gabon, Congo, Cameroon), as well as in western Africa (Sierra Leone, Liberia, The Gambia) and eastern Africa (Congo, Uganda, and Tanzania). Bonobos live in remote and densely forested areas of just one country—the Democratic Republic of Congo. Common chimps live mainly in tropical rain forests but also in woodlands and mixed forest-woodland-grassland areas, such as the

Gombe Stream National Park, Tanzania, where Jane Goodall (1996) and other researchers began to study them in 1960.

There are dietary differences between chimps and gorillas. Gorillas eat large quantities of green bulk vegetation, but chimps, like orangutans and gibbons, prefer fruits. Chimps are actually omnivorous, adding animal protein to their diet by capturing small mammals, birds' eggs, and insects.

Chimps are lighter and more arboreal than gorillas are. The adult male's weight—between

Figure 5.6 **Geographic Distribution of African Apes.**

Chimpanzees and gorillas are primarily rain forest dwellers. However, some chimpanzee populations live in woodland environments. This map shows the ranges of the three species of African apes.

SOURCE: From C. J. Jolly and F. Plog, *Physical Anthropology and Archeology*, 4th ed. (New York: McGraw-Hill, 1986), p. 115.

Most endangered of the apes, the orangutan has the most restricted habitat. The colorful orang is also the least social of the apes. What are the main threats to nonhuman primates such as the orang? What would it take to save the orang from extinction?

Of the three young women recruited in the 1960s by the paleontologist Louis Leakey to study great apes, Dr. Birutá Galdikas, now 53, is the least known. Dr. Leakey's first disciple, Dr. Jane Goodall, who discovered that chimpanzees made tools, has become an international scientific celebrity, and Dr. Dian Fossey, who lived among the gorillas of Rwanda and was killed there in 1985, was played by Sigourney Weaver in the movie *Gorillas in the Mist.*

But the story of Dr. Galdikas, who quietly devoted herself to the study and preservation of the Indonesian orangutan, remains largely unknown. "That's because I have a name nobody can pronounce and because I've been in Borneo all these years, tracking an elusive and solitary animal," Dr. Galdikas, whose name is Lithuanian (pronounced bi-ROO-tay GALD-i-kus), said on a recent morning . . .

Still a resident of Borneo, Dr. Galdikas recently became an Indonesian citizen because "the orangutans are Indonesian and because someone in the government suggested it would be helpful.". . .

Q. Give us a report on the state of the world's orangutans?

A. They are poised on the edge of extinction. It's that simple. We're still seeing orangutans in the forest; they are coming into captivity in enormous numbers. You just know that there can't be that many left in the wild.

Q. How did the orangutans come to be so threatened?

A. The main factor was that until 1988, Indonesia had a forestry minister who was a real forester. In 1988, he was replaced by a forestry minister who was an agriculturist, a

100 and 200 pounds (45 to 90 kilograms)—is about a third that of the male gorilla. There is much less sexual dimorphism among chimps than among gorillas. Females approximate 88 percent of the average male height. This is similar to the ratio of sexual dimorphism in *Homo sapiens.*

Several scientists have studied wild chimps, and we know more about the full range of their behavior and social organization than we do about the other apes (see Wrangham et al. 1994). The long-term research of Jane Goodall and others at Gombe provides especially useful information. Approximately 150 chimpanzees range over Gombe's 30 square miles (80 square kilometers). Goodall (1986, 1996) has described communities of about 50 chimps, all of which know one another and interact from time to time. Communities regularly split up into smaller groups: a mother and her offspring; a few males; males, females, and young; and occasionally solitary animals. Chimp communities are semiclosed. The social networks of males are more closed than are those of females, which are more likely to migrate and mate outside their natal group than males are (Wrangham 1994).

When chimps, which are very vocal, meet, they greet one another with gestures, facial expressions, and calls. They hoot to maintain contact during their daily rounds. Like baboons and macaques, chimps exhibit dominance relationships through attacks and displacement. Some adult females outrank younger adult males, although females do not display as strong dominance relationships among themselves as males do. Males occasionally cooperate in hunting parties.

promoter of plantations. That signaled a shift in government policy from selective logging to clear-cutting of the forest . . . If you selectively log, some animals will survive. But with clear-cutting, the habitat is gone. If that weren't enough, in 1997, there were these horrendous fires that devastated the forests. Moreover, the last three years have been a period of intense political upheaval . . .

After President Suharto stepped down in 1998, there was a vacuum of power in the center. Once people in the provinces understood that, some felt they could do whatever they wanted . . .

At first, only local loggers came in. When nobody stopped them, the bigger commercial loggers followed. Suddenly, there were no more protected parks . . .

We're trying to set up patrols of local men to go out with park rangers so that when they come across illegal loggers, they don't feel totally intimidated. We're working with the Indonesian government to set up new wildlife reserves at expired logging concessions . . .

We have a hospital for 130 orangutans. We have an orphanage for the babies. Eventually, they are released to the wild, though with the fast-disappearing habitat, it's always tough to find a safe place for them.

Q. Tell us what you've learned about orangutans in the nearly 30 years you've been studying them?

A. Well, we've gotten a picture of a very long-lived primate who probably lives 60 to 70 years in the wild. They use a wide variety of foods in the wild, about 400 different kinds, because food is generally scarce for them. The males come and go. They're very, very competitive. Probably very few males are successful at actually impregnating females.

And the females seem to get pregnant about once every eight years. Also, they're very smart. When orangutans have interactions with humans, they use tools at an incredibly rapid pace . . .

SOURCE: http://www.nytimes.com/library/national/science/032100sci-animal-orangutan.html.

BONOBOS

Ancestral chimps, and especially humans, eventually spread out of the forests and into woodlands and more open habitats. Bonobos, which belong to the species *Pan paniscus*, apparently never left the protection of the trees. Up to 10,000 bonobos survive in the humid forests south of the Zaire River, in the Democratic Republic of Congo (DRC). Despite their common name—the pygmy chimpanzee—bonobos can't be distinguished from chimpanzees by size. Adult males of the smallest subspecies of chimpanzee average 43 kilograms (95 pounds), and females average 33 kilograms (73 pounds). These figures are about the same for bonobos (de Waal 1995, 1997).

Although much smaller than the males, female bonobos seem to rule. De Waal (1995, 1997) characterizes bonobo communities as female-centered, peace-loving, and egalitarian. The strongest social bonds are among females, although females also bond with males. The male bonobo's status reflects that of his mother, to whom he remains closely bonded for life.

The frequency with which bonobos have sex—and use it to avoid conflict—makes them exceptional among the primates. Despite frequent sex, the bonobo reproductive rate doesn't exceed that of the chimpanzee. A female bonobo gives birth every five or six years. Then, like chimps, female bonobos nurse and carry around their young for up to five years. Bonobos reach adolescence around seven years of age. Females, which first give birth at age 13 or 14, are full-grown by 15 years.

This photo from the San Diego zoo shows sexual activity involving a male bonobo and a younger female, as two other bonobos embrace. Among bonobos, the strongest social bonds are among females, although females do also bond with males.

It was once thought that face-to-face copulation was a cultural innovation that needed to be taught to nonindustrial peoples (hence the term "missionary position"). Not so—even bonobos engage in face-to-face sex in about one-third of their sexual encounters. This makes them more human-like than are chimpanzees, which rarely have sex face to face. As in human females, the bonobo vulva and clitoris face the front, making the anatomy of their female genitalia adapted for face-to-face activity.

Like baboons and chimps, bonobo females have an estrus cycle. Periodically, females "go into heat" or enter estrus, a period of heightened sexual receptivity. Estrus is signaled by swelling and coloration of the vaginal skin. Female bonobos are receptive during a longer portion of their estrus cycle than female chimps are. This increased sexual receptivity is another similarity with humans. Bonobos have sex in virtually every partner combination imaginable (although they appear to avoid incest). The bonobo's most typical sexual pattern, undocumented in any other primate, is genito-genital rubbing (or GG rubbing) between adult females. Two females embrace in a face-to-face position and rub their genital swellings together, emitting grins and squeals that probably reflect

orgasmic experiences (de Waal 1995, 1997). What about males? Standing back to back, one male may rub his scrotum against the buttocks of another male. Males also practice so-called penis-fencing: Two males hang face to face from a branch while rubbing their erect penises together. Bonobos also engage in occasional oral sex, massage of another individual's genitals, and intense tongue-kissing.

How do we know that bonobos use all this sexual activity to avoid conflict? According to de Waal:

> First, anything, including food, that arouses the interest of more than one bonobo at a time tends to result in sexual contact. If two bonobos approach a cardboard box thrown into their enclosure, they will briefly mount each other before playing with the box. Such situations lead to squabbles in most other species. But bonobos are quite tolerant, perhaps because they use sex to divert attention and to diffuse tension. Second, bonobo sex often occurs in aggressive contexts totally unrelated to food. A jealous male might chase another away from a female, after which the two males reunite and engage in scrotal rubbing. Or after a female hits a juvenile, the latter's mother may lunge at the aggressor, an action that is immediately followed by genital rubbing between the two adults (De Waal 1995, p. 87).

De Waal sees bonobo sexual behavior as a mechanism to displace aggression. Because of this, bonobos' sexual behavior is indistinguishable from their overall social behavior. Given its roles in peacemaking and appeasement, it's not surprising that bonobo sex has so many manifestations.

For more information on bonobos, see the Internet Exercise at your OLC

mhhe ●com /kottak

Endangered Primates

Deforestation poses a special risk for the primates, because 90 percent of the 190 living primate species live in tropical forests—in Africa, Asia, South America, and Central America. Figure 5.7 is a map showing the distribution of primates today. As the earth's human population swells, the populations of the nonhuman primates are shrinking. Accord-

Figure 5.7 **Geographic Distribution of Living Primates.**
SOURCE: From Roger Lewin, *Human Evolution: An Illustrated Introduction*, 3rd ed. (Boston: Blackwell Scientific Publications, 1993), p. 45.

ing to the Convention on International Trade in Endangered Species (ratified in 1973), all nonhuman primates are now endangered or soon to be endangered. The apes (gibbons, gorillas, orangutans, and chimps) are in the "most endangered" category. Mountain gorillas, which once ranged widely in the forested mountains of East Africa, are now limited to a small area near the war-ravaged borders of Rwanda, the DRC, and Uganda. Other severely threatened species include the golden lion tamarin monkey of southeastern Brazil, the cotton-top tamarin of Colombia, the lion-tailed macaque of southern India, the woolly monkeys of Amazonia, and the orangutan of Southeast Asia.

See the Internet Exercise at your OLC

A combination of forestry and forest fires has been deadly to orangutans in Sumatra and Borneo in Indonesia. Sumatra, which is losing 1,000 orangs a year, has an estimated population of 6,000 left. A road for loggers and miners that penetrated the orangutan range in Sumatra led to contact with humans that proved fatal to hundreds of the animals. Borneo was devastated by fires in 1997–98, leaving some 10,000–15,000 orangs, compared with 60,000 in 1980. Habitat destruction and fragmentation can isolate small groups of animals, leaving them vulnerable to extinction due to loss of genetic diversity. Primate populations are slow

to recover from such threats. Ape species, for example, are slow reproducers, rarely having more than three to four offspring over a lifetime (Stern 2000).

Interpret the World
Atlas Map 5

Map 5 in your atlas shows the world geographic distribution of nonhuman primates. Both surviving and extinct primate species are displayed. These include prosimians, New World monkeys, Old World monkeys, gibbons and siamangs, and the Great Apes. Note that primates (what kind?) once thrived in North America, when that continent was warmer and more forested than it is now. Compare maps 3 and 5 to see how primate distribution is related to deforestation. Primates are among the world's most endangered animals. What are some areas of deforestation where you can detect threats to specific primates, such as lemurs or apes (based on maps 3 and 5)?

Although the destruction of their forest habitats is the main reason the primates are disappearing, it isn't the only reason. Another threat is human hunting of primates for bush meat (Viegas 2000). In Amazonia, West Africa, and Central Africa, primates are a major source of food. People kill thousands of monkeys each year. Human hunting is less of a threat to primates in Asia. In India, Hindus avoid monkey meat because the monkey is sacred, while Moslems avoid it because monkeys are considered unclean and not fit for human consumption.

People also hunt primates for their skins and pelts; poachers sell their body parts as trophies and ornaments. Africans use the skins of black-and-white colobus monkeys for cloaks and head-dresses, and American and European tourists buy coats and rugs made from colobus pelts. In Amazonia, ocelot and jaguar hunters shoot monkeys to bait the traps they set for the cats.

Poachers pose the greatest threat to the mountain gorillas, of which there were as few as 250 left in the wild when Fossey started studying them

In Africa, poachers shoot apes with high-powered rifles, then decapitate them and cut off their hands. They sell gorilla heads as trophies and turn the hands into grotesque ashtrays. Is killing a gorilla murder?

(Fossey 1981, 1983). The poachers shoot the apes with high-powered rifles, then decapitate them and cut off their hands. They sell gorilla heads as trophies and turn their hands into grotesque ashtrays. Traps and snares set for antelope and buffalo also endanger gorillas, which sometimes get caught in the traps. Even if they manage to free themselves, they often die from infected wounds. The sad fate (murder and decapitation) of Dian Fossey's favorite gorilla, Digit, is familiar to those who have seen the 1988 film *Gorillas in the Mist*, the story of Fossey, her work with mountain gorillas, and her efforts to save them. Fossey herself was murdered in her cabin at her field site in Rwanda in 1985 (see Roberts 1995). The mystery of her death remains unsolved. The last entry in her diary reads: "When you realize the value of all life, you dwell less on what is past and concentrate on the preservation of the future." Through the efforts of the fund she established, the number of mountain gorillas has increased.

Chimpanzees are also vulnerable to poachers. One famous chimp, Lucy, raised by an American family and taught to use sign language, met a grim fate when she was taken to Africa to live in the wild. In 1986, soon after she had joined an island colony of chimps in The Gambia, Lucy's mutilated corpse was discovered—minus skin, hair, hands, and feet. "We can only speculate that Lucy was killed—probably shot—and skinned. Because of her confidence with humans, she was always the first to confront newcomers to the island. She might have surprised an armed intruder, with fatal consequences" (Carter 1988, p. 47).

Primates also are killed when they are agricultural pests. In some areas of Africa and Asia, baboons and macaques raid the crops on which people depend for subsistence. Between 1947 and 1962, the government of Sierra Leone held annual drives to rid farm areas of monkeys, and between 15,000 and 20,000 primates perished each year.

A final reason for the demise of the primates is the capture of animals for use in labs or as pets. Although this threat is minor compared with deforestation and the hunting of primates for food, it does pose a serious risk to certain endangered species in heavy demand. One of the species most hurt by this trade is the chimpanzee, which has been widely used in biomedical research. One especially destructive way of capturing young primates is to shoot the mother and take her clinging infant.

Human–Primate Similarities

There is a substantial gap between primate society and fully developed human culture. However, studies of primates have revealed many similarities. Scholars used to contend that learned (versus instinctive) behavior separates humans from other animals. We know now that monkeys and apes also rely on learning. Many of the differences between humans and other primates are differences in degree rather than in kind. For example, monkeys learn from experiences, but humans learn much more. Another example: Chimpanzees and orangutans make tools for specific tasks, but human reliance on tools is much greater.

LEARNING

Common to monkeys, apes, and humans is the fact that behavior and social life are not rigidly programmed by the genes. All these animals learn throughout their lives. In several cases, an entire monkey troop has learned from the experiences of some of its members. In one group of Japanese macaques, a three-year-old female monkey started washing dirt off sweet potatoes before she ate them. First her mother, then her age peers, and finally the entire troop began washing sweet potatoes, too. The direction of learning was reversed when members of another macaque troop learned to eat wheat. After the dominant males had tried the new food, within four hours the practice had spread throughout the troop. Changes in learned behavior seem to spread more quickly from the top down than from the bottom up.

For monkeys as for people, the ability to learn, to profit from experience, confers a tremendous adaptive advantage, permitting them to avoid fatal mistakes. Faced with environmental change, primates don't have to wait for a genetic or physiological response. Learned behavior and social patterns can be modified instead.

TOOLS

Anthropologists used to distinguish humans from other animals as tool users, and there is no doubt that Homo does employ tools much more than any other animal does. However, tool use also turns up among several nonhuman species. For example, in the Galápagos Islands off western South America,

Learned behavior among wild chimps includes rudimentary tool manufacture. At Tanzania's Gombe Stream National Park, chimps use specially prepared twigs to "fish" for termites.

there is a "woodpecker finch" that selects twigs to dig out insects and grubs from tree bark. Sea otters use rocks to break open mollusks, which are important in their diet. Beavers are famous for dam construction.

When it became obvious that people weren't the only tool users, anthropologists started contending that only humans make tools with foresight, that is, with a specific purpose in mind. Chimpanzees show that this, too, is debatable, as we saw at the beginning of this chapter in the news story about how chimps living in the Tai rain forest of Ivory Coast make and use stone tools to crack nuts. In 1960, Jane Goodall (1996) began observing wild chimps—including their tool use and hunting behavior—at Gombe Stream National Park in Tanzania, East Africa. From the work of Goodall and many other researchers we know that wild chimps regularly make tools. To get water from places their mouths can't reach, thirsty chimps pick leaves, chew and crumple them, and then dip them into the water. Thus, with a specific purpose in mind, they devise primitive "sponges."

The best studied form of tool making by chimps involves "termiting." Chimps make tools to probe termite hills. They choose twigs, which they modify by removing leaves and peeling off bark to expose the sticky surface beneath. They carry the twigs to termite hills, dig holes with their fingers, and insert the twigs. Finally, they pull out the twigs and dine on termites that were attracted to the sticky surface.

Termiting isn't as easy as it might seem. Learning to termite takes time, and many Gombe chimps never master it. Twigs with certain characteristics must be chosen. Furthermore, once the twig is in the hill and the chimp judges that termites are crawling on its surface, the chimp must quickly flip the twig as it pulls it out so that the termites are on top. Otherwise they fall off as the twig comes out of the hole. This is an elaborate skill that neither all chimps nor human observers have been able to master.

Chimps have other abilities essential to culture. When they are trained by humans, their skills flower, as anyone who has ever seen a movie, circus, or zoo chimp knows. Wild chimps and orangs aim and throw objects. The gorilla, our other nearest relative, lacks the chimp's proclivity for tool making. However, gorillas do build nests, and they throw branches, grass, vines, and other objects. Hominids have considerably elaborated the capacity to aim and throw, which is a homology passed down from the common ancestor of humans and apes. Without it we never would have developed projectile technology and weaponry—or baseball.

PREDATION AND HUNTING

Like tool making and language, hunting has been cited as a distinctive human activity that is not shared with our ape relatives. Again, however, primate research shows that what was previously thought to be a difference of kind is a difference of degree. The diets of other terrestrial primates are not exclusively vegetarian, as was once thought. Baboons kill and eat young antelopes, and researchers have repeatedly observed hunting by chimpanzees.

For several years John Mitani, David Watts, and other researchers have been observing chimpanzees at Ngogo in Uganda's Kibale National Park. This is the largest chimp community ever described in the wild. In 1998 it consisted of 26 adult males, 40 adult females, 16 adolescent males, 5 adolescent females, and 30 infants and juveniles (Mitani and Watts 1999). (Remember that chimp communities have a more stable male than female core membership—adolescent males tend to stay on while adolescent females tend to leave to join other troops.) The large community size permits the formation of large hunting parties, which contributes to hunting success. Hunting parties at Ngogo included an average of 26 individuals (almost always adult and adolescent males). The average hunting time was 19 minutes, varying from 2 to 91 minutes in 29 observed hunts. Most hunts (78 percent) resulted in at least one prey item being caught—a much higher success rate than that among lions (26 percent), hyenas (34 percent), or cheetahs (30 percent). In most hunts (81 percent) the Ngogo chimps managed to catch multiple prey animals (three on average). The favored prey, at Ngogo as in other chimp communities, was the red colobus monkey.

As described by Mitani and Watts (1999), hunting by chimps is both opportunistic and planned. Opportunistic hunting took place when chimps encountered potential prey as they moved about during the day. Other hunts were organized patrols, in which the chimps became silent and moved together in a single file. They would stop, look up into the trees, scan, and change direction several times. Attentive to any arboreal movement, they would stop and search whenever they detected motion. After they spotted a monkey, the chase would begin. Encountering no prey, the chimps would go on patrolling, sometimes for several hours. The Ngogo chimps also collaborate by encircling red colobus groups, blocking potential escape routes, and driving their prey down hill slopes from taller to shorter trees. Chimps may give a specific call, the hunting call, at the start of a hunt, mobilizing hunters into action. Sometimes isolated chimps that encountered a red colobus monkey would give this call, after which other chimps would rush to the site and begin to hunt.

It turns out that chimps eat meat almost as much as some human hunter-gatherers do (Kopytoff 1995; Stanford 1999; Stanford and Bunn, eds. 2001). According to University of Southern California anthropologist Craig Stanford (1999), chimps may consume a quarter pound of meat a day when they hit their hunting stride. This meat intake is comparable to that of some contemporary groups of hunter-gatherers. According to Stanford, male chimps often hunt as a way to gain access to sexually receptive females. Stanford repeatedly observed male chimps dangling monkey meat in front of a sexually swollen female, sharing only after copulation. When in estrus ("heat," or heightened sexual receptivity), female chimps copulate with more than a dozen males each day. The presence of meat in the diet of a female chimpanzee may enhance her offspring's survival chances (Kopytoff 1995). Meat sharing also could increase male reproductive success by making it easier to mate. Stanford found hunting to be seasonal at Gombe—occurring during the dry summer months, precisely the season when females tend to be sexually receptive, and when fruits, leaves, and nuts are scarce.

There appear to be political as well as sexual reasons for meat sharing by chimps. In 1992 the Japanese zoologist Toshisada Nichida described how, in Tanzania's Mahale Mountains, a high-ranking chimp male gave out pieces of meat to allies, while denying them to his enemies (Kopytoff 1995). Stanford observed a similar use of meat to cement alliances at Gombe. Archeological evidence indicates that humans hunted by at least 2.5 million years ago, based on stone meat-cutting tools found at Olduvai Gorge in Tanzania. Given our current understanding of chimp hunting and tool making, we can infer that hominids may have been hunting much earlier than the first archaeological evidence attests. Since chimps seem to devour the monkeys they kill, leaving few remains after their meal, we may never find archaeological evidence for the first hominid hunt, especially if it was done without stone tools.

AGGRESSION AND RESOURCES

The potential for predation and aggression may be generalized in monkeys and apes, but its expression seems to depend on the environment. Jane Goodall specifically linked chimpanzee aggression and predation to human encroachment on their natural habitat. The Gombe chimps are divided into a northern group and a smaller group of southerners. Parties from the north have invaded the southern territory and killed southern chimps. Infant victims were partially eaten by the assailants (Goodall 1986).

John MacKinnon's research (1974) among orangutans on the Indonesian islands of Kalimantan (Borneo) and Sumatra showed that orangutans also have suffered as a result of human encroachment, particularly farming and timbering. On Borneo, in response to nearby human activities, orangs have developed a pattern of extreme sexual antagonism that may further endanger their survival. During MacKinnon's field work, Bornean orangs rarely had sex. Their limited sexual encounters were always brief forced copulations, often with screaming infants clinging to their mothers throughout the ordeal.

As MacKinnon did his field work, logging operations were forcing orangs whose territory was destroyed into his research area, swelling the population it had to support. The response to this sudden overpopulation was a drastic decline in the local orang birth rate. Primates respond in various ways to encroachment and to population pressure. A change in sexual relationships that reduces the birth rate is one way of easing population pressure on resources.

We see that primate behavior is not rigidly determined by the genes. It is plastic (flexible), capable of varying widely as environmental forces change. Among humans, too, aggression increases when resources are threatened or scarce. What we know about other primates makes it reasonable to assume that early hominids were neither uniformly aggressive nor consistently meek. Their aggression and predation reflected environmental variation (see Silverberg and Gray 1992; Wrangham and Peterson 1996).

Human–Primate Differences

The preceding sections have emphasized similarities between humans and other primates. Homo has elaborated substantially on certain tendencies shared with the apes. A unique concentration and combination of characteristics make humans distinct. However, the savanna or open grassland niche in which early humans evolved also selected certain traits that are not so clearly foreshadowed by the apes.

SHARING AND COOPERATION

Early humans lived in small social groups called bands, with economies based on hunting and gathering (foraging). Until fairly recently (12,000 to 10,000 years ago), all humans based their subsistence on hunting and gathering and lived in bands. Some such societies even managed to survive into the modern world, and ethnographers have studied them. From those studies we can conclude that in such societies, the strongest and most aggressive members do not dominate, as they do in a troop of terrestrial monkeys. Sharing and curbing of aggression are as basic to technologically simple humans as dominance and threats are to baboons.

We've seen that bonobos use sex to curb aggression and reduce conflict, and that male chimps cooperate in hunting. But as we saw from the brain response study described in Chapter 3, humans appear to be the most cooperative of the primates—in the food quest and other social activities. Except for meat sharing by chimps, the ape tendency is to forage individually. Monkeys also fend for themselves in getting food. Among human foragers, men generally hunt and women gather. Men and women bring resources back to the camp and share them. Older people who did not engage in the food quest get food from younger adults. Everyone shares the meat from a large animal. Nourished and protected by younger band members, elders live past the reproductive age and are respected for their knowledge and experience. The amount of information stored in a human band is far greater than that in any other primate society. Sharing, cooperation, and language are intrinsic to information storage. Through millions of years of adaptation to an omnivorous diet, hominids have come to rely, more than any other primate, on hunting, food sharing, and cooperative behavior. These are universal features in human adaptive strategies.

MATING AND KINSHIP

Another difference between humans and other primates involves mating. Among baboons, chimpanzees, and bonobos, most mating occurs when females enter estrus, during which they ovulate. Receptive females form temporary bonds with, and mate with, males. Human females, by contrast, lack a visible estrus cycle, and their ovulation is concealed. Neither a woman's sexual receptivity nor her readiness to conceive is physically evident, as it is in chimps and bonobos. Not knowing when ovulation is occurring, humans maximize their reproductive success by mating throughout the year. Human pair bonds for mating tend to be more exclusive and more durable than are those of chimps or bonobos. Related to our more constant sexuality, all human societies have some form of marriage. Marriage gives mating a reliable basis and grants to each spouse special, though not always exclusive, sexual rights in the other.

Marriage creates another major contrast between humans and nonhumans: exogamy and kinship systems. Most cultures have rules of exogamy requiring marriage outside one's kin or local group. Coupled with the recognition of kinship, exogamy confers adaptive advantages. It creates ties between the spouses' groups of origin. Their children have relatives, and therefore allies, in two kin groups rather than just one. The key point here is that ties of affection and mutual support between members of different local groups tend to be absent among primates other than Homo. There is a tendency among primates to disperse at adolescence. Among chimps and gorillas, females tend to migrate, seeking mates in other groups. Both male and female gibbons leave home when they become sexually mature. Once they find mates and establish their own territories, ties

Through millions of years of adaptation to an omnivorous diet, hominids have come to rely on gathering, hunting, and food sharing. These three Batak women from Palawan Island, the Philippines, share wild honeycombs. Locate the Philippines in your atlas.

with their natal groups cease. Among terrestrial monkeys, males leave the troop at puberty, eventually finding places elsewhere. The troop's core members are females. They sometimes form uterine groups made up of mothers, sisters, daughters, and sons that have not yet emigrated. This dispersal of males reduces the incidence of incestuous matings. Females mate with males born elsewhere, which join the troop at adolescence. Although kin ties are maintained between female monkeys, no close lifelong links are preserved through males.

Humans choose mates from outside the natal group, and usually at least one spouse moves. However, *humans maintain lifelong ties with sons and daughters*. The systems of kinship and marriage that preserve these links provide a major contrast between humans and other primates.

Behavioral Ecology and Fitness

According to evolutionary theory, when the environment changes, natural selection starts to modify the *population*'s pool of genetic material. Natural selection has another key feature: the differential reproductive success of *individuals* within the population. **Behavioral ecology** studies the evolutionary basis of social behavior. It assumes that the genetic features of any species reflect a long history of differential reproductive success (that is, natural selection). In other words, biological traits of contemporary organisms have been transmitted across the generations because those traits enabled their ancestors to survive and reproduce more effectively than their competition.

Natural selection is based on *differential* reproduction. Members of the same species may compete to maximize their reproductive fitness—their genetic contribution to future generations. *Individual fitness* is measured by the number of direct descendants an individual has. Illustrating a primate strategy that may enhance individual fitness are cases in which male monkeys kill infants after entering a new troop. Destroying the offspring of other males, they clear a place for their own progeny (Hausfater and Hrdy 1984).

Besides competition, one's genetic contribution to future generations also can be enhanced by cooperation, sharing, and other apparently unselfish behavior. This is because of *inclusive fitness*—reproductive success measured by the genes one shares with relatives. By sacrificing for their kin—even if this means limiting their own direct reproduction—individuals actually may increase their genetic contributions (their shared genes) to the future. Inclusive fitness helps us understand why a female might invest in her sister's offspring, or why a male might risk his life to defend his brothers. If self-sacrifice perpetuates more of their genes than direct reproduction does, it makes sense in terms of behavioral ecology. Such a view can help us understand aspects of primate behavior and social organization.

Maternal care always makes sense in terms of reproductive fitness theory because females know their offspring are their own. But it's harder for males to be sure about paternity. Inclusive fitness theory predicts that males will invest most in offspring when they are surest the offspring are theirs. Gibbons, for example, have strict male–female pair bonding, which makes it almost certain that the offspring are those of both members of the pair. Thus we expect male gibbons to offer care and protection to their young, and they do. However, among species and in situations in which a male can't be sure about his paternity, it may make more sense to invest in a sister's offspring than in a mate's because the niece or nephew definitely shares some of that male's genes.

SUMMARY

1. Humans, apes, monkeys, and prosimians are primates. The primate order is subdivided into suborders, superfamilies, families, genera, species, and subspecies. Organisms in any subdivision (taxon) of a taxonomy are assumed to share more recent ancestry with each other than they do with organisms in other taxa. But it's sometimes hard to tell the difference between homologies, which reflect common ancestry, and analogies, biological similarities that develop through convergent evolution.

2. Prosimians are the older of the two primate suborders. Some 40 million years ago, anthropoids displaced prosimians from niches their ancestors once occupied. Tarsiers and lorises are prosimians that survived by adapting to nocturnal life. Lemurs survived on the isolated island of Madagascar.

3. Anthropoids include humans, apes, and monkeys. All share fully developed primate trends, such as depth and color vision. Other anthropoid traits include a shift in tactile areas to the fingers. The New World monkeys are all arboreal. Old World monkeys include both terrestrial species (e.g., baboons and macaques) and arboreal ones. The great apes are orangutans, gorillas, and chimpanzees. The lesser apes are gibbons and siamangs.

4. Gibbons and siamangs live in Southeast Asian forests. These apes are slight, arboreal animals whose mode of locomotion is brachiation. Sexual dimorphism, slight among gibbons, is marked among orangutans, which are confined to two Indonesian islands. Sexually dimorphic gorillas, the most terrestrial apes, are vegetarians confined to equatorial Africa. Two species of chimpanzees live in the forests and woodlands of tropical Africa. Chimps are less sexually dimorphic, more numerous, and more omnivorous than gorillas are. Terrestrial monkeys (baboons and macaques) live in troops. Baboon males, the troop's main protectors, are twice the size of females.

5. Deforestation poses a special risk for the primates. Most of the 190 living primate species are in tropical forests—in Africa, Asia, South America, and Central America. Primates also are endangered as humans hunt them for food (bush meat) and capture them for zoos and research.

6. There are significant differences between humans and other primates. But similarities are also extensive, and many differences are of degree rather than of kind. A unique concentration and combination of ingredients make humans distinct. Some of our most important adaptive traits are foreshadowed in other primates, particularly in the African apes. Primate behavior and social organization aren't rigidly programmed by the genes. The ability to learn, which is the basis of culture, is an adaptive advantage available to many nonhuman primates. Chimpanzees make tools for several purposes. They also hunt and share meat.

7. Important differences between humans and other primates remain. Aggression and dominance are characteristic of terrestrial monkeys. Sharing and cooperation are equally significant in human bands. Connected with sharing among humans is a traditional division of subsistence labor by age and gender. Only humans have systems of kinship and marriage that permit us to maintain lifelong ties with relatives in different local groups.

8. From the perspective of behavioral ecology, individuals in a population compete to increase their genetic contribution to future generations. Maternal care makes sense from this perspective because females can be sure their offspring are their own. Because it's harder for males to be sure about paternity, evolutionary theory predicts they will invest most in offspring when they are surest the offspring are theirs.

KEY TERMS

See the flash cards

analogies Similarities arising as a result of similar selective forces; traits produced by convergent evolution.

anthropoids Members of Anthropoidea, one of the two suborders of primates; monkeys, apes, and humans are anthropoids.

arboreal Tree-dwelling; arboreal primates include gibbons, New World monkeys, and many Old World monkeys.

behavioral ecology Study of the evolutionary basis of social behavior.

bipedal Two-footed; upright bipedalism is the characteristic human mode of locomotion.

brachiation Under-the-branch swinging; characteristic of gibbons, siamangs, and some New World monkeys.

convergent evolution Independent operation of similar selective forces; the process by which analogies are produced.

estrus Period of maximum sexual receptivity in female baboons, chimpanzees, and other primates, signaled by vaginal area swelling and coloration.

gibbons The smallest apes, natives of Asia; arboreal.

hominids Members of the zoological family that includes fossil and living humans; many scientists now include chimpanzees and gorillas in this family.

hominoids Members of the superfamily including humans and all the apes.

homologies Traits that organisms have jointly inherited from a common ancestor.

opposable thumb A thumb that can touch all the other fingers.

primatology The study of fossil and living apes, monkeys, and prosimians, including their behavior and social life.

prosimians The primate suborder that includes lemurs, lorises, and tarsiers.

sexual dimorphism Marked differences in male and female anatomy and temperament.

taxonomy Classification scheme; assignment to categories (*taxa;* singular, *taxon*).

terrestrial Ground-dwelling; baboons, macaques, and humans are terrestrial primates; gorillas spend most of their time on the ground.

For more self testing, see the self quizzes

CRITICAL THINKING QUESTIONS

1. Give three examples of homologies between humans and apes. Can you think of behavioral as well as biological homologies?

2. Among the primates, give an example of an analogy produced through convergent evolution. Can you think of analogies involving animals other than primates?

3. What are the main trends in primate evolution? Compare a cat or dog with a monkey, ape, or human. What are the main differences in the sensory organs—those that have to do with vision, smell, and touch, for example?

4. Which seems most similar to human social organization, that of baboons, gorillas, or chimpanzees?

5. What are some examples of ways in which nonhuman primates rely on learning to adapt to their environment?

6. How do tools differ with respect to humans and other animals?

7. What environmental conditions might trigger predatory behavior among primates? How about humans?

8. Give three examples of major behavioral differences between humans and other primates.

9. Why is it significant that among primates, only humans maintain ties of affection and mutual support between different local groups?

10. How do behavioral ecology and fitness theory help us understand differences between female and male parental investment strategies?

Atlas Questions

Look at Map 5, "Major Primate Groups."

1. On what continents are there nonhuman primates today? How does this differ from the past? What primate thrives today in North America?

2. What nonhuman primates live on the island of Madagascar? Are they monkeys or what? Where do other members of their suborder live?

3. On what continents can you find apes in the wild today? What continent that used to have apes lacks them today (except, of course, in zoos)?

SUGGESTED ADDITIONAL READINGS

Burton, F. D., and M. Eaton
1995   *The Multimedia Guide to Non-Human Primates.* Upper Saddle River, NJ: Prentice-Hall. A CD-ROM combining photos, illustrations, video, sound, and text—presenting over 200 species of nonhuman primates.

De Waal, F. B. M.
1997   *Bonobo: The Forgotten Ape.* Berkeley: University of California Press. Field-based study of rare and remote apes noted for their similarities to humans and their sexual behavior.

1999   *Chimpanzee Politics: Power and Sex among Apes,* rev. ed. Baltimore: Johns Hopkins University Press. Hierarchy, sex, and alliance among apes, mainly based on zoo observations.

Fedigan, L. M.
1992   *Primate Paradigms: Sex Roles and Social Bonds.* Chicago: University of Chicago Press. Focuses on sex roles in primate social organization.

Fossey, D.
1983   *Gorillas in the Mist.* Boston: Houghton Mifflin. Social organization of the mountain gorilla; basis of the popular film.

Goodall, J.
1996   *My Life with the Chimpanzees.* New York: Pocket Books. Popular account of the author's life among the chimps.

Hinde, R. A.
1983   *Primate Social Relationships: An Integrated Approach.* Sunderland, MA: Sinaeur Associates. Theoretical implications of aspects of social life among various primates.

Montgomery, S.
1991   *Walking with the Great Apes: Jane Goodall, Dian Fossey, Birutá Galdikas.* Boston: Houghton Mifflin. The stories of three primatologists who have worked with, and to preserve, chimpanzees, gorillas, and orangutans.

Morbeck, M. E., A. Galloway, and A. L. Zihlman, eds.
1997   *The Evolving Female: A Life-History Perspective.* Princeton, NJ: Princeton University Press. Primatology and human evolution from a female perspective.

Napier, J. R., and P. H. Napier
1985   *The Natural History of Primates.* Cambridge, MA: The MIT Press. Readable and well-illustrated introduction to the primates.

Roberts, J. L.
1995   *Dian Fossey.* San Diego, CA: Lucent Books. Biography of the gorilla researcher and protector.

Russon, A. E., K. A. Bard, and S. Taylor Parker, eds.

1996   *Reaching into Thought: The Minds of the Great Apes*. New York: Cambridge University Press. Papers examining the intelligence of the apes.

Small, M. F.

1993   *Female Choices: Sexual Behavior of Female Primates*. Ithaca, NY: Cornell University Press. Sexual behavior and characteristics of female apes and monkeys.

Small, M. F., ed.

1984   *Female Primates: Studies by Women Primatologists*. New York: Liss. Differences in female strategies in various primate groups.

Smuts, B. B.

1989   *Sex and Friendship in Baboons*. Cambridge, MA Harvard University Press. Pair bonding, mutual support, and parental investment in baboon social organization, with implications for early human evolution.

Stanford, C. B.

1999   *The Hunting Apes: Meat Eating and the Origins of Human Behavior*. Princeton, NJ: Princeton University Press. The role of meat and hunting in sex and alliance among wild chimps.

Stanford, C. B., and H. T. Bunn, eds.

2001   *Meat-Eating and Human Evolution*. New York: Oxford University Press. Compendium of various recent studies.

Strum, S. C., and L. M. Fedigan, eds.

2000   *Primate Encounters: Models of Science, Gender, and Society*. Chicago: University of Chicago Press. The roles of males and females in primate social organization.

Swindler, D. R.

1998   *Introduction to the Primates*. Seattle: University of Washington Press. Up-to-date survey.

Wrangham, R. W., ed.

1994   *Chimpanzee Cultures*. Cambridge, MA: Harvard University Press.

INTERNET EXERCISES

1. Primate Conflict: Go to the Living Link's video collection at Emory University's Center for the Advanced Study of Ape and Human Evolution website, **http://www.emory.edu/LIVING_LINKS/a/video.html,** and watch the Chimpanzee Conflict Movie, **http://www.emory.edu/LIVING_LINKS/sounds/ram_text/conflict_28k.ram.**

   a. What different kinds of aggression are presented in the movie?

   b. What are the different responses to aggression? Did these responses tend to escalate or terminate the aggressive behavior?

   c. Is aggressive behavior restricted to adults? Does it take on different forms in juveniles?

   d. Which of these aggressive behaviors and responses do humans share with the chimpanzees? For example, do humans use Bluff Display?

2. Endangered Primates: Go to the Living Link's video collection at Emory University's Center for the Advanced Study of Ape and Human Evolution website, **http://www.emory.edu/LIVING_LINKS/a/video.html,** and watch the African Bushmeat Crisis Movie, **http://www.emory.edu/LIVING_LINKS/sounds/ram_text/bushmeat.ram.**

   a. The filmmakers argue that killing primates is similar to murder. Do you agree?

   b. The filmmakers suggest that the roots of the problem lie in those who hunt gorillas, not in those who buy and consume them. Do you think that if Joseph stopped hunting, people would stop eating gorillas?

   c. What other steps would you suggest to help preserve the mountain gorilla populations in Africa?

See Chapter 5 at your McGraw-Hill Online Learning Center for additional review and interactive exercises.

BRINGING IT ALL TOGETHER

Saving the Forests

Deforestation, a problem that faces the world, is also a topic that has attracted the attention of anthropology's four subfields and two dimensions. Anthropology has always been concerned with how environmental forces influence humans and primates and how human activities affect the biosphere and the earth itself. As we saw in Chapter 4, biological anthropologists have examined the relation between farming, deforestation, and the spread of malaria and the gene that causes sickle-cell anemia. Other physical anthropologists—primatologists—see deforestation as a major threat to the animals they study. Paleoanthropologists have suggested a link between climate change, shrinking of forests, and the origin of hominids. Archaeologists have viewed deforestation in the context of resource use by ancient farmers and herders. Linguistic anthropologists have studied how people name and classify plants and forest resources. Cultural anthropologists have documented the varied uses people make of the forest and its products. From the fairy tales of Western Europe (e.g., Hansel and Gretel) to recent Hollywood films (e.g., The *Blair Witch Project*, *AI*), the forest plays a potent symbolic role as a place of mystery, danger, and enchantment. Today applied anthropologists are working to devise culturally appropriate and effective strategies to curb deforestation and preserve biodiversity.

Deforestation is a global concern. Forest loss contributes to greenhouse gas production (CO_2), which has been implicated in global warming. The destruction of tropical forests is also a major factor in the loss of global biodiversity. This is the case because of the many species, often of limited distribution, in forests, especially in the tropics. Tropical forests may contain more than half of earth's species while covering just 6 percent of the planet's land surface. Yet tropical forests are disappearing at the rate of 10 million to 20 million hectares per year (the size of New York state).

Among the tropical animals whose natural habitats are threatened, primates, most of which are forest dwellers, are especially at risk. Consider the Democratic Republic of the Congo (DRC), the country that ranks fourth in the world in terms of greatest biodiversity. Its threatened species include gorillas and bonobos. The major threat to the bonobo, which is found only in the DRC, is forestry and loss of the hardwood forests where most bonobos live (Stern 2000). In Indonesia, deforestation threatens the orangutan. Contact with humans after the opening of a road for loggers and miners proved fatal to hundreds of orangs. Recent Indonesian policy has promoted plantations rather than forest preservation. Government policy has shifted from selective logging, which permits some animals to survive, to clearcutting of the forest, which destroys the habitat (Dreifus 2000). As we hear regularly on the news, forests also have suffered from ancient and modern forest fires.

Cultural factors, including politics, affect the use of the forest and its perceived value to humans. Some governments and administrations are more environment-friendly than others are. And even if a country has strict environmental laws, those laws require enforcement. Consider Brazil's Amazon rain forest, where dozens of primate species live. Brazilian national deforestation policy has to be implemented at the local level, but many local political systems are controlled by ranching and mining interests that oppose environmental regulation.

Physical, archaeological, and cultural anthropologists have all examined how human strategies of adaptation, including economic activities, affect the environment, including use of the forest. The historic shift from foraging (hunting and gather-

Applied anthropology uses anthropological perspectives to identify and solve contemporary problems that affect humans. Deforestation is one such problem. Here children carrying saplings participate in a reforestation project in Sri Lanka.

ing) to food production (farming and herding) first took place in the Middle East some 10,000–12,000 years ago, and again in the Western Hemisphere 5,000 years later. With food production, the rate at which human beings degrade their environments increased. Population increase and the need to expand farming caused deforestation in many parts of the ancient Middle East and Mesoamerica (Mexico, Guatemala, Belize, and Honduras). People cut down trees to plant crops such as wheat in the Middle East and maize (corn) in Mesoamerica. Even today, many farmers think of trees as giant weeds to be removed and replaced with productive fields. Many farmers burn vegetation to remove weeds, then use the ashes for fertilizer. Herders burn to promote the growth of young tender shoots for their livestock. If done too often, as may happen when population grows, these activities result in deforestation. The use of fuel wood by early smelters also took its toll on the forests.

As we'll see in Chapter 11, located in what is now western Honduras, Copán was once a thriving Maya royal center. Its collapse some 1,400 years ago was linked to deforestation, erosion, and soil exhaustion due to overpopulation and overfarm-

ing. Archaeologists have reconstructed hillside farmhouses with debris from erosion at Copán. The erosion started around 750 AD and continued for generations, until the farm sites were abandoned. Some of them eventually were buried by erosion debris. Studies of Copán's paleopathology reveal food stress and malnutrition. Most (80 percent) of the corpses buried there had anemia, due to iron deficiency. Even Copán's nobles were malnourished. One noble skull, known to be such from its carved teeth and cosmetic deformation, has telltale signs of anemia: spongy areas at its rear.

What about forests, their uses and value, and threats to them today? In many parts of the world, forests supply medicinal plants; food products such as honey, game, and fruits; and wood—used to build houses, fences, and animal pens. Forests are also vital parts of watersheds—regions drained by river systems; trees take up and conserve water. By conserving water, forests impede erosion and siltation (mineral deposits) in irrigation canals.

Glen Green (a geologist) and Robert Sussman (a biological anthropologist) (1990) used remote sensing (as discussed in Chapter 3) to study deforestation in the eastern rain forests of Madagascar.

In this area are found several endangered species, including the lemurs discussed in "Beyond the Classroom" in Chapter 5. Green and Sussman found deforestation there to be correlated both with topographic relief (the slope or steepness of the land) and with human population density. Sparsely populated areas and very hilly areas had less forest loss than did densely populated and flat to moderately hilly areas. More than half the forest cover in the sparsely populated regions had survived, compared with just 19 percent in the high-density areas. The Green–Sussman study exposed an important fact for policy makers: Although low relief areas need protection the most, nearly all of Madagascar's forest reserves had been established in hilly areas. What recommendation would an applied anthropologist make for the location of future protected areas?

Often, as in eastern Madagascar, in the ancient Middle East, and at Copán, deforestation is demographically driven—caused by population pressure. Madagascar's population is growing at a rate of 3 percent annually, doubling every generation. Population pressure leads to migration, including rural–urban migration. Madagascar's capital, Antananarivo, had just 100,000 people in 1967, but over 1 million by 1990. Urban growth promotes deforestation if city dwellers rely on fuel wood from the countryside, as has been true in Madagascar.

As forested watersheds disappear, crop productivity declines, as happened at Copán. Madagascar is known as the "great red island," after the color of its soil. On that island, the effects of erosion and runoff are visible to the naked eye. Looking at its rivers, Madagascar appears to be bleeding to death. Increasing runoff of water no longer trapped by trees causes erosion of low-lying rice fields near swollen rivers, as well as siltation in irrigation canals (Kottak, Gezon, and Green 1994).

Besides population pressure, another prominent cause of deforestation is commercial logging, which can degrade forests in several ways. Obviously, logging deforests because it removes trees. Less evident are the destructive effects of road building, tree dragging, and other features of commercial logging. A logging road may cut a swath for erosion. In one village in Madagascar, whose forest had recently been invaded by loggers from outside, villagers told an ethnographer that the loggers killed a dozen trees for every log they dragged out (Kottak, Gezon, and Green 1994).

The global scenarios of deforestation include demographic pressure (from births or immigration) on subsistence economies, commercial logging, road building, cash cropping, fuel wood needs associated with urban expansion, and clearing and burning associated with livestock and grazing. The fact that forest loss has several causes has a policy implication: Different deforestation scenarios require different conservation strategies.

What can be done? On this question applied anthropology weighs in (see Kottak and Costa 1993), spurring policy makers to think about new conservation strategies. The traditional approach has been to restrict access to forested areas designated as parks, then employ park guards and punish violators. Modern strategies are more likely to consider the needs, wishes, and abilities of the people (often impoverished) living in and near the forest. Since effective conservation depends on the cooperation of the local people, their concerns must be addressed in devising conservation strategy.

Typically, forests have substantial economic and cultural utility for the

The causes of deforestation are diverse. In this example from Madagascar, the rain forest has been cut back to enlarge a cattle ranch. What are some other causes of deforestation?

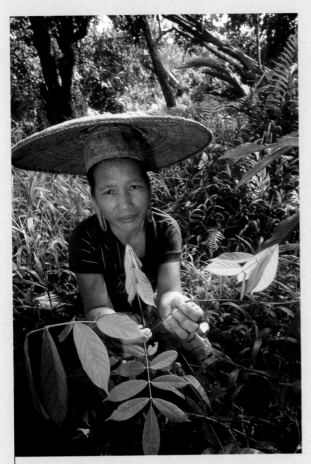

Forests supply medicinal plants, food products, and wood. This woman is collecting medicinal plants in Sarawak, Malaysia.

communities in and near them. Forests supply firewood and wood for house and granary construction, fences, and technology (e.g., oxcarts and mortars and pestles—for pounding grain). Some forests are used for food production, including slash-and-burn or shifting cultivation. Tree crops such as bananas, fruits, and coffee do well in the forest, where foraging for wild products also proceeds. Forests also contain vital cultural products. In Madagascar, for example, these products include medicinal plants and pastes considered essential for the proper growth of children. In one ethnic group rice from a forest field is part of the ceremony used to ensure a successful and fertile marriage. Another ethnic group has its most sacred tombs in the forests. Traditionally, these culturally vital areas of the forest have been tabooed for burning and wood cutting. They are part of a local conservation system that has been in place for generations.

What happens when activities are banned not by the traditional culture but by an external agency? Government-imposed conservation policies may require people to change the way they have been doing things for generations to meet the goals of outside planners rather than those of local people. When communities are asked to give up traditional activities on which they depend for their livelihood, they usually resist. To be successful, conservation schemes must involve local people in planning and implementing the policies and programs that will affect them.

Effective environmentalism requires culturally informed negotiation with political and economic interests at the local, regional, national, and international levels. Here is an arena in which anthropology is fruitfully applied. Conservationists must learn to recognize and build on diverse systems of environmental values—different "ethnoecologies." (An *ethnoecology* is any society's traditional set of environmental perceptions, its ideas about the environment in relation to people and society.) Effective conservation strategy requires extensive and ongoing knowledge of affected areas and the socioeconomic and cultural practices of the local people.

To curb the global deforestation threat, we need conservation strategies that work. Laws and enforcement may help reduce commercially driven deforestation caused by burning and clear-cutting. But local people also use and abuse forested lands. A challenge for the environmentally oriented applied anthropologist is to find ways to make forest preservation attractive to local people and to ensure their cooperation. Successful conservation must be based on culturally appropriate policies, which applied anthropologists can help devise for specific places. To provide locally meaningful incentives, we need good anthropological knowledge of each affected area. Governments and international agencies are likely to fail if they try to impose their goals without considering the practices, customs, rules, laws, beliefs, and values of the people to be affected. Applied anthropologists work to make "good for the globe" good for the people.

6

PRIMATE EVOLUTION

Overview

The primate order evolved by exploiting new opportunities that arose at the end of the Mesozoic era. The age of reptiles yielded to the age of mammals—the Cenozoic era, which began some 65 million years ago. Flowering plants proliferated, along with the insects attracted to them and the animals that preyed on those insects. Primate traits like grasping hands and depth perception aided in the capture of insects and were adaptive in an arboreal environment.

By the Eocene epoch, primates had spread and diversified, mainly in Europe and North America, which were connected at that time. Among primates, the Eocene was the age of prosimians. By the end of the Eocene, the anthropoids had emerged; they eventually displaced the prosimians in most places. In the next

epoch, the Oligocene, the New World monkeys split off from the catarrhines, the ancestors of Old World monkeys, apes, and humans.

The ensuing Miocene epoch, divided into Early, Middle, and Late, witnessed a fluorescence of proto-apes, an amazing variety unlike anything that survives in the contemporary world. Some 16 million years ago, Africa collided with Eurasia. The new land connection allowed African fauna, including apes, to spread into Europe and Asia, where the apes proliferated. The lines leading to the orangutan, on the one hand, and the African apes, on the other, split during the middle Miocene. The common ancestor of humans, chimps, and gorillas—as yet unidentified—lived during the late Miocene, some five to eight million years ago.

Suddenly, Primate Ancestors Pushed Back to Time Dinosaurs Roamed

WASHINGTON POST NEWS BRIEFS

by Guy Gugliotta

April 18, 2002

Fossil evidence confirms that a variety of primates lived, mainly in Europe and North America, during the geological epoch known as the Eocene (54–38 m.y.a.—million years ago). On that basis, many paleontologists suspect that the earliest primates appeared during the previous epoch, the Paleocene (65–54 m.y.a.). The status of several Paleocene fossils as possible primates has been debated, but not resolved. Based on the current *fossil* evidence, it's difficult to believe the first primates might date back even farther—to the age of the dinosaurs, the Mesozoic era, which ended 65 million years ago. Despite what we've seen in the movies, early *humans* did *not* coexist with the dinosaurs. But maybe primates did. Paleontology isn't the only scientific field that studies evolution. For example, significant evolutionary trees have been drawn on the basis of similarities and differences in DNA. As you read this news brief, consider the different techniques scientists use to interpret the past. What analytic techniques support the unorthodox idea that primates may date back 85 million years?

Primates—the mammals from which humans evolved—emerged on Earth much earlier than had been thought, originating perhaps 85 million years ago during the age of the dinosaurs, according to a new analysis. The findings should add fuel to the debate between paleontologists, who place the origin of primates at 55 million years ago, and molecular biologists, who use DNA sequencing to suggest they may be as old as 90 million years.

Paleontologist Robert D. Martin, vice president of academic affairs at Chicago's Field Museum, acknowledged that his team's new research supported the views of the "molecular clock" school, even though the method used by his team did not involve DNA analysis. Instead, the researchers developed a statistical model that builds an evolutionary tree based on the number of primate species alive today (235) and the number of recorded fossil species (396) and their ages. By assuming that each primate species would live approximately 2.5 million years, the team was able to estimate the length of time that elapsed between the oldest known fossil primate, which is 55 million years old, and a hypothetical "last common ancestor" of all primates, 80 million to 85 million years ago. The findings were reported in today's issue of the journal *Nature*. [See Figure 6.1.]

"I've been arguing for years that there's so many gaps in the fossil record that [primates are] probably much older than we thought," Martin said. "You look at how many species there are, and you can estimate the time of the original."

The implications of these findings, if shown to be accurate, could be profound. A primate ancestor 85 million years old would have shared the world with the dinosaurs, which went extinct 65 million years ago, probably in an ecological disaster caused by a meteor hitting the Earth . . . Martin said the earliest primate was probably a lemur-like tree dweller that weighed perhaps two pounds and dined on insects and fruit. Finally, an earlier date for primates would mean that continental drift (in which huge, ancient

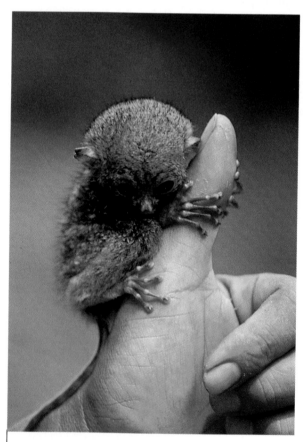

A tarsier from Sumatra, Indonesia, on a human thumb. The first primates were also tiny.

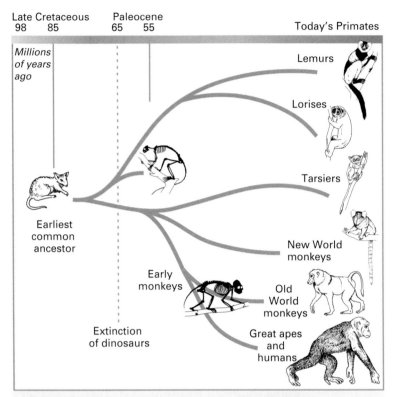

| Late Cretaceous | Paleocene | Today's Primates |
| 98   85 | 65   55 | |

Millions of years ago

Lemurs

Lorises

Tarsiers

Earliest common ancestor

New World monkeys

Early monkeys

Old World monkeys

Extinction of dinosaurs

Great apes and humans

Figure 6.1   A New Evolutionary Tree for Primates, Based on Calculations Reported in This Story.

SOURCE: BBC News, SCI/TECH, "Primate Ancestor Lived with Dinos," http://news.bbc.co.uk/hi/english/sci/tech/newsid_1935000/1935558.stm.

land masses broke up to form what are today's continents) had a significant effect in creating different primate species.

The new findings, however, drew criticism from several paleontologists, who noted that there is little fossil evidence from the dinosaur period that points to primates or indicates that mammals in general were flourishing.

"The primates are a successful group of animals," said K. Christopher Beard, curator of vertebrate paleontology at Pittsburgh's Carnegie Museum of Natural History. . . . "If primates were around and doing well, I suspect we would have found their fossils," Beard continued. "What I would do is issue a challenge and ask them to say where these animals are hiding."

What the fossil record shows is that before the dinosaur extinction, mammals were neither particularly diverse, nor particularly large. Most were rodent-like creatures, and "the biggest was about the

size of a beaver," said Johns Hopkins University paleontologist Kenneth Rose. "There was an explosive radiation of mammals after [the dinosaur] extinction," Rose continued. "It took very little time before we get an animal the size of a steer, and soon we had some truly impressive creatures. With no dinosaurs in the way, there was a lot of open ecological space."

But while everyone agrees that the first unequivocal fossil primate did not appear until 55 million years ago, Martin argues that the record is too skimpy to conclude that the order began only a few million years prior to that.

"Primate paleontologists read the fossil record as if it told us everything," Martin said. "That's reasonable if you have a dense record, but our calculations show we have fossil evidence for only about 5 percent of the extinct primates."

By contrast, molecular biologists analyze DNA to calculate the amount of genetic difference in related species, creating an evolutionary tree that can be projected backward in time to the earliest common ancestor. "Our results actually fit the molecular trees, and they're always much earlier," Martin said. "Several people have generated the tree for mammals," and have come up with dates "around 90 million years." But "there are no fossils that say that," said Michael Novacek, provost and curator of paleontology at New York's American Museum of Natural History, even though "it could be that the record is incomplete." "So what's the truth?" Novacek asked. "I don't know."

Source: *Washington Post* (http://www.washingtonpost.com), April 18, 2002, p. A03. http://www.washingtonpost.com/ac2/wp-dyn?pagename= article&node=&contentId=A4580-2002Apr17.

The fossil record, as we've just seen, provides evidence for only 5 percent of extinct primates. With such small numbers, the fossil record gives us the merest glimpse of the diverse bioforms— living beings—that have existed on earth. In Chapter 3, in the section "Dating the Past," we learned why some areas and times are better represented in the fossil record than others are. Conditions favoring fossilization open special "time windows" for certain places and times, such as western Kenya from 18 to 14 **m.y.a.**—million years ago. Because western Kenya was geologically active then, it has a substantial fossil record. Between 12 and 8 m.y.a., the area was quieter geologically, and there are few fossils. After 8 m.y.a., another time window opens in the Rift Valley area of eastern Kenya. The East African highlands were rising, volcanoes were active, and lake basins were forming and filling with sediments. This time window extends through the present and includes many hominid fossils. Compared with East Africa, West Africa has been more stable geologically and has had few time windows (Jolly and White 1995).

In considering the primate fossil record, we'll see that different geographic areas provide more abundant fossil evidence for different time periods. This doesn't necessarily mean that primates weren't living elsewhere at the same time. The discussions of primate and human evolution must be tentative, because the fossil record is limited and spotty. Much is subject to change as knowledge increases. Recall from Chapter 1 that a key feature of science is to recognize the tentativeness and uncertainty of knowledge. Scientists, including fossil hunters, constantly seek out new evidence, and devise new methods, such as DNA comparison, to improve their understanding, in this case of primate and human evolution.

Chronology

We learned in Chapter 3 that the remains of animals and plants that lived at the same time are found in the same stratum. Based on fossils found in stratigraphic sequences, the history of vertebrate life has been divided into three main eras. The *Paleozoic* was the era of ancient life—fishes, amphibians, and primitive reptiles. The *Mesozoic* was the era of middle life—reptiles, including the dinosaurs. The *Cenozoic* is the era of recent life—birds and mammals. Each era is divided into periods, and the periods are divided into epochs. (See Figure 6.2.)

See the Virtual Exploration

mhhe ● com /kottak

Anthropologists are concerned with the Cenozoic era, which includes two periods: Tertiary and

Era	Period	
Cenozoic	Quaternary	1.8 m.y.a.
	Tertiary	65 m.y.a.
Mesozoic	Cretaceous	146 m.y.a.
	Jurassic	208 m.y.a.
	Triassic	245 m.y.a.
Paleozoic	Permian	286 m.y.a.
	Carboniferous	360 m.y.a.
	Devonian	410 m.y.a.
	Silurian	440 m.y.a.
	Ordovician	505 m.y.a.
	Cambrian	544 m.y.a.
Proterozoic	Neoproterozoic	900 m.y.a.
	Mesoproterozoic	1,600 m.y.a.
	Paleoproterozoic	2,500 m.y.a.
Archaean		3,800 m.y.a.
Hadean		4,500 m.y.a.

Figure 6.2   Geological Time Scales.
The geological time scale, based on stratigraphy. Eras are subdivided into periods, and periods, into epochs. In what era, period, and epoch did *Homo* originate?

Era	Period	Epoch		Climate and Life Forms
Cenozoic	Quaternary	Holocene	11,000 B.P.	Transition to agriculture; emergence of states
		Pleistocene	1.8 m.y.a.	Climatic fluctuations, glaciation; *Homo, A. boisei*
	Tertiary	Pliocene	5 m.y.a.	*A. robustus, A. africanus, A. afarensis, A. anamensis, Ardipithecus ramidus*
		Miocene	23 m.y.a.	Cooler and drier grasslands spread in middle latitudes; Africa collides with Eurasia (16 m.y.a.); *Afropithecus, Ramapithecus, Sivapithecus*
		Oligocene	38 m.y.a.	Cooler and drier in the north; anthropoids in Africa (Fayum); separation of catarrhines and platyrrhines; separation of hylobatids from pongids and hominids
		Eocene	54 m.y.a.	Warm tropical climates become widespread; modern orders of mammals appear; prosimianlike primates; anthropoids appear by late Eocene
		Paleocene	65 m.y.a.	First major mammal radiation

Figure 6.2   **Geological Time Scales—Concluded.**
Periods and Epochs of the Cenozoic Era.

Quaternary. Each of these periods is subdivided into epochs. The Tertiary had five epochs: Paleocene, Eocene, Oligocene, Miocene, and Pliocene. The Quaternary includes just two epochs: Pleistocene and Holocene, or Recent. Figure 6.2 gives the approximate dates of these epochs. Sediments from the Paleocene epoch (65 to 54 m.y.a.) have yielded fossil remains of diverse small mammals, some possibly ancestral to the primates. Prosimian-like fossils abound in strata dating from the Eocene (54 to 36 m.y.a.). The first anthropoid fossils date to the middle to late Eocene and the early Oligocene (36 to 23 m.y.a.). Hominoids became widespread during the Miocene (23 to 5 m.y.a.). Hominids first appeared in the late Miocene or early Pliocene (5 to 2 m.y.a.) (Figure 6.2).

See your OLC Internet Exercises

mhhe com /kottak

Early Primates

When the Mesozoic era ended, and the Cenozoic began, some 65 million years ago, North America was connected to Europe, but not to South America. (The Americas joined some 20 million years ago.) Over millions of years, the continents have "drifted" to their present locations, carried along by the gradually shifting plates of the earth's surface (Figure 6.3).

During the Cenozoic, most land masses had tropical or subtropical climates. The Mesozoic era had ended with a massive worldwide extinction of plants and animals, including the dinosaurs. Thereafter, mammals replaced reptiles as the dominant large land animals. Trees and flowering plants soon proliferated, supplying arboreal foods for the primates that eventually evolved to fill the new niches.

According to the arboreal theory, primates became primates by adapting to arboreal life. The primate traits and trends discussed in the last chapter developed as adaptations to life high up in the trees. A key feature was the importance of sight over smell. Changes in the visual apparatus were adaptive in the trees, where depth perception facilitated leaping. Grasping hands and feet were used to crawl along slender branches. Grasping feet anchored the body as the primate reached for foods at the ends of branches. Early

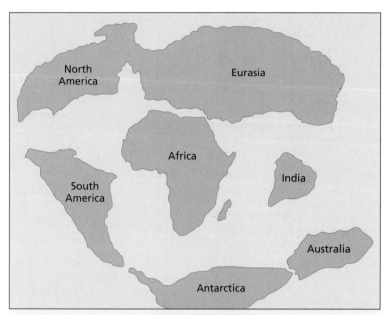

Figure 6.3 **Placement of Continents at the End of the Mesozoic.** When the Mesozoic era ended, and the Cenozoic began, some 65 million years ago, North America was connected to Europe, but not to South America.

According to one theory, binocular vision and manipulative hands developed among primates because they facilitated the capture of insects. What is this theory called? Here a Colombian squirrel monkey uses its hands and eyes to eat a katydid.

primates probably had omnivorous diets based on foods available in the trees, such as flowers, fruits, berries, gums, leaves, and insects. The early Cenozoic era witnessed a proliferation of flowering plants, attracting insects that were to figure prominently in many primate diets.

Matt Cartmill (1974, 1992) notes that although primate traits work well in the trees, they aren't the only possible adaptations to arboreal life. Squirrels, for example, do just fine with claws and snouts and without binocular vision. Something else must have figured in primate evolution, and Cartmill suggests a **visual predation theory**. This is the idea that binocular vision, grasping hands and feet, and reduced claws developed because they facilitated the capture of insects, which figured prominently in the early primate diet. According to this theory, early primates first adapted to bushy forest undergrowth and low tree branches, where they foraged for fruits and insects. Particularly in pursuing insects, early primates would have relied heavily on vision. Close-set eyes permitted binocular vision and depth perception. Such a visual apparatus would have allowed early primates to judge the distance to their prey without moving their heads. They would have hunted like cats and owls. The snout would have been reduced, with a less acute sense of smell, as the eyes came closer together. Early primates would have held on with their grasping feet as they snared their prey with their hands. Several living prosimians retain the small body size and insectivorous diet that may have characterized the first primates. Jurmain (1997) suggests that although key primate traits might have evolved first for life in the lower branches, such traits would have become even more adaptive when bug snatching was done higher up in the trees.

EARLY CENOZOIC PRIMATES

There is considerable fossil evidence that a diversified group of primates lived, mainly in Europe and North America, during the second epoch of the

Compare this line drawing reconstruction of Shoshonius, a member of the Eocene omomyid family, with a modern tarsier from Mindanao in the Philippines. What similarities and differences do you notice?

Cenozoic, the Eocene. On that basis it is likely that the earliest primates lived during the first epoch of the Cenozoic, the Paleocene (65–54 m.y.a.). The status of several fossils as possible Paleocene primates has been debated. As there is no consensus on this matter, such fossils are not discussed here.

The first fossil forms clearly identified as primates lived during the Eocene epoch (54–38 m.y.a.) in North America, Europe, Africa, and Asia. They reached Madagascar from Africa late in the Eocene. The ancestral lemurs must have traveled across the Mozambique Channel, which was narrower then than it is now, on thick mats of vegetation. Such naturally formed "rafts" have been observed forming in East African rivers, then floating out to sea.

In primate evolution, the Eocene was the age of the prosimians, with at least 60 genera in two main families (*Omomyidae* and *Adapidae*). The widely distributed **omomyid** family lived in North America, Europe, and Asia. The omomyids, such as *Shoshonius*, portrayed in the drawing on this page, were squirrel-sized. But unlike squirrels they had grasping hands and feet, used to manipulate objects and to climb by encircling small branches. Early members of the omomyid family may be ancestral to all anthropoids. Later ones may be ancestral to tarsiers.

The **adapid** family was probably ancestral to the lemur–loris line. The only major difference between the Eocene adapids, such as *Smilodectes*, shown in the photo on page 151, and today's lemurs and lorises is that the latter have a dental comb (see Figure 6.4). This structure is formed from the incisor and canine teeth of the lower jaw.

Sometime during the Eocene, ancestral anthropoids branched off from the prosimians by becoming more diurnal (active during the day) and by strengthening the trend favoring vision over smell. Some Eocene prosimians had larger brains and eyes, and smaller snouts, than others did. These were the ancestors of the anthropoids. Anthropoid eyes are rotated more forward when compared with lemurs and lorises. Also, anthropoids have a fully enclosed bony eye socket, which lemurs and lorises lack. And unlike lemurs and lorises, anthropoids lack a rhinarium, a moist nose continuous with the upper lip. Anthropoids have a dry nose, separate from the upper lip. Another distinguishing anthropoid feature has to do with molar cusps—bumps on the teeth. The primitive number of cusps on mammalian lower molars is six. The anthropoids have lost one or two cusps on their lower molars, so as to have four or five.

The oldest probable anthropoid discovered so far is *Eosimias*, from the Eocene of China. The oldest definite anthropoid is *Catopithecus*, from the late Eocene of Egypt. By the end of the Eocene, many prosimian species had become extinct, reflecting competition from the first anthropoids.

Figure 6.4   A Dental Comb.
A dental comb is a derived trait present among contemporary lemurs and lorises but absent in Eocene adapids such as *Smilodectes*.

Source: Robert Jurmain and Harry Nelson, *Introduction to Physical Anthropology*, 6th ed. (Minneapolis: West Publishing, 1994), p. 210.

Oligocene Anthropoids

During the Oligocene epoch (38–23 m.y.a.), anthropoids became the most numerous primates. Most of our knowledge of early anthropoids is based on fossils from Egypt's Fayum deposits. This area is a desert today, but 36–31 million years ago it was a tropical rain forest.

The anthropoids of the Fayum lived in trees and ate fruits and seeds. Compared with prosimians, they had fewer teeth, reduced snouts, larger brains, and increasingly forward-looking eyes. Of the Fayum anthropoid fossils, the *parapithecid* family is the more primitive and is perhaps ancestral to the New World monkeys. The parapithecids were very small (two to three pounds), with similarities to living marmosets and tamarins, small South American monkeys. One genus of this group, *Apidium*, is one of the most common fossils in the Fayum beds.

The *propliopithecid* family seems ancestral to the catarrhines—Old World monkeys, apes, and humans. This family includes *Aegyptopithecus*, which, at 13–18 pounds, was the size of a large domestic cat. The propliopithecids share with the

later catarrhines a distinctive dental formula: 2.1.2.3, meaning two incisors, one canine, two premolars, and three molars. (The formula is based on one-fourth of the mouth, either the right or left side of the upper or lower jaw.) The more primitive primate dental formula is 2.1.3.3. Most other primates, including prosimians and New World monkeys, have the second formula, with three premolars instead of two. Besides the Fayum, Oligocene deposits with primate bones have been found in North and West Africa, southern Arabia, China, Southeast Asia, and North and South America.

The Oligocene was a time of major geological and climatic change. North America and Europe separated and became distinct continents. The Great Rift Valley system of East Africa formed. India drifted into Asia. A cooling trend began, especially in the Northern Hemisphere, where primates disappeared.

Miocene Hominoids

The earliest hominoid fossils date to the Miocene epoch (23–5 m.y.a.), which is divided into three parts: lower, middle, and upper or late. The early Miocene (23–16 m.y.a.) was a warm and wet period, when forests covered East Africa. Recall from the last chapter that *Hominoidea* is the superfamily that includes fossil and living apes and humans. For simplicity's sake, the earliest hominoids are here called proto-apes, or simply apes. Although some of these may be ancestral to living apes, none is identical, or often even very similar, to modern apes.

Proconsul

The superfamily known as *Pliopithecoidea* includes several species of the genus *Proconsul*. The *Proconsul* group represents the most abundant and successful anthropoids of the early Miocene. This group lived in Africa and includes three species: *Proconsul* (*P.*) *africanus*, *P. nyanzae*, and *P. major*. Possibly descended from the Oligocene propliopithecids, these early Miocene proto-apes had teeth with similarities to those of living apes. But their skeleton below the neck was more monkeylike. Some *Proconsul* species were the size of a small monkey; others, the size of a chimpanzee, usually with marked sexual dimorphism. Their dentition suggests they ate fruits and leaves.

Smilodectes was a member of the lemurlike adapid family, which lived during the Eocene. Compare this drawing reconstructing a *Smilodectes* from Wyoming with a modern black lemur (*Eulemur macaco*) from Madagascar.

Their skulls were more delicate than those of modern apes, and their legs were longer than their arms—more like monkeys. *Proconsul* probably moved through the trees like a monkey—on four limbs—and lacked the capacity for suspension and brachiation displayed by modern apes. *Proconsul* probably contained the last common ancestor shared by the Old World monkeys and the apes. By the middle Miocene, *Proconsul* had been replaced by Old World monkeys and apes.

Fossils of Miocene monkeys and prosimians are rare; ape fossils are much more common. Like many living apes, those of the Miocene were forest dwellers and fruit eaters. They lived in areas that, as the forests retreated, monkeys would eventually colonize. By the late Miocene (10–5 m.y.a.) the age of the apes had ended, and monkeys had become the most common anthropoid in the Old World (except for humans, eventually).

Why did the Old World monkeys thrive as the Miocene apes faded? The probable answer was the monkeys' superior ability to eat leaves. Leaves are easier to get than fruits, which are typical ape foods. As the forests retreated at the end of the Miocene, most apes were restricted to the remaining tropical rain forests in areas of (mainly West) Africa and Southeast Asia. Monkeys survived over a wider area. They did so because they could process leaves effectively. Monkey molars developed *lophs*: ridges of enamel that run from side to side between the cusps of the teeth. Old World monkeys have two such lophs, so their molars are called *bilophodont*. Such lophs slice past each other like scissor blades, a good way to shear a leaf.

Some species of *Proconsul* may have been ancestral to the living African apes. *Proconsul* also may be ancestral to the Old World monkeys. *Proconsul* had all the primitive traits shared by apes and Old World monkeys and none of the derived traits of either. *Primitive* traits are those passed on unchanged from an ancestor, such as the five-cusped molars of the apes, which are inherited from an old anthropoid ancestor. *Derived* traits are those that develop in a particular taxon after they split from their common ancestor with another taxon. Examples are bilophodont molars among Old World monkeys. The Old World monkeys have derived bilophodont molars and primitive quadrupedal bodies. The apes have primitive molars and derived brachiating bodies. Proconsul had both primitive teeth and a primitive quadrupedal body.

AFROPITHECUS AND KENYAPITHECUS

During the early Miocene (23–16 m.y.a.), Africa was cut off by water from Europe and Asia. But during the middle Miocene, Arabia drifted into Eurasia, providing a land connection between Africa, Europe, and Asia. Migrating both ways—out of and into Africa—after 16 m.y.a. were various animals, including hominoids. Proto-apes were the most common primates of the middle Miocene (16–10 m.y.a.). Over 20 species have been discovered. (See Figure 6.5.) Their teeth retain the primitive anthropoid five-cusped molar pattern.

During the middle Miocene, the hominoids spread widely, in Europe, Asia, and Africa. East African apes of the middle Miocene include *Afropithecus*, *Equatorius*, and two species of *Kenyapithecus*, one earlier, one later. *Afropithecus* is a large Miocene hominoid from northern Kenya, dated to 18 to 16 m.y.a. (Leakey, Leakey, and Walker 1988). The *Afropithecus* remains consist of skull, jaw, and postcranial (below the head) fragments. *Afropithecus* seems to have been a slow-moving arboreal

Figure 6.5 The Geographic Distribution of Known Miocene Apes.

SOURCE: Robert Jurmain and Harry Nelson, *Introduction to Physical Anthropology*, 6th ed. (Minneapolis: West Publishing, 1994), p. 302.

ape, with large projecting front teeth (similar to those of the modern African apes).

A recent discovery is a 15-million-year-old partial skeleton assigned to a new genus, *Equatorius africanus*. The find, from Kenya, consists of upper incisors, a lower jaw with teeth, and bones from the arm, shoulder, collarbone, chest, wrists, fingers, and vertebrae, all belonging to a single male. In its skeleton *Equatorius* is more modern than earlier hominoids, suggesting that it used the ground more frequently than earlier hominoids did.

There are clear similarities between *Equatorius* and the earlier of the two species of *Kenyapithecus*. Based on these similarities, the discoverers of *Equatorius* have suggested that the earlier *Kenyapithecus* species should be reclassified as *Equatorius*. The two *Kenyapithecus* species that have been recognized traditionally are *K. africanus* (earlier) and *K. wickeri* (later). *Equatorius* and *K. africanus* represent an older pattern. *K. wickeri* illustrates a more modern pattern—more like today's great apes. *K. wickeri*'s dental pattern also is found in the teeth of an unnamed ape from a middle Miocene site in Turkey (Ward et al. 1999).

Equatorius and *Afropithecus* are probable *stem hominoids*: species somewhere on the evolutionary line near the origins of the modern ape group. Stem hominoids are considered too primitive to be the direct ancestors of living apes and humans.

SIVAPITHECUS

Middle and late Miocene apes are often grouped in two families: *Ramapithecidae* and *Dryopithecidae*. The ramapithecids lived during the middle and late Miocene in Europe, Asia, and Africa. There are at least two ramapithecid genera: *Sivapithecus* and *Gigantopithecus*.

Sivapithecus fossils were first found in the Siwalik Hills of Pakistan. They include specimens formerly called "*Ramapithecus*" from that region, along with fossil apes from Turkey, China, and Kenya. A late Miocene find with an almost complete face from Pakistan's Potwar Plateau shows many similarities to the face of the modern orangutan. Because of facial and dental similarities, *Sivapithecus* of the late Miocene is now seen as ancestral to the modern orangutan. The orangutan line appears to have separated from the one leading to the African apes and humans more than 13 million years ago.

Hominids undoubtedly originated from a Miocene ape, but it is unclear which one it might be. "*Ramapithecus*" fossils from Asia and Africa were once viewed as a possible hominid ancestor, based on dental similarities with early hominids: thick tooth enamel, broad molars, and robust jaws. But scientists no longer see a close link between "*Ramapithecus*" or *Sivapithecus* and hominids.

Compare this *Sivapithecus* side view with a contemporary female orangutan.

These dental and jaw characteristics are widely shared with several other middle and late Miocene hominoids, including *Gigantopithecus*.

GIGANTOPITHECUS

Gigantopithecus is almost certainly the largest primate that ever lived. Confined to Asia, it persisted for millions of years, from the Miocene until 400,000 years ago, when it coexisted with members of our own genus, *Homo erectus*. Some people think *Gigantopithecus* is not extinct yet, and that we know it today as the yeti and bigfoot (Sasquatch).

Gigantopithecus was discovered in an unlikely place. In China, druggists sell fossils known as "dragon's" teeth and bones, which are ground up to be used medicinally. In 1935 the anthropologist G. H. R. von Koenigswald recognized that a "dragon's tooth" being sold by a Hong Kong druggist was actually that of an extinct ape. Since then, three jaw bones and more than 1,000 teeth have been recovered, some in drugstores, some at geological sites in China and Vietnam (Pettifor 1995). Some such sites have *Gigantopithecus* remains associated with those of *Homo erectus* (Ciochon et al. 1990), who may have hunted the ape into extinction.

With a fossil record consisting of nothing more than jaw bones and teeth, it is difficult to say for sure just how big *Gigantopithecus* was. Based on ratios of jaw and tooth size to body size in other apes, various reconstructions have been made. One has *Gigantopithecus* weighing 1,200 pounds and standing 10 feet tall (Ciochon et al. 1990). Another puts the height at 9 feet and cuts the weight in half (Simons and Ettel 1970). All agree, however, that *Gigantopithecus* was the largest ape that ever lived. There have been at least two species of *Gigantopithecus*: *G. blacki*, the one that coexisted with *H. erectus* in China and Vietnam, and the much earlier (5 m.y.a.) *G. giganteus*, from northern India.

Given its size, *Gigantopithecus* must have been a ground-dwelling ape rather than an arboreal brachiator. Based on its jaw and dental patterns, it probably ate grasses, fruits, seeds, and especially bamboo. Very large animals, including China's giant panda, need an abundant food source such as bamboo. *Gigantopithecus* molars were adapted to a diet demanding cutting, crushing, and grinding of tough, fibrous matter. The molars are mas-

A reconstruction of *Gigantopithecus* by Russell Ciochon and Bill Munns. Munns is shown here with "Giganto." What would be the likely environmental effects of a population of such large apes?

sive and flat, with low crowns and thick enamel. The premolars are also broad and flat, resembling molars.

See your OLC Internet Exercises

mhhe .com /kottak

Could it be that *Gigantopithecus* did not go extinct, but survives today as the yeti ("abominable snowman" of the Himalayas) or Sasquatch (reportedly sighted in the Pacific Northwest)? Probably not. These creatures are based on legend, not fact. Survival of a species requires a sufficiently large breeding population. Given its dietary demands, *Gigantopithecus* would surely be detectable and have an observable environmental effect. Never have *Gigantopithecus* fossils or teeth been discovered in the Western Hemisphere. Nor are the areas of yeti and Sasquatch sightings ones in which *Gigantopithecus* would fit adaptively.

DRYOPITHECUS

The dryopithecids lived in Europe during the middle and late Miocene. This group probably includes the common ancestor of the lesser apes (gibbons and siamangs) and the great apes. The first fossil member of the *Dryopithecus* group (*Dryopithecus fontani*) was found in France in 1856. The five-cusp and fissure pattern of its molar teeth, known as the Y-5 arrangement, is typical of the dryopithecids and of hominoids in general. Other dryopithecids have been found in Hungary, Spain, and China.

The continental drift that created the land bridge between Africa and Eurasia as the middle Miocene began also triggered mountain building and climatic change. With a cooler, drier climate, forest patches, dry woodlands, and grasslands replaced extensive tropical forests in East Africa and South Asia. The cooling trend continued through the late Miocene (10–5 m.y.a.). As grasslands spread, the stage was set for the divergence of the lines leading to humans, gorillas, and chimps.

OREOPITHECUS

Is upright bipedalism unique to hominids? A recent reanalysis of the fossil remains of an ancient Italian ape suggests otherwise. *Oreopithecus bambolii*, which lived seven to nine million years ago, apparently spent much of its time standing upright and shuffling short distances to collect fruit and other foods. This mode of locomotion contrasts with those of other fossil and living apes, which climb, brachiate, or knuckle-walk. The first *Oreopithecus* fossils were found more than 100 years ago in central Italy. The taxonomic placement and evolutionary significance of *Oreopithecus* have been debated for decades. Similarities have been noted between this Italian ape and both the ramapithecid and the dryopithecid families.

Meike Kohler and Salvador Moya-Sola (1997) recently reanalyzed *Oreopithecus* remains in the Natural History Museum in Basel, Switzerland. These skeletal pieces represented the lower back, pelvis, leg, and foot. The scientists found the creature's lower body to be intermediate between those of apes and early hominids. Like early hominids, *Oreopithecus* had a lower back that

arched forward, a vertically aligned knee joint, and a similar pelvis. All these features are significant for upright walking. However, *Oreopithecus* had a unique foot. Its big toe splayed out 90 degrees from the other toes, all of which were shorter and straighter than those of modern apes. The foot's birdlike, tripod design was probably associated with a short, shuffling stride. Considering the entire postcranium (the area behind or below the head—the skeleton), there are substantial similarities between *Oreopithecus*, *Dryopithecus*, and the living great apes and hominids.

Interpret the World
Atlas Map 6
Look at Map 6, "Evolution of Primates" in your atlas. This map shows the world picture of primate evolution, indicating major sites with taxa and dates. Note that primates at some time have inhabited all the continents except Australia. When did the first primates appear in Asia? Map 6 shows that the geographic distribution of primates has changed through time, with North America prominent during the Eocene, Europe during the Eocene and Miocene, and Africa from the Oligocene through the present. Which of the continents that has wild primates today has the poorest fossil record. Why do you think that is?

A Missing Link?

The idea of "the missing link" goes back to an old notion called the "Great Chain of Being." This was the theological belief that various entities could be placed in a progressive chain. Among life forms, humans were at the top of the chain. Above them stood only angels and divinity. Below them were the apes, most clearly the African apes. But humans seemed too exalted, too different from those apes, to be directly linked to them. Between humans and the apes, there needed to be some form more progressive than the apes—some sort of missing link in the Great Chain of Being. Although modern science does not endorse the Great Chain of Being, it does recognize that our ancestor was a life form that differed from contemporary gorillas and chimps. Humans are not descended from gorillas or chimps. Rather, humans and the African apes share a common

The Great Chain of Being—a powerful visual metaphor for a divinely inspired universal hierarchy ranking all forms of higher and lower life. From Didacus Valades, *Rhetorica Christiana* (1579). What can you tell about the levels in the hierarchy?

orangutan and the gibbon) or with any monkey. All the apes are more closely related to each other—and more physically alike—than they are to monkeys. So why is it human parents at zoos go on saying to their kids "look at the monkey" when they are seeing a chimp, gorilla, or orang? It must be the old idea of our exalted status. We easily detect the monkey in the ape but not the ape in ourselves. Still, the apes fascinate us, to some degree because of their human-like qualities. Gorillas are popular at zoos from San Diego to Atlanta, especially when they are displayed in "family" groups. The antics of orangutans and especially of chimps have been featured in movies and TV shows. The stories of Washoe the chimp and Koko the gorilla, apes that have been taught sign language, have been featured in magazines and on TV. Even the national tabloids on display in the grocery store often turn to apes for their animal stories. Invariably such stories continue the confusion with comments about "monkeying around" or "monkey see, monkey do." Apes aren't monkeys. Apes are a lot closer to humans than they are to monkeys. Imagine a live-action film called *Planet of the Monkeys*. Where could they find actors who could locomote on four legs for an entire movie?

Human ancestors almost certainly diverged from those of chimps and gorillas late in the Miocene epoch, between eight and five million years ago. The evolutionary line leading to orangutans probably split from the one leading to humans, chimps, and gorillas around 13 m.y.a. Around eight million years ago, the common ancestors of humans, chimps, and gorillas started diverging (Fisher 1988*a*). They split up by occupying different environmental niches. Separated in space, they became reproductively isolated from one another—leading to speciation. Ancestral gorillas split off first. They eventually occupied forested zones of the mountains and lowlands of equatorial Africa. They developed a diet based on leaves, shoots, bulk vegetation, and fruits. Humans and chimps share a more recent common ancestor with each other than either does with the gorilla. Chimps evolved into frugivores (fruit eaters) in Africa's forests and woodlands. Ancestral hominids spent more time in Africa's open grasslands, or savannas. Ancestral chimps and humans, like their contemporary

ancestor—a creature that was like chimps and gorillas in some ways, like humans in others. Over time all three species have evolved and have diverged from one another. Is there reason to believe that a chimp ancestor living millions of years ago would look more like a hominid than a contemporary chimp does?

Understanding Ourselves The idea of a huge gap between humans and the apes persists—despite evidence that humans and chimps share about 98.7 percent of their DNA. There's no doubt that humans, chimps, and gorillas share a more recent common ancestor with each other than they do with other apes (e.g., the descendants, may well have added meat to their diet by hunting.

As we have seen, Miocene deposits in Africa, Asia, and Europe have yielded an abundance of hominoid fossils (see Figure 6.5). Some of these may have evolved into modern apes and humans, but others became extinct. Formerly, as was mentioned, certain Asian fossils such as *Sivapithecus* and "*Ramapithecus*" were analyzed as possible common ancestors of humans and the apes. Most scientists have now excluded these Miocene hominoids from the family tree of humans, chimps, and gorillas, considering *Sivapithecus* a probable ancestor of orangs. Discovered in Greece in 1989, the middle to late Miocene ape *Ouranopithecus* lived in Europe some 9–10 m.y.a. This find may be linked to the living African apes and even to hominids (Begun, Ward, and Rose 1997). One distinctive trait that *Ouranopithecus* shares with the modern African apes and humans is the *frontal sinus* (a cavity in the forehead, one of the areas where we get sinus infections and headaches).

On the basis of Miocene finds reported and analyzed during the last decade, some scientists have pondered a new scenario for ape and human evolution. As mentioned, during the middle Miocene, a land bridge connected Africa and Eurasia. This connection enabled hominoids to spread from Africa into Asia and Europe, where they diversified into the groups discussed previously. At the same time, the apes' forest habitat was shrinking in East Africa, and the number of ape species there shrank along with it. In the middle and late Miocene, there appears to have been much more ape diversity in Europe and Asia than there was in Africa. During the late Miocene, Old World monkeys took over from the dwindling African apes in many areas they once inhabited. The new hominoid evolutionary scenario, proposed but hardly established, is that the line leading to the African apes and hominids may have emerged in Europe, with a hominoid such as *Ouranopithecus*. Then there would have been a return migration to Africa, where diversification of ancestral gorillas, chimps, and hominids started around 8 m.y.a. Continued work by fossil hunters, analysts, and taxonomists eventually may reconcile the main issues involving the Miocene apes in relation to their living successors.

Back to Africa for an important recent discovery. In July 2001 anthropologists working in Central Africa—in northern Chad's Djurab desert (Figure 6.6)—unearthed the 6–7-million-year-old skull of the oldest probable or possible human ancestor yet found. This discovery consists of a nearly complete skull, two lower jaw fragments, and three teeth. It dates to the time period when humans and chimps would have been diverging from a common ancestor. "It takes us into another world, of creatures that include the common ancestor, the ancestral human and the ancestral chimp," George Washington University paleobiologist Bernard Wood said (quoted in Gugliotta 2002).

The discovery was made by a 40-member multinational team led by the French paleoanthropologist Michel Brunet. The actual discoverer

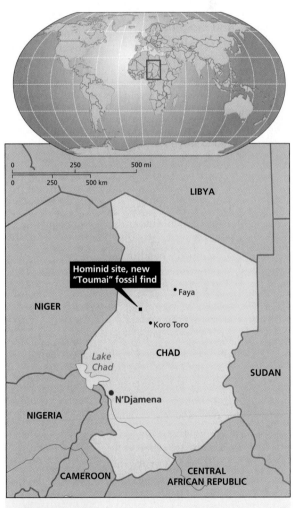

Figure 6.6 Location of Toumai: Discovery.

Beyond the *Classroom*
Maceration of a Canadian Lynx

Background Information

STUDENT:	Barbara Hewitt
SUPERVISING PROFESSOR:	Ariane Burke
SCHOOL:	University of Manitoba
YEAR IN SCHOOL/MAJOR:	Graduated in spring 2000/Anthropology
FUTURE PLANS:	Graduate school in forensic archaeology and osteology in England
PROJECT TITLE:	Maceration of a Canadian Lynx

What is maceration? How might it be useful to archaeologists and biological anthropologists? Would the ethical issues involved be different with primates versus the lynx described here?

In January 2000 I took a Practicum in Archaeology class. We were each to conduct our own research project. I chose to complete a maceration project for our faunal laboratory. The carcass I chose to work with was that of an infirm Canadian lynx, which had been euthanized and donated by the zoo. My objective was to examine the condition of its bones, to determine how its former health would be reflected in its skeleton.

By macerating an animal of known age, with a documented medical history and stable diet, we could compare this animal with one reared in the wild and look at differences in health. To macerate an animal, you remove the pelt and musculature from the bones, then soak the skeleton in chemicals to remove the grease. Once the bones are dry, they are dipped in preservative to keep them from decaying. I examined the bones and teeth for indications of ill health. In this particular lynx,

advanced age had resulted in the ossification of many joints. This would have made extended movement quite painful. I was surprised by the damage to her joints. The excessive development of bone around the joints was like that in humans with osteoarthritis, which gave me a good idea of how painful and debilitating that disease can be. I detected a completely healed break in the right front humerus (upper arm bone), indicating that the animal had been healthy and well nourished when the break happened for the break to have healed so well. Only four teeth remained; this lynx could not eat solid food when she died.

The most challenging aspect of this project was that I worked unassisted. With only an instruction manual to follow, and an occasional consultation with my supervisor, I learned how to most effectively skin and deflesh an animal. The processing and analysis of the skeleton took far longer than I expected. A mistake during processing gave me a deeper appreciation for the people who analyze faunal remains in an archaeological context. The bones had been processed, and were laid out for drying, when another student moved them without moving the

labels as well. After that, each bone had to be indentified again and laid out for relabeling.

The best part of this project was what it taught me about the development of bones and the talent of people who identify and work with them. In trying to reidentify the elements of the lynx skeleton, I realized exactly how tough it would be to pick up a bone (or fragment of a bone) from an archaeological site and determine which bone it is, what species it comes from, and the pathology of that particular animal or person. I think I learned more about the inherent difficulties of faunal identification in an archaeological context from that error than from any other aspect of the project.

The bones of the lynx that I macerated and processed have already proved useful to several faunal analysis classes, and to our zooarchaeologists when asked to identify bones brought to the department for identification.

French paleoanthropologist Michel Brunet holds *Sahelanthropus tchadensis*, nicknamed "Toumai" (on the left) and a modern chimpanzee skull (on the right). If Toumai isn't a human ancestor, what else might it be?

was the university undergraduate Ahounta Djimdoumalbaye, who spied the skull embedded in sandstone. The new fossil was dugged *Sahelanthropus tchadensis*, referring to the northern Sahel region of Chad where it was found. The fossil is also known as "Toumai," a local name meaning "hope of life."

The discovery team identified the skull as that of an adult male with a chimp-sized brain (320–380 cubic centimeters), heavy brow ridges, and a relatively flat, human-like face. Toumai's habitat included savanna, forests, rivers, and lakes—and abundant animal life: elephants, antelope, horses, giraffes, hyenas, hippopotamuses, wild boars,

crocodiles, fish, and rodents. The animal species enabled the team to date the site where Toumai was found (by comparison with radiometrically dated sites with similar fauna).

Was Toumai the "missing link," a common ancestor, a gorilla ancestor (as Wolpoff, Senut, Pickford, and Hawks [2002] suggest), or the earliest hominid known to science? The discovery of Toumai moves scientists close to the time when humans and the African apes diverged from a common ancestor. As we would expect in a fossil so close to the common ancestor, Toumai blends apelike and human characteristics. Although the brain was chimp-sized, the tooth enamel was thicker than a chimp's enamel, suggesting a diet that included not just fruits, but also tougher vegetation of a sort typically found in the savanna. Also, Toumai's snout did not protrude as far as a chimp's—making it more humanlike, and the canine tooth was shorter than those of other apes. "The fossil is showing the first glimmerings of evolution in our direction," according to University of California at Berkeley anthropologist Tim White (quoted in Gugliotta 2002).

The Toumai find is also important because it suggests that human ancestry was not confined to eastern and southern Africa, as had been thought. "To study human origins, you need places where the animals lived," White said. "First you had the South African caves and the East African Rift Valley, and now Brunet has found the Chad Basin and opened up a new area with huge potential" (quoted in Gugliotta 2002). What of the hominids after Toumai? We'll see in the next chapter.

Summary

1. Primates have lived during the past 65 million years, the Cenozoic era, with seven epochs: Paleocene, Eocene, Oligocene, Miocene, Pliocene, Pleistocene, and Recent. The arboreal theory states that primates evolved by adapting to life high up in the trees. The visual predation theory suggests that key primate traits developed because they facilitated the capture of insects.

2. The first fossils clearly identified as primates lived during the Eocene (54–38 m.y.a.), mainly in North America and Europe. The omomyid family may be ancestral to the anthropoids and the tarsier. The adapid family was probably ancestral to the lemur–loris line.

3. During the Oligocene (38–23 m.y.a.), anthropoids became the most numerous primates. The parapithecid family may be ancestral to the New World monkeys. The propliopithecid family, including *Aegyptopithecus,* seems ancestral to the catarrhines—Old World monkeys, apes, and humans.

4. The earliest hominoid fossils are from the Miocene (23–5 m.y.a.). Africa's *Proconsul* group contained the last common ancestor shared by the Old World monkeys and the apes. Since the middle Miocene Africa, Europe, and Asia have been connected. Proto-apes spread beyond Africa and became the most common primates of the middle Miocene (16–10 m.y.a.). East African apes of the middle Miocene include *Afropithecus, Equatorius,* and *Kenyapithecus.* Middle and late Miocene apes are often grouped in two families: *Ramapithecidae* and *Dryopithecidae.* The ramapithecids included at least two genera: *Sivapithecus* and *Gigantopithecus. Sivapithecus* was ancestral to the modern orangutan. Asia's *Gigantopithecus,* the largest primate ever to live, persisted for millions of years, finally coexisting with *Homo erectus.*

5. The dryopithecids, found mainly in Europe, probably include the common ancestor of the lesser apes (gibbons and siamangs) and the great apes. *Oreopithecus bambolii,* which lived 7–9 m.y.a., was an ape that stood upright while collecting fruit and other foods. There are skeletal similarities between *Oreopithecus, Dryopithecus,* and the living great apes and hominids.

6. *Ouranopithecus,* which lived in Europe some 9–10 m.y.a., may be linked to chimps, gorillas, and humans. Anthropologists have yet to identify the fossils of the common ancestors of humans, gorillas, and chimps. However, biochemical evidence strongly suggests that the diversification into ancestral gorillas, chimps, and hominids began in Africa during the late Miocene. A skull found in 2001 in northern Chad, dated at 6–7 m.y.a., officially named *Sahelanthropus tchadensis,* more commonly called "Toumai," may or may not be the earliest hominid yet known.

KEY TERMS

adapids Early (Eocene) primate family ancestral to lemurs and lorises.

arboreal theory Theory that the primates evolved by adapting to life high up in the trees, where visual abilities would have been favored over the sense of smell, and grasping hands and feet would have been used for movement along branches.

dryopithecids Zoological ape family living in Europe during the middle and late Miocene; probably includes the common ancestor of the lesser apes (gibbons and siamangs) and the great apes.

m.y.a. Million years ago.

omomyids Early (Eocene) primate family found in North America, Europe, and Asia; early omomyids may be ancestral to all anthropoids; later ones may be ancestral to tarsiers.

postcranium The area behind or below the head; the skeleton.

Proconsul Early Miocene genus of the pliopithecoid superfamily; the most abundant and successful anthropoids of the early Miocene; the last common ancestor shared by the Old World monkeys and the apes.

Sivapithecus Widespread fossil group first found in Pakistan; includes specimens formerly called *"Ramapithecus"* and fossil apes from Turkey, China, and Kenya; early *Sivapithecus* may contain the common ancestor of the orangutan and the African apes; late *Sivapithecus* is now seen as ancestral to the modern orang.

visual predation theory Theory that the primates evolved in lower branches and undergrowth by developing visual and tactile abilities to aid in hunting and snaring insects.

CRITICAL THINKING QUESTIONS

For more self testing, see the self quizzes

mhhe
●com
/kottak

1. What are the pluses and minuses of relying on the fossil record to reconstruct evolution? Besides fossils, what are other lines of evidence for primate and human evolution?

2. What are some unanswered questions about early primate evolution? What kinds of information would help provide answers?

3. Watch a squirrel move about. How do its movements compare with a monkey's movements? With a cat's movements? With your own? What do these observations suggest to you about that animal's ancestral habitat?

4. What is your opinion about the merits of the arboreal theory versus the visual predation theory of primate origins?

5. There have been reported sightings of "bigfoot" in the Pacific Northwest of North America and of the yeti (abominable snowman) in the Himalayas. What facts about apes lead you to question such reports?

6. Who were the common ancestors of humans, chimps, and gorillas? When and where did they probably live, and what is the fossil evidence for their existence?

7. What's the likelihood that Toumai, the 6–7-million-year-old skull found in 2001 in northern Chad, is a hominid? What else could it be? You might want to check the Internet for the latest on "Toumai."

Atlas Questions

Look at Map 6, "Evolution of Primates."

1. What continent(s) had the earliest primates? What kinds of primates were those?

2. On what continent has the evolution of primates been most continuous? Does this have implications for human evolution?

3. Which continent with several of the earliest primates has the fewest nonhuman primates today?

SUGGESTED ADDITIONAL READINGS

Begun, D. R., C. V. Ward, and M. D. Rose
1997   *Description: Function, Phylogeny, and Fossils: Miocene Hominoid Evolution and Adaptations.* New York: Plenum. A collection of very up-to-date scientific articles on the Miocene apes.

Boaz, N. T.
1999   *Essentials of Biological Anthropology.* Upper Saddle River, NJ: Prentice-Hall. Basic text in physical anthropology, with information on primate evolution and paleoanthropology.

Ciochon, R. L., J. Olsen, and J. James
1990   *Other Origins: The Search for the Giant Ape in Human Prehistory.* New York: Bantam Books. In search of *Gigantopithecus.*

Eldredge, N.
1997   *Fossils: The Evolution and Extinction of Species.* Princeton, NJ: Princeton University Press. What fossils tell us about the natural history of species.

Fleagle, J. G.
1999   *Primate Adaptation and Evolution*, 2nd ed. San Diego: Academic Press. Excellent introduction to adaptation of past and present primate species.

Hrdy, S. B.
1999   *The Woman That Never Evolved*, rev. ed. Cambridge, MA: Harvard University Press. Revised edition of a well-known contribution to primate and human evolution.

Kemp, T. S.

1999   *Fossils and Evolution.* New York: Oxford University Press. Interpreting the fossil record.

Kimbel, W. H., and L. B. Martin, eds.

1993   *Species, Species Concepts, and Primate Evolution.* New York: Plenum. The evolution of primate species.

MacPhee, R. D. E., ed.

1993   *Primates and Their Relatives in Phylogenetic Perspective.* New York: Plenum. Discussion of the primate family tree and its evolution.

Napier, J. R., and P. H. Napier

1985   *The Natural History of the Primates.* Cambridge, MA: MIT Press. The adaptations of primates, past and present.

Park, M. A.

2002   *Biological Anthropology,* 3rd ed. Boston: McGraw-Hill. A concise introduction, with a focus on scientific inquiry.

Wade, N., ed.

2001   *The New York Times Book of Fossils and Evolution,* rev. ed. New York: Lyons Press. Articles on fossils and evolution from the *New York Times.*

INTERNET EXERCISES

1. View Christopher R. Scotese's animation of continental drift **(http://www.scotese.com/pangeanim.htm).**

    a. When did primates first appear?

    b. At that time, which continents were connected? Which continents were isolated?

    c. The article that starts this chapter says that most of the discoveries of the earliest primates were in North America and Europe. Based on the map, does it make sense that similar specimens are being found in both places? Where else can we expect to find fossil evidence of early primates? Which continents are unlikely to have the earliest primates?

2. Bigfoot: Read Lorraine Ahearn's article "Bigfoot Theory: Reality Is What You Make of It," which is a report about a 1999 bigfoot conference **(http://www.n2.net/prey/bigfoot/articles/greens.htm).**

    a. This chapter states that some people (but few scientists) believe bigfoot is a living descendant of *Gigantopithecus blackei.* What are the arguments for and against this claim?

    b. What are some other bigfoot theories presented in this article? How could you go about testing them?

    c. What is your opinion about bigfoot? How would you go about testing it?

See Chapter 6 at your McGraw-Hill Online Learning Center for additional review and interactive exercises.

7

EARLY
HOMINIDS

Overview

Who were the first hominids? Where did they live? What were they like? Did they have big brains? Did they make tools? Did they walk upright? Did they still seek refuge in the trees? How have hominids changed over several million years?

Hominids appeared during the late Miocene, a million or more years before the start of the Pliocene epoch, which began some five million years ago. Most hominid fossils have been dated to the Pliocene, and to the Pleistocene epoch, which began two million years ago. Early hominid remains come mainly from eastern and southern Africa. The first hominids, discovered in Ethiopia, have been assigned to the genus and species *Ardipithecus ramidus*. The australopithecines, members of the hominid genus *Australopithecus*, had evolved by four million years ago. *Ardipithecus* and the early australopithecines shared many features with the apes. The australopithecines had small apelike skulls, slashing front teeth, and marked sexual

dimorphism. Yet they walked on two legs. Upright bipedalism is a fundamental human characteristic that goes back more than five million years.

Remains of two groups, *A. africanus* and *A. robustus*, have been found in South Africa. Both had a powerful chewing apparatus, with large back teeth and robust faces, skulls, and muscle markings. The basis of their diet was savanna vegetation, but these early hominids also hunted small animals and scavenged the kills of predators.

By two million years ago, there were two distinct hominid groups: early *Homo* and *A. boisei*, the "hyperrobust" australopithecines, which became extinct a million years ago. Stone tools dating back 2.5 million years have been found in eastern Africa. Did early *Homo* make them? Or, more likely, did the australopithecines also make and use tools? This chapter examines early human evolution through the advent of *Homo* and the extinction of the australopithecines.

Fossils May Be Earliest Human Link

NEW YORK TIMES NEWS BRIEF

by John Noble Wilford

July 12, 2001

The fossil record grows constantly. Discoveries of possible or probable hominid fossils, such as the Toumai remains discussed in Chapter 6, regularly make the news. The year 2001 was especially good for fossil hunters. "Toumai," also known as *Sahelanthropus tchadensis*, was found that year in northern Chad. Also, fossils that are accepted more generally as hominids, assigned to the genus and species *Ardipithecus ramidus*, were found that year in Ethiopia. A key aspect of the *Ardipithecus* discovery (echoed by the find in northern Chad) is that the earliest hominids didn't live in open grassland (savanna) country, but in wooded areas. As you read this chapter, think about what life in a forested habitat would have been like for early hominids. For what purposes do you imagine they would have used the trees, and the ground? Do you think *Ardipithecus* was more like a modern chimp or more like a modern human? Why?

> An Ethiopian fossil hunter has found the bones and teeth of forest-dwelling creatures who lived as much as 5.8 million years ago, a discovery that appears to . . . extend knowledge of the [human] family tree back close to its roots.
>
> The fossils are the remains of creatures who apparently walked upright. They are more than one million years older than any other fossils definitively established as those of hominids, the group of species that includes humans, their direct ancestors and close relatives.
>
> The new find . . . is especially intriguing . . . because the bones appear to be so . . . apelike and their ages, 5.2 million to 5.8 million years old, put them close to the fateful evolutionary split between the lineage leading to modern humans and the one that produced chimpanzees. . . .
>
> Of particular importance . . . is . . . that these early hominids lived in a relatively wet and cool forest because the prevailing theory had been that hominids evolved in grasslands after forests disappeared. The forest was a hostile environment of shifting terrain, exploding volcanoes and menacing lava flows. . . . The scientist—Yohannes Haile-Selassie . . . —said the state of development of the

fossil teeth included strong clues that the individuals were indeed hominids. And a toe bone, he said, provided evidence that the creature was "a biped when on the ground."

> But the presence of primitive dental and bone characteristics, Mr. Haile-Selassie said, indicated that the species "was phylogenetically close to the common ancestor of chimpanzees and humans." Dr. C. Owen Lovejoy, a paleontologist at Kent State University in Ohio who has examined the fossils, said that he was "in full overall agreement" with the interpretations of Mr. Haile-Selassie and other members of the research project.
>
> Speaking of the relationship between the ancestors of humans and chimpanzees, called pongids, Dr. Lovejoy said: "We are indeed coming very close to that point in the fossil record where we simply will not be able to distinguish ancestral hominids from ancestral pongids because they were so anatomically similar. . . ."
>
> Working with Dr. Tim D. White of Berkeley, one of the most experienced hominid hunters, Mr. Haile-

Yohannes Haile-Selassie of the University of California at Berkeley holds the canine tooth of *Ardipithecus ramidus kadabba*, discovered in 1998.

Selassie and colleagues found the fossils in the Middle Awash River Valley badlands of Ethiopia, about 50 miles from where the "Lucy" skeleton, which is 3.2 million years old, was uncovered 30 years ago. The new find includes 11 specimens, including a jawbone with teeth, hand and foot bones, fragments of arm bones and a piece of collarbone. They represent at least five individuals.

Dr. White said an accurate portrayal of these creatures was not yet possible because an intact skull or limb bones had not been found. The size of the lower jaw and some bones of the skeleton suggests that one of these individuals was about the size of a modern chimpanzee. Until more diagnostic specimens are found, preferably including a skull, the fossils have been tentatively classified as a primitive subspecies, *Ardipithecus ramidus kadabba*. *Kadabba* means "basal family ancestor" in the local language, Afar. The *ramidus* species was discovered in 1994 in 4.4-million-year-old sediments, also in Ethiopia.

The evidence that these creatures lived in forests, as opposed to grasslands, is especially intriguing to scientists. In a separate report on the environmental history of the discovery site, Dr. Giday Wolde Gabriel, a geologist at Los Alamos National Laboratory in New Mexico, and his colleagues concluded that it "seems increasingly likely that early hominids did not frequent open habitats" until after 4.4 million years ago. The *Ardipithecus* hominids at that time also appeared to live in woodlands.

Dr. Stanley H. Ambrose, an anthropologist at the University of Illinois at Urbana, analyzed the chemistry of ancient soil mixed with the fossils. "The expectation was that we would find hominids in savanna grassland sites that date back to about eight million years ago, but that hasn't happened," Dr. Ambrose said. "All older hominids have been found in forested environments."

In that case, the development of upright walking, considered a definitive characteristic of hominids, presumably occurred in a wooded habitat and not as an adaptation to life on the treeless savanna, as had been supposed. . . .

Source: *New York Times*, July 12, 2001, late edition—final, section A, p. 12, column 1, and www.nytimes.com.

Although these *Ardipithecus* discoveries push the hominid lineage back to almost six million years, humans actually haven't been around too long when the age of the earth is considered.

Chronology of Hominid Evolution

If we compare earth's history to a 24-hour day (with one second equaling 50,000 years),

Earth originates at midnight.

The earliest fossils were deposited at 5:45 A.M.

The first vertebrates appeared at 9:02 P.M.

The earliest mammals, at 10:45 P.M.

The earliest primates, at 11:43 P.M.

The earliest hominids (the australopithecines), at 11:58 P.M.

And *Homo sapiens* arrives 36 seconds before midnight (Wolpoff, 1999, p. 10).

For the study of hominid evolution, the Pliocene (5 to 2 m.y.a.), Pleistocene (2 m.y.a. to 10,000 B.P.), and Recent (10,000 B.P. to the present) epochs are most important. Until the end of the Pliocene, the main hominid genus was *Australopithecus*, which lived in sub-Saharan Africa. By the start of the Pleistocene, *Australopithecus* had evolved into *Homo*.

The **Pleistocene** is traditionally and correctly considered the epoch of human life. Its subdivisions are the Lower Pleistocene (2 to 1 m.y.a.), the Middle Pleistocene (1 m.y.a. to 130,000 B.P.), and the Upper Pleistocene (130,000 to 10,000 B.P.). These subdivisions refer to the placement of geological strata containing, respectively, older, intermediate, and younger fossils. The Lower Pleistocene extends from the start of the Pleistocene to the advent of the ice ages in the Northern Hemisphere around one million years ago.

Each subdivision of the Pleistocene is associated with a particular group of hominids. Late *Australopithecus* and early *Homo* lived during the Lower Pleistocene. *Homo erectus* spanned most of the Middle Pleistocene. *Homo sapiens* appeared late in the Middle Pleistocene and was the sole hominid of the Upper Pleistocene. We consider the hominids of the Middle and Upper Pleistocene in the next chapter.

During the second million years of the Pleistocene, there were several ice ages, or **glacials,** major advances of continental ice sheets in Europe and North America. These periods were separated by **interglacials,** long warm periods between the major glacials. (Scientists used to think there were four main glacial advances, but the picture has grown more complex.) With each advance, the world climate cooled and continental ice sheets—massive glaciers—covered the northern parts of Europe and North America. Climates that are temperate today were arctic during the glacials.

During the interglacials, the climate warmed up and the *tundra*—the cold, treeless plain—retreated north with the ice sheets. Forests returned to areas, such as southwestern France, that had had tundra vegetation. The ice sheets advanced and receded several times during the last glacial, the *Würm* (75,000 to 12,000 B.P.). Brief periods of relative warmth during the Würm (and other glacials) are called *interstadials*, in contrast to the longer interglacials. Hominid fossils found in association with animals known to occur in cold or warm climates, respectively, permit us to date them to glacial or interglacial (or interstadial) periods.

The Earliest Hominids

Recent discoveries of fossils and tools have increased our knowledge of early human evolution. The most significant recent discoveries have been made in Africa—Kenya, Tanzania, Ethiopia, and Chad. These finds come from different sites and may be the remains of individuals who lived hundreds of thousands of years apart. Furthermore, geological processes operating over thousands or millions of years inevitably distort fossil remains. Table 7.1 summarizes the major stages of hominid evolution. You should consult it throughout this chapter and the next one.

Climates that are temperate today were arctic during the glacials. The ice-age tundra in Western Europe may have looked like the cold, treeless plain shown here, where Russian Eskimos count on a reindeer herd for their subsistence. Would you expect to find many vegetarians in such an environment?

Table 7.1 Dates and Geographic Distribution of the Major Hominoid and Hominid Fossil Groups

Fossil Group	Dates, m.y.a.	Known Distribution
Hominoids		
Afropithecus	18–16	East Africa
Common ancestor	8–5	East Africa
"Toumai"	7–6	Chad
Hominids		
Ardipithecus ramidus	5.8–4.4	Ethiopia
Australopithecines		
A. anamensis	4.2	Kenya
A. afarensis	3.8–3.0	East Africa (Laetoli, Hadar)
Robusts	2.6–1.2	East and South Africa
A. robustus	2.6?–2.0?	South Africa
A. boisei	2.6?–1.2	East Africa
Graciles		
A. africanus	3.0–2.5?	South Africa
Homo		
H. habilis/H. rudolfensis	2.4?–1.7?	East Africa
H. erectus	1.7?–0.3	Africa, Asia, Europe
Homo sapiens	0.3–present	
Archaic H. sapiens	0.3–0.03 (300,000–30,000)	Africa, Asia, Europe
H. sapiens neanderthalensis	0.13–0.03 (130,000–30,000)	Europe, Middle East
H. sapiens sapiens	0.1?–present (100,000–present)	Worldwide (after 25,000 B.P.)

ARDIPITHECUS AND KENYANTHROPUS

As we saw in the news story at the beginning of this chapter, early hominids assigned to *Ardipithecus ramidus* lived during the late Miocene, between 5.2 and 5.8 million years ago. Our Miocene ancestors eventually evolved into a varied group of Pliocene–Pleistocene hominids known as the australopithecines—for whom we have an abundant fossil record. This term reflects their former classification as members of a distinct subfamily, the "Australopithecinae." Today the distinction between the **australopithecines** and later hominids is made on the genus level. The australopithecines are assigned to the genus *Australopithecus* (A.); later humans, to *Homo* (H.).

Ardipithecus ramidus is generally considered ancestral to early *Australopithecus* and, ultimately, to *Homo*. *Ardipithecus* fossils were first discovered at Kanapoi in Ethiopia by Berhane Asfaw, Gen Suwa, and Tim White. Dating to 4.4 m.y.a., these fossils consisted of the remains of some 17 individuals, with cranial, facial, dental, and upper limb bones. The 2001 news account at the beginning of this chapter discusses even older *Ardipithecus* fossils, dating back as long as 5.8 m.y.a., very near the time of the common ancestor of humans and the African apes. This find consists of 11 specimens, including a jaw bone with teeth, hand and foot bones, fragments of arm bones, and a piece of collarbone. They represent at least five individuals. These creatures were apelike in size, anatomy, and habitat, living in a wooded area rather than the open grassland or savanna habitat where later hominids proliferated. As of this writing, *Ardipithecus ramidus* is recognized as the earliest known hominid, with the Toumai find from Chad, dated to 6–7 m.y.a., possibly an even older hominid.

Presumably, *Ardipithecus ramidus* evolved into *A. anamensis*, a bipedal hominid from Aramis in Kenya, whose fossil remains were first reported by

Maeve Leakey and Alan Walker in 1995. *A. anamensis* consists of 78 fragments from two sites—pieces of skull, jaw bone, teeth, and long bones (Rice 2002). *A. anamensis* then evolved into *A. afarensis*, which usually is considered ancestral to all the later australopithecines (*africanus*, *robustus*, and *boisei*) as well as to *Homo* (Figure 7.1).

Complicating the picture is another recent discovery, which Maeve Leakey has named *Kenyanthropus playtops*, or flat-faced "man" of Kenya. (Actually, the sex hasn't been determined.) This 1999 fossil find—of a nearly complete skull and partial jaw bone—was made by a research team led by Leakey, excavating on the western side of Lake Turkana in northern Kenya. They consider this 3.5-million-year-old find to represent an entirely new branch of the early human family tree.

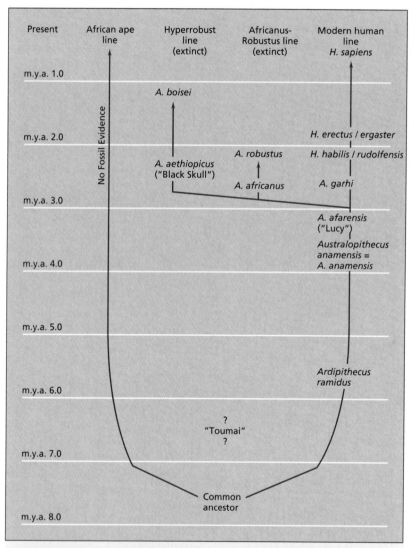

Figure 7.1 **Phylogenetic Tree for African Apes and Hominids.** Their presumed divergence date was between 6 and 8 m.y.a. Branching in later hominid evolution is also shown. For more exact dates, see text.

Maeve Leakey and *Kenyanthropus platyops*, which she discovered in 1999 by Lake Turkana in northern Kenya. What's the significance of *Kenyanthropus?*

Leakey views *Kenyanthropus* as showing that at least two hominid lineages existed as far back as 3.5 million years. One was the well-established fossil species *Australopithecus afarensis* (see below), best known from the celebrated Lucy skeleton. With the discovery of *Kenyanthropus* it would seem that Lucy and her kind weren't alone on the African plain. According to Leakey, Lucy may not be a direct human ancestor after all. The hominid family tree, once drawn with a straight trunk, is beginning to look more like a bush, with branches leading in many directions (Wilford 2001).

Kenyanthropus has a flattened face and small molars that are strikingly different from those of *afarensis*. Ever since its discovery in Ethiopia in 1974 by Donald Johanson, *afarensis* has been regarded as the most likely common ancestor of all subsequent hominids, including humans. In the absence of other hominid fossils between 3.8 million and 3 million years ago, this was the most reasonable conclusion scientists could draw. Undoubtedly, as a result of the *Kenyanthropus* discovery, the place of *afarensis* in human ancestry will now be debated. Taxonomic "splitters" (those

who stress diversity and divergence) will focus on the differences between *afarensis* and *Kenyanthropus* and see it as representing a new taxon (genus and/or species), as Maeve Leakey has done. Taxonomic "lumpers" will focus on the similarities between *Kenyanthropus* and *afarensis* and may try to place them both in the same taxon—probably *Australopithecus*, which is well established.

The Varied Australopithecines

In the scheme followed here, *Australopithecus* had at least five species:

1. *A. anamensis* (4.2 m.y.a.)

2. *A. afarensis* (3.8? to 3.0 m.y.a.)

3. *A. africanus* (3.0? to 2.5? m.y.a.)

4. *A. robustus* (2.6? to 2.0 m.y.a.)

5. *A. boisei* (2.6? to 1.2 m.y.a.)

Before the *Kenyanthropus* discovery, most scholars considered *A. anamensis* and *A. afarensis* to be ancestral to all the later *Australopithecus* species, as well as to *Homo*, which had appeared by 2 m.y.a. Early *Homo* then coexisted for almost a million years with *A. boisei*, which became extinct around 1.2 m.y.a. Thereafter *H. erectus*, our direct ancestors—creators of complex tools, cooperative hunters and gatherers—multiplied, expanded, and eventually colonized the world.

The dates given for each species are approximate because an organism isn't a member of one species one day and a member of another species the next day. Nor could the same dating techniques be used for all the finds. The South African australopithecine fossils (*A. africanus* and *A. robustus*), for example, come from a nonvolcanic area where radiometric dating could not be done. Dating of those fossils has been based mainly on stratigraphy. The hominid fossils from the volcanic regions of East Africa usually have radiometric dates.

AUSTRALOPITHECUS AFARENSIS

The early hominid species known as *A. afarensis* includes fossils found at two sites, Laetoli in northern Tanzania and Hadar in the Afar region of

Ethiopia. Laetoli is earlier (3.8 to 3.6 m.y.a.). The Hadar fossils probably date to between 3.3 and 3.0 m.y.a. Thus, based on the current evidence, *A. afarensis* lived between about 3.8 and 3.0 m.y.a. Research directed by Mary Leakey was responsible for the Laetoli finds. The Hadar discoveries resulted from an international expedition directed by D. C. Johanson and M. Taieb. The two sites have yielded significant samples of early hominid fossils. There are two dozen specimens from Laetoli, and the Hadar finds include the remains of between 35 and 65 individuals. The Laetoli remains are mainly teeth and jaw fragments, along with some very informative fossilized footprints. The Hadar sample includes skull fragments and postcranial material, most notably 40 percent of the complete skeleton of a tiny hominid female, dubbed "Lucy," who lived around 3 m.y.a.

Although the hominid remains at Laetoli and Hadar were deposited half a million years apart, their many resemblances explain their placement in the same species, *A. afarensis*. These fossils, along with the more recently found *Ardipithecus ramidus* and *A. anamensis*, have forced a reinterpretation of the early hominid fossil record. *A. afarensis*, although clearly a hominid, was so similar in many ways to chimps and gorillas that our common ancestry with the African apes must be very recent, certainly no more than 8 m.y.a. *Ardipithecus ramidus* and *A. anamensis* are even more apelike. These discoveries show that hominids are much closer to the apes than the previously known fossil record had suggested. Studies of the learning abilities and biochemistry of chimps and gorillas have taught a valuable lesson about homologies that the fossil record is now confirming.

The *A. afarensis* finds, which have been more completely described than *Ardipithecus ramidus* and *A. anamensis*, make this clear. The many apelike features are surprising in definite hominids that lived as recently as 3 m.y.a. Discussion of hominid fossils requires a brief review of dentition. Moving from front to back, on either side of the upper or lower jaw, humans (and apes) have two incisors, one canine, two premolars, and three molars. Our dental formula is 2.1.2.3, for a total of eight teeth on each side, upper and lower—32 teeth in all—if we have all our "wisdom teeth" (our third molars). Now back to the australopithecines. Like apes, and unlike modern humans, *A. afarensis* had sharp canine teeth that projected

beyond the other teeth. Also like apes, their lower premolar was pointed and projecting to sharpen the upper canine. It had one long cusp and one tiny bump that hints at the bicuspid premolar that eventually developed in hominid evolution.

There is, however, evidence that powerful chewing associated with savanna vegetation was entering the *A. afarensis* feeding pattern. When the coarse, gritty, fibrous vegetation of grasslands and semidesert enters the diet, the back teeth change to accommodate heavy chewing stresses. Massive back teeth, jaws, and facial and cranial structures suggest a diet demanding extensive grinding and powerful crushing. *A. afarensis* molars are large (see Figure 7.2). The lower jaw (mandible) is thick and is buttressed with a bony ridge behind the front teeth. The cheekbones are large and flare out to the side for the attachment of powerful chewing muscles.

Understanding Ourselves What makes us human? When we try to determine whether a fossil is a human ancestor, should we look for traits that make us human today? Maybe; maybe not. Sure, we look for DNA similarities, including mutations shared by certain lineages but not others. But what about our bipedal locomotion, our big brains, our long periods of childhood dependency, and our use of language and tools? Some of those key markers of humanity are fairly recent—or have origins that are impossible to date. Ironically, some of the physical markers that have led scientists to identify certain fossils as hominids rather than apes are features that humans have lost. One example is big back teeth. As they adapted to the savanna, with its gritty, tough, and fibrous vegetation, it was adaptively advantageous for early hominids to have large back teeth and thick tooth enamel. This permitted thorough chewing of tough fibrous vegetation and mixture with salivary enzymes to permit digestion of foods that otherwise would not have been digestible. The churning, rotary motion associated with such chewing also favored reduction of the front teeth, especially the canines and first premolars. These front teeth are much sharper and longer in the apes than in early hominids. The apes use their sharp self-honing teeth to pierce fruits. Males also flash their big sharp canines to intimidate and impress others, including potential mates. Bipedalism seems to have characterized the human lineage since it split from the line

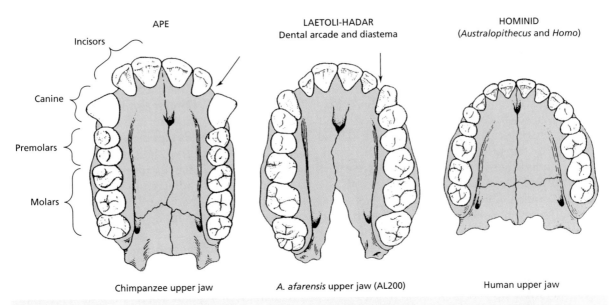

APE

Incisors

Canine

Premolars

Molars

Chimpanzee upper jaw

LAETOLI-HADAR
Dental arcade and diastema

A. afarensis upper jaw (AL200)

HOMINID
(*Australopithecus* and *Homo*)

Human upper jaw

Figure 7.2   Comparison of Dentition in Ape, Human, and A. *afarensis* Palates.

leading to the African apes, but many other "human" features came later. Yet other diagnostic features, such as large back teeth and thick enamel—which we don't have now—offer clues about who was a human ancestor back then.

The skull of *A. afarensis* contrasts with those of later hominids. The brain case is very small. The cranial capacity of 430 cm^3 (cubic centimeters) barely surpasses the chimp average (390 cm^3). The form of the *A. afarensis* skull is like that of the chimpanzee, but the brain/body size ratio was probably larger.

Below the neck, however—particularly in regard to locomotion—*A. afarensis* was unquestionably human. Early evidence of striding bipedalism comes from Laetoli, where volcanic ash, which can be directly dated by the K/A technique, covered a trail of footprints of two or three hominids walking to a water hole. These prints leave no doubt that a small striding biped lived in Tanzania by 3.6 m.y.a. The structure of the pelvic, hip, leg, and foot bones also confirms that upright bipedalism was *A. afarensis*'s mode of locomotion. More recent finds show that bipedalism predated *A. afarensis*. *A. anamensis* (4.2 m.y.a.) was bipedal. Relevant postcranial material from the even older *Ardipithecus ramidus* (5.8–4.4 m.y.a.)

See the Internet Exercises at your OLC

mhhe
●com
/kottak

also suggests a capacity for upright bipedal locomotion. Indeed, it was the shift toward this form of moving around that led to the distinctive hominid way of life.

Bipedalism—upright two-legged locomotion—is the key feature differentiating early hominids from the apes. African fossil discoveries suggest that hominid bipedalism is more than five million years old. This mode of locomotion generally is considered an adaptation to an open grassland or savanna habitat. Scientists have suggested several advantages of bipedalism in such an environment: the ability to see over long grass, to carry items back to a home base, and to reduce the body's exposure to solar radiation. The fossil and archaeological records confirm that upright bipedal locomotion preceded tool manufacture and the expansion of the hominid brain. However, although the earliest hominids could move bipedally through open country during the day, they also preserved enough of an apelike anatomy to make them good climbers. They could take to the trees to sleep at night and to escape terrestrial predators.

One explanation for bipedalism centers on environmental changes that swept Africa more than five million years ago. As the global climate became cooler and drier, grasslands in sub-Saharan Africa expanded. The rain forests contracted, shrinking the habitat available to arboreal primates

The Varied Australopithecines   **173**

(Wilford 1995). Also, at about the same time, a geological shift deepened the Rift Valley, which runs through Ethiopia, Kenya, and Tanzania. The sinking of the valley thrust up mountains. This left the land west of the valley more humid and arboreal, while the east became more arid and dominated by savanna. The common ancestors of hominids and chimpanzees were divided as a result. Those adapting to the humid west became the chimpanzee family. Those in the east had to forge a new life in an open environment (Coppens 1994). At least one branch of the eastern primates ventured more and more into open country, looking for food but retreating to the trees to escape predators and to sleep at night. To move about more efficiently, and perhaps also to keep a lookout above the grasses for food or predators, these primates started standing up and walking on two legs. Presumably, this adaptation enhanced their chances of surviving and passing on genes that favored this stance and gait, leading eventually to bipedal hominids (Wilford 1995).

Yet another factor may have contributed to bipedalism. Early hominids might have found the tropical heat of open country very stressful. Most savanna-dwelling animals have built-in ways of protecting their brains from overheating as their body temperatures rise during the day. This isn't true of humans, nor is it likely to have been true of early hominids. The only way we can protect our brains is by keeping our bodies cool. Could it be that early hominids stood up to cool off? Studies with a scale model of the Lucy skeleton suggest that quadrupedalism exposes the body to 60 percent more solar radiation than does bipedalism. And the upright body could also catch the cooler breeze above the ground (Wilford 1995).

Although bidepal, *A. afarensis* still contrasts in many ways with later homininds. Sexual dimorphism is especially marked. The male–female contrast in jaw size in *A. afarensis* was more marked than in the orangutan. There was a similar contrast in body size. *A. afarensis* females, such as Lucy, stood between three and four feet (91 and 120 centimeters) tall; males might have reached five feet (152 centimeters). *A. afarensis* males weighed perhaps twice as much as the females did (Wolpoff 1999). Table 7.2 below summarizes data on the

Table 7.2   Facts about the Australopithecines

Species	Dates (m.y.a.)	Known Distribution	Important Sites	Body Weight (Mid-sex)	Brain Size (Mid-Sex) (cm³)
Homo sapiens sapiens	100,000 to present			60 kg/132 lbs	1,350
Pan troglodytes (chimpanzee)	Modern			42 kg/93 lbs	390
A. boisei	2.6? to 1.2	E. Africa	Olduvai, East Turkana	39 kg/86 lbs	490
A. robustus	2.6? to 2.0?	S. Africa	Kromdraai, Swartkrans	37 kg/81 lbs	540
A. africanus	3 to 2.5?	S. Africa	Taung, Sterkfontein	36 kg/79 lbs	490
A. afarensis	3.8 to 3.0	E. Africa	Hadar, Laetoli	35 kg/77 lbs	430
A. anamensis	4.2	E. Africa	Aramis	Insufficient data	No published skulls
Ardipithecus ramidus	5.8 to 4.4	E. Africa	Kanapoi	Insufficient data	No published skulls

various australopithecines, including mid-sex body weight and brain size. Mid-sex means midway between the male average and the female average.

Lucy and her kind were far from dainty. Lucy's muscle-engraved bones are much more robust than ours are. With only rudimentary tools and weapons, early hominids needed powerful and resistant bones and muscles. Lucy's arms are longer relative to her legs than are those of later hominids. Here again her proportions are more apelike than ours are. Although Lucy neither brachiated nor knuckle-walked, she was probably a much better climber than modern people are, and she spent some of her day in the trees.

The *A. afarensis* fossils show that as recently as 3.0 m.y.a., our ancestors had a mixture of apelike and hominid features. Canines, premolars, and skulls were much more apelike than most scholars had imagined would exist in such a recent ancestor. On the other hand, the molars, chewing apparatus, and cheekbones foreshadowed later hominid trends, and the pelvic and limb bones were indisputably hominid (Figure 7.3 on page 176). The hominid pattern was being built from the ground up.

Hominids walk with a striding gait that consists of alternating swing and stance phases for each leg and foot. As one leg is pushed off by the big toe and goes into the swing phase, the heel of the other leg is touching the ground and entering the stance phase. Four-footed locomotors such as Old World monkeys are always supported by two limbs. Bipeds, by contrast, are supported by one limb at a time.

The pelvis, the lower spine, the hip joint, and the thigh bone change in accordance with the stresses of bipedal locomotion. Australopithecine pelvises are much more similar (although far from identical) to *Homo*'s than to apes' and show adaptation to bipedalism (Figure 7.4 on page 177). The blades of the australopithecine pelvis (iliac blades) are shorter and broader than are those of the ape. The sacrum, which anchors the pelvis's two side bones, is larger, as in *Homo*. With bipedalism, the pelvis forms a sort of basket that balances the weight of the trunk and supports this weight with less stress. Fossilized spinal bones (vertebrae) show that the australopithecine spine had the lower spine (lumbar) curve characteristic of *Homo*. This curvature helps transmit the weight of the

upper body to the pelvis and the legs. Placement of the *foramen magnum* (the "big hole" through which the spinal cord joins the brain) farther forward in *Australopithecus* and *Homo* than in the ape also represents an adaptation to upright bipedalism (Figure 7.5 on page 177).

In apes, the thigh bone (femur) extends straight down from the hip to the knees. In *Australopithecus* and *Homo*, however, the thigh bone angles into the

An ancient trail of hominid footprints fossilized in volcanic ash. Mary Leakey found this 70-meter trail at Laetoli, Tanzania, in 1979. It dates from 3.6 m.y.a. and confirms that *A. afarensis* was a striding biped.

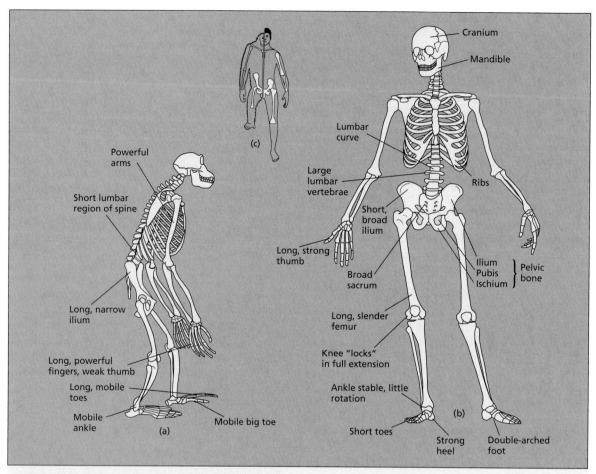

Figure 7.3 **Comparison of *Homo sapiens* and *Pan troglodytes* (the Common Chimp).** (a) Skeleton of chimpanzee in bipedal position; (b) skeleton of modern human; (c) chimpanzee and human "bisected" and drawn to the same trunk length for comparison of limb proportions. The contrast in leg length is largely responsible for the proportional difference between humans and apes.

hip, permitting the space between the knees to be narrower than the pelvis during walking. The pelvises of the australopithecines were similar but not identical to those of *Homo*. The most significant contrast is a narrower australopithecine birth canal (Tague and Lovejoy 1986).

Expansion of the birth canal is a trend in hominid evolution. The width of the birth canal is related to the size of the skull and brain. *A. afarensis* had a small cranial capacity. Even in later australopithecines, the average brain size did not exceed 600 cubic centimeters. Undoubtedly, the australopithecine skull grew after birth to accommodate a growing brain, as it does (much more) in *Homo*. However, the brains of the australop-

ithecines expanded less than ours do. In the australopithecines, the cranial sutures (the lines where the bones of the skull eventually come together) fused relatively earlier in life.

Their patterns of molar eruption (Mann 1975) suggest that australopithecine children, like our own, had a slower maturation rate than do the apes. Young australopithecines must have depended on their parents and kin for nurturance and protection. Those years of childhood dependency would have provided time for observation, teaching, and learning. This may provide indirect evidence for a rudimentary cultural life.

For a quiz on early hominids, see the Interactive Exercise

mhhe
com
/kottak

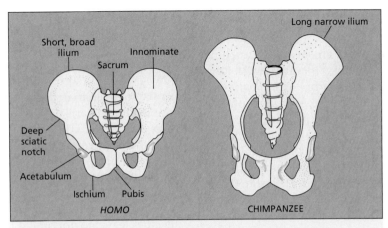

Figure 7.4   A Comparison of Human and Chimpanzee Pelvises.   The human pelvis has been modified to meet the demands of upright bipedalism. The blades (*ilia*; singular, *ilium*) of the human pelvis are shorter and broader than those of the ape. The sacrum, which anchors the side bones, is wider. The australopithecine pelvis is far more similar to that of *Homo* than to that of the chimpanzee, as we would expect in an upright biped.

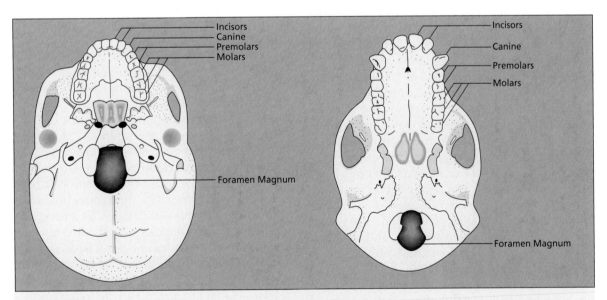

Figure 7.5   A Comparison of the Skull and Dentition (Upper Jaw) of *Homo* and the Chimpanzee.   The *foramen magnum*, through which the spinal cord joins the brain, is located farther forward in *Homo* than in the ape. This permits the head to balance atop the spine with upright bipedalism. The molars and premolars of the ape form parallel rows. Human teeth, by contrast, are arranged in rounded, parabolic form. What differences do you note between human and ape canines? Canine reduction has been an important trend in hominid evolution.

GRACILE AND ROBUST AUSTRALOPITHECINES

The fossils of *A. africanus* and *A. robustus* come from South Africa. In 1924, the anatomist Raymond Dart coined the term *Australopithecus africanus* to describe the first fossil representative of this species, the skull of a juvenile that was found accidentally in a quarry at Taung, South Africa. Radiometric dates are lacking for this non-volcanic region, but the fossil hominids found at the five main South African sites appear (from stratigraphy) to have lived between 3 and 2 m.y.a.

There were two groups of South African australopithecines: **gracile** (*A. africanus*) and robust (*A. robustus*). "Gracile" indicates that members of *A. africanus* were smaller and slighter, less robust, than were members of *A. robustus*. There were also very robust—*hyperrobust*—australopithecines in East Africa. In the classification scheme used here, these have been assigned to *A. boisei*. However, some scholars consider *A. robustus* and *A. boisei* to be regional variants of just one species, usually called *robustus* (sometimes given its own genus, *Paranthropus*).

The relationship between the graciles and the robusts has been debated for generations but has not been resolved. Graciles and robusts probably descend from *A. afarensis* or from a South African version of *A. afarensis*. Some scholars have argued that the graciles lived before (3 to 2.5? m.y.a.) and were ancestral to the robusts (2.6? to 2.0? m.y.a.). Others contend that the graciles and the robusts were separate species that may have overlapped in time. (Classifying them as members of different species implies they were reproductively isolated from each other in time or space.) Other paleoanthropologists view the gracile and robust australopithecines as different ends of a continuum of variation in a single *polytypic species*—one with considerable phenotypic variation. The range of *Australopithecus* sites in East and South Africa is shown in Figure 7.6 (on page 179).

The trend toward enlarged back teeth, chewing muscles, and facial buttressing, which is already noticeable in *A. afarensis*, continues in the South African australopithecines. However, the canines are reduced, and the premolars are fully bicuspid. Dental form and function changed as dietary needs shifted from cutting and slashing to chewing and grinding. The mainstay of the aus-

tralopithecine diet was the vegetation of the savanna.

These early hominids also might have hunted small and slow-moving game. Archaeological analyses of animal remains at australopithecine camps suggest that these hominids scavenged, bringing home parts of kills made by large cats and other carnivores. The camp sites of early hominids in East Africa include the remains of small animals and scavenged parts of carnivores' kills. However, the ability to hunt large animals was an achievement of *Homo* and is discussed later.

The skulls, jaws, and teeth of the australopithecines leave no doubt that their diet was mainly vegetarian. Natural selection modifies the teeth to conform to the stresses associated with a particular diet. Massive back teeth, jaws, and associated facial and cranial structures confirm that the australopithecine diet required extensive grinding and powerful crushing.

In the South African australopithecines, both deciduous ("baby") and permanent molars and premolars are massive, with multiple cusps. The later australopithecines had bigger back teeth than did the earlier ones. However, this evolutionary trend ended with early *Homo*, which had much smaller back teeth, reflecting a dietary change that will be described later.

Contrasts with *Homo* in the front teeth are less marked. But they are still of interest because of what they tell us about sexual dimorphism. *A. africanus*'s canines were more pointed, with larger roots, than *Homo*'s are. Still, the *A. africanus* canines were only 75 percent the size of the canines of *A. afarensis*. Despite this canine reduction, there was just as much canine sexual dimorphism in *A. africanus* as there had been in *A. afarensis* (Wolpoff 1999). Sexual dimorphism in general was much more pronounced among the early hominids than it is among *Homo sapiens*. *A. africanus* females were about four feet (120 centimeters), and males five feet (150 centimeters), tall. The average female probably had no more than 60 percent the weight of the average male (Wolpoff 1980*a*). (That figure contrasts with today's average female/male weight ratio of about 88 percent.)

Teeth, jaw, face, and skull changed to fit a diet based on tough, gritty, fibrous grasslands vegetation. A massive face housed large upper teeth and provided a base for the attachment of powerful chewing muscles. Australopithecine cheekbones were elongated and massive structures (Figure 7.7

Figure 7.6
***Australopithecus* Sites in Africa.** These sites fall into two major clusters: the open, mostly lake bed deposits in and around the East African rift valleys and the limestone cave sites of South Africa.

Members of an *A. robustus* band brandish limbs to defend their territory. This painting imagines a time of drying, with forests turning to grassland. What was the basis of the *A. robustus* diet? What kind of social organization is suggested by this image?

on page 181) that anchored large chewing muscles running up the jaw. Another set of robust chewing muscles extended from the back of the jaw to the sides of the skull.

In the more robust australopithecines (*A. robustus* in South Africa and *A. boisei* in East Africa), these muscles were strong enough to produce a *sagittal crest*, a bony ridge on the top of the skull. Such a crest forms as the bone grows. It develops from the pull of the chewing muscles as they meet at the midline of the skull.

Overall robustness, especially in the chewing apparatus, increased through time among the australopithecines. This trend was most striking in *A. boisei*, which survived through 1.2 m.y.a in East Africa. Compared with their predecessors, the later australopithecines tended to have larger overall size, skulls, and back teeth. They also had thicker faces, more prominent crests, and more rugged muscle markings on the skeleton. By contrast, the front teeth stayed the same size.

Brain size (measured as cranial capacity, in cubic centimeters—cm³) increased only slightly between *A. afarensis* (430 cm³), *A. africanus* (490 cm³), and *A. robustus* (540 cm³) (Wolpoff 1999).

These figures can be compared with an average cranial capacity of 1,350 cm³ in *Homo sapiens*. The modern range goes from less than 1,000 cm³ to more than 2,000 cm³ in normal adults. The cranial capacity of chimps (*Pan troglodytes*) averages 390 cm³ (see Table 7.2). The brains of gorillas (*Gorilla gorilla*) average around 500 cm³, which is within the australopithecine range, but gorilla body weight is much greater.

Casts of the inside of a skull (endocranial casts) provide information about the brain's size, proportions, and shape, and the areas devoted to particular functions—such as motor activities, speech, memory, sensory integration, and vision. Australopithecine endocranial casts are more human than apelike, as we would expect in an organism that relied more on learning, memory, and intellectual association.

Given the tool-making abilities of the apes, there is no reason to doubt that the australopithecines relied on rudimentary cultural means of adaptation. Animal bones that are sharpened and scratched, as they might have been if used for digging, were found at one South African australopithecine site. The earliest known stone tools come

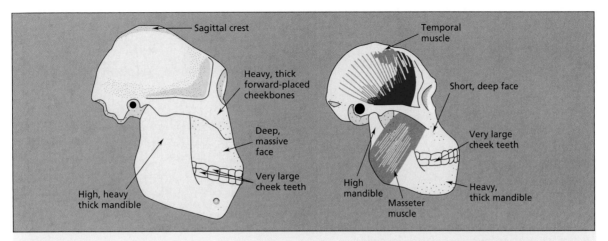

Figure 7.7   Skulls of Robust (Left) and Gracile (Right) Australopithecines, Showing Chewing Muscles.   Flaring cheek arches and, in some robusts, a sagittal crest supported this massive musculature. The early hominid diet—coarse, gritty vegetation of the savanna—demanded such structures. These features were most pronounced in *A. boisei.*

from East Africa, with radiometric dates of 2 to 2.5 m.y.a. (Asfaw, White, et al. 1999; Jolly and White 1995). Additional evidence for early hominid tool use and manufacture is discussed below.

The Australopithecines and Early *Homo*

Between 3 and 2 m.y.a., the ancestors of *Homo* split off and became reproductively isolated from the later australopithecines, such as *A. boisei*, which coexisted with *Homo* until around 1.2 m.y.a. The first evidence for speciation is dental. The fossil sample of hominid teeth dated to 2 m.y.a. has two clearly different sizes of teeth. One set is huge, the largest molars and premolars in hominid evolution; these teeth belong to *A. boisei*. The other group of (smaller) teeth belonged to our probable ancestor, *H. habilis*, the first exemplar of the genus *Homo*.

By 1.7 m.y.a., the difference was even more evident. Two hominid groups occupied different environmental niches in Africa. One of them, *Homo*—by then *Homo erectus*—had a larger brain and a reproportioned skull; it had increased the areas of the brain that regulate higher mental functions. These were our ancestors, hominids with greater capacities for culture than the australopithecines had. *H. erectus* hunted and gathered,

made sophisticated tools, and eventually displaced its sole surviving cousin species, *A. boisei*.

A. boisei of East Africa, the hyperrobust australopithecines, had mammoth back teeth. *A. boisei* females had bigger back teeth than did earlier australopithecine males. *A. boisei* became ever more specialized with respect to one part of the traditional australopithecine diet, concentrating on coarse vegetation with a high grit content.

The separation that led to speciation between *A. boisei* and early *Homo* took time. And why, if two new *species* were forming, is one of them assigned to a new genus, *Homo*? This classification is done in retrospect, since we know that one species survived and evolved into a contemporary descendant whereas the other one became extinct. Hindsight shows us their very different lifeways, which suggest their placement in different genera.

We still don't know why, how, and exactly when the split between *Australopithecus* and *Homo* took place. Scholars have defended many different models, or theoretical schemes, to interpret the early hominid fossil record. Because new finds have so often forced reappraisals, most scientists are willing to modify their interpretation when given new evidence.

The model of Johanson and White (1979), who coined the term *A. afarensis*, proposes that *A. afarensis* split into two groups. One group, the ancestors of *Homo*, became reproductively isolated

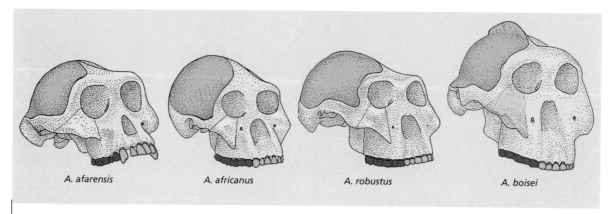

Shown from left to right are *A. afarensis*, *A. africanus*, *A. robustus*, and *A. boisei*. What are the main differences you notice among these four types of early hominids?

Palates of *Homo sapiens* (left) and *A. boisei* (right), a late, hyperrobust australopithecine. In comparing them, note the australopithecine's huge molars and premolars. What other contrasts do you notice? The large back teeth represent an extreme adaptation to a diet based on coarse, gritty savanna vegetation. Reduction in tooth size during human evolution applied to the back teeth much more than to the front.

from other hominids between 3 and 2 m.y.a. This group appeared as *Homo habilis,* a term coined by L. S. B. and Mary Leakey for the first members of the genus *Homo* and the immediate ancestors of *H. erectus. H. habilis* lived between 2 m.y.a. and about 1.7 m.y.a., by which time it had evolved into *H. erectus.* Other members of *A. afarensis* evolved into the various kinds of australopithecines (*A.*

africanus, A. robustus, and hyperrobust *A. boisei,* the last member to become extinct).

In 1985, the paleoanthropologist Alan Walker made a significant find near Lake Turkana in northern Kenya. Called the "black skull" because of the blue-black sheen it bore from the minerals surrounding it, the fossil displayed a "baffling combination of features" (Fisher 1988a). The jaw was ape-

The "black skull," dated to 2.6 m.y.a., was discovered by Alan Walker in 1985 near Lake Turkana. It gets its name from the blue-black sheen it acquired from the minerals surrounding it. The jaw is apelike and the brain is small, and there is a massive bony sagittal crest, as in *A. boisei*. Some consider the black skull to be a very early hyperrobust *A. boisei*. Others assign it to its own species, *A. aethiopicus*.

like and the brain was small (as in *A. afarensis*), but there was a massive bony crest atop the skull (as in *A. boisei*). Walker and Richard Leakey (Walker's associate on the 1985 expedition) view the black skull (dated to 2.6 m.y.a.) as a very early hyperrobust *A. boisei*. Others (e.g., Jolly and White 1995) assign the black skull to its own species, *A. aethiopicus*. The black skull shows that some of the anatomical features of the hyperrobust australopithecines (2.6? to 1.2 m.y.a.) did not change very much during well over one million years.

Interpret the World   Map 7, "Early Homi-
Atlas Map 7   nids," in your atlas
                     shows African sites
from Chad to East and South Africa. Map 7 is accompanied by a time line running from 6 million to 10,000 years ago. How might you use the data in Map 7 and the time line to interpret human evolution? Can you detect patterns of origin and dispersal? Some areas, such as Tanzania, appear to have been occupied more continuously than others. However, lack of fossil evidence for continuous occupation may reflect deficiencies in the fossil record rather than absence of occupation. What factors favor or hinder the preservation and discovery of fossils, and thus produce a map like this?

Regardless of when the split between *Homo* and *Australopithecus* occurred, there is good fossil evidence that *Homo* and *A. boisei* coexisted in East Africa. *A. boisei* seems to have lived in very arid areas, feeding on harder-to-chew vegetation than had any previous hominid. This diet would explain the hyperrobusts' huge back teeth, jaws, and associated areas of the face and skull.

H. RUDOLFENSIS AND *H. HABILIS*

In 1972, in an expedition led by Richard Leakey, Bernard Ngeneo unearthed a skull designated KNM-ER 1470. The name comes from its catalogue number in the Kenya National Museum (KNM) and its discovery location (East Rudolph—ER)— east of Lake Rudolph, at a site called Koobi Fora. The 1470 skull attracted immediate attention because of its unusual combination of a large brain (775 cc) and very large molars. Its brain size was more human than australopithecine, but its molars recalled those of a hyperrobust australopithecine. Some paleoanthropologists attributed the large skull and teeth to a very large body, assuming that this had been one *big hominid*. But no postcranial remains were found with 1470, nor have they been found with any later discovery of a 1470-like specimen.

How to interpret KNM-ER 1470? On the basis of its brain size, it seemed to belong in *Homo*. On the basis of its back teeth, it seemed more like *Australopithecus*. There are also problems with dating. The best dating guess is 1.8 m.y.a., but another estimate suggests that 1470 may be as old as 2.4 m.y.a. Originally, some paleoanthropologists assigned 1470 to *H. habilis*, while others saw it as an unusual australopithecine. In 1986, it received its own species name, *Homo rudolfensis*, from the lake near which it was found. This label has stuck—although it isn't accepted by all paleoanthropologists. Those who find *H. rudolfensis* to be a valid species emphasize its contrasts with *H. habilis*. Note the contrasts in the two skulls in the photos on page 184. KNM-ER 1813, on the left, is considered *H. habilis*; KNM-ER 1470, on the right, is *H. rudolfensis*. The *habilis* skull has a more marked brow ridge and a depression behind it, whereas 1470 has a less pronounced brow ridge and a longer, flatter face. Some think that *rudolfensis* lived earlier than and is ancestral to *habilis*. Some think that *rudolfensis* and *habilis* are simply male and female members of the same

Meet two kinds of early *Homo*. On the left KNM-ER 1813. On the right KNM-ER 1470. The latter (1470) has been classified as *H. rudolfensis*. What's the classification of 1813?

species—*H. habilis*. Some think they are separate species that coexisted in time and space (from about 2.4 m.y.a. to about 1.7 m.y.a.). Some think that one or the other gave rise to *H. erectus* (also known in Africa as *H. ergaster*). The debate continues. The only sure conclusion is that several different kinds of hominid lived in Africa before and after the advent of *Homo*.

Tools

It may have been *Homo*'s increasing hunting proficiency that forced *A. boisei* into becoming an ever-more-specialized vegetarian. Tool making also might have had something to do with the split. The simplest obviously manufactured tools were discovered in 1931 by L.S.B. and Mary Leakey at Olduvai Gorge. This site gave the tools their name—**Oldowan pebble tools.** The oldest tools from Olduvai are about 1.8 million years old. Richard Leakey also has found tools that old at East Turkana. Still older (2.5 to 2 m.y.a.) tools have been found in Ethiopia, Zaire, and Malawi (Asfaw, White, et al. 1999; Lemonick and Dorfman 1999).

Oldowan pebble tools (Figure 7.8) are pieces of stone about the size of a tennis ball. Flakes were struck off both sides to form a cutting edge. Stone is more durable than bone, horn, and wood are. Although there were probably early tools made of those materials, these substances are less likely to survive than stone is. Early hominids probably also used tools they did not make, for example, naturally chipped or cracked rocks or flakes. We can tell that early pebble tools were manufactured because their cutting edges are flaked on both sides, whereas rocks that are fractured by natural forces usually have flakes removed from just one side. Other evidence for manufacture is that some tools were made from rocks that were not locally available. They must have been brought to the site from elsewhere (Isaac 1978).

For more information on stone tool production, see the Virtual Exploration

A. *GARHI* AND EARLY STONE TOOLS

In 1999 an international team reported the discovery, in Ethiopia, of a new species of hominid, along with the earliest traces of animal butchery (Asfaw, White, et al. 1999). These new fossils, dating to 2.5 m.y.a., may be the remains of a direct human

Figure 7.8   Evolution in Tool Making.   Finds at Olduvai Gorge and elsewhere show how pebble tools (the first tool at the left) evolved into the Acheulian hand ax of *H. erectus*. This drawing begins with an Oldowan pebble tool and moves through crude hand axes to fully developed Acheulian tools. The oldest tools date back to about 2.5 m.y.a. With the split between *Homo* (*habilis*, then *erectus*) and *A. boisei*, stone-tool manufacture rapidly grew more sophisticated. The Acheulian techniques of *H. erectus* are described in the following chapter.

ancestor and an evolutionary link between *Australopithecus* and the genus *Homo*. At the same site was evidence that antelopes and horses had been butchered with the world's earliest stone tools. When scientists excavated these hominid fossils, they were shocked to find a combination of unforeseen skeletal and dental features. They named the specimen *Australopithecus garhi*. The word *garhi* means "surprise" in the Afar language.

For more on early stone tools, see the Internet Exercises at your OLC

Tim White, coleader of the research team, viewed the discoveries as important for three reasons. First, they add a new potential ancestor to the human family tree. Second, they show that the thigh bone (femur) had elongated by 2.5 million years ago, a million years before the forearm shortened—to create our current human proportions. Third, evidence that large mammals were being butchered shows that early stone technologies were aimed at getting meat and marrow from big game. This signals a dietary revolution that eventually may have allowed an invasion of new habitats and continents (Berkleyan 1999).

In 1997 the Ethiopian archaeologist Sileshi Semaw announced he had found the world's earliest stone tools, dating to 2.5 m.y.a., at the nearby Ethiopian site of Gona. But which human ancestor had made these tools, he wondered, and what were they used for? The 1999 discoveries by Asfaw, White, and their colleagues provided answers, identifying *A. garhi* as the best candidate for toolmaker (Berkleyan 1999).

Is it surprising that australopithecines made stone tools? A series of anatomic features strongly suggest the existence of australopithecine culture. These features include upright locomotion and evidence of a long period of infant and childhood dependency. Upright bipedalism would have permitted the use of tools and weapons against predators and competitors in an open grassland habitat. Bipedal locomotion also allowed early hominids to carry things, such as scavenged parts of carnivore kills. We know that primates have generalized abilities to adapt through learning. It would be amazing if the australopithecines, who are much more closely related to us than the apes are, didn't have even greater cultural abilities than contemporary apes have.

The association, in the same area at the same time, of *A. garhi*, animal butchery, and the earliest stone tools suggests that the australopithecines were

Beyond the *Classroom*

Hydrodynamic Sorting of Avian Skeletal Remains

Background Information

STUDENT:	Josh Trapani
SUPERVISING PROFESSOR:	Peter Stahl
SCHOOL:	State University of New York at Binghamton
YEAR IN SCHOOL/MAJOR:	Senior/Anthropology
FUTURE PLANS:	Graduate school
PROJECT TITLE:	Hydrodynamic Sorting of Avian Skeletal Remains

People have dietary preferences for particular animal parts. Archaeologists typically encounter remains of animals that humans may have hunted and eaten. At a given site, certain kinds of bones may be more common than others are. How can we know whether humans choose some preferred parts to take away, while leaving others, or whether natural processes were responsible? This project examines the effects of water current in sorting avian (bird) bones. Some parts (e.g., skulls) are more likely than others are to have been moved by water, and this helps to determine whether humans played a role in the selection of animal parts at the site.

Taphonomy is the study of the processes that affect preservation of organic remains. Specific taphonomic factors may bias (i.e., alter the preservation, condition, and identifiability of) archaeological and paleontological faunal assemblages in specific ways. It is necessary to understand the taphonomic biases an assemblage has been subjected to so that accurate interpretations about that assemblage can be made.

One important taphonomic agent is sorting by current. Many archaeological sites are located near water, and current action may alter their faunal assemblages. Currents sort bones in the same way they sort sediment: by selectively removing certain bones from a site while leaving others behind. Archaeologists often attribute relative frequencies of different skeletal elements at a site to human agency (e.g., dietary preference for certain parts of an animal over others). But if the assemblage has been subjected to sorting by current (or any of a number of other taphonomic factors), such interpretations may be erroneous.

Previous studies examined the way mammal and turtle bones sort in a current. However, a study with avian material had never been done before. Bird bones are structurally different from bones of other vertebrates and they often comprise an important component of human diet. I partially and completely skele-

toolmakers, with some capacity for culture. Nevertheless, cultural abilities developed exponentially with *Homo*'s appearance and expansion. With increasing reliance on hunting, tool making, and other cultural abilities, *Homo* eventually became the most efficient exploiter of the savanna niche. The last surviving members of *A. boisei* may have been forced into ever-more-marginal areas. They eventually became extinct. By 1 m.y.a., a single species of hominid, *H. erectus*, not only had rendered other hominid forms extinct but also had expanded the hominid range to Asia and Europe. An essentially human strategy of adaptation, incorporating hunting as a fundamental ingredient of a generalized foraging economy, had emerged. Despite regional variation, it was to be the basic economy for our genus until 11,000 years ago. We turn now to the fossils, tools, and life patterns of the various forms of *Homo*.

tonized several domestic pigeons (*Columba livia*) and studied the way their bones sorted in a current.

I conducted the experiments in a flume, which is a large tank that simulates conditions inside a natural channel but allows for control of many variables. The bottom may be lined with sediment, and an adjustable current flows from one end to another. I examined the order that the bones moved in, how they moved, and how likely they were to be buried. I also examined transport of partially skeletonized birds to compare behavior of individual bones with articulated skeletal units. Repeated observations under a number of different flow conditions (e.g., current velocities, bedform types) allowed me to determine a general order in which bones were expected to move.

This "sorting sequence" is useful as a general guide to whether an avian assemblage has been sorted by a current. For example, an assemblage containing skulls (most likely to be moved) and scapulae or shoulder blades (least likely to be moved) was probably not subjected to sorting. However, if an assemblage contains many easily-moved bones and few "lag" bones (or vice versa), it becomes necessary to rule out current sorting before attributing observed relative frequencies to human (or other) agency.

I also attempted to establish correlations between sorting behavior and bone size, shape, and density. Finally, I noted similarities and differences between sorting sequences for the pigeon and already-published sequences for other vertebrates.

Hopefully, this research constitutes a small step in the direction of understanding how current sorting operates as a taphonomic bias. This knowledge may aid our interpretations of site formation and thus allow greater insight into past human behavior and practices.

SUMMARY

1. Hominids lived during the late Miocene, Pliocene (5 to 2 m.y.a.), and Pleistocene (2 m.y.a. to 10,000 B.P.) epochs. The australopithecines had appeared by 4.2 m.y.a. The five species of *Australopithecus* were *A. anamensis* (4.2 m.y.a.), *A. afarensis* (3.8 to 3.0 m.y.a.), *A. africanus* (3.0 to 2.5 m.y.a.), *A. robustus* (2.5? to 2 m.y.a.), and *A. boisei* (2.6 to 1.0 m.y.a.). The earliest identifiable hominid remains date to between 7 m.y.a. and 5.8 m.y.a. The "Toumai" find from northern Chad is a possible early hominid. More generally accepted hominid remains from Ethiopia are classified as *Ardipithecus ramidus.* Next comes *A. anamensis,* then a group of fossils from Hadar, Ethiopia, and Laetoli, Tanzania, classified as *A. afarensis.*

2. These early finds suggest that the common ancestor of humans and the African apes lived more recently than had been thought. These earliest hominids shared many primitive features, including slashing canines, elongated premolars, a small apelike skull, and marked sexual dimorphism. Still, *A. afarensis* and its recently discovered predecessors were definite hominids. In *A. afarensis* this is confirmed by large molars and, more important, by skeletal evidence (e.g., in Lucy) for upright bipedalism.

3. Remains of two later groups, *A. africanus* (graciles) and *A. robustus* (robusts), were found in South Africa. Both groups show the australopithecine trend toward a powerful chewing apparatus. They had large molars and premolars and large and robust faces, skulls, and muscle markings. All these features are more pronounced in the robusts than they are in the graciles. The basis of the australopithecine diet was savanna vegetation. These early hominids also hunted small animals and scavenged the kills of predators.

4. Early *Homo, H. habilis* (2? to 1.7 m.y.a.), evolved into *H. erectus* (1.7 m.y.a. to 300,000 B.P.). By 2 m.y.a. there is ample evidence for two distinct hominid groups: early *Homo* and *A. boisei,* the hyperrobust australopithecines. The latter eventually became extinct around 1 m.y.a. *A. boisei* became increasingly specialized, dependent on tough, coarse, gritty, fibrous savanna vegetation. The australopithecine trend toward dental, facial, and cranial robustness continued with *A. boisei,* but these structures were reduced as *H. habilis* evolved into *H. erectus.*

5. Pebble tools dating to between 2.5 and 2 m.y.a. have been found in Ethiopia, Zaire, and Malawi. Scientists have disagreed about their maker, some arguing that only early *Homo* could have made them. Evidence has been presented that *A. garhi* made pebble tools around 2.5 m.y.a. Cultural abilities developed exponentially with *Homo*'s appearance and evolution.

KEY TERMS

See the flash cards

/kottak

australopithecines Varied group of Pliocene–Pleistocene hominids. The term is derived from their former classification as members of a distinct subfamily, the Australopithecinae; now they are distinguished from *Homo* only at the genus level.

glacials The four or five major advances of continental ice sheets in northern Europe and North America.

gracile Opposite of robust; "gracile" indicates that members of *A. africanus* were a bit smaller and slighter, less robust, than were members of *A. robustus.*

Homo habilis Term coined by L. S. B. and Mary Leakey; immediate ancestor of *H. erectus;* lived from about 2 to 1.7 m.y.a.

interglacials Extended warm periods between such major glacials as Riss and Würm.

Oldowan pebble tools Earliest (2 to 2.5 m.y.a.) stone tools; first discovered in 1931 by L. S. B. and Mary Leakey at Olduvai Gorge.

Pleistocene Epoch of *Homo*'s appearance and evolution; began 1.8 million years ago; divided into Lower, Middle, and Upper.

robust Large, strong, sturdy; said of skull, skeleton, muscle, and teeth; opposite of gracile.

CRITICAL THINKING QUESTIONS

For more self testing, see the self quizzes

/kottak

1. What are some of the unanswered questions about early hominid evolution? What kinds of information would help provide answers?

2. If you found a new hominoid fossil in East Africa, dated to five million years ago, would it most likely be an ape ancestor or a human ancestor? How would you tell the difference?

3. What was the first species of *Australopithecus*? Where and when did it live? What hominid lived before it?

4. What are some different ways of interpreting the relationships among the early hominids, from *Australopithecus* to *Homo*? That is, which were ancestral to *Homo,* and which were sidelines in human evolution?

5. What is the significance of the black skull?

6. Do you think that *Australopithecus* or *Homo* made the first tools? What's the basis of your opinion?

Atlas Questions

Look at Map 7, "Early Hominids: Origins and Diffusion"

1. How many African countries have hominid sites? How many have sites from the Miocene? From the Pliocene? And from the Pleistocene?

2. Compare the African distribution of nonhuman primates in Map 6 (discussed in Chapter 6) with the distribution of early hominids in Map 7. Which fossil record is better—the one for nonhuman primates or the one for hominids?

3. Compare the distribution of the African apes, as shown in Map 5 (Chapter 5) with the distribution of early hominid sites in Map 7. Also look at the distribution of extinct African apes in Map 6 (Chapter 6). What patterns do you notice? Where did early hominids overlap with the African apes (extinct and contemporary)? Where were there apes but no known early hominids, and vice versa?

SUGGESTED ADDITIONAL READINGS

Boaz, N. T.

1999   *Essentials of Biological Anthropology*. Upper Saddle River, NJ: Prentice-Hall. Basic text in physical anthropology, with information on paleoanthropology.

Bogin, B.

2001   *The Growth of Humanity*. New York: Wiley. Human growth in relation to human evolution.

Brace, C. L.

1995   *The Stages of Human Evolution*, 5th ed. Englewood Cliffs, NJ: Prentice-Hall. Brief introduction to the hominid fossil record.

2000   *Evolution in an Anthropological View*. Walnut Creek, CA: AltaMira. Essays on human evolution.

Campbell, B. G.

1998   *Human Evolution: An Introduction to Man's Adaptations*, 4th ed. New York: Aldine de Gruyter. Basic paleoanthropology text.

Campbell, B. G., and J. D. Loy, eds.

2000   *Humankind Emerging*, 8th ed. New York: Longman. Well-illustrated survey of physical anthropology, particularly the fossil record.

Cole, S.

1975   *Leakey's Luck: The Life of Louis Bazett Leakey, 1903–1972*. New York: Harcourt Brace Jovanovich. The personal and professional life of anthropology's greatest fossil finder, written by an archaeologist.

Johanson, D. C., and B. Edgar

1996   *From Lucy to Language*. New York: Simon & Schuster. Popular account of human evolution by a prominent contributor to understanding the fossil record.

Lewin, R.

1999   *Human Evolution: An Illustrated Introduction*, 4th ed. Malden, MA: Blackwell Science. Readable and well-illustrated introduction.

Park, M. A.

2002   *Biological Anthropology*, 3rd ed. Boston: McGraw-Hill. A concise introduction, with a focus on scientific inquiry.

Poirier, F. E., and J. K. McKee

1999   *Understanding Human Evolution*, 4th ed. Upper Saddle River, NJ: Prentice-Hall. Principles of human evolution.

Relethford, J. H.

2000   *The Human Species: An Introduction to Biological Anthropology*. 4th ed. Boston: McGraw-Hill. Up-to-date text in biological anthropology.

Wolpoff, M. H.

1999   *Paleoanthropology*, 2nd ed. Boston: McGraw-Hill. Thorough introduction to the hominid and pre-hominid fossil record.

INTERNET EXERCISES

1. Early Hominid Skulls: Visit Philip L. Walker and Edward H. Hagen's "Human Evolution: The Fossil Evidence in 3D" **(http://www.anth.ucsb.edu/projects/human/#).**

   Then click the link to enter the gallery.

   a. Click on the human figure labeled "Human origins" and then click on the skull labeled "Australopithecine radiation." You now have a three-dimensional view of an *Australopithecus afarensis* skull, and you can use the mouse to rotate the skull. Compare it with a modern human skull. What are some of the differences you notice? What do these differences mean about diet, environment, and brain size?

   b. Go back and view the *Paranthropus boisei* (equivalent to *Australopithecus boisei* in this text) and *Australopithecus africanus* skulls. What are the major differences between the two, and what do these differences say about diet, environment, and brain size?

2. Paleoanthropologist Fieldwork in Kenya: Go to the Human Origins Field Projects in Kenya page of the Human Origins Program at the Smithsonian, **http://www.mnh.si.edu/anthro/humanorigins/aop/aop_ken.html.**

   Explore the pages describing the field work and methods (press Continue to Next Page).

   a. The site shows pictures of the modern environment of Kenya. How much has the environment changed since early hominids lived there?

   b. Did the field work just involve excavating fossils? What other types of data are researchers gathering to understand early hominids?

   c. Make sure to read the dispatches from the researchers working at Olorgesailie in 1999, **http://www.mnh.si.edu/anthro/humanorigins/aop/Olorgesailie/dispatch/start.html.**

   Read some of the diary entries. What is a day in the field of a paleoanthropologist like?

   See Chapter 7 at your McGraw-Hill Online Learning Center for additional review and interactive exercises.

8

MODERN
HUMANS

Overview

This chapter begins around two million years ago, with the advent of the genus *Homo*. It ends with the much more recent past, when anatomically modern people were painting artistic masterpieces on cave walls in France and Spain. We focus here on the biological and cultural changes that led from early *Homo*, through intermediate forms, to anatomically modern humans—*Homo sapiens sapiens*.

The earliest member of our genus, *Homo habilis*, evolved into *Homo erectus* around 1.8 million years ago. With *H. erectus*, average cranial capacity doubled, compared with the australopithecines. *H. erectus* extended the human range out of Africa. Complex tools and cooperative hunting suggest a long period of enculturation and learning. Fire permitted expansion into cooler areas, as well as cooking and cave life. *H. erectus* had evolved into archaic *H. sapiens* by 300,000 years ago.

The Neandertals were a form of archaic *H. sapiens* that lived in Western Europe (and elsewhere) early in the last glacial period. Scientists tend to exclude the Neandertals as ancestors of modern humans. The ancestry of modern humans lies among other archaic *H. sapiens* groups, most probably those in Africa. Modern people had reached Western Europe by 31,000 years ago.

As glacial ice melted, the Western European food quest was generalized to include fish, fowl, and plants, in addition to the diminishing herds of big game. The start of such a diversified economy coincided with an intensification of Upper Paleolithic cave art. On limestone cave walls, prehistoric hunters painted animals important in their lives. Explanations of such cave paintings link them to hunting magic, ceremonies, and initiation rites.

Skulls in Caucasus Linked to Early Humans in Africa

NY TIMES NEWS BRIEF

by John Noble Wilford

May 12, 2000

The contrasting skulls of *H. erectus* or *H. ergaster* found at Dmanisi, Republic of Georgia.

Without doubt, the origins of all humans can be traced to Africa. But when did hominids first leave that continent, and what kind of creatures were those first colonists? This account tells of the discovery of an early form of human, here dubbed *Homo ergaster* but usually called early *Homo erectus*, that had reached the former Soviet Republic of Georgia by 1.7 million years ago. The *H. ergaster* or *erectus* skulls described here are remarkably similar to comparably dated fossils found in East Africa, which have been identified as being either *H. ergaster* or an early form of *H. erectus*. Other finds at the Georgian town of Dmanisi show that the hominids living there around 1.7 m.y.a. were remarkably varied. Besides the two skulls discussed in this news story, a large jaw bone (mandible) had been found previously. The most recent (2001) discovery was of a skull with some very primitive characteristics—such as large canine teeth and a small cranial capacity (Vekua and Lordkipanidze 2002). This skull may be that of a teenage girl whose skull had not yet reached full size—but whose canines had. The simplest explanation for the anatomical differences observed at Dmanisi is that *Homo erectus* was at least as variable a species as is *Homo sapiens*. In terms of size and anatomy, who are the two most different people you can think of? Imagine the interpretations that might be offered if they were found as fossils in the same stratigraphic layer.

In a discovery with profound implications for the study of early human history, scientists digging in the nation of Georgia have found 1.7-million-year-old fossil human skulls that show clear signs of African ancestry and so may represent the species that first migrated out of Africa.

The two relatively complete skulls, being described today in the journal *Science*, begin to put a face, in a sense, to the ancestors who responded to opportunity and necessity by leaving Africa and spreading out over much of the rest of the world.

Many paleoanthropologists hailed the discovery as a major advance in their field, and said the skulls were probably the most ancient undisputed human fossils outside Africa . . . .

The international discovery team, led by Dr. Leo Gabunia of the Georgia National Academy of Sciences, concluded that the age and skeletal characteristics of the skulls linked them to the early human species *Homo ergaster*, who lived from 1.9 million to 1.4 million years ago and who some researchers think is the African version of *Homo erectus* . . . .

Dr. Susan C. Anton, . . . a member of the discovery team, said that by this time human ancestors had become more carnivorous and their diets pushed them to expand their home range to match the wider ranges of the animals they preyed on.

"With the appearance of *Homo*, we see bigger bodies that require more energy to run, and therefore need these higher quality sources of protein as fuel," Dr. Anton said of the adaptation to meat-rich diets.

As long as early human ancestors had smaller bodies and brains . . . they lived mainly on plants and confined themselves to a limited range at the edge of forests, not too deep in or too exposed far out on the savanna.

Once they had stronger bodies and high-protein meat diets, they were able to spread out geographically and ecologically.

Dr. Alan Walker, a paleoanthropologist at Pennsylvania State University who specializes in searching for human fossils in Kenya, said he agreed with the interpretation of the Georgian skulls. "The new fossils look exactly like early *Homo* skulls from Kenya," Dr. Walker said.

He said the implications of the new findings for human dispersal from Africa supported an idea he and his wife, Dr. Pat Shipman, an anthropologist, proposed in 1989.

They suggested that once the more apelike *australopithecines* evolved into the genus *Homo* and became carnivorous, they were forced to expand their home territory.

"Herbivores are restricted to where the plants are that they eat," Dr. Walker said. "Carnivores are not so restricted. Meat is meat, and you often have to travel far to find it."

The two skulls were uncovered last summer at Dmanisi, on a slope of the Caucasus Mountains 55 miles southwest of Tbilisi, the Georgian capital. At the same site in 1991, paleontologists found a jawbone of what was identified as a *Homo erectus*.

Finding the craniums—one of a young adult male and the other of a female adolescent—has seemed to quiet skeptics who had disputed the jawbone dating.

The discovery team included scientists from France, Germany and the United States, as well as Georgia . . . .

Dr. Philip Rightmire, a specialist in *Homo erectus* at the State University of New York at Binghamton, said he was impressed by the new discovery's implications for "a pretty quick, really wholesale dispersal of these people, along with other animals," from the time the new species emerged in East Africa . . . .

Unlike some scientists, Dr. Rightmire classifies the African ergaster together with the Asian erectus in the same species. To him and many others, they are regional variants of the same species . . . .

The fact that *Homo* was living and hunting in Africa by 1.7 million years ago isn't newsworthy; it's been known for decades. What's interesting here is evidence for the spread of early *Homo* beyond Africa by such an early date. As we saw in Chapter 7, at two million years ago there is African evidence for two distinct hominid groups: early *Homo* and *A. boisei*, the hyperrobust australopithecines, which became extinct around 1.2 m.y.a. *A. boisei* became increasingly specialized, dependent on tough, coarse, gritty, fibrous savanna vegetation. The australopithecine trend toward den-

tal, facial, and cranial robustness continued with *A. boisei*. However, these structures were reduced as early forms of *Homo* evolved into *H. ergaster* (or early *H. erectus*) by 1.8–1.7 m.y.a. By that date *Homo* had generalized the subsistence quest to the hunting of large animals to supplement the gathering of vegetation and scavenging.

Early *Homo*

L.S.B. and Mary Leakey gave the name *Homo habilis* to the earliest members of our genus, first found at Olduvai Gorge in Tanzania. Olduvai's oldest layer, Bed I, dates to 1.8 m.y.a. This layer has yielded both small-brained *A. boisei* (average 490 cm^3) fossils and *H. habilis* skulls, with cranial capacities between 600 and 700 cm^3.

Another important *habilis* find was made in 1986 by Tim White of the University of California, Berkeley. OH62 (Olduvai Hominid 62) is the partial skeleton of a female *H. habilis* from Olduvai Bed I. This was the first find of a *H. habilis* skull with a significant amount of skeletal material. OH62, dating to 1.8 m.y.a., consists of parts of the skull, the right arm, and both legs. This fossil was surprising because of its small size and its apelike limb bones. Scientists had assumed that *H. habilis* would be taller than Lucy (*A. afarensis*), moving gradually in the direction of *H. erectus*. According to expectations, even a female *H. habilis* should have stood somewhere between Lucy's three feet and the five to six feet of *H. erectus*. However, not only was OH62 just as tiny as Lucy, its arms were longer and more apelike than expected. The limb proportions suggested greater tree-climbing ability than later hominids had. *H. habilis* may still have sought occasional refuge in the trees.

The small size and primitive proportions of *H. habilis* were unexpected given what was already known about early *H. erectus* in East Africa. (Some paleoanthropologists use the term *Homo ergaster* to refer to the earliest *H. erectus* fossils in Africa. Here I follow the more traditional scheme of calling them *Homo erectus*.) In deposits near Lake Turkana, Richard Leakey had uncovered two *H. erectus* skulls dating to 1.6 m.y.a. By that date, *H. erectus* had already attained a cranial capacity of 900 cm^3, along with a modern body shape and height. An

Drawing of a *Homo habilis* band, as it might have existed some two million years ago. Besides gathering and hunting small, slow animals, early *Homo* probably scavenged the prey of stronger, faster carnivores such as leopards. What's going on in this photo? Is there any evidence of rudimentary culture?

"What a find, Williams! The fossilized footprint of a brachiosaurus! ... And a *Homo habilus* thrown in to boot!"

What's wrong with this picture, besides the spelling of habilis?

amazingly complete young male *H. erectus* fossil (WT15,000) found at West Turkana in 1984 by Kimoya Kimeu, a collaborator of the Leakeys, has confirmed this. WT15,000, also known as the Nariokotome boy, was a 12-year-old male who had already reached 168 cm (5 feet 5 inches). He might have grown to six feet had he lived.

The sharp contrast between the OH62 *H. habilis* (1.8 m.y.a.) and early *H. erectus* (1.7–1.6 m.y.a.) suggests an acceleration in hominid evolution during that 100,000–200,000-year period. This fossil evidence may support a punctuated equilibrium model of the early hominid fossil record. In this view, long periods of equilibrium, during which species change little, are interrupted (punc-tuated) by sudden changes—evolutionary jumps. Apparently hominids changed very little below the neck between Lucy (*A. afarensis*) and *H. habilis*. Then, between 1.8 and 1.6 m.y.a., a profound change—an evolutionary leap—took place. *H. erectus* looks much more human than *H. habilis* does.

GRADUAL AND RAPID CHANGE

Charles Darwin saw life forms as arising from others gradually over time, in a slow and orderly fashion. Small modifications, accumulating over many generations, add up to major changes after thousands of years. Gradualists like Darwin cite intermediate or "mixed-trait" fossils as evidence for

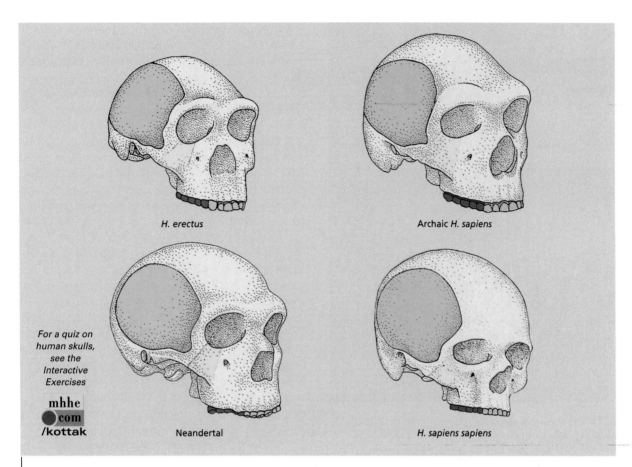

For a quiz on human skulls, see the Interactive Exercises

mhhe
com
/kottak

Compare these drawings (left to right) of *H. erectus*, archaic *H. sapiens*, Neandertal, and *H. sapiens sapiens*. What are the main differences you notice? Is the Neandertal more like *H. erectus* or *H. sapiens sapiens*?

their position. They contend we would see even more transitional forms if it weren't for gaps in the fossil record.

Advocates of the punctuated equilibrium model (see Eldredge 1985; Gould 1999) believe that long periods of stasis (stability), when species change little, are interrupted by evolutionary leaps. One reason for such jumps in the fossil record may be extinction followed by invasion by a closely related species. For example, a sea species may die out when a shallow body of water dries up, while a closely related species survives in deeper waters. Later, when the sea reinvades the first locale, the protected species will extend its range to the first area. Another possibility is that when barriers are removed, a group may replace, rather than succeed, a related one because it has a

trait that makes it adaptively fitter in the environment they now share.

When there is a sudden environmental change, one possibility is for the pace of evolution to increase. Another possibility is extinction. The earth has witnessed several mass extinctions—worldwide catastrophes affecting multiple species. The biggest one divided the era of "ancient life" (the Paleozoic) from the era of "middle life" (the Mesozoic). This mass extinction occurred 245 m.y.a., when 4.5 million of the earth's estimated 5 million species (mostly invertebrates) were wiped out. The second biggest extinction, around 65 million years ago, destroyed the dinosaurs. One explanation for the extinction of the dinosaurs is that a massive, long-lasting cloud of gas and dust arose from the impact of a giant meteorite. The cloud blocked solar

This photo shows the early (1.6 m.y.a) *Homo erectus* WT15,000, or Nariokotome boy, found in 1984 near Lake Turkana, Kenya. This is the most complete *Homo erectus* ever found.

cated soon after the advent of *Homo erectus* in Africa. Out of the crude tools in Bed I evolved better-made and more varied tools. Edges were straighter, for example, and differences in form suggest functional differentiation—that is, the tools were being made and used for different jobs, such as smashing bones or digging for tubers.

The more sophisticated tools aided in hunting and gathering. With the new tools, *Homo* could obtain meat on a more regular basis and dig and process tubers, roots, nuts, and seeds more efficiently. New tools that could batter, crush, and pulp coarse vegetation also reduced chewing demands.

With changes in the types of foods consumed, the burden on the chewing apparatus eased. Chewing muscles developed less, and supporting structures, such as jaws and cranial crests, also were reduced. With less chewing, jaws developed less, and so there was no place to put large teeth. The size of teeth, which form before they erupt, is under stricter genetic control than jaw size and bone size are. Natural selection began to operate against the genes that caused large teeth. In smaller jaws, large teeth now caused dental crowding, impaction, pain, sickness, fever, and sometimes death (there were no dentists).

Some of the main contrasts between *Australopithecus* and early *Homo* are in dentition. *H. erectus* back teeth are smaller; and the front teeth, relatively larger than australopithecine teeth. *H. erectus* used its front teeth to pull, twist, and grip objects. A massive ridge over the eyebrows (a *superorbital torus*) provided buttressing against the forces exerted in these activities.

As hunting became more important to *H. erectus*, encounters with large animals increased. Individuals with stronger skulls had better-protected brains and better survival rates. Given the dangers associated with larger prey, and without sophisticated spear or arrow technology, which developed later, natural selection favored the thickening of certain areas for better protection. The base of the skull expanded dramatically, with a ridge of spongy bone (an *occipital bun*) across the back, for the attachment of massive neck muscles. The frontal and parietal (side) areas of the skull also increased, indicating expansion in those areas of the brain. Finally, average cranial capacity expanded from about 500 cm^3 in the australopithecines to 1,000 cm^3 in *H. erectus*, which is within the modern range of variation.

radiation and therefore photosynthesis, ultimately destroying most plants and the chain of animals that fed on them.

The hominid fossil record exemplifies both gradual and rapid change. Evolution can be slow or fast depending on the rate of environmental change, the speed with which geographic barriers rise or fall, and the effectiveness of the group's adaptive response. There is no doubt that the pace of hominid evolution sped up around 1.8 m.y.a. This spurt resulted in the emergence (in less than 200,000 years) of *H. erectus*. This was followed by a long period of relative stability. One possible key to the rapid emergence of *H. erectus* was a dramatic change in adaptive strategy: greater reliance on hunting through larger body size, along with improved tools and other cultural means of adaptation.

Significant changes in technology occurred during the 200,000-year evolutionary spurt between Bed I (1.8 m.y.a.) and Lower Bed II (1.6 m.y.a) at Olduvai. Tool making got more sophisti-

Out of Africa

Biological and cultural changes enabled *Homo erectus* to exploit a new adaptive strategy—gathering and hunting. *H. erectus* pushed the hominid range beyond Africa—to Asia and Europe. Small groups broke off from larger ones and moved a few miles away. They foraged new tracts of edible vegetation and carved out new hunting territories. Through population growth and dispersal, *H. erectus* gradually spread and changed. Hominids were following an essentially human life style based on hunting and gathering. This basic pattern survived until recently in marginal areas of the world, although it is now fading rapidly.

This chapter begins around two million years ago, with the transition to *Homo*. It ends in the less distant past, when anatomically modern humans were painting artistic masterpieces on cave walls in France and Spain. We focus in this chapter on the biological and cultural changes that led from early *Homo*, through intermediate forms, to anatomically modern humans—*Homo sapiens sapiens*.

PALEOLITHIC TOOLS

For more on Oldowan tools see the Virtual Exploration

mhhe
●com
/kottak

The stone-tool-making techniques that evolved out of the Oldowan, or pebble tool, tradition and that lasted until about 15,000 years ago are described by the term **Paleolithic** (from Greek roots meaning "old" and "stone"). The Paleolithic, or Old Stone Age, has three divisions: Lower (early), Middle, and Upper (late). Each part is roughly associated with a particular stage in human evolution. The Lower Paleolithic is roughly associated with *H. erectus*; the Middle Paleolithic with archaic *H. sapiens*, including the Neandertals of Western Europe and the Middle East; and the Upper Paleolithic with early members of our own subspecies, *H. sapiens sapiens*, anatomically modern humans.

The best stone tools are made from rocks such as flint that fracture sharply and in predictable ways when hammered. Quartz, quartzite, chert, and obsidian are also suitable. Each of the three main divisions of the Paleolithic had its typical *tool-making traditions*—coherent patterns of tool manufacture. The main Lower Paleolithic tool-making tradition used by *Homo erectus* was the **Acheulian**, named after the French village of St. Acheul, where it was first identified.

Like Oldowan tools, the characteristic Acheulian tool, the hand ax, consisted of a modified core of rock. Flakes removed from the core when it was struck with a hammerstone also were used as tools. Flakes, smaller tools with finer cutting edges, became progressively more important in human evolution, particularly in Middle and Upper Paleolithic tool making.

Acheulian tools were an advance over pebble tools in several ways. Early hominids had made simple tools by picking up pebbles the size of tennis balls and chipping off a few flakes from one end to form a rough and irregular edge. They used these pebble tools (and probably some of the flakes as well) for a variety of purposes, such as smashing animal bones to extract marrow. The Acheulian technique involved chipping the core all over rather than at one end only. The core was converted from a round piece of rock into a flattish oval hand ax about 15 centimeters (6 inches) long. Its cutting edge was far superior to that of the pebble tool.

Hand axes, along with digging sticks made of bone, horn, and wood, were used to dig edible roots and other foods from the ground. Hunters made tools with a sharper cutting edge to skin and cut up their prey. Cleavers—core tools with a straight edge at one end—were used for heavy chopping and hacking at the sinews of larger animals. Flakes were used to make incisions and for finer work. The Acheulian tradition illustrates trends in the evolution of technology: greater efficiency, manufacture of tools for specific tasks, and an increasingly complex technology. These trends became even more obvious with the advent of *H. sapiens*.

ADAPTIVE STRATEGIES OF *HOMO ERECTUS*

Interrelated changes in biology and culture have increased human adaptability—the capacity to live in and modify an ever-wider range of environments. Acheulian tools helped *H. erectus* increase its range. Biological changes also increased hunting efficiency. *H. erectus* had a rugged but essentially modern skeleton that permitted long-distance stalking and endurance during the hunt. The *H. erectus* body was much larger and longer-legged than those of previous hominids, permitting longer-distance hunting of large prey. There is archaeological evidence of *H. erectus*'s success in hunting elephants, horses, rhinos, and giant baboons.

An increase in cranial capacity has been a trend in human evolution. The average *H. erectus* brain (about 1,000 cm³) doubled the australopithecine average. The capacities of *H. erectus* skulls range from 800 to 1,250 cm³, well above the *H. sapiens sapiens* minimum.

Understanding Ourselves Now we can understand why our children, compared with the young of other primates, are so dependent for so long—it's because of our big brains and our bipedal locomotion. As was noted in Chapter 7, larger skulls demand larger birth canals. However, the requirements of upright bipedalism impose limits on the expansion of the pelvic opening. If the opening is too large, the pelvis doesn't provide sufficient support for the trunk. Locomotion suffers, and posture problems develop. If, by contrast, the birth canal is too narrow, mother and child (without the modern option of Caesarean section) may die. Natural selection has struck a balance between the structural demands of upright posture and the tendency toward increased brain size—the birth of immature and dependent children whose brains and skulls grow dramatically after birth.

The interrelation between immature birth, childhood dependency, and social nurturance applies with greater force to *H. erectus* than it did to the australopithecines. During a long period of dependence, growth, and maturation, children can absorb the traditions and cultural directives of parents and other members of the group. Extended enculturation helps explain increasing complexity in tool manufacture and increasingly efficient coordination of hunting among *H. erectus*. These observations, of course, apply even more strongly to—and help us understand—our own systems of cultural transmission, as modern members of *Homo sapiens*.

H. erectus had an essentially modern, though very robust, skeleton with a brain and body closer in size to *H. sapiens* than to *Australopithecus*. Still, several anatomical contrasts, particularly in the cranium, distinguish *H. erectus* from modern humans. Compared with moderns, *H. erectus* had a lower and more sloping forehead accentuated by a large brow ridge above the eyes. Skull bones were thicker, and, as noted, average cranial capacity was smaller. The braincase was lower and flatter than in *H. sapiens*, with spongy bone development at the lower rear of the skull. Seen from behind, the *H. erectus* skull has a broad-based angular shape that has been compared to a half-inflated football (Jolly and White 1995) (Figure 8.1). The *H. erectus* face, teeth, and jaws were larger than those in contemporary humans but smaller than those in *Australopithecus*. The front teeth were especially large, but molar size was well below the australopithecine average. Presumably, this reduction reflected changes in diet or food processing.

Taken together, the *H. erectus* skeleton and chewing apparatus provide biological evidence of a fuller commitment to hunting and gathering,

Homo erectus (Java)

Homo erectus (Zhoukoudian)

Homo erectus (Ngandong XI)

Homo sapiens (Neandertal from La Chapelle-aux-Saints)

Figure 8.1   Rear Views of Three Skulls of *H. erectus* and One of "Archaic" *Homo sapiens* (a Neandertal).   Note the more angular shape of the *H. erectus* skulls, with the maximum breadth low down, near the base.
SOURCE: From *Physical Anthropology and Archaeology*, 5th edition, by C. J. Jolly and R. White (New York: McGraw-Hill, 1995), p. 271.

which was *Homo*'s only adaptive strategy until plant cultivation and animal domestication emerged some 10,000 to 12,000 years ago. Archaeologists have found and studied several sites of *H. erectus* activity, including cooperative hunting. At one of these sites, Terra Amata, overlooking Nice in southern France, archaeologists have documented activities of late *H. erectus* (or more probably, early archaic *H. sapiens*) populations from around 300,000 years ago. Small bands of hunters and gatherers consisting of 15 to 25 people made regular visits during the late spring and early summer to Terra Amata, a sandy cove on the coast of the Mediterranean.

Archaeologists determined the season of occupation by examining fossilized human excrement, which contained pollen from flowers that are known to bloom in late spring. There is evidence for 21 such visits. Four groups camped on a sand bar, 6 on the beach, and 11 on a sand dune. Archaeologists surmise that the 11 dune sites represent that number of annual visits by the same band (deLumley 1969/1976).

From a camp atop the dune, these people looked down on a river valley where animals were abundant. Bones found at Terra Amata show that their diet included red deer, young elephants, wild boars, wild mountain goats, an extinct variety of rhinoceros, and wild oxen. The Terra Amata people also hunted turtles and birds and collected oysters and mussels. Fish bones also were found at the site.

The arrangement of postholes shows that these people used saplings to support temporary huts. There were hearths—sunken pits and piled stone fireplaces—within the shelters. Stone chips inside the borders of the huts show that tools were made from locally available rocks and beach pebbles. Thus, at Terra Amata, hundreds of thousands of years ago, people were already pursuing an essentially human life style, one that survived in certain coastal regions into the 20th century.

The hearths at Terra Amata and other sites confirm that fire was part of the human adaptive kit by this time. Fire provided protection against cave bears and saber-toothed tigers. It permitted *H. erectus* to occupy cave sites, including Zhoukoudian, near Beijing in China, which has yielded the remains of more than 40 specimens of *H. erectus*. Fire widened the range of climates open to human colonization. Its warmth enabled people to survive winter cold in temperate regions. Human control over fire offered other advantages, such as cooking, which breaks down vegetable fibers and tenderizes meat. Cooking kills parasites and makes meat more digestible, thus reducing strain on the chewing apparatus.

Could language (fireside chats, perhaps) have been an additional advantage available to *H. erectus*? Archaeological evidence confirms the cooperative hunting of large animals and the manufacture of complicated tools. These activities might have been too complex to have gone on without some kind of language. Speech would have aided coordination, cooperation, and the learning of traditions, including tool making. Words, of course, aren't preserved until the advent of writing. However, given the potential for language-based communication—which even chimps and gorillas share with *H. sapiens*—and given brain size within the low *H. sapiens* range, it seems plausible to assume that *H. erectus* had rudimentary speech. For contrary views, see Binford (1981), Fisher (1988b), and Wade (2002).

THE EVOLUTION AND EXPANSION OF *HOMO ERECTUS*

The archaeological record of *H. erectus* activities can be combined with the fossil evidence to provide us with a more complete picture of our Lower Paleolithic ancestors. We now consider some of the fossil data, whose geographic distribution is shown in Figure 8.2. Early *H. erectus* remains, found by Richard Leakey's team at East and West Turkana, Kenya, and dated to around 1.6 m.y.a., including the Nariokotome boy, have been discussed previously.

One fairly complete skull, one large mandible, and two partial skulls—one of a young adult male (780 cm^3) and one of an adolescent female (650 cm^3)—have been found recently at the Dmanisi site in the former Soviet Republic of Georgia (see the news story at the start of this chapter). They have been assigned a date of 1.7–1.75 m.y.a. There are notable similarities between the two partial skulls and that of the Narikotome boy (1.6 m.y.a.) found near Kenya's Lake Turkana. Tools of comparable age associated with the Kenyan and Georgian fossils also are similar. Some paleoanthropologists assign the Nariokotome and Dmanisi finds to a new species, *Homo ergaster*, intermediate between *H. habilis* and *H. erectus*. The most recent

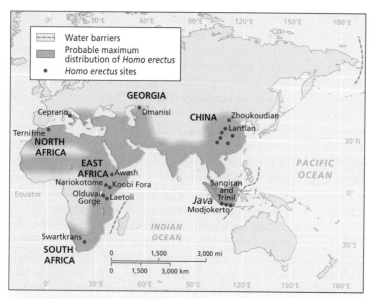

Figure 8.2 **The Sites of Discovery of *Homo erectus* and Its Probable Maximum Distribution.**

SOURCE: From *Physical Anthropology and Archaeology*, 5th edition, by C. J. Jolly and R. White (New York: McGraw-Hill, 1995), p. 268.

Later *H. erectus* remains come from Upper Bed II at Olduvai, Tanzania. Those fossils, about a million years old, were associated with Acheulian tools. Besides Kenya and Tanzania, African *H. erectus* fossils have been found in Ethiopia, Eritrea, and South Africa. The time span of *H. erectus* in East Africa was long. *H. erectus* fossils also have been found in Bed IV at Olduvai, dating to 500,000 B.P.

In 1891, the Indonesian island of Java yielded the first *H. erectus* fossil find, popularly known as "Java man." Eugene Dubois, a Dutch army surgeon, had gone to Java to discover a transitional form between apes and humans. Of course, we now know that the transition to hominid had taken place much earlier than the *H. erectus* period and occurred in Africa. However, Dubois's good luck did lead him to the most ancient human fossils discovered at that time. Excavating near the village of Trinil, Dubois found parts of a *H. erectus* skull and a thigh bone. During the 1930s and 1940s, excavations in Java uncovered additional remains.

The Indonesian *H. erectus* fossils date back at least 700,000, and maybe more than a million, years. Fragments of a skull and a lower jaw found in northern China at Lantien may be about the same age.

(2001) skull find, with its large canines and small brain size, looks more like *H. habilis* than do the other fossils from Dmanisi. Others simply consider all these Dmanisi fossils early *H. erectus*. The Dmanisi finds suggest a rapid spread, by 1.7 m.y.a., of early *Homo* out of Africa and into Eurasia (Figure 8.3).

Meet *Homo erectus*. On the left is a reconstruction of one of the *H. erectus* skulls from Zhoukoudian, China. On the right, an attempt to render *H. erectus* in the flesh.

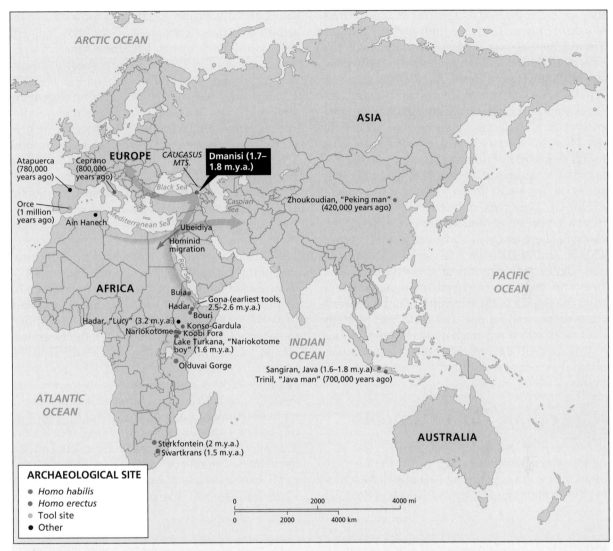

Figure 8.3 **The Expansion of *H. erectus* out of Africa around 1.7 m.y.a.**

Other *H. erectus* remains, of uncertain date, have been found in Algeria and Morocco in North Africa.

The largest group of *H. erectus* fossils was found in the Zhoukoudian cave in China. The Zhoukoudian ("Peking"—now Beijing—"man") site, excavated from the late 1920s to the late 1930s, was a major find for the human fossil record. Zhoukoudian yielded remains of tools, hearths, animal bones, and more than 40 hominids, including five skulls. The analysis of these remains led to the conclusion that the Java and Zhoukoudian fossils were examples of the same broad stage of human evolution. Today they are commonly classified together as *H. erectus*.

The Zhoukoudian individuals lived more recently than did the Javanese *H. erectus*, between 500,000 and 350,000 years ago, when the climate in China was colder and moister than it is today. The inference about the climate has been made on the basis of the animal remains found with the human fossils. The people at Zhoukoudian ate venison, and seed and plant remains suggest they were both gatherers and hunters.

What about Europe? A cranial fragment found at Ceprano, Italy, in 1994, has been assigned a date of 800,000 B.P. Other probable *H. erectus* remains have been found in Europe, but their dates are uncertain. All are later than the Ceprano skull, and they are usually classified as late *H. erectus*, or transitional between *H. erectus* and early *H. sapiens*. There have been recent fossil discoveries at two sites in northern Spain's Atapuerca mountains. The site of Gran Dolina has yielded the remains of 780,000-year-old hominids that Spanish researchers see as a possible common ancestor of *H. sapiens sapiens* and the Neandertals. At the nearby cave of Sima dos Huesos a team led by Juan Luis Arsuaga has found thousands of fossils representing at least 33 hominids of all ages. Almost 300,000 years old, they appear to represent an early stage of Neandertal evolution (Lemonick and Dorfman 1999). A jaw from a gravel pit at Mauer near Heidelberg, Germany, has been assigned a broad time span between 450,000 and 250,000 B.P. Archaeological evidence also suggests the presence of *H. erectus* in Europe. *H. erectus* therefore extended the hominid range from the tropics to the subtropical and temperate zones of Asia and Europe. The stone tools typically used by *H. erectus* are much more widespread than the fossils are. The combination of fossil and archaeological evidence confirms the adaptability of *H. erectus*.

Archaic *Homo sapiens*

Africa, which was center stage during the australopithecine period, is joined by Asia and Europe during the *H. erectus* and *H. sapiens* periods of hominid evolution. European fossils and tools have contributed disproportionately to our knowledge of early (archaic) *H. sapiens*. This doesn't mean that *H. sapiens* evolved in Europe, that most early *H. sapiens* lived in Europe, or that comparable changes in biology and culture were not occurring elsewhere. Indeed, the fossil evidence suggests that parallel physical changes and cultural advances were proceeding in Asia and especially in Africa (Wolpoff 1999). There were probably many more people in the tropics than in Europe during the ice ages. We merely *know more* about recent human evolution in Europe because archaeology and fossil hunting—not human evolution—have been going on longer there than in Africa and Asia.

Recent discoveries, along with reinterpretation of the dating and the anatomical relevance of some earlier finds, are filling in the gap between *H. erectus* and archaic *H. sapiens*. **Archaic *H. sapiens*** (300,000 to 30,000 B.P.) encompasses the earliest members of our species, along with the **Neandertals** (*H. sapiens neanderthalensis*—130,000 to 30,000 B.P.) of Europe and the Middle East and their Neandertal-like contemporaries in Africa and Asia. Brain size in archaic *H. sapiens* was within the modern human range. (The modern average, remember, is about 1,350 cm^3.) (See Table 8.1.) A rounding out of the brain case was associated with the increased brain size. As Jolly and White (1995) put it, evolution was pumping more brain into the *H. sapiens* cranium—like filling a football with air.

Table 8.1 **Summary of Data on *Homo* Fossil Groups.** Fossil representatives of the genus *Homo*, compared with modern humans (*Homo sapiens sapiens*) and chimps (*Pan troglodytes*).

Species	Dates	Known Distribution	Important Sites	Brain Size (in cm^3)
Homo sapiens sapiens	100,000 B.P. to present	Worldwide	Beijing, New York, Paris, Nairobi	1350
Homo sapiens neanderthalensis	130,000 to 30,000 B.P.	Europe, southwestern Asia	La Chapelle-aux-Saints	1430
Archaic *Homo sapiens*	300,000 to 30,000 B.P.	Africa, Europe, Asia	Kabwe, Arago, Dali, Mount Carmel caves	1135
Homo erectus	1.7 m.y.a. to 300,000 B.P.	Africa, Asia, Europe	East + West Turkana, Olduvai, Zhoukoudian, Java, Ceprano	900
Pan troglodytes	Modern	Central Africa	Gombe, Mahale	390

Archaic *H. sapiens* lived during the last part of the *Middle Pleistocene*—during the *Mindel* (second) glacial, the interglacial that followed it, and the following *Riss* (third) glacial. The distribution of the fossils and tools of archaic *H. sapiens*, which have been found in Europe, Africa, and Asia, shows that *Homo*'s tolerance of environmental diversity had increased. For example, the Neandertals and their immediate ancestors managed to survive extreme cold in Europe. Archaic *H. sapiens* occupied the Arago cave in southeastern France at a time when Europe was bitterly cold. The only Riss glacial site with facial material, Arago, was excavated in 1971. It produced a partially intact skull, two jaw bones, and teeth from a dozen individuals. With an apparent date of about 200,000 B.P., the Arago fossils have mixed features that seem transitional between *H. erectus* and the Neandertals.

The Neandertals

See the Internet Exercises at your OLC

mhhe
com
/kottak

Neandertals were first discovered in Western Europe. The first one was found in 1856 in a German valley called Neander Valley—*tal* is the German word for valley. Scientists had trouble interpreting the discovery. It was clearly human and similar to modern Europeans in many ways, yet different enough to be considered strange and abnormal. This was, after all, 35 years before Dubois discovered the first *Homo erectus* fossils in Java and almost 70 years before the first australopithecine was found in South Africa. Darwin's *On the Origin of Species*, published in 1859, had not yet appeared to offer a theory of evolution through natural selection. There was no framework for understanding human evolution. Over time, the fossil record filled in, along with evolutionary theory. Subsequent discoveries of Neandertals in Europe and the Middle East and of archaic human fossils with comparable features in Africa and Asia confirmed this stage of human evolution as geographically widespread. With the discovery of earlier and later hominid fossils, the similarities and differences between Neandertals and other members of *Homo sapiens* have become clearer.

Fossils that are not Neandertals but that have similar features (such as large faces and brow ridges) have been found in Africa and Asia. The Kabwe skull from Zambia (130,000 B.P.) is an archaic *H. sapiens* with a Neandertal-like brow ridge. Archaic Chinese fossils with Neandertal-like features have been found at Maba and Dali. Neandertals have been found in Central Europe and the Middle East. For example, Neandertal fossils found at the Shanidar cave in northern Iraq date to around 60,000 B.P., as does a Neandertal skeleton found at Israel's Kebara cave (Shreeve 1992). At the Israeli site of Tabun on Mount Carmel, a Neandertal female skeleton was excavated in 1932. She was a contemporary of the Shanidar Neandertals, and her brow ridges, face, and teeth show typical Neandertal robustness.

COLD-ADAPTED NEANDERTALS

By 75,000 B.P., after an interglacial interlude, Western Europe's hominids (Neandertals, by then) again faced extreme cold as the Würm glacial began. To deal with this environment, they wore clothes, made more elaborate tools, and hunted reindeer, mammoths, and woolly rhinos.

The Neandertals were stocky, with large trunks relative to limb length—a phenotype that minimizes surface area and thus conserves heat. Another adaptation to extreme cold was the Neandertal face, which has been likened to a *H. erectus* face that has been pulled forward by the nose. This extension increased the distance between outside air and the arteries that carry blood to the brain and was adaptive in a cold climate. The brain is sensitive to temperature changes and must be kept warm. The massive nasal cavities of Neandertal fossils suggest long, broad noses. This would expand the area for warming and moistening air.

Neandertal characteristics also include huge front teeth, broad faces, and large brow ridges, and ruggedness of the skeleton and musculature. What activities were associated with these anatomical traits? Neandertal teeth probably did many jobs later done by tools (Brace 1995; Rak 1986). The front teeth show heavy wear, suggesting that they were used for varied purposes, including chewing animal hides to make soft winter clothing out of them. The massive Neandertal face showed the stresses of constantly using the front teeth for holding and pulling.

Comparison of early and later Neandertals shows a trend toward reduction of their robust features. Neandertal technology, a Middle Pale-olithic tradition called **Mousterian**, improved considerably during the Würm glacial. Tools assumed many burdens formerly placed on the anatomy. For example, tools took over jobs once done by the front teeth. Through a still imperfectly understood mechanism, facial muscles and supporting structures developed less. Smaller front teeth—perhaps because of dental crowding—were favored. The projecting face reduced, as did the brow ridge, which had provided buttressing against the forces generated when the large front teeth were used for environmental manipulation.

THE NEANDERTALS AND MODERN PEOPLE

Scientists disagree about whether the Neandertals were ancestral to modern Western Europeans. The current prevailing view, denying this ancestry, proposes that *H. erectus* split into separate groups, one ancestral to the Neandertals and the other ancestral to *H. sapiens sapiens*—**anatomically modern humans (AMHs)** who appeared in Western Europe after 40,000 B.P. (Early AMHs in Western Europe often are referred to as *Cro-Magnon*, after the earliest fossil find of an anatomically modern human, in France's Les Eyzies region, Dordogne Valley, in 1868.) In different versions of this view, modern humans evolved in Africa, Asia, Central Europe, or the Middle East. They eventually colonized Western Europe, displacing the Neandertals there. In this interpretation, the Neandertals who lived in Western Europe during the Ice Age were too anatomically specialized to evolve into modern Europeans.

What were the contrasts between the Neandertals and AMHs? Like *H. erectus* before them, the Neandertals had heavy brow ridges and slanting foreheads. However, average Neandertal cranial capacity (more than 1,400 cm^3) exceeded the modern average. Neandertal jaws were large, providing support for huge front teeth, and their faces were massive. The bones and skull were generally more rugged and had greater sexual dimorphism—particularly in the face and skull—than do those of AMHs. In some Western European fossils, these contrasts between Neandertals and AMHs are accentuated—giving a stereotyped, or *classic Neandertal*, appearance.

Some scientists believe only the classic Neandertals were too different to be ancestors of AMHs. They contend that outside Western Europe, the anatomical differences were fewer and the people who lived there were not really Neandertals but merely Neandertal-like in some respects. Actually, the European Neandertals were variable, and many lacked the "classic" constellation of features.

Doubt about the Neandertal ancestry of Western Europeans is partly due to the history of fossil discoveries. As mentioned, the first Neandertal remains were found in 1856; and the first *H. erectus* ("Java man"), in 1891. The inclusion of "Java man" in the human evolutionary tree was debated for decades. Nor was the first australopithecine skull, uncovered in 1924, immediately accepted as a hominid. Without these earlier hominids, which were much more different from AMHs than the Neandertals were, the differences between Neandertals and moderns stood out and were emphasized.

The interpretation of one fossil contributed most to the scientific rejection of Neandertal ancestry (and to the popular stereotype of the slouching caveman). This was the complete human skeleton

In a wilderness survival school in the mountains of central Spain, Mikel Aguirre flakes a flint knife. Manufactured in four minutes, the razor-sharp blade will be used to butcher a goat.

The skull of the classic Neandertal found in 1908 at La Chapelle-aux-Saints. This was the first Neandertal to be discovered with the whole skull, including the face, preserved. Later finds showed that La Chapelle wasn't a typical Neandertal but an extreme form. What was atypical about this fossil?

What images would you have if you heard someone described as "a Neandertal"? The European Neandertals were a variable population, but they have been stereotyped as subhuman brutes. The Neandertal Museum in Erkrath, Germany, near the original fossil discovery site, offers different representations of Neandertals, from a beast to "just a guy in a suit."

discovered in 1908 at La Chapelle-aux-Saints in southwestern France, in a layer containing the characteristic Mousterian tools made by Neandertals. This was the first Neandertal to be discovered with the whole skull, including the face, preserved.

The skeleton was given for study to the French paleontologist Marcellin Boule. His analysis of the fossil helped create the stereotype of Neandertals as brutes who had trouble walking upright. Boule argued that La Chapelle's brain, although larger than the modern average, was inferior to modern brains. Further, he suggested that the Neandertal head was slung forward like an ape's. To round out the primitive image, Boule proclaimed that the Neandertals were incapable of straightening their legs for fully erect locomotion. However, later fossil finds show that the La Chapelle fossil wasn't a typical Neandertal but an extreme one. Also, this much-publicized "classic" Neandertal turned out to be an aging man whose skeleton had been distorted by osteoarthritis. Hominids, after all, have been erect bipeds for millions of years. European Neandertals were a variable population. Other Neandertal finds lack La Chapelle's combination of extreme features and are more acceptable ancestors for AMHs.

Advocates of the Neandertal ancestry of modern Europeans cite certain fossils to support their view. For example, the Central European site of Mladeč (31,000 to 33,000 B.P.) has yielded remains of several hominids that combine Neandertal robustness with modern features. Wolpoff (1999) also notes modern features in the late Neandertals found at l'Hortus in France and Vindija in Croatia. A recently reported (1999) find of a four-year-old boy in Portugal, dated to 24,000 B.P., also shows mixed Neandertal and modern features.

Fossils from Israel's Mount Carmel site of Skhūl also combine archaic and modern features. But most analyses stress the "modernness" of the Skhūl fossils, which date to 100,000 B.P. Another group of modern-looking and similarly dated (92,000 B.P.) skulls comes from the Israeli site of Qafzeh. The Skhūl and Qafzeh fossils would seem to cast serious doubt on the Neandertal ancestry of AMHs in Europe and the Middle East. The skulls from Skhūl (Figure 8.4) and Qafzeh have a modern, rather than a Neandertal, shape and are classified as AMHs. Their brain cases are higher, shorter, and rounder than Neandertal skulls. There

Figure 8.4 Skhūl V.

This anatomically modern human with some archaic features was recently redated to 100,000 B.P. This is one of several fossils found at Skhūl, Israel. Formerly dated to 32,000 B.P., this fossil group once seemed transitional between Neandertals and *H. sapiens sapiens*.

dertals spread east and south (and into the Middle East) as part of a general southward expansion of cold-adapted fauna. AMHs, in turn, followed warmer-climate fauna south into Africa, returning to the Middle East once the Würm ended.

Most current interpretations of the fossil evidence and dating favor the replacement hypothesis, which denies the Neandertal ancestry of AMHs in Western Europe and the Middle East. AMHs seem likely to have evolved from an archaic *H. sapiens* African ancestor. In Africa, as in the Middle East and Asia, the archaic *H. sapiens* fossils generally had flatter, less projecting faces than the Neandertals did. Eventually, AMHs spread to other areas, including Western Europe, where they replaced, or interbred with, the Neandertals, whose robust traits eventually disappeared (Figure 8.5).

About Eve   In 1987 a group of molecular geneticists at the University of California at Berkeley offered support for the idea that *H. sapiens sapiens* (anatomically modern humans or AMHs) arose fairly recently in Africa, then spread out and colonized the world. Rebecca Cann, Mark Stoneking, and Allan C. Wilson (1987) analyzed genetic markers in placentas donated by 147 women whose ancestors came from Africa, Europe, the Middle East, Asia, New Guinea, and Australia.

The researchers focused on mitochondrial DNA (mtDNA). This genetic material is located in the cytoplasm (the outer part—not the nucleus) of cells. Ordinary DNA, which makes up the genes that determine most physical traits, is found in the nucleus and comes from both parents. But only the mother contributes mitochondrial DNA (cloned from her own mtDNA) to the fertilized egg. The father plays no part in mtDNA transmission, just as the mother has nothing to do with the transmission of the Y chromosome, which comes from the father and determines the sex of the child. Because mtDNA is cloned, its genetic pattern is usually an exact replica of the mother's, except when mutations occur.

To establish a "genetic clock," the Berkeley researchers measured the variation in mtDNA in their 147 tissue samples. They cut each sample into segments to compare with the others. By estimating the number of mutations that had taken place in each sample since its common origin with the 146 others, the researchers drew an evolutionary tree with the help of a computer.

is a more filled-out forehead region, which rises more vertically above the brows. A marked chin is another modern feature. Still, these early AMHs do retain distinct brow ridges, though reduced from their archaic *H. sapiens* ancestor.

Dated to 100,000 and 92,000 B.P., the Skhūl and Qafzeh findings suggest that archaic *H. sapiens* was evolving directly into AMHs in the Middle East more than 50,000 years before the demise of the Western European Neandertals. Neandertals and AMHs, therefore, overlapped in time rather than being ancestor and descendant. AMHs even may have inhabited the Middle East before the Neandertals did. Ofer Bar-Yosef (1987) suggests that during the last (Würm) glacial period, which began around 75,000 B.P., Western European Nean-

That tree started in Africa and then branched in two. One group remained in Africa, while the other one split off, carrying its mtDNA to the rest of the world. The variation in mtDNA was greatest among Africans. This suggests that they have been evolving the longest. In fact, some of the earliest dated AMH fossils have been found on the African continent. AMH fossils and associated tools that may date back 100,000 years have been found at two South African cave sites, as well as at Qafzeh and Skhūl, Israel, as described previously.

The Berkeley researchers concluded that everyone alive today has mtDNA that descends from a woman (dubbed "Eve") who lived in sub-Saharan Africa around 200,000 years ago. Eve was not the only woman alive then; she was just the only one whose descendants have included a daughter in each generation through the present. Because mtDNA passes exclusively through females, mtDNA lines disappear whenever a woman has no children or has only sons. The details of the Eve theory suggest that her descendants left Africa no more than 135,000 years ago. They eventually displaced the Neandertals in Western Europe and went on to colonize the rest of the world.

Recent DNA Evidence   Additional DNA comparisons have been used to support the view that the Neandertals and AMHs were distinct groups, rather than ancestor and descendant. In 1997, ancient DNA was extracted from one of the Neandertal bones originally found in Germany's Neander Valley in 1856. This DNA, from an upper arm bone (humerus), has been compared with the DNA of modern humans. The kinds of matches we would expect in closely related humans did not occur. Thus, there were 27 differences between the Neandertal DNA and a reference sample of modern DNA. By contrast, samples of DNA from modern populations worldwide show only five to eight differences with the reference sample.

See the Internet Exercises at your OLC

Figure 8.5   **The Known Distribution of Human Populations Approximately 130,000 to 28,000 B.P.**

According to some scholars, Neandertals and moderns may have mixed in the East Mediterranean hybrid zone. In your opinion, would that have been possible?

SOURCE: From *Physical Anthropology and Archaeology*, 5th edition, by C. J. Jolly and R. White (New York: McGraw-Hill, 1995), p. 277.

This was the first time that DNA of a premodern human had been recovered. The original analysis was done by Svante Pääbo of the University of Munich. The findings were then duplicated by Mark Stoneking and Anne Stone at Pennsylvania State University. The researchers again focused on mitochondrial DNA. Using a "genetic clock" again, these scientists interpreted their results to mean that Neandertals and moderns separated over 550,000 years ago.

We know that the Neandertals coexisted with modern humans in the Middle East for thousands of years. At certain Israeli sites, modern humans date back 100,000 years. Middle Eastern Neandertals date back 40,000 to 60,000 years. In Western Europe, Neandertals survived perhaps through 28,000 years ago. To what extent did Neandertals and AMHs interact? Did they trade or interbreed? Were the Neandertals outcompeted by modern humans or killed off by them? Were they absorbed into the AMH population and genetically swamped (Rose 1997)?

MULTIREGIONAL EVOLUTION

There are two competing theories about the origin of anatomically modern humans. One is the **Eve theory** (based on the molecular study discussed previously). The other is **multiregional evolution**. According to the first theory, a small group of modern people arose recently in one place (Africa), then spread out and occupied the rest of the world. Somehow they replaced the native, and more archaic, populations of all other regions. The multiregional model (Wolpoff 1999; Wolpoff and Caspari 1997) proposes that the evolution was more inclusive. Ever since *H. erectus* spread beyond Africa, human bands have always maintained relations with their neighbors, including interbreeding. Linked by gene flow, humans in every region could and would share any beneficial mutation that arose in any one place. If a genetic change conferred a substantial selective advantage, it would spread rapidly from one group to all the others—across the entire human range. In this way human groups in Africa, Asia, and Europe would have come to share the features and behaviors of modern humans.

Advocates of multiregional evolution believe the fossil evidence contradicts the theory of an Eve who lived as recently as 200,000 B.P. Fossils show that certain physical features have persisted in particular regions for hundreds of thousands of years. For example, there are striking similarities between fossils dating back 750,000 to 500,000 years in Australasia (Indonesia and Australia), China, and Europe and the people who live in each of those regions today. One example is the facial similarity between modern Chinese people and the "vertical flat face" (Fenlason 1990) of *H. erectus* fossils found near Beijing. Another example is the "protruding face with large teeth and heavy brows," which is characteristic of both Indonesian *H. erectus* fossils and modern Native Australians. A third example is the prevalence among both ancient and modern Europeans of "angular faces with large projecting noses."

These unique regional features appeared (in *H. erectus*) long before the proposed migration of Eve's descendants. These traits probably arose through the founder effect (random genetic drift). By chance, the ancient founders of each regional population happened to have flat, protruding, or angular faces. After the founders settled each region, some of their unique physical features became common among their descendants.

If Eve's descendants arrived later than these fossils lived, and wiped out the previous inhabitants of China, Australasia, and Europe, these specific physical similarities between the fossils and the modern people of each region wouldn't exist. Rather than the Eve hypothesis, Milford Wolpoff proposes a model of multiregional evolution, in which *H. erectus* evolved into modern *H. sapiens* in each region (Africa, Europe, northern Asia, and Australasia). As the regional populations evolved, gene flow always connected them, so that beneficial mutations would spread rapidly from one group to all the others since they always belonged to the same species. Wolpoff agrees that a mitochondrial Eve might have existed, but much earlier than the Berkeley researchers suggest. Many anthropologists doubt that Eve could have lived as recently as 200,000 B.P. However, most anthropologists would have no trouble accepting a *H. erectus* Eve. Assuming the mtDNA mutation rate was much slower than the Berkeley researchers estimated, our common African mother could have been a member of one of the first hominid groups to migrate out of Africa more than 1.7 million years ago.

Advances in Technology

Early *H. sapiens sapiens* (AMHs) made tools in a variety of traditions, collectively known as **Upper Paleolithic** because of the tools' location in the upper, or more recent, layers of sedimentary deposits. Some cave deposits have Mousterian tools (made by Neandertals) at lower levels and increasing numbers of Upper Paleolithic tools at higher levels.

Although the Neandertals are remembered more for their physiques than for their manufacturing abilities, their tool kits were sophisticated. Mousterian technology included at least 14 categories of tools designed for different jobs. The Neandertals elaborated on a revolutionary technique of flake-tool manufacture invented in southern Africa around 200,000 years ago, which spread widely throughout the Old World. Uniform flakes were chipped off a specially prepared core of rock. Additional work on the flakes produced such special-purpose tools as those shown in Figure 8.6.

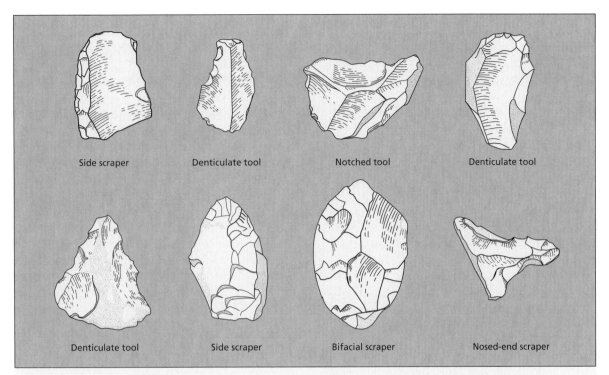

Figure 8.6 **Middle Paleolithic Tools of the Mousterian Tool-Making Tradition.**
The manufacture of diverse tool types for special purposes confirms Neandertal sophistication.

Scrapers were used to prepare animal hides for clothing. And special tools also were designed for sawing, gouging, and piercing (Binford and Binford 1979).

The Upper Paleolithic traditions of early *H. sapiens sapiens* all emphasized **blade tools**. Blades were hammered off a prepared core, as in Mousterian technology, but a blade is longer than a flake—its length is more than twice its width. Blades were chipped off cores four to six inches high by hitting a punch made of bone or antler with a hammerstone (Figure 8.7). Blades were then modified to produce a variety of special-purpose implements. Some were composite tools that were made by joining reworked blades to other materials.

The blade-core method was faster than the Mousterian and produced 15 times as much cutting edge from the same amount of material. More efficient tool production might have been especially valued by people whose economy depended on cooperative hunting of mammoths, woolly rhinoceroses, bison, wild horses, bears, wild cattle, wild boars, and—principally—reindeer. It has been estimated that approximately 90 percent of

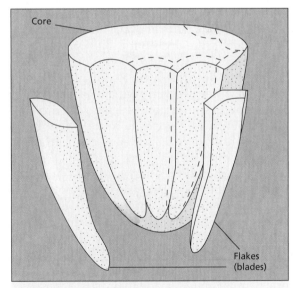

Figure 8.7 **Upper Paleolithic Blade-Tool Making.** Blades are flakes that are detached from a specially prepared core. A punch (usually a piece of bone or antler) and a hammerstone (not shown here) were used to knock the blade off the core.

the meat eaten by Western Europeans between 25,000 and 15,000 B.P. came from reindeer.

Trends observable throughout the entire archaeological record also mark the changeover from the Mousterian to the Upper Paleolithic. First, the number of distinct tool types increased. This trend reflected functional specialization—the manufacture of special tools for particular jobs. A second trend was increasing standardization in tool manufacture. The form and inventory of tools reflect several factors: the jobs tools are intended to perform, the physical properties of the raw materials from which they are made, and distinctive cultural traditions about how to make tools. Furthermore, accidental or random factors also influenced tool forms and the proportions of particular tool types (Isaac 1972). However, Mousterian and Upper Paleolithic tools were more standardized than those of *H. erectus* were.

Other trends include growth in *Homo*'s total population and geographic range and increasing local cultural diversity as people specialized in particular economic activities. Illustrating increasing economic diversity are the varied special-purpose tools made by Upper Paleolithic populations. Scrapers were used to hollow out wood and bone, scrape animal hides, and remove bark from trees. Burins, the first chisels, were used to make slots in bone and wood and to engrave designs on bone. Awls, which were drills with sharp points, were used to make holes in wood, bone, shell, and skin.

Upper Paleolithic bone tools have survived: knives, pins, needles with eyes, and fishhooks. The needles suggest that clothes sewn with thread—made from the sinews of animals—were being worn. Fishhooks and harpoons confirm an increased emphasis on fishing.

Different tool types may represent culturally distinct populations that made their tools differently because of different ancestral traditions. Archaeological sites also may represent different activities carried out at different times of the year by a single population. Some sites, for example, are obviously butchering stations, where prehistoric people hunted, made their kills, and carved them up. Others are residential sites, where a wider range of activities was carried out. The major fossils and hominid types found in the Old World through the Upper Paleolithic are summarized in Figure 8.8.

Interpret the World
Atlas Map 8

With increasing technological differentiation, specialization, and efficiency, humans have become increasingly adaptable. Through heavy reliance on cultural means of adaptation, *Homo* has become (in numbers and range) the most successful primate by far. The hominid range expanded significantly in Upper Paleolithic times with the colonization of two new continents—North America and South America—a story told in Chapter 10. (Australia was colonized by at least 50,000 B.P.) Look at Map 8, "Origins and Distribution of *Homo sapiens sapiens*," in your atlas. The map shows water, land, and glacial ice cover and indicates the major finds of *H. sapiens sapiens* (AMHs), with dates of sites and fossils and approximate dates of migrations. On Map 8 can you locate three major migrations and their dates?

Glacial Retreat

Consider now one regional example, Western Europe, of the consequences of glacial retreat. The Würm glacial ended in Europe between 17,000 and 12,000 years ago, with the melting of the ice sheet in northern Europe (Scotland, Scandinavia, northern Germany, and Russia). As the ice retreated, the tundra and steppe vegetation grazed by reindeer and other large herbivores gradually moved north. Some people moved north, too, following their prey.

Shrubs, forests, and more solitary animals appeared in southwestern Europe. With most of the big-game animals gone, Western Europeans were forced to use a greater variety of foods. To replace specialized economies based on big game, more generalized adaptations developed during the 5,000 years of glacial retreat.

As water flowed from melting glacial ice, sea levels all over the world started rising. Today, off most coasts, there is a shallow-water zone called the *continental shelf*, over which the sea gradually deepens until the abrupt fall to deep water, which is known as the *continental slope*. During the ice ages, so much water was frozen in glaciers that most continental shelves were exposed. Dry land extended right up to the slope's edge. The waters right off-

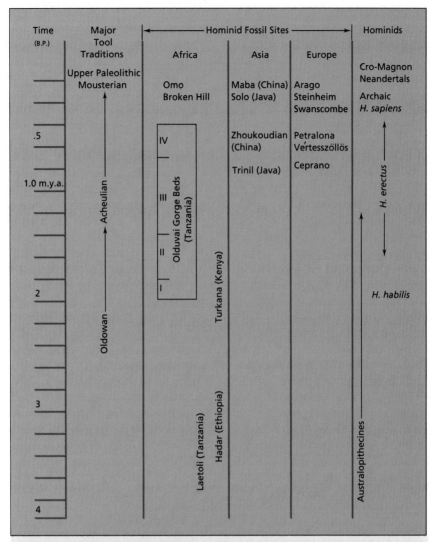

Figure 8.8 **Chronology of Evolution in Human Biology and Tool Making over the Past Four Million Years.**
See the text for particular fossils found at the different sites.

shore were deep, cold, and dark. Few species of marine life could thrive in this environment.

How did people adapt to the postglacial environment? As seas rose, conditions more encouraging to marine life developed in the shallower, warmer offshore waters. The quantity and variety of edible species increased tremendously in waters over the shelf. Furthermore, because rivers now flowed more gently into the oceans, fish such as salmon could ascend rivers to spawn. Flocks of birds that nested in seaside marshes migrated across Europe during the winter. Even inland

Europeans could take advantage of new resources, such as migratory birds and springtime fish runs, which filled the rivers of southwestern France.

Although hunting remained important, southwestern European economies became less specialized. A wider range, or broader spectrum, of plant and animal life was being hunted, gathered, collected, caught, and fished. This was the beginning of what anthropologist Kent Flannery (1969) has called the *broad-spectrum revolution*. It was revolutionary because, in the Middle East, it led to food production—human control over the reproduction of plants and animals. In a mere 10,000 years—after more than a million years during which hominids had subsisted by foraging for natural resources—food production based on plant cultivation and animal domestication replaced hunting and gathering in most areas.

Cave Art

It isn't the tools or the skeletons of Upper Paleolithic people but their art that has made them most familiar to us. Most extraordinary are the cave paintings, the earliest of which dates back some 30,000 years. More than a hundred cave painting sites are known, mainly from a limited area of southwestern France and adjacent northeastern Spain. The most famous site is Lascaux, found in 1940 in southwestern France by a dog and his young human companions.

The paintings adorn limestone walls of true caves located deep in the earth. Over time, the paintings have been absorbed by the limestone and thus preserved. Prehistoric big-game hunters painted their prey: woolly mammoths, wild cattle and horses, deer, and reindeer. The largest animal image is 18 feet long (see "Interesting Issues").

Most interpretations associate cave painting with magic and ritual surrounding the hunt. For example, because animals are sometimes depicted with spears in their bodies, the paintings might have been attempts to ensure success in hunting. Artists might have believed that by capturing the animal's image in paint and predicting the kill, they could influence the hunt's outcome.

Another interpretation sees cave painting as a magical human attempt to control animal reproduction. Something analogous was done by Native Australian (Australian aboriginal) hunters and gatherers, who held annual *ceremonies of increase* to honor and to promote, magically, the fertility of the plants and animals that shared their homeland. Australians believed that ceremonies were necessary to perpetuate the species on which humans depended. Similarly, cave paintings might have been part of annual cere-

monies of increase. Some of the animals in the cave murals are pregnant, and some are copulating. Did Upper Paleolithic people believe they could influence the sexual behavior or reproduction of their prey by drawing them? Or did they perhaps think that animals would return each year to the place where their souls had been captured pictorially?

Paintings often occur in clusters. In some caves, as many as three paintings have been drawn over the original, yet next to these superimposed paintings stand blank walls never used for painting. It seems reasonable to speculate that an event in the outside world sometimes reinforced a painter's choice of a given spot. Perhaps there was an especially successful hunt soon after the painting had been done. Perhaps members of a social subdivision significant in Upper Paleolithic society customarily used a given area of wall for their drawings.

Cave paintings also might have been a kind of pictorial history. Perhaps Upper Paleolithic people, through their drawings, were reenacting the hunt after it took place, as hunters of the Kalahari Desert in southern Africa still do today. Designs and markings on animal bones may indicate that Upper Paleolithic people had developed a calendar based on the phases of the moon (Marshack 1972). If this is so, it seems possible that late Stone Age hunters, who were certainly as intelligent as

Landscape of the Dordogne region of southwestern France. In this town, Les Eyzies, you can stay at the Cro-Magnon Hotel. You can also visit nearby sites of cave painting. Note the limestone cliffs. What is the significance of this area for prehistory?

In the mountains of southern France, where human beings have habitually hunted, loved and produced art, explorers have discovered an underground cave full of Stone Age paintings, so beautifully made and well preserved that experts are calling it one of the archeological finds of the century.

The enormous underground cavern [see Figure 8.9], which was found on Dec. 18, 1994, in a gorge near the town of Vallon-Pont-d'Arc in the Ardèche region, is studded with more than 300 vivid images of animals and human hands that experts believe were made some 20,000 years ago.

In this great parade of beasts appear woolly-haired rhinos, bears, mammoths, oxen and other images from the end of the Paleolithic era, creatures large and small and variously drawn in yellow ochre, charcoal and hematite. The murals have surprised specialists because they also include a rare image of a red, slouching hyena and the era's first-ever recorded paintings of a panther and several owls. Specialists say this ancient art gallery surpasses in size that of the famous caves of Lascaux and Altamira, which are widely held to be Western Europe's finest collection of Stone Age art.

Archeologists said they were thrilled not only by the number and the quality of the images but also by the discovery that the great underground site, sealed by fallen debris, appears to have been left undisturbed for thousands of years. They see this as tantamount to finding a time capsule full of hidden treasures.

One remarkable find, they said, was the skull of a bear, placed on a large rock set in the middle of one gallery against a backdrop of bear paintings.

"Is this some kind of altar? Someone placed the skull there for a reason," said Jean Clottes, France's leading rock art specialist. Many other skulls and bones of cave-bears were found in the underground warren, along with bones, flint knives, footprints and remains of fireplaces, all of which archeologists hope will provide important clues to the questions: What was the purpose of these paintings? What did their makers have in mind? . . .

The known part of the cavern consists of four great halls, up to 70 yards long and 40 yards wide, which are connected by smaller galleries roughly five by four yards, according [to] a report issued by the Ministry of Culture. The more than 300 paintings and engravings vary in size between 2 feet and 12 feet long. Some stand alone, while others are clustered in panels or painted with some cohesion, such as two rhinos head-to-head as if in a fight. As Mr. Clottes showed a videotape revealing a panel with four horses' heads close together, drawn in charcoal, he said: "These are one of the great marvels of prehistoric art." The artist or artists, he continued, made use of the natural colors of the rock

Figure 8-9 Location of Chauvet Cave.
Source: From *The New York Times.*

and of natural stone relief to give form and bulges to the animals.

Archeologists have long believed that the deep prehistoric caves were used not as habitats, because they were too dark, but for religious services or cults about which next to nothing is known. Some specialists believe that initiation rites were held in the caves and that the drawings of the humans' hands from the Paleolithic found here and elsewhere were a token of membership in a cult or community . . .

SOURCE: Marlise Simons, "Prehistoric Art Treasure Is Found in French Cave," *New York Times,* January 19, 1995, pp. A1, A5.

Aboriginal wall painting by the Tjapukal people of Kuranda, Queensland, Australia. Like Upper Paleolithic Europeans, Native Australians made both cave painting and petroglyphs, carvings on stone.

we are, would have been interested in recording important events in their lives.

It is worth noting that the *late* Upper Paleolithic, when many of the most spectacular multicolored cave paintings were done and Paleolithic artistic techniques were perfected, coincides with the period of glacial retreat. An intensification of cave painting for any of the reasons connected with hunting magic could have been caused by concern about decreases in herds as the open lands of southwestern Europe were being replaced by forests.

The Mesolithic

The broad-spectrum revolution in Europe includes the late Upper Paleolithic and the **Mesolithic**, which followed it. Again, because of the long history of European archaeology, our knowledge of the Mesolithic (particularly in southwestern Europe and the British Isles) is extensive. According to the traditional typology that distinguishes between Old, Middle, and New Stone Ages, the Middle Stone Age, the Mesolithic, had a characteristic tool type—the *microlith* (Greek for "small stone"). Of interest to us is what an abundant

inventory of small and delicately shaped stone tools can tell us about the total economy and way of life of the people who made them.

By 12,000 B.P., there were no longer subarctic animals in southwestern Europe. By 10,000 B.P. the glaciers had retreated to such a point that the range of hunting, gathering, and fishing populations in Europe extended to the formerly glaciated British Isles and Scandinavia. The reindeer herds had gradually retreated to the far north, with some human groups following (and ultimately domesticating) them. Europe around 10,000 B.P. was forest rather than treeless steppe and tundra. Europeans were exploiting a wider variety of resources and gearing their lives to the seasonal appearance of particular plants and animals.

People still hunted, but their prey were solitary forest animals, such as the roe deer, the wild ox, and the wild pig, rather than herd species. This led to new hunting techniques: solitary stalking and trapping, similar to more recent practices of many American Indian groups. The coasts and lakes of Europe and the Middle East were fished intensively. Some important Mesolithic sites are Scandinavian shell mounds—the garbage dumps of prehistoric oyster collectors. Microliths were used as fishhooks and in harpoons. Dugout canoes were used for fishing and travel. The process of preserving meat and fish by smoking and salting grew increasingly important. (Meat preservation had been less of a problem in a subarctic environment since winter snow and ice, often on the ground nine months of the year, offered convenient refrigeration.) The bow and arrow became essential for hunting water fowl in swamps and marshes. Dogs were domesticated, as retrievers, by Mesolithic people (Champion and Gamble 1984). Woodworking was important in the forested environment of northern and Western Europe. Tools used by Mesolithic carpenters appear in the archaeological record: new kinds of axes, chisels, and gouges.

Big-game hunting and, thereafter, Mesolithic hunting and fishing were important in Europe, but

Background Information

STUDENT:	Kelsey Foster
SUPERVISING PROFESSOR:	Dr. James G. Enloe
SCHOOL:	University of Iowa
YEAR IN SCHOOL/MAJOR:	Senior/Anthropology
FUTURE PLANS:	Marine Archaeology Internship/Graduate School
PROJECT TITLE:	Meat and Marrow: Paleolithic Butchering at Verberie

---

How can the analysis of animal bones provide evidence for specific kinds of human activity? What kinds of animals were hunted at this Paleolithic site? What kind of eating behavior went on at the site?

The Paleolithic archaeological site of Verberie le Buisson Campin is located along the banks of the Oise River in Northern France. It was the site of repeated occupation by a small band of Paleolithic hunters to mass-kill reindeer, which make up over 98% of the faunal assemblage. Examinations of the faunal material indicate that the reindeer were killed during the fall of the year, which corresponds with the yearly migration of the reindeer herds. Dental analysis and postcranial measurements served to determine that the majority of the reindeer remains were from sub-adult males. This shows great selectivity on the part of the Paleolithic hunters for large, healthy prey.

My research focuses on furthering the existing knowledge of Verberie by attempting to determine the butchering pattern used by the Paleolithic hunters at the site. I examined the faunal remains from the entire upper occupation level (Level II1) for any indication of human modification of bone, which is indicated by the presence of stone tool cut marks and/or impact cones. Stone tool cut marks are produced during the filleting of meat from the bones and during the dismemberment of the carcass. The impact cones are the result of the cracking of bones in order to remove the marrow.

During my research I examined 1,133 specimens of reindeer bone fragments to investigate butchering practices at Verberie. Using Lewis Binford's Meat Utility Index and Marrow Utility Index numbers for the nutritive value of reindeer limb elements, I found that the elements with high marrow index values composed a greater percentage of the assemblage, while the elements with high meat index values were much less represented.

I then compared the numbers and degree of human modification between each element and found that the higher marrow utility elements showed a higher degree of exploitation for marrow cracking than did the lower marrow utility elements. This identified the systematic processing of marrow at Verberie. Conversely, the stone tool cut marks present on the assemblage were predominately the result of dismemberment and not the result of meat removal.

I finally compared the percentages of the elements with a similar ethnoarchaeologic study performed on the remains from a known marrow processing event at a Nunamuit (Alaskan Eskimos, or Inuit) residential site. The extreme similarity between these two assemblages solidified the claim of extensive marrow processing at Verberie.

When all this information is taken together, the butchering sequence at Verberie becomes clear. The butchering practice of Verberie consisted of primary dismemberment of the carcass into smaller units, with intentional snacking on the high marrow utility elements. The lack of filleting marks indicates that minimal, if any, meat exploitation occurred at the hunting camp. Therefore, if the high meat utility elements were not eaten at Verberie, they were transported to a larger residential camp for later consumption.

other foraging strategies were used by prehistoric humans in Africa and Asia. Among contemporary foragers in the tropics, gathering is the dietary mainstay (Lee 1968/1974). Although herds of big-game animals were more abundant in the tropics in prehistory than they are today, gathering has probably always been at least as important as hunting for tropical foragers (Draper 1975).

Generalized, broad-spectrum economies persisted about 5,000 years longer in Europe than in the Middle East. Whereas Middle Easterners had begun to cultivate plants and breed animals by 10,000 B.P., food production came to Western Europe only around 5000 B.P. (3000 B.C.) and to northern Europe 500 years later. In Chapter 10, we will shift our focus to the Middle East, where the origin of food production took place.

Summary

1. Dental, facial, and cranial robustness was reduced as *H. habilis* evolved into *H. erectus*, who extended the hominid food quest to the hunting of large animals. *H. erectus*, with a much larger body, had smaller back teeth but larger front teeth and supporting structures, including a massive eyebrow ridge. The Lower Paleolithic Acheulian tradition provided *H. erectus* with better tools. *H. erectus*'s average cranial capacity doubled the australopithecine average. Tool complexity and archaeological evidence for cooperative hunting suggest a long period of enculturation and learning. *H. erectus* extended the hominid range beyond Africa to Asia and Europe.

2. The oldest *H. erectus* skulls yet found come from Kenya and Georgia (in Eurasia) and date back some 1.75–1.6 million years. At Olduvai Gorge, Tanzania, geological strata spanning more than a million years demonstrate a transition from Oldowan tools to the Archeulian implements of *H. erectus*. *H. erectus* persisted for more than a million years, evolving into archaic *H. sapiens* by the Middle Pleistocene epoch, some 300,000 years ago. Fire allowed *H. erectus* to expand into cooler areas, to cook, and to live in caves.

3. The classic Neandertals, who inhabited Western Europe during the early part of the Würm glacial, were among the first hominid fossils found. With no examples of *Australopithecus* or *H. erectus* yet discovered, the differences between them and modern humans were accentuated. Even today, anthropologists tend to exclude the classic Neandertals from the ancestry of Western Europeans. The ancestors of AMHs (anatomically modern humans) were other archaic *H. sapiens* groups, most probably those in Africa. AMH fos-

sil finds such as Skhūl (100,000 B.P.) and Qafzeh (92,000 B.P.) are cited to support the contention that the Neandertals (130,000 to 30,000 B.P.) and AMHs were contemporaries, rather than ancestor and descendant.

4. The classic Neandertals adapted physically and culturally to bitter cold. Their tool kits were much more complex than those of preceding humans. Their front teeth were among the largest to appear in human evolution. The Neandertals manufactured Mousterian flake tools. *H. sapiens sapiens* made Upper Paleolithic blade tools. The changeover from Neandertal to modern appears to have occurred in Western Europe by 28,000 B.P.

5. As glacial ice melted, foraging patterns were generalized, adding fish, fowl, and plant foods to the diminishing big-game supply. The beginning of a broad-spectrum economy in Western Europe coincided with an intensification of Upper Paleolithic cave art. On limestone cave walls, prehistoric hunters painted images of animals important in their lives. Explanations of cave paintings link them to hunting magic, ceremonies of increase, and initiation rites.

6. By 10,000 B.P., people were pursuing broad-spectrum economies in the British Isles and Scandinavia. Tool kits adapted to a forested environment included small, delicately shaped stone tools called microliths. The Mesolithic, or Middle Stone Age, had begun. The broad-spectrum revolution, based on a wide variety of dietary resources, began in the Middle East somewhat earlier than in Europe. As we will see in Chapter 10, it culminated in the first food-producing economies in the Middle East around 10,000 B.P.

KEY TERMS

See the flash cards

Acheulian Derived from the French village of St. Acheul, where these tools were first identified; Lower Paleolithic tool tradition associated with *H. erectus*.

anatomically modern humans (AMHs) Including the Cro-Magnons of Europe (31,000 B.P.) and the older fossils from Skhūl (100,000) and Qafzeh (92,000); continue through the present; also known as *H. sapiens sapiens*.

archaic *Homo sapiens* Early *H. sapiens*, consisting of the Neandertals of Europe and the Middle East, the Neandertal-like hominids of Africa and Asia, and the immediate ancestors of all these hominids; lived from about 300,000 to 30,000 B.P.

blade tool The basic Upper Paleolithic tool type, hammered off a prepared core.

Eve theory Theory that a small group of anatomically modern people arose recently, probably in Africa, from which they spread and replaced the native and more archaic populations of other inhabited areas.

Mesolithic Middle Stone Age, whose characteristic tool type was the microlith; broad-spectrum economy.

Mousterian Middle Paleolithic tool-making tradition associated with Neandertals.

multiregional evolution Theory that *H. erectus* gradually evolved into modern *H. sapiens* in all regions inhabited by humans (Africa, Europe, northern Asia, and Australasia). As the regional populations evolved, gene flow always connected them, and so they always belonged to the same species. This theory opposes replacement models such as the Eve theory.

Neandertals *H. sapiens neanderthalensis*, representing an archaic *H. sapiens* subspecies, lived in Europe and the Middle East between 130,000 and 30,000 B.P.

Paleolithic Old Stone Age (from Greek roots meaning "old" and "stone"); divided into Lower (early), Middle, and Upper (late).

punctuated equilibrium Model of evolution; long periods of equilibrium, during which species change little, are interrupted by sudden changes—evolutionary jumps.

Upper Paleolithic Blade-tool-making traditions associated with early *H. sapiens sapiens*; named from their location in upper, or more recent, layers of sedimentary deposits.

For more self testing, see the self quizzes

CRITICAL THINKING QUESTIONS

1. What were the main differences between the two earliest species of *Homo*? Was *Homo habilis* more like *Homo erectus*, or more like the australopithecines?

2. How do you evaluate the evidence for a punctuated equilibrium model of hominid evolution?

3. How do you evaluate the evidence for a gradualist model of hominid evolution?

4. What were the main trends in the evolution of technology during the Paleolithic? Do these trends continue today?

5. How does the geographic distribution of *H. erectus* differ from that of the australopithecines? What did culture have to do with this difference?

6. Was *Homo erectus* more like *Homo habilis* or more like *Homo sapiens sapiens*? What evidence do you offer for your opinion?

7. Do you think *H. erectus* had language? Why or why not? How about the Neandertals?

8. Do you think that *Homo sapiens sapiens* has Neandertal ancestry? Why? Can you think of ways in which the different theories about the origin of *H. sapiens sapiens* might be reconciled?

9. What cultural changes accompanied glacial retreat in Europe during the late Upper Paleolithic and the Mesolithic? Does anything happening today remind you of the effects of glacial retreat?

Atlas Questions

Look at Map 8, "Origins and Distribution of *Homo sapiens sapiens*,"

1. When and from where was Australia first settled?

2. When and from where was North America first settled? How many migrations are shown as figuring in the settlement of North America? How were these migrations related to the glacial ice cover? Did they all follow the same route?

3. What and when are the earliest *Homo sapiens sapiens* sites in Europe? How about Asia? How about Africa? Which continent has the oldest sites?

SUGGESTED ADDITIONAL READINGS

Cunliffe, B., ed.

1998   *Prehistoric Europe: An Illustrated History*. New York: Oxford University Press. An Oxford illustrated history book.

Dibble, H. L., S. P. McPherron, and B. J. Roth

2000   *Virtual Dig: A Simulated Archaeological Excavation of a Middle Paleolithic Site in France*. Boston: McGraw-Hill. Interactive computer excavation of a Middle Paleolithic site.

Fagan, B. M.

2000   *People of the Earth: A Brief Introduction to World Prehistory*, 10th ed. Upper Saddle River, NJ: Prentice-Hall. Prehistoric peoples and civilizations.

2002   *World Prehistory: A Brief Introduction*, 5th ed. New York: Longman. From the Paleolithic to the Neolithic around the world.

Gamble, C.

1999   *The Palaeolithic Societies of Europe*. New York: Cambridge University Press. Survey mainly of the Middle and Upper Paleolithic in Europe.

Klein, R. G.

1999   *The Human Career: Human Biological and Cultural Origins*, 2nd ed. Chicago: University of Chicago Press. Hominid fossils, origins, and evolution.

Klein, R. G., with B. Edgar

2002   *The Dawn of Human Culture*. New York: Wiley. Becoming modern, physically and culturally.

Knecht, H., A. Pike-Tay, and R. White, eds.

1993   *Before Lascaux: The Complex Record of the Early Upper Paleolithic*. Boca Raton, FL: CRC Press. Before cave art.

Lieberman, P.

1998   *Eve Spoke: Human Language and Human Evolution*. New York: W. W. Norton. Language and behavior in human evolution.

Oakley, K. P.

1976   *Man the Tool-Maker*, 6th ed. Chicago: University of Chicago Press. Classic, brief introduction to tool making.

Rightmire, G. P.

1990   *The Evolution of* Homo erectus: *Comparative Anatomical Studies of an Extinct Human Species*. New York: Cambridge University Press. Thorough review of the fossil evidence for the H. erectus period of human evolution.

Tattersall, Ian

1998   *Becoming Human: Evolution and Human Uniqueness*. New York: Harcourt Brace. Human evolution, including primates, fossil hominids, and social evolution.

1999   *The Last Neandertal: The Rise, Success, and Mysterious Extinction of Our Closest Human Relatives*, rev. ed. Boulder, CO: Westview. One view of what happened to the Neandertals.

Ucko, P., and A. Rosenfeld
1967   *Paleolithic Cave Art*. London: Weidenfeld and Nicolson. A survey, including finds and interpretations.

Wenke, R. J.
1996   *Patterns in Prehistory: Mankind's First Three Million Years*, 4th ed. New York: Oxford University Press. Very thorough survey of fossil and archaeological reconstruction of human evolution.

INTERNET EXERCISES

1. Visit the home page of the Chauvet-Pont-d'Arc cave (**http://www.culture.gouv.fr/culture/arcnat/chauvet/en/index.html**). Read about the discovery and authentication of the cave (under "The Cave Today") and about the archaeological context, dating, and significance of the cave (under "Time and Space").

   a. How was the cave found? How do they know the paintings are as old as they claim?

   b. When was the cave occupied? What kind of hominids were using the cave?

   c. What makes the Chauvet-Pont-d'Arc cave different from other caves used during a similar time period? What do archaeologists know about the people who occupied the cave and made the paintings?

2. Modern Hominid Origins: Visit Philip L. Walker and Edward H. Hagen's "Human Evolution: The Fossil Evidence in 3D" (**http://www.anth.ucsb.edu/projects/human/#**). Then click the link to enter the gallery.

   a. Click on the human figure labeled "Human origins" and then click on the skull labeled "Homo erectus." You now have a three-dimensional view of a *Homo erectus* skull, and you can use the mouse to rotate the skull. Compare it with a modern human skull. What are some of the prominent features that differentiate a *Homo erectus* skull from a modern human skull? From the image, is it clear who has the bigger brain?

   b. Go back and look at the *Homo neanderthalensis* skull. Rotate the skulls to look at a profile or side view. Which skull has a large brow ridge; a low, elongated skull; and a bun on the back of the skull? From the image, is it clear who has the bigger brain? Some people have argued that modern Europeans descended from Neanderthals. Based on these skulls, do you think this is possible?

See Chapter 8 at your McGraw-Hill Online Learning Center for additional review and interactive exercises.

BRINGING IT ALL TOGETHER

See your OLC Bringing It All Together links

mhhe.com /kottak

When Did Humans Start Acting Like Humans?

Let's summarize what we've learned in the last few chapters and try to bring it all together. As you read this account, note how anthropologists draft hypotheses and use evidence from artifacts, art, language, and other aspects of culture, as well as genetics, anatomy, and animal remains, to reconstruct our past.

Scientists agree that (1) between 7 and 5 million years ago, our hominid ancestors originated in Africa, as apelike creatures became habitual bipeds; (2) by 2.5 million years ago, still in Africa, hominids were making crude stone tools; and (3) by 1.7 million years ago, hominids had spread from Africa into Asia and eventually into Europe.

Most scientists agree on those three points. A smaller majority—but still a majority—of scientists think that anatomically modern humans (AMHs, or *H. sapiens sapiens*) had evolved by 130,000 years ago from ancestors who had remained in Africa. Like earlier hominids (*H. erectus* or *ergaster*), they too spread out from Africa. Eventually they replaced—perhaps in some cases interbreeding with—nonmodern human types, such as the Neandertals in Europe and parts of Asia and the successors of *H. erectus* in the Far East.

Disagreement remains about when, where, and how these early AMHs achieved *behavioral modernity*—relying on symbolic thought, elaborating cultural creativity, and, as a result, becoming fully human in behavior as well as in anatomy. Was it 90,000 or 40,000 years ago? Was it in Africa, the Middle East, or Europe? Was it population increase, competition with nonmodern humans, or a genetic mutation that triggered the change? The traditional view has been that modern behavior originated fairly recently, around 40,000 years ago, and only after *H. sapiens* had pushed into Europe. This theory of a "creative explosion" is based on evidence such as the impressive cave paintings at Lascaux and Chauvet (Wilford 2002).

Some researchers think this theory reflects Eurocentrism, in that anthropologists were more likely to believe evidence for early creativity in Western Europe. But when they found signs of early behavioral complexity in Africa or the Middle East, they discounted it. In fact, recent discoveries outside Europe do suggest an older, more gradual evolution of modern behavior, rather than its sudden appearance in Europe.

British archaeologist Clive Gamble observes, "Europe is a little peninsula that happens to have a large amount of spectacular archaeology. But the European grip of having all the evidence is beginning to slip. We're finding wonderful new evidence in Africa and other places. And in the last two or three years, this has changed and widened the debate over modern human behavior" (quoted in Wilford 2002).

Uncertainty about the origin of modern behavior reflects the long lag between the time when the species first looked modern (130,000–100,000 B.P.) and the time when it started acting modern (90,000–40,000 B.P.) (Wilford 2002). Did the capacity for behavioral modernity lie latent in early *H. sapiens* until it was needed for survival? According to archaeologist Sally McBrearty of the University of Connecticut, "the earliest *Homo sapiens* probably had the cognitive capability to invent Sputnik, but they didn't yet have the history of invention or a need for those things" (quoted in Wilford 2002). Did the need for behavioral modernity arise gradually, in the context of new social conditions, environmental change, or competition with other early human types? Or did the capacity for modern behavior develop late, reflecting some kind of genetic transformation? Mary Stiner of the University of Arizona reduces the matter to one key question: "Was there some fundamental shift in brain wiring or some change in conditions of life?" (quoted in Wilford 2002).

According to John Noble Wilford (2002), Richard G. Klein, a Stanford archaeologist, is the main advocate for the idea that human creativity dawned suddenly, in Europe around 40,000 years ago. Before this "dawn of human culture" (Klein with Edgar 2002), *Homo* had changed very slowly—and more or less simultaneously in anatomy and behavior. After this "dawn of culture," human anatomy changed little, but behavior started changing dramatically. The pace of cultural change has been accelerating ever since 40,000 B.P.

In this traditional view, it was in Europe that modern *H. sapiens* made the first tools that confirm a pattern of abstract and symbolic thought. There, humans who were behaviorally, as well as anatomically, modern also buried their dead with ceremonies, adorned their bodies with pigments and jewelry, and fashioned figurines of fertile females. Their cave paintings expressed images from their minds, as they remembered the hunt and events and symbols associated with it.

To explain such a flowering of creativity, Klein proposes a neurological hypothesis. About 50,000 years ago, he thinks, a genetic mutation acted to rewire the human brain, possibly allowing for an advance in language. Improved communication, in Klein's view, could have given people "the fully modern ability to invent and manipulate culture" (quoted in Wilford 2002). Klein thinks this genetic change probably happened in Africa and then allowed "human populations to colonize new and challenging environments" (quoted in Wilford 2002). Reaching Europe, the rewired modern humans, the AMH Cro-Magnons, met and eventually replaced the resident Neandertals.

Klein recognizes that his genetic hypothesis "fails one important measure of a proper scientific hypothesis—it cannot be tested or falsified by experiment or by examination of relevant human fossils" (quoted in Wilford 2002). AMH skulls from the time period in question show no change in brain size or function. According to Wilford (2002), Klein's critics object that his concepts of "the dawn of creativity" and of an abrupt "human revolution" are too simplistic, as well as unprovable.

Other archaeologists think it inappropriate and outdated to link the origin of human behavioral modernity so closely to the European evidence. Such thinking was more understandable when few relevant sites were known elsewhere.

But in the last 30 years, archaeologists working in Africa and the Middle East have found considerable evidence for early modern behavior, in the form of finely made stone and bone tools, long-distance trade, dietary changes, self-ornamentation, and abstract carvings.

In a survey of African archeological sites dating to between 300,000 and 30,000 years ago, Sally McBrearty and Alison Brooks (2000) conclude that artifacts thought to indicate the "human revolution" of the Upper Paleolithic in Europe—where they appear abruptly about 40,000 years ago—are found in Africa, much earlier but not all at the same time. In other words, what might appear to be a sudden event outside Africa was a slow process of accumulation within Africa. Given the genetic evidence that AMHs came from Africa, this makes good sense. There was a period of gradual cultural development in Africa for thousands of years, followed by migration out of Africa with a fairly developed culture. The implication is that humans were fully "human" long before the Upper Paleolithic and that we do not need to postulate a genetic change 50,000 years ago (e.g., a mutation "for language") to account for the "human revolution."

At South Africa's Blombos Cave, an archaeological team led by Christopher Henshilwood found evidence that AMHs were making bone

At South Africa's Blombos Cave, anatomically modern humans were making bone awls and weapon points more than 70,000 years ago. Shown here--some of the more than 100,000 artifacts that have been found in the cave.

awls and weapon points more than 70,000 years ago. Three weapon points had been shaped with a stone blade and then finely polished. Henshilwood thinks these artifacts indicate symbolic behavior and artistic creativity—people trying to make beautiful objects. In January 2002, Henshilwood reported additional evidence from Blombos Cave for early symbolic thought: two small pieces of ocher (a soft red iron oxide stone) with inscribed triangles and horizontal lines, dating back 77,000 years (Wilford 2002).

Earlier excavations in Congo's Katanda region had uncovered barbed bone harpoon points dating back 80,000 to 90,000 years (Yellen, Brooks, and Cornelissen 1995). Archaeologists Alison Brooks and John Yellen contend that these ancient people "not only possessed considerable technological capabilities at this time, but also incorporated symbolic or stylistic content into their projectile forms" (quoted in Wilford 2002).

Some scientists still challenge the idea of early behavioral modernity in Africa (Wilford 2002). The doubters wonder why, if the artifacts are that old and represent a basic change in human behavior,

they aren't more common and widespread. John Yellen counters that AMH populations at places such as Blombos Cave and Katanda were probably small and scattered. Low population density would have been a barrier to the spread of ideas and cultural practices between groups (Wilford 2002).

In Turkey and Lebanon, Steven Kuhn, Mary Stiner, and David Reese (2001) found evidence that, around 43,000 years ago, coastal people made and wore beads and shell ornaments with repetitive designs. Some of the shells were rare varieties, white or brightly colored. The bone of a large bird was incised for use as a pendant. The Mediterranean coastal sites of Ucagizli Cave in Turkey and Ksar Akil in Lebanon are located in a corridor of ancient migrations from Africa into Europe and Asia. There the archaeologists also found remains of animal bones that offered evidence for a dietary change. Over time, the people ate fewer deer, wild cattle, and other large animals. They also hunted fewer of the slower-reproducing, easier-to-catch animals, such as shellfish and tortoises, and more of the more agile animals such as birds and hares (Kuhn, Stiner, and Reese 2001).

Body ornamentation—a sign of behavioral modernity. On the left, a man from Irian Jaya, Indonesia (island of New Guinea—see your atlas). On the right, a man photographed at Finsbury Park, England. What are the social functions of such ornamentation?

Kuhn, Stiner, and Reese (2001) suggest that population increase could have caused changes in the living conditions of these AMHs—putting pressure on their resources and forcing experimentation with diet and subsistence strategies. Even a modest increase in the population growth rate could double or triple the numbers and populations of small AMH bands, forcing people to vary their subsistence strategies. People would be living nearer to one another, with more opportunities to interact. Body ornaments could have been part of a system of communication, signaling group identity and social status. The archaeologists note that such standardized ornaments first appeared at about the same time at two other widely separated sites, in Kenya and Bulgaria. Such reliance on communication through ornamentation probably implies "the existence of certain cognitive capacities and that these evolved relatively late in prehistory" (Stiner and Kuhn, quoted in Wilford 2002; Kuhn, Stiner, and Reese 2001).

Such capacities probably were not the result of a sudden genetic mutation. "The fact that traditions of ornament making emerged almost simultaneously in the earliest Upper Paleolithic/Late Stone Age on three continents argues strongly against their corresponding to a specific event in the cognitive evolution of a single population," according to Stiner and Kuhn (quoted in Wilford 2002).

Clive Gamble attributes the rise of behavioral modernity more to increasing social competition than to population increase. Competing with neighboring populations, including, in Europe, the Neandertals, could have produced new subsistence strategies, along with new ways of sharing ideas and organizing society. Such innovations would have advantaged AMH bands as they occupied new lands and faced new circumstances, including contact with nonmodern humans.

According to archaeologist Randall White of New York University, an expert on Cro-Magnon creativity, early personal adornment in Africa and the Middle East shows that the human creative capacity was latent in AMHs long before they reached Europe (Wilford 2002). Facing new circumstances, including competition, AMHs honed their cultural abilities, which enabled them to maintain a common identity, communicate ideas, and organize their societies into "stable, enduring regional groups" (quoted in Wilford 2002). Symbolic thought and cultural advances, expressed most enduringly in artifacts, ornamentation, and art, gave them the edge over the Neandertals, with whom they may have interbred, but whom they eventually replaced in Europe.

The origin of behavioral modernity continues to be debated. We see, however, that archaeological work in many world areas suggests strongly that neither anatomical modernity nor behavioral modernity was a European invention. Africa's role in the origin and development of humanity is prominent yet again.

9

HUMAN DIVERSITY AND "RACE"

Overview

Scientists have approached the study of human biological diversity in two main ways: racial classification, an approach that has been rejected, and the current explanatory approach. It is not possible to define human races biologically. Because of a range of problems involved in classifying humans into racial categories, biologists now focus on specific biological differences and try to explain them.

Race is a cultural category, not a biological reality. "Races" derive from contrasts perceived in particular societies, rather than from scientific classification. In American culture, one acquires a racial identity at birth. But in the final analysis, race in the United States isn't based on genetics or appearance. Children of mixed unions, no matter what they look like,

are usually classified with the minority-group parent. Other cultures have different ways of assigning racial labels, of socially constructing race.

Latin American countries deal with race differently. In Brazil, for example, full siblings may belong to different races if they look different. Brazilians recognize many more races than Americans do. A person's racial identity can change during his or her lifetime. It also varies depending on who is doing the classifying.

Environmental variables involving educational, economic, and social backgrounds provide better explanations for performance on intelligence tests by races, classes, and ethnic groups than do genetic differences in learning ability.

A Hemings Family Turns from Black, to White, to Black

NEW YORK TIMES NEWS BRIEF

by Brent Staples

December 17, 2001

Race is a reality of everyday life, right? Maybe not. Are races real, and in what sense? What entitles someone to belong to one race rather than another? Genes, ancestry, physical appearance? This chapter shows that races are social categories rather than biological facts. North American racial categories are socially constructed. That is, races are defined by society and culture, not by science. Consider this account of the descendants of Eston Hemings, a son of Thomas Jefferson, who was white, and Sally Hemings, an African-American woman with light skin. What should Eston's race have been? Was he right in changing it? Are his descendants, who have intermarried with whites across several generations, white or black? All of us have African roots. How recent must those roots be to turn a "white" person into a "black" person? How do you know whether Julia Jefferson, discussed in this article, is "black" or "white"? How do you know what your race is?

The Census Bureau is poking and prodding the nearly seven million people who described themselves as belonging to more than one race in the 2000 census . . . . Are some of them about to quit one race and join another? Given the slippery history of race in the census, the answer is probably "yes."

Historians who study the 19th century commonly turn up people who appear as "black" or "mulatto" in one census and "white" in another. These judgments were made by census workers who behaved essentially as race police, counting people as either black or white depending on what they looked like or on the race of the people who lived nearest to them. White people who either lived with or married blacks were magically rendered black in the census. This came at a time when blacks were sometimes barred from voting, from public school and from testifying in court. Fair-skinned blacks escaped the penalties of race by moving to places where no one knew them and taking up lives among the white folk. They lived in terror of discovery. To protect their new identities, they often broke ties with their black families.

Descendants of Thomas Jefferson and descendants of Sally Hemings pose for a group shot in 1999 in front of Jefferson's plantation.

The number of black people who passed into whiteness is difficult to determine. A provocative 1958 study cited in Supreme Court records estimated that as many as 15,000 blacks slipped across the line to live and sometimes marry as white every year in the 1940's alone. The study, by the sociologist Robert Stuckert, concluded that by the close of that decade, one in five Americans who were recorded as white in the census had an unacknowledged black ancestor within the previous four generations. . . .

The 40's found young Julia Jefferson entering her teens in a white, suburban household with parents who admonished her to avoid black people and play only with "her own kind." When she bicycled off to meet a black friend she'd met in Bible school, her parents followed her in the car, put the bicycle in the trunk and told her never to do that again. . . .

Julia's father was descended from Eston Hemings, a son of the enslaved woman Sally Hemings and Thomas Jefferson. A genetic study in 1998 established a match on the Y chromosome markers between Thomas Jefferson's descendants and Eston Hemings's. . . . The emerging consensus is that Thomas Jefferson and Sally Hemings became lovers when she was little more than a child and remained involved for nearly 40 years. The evidence suggests that the former president fathered several, if not all, of Sally's children.

Three of the Hemings children slipped off into whiteness, leaving the family and their black identities behind. Beverly and Harriet Hemings seem to have made a clean getaway, leaving little evidence that would have allowed people to track them down. But the Hemings records and oral histories show that Eston's journey into whiteness was painful. Freed in Thomas Jefferson's will in 1827, Eston and his brother Madison lived for a time in the mixed-race community of Charlottesville, Va., but were forced to abandon the state by a vicious campaign aimed at purging Virginia of free people of color. The two brothers moved to Ohio, where Madison lived as black for the remainder of his days.

Driven perhaps by the "black codes" that forbade him from educating his children or testifying in court, Eston moved with his wife and three teenaged children to Wisconsin. There he dropped the "black" Hemings name and became the "white" E. H. Jefferson. Turning white allowed Eston's children and grandchildren to fare well professionally. But they often exhibited signs of distress, including early deaths and a possible suicide that may have been related to the stress of passing for white. . . .

Julia learned about Sally Hemings during the 1970's, after the historian Fawn Brodie published a steamy biography of Jefferson, which included speculation about the love affair. The subterfuge and deceit of the cover-up have come pouring back to Julia in recent years, as the story became steadily more public and the white and the black Jeffersons began to discover each other and make common cause.

Meeting the black Jeffersons has had a profound effect on Julia. . . . She has examined her own prejudices and found the exercise "very painful." Everyone in the family was aware of her journey. But they were probably surprised when this 67-year-old grandmother announced her plan to declare herself "black" on the 2000 census. Julia says her children are fine with the decision. But another relative said it was a bad idea to pass blackness down through the generations and said that Eston had sacrificed a lot for the advantages Julia was "throwing out the window."

Julia responded that "these are different times." When people ask her why a middle-class woman who has lived all of her life as white would check "black" on the census, Julia sometimes gives them the smart-alecky answer "Because I can." Then she tells them the real reasons. She wants the government to support affirmative action and believes that goal will be easier to achieve if more people are counted as black. Most important, she says, "I want to show people that I am not afraid to be black."

SOURCE: Brent Staples, "A Hemings Family Turns from Black, to White, to Black," *New York Times*, December 17, 2001, late edition—final, section A, p. 20, column 1.

The classification of human beings into races is arbitrary. Racial classification varies among societies, and it varies through time in the same society, as we've just seen in this discussion of American census categories. Human biological diversity is real, but discrete (separate and clearly demarcated) human races don't exist. Historically, scientists have approached the study of human biological variation from two main directions: (1) racial classification, an approach that has been rejected, and (2) the current explanatory approach, which focuses on understanding specific differences. I'll review each approach briefly, first considering the problems with racial classification and then providing an example of the explanatory approach to human biological diversity. Biological differences are real, important, and apparent to us all. Modern scientists seek to explain this diversity, rather than trying to pigeonhole humanity into discrete categories called races.

Race: A Discredited Concept in Biology

In theory, a biological race would be a geographically isolated subdivision of a species. Such a *subspecies* would be capable of interbreeding with other subspecies of the same species, but it would not actually do so because of its geographic isolation. Subspecies that remain separate and reproductively isolated long enough eventually can develop into different species. Some biologists also use "race" to refer to "breeds," as of dogs or roses. Thus, a pit bull and a chihuahua would be different races of dogs. Such domesticated "races" have been carefully bred by humans for generations. However, human populations have not been isolated enough from one another to develop into discrete races. Nor have

The photos in this chapter illustrate only a small part of the range of human biological diversity. Shown here is a Bai minority woman, from Shapin, in China's Yunnan province.

humans experienced controlled breeding like that which has created the various kinds of dogs and roses. Humans vary biologically, for example, in their genetic attributes, but there are no sharp breaks between human populations of the sort we might associate with discrete subspecies or races. We can observe gradual, rather than abrupt, shifts in gene frequencies between neighboring human populations. Such gradual shifts are called **clines**. We do not, however, find the sharp shifts in genes and other biological features we would associate with discrete races.

Racial classification has fallen out of favor in biology for several reasons. The main reason is that scientists have trouble grouping people into distinct racial units. A race is supposed to reflect shared *genetic* material (inherited from a common ancestor), but early scholars used *phenotypical* traits (usually skin color) for racial classification. **Phenotype** refers to an organism's evident traits, its "manifest biology"—anatomy and physiology. There are thousands of evident (detectable) physical traits. They range from skin color, hair form, and eye color (which are visible) to blood type, color blindness, and enzyme production (which become evident through testing).

There are several problems with a phenotypical approach to race. First, which traits should be primary in assigning people to different races? Should races be defined by height, weight, body shape, facial features, teeth, skull form, or skin color? Like their fellow citizens, early European and American scientists gave priority to skin color. The phenotypic features that were most apparent to those early scientists, for example, skin color, were also the very characteristics that had been assigned arbitrary cultural value for purposes of discrimination. Genetic variations (e.g., differences in blood types) that were not directly observable were not used in early racial classification.

Many school books and encyclopedias still proclaim the existence of three great races: the white, the black, and the yellow. This simplistic classification was compatible with the political use of race during the colonial period of the late 19th and early 20th centuries. The tripartite scheme kept white Europeans neatly separate from their African, Asian, and Native American subjects. (See "Interesting Issues" for the "American Anthropological Association [AAA] Statement on 'Race.'") Colonial empires began to break up, and scientists began to question established racial categories, after World War II.

RACES ARE NOT BIOLOGICALLY DISTINCT

History and politics aside, one obvious problem with "color-based" racial labels is that the terms don't accurately describe skin color. "White" people are more pink, beige, or tan than white. "Black" people are various shades of brown, and "yellow" people are tan or beige. But these terms have also been dignified by more scientific-*sounding* synonyms: Caucasoid, Negroid, and Mongoloid.

Another problem with the tripartite scheme is that many populations don't neatly fit into any one of the three "great races." For example, where would one put the Polynesians? *Polynesia* is a triangle of South Pacific islands formed by Hawaii to the north, Easter Island to the east, and New Zealand to the southwest. Does the "bronze" skin color of Polynesians connect them to the Caucasoids or to the Mongoloids? Some scientists, recognizing this problem, enlarged the original tripartite scheme to include the Polynesian "race." Native Americans presented a similar problem.

A Native American:
a Chiquitanos Indian woman
from Bolivia.

Were they red or yellow? Some scientists added a fifth race—the "red," or Amerindian—to the major racial groups.

Many people in southern India have dark skins, but scientists have been reluctant to classify them with "black" Africans because of their "Caucasoid" facial features and hair form. Some, therefore, have created a separate race for these people. What about the Australian aborigines, hunters and gatherers native to what has been, throughout human history, the most isolated continent? By skin color, one might place some Native Australians in the same race as tropical Africans. However, similarities to Europeans in hair color (light or reddish) and facial features have led some scientists to classify them as Caucasoids. But there is no evidence that Australians are closer genetically or historically to either of these groups than they are to Asians. Recognizing this problem, scientists often regard Native Australians as a separate race.

Finally, consider the San ("Bushmen") of the Kalahari Desert in southern Africa. Scientists have perceived their skin color as varying from brown to yellow. Some who regard San skin as "yellow" have placed them in the same category as Asians. In theory, people of the same race share more recent common ancestry with each other than they do with any others. But there is no evidence for recent common ancestry between San and Asians. Somewhat more reasonably, some scholars assign the San to the Capoid race (from the Cape of Good Hope), which is seen as being different from other groups inhabiting tropical Africa.

Similar problems arise when any single trait is used as a basis for racial classification. An attempt to use facial features, height, weight, or any other phenotypical trait is fraught with difficulties. For example, consider the *Nilotes*, natives of the upper Nile region of Uganda and Sudan. Nilotes tend to be tall and to have long, narrow noses. Certain Scandinavians are also tall, with similar noses. Given the distance between their homelands, to classify them as members of the same race makes little sense. There is no reason to assume that Nilotes and Scandinavians are more closely related to each other than either is to shorter and nearer populations with different kinds of noses.

Would it be better to base racial classifications on a combination of physical traits? This would avoid some of the problems mentioned above, but others would arise. First, skin color, stature, skull form, and facial features (nose form, eye shape, lip thickness) don't go together as a unit. For example, people with dark skin may be tall or short and have hair ranging from straight to very curly. Dark-haired populations may have light or dark skin, along with various skull forms, facial features, and body sizes and shapes. The number of

A Native Australian.

Interesting *Issues*

American Anthropological Association (AAA) Statement on "Race"

As a result of public confusion about the meaning of "race," claims as to major biological differences among "races" continue to be advanced. Stemming from past AAA actions designed to address public misconceptions on race and intelligence, the need was apparent for a clear AAA statement on the biology and politics of race that would be educational and informational.

The following statement was adopted by the Executive Board of the American Anthropological Association in May 1998, based on a draft prepared by a committee of representative anthropologists. The Association believes that this statement represents the thinking and scholarly positions of most anthropologists.

In the United States both scholars and the general public have been conditioned to viewing human races as natural and separate divisions within the human species based on visible physical differences. With the vast expansion of scientific knowledge in this century, however, it has become clear that human populations are not unambiguous, clearly demarcated, biologically distinct groups. Evidence from the analysis of genetics (e.g., DNA) indicates that most physical variation, about 94%, lies within so-called racial groups. Conventional geographic "racial" groupings differ from one another only in about 6% of their genes. This means that there is greater variation within "racial" groups than between them. In neighboring populations there is much overlapping of genes and their phenotypic (physical) expres-

sions. Throughout history whenever different groups have come into contact, they have interbred. The continued sharing of genetic materials has maintained all of humankind as a single species.

Physical variations in any given trait tend to occur gradually rather than abruptly over geographic areas. And because physical traits are inherited independently of one another, knowing the range of one trait does not predict the presence of others. For example, skin color varies largely from light in the temperate areas in the north to dark in the tropical areas in the south; its intensity is not related to nose shape or hair texture. Dark skin may be associated with frizzy or kinky hair or curly or wavy or straight hair, all of which are found among different indigenous peoples in tropical regions. These facts render any attempt to establish lines of division among biological populations both arbitrary and subjective.

Historical research has shown that the idea of "race" has always carried more meanings than mere physical differences; indeed, physical variations in the human species have no meaning except the social ones that humans put on them. Today scholars in many fields argue that "race" as it is understood in the United States of America was a social mechanism invented during the 18th century to refer to those populations brought together in colonial America: the English and other European settlers, the conquered Indian peoples, and those peoples of Africa brought in to provide slave labor.

From its inception, this modern concept of "race" was modeled after an ancient theorem of the Great Chain of Being, which posited natural categories on a hierarchy established by God or nature. Thus "race" was a mode of classification linked specifically to peoples in the colonial situation. It subsumed a growing ideology of inequality devised to rationalize European attitudes and treatment of the conquered and enslaved peoples. Proponents of slavery in particular during the 19th century used "race" to justify the retention of slavery. The ideology magnified the differences among Europeans, Africans, and Indians, established a rigid hierarchy of socially exclusive categories, underscored and bolstered unequal rank and status differences, and provided the rationalization that the inequality was natural or God-given. The different physical traits of African-Americans and Indians became markers or symbols of their status differences.

As they were constructing US society, leaders among European-Americans fabricated the cultural/behavioral characteristics associated with each "race," linking superior traits with Europeans and negative and inferior ones to blacks and Indians. Numerous arbitrary and fictitious beliefs about the different peoples were institutionalized and deeply embedded in American thought . . .

Ultimately "race" as an ideology about human differences was subsequently spread to other areas of the world. It became a strategy for dividing, ranking, and controlling colonized people used by colonial

Roma, or Gypsies, such as these women at the central market in Athens, Greece, have faced discrimination in many nations. During World War II, the Nazis led by Adolph Hitler murdered 11 million Jews, Gypsies, Africans, homosexuals, and others.

powers everywhere. But it was not limited to the colonial situation. In the latter part of the 19th century it was employed by Europeans to rank one another and to justify social, economic, and political inequalities among their peoples. During World War II, the Nazis under Adolf Hitler enjoined the expanded ideology of "race" and "racial" differences and took them to a logical end: the extermination of 11 million people of "inferior races" (e.g., Jews, Gypsies, Africans, homosexuals, and so forth) and other unspeakable brutalities of the Holocaust.

"Race" thus evolved as a world view, a body of prejudgments that distorts our ideas about human differences and group behavior. Racial beliefs constitute myths about the diversity in the human species and about the abilities and behavior of people homogenized into "racial" categories. The myths fused behavior and physical features together in the public mind, impeding our comprehension of both biological variations and cultural behavior, implying that both are genetically determined. Racial myths bear no relationship to the reality of human capabilities or behavior . . .

We now understand that human cultural behavior is learned, conditioned into infants beginning at birth, and always subject to modification. No human is born with a built-in culture or language. Our temperaments, dispositions, and personalities, regardless of genetic propensities, are developed within sets of meanings and values that we call "culture" . . .

It is a basic tenet of anthropological knowledge that all normal human beings have the capacity to learn any cultural behavior. The American experience with immigrants from hundreds of different language and cultural backgrounds who have acquired some version of American culture traits and behavior is the clearest evidence of this fact. Moreover, people of all physical variations have learned different cultural behaviors and continue to do so as modern transportation moves millions of immigrants around the world.

How people have been accepted and treated within the context of a given society or culture has a direct impact on how they perform in that society. The "racial" world view was invented to assign some groups to perpetual low status, while others were permitted access to privilege, power, and wealth. The tragedy in the United States has been that the policies and practices stemming from this world view succeeded all too well in constructing unequal populations among Europeans, Native Americans, and peoples of African descent. Given what we know about the capacity of normal humans to achieve and function within any culture, we conclude that present-day inequalities between so-called "racial" groups are not consequences of their biological inheritance but products of historical and contemporary social, economic, educational, and political circumstances.

NOTE: For further information on human biological variations, see the statement prepared and issued by the American Association of Physical Anthropologists, 1996 (*American Journal of Physical Anthropology* 101, pp. 569–70).

A man from Afghanistan. How would he look without the turban?

EXPLAINING SKIN COLOR

Traditional racial classification assumed that biological characteristics were determined by heredity and that they were stable (immutable) over long periods of time. We now know that a biological similarity doesn't necessarily indicate recent common ancestry. Dark skin color, for example, can be shared by tropical Africans and Native Australians for reasons other than common ancestry. It is not possible to *define races* biologically. Still, scientists have made much progress in *explaining* variation in human skin color, along with many other expressions of human biological diversity. We shift now from classification to *explanation*, in which natural selection plays a key role.

As recognized by Charles Darwin and Alfred Russel Wallace, **natural selection** is the process by which nature selects the forms most fit to survive and reproduce in a given environment—such as the tropics. Over the years, the less fit organisms die out, and the favored types survive by producing more offspring. The role of natural selection in producing variation in skin color will illustrate the explanatory approach to human biological diversity. Comparable explanations have been provided for many other aspects of human biological variation.

combinations is very large, and the amount that heredity (versus environment) contributes to such phenotypical traits is often unclear.

There is a final objection to racial classification based on phenotype. The phenotypical characteristics on which races are based supposedly reflect genetic material that is shared and that has stayed the same for long time periods. But phenotypical similarities and differences don't necessarily have a genetic basis. Because of changes in the environment that affect individuals during growth and development, the range of phenotypes characteristic of a population may change without any genetic change. There are several examples. In the early 20th century, the anthropologist Franz Boas (1940/1966) described changes in skull form (e.g., toward rounder heads) among the children of Europeans who had migrated to North America. The reason for this was not a change in genes, for the European immigrants tended to marry among themselves. Also, some of their children had been born in Europe and merely raised in the United States. Something in the environment, probably in the diet, was producing this change. We know now that changes in average height and weight produced by dietary differences in a few generations are common and may have nothing to do with race or genetics.

Before the 16th century, almost all the very dark-skinned populations of the world lived in the tropics, as does this Samburu woman from Kenya.

Skin color is a complex biological trait. That means it is influenced by several genes. Just how many isn't known. **Melanin**, the primary determinant of human skin color, is a chemical substance manufactured in the epidermis, or outer skin layer. The melanin cells of darker-skinned people produce more and larger granules of melanin than do those of lighter-skinned people. By screening out ultraviolet radiation from the sun, melanin offers protection against a variety of maladies, including sunburn and skin cancer.

Interpret the World
Atlas Map 9

Prior to the 16th century, most of the world's very dark-skinned peoples lived in the **tropics**, a belt extending about 23 degrees north and south of the equator, between the Tropic of Cancer and the Tropic of Capricorn. Look at Map 9, "Human Variations: Skin Color," in your atlas. Using a skin-color index (Biasutti's index), Map 9 shows the relationship between human skin color (melanin production) and ultraviolet radiation from the sun. Note that the association between dark skin color and a tropical habitat existed throughout the Old World, where humans and their ancestors have lived for millions of years. The darkest populations of Africa evolved not in shady equatorial forests but in sunny open grassland, or savanna, country.

Outside the tropics, skin color tends to be lighter. Moving north in Africa, for example, there is a gradual transition from dark brown to medium brown. Average skin color continues to lighten as one moves through the Middle East, into southern Europe, through central Europe, and to the north. South of the tropics skin color is also lighter. In the Americas, by contrast, tropical populations do not have very dark skin. This is because the settlement of the New World, by light-skinned Asian ancestors of Native Americans, was relatively recent, probably dating back no more than 20,000 years.

How, aside from migrations, can we explain the geographic distribution of skin color? Natural selection provides an answer. In the tropics, there is intense ultraviolet radiation from the sun. Unprotected humans there face the threat of severe sunburn, which can increase susceptibility to disease. This confers a selective *dis*advantage (i.e., less success in surviving and reproducing) on lighter-skinned people in the tropics (unless they stay indoors or use cultural products, like umbrellas or lotions, to screen sunlight). Sunburn also impairs the body's ability to sweat. This is a second reason why light skin color, given tropical heat, can diminish the human ability to live and work in equatorial climates. A third disadvantage of having light skin color in the tropics is that exposure to ultraviolet radiation can cause skin cancer (Blum 1961).

A fourth factor affecting the geographic distribution of skin color is vitamin D production by the body. W. F. Loomis (1967) focused on the role of ultraviolet radiation in stimulating the manufacture of vitamin D by the human body. The unclothed human body can produce its own vitamin D when exposed to sufficient sunlight. But in a cloudy environment that is also so cold that people have to dress themselves much of the year (such as northern Europe, where very light skin color evolved), clothing interferes with the body's manufacture of vitamin D. The ensuing shortage of vitamin D diminishes the absorption of calcium in the intestines. A nutritional disease known as **rickets**, which softens and deforms the bones, may

Very light skin color, illustrated in this photo of a blond, blue-eyed North Sea German fisherman, maximizes absorption of ultraviolet radiation by those few parts of the body exposed to direct sunlight during northern winters. This helps prevent rickets.

Student: Heather Norton
Supervising Professors: Jonathan Friedlaender, Temple University; Andy Merriwether, University of Michigan; and Mark Shriver, Pennsylvania State University
School: Pennsylvania State University
Year in School:/Major: Graduated in spring 2000 with a BA in anthropology
Future Plans: Field work in Melanesia (the Solomon Islands) tentatively in spring 2001.
Project Title: Skin Pigmentation in Papua New Guinea.

What aspects of human biological variation are addressed in this study? Are they genotypic or phenotypic?

In summer 2000, following my senior year at Penn State, I spent five weeks in Papua New Guinea studying variation in skin pigmentation. I was part of a larger research effort led by Dr. Jonathan Friedlaender and Dr. Andy Merriwether. The goal was to examine variation in mitochondrial and Y-chromosome DNA sequences in an attempt to identify patterns of migration to the islands of Melanesia. Skin pigmentation is a phenotypic trait that shows extensive variation around the world.

Skin color is primarily determined by the pigment melanin, although others, such as hemoglobin, may also contribute. One way to measure skin pigmentation is to use reflectometry, the controlled illumination of an object and the precise measurement of the light that is reflected from it. The narrow-band spectrophotometer that I used estimates the concentration of hemoglobin and melanin by taking reflectance readings. The resulting measurements are known as the melanin index (M), and the erythema index (E). The more darkly pigmented an individual, the greater their M-index measurement. I took

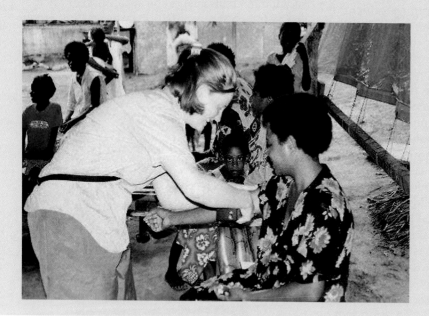

develop. In women, deformation of the pelvic bones from rickets can interfere with childbirth. During northern winters, light skin color maximizes the absorption of ultraviolet radiation and the manufacture of vitamin D by the few parts of the body that are exposed to direct sunlight. There has been selection against dark skin color in northern areas because melanin screens out ultraviolet radiation.

Considering vitamin D production, light skin is an advantage in the cloudy north, but a disadvantage in the sunny tropics. Loomis suggested that in the tropics, dark skin color protects the body against an *overproduction* of vitamin D by

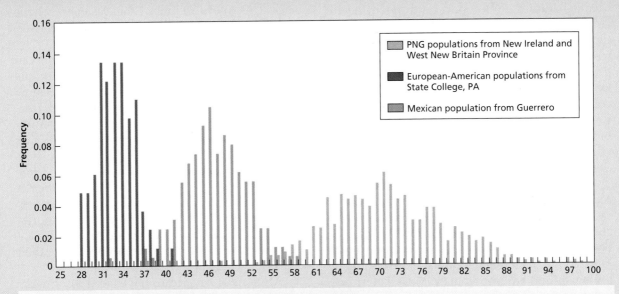

Skin Pigmentation among Various Human Groups.

M = Index of PNG, European-American, and Mexican Populations

multiple measurements on both of the inner arms of each subject, as well as measurements of their hair color.

I chose to study pigmentation in Melanesia because of its variability among individuals there. In two weeks I was able to obtain samples from Bougainvillians, whose skin contains large amounts of melanin, as well as from lighter-skinned individuals from the Sepik region of Papua New Guinea. This area of the world is also interesting from a pigmentation perspective in terms of hair color. Individuals from Papua New Guinea

and other Melanesian islands, as well as Australian aborigines, display a trait known as blondism. This refers to very blond hair, similar to someone of European descent, with darkly pigmented skin. This histogram shows the wide range of pigmentation found on the two islands—individuals at the upper end of the scale are from Bougainville, while those at the lower end are from areas such as the Sepik.

I am currently doing statistical analyses to see if differences in skin color are associated in any way with language. Although close to 1,000 languages are spoken in Papua New

Guinea, they belong to two main groups, Austronesian and non-Austronesian. The non-Austronesian speakers appear to have migrated to New Guinea first, followed by a second wave of Austronesian-speaking groups. Current mitochondrial DNA evidence supports this theory. If significant skin color differences between the two groups can be shown, it may help lend support to that argument. I hope to return to Melanesia in the spring of 2001 to continue my study of pigmentation variation, this time in the neighboring Solomon Islands.

screening out ultraviolet radiation. Too much vitamin D can lead to a potentially fatal condition (**hypervitaminosis D**), in which calcium deposits build up in the body's soft tissues. The kidneys may fail. Gallstones, joint problems, and circulation problems are other symptoms of hypervitaminosis D.

This discussion of skin color shows that common ancestry, the presumed basis of race, is not the only reason for biological similarities. We see that natural selection has made a major contribution to our understanding of human biological differences and similarities.

Social Race

Medical studies often report on different health risks and conditions of blacks and whites. Next time you see such a study, think about how the results might have differed if people had been grouped, say, as light-skinned versus dark-skinned, or assessed along a continuum of skin color, rather than simply classified as black or white. Do you imagine that blue-eyed people and brown-eyed people are prone to different health risks and medical conditions? Do they belong to different races?

We have seen that it is not possible to define races biologically. Only cultural constructions of race are possible—even though the average citizen conceptualizes "race" in biological terms. The belief that races exist and are important is much more common among the public than it is among biologists and anthropologists. Most Americans, for example, believe that their population includes biologically based "races" to which various labels have been applied. These labels include "white," "black," "yellow," "red," "Caucasoid," "Negroid," "Mongoloid," "Amerindian," "Asian-American," "African-American," "Euro-American," and "Native American."

The races we hear about every day are culturally constructed categories that may have little to do with actual biological differences. In Charles Wagley's terms (Wagley 1959/1968), they are **social races** (groups assumed to have a biological basis but actually defined in a culturally arbitrary, rather than a scientific manner). Many Americans mistakenly assume that "whites" and "blacks," for example, are biologically distinct and that these terms stand for discrete races. But these labels, like racial terms used in other societies, really designate culturally defined and perceived, rather than biologically based, groups.

HYPODESCENT: RACE IN THE UNITED STATES

How is race culturally constructed in the United States? In American culture, one acquires his or her racial identity at birth, but race isn't based on biology or on simple ancestry. Take the case of the child of a "racially mixed" marriage involving one black and one white parent. We know that 50 per-

cent of the child's genes come from one parent and 50 percent from the other. Still, American culture overlooks heredity and classifies this child as black. This rule is arbitrary. From *genotype* (genetic composition), it would be just as logical to classify the child as white.

American rules for assigning racial status can be even more arbitrary. In some states, anyone known to have any black ancestor, no matter how remote, is classified as a member of the black race. This is a rule of **descent** (it assigns social identity on the basis of ancestry), but of a sort that is rare outside the contemporary United States. It is called **hypodescent** (Harris and Kottak 1963) (hypo means "lower") because it automatically places the children of a union or mating between members of different groups in the minority group. Hypodescent helps divide American society into groups that have been unequal in their access to wealth, power, and prestige.

Millions of Americans have faced discrimination because one or more of their ancestors happened to belong to a minority group. The following case from Louisiana is an excellent illustration of the arbitrariness of the hypodescent rule. It also illustrates the role that governments (federal, or state in this case) play in legalizing, inventing, or eradicating race and ethnicity (Williams 1989). Susie Guillory Phipps, a light-skinned woman with "Caucasian" features and straight black hair, discovered as an adult that she was "black." When Phipps ordered a copy of her birth certificate, she found her race listed as "colored." Since she had been "brought up white and married white twice," Phipps challenged a 1970 Louisiana law declaring anyone with at least one-thirty-second "Negro blood" to be legally black. In other words, having 1 "Negro" great-great-great-grandparent out of 32 is sufficient to make one black. Although the state's lawyer admitted that Phipps "looks like a white person," the state of Louisiana insisted that her racial classification was proper (Yetman 1991, pp. 3–4).

Cases like Phipps's are rare, because "racial" and ethnic identities are usually ascribed at birth and usually don't change. The rule of hypodescent affects blacks, Asians, Native Americans, and Hispanics differently. It's easier to negotiate Indian or Hispanic identity than black identity. The ascription rule isn't as definite, and the assumption of a biological basis isn't as strong.

To be considered "Native American," one ancestor out of eight (great-grandparents) or four (grandparents) may suffice. This depends on whether the assignment is by federal or state law or by an Indian tribal council. The child of a Hispanic may (or may not, depending on context) claim Hispanic identity. Many Americans with an Indian or Latino grandparent consider themselves "white" and lay no claim to minority-group status.

The controversy that erupted in 1990–91 over the casting of the Broadway production of the musical *Miss Saigon* also illustrates the cultural construction of race in the United States. The musical had opened a few years earlier in London, where the Filipina actress Lea Salonga had played Kim, a young Vietnamese woman. Another major role is that of the Eurasian (half-French, half-Vietnamese) pimp known as the "Engineer." For the New York production, the producer wanted Salonga to play Kim and the English actor Jonathan Pryce, who had originated the part in London, to play the Engineer. Actors' Equity must approve the casting of foreign stars in New York productions. The union initially ruled that Pryce, a "Caucasian," could not play a Eurasian. The part had to go to an "Asian" instead. (Actors' Equity eventually reconsidered its position and allowed Pryce to open in the musical.)

In this case the American hypodescent rule was being extended from the offspring of black–white unions to "Eurasians" (in this case French–Vietnamese). Again, the cultural construction of race is that children get their identity from the minority parent—Asian rather than European. This notion also assumes that all Asians (e.g., Vietnamese, Chinese, and Filipinos) are equivalent. Thus it's okay for someone from the Philippines to play a Vietnamese (or even a Eurasian), but an Englishman can't play a half-French Eurasian.

The culturally arbitrary rule of hypodescent is behind the idea that an Asian is more appropriate to play a Eurasian than a "Caucasian" is. Hypodescent governs racial and ethnic ascription in the United States. This rule of descent channels discrimination against offspring of mixed unions, who are assigned minority status. But, as the case of *Miss Saigon* illustrates, a cultural rule that has been used against a group also can be used to promote the interests of that group. There has been a shortage of parts for Asian and Asian American actors. In this case, the hypodescent rule was used to stake a claim for Asians and Asian-Americans to have prime access to "Eurasian" as well as "Asian" parts.

RACE IN THE CENSUS

In this 1997 photo, Tiger Woods tees off at Ponte Vedra Beach, Florida. The number of interracial marriages and children is increasing, which has implications for the traditional American system of racial classification.

For more about race and the census, see the Virtual Exploration

mhhe ●com /kottak

The U.S. Census Bureau has gathered data by race since 1790. Initially this was done because the Constitution specified that a slave counted as three-fifths of a white person and because Indians were not taxed. The racial categories specified in the U.S. census include White, Black or Negro, Indian (Native American), Eskimo, Aleut or Pacific Islander, and Other. A separate question asks about Spanish-Hispanic heritage. Check out Figure 9.1 for the racial categories in the 2000 census. What changes do you notice?

An attempt by social scientists and interested citizens to add a "multiracial" census category has

5. Is this person Spanish/Hispanic/Latino? *Mark* $\boxed{X}$ *the "No" box if not Spanish/Hispanic/Latino.*

- ☐ **No,** not Spanish/Hispanic/Latino
- ☐ Yes, Mexican, Mexican Am., Chicano
- ☐ Yes, other Spanish/Hispanic/Latino — *Print group.* ↗
- ☐ Yes, Puerto Rican
- ☐ Yes, Cuban

[ ][ ][ ][ ][ ][ ][ ][ ][ ][ ][ ][ ][ ][ ][ ][ ][ ]

5. What is this person's race? *Mark* $\boxed{X}$ *one or more races to indicate what this person considers himself/herself to be.*

- ☐ White
- ☐ Black, African Am., or Negro
- ☐ American Indian or Alaska Native — *Print name of enrolled or principal tribe.* ↗

[ ][ ][ ][ ][ ][ ][ ][ ][ ][ ][ ][ ][ ][ ][ ][ ][ ]

- ☐ Asian Indian
- ☐ Chinese
- ☐ Filipino
- ☐ Other Asian — *Print race.* ↗
- ☐ Japanese
- ☐ Korean
- ☐ Vietnamese
- ☐ Native Hawaiian
- ☐ Guamanian or Chamorro
- ☐ Samoan
- ☐ Other Pacific Islander — *Print race.* ↗

[ ][ ][ ][ ][ ][ ][ ][ ][ ][ ][ ][ ][ ][ ][ ][ ][ ]

- ☐ Some other race — *Print race.* ↗

[ ][ ][ ][ ][ ][ ][ ][ ][ ][ ][ ][ ][ ][ ][ ][ ][ ]

Figure 9.1 **Reproduction of Questions on Race and Hispanic Origin from Census 2000.**
SOURCE: U.S. Census Bureau, Census 2000 questionnaire.

been opposed by the National Association for the Advancement of Colored People (NAACP) and the National Council of La Raza (a Hispanic advocacy group). As the *Miss Saigon* incident demonstrates, racial classification is a political issue. It involves access to resources, including parts, jobs, voting districts, and federal funding of programs aimed at minorities. The hypodescent rule results in all the population growth being attributed to the minority category. Minorities fear their political clout will decline if their numbers go down.

But things are changing. Choice of "some other race" in the U.S. Census more than doubled from 1980 (6.8 million) to 2000 (over 15 million)—suggesting imprecision in and dissatisfaction with the existing categories (Mar 1997). In the year 2000, 274.6 million Americans (out of 281.4 million censused) reported they belonged to just one race, as shown in Table 9.1.

Hispanics totaled 35.3 million, or about 13 percent, of the total U.S. population. Nearly 48 percent of Hispanics identified as White alone, and about 42 percent as "some other race" alone. In the 2000 census, 2.4 percent of Americans, or 6.8 million people, chose a first-ever option of identifying themselves as belonging to more than one race. About 6 percent of Hispanics reported two or more races, compared with less than 2 percent of non-Hispanics (http://www.census.gov/Press-Release/www/2001/cb01cn61.html).

The number of interracial marriages and children is increasing, with implications for the traditional system of American racial classification. "Interracial," "biracial," or "multiracial" children who grow up with both parents undoubtedly identify with particular qualities of either parent. It is troubling for many of them to have so important an identity as race dictated by the arbitrary rule of hypodescent. It may be especially discordant when racial identity doesn't parallel gender identity, for example, a boy with a white father and a black mother, or a girl with a white mother and a black father.

How does the Canadian census compare with the American census in its treatment of race? Currently, the most recent Canadian census data, gathered every five years, are for 1996. Rather than race, the Canadian census asks about "visible minorities." That country's Employment Equity Act defines such groups as "persons, other than Aboriginal peoples [a.k.a. First Nations in Canada, Native Americans in the United States], who are non-Caucasian in race or non-white in colour" (Statistics Canada 2001). The 1996 census was the first to gather systematic data on visible minorities—for the purpose of assessing employment equity. Similar to affirmative action in the United States, Canada's Employment Equity Act was a response to the political organization of diversity in that country. Table 9.2 shows that "Chinese" and "South Asian" are Canada's largest visible minorities. Note that Canada's total visible minority population of 11.2 percent contrasts with a figure of about 25 percent for the United States in the 2000 Census. In particular, Canada's Black 2 percent population contrasts with the American figure of 12.3 percent for African Americans, while Canada's Asian population is significantly higher than the U.S. figure of 3.6 percent on a percentage

Table 9.1 Americans Reporting They Belonged to Just One Race	
White	75.1%
Black or African-American	12.3%
American Indian and Alaska Native	0.9%
Asian	3.6%
Native Hawaiian and Other Pacific Islander	0.1%
Some other race	5.5%

SOURCE: http://www.census.gov/Press-Release/www/2001/cb01cn61.html.

Table 9.2 Visible Minority Population of Canada, 1996 Census

	Number	Percent
Total population	28,528,125	100.0
Total visible minority population	3,197,460	11.2
Chinese	860,150	3.0
South Asian	670,590	2.4
Black	573,860	2.0
Arab/West Asian	244,665	0.8
Filipino	234,195	0.8
Southeast Asian	172,765	0.6
Latin American	176,970	0.6
Japanese	68,135	0.2
Korean	64,835	0.2
Other visible minority	69,745	0.2
Multiple visible minority	61,575	0.2
Nonvisible minority	25,330,645	88.8

SOURCE: Statistics Canada 2001.

basis. Only a tiny fraction of the Canadian population (0.2 percent) claimed multiple visible minority affiliation, compared with 2.4 percent claiming "more than one race" in the United States in 2000.

NOT US: RACE IN JAPAN

See the Internet Exercises at your OLC

mhhe.com /kottak

American culture ignores considerable diversity in biology, language, and geographic origin as it socially constructs race within the United States. North Americans also overlook diversity by seeing Japan as a nation that is homogeneous in race, ethnicity, language, and culture—an image the Japanese themselves cultivate. Thus in 1986, former Prime Minister Nakasone created an international furor by contrasting his country's supposed homogeneity (responsible, he suggested, for Japan's success in international business) with the ethnically mixed United States. To describe Japanese society, Nakasone used *tan'itsu minzoku*, an expression connoting a single ethnic-racial group (Robertson 1992).

Japan is hardly the uniform entity Nakasone described. Some dialects of the Japanese language are mutually unintelligible. Scholars estimate that 10 percent of Japan's population are minorities of various sorts. These include aboriginal Ainu, annexed Okinawans, outcast *burakumin*, children of mixed marriages, and immigrant nationalities, especially Koreans, who number more than 700,000 (De Vos et al. 1983).

Americans tend to see Japanese and Koreans as alike, but the Japanese stress the difference between themselves and Koreans. To describe racial attitudes in Japan, Jennifer Robertson (1992) uses Kwame Anthony Appiah's (1990) term *intrinsic racism*—the belief that a (perceived) racial difference is a sufficient reason to value one person less than another.

In Japan, the valued group is majority ("pure") Japanese, who are believed to share "the same blood." Thus, the caption to a printed photo of a Japanese-American model reads: "She was born in Japan but raised in Hawaii. Her nationality is American but no foreign blood flows in her veins" (Robertson 1992, p. 5). Something like hypodescent also operates in Japan, but less precisely than in the United States, where mixed offspring automatically become members of the minority group. The children of mixed marriages between majority Japanese and others (including Euro-Americans) may not get the same "racial" label as the minority parent, but they are still stigmatized for their non-Japanese ancestry (De Vos and Wagatsuma 1966).

How is race culturally constructed in Japan? The (majority) Japanese define themselves by opposition to others, whether minority groups in their own nation or outsiders—anyone who is "not us." Aspects of *phenotype* (detectable physical traits, such as perceived body odor) are considered part of being *racially different by opposition*. Other races don't smell as "we" do. The Japanese stigmatize Koreans by saying they smell different (as Europeans also do). Japanese also stereotype their minorities with behavioral and psychological traits. Koreans are stereotyped as underachievers, crime-prone, and working class. They are placed in opposition to dominant Japanese, who are positively stereotyped as harmonious, hard-working, and middle class (Robertson 1992).

The "not us" should stay that way; assimilation is generally discouraged. Cultural mechanisms, especially residential segregation and taboos on "interracial" marriage, work to keep minorities "in their place." (Still, many marriages between minorities and majority Japanese do occur.) However, perhaps to give the appearance of homogeneity, people (e.g., Koreans) who become Japanese citizens are expected to take Japanese-sounding names (Robertson 1992; De Vos et al. 1983).

In its construction of race, Japanese culture regards certain ethnic groups as having a biological basis, when there is no evidence that they do. The best example is the *burakumin*, a stigmatized group of at least four million outcasts. They are sometimes compared to India's untouchables. The *burakumin* are physically and genetically indistinguishable from other Japanese. Many of them "pass" as (and marry) majority Japanese, but a deceptive marriage can end in divorce if *burakumin* identity is discovered (Aoki and Dardess 1981).

Burakumin are perceived as standing apart from the majority Japanese lineage. Through ancestry and descent (and thus, it is assumed, "blood," or genetics), *burakumin* are "not us." Majority Japanese try to keep their lineage pure by discouraging mixing. The *burakumin* are residentially segregated in neighborhoods (rural or urban) called *buraku*, from which the racial label is derived. Compared with majority Japanese, the *burakumin* are less likely to attend high school and college. When *burakumin* attend the same schools as majority Japanese, they face discrimination. Majority children and teachers may refuse to eat with them because *burakumin* are considered unclean.

In applying for university admission or a job, and in dealing with the government, Japanese must list their address, which becomes part of a household or family registry. This list makes residence in a *buraku*, and likely *burakumin* social status, evident. Schools and companies use this information to discriminate. (The best way to pass is to move so often that the *buraku* address eventually disappears from the registry.) Majority Japanese also limit "race" mixture by hiring marriage mediators to check out the family histories of prospective spouses. They are especially careful to check for *burakumin* ancestry (De Vos et al. 1983).

The origin of the *burakumin* lies in a historic system of stratification (from the Tokugawa period: 1603–1868). The top four ranked categories were warrior-administrators (*samurai*), farmers, artisans, and merchants. The ancestors of the *burakumin* were below this hierarchy. An outcast group, they did unclean jobs, like animal slaughter and disposal of the dead. *Burakumin* still do related jobs, including work with animal products, like leather. The *burakumin* are more likely than majority Japanese to do manual labor (including farm work) and to belong to the national lower class. *Burakumin* and other Japanese minorities are also more likely to have careers in crime, prostitution, entertainment, and sports (De Vos et al. 1983).

Like blacks in the United States, the *burakumin* are class-stratified. Because certain jobs are reserved for the *burakumin*, people who are successful in those occupations (e.g., shoe factory owners) can be wealthy. *Burakumin* also have found jobs as government bureaucrats. Financially successful *burakumin* can temporarily escape their stigmatized status by travel, including foreign travel.

Today, most discrimination against the *burakumin* is *de facto* rather than *de jure*. It is strikingly like the discrimination that blacks have faced in the United States. The *burakumin* often live in villages and neighborhoods with poor housing and sanitation. They have limited access to education, jobs, amenities, and health facilities. In response to *burakumin* political mobilization, Japan has dismantled the legal structure of discrimination against *burakumin* and has worked to improve conditions in the *buraku*. Still, Japan has not instituted American-style affirmative action programs for education and jobs. Discrimination against nonmajority Japanese is still the rule in companies. Some employers say that hiring *burakumin* would

Japan's stigmatized *burakumin* are physically and genetically indistinguishable from other Japanese. In response to *burakumin* political mobilization, Japan has dismantled the legal structure of discrimination against *burakumin*. This Sports Day for *burakumin* children is one kind of mobilization.

born in Japan and living there three successive years (Robertson 1992).

Like the *burakumin*, many Koreans (who by now include third and fourth generations) fit physically and linguistically into the Japanese population. Most Koreans speak Japanese as their primary language. Many of them pass as majority Japanese. Still, they tend to be segregated residentially. Often they live in the same neighborhoods as *burakumin*, with whom they sometimes intermarry. Koreans maintain strong kin ties and a sense of ethnic identity with other Koreans, especially in their neighborhoods. Most Japanese Koreans who qualify for citizenship choose not to take it because of Japan's policy of forced assimilation. Anyone who naturalizes is strongly encouraged to take a Japanese name. Many Koreans feel that to do so would cut them off from their kin and ethnic identity. Knowing they can never become majority Japanese, they choose not to become "not us" twice.

give their companies an unclean image and thus create a disadvantage in competing with other businesses (De Vos et al. 1983).

Burakumin are citizens of Japan. Most Japanese Koreans, who form one of the nation's largest minorities (about 750,000 people), are not. As resident aliens, Koreans in Japan face discrimination in education and jobs. They lack citizens' healthcare and social-service benefits. Government and company jobs don't usually go to non-Japanese.

Koreans started arriving in Japan, mainly as manual laborers, after Japan conquered Korea in 1910 and ruled it through 1945. During World War II, there were more than two million Koreans in Japan. They were recruited to replace Japanese farm workers who left the fields for the imperial army. Some Koreans were women (numbering from 70,000 to 200,000) forced to serve as prostitutes ("comfort women") for Japanese troops. By 1952, most Japanese Koreans had been repatriated to a divided Korea. Those who stayed in Japan were denied citizenship. They became "resident aliens," forced, like Japanese criminals, to carry an ID card, which resentful Koreans call a "dog tag." Unlike most nations, Japan doesn't grant automatic citizenship to people born in the country. One can become Japanese by having one parent

PHENOTYPE AND FLUIDITY: RACE IN BRAZIL

There are more flexible, less exclusionary ways of constructing social race than those used in the United States and Japan. Along with the rest of Latin America, Brazil has less exclusionary categories, which permit individuals to change their racial classification. Brazil shares a history of slavery with the United States, but it lacks the hypodescent rule. Nor does Brazil have racial aversion of the sort found in Japan. The history of Brazilian slavery dates back to the 16th century, when Africans were brought as slaves to work on sugar plantations in northeastern Brazil. Later, Brazilians used slave labor in mines and on coffee plantations. The contributions of Africans to Brazilian culture have been as great as they have been to North American culture. Today, especially in areas of Brazil where slaves were most numerous, African ancestry is evident.

The system that Brazilians use to classify biological differences contrasts with those used in the United States and Japan. First, Brazilians use many

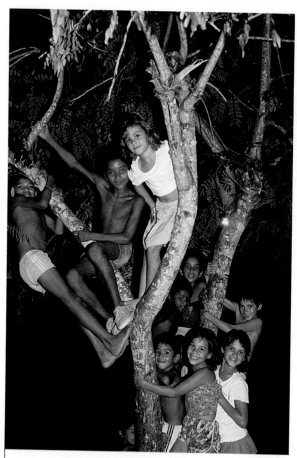

Families migrate to the Amazon from many parts of
Brazil. Notice the phenotypical diversity in this photo.
How might it be reflected in racial classification?

by hypodescent and doesn't usually change. In
Japan, race also is ascribed at birth, but it can
change when, say, a *burakumin* or a naturalized
Korean passes as a majority Japanese. In Brazil,
racial identity is less automatic and more flexible.
Brazilian racial classification pays attention to phenotype. A Brazilian's phenotype, and racial label,
may change due to environmental factors, such as
the tanning rays of the sun.

For historical reasons, darker-skinned Brazilians tend to be poorer than lighter-skinned Brazilians are. When Brazil abolished slavery in 1889,
the freed men and women received no land or
other reparations. They took what jobs were available. For example, the freed slaves who founded
the village of Arembepe, which I have been studying since 1962, turned to fishing. Many Brazilians
(including slave descendants) are poor because
they lack a family history of access to land or commercial wealth and because upward social mobility is difficult. Continuing today, especially in
cities, it is poor, dark-skinned Brazilians, on average, who face the most intense discrimination.

Given the correlation between poverty and
dark skin, one's class status affects one's racial
classification in Brazil. Thus, someone who has
light skin and is poor will be perceived and classified as darker than a comparably colored person
who is rich. The racial term applied to a wealthy
person with dark skin will tend to "lighten" his or
her skin color. This gives rise to the Brazilian
expression "money whitens." In the United States,
by contrast, race and class are correlated, but racial
classification isn't changed by class. Because of
hypodescent, racial identity in the United States is
fixed and lifelong, regardless of phenotype or economic status. One illustration of the absence of
hypodescent in Brazil is the fact that (unlike the
United States) full siblings there may belong to different races (if they are phenotypically different).

Arembepe has a mixed and physically diverse
population, reflecting generations of immigration
and intermarriage between its founders and outsiders. Some villagers have dark, others light, skin
color. Facial features, eye and hair color, and hair
type also vary. Although physically heterogeneous, until recently Arembepe was economically
homogeneous: local residents had not risen out of
the national lower class. Given such economic uniformity, wealth contrasts do not affect racial classification, which Arembepeiros base on the physical

more racial labels (over 500 have been reported
[Harris 1970]) than North Americans or Japanese
do. In northeastern Brazil, I found 40 different
racial terms in use in Arembepe, a village of only
750 people (Kottak 1999). Through their classification system, Brazilians recognize and attempt to
describe the physical variation that exists in their
population. The system used in the United States,
by recognizing only three or four races, blinds
North Americans to an equivalent range of evident
physical contrasts. Japanese races, remember, don't
even originate in physical contrasts. *Burakumin* are
physically indistinguishable from other Japanese
but are considered to be biologically different.

The system that Brazilians use to construct
social race has other special features. In the United
States, one's race is assigned automatically at birth

differences they perceive between individuals. As physical characteristics change (sunlight alters skin color, humidity affects hair form), so do racial terms. Furthermore, racial differences have been so insignificant in structuring community life that people often forget the terms they have applied to others. Sometimes they even forget the ones they've used for themselves. To reach this conclusion, I made it a habit to ask the same person on different days to tell me the races of others in the village (and my own). In the United States, I am always "white" or "Euro-American," but in Arembepe I got lots of terms besides *branco* ("white"). I could be *claro* ("light"), *louro* ("blond"), *sarará* ("light-skinned redhead"), *mulato claro* ("light mulatto"), or *mulato* ("mulatto"). The racial term used to describe me or anyone else varied from person to person, week to week, even day to day. My best local friend, a man with very dark skin color, changed the term he used for himself all the time—from *escuro* ("dark") to *preto* ("black") to *moreno escuro* ("dark brunet").

The North American and Japanese racial systems are creations of particular cultures. They are not scientific—or even accurate—descriptions of human biological differences. Brazilian racial classification is also a cultural construction. However, Brazilians have devised a way of describing human biological diversity that is more detailed, fluid, and flexible than the systems used in most cultures. Brazil lacks Japan's racial aversion. It also lacks a rule of descent like that which ascribes racial status in the United States (Degler 1970; Harris 1964).

The operation of the hypodescent rule helps us understand why the populations labeled "black" and "Indian" (Native American) are growing in the United States but shrinking in Brazil. North American culture places all "mixed" children in the minority category, which therefore gets all the resultant population increase. Brazil, by contrast, assigns the offspring of mixed marriages to intermediate categories, using a larger set of ethnic and racial labels. A Brazilian with a "white" (*branco*) parent and a "black" (*preto*) parent will almost never be called *branco* or *preto* but instead by some intermediate term (of which dozens are available). The United States lacks fully functional intermediate categories, but it is those categories that are swelling in Brazil. Brazil's assimilated Indians are called *cabôclos* (rather than *indíos*, or a specific tribal name, like *Kayapó* or Yanomami). With

hypodescent, by contrast, someone may have just one of four or eight Indian grandparents or great-grandparents and still "feel Indian," be so classified, and even have a tribal identity.

For centuries, the United States and Brazil each has had mixed populations, with ancestors from Native America, Europe, Africa, and Asia. Although these populations have mixed in both countries, Brazilian and North American cultures have constructed the results differently. The historic reasons for this contrast lie mainly in the different characteristics of the settlers of the two countries. The mainly English early settlers of the United States came as women, men, and families. Brazil's Portuguese colonizers, by contrast, were mainly men—merchants and adventurers. Many of these Portuguese men married Native American women and recognized their "racially mixed" children as their heirs. Like their North American counterparts, Brazilian plantation owners had sexual relations with their slaves. But the Brazilian landlords more often freed the children that resulted—for demographic and economic reasons. (Sometimes these were their only children.) Freed offspring of master and slave became plantation overseers and foremen and filled many intermediate positions in the emerging Brazilian economy. They were not classed with the slaves, but allowed to join a new intermediate category. No hypodescent rule ever developed in Brazil to ensure that whites and blacks remained separate (see Degler 1970; Harris 1964).

Stratification and "Intelligence"

See the Internet Exercises at your OLC

Over the centuries groups with power have used racial ideology to justify, explain, and preserve their privileged social positions. Dominant groups have declared minorities to be *innately*, that is, biologically, inferior. Racial ideas have been used to suggest that social inferiority and presumed shortcomings (in intelligence, ability, character, or attractiveness) are immutable and are passed across the generations. This ideology defends stratification as inevitable, enduring, and "natural"—based in biology rather than society. Thus, the Nazis argued for

mhhe.com/kottak

the superiority of the "Aryan race," and European colonialists asserted the "white man's burden." South Africa institutionalized *apartheid*. Again and again, to justify the exploitation of minorities and native peoples, those in control have proclaimed the innate inferiority of the oppressed. In the United States the supposed superiority of whites was once standard segregationist doctrine. Belief in the biologically based inferiority of Native Americans has been an argument for their slaughter, confinement, and neglect.

However, anthropologists know that most of the behavioral variation among human groups rests on culture rather than biology. The cultural similarities revealed through thousands of ethnographic studies leave no doubt that capacities for cultural evolution are equivalent in all human populations. There is also excellent evidence that within any stratified (class-based) society, differences in performance between economic, social, and ethnic groups reflect their different experiences and opportunities. (Stratified societies are those with marked differences in wealth, prestige, and power between social classes.)

Stratification, political domination, prejudice, and ignorance continue to exist. They propagate the mistaken belief that misfortune and poverty result from lack of ability. Occasionally, doctrines of innate superiority are even set forth by scientists, who, after all, tend to come from the favored stratum of society. One of the best-known examples is Jensenism, named for the educational psychologist Arthur Jensen (Jensen 1969; Herrnstein 1971), its leading proponent. Jensenism is a highly questionable interpretation of the observation that African Americans, on average, perform less well on intelligence tests than Euro-Americans and Asian Americans do. Jensenism asserts that blacks are hereditarily incapable of performing as well as whites do. Writing with Charles Murray, Richard Herrnstein made a similar argument in the 1994 book *The Bell Curve*, to which the following critique also applies (see also Jacoby and Glauberman, eds. 1995). It should be noted that Jensen, Herrnstein, and Murray have no special training or expertise in genetics or evolution.

Environmental explanations for test scores are much more convincing than are the genetic arguments of Jensen, Herrnstein, and Murray. An environmental explanation does not deny that some

people may be smarter than others. In any society, for many reasons, genetic and environmental, the talents of individuals vary. An environmental explanation does deny, however, that these differences can be generalized to whole populations. Even when talking about individual intelligence, however, we have to decide which of several abilities is an accurate measure of intelligence.

Psychologists have devised various kinds of tests to measure intelligence, but there are problems with all of them. Early intelligence tests required skill in manipulating words. Such tests do not measure learning ability accurately for several reasons. For example, individuals who have learned two languages as children—bilinguals—don't do as well, on average, on verbal intelligence tests as do those who have learned a single language. It would be absurd to suppose that children who master two languages have inferior intelligence. The explanation seems to be that because bilinguals have vocabularies, concepts, and verbal skills in both languages, their ability to manipulate either one suffers a bit. This would seem to be offset by the advantage of being fluent in two languages.

Understanding Ourselves   Are you bilingual? Probably not. Most Americans aren't— even many people raised in homes where two languages are spoken. Do you come from, or know someone who comes from, such a home? Is that person bilingual? What do you think of bilingual people? In public are you, or would you be, embarrassed to speak a language other than English? When you hear someone speaking a foreign language in public, what do you think?

One explanation for why bilinguals do less well on IQ tests than monolinguals do has been suggested in the text. Can you think of others? Do you think that North American culture discriminates against bilinguals—or, more generally, against people who speak foreign languages? Is American culture intolerant of, perhaps even phobic about, foreign languages? How can we learn about other cultures if we avoid learning their languages? Do American attitudes about foreign languages help us understand why American intelligence agencies did not anticipate the September 11, 2001, attacks against the World Trade Center and the Pentagon? More widespread and effective knowledge of Middle Eastern languages, such as Arabic, and of Central Asian languages, such as Persian (spoken in Iran) and Pashto (spoken in Afghanistan), would seem indicated as the United States claims interests in those world areas.

Tests reflect the experience of the people who devise them, who tend to be educated people in Europe and North America. It isn't surprising that middle- and upper-class children do best, because they are more likely to share the test makers' educational background, knowledge, and standards. Numerous studies have shown that performance on the Scholastic Achievement Test (SAT) can be improved by coaching and preparation. Parents who can afford hundreds of dollars for an SAT preparation course enhance their children's chances of getting high scores. Standardized college entrance exams are similar to IQ tests in that they have claimed to measure intellectual aptitude. They may do this, but they also measure type

and quality of high school education, linguistic and cultural background, and parental wealth. No test is free of bias based on class and culture.

Tests can only measure phenotypical intelligence, the product of a particular learning history, rather than genetically determined learning potential. IQ tests use middle-class experience as a standard for determining what should be known at a given chronological age. Furthermore, tests usually are administered by middle-class white people who give instructions in a dialect or language that may not be totally familiar to the child being tested. Test performance improves when the cultural, socioeconomic, and linguistic backgrounds of takers and examiners are similar (Watson 1972).

Links between social, economic, and educational environment and test performance show up in comparisons of American blacks and whites. At the beginning of World War I, intelligence tests were given to approximately one million American army recruits. Blacks from some northern states had higher average scores than did whites

At South Carolina's Clemson University in 1998, high school juniors take the SAT as part of a career enrichment program for minority students. How did you prepare for the SAT?

from some southern states. At that time northern blacks got a better public education than many southern whites did, and so their superior performance wasn't surprising. The fact that southern whites did better, on average, than southern blacks did also was expectable, given the unequal school systems then open to whites and blacks in the South.

Racists tried to dismiss the environmental explanation for the superior performance of northern blacks compared with southerners by suggesting selective migration, saying that smarter blacks had moved north. However, it was possible to test this hypothesis, which turned out to be false. If smarter blacks had moved north, their superior intelligence should have been evident in their school records while they were still living in the South. It was not. Furthermore, studies in New York, Washington, and Philadelphia showed that as length of residence in those cities increased, test scores also rose.

Studies of identical twins raised apart also illustrate the impact of environment on identical heredity. In a study of 19 pairs of twins, IQ scores varied directly with years in school. The average difference in IQ was only 1.5 points for the eight twin pairs with the same amount of schooling. It was 10 points for the 11 pairs with an average of five years' difference. One subject, with 14 years' more education than his twin, scored 24 points higher (Bronfenbrenner 1975).

These and similar studies provide overwhelming evidence that test performance measures background and education rather than genetically determined intelligence. For centuries, Europeans and their descendants have extended their political and economic control over much of the world. They colonized and occupied environments that they reached in their ships and conquered with their weapons. Most people in the most powerful contemporary nations—located in North America, Europe, and Asia—have light skin color. Some people in these currently powerful countries may incorrectly assert and believe that their position rests on innate biological superiority. Remember (as we saw in a previous section) that a prime minister of Japan has made such a claim.

We are living in and interpreting the world at a particular time. In the past there were far different associations between centers of power and human physical characteristics. When Europeans were barbarians, advanced civilizations thrived in the Middle East. When Europe was in the Dark Ages, there were civilizations in West Africa, on the East African coast, in Mexico, and in Asia. Before the Industrial Revolution, the ancestors of many white Europeans and North Americans were living more like precolonial Africans than like current members of the American middle class. Do you think preindustrial Europeans would excel on contemporary IQ tests?

SUMMARY

1. How do scientists approach the study of human biological diversity? Because of a range of problems involved in classifying humans into racial categories, contemporary biologists focus on specific differences and try to explain them. Biological similarities between groups may reflect—rather than common ancestry—similar but independent adaptation to similar natural selective forces.

2. Race is a cultural category, not a biological reality. "Races" derive from contrasts perceived in particular societies, rather than from scientific classifications based on common genes. In the United States, "racial" labels like "white" and "black" designate social races—categories defined by American culture. In American culture, one acquires his or her racial identity at birth. But American racial classification, gov-

erned by the rule of hypodescent, is based on neither phenotype nor genes. Children of mixed unions, no matter what their appearance, are classified with the minority-group parent.

3. Ten percent of Japan's people are minorities: Ainu, Okinawans, *burakumin*, children of mixed marriages, and immigrant nationalities, especially Koreans. Racial attitudes in Japan illustrate "intrinsic racism"—the belief that a perceived racial difference is a sufficient reason to value one person less than another. The valued group is majority ("pure") Japanese, who are believed to share "the same blood." Majority Japanese define themselves by opposition to others. These may be minority groups in Japan or outsiders—anyone who is "not us." Residential segregation and taboos on "interracial" marriage work

against minorities. Japanese culture regards certain ethnic groups as having a biological basis when there is no evidence that they do. The *burakumin* are physically and genetically indistinguishable from other Japanese, but they still face discrimination as a social race.

4. Such exclusionary racial systems are not inevitable. Although Brazil shares a history of slavery with the United States, it lacks the hypodescent rule. Full siblings who are phenotypically different can belong to different races. Brazilian racial identity is more of an achieved status. It can change during someone's lifetime, reflecting phenotypical changes. Given the correlation between poverty and dark skin, the class structure affects Brazilian racial classification. Someone with light skin who is poor will be classified as darker than a comparably colored person who is rich.

5. Some people assert genetic differences in the learning abilities of "races," classes, and ethnic groups. However, environmental variables (particularly educational, economic, and social background) provide better explanations for performance on intelligence tests by such groups. Intelligence tests reflect the life experiences of those who develop and administer them. All tests are to some extent culture-bound. Equalized environmental opportunities show up in test scores.

KEY TERMS

See the flash cards

**mhhe
com
/kottak**

cline   A gradual shift in gene frequencies between neighboring populations.

descent   Rule assigning social identity on the basis of some aspect of one's ancestry.

hypervitaminosis D   Condition caused by an excess of vitamin D; calcium deposits build up in the body's soft tissues, and the kidneys may fail; symptoms include gallstones and joint and circulation problems; may affect unprotected light-skinned individuals in the tropics.

hypodescent   Rule that automatically places the children of a union or mating between members of different socioeconomic groups in the less-privileged group.

melanin   Substance manufactured in specialized cells in the lower layers of the epidermis (outer skin layer); melanin cells in dark skin produce more melanin than do those in light skin.

natural selection   As formulated by Charles Darwin and Alfred Russel Wallace, the process by which nature selects the forms most fit to survive and reproduce in a given environment.

phenotype   An organism's evident traits, its "manifest biology"—anatomy and physiology.

rickets   Nutritional disease caused by a shortage of vitamin D; interferes with the absorption of calcium and causes softening and deformation of the bones.

social race   A group assumed to have a biological basis but actually perceived and defined in a social context, by a particular culture rather than by scientific criteria.

tropics   Geographic belt extending about 23 degrees north and south of the equator, between the Tropic of Cancer (north) and the Tropic of Capricorn (south).

For more self testing, see the self quizzes

**mhhe
com
/kottak**

CRITICAL THINKING QUESTIONS

1. If race is a discredited term in biology, what has replaced it?

2. What are the main problems with racial classification based on phenotype?

3. Besides those given in the text, can you think of other reasons why "race" is problematic?

4. What does racism mean if race has no biological basis?

5. What are three examples of ways in which the hypodescent rule affects American racial classification?

6. What are the main physical differences between majority Japanese, on the one hand, and *burakumin*, on the other?

7. What kind of racial classification system operates in the community where you grew up or now live? Does it differ from the racial classification system described for American culture in this chapter?

8. What is the difference between race and skin color in contemporary American culture? Are the social identities of Americans and discrimination against some Americans based on one or both of these attributes?

9. When medical studies find differences between blacks and whites, are those differences best explained by sociocultural or biological factors? Could such studies be more accurate if they abandoned the labels "black" and "white" in favor of other measures of biological variation, such as actual skin color or body fat?

10. If you had to devise an ideal system of racial categories, would it be more like the North American, the Japanese, or the Brazilian system? Why?

11. What kinds of environmental variables explain differential performance on intelligence tests by races, classes, and ethnic groups?

Atlas Questions

Look at Map 9, "Human Variations: Skin Color."

1. Where are the Native Americans with the darkest skin color located? What factors help explain this distribution?

2. In both western and eastern hemispheres, is the lightest skin color found in the north or the south? Outside Asia, where do you find skin color closest to northern Asian skin color? Is this surprising given what you have read about migrations and settlement history?

3. Where are skin colors darkest? How do you explain this distribution? Are there any areas that don't fit the explanations for skin color distribution given in the textbook?

SUGGESTED ADDITIONAL READINGS

Cohen, M.

1998   *Culture of Intolerance: Chauvinism, Class, and Racism.* New Haven, CT: Yale University Press. Various forms of intolerance, prejudice, and discrimination are examined.

Degler, C.

1970   *Neither Black nor White: Slavery and Race Relations in Brazil and the United States.* New York: Macmillan. The main contrasts between Brazilian and North American race relations and the historic, economic, and demographic reasons for them.

De Vos, G. A., and H. Wagatsuma

1966   *Japan's Invisible Race: Caste in Culture and Personality.* Berkeley: University of California Press. Considers many aspects of the *burakumin* (and other minorities) and their place in Japanese society and culture, including psychological factors.

Diamond, J. M.

1997   *Guns, Germs, and Steel: The Fates of Human Societies.* New York: W.W. Norton. An ecological approach to expansion and conquest in world history by a non-anthropologist.

Goldberg, D. T.

1997   *Racial Subjects: Writing on Race in America.* New York: Routledge. Survey of treatments of race in the United States.

2001   *The Racial State.* Malden, MA: Blackwell. Governments, racial policies, and racism.

Goldberg, D. T., ed.

1990   *Anatomy of Racism.* Minneapolis: University of Minnesota Press. Collection of articles on race and racism.

Harris, M.

1964   *Patterns of Race in the Americas.* New York: Walker. Reasons for different racial and ethnic relations in North and South America and the Caribbean.

Molnar, S.

2001   *Human Variation: Races, Types, and Ethnic Groups,* 5th ed. Upper Saddle River, NJ: Prentice-Hall. Links between biological and social diversity.

Montagu, A.

1981   *Statement on Race: An Annotated Elaboration and Exposition of the Four Statements on Race Issued by the United Nations Educational, Scientific, and Cultural Organization.* Westport, CT: Greenwood. United Nations positions on race analyzed.

Montagu, A., ed.

1997   *Man's Most Dangerous Myth: The Fallacy of Race,* 6th ed. Walnut Creek, CA: AltaMira. Revision of classic book.

1999   *Race and IQ,* expanded ed. New York: Oxford University Press. Revision of a classic volume of essays.

Shanklin, E.

1994   *Anthropology and Race.* Belmont, CA: Wadsworth. A concise introduction to the race concept from the perspective of anthropology.

Wade, P.

2002   *Race, Nature, and Culture: An Anthropological Perspective.* Sterling, VA: Pluto Press. A processual approach to human biology and race.

INTERNET EXERCISES

1. Go to the U.S. Census page entitled "Mapping Census 2000: The Geography of US Diversity," pp. 20–23 (**http://www.census.gov/population/cen2000/atlas/censr01-104.pdf**). Examine all four maps showing aspects of racial and ethnic diversity by county in the United States. Try to explain the historic processes that have produced, and are now producing, the patterns of diversity and density of specific groups.

   a. The first map shows the ethnic group with the highest percentage of population for all U.S. counties. What is the closest county to you with a high proportion of Native Americans? How about Hispanics?

   b. Examine Maps 1 and 2 for clusters of African Americans. Why are so many African Americans clustered in the southeastern part of the United States?

   c. Examine Map 2 for clusters of Hispanics. How do you explain high concentrations of Hispanics in the Pacific Northwest, in the Midwest, and on the East Coast?

   d. On Maps 1 and 2 determine where you find the highest concentrations of Asian Americans. Why are the concentrations of Asian Americans so different from those of other ethnic groups?

   e. Examine Map 3 to see which states were the most diverse in 2000. Examine Map 4 to see which states increased most in diversity between 1990 and 2000. Give a brief definition of the diversity index used in the map calculations.

2. Race and the Census: Read Gregory Rodriguez's article in *Salon* magazine entitled "Do the Multiracial Count?" (**http://www.salon.com/news/feature/2000/02/15/census/index.html**).

   a. What was the problem that some people had with the original census? How does this reflect American notions of race as described in this chapter?

   b. What was the compromise that the Clinton administration presented? What are its ramifications?

   c. In this case what role does the federal government play in our society's notions of race? Is the federal government merely responding to changing conceptions of race of the American people, or is it trying to shape the way the American public thinks about race?

   d. Based on this chapter, how do you think this kind of question on the census form would be handled in Brazil? In Japan?

See Chapter 9 at your McGraw-Hill Online Learning Center for additional review and interactive exercises.

10
THE FIRST FARMERS

Overview

Food production encompasses the domestication of plants and animals and the farming and herding economies that result. This new economy developed out of foraging, as people gradually added domesticates to the broad spectrum of resources used for subsistence. By 10,000 B.P. ancient Middle Easterners, the first farmers, were cultivating wheat and barley and influencing the reproduction of goats and sheep. It took a few thousand years, however, for them to become full-time food producers.

There were seven independent inventions of food production: in the Middle East, sub-Saharan Africa, northern and southern China, Mesoamerica, the south central Andes, and the eastern United States. They occurred at different times and were based on different sets of crops. In

Mesoamerica between 7000 and 4000 B.P., maize and other domesticates were gradually added to a broad-spectrum foraging economy. The first permanent farming communities arose in the lowlands and in a few frost-free areas of the highlands. In the Valley of Mexico, quick-growing maize eventually made year-round village life possible. This paved the way for the emergence of the state and city life at Teotihuacan (A.D. 100 to A.D. 700) and Tenochtitlan, the Aztec capital (1325 to 1520).

Food production and the social and political systems it supported brought advantages and disadvantages. The advantages included many discoveries and inventions. The disadvantages included harder work, poorer health, crime, war, social inequality, and environmental degradation.

Gene Study Traces Cattle Herding in Africa

NATIONAL GEOGRAPHIC NEWS BRIEF

by Ben Harder

April 11, 2002

Plant cultivation and animal domestication, which are basic to farming and herding, respectively, are the two key forms of food production. They arose together in the Middle East, home of the world's first farmers and herders, but they don't always go together. In Mesoamerica (Mexico, Guatemala, and Belize), for example, there was farming but no herding. And in sub-Saharan Africa, where cattle have tremendous economic, social, and symbolic value, some areas had herding without farming. This news brief describes recent research showing that the domestication of cattle in Africa was independent of the domestication of cattle in the Middle East and South Asia. Where in Africa were cattle originally domesticated? Were sheep and goats also domesticated in Africa, or were they brought in through trade and migration? The article also discusses a trend in which native African cattle are being displaced by larger cattle with external origins. What subfields of anthropology help us understand the origin and significance of herding in Africa?

African herders rely on cattle for food and other basic needs, and as beasts of burden. But how cattle domestication occurred in Africa has been obscured by long-ago migrations and trade.

Now, by studying the DNA of cattle in 23 countries, an international team of scientists is filling in the picture.

An extensive new study of genetic variation in African cattle sheds light on how the domestication of cattle unfolded differently in Africa than elsewhere in the world.

Evidence suggests that sheep and goats, first domesticated in the Near East, were imported into Africa through colonization and ocean-going trade. Scientists have long speculated that the domestication of cattle also occurred first in the Near East and that the practice of herding cattle was similarly imported.

But new evidence, reported in the April 12 [2002] issue of the journal *Science*, suggests that Africans independently domesticated cattle.

Belgian geneticist Olivier Hanotte, who headed the new study, said the research "reconciles the two

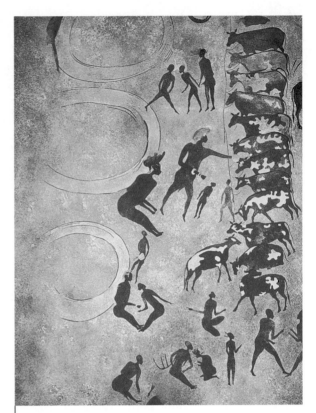

A close relationship between African societies and cattle, as depicted in this rock art from Algeria, is thousands of years old. Over the centuries, indigenous African cattle have interbred with cattle from outside.

schools of thought" about how cattle domestication occurred in Africa.

"There were Near Eastern influences" on African herds, he said, "but they came after local domestication." Since then, there has been considerable mixing of African and Asian breeds . . .

In many parts of Africa, people herded cattle long before agriculture was introduced from the Near East and south Asia. Some African groups that have herded cattle for centuries have never adopted agriculture at all, or have done so only recently. One example is the Masai of eastern Africa, who rarely slaughter cattle but instead mix the milk and blood of the animals to create a staple of their diet.

Intrigued by the uncommon pattern of cattle domestication in Africa, Hanotte moved to Kenya in 1995 in an effort to explain the development. He and other researchers in Europe began untangling layers of genetic information in cattle DNA to help answer major questions about the history of herding in Africa.

Their findings offer scientists and herders a virtual history book describing how cattle, crucial to so many Africans, came to be so genetically diverse. The research also underscores why preserving that variety is essential.

[For each animal], Hanotte and his colleagues analyzed more than a dozen segments of . . . DNA [from] cattle belonging to 50 different herds in 23 African nations . . .

The samples of cattle DNA . . . revealed a telling geographic pattern [of variation among] cattle from West Africa, Central Africa, and southern Africa. The greatest amount of genetic diversity was found among herds in Central Africa. Based on the data, Hanotte and his colleagues concluded that people living in Central Africa developed cattle domestication on their own, and that the techniques—or the herders themselves—gradually migrated toward the west and the south, spreading domestication across the continent.

In looking at the wide genetic variation among African cattle, the researchers [also] found evidence of interbreeding between cattle native to Africa and an imported breed.

Most modern African herds represent mixtures of two breeds: Africa's native cattle, called taurines (*Bos taurus*), and a slightly larger Asian breed, known as zebu (*Bos indicus*), which was domesticated before it arrived in Africa.

Long-distance trade across the Indian Ocean brought many domesticated plants and animals to Africa . . . Presumably, Hanotte said, trade also brought zebu bulls that farmers interbred with domesticated taurine cows, producing the mixed herds of today . . .

For thousands of years, animal farmers have gradually improved their livestock by selectively breeding animals with . . . desired traits to endow the offspring with valuable combinations of traits.

Resistance to sleeping sickness is one trait that potentially could spread through selective breeding. Taurine cattle in one region of western Africa, unlike most livestock, are resistant to the parasite that causes the deadly disease.

But the number of animals with the protective adaptation is dwindling, as local farmers give up their taurine herds for large zebu animals.

Hanotte, along with other people, is worried by this trend. "The starting material for selective breeding is diversity," he said. "We can't afford to lose it."

SOURCE: http://news.nationalgeographic.com/news/2002/04/0411_020411_africacattle.html.

In Chapter 8 we saw that Europeans of the Upper Paleolithic painted big game, including wild cattle, on cave walls. African rock art also celebrates cattle—presumably the domesticated variety. Various cereals were domesticated in Africa some 6,000 years later than the earliest food production in the Middle East. African food production—crops and herds—was both independently invented and borrowed and differed substantially from the earliest food-producing economies in the Middle East, whose development we now examine.

In Chapter 8, we also considered the economic implications of the end of the Ice Age in Europe. With glacial retreat, foragers pursued a more generalized economy, focusing less on large animals. This was the beginning of what Kent Flannery (1969) has called the **broad-spectrum revolution**. This refers to the period beginning around 15,000 B.P. in the Middle East and 12,000 B.P. in Europe, during which a wider range, or broader spectrum, of plant and animal life was hunted, gathered, collected, caught, and fished. It was revolutionary because, in the Middle East, it led to **food production**—human control over the reproduction of plants and animals.

After 15,000 B.P., throughout the inhabited world, as the big-game supply diminished, foragers had to pursue new resources. Human attention shifted from large-bodied, slow reproducers (such as mammoths) to species such as fish, mollusks, and rabbits that reproduce quickly and prolifically (Hayden 1981).

For example, archaeologist David Lubell and his colleagues have reconstructed a pattern of intensive snail collecting at Kef Zoura, eastern Algeria. Dozens of sites in and around the Kef Zoura valley were occupied between 10,000 and 7,000 years ago by members of the Capsian culture. The *Capsians* were a Mesolithic people who based much of their subsistence on land snails, including the modern species the French call *escargot*. The Kef Zoura site has yielded millions of snail shells. The Capsians were nomadic, shifting camp sites after depleting the local snail supply. They also ate plants, including various grasses, acorns, pine nuts, and pistachio nuts (Bower and Lubell 1988).

Spirit Cave in northwestern Thailand has yielded the earliest plant remains from Southeast Asia (Gorman 1969). Between about 9200 and about 8600 B.P., the people at Spirit Cave ate wild nuts, gourds, water chestnuts, black pepper, and cucumbers. Although these plants were not yet domesticated, their association at the same site does indicate a diverse diet and a broad-spectrum pattern that eventually led to food production.

The Japanese site of Nittano (Akazawa 1980), on an inlet near Tokyo, offers additional evidence for the widespread importance of broad-spectrum foraging. Nittano was occupied several times between 6000 and 5000 B.P. by members of the *Jomon* culture, for which 30,000 sites are known in Japan. The Jomon people hunted deer, pigs, bears, and antelope. They also ate fish, shellfish, and plants. Jomon sites have yielded the remains of 300 species of shellfish and 180 species of edible plants (including berries, nuts, and tubers) (Akazawa and Aikens 1986).

We've just examined intensified and diversified resource use, in the form of broad-spectrum collecting, hunting, and gathering, in Algeria, Thailand, and Japan. Early experiments in food production illustrate another, and the most significant, form of intensified resource use in the post–Ice Age world. By 10,000 B.P., a major economic shift was under way in the Middle East (Turkey, Iraq, Iran, Syria, Jordan, and Israel). People started intervening in the reproductive cycles of the plants and animals their ancestors had foraged for generations. Middle Easterners eventually became the world's first farmers and herders (Moore 1985). No longer simply harvesting nature's bounty, they grew their own food and modified the biological characteristics of the plants and animals in their diet. By 10,000 B.P., domesticated plants and animals were part of the broad spectrum of resources used by Middle Easterners. By 7500 B.P., most Middle Easterners were moving away from a broad-spectrum foraging pattern toward more specialized economies based on fewer species, which were domesticates. They were becoming farmers and herders.

Kent Flannery (1969) has proposed a series of eras during which the Middle Eastern transition to farming and herding took place (Table 10.1). The era of seminomadic hunting and gathering (12,000 to 10,000 B.P.) encompasses the last stages of broad-spectrum foraging. This was the period just before the first domesticated plants (wheat and barley) and animals (goats and sheep) were added to the diet. Next came the era of early dry farming (of wheat and barley) and caprine domestication (10,000 to 7500 B.P.). *Dry farming* refers to farming without irrigation; such farming depended on rainfall. *Caprine* (from *capra*, Latin for "goat") refers to goats and sheep, which were domesticated during this era.

During the era of increasing specialization in food production (7500 to 5500 B.P.), new crops were added to the diet, along with more productive varieties of wheat and barley. Cattle and pigs were domesticated. By 5500 B.P., agriculture extended to the alluvial plain of the Tigris and Euphrates rivers (Figure 10.1), where early Mesopotamians lived in walled towns, some of which grew into cities. Metallurgy and the wheel were invented. After two million years of stone-tool making, *H. sapiens* was living in the Bronze Age.

The archaeologist V. Gordon Childe (1951) used the term *Neolithic Revolution* to describe the origin and impact of food production—plant cultivation and animal domestication. **Neolithic**, which means "New Stone Age," was coined to refer to techniques of grinding and polishing stone tools. However, the main significance of the Neolithic was the new total economy rather than just the tool-making techniques. *Neolithic* now

Table 10.1 The Transition to Food Production in the Middle East

Era	Dates (B.P.)
Origin of state (Sumer)	5500
Increasing specialization in food production	7500–5500
Early dry farming and caprine domestication	10,000–7500
Seminomadic hunting and gathering (e.g., Natufians)	12,000–10,000

"Neolithic" was coined to refer to techniques of grinding and polishing stone tools, like these axes and hammers from Austria, Hungary, and the Czech Republic. Was the new tool-making style the most significant thing about the Neolithic?

refers to the first cultural period in a given region in which the first signs of domestication are present. The Neolithic economy based on food production produced substantial changes in human life styles. The pace of social and cultural change increased enormously.

The First Farmers and Herders in the Middle East

Middle Eastern food production arose in the context of four environmental zones. From highest to lowest, they are plateau (5,000 feet, or 1,500 meters), Hilly Flanks, steppe (treeless plain), and alluvial plain of the Tigris and Euphrates rivers (100 to 500 feet, or 30 to 150 meters). The **Hilly Flanks** is a subtropical woodland zone that flanks those rivers to the north (Figures 10.1 and 10.2).

It was once thought that food production began in oases in the alluvial plain. (*Alluvial* describes rich, fertile soil deposited by rivers and streams.) This arid region was where Mesopotamian civilization arose later. Today, we know that although the world's first civilization (Mesopotamian) did indeed develop in this zone, irrigation, a late (7000 B.P.) invention, was necessary to farm the alluvial river plain, a desert area. Plant cultivation and animal domestication started not in the arid river zone but in areas with reliable rainfall.

The archaeologist Robert J. Braidwood (1975) proposed instead that food production started in the Hilly Flanks, or subtropical woodland, zone, where wild wheat and barley would have been most abundant (see Figures 10.1 and 10.2). In 1948, a team headed by Braidwood started excavations at Jarmo, an early food-producing village inhabited between 9000 and 8500 B.P., located in the Hilly Flanks. We now know, however, that there were farming villages earlier than Jarmo (Figure 10.1) in zones adjacent to the Hilly Flanks. One example is Ali Kosh (Figure 10.1), a village in the foothills (piedmont steppe) of the Zagros mountains. By 9000 B.P., the people of Ali Kosh were herding goats, intensively collecting various wild plants, and harvesting wheat during the late winter and early spring (Hole, Flannery, and Neely 1969).

Climate change played a role in the origin of food production (Smith 1995). The end of the Ice Age brought greater regional and local variation in climatic conditions. Lewis Binford (1968) proposed that in certain areas of the Middle East (such as the Hilly Flanks), local environments were so rich in resources that foragers could adopt **sedentism**—sedentary (settled) life in villages. Binford's prime example is the widespread Natufian culture (12,500 to 10,500 B.P.), based on broad-spectrum foraging. The **Natufians**, who collected wild cereals and hunted gazelles, had year-round villages. They were able to stay in the same place (early villages) because they could harvest nearby wild cereals for six months.

Donald Henry (1989, 1995) documented a climate change toward warmer, more humid conditions just before the Natufian period. This expanded the altitude range of wild wheat and

Figure 10.1   The Ancestors of Wheat and Barley Grew Wild in the Subtropical Woodland Zone.   Food production emerged on the margins of the subtropical woodland zone, at places such as Ali Kosh, rather than within it, at places such as Jarmo. Food production did not reach the alluvial desert lowlands near the Tigris and Euphrates rivers (see Figure 10.2), where Mesopotamian civilization arose around 5500 B.P., until irrigation was invented, much later.

barley, thus enlarging the available foraging area and allowing a longer harvest season. Wheat and barley ripened in the spring at low altitudes, in the summer at middle altitudes, and in the fall at high altitudes. As locations for their villages, the Natufians chose places where they could harvest wild cereals in all three zones.

Around 11,000 B.P., this favorable foraging pattern was threatened by a second climate change—to drier conditions. As many wild cereal habitats dried up, the optimal zone for foraging shrank. Natufian villages were now restricted to areas with permanent water. As population continued to grow, some Natufians attempted to maintain productivity by transferring wild cereals to well-watered areas, where they started cultivating.

In the view of many scholars, the people most likely to adopt a new subsistence strategy, such as food production, would be those having the most trouble in following their traditional subsistence strategy (Binford 1968; Flannery 1973; Wenke 1996). Thus, those ancient Middle Easterners living outside the area where wild foods were most abundant would be the most likely to experiment and to adopt new subsistence strategies. This would have been especially true as the climate dried up. Recent archaeological finds support this hypothesis that food production began in *marginal areas*, such as the piedmont steppe, rather than in the optimal zones, such as the Hilly Flanks, where traditional foods were most abundant.

Even today, wild wheat grows so densely in the Hilly Flanks that one person working just an hour with Neolithic tools can easily harvest a kilogram of wheat (Harlan and Zohary 1966). People would have had no reason to invent cultivation when wild grain was ample to feed them. Wild wheat ripens rapidly and can be harvested over a three-week period. According to Flannery, over that time period, a family of experienced plant collectors could harvest enough grain—2,200 pounds (1,000 kilograms)—to feed themselves for a year. But after harvesting all that wheat, they'd need a place to put it. They could no longer maintain a nomadic life style, since they'd need to stay close to their wheat.

Sedentary village life thus developed before farming and herding in the Middle East. The Natufians and other Hilly Flanks foragers had no choice but to build villages near the densest stands of wild grains. They needed a place to keep their grain. Furthermore, sheep and goats came to graze on the stubble that remained after humans had harvested the grain. The fact that basic plants and animals were available in the same area also favored village life. Hilly Flanks foragers built houses, dug storage pits for grain, and made ovens to roast it.

Natufian settlements, occupied year-round, show permanent architectural features and evidence for the processing and storage of wild grains. One such site is Abu Hureyra, Syria (see Figure 10.1), which was initially occupied by Natufians around 11,000 to 10,500 B.P. Then it was abandoned—to be reoccupied later by food producers, between 9500 and 8000 B.P. From the Natufian period, Abu Hureyra has yielded the remains of grinding stones, wild plants, and 50,000 gazelle bones, which represent 80 percent of all the bones recovered at the site (Jolly and White 1995).

Prior to domestication, the favored Hilly Flanks zone had the densest human population. Eventually, its excess population started to spill over into adjacent areas. Colonists from the Flanks tried to maintain their traditional broad-spectrum foraging in these marginal zones. But with sparser resources available, they had to experiment with new subsistence strategies. Eventually, population pressure on more limited resources forced people in the marginal zones to become the first food producers (Binford 1968; Flannery 1969). *Early cultivation began as an attempt to copy, in a less favorable environment, the dense stands of wheat and barley that grew wild in the Hilly Flanks.*

The Middle East, along with certain other world areas where food production originated, is a region that for thousands of years has had a *vertical economy*. (Other examples include Peru and **Mesoamerica**—Middle America, including Mexico, Guatemala, and Belize.) A vertical economy exploits environmental zones that, although close together in space, contrast with one another in altitude, rainfall, overall climate, and vegetation (Figure 10.2). Such a close juxtaposition of varied environments allowed broad-spectrum foragers to use different resources in different seasons.

Early seminomadic foragers in the Middle East had followed game from zone to zone. In winter they hunted in the piedmont steppe region, which had winter rains rather than snow and provided

Some 12,000 to 10,000 years ago, ancient Middle Easterners followed the availability of plants and animals, from lower to higher zones. With domestication, this pattern evolved into nomadic herding (pastoralism). Contemporary Middle Eastern herders still take their flocks to grazing areas at different elevations. This 1997 photo shows a Bedouin shepherd in the hills near Bethlehem, West Bank, Israel.

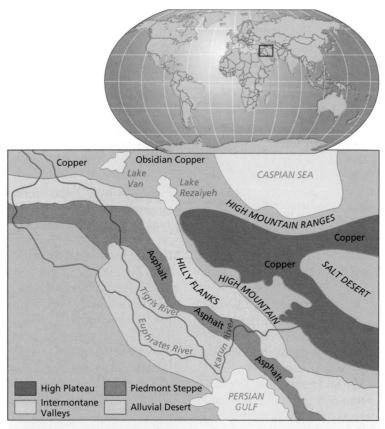

Figure 10.2 **The Vertical Economy of the Ancient Middle East.** Geographically close but contrasting environments were linked by seasonal movements and trade patterns of broad-spectrum foragers. Traded resources included copper, obsidian, and asphalt, located in particular zones. As people traveled and traded, they removed plants from the zones where they grew wild in the Hilly Flanks into adjacent zones where humans became agents of selection.

winter pasture for game animals 12,000 years ago. (Indeed it is still used for winter grazing by herders today.) When winter ended, the steppe dried up. Game moved up to the Hilly Flanks and high plateau country as the snow melted. Pasture land became available at higher elevations. Foragers gathered as they climbed, harvesting wild grains that ripened later at higher altitudes. Sheep and goats followed the stubble in the wheat and barley fields after people had harvested the grain.

The four Middle Eastern environmental zones shown in Figure 10.2 also were tied together through trade. Certain resources were confined to specific zones. Asphalt, used as an adhesive in the manufacture of sickles, came from the steppe.

Copper and turquoise sources were located in the high plateau. Contrasting environments were therefore linked in two ways: by foragers' seasonal migration and by trade.

The movement of people, animals, and products between zones—plus population increase supported by highly productive broad-spectrum foraging—was a precondition for the emergence of food production. As they traveled between zones, people carried seeds into new habitats. Mutations, genetic recombinations, and human selection led to new kinds of wheat and barley. Some of the new varieties were better adapted to the steppe and, eventually, the alluvial plain than the wild forms had been.

GENETIC CHANGES AND DOMESTICATION

See the Virtual Exploration

mhhe
●com
/kottak

What are the main differences between wild and domesticated plants? The seeds of domesticated cereals, and often the entire plant, are larger. Compared with wild plants, crops produce a higher yield per unit of area. Domesticated plants also lose their natural seed dispersal mechanisms. Cultivated beans, for example, have pods that hold together, rather than shattering as they do in the wild. Domesticated cereals have tougher connective tissue holding the seedpods to the stem.

Grains of wheat, barley, and other cereals occur in bunches at the end of a stalk (Figure 10.3). The grains are attached to the stalk by an *axis*, plural *axes*. In wild cereals, this axis is brittle. Sections of the axis break off one by one, and a seed attached to each section falls to the ground. This is how wild cereals spread their seeds and propagate their species. But a brittle axis is a problem for people. Imagine the annoyance experienced by broad-spectrum foragers as they tried to harvest wild wheat, only to have the grain fall off or be blown away.

In very dry weather, wild wheat and barley ripen—their axes totally disintegrating—in just three days (Flannery 1973). The brittle axis must have been even more irritating to people who planted the seeds and waited for the harvest. But fortunately, certain stalks of wild wheat and barley happened to have tough axes. These were the ones whose seeds people saved to plant the following year.

Another problem with wild cereals is that the edible portion is enclosed in a tough husk. This husk was too tough to remove with a pounding stone. Foragers had to roast the grain to make the husk brittle enough to come off. However, some wild plants happened to have genes for brittle husks. Humans chose the seeds of these plants (which would have germinated prematurely in nature) because they could be more effectively prepared for eating.

People also selected certain features in animals (Smith 1995). Some time after sheep were domesticated, advantageous new phenotypes arose. Wild sheep aren't woolly; wool coats were products of domestication. Although it's hard to imagine, a wool coat offers protection against extreme heat. Skin temperatures of sheep living in very hot areas

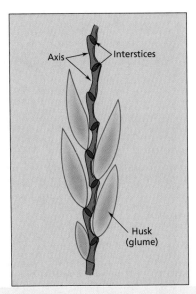

Figure 10.3   A Head of Wheat or Barley.   In the wild, the axis comes apart as its parts fall off one by one. The connecting parts (interstices) are tough and don't come apart in domesticated grains. In wild grains, the husks are hard. In domestic plants, they are brittle, which permits easy access to the grain. How did people deal with hard husks before domestication?

are much lower than temperatures on the surface of their wool. Woolly sheep, but not their wild ancestors, could survive in hot, dry alluvial lowlands. Wool had an additional advantage: its use for clothing.

What are some of the differences between wild and domesticated animals? Plants got larger with domestication, while animals got smaller, probably because smaller animals are easier to control. Middle Eastern sites document changes in the horns of domesticated goats. Such change may have been genetically linked to some other desirable trait that has left no skeletal evidence behind.

FOOD PRODUCTION AND THE STATE

The shift from foraging to food production was gradual. The knowledge of how to grow crops and breed livestock didn't immediately convert Middle Easterners into full-time farmers and herders. Domesticated plants and animals began as minor parts of a broad-spectrum economy. Foraging for fruits, nuts, grasses, grains, snails, and insects continued.

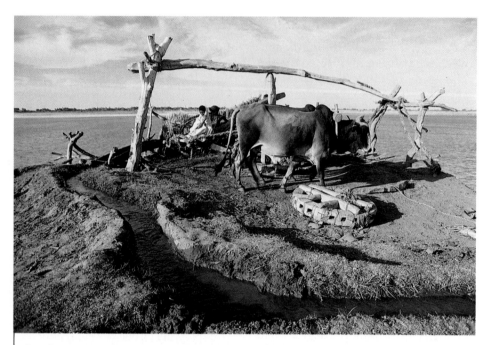

Simple irrigation systems were being used in the Middle East by 7000 B.P. By 6000 B.P., complex irrigation techniques made agriculture possible in the arid lowlands of southern Mesopotamia. Here in Sudan, we see a fairly simple, ox-powered irrigation system.

Over time, Middle Eastern economies grew more specialized, geared more exclusively toward crops and herds. The former marginal zones became centers of the new economy and of population increase and emigration. Some of the increasing population spilled back into the Hilly Flanks, where people eventually had to intensify production by cultivating. Domesticated crops could now provide a bigger harvest than could the grains that grew wild there. Thus, in the Hilly Flanks, too, farming eventually replaced foraging as the economic mainstay.

Farming colonies spread down into drier areas. By 7000 B.P., simple irrigation systems had developed, tapping springs in the foothills. By 6000 B.P., more complex irrigation techniques made agriculture possible in the arid lowlands of southern Mesopotamia. In the alluvial desert plain of the Tigris and Euphrates rivers, a new economy based on irrigation and trade fueled the growth of an entirely new form of society. This was the *state*, a social and political unit featuring a central government, extreme contrasts of wealth, and social classes. The process of state formation is examined in the next chapter.

We now understand why the first farmers lived neither in the alluvial lowlands, where the Mesopotamian state arose around 5500 B.P., nor in the Hilly Flanks, where wild plants and animals abounded. Food production began in marginal zones, such as the piedmont steppe, where people experimented at reproducing, artificially, the dense grain stands that grew wild in the Hilly Flanks. As seeds were taken to new environments, new phenotypes were favored by a combination of natural and human selection. The spread of cereal grains outside their natural habitats was part of a system of migration and trade between zones, which had developed in the Middle East during the broad-spectrum period. Food production also owed its origin to the need to intensify production to feed an increasing human population—the legacy of thousands of years of productive foraging.

Other Old World Farmers

The path from foraging to farming was one that people followed independently in at least seven world areas. As we'll see later in this chapter, three were in the Americas. Four were in the Old World, including the very first farmers and herders in the Middle East. In each of these seven centers, people independently invented domestication—albeit of different sets of crops and animals.

Food production also spread out from the Middle East and other centers of domestication. This happened through trade, through diffusion of plants, animals, products and information, and through the actual migration of farmers, who in some cases displaced native foragers. The crops and livestock that were originally domesticated in the Middle East spread westward to northern Africa, including Egypt's Nile Valley, and into Europe (Price 2000). Trade also extended eastward from the Middle East to India and Pakistan. In Egypt, an agricultural economy based on plants and animals originally domesticated in the Middle East led to a pharaonic civilization. Another early civilization eventually arose in western Pakistan.

Interpret the World Around 8,000 B.P., com-
Atlas Map 10 munities on Europe's Mediterranean shores, in Greece, Italy, and France, started shifting from foraging to farming, using imported species. By 7000 B.P., there were fully sedentary farming villages in Greece and Italy. By 6000 B.P., there were thousands of farming villages as far east as Russia and as far west as northern France. In your atlas, look at Map 10, "Early Neolithic Sites of the Middle East and Europe," which shows major archaeological sites there and also indicates the dates and directions of diffusion of food production from the Mediterranean and Middle East to Europe. Also note the symbols used to show plant and animal domesticates. Which plants and animals were most widely diffused in Europe? By chance, we can even meet a man from one of those European Neolithic villages. The "Iceman" discovered in the Italian Alps in 1991 (see "Interesting Issues" on pp. 264–265) came from a village of farmers who raised wheat, barley, sheep, and goats.

Compared with the Middle East, less is known about early farmers in such Old World areas as sub-Saharan Africa, South and Southeast Asia, and China. Partly this reflects the poorer preservation of archaeological remains in hot, moist habitats. Mostly it reflects the need for more archaeological research in such areas. In Pakistan's Indus River Valley, ancient cities (Harappa and Mohenjo-daro) emerged slightly later than did the first Mesopotamian city-states. Domestication and state formation in the Indus Valley were probably influenced by developments in, and trade with, the Middle East. Still, archaeological research confirms the early (8000 B.P.) presence of domesticated goats, sheep, cattle, wheat, and barley in Pakistan (Meadow 1991).

China was also one of the first world areas to develop farming, based on millet and rice. Millet is a tall, coarse cereal grass still grown in northern China. This grain, which today feeds a third of the world's population, is used in contemporary North America mainly as birdseed. By 7500 B.P., two varieties of millet supported early farming communities in northern China, along the Yellow River. Millet cultivation paved the way for widespread village life and eventually for Shang dynasty civilization, based on irrigated agriculture, between 3600 and 3100 B.P. (See Chapter 11.) The northern Chinese also had domesticated dogs, pigs, and possibly cattle, goats, and sheep by 7000 B.P. (Chang 1977).

Millet, being harvested here on a Chinese plateau, was grown in the Hwang-Ho (Yellow River) Valley by 7000 B.P. This grain supported early farming communities in northern China. What was being grown in southern China at the same time?

The glacially preserved "Iceman" found in the Italian Alps in 1991 was a Neolithic Alpine European. The find is significant because of its age, its state of preservation, and its combination of a human cadaver with clothing and possessions, including stone and metal (copper) tools. The Iceman probably came from an Alpine farming village. He was on an autumn hunting trip when he was killed and eventually frozen. DNA analysis of the contents of his stomach shows he ate red deer for his last meal (Fountain 2002). The Neolithic, which began some 10,000 years ago in the Middle East, had spread to Western Europe by 6500 B.P.

The "Iceman," who scientists now know lived about 5,300 years ago, had been in the ice 1,000 years when the Egyptians built the pyramids at Giza, more than 3,000 years when Jesus was born. Yet he was found with a remarkable array of clothing, weapons, and equipment, including some mysterious objects of types never seen before.

Some—including the man's fur hat, the oldest known in Europe—were found . . . near the Austrian–Italian border . . .

The man's body was found not in a grave, the usual source of ancient remains, but at a campsite he made during a sojourn in the mountains . . . [S]now and ice covered him and his things, preserving them almost perfectly.

His perishable belongings—items made of wood, leather, grass, and apparently even food and medicines—have come out of the ice virtually intact, providing scientists with the most intimate picture ever seen of the daily life of a prehistoric man.

For example, his ax, which has a copper head, looks and feels as new and dangerous as on the fall day in about 3300 B.C. [5,300 B.P.], when the man leaned it against a rock before bedding down for his last night. It is among the oldest copper axes known and one of the best made, dating from the dawn of the use of metals.

Archaeologists know that fateful night was in the autumn, because frozen with him was a ripe blackthorn fruit, the plumlike berry also called sloe, which grows at lower altitudes and ripens in the fall.

The man's body is startlingly well preserved—by far the most lifelike from prehistoric times. . .

The body was naturally freeze-dried and is in such good condition that pores in the skin look normal. Even his eyeballs can still be seen behind lids frozen open, and CT scans show the brain and other internal organs in place.

"We have never had a prehistoric discovery as complete as this," said Andreas Lippert, a University of Vienna archaeologist who led the expedition to the site . . . The group found more than 400 objects, most of them parts of the man's clothing.

Yet several key questions remain. What was he doing so high in the mountains? How did he die? And, most intriguing to archaeologists, did he come from one of the known prehistoric cultures of the region, or does he represent something entirely new?

What is clear is that he lived during one of the more critical transitions in the development of human culture, when stone tools were beginning to give way to metal.

Farming, which began in the Middle East about 5,000 years ear-lier, had spread to much of Eurasia by 5,300 years ago. The man probably came from a village of farmers who raised wheat, barley, and oats and herded sheep and goats.

The man in the ice was discovered Sept. 19, 1991, by Helmut and Erika Simon, a German couple hiking in the Alps. Near the 10,500-foot-high ridge that defines the Austrian–Italian border they were tramping over the snow and ice of a commonly used pass when they saw a human head and shoulders sticking out of the ice. The body was lying face down, its skin a tawny color and the head hairless. The Simons reported it to police in the Italian state of South Tirol.

The local Carabinieri, Italian police familiar with the common problem of retrieving bodies of modern climbers, insisted that this time the site was in Austria and not their problem.

Two days later the Austrian police from north Tirol arrived with a helicopter and—not realizing the site's importance—used an air hammer to hack the body out of the ice. They accidentally cut into the man's hip, but his legs stayed stuck. Forensic officials spotted the copperbladed ax on a nearby rock and, presuming foul play in the man's death, took it as "evidence."

Bad weather forced a temporary retreat. But word of the find encouraged curious hikers to trek to the body, and several tried to chop it free.

On Sept. 23, four days after the find, a forensic team from the University of Innsbruck helicoptered to the site, found that meltwater had refrozen around the body and began again to chop. When they pulled out the prone body, it was later realized,

Meet the Iceman. Since his frozen body emerged from a glacier in the Italian Alps in 1991, scientists have come to realize he is the closest we may ever come to meeting a real person from the Stone Age. How would you evaluate his state of preservation?

the man's penis remained embedded in the ice.

Workers also gathered up some pieces of fur and leather clothing, string, a leather bag and a flint dagger. A long stick, apparently a bow, was still partly embedded in ice, so workers broke off part and took that, too.

Hikers and skiers had been lost in the Alps many times, but they usually emerged a few decades later when the flow of the glaciers transported them to lower altitudes where they melted out. Moreover, these "young" bodies were usually horribly transformed into misshapen blobs of "fat wax." This man in the ice, though dried and somewhat shriveled like a mummy, looked too good to be very old.

A team of glaciologists soon resolved the question with another visit to the site. They found that the body had lain at the bottom of a narrow ravine. Snow could have filled the 6-to-10-foot-deep crevice, but the resulting ice was trapped.

The glaciologists also found evidence to support the man's antiquity—his quiver, which contained 14 arrows, two of them fitted with flint arrowheads, hardly the choice of any bowman who lived since the Iron Age swept Eurasia more than 3,000 years ago.

And the glaciologists explained why the body had only just emerged. Earlier in 1991 great storms had blown dust from North Africa into the Alps, darkening the snow cover.

The dust absorbed solar heat, causing more than the usual amount of snow to melt during the summer of 1991, exposing the body.

Years after the original discovery, which turned out actually to have been in Italy rather than Austria, new imaging techniques detected an arrow point in the Iceman's shoulder. This suggests that he may have died in a weakened condition after an attack. The Iceman currently resides in Bolzano, Italy, in a museum established in his honor.

SOURCE: Boyce Rensberger, "A Man Who Lived 5,300 Years Ago," *The Washington Post*, November 26, 1992, p. E1.

Recent discoveries by Chinese archaeologists suggest that rice was domesticated in the Yangtze River corridor of southern China as early as 8400 B.P. (Smith 1995). Other early rice comes from the 7,000-year-old site Hemudu, on Lake Dongting in southern China. The people of Hemudu used both wild and domesticated rice, along with domesticated water buffalo, dogs, and pigs. They also hunted wild game (Jolly and White 1995).

China seems to have been the scene of two independent transitions to food production, based on different crops grown in strikingly different climates. Southern Chinese farming was rice aquaculture in rich subtropical wetlands. Southern winters were mild; and summer rains, reliable. Northern China, by contrast, had harsh winters, with unreliable rainfall during the summer growing season. This was an area of grasslands and temperate forests. Still, in both areas by 7500 B.P., food production supported large and stable villages. Based on the archaeological evidence, early Chinese villagers had architectural expertise. They lived in substantial houses, made elaborate ceramic vessels, and had rich burials.

At Nok Nok Tha in central Thailand, pottery made more than 5,000 years ago has imprints of husks and grains of domesticated rice (Solheim 1972/1976). Animal bones show that the people of Nok Nok Tha also had humped zebu cattle similar to those of contemporary India. Rice might have been cultivated at about the same time in the Indus River Valley of Pakistan and adjacent western India.

It appears that food production arose independently as many as seven times in different world areas. Figure 10.4 is a map highlighting those seven areas: the Middle East, north China, south China, sub-Saharan Africa, central Mexico, the south central Andes, and the eastern United States. A different set of major foods was domesticated, at different times, in each area, as we see in Table 10.2. Some grains, such as millet and rice, were domesticated more than once. Millet grows wild in China and Africa, where it became an important food crop, as well as in Mexico, where it did not. Indigenous African rice, grown only in West Africa, belongs to the same genus as Asian rice. Pigs and possibly cattle were independently domesticated in the Middle East, China, and sub-Saharan Africa. Independent domestication of the dog was virtually a worldwide phenomenon, including the Western Hemisphere. We turn now to archaeological sequences in the Americas.

The First American Farmers

Homo did not, of course, originate in the Western Hemisphere. Never have fossils of Neandertals or earlier hominids been found in North or South America. The settlement of the Americas was one of the major achievements of *H. sapiens sapiens*. This colonization continued the trends toward population increase and expansion of geographic range that have marked human evolution generally.

AMERICA'S FIRST IMMIGRANTS

See the Internet Exercises at your OLC

The original settlers of the Americas came from Northeast Asia. They were the ancestors of American Indians. They entered North America via the Bering land bridge, *Beringia*, which connected North America and Siberia several times during the ice ages. Beringia, which today lies under the Bering Sea, was a dry land area several hundred miles wide, exposed during the glacial advances (Figure 10.5).

Living in Beringia thousands of years ago, the ancestors of Native Americans didn't realize they were embarking on the colonization of a new continent. They were merely big-game hunters who, over the generations, moved gradually eastward as they spread their camps and followed their prey—woolly mammoths and other tundra-adapted herbivores. Other ancient hunters entered North America along the shore by boat, fishing and hunting sea animals.

This was truly a "new world" to its earliest colonists, as it would be to the European voyagers who rediscovered it thousands of years later. Its natural resources, particularly its big game, had never before been exploited by humans. Early bands followed the game south. Although ice sheets covered most of what is now Canada, colonization gradually penetrated the heartland of what is now the United States. Successive generations of hunters followed game through unglaciated corridors, breaks in the continental ice sheets. Others spread by boat down the Pacific coast.

In North America's rolling grasslands, early American Indians, *Paleoindians*, hunted horses, camels, bison, elephants, mammoths, and giant sloths. The **Clovis tradition**—a sophisticated stone

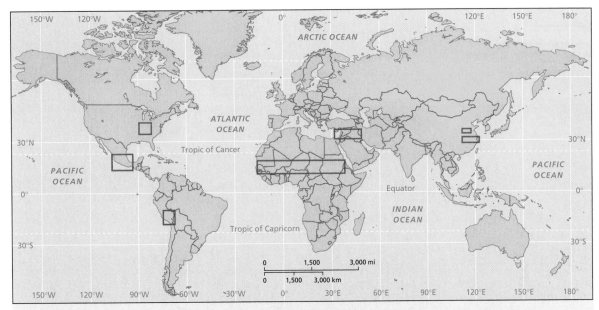

Figure 10.4 **Seven World Areas Where Food Production Was Independently Invented.** Do any of these areas surprise you?

SOURCE: B. D. Smith, *The Emergence of Agriculture* (New York: Scientific American Library, W. H. Freeman, 1995), p. 12.

See the Interactive Exercise for a quiz

/kottak

Table 10.2 Seven World Areas Where Food Production Was Independently Invented

World Area	Major Domesticated Plants/Animals	Earliest Date (B.P.)
Middle East	Wheat, barley Sheep, goats, cattle, pigs	10,000
South China (Yangtze River corridor)	Rice Water buffalo, dogs, pigs	8500–6500
North China (Yellow River)	Millet Dogs, pigs, chickens	7500
Sub-Saharan Africa	Sorghum, pearl millet, African rice	4000
Central Mexico	Maize, beans, squash Dogs, turkeys	4700
South Central Andes	Potato, quinoa, beans Camelids (llama, alpaca), guinea pigs	4500
Eastern United States	Goosefoot, marsh elder, sunflower, squash	4500

SOURCE: Data compiled from B. D. Smith, *The Emergence of Agriculture* (New York: Scientific American Library, W. H. Freeman, 1995).

Overland migrations from Asia ended when rising sea levels flooded Beringia, leaving a landscape of ice, ocean, and jagged peaks. How might later Asian migrants have entered North America? How might archaeologists find out more about the people who lived in Beringia?

technology based on a point that was fastened to the end of a hunting spear (Figure 10.6)—flourished between 12,000 and 11,000 B.P. in the Central Plains, on their western margins, and over a large area of what is now the eastern United States. The Monte Verde archaeological site in south central Chile has been firmly dated to 12,000 B.P. (Smith 1995). This evidence for the early occupation of southern South America suggests that the first migration of humans into the Americas may date back 20,000 years.

Reinforcing this idea is work done by archaeologist Joseph M. McAvoy, whose team has studied an early human settlement in Virginia, located on a sandy slope called Cactus Hill, 45 miles south of Richmond. McAvoy has worked since 1989 at Cactus Hill, located near the Nottoway River, where Clovis tools had been found. Beneath the Clovis- era site, McAvoy's team found tools dating back 15,000 to 17,000 years. These toolmakers, who lived in Virginia before the Clovis era, may have foraged eastern mud turtles and whitetail deer, burned remains of which were found by the archaeologists. The Americas probably were not populated by a single mass migration but rather in spurts, perhaps starting around 20,000 years ago, as small groups of nomadic foragers made their way to North America at various times, following different routes (Todt 2000).

THE FOUNDATIONS OF FOOD PRODUCTION

As hunters benefiting from the abundance of big game, bands of foragers gradually spread through the Americas. As they moved, these early Americans learned to cope with a great diversity of environments. Thousands of years later, their descendants independently invented food production, paving the way for the emergence of states based on agriculture and trade in Mexico and Peru. New World food production emerged 3,000 to 4,000 years later than in the Middle East, as did the first states.

The most significant contrast between Old and New World food production involved animal domestication, which was much more important in the Old World than in the New World. The animals that had been hunted during the early American big-game tradition either became extinct before people could domesticate them or were not domes-

Figure 10.6
A Clovis Spear Point.
Such points were attached to spears used by Paleoindians of the North American plains between 12,000 and 11,000 B.P. Are there sites with comparable ages in South America?

Figure 10.5   The Ancestors of Native Americans Came to North America as Migrants from Asia.   They followed big-game herds across Beringia, an immense stretch of land exposed during the ice ages. Was their settlement of the Americas intentional? When did it probably happen? Other migrants reached North America along the shore by boat, fishing and hunting sea animals.

Ice cap
Glaciers
Ice-free corridor
Present-day shore lines
Formerly exposed land areas

ticable. The largest animal ever domesticated in the New World (in Peru, around 4,500 B.P.) was the llama. Early Peruvians and Bolivians ate llama meat and used that animal as a beast of burden (Flannery, Marcus, and Reynolds 1989). They bred the llama's relative, the alpaca, for its wool. (Llamas and alpacas are members of the *camelid* family.) Peruvians also added animal protein to their diet by raising and eating guinea pigs and ducks.

The turkey was domesticated in Mesoamerica and in the southwestern United States. Lowland South Americans domesticated a type of duck. The dog is the only animal that was domesticated throughout the New World. There were no cattle, sheep, or goats in the areas where food production

arose. As a result, neither herding nor the kinds of relationships that developed between herders and farmers in many parts of the Middle East, Europe, Asia, and Africa emerged in the precolonial Americas. The New World crops were different, although staples as nutritious as those of the Old World were domesticated from native wild plants.

Understanding Ourselves   Differences in early food production between the Old World and the Americas help us understand their subsequent histories. Domesticable animals were a key ingredient in the origin of food production in the Middle East. Animals and crops thrived together in most regions of early food production in the Old World, including the Middle East, Africa, Europe, and Asia. Not so in the Americas, where wild oxen, horses, pigs, and camels once lived, but went extinct (probably due to a combination of hunting by humans and climatic changes) long before the first crops were cultivated. In the Middle East a mutually supportive relationship could develop between farming and herding. Animals could feed on stubble left in wheat fields after the crops were harvested. Crops could be grown to feed sheep, goats, and eventually cattle, pigs, horses, and donkeys. Animals could be used as beasts of burden, attached to sleds, rollers, and eventually wheeled vehicles.

Early Peruvians and Bolivians ate llama meat, harnessed llamas as beasts of burden (as is shown here), and used llama dung to fertilize their fields. What was the largest animal domesticated in the New World?

The widespread use of wheeled vehicles, as diverse as oxcarts, chariots, and carriages, fueled the growth of trade, travel, and transport in the Old World. Advances in transportation led to an eventual "age of discovery" and the European conquest of the Americas. Early farmers in Mesoamerica had no trouble coming up with the idea of the wheel, which they sometimes attached to toys. But how could they have oxcarts or chariots without the appropriate animals to pull them? Dogs do pull sleds in the Arctic (never a center of food production), but dogs and turkeys can't match horses, donkeys, or oxen as beasts of burden. The lack of animal domestication in Mesoamerica is more than a textbook fact to be memorized for a test. It's a key factor in world history, helping us understand the divergent development of societies on different sides of the oceans.

Three *caloric staples*, major sources of carbohydrates, were domesticated by Native American farmers. **Maize**, or corn, first domesticated in highland Mexico, became the caloric staple in Mesoamerica and Central America; it eventually spread to coastal Peru. The other two staples were root crops: white ("Irish") potatoes, first domesticated in the Andes, and **manioc**, or cassava, a tuber first cultivated in the South American lowlands. Other crops added variety to New World diets and made them nutritious. Beans and squash, for example, provided essential proteins, vitamins, and minerals. Maize, beans, and squash were the basis of the Mesoamerican diet.

Food production was independently invented in three areas of the Americas: Mesoamerica, the eastern United States, and the south central Andes. Mesoamerica is discussed in detail in the next section. Food plants known as goosefoot and marsh elder, along with the sunflower and a species of squash, were domesticated by Native Americans in the eastern United States by 4500 B.P. These crops supplemented a diet based mainly on hunting and gathering. They never became caloric staples like maize, wheat, rice, millet, manioc, and potatoes. Eventually maize diffused from Mesoamerica into what is now the United States, reaching both the Southwest and the eastern area just mentioned. Maize provided a more reliable caloric staple for Native North American farming. In what is now Peru and Bolivia, six species appear to have been domesticated more or less together in the highland valleys and basins of the south central Andes between 5000 and 4000 B.P. These domesticates were the potato, quinoa (a cereal grain), beans, llamas, alpacas, and guinea pigs (Smith 1995).

EARLY FARMING IN THE MEXICAN HIGHLANDS

Long before Mexican highlanders developed a taste for maize, beans, and squash, they hunted as part of a pattern of broad-spectrum foraging. Mammoth remains dated to 11,000 B.P. have been

By diffusion, manioc or cassava, originally domesticated in lowland South America, has become a caloric staple in the tropics worldwide. This young Thai farmer displays his manioc crop.

found along with spear points in the basin that surrounds Mexico City. However, small animals were more important than big game, as were the grains, pods, fruits, and leaves of wild plants.

In the *Valley of Oaxaca*, in Mexico's southern highlands, between 10,000 and 4000 B.P., foragers concentrated on certain wild animals—deer and rabbits—and plants—cactus leaves and fruits, and tree pods, especially mesquite (Flannery 1986). Those early Oaxacans dispersed to hunt and gather in fall and winter. But they came together in late spring and summer, forming larger groups to harvest seasonally available plants. Cactus fruits appeared in the spring. Since summer rains would reduce the fruits to mush and since birds, bats, and rodents competed for them, cactus collection required hard work by large groups of people. The edible pods of the mesquite, available in June, also required intensive gathering.

In fall, these early Oaxacan foragers gathered a wild grass known as **teocentli**, or *teosinte*, the wild ancestor of maize. Sometime between 7000 and 4000 B.P., teocentli-maize underwent a series of genetic changes like those described earlier for Middle Eastern wheat and barley. These changes included increases in the number of kernels per cob, cob size, and the number of cobs per stalk (Flannery 1973). Such steps toward domestication made it increasingly profitable to collect wild maize and eventually to plant maize.

Undoubtedly, some of the mutations necessary for domesticated maize had occurred in wild teocentli before people started growing it. However, since teocentli was well adapted to its natural niche, the mutations offered no advantage and didn't spread. But once people started harvesting wild maize intensively, they became selective agents. As foragers wandered during the year, they carried teocentli to environments different from its natural habitat.

Furthermore, as people harvested teocentli, they took back to camp a greater proportion of plants with tough axes and stalks. These were the plants most likely to hold together during harvesting and least likely to disintegrate on the way back home. Now teocentli depended on humans for its survival, since it lacked the natural means of dispersal—a brittle axis or stalk. If humans chose plants with tough axes inadvertently, their selection of plants with soft husks must have been intentional. Their selection of corn ears with larger cobs, more kernels per cob, and more cobs per plant was also intentional.

Eventually, people started planting maize in the alluvial soils of valley floors. This was the zone where foragers had traditionally congregated for the annual summer harvest of mesquite pods. By 4000 B.P., a type of maize had been developed that provided more food than the mesquite pods did. Once that happened, people started cutting down mesquite trees and replacing them with corn fields.

Farming triggered a population explosion and adaptive radiation throughout Mesoamerica. Yet again, changes were gradual. In the Middle East, thousands of years intervened between the first experiments in domestication and the appearance of the state. The same was true in Mesoamerica.

See the Internet Exercises at your OLC for information on the domestication of chocolate

mhhe
●com
/kottak

FROM EARLY FARMING TO THE STATE

Eventually, food production led to the *early village farming community*. Permanent villages sustained by farming were occupied year-round. The earliest

As maize cultivation spread, genetic changes led to higher yields and more productive farming. Pressures to intensify cultivation helped improve water-control systems, such as the canal irrigation shown in this mural by Diego Rivera.

such settlements in Mesoamerica developed around 3500 B.P., in two kinds of environment. One was humid lowlands, along the Gulf Coast of Mexico and the Pacific Coast of Mexico and Guatemala. Here, maize farming in rich soils was combined with gathering and hunting of several species of wild plants and animals.

Early village farming communities also emerged in one part of the Mexican highlands. In the Valley of Oaxaca in southern Mexico, winter frosts are absent, and simple irrigation permitted the establishment of early permanent villages based on maize farming. Water close to the surface allowed early farmers to dig wells right in their corn fields. Using pots, they dipped water out of these wells and poured it on their growing plants, a technique known as *pot irrigation*. The earliest year-round Mesoamerican farming depended on reliable rainfall, pot irrigation, or access to humid river bottomlands.

The subsequent spread of maize farming resulted in further genetic changes, higher yields, higher human populations, and more intensive farming. Pressures to intensify cultivation led to improvements in early water-control systems. New varieties of fast-growing maize eventually appeared, expanding the range of areas that could be cultivated. Increasing population and irrigation also helped spread maize farming.

The gradual transformation of broad-spectrum foraging into intensive cultivation laid the foundation for the emergence of the state in Mesoamerica—some 3,000 years later than in the Middle East (Table 10.3). A state is a form of social and political organization that has a formal, central government and a division of society into classes. Chiefdoms are precursors to states; they have privileged and effective leaders—chiefs—but they lack the sharp class divisions that characterize states. Evidence of what archaeologists call the *elite level*, indicating a chiefdom or a state, appears around 3500 B.P. An early example comes from Mexico's Gulf Coast, where, between 3200 and 2500 B.P., the *Olmecs* (a chiefdom) built several ritual centers. Large earthen mounds, presumably dedicated to religion, document the ability of Olmec elites to marshal labor. The Olmecs also sculpted massive stone heads, which may be representations of their chiefs.

By 2500 B.P., Olmec culture had dimmed, but the elite level was spreading throughout Mesoamerica. By A.D. 1 (2000 B.P.), the highlands, particularly the Valley of Mexico, moved to center stage in the Mesoamerican transformation. It was in the Valley of Mexico that the city and state of Teotihuacan flourished between 1900 and 1300 B.P. (A.D. 100 and A.D. 700). The Aztec state, which lasted until the Spanish conquest in 1521, arose in the valley around 1325. (The Classic Maya state thrived in Mexico's Yucatán peninsula and in neighboring areas of what are now Guatemala and Belize from A.D. 200 to 900.) The process of state formation in Mesoamerica is examined further in the next chapter.

Costs and Benefits

Food production brought advantages and disadvantages. Among the advantages were discoveries and inventions. People learned to spin and weave; to make pottery, bricks, and arched masonry; and to smelt and cast metals. They developed trade and commerce by land and sea. By 5500 B.P., Middle

Table 10.3 The Rise of Food Production and the State in Mesoamerica

These developments, from early corn domestication to the fall of the Aztec state, are organized here according to period names. Elite-level societies (beginning with the Olmecs, through the Spanish Conquest of the Aztecs) are described as Preclassic (Olmecs and Oaxaca). Next come Classic (Oaxaca continues, along with Teotihuacan and the Maya area) and Postclassic (Toltecs and Aztecs).

Period	Date (B.P.)	Area/Sites	Settlement Types	Ranking/Stratification System
Conquest (Cortez)	A.D. 1521	Mexico	Colony of Spain	Spanish domination; world system
Postclassic	1150–500 (A.D. 1000–1200) (A.D. 1325–1521)	Toltec Increased militarism Aztec	Cities, social unrest Empire More secular rule Expanded trade	State Empire
Classic	1750–1150	Teotihuacan Oaxaca Maya	Cities Trade, crafts expand	Stratification, states
Preclassic (Formative)	3500–1750	Olmec Oaxaca	Ceremonial centers Writing (by end)	Ranking, chiefdoms Stratification (by end)
Early food production	4000–3500	Oaxaca Pacific Coast Gulf Coast	Village farming community	Ranking
Earliest domestication	5000	Tehuacan Oaxaca	Seminomadic bands	Egalitarian

Easterners were living in vibrant cities with markets, streets, temples, and palaces. They created sculpture, mural art, writing systems, weights, measures, mathematics, and new forms of political and social organization (Jolly and White 1995).

Because it increased economic production and led to new social, scientific, and creative forms, food production is often considered an evolutionary advance. But the new economy also brought hardships. For example, food producers typically work harder than foragers do—and for a less adequate diet. Because of their extensive leisure time, foragers have been characterized as living in "the original affluent society" (Sahlins 1972). Certain foragers have survived into recent times and have been studied by anthropologists. Among foragers living in the Kalahari Desert of southern Africa, only part of the group needed to hunt and gather, maybe 20 hours a week, to provide an adequate diet for the entire group. Women gathered, and adult men hunted. Their labor supported older people and children. Early retirement from the food quest was possible, and forced child labor was unknown.

With food production, yields are more reliable, but people work much harder. Herds, fields, and irrigation systems need care. Weeding can require hours of arduous bending. No one has to worry about where to keep a giraffe or a gazelle, but pens and corrals are built and maintained for livestock. Trade takes men, and sometimes women, away from home, leaving burdens for those who stay behind. For several reasons, food producers tend to have more children than foragers do. This means greater child care demands, but child labor also tends to be more needed and valued than it is among foragers. Many tasks in farming and herding can be done by children. The division of economic labor grows more complex, so that children and older people have assigned economic roles.

Not only does the new economy require hard work, so do the social and political systems supported by food production (See Chapter 11). States

Beyond the *Classroom*
Late Postclassic Economy in Northern Belize

Background Information

STUDENT: Maxine H. Oland
SUPERVISING PROFESSOR: Marilyn A. Masson
SCHOOL: State University of New York–Albany
YEAR IN SCHOOL/MAJOR: Senior/Anthropology
FUTURE PLANS: Graduate school in anthropology
PROJECT TITLE: Late Postclassic Economy in Northern Belize: Stone Tools and Raw Materials from the Freshwater Creek Drainage

---

What techniques were used to distinguish between locally made and imported tools? Does it surprise you that a food-producing state-level society such as the Maya would be using stone tools?

Laguna de On is a small archaeological site located on an island in Honey Camp Lagoon in Northern Belize. The Maya village site dates to the Postclassic Period (A.D. 900–1500). In order to better understand the economy of the region during this epoch, I sought to define patterns of local exchange regarding stone tools and raw materials. The project was funded by the National Science Foundation Research Experience for Undergraduates Award. It was completed during a field school run by the University at Albany.

It was already known that many of the tools at Laguna de On were made at Colha, a specialized lithic (stone tool) manufacturing center only 10 km away. Archaeological data at Colha indicate mass production of uniform stone tools made of highly distinctive chert. My project was concerned with the extent to which the inhabitants of Laguna de On were using local stone resources, and for what purposes.

In order to recognize those raw materials immediately available to the residents of Laguna de On, a survey was conducted of the region surrounding the lagoon. Various coarse cherts, chalcedonies, and quartz-blend materials were found outcropping naturally in sugar cane fields, road-cuts, and back yards. Every locality from which samples were collected was plotted on a map of Belize with the use of a global positioning system. The survey was purely geological, although one archaeological quarry was discovered in the process. This locality showed a surprising variety of fine chalcedonies in a concentrated area, as well as ample evidence for human modification of the materials.

In the field laboratory small samples were made of each material, using a geologist's hammer to create flakes from each nodule. These samples were labeled by locality and type (A, B, C, etc.) within the locality. They were then photographed to provide a visual record.

In the archaeology labs of the University at Albany a separate analysis of the stone tools was completed, classifying each artifact by raw material and tool type. Of the 417 stone tools examined in the study, 42 percent were made from Colha chert, which implies a heavy reliance on tools from Colha. Locally available materials made up the remaining 58 percent. An examination of tool type showed that formal tools (oval bifaces, stemmed blades) were almost exclusively acquired from Colha, while local resources were used for expedient (immediate use) tools (flakes, hammerstones).

Future work will build upon this research by comparing these findings to other nearby Postclassic sites of Northern Belize. A continuation of the raw material survey is planned, as the identification of more outcrops is essential to truly understanding procurement systems.

The labor demands of food production far exceed those associated with foraging. Here, in India's Andra Pradesh, these Banjara women are pounding grain. Such processing of food is just one step in getting the grain from the fields into people's mouths. What are some of the other steps?

may have mathematicians, artists, astronomers, priests, and kings, but ordinary people have to sweat in the fields to grow food for the elites and specialists. Unlike foragers, food producers have bosses. The elites conscript labor to build temples and pyramids, to move stone for enduring monuments. In states, people have to pay taxes and get drafted for work or war. It is a myth that leisure time increases with civilization. For some, there is leisure and privilege; for most, there is work and obligation.

And public health declines. Diets based on crops and dairy products tend to be less varied, less nutritious, and less healthful than foragers' diets, which are usually higher in proteins and lower in fats and carbohydrates. With the shift to food production, the physical well-being of the population often declines. Communicable diseases, protein deficiency, and dental caries increase (Cohen and Armelagos 1984). Greater exposure to pathogens comes with food production.

Compared with a seminomadic foraging band, food producers tend to be sedentary. Their populations are denser, which makes it easier to transmit and maintain diseases. We saw in Chapter 4 that malaria and sickle-cell anemia spread along with food production. Population concentrations, especially cities, are breeding grounds for epidemic diseases. People live nearer other people and animals and their wastes, which also affect public health (Diamond 1997). Compared with farmers, herders, and city dwellers, foragers were relatively disease-free, stress-free, and well nourished.

Other hardships and stresses accompanied food production and the state. Social inequality and poverty increased. Elaborate systems of social stratification eventually replaced the egalitarianism of the past. Resources were no longer common goods, open to all, as they tend to be among foragers. Property distinctions proliferated. Slavery and other forms of human bondage were invented. Crime, war, and human sacrifice became widespread.

The rate at which human beings degraded their environments also increased with food production. The environmental degradation in today's world, including air and water pollution and deforestation, is on a much larger scale, compared with early villages and cities, but modern trends are foreshadowed. After food production, population increase and the need to expand farming led to deforestation in the Middle East. Even today, many farmers think of trees as giant weeds to be cut down to make way for productive fields. Previously, we saw how early Mesoamerican farmers cut down mesquite trees for maize cultivation in the Valley of Oaxaca.

Many farmers and herders burn trees, brush, and pasture. Farmers burn to remove weeds; they also use the ashes for fertilizer. Herders burn to promote the growth of new tender shoots for their livestock. But such practices do have environmental costs, including air pollution. Smelting and other chemical processes basic to the manufacture of metal tools also have environmental costs. As modern industrial pollution has harmful effluents, early chemical processes had by-products that polluted

Table 10.4 The Benefits and Costs of Food Production (Compared with Foraging)

Do the costs outweigh the benefits?

Benefits	Costs
Discoveries and inventions	Harder work
New social, political, scientific, and creative forms (e.g., spinning, weaving, pottery, bricks, metallurgy)	Less nutritious diets
	Child labor and child care demands
Monumental architecture, arched masonry, sculpture	Taxes and military drafts
Writing	Public health declines (e.g., more exposure to pathogens, including communicable and epidemic diseases)
Mathematics, weights, and measures	Rise in protein deficiency and dental caries
Trade and markets	Greater stress
Urban life	Social inequality and poverty
Increased economic production	Slavery and other forms of human bondage
More reliable crop yields	Rise in crime, war, and human sacrifice
	Increased environmental degradation (e.g., air and water pollution, deforestation)

air, soils, and waters. Salts, chemicals, and microorganisms accumulate in irrigated fields. These and other pathogens and pollutants, which were by and large nonissues during the Paleolithic, endanger growing human populations. To be sure, food production had benefits. But its costs are just as evident. Table 10.4 summarizes the costs and benefits of food production. We see that progress is much too optimistic a word to describe food production, the state, and many other aspects of the evolution of society.

SUMMARY

1. After 15,000 B.P., as the big-game supply diminished, foragers sought out new foods. By 10,000 B.P., domesticated plants and animals were part of a broad spectrum of resources used by Middle Easterners. By 7500 B.P., most Middle Easterners were moving away from broad-spectrum foraging toward more specialized food-producing economies. *Neolithic* refers to the period when the first signs of domestication appeared.

2. Braidwood proposed that food production started in the Hilly Flanks zone, where wheat and barley grew wild. Others questioned this: The wild grain supply in that zone already provided an excellent diet for the Natufians and other

ancient Middle Easterners. There would have been no incentive to domesticate. Other scholars view the origin of food production in the context of increasing population and climate changes.

3. Ancient Middle Eastern foragers migrated seasonally in pursuit of game. They also collected wild plant foods as they ripened at different altitudes. As they moved about, these foragers took grains from the Hilly Flanks zone where they grew wild, to adjacent areas. Humans became agents of selection, preferring plants with certain attributes. Population spilled over from the Hilly Flanks into adjacent areas like the piedmont steppe. In such marginal zones people started

cultivating plants. They were trying to duplicate the dense wild grains of the Hilly Flanks.

4. After the harvest, sheep and goats fed off the stubble of these wild plants. Animal domestication occurred as people started selecting certain features and behavior and guiding the reproduction of goats, sheep, cattle, and pigs. Gradually, food production spread into the Hilly Flanks. Later, with irrigation it spread down into Mesopotamia's alluvial desert, where the first cities, states, and civilizations developed by 5500 B.P. Food production then spread west from the Middle East into North Africa and Europe and east to India and Pakistan.

5. There were seven independent inventions of food production: in the Middle East, sub-Saharan Africa, northern and southern China, Mesoamerica, the south central Andes, and the eastern United States. Millet was domesticated by 7000 B.P. in northern China; and rice, by 8000 B.P. in southern China.

6. The transition to food production took place thousands of years later in the New World. Humans entered the Americas some 20,000 years ago. Pursuing big game or moving by boat along the North Pacific Coast, they gradually moved into North America. Adapting to different environments, Native Americans developed a variety of cultures. Some continued to rely on big game. Others became broad-spectrum foragers.

7. In the New World the most important domesticates were maize, potatoes, and manioc. The llama of the central Andes was the largest animal domesticated in the New World, where herding traditions analogous to those of the Old World did not develop. Economic similarities between the hemispheres must be sought in foraging and farming.

8. The earliest New World farming was in Mesoamerica. At Oaxaca, in Mexico's southern highlands, maize was gradually added to a broad-spectrum diet between 7000 and 4000 B.P. The first permanent villages, supported by maize cultivation, arose in the lowlands and in a few frost-free areas of the highlands. In the Valley of Mexico, quick-growing maize made year-round village life possible and paved the way for the emergence of civilization and city life.

9. Food production and the social and political system it supported brought advantages and disadvantages. The advantages included discoveries and inventions. The disadvantages included harder work, poorer health, crime, war, social inequality, and environmental degradation.

KEY TERMS

broad-spectrum revolution Period beginning around 15,000 B.P. in the Middle East and 12,000 B.P. in Europe, during which a wider range, or broader spectrum, of plant and animal life was hunted, gathered, collected, caught, and fished; revolutionary because it led to food production.

Clovis tradition Stone technology based on a projectile point that was fastened to the end of a hunting spear; it flourished between 12,000 and 11,000 B.P. in North America.

food production Human control over the reproduction of plants and animals.

Hilly Flanks Woodland zone that flanks the Tigris and Euphrates rivers to the north; zone of wild wheat and barley and of sedentism (settled, nonmigratory life) preceding food production.

maize Corn; domesticated in highland Mexico.

manioc Cassava; a tuber domesticated in the South American lowlands.

Mesoamerica Middle America, including Mexico, Guatemala, and Belize.

Natufians Widespread Middle Eastern culture, dated to between 12,500 and 10,500 B.P.; subsisted on intensive wild cereal collecting and gazelle hunting and had year-round villages.

Neolithic "New Stone Age," coined to describe techniques of grinding and polishing stone tools; the first cultural period in a region in which the first signs of domestication are present.

sedentism Settled (sedentary) life; preceded food production in the Old World and followed it in the New World.

teocentli Or *teosinte*, a wild grass; apparent ancestor of maize.

CRITICAL THINKING QUESTIONS

For more self
testing, see the
self quizzes

mhhe
● com
/kottak

1. How would you explain the origin of food production? Would your explanation for the first farming in the Middle East also apply to Mesoamerica?

2. What environmental and demographic conditions contributed to the origin of food production in the Middle East? Did they also apply in Mesoamerica?

3. Is your own diet more like that of a forager or that of an early farmer? How so?

4. What were the main similarities and differences between early food production in the Middle East and in Mesoamerica?

5. For the Old World, name four caloric staples. Name three for the New World. Where was each domesticated? For each staple, is it part of your diet? What's the most important caloric staple in your diet?

6. What evidence supports the statement that transitions to food production were gradual and evolutionary?

7. Do you think it's likely that food production originated independently in south China and north China? Why?

8. Was the origin of food production good or bad? Why?

Atlas Questions

Look at Map 10, "Early Neolithic Sites of the Middle East and Europe."

1. What countries were the first to receive Middle Eastern domesticates? What countries were the last to receive these plants and animals?

2. Did Ireland receive Middle Eastern domesticates? See the text to learn the origin of the "Irish potato," which became, much later, the caloric basis of Irish subsistence.

3. Which diffused most widely, plants or animals, from the Middle East? Is the European Neolithic distribution the same for sheep, goats, cows, and pigs?

SUGGESTED ADDITIONAL READINGS

Ashmore, W., and R. Sharer

2000   *Discovering Our Past: A Brief Introduction to Archaeology*, 3rd ed. Boston: McGraw-Hill. Good introduction.

Cohen, M. N., and G. J. Armelagos, eds.

1984   *Paleopathology at the Origins of Agriculture.* New York: Academic Press. Some of the negative consequences of food production for human health.

Diamond, J. M.

1997   *Guns, Germs, and Steel: The Fates of Human Societies.* New York: W. W. Norton. Disease, tools, and environmental forces and effects throughout human history.

Fagan, B. M.

2000   *Ancient Lives: An Introduction to Method and Theory in Archaeology.* Upper Saddle River, NJ: Prentice-Hall. How archaeologists do what they do.

2002   *World Prehistory: A Brief Introduction*, 5th ed. New York: Longman. Major events in human prehistory, including the emergence of food production and the state in various locales.

Feinman, G. M., and T. D. Price

2001   *Archaeology at the Millennium: A Sourcebook.* New York: Kluwer Academic/Plenum. Prospects and new directions in archaeology.

Gamble, C.

2000   *Archaeology, the Basics*. New York: Routledge. The title says it all.

Henry, D. O.

1995   *Prehistoric Cultural Ecology and Evolution: Insights from Southern Jordan*. New York: Plenum Press. The origin of food production in the Middle East, with reference to environmental factors.

Kent, S., ed.

1998   *Gender in African Prehistory*. Walnut Creek, CA: AltaMira Press. Women and men in the African past.

Price, T. D., ed.

2000   *Europe's First Farmers*. New York: Cambridge University Press. The expansion of farming into Europe.

Price, T. D., and G. M. Feinman

2001   *Images of the Past*, 3rd ed. Boston: McGraw-Hill. Introduction to prehistory, including the origin of food production.

Price, T. D., and A. B. Gebauer, eds.

1995   *Last Hunters, First Farmers: New Perspectives on the Prehistoric Transition to Agriculture*. Santa Fe, NM: School of American Research Press. Recent ideas on the origin of food production.

Renfrew, C., and P. Bahn

2000   *Archaeology: Theories, Methods, and Practives*, 3rd ed. New York: Thames and Hudson. Basic methods text.

Smith, B. D.

1995   *The Emergence of Agriculture*. New York: Scientific American Library, W. H. Freeman. The first farmers and herders in several world areas.

Staeck, J.

2002   *Back to Earth: An Introduction to Archaeology*. Boston: McGraw-Hill. Introduction to the field.

Wenke, R.

1996   *Patterns in Prehistory: Humankind's First Three Million Years*, 4th ed. New York: Oxford University Press. Rise of food production and the state throughout the world; thorough, useful text.

INTERNET EXERCISES

1. Read the article by Jack Challum in *The Nutrition Reporter* entitled "Paleolithic Nutrition: Your Future Is in Your Dietary Past" **(http://www.nutritionreporter.com/stone_age_diet.html)**.

   a. What kinds of foods typified the Paleolithic diet? What kinds of foods typify the modern American diet?

   b. What changes have occurred to the number and kind of foods consumed by humans? Why are our foods higher in saturated fats? What changes have occurred in vitamin intake?

   c. Despite the fact that humans may not be completely adapted to an agricultural diet, what are the physical and cultural advantages of agriculture?

2. Read the history of maize written by Ricardo J. Salvador **(http://maize.agron.iastate.edu/maizearticle.html)**.

   a. When and where was maize domesticated?

   b. Maize is a very important source of carbohydrates and is one of the top three cereal crops in the world (along with rice and wheat). However, what are its nutritional deficiencies? How did Native Americans respond to this deficiency?

   c. When did maize first arrive in Europe? How was it carried there? Where else did it spread?

See Chapter 10 at your McGraw-Hill Online Learning Center for additional review and interactive exercises.

11

THE FIRST CITIES AND STATES

Overview

The spread and intensification of food production, which was discussed in Chapter 10, paved the way for state formation. The first states developed in Mesopotamia by 5500 B.P. and in Mesoamerica some 3,000 years later. Chiefdoms were precursors to states, with privileged and effective leaders—chiefs—but lacking the sharp class divisions that characterize states. By 7000 B.P. in the Middle East and 3200 B.P. in Mesoamerica, there is evidence for what archaeologists call the elite level, indicating a chiefdom or a state. By 3200 B.P. many different chiefdoms existed in Mesoamerica, one of which was the Olmec. Chapter 10 cited the Olmec, which thrived between 3200 and 2500 B.P. on Mexico's Gulf Coast, as an example of the elite level. The Olmec were neither the first nor the most elaborate of the early Mexican chiefdoms,

and they never developed into a state. Other Mexican chiefdoms, such as the ones in Oaxaca and the Valley of Mexico, did develop into states.

Like food production, states emerged in several world areas. The very first states arose in Mesopotamia (between the Tigris and Euphrates rivers) by 5500 B.P. and in the Nile Valley by 5250 B.P. Another state flourished between 4,600 and 3,900 years ago in the Indus River Valley of Pakistan and western India. The Shang dynasty state arose in the Huang He (Yellow) River valley of northern China around 3,750 years ago. By 2200 B.P., the process of state formation had accelerated in Mesoamerica and the Andes. Early states built on the social, political, and economic hierarchies and flamboyant art styles and architecture of the chiefdoms that preceded them.

Ancient Peru Torture Deaths: Sacrifices or War Crimes?

NATIONAL GEOGRAPHIC NEWS BRIEF

by Ben Harder

April 29, 2002

Codes of conduct apply to warfare as they do to other aspects of culture. How do the perpetrators of brutality—illustrated by the possible "war crimes" described in this account—justify their behavior? Do they kill and mutilate for revenge, punishment, or desecration, or as part of a ritual? Warfare was common in ancient cities and states, as well as in the chiefdoms that preceded them. Did ancient warriors mainly kill members of their own group or members of other societies? Read this story to discover at least one way in which anthropologists go about answering this question.

Forensic anthropologist John Verano of Tulane University in New Orleans has been investigating a series of grisly executions in the arid valleys of lowland Peru. Evidence from the skeletal remains shows that the victims, who lived during the Moche civilization nearly two thousand years ago, suffered shockingly brutal deaths . . .

When the graves at a Moche temple complex in northern Peru were uncovered, the human remains showed many clear marks of violence. Various theories arose to explain it. One proposes that the Moche sacrificed some of their own people to appease the gods and improve the fertility of their land. Another suggests that the victims were . . . losers of fierce power struggles between competing prehistoric city-states . . .

So far, the scientists have unearthed more than 100 skeletons buried at different sites between about A.D. 150 and A.D. 650 . . .

The grim events revealed by the archaeological findings have long been familiar to scholars from finely rendered pottery and murals of the Moche people. Scenes embellished with abundant bloodshed show victims being humiliated, abused, and executed.

Some people have interpreted these frightening scenes as exaggerated fictions concocted by the Moche to scare enemies. The recent analysis, however, suggests that the events depicted were horrifyingly real and not figments of artists' imagination.

The revelation of gruesome forms of torture is puzzling in part because the Moche developed a vibrant and highly advanced culture. These pre-Inca Peruvians were renowned builders, artists, and warriors. Their technological advances included, for example, techniques of irrigation that made their valleys even more productive than the same land is today . . .

Combat was a prevalent theme of Moche art. The detailed scenes on pottery and murals form what UCLA anthropologist Christopher B. Donnan calls a rich "warrior narrative."

Donnan has been studying Moche art for 35 years, and his interpretation of the disturbing executions is that they were part of ritual combat among Moche elites. "From all the artistic depictions we have, these are Moche against Moche, not warfare with some other group," he said.

Combat was a prevalent theme in the life, and art—as is illustrated here—of Peru's Moche period.

In the Moche scenes of battle, each combatant wore a loincloth, patterned tunic, and conical helmet, and hung a trapezoidal metal flap from the back of his belt. Along with their other accessories, the warriors' elaborate dress suggests that they brought both wealth and pageantry to combat, which Donnan likens to medieval jousts.

Various panels show warriors squaring off, locked in combat, or in the aftermath of battle.

"A few [panels] show a warrior triumphing over another, but not striking the loser on the ground"—a sign that battles were not fought to the death, said Donnan.

Instead, the art suggests that a victorious warrior took the weapons and belongings of the loser, tied a rope around the vanquished fighter's neck, and led him away naked.

The captives were subsequently sacrificed in a bloody ritual, and their bodies—or parts of them—scattered . . . Why were the bodies . . . so mutilated and cast aside . . . ?

Verano's latest finds . . . undermine the notion that these scenes were merely a part of ritual combat. Some of the recently unearthed skeletons . . . show marks indicating that the bones were stripped of flesh . . .

Such practices of defleshing victims don't appear in Moche art, said Donnan. "This makes it extremely enigmatic," he said. "It's hard to fit it into the warrior narrative."

"These people were clearly denied proper burial," and were instead left in open pits to be preyed on by vultures and flies, Verano said. "They were desecrated. The closest analogy would be war crimes today." He thinks the victims were war prisoners, not losers of ritual combat among the elite of a particular city. "They may be Moche," he said, "but from other valleys."

One clue is that some of their wounds had time to heal before they died, perhaps an indication that they were rounded up after battle and marched back to the city where they were ultimately killed.

Other clues also hint that the victims hailed from different regions . . .

By analyzing the chemical composition of the victims' hair, Verano and his colleagues determined that some of the dead had a diet rich in seafood, indicating that they lived along the coast, while others appeared to have lived at higher elevations . . .

The victims were buried individually or in small groups, not in true mass graves. To Verano, this suggests that the victims represent "a few principal captives from each episode" of conflict between the city and its enemies . . .

SOURCE: http://news.nationalgeographic.com/news/2002/04/0425_020426_mochekillings.html.

In coastal Peru, as in many ancient states, the population pressure triggered by productive farming fueled a pattern of warfare aimed at the acquisition of scarce resources, such as land and labor. The vanquished had to pay tribute to their conquerors. To do this, they intensified production, perfecting techniques, such as irrigation, to produce more food. Eventually, through a series of conquests, expansive states, like that of the Moche, with its famous Mochica pottery, extended their rule over entire regions. Warfare is associated with all ancient states—as, too, are impressive artistic and scientific achievements. What are other attributes of states?

Attributes of States

A **state** is a society with a formal, central government and a division of society into classes. Certain attributes distinguish states from earlier forms of society:

1. A state controls a specific regional territory, such as the Nile Valley or the Valley of Mexico. The regional expanse of a state contrasts with the much smaller territories controlled by kin groups and villages in prestate societies. Early states were expansionist; they arose from competition among chiefdoms, as the most powerful chiefdom conquered others, extended its rule over a larger territory, and managed to hold on to, and rule, the land and people acquired through conquest.

2. Early states had productive farming economies, supporting dense populations, often in cities. The agricultural economies of early states usually involved some form of water control or irrigation.

3. Early states used tribute and taxation to accumulate, at a central place, resources needed to support hundreds, or thousands, of specialists. These states had rulers, a military, and control over human labor.

4. States are stratified into social classes. In the first states, the non-food-producing population consisted of a tiny elite, plus artisans, officials, priests, and other specialists. Most people were commoners. Slaves and prisoners constituted the lowest rung of the social ladder. Rulers stayed in power by combining personal ability, religious authority, economic control, and force.

5. Early states had imposing public buildings and monumental architecture, including temples, palaces, and storehouses.

6. Early states developed some form of record-keeping system, usually a written script (Fagan 1996).

State Formation in the Middle East

In the last chapter we saw that food production arose in the ancient Middle East around 10,000 B.P. In the ensuing process of change, the center of population growth shifted from the zone where wheat and barley grew wild (Hilly Flanks) to adjacent areas (steppe) where those grains were first domesticated. By 6000 B.P., population was increasing most rapidly in the alluvial plain of southern Mesopotamia. (**Mesopotamia** refers to the area between the Tigris and Euphrates rivers in what is now southern Iraq and southwestern Iran.) This growing population supported itself through irrigation and intensive river valley agriculture. By 5500 B.P. towns had grown into cities. The earliest city-states were Sumer (southern Iraq) and Elam (southwestern Iran), with their capitals at Uruk (Warka) and Susa, respectively.

URBAN LIFE

The first towns arose around 10,000 years ago in the Middle East. Over the generations houses of mud brick were built and rebuilt in the same place.

Substantial tells or mounds arose from the debris of a succession of such houses. The Middle East and Asia have hundreds or thousands of such mounds, only a few of which have been excavated. These sites have yielded remains of ancient community life, including streets, buildings, terraces, courtyards, wells, and other artifacts.

The earliest known town was Jericho, located in what is now Israel, below sea level at a well-watered oasis a few miles northwest of the Dead Sea (Figure 11.1). From the lowest (oldest) level, we know that around 11,000 years ago, Jericho was first settled by Natufian foragers. Occupation continued thereafter, through and beyond biblical times, when "Joshua fit the battle of Jericho, and the walls came tumbling down."

During the phase just after the Natufians, the earliest known town appeared. It was an unplanned, densely populated settlement with round houses and some 2,000 people. At this time, well before the invention of pottery, Jericho was surrounded by a sturdy wall, with a massive tower. The wall may have been built initially as a flood barrier rather than for defense. Around 9000 B.P. Jericho was destroyed, to be rebuilt later. The new occupants lived in square houses with finished plaster floors. They buried their dead beneath their homes, a pattern seen at other sites, such as Çatal Hüyük in Turkey (see below). Pottery reached Jericho around 8000 B.P. (Gowlett 1993).

Long-distance trade, especially of obsidian, a volcanic glass used to make tools and ornaments, became important in the Middle East between 9500 and 7000 B.P. One town that prospered from this trade was Çatal Hüyük in Anatolia, Turkey (DeMarco 1997). A grassy mound 65 feet high holds the remains of this 9,000-year-old town, probably the largest settlement of the Neolithic age. Çatal Hüyük was located on a river, which deposited rich soil for crops, created a lush environment for animals, and was harnessed for irrigation by 7000 B.P. Over the mound's 32 acres (12.9 hectares), up to 10,000 people once lived in crowded mud-brick houses packed so tight that residents entered from their roofs.

Shielded by a defensive wall, Çatal Hüyük flourished between 8000 and 7000 B.P. Its individual mud-brick dwellings, rarely larger than a suburban American bedroom, had separate areas reserved for ritual and secular uses. In a given house, the ritual images were placed along the

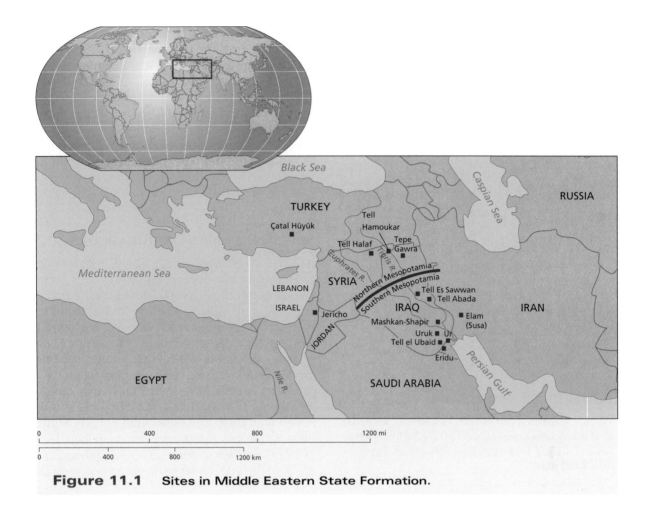

Figure 11.1 Sites in Middle Eastern State Formation.

walls that faced north, east, or west, but never south. That area was reserved for cooking and other domestic tasks. The ritual areas were originally identified as shrines, but ritual appears now to have been organized at the household level rather than by religious specialists. Priests appeared later in Middle Eastern history.

The ritual spaces were decorated with wall paintings, sculpted ox heads, bull horns, and relief models of bulls and rams. The paintings showed bulls surrounded by stick figures running, dancing, and sometimes throwing stones. Vultures attacked headless humans. One frieze had human hand prints painted below mounted bull horns. These images and their placement are reminiscent of Paleolithic cave art. The dwellings at Çatal Hüyük were entered through the roof, and people had to crawl through holes from room to room, somewhat like moving between chambers of a cave. The deeper down one went, the richer the art

became. The town's spiritual life seems to have revolved around a preoccupation with animals, danger, and death, perhaps related to the site's recent hunter-gatherer past.

Two or three generations of a family were buried beneath their homes. In one dwelling, archaeologists found remains of 17 individuals, mostly children. After two or three generations of family burials, the ritual art was removed; and the dwelling, burned. The site was then covered with fine dirt, and a floor laid for a new dwelling.

Çatal Hüyük's residents, though living in a town, acted independently in family groups without any apparent control by a priestly or political elite. The town never became a full-fledged city with centralized organization. Just as it lacked priests, Çatal Hüyük never had leaders who controlled or managed trade and production (Fagan 1996). Food was not stored and processed collectively, but on a smaller, domestic, scale (DeMarco 1997).

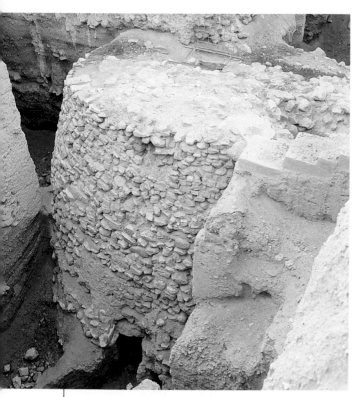

The world's earliest known town was Jericho, located in what is now Israel. Jericho was first settled by Natufian foragers around 11,000 B.P. This round tower dates back 8,000 years.

THE ELITE LEVEL

The first pottery (ceramics) dates back a bit more than 8,000 years, when it first reached Jericho. Before that date, the Neolithic is called the prepottery Neolithic. By 7000 B.P., pottery had become widespread in the Middle East. Archaeologists consider pottery shape, finishing, decoration, and type of clay as features used for dating. The geographic distribution of a given pottery style may indicate trade or alliance spanning a large area at a particular time.

An early and widespread pottery style, the **Halafian**, was first found at Tell Halaf in the mountains of northern Syria. Halafian (7500–6500 B.P.) refers to a delicate ceramic style. It also describes the period during which the elite level and the first chiefdoms emerged. The low number of Halafian ceramics suggests they were luxury goods associated with a social hierarchy.

By 7000 B.P. ranked chiefdoms had emerged in the Middle East. The Ubaid period (7000–6000 B.P.) is named for a southern Mesopotamian pottery type first discovered at a small site, Tell el-Ubaid, located near the major city of Ur in southern Iraq. Similar pottery has been discovered in the deep levels of the Mesopotamian cities of Ur, Uruk, and Eridu. Ubaid pottery is associated with advanced chiefdoms and perhaps the earliest states. It diffused rapidly over a large area, becoming more widespread than earlier ceramic styles such as the Halafian.

SOCIAL RANKING AND CHIEFDOMS

It is easy for archaeologists to identify early states. Evidence for state organization includes monumental architecture, central storehouses, irrigation systems, and written records. In Mesoamerica, even chiefdoms are easy to detect archaeologically. Ancient Mexican chiefdoms left behind stone works, such as temple complexes and the huge carved Olmec heads. Mesoamericans also had a penchant for marking their elites with durable ornaments and prestige goods, including those buried with chiefs and their families. Early Middle Eastern chiefs were less ostentatious in their use of material markers of prestige, making their chiefdoms somewhat harder to detect archaeologically (Flannery 1999).

On the basis of the kinds of status distinctions within society, the anthropologist Morton Fried (1959) divided societies into three types: egalitarian, ranked, and stratified (Table 11.1). An **egalitarian society**, most typically found among foragers, lacks status distinctions except for those based on age, gender, and individual qualities, talents, and achievements. Thus, depending on the society, adult men, elder women, talented musicians, or ritual specialists might receive special respect for their activities or knowledge. In egalitarian societies, status distinctions are not usually inherited. The child of a respected person will not receive special recognition because of his or her parent, but must earn such respect.

Ranked societies, in contrast, do have hereditary inequality. But they lack **stratification** (sharp social divisions—*strata*—based on unequal access to wealth and power) into noble and commoner classes. In ranked societies, individuals tend to be ranked in terms of their genealogical distance from

Table 11.1 Egalitarian, Ranked, and Stratified Societies

Kind of Status Distinction	Nature of Status	Common Form of Subsistence Economy	Common Forms of Social Organization	Examples
Egalitarian	Status differences are not inherited. All status is based on age, gender, and individual qualities, talents, and achievements.	Foraging	Bands and tribes	Inuit, Ju/'hoansi San, and Yanomami
Ranked	Status differences are inherited and distributed along a continuum from the highest-ranking member (chief) to the lowest without any breaks.	Horticulture, pastoralism, and some foraging groups	Chiefdoms and some tribes	Native American groups of the Pacific Northwest (for example, Salish and Kwakiutl), Natchez, Halaf and Ubaid Period polities, Olmec
Stratified	Status differences are inherited and divided sharply between distinct noble and commoner classes.	Agriculture	States	Teotihuacan, Uruk Period states, Inca, Shang dynasty, Rome, U.S., Great Britain

the chief. Closer relatives of the chief have higher rank or social status than more distant ones do. But there is a continuum of status, with many individuals and kin groups ranked about equally, which can lead to competition for positions of leadership.

Not all ranked societies are chiefdoms. Robert Carneiro (1991) has distinguished between two kinds of ranked societies, only the second of which is a chiefdom. In the first type, exemplified by some Indians of North America's Pacific Northwest, there were hereditary differences in rank, but villages were independent of one another. Exemplifying the second type were the Cauca of Colombia and the Natchez of the eastern United States. These ranked societies had become **chiefdoms**, societies in which relations among villages as well

as among individuals were unequal. The smaller villages had lost their autonomy and were under the authority of leaders who lived at larger villages. According to Kent Flannery (1999), *only those ranked societies with such loss of village autonomy should be called chiefdoms*. In chiefdoms, there is always inequality—differences in rank—among both individuals and communities.

In Mesopotamia, Mesoamerica, and Peru, chiefdoms were precursors to **primary states** (states that arose on their own, and not through contact with other state societies—see Wright 1994). Primary states emerged from competition among chiefdoms, as one chiefdom managed to conquer its neighbors and to make them part of a larger political unit (Flannery 1995).

Unlike states, such as Japan, whose emperor and empress are shown here, egalitarian societies lack inherited wealth and status and succession to political office. How are inherited status distinctions marked in your society?

Archaeological evidence for chiefdoms in Mesoamerica, where several states arose between 2,500 and 1,600 years ago, dates back more than 3,000 years. Mesoamerican chiefdoms are easy to detect archaeologically because they were flamboyant in the way they marked their aristocracy. High-status families deformed the heads of their infants and buried them with special symbols and grave goods. In burials, prestige goods show a continuum from graves with many, to less, to none, of precious materials, such as jade and turquoise (Flannery 1999).

The first Middle Eastern states developed between 6000 and 5500 B.P. The first societies based on rank, including the first chiefdoms, emerged during the preceding 1,500 years. In the Middle East, the archaeological record of the period after 7300 B.P. reveals behavior typical of chiefdoms, including exotic goods used as markers of status,

along with raiding and political instability. Early Middle Eastern chiefdoms included both the Halafian culture of northern Iraq and the Ubaid culture of southern Iraq, which eventually spread north.

As in Mesoamerica, ancient Middle Eastern chiefdoms had cemeteries where chiefly relatives were buried with distinctive items: vessels, statuettes, necklaces, and high-quality ceramics. Such goods were buried with children too young to have earned prestige on their own, but who happened to be born into elite families. In the ancient village of Tell es-Sawwan, infant graves show a continuum of richness from six statuettes, to three statuettes, to one statuette, to none. Such signs of slight gradations in social status are exactly what one expects in ranked societies (Flannery 1999).

Such burials convince Flannery (1999) that hereditary status differences were present in the Middle East by 7000 B.P. But had the leaders of large villages extended their authority to the smaller villages nearby? Is there evidence for the loss of village autonomy, converting simple ranked societies into chiefdoms? One clue that villages were linked in political units is the use of a common canal to irrigate several villages. This suggests a way of resolving disputes among farmers over access to water, for example, by appeal to a strong leader. By later Halafian times in northern Mesopotamia, there is evidence for such multivillage alliances (Flannery 1999). Another clue to the loss of village autonomy is the emergence of a two-tier settlement hierarchy, with small villages clustering around a large village, especially one with public buildings. There is evidence for this pattern in northern Mesopotamia during the Halafian (Watson 1983).

HOW ETHNOGRAPHY HELPS IN INTERPRETING THE ARCHAEOLOGICAL RECORD

When they excavate sites, how do archaeologists know whether they've found a chiefdom, or some less complex form of society? Grave goods and settlement hierarchy offer clues. Also, studying ethnography helps archaeologists interpret the past.

Thus, to infer the archaeological characteristics of ancient Middle Eastern chiefdoms, Kent Flannery (1999) looks to recent chiefdoms that

This funerary chamber from Sipan, Peru (a Moche site), contains gold jewelry, pottery, and other artifacts. In chiefdoms and states, high-status families often bury their dead with distinctive symbols and grave goods.

ancient Middle Eastern chiefdom, archaeologists should look not for one unique residence but also for the nearby houses of chiefly kin. Such homes would be large enough to entertain many visitors (perhaps with a spacious central court). They might have a large kitchen and storerooms for food staples and craft products used as gifts. Indeed, prehistoric houses fitting this description have been found (Jasim 1985).

According to Robert Carneiro (1991), raiding is especially common in chiefdoms. Illustrating such raiding, early chiefdoms in Mexico and Peru had public art featuring enemy corpses, mutilated prisoners, and trophy heads (Marcus 1992). Middle Eastern chiefdoms lacked this kind of art. But their sites did have defensive walls, ditches, and watchtowers comparable to those of Mesoamerica. Political alliance also offered some protection against raiding.

Despite their defenses and alliances, prehistoric chiefdoms were still raided. There is archaeological evidence that large houses, belonging to community leaders, were sacked and burned during raids in the Halafian and Ubaid periods. Consider Tepe Gawra, a site dating to the late Ubaid period (Tobler 1950). This densely packed town was defended by its position atop a mound, and by a watchtower. Its largest residence had an inner court that illustrates the kind of large, elegant reception space Flannery (1999) expects to find in the home of a chief who hosted many subordinates and visitors. There was also a large kitchen.

On the same street was a slightly less impressive residence, supporting the belief that archaeologists should look for multiple elite houses in chiefly neighborhoods. This town had been raided and partly burned. At least four victims—a baby and three youths—were left unburied in the ruins. The building hardest hit was that with the largest inner court, confirming that, as is usual, the chiefly family was the raid's main target.

From such clues—archaeological and ethnographic—we infer that chiefly families and a pattern of raiding one's rivals were present in the Middle East between 7300 and 5800 B.P.

have been studied ethnographically in that region. One example is the Basseri, a population of 16,000 migratory herders in Iran (Barth 1964). The Basseri had a large grazing territory, but some of their chiefly families also owned farming villages and city homes. Leading the Basseri was a chief, whose brothers, cousins, uncles, and nephews vied for leadership during "periods of confusion" (Barth 1964). Such political rivalry among close kin is typical of chiefdoms worldwide.

Using the Basseri as an ethnographic analogy, Flannery (1999) suggests likely characteristics of an ancient Middle Eastern chiefdom. Such an ancient confederacy of several thousand people would have had a hereditary aristocracy, but no capital city. There would have been no palace, no temples, no clear territorial boundaries. Its thousands of tents would barely leave a trace archaeologically. But by analogy with the Basseri, we might find remains of a few chiefly houses in mud-walled cities.

According to Barth (1964), a Basseri chief's home was large—to entertain visitors. The chief gave substantial gifts to his prominent subjects, who were expected to reciprocate. The chief's close kinsmen were almost as privileged as he was. By analogy, Flannery (1999) suggests, to identify an

ADVANCED CHIEFDOMS

In northeastern Syria, near the border with Iraq, archaeologists have been excavating an ancient settlement that once lay on a major trade route. This large site, Tell Hamoukar, dates back more than 5,500 years (Wilford 2000). Its remains suggest that advanced chiefdoms arose in northern areas of the Middle East independently of the better-known city-states of southern Mesopotamia, in southern Iraq (Wilford 2000).

The oldest layer yet uncovered at Tell Hamoukar contains traces of villages dating back 6,000 years. By 5700 B.P. the settlement was a prosperous town of 32 acres, enclosed by a defensive wall 10 feet high and 13 feet wide. The site had fine pottery and large ovens—evidence of food preparation on an institutional scale. The site has yielded pieces of large cooking pots, animal bones, and traces of wheat, barley, and oats for baking and brewing. The archaeologist McGuire Gibson, one of the excavators, believes that food preparation on this scale is evidence of a rank society in which elites were organizing people and resources (Wilford 2000). Most likely they were hosting and entertaining in a chiefly manner (as discussed in the preceding section).

Also providing evidence for social ranking are the seals used to mark containers of food and other goods. Some of the seals are small, with only simple incisions or cross-hatching. Others are larger and more elaborate, presumably for higher officials to stamp more valuable goods. Gibson suspects the larger seals with figurative scenes were held by the few people who had greater authority. The smaller, simply incised seals were used by many more people with less authority (Wilford 2000).

THE RISE OF THE STATE

See the Virtual Exploration for information about early writing in the Indus Valley

In southern Mesopotamia at this time (5700 B.P.), an expanding population and increased food production from irrigation were changing the social landscape even more drastically than in the north. Irrigation had allowed Ubaid communities to spread along the Euphrates River. Travel and trade were expanding, with water serving as the highway system. Such raw materials as hardwood and stone, which southern Mesopotamia lacked, were imported via river routes. Population density increased as new settlements appeared. Social and economic networks now linked communities on the rivers in the south and in the foothills to the north. Settlements spread north into what is now Syria. Social differentials also increased. Priests and political leaders joined expert potters and other specialists. These non-food-producers were supported by the larger population of farmers and herders (Gilmore-Lehne 2000).

Economies were being managed by central leadership. Agricultural villages had grown into cities, some of which were ruled by local kings. The Uruk period (6000–5200 B.P.), which succeeded the Ubaid period, takes it name from a prominent southern city-state located more than 400 miles south of Tell Hamoukar (Table 11.2). The Uruk period established Mesopotamia as "the cradle of civilization" (see Pollock 1999).

There is no evidence of Uruk influence at Tell Hamoukar until 5200 B.P., when some Uruk pottery showed up. When southern Mesopotamians expanded north, they found advanced chiefdoms, which were not yet states. The fact that writing

Illustrating pictographic writing is this limestone tablet from the proto-urban period of lower Mesopotamia. This Sumerian script records proper names, including that of a landowner—symbolized by the hand—who commissioned the tablet.

Table 11.2 Archaeological Periods in Middle Eastern State Formation

Dates	Period	Age
3000–2539 B.P.	Neo-Babylonian	Iron Age
3600–3000 B.P.	Kassite	
4000–3600 B.P.	Old Babylonian	Bronze Age
4150–4000 B.P.	Third Dynasty of Ur	
4350–4150 B.P.	Akkadian	
4600–4350 B.P.	Early Dynastic III	
4750–4600 B.P.	Early Dynastic II	
5000–4750 B.P.	Early Dynastic I	
5200–5000 B.P.	Jemdet Nasr	
6000–5200 B.P.	Uruk	Chalcolithic
7500–6000 B.P.	Ubaid (southern Mesopotamia)–Halaf (northern Mesopotamia)	
10,000–7000 B.P.		Neolithic

Early Mesopotamian scribes used a stylus to scrawl symbols on raw clay. This writing, called *cuneiform*, left a wedge-shaped impression on the clay. What languages were written in cuneiform?

originated in Sumer, in southern Mesopotamia, indicates a more advanced, state-organized society there. The first writing presumably developed to handle record keeping for a centralized economy.

Writing was initially used to keep accounts, reflecting the needs of trade. Rulers, nobles, priests, and merchants were the first to benefit from it. Writing spread from Mesopotamia to Egypt by 5000 B.P. The earliest writing was pictographic, for example, with pictorial symbols of horses used to represent them.

Early Mesopotamian scribes used a stylus (writing implement) to scrawl symbols on raw clay. This writing left a wedge-shaped impression on the clay, called **cuneiform** writing, from the Latin word for wedge. Both the Sumerian (southern Mesopotamia) and Akkadian (northern Mesopotamia) languages were written in cuneiform (Gowlett 1993).

Writing and temples played key roles in the Mesopotamian economy. For the historic period after 5600 B.P., when writing was invented, there are temple records of economic activities. States can exist without writing, but literacy facilitates the flow and storage of information. We know that Mesopotamian priests managed herding, farming, manufacture, and trade. Temple officials allotted fodder and pasture land for cattle and donkeys, which were used as plow and cart animals. As the economy expanded, trade, manufacture, and grain

Beyond the *Classroom*
The Akhenaten Temple Project

Background Information

STUDENT:	Jerusha Achterberg
SUPERVISING PROFESSOR:	Donald Redford
SCHOOL:	The Pennsylvania State University
YEAR IN SCHOOL/MAJOR:	Senior/Anthropology
MINORS:	Mathematics/Education Policy Studies Future
PLANS:	Graduate school
PROJECT TITLE:	The Akhenaten Temple Project

What is the nature of the student work described here? How independent was this research?

My first archaeological field-work experience was in Egypt, where I worked as a site supervisor on the 10th round of excavations at Mendes (Tel er-Rub'a), on Middle Kingdom levels of that site in summer 2000. As a newcomer to the field, many techniques were unfamiliar to me. But the most difficult things for me to adapt to were the working conditions. Egyptian weather in July was not what my body was used to, and I was unprepared for what it would be like to work primarily with a team of native workers with whom I shared very little language. I was assigned a dig site, and a team of Egyptian workers including a Kufdi, who essentially guided the team, two pickmen and four basket-girls who removed the dirt after excavation. Rather than my primary job being the digging, as site supervisor, I recorded, measured, and mapped all our finds and loci. I was also responsible for making on-the-spot decisions about the course of our progress.

Because I had done no hands-on archeology before my arrival in Egypt, I was surprised by how quickly I learned the techniques we used. I kept constant records of every find in my site, as well as of the soil type. For those who have not worked in Egypt, it is hard to imagine the sheer volume of pottery that is found at the sites. Every piece had to be sorted and catalogued following excavation. As a result, after excavating from 6 A.M.–1 P.M., we spent the afternoons sorting and washing pottery. On occasion I was able to participate in the more specialized tasks, such as tracing the stance of representative pottery fragments and sorting through the small finds collection.

One job in which I found particular skill was rebuilding pottery vessels from the excavated fragments. This job is important, although too tedious for most people's patience. I found the repetitiveness of the work relaxing compared to the excavation work of the morning. Also, because of my past work in mathematics I found I was good at profiling the excavation site stratigraphy, and drawing spatial representations of the architecture and finds. This work was usually done with a partner. One person called out measurements from a baseline, while the other plot-ted the information on a grid. This was later fleshed out with information about the materials involved, orientation, and presence of particular features. Prior to going to Egypt, I was concerned about handling human remains. I had never had a problem considering the idea while sitting in a classroom, but I worried that the hands-on work might be different. Recalling this worry was humorous after several hours of cleaning off a human skull. I had become so involved with the work and the satisfaction of slowly revealing the fragile bone, it hadn't occurred to me to be concerned about handling the remains. In fact, it seemed as though the care I was granting the skull was more respectful than leaving it in the ground to weather further. My reaction, or lack thereof, came as a surprise to me, but a welcome one. Overall, I'm very proud of the work I did in Egypt and the help I provided to the ongoing work at Mendes.

storage were centrally managed. Temples collected and distributed meat, dairy products, crops, fish, clothing, tools, and trade items. Potters, metal workers, weavers, sculptors, and other artisans perfected their crafts.

Prior to the invention of **metallurgy** (knowledge of the properties of metals, including their extraction and processing and the manufacture of metal tools), raw copper was shaped by hammering. If copper is hammered too long, it hardens and becomes brittle, with a risk of cracking. But once heated (annealed) in a fire, copper becomes malleable again. Such annealing of copper was an early form of metallurgy. A vital step for metallurgy was the discovery of **smelting**, the high-temperature process by which pure metal is produced from an ore. Ores, including copper ore, have a much wider distribution than does native copper, which was initially traded as a luxury good because of its rarity (Gowlett 1993).

When and how smelting was discovered is unknown. But after 5000 B.P., metallurgy evolved rapidly. The Bronze Age began when alloys of arsenic and copper, or tin and copper (in both cases known as **bronze**), became common and greatly extended the use of metals. Bronze flows more easily than copper does when heated to a similar temperature, so bronze was more convenient for metal casting. Early molds were carved in stone, as shaped depressions to be filled with molten metal. A copper ax cast from such a mold has been found in northern Mesopotamia and predates 5000 B.P. Thereafter, other metals came into common use. By 4500 B.P. golden objects were found in royal burials at Ur.

Iron ore is distributed more widely than is copper ore. Iron, when smelted, can be used on its own; there is no need for tin or arsenic to make a metal alloy (bronze). The Iron Age began once high-temperature iron smelting was mastered. In the Old World after 3200 B.P., iron spread rapidly. Formerly valued as highly as gold, iron crashed in value when it became plentiful (Gowlett 1993).

The Mesopotamian economy, based on craft production, trade, and intensive agriculture, spurred population growth and an increase in urbanism. Sumerian cities were protected by a fortress wall and surrounded by a farming area. By 4800 B.P., Uruk, the largest early Mesopotamian city, had a population of 50,000. As irrigation and the population expanded, communities fought over water. People sought protection in the fortified cities (Adams 1981), which defended themselves when neighbors or invaders threatened.

By 4600 B.P., secular authority had replaced temple rule. The office of military coordinator developed into kingship. This change shows up architecturally in palaces and royal tombs. The palace raised armies and supplied them with armor, chariots, and metal armaments. At Ur's royal cemetery, by 4600 B.P. monarchs were being buried with soldiers, charioteers, and ladies in waiting. These subordinates were killed at the time of royal burial to accompany the monarch to the afterworld.

Agricultural intensification made it possible for the number of people supported by a given area to increase. Population pressure on irrigated fields helped create a stratified society. Land became scarce private property that was bought and sold. Some people amassed large estates, and their wealth set them off from ordinary farmers. These landlords joined the urban elite, while sharecroppers and serfs toiled in the fields. By

This ziggurat, or temple tower, at Ur, Iraq, dates back to 4100 B.P. [2100 B.C.]. Temples and their officials played key roles in the Mesopotamian economy. Who handles such duties in our own society?

4600 B.P., Mesopotamia had a well-defined class structure, with complex stratification into nobles, commoners, and slaves.

Other Early States

For more on state formation in Africa, see the Internet Exercises at your OLC

mhhe
●com
/kottak

In northwestern India and Pakistan, the Indus River Valley (or *Harappan*) state, with major cities at Harappa and Mohenjo-daro, takes its name from the river valley along which it extended. (Figure 11.2 maps the four great early river valley states of the Old World: Mesopotamia, Egypt, India/Pakistan, and northern China.) Trade and the spread of writing from Mesopotamia may have played a role in the emergence of the Harappan state around 4600 B.P. Located in Pakistan's Punjab Province, the ruins of Harappa were the first to be identified as part of the Indus River Valley civilization. At its peak, the Indus River Valley state incorporated 1,000 cities, towns, and villages, spanning 280,000 square miles (725,000 square kilometers). This state flourished between 4600 and 3900 B.P. It displayed such features of state organization as urban planning, social stratification, and an early writing system, which remains undeciphered. The Harappans maintained a uniform system of weights, and their cites had carefully planned residential areas with wastewater systems. An array of products from sophisticated craft industries included ceramic vessels made on potter's wheels (Meadow and Kenoyer 2000).

Figure 11.2   The Four Great Early River Valley States of the Old World.

By approximately 4,000 B.P. urban life had been established along the Tigris and Euphrates rivers in Mesopotamia, the Nile River in Egypt, the Indus and Ganges rivers in India/Pakistan, and the Yellow River in China.

SOURCE: Based on Map 1-1, Chapter 1, "Birth of Civilization." In Albert M. Craig, *The Heritage of World Civilizations*, *Volume I, to 1650*, 4th ed. Upper Saddle River, NJ: Prentice-Hall, 1997.

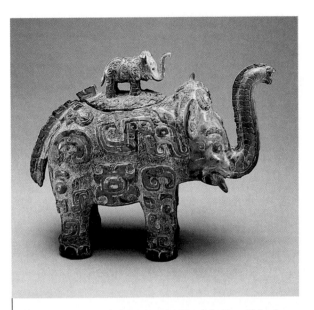

This bronze vessel was commissioned during China's Shang dynasty. The small elephant on top forms the handle of the lid. Wine was poured through the spout formed by the big elephant's trunk. Three notable features of the Shang dynasty were bronze, writing, and social stratification.

The first Chinese state, dating to 3750 B.P., was that of the Shang dynasty. It arose in the Huang He (Yellow) River area of northern China, where wheat, rather than rice, was the dietary staple. This state was characterized by urbanism, palatial (as well as domestic) architecture, human sacrifice, and a sharp division between social classes. Burials of the aristocracy were marked by ornaments of stone, including jade. The Shang had bronze metallurgy and an elaborate writing system. In warfare they used chariots and took prisoners (Gowlett 1993).

Like Mesopotamia and China, many early civilizations came to rely on metallurgy. At Nok Nok Tha in northern Thailand, metalworking goes back 6,000 years. In Peru's Andes metalworking appeared around 4000 B.P. The ancient inhabitants of the Andes were skilled workers of bronze, copper, and gold. They are also well known for their techniques of pottery manufacture. Their arts, crafts, and agricultural knowledge compared well with those of Mesoamerica at its height, to which we now turn. Note that both Mesoamerican and Andean state formation were truncated by Spanish conquest. The Aztecs of Mexico were conquered in A.D. 1519; and the Inca of Peru, in 1532.

The Indus River Valley state collapsed, apparently through warfare, around 3900 B.P. Its cities became largely depopulated. Skeletons of massacre victims have been found in the streets of Mohenjo-daro. Harappa continued to be occupied, but on a much smaller scale than previously (Meadow and Kenoyer 2000). (For more on the ongoing Harappa Archaeological Research Project, visit www.harappa.com.)

Interpret the World
Atlas Map 11

In your atlas, look at Map 11, "Ancient Civilizations of the Old World," which shows the locations of ancient civilizations (archaic states) in Europe, Africa, and Asia and also indicates the date when each state first appeared. What's the chronological order in which these states appeared? Compare Map 11 in your atlas with Figure 11.2 in the text. Figure 11.2 shows the four great early river valley states of the Old World, whereas Map 11 shows other states as well. Name some states that originated outside river valleys.

State Formation in Mesoamerica

See the Internet Exercises at your OLC

/kottak

In the last chapter we examined the independent inventions of farming in the Middle East and Mesoamerica. The processes of state formation that took place in these areas were also comparable, beginning with ranked societies and chiefdoms, and ending with fully formed states and empires.

The first monumental buildings (temple complexes) in the Western Hemisphere were constructed by Mesoamerican chiefdoms in many areas, from the Valley of Mexico to Guatemala. These chiefdoms influenced one another as they traded materials, such as obsidian, shells, jade, and pottery. (Figure 11.3 maps major sites in the emergence of Mesoamerican food production, chiefdoms, and states. See Table 10.3 on p. 273 of Chapter 10 for a chronology of Mesoamerican state formation.)

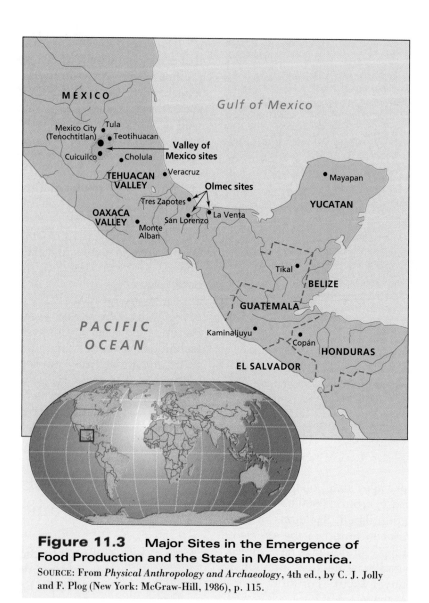

Figure 11.3 **Major Sites in the Emergence of Food Production and the State in Mesoamerica.**

SOURCE: From *Physical Anthropology and Archaeology*, 4th ed., by C. J. Jolly and F. Plog (New York: McGraw-Hill, 1986), p. 115.

EARLY CHIEFDOMS AND ELITES

The Olmec built a series of ritual centers on Mexico's southern Gulf Coast between 3,200 and 2,500 years ago. Three of these centers, each from a different century, are known. Earthen mounds were grouped into plaza complexes, presumably for religious use. Such centers show that Olmec chiefs could marshal human labor to construct such mounds. The Olmec were also master sculptors; they carved massive stone heads, perhaps as images of their chiefs or their ancestors, such as on Polynesia's Easter Island (see the chapter-opening photo).

There is evidence, too, that trade routes linked the Olmec with other parts of Mesoamerica, such as the Valley of Oaxaca in the southern highlands and the Valley of Mexico (see Figure 11.3). By 3000 B.P. a ruling elite had emerged in Oaxaca. The items traded at that time between Oaxaca and the Olmec were for elite consumption. High-status Oaxacans wore ornaments made of mussel shells from the coast. In return, the Olmec elite imported mirrors and jade made by Oaxacan artisans. Chiefdoms in Oaxaca developed canal and well irrigation, exported magnetite mirrors, and were precocious in their use of adobes (mud bricks), stucco, stone masonry, and architecture. Chiefdoms in the Olmec area farmed river levees, built mounds of earth, and carved colossal stone heads.

The Olmec are famous for their huge carved stone heads, but other early Mexican chiefdoms also had accomplished artists and builders, using adobes and lime plaster and constructing stone buildings, precisely oriented 8 degrees north of east.

The period between 3,200 and 3,000 B.P. was one of rapid social change in Mexico. All or almost all of Mesoamerica's chiefdoms were linked by trade and exchange. Many competing chiefly centers were concentrating labor power, intensifying agriculture, exchanging trade goods, and borrowing ideas, including art motifs and styles, from each other. Archaeologists now believe it was the *intensity of competitive interaction*—rather than the supremacy of any one chiefdom—that made social change so rapid. The social and political landscape of Mexico around 3000 B.P. was one in which 25 or so chiefly centers were (1) sufficiently separate and autonomous to adapt to local zones and conditions and (2) sufficiently interacting and competitive to borrow and incorporate new ideas and innovations as they arose in other regions (Flannery and Marcus 2000).

It used to be thought that a single chiefdom could become a state on its own. Archaeologists know now that state formation involves one chiefdom's incorporating several others into the emerging state it controls, and making changes in its own infrastructure as it acquires and holds on to new territories, followers, and goods. Warfare and attracting followers are two key elements in state formation.

Many chiefdoms have dense populations, intensive agriculture, and settlement hierarchies that include hamlets, villages, and perhaps towns. These factors pave the way for greater social and political complexity. Political leaders emerge, and military success (in raiding) often solidifies their position. Such figures attract lots of followers, who are loyal to their leader. Warfare enables leaders to incorporate new lands and people. Success in warfare leads to states' becoming even more densely occupied and in control of new lands. States, in contrast to chiefdoms, can acquire labor and land and hold on to them. States have armies, warfare, developed political hierarchies, law codes, and military force, which can be used in fact or as a threat.

The Olmec and Oaxaca were just two of many flamboyant early Mexican chiefdoms that once thrived in the area from the Valley of Mexico to Guatemala. Oaxaca went on to develop a state as early as the Teotihuacan state in the Valley of Mexico. Oaxaca and other highland areas came to overshadow the Olmec area and the Mesoamerican lowlands in general. By 2500 B.P. the Zapotec state at Oaxaca had developed a distinctive art style, perfected at its capital city of Monte Alban. The Zapotec state lasted almost 2,000 years, until it—along with the rest of Mexico—was conquered by Spain (see Blanton 1999; Marcus and Flannery 1996).

As the Olmec chiefdoms were declining, the elite level was spreading throughout Mesoamerica. By A.D. 1 (2000 B.P.), the Valley of Mexico, located in the highlands where Mexico City now stands, came to prominence in Mesoamerican state formation. In this large valley **Teotihuacan** flourished between 1900 and 1300 B.P. (A.D. 100 and 700).

STATES IN THE VALLEY OF MEXICO

The Valley of Mexico is a large basin surrounded by mountains. The valley has rich volcanic soils, but rainfall isn't always reliable. The northern part of the valley, where the huge city and state of Teotihuacan

This colossal Olmec head, carved from basalt, is displayed at the La Venta Archaeology Museum in Tabasco state, Mexico, in a setting designed to recall its original site. What is the significance of such a massive artifact?

eventually arose, is colder and drier than the south. Frosts there limited farming until quick-growing varieties of maize were developed. Until 2500 B.P., most people lived in the warmer and wetter southern part of the valley, where rainfall made farming possible. After 2500 B.P., new maize varieties and small-scale irrigation appeared. Population increased and began to spread north.

By A.D. 1 Teotihuacan was a town of 10,000 people. It governed a territory of a few thousand square kilometers and perhaps 50,000 people (Parsons 1974). Teotihuacan's growth reflected its agricultural potential. Perpetual springs permitted irrigation of a large alluvial plain. Rural farmers supplied food for the growing urban population.

By this time, a clear **settlement hierarchy** had emerged. This is a ranked series of communities that differ in size, function, and building types. The settlements at the top of the hierarchy were political and religious centers. Those at the bottom were rural villages. Such a three-level settlement hierarchy (capital city, smaller urban centers, and rural villages) provides archaeological evidence of state organization (Wright and Johnson 1975). How many levels indicate a chiefdom?

Along with state organization went large-scale irrigation, status differentiation, and complex architecture. Teotihuacan thrived between A.D. 100 and 700. It grew as a planned city built on a grid pattern, with the Pyramid of the Sun at its center. By A.D. 500, the population of Teotihuacan had reached 130,000, making it larger than imperial Rome. Farmers were one of its diverse specialized groups, along with artisans, merchants, and political, religious, and military personnel.

After A.D. 700 Teotihuacan declined in size and power. By A.D. 900 its population had shrunk to 30,000. Between A.D. 900 and 1200, the Toltec period, the population scattered, and small cities and towns sprang up throughout the valley. People also left the Valley of Mexico to live in larger cities—like Tula, the Toltec capital—on its edge (see Figure 11.3).

Population increase (including immigration by the ancestors of the Aztecs) and urban growth returned to the Valley of Mexico between A.D. 1200 and 1520. During the **Aztec** period (A.D. 1325 to 1520) there were several cities, the largest of which—Tenochtitlan, the capital—may have surpassed Teotihuacan at its height. A dozen Aztec towns had more than 10,000 people. Fueling this population growth was intensification of agriculture, particularly in the southern part of the valley, where the drainage of lake bottoms and swamps added new cultivable land (Parsons 1976).

Another factor in the renaissance of the Valley of Mexico was trade. Local manufacture created products for a series of markets. The major towns and markets were located on the lake shores, with easy access to canoe traffic. The Aztec capital stood on an island in the lake. In Tenochtitlan, the production of luxury goods was more prestigious and

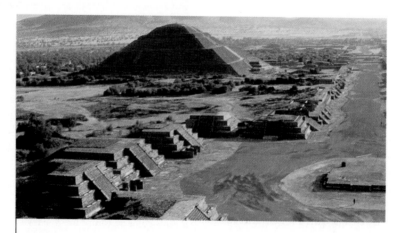

The Pyramid of the Sun, Teotihuacan's largest structure, is shown in the upper part of the photo. At its height around A.D.500, Teotihuacan was larger than imperial Rome. The mobilization of manual labor to build such structures is one of the costs of state organization.

The Aztecs played the board game of patolli, as represented here in the Codex Magliabecchiano, housed in the National Library in Florence, Italy.

more highly organized than that of pottery, basket making, and weaving. Luxury producers, such as stone workers, feather workers, and gold- and silversmiths, occupied a special position in Aztec society. The manufacture of luxury goods for export was an important part of the economy of the Aztec capital (Hassig 1985; Santley 1985).

The Origin of the State

Early states were often multivalley (extensive territorial units), whereas chiefdoms might occupy different sections of a single valley. Chiefs often could take captives from other chiefdoms and raid villages for booty. Early states, by contrast, could acquire and *hold on to* new land and people. State control is more permanent, effective, and secure than chiefly control. Early states were often extensive because they could expand against less politically developed chiefdoms. This was true of the Zapotec, Maya, and Teotihuacan states. In fact, the most extensive territorial control was achieved by some of the earliest states. Later, some of their incorporated units broke away and became independent. Some of them went on to forge new expansionist states. **Empires** are mature, territorially large, and expansive states that are typically multiethnic, multilinguistic, and more militaristic, with better developed bureaucracy than earlier states.

How and why did states originate? The state develops to handle regulatory problems encountered as the population grows and/or the economy increases in scale and diversity. Anthropologists and historians have identified the causes of state formation and have reconstructed the rise of several states. Many factors always contribute to state formation, with the effects of one magnifying those of the others. Although some contributing factors appear again and again, no single one is always present. In other words, state formation has generalized rather than universal causes.

See the Interactive Exercise for a Quiz

**mhhe
●com
/kottak**

Furthermore, because state formation may take centuries, people experiencing the process at any time rarely perceive the significance of the long-term changes. Later generations find themselves dependent on government institutions that took generations to develop.

Understanding Ourselves State formation is the subject of numerous anthropology books. Ancient states developed out of competing chiefdoms. Chiefdoms or states conquered

The Origin of the State **299**

others and created new states in the process. Although the causes of state formation are always multiple, all states have certain features (e.g., central government, political and settlement hierarchies, stratification, taxation, a military) that define them as states. States also need economies and demographic characteristics that sustain them. Even in the modern world, can a political unit that is sparsely populated by nomadic herders be governed as easily as can one with a dense population supported by irrigation and sedentary farming? Settled farmers are easier to subject to state control than are pastoral nomads or hunters and gatherers. Given their economies, we'd expect to find more stable and enduring states in China and India than in Afghanistan, Sudan, or Somalia. We'd expect to find tighter political control in river basins with irrigated agriculture than in hilly areas of slash-and-burn farming.

The world has changed substantially since ancient times, and the pace of change has increased. Nevertheless, knowledge of a state's foundation—of the correlations between economic and political types that anthropologists study—can help us understand the stability and instability of states in today's world. Anthropological knowledge of the past, especially of political history and of economic and demographic features, supports predictions about the contemporary countries in which we'd expect nation building to be more, or less, successful. Care to offer some predictions?

HYDRAULIC SYSTEMS

One suggested cause of state formation is the need to regulate *hydraulic* (water-based) agricultural economies (Wittfogel 1957). In certain arid areas, states have emerged to manage systems of irrigation, drainage, and flood control. However, hydraulic agriculture is neither a sufficient nor a necessary condition for the rise of the state. That is, many societies with irrigation never experienced state formation, and states have developed without hydraulic systems.

But hydraulic agriculture does have certain implications for state formation. Water control increases production in arid lands, such as ancient Mesopotamia and Egypt. Because of its labor demands and its ability to feed more people, irrigated agriculture fuels population growth. This in

turn leads to enlargement of the system. The expanding hydraulic system supports larger and denser concentrations of people. Interpersonal problems increase, and conflicts over access to water and irrigated land become more frequent. Political systems may arise to regulate interpersonal relations and the means of production.

Large hydraulic works can sustain towns and cities and become essential to their subsistence. Regulators protect the economy by mobilizing crews to maintain and repair the hydraulic system. These life-and-death functions enhance the authority of state officials. Thus, growth in hydraulic systems is often (as in Mesopotamia, Egypt, and the Valley of Mexico), but not always, associated with state formation.

LONG-DISTANCE TRADE ROUTES

Another theory is that states develop at strategic locations in regional trade networks. These sites include points of supply or exchange, such as crossroads of caravan routes, and places (e.g., mountain passes and river narrows) situated so as to threaten or halt trade between centers. Here again, however, the cause is generalized but neither necessary nor sufficient. Long-distance trade has been important in the evolution of many states, including Mesopotamia and Mesoamerica. Such exchange does eventually develop in all states, but it can follow rather than precede state formation. Furthermore, long-distance trade also occurs in societies such as those of Papua New Guinea, where no states developed.

POPULATION, WAR, AND CIRCUMSCRIPTION

Carneiro (1970) proposed a theory that incorporates three factors working together instead of a single cause of state formation. (We call a theory involving multiple factors or variables a **multivariate** theory.) Wherever and whenever *environmental circumscription* (or *resource concentration*), *increasing population*, and *warfare* exist, says Carneiro, state formation will begin. Environmental circumscription may be physical or social. Physically circumscribed environments include small islands and, in arid areas, river plains, oases, and valleys with streams. Social circumscription exists when neighboring societies block expansion, emigration, or access to resources. When strategic resources are concentrated in limited areas—even when no obstacles to migration exist—the effects are similar to those of circumscription.

Coastal Peru, one of the world's most arid areas, illustrates the interaction of environmental circumscription, warfare, and population increase. Early cultivation was limited to valleys with springs. Each valley was circumscribed by the Andes Mountains to the east, the Pacific Ocean to the west, and desert regions to the north and south. The transition from foraging to food production triggered population increase (Figure 11.4). In each valley, villages got bigger. Colonists split off from the old villages and founded new ones. Rivalries and raiding developed between villages in the same valley. As villages proliferated and the valley population grew, a scarcity of land developed.

Population pressure and land shortages were developing in all the valleys. Because the valleys were circumscribed, when one village conquered another, the losers had to submit to the winners—they had nowhere else to go. Conquered villagers could keep their land only if they agreed to pay tribute to their conquerors. To do this, they had to intensify production, using new techniques to produce more food. By working harder, they managed to pay tribute while meeting their own subsistence needs. Villagers brought new areas under cultivation by means of irrigation and terracing.

Those early inhabitants of the Andes didn't work harder because they chose to do so. They were *forced* to pay tribute, accept political domination, and intensify production by factors beyond their control. Once established, all these trends accelerated. Population grew, warfare intensified, and villages were eventually united in chiefdoms. The first states developed when one chiefdom in a valley conquered the others (Carneiro 1990). Eventually, different valleys began to fight. The winners brought the losers into growing states and empires, which eventually expanded from the coast to the highlands. By the 16th century, from their capital, Cuzco, in the high Andes, the Inca ruled one of the major empires of the tropics.

Carneiro's theory is very useful, but again, the association between population density and state organization is generalized rather than universal. States do tend to have large and dense populations (Stevenson 1968). However, population increase

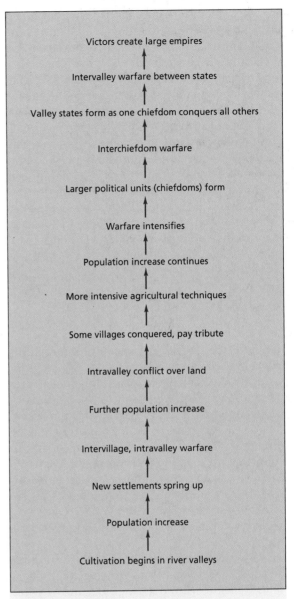

Figure 11.4 Carneiro's Multivariate Approach to the Origin of the State as Applied to Coastal Peru. In this very arid area, food production developed in narrow river valleys where water for cultivation was available (resource concentration). With cultivation, the population increased. Population pressure on land led to warfare, and some villages conquered others. Physical circumscription meant that the losers had no way to escape. The process accelerated as the population grew and as warfare and cultivation intensified. Chiefdoms, states, and empires eventually developed.

and warfare within a circumscribed environment did not trigger state formation in highland Papua New Guinea. Certain valleys there are socially or physically circumscribed and have population densities similar to those of many states. Warfare also was present, but no states emerged. Again we are dealing with an important theory that explains many but not all cases of state formation.

Early states arose in different areas for many reasons. In each case, interacting causes (often comparable ones) magnified each other's effects. To explain any instance of state formation, we must search for the specific changes in access to resources and in regulatory problems that fostered stratification and state machinery. The opposite of state formation is state decline.

Why States Collapse

States can be fragile and decomposable, falling apart along the same cleavage lines (e.g., regional political units) that were forged together to form the state originally. Various factors could threaten their economies and political institutions. Invasion, disease, famine, or prolonged drought could upset the balance. A state's citizens might harm the environment, usually with economic costs. For example, farmers and smelters might cut down trees. Such deforestation promotes erosion and leads to a decline in the water supply. Overuse of land may deplete the soil of the nutrients needed to grow crops.

We've just considered theories for the origin of the state. If factors such as irrigation help create states to begin with, does their decline or failure explain the fall of the state? Irrigation does have costs as well as benefits. In ancient Mesopotamia, irrigation water came from the Tigris and Euphrates rivers. Because sediment (silt) had accumulated in those rivers, their beds were higher than the alluvial plain and fields they irrigated. Canals channeled river water as it flowed down into the fields by gravity. As the water evaporated, water-borne mineral salts remained in the fields, eventually creating a poisonous environment for plants.

One of the worst droughts of the last 10,000 years, perhaps global in scale, began around 4300 B.P. and lasted three centuries. According to

Richard Kerr (1998), this long dry spell contributed to the fall of northern Mesopotamia's Akkadian empire. By 4200 B.P., overall agricultural production in Mesopotamia had fallen to a fraction of what it once had been. Many fields were abandoned as useless. The drought probably played a role. So did the buildup of mineral salts in the irrigated fields.

Mashkan-shapir was a Mesopotamian city located about 20 miles from the Tigris, to which it was connected by a network of canals. This city was abandoned just 20 years after it was settled. Destruction of its fields by mineral salts seems to have been a prime factor in its collapse (see Annenberg/CPB Exhibits at http://www.learner.org/exhibits/collapse/mesopotamia.html).

One key role of the state is regulation, whether of the economy or of relations between individuals and groups. Subsistence needs must be met, and chiefdoms and states may offer greater food security than do less centralized forms of society. Political leaders often maintain storehouses or central supplies of food and other goods, which may be distributed to the people in times of need. For example, tribute collected by Mexico's Aztec rulers was used for several purposes: (1) to appease troublesome nobles and otherwise to reward the elite establishment, (2) to support royal craftsmen, and (3) to be stored in royal granaries for distribution to the urban population in times of acute food stress (Santley 1985).

States may collapse when they fail to do what they are supposed to do, such as maintain social order, protect themselves against outsiders, and allow their people to meet subsistence needs. If the economy collapses, the political structure is likely to disintegrate as well. When a state declines, basic skills typically survive, but more refined levels of knowledge, shared by fewer people, tend to be lost (Gowlett 1993).

THE MAYAN DECLINE

Generations of scholars have debated the decline of classic Mayan civilization around A.D. 900 (1700–1100 B.P.). Classic Mayan culture, featuring several competing states, flourished between A.D. 300 and 900 in parts of what are now Mexico, Honduras, El Salvador, Guatemala, and Belize. The ancient Maya are known for their monuments (temples and pyramids), calendars, mathematics, and hieroglyphic writing.

Archaeological clues to Mayan decline have been found at Copán, in western Honduras. This classic Maya royal center, the largest site in the southeastern part of the Maya area, covered 29 acres. It was built on an artificial terrace overlooking the Copán river. Its rulers inscribed their monuments with accounts of their coronation, their lineage history, and reports of important battles. The Maya dated their monuments with the names of kings and when they reigned. One monument at Copán was intended to be the ruler's throne platform, but only one side had been finished. The monument bears a date, A.D. 822, in a section of unfinished text. Copán has no monuments with later dates. The site probably was abandoned by A.D. 830.

Environmental factors implicated in Copán's demise may have included erosion and soil exhaustion due to overpopulation and overfarming. Overfarming contributes to deforestation and erosion. Hillside farmhouses in particular had debris from erosion—probably caused by overfarming of the hillsides. This erosion began as early as A.D. 750—until these farm sites were abandoned, with some eventually buried by erosion debris. For the classic Maya in general, William Sanders (1972, 1973) has attributed state decline to overfarming, leading to environmental degradation through grass invasion and erosion.

Food stress and malnutrition were clearly present at Copán, where 80 percent of the buried skeletons display signs of anemia, due to iron deficiency. One skull shows anemia severe enough to have been the cause of death. Even the nobility were malnourished. One noble skull, known to be such from its carved teeth and cosmetic deformation, also has telltale signs of anemia: spongy areas at its rear (Annenberg/CPB Exhibits).

About as many people (25,000) live in the Copán valley today as lived there in A.D. 822. Like the ancient Maya, their subsistence depends on maize farming. Today's farmers cultivate the land year after year, with no fallow or resting period, and they complain of declining harvests. That yields are falling suggests the land could use fallow time to recoup the nutrients needed for successful farming (Annenberg/CPB Exhibits).

Just as the origins of states, and their causes, are diverse, so are the reasons for state decline. The Mayan state was not as powerful as was once assumed; it was fragile and vulnerable. Increased warfare and political competition destabilized many of its dynasties and governments. Archaeologists now stress the role of warfare in Mayan state

Ruins at Copán, a center of Classic Mayan royalty in western Honduras.

Interesting *Issues*
Pseudo-Archaeology

The 1998 film *The X-Files* opens with a scene purportedly dating to 35,000 B.C. Two prehistoric men trek across a glacial landscape in North Texas. Soon they have an alien encounter. Who's more likely to have been in Texas back then: the humans or the aliens? The study of prehistory has spawned popular-culture creations, including movies, TV programs, and books. In these fictional works, the anthropologists (and the natives as well) usually don't bear much resemblance to their real-life counterparts. Unlike Indiana Jones, normal and reputable archaeologists don't have nonstop adventures—fighting Nazis, lashing whips, or rescuing antiquities. The archaeologist's profession isn't a matter of raiding lost arks or of going on crusades but of reconstructing lifeways through the analysis of material remains, in order to understand culture and human behavior.

Much of the popular nonfiction dealing with prehistory is also suspect. Through books and the mass media, we have been exposed to the ideas of popular writers such as Thor Heyerdahl and Erich von Daniken. Heyerdahl, a well-known diffusionist, believes that developments in one world area are usually based on ideas borrowed from another. Von Daniken carries diffusionism one step further, proposing that major human achievements have been borrowed from beings from space who have visited us at various periods of our past. Heyerdahl and von Daniken seem to share (with some science-fiction writers) a certain contempt for human inventiveness and originality. They take the position that major changes in ancient human life styles were the results of outside instruction or interference rather than the achievements of the natives of the places where the changes took place.

In *The Ra Expeditions* (Heyerdahl 1971), for example, world traveler and adventurer Heyerdahl argued that his voyage in a papyrus boat from the Mediterranean to the Caribbean demonstrates that ancient Egyptians could have navigated to the New World. (The boat was modeled on an ancient Egyptian vessel, but Heyerdahl and his crew took along such modern conveniences as a radio and canned goods.) Heyerdahl maintained that given the possibility of ancient transatlantic voyages, Old World people could have influenced the emergence of civilization in the Americas.

What is the scientific evaluation of Heyerdahl's contention? Even if Old World ancients had reached the New World, they couldn't have done much to propel Native Americans toward state organization because the New World wasn't yet ready for food production and the state. When Egypt became a major power capable of sending scouts across the seas, around 5,000 years ago, Mexicans were broad-spectrum foragers. Had they even started cultivating corn? (See the text for the answer.) The gradual nature of the Mesoamerican transition from foraging to food production is clearly demonstrated by archaeological sequences in such sites as Oaxaca and the Valley of Mexico. Had foreign inputs been important, they would have shown up in the material remains that constitute the archaeological record.

Beginning some 2,000 years ago, states fully comparable to those of Mesopotamia and Egypt began to rise and fall in the Mexican highlands. This occurred more than 1,000 years after the height of ancient Egyptian influence, between 3600 and 3400 B.P. Had Egypt or any other ancient Old World state contributed to the rise or the fall of Mesoamerican civilization, we would expect this influence to have been exerted during Egypt's heyday as an ancient power—not 1,500 years later.

decline. Hieroglyphic texts document increased warfare among many Mayan cities. From the period just before the collapse, there is archaeological evidence for increased concern with fortifications (moats, ditches, walls, and palisades) and moving to defensible locations. Archaeologists have evidence of the burning of structures, the projectile points from spears, and some of the bodies of those killed. Some sites were abandoned, with the people fleeing into the forests to occupy perishable huts. (Copán, as we have seen, was depopulated after A.D. 822.) Archaeologists now believe that social, political, and military upheaval and competition had as much as or more to do

How much does Indiana Jones tell us about real archaeologists? The photo is from *Indiana Jones and the Temple of Doom.*

There is abundant archaeological evidence for the gradual, evolutionary emergence of food production and the state in the Middle East, in Mesoamerica, and in Peru. This evidence effectively counters the diffusionist theories about how and why human achievements, including farming and the state, began. Popular theories to the contrary, changes, advances, and setbacks in ancient American social life were the products of the ideas and activities of the Native Americans themselves.

There are certain unresolved issues, to be sure, in explaining why Mesoamerican civilizations rose and fell. Archaeologists are still unraveling the causes of the collapse around A.D. 900 of the Mayan culture of Mexico and Guatemala. However, there is simply no valid evidence for Old World interference before the European Age of Discovery, which began late in the 15th century. Francisco Pizzaro conquered Peru's Inca state in 1532, 11 years after its Mesoamerican counterpart, Tenochtitlan, the Aztec capital, fell to Spanish conquistadores in 1521. (We do have abundant archaeological, as well as written, evidence for this recent, historically known contact between Europeans and Native Americans.)

The archaeological record also casts doubt on contentions that the advances of earthlings came with extraterrestrial help, as Erich von Daniken argued in his book *Chariots of the Gods* (1971), and as Discovery-type TV sometimes suggests. Abundant, well-analyzed archaeological data from the Middle East, Mesoamerica, and Peru tell a clear story.

Plant and animal domestication, the state, and city life were not brilliant discoveries, inventions, or secrets that humans needed to borrow from extraterrestrials. They were long-term, gradual processes, developments with down-to-earth causes and effects. They required thousands of years of orderly change, not some chance meeting in the high Andes between an ancient Inca chief and a beneficent Johnny Appleseed from Aldebaran.

This is not to deny, by the way, that intelligent life and civilizations at a variety of technological levels—some more, some less advanced than earth—may exist throughout the galaxy or even that extraterrestrials may have occasionally ventured into this relatively isolated outer spiral arm of the Milky Way galaxy and even visited earth itself. However, even if extraterrestrials have been on earth, archaeological evidence suggests that their starship commanders observed a prime directive of noninterference in the affairs of less-advanced planets. There is no scientifically valid evidence for the rapid kind of change that sustained extraterrestrial intervention would have produced. What would constitute such evidence?

with the Mayan decline and abandonment of cities than did natural environmental factors (Marcus, personal communication).

Formerly archaeologists tended to explain state origin and decline mainly in terms of natural environmental factors, such as climate change, habitat destruction, and demographic pressure. Archaeologists now see state origins and declines more fully—in social and political terms—because we can read the texts. And the Mayan texts document competition and warfare between dynasties jockeying for position and power. Warfare was indeed a creator and a destroyer of ancient chiefdoms and states. What's its role in our own?

SUMMARY

1. A state is a society with a formal, central government and a division of society into classes. The first cities and states, supported by irrigated farming, developed in southern Mesopotamia between 6000 and 5500 B.P. Evidence for early state organization includes monumental architecture, central storehouses, irrigation systems, and written records.

2. Towns predate pottery in the Middle East. The first towns grew up 10,000 to 9,000 years ago. The first pottery dates back just over 8,000 years. Halafian (7500–6500 B.P.) refers to a pottery style and to the period when the first chiefdoms emerged. Ubaid pottery (7000–6000 B.P.) is associated with advanced chiefdoms and perhaps the earliest states. Most state formation occurred during the Uruk period (6100–5100 B.P.).

3. Based on the status distinctions they include, societies may be divided into egalitarian, ranked, and stratified. In egalitarian societies, status distinctions are not usually inherited. Ranked societies have hereditary inequality, but they lack stratification. Stratified societies have sharp social divisions—social classes or *strata*—based on unequal access to wealth and power. Ranked societies with loss of village autonomy are chiefdoms. The first chiefdoms appeared between 7,300 and 5,800 years ago. Chiefdoms feature political instability, raiding, and exotic goods used to mark status.

4. Mesopotamia's economy was based on craft production, trade, and intensive agriculture. Writing, invented by 5600 B.P., was first used to keep accounts for trade. With the invention of smelting, the Bronze Age began just after 5000 B.P.

5. In northwestern India and Pakistan, the Indus River Valley state flourished from 4600 to 3900 B.P. The first Chinese state, dating to 3750 B.P., was that of the Shang dynasty in northern China. The major early states of the Western Hemisphere were in Mesoamerica and Peru.

6. States arose between 2500 and 1600 B.P. (500 B.C. and A.D. 400) in Mesoamerica. Previously, Olmec chiefdoms had built ritual centers on Mexico's southern Gulf Coast between 3,200 and 2,500 years ago. Between 3,200 and 3,000 B.P., intense competitive interaction among the many chiefdoms in Mesoamerica at that time fueled rapid social change. Some chiefdoms would develop into states (e.g., Oaxaca, Valley of Mexico). Others (e.g., Olmec) would not. By A.D. 1 (2000 B.P.), the Valley of Mexico had come to prominence. In this large valley in the highlands, Teotihuacan thrived between A.D. 100 and 700. Tenochtitlan, the capital of the Aztec state (A.D. 1325 to 1520), may have surpassed Teotihuacan at its height.

7. States develop to handle regulatory problems as the population grows and the economy gets more complex. Multiple factors contribute to state formation. Some appear repeatedly, but no single factor is always present. Among the most important factors are irrigation and long-distance trade. Coastal Peru, a very arid area, illustrates how environmental circumscription, population growth, and warfare may contribute to state formation.

8. Early states faced various threats: invasion, disease, famine, drought, soil exhaustion, erosion, and the buildup of irrigation salts. States may collapse when they fail to keep social and economic order or to protect themselves against outsiders. The Mayan state fell in the face of increased warfare among competing dynasties.

KEY TERMS

See the flash cards

Aztec Last independent state in the Valley of Mexico; capital was Tenochtitlan. Thrived between A.D. 1325 and the Spanish Conquest in 1520.

bronze An alloy of arsenic and copper or of tin and copper.

chiefdom A ranked society in which relations among villages as well as among individuals are unequal, with smaller villages under the authority of leaders in larger villages; has a two-level settlement hierarchy.

cuneiform Early Mesopotamian writing that used a stylus (writing implement) to write wedge-shaped impressions on raw clay; from the Latin word for wedge.

egalitarian society A type of society, most typically found among hunter-gatherers, that lacks status distinctions except for those based on age, gender, and individual qualities, talents, and achievements.

empire A mature, territorially large, and expansive, state; empires are typically multiethnic, multilinguistic, and more militaristic, with better developed bureaucracy than earlier states.

Halafian An early (7500–6500 B.P.) and widespread pottery style, first found in northern Syria; refers to a delicate ceramic style and to the period when the first chiefdoms emerged.

Mesopotamia The area between the Tigris and Euphrates rivers in what is now southern Iraq and southwestern Iran; location of the first cities and states.

metallurgy Knowledge of the properties of metals, including their extraction and processing and the manufacture of metal tools.

multivariate Involving multiple factors, causes, or variables.

primary states States that arise on their own (through competition among chiefdoms), and not through contact with other state societies.

ranked society A type of society with hereditary inequality but not social stratification; individuals are ranked in terms of their genealogical closeness to the chief, but there is a continuum of status, with many individuals and kin groups ranked about equally.

settlement hierarchy A ranked series of communities differing in size, function, and type of building; a three-level settlement hierarchy indicates state organization.

smelting The high-temperature process by which pure metal is produced from an ore.

state A form of social and political organization with a formal, central government and a division of society into classes.

stratification A stratified society has sharp social divisions—*strata*—based on unequal access to wealth and power, e.g., into noble and commoner classes.

Teotihuacan A.D. 100 to 700; first state in the Valley of Mexico and earliest major Mesoamerican empire.

CRITICAL THINKING QUESTIONS

For more self testing, see the self quizzes

mhhe
●com
/kottak

1. What were the main similarities and differences in the processes of state formation in the Middle East and in Mesoamerica?
2. Was the origin of the state good or bad? Why?
3. Can you think of three reasons to build walls around a town or a city? What is probably the most common reason? Does Çatal Hüyük remind you of an Upper Paleolithic cave site? Why and why not?
4. Imagine yourself transported back in time to an early chiefdom of your choice. Would it be in the Middle East or Mesoamerica? Why?
5. What would be the advantages and disadvantages of being an early chief in the Middle East? Would you rather be the chief or a chief's close relative?
6. Imagine yourself an archaeologist trying to identify ancient chiefdoms in the Middle East after excavating Mesoamerican chiefdom sites. What similar and different lines of evidence for ranking and political alliance might you find in the two hemispheres?
7. Imagine yourself transported back in time to an early state of your choice. Where would it be and why?
8. Would you feel more secure in an ancient chiefdom or an ancient state? How about those societies compared with the more egalitarian societies of prehistoric hunters and gatherers?
9. Is it harder to tell the difference between a chiefdom and a state in the ancient Middle East or in Mesoamerica. Why?

10. What kind of economic roles were available in early states, as compared with the earliest food-producing societies?

11. Why do you think the earliest states developed about 3,000 years later in Mesoamerica than in the Middle East? Imagine what might have happened if those states had developed at the same time.

12. Compare the origin of the United States or Canada with the origin of ancient states. Do any of the theories for the origin of the state apply to your country?

13. If our own state declined, what would be the most likely cause(s)? Do you view our government as stronger or weaker than it was a generation ago? How about a century ago? What is the likely reason for this strength or weakness?

14. Do you view our government as stronger or weaker than those of ancient states? What are the main reasons for this strength or weakness?

Atlas Questions

Look at Map 11, "Ancient Civilizations of the Old World."

1. What contemporary nations would you have to visit if you wanted to see all the places where ancient civilizations developed in the Old World? Would some countries be off limits for political reasons? How do you think such limitations have affected the archaeological record? Have the limitations been as substantial in the western hemisphere as in the Old World?

2. Of the ancient states shown on Map 11, which developed latest? Did other states develop even later that are not shown on Map 11? If so, give some examples, indicating where and when they appeared.

3. In which of the ancient states shown on Map 11 were Middle Eastern domesticates basic to the economy? In which states shown on Map 11 were other domesticates basic to the economy?

SUGGESTED ADDITIONAL READINGS

Blanton, R. E.

1999   *Ancient Oaxaca: The Monte Alban State.* New York: Cambridge University Press. The story of an early—and enduring—area of Mesoamerican state formation.

Blanton, R. E., S. A. Kowalewski, G. M. Feinman, and L. M. Finsten, eds.

1993   *Ancient Mesoamerica: A Comparison of Change in Three Regions,* 2nd ed. New York: Cambridge University Press. This book synthesizes research on three well-studied regions of Mesoamerica: the Valley of Oaxaca, the Valley of Mexico, and the Maya lowlands.

Diamond, J. M.

1997   *Guns, Germs, and Steel: The Fates of Human Societies.* New York: W.W. Norton. Disease, tools, and environmental forces and effects throughout human history.

Fagan, B. M.

2002   *World Prehistory: A Brief Introduction,* 5th ed. New York: Longman. Major events in human prehistory, including the emergence of the state in various locales.

Feinman, G. M., and J. Marcus, eds.

1998   *Archaic States.* Santa Fe, NM: School of American Research Press. Features of early states, in general and in particular world areas.

Joyce, R. A.

2000   *Gender and Power in Prehispanic Mesoamerica.* Austin, TX: University of Texas Press. Issues of gender and power in Mesoamerica before the Spanish Conquest.

Pollock, S.

1999   *Ancient Mesopotamia: The Eden That Never Was.* Cambridge, England: Cambridge University Press. Mesopotamia state formation—a new synthesis.

Smith, M. E., and M. A. Masson, eds.

2000   *The Ancient Civilizations of Mesoamerica: A Reader.* Malpen, MA: Blackwell. Explores the diversity of Mesoamerican chiefdoms and states.

Trigger, B. G.

1993   *Early Civilizations: Ancient Egypt in Context.* New York: Columbia University Press. Considers the Incas (Inka); the Shang and western Chou of China; the Aztecs and Mayas of Mesoamerica; the Yoruba and Benin of West Africa; Mesopotamia; and ancient Egypt.

Wenke, R.

1996   *Patterns in Prehistory: Humankind's First Three Million Years,* 4th ed. New York: Oxford University Press. Rise of food production and the state throughout the world; thorough, useful text.

INTERNET EXERCISES

1. Early Cities in Mesoamerica: Read *Archaeology* magazine's article on the New Tomb Found at Teotihuacan, **http://www.archaeology.org/online/features/mexico/index.html**.

   a. Where was the tomb found at Teotihuacan, and how old is it? Was the tomb created early or late in the history of this city? How does the tomb help us to understand the history of Teotihuacan?

   b. What was found in the tomb? What do they signify?

   c. As an example of a state, what are some of the institutions that you think may have existed at Teotihuacan? For example, do you think they had military and professional religion practitioners?

2. Indus Valley Civilization: Go to Mark Kenyoyer's "Around the Indus in 90 Slides" presentation, **http://www.harappa.com/indus/indus0.html**, and read his Essay about the Indus civilization, **http://www.harappa.com/indus/indus1.html**.

   a. Where is the Indus? When did its first cities arise? What are the names of some of the cities?

   b. What are some of the characteristics of Indus cities? Are those characteristic of a state?

   c. What are some of the common misconceptions about the origins of Indus civilization?

   d. The Indus had a form of writing. What did they write on? What are some of the common images and motifs associated with the inscriptions?

See Chapter 11 at your McGraw-Hill Online Learning Center for additional review and interactive exercises.

See
your
OLC
*Bringing
It All
Together*
links

mhhe
● com
/kottak

Bringing It All Together

The Peopling of the Pacific

On April 28, 1947, the adventurer Thor Heyerdahl and five others set out from Peru, aboard a balsa raft, on a voyage they hoped would end on Polynesia's Easter Island. (They actually reached Raroia, French Polynesia.) Contrary to scientific opinion then and now, Heyerdahl sought to prove that Native South Americans could have rafted to, and then colonized, Polynesia. No scientific evidence has ever been found to support the hypothesis that Polynesia was settled by Native Americans.

Who did settle the vast Pacific? Today, when archaeologists dig in Australia, Papua New Guinea, and the neighboring islands of the southwest Pacific (consult the map on page 311 throughout this discussion), they find traces of humankind more than 30,000 years old. Humans reached northern Australia between 50,000 and 60,000 years ago. People even reached the islands north of Australia, as far as the Solomon Islands, more than 30,000 years ago (Terrell 1998).

And there they stayed. Based on current evidence, people waited thousands of years before they risked sailing farther eastward on the open sea. Until 3000 B.P., the Solomon Islands formed the eastern edge of the inhabited Pacific. The deep-sea crossings and colonization that began around 3000 B.P. was linked to the rapid spread of the earliest pottery found in Oceania, an ornately decorated ware with geometric designs called Lapita.

The first Lapita potsherds were excavated in 1952. The name Lapita comes from the discovery site on the Melanesian island of New Caledonia. (Locate New Caledonia the map on page 311. Where does New Caledonia lie in relation to the Solomon Islands, the Bismarck Archipelago, Tonga, and Samoa?) The oldest Lapita artifacts, dating back some 3,500 years, have been found in the Bismarck Archipelago, northeast of New Guinea. Many scholars see this ornate ware as the product of an ethnically distinct people, and think the Lapita "cultural complex" was carried into the Pacific by a migration of racially distinct newcomers from Asia.

No one knows why people with Lapita pottery left home and risked sailing in deeper waters. Was it for reasons of wanderlust, a pioneering spirit, or improvements in canoe building and navigation? Some experts think the domestication of certain plants and animals thought to be of Asian origin—such as dogs, pigs, and chickens—somehow fueled Lapita's expansion (Terrell 1998).

Archaeologist John Terrell has excavated a site dated to 3000 B.P. on the Sepik (midnorthern) coast of Papua New Guinea. At that time, according to Terrell (1998), newly stabilized coastal lagoons were producing an abundance of (mainly wild) foods, fueling human population growth. Like the

Lapita pottery fragments from the Solomon Islands, dated to 3000 B.P.

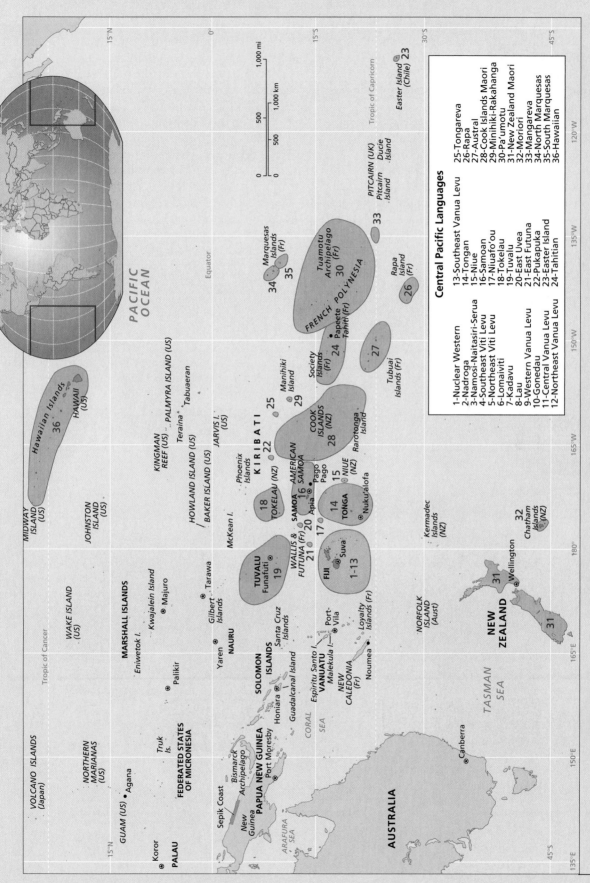

Central Pacific Languages

1-Nuclear Western	13-Southeast Vanua Levu	25-Tongareva
2-Nadroga	14-Tongan	26-Rapa
3-Namosi-Naitasiri-Serua	15-Niue	27-Austral
4-Southeast Viti Levu	16-Samoan	28-Cook Islands Maori
5-Northeast Viti Levu	17-Niuafo'ou	29-Minihiki-Rakahanga
6-Lomaiviti	18-Tokelau	30-Pa'umotu
7-Kadavu	19-Tuvalu	31-New Zealand Maori
8-Lau	20-East Uvea	32-Moriori
9-Western Vanua Levu	21-East Futuna	33-Mangareva
10-Gonedau	22-Pukapuka	34-North Marquesas
11-Central Vanua Levu	23-Easter Island	35-South Marquesas
12-Northeast Vanua Levu	24-Tahitian	36-Hawaiian

Polynesian islands are shaded khaki. Other Central Pacific languages outside of Polynesia are spoken in the area shaded orange, which includes Fiji.

broad-spectrum economies discussed in Chapter 10, the resource base of the early Lapita pottery makers included diverse foods, some wild and some (e.g., yams, taro, pigs, chickens) domesticated and carefully managed.

Archaeologist David Burley uncovered early Lapita shards (potsherds) at Fanga'uta lagoon on the island of Tongatapu in the Polynesian kingdom of Tonga. Early outrigger canoes reached that lagoon after traveling hundreds, and perhaps more than a thousand, miles from the west. Radiocarbon dating of charcoal among the shards showed that seafarers reached Tonga between 2,950 and 2,850 years ago. *This is the earliest known settlement in Polynesia*. Burley thinks that Tongatapu "probably served as the initial staging point for population expansion" to other islands of Tonga, then to Samoa, and then on to the rest of Polynesia (quoted in Wilford 2002*a*).

Improvements in their outrigger canoes allowed Lapita navigators to sail across large stretches of open sea, thus propelling the Polynesian diaspora. The larger canoes could have carried dozens of people, plus pigs and other cargo. Polynesian seafarers eventually reached Tahiti to the east, and Hawaii—located more than 2,500 miles northeast of Tonga and Samoa. Later voyages carried the Polynesian diaspora south to New Zealand, and farther east to Easter Island. Covering one-fourth of the Pacific, Polynesia became the last large area of the world to be settled by humans.

The Lapita pottery found at Tongatapu offered clues about where the seafarers originated. Analyzing bits of the shards, William Dickinson, a University of Arizona geologist, found sandy minerals from outside Tonga. Some of the pots had been brought there from elsewhere. It turned out that the artifacts were made of minerals found only on the Santa Cruz Islands in Melanesia, some 1,200 miles to the west of Tonga, and just east of the Solomon Islands (Burley and Dickinson 2001). The shards from Tongatapu provided the first physical evidence linking the voyages of the Lapita people between the western and eastern parts of the Pacific. This evidence may mean that Tonga was first settled by people who came directly from central Melanesia (Wilford 2002*a*).

Anthropologists from all four subfields— archaeologists and physical, cultural, and linguistic anthropologists—have considered questions

Traditional Maori (New Zealand) oceangoing vessel. The Lapita people reached and colonized vast areas of the Pacific in their outrigger canoes.

about Polynesian origins. Who made Lapita pottery, along with the distinctive stone tools, beads, rings, and shell ornaments often found with it? Were they an ethnically distinct society of newcomers? Or did they consist of several cultural groups that came to share a handicraft style through diffusion or borrowing? How were the Lapita pottery makers linked to earlier settlers of the Pacific—the original colonists of Australia, New Guinea, and nearby islands? Did the Lapita complex originate with indigenous dark-skinned Melanesians, assumed to descend from the first settlers of the Pacific? Or was it introduced by new, lighter-skinned arrivals from Southeast Asia? Did lighter- and darker-skinned groups intermarry in Melanesia, forming a hybrid population that created the Lapita complex and eventually colonized Polynesia?

In the 18th century, the explorer Captain James Cook was struck by how similar were the appearance and customs of light-skinned Polynesians living on islands thousands of miles apart, such as Tonga, Hawaii, New Zealand, and Easter Island. Cook thought that the Polynesians originally had come from Malaysia or Micronesia. French navigators stressed the physical and cultural differences between the Polynesians and the darker-skinned Melanesians who lived near New Guinea, and who resembled the indigenous peoples of Papua New Guinea.

As in the tripartite classification of human races in vogue during the 19th century (see Chapter 9), Europeans grouped Pacific "races" into three: Polynesians ("many islands"), Melanesians ("dark islands"), and Micronesians ("little islands"). Until recently, anthropologists supposed that the ancestors of the Polynesians originated in mainland China and/or Taiwan, which they left between 3,600 and 6,000 years ago. They were seen as spreading rapidly through the Pacific, largely bypassing Melanesia. This would explain why the Polynesians are not dark-skinned and why they speak Austronesian languages, rooted in Taiwan, rather than Papuan languages, spoken in parts of Melanesia. This view now seems discredited by the fact that nothing resembling Lapita pottery has ever been found in Taiwan or southern China. Lapita features first show up in Melanesia, on islands of the Bismarck Archipelago. Recent genetic studies also suggest that ancestral Polynesians stopped off in Melanesia. Interbreeding between early Polynesians and Melanesians has

On the left, a Polynesian woman from Tahiti, Society Islands, French Polynesia. On the right, a Melanesian woman from Madang, Papua New Guinea. What differences and similarities do you notice between these two women?

left clear genetic markers in today's Polynesians. The debate now focuses on where the interbreeding took place and how extensive it was.

DNA evidence has convinced Mark Stoneking, a molecular anthropologist, that the ancestors of the Polynesians were indeed Austronesians. (The Austronesian, or Malayo-Polynesian, language family covers a large area of the world. Austronesian languages are the main languages of Polynesia [e.g., Hawaiian], Indonesia, and Malaysia, and even of Madagascar, located just off the African coast.) Stoneking thinks that the ancestral Polynesians left Southeast Asia—not necessarily Taiwan—and sailed to, then expanded along, the coast of New Guinea. They intermingled with Melanesians there and then started voyaging eastward into the Pacific. Interacting with other human groups, ancestral Polynesians exchanged genes and cultural traits (Gibbons 2001; Wilford 2002a).

Excavating in Melanesia's Bismarck Archipelago, archaeologist Patrick Kirch found evidence that newcomers from the islands of southeast Asia had reached Melanesia by 3500 B.P. They built their houses on stilts, as in houses still found in Southeast Asia. They sailed in outrigger canoes and brought agricultural plants along with them. There was mixing between the newcomers and the Melanesians. Out of their contact and interaction emerged the Lapita pottery style. Archaeologists aren't sure if Lapita pottery was first developed where the oldest specimens have been found, in the Bismarcks, or if it was introduced there by seafarers from the west (see Kirch 2000).

Why don't Polynesians resemble their presumed Melanesian cousins, or any Asian forebears? Can we explain the physical differences between Polynesians and Melanesians? Might the Polynesian population have originated in what geneticists call a founder event? In such an event, just a few people, whose physical traits do not randomly sample the larger population from which they came, happen to give rise to a very large diaspora. A very small number of people, say, a few canoeloads reaching Tonga's Fanga 'Uta Lagoon, may have given rise to the entire, geographically dispersed Polynesian population. The physical traits of such a small founding group could not fully represent the population from which they came. Whatever traits the founders happened to have, such as light skin color, would be transmit-

ted to their descendants. This may explain why the Polynesians look so different from Melanesians, even though they share DNA in common.

Whatever their roots, the Lapita people, whose pottery marked their eastward migrations, eventually abandoned the elaborate Lapita style. On Tonga and Samoa, the decorative ceramics soon disappeared in favor of plain, functional bowls, cups, and storage vessels. Nor did the seafarers take Lapita pottery on their later voyages to the rest of Polynesia. (How might you explain this change in pottery style?)

By 2000 B.P., according to Patrick Kirch (2000), the people of Tonga had developed a significant new technology: the double-hull sailing canoe. Even though they could not spot other islands on the distant horizon, as their ancestors had been able to do in the Southwestern Pacific, the notion that the ocean was full of islands endured. Once they could more securely travel long distances—with the new canoe—they set forth. These weren't all accidental voyages and discoveries, as once was thought. These ancient sailors tacked against the prevailing east-to-west winds, knowing that, if necessary, they could ride a following wind back home. Anthropologists have learned from oral tradition that these societies had a social structure with status ranked by birth order. Many of the Polynesian island societies developed into chiefdoms, of the sort discussed in Chapter 11. According to Kirch, the Polynesian islanders "were descendants of settlers who were junior siblings and their own explorations were very often conducted by junior siblings . . . They were the ones with a reason to explore, to find new land and claim that for themselves" (quoted in Wilford 2002a). (There was a similar pattern in the early settlement of British North America.)

Long ago, the anthropologist Alexander Lesser disputed what he saw as the "myth of the primitive isolate" (quoted in Terrell 1998)—the idea that ancient peoples lived in closed societies, each one out of contact with others. It is doubtful that the human world has ever been one of distinct societies, sealed cultures, or isolated ethnic groups. Even on the small islands and atolls of the vast Pacific Ocean lived societies that contradicted the "primitive isolate." The adventurous and interconnected peoples of the Pacific and their prehistoric past reveal that human diversity is as much a product of contact as of isolation (Terrell 1998).

Part Three

Cultural Diversity

In Part III, we'll explore cultural anthropology and linguistic anthropology, which, along with physical anthropology and archaeology, complete anthropology's four subfields. A common interest in diversity in time and particularly in space (i.e., geographic location and social context) unites these two subfields. Among its many research interests, linguistic anthropology explores how language and its uses are linked to cultural contrasts and social variation. The main chapter on linguistic anthropology is Chapter 15, "Language and Communication." In Part III, the focus will be on cultural anthropology, as is also true of Part IV, "The Changing World." The remaining chapters from here to the end of the book examine topics and issues in cultural anthropology.

In Chapter 12, we'll consider some of the ethical contexts in which cultural and linguistic anthropologists operate, along with field methods in cultural anthropology. Chapter 15 discusses linguistic methods. Chapter 13 examines the key concept of culture—its nature, transmission, and variety. Chapter 14 considers ethnicity, based on cultural similarities and differences within and among nations. Chapter 15, on language and communication, describes basic linguistic principles and techniques. It also shows how linguistic diversity is related to other aspects of social and cultural diversity, including gender and ethnicity.

Chapter 16 examines how various human groups make their living, surveying the main economic types in nonindustrial societies, such as foraging, cultivating, and herding. It also considers the principles that govern economic exchanges cross-culturally. Chapter 17 surveys the types of political units, systems, and relations found in societies ranging from hunting and gathering bands to state-organized societies. Chapter 17 also discusses correlations between economic and political systems. In Chapter 18, we turn to families, kinship, and descent—institutions that play a prominent role in nonindustrial societies, where they often structure the political system, as does marriage, the topic of Chapter 19. That chapter considers definitions of marriage and variation in marriage practices in different societies. The focus of Chapter 20 is gender roles and ideologies and how they are linked to economy, politics, and systems of kinship and marriage.

In Chapter 21, we consider diversity in religious beliefs and behavior in various societies. We also discuss the major world religions, as well as how religion contributes to social control, stability, and change. In Chapter 22, we look at the arts in cross-cultural perspective, considering how they are distinguished from other aspects of culture, and how they vary among societies. Having explored diversity in the major domains of human cultural life in Part III, we examine their transformations and expressions in the modern world in Part IV.

12

Ethics and Methods in Cultural Anthropology

Overview

Increasingly aware of the ethical and legal contexts of their work, anthropologists know they can't study something simply because it's interesting or has scientific value. Cultural and linguistic anthropologists typically study living people, and the anthropologist's deepest ethical commitment is to the people he or she studies. This chapter focuses mainly on cultural anthropology. Linguistic methods are discussed in Chapter 15.

Traditionally, doing cultural anthropology has required field work in another society. The firsthand, personal study of local cultural settings is ethnography. Ethnographers work in natural communities. They form personal relationships with local people as they study those people's lives. Interview schedules may be used to guide interviews, ensuring that the ethnographer collects comparable information from everyone. Ethnographers work closely with key cultural consultants on particular areas

of local life. Life histories document personal experiences with culture and culture change. Genealogical information is particularly important in societies in which principles of kinship, descent, and marriage organize social life. Longitudinal research, often done by a team, is the systematic study of an area or field site over time.

Traditionally, cultural anthropologists worked in small-scale societies; sociologists, in modern nations. How does survey research, which typifies sociology, differ from ethnography? With more literate respondents, survey researchers use questionnaires, which research subjects fill out. Sociologists study samples to make inferences about a larger population. The diversity of social life in modern nations requires that even anthropologists adopt some survey procedures. However, anthropologists also retain the intimacy and firsthand investigation characteristic of ethnography.

Anthropological Association's Report Criticizes Yanomami Researchers and Their Accuser

CHRONICLE OF HIGHER EDUCATION NEWS BRIEF

By David Glenn

July 2, 2002

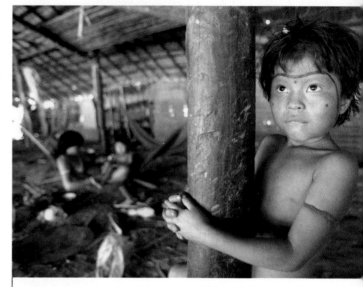

A Yanomami child at home in Demini, Brazil, in 1998.

In 2000 anthropology was rocked by news-grabbing accusations against researchers who had done field work among the Yanomami Indians of Venezuela and Brazil. In a book titled *Darkness in El Dorado*, Patrick Tierney, an investigative journalist, accused, among others, the late James Neel, a respected physician and geneticist, and Napoleon Chagnon, a well-known anthropologist, of research improprieties. Tierney contended that Neel had knowingly used a dangerous measles vaccine, which, Tierney claimed, harmed rather than helped the Yanomami, and that Neel withheld medical treatment to Indians in order to preserve the integrity of his research design.

The American Anthropological Association (AAA) organized a task force to look into Tierney's charges. The following article discusses the final report of that panel, which was issued on July 1, 2002. On the question as to whether Dr. Neel should be censured for the measles vaccinations given to the Yanomami, the Task Force Report determined that the vaccinations "unquestionably . . . saved many lives" and were "a beneficial measure." The AAA report also found many of the charges against Chagnon false, unverifiable, exaggerated, or illustrating bad judgment rather than ethical misconduct. In some cases, Tierney's allegations had been based not on an independent investigation by Tierney but on material that Chagnon himself had published in a series of books and articles on the Yanomami.

Tierney's book, and the reactions of various anthropologists to it, created a furor in the profession of anthropology. Physicians, geneticists, and several prominent anthropologists flocked to Neel's defense. Many anthropologists also defended Chagnon, identifying specific flaws in Tierney's account. Others were willing to believe the worst about Chagnon—based perhaps on suspicion aroused by his own swashbuckling accounts, in books and films, of his Yanomami ethnography. Many anthropologists saw Chagnon's accounts, particularly his tendency to draw on biological models to explain human aggression, as flawed and unconvincing. Many others thought Chagnon's work had been singled out for unfair criticism because of his unorthodox theoretical views or out of professional jealousy. There was also criticism of the composition of the AAA task force, which some saw as biased against Chagnon and his views, and therefore unlikely to reach an impartial conclusion. The full final report is available at the AAA website (http://www.aaanet.org/edtf/index.htm). As you read this article, see how you react to the conclusions of the task force and to the severity of the various allegations. Do you think Tierney's book was good for anthropology?

A two-year-old controversy within anthropology has been brought to a conclusion—or at least to a new plateau. On Monday [July 1, 2002], the American Anthropological Association released the final report of a panel charged with reviewing accusations of unethical behavior by prominent anthropologists who studied the Yanomami people in the Amazon River basin in the late 1960s. Alongside its factual dissections, in which it criticizes both the accused anthropologists and their accuser, the 304-page report contains reflective essays that are intended to improve ethical practices among anthropologists who work with indigenous communities.

Patrick Tierney's 2000 book, *Darkness in El Dorado* (W.W. Norton), revolved around anthropologists' work among the Yanomami, an indigenous ethnic group in remote areas of Brazil and Venezuela. Mr. Tierney charged that during the late 1960s, Napoleon Chagnon, now a professor emeritus of anthropology at the University of California at Santa Barbara, and the late James V. Neel, a longtime professor of human genetics at the University of Michigan at Ann Arbor, had recklessly endangered the communities they studied. Among the most serious accusations: that Mr. Chagnon had subtly encouraged murderous violence among the Yanomami, and that Mr. Neel's efforts to administer measles vaccines among the Yanomami were driven more by scientific curiosity than by sound medical practice.

Critics of Mr. Tierney's book have strongly denied these charges, and two previous reports—by the American Society of Human Genetics and the University of California at Santa Barbara—have found the accusations to be unwarranted.

In a short preface to the report, the association's executive board declares that Mr. Tierney's book "contains numerous unfounded, misrepresented, and sensationalistic accusations about the conduct of anthropology among the Yanomami." But the report also says that the book, though "deeply flawed . . . [presents] ethical issues that we must confront." Among them:

The representation of the Yanomami in the mass media. The report finds that Mr. Chagnon failed to intervene when news organizations presented simplistic, caricatured portrayals of the Yanomami as highly warlike—as "fierce people," in Mr. Chagnon's phrase.

The failure to obtain informed consent when obtaining Yanomami blood samples. The report concludes that Mr. Neel and his colleagues failed to explain to the Yanomami that certain blood-taking procedures "would yield no immediate health benefit." This practice, the anthropology association's panel contends, failed to meet the informed-consent standards that had been established by the late 1960s . . .

The report also includes a number of essays about the El Dorado controversy's implications for anthropology's broader ethical guidelines. One such essay was drafted by Joe E. Watkins, an archaeologist with the U.S. Bureau of Indian Affairs, who also is head of the association's Committee on Ethics. Mr. Watkins writes that the Yanomami affair should prompt the field to revisit and strengthen its guidelines on informed consent [and] gift-giving between anthropologists and the people they study . . .

Initial response to the report was mixed. Michael D. Fischer, a senior lecturer in anthropology at the University of Kent, in England, said in an e-mail message that he commends the panel's members for being explicit about their failure to reach consensus on several questions of fact and interpretation.

A more skeptical assessment came from Raymond Hames, a professor of anthropology at the University of Nebraska at Lincoln . . . Mr. Hames said Monday that he is puzzled by the report's emphasis on media representations of the Yanomami. The report, he said, does not spell out exactly what sort of damage has allegedly been done to the Yanomami by caricatures of them in the North American media. Perhaps, he said, the committee's concern is that such caricatures have been used as rationales by mining and logging interests who hope to dispossess the Yanomami of their land. But Mr. Hames believes that those commercial interests would find ways to demonize the Yanomami with or without the aid of media distortions of anthropological studies. Because the report's account of these questions is vague, he said, it is hard for the reader to assess exactly how the Yanomami's condition might be different if Mr. Chagnon had prevented the news media from caricaturing his work.

James S. Boster, a professor of anthropology at the University of Connecticut, said that it was foolish for the committee to expend so much energy once it became clear that Mr. Tierney's most sensational allegations were false. "Chagnon was accused of capital murder, and it appears that he's now been convicted of a parking violation."

Robert Borofsky, a professor of anthropology at Hawaii Pacific University, said he believes the committee "made significant progress since the November meeting." At that meeting of the association, the committee released a preliminary report that was quickly enveloped in controversy. Two members of the committee said that they hadn't approved certain language, and asked that the report be withdrawn.

Mr. Borofsky said he was sharply disappointed, however, that the final report did not include a series of critical commentaries on the committee's work that have been posted on the association's Web site since

November. The report includes instructions for finding such commentaries online, but does not include them in its own text.

Source: David Glenn, "Anthropological Association's Report Criticizes Yanomami Researchers and Their Accuser," *Chronicle of Higher Education*, July 2, 2002. http://chronicle.com/free/2002/07/2002070202n.htm.

Unlike certifying organizations in medicine and law, the AAA lacks the authority to punish ethical misconduct. The AAA can, however, investigate allegations of such conduct and publicize its findings, as was done in the case you just read about. Discussions of ethics, including hypothetical cases that raise ethical issues, have appeared regularly in the AAA's monthly newsletter. In Chapter 2, you read parts of the AAA's Code of Ethics, offered by the association to provide guidelines for anthropologists as they plan and conduct their research, and as they deal with colleagues at home and abroad.

This chapter examines ethics and methods in cultural and linguistic anthropology. Many ethical considerations are common to cultural and linguistic anthropology, to the extent that both work with living people. The discussion of methods later in this chapter will focus on cultural anthropology, especially on ethnography. Methods in linguistics and in linguistic anthropology are discussed in Chapter 15.

Ethics

Ethnographers (field workers in cultural anthropology) typically have done field work outside their nations of origin. In the host country, the ethnographer seeks permissions, cooperation, and knowledge from government officials, scholars, and many others, most importantly the people of the community being studied. Cultural sensitivity is paramount when the research subjects are living people into whose lives the anthropologist intrudes. Anthropologists need to establish and maintain appropriate, collaborative, and nonexploitative relationships with colleagues and communities in the host country.

The AAA advises anthropologists to be guided by its Code of Ethics. Remember (from Chapter 2) that the Code states that anthropologists have obligations to their scholarly field, to the wider society and culture, and to the human species, other species, and the environment. You may want to review that Code to fill out this discussion.

To work in a host country and community, researchers must inform officials and colleagues there about the purpose and funding, and the anticipated results and impacts, of the research. Researchers have to gain the informed consent of all affected parties—from the authorities who control access to the field site to the members of the community to be studied. Before the research begins, people should be told about the purpose, nature, and procedures of the research and its potential costs and benefits to them. Informed consent (agreement to take part in the research) should be obtained from anyone who provides information or who might be affected by the research.

See the Internet Exercises at your OLC for examples of ethical dilemmas in anthropology

A process of culturally appropriate networking, which will vary from country to country, is necessary before field work can begin. As an example, consider how I prepared for my first field work in Madagascar, which began in 1966. Before arriving in Madagascar I obtained a visa to do research there from Madagascar's embassy in France, where I spent six months on language preparation. Once I reached Antananarivo, Madagascar's capital, I visited university anthropologists there to draw on their expertise and get their advice about my plans. Later, when I arrived in the territory of the ethnic group (Betsileo) I planned to study, I met with the province chief (Figure 12.1). Eventually I met with the heads of all the lower-level administrative units where I would be working. Next, I became friendly with knowledgeable people in the small town where I first settled. Townfolk have social networks that extend to rural areas—where I would be doing the bulk of my ethnographic field work. Through personal contacts, I created a network that eventually enabled me to work in several rural villages, one of which was my primary field site. Throughout my stay in Madagascar, I tried to stay in touch with the scholars and officials who had helped me at the outset. When I later applied for grants to return to Madagascar, I

Figure 12.1 Location of the Betsileo in Madagascar.

Proposing Research

Anthropologists need funding (research grants) for their research. The National Science Foundation (NSF) and the Wenner-Gren Foundation for Anthropological Research fund research across anthropology's four subfields. The Social Science Research Council (SSRC) supports research in cultural anthropology, as do various government agencies and programs. Before accepting a research proposal, all federal agencies require a "human subjects review." University panels review proposals to make sure that the research won't put the people being studied at risk.

A good proposal should answer several key questions. (College students should use these questions as guidelines if they are planning to do research beyond the classroom.) What's the topic or problem to be investigated? Why is the research important? Where and when will it happen? What's going to be tested and how? Is the person proposing it qualified to do it?

Funding agencies decide which research projects are worthy of support. Grant writers must show why their topic is more important than other topics being proposed for funding at the same time. Some projects make sense in certain locales but not in others; the grant writer has to show the connection. Thus, it was easy for me to justify my research on the cultural impact of television in Brazil because that country has the world's most watched commercial television network, with national penetration. By contrast, it wouldn't have made much sense for me to study television in Madagascar, where sets and transmissions reach a limited audience.

As the number of anthropologists increases, it isn't uncommon to come across two people who want to study similar topics in the same country. Especially in that event, but in any case, it's important to identify the special qualifications of the person who proposes to do research in a particular place. Relevant here are such background factors as a history of residing in the country, language training or fluency, relevant pilot (preliminary) research, and experience elsewhere with the topic or method.

Discussions of the methods to be used and the hypotheses to be tested in the research are important. Books such as *Anthropological Research: The*

included two of those scholars as funded participants in the research.

According to the AAA Code, anthropologists have a debt to the people they work with in the field, and they should reciprocate in appropriate ways. For example, it is highly appropriate for North American anthropologists working in another country to (1) include host country colleagues in their research plans and funding requests, (2) establish collaborative relationships with those colleagues and their institutions, and (3) include host country colleagues in publication of the research results. Of course, in cultural and linguistic anthropology, as in all the subfields, anthropologists' primary ethical obligation is to the people being studied. Their welfare and interests come first.

Structure of Inquiry by Pertti and Gretel Pelto (1978) and especially H. Russell Bernard's *Research Methods in Anthropology: Qualitative and Quantitative Methods* (2002) have allowed anthropology methods courses to burgeon in colleges and universities. Another good source is *The Handbook of Methods in Cultural Anthropology* (Bernard ed. 1998).

Methods—Ethnography

Cultural anthropology started to separate from sociology around the turn of the 20th century. Early students of society, such as the French scholar Émile Durkheim, were among the founders of both sociology and anthropology. Theorizing about the organization of simple and complex societies, Durkheim drew on written accounts of the religions of Native Australia (Durkheim 1912/1961) as well as considering mass phenomena (such as suicide rates) in modern nations (Durkheim 1897/1951). Eventually anthropology would specialize in the former, sociology in the latter.

Anthropology developed into a separate field as early scholars worked on Indian (Native American) reservations and traveled to distant lands to study small groups of foragers and cultivators. This type of firsthand personal study of local settings is called ethnography. Traditionally, the process of becoming a cultural anthropologist has required field experience in another society. Early ethnographers lived in small-scale, relatively isolated societies with simple technologies and economies.

Ethnography thus emerged as a research strategy in societies with greater cultural uniformity and less social differentiation than are found in large, modern industrial nations. In such nonindustrial settings, ethnographers have needed to consider fewer paths of enculturation (the process by which one acquires cultural knowledge) to understand social life. Traditionally, ethnographers have tried to understand the whole of a particular culture (or, more realistically, as much as they can, given limitations of time and perception). To pursue this goal, ethnographers adopt a free-ranging strategy for gathering information. In a given society or community, the ethnographer moves from setting to setting, place to place, and subject to subject to discover the totality and interconnectedness of social life.

By expanding our knowledge of the range of human diversity, ethnography provides a foundation for generalizations about human behavior and social life. Chapter 1 pointed out that ethnography involves field work in a particular society, whereas *ethnology* is the comparative aspect of cultural anthropology. The goals of ethnology are to identify, compare, and explain cultural differences and similarities, and to build theory about how social and cultural systems work. You might want to review the section of Chapter 1 titled "Science, Explanation, and Hypothesis Testing." That section discusses how ethnographic data, gathered through the techniques discussed here, can be used to compare and contrast, and to make generalizations about, societies and cultures.

In this chapter we focus on ethnographic field techniques. Ethnographers draw on a variety of techniques to piece together a picture of otherwise alien life styles. Anthropologists usually employ several (but rarely all) of the techniques discussed here.

Ethnographic Techniques

The characteristic *field techniques* of the ethnographer include the following:

1. Direct, firsthand observation of daily behavior, including *participant observation*.

2. Conversation with varying degrees of formality, from the daily chitchat that helps maintain rapport and provides knowledge about what is going on to prolonged *interviews*, which can be unstructured or structured. Formal, printed *interview schedules* or questionnaires may be used to ensure that complete, comparable information is available for everyone of interest to the study.

3. The *genealogical method*.

4. Detailed work with *key consultants* about particular areas of community life.

5. In-depth interviewing, often leading to the collection of *life histories* of particular people (narrators).

6. Discovery of local beliefs and perceptions, which may be compared with the ethnographer's own observations and conclusions.

7. Problem-oriented research of many sorts.

8. Longitudinal research—the continuous long-term study of an area or site.

9. Team research—coordinated research by multiple ethnographers.

OBSERVATION AND PARTICIPANT OBSERVATION

See the Internet Exercises at your OLC for an ethnographic experience

mhhe
●com
/kottak

Ethnographers get to know their hosts and usually take an interest in the totality of their lives. Ethnographers must pay attention to hundreds of details of daily life, seasonal events, and unusual happenings. They must observe individual and collective behavior in varied settings. They should record what they see as they see it. Things will never seem quite as strange as they do during the first few days and weeks in the field. The ethnographer eventually gets used to, and accepts as normal, cultural patterns that were initially alien. Ethnographers typically spend more than a year in the field. This permits them to observe the entire annual cycle. Staying a bit more than a year allows the ethnographer to repeat the season of his or her arrival, when certain events and processes may have been missed because of initial unfamiliarity and culture shock.

Many ethnographers record their impressions in a personal *diary*, which is kept separate from more formal *field notes*. Later, this record of early impressions will help point out some of the most basic aspects of cultural diversity. Such aspects include distinctive smells, noises people make, how they cover their mouths when they eat, and how they gaze at others. These patterns, which are so basic as to seem almost trivial, are part of what Bronislaw Malinowski called "the imponderabilia of native life and of typical behavior" (Malinowski 1922/1961, p. 20). These features of culture are so fundamental that local people take them for granted. They are too basic even to talk about, but the unaccustomed eye of the fledgling anthropologist picks them up. Thereafter, becoming familiar, they fade to the edge of consciousness. Initial impressions are valuable and should be recorded.

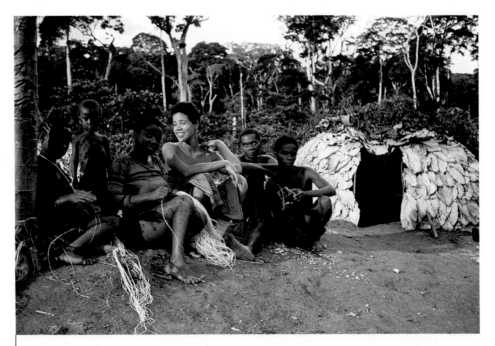

Ethnographers strive to establish rapport—a friendly relationship based on personal contact—with the people they study. Here anthropologist Nadine Peacock works among the Efe of Congo. What research method does this photo suggest?

First and foremost, ethnographers should be accurate observers, recorders, and reporters of what they see in the field.

Ethnographers don't study animals in laboratory cages. The experiments that psychologists do with pigeons, chickens, guinea pigs, and rats are very different from ethnographic procedure. Anthropologists don't systematically control subjects' rewards and punishments or their exposure to certain stimuli. Our subjects are not speechless animals but human beings. It is not part of ethnographic procedure to manipulate them, control their environments, or experimentally induce certain behaviors.

Ethnographers strive to establish *rapport*—a good, friendly working relationship based on personal contact—with our hosts. One of ethnography's most characteristic procedures is *participant observation*, which means that we take part in community life as we study it. As human beings living among others, we cannot be totally impartial and detached observers. We also must take part in many of the events and processes we are observing and trying to comprehend. By participating, we may learn how and why natives find such events meaningful, as well as see how they are organized and conducted.

To exemplify participant observation, let me describe aspects of my own ethnographic field work in Madagascar, a large island off the southeastern coast of Africa, and in Brazil. During the 14 months I lived in Madagascar in 1966–67, I observed and participated in many occasions in Betsileo life. I helped out at harvest time, joining other people who climbed atop—in order to stomp down on and compact—accumulating stacks of rice stalks. One September, for a reburial ceremony, I bought a silk shroud for a village ancestor. I entered the village tomb and watched people rewrap the bones and decaying flesh of their ancestors. I accompanied Betsileo peasants to town and to market. I observed their dealings with outsiders and sometimes offered help when problems arose.

In Arembepe, Brazil (see Chapter 1, pp. 12–13), I learned about fishing by sailing on the Atlantic in sim-

ple boats with local fishermen. I gave Jeep rides into the capital to malnourished babies, to pregnant mothers, and once to a teenage girl possessed by a spirit. All those people needed to consult specialists outside the village. I danced on Arembepe's festive occasions, drank libations commemorating new births, and became a godfather to a village girl. Most anthropologists have similar field experiences. The common humanity of the student and the studied, the ethnographer and the research community, makes participant observation inevitable.

CONVERSATION, INTERVIEWING, AND INTERVIEW SCHEDULES

Participating in local life means that ethnographers constantly talk to people and ask questions about what they observe. As their knowledge of the local language increases, they understand more. There are several stages in learning a field language. First is the naming phase—asking name after name of the objects around us. Later we are able to pose more complex questions and understand the replies. We begin to understand simple conversations between two villagers. If our language expertise proceeds far enough, we eventually become able to comprehend rapid-fire public discussions and group conversations.

A young interviewer at work on the campus of the University of Southern California (USC). Does this strike you as a formal or an informal interview?

One data-gathering technique I have used in both Arembepe and Madagascar involves an ethnographic survey that includes an interview schedule. In 1964, my fellow field workers and I attempted to complete an interview schedule in each of Arembepe's 160 households. We entered almost every household (fewer than 5 percent refused to participate) to ask a set of questions on a printed form.

Our results provided us with a census and basic information about the village. We wrote down the name, age, and sex of each household member. We gathered data on family type, political party, religion, present and previous jobs, income, expenditures, diet, possessions, and many other items on our eight-page form.

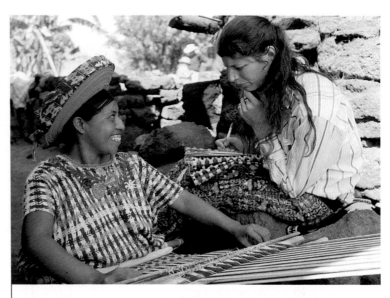

Anthropologists such as Christie Kiefer typically form personal relationships with their cultural consultants, such as this Guatemalan weaver.

Although we were doing a survey, our approach differed from the survey research design routinely used by sociologists and other social scientists working in large, industrial nations. That survey research, discussed below, involves sampling (choosing a small, manageable study group from a larger population) and impersonal data collection. We did not select a partial sample from the total population. Instead, we tried to interview all households in the community we were studying (that is, to have a total sample). We used an interview schedule rather than a questionnaire. With the **interview schedule**, the ethnographer talks face to face with people, asks the questions, and writes down the answers. **Questionnaire** procedures tend to be more indirect and impersonal; the respondent often fills in the form.

Our goal of getting a total sample allowed us to meet almost everyone in the village and helped us establish rapport. Decades later, Arembepeiros still talk warmly about how we were interested enough in them to visit their homes and ask them questions. We stood in sharp contrast to the other outsiders the villagers had known, who considered them too poor and backward to be taken seriously.

Like other survey research, however, our interview-schedule survey did gather comparable quantifiable information. It gave us a basis for assessing patterns and exceptions in village life. Our schedules included a core set of questions that were posed to everyone. However, some interesting side issues often came up during the interview, which we would pursue then or later.

We followed such leads into many dimensions of village life. One woman, for instance, a midwife, became the key cultural consultant we sought out later when we wanted detailed information about local childbirth. Another woman had done an internship in an Afro-Brazilian cult (*candomblé*) in the city. She still went there regularly to study, dance, and get possessed. She became our *candomblé* expert.

Thus, our interview-schedule survey provided a structure that *directed but did not confine* us as researchers. It enabled our ethnography to be both quantitative and qualitative. The quantitative part consisted of the basic information we gathered and later analyzed statistically. The qualitative dimension came from our follow-up questions, open-ended discussions, pauses for gossip, and work with key consultants.

THE GENEALOGICAL METHOD

As ordinary people, many of us learn about our own ancestry and relatives by tracing our genealogies. Computer programs such as Brother's Keeper allow us to trace our "family trees" and degrees of relationship. The **genealogical method** is a well-established ethnographic technique.

Early ethnographers developed notation and symbols (see the chapter on "Families, Kinship, and Descent") to deal with kinship, descent, and marriage. Genealogy is a prominent building block in the social organization of nonindustrial societies, where people live and work each day with their close kin. Anthropologists need to collect genealogical data to understand current social relations and to reconstruct history. In many nonindustrial societies, kin links are basic to social life. Anthropologists even call such cultures "kin-based societies." Everyone is related to each other and spends most of his or her time with relatives. Rules of behavior attached to particular kin relations are basic to everyday life. Marriage is also crucial in organizing nonindustrial societies because strategic marriages between villages, tribes, and clans create political alliances.

KEY CULTURAL CONSULTANTS

Every community has people who by accident, experience, talent, or training can provide the most complete or useful information about particular aspects of life. These people are **key cultural consultants**. In Ivato, the Betsileo village where I spent most of my time, a man named Rakoto was particularly knowledgeable about village history. However, when I asked him to work with me on a genealogy of the 50 to 60 people buried in the village tomb, he called in his cousin Tuesdaysfather, who knew more about this subject. Tuesdaysfather had survived an epidemic of influenza that ravaged Madagascar, along with much of the world, around 1919. Immune to the disease himself, Tuesdaysfather had the grim job of burying his kin as they died. He kept track of everyone buried in the tomb. Tuesdaysfather helped me with the tomb genealogy. Rakoto joined him in telling me personal details about the deceased villagers.

LIFE HISTORIES

In nonindustrial societies as in our own, individual personalities, interests, and abilities vary. Some villagers prove to be more interested in the ethnographer's work and are more helpful, interesting, and pleasant than others. Anthropologists develop

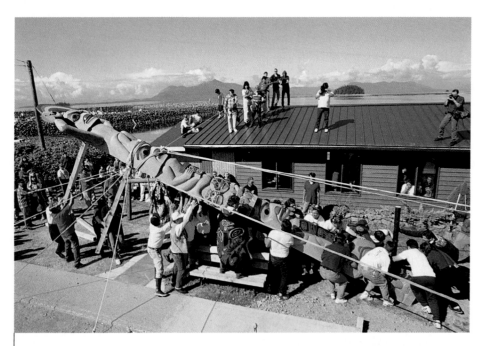

Kinship and descent are vital social building blocks in nonindustrial cultures. Without writing, genealogical information may be preserved in material culture, such as this totem pole being raised in Metlakatla, Alaska. What do you think is the significance of the images on the totem pole?

likes and dislikes in the field as we do at home. Often, when we find someone unusually interesting, we collect his or her **life history**. This recollection of a lifetime of experiences provides a more intimate and personal cultural portrait than would be possible otherwise. Life histories, which may be recorded or videotaped for later review and analysis, reveal how specific people perceive, react to, and contribute to changes that affect their lives. Such accounts can illustrate diversity, which exists within any community, since the focus is on how different people interpret and deal with some of the same problems.

Local Beliefs and Perceptions, and the Ethnographer's

One goal of ethnography is to discover local views, beliefs, and perceptions, which may be compared with the ethnographer's own observations and conclusions. In the field, ethnographers typically combine two research strategies, the emic (local-oriented) and the etic (scientist-oriented). These terms, derived from linguistics, have been applied to ethnography by various anthropologists. Marvin Harris (1968) has popularized the following meanings of the terms. An **emic** approach investigates how local people think. How do they perceive and categorize the world? What are their rules for behavior? What has meaning for them? How do they imagine and explain things? Operating emically, the ethnographer seeks the "local viewpoint," relying on local people to explain things and to say whether something is significant or not. The term **cultural consultant** refers to individuals the ethnographer gets to know in the field, the people who teach him or her about their culture, who provide the emic perspective.

The **etic** (scientist-oriented) approach shifts the focus from local categories, expressions, explanations, and interpretations to those of the anthropologist. The etic approach realizes that members of a culture are often too involved in what they are doing to interpret their cultures impartially. Operating etically, the ethnographer emphasizes what he or she (the observer) notices and considers important. As a trained scientist, the ethnographer should try to bring an objective and comprehensive viewpoint to the study of other cultures. Of course, the ethnographer, like any other scientist, is also a human being with cultural blinders that prevent complete objectivity. As in other sciences, proper training can reduce, but not totally eliminate, the observer's bias. But anthropologists do have special training to compare behavior between different societies.

Understanding Ourselves How does the emic–etic distinction help us understand ourselves? To exemplify an emic versus an etic perspective, consider our holidays. For North Americans, Thanksgiving Day has special significance. In our view (emically), it's a unique cultural celebration that commemorates particular historical themes. But a wider, etic, perspective sees Thanksgiving as just one more example of the postharvest festivals held in many societies. Another example: Laypeople (including many Americans) may believe that chills and drafts cause colds, which scientists know are caused by germs. In cultures that lack the germ theory of disease, illnesses are emically explained by various causes, ranging from spirits, to ancestors, to witches. *Illness* refers to a culture's (emic) perception and explanation of bad health, whereas *disease* refers to the scientific—etic—explanation of poor health, involving known pathogens. Like people raised in any culture, we suffer both from illness (what we think we have) and from disease (what we really have), which may not be the same. Bad health has both emic and etic roots.

Another example is the emics and etics of color terminology, to which we return in the chapter on language. In different cultures, people label colors differently. Some cultures have only 2 basic color terms—for light and dark—whereas others have all 11 primary color terms, plus a series of additional ones that recognize finer discriminations of shade and hue. Etically, the color spectrum exists everywhere, but emically, people interpret and classify it differently in different societies.

Ethnographers typically combine emic and etic strategies in their field work. Local statements, perceptions, categories, and opinions help ethnographers understand how cultures work. Local beliefs are also interesting and valuable in themselves. However, local people often don't admit, or even recognize, certain causes and consequences of their behavior. This is as true of North Americans as it is of people in other societies. To describe and interpret culture, ethnographers should recognize biases that come from their own culture as well as those of the people being studied.

THE EVOLUTION OF ETHNOGRAPHY

The Polish anthropologist Bronislaw Malinowski (1884–1942), who spent most of his professional life in England, is generally considered the father of ethnography. Like most anthropologists of his time, Malinowski did *salvage ethnography*, in the belief that the ethnographer's job is to study and record cultural diversity threatened by westernization. Early ethnographic accounts (*ethnographies*), such as Malinowski's classic *Argonauts of the Western Pacific* (1922/1961), were similar to earlier traveler and explorer accounts in describing the writer's discovery of unknown people and places. However, the *scientific* aims of ethnographies set them apart from books by explorers and amateurs.

The style that dominated "classic" ethnographies was *ethnographic realism*. The writer's goal was to present an accurate, objective, scientific account of a different way of life, written by someone who knew it firsthand. This knowledge came from an "ethnographic adventure" involving

Bronislaw Malinowski (1884–1942), seated with villagers in the Trobriand Islands. A Polish anthropologist who spent most of his professional life in England, Malinowski is generally considered the father of ethnography. Does this photo suggest anything about Malinowski's relationship with the villagers?

immersion in an alien language and culture. Ethnographers derived their authority—both as scientists and as voices of "the native" or "the other"—from this personal research experience.

Malinowski's ethnographies were guided by the assumption that aspects of culture are linked and intertwined. Beginning by describing a Trobriand sailing expedition, the ethnographer then follows the links between that entry point and other areas of the culture, such as magic, religion, myths, kinship, and trade. Compared with Malinowski, today's ethnographies tend to be less inclusive and holistic, focusing on particular topics, such as kinship or religion.

According to Malinowski, a primary task of the ethnographer is "to grasp the native's point of view, his relation to life, to realize *his* vision of *his* world" (1922/1961, p. 25—Malinowski's italics). This is a good statement of the need for the emic perspective, as was discussed earlier. Since the 1970s, *interpretive anthropology* has considered the task of describing and interpreting that which is meaningful to natives. Interpretivists such as Clifford Geertz (1973) view cultures as meaningful texts that natives constantly "read" and ethnographers must decipher. According to Geertz, anthropologists may choose anything in a culture that interests them, fill in details, and elaborate to inform their readers about meanings in that culture. Meanings are carried by public symbolic forms, including words, rituals, and customs.

A current trend in ethnographic writing is to question traditional goals, methods, and styles, including ethnographic realism and salvage ethnography (Clifford 1982, 1988; Marcus and Cushman 1982). Marcus and Fischer argue that experimentation in ethnographic writing is necessary because all peoples and cultures have already been "discovered" and must now be "*re*discovered . . . in changing historical circumstances" (1986, p. 24).

In general, experimental anthropologists see ethnographies as works of art as well as works of science. Ethnographic texts may be viewed as literary creations in which the ethnographer, as mediator, communicates information from the "natives" to readers. Some experimental ethnographies are "dialogic," presenting ethnography as a dialogue between the anthropologist and one or more native informants (e.g., Dwyer 1982; Behar 1993). These works draw attention to ways in which ethnographers, and by extension their readers, communicate with other cultures. However, some such ethnographies have been criticized for spending too much time talking about the anthropologist and too little time describing the natives and their culture.

The dialogic ethnography is one genre within a larger experimental category—that is, *reflexive ethnography*. Here the ethnographer-writer puts his or her personal feelings and reactions to the field situation right in the text. Experimental writing strategies are prominent in reflexive accounts. The ethnographer may adopt some of the conventions of the novel, including first-person narration, conversations, dialogues, and humor. Experimental ethnographies, using new ways of showing what it means to be a Samoan or a Brazilian, may convey to the reader a richer and more complex understanding of human experience.

Interpret the World
Atlas Map 12

Linked to salvage ethnography was the idea of the *ethnographic present*—the period before westernization, when the "true" native culture flourished. This notion often gives classic ethnographies an unrealistic timeless quality. Providing the only jarring note in this idealized picture are occasional comments by the author about traders or missionaries, suggesting that in actuality the natives were already part of the world system. Map 12 in your atlas, "Ethnographic Study Sites Prior to 1950," locates sites where important ethnographic studies were done prior to 1950. Note that several sites of Native American societies are located within North America. How would you describe the distribution of ethnographic studies prior to 1950? Read the text to see how the sites and topics of ethnographic research have evolved since 1950.

Anthropologists now recognize that the ethnographic present is a rather unrealistic construct. Cultures have been in contact—and have been changing—throughout history. Most native cultures had at least one major foreign encounter before any anthropologist ever came their way. Most of them had already been incorporated in some fashion into nation-states or colonial systems.

Contemporary ethnographies usually recognize that cultures constantly change and that an ethnographic account applies to a particular moment. A current trend in ethnography is to focus on the ways in which cultural ideas serve political and economic interests. Another trend is to describe how various particular "natives" participate in broader historical, political, and economic processes (Shostak 1981).

PROBLEM-ORIENTED ETHNOGRAPHY

We see, then, a tendency to move away from holistic accounts toward more problem-focused and experimental ethnographies. Although anthropologists are interested in the whole context of human behavior, it is impossible to study everything, and field research usually addresses specific questions. Most ethnographers now enter the field with a specific problem to investigate, and they collect data about variables deemed relevant to that problem. And local people's answers to questions are not the only data source. Anthropologists also gather information on factors such as population density, environmental quality, climate, physical geography, diet, and land use. Sometimes this involves direct measurement—of rainfall, temperature, fields, yields, dietary quantities, or time allocation (Bailey 1990; Johnson 1978). Often it means that we consult government records or archives.

The information of interest to ethnographers is not limited to what local people can and do tell us. In an increasingly interconnected and complicated world, local people lack knowledge about many factors that affect their lives. Our local consultants may be as mystified as we are by the exercise of power from regional, national, and international centers.

LONGITUDINAL RESEARCH

Geography limits anthropologists less now than in the past, when it could take months to reach a field site and return visits were rare. New systems of transportation allow anthropologists to widen the area of their research and to return repeatedly. Ethnographic reports now routinely include data from two or more field stays. **Longitudinal research** is the long-term study of a community, region, society, culture, or other unit, usually based on repeated visits. One example of such research is the longitudinal study of Gwembe District, Zambia (Figure 12.2). This study, planned in 1956 as a longitudinal project by Elizabeth Colson and Thayer Scudder, continues with Colson,

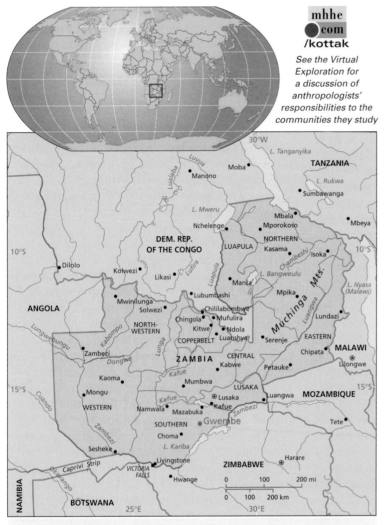

mhhe
.com
/kottak

See the Virtual
Exploration for
a discussion of
anthropologists'
responsibilities to the
communities they study

Figure 12.2   Location of Gwembe in Zambia.

Zambian assistants keep records of local events, as well as diaries of foods bought and eaten. Shifts in preferences for products are documented by shopping lists provided by villagers. Field notes describe attendance at courts, meetings, church services, funerals, and ceremonies. This information is supplemented by interviews with political leaders, officials, traders, technical workers, and foreigners who work for religious missions and *nongovernmental organizations* (NGOs). The anthropologists also consult government archives and other records. Zambian social scientists working in the district also provide insights about the changes taking place.

A series of different research questions have emerged, while basic data on communities and individuals continue to be collected. The first focus of study was the impact of a large hydroelectric dam, which subjected the Gwembe people to forced resettlement. The dam also spurred road building and other activities that brought the people of Gwembe more closely in touch with the rest of Zambia (Colson 1971; Scudder 1982; Scudder and Habarad 1991).

In the late 1960s, education became the research focus. Scudder and Colson (1980) examined how education provided access to new opportunities as it also widened a social gap between people with different educational levels. A third major study then examined a change in brewing and drinking patterns, including a rise in alcoholism, in relation to changing markets, transportation, and exposure to town values (Colson and Scudder 1988).

TEAM RESEARCH

As mentioned, longitudinal research is often team research. My own field site of Arembepe, Brazil, for example, first entered the world of anthropology as a field-team village in the 1960s. It was one of four sites for the now defunct Columbia–Cornell–Harvard–Illinois Summer Field Studies Program in

Scudder, and their associates of various nationalities. Thus, as is often the case with longitudinal research, the Gwembe study also illustrates team research—coordinated research by multiple ethnographers. The Gwembe research project is both longitudinal (multitime) and multisite (considering several field sites) (Colson and Scudder 1975; Scudder and Colson 1980). Four villages, in different areas, have been followed for five decades. Periodic village censuses provide basic data on population, economy, kinship, and religious behavior. Censused people who have moved are traced and interviewed to see how their lives compare with those of people who have stayed in the villages.

Anthropology. For at least three years, that program sent a total of about 20 undergraduates annually, the author included, to do brief summer research. We were stationed in rural communities in four countries: Brazil, Ecuador, Mexico, and Peru. Since my wife, Isabel Wagley Kottak, and I began studying it in 1962, Arembepe has become a longitudinal field site. There generations of researchers have monitored various aspects of change and development. The community has changed from a village into a town. Its economy, religion, and social life have been transformed.

Brazilian and American researchers worked with us on team research projects during the 1980s (on television's impact) and the 1990s (on ecological awareness and environmental risk perception). Graduate students from the University of Michigan have drawn on our baseline information from the 1960s as they have studied various topics in Arembepe. In 1990, Doug Jones, a Michigan student doing biocultural research, used Arembepe as a field site to investigate standards of physical attractiveness. In 1996–97, Janet Dunn studied family planning and changing female reproductive strategies (Dunn 2000). Chris O'Leary, who first visited Arembepe in summer 1997, has investigated a striking aspect

of religious change in Arembepe—the arrival of Protestantism. Later he did a study of changing food preferences (O'Leary 2002).

Arembepe is thus a site where various field workers have worked as members of a longitudinal team. The more recent researchers have built on prior contacts and findings to increase knowledge about how local people meet and manage new circumstances. I think that scholarship should be a community enterprise. The information we gathered in the past is there for new generations to use. To monitor changing attitudes and to understand the relation between television and family planning, Janet Dunn reinterviewed many of the women we had interviewed in the 1980s. Similarly, Chris O'Leary, who compared food habits and nutritional status in Arembepe and another Brazilian town, had access to dietary information from our 1964 interviews.

Contemporary forces of change are too pervasive and complex to be understood fully by a "lone ethnographer"—a researcher who starts from scratch and works alone, for a limited period of time, and who views his or her field site as relatively discrete and isolated. No longer can any ethnographer imagine that his or her field site represents some sort of pristine or autonomous entity. Nor should the ethnographer assume that he or she has exclusive (owner's) rights to the site, or even to the data gathered there. That information, after all, has been produced in friendship, cooperation, and consultation with local people. More and more anthropological field sites, including Malinowski's Trobriand Islands, have been restudied. Ideally, later ethnographers collaborate with and build on the work of their predecessors. Compared with the lone ethnographer model, team work across time (as in Arembepe) and space (as in our comparative studies in various Brazilian towns) produces better understanding of cultural change and social complexity.

Survey Research

As anthropologists work increasingly in large-scale societies, they have developed innovative ways of blending ethnography and survey research (Fricke 1994). Before considering such combinations of field methods, I must describe

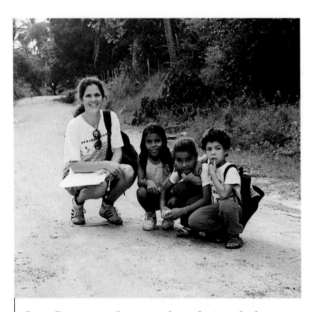

Janet Dunn, one of many anthropologists who have worked in Arembepe. Where is Arembepe, and what kinds of research have been done there?

survey research and the main differences between survey research and ethnography as traditionally practiced. Working mainly in large, populous nations, sociologists, political scientists, and economists have developed and refined the **survey research** design, which involves sampling, impersonal data collection, and statistical analysis. Survey research usually draws a **sample** (a manageable study group) from a much larger population. By studying a properly selected and representative sample, social scientists can make accurate inferences about the larger population.

In smaller-scale societies, ethnographers get to know most of the people, but given the greater size and complexity of nations, survey research cannot help being more impersonal. Survey researchers call the people they study *respondents*. These are people who respond to questions during a survey. Sometimes survey researchers personally interview them. Sometimes, after an initial meeting, they ask respondents to fill out a questionnaire. In other cases, researchers mail printed questionnaires to randomly selected sample members or have graduate students interview or telephone them. (In a **random sample**, all members of the population have an equal statistical chance of being chosen for inclusion. A random sample is selected by randomizing procedures, such as tables of random numbers, which are found in many statistics textbooks.) Table 12.1 summarizes the main differences between ethnography and survey research.

Anyone who has grown up recently in the United States or Canada has heard of sampling. Probably the most familiar example is the polling used to predict political races. The media hire agencies to estimate outcomes and do exit polls to find out what kinds of people voted for which candidates. During sampling, researchers gather information about age, gender, religion, occupation, income, and political party preference. These characteristics (**variables**—attributes that vary among members of a sample or population) are known to influence political decisions.

The number of variables influencing social identity and behavior increases with, and can be considered a measure of, social complexity. Many more variables affect social identities, experiences, and activities in a modern nation than is the case in the small communities where ethnography grew up. In contemporary North America, hundreds of factors influence our social behavior and attitudes. These social predictors include our religion; the region of the country in which we grew

Table 12.1 Ethnography and Survey Research Contrasted	
Ethnography	**Survey Research**
Studies whole, functioning communities	Studies a small sample of a larger population
Is usually based on firsthand field work, during which information is collected after rapport, based on personal contact, is established between researcher and hosts	Is often conducted with little or no personal contact between study subjects and researchers, as interviews are frequently conducted by assistants over the phone or in printed form
Is generally interested in all aspects of local life (holistic)	Usually focuses on a small number of variables, e.g., factors that influence voting, rather than on the totality of people's lives
Has been traditionally conducted in nonindustrial, small-scale societies, where people often do not read and write	Is normally carried out in modern nations, where most people are literate, permitting respondents to fill in their own questionnaires
Makes little use of statistics, because the communities being studied tend to be small, with little diversity besides that based on age, gender, and individual personality variation	Is heavily dependent on statistical analyses to make inferences regarding a large and diverse population, based on data collected from a small subset of that population

A population census taker surrounded by villagers in Paro, Bhutan. Is the technique of gathering information illustrated here more like ethnography or survey research?

up; whether we come from a town, suburb, or city; and our parents' professions, ethnic origins, and income levels. Because survey research deals with large and diverse groups and with samples and probability, its results must be analyzed statistically.

Ethnography can be used to supplement and fine-tune survey research. Anthropologists can transfer the personal, firsthand techniques of ethnography to virtually any setting that includes human beings. A combination of survey research and ethnography can provide new perspectives on life in **complex societies** (large and populous societies with social stratification and central governments). Preliminary ethnography also can help develop relevant and culturally appropriate questions for inclusion in surveys.

A Brazilian boy forages for valuables in a sidewalk drain outside a restaurant on Copacabana beach, Rio de Janeiro. Anthropologists have studied street children in Brazil and elsewhere. What techniques do you imagine they use for such studies?

Background Information

STUDENT: **Angela C. Stuesse**
SUPERVISING PROFESSOR: **Allan F. Burns**
SCHOOL: **University of Florida**
YEAR IN SCHOOL/MAJOR: **Senior/Anthropology**
FUTURE PLANS: **Master's in Latin American Studies**

PROJECT TITLE: **The *Patrona-Empleada** Relationship Revealed: Stories from Women Domestics of the Yucatán**

What research techniques are illustrated in this account of undergraduate research? Think about this student's approach in terms of the issues raised in the section on the evolution of ethnography.

My fascination with anthropology sprang to life in early 1996, during a semester of study abroad in the Yucatán of Mexico. It was also there that I first came into contact with domestic workers of Latin America. Witness to the daily interactions between my host-family and their servant, I became intrigued by the complex nature of their relationship and decided to return the following year to do research for my honors thesis.

The testimonial of a domestic worker is often the story of both her personal and professional life. This is because she works not in an office, but rather in her *patrona's* home. Over time, the distinction between employee and family member blurs. The indefinite relationship that results gives rise to many questions: To what extent is the servant influenced by the values and attitudes of her *patrona*? How does the way she perceives her own life compare with the way her *patrona* sees her? Under what conditions does their bond become less work-related and more analogous to family? What causes their association to be hierarchical in nature, and in what ways is this verticality expressed and/or mediated? These themes were the driving force of my investigations.

Through personal contacts, I met four domestic workers who agreed to participate in my research. They ranged in age from 17 to 70 years old, and had between 5 and 50 years of experience. Research methods included auto-photography, unstructured and semi-structured interviews, and participant observation. Our conversations were sometimes lighthearted, sometimes very serious, and always key to a deeper understanding of each individual. Apart from listening and discussing, I also learned from these women by watching and doing. I helped them hang the laundry, set the table, sweep the patio, and fill the swimming pool. I visited their pueblos and met their families. We spent hours exchanging thoughts and discussing life. I laughed along with many and I held a hand as one woman cried. It was by participating in simple events like these that I began to understand the profundity and strength of these unique women. By interviewing and getting to know their *patronas* as well, I was able to analyze the nature of their relationships and place them within the context of existing ethnographic literature and theory.

The resulting thesis gives identity to the faceless numbers common in survey and demographic research. Through my writing I have attempted to let these women speak, to give them decision, control, and value. I also have explored the genre known as "narrative ethnography," which, by including first-person experiences, rejects the idea that a valid, professional study must be "objective" and "scientific." My research adds to the growing body of narrative ethnographic, testimonial, and introspective literature about women domestics and change in the Yucatán and Latin America. With each new study we are a few steps closer to a greater cultural understanding.

*Patrona literally means patron or boss, referring to the female head of the household who oversees the domestic servants.

Empleada literally means employee, here referring to the female domestic servant.

In my own courses in Ann Arbor, Michigan, undergraduates have done ethnographic research on sororities, fraternities, teams, campus organizations, and the local homeless population. Other students have systematically observed behavior in public places. These include racquetball courts, restaurants, bars, football stadiums, markets, malls, and classrooms. Other "modern anthropology" projects use anthropological techniques to interpret and analyze mass media. Anthropologists have been studying their own cultures for decades, and anthropological research in the United States and Canada is booming today. Wherever there is patterned human behavior, there is grist for the anthropological mill.

In any complex society, many predictor variables (*social indicators*) influence behavior and opinions. Because we must be able to detect, measure, and compare the influence of social indicators, many contemporary anthropological studies have a statistical foundation. Even in rural field work, more anthropologists now draw samples, gather quantitative data, and use statistics to interpret them (see Bernard 1994). Quantifiable information may permit a more precise assessment of similarities and differences between communities. Statistical analysis can support and round out an ethnographic account of local social life.

However, in the best studies, the hallmark of ethnography remains: Anthropologists enter the community and get to know the people. They participate in local activities, networks, and associations, in the city or in the countryside. They observe and experience social conditions and problems. They watch the effects of national policies and programs on local life. I believe that the ethnographic method and the emphasis on personal relationships in social research are valuable gifts that cultural anthropology brings to the study of a complex society.

SUMMARY

1. A code of ethics guides anthropologists' research and other professional activities. Anthropologists need to establish and maintain appropriate, collaborative, and nonexploitative relationships with colleagues and communities in the host country. Researchers must gain the informed consent of all affected parties—from the authorities who control access to the field site to the members of the community being studied.

2. Several agencies support research in anthropology. A research proposal should answer certain key questions: What's the topic/problem? Why is the research important? Where and when will it happen? Is the person proposing it qualified to do it? How will he or she do it?

3. Ethnographic methods include observation, rapport building, participant observation, interviewing, genealogies, work with key consultants, life histories, and longitudinal research. Ethnographers do not systematically manipulate their subjects or conduct experiments. Rather, they work in actual communities and form personal relationships with local people as they study their lives.

4. An interview schedule is a form that an ethnographer completes as he or she visits a series of households. The schedule organizes and guides each interview, ensuring that comparable information is collected from everyone. Key cultural consultants teach about particular areas of local life. Life histories dramatize the fact that culture bearers are individuals. Such case studies document personal experiences with culture and culture change. Genealogical information is particularly useful in societies in which principles of kinship and marriage organize social and political life. Emic approaches focus on native perceptions and explanations. Etic approaches give priority to the ethnographer's own observations and conclusions. Longitudinal research is the systematic study of an area or site over time. Forces of change are often too pervasive and complex to be understood by a lone ethnographer. Anthropological research may be done by teams.

5. Traditionally, anthropologists worked in small-scale societies; sociologists, in modern nations. Different techniques were developed to study such different kinds of societies. Social scientists working in complex societies use survey research to sample variation. Anthropologists do their field work in communities and study the totality of social life. Sociologists study samples to make inferences about a larger population. Sociologists often are interested in causal relations among a very small number of variables. Anthropologists more typically are concerned with the interconnectedness of all aspects of social life.

6. The diversity of social life in modern nations and cities requires social survey procedures. However, anthropologists add the intimacy and direct investigation characteristic of ethnography. Anthropologists may use ethnographic procedures to study urban life. But they also make greater use of survey techniques and analysis of the mass media in their research in contemporary nations.

KEY TERMS

See the flash cards

mhhe
●com
/kottak

complex societies Nations; large and populous, with social stratification and central governments.

cultural consultants Subjects in ethnographic research; people the ethnographer gets to know in the field, who teach him or her about their culture.

emic The research strategy that focuses on local explanations and criteria of significance.

etic The research strategy that emphasizes the ethnographer's rather than the locals' explanations, categories, and criteria of significance.

genealogical method Procedures by which ethnographers discover and record connections of kinship, descent, and marriage, using diagrams and symbols.

interview schedule Ethnographic tool for structuring a formal interview. A prepared form (usually printed or mimeographed) that guides interviews with households or individuals being compared systematically. Contrasts with a *questionnaire* because the researcher has personal contact with the local people and records their answers.

key cultural consultant Person who is an expert on a particular aspect of local life.

life history Of a key consultant or narrator; provides a personal cultural portrait of existence or change in a culture.

longitudinal research Long-term study of a community, region, society, culture, or other unit, usually based on repeated visits.

questionnaire Form (usually printed) used by sociologists to obtain comparable information from respondents. Often mailed to and filled in by research subjects rather than by the researcher.

random sample A sample in which all members of the population have an equal statistical chance of being included.

sample A smaller study group chosen to represent a larger population.

survey research Characteristic research procedure among social scientists other than anthropologists. Studies society through sampling, statistical analysis, and impersonal data collection.

variables Attributes (e.g., sex, age, height, weight) that differ from one person or case to the next.

CRITICAL THINKING QUESTIONS

For more self testing, see the self quizzes

mhhe
com
/kottak

1. What kinds of problems—practical, personal, and ethical—can you imagine arising during ethnographic field work?

2. How might ethical issues and concerns differently affect cultural, biological, and archaeological anthropologists?

3. Imagine yourself a foreign ethnographer starting field work in the United States. Where would you locate? What would be some of the imponderabilia of typical life that you'd notice during the first few weeks of your research?

4. If you were an anthropologist planning a field trip, what kinds of preparations would you have to make before and after you planned your research and arrange funding? How would your preparations differ depending on whether you planned to work in an industrial or a nonindustrial society?

5. How might the genealogical method be used in subfields of anthropology other than cultural anthropology?

6. If you were planning to use a life history approach to ethnography and had a year to spend in the field, how many consultants do you think you'd need to interview, and why? What sorts of people would you seek out as key cultural consultants?

7. Using your own society as an example, can you think of additional examples of the emic–etic distinction? What are some folk beliefs for which science has provided more satisfactory explanations? Why do folk beliefs persist if science does such a good job of explaining things?

8. How do you think the subfields of anthropology differ with respect to field work? Are some subfields more likely to use a team approach than others are? What about the equipment needs of the different subfields?

9. What do you see as the strengths and weaknesses of ethnography compared with survey research? Which provides more accurate data? Might one be better for finding questions, while the other is better for finding answers? Or does it depend on the context of the research?

10. How might the grant proposal guidelines in this chapter help you plan your own field research on campus or nearby?

Atlas Questions

Look at Map 12, "Ethnographic Study Sites Prior to 1950."

1. Anthropology originated as the scientific study of nonwestern peoples and cultures. Yet Map 12 shows that many anthropological studies conducted prior to 1950 were done in North America. What societies were being studied in North America? Were they considered western or nonwestern? What does this tell us about the concept of "western"?

2. How would you describe the range of ethnographic sites prior to 1950? Were some world areas being neglected, such as the Middle East or mainland Asia? What might be the reasons for such omissions?

3. Think about how changes in transportation and communication have affected the way anthropologists do their research. How might a list of contemporary ethnographic sites contrast with the distribution shown in Map 12. See the chapter "Culture" for a discussion of longitudinal research. How has longitudinal research been affected by changes in transportation and communication?

Suggested Additional Readings

Agar, M. H.

1996 *The Professional Stranger: An Informal Introduction to Ethnography*, 2nd ed. San Diego: Academic Press. Basics of ethnography, illustrated by the author's field experiences in India and among heroin addicts in the United States.

Angrosino, M. V., ed.

2002 *Doing Cultural Anthropology: Projects for Ethnographic Data Collection.* Prospect Heights, IL: Waveland. How to get ethnographic data.

Berg, B. L.

2001 *Qualitative Research Methods for the Social Sciences*, 4th ed. Boston: Allyn and Bacon. How ethnography and other qualitative procedures may be extended across the range of social sciences; very thorough survey of qualitative methods.

Bernard, H. R.

2002 *Research Methods in Anthropology: Qualitative and Quantitative Methods*, 3rd ed. Walnut Creek, CA: Altamira. Expansion of a classic text on research methods in cultural anthropology.

Bernard, H. R., ed.

1998 *The Handbook of Methods in Cultural Anthropology.* Walnut Creek, CA: Altamira. Various authors describe a series of methods in cultural anthropology.

Chiseri-Strater, E., and B. S. Sunstein

2002 *Fieldworking: Reading and Writing Research*, 2nd ed. Upper Saddle River, NJ: Prentice-Hall. Ways of evaluating and presenting research data.

Crane, J. G., and M. V. Angrosino

1992 *Field Projects in Anthropology: A Student Handbook*, 3rd ed. Prospect Heights, IL: Waveland. Methods and key issues in doing field work.

DeVita, P. R., and J. D. Armstrong, eds.

2002 *Distant Mirrors: America as a Foreign Culture*, 3rd ed. Belmont, CA: Wadsworth. The social life, customs, and popular culture of the United States as viewed and interpreted by outsiders.

Kottak, C. P., ed.

1982 *Researching American Culture: A Guide for Student Anthropologists.* Ann Arbor: University of Michigan Press. Advice for college students doing field work in the United States. Includes papers by undergraduates and anthropologists on contemporary American culture.

Kutsche, P.

1998 *Field Ethnography: A Manual for Doing Cultural Anthropology.* Upper Saddle River, NJ: Prentice-Hall. Useful guide for fledgling ethnographers.

Michrina, B. P., and C. Richards

1996 *Person to Person: Fieldwork, Dialogue, and the Hermeneutic Method.* Albany: State University of New York Press. Discusses some of the experimental and interpretive ethnographic procedures discussed in this chapter.

Pelto, P. J., and G. H. Pelto

1978 *Anthropological Research: The Structure of Inquiry*, 2nd ed. New York: Cambridge University Press. Discusses data collection and analysis, including the relationship between theory and field work, hypothesis construction, sampling, and statistics.

Spradley, J. P.

1979 *The Ethnographic Interview.* New York: Harcourt Brace Jovanovich. Discussion of the ethnographic method, with emphasis on discovering native viewpoints.

INTERNET EXERCISES

1. Ethnographic Field Work: Look at this collection of papers from the page entitled "Ethnographic Research Done in the Southern Appalachians," **http://www.acs.appstate.edu/dept/anthro/ ebooks/ethno97/title.html**.

   a. Read the Preface. What skills were the students able to develop in the field that cannot be taught in a lecture course?

   b. Go to the paper entitled Women's Work in Allegheny County, NC, **http://www.acs. appstate.edu/dept/anthro/ebooks/ethno97/ efird.html**. Skim the paper, paying special attention to the introduction, conclusion, and appendices. What did the student learn? How different are the women portrayed in this article from the women in your own community?

   c. Look specifically at the student's appendices. How did she collect the information she needed to make her conclusions? Are there questions you would have added? Why?

   d. Skim at least one other chapter, focusing on the introduction and conclusion. What are the advantages of doing research as a team? If there were only one person doing work on this project in the Appalachians, how do you think the results might be different? Do you think it is possible for a single ethnographer to fully understand a community?

2. Read the short article by Barbara Schneider entitled "The Role of Field Notes in Constructing Ethnographic Knowledge" (**http://www. stthomasu.ca/inkshed/nlett500/schneidr.htm**).

   a. What kind of research methods did the anthropologist employ?

   b. What was the subject of the anthropologist's research? How did the topic of research change over time?

   c. What is the author's concern about how ethnographic material is interpreted? How can anthropologists avoid these problems?

See Chapter 12 at your McGraw-Hill Online Learning Center for additional review and interactive exercises.

13
CULTURE

Overview

Culture is learned, and is passed from one generation to the next, through the process of enculturation. Only humans have cultural learning, which depends on symbols. Symbols have a particular meaning and value for people who share the same culture. Experiences, memories, values, and beliefs are shared as a result of common enculturation. Cultural traditions take natural phenomena, including biologically based urges, and channel them in particular directions. Everyone is cultured, not just people with elite educations. Societies are integrated and patterned through their dominant economic forces, social patterns, key symbols, and core values. Cultural rules don't always dictate behavior. There is room for creativity, flexibility, diversity, and disagreement within societies. Cultural means

of adaptation have been crucial in human evolution. However, aspects of culture also can be maladaptive.

There are different levels of cultural systems. Diffusion and migration carry the same cultural traits and patterns to different areas. Such features are therefore shared across national boundaries. Nations also have internal cultural diversity associated with ethnicity, region, and social class. Some cultural features are universal. Others are widespread or generalized. Still others are unique and distinctive to particular societies. Mechanisms of cultural change include diffusion, acculturation, and independent invention. Globalization describes a series of processes that promote change in a world whose nations and people are increasingly linked.

343

Culture Clash: Makah Say Whale Hunt Opponents Debase Indian Culture

ABC NEWS BRIEF

by Dean Schabner

May 29, 2002

Makah Indians kill a gray whale in May 1999. More than 500 Makah Indians attended the traditional ceremony of the whale hunt.

Consider this definition: "Culture . . . is that complex whole which includes knowledge, belief, arts, morals, law, custom, and any other capabilities and habits acquired by man as a member of society" (Tylor 1871/1958, p. 1). Tylor's definition focuses on attributes that people acquire by growing up in a particular society, where they are exposed to a specific cultural tradition. Contemporary indigenous peoples must heed not only their own customs but also laws and agencies operating at the national and international levels. As you read the following account and this chapter on culture, pay attention to the various kinds of rights being asserted—for example, animal rights versus cultural rights. Also consider the levels of culture and of political regulation (local, regional, national, and global) that determine how contemporary people live their lives and maintain their traditions.

The Fund for Animals, the Humane Society of the United States and other groups have been waging a legal battle to keep the Makah, an American Indian tribe who live along the coasts of the Olympic Peninsula in Washington state, from rowing out from the shore in traditional dugout canoes and hunting whales . . . the way their ancestors did.

Opponents of the hunt say the Makah should not be allowed to kill whales because, unlike some tribes in Alaska and northern Canada and the indigenous people of parts of Russia, they do not need whale meat to survive. They characterize the Makah hunt as sport or recreation, and discount the tribe's claim that whaling is culturally important to them.

"That's incredibly insulting and racist," said Janine Bowechop, the director of the Makah museum. "For them to determine what it means to us brings us back to the last century when it was thought that Indians could not speak for themselves and determine what things mean to us. I would not pretend to determine what something means to another culture."

She said that despite the 70 years when the tribe did not have a whale hunt, it is still "a regular and important part of our lives." "There are lots of strengthening values associated with whaling," she said. "There are lots of spiritual values that feed sharing and cooperation among our community. And it connects us with the ocean in ways that Makahs have always been connected with the ocean."

In the five years since the Makah have been allowed to resume their hunt, they have caught one whale, and have spent more time navigating turbulent legal waters in the courts than fighting ocean waves in their dugout canoes.

The Makah may be nearing the end of their legal fight, though. On May 17, a federal judge in Tacoma, Wash., refused to . . . stop the Makah from whaling until a decision is reached in the animal rights groups' lawsuit against the . . . agencies that cleared the way for the tribe to resume the hunt. . . .

Another potential obstacle to the Makah resuming their hunt was removed Friday when the International Whaling Commission, meeting in Shimonoseki, Japan, approved a U.S. request to allow the tribe to kill four gray whales a year—in a re-vote after the proposal was voted down on Thursday.

The commission turned down another request by the United States to allow Eskimos to take 55 bowhead whales over five years, and one from Russia to allow the Chukotka to hunt 120 whales per year.

The Eskimo tribes and the Chukotka both depend on whale as a major food source.

According to some observers, the vote to deny the requests was orchestrated by Japan in retaliation for international efforts to maintain the commercial whaling moratorium imposed on Japanese coastal communities.

"Japan essentially took the interests of arctic communities who aren't really part of this political process and held them hostage to try and get a relaxation of the commercial moratorium on whaling," World Wildlife Fund vice president Richard Mott said. As much as the animal rights groups are concerned about the situation around the Washington coast, they are equally concerned that if the Makah are allowed to hunt whales, it will set a precedent for other tribes without a subsistence need to resume whale hunts of their own and for the resumption of large-scale commercial whaling by countries like Japan and Norway. . . .

What allowed the Makah to even test the waters after some 70 years of not hunting whales was the decision in 1994 to remove the gray whale, which migrates along the West Coast of the United States, from the endangered species list. Their right to hunt whales was recognized by the U.S. government in an 1855 treaty, under which the tribe ceded a portion of its lands to the government . . .

The Makah say that the question of whether the hunt will have a negative effect on the overall whale population has already been answered.

"This hunt presents fewer concerns than most, if not any other hunt, because of the limited nature of the hunt, the limited number of shots that are going to be fired, the training requirements, the presence of a safety officer," Makah attorney Mark Slonim said.

According to a statement from the tribe, as little as one whale a year could satisfy the "traditional subsistence or cultural need for whale in the community," which is a requirement for a hunt to take place. . . .

"The anti-whaling community is very well organized and very well financed and puts out a steady stream of propaganda designed to denigrate our culture and play on human sympathy for all animals," the statement says. "Perhaps what is lost in all of their rhetoric is an appreciation of the value of preserving the culture of an American Indian Tribe— a culture which has always had to struggle against the assumption by some non-Indians that their values are superior to ours.

"But our opponents would have us abandon this part of our culture and restrict it to a museum. To us this means a dead culture. We are trying to maintain a living culture. We can only hope that those whose opposition is most vicious will be able to recognize their ethnocentrism—subordinating our culture to theirs." The groups opposed to the hunt say the issue goes beyond cultural concerns, though.

Source: http://abcnews.go.com/sections/us/DailyNews/makah020529.html.

Are the animal rights activists ethnocentric? **Ethnocentrism** is the tendency to view one's own cultural beliefs as superior and to apply one's own values in judging the behavior and beliefs of people raised in other cultures. Ethnocentrism contributes to social solidarity, a sense of value and community, among people who share the same beliefs. But it also fuels clashes among cultures, especially when their different beliefs, values, and practices come into direct conflict.

What Is Culture

More than a century ago, in his book *Primitive Culture* (1871), the British anthropologist Sir Edward Burnett Tylor proposed that cultures—systems of human behavior and thought—obey natural laws and therefore can be studied scientifically. In that book he also offered his now-famous definition of culture, which was quoted in the introduction to the news story. When Tylor thought of culture and cultures, he had in mind more autonomous units than the interlinked cultural entities that anthropologists study today. But his definition of culture, which focuses on attributes that people acquire not through biological inheritance but by growing up in a particular society where they are exposed to a specific cultural tradition, remains useful. **Enculturation** is the process by which a child *learns* his or her culture.

CULTURE IS LEARNED

The ease with which children absorb any cultural tradition rests on the uniquely elaborated human capacity to learn. Other animals may learn from experience; for example, they avoid fire after discovering that it hurts. Social animals also learn from other members of their group. Wolves, for instance, learn hunting strategies from other pack members. Such social learning is particularly important among monkeys and apes, our closest biological relatives. But our own *cultural learning* depends on the uniquely developed human capacity to use **symbols**, signs that have no necessary or natural connection to the things they signify or for which they stand.

On the basis of cultural learning, people create, remember, and deal with ideas. They grasp and apply specific systems of symbolic meaning. Anthropologist Clifford Geertz defines culture as ideas based on cultural learning and symbols. Cultures have been characterized as sets of "control mechanisms—plans, recipes, rules, instructions, what computer engineers call programs for the governing of behavior" (Geertz 1973, p. 44). These programs are absorbed by people through enculturation in particular traditions. People gradually internalize a previously established system of meanings and symbols. They use this cultural system to define their world, express their feelings, and make their judgments. This system helps guide their behavior and perceptions throughout their lives.

Every person begins immediately, through a process of conscious and unconscious learning and interaction with others, to internalize, or incorporate, a cultural tradition through the process of enculturation. Sometimes culture is taught directly, as when parents tell their children to say "thank you" when someone gives them something or does them a favor.

Culture also is transmitted through observation. Children pay attention to the things that go on around them. They modify their behavior not just because other people tell them to but as a result of their own observations and growing awareness of what their culture considers right and wrong. Culture also is absorbed unconsciously. North Americans acquire their culture's notions about how far apart people should stand when they talk (see "Interesting Issues" on pages 348 and 349) not by being directly told to maintain a certain distance but through a gradual process of observation, experience, and conscious and unconscious behavior modification. No one tells Latins to stand closer together than North Americans do, but they learn to do so anyway as part of their cultural tradition.

See the Virtual Exploration for an example of how cultural values are learned

Anthropologists agree that cultural learning is uniquely elaborated among humans and that all humans have culture. Anthropologists also accept a doctrine named in the 19th century as "the psychic unity of man." This means that although *individuals* differ in their emotional and intellectual tendencies and capacities, all human *populations* have equivalent capacities for culture. Regardless of their genes or their physical appearance, people can learn *any* cultural tradition.

To understand this point, consider that contemporary Americans and Canadians are the genetically mixed descendants of people from all over the world. Our ancestors were biologically varied, lived in different countries and continents, and participated in hundreds of cultural traditions. However, early colonists, later immigrants, and their descendants have all become active participants in American and Canadian life. All now share a national culture.

Culture Is Shared

See the Internet Exercises at your OLC

Culture is an attribute not of individuals per se but of individuals as members of *groups*. Culture is transmitted in society. Don't we learn our culture by observing, listening, talking, and interacting with many other people? Shared beliefs, values, memories, and expectations link people who grow up in the same culture. Enculturation unifies people by providing us with common experiences.

Understanding Ourselves

People in the United States sometimes have trouble understanding the power of culture because of the value American culture places on the idea of the *individual*. Americans are fond of saying that everyone is unique and special in some way. In American culture, individualism itself is a distinctive *shared* value, a feature of culture. Individualism is transmitted through hundreds of statements and settings in our daily lives. Watch a morning TV show, such as *Today*, for an hour. Count how many stories focus on individuals, especially their achievements. Contrast that with the number of stories that focus on the achievements of communities. From daytime TV's Mr. Rogers to "real-life" parents, grandparents, and teachers, our enculturative agents insist we are all "someone special." That is, we are individuals first and members of groups second. This is the opposite of the lesson being taught in this chapter about culture. Without doubt we have distinctive features because we are individuals, but we have other distinct attributes because we are members of groups.

Today's parents were yesterday's children. If they grew up in North America, they absorbed certain values and beliefs transmitted over the generations. People become agents in the enculturation of their children, just as their parents were for them. Although a culture constantly changes, certain fundamental beliefs, values, worldviews, and child-rearing practices endure. Consider a simple American example of enduring shared enculturation. As children, when we didn't finish a meal, our parents reminded us of starving children in some foreign country, just as our grandparents had done a generation earlier. The specific country changes (China, India, Bangladesh, Ethiopia, Somalia, Rwanda—what was it in your home?). Still, American culture goes on transmitting the idea that by eating all our brussels sprouts or broccoli, we can justify our own good fortune, compared to a hungry Third World child.

Despite characteristic American notions that people should "make up their own minds" and "have a right to their opinion," little of what we think is original or unique. We share our opinions and beliefs with many other people. Illustrating the power of shared cultural background, we are most likely to agree with and feel comfortable with people who are socially, economically, and culturally similar to ourselves. This is one reason why Americans abroad tend to socialize with each other, just as French and British colonials did in their overseas empires. Birds of a feather flock together, but for people, the familiar plumage is culture.

CULTURE IS SYMBOLIC

Symbolic thought is unique and crucial to humans and to cultural learning. Anthropologist Leslie White defined culture as

> dependent upon symbolling . . . Culture consists of tools, implements, utensils, clothing, ornaments, customs, institutions, beliefs, rituals, games, works of art, language, etc. (White 1959, p. 3)

For White, culture originated when our ancestors acquired the ability to use symbols, that is, to originate and bestow meaning on a thing or event, and, correspondingly, to grasp and appreciate such meanings (White 1959, p. 3).

A symbol is something verbal or nonverbal, within a particular language or culture, that comes to stand for something else. There is no obvious, natural, or necessary connection between the symbol and what it symbolizes. A pet that barks is no more naturally a *dog* than a *chien*, *Hund*, or *mbwa*, to use the words for the animal we call "dog" in French, German, and Swahili. Language is one of the distinctive possessions of *Homo sapiens*. No other animal has developed anything approaching the complexity of language.

Symbols are usually linguistic. But there are also nonverbal symbols, such as flags, that stand for countries, as arches do for a hamburger chain. Holy water is a potent symbol in Roman Catholi-

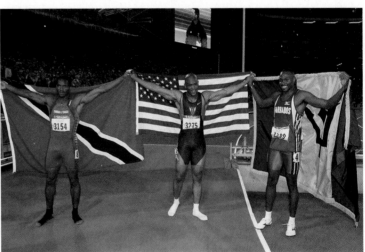

Three winners of the men's 100-meter sprint at the 2000 Sydney Olympics. American gold medalist Maurice Greene is at the center, silver medalist Ato Bolden of Trinidad and Tobago is on the left, and bronze medalist Obadele Thompson of Barbados stands to the right. What are the symbols in this photo and caption?

Interesting *Issues*
Touching, Affection, Love, and Sex

Comparing the United States to Brazil—or virtually any Latin nation—we can see a striking cultural contrast between a culture that tends to discourage physical contact and demonstrations of affection and one in which the contrary is true.

"Don't touch me." "Take your hands off me." Such statements are not uncommon in North America, but they are virtually never heard in Brazil, the Western Hemisphere's second most populous country. Brazilians like to be touched (and kissed) more than North Americans do. The world's cultures have strikingly different notions about displays of affection and about matters of personal space. When North Americans talk, walk, and dance, they maintain a certain distance from others—their personal space. Brazilians, who maintain less physical distance, interpret this as a sign of coldness. When conversing with a North American, the Brazilian characteristically moves in as the North American "instinctively" retreats. In these body movements, neither Brazilian nor North American is try-ing consciously to be especially friendly or unfriendly. Each is merely executing a program written on the self by years of exposure to a partic-ular cultural tradition. Because of different ideas about proper social space, cocktail parties in interna-tional meeting places such as the United Nations can resemble an elab-orate insect mating ritual as diplo-mats from different cultures advance, withdraw, and sidestep.

One easily evident difference between Brazil and the United States involves kissing, hugging, and touching. Middle-class Brazilians teach their kids—both boys and girls—to kiss (on the cheek, two or three times, coming and going) every adult relative they ever see. Given the size of Brazilian extended fami-lies, this can mean hundreds of peo-ple. Females continue kissing throughout their lives. They kiss male and female kin, friends, rela-tives of friends, friends of relatives, friends of friends, and, when it seems appropriate, more casual acquaintances. Males go on kissing their female relatives and friends. Until they are adolescents, boys also kiss adult male relatives. Brazilian men typically greet each other with hearty handshakes and a traditional male hug (*abraço*). The closer the relationship, the tighter and longer-lasting the embrace. These com-ments apply to brothers, cousins, uncles, and friends. Many Brazilian men keep on kissing their fathers and uncles throughout their lives. Could it be that homophobia (fear of homosexuality) prevents American men from engaging in such displays of affection with other men? Are American women more likely to show affection with each other than American men are?

Like other North Americans who spend time in a Latin culture, I miss the numerous kisses and hand-shakes when I get back to the United States. After several months in Brazil, I find North Americans rather cold and impersonal. Many Brazilians share this opinion. I have heard similar feelings expressed by Italian-Americans as they describe North Americans with different eth-nic backgrounds.

---

cism. As is true of all symbols, the association between a symbol (water) and what is symbol-ized (holiness) is arbitrary and conventional. Water is not intrinsically holier than milk, blood, or other natural liquids. Nor is holy water chem-ically different from ordinary water. Holy water is a symbol within Roman Catholicism, which is part of an international cultural system. A nat-ural thing has been arbitrarily associated with a particular meaning for Catholics, who share common beliefs and experiences that are based on learning and that are transmitted across the generations.

For hundreds of thousands of years, humans have shared the abilities on which culture rests. These abilities are to learn, to think symbolically, to manipulate language, and to use tools and other cultural products in organizing their lives and cop-ing with their environments. Every contemporary human population has the ability to use symbols and thus to create and maintain culture. Our near-est relatives—chimpanzees and gorillas—have rudimentary cultural abilities. However, no other animal has elaborated cultural abilities—to learn, to communicate, and to store, process, and use information—to the extent that *Homo* has.

Cultures have strikingly different standards of personal space, such as how far apart people should stand in normal encounters and interactions. Contrast the distance between the American businessmen and the closeness (including touching) of the two rabbis in Jerusalem. Have you noticed such differences in your own interactions with others?

Question: *Ethnocentrism* is the tendency to view one's own culture as superior and to apply one's own cultural values in judging the behavior and beliefs of people from other cultures (see pages 345 and 353). Do you have an ethnocentric position on the matter of displays of affection?

According to clinical psychologist David E. Klimek, who has written about intimacy and marriage in the United States, "in American society, if we go much beyond simple touching, our behavior takes on a minor sexual twist" (Slade 1984). North Americans define demonstrations of affection between males and females with reference to marriage. Love and affection are supposed to unite the married pair, and they blend into sex.

When a wife asks her husband for "a little affection," she may mean, or he may think she means, sex.

A certain lack of clarity in North American definitions of love, affection, and sex is evident on Valentine's Day, which used to be just for lovers. Valentines used to be sent to wives, husbands, girlfriends, and boyfriends. Now, after years of promotion by the greeting card industry, they also go to mothers, fathers, sons, daughters, aunts, and uncles. There is a blurring of sexual and nonsexual affection. In Brazil, Lovers' Day retains its autonomy. Mother, father, and children have their own separate days of recognition.

It's true, of course, that in a good marriage love and affection exist alongside sex. Nevertheless, affection does not necessarily imply sex. The Brazilian culture shows that there can be rampant kissing, hugging, and touching without sex—or fears of improper sexuality. In Brazilian culture, physical demonstrations help cement many kinds of close personal relationships that have no sexual component.

CULTURE AND NATURE

Culture takes the natural biological urges we share with other animals and teaches us how to express them in particular ways. People have to eat, but culture teaches us what, when, and how. In many cultures people have their main meal at noon, but most North Americans prefer a large dinner. English people may eat fish for breakfast, while North Americans may prefer hot cakes and cold cereals. Brazilians put hot milk into strong coffee, whereas North Americans pour cold milk into a weaker brew. Midwesterners dine at 5 or 6 PM, Spaniards at 10 PM.

Cultural habits, perceptions, and inventions mold "human nature" in many directions. People have to eliminate wastes from their bodies. But some cultures teach people to defecate squatting, while others tell them to do it sitting down. A generation ago, in Paris and other French cities, it was customary for men to urinate almost publicly, and seemingly without embarrassment, in barely shielded *pissoirs* located on city streets. Our "bathroom" habits, including waste elimination, bathing, and dental care, are parts of cultural traditions that have converted natural acts into cultural customs.

Our culture—and cultural changes—affect the ways in which we perceive nature, human nature, and "the natural." Through science, invention, and discovery, cultural advances have overcome many "natural" limitations. We prevent and cure diseases such as polio and smallpox that felled our ancestors. We use Viagra to restore sexual potency. Through cloning, scientists have altered the way we think about biological identity and the meaning of life itself. Culture, of course, has not freed us from natural threats. Hurricanes, floods, earthquakes, and other natural forces regularly challenge our wishes to modify the environment through building, development, and expansion. Can you think of other ways in which nature strikes back at people and their products?

CULTURE IS ALL-ENCOMPASSING

For anthropologists, culture includes much more than refinement, taste, sophistication, education, and appreciation of the fine arts. Not only college graduates but all people are "cultured." The most interesting and significant cultural forces are those that affect people every day of their lives, particularly those that influence children during enculturation. *Culture*, as defined anthropologically, encompasses features that are sometimes regarded as trivial or unworthy of serious study, such as "popular" culture (see the appendix). To understand contemporary North American culture, we must consider television, fast-food restaurants, sports, and games. As a cultural manifestation, a rock star may be as interesting as a symphony conductor, a comic book as significant as a book-award winner.

CULTURE IS INTEGRATED

Cultures are not haphazard collections of customs and beliefs. Cultures are integrated, patterned systems. If one part of the system (e.g., the economy) changes, other parts change as well. For example, during the 1950s, most American women planned domestic careers as homemakers and mothers. Most of today's college women, by contrast, expect to get paid jobs when they graduate.

What are some of the social repercussions of the economic change? Attitudes and behavior regarding marriage, family, and children have changed. Late marriage, "living together," and divorce have become more common. The average age at first marriage for American women rose from 20 in 1955

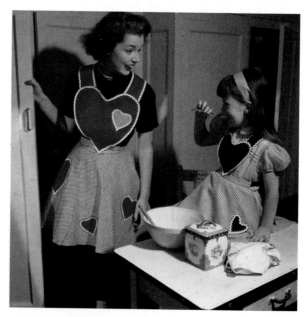

Cultures are integrated systems. When one behavior pattern changes, others also change. During the 1950s most American women expected to have domestic careers. But as more and more women have entered the work force, attitudes toward work and family have changed. Contrast the "fifties Mom" with a modern career woman. The twice-elected U.S. Senator Patty Murray of Washington State originally ran as a "mom in tennis shoes." Which of these women is more like your mother?

to 25 in 2000 (Fields 2001; Saluter 1996). The comparable figures for men were 23 and 27 (Fields 2001). The number of currently divorced Americans quadrupled from 4 million in 1970 to more than 19 million in 1998 (Lugaila 1999). Work competes with marriage and family responsibilities and reduces the time available to invest in child care.

Cultures are integrated not simply by their dominant economic activities and related social patterns but also by sets of values, ideas, symbols, and judgments. Cultures train their individual members to share certain personality traits. A set of characteristic central or **core values** (key, basic, or central values) integrates each culture and helps distinguish it from others. For instance, the work ethic and individualism are core values that have integrated American culture for generations. Different sets of dominant values influence the patterns of other cultures.

PEOPLE USE CULTURE ACTIVELY

Although cultural rules tell us what to do and how to do it, people don't always do what the rules say should be done. People use their culture actively and creatively, rather than blindly following its dictates. We are not passive beings who are doomed to follow our cultural traditions like programmed robots. Instead, people can learn, interpret, and manipulate the same rule in different ways. Also, culture is contested. That is, different groups in society often struggle with one another over whose ideas, values, and beliefs will prevail. Even common symbols may have radically different *meanings* to different people and groups in the same culture. Golden arches may cause one person to salivate while another plots a vegetarian protest. The flag is a national symbol for the United States, but its meaning also varies among Americans.

Even if they agree about what should and shouldn't be done, people don't always do as their culture directs or as other people expect. Many rules are violated, some very often (for example, automobile speed limits). Some anthropologists find it useful to distinguish between ideal and real culture. The *ideal culture* consists of what people say they should do and what they say they do. *Real culture* refers to their actual behavior as observed by the anthropologist. This contrast is like the emic–etic contrast discussion in the last chapter.

Culture is both public and individual, both in the world and in people's minds. Anthropologists are interested not only in public and collective behavior but also in how *individuals* think, feel, and act. The individual and culture are linked because human social life is a process in which individuals internalize the meanings of *public* (i.e., cultural) messages. Then, alone and in groups, people influence culture by converting their private understandings into public expressions (D'Andrade 1984).

CULTURE CAN BE ADAPTIVE AND MALADAPTIVE

As we saw in Chapter 1, humans have both biological and cultural ways of coping with environmental stresses. Besides our biological means of adaptation, we also use "cultural adaptive kits," which contain customary activities and tools. Although humans continue to adapt biologically, reliance on social and cultural means of adaptation has increased during human evolution.

Understanding Ourselves Think about the earlier discussion of the value American culture places on the individual rather than the group. One word that applies to groups is *collective*, as when people collectively reach an opinion—or consensus. Yet when many Americans hear the word *collective*, they may think of collective farms and other features of Soviet communism. And we collectively stereotype communism as valuing the group above the individual.

In this discussion of the adaptive and maladaptive features of our cultural behavior, let's recognize that what's good for the individual isn't necessarily good for the group. Sometimes adaptive behavior that offers short-term benefits to particular individuals may harm the environment and threaten the group's long-term survival. Economic growth may benefit some people while it also depletes resources needed for society at large or for future generations (Bennett 1969, p. 19). Despite the crucial role of cultural adaptation in human evolution, cultural traits, patterns, and inventions also can be *maladaptive*, threatening the group's continued existence (survival and reproduction). Air conditioners help us deal with heat, as fires and furnaces protect us against the cold. Automobiles permit us to make a living by getting us from home to workplace. But the by-products of such "beneficial" technology often create new problems. Chemical emissions increase air pollution, deplete the ozone layer, and contribute to global warming. Many cultural patterns, such as overconsumption and pollution, appear to be maladaptive in the long run.

LEVELS OF CULTURE

Of increasing importance in today's world are the distinctions between different levels of culture: national, international, and subcultural. **National culture** refers to the beliefs, learned behavior patterns, values, and institutions shared by citizens of the same nation. **International culture** is the term for cultural traditions that extend beyond and across national boundaries. Because culture is transmitted through learning rather than genetically, cultural traits can spread through borrowing or *diffusion* from one group to another.

Because of borrowing, migration, and multinational organizations, many cultural traits and patterns have international scope. For example, Roman Catholics in many different countries share beliefs, symbols, experiences, and values transmitted by their church. The contemporary United States, Canada, Great Britain, and Australia share cultural traits they have inherited from their common linguistic and cultural ancestors in Great Britain. The World Cup has become an international cultural event, as people in many countries know the rules of, play, and follow soccer.

Cultures also can be smaller than nations. Although people who live in the same country share a national cultural tradition, all cultures also contain diversity. Individuals, families, communities, regions, classes, and other groups within a culture have different learning experiences as well as shared ones. **Subcultures** are different symbol-based patterns and traditions associated with particular groups in the same complex society. In a large nation like the United States or Canada, subcultures originate in region, ethnicity, language, class, and religion. The religious backgrounds of Jews, Baptists, and Roman Catholics create subcultural differences between them. While sharing a common national culture, U.S. northerners and southerners also differ in aspects of their beliefs, values, and customary behavior as a result of regional variation. French-speaking Canadians

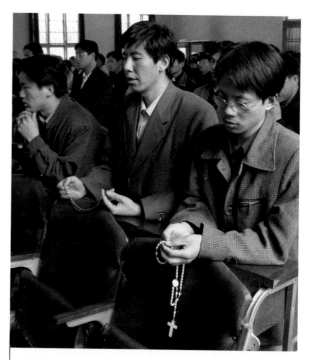

Illustrating the international level of culture, Roman Catholics in different nations share knowledge, symbols, beliefs, and values transmitted by their church. Shown here is a Catholic seminary in Xian, China. Besides religious conversion, what other forces work to spread international culture?

contrast with English-speaking people in the same country. Italian Americans have ethnic traditions different from those of Irish, Polish, and African Americans. Using sports and foods, Table 13.1 gives some examples of international, national, and subculture. Soccer and basketball are played internationally. Monster-truck rallies are held throughout the United States. Bocci is a bowling-like sport from Italy still played in some Italian-American neighborhoods.

Nowadays, many anthropologists are reluctant to use the term *subculture*. They feel that the prefix "sub-" is offensive because it means "below." "Subcultures" may thus be perceived as "less than" or somehow inferior to a dominant, elite, or national culture. In this discussion of levels of culture, I intend no such implication. My point is simply that nations may contain many different culturally defined groups. As mentioned earlier, culture is contested. Various groups may strive to promote the correctness and value of their

Table 13.1 Levels of Culture, with Examples from Sports and Foods

Level of Culture	Sports Examples	Food Examples
International	Soccer, basketball	Pizza
National	Monster-truck rallies	Apple pie
Subculture	Bocci	Big Joe Pork Barbeque (South Carolina)

own practices, values, and beliefs in comparison with those of other groups, or the nation as a whole.

ETHNOCENTRISM, CULTURAL RELATIVISM, AND HUMAN RIGHTS

Ethnocentrism is the tendency to view one's own culture as superior and to apply one's own cultural values in judging the behavior and beliefs of people raised in other cultures. Ethnocentrism is a cultural universal. It contributes to social solidarity, a sense of value and community, among people who share a cultural tradition. People everywhere think that their familiar explanations, opinions, and customs are true, right, proper, and moral. They regard different behavior as strange, immoral, or savage. The tribal names that appear in anthropology books often come from the native word for *people*. "What are you called?" asks the anthropologist. "Mugmug," reply informants. *Mugmug* may turn out to be synonymous with *people*, but it also may be the only word the natives have for themselves. Other tribes are not considered fully human. The not-quite-people in neighboring groups are not classified as *Mugmug*. They are given different names that symbolize their inferior humanity. Neighboring tribes may be ridiculed and insulted because of their customs and preferences. They may be castigated as cannibals, thieves, or people who do not bury their dead.

In the Trans-Fly region of Papua New Guinea live several tribes in which homosexual activities are valued over heterosexual ones (see the chapter on gender). Men who grow up in the Etoro tribe (Kelly 1976) favor oral sex between men, while their neighbors, the Marind-anim, encourage men to engage in anal sex. (In both groups, heterosexual coitus is stigmatized and allowed only for reproduction.) Etoro men consider Marind-anim anal sex to be disgusting, while seeing nothing abnormal about their own oral practices.

Opposing ethnocentrism is **cultural relativism**, the argument that behavior in one culture should not be judged by the standards of another culture. This position also can present problems. At its most extreme, cultural relativism argues that there is no superior, international, or universal morality, that the moral and ethical rules of all cultures deserve equal respect. In the extreme relativist view, Nazi Germany would be evaluated as nonjudgmentally as Athenian Greece.

In today's world, human rights advocates challenge many of the tenets of cultural relativism. For example, several cultures in Africa and the Middle East have traditions of female genital modification. *Clitoridectomy* is the removal of a girl's clitoris. *Infibulation* involves sewing the lips (labia) of the vagina so as to constrict the vaginal opening. Both procedures reduce female sexual pleasure and, it is believed in some cultures, the likelihood of adultery. One or both of the procedures have been traditional in several societies, but such practices, characterized as female genital mutilation, have been opposed by human rights advocates, especially women's rights groups. The idea is that the tradition infringes on a basic human right: disposition over one's body and one's sexuality. Although such practices continue in certain areas, they are fading as a result of worldwide attention to the problem and changing sex-gender roles. Some African countries have banned or otherwise discouraged the procedures, as have Western nations that receive immigration from such cultures. Similar issues arise with circumcision and other male genital operations. Is it right for a baby boy to be circumcised without his knowledge and permission, as has been routinely done in the United States? Is it proper to require adolescent boys to undergo collective circumcision to fulfill cultural tradition, as is done traditionally in parts of Africa and Australia?

The idea of **human rights** challenges cultural relativism by invoking a realm of justice and morality beyond and superior to particular countries, cultures, and religions. Human rights, usually seen as vested in individuals, include the right to speak freely, to hold religious beliefs without persecution, and to not be murdered, injured, enslaved, or imprisoned without charge. These rights are not ordinary laws that particular governments make and enforce. Human rights are seen as *inalienable* (nations cannot abridge or terminate them) and international (larger than and superior to individual nations and cultures). Four United Nations documents describe nearly all the human rights that have been internationally recognized. Those documents are the UN Charter; the Universal Declaration of Human Rights; the Covenant on Economic, Social and Cultural Rights; and the Covenant on Civil and Political Rights.

Alongside the human rights movement has arisen an awareness of the need to preserve cultural rights. Unlike human rights, **cultural rights** are vested not in individuals but in *groups*, such as religious and ethnic minorities and indigenous societies. Cultural rights include a group's ability to preserve its culture, to raise its children in the ways of its forebears, to continue its language, and not to be deprived of its economic base by the nation in which it is located (Greaves 1995). Many countries have signed pacts endorsing, for cultural minorities within nations, such rights as self-determination; some degree of home rule; and the right to practice the group's religion, culture, and language. The related notion of indigenous intellectual property rights (**IPR**) has arisen in an attempt to conserve each society's cultural base—its core beliefs and principles. IPR are claimed as a cultural right, allowing indigenous groups to control who may know and use their collective knowledge and its applications. Much traditional cultural knowledge has commercial value. Examples include ethnomedicine (traditional medical knowledge and techniques), cosmetics, cultivated plants, foods, folklore, arts, crafts, songs, dances, costumes, and rituals. According to the IPR concept, a particular group may determine how indigenous knowledge and its products may be used and distributed, and the level of compensation required.

The notion of cultural rights is related to the idea of cultural relativism, and the problem discussed previously arises again. What does one do

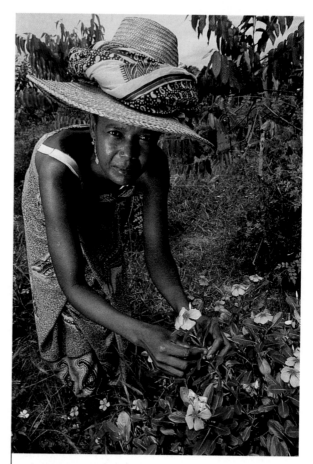

The notion of indigenous intellectual property rights (IPR) has arisen in an attempt to conserve each society's cultural base, which may have commercial value. One example is ethnomedicine—traditional medical knowledge and techniques, including the use of medicinal plants, such as Madagascar's rosy periwinkle. Can you think of another example of IPR?

about cultural rights that interfere with human rights? I believe that anthropology's main job is to present accurate accounts and explanations of cultural phenomena. The anthropologist doesn't have to approve customs such as infanticide, cannibalism, and torture to record their existence and determine their causes. However, each anthropologist has a choice about where he or she will do field work. Some anthropologists choose not to study a particular culture because they discover in advance or early in field work that behavior they consider morally repugnant is practiced there. Anthropologists respect human diversity. Most ethnographers try to be objective, accurate, and sensitive in their accounts of other cultures. However, objectivity, sensitivity, and a cross-cultural perspective don't mean that anthropologists have to ignore international standards of justice and morality. What do you think?

Universality, Generality, and Particularity

In studying human diversity in time and space, anthropologists distinguish among the universal, the generalized, and the particular. Certain biological, psychological, social, and cultural features are **universal**, found in every culture. Others are merely **generalities**, common to several but not all human groups. Still other traits are **particularities**, unique to certain cultural traditions.

UNIVERSALITY

Universal traits are the ones that more or less distinguish *Homo sapiens* from other species (see Brown 1991). Biologically based universals include a long period of infant dependency, year-round (rather than seasonal) sexuality, and a complex brain that enables us to use symbols, languages, and tools. Psychological universals involve common ways in which humans think, feel, and process information. Most such universals probably reflect human biological universals, such as the structure of the human brain or certain physical differences between men and women, or children and adults.

Among the social universals is life in groups and in some kind of family. In all human societies, culture organizes social life and depends on social interactions for its expression and continuation. Family living and food sharing are universals. Among the most significant cultural universals are exogamy and the *incest taboo* (prohibition against marrying or mating with a close relative). All cultures consider some people (various cultures differ about *which* people) too closely related to mate or marry. The violation of this taboo is *incest*, which is discouraged and punished in a variety of ways in different cultures. If incest is prohibited, *exogamy*—marriage outside one's group—is inevitable. Because it links human groups together into larger networks, exogamy has been crucial in

human evolution. Exogamy elaborates on tendencies observed among other primates. Recent studies of monkeys and apes show that these animals also avoid mating with close kin and often mate outside their native groups.

GENERALITY

Between universals and uniqueness (see the next section) is a middle ground that consists of cultural generalities. These are regularities that occur in different times and places but not in all cultures. One reason for generalities is diffusion. Societies can share the same beliefs and customs because of borrowing or through (cultural) inheritance from a common cultural ancestor. Speaking English is a generality shared by North Americans and Australians because both countries had English settlers. English also has spread through diffusion to many countries, as it has become the world's foremost language for business and travel. Cultural generalities also can arise through independent invention of the same cultural trait or pattern in two or more different cultures. For example, farming arose through independent invention in the Eastern (e.g., the Middle East) and Western (e.g., Mexico) Hemispheres. Similar needs and circumstances have led people in different lands to innovate in parallel ways. They have independently come up with the same cultural solution to a common problem.

One cultural generality that is present in many but not all societies is the *nuclear family*, a kinship group consisting of parents and children. Although many middle-class Americans ethnocentrically view the nuclear family as a proper and "natural" group, it is not universal. It is absent, for example, among the Nayars, who live on the Malabar Coast of India. The Nayars live in female-headed households, and husbands and wives do not live together. In many other societies, the nuclear family is submerged in larger kin groups, such as extended families, lineages, and clans. However, the nuclear family is prominent in many of the technologically simple societies that live by hunting and gathering. It is also a significant kin group among contemporary middle-class North Americans and Western Europeans. Later, an explanation of the nuclear family as a basic kinship unit in specific types of society will be given.

PARTICULARITY

See the Internet Exercises at your OLC on cultural insults

mhhe
com
/kottak

Many cultural traits are widely shared because of diffusion and independent invention and as cultural universals. Nevertheless, different cultures emphasize different things. Cultures are integrated and patterned differently and display tremendous variation and diversity. Uniqueness and particularity stand at the opposite extreme from universality.

Unusual and exotic beliefs and practices lend distinctiveness to particular cultural traditions. Many cultures ritually observe such universal life-cycle events as birth, puberty, marriage, parenthood, and death. However, cultures vary in just which event merits special celebration. Americans regard expensive weddings as more socially appropriate than lavish funerals. However, the Betsileo of Madagascar take the opposite view. The marriage ceremony is a minor event that brings together just the couple and a few close relatives. However, a funeral is a measure of the deceased person's social position and lifetime achievement, and it may attract a thousand people. Why use money on a house, the Betsileo say, when one can use it on the tomb where one will spend eternity in the company of dead relatives? How different from contemporary Americans' preference for quick and inexpensive funerals and cremation, which would horrify the Betsileo, whose ancestral bones and relics are important ritual objects.

What are some of the particularities of modern American culture? Although the mass media and a consumers' culture are spreading (diffusing) globally, these trends are most advanced in contemporary North America. They pervade all aspects of our culture. The fact that TVs outnumber toilets in American households is a significant cultural fact that anthropologists can't afford to ignore. My own research on Michigan college students is probably generalizable to other young Americans. They visit fast-food restaurants more often than they visit houses of worship. Almost all have seen a Walt Disney movie and have attended rock concerts and football games. Such shared experiences are major features of American enculturation patterns. Certainly any extraterrestrial anthropologist doing field work in the United States would stress them as prominent patterns of contemporary American national culture.

Cultures vary tremendously in their beliefs, practices, integration, and patterning. By focusing on and trying to explain alternative customs, anthropology forces us to reappraise our familiar ways of thinking. In a world full of cultural diversity, contemporary American culture is just one cultural variant, more powerful perhaps, but no more natural, than the others.

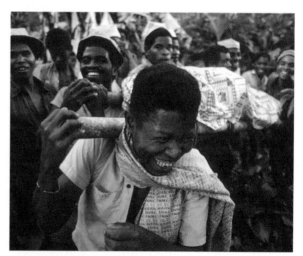

Cultures use rituals to mark such universal life-cycle events as birth, puberty, marriage, parenthood, and death. But particular cultures differ as to which event merits special celebration and in the emotions expressed during their rituals. Compare the wedding party (left) in Bali, Indonesia with the funeral (right) among the Tanala of eastern Madagascar. How would you describe the emotions suggested by the photos?

Africa. In
Language
shows th
guages. Lo
when they
and langu

Indep
which hu
tions to p
tural chan
and challe
innovatec
one reaso
ple is the
the Middl
human hi
the expen
tion, such
quent inte
lutions h
Thus, in b
ture led
changes,
tinctions i

The term
processes
working
nations ar
mutually
economic
systems o
forces of g
merce, tra
the medi

SUM

1. Cultur
to cus
passe
on the
ture er

Background Information

Student:	Mark Dennis
Supervising Professor:	Usher Fleising
School:	University of Calgary
Year in School/Major:	Fifth-Year Senior/Social Anthropology
Future Plans:	Graduate school, traveling
Project Title:	Folklore Reveals Ethos of Heating Plant Workers

What role does folklore play among the workers described in this account? What functions do common tales serve in enabling workers to adapt to their work setting? What attributes of culture are represented here?

At the periphery of the University of Calgary campus exists a place, ironically called the central heating and cooling plant. Housed within its four walls and three levels are the industrial machinery and a tangle of pipes that snake through an eight-mile tunnel system in the bowels of the earth, bringing heat and cooling to a campus of 21,000.

Folklore is an oral form of knowledge shared by a cultural group. The objective of my research was to reveal the social and cultural manifestations of folklore among the University Central Heating and Cooling Plant (CHCP) employees. In an isolated control room, a fieldworker finds plant employees engaged in a social atmosphere filled with storytelling and humor. Accustomed to the mental and physical distance from the rest of the university, the men of the CHCP were glad to share their knowledge and folklore with me.

In addition to simple observations and document analysis, my research method consisted primarily of unstructured interviews. Using this technique I was able to control the direction of the conversation while still giving the informants (cultural consultants, community members) freedom to express themselves.

Folklore at the CHCP was passed on between employees during their shifts or during shift changes. Most stories were known by all employees. The themes included slapstick humor, disaster stories, tales about eccentric characters, practical jokes, and stories about complaints. The folklore was based entirely on oral history, with no written documentation ever produced.

During the course of fieldwork, I found that folklore functioned as an organic mechanism adapting to the needs of the employees by providing stress relief. Folklore helped them to deal constructively with job frustrations, and it created social cohesion among employees.

The last six years at the CHCP have been turbulent because of a management change. Conflicting working methods and rapid changes in technology made it hard for many employees to adapt. In this context the humor that folklore provided not only lightened the mood, but it also brought back fond memories of the easy-going past.

The CHCP has a unique working environment. At its worst, days can be filled with isolation and mundane activity, leaving the employees feeling that no one cares about the important work they do. Folklore is a healthy way of dealing with the isolation and ignorance of others. Workers share stories of the prestigious visitors, like university presidents, who have visited the plant over the years. By telling these stories the plant workers can see that there is hope for educating people about what they do. Such stories affirm that their jobs are very important.

Finally, folklore is a cohesive force whereby plant workers both old and new can celebrate the shared knowledge and unique work environment that surrounds them, leading to a happier and more productive work environment. Folklore is an interesting starting point from which to analyze subcultures and their social relations. The study of the Central Heating and Cooling Plant at the University of Calgary was one application of folklore as a theoretical basis for social analysis.

on things and events. By convention, a symbol stands for something with which it has no necessary or natural relation. Symbols have special meaning for people who share memories, values, and beliefs because of common enculturation. People absorb cultural lessons consciously and unconsciously.

3. Cultural traditions mold biologically based desires and needs in particular directions. Everyone is cultured, not just people with elite educations. Cultures may be integrated and patterned through economic and social forces, key symbols, and core values. Cultural rules don't rigidly dictate our behavior. There is room for creativity, flexibility, diversity, and disagreement within societies. Cultural means of adaptation have been crucial in human evolution. Aspects of culture also can be maladaptive.

4. There are levels of culture, which can be larger or smaller than a nation. Diffusion and migration carry cultural traits and patterns to different areas. Such traits are shared across national boundaries. Nations also include cultural differences associated with ethnicity, region, and social class.

5. Using a comparative perspective, anthropology examines biological, psychological, social, and cultural universals and generalities. There are also unique and distinctive aspects of the human condition. North American cultural traditions are no more natural than any others. Mechanisms of cultural change include diffustion, acculturation, and independent invention. Globalization describes a series of processes that promote change in a world in which nations and people are interlinked and mutually dependent.

KEY TERMS

See the flash cards

mhhe
● **com**
/kottak

acculturation The exchange of cultural features that results when groups come into continuous firsthand contact; the cultural patterns of either or both groups may be changed, but the groups remain distinct.

core values Key, basic, or central values that integrate a culture and help distinguish it from others.

cultural relativism The position that the values and standards of cultures differ and deserve respect. Extreme relativism argues that cultures should be judged solely by their own standards.

cultural rights Doctrine that certain rights are vested in identifiable groups, such as religious and ethnic minorities and indigenous societies. Cultural rights include a group's ability to preserve its culture, to raise its children in the ways of its forebears, to continue its language, and not to be deprived of its economic base by the nation-state in which it is located.

diffusion Borrowing of cultural traits between societies, either directly or through intermediaries.

enculturation The social process by which culture is learned and transmitted across the generations.

ethnocentrism The tendency to view one's own culture as best and to judge the behavior and beliefs of culturally different people by one's own standards.

generality Culture pattern or trait that exists in some but not all societies.

globalization The accelerating interdependence of nations in a world system linked economically and through mass media and modern transportation systems.

human rights Doctrine that invokes a realm of justice and morality beyond and superior to particular countries, cultures, and religions. Human rights, usually seen as vested in individuals, would include the right to speak freely, to hold religious beliefs without persecution, and to not be murdered, injured, enslaved, or imprisoned without charge.

independent invention Development of the same cultural trait or pattern in separate cultures as a result of comparable needs, circumstances, and solutions.

international culture Cultural traditions that extend beyond national boundaries.

Me

Why and
diffusion,
Such exch
gone on tl
tures hav
between r
and has ex
Diffusion
marry, or
forced whe
imposes it:
fusion is *in*
group C vi
between A
sist of trac
from a vari
B might be
C, so that v
in C, and

IPR Intellectual property rights, consisting of each society's cultural base—its core beliefs and principles. IPR are claimed as a group right—a cultural right, allowing indigenous groups to control who may know and use their collective knowledge and its applications.

national culture Cultural experiences, beliefs, learned behavior patterns, and values shared by citizens of the same nation.

particularity Distinctive or unique culture trait, pattern, or integration.

subcultures Different cultural traditions associated with subgroups in the same complex society.

symbol Something, verbal or nonverbal, that arbitrarily and by convention stands for something else, with which it has no necessary or natural connection.

universal Something that exists in every culture.

For more self testing, see the self quizzes

mhhe
●com
/kottak

CRITICAL THINKING QUESTIONS

1. How does human learning differ from animal learning? What and how much can you teach a cat? A dog? An ape? A child?

2. What cultural symbols have the most meaning for you? For your family? For your nation?

3. What are some cultural features that you share just with members of your hometown?

4. What are the key symbols and values that work to unite your religious group or other organization to which you belong?

5. Give some examples of cultural practices that are adaptive in the short run but probably maladaptive in the long run.

6. To how many cultures do you belong? Do you participate in an international culture and a subculture in addition to a national culture?

7. Do you feel you have multiple cultural identities? If so, how do you handle them?

8. What are some issues about which you find it hard to be culturally relativistic?

9. What are some issues about which you find it easy to be culturally relativistic?

10. Besides the examples discussed in the text, what are some other cultural universals? Is religion a cultural universal?

11. Besides the ones discussed in the text, are there other particularities in contemporary American (or Canadian) culture?

12. Think of three ways in which globalization has affected you in the past week.

Atlas Questions

Look at Map 13, "Invented Languages: Pidgins, Jargons, and Creoles."

1. Where and when did French creole languages develop? See the Chapter "Language and Communication" to learn the difference between a pidgin and a creole. Are there French-derived pidgins shown on Map 13—or just creoles?

2. Compare the distribution of pidgins and creoles in which English played a role with the distribution of invented languages in which French played a role. Are there creoles spoken in the United States—where and derived from what languages? Which is more widespread—French or English influence on invented languages? Why do you think this is?

3. Besides French and English, what are some other European languages that have been blended to form pidgins and creoles? What are some of the non-European languages that have contributed to invented languages?

SUGGESTED ADDITIONAL READINGS

Archer, M. S.

1996   *Culture and Agency: The Place of Culture in Social Theory*, rev. ed. Cambridge, England: Cambridge University Press. Examines interrelations among individual action, social structure, culture, and social integration.

Bohannan, P.

1995   *How Culture Works*. New York: Free Press. A consideration of the nature of culture.

Brown, D.

1991   *Human Universals*. New York: McGraw-Hill. Surveys the evidence for "human nature" and explores the roles of culture and biology in human variation.

Geertz, C.

1973   *The Interpretation of Cultures*. New York: Basic Books. Essays about culture viewed as a system of symbols and meaning.

Hall, E. T.

1990   *Understanding Cultural Differences*. Yarmouth, ME: Intercultural Press. Focusing on business and industrial management, this book examines the role of national cultural contrasts among France, Germany, and the United States.

1992   *An Anthropology of Everyday Life: An Autobiography*. New York: Doubleday. A prominent student of language and culture examines his own life in the context of intercultural communication.

Kroeber, A. L., and C. Kluckhohn

1963   *Culture: A Critical Review of Concepts and Definitions*. New York: Vintage. Discusses and categorizes more than a hundred definitions of culture.

Lindholm, C.

2001   *Culture and Identity: The History, Theory, and Practice of Psychological Anthropology*. New York: McGraw-Hill. An introduction to psychological anthropology, with special attention to the roles of culture and the individual.

Naylor, L. L.

1996   *Culture and Change: An Introduction*. Westport, CT: Bergin and Garvey. Anthropology, culture, and change.

Scholte, J. A.

2000   *Globalization: A Critical Introduction*. New York: St. Martin's. International relations, culture contact, and change in the era of globalization.

Van der Elst, D., and P. Bohannan

1999   *Culture as Given, Culture as Choice*. Prospect Heights, IL: Waveland. Culture and individual choices.

Wagner, R.

1981   *The Invention of Culture*, rev. ed. Chicago: University of Chicago Press. Culture, creativity, society, and the self.

Wilson, R., ed.

1996   *Human Rights: Culture and Context: Anthropological Perspectives*. Chicago: Pluto. Issues of cultural relativism and cross-cultural studies of human rights issues.

INTERNET EXERCISES

1. *Acculturation:* Go and read Cyndi Patee's article "Pidgins and Creoles," **http://logos.uoregon. edu/explore/socioling/pidgin.html**.

   a. What are pidgins and creoles? How are they examples of acculturation?

   b. What role did colonialism play in the development of pidgins and creoles?

   c. Take the quiz at the end of the page. Which sentences were easiest for you to read? Which were hardest? Look at the answers. Does the substrate language explain your ability or inability to understand?

2. *The Kiss:* Read Washington State University's page on "The Kiss," **http://www.wsu.edu:8001/ vcwsu/commons/topics/culture/behaviors/ kissing/kissing-essay.html**.

   a. Is kissing an instinctive human display of affection? Or is it learned?

   b. What is the history of the kiss?

   c. Is there a single, universal meaning for a kiss? How and why can the meanings change by culture and situation?

See Chapter 13 at your McGraw-Hill Online Learning Center for additional review and interactive exercises.

14
ETHNICITY

Overview

"Ethnic group" describes a specific culturally defined group in a nation or region that contains others. Ethnicity is based on cultural similarities (among members of the same ethnic group) and differences (between that group and others). Ethnicity can be said to exist when people claim a certain ethnic identity for themselves and are defined by others as having that identity. Ethnic distinctions can be associated with language, religion, history, geography, kinship, or "race." A race is an ethnic group that is assumed to have a biological basis.

The global scale of modern migration introduces unparalleled ethnic variety to host nations. Because of migration, conquest, and colonialism, most nation-states are not ethnically homogeneous. Assimilation is a process an ethnic group may

experience when it moves to a country where another cultural tradition dominates. By assimilating, the minority adopts the patterns and norms of its host nation. Multiculturalism contrasts with assimilation, in which minorities are expected to abandon their cultural traditions. A multicultural society socializes individuals not only into the dominant (national) culture but also into an ethnic culture.

Ethnicity can be expressed in peaceful multiculturalism, or in discrimination or violent confrontation. Ethnic conflict often arises in relation to prejudice (attitudes and judgments) or discrimination (action). A dominant group may try to destroy certain ethnic practices (ethnocide). Or it may attempt to force ethnic group members to adopt the dominant culture (forced assimilation).

Sosa vs. McGwire: It's a Race, but Is It Also about Race?

NEW YORK TIMES NEWS BRIEF

By Bill Dedman

August 7, 1998

Racial, ethnic, and national identities affected the way different Americans rooted for Mark McGwire or Sammy Sosa during their memorable 1998 home run race. This account reports on fan reaction as the contest, which McGwire eventually won with 70 home runs, was nearing its close. Do you think the fans who rooted for one or the other because of his race, ethnicity, or national origin were prejudiced? What is Sammy Sosa's race? What's his ethnicity? What's his national origin? What's his nationality? How about Mark McGwire? In 2001 Barry Bonds beat McGwire's short-lived home run record. How did you feel about that? Do you think race or ethnicity had anything to do with your reaction?

All across the country, Americans are talking baseball and home runs. Or more specifically, Mark McGwire and Sammy Sosa. Take a seat at the bar in Denver, or at a hamburger joint in Los Angeles. The questions are simple: Who are you rooting for in the home run race? And why?

The answers are not so simple. It does not take long for the vexing issues of race and national origin to creep onto the field. In Atlanta or Boston, in Houston or Miami, awkward pauses and disagreements renew the long, uncomfortable relationship between the national pastime and the national enigma.

With only one week to go in the Home Run Derby of 1998, with two players already past Roger Maris's record of 61 home runs in a season, the overwhelming reaction of sports fans and nonfans has been delight at the simple joy of the competition. McGwire of the St. Louis Cardinals, who had 64 home runs going into yesterday's games, and Sosa of the Chicago Cubs, who had 63, are seen as embodiments of power, sportsmanship and grace.

And yet a fact remains, mentioned frequently by fans: one of the sluggers, McGwire, happens to be a white, red-headed Californian, a European American. The other, Sosa, is a dark-skinned, Spanish-speaking Dominican, a Latin American.

In dozens of conversations in 10 cities in recent days, the complexities of race emerged from the simplest questions about the home run race. The

In St. Louis, Missouri, on August 7, 1998, Mark McGwire, the eventual winner of the 1998 home run derby, greets his rival, Sammy Sosa.

answers raise more questions, unsettled and unsettling: If it is a matter of pride for Latinos to root for Sosa, why would many consider it racist for whites to root for McGwire because he is white? And how precise are the racial labels anyway? Which group may claim Sosa as a hero? And what of citizenship? Will an immigrant, an American citizen, be considered by everyone an American hero if he wins? . . .

For those who are picking a champion, race often seems to play a role. Latinos, whites and blacks speak of choosing "one of our own" or "someone like us." This allegiance causes some to flinch, and fills others with pride.

In Latino neighborhoods across the country, Dominican flags are flying, and Latinos of every origin are soaping Sosa's name and uniform No. 21 onto windows. In South Florida, Cuban radio stations have been preaching that all Hispanics should support Sosa . . .

In San Diego last week, 12-year-old Armando Flores 3d went to a Padres–Cubs game to see Sosa. "I've never hit a home run, so I like to look up to Sammy and see how he does it, how he feels hitting a home run," said Flores, a Mexican-American. "My team won the district, and I'm a shortstop, and I want to be a major league player.

"I think because he is the same color of skin as me, I like that . . ."

Sometimes the racial labels are hard to keep straight. In Atlanta, with a large African-American population, Sosa is often considered a black man. In Miami and Los Angeles, with larger Hispanic populations, he is a Latino man, and the black label is rejected as robbing Hispanics of a hero.

And in all precincts, nationality is up for grabs. McGwire is often referred to as "the American," and Sosa as "the foreigner." Hardly anyone seems to know that Sosa has been an American citizen for three years.

"Personally, I pull for McGwire because he's an American," said Ethon Vivion, 27, a black man, director of health and fitness for a Boys Club in Atlanta. "Sosa's a brother, and I'm a brother. But McGwire's an American." . . .

Source: Copyright 1998 The New York Times Company, September 20, 1998. By Bill Dedman (excerpted).

In this discussion of the Sosa–McGwire competition, do you detect any confusion about race and ethnicity? We hear the words *ethnicity* and *race* frequently, but American culture doesn't draw a very clear line between them. As an illustration, consider two articles in *The New York Times* of May 29, 1992.

"Hispanic" and "Latino" are ethnic categories that crosscut "racial" contrasts such as that between "black" and "white." Note the physical diversity exemplified by these Latina teenagers.

One, discussing the changing ethnic composition of the United States, states (correctly) that Hispanics "can be of any race" (Barringer 1992, p. A12). In other words, "Hispanic" is an ethnic category that crosscuts "racial" contrasts such as that between "black" and "white." The other article reports that during the Los Angeles riots of spring 1992, "hundreds of Hispanic residents were interrogated about their immigration status on the basis of their *race* alone [emphasis added]" (Mydans 1992*a*, p. A8). Use of "race" here seems inappropriate because "Hispanic" usually is perceived as referring to a linguistically based (Spanish-speaking) ethnic group, rather than a biologically based race. Since these Los Angeles residents were being interrogated because they were Hispanic, the article is actually reporting on ethnic, not racial, discrimination. However, given the lack of a precise distinction between race and ethnicity, it is probably better to use the term "ethnic group" instead of "race" to describe *any* such social group, for example, African Americans, Asian Americans, Irish Americans, Anglo Americans, or Hispanics.

Ethnic Groups and Ethnicity

According to Fredrik Barth (1969), ethnicity can be said to exist when people claim a certain ethnic identity for themselves and are defined by others as having that identity. Members of an ethnic group may define themselves—and/or be defined by others—as different and special because of their language, religion, geography, history, ancestry, or physical traits. When an ethnic group is assumed to have a biological basis (shared "blood" or genetic material), it is called a *race*. Today, some people think that "ethnic group" and "ethnicity" are just politically correct ways of talking about race. That's not so. Ethnicity is based on common cultural traditions—not mainly on assumed biological traits, as race is. The complex issues of race have been discussed at greater length in the chapter "Human Diversity and 'Race'" (see also Scupin 2003).

Table 14.1 Racial/Ethnic Identification in the United States, 2000 Census

Claimed Identity	Millions of People
African Americans	34.7
Asians and Pacific Islanders	10.6
American Indians, Eskimos, and Aleuts	2.5
Hispanics (any "race")	35.3
Two or more "races"	6.8
Non-Hispanic whites	176.1
Others	15.4
Total population	281.4

Source: Census 2000, www.census.gov.

We know from the "Culture" chapter that culture is learned, shared, symbolic, integrated, and all-encompassing, and that it can be adaptive or maladaptive. Ethnicity is based on cultural similarities and differences—which may be claimed, perceived, assumed, or actual—in a nation or region. The similarities are with members of the same ethnic group; the differences are between that group and others. The term "ethnic group" refers to a particular culturally defined group in a nation or region that contains others. Ethnic diversity is associated with group boundaries and varied cultural patterns and traditions within and among nations. Ethnic groups must deal with other such groups in the nation or region they inhabit, so that interethnic relations are important in the study of that nation or region. (Table 14.1 lists American ethnic groups, as given in the 2000 census.)

ETHNIC MARKERS, IDENTITIES, AND STATUSES

As with any culturally defined group, members of an **ethnic group** have *shared* beliefs, values, customs, and norms—which are actual and perceived. Members of a given ethnic group define themselves as special and different from other such groups because of cultural features. They may speak a common language, observe the same religion, or share historic experience. Markers of an ethnic group may include a collective name, belief in common ancestry, a sense of solidarity, and an association with a specific territory, such as a homeland, that the group may or may not hold (Ryan 1990, pp. xiii, xiv).

Ethnicity means identifying with, and feeling part of, a socially recognized ethnic group. Ethnicity also means being excluded from other such groups because of one's ethnic identity. Ethnic feeling varies in intensity within ethnic groups and countries and over time. A change in the importance attached to an ethnic identity may reflect a political change. For example, with the fall of the Soviet Union, ethnic feeling rose in many areas of the former U.S.S.R. where ethnic expression previously had been discouraged. The importance of an ethnic identity also may change during the individual life cycle. For example, young people may relinquish, or old people reclaim, an ethnic background.

Ethnic differences have been around for a long time. Archaeologists find evidence that different ethnic groups participated in the same social system thousands of years ago. For example, around 1,500 years ago, traders from different regions and ethnic groups regularly visited the monumental Mexican site of Teotihuacan to sell their products in its markets. Variation in material remains such as pottery, ornaments, statuary, and building styles can point to ethnic differences in an ancient city.

We saw in the "Culture" chapter that people participate in various levels of culture. Groups within the same society (including ethnic groups in a nation) have different learning experiences as well as shared ones. Subcultures may originate in ethnicity, class, region, or religion. Individuals often have more than one group identity. Depending on circumstances, people may identify with their neighborhood, school, town, state or province, region, nation, continent, religion, ethnic group, gender, profession, or interest group. In the chapter "Human Diversity and `Race'," we saw how racial classification varies cross-culturally and how race is socially constructed. *Individuals* also construct their own social identities, depending on context and their interests. In a complex society such as the United States or Canada, people constantly negotiate their social identities. All of us "wear different hats," presenting ourselves sometimes as one thing, sometimes as another.

In daily conversation, we hear the term "status" used as a synonym for prestige. In this context, "She's got a lot of status" means she's got a lot of prestige; people look up to her. Among social scientists, that's not the primary meaning of "status." Social scientists use *status* more neutrally—for any position, no matter what the prestige, that someone occupies in society. In this sense, **status** encompasses the various positions that people occupy in society. Parent is a social status. So are professor, student, factory worker, Democrat, shoe salesperson, homeless person, labor leader, ethnic-group member, and thousands of others. People always occupy multiple statuses (e.g., Hispanic, Catholic, infant, brother). Among the statuses we occupy, particular ones dominate in particular settings, such as son or daughter at home and student in the classroom.

Some statuses are **ascribed**: People have little or no choice about occupying them. Age is an ascribed status; we can try to maintain a youthful—or a mature—attitude and appearance, but we can't choose not to age. Race and gender usually are ascribed; people are born members of a certain group and remain so all their lives. **Achieved statuses**, by contrast, aren't automatic; they come through choices, actions, efforts, talents, and accomplishments (Figure 14.1). Examples of achieved statuses include physician, senator, salesperson, union member, father, and college student. Our kinship statuses are partly ascribed, partly achieved. As we'll see in the chapter "Families, Kinship, and Descent," most of us are born into a *family of orientation* consisting of our parents and siblings. The relatives who came before us will be our kin forever. Our relationship to them is an ascribed status. But we choose to marry or not, and to have children or not, so that our status as spouse or parent is achieved.

A status may be associated with a position in a social or political hierarchy. Certain groups, called *minority groups*, are subordinate. That means they have less power and less secure access to resources than do *majority groups* (which are superordinate or dominant). Minorities need not have fewer members than the majority group does. Women in the United States and blacks in South Africa have been numerical majorities but minorities in terms of income, authority, and power. Often, ethnic groups, which are based on a combination of ascribed and achieved status, are minorities.

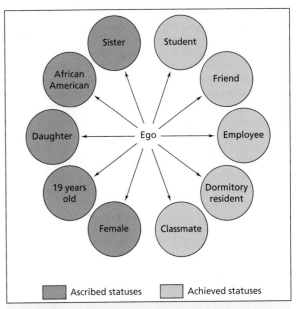

Figure 14.1 **Social Statuses.**
The person in this figure—"ego," or "I"—occupies many social statuses. The green circles indicate ascribed statuses; the yellow circles represent achieved statuses.

STATUS SHIFTING

Sometimes statuses, especially ascribed ones, are mutually exclusive. It's hard to bridge the gap between black and white, or male and female (although some rock stars seem to be trying to do so). Sometimes, assuming a status or joining a group requires a conversion experience. One acquires a new and meaningful identity, such as "coming out" as gay or becoming a "born again" Christian.

Understanding Ourselves   How do we determine who (what kind of a person) we are, and who others are? What kinds of identity cues and clues do people use to figure out who they are dealing with, and how to act in social situations? Part of human adaptive flexibility is our ability to shift statuses, varying our claimed identities in response to context. Many of the social statuses we occupy, the "hats" we wear, depend on the situation. People (e.g., Sammy Sosa, discussed at the beginning of this chapter) can be both black and Hispanic, or both a father and a ballplayer. One identity is claimed or perceived in certain settings, another in different ones. Among African Americans Sosa might be black; among Hispanics, Hispanic. When claimed or perceived identity varies depending on the audience, this is called the *situational negotiation of social identity*. As an illustration, the same man might declare any of the following, depending on the situation: "I'm Jimmy's father." "I'm your boss." "I'm African American." "I'm your professor."

We'll see in the next chapter that we vary the way we talk, as well as act, depending on our audience. In face-to-face encounters, other people can see who we are. They may expect us to think and act in certain ways based on their visual judgment of our identity, and their stereotypes about how people with that identity act. Although we can't know which aspect of identity they'll focus on (e.g., race, age, or gender), face to face it's hard to be anonymous or to be someone else. That's what masks and costumes are for.

But we don't just interact face to face. We phone, write, and—more than ever—use the Internet. Cyberspace communication is changing notions of identity and the self. Virtual worlds, such as computer role-playing games, are ways of extending ourselves into various forms of cyber-social interaction (Escobar 1994). People choose and vary their identities by using different "handles," multiple names in cyberspace. People may manipulate ("lie about") their ages and genders and create their own cyberfantasies. Of course there are subtle clues, revealed in writing. A greeting of "Dude" suggests a male. Linguistic (e.g., foreign language) background and class (educational) status may be evident in written expression. In psychology, multiple personalities are abnormal, but in anthropology, multiple identities are more and more the norm.

When ethnic identity is flexible and situational (Moerman 1965), it becomes an achieved status. Ethnicity, like race, is socially constructed—claimed, performed, and demonstrated in society (see Leman 2001). Hispanics, for instance, may shift ethnic affiliations as they negotiate their identities. "Hispanic" is an ethnic category based mainly on language. It includes whites, blacks, and "racially" mixed Spanish speakers and their ethnically conscious descendants. (There are also "Native American," and even "Asian," Hispanics). "Hispanic" lumps together millions of people of diverse geographic origin. Hispanic locales include Puerto Rico, Mexico, Cuba, El Salvador, Guatemala, the Dominican Republic, and other Spanish-speaking countries of Central and South America and the Caribbean. "Latino" is a broader category, which also can include Brazilians (who speak Portuguese).

A 53 percent increase in the number of Mexican Americans fueled a 13 million rise in the number of Hispanic Americans between 1990 and 2000. The national origins of American Hispanics/Latinos in 2000 were as follows:

National Origin	Millions of People
Mexican American	20.6
Puerto Rican	3.4
Cuban	1.2
Central American	1.7
South American	1.4
Dominican	0.8
Other Hispanic/Latino Origin	6.1
Total	35.3

Source:http://www.census.gov/Press-Release/www/2001/cb01-81.html.

Mexican Americans (Chicanos), Cuban Americans, and Puerto Ricans may join together as "Hispanics" to promote general Hispanic issues (e.g., opposition to "English-only" laws), but act as three separate interest groups in other contexts. Cuban Americans are richer on average than Chicanos and Puerto Ricans are, and their class interests and voting patterns differ. Cubans often vote Republican. Puerto Ricans and Chicanos tend to favor Democrats. Some Mexican Americans whose families have lived in the United States for generations have little in common with new Hispanic immigrants, such as those from Central America. Many Americans (especially those who are fluent in English) claim Hispanic ethnicity in some contexts but shift to a general "American" identity in others. As discussed in the chapter "Language and Communication," bilingual people may manage an ethnic identity while also participating in a national culture.

Ethnic Groups, Nations, and Nationalities

See the Internet Exercises at your OLC for information on ethnicity in Nigeria

mhhe
com
/kottak

The term **nation** was once synonymous with "tribe" or "ethnic group"—what today we might call a cultural community. All these terms have been used to refer to a single ethnic unit, living together or apart, sharing perhaps a common language, religion, history, territory, ancestry, or genealogy. Thus, one could speak interchangeably of the Seneca (American Indian) nation, tribe, or ethnic group. Now, in our everyday language, nation has come to mean a **state**—an independent, centrally organized political unit—a government. Nation and state have become synonymous. Combined in **nation-state**, they refer to an autonomous political entity, a "country"—like the United States, "one nation, indivisible." "Nation" and "state" probably have become synonymous because of the prevalence of the idea of self-determination—that each group of people should have its own state.

Interpret the World
Atlas Map 14

Because of migration, conquest, and colonialism, most nation-states are ethnically heterogeneous. Of 132 nation-states existing in 1971, Connor (1972) found only 12 (9 percent) to be ethnically homogeneous. In another 25 countries (19 percent), a single ethnic group accounted for more than 90 percent of the population. Forty percent of the countries had more than five significant ethnic groups. In a later study, Nielsson (1985) found that in only 45 of 164 states (27 percent) did a single ethnic group have more than 95 percent of the population. In your atlas Map 14, "Global Distribution of Minority Groups," shows the percentage of each country's population that belongs to minority ethnic or "racial" groups. Notice that most African countries, reflecting the legacy of colonialism, have considerable ethnic heterogeneity. What are some of the countries in which a single (majority) eth-nic group accounts for more than 90 percent of the population?

NATIONALITIES AND IMAGINED COMMUNITIES

Groups that now have, or wish to have or regain, autonomous political status (their own country) are called **nationalities**. In the words of Benedict Anderson (1991), nationalities are "imagined communities." Their members do not form an actual face-to-face community. They can only imagine that they all belong to and participate in the same group. Even when they become nation-states, they remain imagined communities, because most of their members, though feeling strong comradeship, will never meet (Anderson 1991, pp. 6–10).

Anderson traces Western European nationalism, which arose in imperial powers such as England, France, and Spain, back to the 18th century. He stresses that language and print played a crucial role in the growth of European national consciousness. (See "Interesting Issues" on pages 372–373 for a modern illustration.) The novel and the newspaper were "two forms of imagining" communities that flowered in the 18th century

World War I split the Kurds, who form a majority in no state. They are a minority group in Turkey, Iran, Iraq, and Syria. This is an April 1991 photo of a Kurdish woman and baby near the Iran/Iraq border. There was an exodus of Kurd refugees from Iraq during the Gulf War of 1991.

The Socialist Federal Republic of Yugoslavia was a nonaligned country outside the former Soviet Union (U.S.S.R.). Like the U.S.S.R., Yugoslavia fell apart, mainly along ethnic and religious lines, in the early 1990s. Among Yugoslavia's ethnic groups were Roman Catholic Croats, Eastern Orthodox Serbs, Muslim Slavs, and ethnic Albanians. Citing ethnic and religious differences, several republics broke away from Yugoslavia in 1991–92. These republics included Slovenia, Croatia, and Bosnia-Herzegovina (see Figure 14.2). Serbia and Montenegro are the two remaining republics within Yugoslavia. In Kosovo, which is a province in Serbia, but one whose population is 90 percent ethnic Albanian, there has been a strong movement for independence, led by the Kosovo Liberation Army.

Much of the ethnic differentiation in Yugoslavia has been based on religion, culture, political and military history, and some differences involving language. Serbo-Croatian is a Slavic language spoken, with dialect variation, by Serbs, Croats, and Muslim Slavs alike. (Albanian is a separate language.) Croats and Serbs use different alphabets. The Croats have adopted the Roman alphabet, but the Serbs use the Cyrillic alphabet, which they share with Russia and Bulgaria. The two alphabets help promote ethnic differentiation and nationalism. Serbs and Croats, who share speech, are divided by writing—by literature, newsprint, and political manifestos.

The Yugoslav Serbs reacted violently—with military intervention—after a 1992 vote for the independence of Muslim-led Bosnia-Herzegovina, whose population is one-third Serbian. In Bosnia, the Serbs initiated a policy of forced expulsion—"ethnic purification"—against Croats, but mainly against Muslim Slavs. Serbs in Yugoslavia, who controlled the national army, lent their support to the Bosnian Serbs in their "ethnic-cleansing" campaign.

For more on Bosnia see the Virtual Exploration and the Internet Exercises at your OLC

mhhe
●com
/kottak

Backed by the Yugoslav army, Bosnian Serb militias rounded up Bosnian Muslims, killed groups of them, and burned and looted their homes. Thousands of Slavs fled. Hundreds of thousands of Muslims became involuntary refugees in tent camps, school gyms, and parks.

The Serbs had no use for the ethnic coexistence that the previous Yugoslav socialist government had encouraged. The Serbs also wished

Figure 14.2 **Former Yugoslavia, with Province and Republics**

The former Yugoslavia, although a socialist nation, was a nonaligned country outside the former Soviet Union. Like the U.S.S.R., Yugoslavia disintegrated in the early 1990s. The breakaway portions included Slovenia, Croatia, and Bosnia-Herzegovina.

Former Yugoslav president Slobodan Milosovic on trial in the Hague, Netherlands, in 2002. What would justify the charge of war crimes against the president of a country?

to avenge historic affronts by Muslims and Croats. In the 15th century, Muslim Turks had overthrown a Serbian ruler, persecuted the Serbs, and—eventually—converted many local people to Islam during their centuries of rule in this area. Bosnian Serbs still resent Muslims—including the descendants of the converts—for the Turkish conquest.

Bosnian Serbs claimed to be fighting to resist the Muslim-dominated government of Bosnia-Herzegovina. They feared that a policy of Islamic fundamentalism might arise and threaten the Serbian Orthodox Church and other expressions of Serbian identity. The Serbs' goal was to carve up Bosnia along ethnic lines, and they wanted two-thirds of it for themselves. A stated aim of Bosnia's ethnic purification was to ensure that the Serbs would

never again be dominated by another ethnic group (Burns 1992a).

Although the Croats and the Muslim Slavs also carried out forced deportations in other parts of the former Yugoslavia, the Serbian campaign in Bosnia was the widest and the most systematic. More than 200,000 people were killed during the Bosnian conflict (Cohen 1995). With Bosnia's capital, the multiethnic city of Sarajevo, under siege, the conflict was suspended after a December 1995 peace settlement signed in Dayton, Ohio.

In spring 1999 NATO began a 78-day bombing campaign against Yugoslavia in retaliation for Serbian atrocities against ethnic Albanians in the separatist province of Kosovo. In May 1999 the then Yugoslav president, Slobodan Milosevic, was indicted for abuses against the

Kosovar Albanian population by the war crimes tribunal in the Hague, Netherlands. By June 1999, accords ending 78 days of NATO bombing placed Kosovo under international control, enforced by NATO peacekeepers, who remain there as of this writing (November 2002). In the year 2000 Yugoslavia itself took several steps toward democracy. In September 2000, Milosevic was voted out of office and replaced by a new president, Vajislav Kostinica. Parliamentary elections in December 2000 removed the last vestiges of power Milosevic had built up during the previous decade. On June 28, 2001, Milosevic was transferred from a Belgrade jail to a prison cell in the Hague, Netherlands, for eventual trial by the United Nations war crimes tribunal there.

How can we explain Yugoslavia's ethnic conflict? Ethnic distinctions represent people's perceptions of cultural differences, and people may overlook even very strong cultural similarities when circumstances make their differences more important. According to Fredrik Barth (see pages 375–376), ethnic differences are most secure and enduring in places where the groups occupy different ecological niches: They make their living in different ways or places, don't compete, and are mutually dependent. In Bosnia, the Serbs, the Croats, and the Muslim Slavs were more mixed than they were in any other former Yugoslav republic (Burns 1992b). Is it possible that the boundaries among the three groups were not sharp enough to keep them together by keeping them apart?

(Anderson 1991, pp. 24–25). Such communities consisted of people who read the same sources and thus witnessed the same events.

Making a similar point, Terry Eagleton (1983, p. 25) describes the role of the novel in promoting English national consciousness and identity. The novel gave the English "a pride in their national language and literature; if scanty education and extensive hours of labor prevented them personally from producing a literary masterpiece, they could take pleasure in the thought that others of their kind—English people—had done so."

Political upheavals and wars have divided many nationalities. The German and Korean homelands were artificially divided after wars, and according to socialist and capitalist ideologies. World War I split the Kurds, who form a majority in no state. They are a minority group in Turkey, Iran, Iraq, and Syria. Similarly, Azerbaijanis, who are related to Turks, were a minority in the former Soviet Union, as they still are in Iran. Geographically dispersed 20th century Jews imagined the modern nation of Israel long before its creation.

Migration is another reason certain nationally based ethnic groups now live in different nation-states. Massive migration in the decades before and after 1900 brought Germans, Poles, and Italians to Brazil, Canada, and the United States. Chinese, Senegalese, Lebanese, and Jews have spread all over the world. Some such people (e.g., descendants of Germans in Brazil and the United States) have assimilated to their host nations and no longer feel part of the imagined community of their origin. Such dispersed populations, which have spread out, voluntarily or not, from a common center or homeland, are called *diasporas*. The African diaspora, for example, encompasses descendants of Africans worldwide, such as in the United States, the Caribbean, and Brazil.

In creating multiethnic states, former colonial powers such as France and England often erected boundaries that corresponded poorly with preexisting cultural divisions. **Colonialism** refers to the political, social, economic, and cultural domi-

nation of a territory and its people by a foreign power for an extended time. Often, the colonial powers followed a "divide and rule" policy. They split up an ethnic group between colonies to dilute its strength in numbers. Or they stirred up rivalries among different ethnic groups in the same colony in order to strengthen allegiance to the colonial power. Still, interethnic contacts fostered by colonial institutions also helped create new "imagined communities" beyond nations. One example is the idea of *négritude* ("black association and identity"). This concept was developed by dark-skinned intellectuals from the Francophone (French-speaking) colonies of West Africa and the Caribbean. (Günther Schlee, ed. [2002] provides cases illustrating the role of "imagined differences" in ethnic conflict—the dark side of imagining communities.)

Peaceful Coexistence

Ethnic diversity may be associated with positive group interaction and coexistence or with conflict—which is discussed in the next section. In many nations, multiple cultural groups live

German, Italian, Japanese, Middle Eastern, and Eastern European immigrants have assimilated, culturally and linguistically, to a common Brazilian culture. Here a Brazilian of Japanese ancestry celebrates the election, in October 2002, of Luis Inácio da Silva (Lula) as president of Brazil. More that 220,000 people of Japanese descent live in Brazil, mostly in and around the city of São Paulo, shown here. Does this photo suggest assimilation or multiculturalism?

together in reasonable harmony. Three ways of realizing such peaceful coexistence are assimilation, the plural society, and multiculturalism.

ASSIMILATION

Assimilation describes the process of change that a minority ethnic group may experience when it moves to a country where another culture dominates. By assimilating, the minority adopts the patterns and norms of its host culture. It is incorporated into the dominant culture to the point that it no longer exists as a separate cultural unit. This is the "melting pot" model; ethnic groups give up their own cultural traditions as they blend into a common national stew. Some countries, such as Brazil, are more assimilationist than others are. Germans, Italians, Japanese, Middle Easterners, and East Europeans started migrating to Brazil late in the 19th century. These immigrants have assimilated to a common Brazilian culture, which has Portuguese, African, and Native American roots. The descendants of these immigrants speak the national language (Portuguese) and participate in national culture. (During World War II, Brazil, which was on the Allied side, forced assimilation by banning instruction in any language other than Portuguese—especially in German.)

Brazil has been more of a melting pot than have the United States and Canada, in which ethnic groups retain more distinctiveness and self-identity (see Table 14.2). I remember my first visit to the southern Brazilian city of Porto Alegre, the site of mass migration by Germans, Poles, and Italians. Transferring an expectation derived from my North American culture to Porto Alegre, I asked my tour guide to show me his city's ethnic neighborhoods. He couldn't understand what I was talking about. Except for a Japanese-Brazilian neighborhood in the city of São Paulo, the idea of an ethnic neighborhood is alien to Brazil.

THE PLURAL SOCIETY

Assimilation isn't inevitable, and there can be ethnic harmony without it. Ethnic distinctions can be maintained, rather than assimilated, despite decades, or even generations, of interethnic contact. Through a study of three ethnic groups in Swat, Pakistan, Fredrik Barth (1958/1968) challenged an old idea that interaction always leads to assimilation. He showed that ethnic groups can be

Table 14.2 Top 25 Ethnic Origins in Canada, 1996[*]

Total population	28,528,125
1. Canadian	8,806,275
2. English	6,832,095
3. French	5,597,845
4. Scottish	4,260,840
5. Irish	3,767,610
6. German	2,757,140
7. Italian	1,207,475
8. Aboriginal	1,101,955
9. Ukrainian	1,026,475
10. Chinese	921,585
11. Dutch	916,215
12. Polish	786,735
13. South Asian	723,345
14. Jewish	351,705
15. Norwegian	346,310
16. Welsh	338,905
17. Portuguese	335,110
18. Swedish	278,975
19. Russian	272,335
20. Hungarian	250,525
21. Filipino	242,880
22. American	211,790
23. Spanish	204,360
24. Greek	203,345
25. Jamaican	188,770

[*]Includes single and multiple responses.
Source: http://www.statcan.ca/english/census96/feb17/eo1can.pdf.

In the United States and Canada, multiculturalism is of growing importance. Especially in large cities like Toronto (shown here), people of diverse backgrounds attend ethnic fairs and festivals and feast on ethnic foods. What are some other expressions of multiculturalism in your society?

in contact for generations without assimilating and that they can live in peaceful coexistence.

Barth (1958/1968, p. 324) defines a **plural society** as a society combining ethnic contrasts, ecological specialization (that is, use of different environmental resources by each ethnic group), and the economic interdependence of those groups. Consider his description of the Middle East (in the 1950s): "The `environment' of any one ethnic group is not only defined by natural conditions, but also by the presence and activities of the other ethnic groups on which it depends. Each group exploits only part of the total environment, and leaves large parts of it open for other groups to exploit."

In Barth's view, ethnic boundaries are most stable and enduring when the groups occupy different ecological niches. That is, they make their living in different ways and don't compete. Ideally, they should depend on each other's activities and exchange with one another. Under such conditions, ethnic diversity can be maintained, although the specific cultural features of each group may change. By shifting the analytic focus from specific cultural practices and values to the *relations* between ethnic groups, Barth (1958/1968 and 1969) has made important contributions to ethnic studies.

MULTICULTURALISM

Multiculturalism views cultural diversity in a country as something desirable and to be encouraged. The multicultural model contrasts sharply with the assimilationist model, in which minorities are expected to abandon their traditions, replacing them with those of the majority population. Multiculturalism encourages the perception and practice of many ethnic traditions. A multicultural society socializes individuals not only into the dominant (national) culture but also into an ethnic culture. Thus, in the United States, millions of people speak both English and another language. They eat both "American" foods (apple pie, steak, hamburgers) and "ethnic" cuisine (e.g., Chinese, Cambodian, Armenian). They celebrate both national (July 4, Thanksgiving) and ethnic-religious holidays. And they study both national and

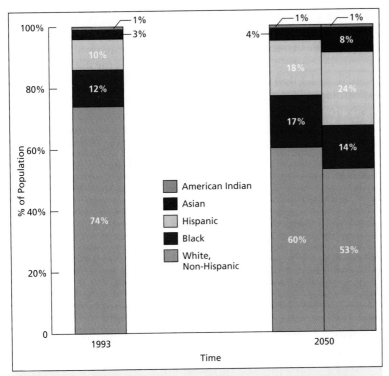

Figure 14.3 **Ethnic Composition of the United States.** The proportion of the American population that is white and non-Hispanic is declining. Consider two projections of the ethnic composition of the United States in AD 2050. The first assumes an annual immigration rate of zero; the second assumes continuation of the current level of immigration—about 880,000 immigrants per year. With either projection, the non-Hispanic white portion of the population declines dramatically.
Source: U.S. Census data.

ethnic-group histories. Multiculturalism works best in a society whose political system promotes free expression and in which there are many and diverse ethnic groups.

In the United States and Canada, multiculturalism is of growing importance. This reflects awareness that the number and size of ethnic groups have grown dramatically in recent years. If this trend continues, the ethnic composition of the United States will change dramatically. See Figure 14.3.

Because of immigration and differential population growth, whites are now outnumbered by minorities in many urban areas. For example, of the 8,008,278 residents of New York City in 2000, 27 percent were black, 27 percent Hispanic, 10 percent Asian, and 36 percent other—including non-

Hispanic whites. The comparable figures for Los Angeles (3,694,820 people) were 11 percent black, 47 percent Hispanic, 9 percent Asian, and 33 percent other—including non-Hispanic whites (Census 2000, www.census.gov).

One response to ethnic diversity and awareness has been for whites to claim or reclaim ethnic identities (Italian, Albanian, Serbian, Lithuanian, etc.) and to join ethnic associations (clubs, gangs). Some such groups are new. Others have existed for decades, although they lost members during the assimilationist years of the 1920s through the 1950s. Even "whiteness" has entered the domain of ethnicity. Today's political and academic environments include particular ethnic movements and studies, such as the Latino movement and Latino studies. In this context, there has emerged an increasing debate—as yet far from resolved—about what it means to be white. Relevant questions include: What kinds of people are considered white today versus a century ago? What kind of identity is conferred by the simple label "white"? What is the range of variation among people who are classified as "white"? How is the label related to cultural practices?

Multiculturalism seeks ways for people to understand and interact that don't depend on sameness but on respect for diversity. Multiculturalism assumes that each group has something to offer and to learn from the others. We see evidence of multiculturalism all around us. Seated near you in the classroom (perhaps in your chair!) are students whose parents were born in other countries. Islamic mosques have joined synagogues and churches in American cities. To help in exam scheduling, colleges inform professors about the main holidays of many religions. You can attend ethnic fairs and festivals, watch ethnically costumed dancers on TV, eat ethnic foods, and buy such foods at your supermarket. Some foods (e.g., bagels, pasta, tacos) have become so familiar that their ethnic origin has faded from our memories. (From the perspective of other countries, the United States has its own ethnic foods. Hamburgers, hot dogs, fried chicken, and apple pies are foods that are considered typical of American meals. These have been diffused widely by international chains such as McDonald's, Burger King, and KFC.) Popular shrines celebrate the union of ethnic diversity and globalization: At Disneyland and Walt Disney World, a chorus of ethnically costumed dolls drone on that "it's a small world after all."

Several forces have propelled North America away from assimilation toward multiculturalism. First, multiculturalism reflects the fact of recent large-scale migration, particularly from the "less-developed countries" to the "developed" nations of North America and Western Europe. The global scale of modern migration introduces unparalleled ethnic variety to host nations. People use modern means of transportation to migrate to nations whose life styles they learn about through the media and from tourists who increasingly visit their countries.

Migration also is fueled by rapid population growth, coupled with insufficient jobs, in the less-developed countries. As traditional rural economies decline or mechanize, displaced farmers move to cities, where they and their children are often unable to find jobs. As people in the less-developed countries get better educations, they seek more skilled employment. They hope to partake in an international culture of consumption that includes such modern amenities as refrigerators, televisions, and automobiles.

Contrary to popular belief, many of the people who migrate to the United States or to Canada are not poor and unskilled but middle-class and fairly well educated. Educated people migrate for several reasons. Often they can't find jobs to match their skills in their countries of origin (Grasmuck and Pessar 1991; Margolis 1994). Also, they are knowledgeable enough to deal with international rules and regulations. Arriving in North America or Western Europe, immigrants find themselves in democracies whose citizens are allowed, even encouraged, to organize for a "fair share" of resources, political influence, and cultural respect. Educated immigrants often become political organizers and particularly effective advocates of multiculturalism.

Often, people claim and express ethnic identities for political and economic reasons. Michel Laguerre's (1984) study of Haitian immigrants in New York City shows that they mobilize to deal with discrimination against black people, such as themselves, in American society. Ethnicity (their common Haitian Creole language and cultural background) is an evident basis for their mobilization. Haitian ethnicity then helps distinguish them from African Americans and other ethnic groups who may be competing for the same resources. In studying ethnic relations, it is not enough to look just at skin color—or at the cultural practices and values of the ethnic group. Equally important is the political and economic context in which ethnic diversity exists.

Much of the world is experiencing an "ethnic revival." A new assertiveness by long-resident ethnic groups is seen among the Basques and Catalans in Spain, the Bretons and Corsicans in France, and the Welsh and Scots in the United Kingdom. The United States and Canada have become increasingly multicultural, focusing on their internal diversity. "Melting pots" no longer, they are better described as ethnic "salads" (each ingredient remains distinct, although in the same bowl, with the same dressing).

A document of the University of Michigan Program in American Culture offers a good exposition of the multicultural model. It recognizes "the multiplicity of American cultures." It presents multiculturalism as a new approach to the central question in American studies: What does it mean to be an American? The document suggests a shift from the study of core myths and values (see the appendix), and people's relationships to them as generalized Americans, to "recognizing that 'America' includes people of differing community, ethnic, and cultural histories, different points of view and degrees of empowerment." Such a perspective spurs studies of specific ethnic groups rather than the country as a whole (Internal Review document of the Program in American Culture of the University of Michigan—March 12, 1992).

Roots of Ethnic Conflict

Ethnicity can be expressed in peaceful multiculturalism, or in discrimination or violent interethnic confrontation. Culture is both adaptive and maladaptive (see the "Culture" chapter). The perception of cultural differences can have disastrous effects on social interaction. The roots of ethnic

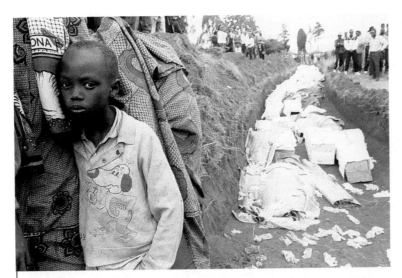

Genocide is the deliberate elimination of a group through mass murder. In Burundi, on July 20, 1996, 312 Tutsi living in a refugee camp at Bugendana were murdered by Hutu rebels. Here the victims are buried at that camp.

American minorities tend to get from the police and the judicial system. Such unequal treatment isn't legal, but it happens anyway. Segregation in the southern United States and *apartheid* in South Africa provide two examples of *de jure* discrimination, which are no longer in existence. In the United States, *de jure* segregation has been illegal since the 1960s. The South African *apartheid* system was abandoned in 1991. In both systems, by law, blacks and whites had different rights and privileges. Their social interaction ("mixing") was legally curtailed. Slavery is the most extreme form of legalized inequality; people are treated as property.

We also can distinguish between attitudinal and institutional discrimination. With *attitudinal discrimination*, people discriminate against members of a group because they are prejudiced against that group. For example, in the United States, members of the Ku Klux Klan have expressed their prejudice against blacks, Jews, and Catholics through verbal, physical, and psychological harassment.

The most extreme form of ethnic discrimination is genocide, the deliberate elimination of a group through mass murder. The United Nations defines *genocide* as acts "committed with intent to destroy, in whole or in part, a national, ethnical, racial, or religious group, as such" (Ryan 1990, p. 11). Genocide has been directed against people viewed as "standing in the way of progress" (e.g., Native Americans) and people with jobs that the dominant group wants (e.g., Jews in Hitler's Germany). In Africa, as recently as the late 1990s, the countries of Rwanda and Burundi have witnessed genocidal conflict between groups known as Tutsi and Hutu. The difference between Tutsi (the numeric minority, but socioeconomically favored stratum) and Hutu is one of different social strata, rather than language, "race," or culture. Civil wars have ravaged Rwanda and Burundi after generations of intermarriage that make physical contrasts between Tutsi (stereotyped as taller) and Hutu all but indistinguishable.

Institutional discrimination refers to laws, policies, and arrangements that deny equal rights to,

conflict can be political, economic, religious, linguistic, cultural, or "racial." Why do ethnic differences often lead to conflict and violence? The causes include a sense of injustice because of resource distribution, economic or political competition, and reaction to prejudice or discrimination (Ryan 1990, p. xxvii).

PREJUDICE AND DISCRIMINATION

Ethnic conflict may arise in the context of prejudice (attitudes and judgments) and/or discrimination (action). **Prejudice** means devaluing (looking down on) a group because of its assumed behavior, values, abilities, or attributes. People are prejudiced when they hold stereotypes about groups and apply them to individuals. (*Stereotypes* are fixed ideas—often unfavorable—about what the members of a group are like.) Prejudiced people assume that members of the group will act as they are "supposed to act," according to the stereotype. They interpret a wide range of individual behaviors as evidence of the stereotype. They use this behavior to confirm their stereotype (and low opinion) of the group.

Discrimination refers to policies and practices that harm a group and its members. Discrimination may be *de facto* (practiced, but not legally sanctioned) or *de jure* (part of the law). An example of *de facto* discrimination is the harsher treatment that

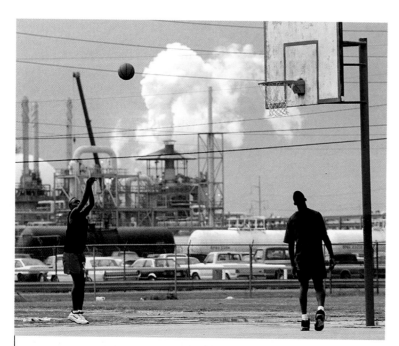

"Environmental racism" refers to policy decisions that locate a disproportionate share of environmental hazards in minority communities. Here in Norco, Louisiana, neighborhood residents play basketball at a park across from a Shell oil refinery. Why, in your opinion, do poor neighborhoods have a higher concentration of hazards than richer ones do?

move out. Poorer people, often minorities, move in, to suffer the consequences of living in a hazardous environment.

CHIPS IN THE MULTICULTURAL MOSAIC

Although multiculturalism is increasingly prominent in North America, ethnic competition and conflict also are evident. Enmity may develop between new arrivals, such as Central Americans and Koreans, and long-established ethnic groups, such as African Americans. Ethnic antagonism flared in South-Central Los Angeles in spring 1992. Rioting followed the acquittal of four white police officers who had been tried for the videotaped beating of an African-American motorist, Rodney King.

Angry blacks attacked whites, Koreans, and Hispanics. This violence expressed the frustration of African Americans about their prospects in an increasingly multicultural society. A *New York Times*/CBS News poll conducted just after the Los Angeles riots found that blacks had a bleaker outlook than whites did about the effects of immigration on their lives. Only 23 percent of the blacks felt they had more opportunities than recent immigrants, compared with twice that many whites (Toner 1992).

South-Central Los Angeles, where the 1992 rioting took place, is an ethnically mixed area. It used to be mainly African American. As blacks have moved out, there has been an influx of Mexicans and Central Americans. The Hispanic population of South-Central Los Angeles increased by 119 percent in a decade, while the number of blacks there declined by 17 percent. By 1992, the neighborhood had become 45 percent Hispanic and 48 percent black. Also, many store owners in South-Central Los Angeles are Korean immigrants (see Abelmann and Lie 1995).

Korean stores were hard hit during the 1992 riots, and more than a third of the businesses destroyed were Hispanic-owned. A third of those who died in the riots were Hispanics. These

or differentially harm, members of particular groups. Historical examples, already mentioned, include South African *apartheid* and segregationist policies in the American South. Both of those forms of institutional discrimination treated blacks as lesser citizens with fewer rights and protections under the law than whites enjoyed. Another, less formal, example of institutional discrimination is what Bunyan Bryant and Paul Mohai (1991, p. 4) call *environmental racism*: "the systematic use of institutionally based power . . . to formulate policy decisions that will lead to the disproportionate burden of environmental hazards in minority communities." Thus, toxic waste dumps tend to be located in areas with nonwhite populations.

Environmental racism is discriminatory but not always intentional. Sometimes, toxic wastes *are* deliberately dumped in areas whose residents are considered unlikely to protest because they are poor, "disorganized," or "uneducated." In other cases, property values fall after toxic waste sites are located in an area. The wealthier people

These Afghan refugees fled from Kabul, Afghanistan to Peshawar, Pakistan after September 11, 2001. Why do people become refugees?

1999). Family members work together in small grocery stores, like those in South-Central Los Angeles. They pool their labor and their wealth. In our high-tech society, good jobs demand education beyond high school. Korean "family values" and support systems encourage children to study and work hard, with eventual careers in mind. These values also fit certain general American ideals. Work, achievement, and the need to save for a college education were American values that the Korean Americans being interviewed invoked to explain their practice of using family labor, rather than hiring people from the neighborhood. The Koreans said they couldn't succeed financially if they had to hire nonrelatives. (Family solidarity is also a general American value, but the specific meaning of "family" varies between groups.) Note that both African Americans and Korean Americans appealed to a national set of values as they discussed reasons for their behavior and attitude toward other groups.

mainly recent migrants lacked deep roots to the neighborhood and, as Spanish speakers, faced language barriers (Newman 1992). Many Koreans also had trouble with English.

Koreans interviewed on ABC's *Nightline* on May 6, 1992, recognized that blacks resented them and considered them unfriendly. One man explained, "It's not part of our culture to smile." African Americans interviewed for the same program complained about Korean unfriendliness. "They come into our neighborhoods and treat us like dirt." These comments suggest a shortcoming of the multicultural perspective: Ethnic groups (blacks here) expect other ethnic groups in the same nation to assimilate to some extent to a shared (national) culture. The African Americans' comments invoked a general American value system that includes friendliness, openness, mutual respect, community participation, and "fair play." Los Angeles blacks wanted their Korean neighbors to act more like generalized Americans, and good neighbors.

One way in which Koreans in cities like New York and Los Angeles have succeeded economically is through family enterprise (see Laguerre

AFTERMATHS OF OPPRESSION

Among the factors that fuel ethnic conflict are forced assimilation, ethnocide, and cultural colonialism. A dominant group may try to destroy the cultures of certain ethnic groups (*ethnocide*) or force them to adopt the dominant culture (*forced assimilation*). Many countries have penalized or banned the language and customs of an ethnic group (including its religious observances). One example of forced assimilation is the anti-Basque campaign that the dictator Francisco Franco (who ruled between 1939 and 1975) waged in Spain. Franco banned Basque books, journals, newspapers, signs, sermons, and tombstones. He imposed fines for using the Basque language in schools. His policies led to the formation of a Basque terrorist group and spurred strong nationalist sentiment in the Basque region (Ryan 1995).

A policy of ethnic expulsion aims at removing groups that are culturally different from a country.

Recent examples include Bosnia-Herzegovina and Kosovo in the 1990s (see "Interesting Issues," pages 372–373). Uganda expelled 74,000 Asians in 1972. The neofascist parties of contemporary Western Europe advocate repatriation (expulsion) of immigrant workers (West Indians in England, Algerians in France, and Turks in Germany) (Ryan 1995). A policy of expulsion may create *refugees*—people who have been forced (involuntary refugees) or who have chosen (voluntary refugees) to flee a country, to escape persecution or war.

Colonialism, another form of oppression, is the domination of a territory and its people by a foreign power for an extended time (Bell 1981). The British and French colonial empires are familiar examples of colonialism. The United States has been like a colonial power with respect to Native Americans. We also can extend the term to the former Soviet empire, formerly known as "the Second World."

Using the labels "First World," "Second World," and "Third World" is a common, although clearly ethnocentric, way of categorizing nations. The *First World* refers to the "democratic West"—traditionally conceived in opposition to a "Second World" ruled by "communism." The First World includes Canada, the United States, Western Europe, Japan, Australia, and New Zealand. The *Second World* refers to the Warsaw Pact nations, including the former Soviet Union and the socialist and once-socialist countries of Eastern Europe and Asia. Proceeding with this classification, the "less-developed countries" or "developing nations" make up the *Third World*. See Figure 14.4.

The frontiers imposed by colonialism were not usually based on, and often didn't reflect, preexisting cultural units. In many countries, colonial nation building left ethnic strife in its wake. Thus, over a million Hindus and Moslems were killed in the violence that accompanied the division of the Indian subcontinent into India and Pakistan. Problems between Arabs and Jews in Palestine began during the British mandate period, before the cre-

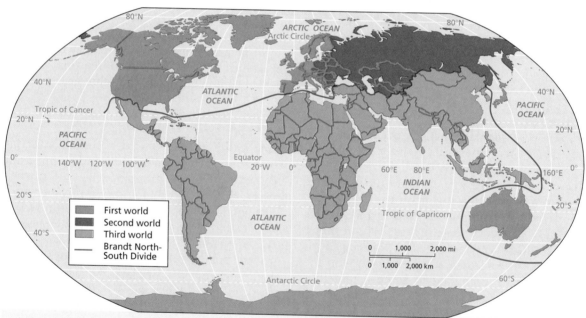

Figure 14.4 **"First," "Second," and "Third" Worlds.** Use of "First World," "Second World," and "Third World" is a common, albeit ethnocentric, way of categorizing nations. "First World" refers to the "democratic West"—traditionally conceived in opposition to a "Second World" ruled by "communism." The "less-developed countries" or "developing nations" make up the "Third World." Another way of viewing the world in terms of differential economic and political influence is the Brandt North–South divide. This division classifies Australia and New Zealand as northern nations even though they are in the Southern Hemisphere. The map shows both divisions.

ation of the independent state of Israel. Ethnic conflicts in the less-developed countries have proliferated since the early 1960s, when decolonization (the end of colonialism and the rise of independence) reached its height. There have been bitter ethnic conflicts in Congo, Nigeria, Bangladesh, Sudan, India, Sri Lanka, Ethiopia, Uganda, Lebanon, and Cyprus. Many of these remain unresolved (see Friedman, ed. 2002).

Multiculturalism may be growing in the United States and Canada, but the opposite is happening in the disintegrating Second World, where ethnic groups (nationalities) want their own nation-states. The rise of ethnic feeling and conflict as the Soviet empire disintegrated illustrates that years of political repression and ideology provide insufficient "common ground" for lasting unity.

Cultural colonialism refers to internal domination—by one group and its culture/ideology over others. One example is the domination over the former Soviet empire by Russian people, language, and culture, and by socialist ideology. The dominant culture makes itself the official culture. This is reflected in schools, the media, and public interaction. Under Soviet rule, ethnic minorities had limited self-rule in republics and regions controlled by Moscow. All the republics and their peoples were to be united by the oneness of "socialist internationalism."

One common technique in cultural colonialism is to flood ethnic areas with members of the dominant ethnic group. Thus, in the former Soviet Union, ethnic Russian colonists were sent to many areas, such as Tajikistan (see Figure 14.5), to diminish the cohesion and clout of the local people. Tajikistan is a small, poor state (and former Soviet republic) in central Asia, near Afghanistan, with 5.1 million people. In Tajikistan, as in central Asia generally, most people are Muslims. Today, Islam, as an alternative way of ordering spiritual and social life, is replacing socialist ideology. This comes after more than 70 years of official atheism

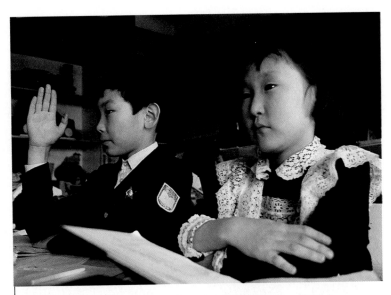

An example of cultural colonialism was the domination of the former Soviet empire by Russian people, language, and culture. Ethnic minorities had very limited self-rule in republics and regions controlled by Moscow. These Siberian children are trained to be model Soviet (Russian) citizens. Can you think of examples of cultural colonialism in your own country?

and suppression of religion. The Soviets destroyed mosques and discouraged religious practice by the young, while allowing it for old people. Still, Islam was taught at home, around the kitchen table, so it has been called "kitchen Islam."

Now, as the Russians leave Tajikistan, the force of Russian culture and language is receding. Islamic influence is growing. Women have started covering their arms, legs, and hair. More and more people speak and pray in Tajik, a language related to Persian (which is spoken in Iran) (Erlanger 1992).

"The Commonwealth of Independent States" is all that remains of the former Soviet Union. In this group of new nations, ethnic groups (nationalities) like the Tajiks and Chechens are seeking to establish separate and viable nation-states based on cultural, including religious, boundaries. This celebration of ethnic autonomy is a reaction to the Soviet Union's decades of suppressing diversity: historic, national, linguistic, ethnic, cultural, and religious. It is part of an ethnic florescence that—as surely as globalization—is a trend at the new millennium.

Figure 14.5 Former Soviet Socialist Republics of Central Asia, Including Tajikistan.

SUMMARY

1. An "ethnic group" refers to a particular culture in a nation or region that contains others. Ethnicity is based on perceived cultural similarities (among members of the same ethnic group) and differences (between that group and others). Ethnic distinctions can be based on language, religion, history, geography, kinship, or "race." A race is an ethnic group assumed to have a biological basis.

2. The term *nation* was once synonymous with "ethnic group." Now *nation* has come to mean a state—a centrally organized political unit. *Nation* and *state* have become synonymous. Combined in *nation-state,* they refer to such a political entity, a "country." Because of migration, conquest, and colonialism, most nation-states are not ethnically homogeneous. Ethnic diversity may be associated with harmony or conflict. In creating multi-tribal and multiethnic states, colonial regimes often erected boundaries that corresponded poorly with preexisting cultural divisions. Ethnic groups that seek autonomous political status (their own country) are *nationalities*. Political upheavals, wars, and migrations have divided many imagined national communities.

3. *Assimilation* describes the process of change an ethnic group may experience when it moves to a country where another culture dominates. By assimilating, the minority adopts the patterns and norms of its host culture. Assimilation isn't inevitable, and there can be ethnic harmony without it. A plural society combines ethnic contrasts and economic interdependence between ethnic groups. The view of cultural diversity in a nation-state as good and desirable is multiculturalism. A multicultural society socializes individuals not only into the dominant (national) culture but also into an ethnic one.

4. Ethnicity can be expressed in peaceful multiculturalism, or in discrimination or violent confrontation. Ethnic conflict often arises in reaction to prejudice (attitudes and judgments) or discrimination (action). *Prejudice* means devaluing (looking down on) a group because of its assumed attributes. *Discrimination* refers to policies that harm a group and its members. Discrimination may be *de facto* (practiced, but not legally sanctioned or *de jure* (part of the law). The most extreme form of anti-ethnic discrimination is genocide, the deliberate elimination of a group through mass murder.

5. A dominant group may try to destroy certain ethnic practices (ethnocide) or to force ethnic-group members to adopt the dominant culture (forced assimilation). A policy of ethnic explusion may create refugees. *Colonialism* refers to the political, social, economic, and cultural domination of a territory and its people by a foreign power for an extended time. *Cultural colonialism* refers to internal domination—by one group and its culture and/or ideology over others. One example is the domination of the former Soviet empire by the Russian people, language, and culture.

KEY TERMS

See the flash cards

mhhe.com/kottak

achieved status Social status that comes through talents, choices, actions, and accomplishments, rather than ascription.

ascribed status Social status (e.g., race or gender) that people have little or no choice about occupying.

assimilation The process of change that a minority group may experience when it moves to a country where another culture dominates; the minority is incorporated into the dominant culture to the point that it no longer exists as a separate cultural unit.

colonialism The political, social, economic, and cultural domination of a territory and its people by a foreign power for an extended time.

discrimination Policies and practices that harm a group and its members.

ethnic group Group distinguished by cultural similarities (shared among members of that group) and differences (between that group and others); ethnic-group members share beliefs, customs, and norms, and, often, a common language, religion, history, geography, and kinship.

ethnicity Identification with, and feeling part of, an ethnic group, and exclusion from certain other groups because of this affiliation.

multiculturalism The view of cultural diversity in a country as something good and desirable; a multicultural society socializes individuals not only into the dominant (national) culture but also into an ethnic culture.

nation Once a synonym for "ethnic group," designating a single culture sharing a language, religion, history, territory, ancestry, and kinship; now usually a synonym for state or *nation-state*.

nationalities Ethnic groups that once had, or wish to have or regain, autonomous political status (their own country).

nation-state An autonomous political entity; a country like the United States or Canada.

négritude Black association and identity—an idea developed by dark-skinned intellectuals in Francophone (French-speaking) West Africa and the Caribbean.

plural society A society that combines ethnic contrasts and economic interdependence of the ethnic groups.

prejudice   Devaluing (looking down on) a group because of its assumed behavior, values, abilities, or other attributes.

state   An independent, centrally organized political unit; a government.

status   Any social position that someone occupies; may be ascribed or achieved.

CRITICAL THINKING QUESTIONS

For more self testing, see the self quizzes

**mhhe
●com
/kottak**

1. What's the difference between a culture and an ethnic group? In what culture(s) do you participate? To what ethnic group(s) do you belong? What is the basis of your primary cultural identity?
2. Name five social statuses you currently occupy. Which of those statuses are ascribed, and which ones are achieved?
3. Are your ascribed statuses more important to you than your achieved statuses, or vice versa?
4. Is ethnicity an achieved status? If so, give an example.
5. What is a minority group? Must it be a numerical minority? What are some minority groups in contemporary North America?
6. What are some of the forces that help forge and maintain imagined communities in the world today?
7. Do perceived linguistic and cultural similarities between ethnic groups tend to produce ethnic harmony or conflict?
8. How does multiculturalism differ from assimilation? Which process do you favor for your country?

9. How does prejudice differ from discrimination? Give three examples of each.
10. Give a few examples of "ethnic florescence" in today's world.

Atlas Questions

Look at Map 14, "Global Distribution of Minority Groups."

1. What is the extent of ethnic diversity in the United States and Canada? What factors have created this diversity.
2. China has several minority populations, but, according to Map 14, do they account for more than 10 percent of the Chinese population? Name two other countries that are similar to China in their degree of ethnic homogeneity.
3. What continent would you say has the most ethnic diversity? How would you attempt to explain this diversity? What continent would you say has the least ethnic diversity? How might you explain this relative homogeneity?

SUGGESTED ADDITIONAL READINGS

Abelmann, N., and J. Lie
1995   *Blue Dreams: Korean Americans and the Los Angeles Riots*. Cambridge, MA: Harvard University Press. Some of the roots of ethnic conflict in Los Angeles today.

Anderson, B.
1991   *Imagined Communities: Reflections on the Origin and Spread of Nationalism*, rev. ed. London: Verso. The origins of nationalism in Europe and its colonies, with special attention to the role of print, language, and schools.

1998   *The Spectre of Comparisons: Nationalism, Southeast Asia, and the World*. New York: Verso. A regional and international focus on nationalism.

Barth, F.

1969   *Ethnic Groups and Boundaries: The Social Organization of Cultural Difference.* London: Allyn and Unwin. Classic discussion of the prominence of differentiation and boundaries (versus cultural features per se) in interethnic relations.

Delamont, S.

1995   *Appetites and Identities: An Introduction to the Social Anthropology of Western Europe.* London: Routledge. An anthropological account of national cultures and ethnic variation in Western Europe.

Fox, R. G., ed.

1990   *Nationalist Ideologies and the Production of National Cultures.* American Ethnological Society Monograph Series, no. 2. Washington, DC: American Anthropological Association. A series of papers about ethnicity and nationalism in Israel, Romania, India, Guatemala, Guyana, Burundi, and Tanzania.

Friedman, J.

1994   *Cultural Identity and Global Process.* Thousand Oaks, CA: Sage. Issues of ethnic and cultural identity in the face of globalization.

Friedman, J., ed.

2002   *Globalization, the State, and Violence.* Walnut Creek, CA: Altamira. Essays by prominent anthropologists focusing on violence in the context of globalization.

Gellner, E.

1997   *Nationalism.* New York: New York University Press. Up-to-date comments from a longtime anthropological student of nationalism.

Hastings, A.

1997   *The Construction of Nationhood: Ethnicity, Religion, and Nationalism.* New York: Cambridge University Press. Beliefs, identities, and nation-building.

Hobsbawm, E. J.

1992   *Nations and Nationalism since 1780: Programme, Myth, Reality,* 2nd ed. New York: Cambridge University Press. The making of modern nation-states.

Kottak, C. P., and K. A. Kozaitis

2003   *On Being Different: Diversity and Multiculturalism in the North American Mainstream,* 2nd ed. New York: McGraw-Hill. Aspects of diversity in the United States and Canada, plus an original theory of multiculturalism.

Laguerre, M. S.

1998   *Diasporic Citizenship: Haitian Americans in Transnational America.* New York: St. Martin's Press. Haitians in today's America.

1999   *The Global Ethnopolis: Chinatown, Japantown, and Manilatown in American Society* New York: St. Martin's Press. Asian-American urban enclaves, with a focus on San Francisco.

Leman, J.

2001   *The Dynamics of Emerging Ethnicities: Immigrant and Indigenous Ethnogenesis in Confrontation.* New York: Peter Lang. The creation and negotiation of ethnicity.

Maybury-Lewis, D.

2002   *Indigenous Peoples, Ethnic Groups, and the State,* 2nd ed. Boston: Allyn and Bacon. Studies of cultural survival, ethnicity, and social change.

Ryan, S.

1995   *Ethnic Conflict and International Relations,* 2nd ed. Brookfield, MA: Dartmouth. Cross-national review of the roots of ethnic conflict.

Schlee, G., ed.

2002   *Imagined Differences: Hatred and the Construction of Identity.* New York: Palgrave. The dark side of imagining communities.

Scupin, R.

2003   *Race and Ethnicity: An Anthropological Focus on the United States and the World.* Upper Saddle River, NJ: Prentice-Hall. Broad survey of race and ethnic relations.

Yetman, N., ed.

1999   *Majority and Minority: The Dynamics of Race and Ethnicity in American Life,* 6th ed. Boston: Allyn and Bacon. A wide-ranging anthology focusing on the United States.

INTERNET EXERCISES

1. *Ethnicity on the Border*: Read Gregory Rodriguez's article "We're Patriotic Americans because We're Mexican" in *Salon Magazine* **http://archive.salon.com/news/feature/2000/02/24/laredo/.**

  a. Who is participating in the celebration of George Washington's Birthday?

  b. How does this celebration reflect the influence of Mexican and American cultures? Since it is a mixture, is this celebration any less "pure"?

  c. Do you think a multiethnic identity is incompatible with a single national identity?

  d. What factors would cause a border community to invest so much energy in recognizing a day such as Washington's Birthday that so many other Americans ignore? Do you think it is more important for communities living on the border to assert their nationality than for communities living in the heartland?

2. *The Marketing of Ethnicity*: Read Marilyn Halter's article in the *Washington Post* entitled "Ethnicity for Sale," **http://washingtonpost.com/wp-dyn/print/sunday/outlook/inside/A48082-2000 Jul15.html.**

  a. In the past what were the predominant American attitudes toward ethnic minorities? How have they changed?

  b. How are these new attitudes toward ethnic minorities reflected in American business? What are some examples?

  c. How has the "Roots" phenomenon influenced the St. Patrick's Day celebration?

  d. How do you predict America's attitude toward ethnic minorities will change in the future?

See Chapter 14 at your McGraw-Hill Online Learning Center for additional review and interactive exercises.

15

LANGUAGE AND COMMUNICATION

Overview

Linguistic anthropology shares the field's general interest in diversity in time and space. Linguistic anthropology examines language structure and use, linguistic change, and relations among language, society, and culture.

In the wild, nonhuman primates use limited call systems to communicate. The call systems of our hominid ancestors eventually grew too complicated for genetic transmission. The hominids began to rely on learning, and the call systems evolved into language, our main system of communication. But humans also continue to use nonverbal communication, such as facial expressions and gestures. No language includes all the sounds the human vocal apparatus can make. Phonol-

ogy, the study of speech sounds, focuses on sounds that make a difference in a given language.

Sociolinguistics investigates relationships between social and linguistic variation. How do different kinds of people use language? Do men and women speak differently? How about classes, professions, and ethnic groups? People vary their speech on different occasions, shifting styles, dialects, even languages.

Historical linguistics is useful for anthropologists interested in historical relationships. Linguistic clues can suggest past contacts between cultures. Relationships between languages don't necessarily mean there are biological ties between their speakers, because people can learn new languages.

How Languages Came to Be, and Change: A Conversation with John McWhorter

NEW YORK TIMES NEWS BRIEF

by Claudia Dreifus

October 30, 2001

Several key issues in language and communication are highlighted in this interview with Professor John H. McWhorter of the University of California at Berkeley, who is an expert on language change and evolution. While some scholars think that language may be even older, McWhorter speculates that language arose with *Homo sapiens* in Africa, some 150,000 years ago. From there it diversified and spread as anatomically modern humans colonized the rest of the world. Among the interesting claims in this article is that small, isolated societies tend to have more complex languages than do larger societies that are in regular contact with others. Linguistic simplification, illustrated by pidgins and Creole languages, occurs in the context of contact between people who speak different languages, yet have to learn to communicate with each other.

Q. In [your book] "The Power of Babel," you write, "The first human language emerged roughly 150,000 years ago in East Africa." How can you know this?

A. . . . The fossil evidence of *Homo sapiens* goes back to about 150,000 years ago. So we may assume that part of what distinguished the species when it arose was speech . . . The first vocabulary must have corresponded closely with the life experience of the people in question . . . They would certainly have had words for animals and plants. If you look at contemporary hunter-gatherer societies, we find their vocabularies correspond closely to their life experiences. Of course, they spoke about the sorts of things that all humans have always spoken about, such as love, food, pain and the future.

Q. The late Dr. Joseph Greenberg of Stanford tried to reconstruct pieces of what he believed to be the original human language. Was he guessing when he tried to do that?

A. He was making thoroughly educated guesses based on comparing words from the ancestors of certain groups of languages that we can reconstruct now. However, there's a problem to this method: language is always changing. In 150,000 years, every word has been turned inside out so many times that there's no way of going back to what the words might have been . . . There's a second problem: there's no record. We can know what some ancient creatures looked like because they've left behind a fossil record. There's no record of language until the advent of writing . . .

Q. Do we know how the original East African language proliferated into the thousands we have today?

A. We know it happened because of the process of change. Change is the central reality of human language. The shapes of words, and the structures of languages, are always changing . . . As soon as there were separate populations of human beings, there were bound to be whole separate languages. And then, once *Homo sapiens* coated the world, there were thousands of languages.

Q. Do languages evolve in the same way living organisms do?

A. Very much. In organisms, a species develops subspecies. Similarly, a language develops dialects. Today, there are maybe 5,000 languages on earth. Michael Krauss of the University of Alaska estimates we'll have 500 within 100 years. Minority languages are being killed off along with minority cultures.

Although minority languages are being killed off along with minority cultures, efforts are underway to preserve linguistic diversity. Here, in April 2002, Ryan Branstetter (*left*) learns the Walla Walla language of his ancestors from seventy-eight-year-old Cecilia Bearchum on Oregon's Umatilla Indian reservation.

Q. Should we be organizing conservation programs for endangered languages in the same way we do for wildlife and plants?

A. Ideally we'd like to keep all 5,000 languages. Just as every creature is this marvelous repository of nature's wonders, if you look at any language, you are dazzled by its richness and complexity. This is especially true if you go way off into the jungle and find a language spoken by some 300 people. That language is going to be unbelievably complex because it has had thousands of years in isolation to get that way . . . To the extent third-world people are joining the globalized world, it seems that many of these languages are doomed, at least in their spoken form. What I urge is that these languages be recorded so that we will always know what they were like . . .

Q. In your book, you assert that the more complex a society is, the simpler its language. Can you explain how that works?

A. I also say that the more isolated the society, the more complex the language. In large cosmopolitan societies, you have new people constantly coming in, learning the language as a second language, and for that reason, constantly simplifying it. If a language is spoken over millennia by a group of 500 people and newcomers aren't learning it as a second language, then you don't have people shaving it down to its simplest form. Thus, it will get very complex, arbitrary, full of bells and whistles and needless gunk.

Q. You are, among other things, an expert in pidgin and Creole languages. What drew you to this?

A. One thing I really like about Creole languages is that they are a testament to the hybridicity of human nature and the fact that hybridicity creates not sterile creatures but brand-new living things. Another thing about Creoles is that I suspect that they most approximate some of the early languages. Creoles begin as pidgin languages. They start when adults from different places come together in a situation such as slavery and have to learn a particular language very quickly, without formal teaching. They still are speaking their native language most of the time, but in their work, they speak this pidgin language. Now, if these people remain isolated in that situation for all their lives, they and their children will often expand the pidgin into a brand-new language, a Creole-Jamaican patois, for instance . . .

Q. Can animals have language?

A. They have some. Nothing remotely as rich or complex as ours. On a primitive symbolic level, yeah. It's been shown that if you say to a chimpanzee, "Go get the banana that's in the trough on the left," he'll understand enough to actually go get it. However, there's no way to communicate to an animal, "I've seen the carcass of a giant squid washed up on a beach missing an eye," and have him get that . . .

Source: Claudia Dreifus, *A Conversation with John McWhorter: How Languages Came to Be, and Change*, *The New York Times*, October 30, 2001, late edition, section f, p. 3, column 1.

Language, which may be spoken (*speech*) or written (*writing*), is our primary means of communication. Writing has existed for about 6,000 years. Language originated thousands of years before that, but no one can say exactly when. Like culture in general, of which language is a part, language is transmitted through learning, as part of enculturation. Language is based on arbitrary, learned associations between words and the things for which they stand. As McWhorter suggests in the interview you just read, the complexity of language—absent in the communication systems of other animals—allows us to conjure up elaborate images, to discuss the past and the future, to share our experiences with others, and to benefit from their experiences.

Anthropologists study language in its social and cultural context. Linguistic anthropology illustrates anthropology's characteristic interest in comparison, variation, and change. As McWhorter notes, a key feature of language is that it is always changing. Some linguistic anthropologists reconstruct ancient languages by comparing their contemporary descendants and in so doing make discoveries about history. Others study linguistic differences to discover the varied worldviews and patterns of thought in a multitude of cultures. Sociolinguists examine dialects and styles in a single language to show how speech reflects social differences (Fasold 1990; Labov 1972a,b). Linguistic anthropologists also explore the role of language in colonization and in the expansion of the world economy (Geis 1987).

Animal Communication

CALL SYSTEMS

Only humans speak. No other animal has anything approaching the complexity of language. The natural communication systems of other primates (monkeys and apes) are **call systems**. These vocal systems consist of a limited number of sounds—*calls*—that are produced only when particular environmental stimuli are encountered. Such calls may be varied in intensity and duration, but they are much less flexible than language because they are automatic and can't be combined. When primates encounter food and danger simultaneously, they can make only one call. They can't combine the calls for food and danger into a single utterance, indicating that both are present. At some point in human evolution, however, our ancestors began to combine calls and to understand the combinations. The number of calls also expanded, eventually becoming too great to be transmitted even partly through the genes. Communication came to rely almost totally on learning.

Although wild primates use call systems, the vocal tract of apes is not suitable for speech. Until the 1960s, attempts to teach spoken language to apes suggested that they lack linguistic abilities. In the 1950s, a couple raised a chimpanzee, Viki, as a member of their family and systematically tried to teach her to speak. However, Viki learned only four words ("mama," "papa," "up," and "cup").

SIGN LANGUAGE

More recent experiments have shown that apes can learn to use, if not speak, true language (Miles 1983). Several apes have learned to converse with people through means other than speech. One such communication system is American Sign Language, or ASL, which is widely used by deaf and mute Americans. ASL employs a limited number of basic gesture units that are analogous to sounds in spoken language. These units combine to form words and larger units of meaning.

The first chimpanzee to learn ASL was Washoe, a female. Captured in West Africa, Washoe was acquired by R. Allen Gardner and Beatrice Gardner, scientists at the University of Nevada in Reno, in 1966, when she was a year old. Four years later, she moved to Norman, Oklahoma, to a converted farm that had become the Institute for Primate Studies. Washoe revolutionized the discussion of the language-learning abilities of apes. At first she lived in a trailer and heard no spoken language. The researchers always used ASL to communicate with each other in her presence. The chimp gradually acquired a vocabulary of more than 100 signs representing English words (Gardner, Gardner, and Van Cantfort 1989). At the age of two, Washoe began to combine as many as five signs into rudimentary sentences such as "you, me, go out, hurry."

The second chimp to learn ASL was Lucy, Washoe's junior by one year. Lucy died, or was murdered by poachers, in 1986, after having been introduced to "the wild" in Africa in 1979 (Carter

Apes, such as these Congo chimpanzees, use call systems to communicate in the wild. Their vocal systems consist of a limited number of sounds—*calls*—that are produced only when particular environmental stimuli are encountered.

1988). From her second day of life until her move to Africa, Lucy lived with a family in Norman, Oklahoma. Roger Fouts, a researcher from the nearby Institute for Primate Studies, came two days a week to test and improve Lucy's knowledge of ASL. During the rest of the week, Lucy used ASL to converse with her foster parents. After acquiring language, Washoe and Lucy exhibited several human traits: swearing, joking, telling lies, and trying to teach language to others (Fouts 1997).

When irritated, Washoe has called her monkey neighbors at the institute "dirty monkeys." Lucy insulted her "dirty cat." On arrival at Lucy's place, Fouts once found a pile of excrement on the floor. When he asked the chimp what it was, she replied, "dirty, dirty," her expression for feces. Asked whose "dirty, dirty" it was, Lucy named Fouts's coworker, Sue. When Fouts refused to believe her about Sue, the chimp blamed the excrement on Fouts himself.

Cultural transmission of a communication system through learning is a fundamental attribute of language. Washoe, Lucy, and other chimps have tried to teach ASL to other animals, including their own offspring. Washoe has taught gestures to other institute chimps, including her son Sequoia, who died in infancy (Fouts, Fouts, and Van Cantfort 1989).

Because of their size and strength as adults, gorillas are less likely subjects than chimps for such experiments. Lean adult male gorillas in the wild weigh 400 pounds (180 kilograms), and full-grown females can easily reach 250 pounds (110 kilograms). Because of this, psychologist Penny Patterson's work with gorillas at Stanford University seems more daring than the chimp experiments. Patterson raised her now full-grown female gorilla, Koko, in a trailer next to a Stanford museum. Koko's vocabulary surpasses that of any chimp. She regularly employs 400 ASL signs and has used about 700 at least once.

Koko and the chimps also show that apes share still another linguistic ability with humans: **productivity**. Speakers routinely use the rules of their language to produce entirely new expressions that are comprehensible to other native speakers. I can, for example, create "baboonlet" to refer to a baboon infant. I do this by analogy with English words in which the suffix -*let* designates the young of a species. Anyone who speaks English immediately understands the meaning of my new word. Koko, Washoe, Lucy, and others have shown that apes also are able to use language productively. Lucy used gestures she already knew to create "drinkfruit" for watermelon. Washoe, seeing a swan for the first time, coined "waterbird." Koko, who knew the gestures for "finger" and "bracelet," formed "finger bracelet" when she was given a ring.

Chimps and gorillas have a rudimentary capacity for language. They may never have invented a meaningful gesture system in the wild. However, given such a system, they show many humanlike abilities in learning and using it. Of course, language use by apes is a product of human intervention and teaching. The experiments mentioned here do not suggest that apes can invent language (nor are human children ever faced with that task). However, young apes have managed to learn the basics of gestural language. They can employ it productively and creatively, although not with the sophistication of human ASL users.

Apes, like humans, also may try to teach their language to others. Lucy, not fully realizing the difference between primate hands and feline paws, once tried to mold her pet cat's paw into ASL signs. Koko taught gestures to Michael, a male gorilla six years her junior.

Apes also have demonstrated linguistic **displacement**. Absent in call systems, this is a key ingredient in language. Normally, each call is tied to an environmental stimulus such as food. Calls

(Cartoon by Sidney Harris)

Table 15.1 Language Contrasted with Call Systems

Human Language	Primate Call Systems
Has the capacity to speak of things and events that are not present (displacement).	Are stimuli-dependent; the food call will only be made in the presence of food; it cannot be faked.
Has the capacity to generate new expressions by combining other expressions (productivity).	Consist of a limited number of calls that cannot be combined to produce new calls.
Is group specific in that all humans have the capacity for language, but each linguistic community has its own language, which is culturally transmitted.	Tend to be species specific, with little variation among communities of the same species for each call.

are uttered only when that stimulus is present. Displacement means that humans can talk about things that are not present. We don't have to see the objects before we say the words. Human conversations are not limited by place. We can discuss the past and future, share our experiences with others, and benefit from theirs.

Patterson has described several examples of Koko's capacity for displacement (Patterson 1978). The gorilla once expressed sorrow about having bitten Penny three days earlier. Koko has used the sign "later" to postpone doing things she doesn't want to do. Table 15.1 summarizes the contrasts between language, whether sign or spoken, and the call systems that primates use in the wild.

Certain scholars doubt the linguistic abilities of chimps and gorillas (Sebeok and Umiker-Sebeok 1980; Terrace 1979). These people contend that Koko and the chimps are comparable to trained circus animals and don't really have linguistic ability. However, in defense of Patterson and the other researchers (Hill 1978; Van Cantfort and Rimpau 1982), only one of their critics has worked with an ape. This was Herbert Terrace, whose experience teaching a chimp sign language lacked the continuity and personal involvement that have contributed so much to Patterson's success with Koko.

No one denies the huge difference between human language and gorilla signs. There is a major gap between the ability to write a book or say a prayer and the few hundred gestures employed by a well-trained chimp. Apes aren't people, but they aren't just

See the Internet Exercises at your OLC for more on primate language ability

mhhe
●com
/kottak

animals either. Let Koko express it: When asked by a reporter whether she was a person or an animal, Koko chose neither. Instead, she signed "fine animal gorilla" (Patterson 1978).

THE ORIGIN OF LANGUAGE

The capacity to remember and combine linguistic expressions seems to be latent in the apes (Miles 1983). In human evolution, the same ability flowered into language. Language did not appear miraculously at a certain moment in human history. It developed over hundreds of thousands of years, as our ancestors' call systems were gradually transformed. Language offered a tremendous adaptive advantage to *Homo*. Language permits the information stored by a human society to exceed by far that of any nonhuman group. Language is a uniquely effective vehicle for learning. Because we can speak of things we have never experienced, we can anticipate responses before we encounter the stimuli. Adaptation can occur more rapidly in *Homo than in the other primates because our adaptive means are more flexible.*

Nonverbal Communication

Language is our principal means of communicating, but it isn't the only one we use. We communicate when we transmit information about ourselves to others and receive such information from them. Our facial expressions, bodily stances, gestures, and movements, even if unconscious, convey information and are part of our communication

Men and women differ in their phonology, grammar, and vocabulary, and in the body stances and movements that accompany speech. What differences do you note in the communication styles of the two women in the foreground, compared with the several men in the background?

styles. Deborah Tannen (1990) discusses differences in the communication styles of American men and women, and her comments go beyond language. She notes that girls and women tend to look directly at each other when they talk, whereas boys and men do not. Males are more likely to look straight ahead rather than to turn and make eye contact with someone, especially another man, seated beside them. Also, in conversational groups, men tend to relax and sprawl out. Women may adopt a similar relaxed posture in all-female groups, but when they are with men, they tend to draw in their limbs and adopt a tighter stance.

Kinesics is the study of communication through body movements, stances, gestures, and facial expressions. Related to kinesics is the examination of cultural differences in personal space and displays of affection discussed in the chapter "Culture." Linguists pay attention not only to what is said but to how it is said, and to features besides language itself that convey meaning. A speaker's enthusiasm is conveyed not only through words, but also through facial expressions, gestures, and other signs of animation. We use gestures, such as

a jab of the hand, for emphasis. We use verbal and nonverbal ways of communicating our moods: enthusiasm, sadness, joy, regret. We vary our intonation and the pitch or loudness of our voices. We communicate through strategic pauses, and even by being silent. An effective communication strategy may be to alter pitch, voice level, and grammatical forms, such as declaratives ("I am . . ."), imperatives ("Go forth . . ."), and questions ("Are you . . . ?"). Culture teaches us that certain manners and styles should accompany certain kinds of speech. Our demeanor, verbal and nonverbal, when our favorite team is winning would be out of place at a funeral, or when a somber subject is being discussed.

Understanding Ourselves Some of our facial expressions reflect our primate heritage. We can see them in monkeys and especially in the apes. How "natural" and universal are the meanings conveyed by facial expressions? Throughout the world, smiles, laughs, frowns, and tears tend to have similar meanings, but culture does intervene. In some cultures, people smile less than in others. In a given culture, men may smile less than women; and adults, less than children. A lifetime of smiling and frowning marks the face, so that smile lines and frown furrows develop. In North America, smile lines may be more marked in women than men. Margaret Mead focused on kinesics in her studies of infant care in different cultures. She noted differences in mother–child interactions, finding that patterns of holding, releasing, and playing varied from culture to culture. In some cultures, babies were held more securely than in others. Mead thought that patterns of infant and child care played an important role in forming adult personality.

Culture always plays a role in shaping the "natural." Animals communicate through odors, using scent to mark territories, a chemical means of communication. Among modern North Americans, the perfume, mouthwash, and deodorant industries are based on the idea that the sense of smell plays a role in communication and social interaction. But different cultures are more tolerant of "natural" odors than ours is. Cross-culturally, nodding does not always mean affirmative, nor does head shaking from side to side always mean negative. Brazilians wag a finger to mean no. Americans say "uh huh" to affirm, whereas in Madagascar a similar sound is made to deny. Americans point with their fingers; the people of Madagascar point with their lips. Patterns of "lounging around" vary, too. Outside, when resting, some people may sit or lie on the ground; others squat; others lean against a tree.

Body movements communicate social differences. Lower-class Brazilians, especially women, offer limp handshakes to their social superiors. In many cultures, men have firmer handshakes than women do. In Japan, bowing is a regular part of social interaction, but different bows are used depending on the social status of the people who are interacting. In Madagascar and Polynesia, people of lower status should not hold their heads above those of people of higher status. When one approaches someone older or of higher status, one bends one's knees and lowers one's head as a sign of respect. In Madagascar, one always does this, for politeness, when passing between two people. Although our gestures, facial expressions, and body stances have roots in our primate heritage, and can be seen in the monkeys and the apes, they have not escaped the cultural shaping described in previous chapters. Language, which is so highly dependent on the use of symbols, is the domain of communication, in which culture plays the strongest role.

The Structure of Language

The scientific study of a spoken language (*descriptive linguistics*) involves several interrelated areas of analysis: phonology, morphology, lexicon, and syntax. **Phonology**, the study of speech sounds, considers which sounds are present and significant in a given language. **Morphology** studies the forms in which sounds combine to form *morphemes*—words and their meaningful parts. Thus, the word *cats* would be analyzed as containing two morphemes: *cat*, the name for a kind of animal, and *-s*, a morpheme indicating plurality. A language's **lexicon** is a dictionary containing all its morphemes and their meanings. **Syntax** refers to the arrangement and order of words in phrases and sentences. Syntactic questions include whether nouns usually come before or after verbs, or whether adjectives normally precede or follow the nouns they modify.

SPEECH SOUNDS

From the movies and TV, and from actually meeting foreigners, we know something about foreign accents and mispronunciations. We know that someone with a marked French accent doesn't pronounce *r* the same way an American does. But at least someone from France can distinguish between "craw" and "claw," which someone from Japan may not be able to do. The difference between *r* and *l* makes a difference in English and in French, but it doesn't in Japanese. In linguistics, we say that the difference between *r* and *l* is *phonemic* in English and French but not in Japanese; that is, *r* and *l* are phonemes in English and French but not in Japanese. A **phoneme** is a sound contrast that makes a difference, that differentiates meaning.

We find the phonemes in a given language by comparing *minimal pairs*, words that resemble each other in all but one sound. The words have totally different meanings, but they differ in just one sound. The contrasting sounds are therefore phonemes in that language. An example in English is the minimal pair *pit/bit*. These two words are distinguished by a single sound contrast between /p/ and /b/ (we enclose phonemes in slashes). Thus /p/ and /b/ are phonemes in English. Another example is the different vowel sound of *bit* and *beat* (see Figure 15.1). This contrast serves to distinguish these two words and the two vowel phonemes written /I/ and /i/ in English.

Standard (American) English (SE), the "region-free" dialect of TV network newscasters, has about 35 phonemes: at least 11 vowels and 24 consonants. The number of phonemes varies from language to language—from 15 to 60, averaging between 30 and 40. The number of phonemes also varies between dialects of a given language. In American English,

for example, vowel phonemes vary noticeably from dialect to dialect (see "Interesting Issues" on page 400). Readers should pronounce the words in Figure 15.1, paying attention to (or asking someone else) whether they distinguish each of the vowel sounds. Most Americans don't pronounce them all.

Phonetics is the study of speech sounds in general, what people actually say in various languages, like the differences in vowel pronunciation described in "Interesting Issues." **Phonemics** studies only the *significant* sound contrasts (phonemes) of a given language. In English, like /r/ and /l/ (remember *craw* and *claw*), /b/ and /v/ are also phonemes, occurring in minimal pairs like *bat* and *vat*. In Spanish, however, the contrast between [b] and [v] doesn't distinguish meaning, and they are therefore not phonemes (we enclose sounds that are not phonemic in brackets). Spanish speakers normally use the [b] sound to pronounce words spelled with either *b* or *v*.

In any language, a given phoneme extends over a phonetic range. In English, the phoneme /p/ ignores the phonetic contrast between the [pʰ] in *pin* and the [p] in *spin*. Most English speakers don't even notice that there is a phonetic difference. [pʰ] is aspirated, so that a puff of air follows the [p]. The [p] in *spin* is not. (To see the difference, light a match, hold it in front of your mouth, and watch the flame as you pronounce the two words.) The contrast between [pʰ] and [p] is phonemic in some languages, such as Hindi (spoken in India). That is, there are words whose meaning is distinguished only by the contrast between an aspirated and an unaspirated [p].

Native speakers vary in their pronunciation of certain phonemes, such as the /e/ phoneme discussed in "Interesting Issues." This variation is important in the evolution of language. With no shifts in pronunciation, there can be no linguistic change. The section on sociolinguistics below considers phonetic variation and its relationship to social divisions and the evolution of language.

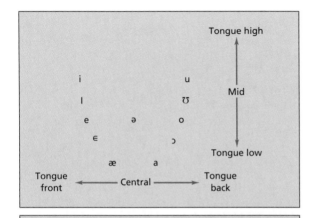

High front (spread)	[i]	as in *beat*
Lower high front (spread)	[I]	as in *bit*
Mid front (spread)	[e]	as in *bait*
Lower mid front (spread)	[ɛ]	as in *bet*
Low front	[æ]	as in *bat*
Central	[ə]	as in *butt*
Low back	[a]	as in *pot*
Lower mid back (rounded)	[ɔ]	as in *bought*
Mid back (rounded)	[o]	as in *boat*
Lower high back (rounded)	[ʊ]	as in *put*
High back (rounded)	[u]	as in *boot*

Figure 15.1 Vowel Phonemes in Standard American English

The phonemes are shown according to height of tongue and tongue position at front, center, or back of mouth. Phonetic symbols are identified by English words that include them; note that most are minimal pairs.

Source: Adaptation of excerpt and figure 2–1 from *Aspects of Language*, third edition, by Dwight Bollinger and Donald Sears, copyright © 1981 by Harcourt Brace Jovanovich, Inc., reprinted by permission of the publisher.

Language, Thought, and Culture

The well-known linguist Noam Chomsky (1955) has argued that the human brain contains a limited set of rules for organizing language, so that

Depending on where we live, Americans have certain stereotypes about how people in other regions talk. Some stereotypes, spread by the mass media, are more generalized than others. Most Americans think they can imitate a "southern accent." We also have nationwide stereotypes about speech in New York City (the pronunciation of *coffee*, for example) and Boston ("I pahked the kah in Hahvahd Yahd").

Many Americans also believe that midwesterners don't have accents. This belief stems from the fact that midwestern dialects don't have many stigmatized linguistic variants—speech patterns that people in other regions recognize and look down on, such as *r*lessness and *dem*, *dese*, and *dere* (instead of *them*, *these*, and *there*).

Actually, regional patterns influence the way all Americans speak. Midwesterners do have detectable accents. College students from out of state easily recognize that their in-state classmates speak differently. In-state students, however, have difficulty hearing their own speech peculiarities, because they are accustomed to them and view them as normal.

Far from having no accents, midwesterners, even in the same high school, exhibit linguistic variation (see Eckert 1989, 2000). Furthermore, dialect differences are immediately obvious to people, like myself, who come from other parts of the country. One of the best examples of variable midwestern pronunciation, involving vowels, is the /e/ phoneme, which occurs in words like *ten*, *rent*, *French*, *section*, *lecture*, *effect*, *best*, and *test*. In southeastern Michigan, where I live and teach, there are four different ways of pronouncing this phoneme. Speakers of Black English and immigrants from Appalachia often pronounce *ten* as *tin*, just as southerners habitually do. Some Michiganders say *ten*, the correct pronunciation in Standard English. However, two other pronunciations are more common. Instead of *ten*, many Michiganders say *tan*, or *tun* (as though they were using the word *ton*, a unit of weight).

My students often astound me with their pronunciation. One day I met one of my Michigan-raised teaching assistants in the hall. She was deliriously happy. When I asked why, she replied, "I've just had the best suction."

"What?" I said.

"I've just had a wonderful suction," she repeated.

"What?" I still wasn't understanding.

She finally spoke more precisely. "I've just had the best saction." She considered this a clearer pronunciation of the word *section*.

Another TA complimented me, "You luctured to great effuct today." After an exam, a student lamented that she hadn't been able to do her "bust on the tust." Once I lectured about uniformity in fast-food restaurant chains. One of my students had just vacationed in Hawaii, where, she told me, hamburger prices were higher than they were on the mainland. It was, she said, because of the runt. Who, I wondered, was this runt? The very puny owner of Honolulu's McDonald's franchise? Perhaps he advertised on television, "Come have a hamburger with the runt." Eventually I figured out that she was talking about the high cost of *rent* on those densely packed islands.

all languages have a common structural basis. (Chomsky calls this set of rules *universal grammar*.) The fact that people can learn foreign languages and that words and ideas can be translated from one language into another tends to support Chomsky's position that all humans have similar linguistic abilities and thought processes. Another line of support comes from creole languages. Such languages develop from pidgins, languages that form in situations of acculturation, when different societies come into contact and must devise a system of communication. As mentioned in the "Culture" chapter, pidgins based on English and native languages developed in the context of trade and colonialism in China, Papua New Guinea, and West Africa. Eventually, after generations of being spoken, pidgins may develop into *creole languages*. These are more mature languages, with developed grammatical rules and native speakers (that is, people who learn the language as their primary means of communication during enculturation). Creoles are spoken in several Caribbean societies. Gullah, which is spoken by African Americans on coastal islands in South Carolina and Georgia, is also a creole language. Supporting the idea that creoles are based on universal grammar is the fact that such languages all share certain features. Syntactically, all use particles (e.g., will, was) to form future and past tenses and multiple negation to deny or negate (e.g., he don't got none). Also, all form questions by changing inflection rather than by changing word order. For example, "You're going home for the holidays?" (with a rising tone at the end) rather than "Are you going home for the holidays?"

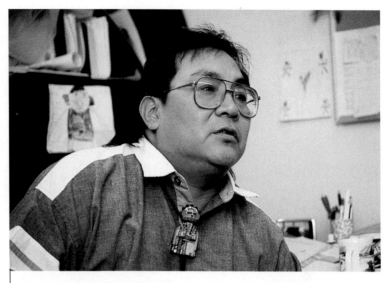

Shown here in 1995 is Leigh Jenkins, who was or is Director of Cultural Preservation for the Hopi tribal council. Would the Hopi language have to distinguish between *was* and *is* in that sentence?

THE SAPIR-WHORF HYPOTHESIS

Other linguists and anthropologists take a different approach to the relation between language and thought. Rather than seeking universal linguistic structures and processes, they believe that different languages produce different ways of thinking. This position is sometimes known as the **Sapir-Whorf hypothesis** after Edward Sapir (1931) and his student Benjamin Lee Whorf (1956), its prominent early advocates. Sapir and Whorf argued that the grammatical categories of different languages lead their speakers to think about things in particular ways. For example, the third-person singular pronouns of English (*he, she; him, her; his, hers*) distinguish gender, whereas those of the Palaung, a small tribe in Burma, do not (Burling 1970). Gender exists in English, although a fully developed noun-gender and adjective-agreement system, as in French and other Romance languages (*la belle fille, le beau fils*), does not. The Sapir-Whorf hypothesis therefore might suggest that English speakers can't help paying more attention to differences between males and females than do the Palaung and less than do French or Spanish speakers.

English divides time into past, present, and future. Hopi, a language of the Pueblo region of the Native American Southwest, does not. Rather, Hopi distinguishes between events that exist or have existed (what we use present and past to discuss) and those that don't or don't yet (our future events, along with imaginary and hypothetical events). Whorf argued that this difference leads Hopi speakers to think about time and reality in different ways than English speakers do. A similar example comes from Portuguese, which employs a future subjunctive verb form, introducing a degree of uncertainty into discussions of the future. In English, we routinely use the future tense to talk about something we think will happen. We don't feel the need to qualify "The sun'll come out tomorrow," by adding "if it doesn't go supernova." We don't hesitate to proclaim "I'll see you next year," even when we can't be absolutely sure we will. The Portuguese future subjunctive qualifies the future event, recognizing that the future can't be certain. Our way of expressing the future as certain is so ingrained that we don't even think about it, just as the Hopi don't see the need to distinguish between present and past, both of which are real, while the future remains hypothetical. It would seem, however, that language does not tightly restrict thought, because cultural changes can produce changes in thought and in language, as we shall see in the next section.

Olives, but what kinds? Undoubtedly the olive vendor has a more elaborate focal vocabulary for what he sells than you or I do.

FOCAL VOCABULARY

A lexicon (or vocabulary) is a language's dictionary, its set of names for things, events, and ideas. Lexicon influences perception. Thus, Eskimos have several distinct words for different types of snow that in English are all called *snow*. Most English speakers never notice the differences between these types of snow and might have trouble seeing them even if someone pointed them out. Eskimos recognize and think about differences in snow that English speakers don't see because our language provides us with just one word.

Similarly, the Nuer of Sudan have an elaborate vocabulary to describe cattle. Eskimos have several words for snow and Nuer have dozens for cattle because of their particular histories, economies, and environments (Brown 1958; Eastman 1975). When the need arises, English speakers also can elaborate their snow and cattle vocabularies. For example, skiers name varieties of snow with words that are missing from the lexicons of Florida retirees. Similarly, the cattle vocabulary of a Texas rancher is much more ample than that of a salesperson in a New York City department store. Such specialized sets of terms and distinctions that are particularly important to certain groups (those with particular foci of experience or activity) are known as **focal vocabulary**.

Vocabulary is the area of language that changes most readily. New words and distinctions, when needed, appear and spread. For example, who would have "faxed" or e-mailed anything a generation ago? Names for items get simpler as they become common and important. A television has become a *TV*, an automobile a *car*, and a videocassette recorder a *VCR*.

Language, culture, and thought are interrelated. However, and in opposition to the Sapir-Whorf hypothesis, it would be more reasonable to say that changes in culture produce changes in language and thought than the reverse. Consider differences between female and male Americans in regard to the color terms they use (Lakoff 1975). Distinctions implied by such terms as *salmon, rust, peach, beige, teal, mauve, cranberry,* and *dusky orange* aren't in the vocabularies of most American men. However, many of them weren't even in American women's lexicons 50 years ago. These changes reflect changes in American economy, society, and culture. Color terms and distinctions have increased with the growth of the fashion and cosmetic industries. A similar contrast (and growth) in Americans' lexicons shows up in football, basketball, and hockey vocabularies. Sports fans, more often males than females, use more terms in reference to, and make more elaborate distinctions between, the games they watch,

How would a hockey insider use focal vocabulary to describe the items shown in this photo? How would you describe them?

Table 15.2 **Focal Vocabulary for Hockey** Insiders have special terms for the major elements of the game.

Elements of Hockey	Insiders' Term
puck	biscuit
goal/net	pipes
penalty box	sin bin
hockey stick	twig
helmet	bucket
space between a goalie's leg pads	five hole

ceive. **Ethnosemantics** studies such classification systems in various languages. Well-studied ethnosemantic *domains* (sets of related things, perceptions, or concepts named in a language) include kinship terminology and color terminology. When we study such domains, we are examining how those people perceive and distinguish between kin relationships or colors. Other such domains include ethnomedicine—the terminology for the causes, symptoms, and cures of disease (Frake 1961); ethnobotany—native classification of plant life (Berlin, Breedlove, and Raven 1974; Conklin 1954); and ethnoastronomy (Goodenough 1953).

The ways in which people divide up the world—the contrasts they perceive as meaningful or significant—reflect their experiences. Anthropologists have discovered that certain lexical domains and vocabulary items evolve in a determined order. For example, after studying color terminology in more than 100 languages, Berlin and Kay (1991/1999) discovered 10 basic color terms: *white, black, red, yellow, blue, green, brown, pink, orange,* and *purple* (they evolved in more or less that order). The number of terms varied with cultural complexity. Representing one extreme were Papua New Guinea cultivators and Australian hunters and gatherers, who used only two basic terms, which translate as *black* and *white* or *dark* and *light*. At the other end of the continuum were European and Asian languages with all the color terms. Color terminology was most developed in areas with a history of using dyes and artificial coloring.

such as hockey (see Table 15.2). Thus, cultural contrasts and changes affect lexical distinctions (for instance, peach versus salmon) within semantic domains (for instance, color terminology). **Semantics** refers to a language's meaning system.

MEANING

Speakers of particular languages use sets of terms to organize, or categorize, their experiences and perceptions. Linguistic terms and contrasts encode (embody) differences in meaning that people per-

Sociolinguistics

No language is a uniform system in which everyone talks just like everyone else. Linguistic *performance* (what people actually say) is the concern of sociolinguists. The field of **sociolinguistics** investigates relationships between social and linguistic variation, or language in its social context (Eckert and Rickford 2001). How do different speakers use a given language? How do linguistic features correlate with social stratification, including class, ethnic, and gender differences (Tannen 1990, 1993)? How is language used to express, reinforce, or resist power (Geis 1987; Thomas 1999)?

Sociolinguists don't deny that the people who speak a given language share knowledge of its basic rules. Such common knowledge is the basis of mutually intelligible communication. However, sociolinguists focus on features that vary systematically with social position and situation. To study variation, sociolinguists must do field work. They must observe, define, and measure variable use of language in real-world situations. To show that linguistic features correlate with social, economic, and political differences, the social attributes of speakers also must be measured and related to speech (Fasold 1990; Labov 1972a; Trudgill 2000).

Variation within a language at a given time is historic change in progress. The same forces that, working gradually, have produced large-scale linguistic change over the centuries are still at work today. Linguistic change doesn't occur in a vacuum but in society. When new ways of speaking are associated with social factors, they are imitated, and they spread. In this way, a language changes.

LINGUISTIC DIVERSITY

See the Internet Exercises at your OLC for information on the extinction of languages

mhhe
com
/kottak

As an illustration of the linguistic variation that is encountered in all nations, consider the contemporary United States. Ethnic diversity is revealed by the fact that millions of Americans learn first languages other than English. Spanish is the most common. Most of those people eventually become bilinguals, adding English as a second language. In many multilingual (including colonized) nations, people use two languages on different occasions: one in the home, for example, and the other on the job or in public.

Whether bilingual or not, we all vary our speech in different contexts; we engage in **style shifts** (see Eckert and Rickford, eds. 2001). In certain parts of Europe, people regularly switch dialects. This phenomenon, known as **diglossia**, applies to "high" and "low" variants of the same language, for example, in German and Flemish (spoken in Belgium). People employ the "high" variant at universities and in writing, professions, and the mass media. They use the "low" variant for ordinary conversation with family members and friends.

Just as social situations influence our speech, so do geographic, cultural, and socioeconomic differences. Many dialects coexist in the United States with Standard (American) English (SE). SE itself is a dialect that differs, say, from "BBC English," which is the preferred dialect in Great Britain. According to the principle of *linguistic relativity*, all dialects are equally effective as systems of communication, which is language's main job. Our tendency to think of particular dialects as cruder or more sophisticated than others is a social rather than a linguistic judgment. We rank certain speech patterns as better or worse because we recognize that they are used by groups that we also rank. People who say *dese*, *dem*, and *dere* instead of *these*, *them*, and *there* communicate perfectly well with anyone who recognizes that the *d* sound systematically replaces the *th* sound in their speech. However, this form of speech has become an indicator of low social rank. We call it, like the use of *ain't*, "uneducated speech." The use of *dem*, *dese*, and *dere* is one of many phonological differences that Americans recognize and look down on.

GENDER SPEECH CONTRASTS

Comparing men and women, there are differences in phonology, grammar, and vocabulary, as well as in the body stances and movements that accompany speech (Baron 1986; Eckert and McConnell-Ginet 2003; Tannen 1990). In phonology, American women tend to pronounce their vowels more peripherally ("rant," "rint"), whereas men tend to pronounce theirs more centrally ("runt"—in all cases when saying the word "rent"). In public contexts, Japanese women tend to adopt an artificially high voice, for the sake of politeness, according to their traditional culture (Kristof 1995). In North America and Great Britain, women's speech tends to be more similar to the standard dialect than men's is. Consider the data in Table 15.3, gathered in Detroit. In all social classes, but particularly in the working class, men were more apt to use double negatives (e.g., "I don't want none"). Women tend to be more careful about "uneducated speech." This trend shows up in both the United States and England. Men may adopt working-class speech because they associate it with masculinity. Perhaps women pay more attention to the media, where standard dialects are employed.

According to Robin Lakoff (1975), the use of certain types of words and expressions has been

Table 15.3   Multiple Negation ("I don't want none") According to Gender and Class (in Percentages)

	Upper Middle Class	Lower Middle Class	Upper Working Class	Lower Working Class
Male	6.3	32.4	40.0	90.1
Female	0.0	1.4	35.6	58.9

Source: From *Sociolinguistics: An Introduction to Language and Society* by Peter Trudgill (London: Pelican Books, 1974, revised edition 1983), p. 85, copyright © Peter Trudgill, 1974, 1983. Reproduced by permission of Penguin Books Ltd.

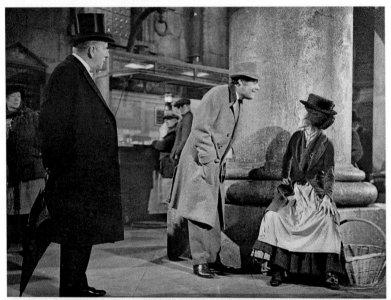

Certain dialects are stigmatized, not because of actual linguistic deficiencies, but because of a symbolic association between a certain way of talking and low social status. In this scene from *My Fair Lady*, Professor Henry Higgins (Rex Harrison) encounters Eliza Doolittle (Audrey Hepburn), a Cockney flower girl. Higgins will teach Doolittle how to speak like an English aristocrat.

likely to use such adjectives as *adorable*, *charming*, *sweet*, *cute*, *lovely*, and *divine* than men are.

Let's return to the previously discussed domains of sports and color terminology for additional illustration of differences in lexical (vocabulary) distinctions that men and women make. Men typically know more terms related to sports, make more distinctions among them (e.g., runs versus points), and try to use the terms more precisely than women do. Correspondingly, influenced more by the fashion and cosmetics industries than men are, women use more color terms and attempt to use them more specifically than men do. Thus, when I lecture on sociolinguistics, and to make this point, I bring an off-purple shirt to class. Holding it up, I first ask women to say aloud what color the shirt is. The women rarely answer with a uniform voice, as they try to distinguish the actual shade (mauve, lilac, lavender, wisteria, or some other purplish hue). I then ask the men, who consistently answer as one, "PURPLE." Rare is the man who on the spur of the moment can imagine the difference between *fuchsia* and *magenta* or *grape* and *aubergine*.

associated with women's traditional lesser power in American society (see also Coates 1986; Tannen 1990). For example, *Oh dear*, *Oh fudge*, and *Goodness!* are less forceful than *Hell* and *Damn*. Men's customary use of "forceful" words reflects their traditional public power and presence. Watch the lips of a disgruntled athlete in a televised competition, such as a football game. What's the likelihood he's saying "Phooey on you"? Women are more

Understanding Ourselves   How does gender help us understand differences in communication styles? Differences in the linguistic strategies and behavior of men and women are examined in several books by the well-known sociolinguist Deborah Tannen (1990, 1993). Tannen (1990) uses the terms "rapport" and "report" to contrast women's and men's overall linguistic styles. Women, says Tannen, typically use language and the body movements that accompany it to build rapport, social connections with others. Men, on the other hand, tend to make reports, reciting information that serves to establish a place for themselves in a hierarchy, as they also attempt to determine the relative ranks of their conversation mates.

STRATIFICATION

We use and evaluate speech in the context of *extralinguistic* forces—social, political, and economic. Mainstream Americans evaluate the speech of low-status groups negatively, calling it "uneducated." This is not because these ways of speaking are bad in themselves but because they have come to symbolize low status. Consider variation in the pronunciation of *r*. In some parts of the United States, *r* is regularly pronounced, and in other (*r*less) areas, it is not. Originally, American *r*less speech was modeled on the fashionable speech of England. Because of its prestige, *r*lessness was adopted in many areas and continues as the norm around Boston and in the South.

A debutante ball at the Hotel de Crillon in Paris, France. See the movie *Metropolitan* for an illustration of how American debutantes, and their male escorts, talk. From your own experience, can you think of ways in which language varies with social class?

New Yorkers sought prestige by dropping their *r*'s in the 19th century, after having pronounced them in the 18th. However, contemporary New Yorkers are going back to the 18th-century pattern of pronouncing *r*'s. What matters, and what governs linguistic change, is not the reverberation of a strong midwestern *r* but *social* evaluation, whether *r*'s happen to be "in" or "out."

Studies of *r* pronunciation in New York City have clarified the mechanisms of phonological change. William Labov (1972*b*) focused on whether *r* was pronounced after vowels in such words as *car*, *floor*, *card*, and *fourth*. To get data on how this linguistic variation correlated with social class, he used a series of rapid encounters with employees in three New York City department stores, each of whose prices and locations attracted a different socioeconomic group. Saks Fifth Avenue (68 encounters) catered to the upper middle class, Macy's (125) attracted middle-class shoppers, and S. Klein's (71) had predominantly lower-middle-class and working-class customers. The class origins of store personnel tended to reflect those of their customers.

Having already determined that a certain department was on the fourth floor, Labov approached ground-floor salespeople and asked where that department was. After the salesperson had answered, "Fourth floor," Labov repeated his "Where?" in order to get a second response. The second reply was more formal and emphatic, the salesperson presumably thinking that Labov hadn't heard or understood the first answer. For each salesperson, therefore, Labov had two samples of /r/ pronunciation in two words.

Labov calculated the percentages of workers who pronounced /r/ at least once during the interview. These were 62 percent at Saks, 51 percent at Macy's, but only 20 percent at S. Klein's. He also found that personnel on upper floors, where he asked "What floor is this?" (and where more expensive items were sold), pronounced /r/ more often than ground-floor salespeople did.

In Labov's study, summarized in Table 15.4, r pronunciation was clearly associated with prestige. Certainly the job interviewers who had hired the salespeople never counted r's before offering employment. However, they did use speech evaluations to make judgments about how effective

Table 15.4 Pronunciation of *r* in New York City Department Stores		
Store	Number of Encounters	% *r* Pronunciation
Saks Fifth Avenue	68	62
Macy's	125	51
S. Klein's	71	20

certain people would be in selling particular kinds of merchandise. In other words, they practiced sociolinguistic discrimination, using linguistic features in deciding who got certain jobs.

Our speech habits help determine our access to employment and other material resources. Because of this, "proper language" itself becomes a strategic resource—and a path to wealth, prestige, and power (Gal 1989). Illustrating this, many ethnographers have described the importance of verbal skill and oratory in politics (Beeman 1986; Bloch, 1975; Brenneis 1988; Geis 1987). Ronald Reagan, known as a "great communicator," dominated American society in the 1980s as a two-term president. Another twice-elected president, Bill Clinton, despite his southern accent, was known for his verbal skills in certain contexts (e.g., televised debates and town-hall meetings). Communications flaws may have helped doom the presidencies of Gerald Ford, Jimmy Carter, and George Bush (the elder) ("Couldn't do that; wouldn't be prudent.").

The French anthropologist Pierre Bourdieu views linguistic practices as *symbolic capital* that properly trained people may convert into economic and social capital. The value of a dialect—its standing in a "linguistic market"—depends on the extent to which it provides access to desired positions in the labor market. In turn, this reflects its legitimacy by formal institutions: educational institutions state, church, and prestige media. Even people who don't use the prestige dialect accept its authority and correctness, its "symbolic domination" (Bourdieu 1982, 1984). Thus, linguistic forms, which lack power in themselves, take on the power of the groups they symbolize. The education system, however (defending its own worth), denies this, misrepresenting prestige speech as being inherently better. The linguistic insecurity often felt by lower-class and minority speakers is a result of this symbolic domination.

BLACK ENGLISH VERNACULAR (BEV), A.K.A. "EBONICS"

No one pays much attention when someone says "runt" instead of "rent." But some nonstandard speech carries more of a stigma. Sometimes stigmatized speech is linked to region, class, or educational background; sometimes it is associated with ethnicity or "race."

A national debate involving language, race, and education was triggered by a vote on December 18, 1996, by the Oakland, California, school board. The board unanimously declared that many black students did not speak Standard English but instead spoke a distinct language called "ebonics" (from "ebony" and "phonics"), with roots in West African languages. Soon disputing this claim were the poet Maya Angelou, the Reverend Jesse Jackson, and the Clinton administration, along with virtually all professional linguists, who see ebonics as a dialect of English rather than a separate language. Linguists call ebonics BEV (Black English Vernacular) or AAEV (African-American English Vernacular) (Rickford 1999; Rickford and Rickford 2000).

Some saw the Oakland resolution as a ploy designed to permit the school district to increase its access to federal funds available for bilingual programs for Hispanic and Asian students. According to federal law, Black English is not a separate language eligible for Title 7 funds. Funds for bilingual education (itself a controversial issue, especially in California politics) have been available to support the education of immigrant students (Golden 1997). Some educators have argued that similar support should be available to blacks. If ebonics were accepted as a foreign language, teachers could receive merit pay for studying Black English and for using their knowledge of it in their lessons (Applebome 1996).

Early in 1997, responding to the widespread negative reaction to its original resolution, the Oakland educational task force proposed a new resolution. This one required only the recognition

Rap and hip-hop music weave BEV into musical expression. Here rapster Ludacris and his "posse" arrive at the Source Hip Hop Music Awards in Miami, Florida, in August 2001.

of language differences among black students, in order to improve their proficiency in English. School officials emphasized that they had never intended to teach black students in ebonics. They just sought to employ some of the same tools used with students brought up speaking a foreign language to help black students improve their English-language skills. The Oakland school board planned to expand its 10-year-old pilot program for black students, which taught the phonetic and grammatical differences between Standard English and what the students spoke outside the classroom (Golden 1997).

Linguists view ebonics as a dialect rather than a separate language, and they more often trace its roots to southern English than to Africa. Still, most linguists see nothing wrong with the Oakland schools' goal of understanding the speech patterns of black students and respecting that speech while teaching Standard English. Indeed, this is policy and teaching strategy in many American school districts. The Linguistic Society of America (LSA) considers ebonics or Black English to be "systematic and rule-governed" (Appleborne 1997).

What about ebonics as a linguistic system? William Labov and several associates, both white and black, have conducted detailed studies of what they call **Black English Vernacular (BEV)**. (*Vernacular* means ordinary, casual speech.) BEV is the "relatively uniform dialect spoken by the majority of black youth in most parts of the United

States today, especially in the inner city areas of New York, Boston, Detroit, Philadelphia, Washington, Cleveland, . . . and other urban centers. It is also spoken in most rural areas and used in the casual, intimate speech of many adults" (Labov 1972*a*, p. xiii).

BEV isn't an ungrammatical hodgepodge. Rather, BEV is a complex linguistic system with its own rules, which linguists have described. The phonology and syntax of BEV are similar to those of southern dialects. This reflects generations of contact between southern whites and blacks, with mutual influence on each other's speech patterns. Many features that distinguish BEV from SE (Standard English) also show up in southern white speech, but less frequently than in BEV.

Linguists disagree about exactly how BEV originated (Rickford 1997). Smitherman (1977) calls it an Africanized form of English reflecting both an African heritage and the conditions of servitude, oppression, and life in America. She notes certain structural similarities between West African languages and BEV. African linguistic backgrounds no doubt influenced how early African Americans learned English. Did they restructure English to fit African linguistic patterns? Or did they quickly learn English from whites, with little continuing influence from the African linguistic heritage? Or, possibly, in acquiring English, did African slaves fuse English with African languages to make a pidgin or creole, which influenced the subsequent development of BEV? Creole speech may have been brought to the American colonies by the many slaves who were imported from the Caribbean during the 17th and 18th centuries. Some slaves may even have learned, while still in Africa, the pidgins or creoles spoken in West African trading forts (Rickford 1997).

Origins aside, there are phonological and grammatical differences between BEV and SE. One phonological difference between BEV and SE is that BEV speakers are less likely to pronounce *r* than SE speakers are. Actually, many SE speakers don't pronounce *r*'s that come right before a consonant (ca*r*d) or at the end of a word (car). But SE speakers do usually pronounce an *r* that comes right before a vowel, either at the end of a word (fou*r* o'clock) or within a word (Ca*r*ol). BEV speakers, by contrast, are much more likely to omit such intervocalic (between vowels) *r*'s. The result is that speakers of the two dialects have different *homonyms* (words that sound the same but have different meanings). BEV speakers who don't pronounce intervocalic *r*'s have the following homonyms: Carol/Cal; Paris/pass.

Observing different phonological rules, BEV speakers pronounce certain words differently than SE speakers do. Particularly in the elementary school context, where the furor over ebonics has raged, the homonyms of BEV-speaking students typically differ from those of their SE-speaking teachers. To evaluate reading accuracy, teachers should determine whether students are recognizing the different meanings of such BEV homonyms as *passed*, *past*, and *pass*. Teachers need to make sure students understand what they are reading, which is probably more important than whether they are pronouncing words correctly according to the SE norm.

The phonological contrasts between BEV and SE speakers often have grammatical consequences. One of these is *copula deletion*, which means the absence of SE forms of the copula—the verb *to be*. For example, SE and BEV may contrast as follows:

SE	SE Contraction	BEV
you are tired	you're tired	you tired
he is tired	he's tired	he tired
we are tired	we're tired	we tired
they are tired	they're tired	they tired

In its deletion of the present tense of the verb *to be*, BEV is similar to many languages, including Russian, Hungarian, and Hebrew. BEV's copula deletion is simply a grammatical result of its phonological rules. Notice that BEV deletes the copula where SE has contractions. BEV's phonological rules dictate that *r*'s (as in *you're*, *we're*, and *they're*) and word-final *s*'s (as in *he's*) be dropped. However, BEV speakers do pronounce *m*, so that the BEV first-per-

son singular is "I'm tired," just as in SE. Thus, when BEV omits the copula, it merely carries contraction one step further, as a result of its phonological rules.

Also, phonological rules may lead BEV speakers to omit *-ed* as a past-tense marker and *-s* as a marker of plurality. However, other speech contexts demonstrate that BEV speakers do understand the difference between past and present verbs, and between singular and plural nouns. Confirming this are irregular verbs (e.g., *tell*, *told*) and irregular plurals (e.g., *child*, *children*), in which BEV works the same as SE.

SE is not superior to BEV as a linguistic system, but it does happen to be the prestige dialect—the one used in the mass media, in writing, and in most public and professional contexts. SE is the dialect that has the most "symbolic capital." In areas of Germany where there is diglossia, speakers of Plattdeusch (Low German) learn the High German dialect to communicate appropriately in the national context. Similarly, upwardly mobile BEV-speaking students learn SE.

Historical Linguistics

Sociolinguists study contemporary variation in speech—language change in progress. **Historical linguistics** deals with longer-term change. Historical linguists can reconstruct many features of past languages by studying contemporary **daughter languages**. These are languages that descend from the same parent language and that have been changing separately for hundreds or even thousands of years. We call the original language from which they diverge the **protolanguage**. Romance languages such as French and Spanish, for example, are daughter languages of Latin, their common protolanguage. German, English, Dutch, and the Scandinavian languages are daughter languages of proto-Germanic. Historical linguists classify languages according to their degree of relationship (see Figure 15.2).

Interpret the World Look at Map 15, "World Languages," in your atlas. Map 15 shows major global language families with predominant subfamilies also indicated. Thus the Germanic language family, which contains Eng-

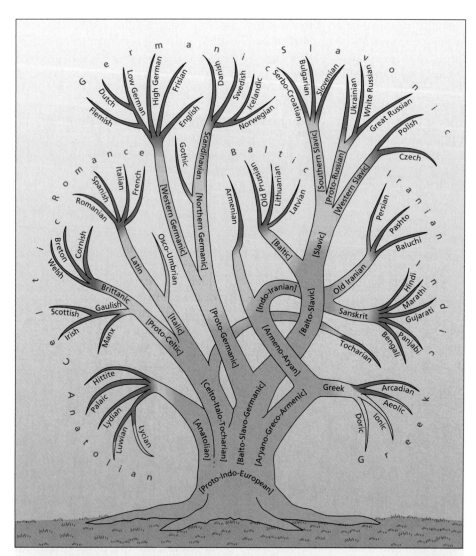

Figure 15.2   PIE Family Tree.

This is a family tree of the Indo-European languages. All can be traced back to a protolanguage, Proto-Indo-European (PIE), spoken more than 6,000 years ago. PIE split into dialects that eventually evolved into separate languages, which, in turn, evolved into languages such as Latin and proto-Germanic, which are ancestral to dozens of modern daughter languages. To what branch—Germanic, Romance, Slavonic—does your parents' native language(s) belong? How about English? What are the closest linguistic relatives of English (i.e., its sister languages)?

lish, Dutch, and German, is itself a member of the larger Indo-European language family. The Romance languages and the Germanic languages all belong to the Indo-European language family. Their common protolanguage is called PIE, Proto-Indo-European. Which language family spans the largest number of continents?

For more on PIE, see the Virtual Exploration

**mhhe
●com
/kottak**

Language changes over time. It evolves—varies, spreads, divides into **subgroups** (languages within a taxonomy of related languages that are most closely related). Dialects of a single parent language become distinct daughter languages, especially if they

Beyond the *Classroom*
Cybercommunication in Collegespace

Background Information

STUDENT:	Jason A. DeCaro
SUPERVISING PROFESSOR:	Robert Herbert
SCHOOL:	State University of New York at Binghamton
YEAR IN SCHOOL/MAJOR:	Senior/Anthropology and Biochemistry dual major
FUTURE PLANS:	Ph.D. in Biological Anthropology; career in academics or public health
PROJECT TITLE:	Cybercommunication in Collegespace: The Electronic/ Personal Juncture in a Campus Living Community

How is on-line communication related to face-to-face communication and to social interaction? On the basis of this research, is electronic communication good or bad for community formation?

Why do people who live in face-to-face proximity communicate using their computers? What is the interaction between their social lives "on-" and "off-line"? How does this affect their sense of community? I conducted research to address these questions through an anthropological case study.

The Internet has been interpreted as personalizing or depersonalizing, as highly democratic or merely chaotic, and as vitalizing or damaging to American "community." Some theorists suppose that electronic communication extends the pool of individuals with whom one maintains contact. However, others suggest that this merely creates an electronic "pseudocommunity" with shifting membership and superficial social ties. If this "pseudocommunity" competes for members' time and energy, it may be detrimental to their face-to-face interaction. Despite the active theoretical debate, very few studies have examined the interaction between electronic and face-to-face community in a geographically local group of individuals.

I observed a group of students of mixed gender who live in close proximity on a college campus. These students chose their living arrangement on the basis of common interest in computers, robotics, and engineering. Not all are computer scientists; some pursue majors such as creative writing and chemistry. Roughly a dozen alumni, some of whom no longer live in the local area, remain integral to the organization.

I am an alumnus; thus, I have a personal as well as a professional interest. One of my most challenging jobs was to avoid unintentional manipulation—even distancing myself from the group would have changed it! Yet, by remaining an "insider," I received tremendous access, and had a great deal of fun.

Members maintain face-to-face social activity and a busy electronic mailing list. The "real" and "virtual" communities thus created have overlapping but nonidentical membership. Most members who communicate exclusively within the "virtual" electronic domain are alumni. Students vary with respect to the form of communication that they favor. A few shun the electronic medium entirely and thereby opt out of the "virtual" community.

I distributed questionnaires, analyzed one year's mailing list traffic, and remained a participant in face-to-face social life. I found that conversations sometimes flow on and off the mailing list, and members do organize face-to-face social activities on-line. However, most people segregate the electronic and face-to-face domains, and most messages serve no explicit organizational purpose. Messages in this latter category allow contact between people who are not local, or strengthen bonds between individuals who see each other regularly.

Those who dedicate considerable time and energy to the virtual community put the mailing list to its widest range of uses. However, there is little evidence that electronic communication detracts from face-to-face interaction. Most people who are highly social on-line are highly social off-line as well. I suspect that individuals supplement, rather than replace, their face-to-face social lives with electronic communication. This is particularly valuable to those who do not live locally, or are less than comfortable with face-to-face communication. Thus, on the whole, members are integrated far more than they are alienated by the mailing list.

are isolated from one another. Some of them split, and new "granddaughter" languages develop. If people remain in the ancestral homeland, their speech patterns also change. The evolving speech in the ancestral homeland should be considered a daughter language like the others.

A close relationship between languages does not necessarily mean that their speakers are closely related biologically or culturally, because people can adopt new languages. In the equatorial forests of Africa, "pygmy" hunters have discarded their ancestral languages and now speak those of the cultivators who have migrated to the area. Immigrants to the United States and Canada spoke many different languages on arrival, but their descendants now speak fluent English.

Knowledge of linguistic relationships is often valuable to anthropologists interested in history, particularly events during the past 5,000 years. Cultural features may (or may not) correlate with the distribution of language families. Groups that speak related languages may (or may not) be more culturally similar to each other than they are to groups whose speech derives from different linguistic ancestors. Of course, cultural similarities aren't limited to speakers of related languages. Even groups whose members speak unrelated languages have contact through trade, intermarriage, and warfare. Ideas and inventions diffuse widely among human groups. Many items of vocabulary in contemporary English come from French. Even without written documentation of France's influence after the Norman Conquest of England in

The Book of Kells, an illustrated manuscript, was created at Kells, the ancient Irish monastery shown here. The book, which now resides in the Trinity College library in Dublin, Ireland, is displayed here on a laptop computer. Such documents provide historical linguists with information on how languages change.

1066, linguistic evidence in contemporary English would reveal a long period of important firsthand contact with France. Similarly, linguistic evidence may confirm cultural contact and borrowing when written history is lacking. By considering which words have been borrowed, we also can make inferences about the nature of the contact.

SUMMARY

1. Wild primates use call systems to communicate. Environmental stimuli trigger calls, which cannot be combined when multiple stimuli are present. Contrasts between language and call systems include displacement, productivity, and cultural transmission. Over time, our ancestral call systems grew too complex for genetic transmission, and hominid communication began to rely on learning. Humans still use nonverbal communication, such as facial expressions, gestures, and body stances and movements. But language is the main system humans use to communicate. Chimps and gorillas can understand and manipulate nonverbal symbols based on language.

2. No language uses all the sounds the human vocal tract can make. Phonology—the study of speech sounds—focuses on sound contrasts (phonemes) that distinguish meaning. The grammars and lexicons of particular languages can lead their speakers to perceive and think in certain ways. Studies of domains such as kinship, color terminologies, and pronouns show that speakers of different languages categorize their experiences differently.

3. Linguistic anthropologists share anthropology's general interest in diversity in time and space. Sociolinguistics investigates relationships between social and linguistic variation by focusing on the actual use of language. Only when features

of speech acquire social meaning are they imitated. If they are valued, they will spread. People vary their speech, shifting styles, dialects, and languages. As linguistic systems, all languages and dialects are equally complex, rule-governed, and effective for communication. However, speech is used, is evaluated, and changes in the context of political, economic, and social forces. Often the linguistic traits of a low-status group are negatively evaluated. This devaluation is not because of *linguistic* features per se. Rather, it reflects the association of such features with low *social* status. One dialect, supported by the dominant institutions of the state, exercises symbolic domination over the others.

4. Historical linguistics is useful for anthropologists interested in historic relationships among populations. Cultural similarities and differences often correlate with linguistic ones. Linguistic clues can suggest past contacts between cultures. Related languages—members of the same language family—descend from an original proto-language. Relationships between languages don't necessarily mean that there are biological ties between their speakers, because people can learn new languages.

KEY TERMS

See the flash cards

mhhe
com
/kottak

Black English Vernacular (BEV) A rule-governed dialect of American English with roots in southern English. BEV is spoken by African-American youth and by many adults in their casual, intimate speech—sometimes called "ebonics."

call systems Systems of communication among nonhuman primates, composed of a limited number of sounds that vary in intensity and duration. Tied to environmental stimuli.

cultural transmission A basic feature of language; transmission through learning.

daughter languages Languages developing out of the same parent language; for example, French and Spanish are daughter languages of Latin.

diglossia The existence of "high" (formal) and "low" (informal, familial) dialects of a single language, such as German.

displacement A basic feature of language; the ability to speak of things and events that are not present.

ethnosemantics The study of lexical (vocabulary) contrasts and classifications in various languages.

focal vocabulary A set of words and distinctions that are particularly important to certain groups (those with particular foci of experience or activity), such as types of snow to Eskimos or skiers.

historical linguistics Subdivision of linguistics that studies languages over time.

kinesics The study of communication through body movements, stances, gestures, and facial expressions.

language Human beings' primary means of communication; may be spoken or written; features productivity and displacement and is culturally transmitted.

lexicon Vocabulary; a dictionary containing all the morphemes in a language and their meanings.

morphology The study of form; used in linguistics (the study of morphemes and word construction) and for form in general—for example, biomorphology relates to physical form.

phoneme Significant sound contrast in a language that serves to distinguish meaning, as in minimal pairs.

phonemics The study of the sound contrasts (phonemes) of a particular language.

phonetics The study of speech sounds in general; what people actually say in various languages.

phonology The study of sounds used in speech.

productivity A basic feature of language; the ability to use the rules of one's language to create new expressions comprehensible to other speakers.

protolanguage   Language ancestral to several daughter languages.

Sapir-Whorf hypothesis   Theory that different languages produce different ways of thinking.

semantics   A language's meaning system.

sociolinguistics   Study of relationships between social and linguistic variation; study of language (performance) in its social context.

style shifts   Variations in speech in different contexts.

subgroups   Languages within a taxonomy of related languages that are most closely related.

syntax   The arrangement and order of words in phrases and sentences.

For more self testing, see the self quizzes

mhhe
●**com**
/kottak

CRITICAL THINKING QUESTIONS

1. Based on your own knowledge of one or more languages, can you think of additional examples of ways in which language can influence perception and thought?

2. Give some additional examples of nonverbal communication. Check out your classmates during a discussion and see what examples you notice.

3. During a class discussion, what examples do you notice of sociolinguistic variation—say, between men and women, the professor and students, and so forth?

4. List some stereotypes about how different sorts of people speak. Are those real differences, or just stereotypes? Are the stereotypes positive or negative? Why do you think those stereotypes exist?

5. Based on your own experience and observations, list five ways in which young children and adults differ in their communication styles. Now classify these differences as kinesic, phonological, grammatical, lexical—or other.

6. Based on your own experience and observations, list five ways in which men and women differ in their use of language. Now classify these differences as kinesic, phonological, grammatical, lexical—or other.

7. What can historical linguistics tell us about history?

8. Do you agree with the principle of linguistic relativity? If not, why not? What dialects and languages do you speak? Do you tend to use different dialects, languages, or speech styles in different contexts? Why?

9. How do you use cyberspace? Jot down and try to categorize the places you visit via computer in a given week. Does use of the computer make you feel less or more isolated from other people?

Atlas Questions

Look at Map 15, "World Languages."

1. Name three language families or subfamilies that are spoken on more than one continent. How do you explain this distribution?

2. Where are the Austronesian languages spoken? How might one explain this distribution?

3. What language families are spoken on the African continent? Locate the Niger-Congo language family, of which the Bantu languages comprise a subfamily.

Suggested Additional Readings

Baron, D.

1986   *Grammar and Gender*. New Haven, CT: Yale University Press. Differences in grammatical patterns and strategies of men and women.

Bonvillain, N.

2003   *Language, Culture, and Communication: The Meaning of Messages*, 4th ed. Upper Saddle River, NJ: Prentice-Hall. Up-to-date text on language and communication in cultural context.

Downes, W.

1998   *Language and Society*, 2nd ed. New York: Cambridge University Press.

Eckert, P.

2000   *Linguistic Variation as Social Practice: The Linguistic Construction of Identity in Belten High*. Malden, MA: Blackwell. How speech correlates with high school social networks and cliques.

Eckert, P., and S. McConnell-Ginet

2003   *Language and Gender*. New York: Cambridge University Press. The sociolinguistics of male and female speech.

Eckert, P., and J. R. Rickford, eds.

2001   *Style and Sociolinguistic Variation*. New York: Cambridge University Press. The social context of style shifts.

Fasold, R. W.

1990   *The Sociolinguistics of Language*. Oxford: Basil Blackwell. Recent text with up-to-date examples.

Foley, W. A.

1997   *Anthroplogical Linguistics: An Introduction*. Cambridge, MA: Blackwell Publishers. Language, society, and culture.

Fouts, R.

1997   *Next of Kin: What Chimpanzees Have Taught Me about Who We Are*. New York, William Morrow. A teacher of Washoe, Lucy, and other signing chimps tells what he's learned from them.

Geis, M. L.

1987   *The Language of Politics*. New York: Springer-Verlag. Thorough examination of political uses of speech and oratory and the manipulation of language in power relations.

Gumperz, J., and S. C. Levinson, eds.

1996   *Rethinking Linguistic Relativity*. New York: Cambridge University Press. Essays on thought and thinking, language and culture.

Hanks, W. F.

1996   *Language and Communicative Practices*. Boulder, CO: Westview. The nature and role of language in communication and society.

Lakoff, R.

1975   *Language and Woman's Place*. New York: Harper & Row. Influential nontechnical discussion of how women use and are treated in Standard American English.

2000   *Language War*. Berkeley: University of California Press. Politics and language in the United States today.

Rickford, J. R.

1999   *African American Vernacular English: Features, Evolution, Educational Implications*. Malden, MA: Blackwell. An introduction to BEV and its social significance.

Rickford, J. R., and R. J. Rickford

2000   *Spoken Soul: The Story of Black English*. New York: Wiley. Readable account of the history and social meaning of BEV.

Romaine, S.

1999   *Communicating Gender*. Mahwah, NJ: L. Erlbaum Associates, 1999 Gender and language.

2000   *Language in Society: An Introduction to Sociolinguistics*, 2nd ed. New York: Oxford University Press. An introduction to sociolinguistics.

Salzmann, Z.

1998   *Language, Culture, and Society: An Introduction to Linguistic Anthropology*, 2nd ed. Boulder, CO: Westview. The function of language in culture and society.

Tannen, D.

1990   *You Just Don't Understand: Women and Men in Conversation*. New York: Ballantine. Popular book on gender differences in speech and conversational styles.

Tannen, D., ed.

1993   *Gender and Conversational Interaction*. New York: Oxford University Press. Twelve papers about conversational interaction illustrate the complexity of the relationship between gender and language use.

Thomas, L., and S. Wareing, eds.

1999   *Language, Society and Power*. New York: Routledge. Political dimensions and use of language.

Trudgill, P.

2000   *Sociolinguistics: An Introduction to Language and Society*, 4th ed. New York: Penguin. Readable short introduction to the role and use of language in society.

INTERNET EXERCISES

1. *Politeness Strategies*: Go and read Cyndi Patee's article "Linguistic Politeness Strategies," **http://logos.uoregon.edu/explore/socioling/politeness.html.**

   a. What kind of strategy do you most often use? Do your strategies change when you are talking to different people (i.e., your friend, your parent, your professor)?

   b. What kind of politeness strategy do you like other people to use with you? Would you prefer people to sacrifice politeness for directness?

   c. Pay attention to what politeness strategies are being used around you in class, at home, and with friends. Can you identify any patterns in the way people select politeness strategies?

2. Urban Legends: Read the Urban Legends information page at About.com, **http://urbanlegends. about.com/science/urbanlegends/library/weekly/aa082497.htm.** Make sure to read some of the examples of urban legends that are provided.

   a. What constitutes an urban legend?

   b. Why are urban legends so popular? Many of them are not true, so why do they continue to be shared?

   c. What role does the Internet play in propagating urban legends?

   d. After reading this page, are you going to be more or less skeptical the next time a friend relates a story to you?

See Chapter 15 at your McGraw-Hill Online Learning Center for additional review and interactive exercises.

BRINGING IT ALL TOGETHER

See your OLC Bringing It All Together links

mhhe
com
/kottak

Canada: Unity and Diversity in Culture and Language

There are levels of culture, as was pointed out in the chapter "Culture." National culture consists of the beliefs, values, behavior patterns, and institutions that people share through growing up in a given nation. Cultures also can be smaller than nations. Such "subcultures" may originate in region, ethnicity, language, class, or religion. Thus, the religious backgrounds of American Jews, Baptists, Roman Catholics, and Muslims create subcultural differences among them. French-speaking Canadians contrast with English-speaking people in the same country.

Studying a modern nation, anthropologists may focus on either unity or diversity—on what is common or what is different. A focus on unity would examine themes, values, behavior, institutions, and experiences that transcend regions and social divisions. A focus on diversity would look at the cultures within the national culture.

The two approaches shouldn't be mutually exclusive. Despite diversity, we can still detect a series of nationally relevant institutions, norms, and expectations. As we saw in the chapter "Ethnicity," the pressure on members of an ethnic group to observe a set of common national values comes not only from the national culture, but also from other ethnic groups. We saw, for example, that African Americans in Los Angeles, after that city's 1992 riots, complained about their Korean neighbors. In doing so they referred to such general American values as openness, mutual respect, community participation, and "fair play." They saw their Korean neighbors as deficient in these traits. The Koreans countered by stressing another set of American national values, involving education, family unity, discipline, hard work, and achievement.

We focus now on unity and diversity in Canada. (American national culture is examined in the appendix.) One key feature of Canadian national consciousness is the contrast with the United States. Canadians, when traveling internationally, often are taken for Americans, which emphatically they are not. To be sure, Canada and the United States share many cultural traits. Some reflect the shared English-language heritage of most Canadians and Americans. Some reflect common experiences in the colonization of North America. Still others reflect participation in a global system, or diffusion of products and information across porous borders.

The media, especially television, have helped bring nationalism and its symbols, including cultural contrasts with the United States, to prominence in Canada. In spring 2000, a TV commercial produced in Toronto for Molson Canadian beer gained instantaneous national prominence. The ad featured the character Joe Canadian, delivering what came to be known as The Rant, soon to become a nationalist mantra for 30 million Canadians:

"I'm not a lumberjack or a fur trader; I don't live in an igloo, eat blubber or own a dogsled."

Jeff Douglas, who plays Joe Canadian, delivers "The Rant" in Ottawa, Ontario, on Canada Day—July 1, 2000.

417

"I have a prime minister, not a president. I speak English and French, not American."

"I can proudly sew my country's flag on my backpack." (This refers to Canada's gender-neutral school curriculum, in which sewing is taught both to boys and girls.)

"I believe in peacekeeping, not policing; diversity, not assimilation."

Images of maple leaves and beavers flashed on the screen as Joe reached his climax:

"Canada is the second-largest land mass, the first nation of hockey and the best part of North America. My name is Joe and I am Canadian" (Quoted in Brooke 2000).

The Rant spurred the government of Ontario, Canada's most populous province, to announce that starting in September 2000, each student would start the day by singing "O Canada," and pledging allegiance to the queen (since Canada is a member of the British Commonwealth). Although The Rant was recited by ordinary Canadians from Vancouver to Halifax, one province did not join in this affirmation of national identity. In French-speaking Quebec, which has been governed by the separatist Parti Quebecois since 1994, Canadian national symbols such as the flag and the anthem are officially ignored, and Molson Canadian beer is not even marketed (Brooke 2000).

The contrast between Quebec and the rest of Canada is the most dramatic, jarring, and politically problematic in a nation that prides itself on diversity in language and culture. Few countries rival Canada in cultivating a national image of a bilingual, multicultural society. According to a Government of Canada website:

Canada's experience with diversity distinguishes it from most other countries. Our 30 million inhabitants reflect a cultural, ethnic and linguistic makeup found nowhere else on earth . . . Diversity has been a fundamental characteristic of Canada since its beginnings (http://www.pch.gc.ca/progs/multi/respect_e.cfm).

Unlike the United States, which is suspicious of linguistic difference, bilingualism (with English and French as official languages) lies at the root of the Canadian federation.

Jean Chretien, Canada's prime minister, proclaimed in June 2000 that Canada has become a post-national, multicultural society. It contains the globe within its borders, and Canadians have learned that their two international languages and their diversity are a comparative advantage and a source of continuing creativity and innovation. Canadians are, by virtue of history and necessity, open to the world (http://www.pch.gc.ca/progs/multi/respect_e.cfm).

The longest-standing test of Canada's capacity to balance unity and diversity is the challenge of linguistic duality. When the Canadian Confederation was established in 1867, English and French were accorded official, constitutional status. Substantial powers were granted to Canada's constituent provinces. In one of those provinces, Quebec, French-speaking Canadians formed a large majority. They used their constitutional powers to protect and develop a regional culture based

Canada is officially bilingual, but French language and culture dominate in the province of Quebec. Shown here on March 2, 2001, is Bernard Landry, who became the new Prime Minister of Quebec.

on French language and culture and French-Canadian heritage. Elsewhere in Canada, the French language was swamped by immigrants who either were of English origin or were encouraged to speak English. In 1996 (the year of the most recent census data available as of this writing), 86 percent of Canada's native French speakers (Francophones) lived in Quebec, where they made up 82 percent of the population.

The national dominance of English is troubling to French Canadians. Illustrating a power imbalance that tilts toward English is the fact that there are five times as many bilingual Francophones as Anglophones (native English speakers). Francophones need to learn English more than Anglophones need to learn French.

Because of immigration, linguistic diversity in Canada is increasing. In 1996, 4.7 million Canadians reported a mother tongue (language learned in the home in childhood) other than English or French. Anglophone Canadians accounted for 60 percent of the population, versus 24 percent for Francophones. One-tenth of Canadians habitually spoke a language other than English or French. Chinese was the third most common, followed by Italian, German, Spanish, Portuguese, Polish, Punjabi, Ukrainian, Arabic, Tagalog (Filipino), and aboriginal languages. (What are the clearest contrasts between Canada and the United States in terms of languages spoken at home?)

English-French bilingualism (people speaking both English and French) has increased. In 1996, 17 percent of the population could speak both official languages, compared with 13 percent in 1971. Note that both Canada and Canadians illustrate increased linguistic diversity. Is this also true of the United States?

In 1950, 92 percent of Canada's population growth was from births to Canadians. Today, with 200,000 people moving to Canada each year, immigration accounts for 53 percent of the overall population growth. Canada has been called "the global village in one country." By 2006, Toronto, Canada's largest city, in its largest province, will be the world's most multicultural city, ahead of New York and London.

Canada has always relied on immigrants to supply settlers and labor. During the late 19th and early 20th centuries, Canada's immigration policy had as its primary objective supplying a labor pool, first for settlement and agriculture and then

Unity and diversity in Canada. On July 1, 2002, Patricia Richard holds up the Canadian and Quebecois flags as she watches the Canada Day parade in Montreal, Quebec.

to support industrialization. In 1960, a Canadian Bill of Rights barred discrimination by federal agencies based on national origin, race, color, religion, or sex. In 1962 a revised Canadian Immigration Act stated that any qualified person from any part of the world could be considered for immigration. The mix of source countries soon shifted from northern Europe to southern Europe, Asia, the West Indies, and the Middle East.

In 1971, Canada became the world's first country to adopt an official Multiculturalism Policy. According to the government's multiculturalism website:

Canada's approach to diversity is based on the belief that the common good is best served when everyone is accepted and respected for who they are, and that this ultimately makes for a resilient, more harmonious and more creative society. This faith in the value of diversity recognizes that respect

419

for cultural distinctiveness is intrinsic to an individual's sense of self worth and identity, and a society that accommodates everyone equally is a society that encourages achievement, participation, attachment to country and a sense of belonging (http://www.pch.gc.ca/progs/multi/respect_e.cfm).

Despite its admirable ideology of respect, Canada hasn't totally avoided discrimination. Abuses of the rights of aboriginal peoples, for example, can be traced back to Canada's beginnings. Aboriginal Canadians still have more poverty, poorer health, higher death and suicide rates, and more unemployment than their fellow citizens do. To its credit, the Canadian government had taken many steps to correct past mistakes and to address the needs of aboriginal peoples. For example, in 1973 Canada's Supreme Court recognized land rights based on an aboriginal group's traditional use and occupancy of land. And in 1982, the government affirmed the treaty rights of aboriginal peoples to protect their cultures, customs, traditions and languages.

In 1996 some 800,000 Canadians (2.8 percent of the national population) claimed aboriginal identity as North American Indians (First Nations), *métis* (mixed), or Inuit. A quarter of the aboriginal population reported an aboriginal language as the mother tongue. At the time of European settlement, Canada had more than 56 aboriginal nations speaking more than 30 languages. Among aboriginal languages reported as mother tongues in 1996, the three largest were Cree (87,500 people), Inuktitut (spoken by Inuit—27,800), and Ojibway (25,900).

The chapter "Human Biological Diversity and 'Race'" discussed the social construction of race in the United States, Japan, and Brazil. Canada constructs race and ethnicity differently from any of those three countries, although there are similarities. For example, the classification of people who claim a *métis* (mixed) identity as Aboriginal People

hints of the American hypodescent rule. Rather than race, the Canadian census asks about "visible minorities." That country's Employment Equity Act defines such groups as "persons, other than Aboriginal peoples, who are non-Caucasian in race or non-white in colour" (Statistics Canada 2001). Unlike the United States, the Canadian census would seem to assume that racial differences lie in the minds (and eyes) of the beholder rather than being self-identified.

Canada's 1996 census was the first to gather systematic data on visible minorities—for the purpose of assessing employment equity. Like affirmative action in the United States, Canada's Employment Equity Act was a response to evidence of discrimination.

"Chinese" and "South Asian" are Canada's largest visible minorities. Note that Canada's total visible minority population of 11.2 percent contrasts with a comparable figure of about 25 percent for the United States in the 2000 census. In particular, Canada's 2 percent black population contrasts with the American figure of 12.3 percent for African Americans. Canada's Asian population is significantly higher than the U.S. figure of 3.6 percent. Only a tiny fraction of the Canadian population (0.2 percent) claimed multiple visible minority affiliations, compared with 2.4 percent claiming "more than one race" in the United States in 2000.

Having read this essay, think about the main similarities and differences between the United States and Canada in terms of racial classification, ethnicity and multiculturalism, and linguistic diversity. What are key symbols of Canadian national culture—and of the national culture of the United States?

(The statistical information on which this essay is based can be found at: http://canadaonline.about.com/gi/dynamic/offsite.htm?site=http%3A%2F%2Fwww.statcan.ca%2Fenglish%2FPgdb%2Fdemo25a.htm.)

16
MAKING A LIVING

Overview

Four basic economic types are found in nonindustrial societies: foraging, horticulture, agriculture, and pastoralism. Food production eventually supplanted foraging in most world areas. Among foragers the band is a basic social unit. Ties of kinship and marriage link its members. Men usually hunt and fish. Women usually gather.

Horticulture and agriculture are two forms of farming, representing different ends of a continuum based on land and labor use. Horticulture always has a fallow period, but agriculturalists farm the same land year after year. Agriculturalists also use labor intensively, in irrigation and terracing, and by maintaining domesticated animals. The mixed nature of pastoralism, based on herding, is evident. Nomadic pastoralists trade with farmers. Among transhumant pastoralists, part of the population farms, while another part takes the herds to pasture.

Economic anthropologists study systems of production, distribution (exchange), and consumption. Economics has been defined as the science that studies the allocation of scarce means to alternative ends. Western economists assume that the idea of scarcity is universal—which it isn't—and that in making choices, people strive to maximize personal profit. However, people may and do maximize values other than individual profit.

There are three forms of exchange. Market exchange is based on impersonal purchase and sale, motivated by profit. With redistribution, goods are collected at a central place, with some eventually given back to the people. Reciprocity governs exchanges between social equals. Reciprocity, redistribution, and the market principle may coexist in the same society. The primary exchange mode in a society is the one that allocates the means of production.

423

Reindeer Herders, at Home on a (Very Cold) Range

NEW YORK TIMES NEWS BRIEF

By Warren Hoge

March 26, 2001

Occupational titles are proliferating today, but some professions have been around for millennia. In Norway, Sweden, and Finland, the Samis (also known as Lapps or Laplanders) domesticated reindeer, which their ancestors used to hunt, in the 16th century. Yet, like other herders, they still follow their animals as they make an annual trek, in this case from coast to interior. Their environment may be harsher, but the Samis, like other herders, live in nation-states and must deal with outsiders, including government officials, as they follow their herds and make their living through animal husbandry, trade, and sales.

KAUTOKEINO, Norway—Johan Martin Eira stepped from his front door into the Arctic dawn and studied the snowbound valley dotted with cozy homes and cabins.

"When the smoke rises straight up from the chimneys like that," he said, "you know it's really cold."

Really cold this February morning meant minus 40 degrees, and presumably even the wind had gone into deep freeze . . .

Mr. Eira, 31, was born and raised in this town, 200 miles north of the Arctic Circle, and has spent his life with creatures who are as comfortable in polar climes as he and his fellow reindeer herders seem to be.

For the indigenous Samis, like Mr. Eira, reindeer can be everything. Samis, also known as Lapps or Laplanders, raise them, sell them, race them, eat them, capture their images in their art, make jewelry from their bones, decorate barn walls with their pelts and use their hides to make coats, boots, leggings, hats and gloves. Economic and cultural activity centers on reindeer . . .

Reindeer husbandry has existed here since the end of the Ice Age. Reindeer followed the ice as it receded, the story goes, and the people followed the reindeer.

These animals are so much a part of the landscape that hundreds huddle silently on a hillside several miles out of town, barely spottable, the pewter color of their skins camouflaging them against the grey sky, white birch and snowy fields. In this cold, they stand unmoving as statues, eager to conserve their energy.

"I can't say they really like it outside in this temperature, but they can survive it," Mr. Eira said. They have a natural interior heating system, warming air in their mouths and lungs and then spreading it through their bodies. Their hairs are hollow, providing insulation . . .

Norway has an estimated 190,000 reindeer, and about 40 percent of the country's land is used for grazing and calving. In the 16th century, there was a gradual transition from hunting wild reindeer to herding, and the Samis became a nomadic people in what is now Europe's last wilderness. Of the 80,000 Samis in Norway, Sweden and Finland, about 10 percent are still reindeer herders. The largest number, about 50,000, live in Norway, where laws passed the last 25 years have given them exclusive right to the trade.

Mr. Eira, his four brothers and their father all mind the family herd of 3,500 animals, and though they have traded in their sleds for snowmobiles, and their wagons for four-wheel-drive vehicles, their lives follow ancient traditions.

Throughout the winter, the herds move across the slopes and valleys, feeding on moss and lichen the

In northern Norway a Sami herder uses a snow scooter to drive his migrating reindeer.

animals dig from beneath the snow and shreds of bark from scrubby trees that poke above the drifts. In the spring they move to milder areas for calving and then to the coast, where they fatten up for the winter on grass, shrubs and mushrooms. They are beasts of rigid habit.

"They're patterned from ancient times," Mr. Eira said, "and when they decide they want to move, they just turn and go . . ." . . .

Each siida, a Sami family cooperative that owns and cares for its herd, has a distinguishing design that is cut into a reindeer's ear at birth to identify it . . .

Predators are by far the greatest worry: bear, wolves, wolverines, lynxes, eagles. An eagle can lift a 40-pound animal and spirit it away for the kill. Losses can approach 40 percent of the herd, and Samis are locked in a dispute over the issue with government conservationists who want to protect large carnivores and see the wolf population grow. When a herder is not there to protect the herd, trained huskies mind the animals, intimidating them into remaining bunched together and trying to scare off tormentors.

In recent years the government has become more active in trying to regulate the reindeer industry, ending traditional slaughtering on the snow and directing it toward large government abattoirs, providing subsidies to herders who will sell at lower prices. The Samis complain that this interference has hurt their business. The quality of the meat has declined with the greater distances the animals have to be trucked to slaughter, prices have dropped by 50 percent and the reindeer folk have been outflanked by the better organized and far larger beef industry.

The supply has also fallen. Reindeer meat is scarce everywhere, from local food stores to Oslo restaurants, where it was long considered a delicacy. In addition, herders must give the entire carcasses to the slaughterhouse and cannot put other parts of the animals to traditional uses, ranging from soup to clothing.

"Agricultural politics have hit the reindeer industry and ruined it," said Erik S. Reinert, an Oslo economist and anthropologist who negotiates for the Samis. "These are the last tribal people of Europe, and they have a unique thing going for them—they have a luxury product." Reindeer meat, aside from being tasty, is fat free.

Mr. Reinert argued that at a time when Europeans are panicked about the quality and safety of their food, meat from reindeer raised in unpolluted surroundings on natural feed ought to command a growing market . . .

SOURCE: Warren Hoge, "Kautokeino Journal; Reindeer Herders, at Home on a (Very Cold) Range," *New York Times*, March 26, 2001, late edition—final, section A, p. 4, column 3. Copyright 2002 The New York Times Company.

Today's Samis are herders, caretakers of domesticated animals, who use modern technology, such as snowmobiles and four-wheel-drive vehicles, to accompany their herds on their annual nomadic trek. And, as the article shows, the Samis, like other indigenous peoples, face increasing government interference in their lives. In the contemporary world, communities and societies are being incorporated, at an accelerating rate, into larger systems, just as the Samis face increased regulation of their economic adaptation—reindeer herding—by the government of Norway. Historically, the origin and spread of food production (animal domestication and plant cultivation) led to the formation of larger social and political systems, such as states. Compared with hunting and gathering, food production led to major changes in human life. The pace of cultural transformation increased enormously. This chapter provides a framework for understanding a variety of human adaptive strategies and economic systems—ranging from hunting and gathering to farming and herding.

Adaptive Strategies

The anthropologist Yehudi Cohen (1974b) used the term *adaptive strategy* to describe a group's system of economic production. Cohen argued that the most important reason for similarities between two (or more) unrelated societies is their possession of a similar adaptive strategy. For example, there are clear similarities among societies that have a foraging (hunting and gathering) strategy. Cohen developed a typology of societies based on correlations between their economies and their social features. His typology includes these five adaptive strategies:

foraging, horticulture, agriculture, pastoralism, and industrialism. Industrialism is discussed in the chapter "The Modern World System." The present chapter focuses on the first four adaptive strategies.

Foraging

Until 10,000 years ago, people everywhere were foragers, also known as hunter-gatherers. However, environmental differences did create contrasts among the world's foragers. Some, such as the people who lived in Europe during the ice ages, were big-game hunters. Today, hunters in the Arctic still focus on large animals and herd animals; they have much less vegetation and variety in their diets than do tropical foragers. In general, as one moves from colder to warmer areas, there is an increase in the number of species. The tropics contain tremendous biodiversity, a great variety of plant and animal species, many of which have been used by human foragers. Tropical foragers typically hunt and gather a wide range of plant and animal life. The same may be true in temperate areas, such as the North Pacific Coast of North America, where Native American foragers could draw on a variety of land and sea resources, including salmon, other fish species, berries, mountain goats, seals, and sea mammals. Nevertheless, despite differences due to environmental variation, all foraging economies have shared one essential feature: People rely on nature to make their living.

Animal domestication (initially of sheep and goats) and plant cultivation (of wheat and barley) began 10,000 to 12,000 years ago in the Middle East. Cultivation based on different crops, such as maize, manioc (cassava), and potatoes, arose independently some 3,000 to 4,000 years later in the Americas. In both hemispheres the new economy spread rapidly. Most foragers eventually turned to food production. Today, almost all foragers have at least some dependence on food production or on food producers (Kent 1992).

The foraging way of life survived in certain environments (see Figure 16.1), including a few islands and forests, along with deserts and very cold areas—places where food production was not practicable with simple technology (see Lee and Daly 1999). In many areas, foragers had been exposed to the "idea" of food production but never adopted it because their own economies provided a perfectly adequate and nutritious diet—with a lot less work. In some areas, people reverted to foraging after trying food production and abandoning it. In most areas where hunter-gatherers did survive, foraging should be described as "recent" rather than "contemporary." All modern foragers live in nation-states, depend to some extent on government assistance, and have contacts with food-producing neighbors, as well as missionaries and other outsiders. We should not view contemporary foragers as isolated or pristine survivors of the Stone Age. Modern foragers are influenced by regional forces (e.g., trade and war), national and international policies, and political and economic events in the world system.

Although foraging is disappearing as a way of life, the outlines of Africa's two broad belts of recent foraging remain evident. One is the Kalahari Desert of southern Africa. This is the home of the *San* (Bushmen), who include the *Ju/'hoansi* (see Kent 1996; Lee 1993). The other main African foraging area is the equatorial forest of central and eastern Africa, home of the Mbuti, Efe, and other "pygmies" (Bailey et al. 1989; Turnbull 1965).

People still do subsistence foraging in certain remote forests in Madagascar; in Southeast Asia, including Malaysia and the Philippines; and on certain islands off the Indian coast (Lee and Daly 1999). Some of the best-known recent foragers are the aborigines of Australia. Those Native Australians lived on their island continent for more than 40,000 years without developing food production.

The Western Hemisphere also had recent foragers. The Eskimos, or Inuit, of Alaska and Canada are well-known hunters. These (and other) northern foragers now use modern technology, including rifles and snowmobiles, in their subsistence activities (Pelto 1973). The native populations of California, Oregon, Washington, British Columbia, and Alaska were all foragers, as were those of inland subarctic Canada and the Great Lakes. For many Native Americans, fishing, hunting, and gathering remain important subsistence (and sometimes commercial) activities.

Coastal foragers also lived near the southern tip of South America, in Patagonia. On the grassy plains of Argentina, southern Brazil, Uruguay, and Paraguay, there were other hunter-gatherers. The contemporary Aché of Paraguay are usually called

Figure 16.1 Worldwide Distribution of Recent Hunter-Gatherers.

SOURCE: Adapted from a map by Ray Sim, in Göran Burenhult, ed., *Encyclopedia of Humankind: People of the Stone Age* (McMahons Point, NSW, Australia: Weldon Owen Pty Ltd., 1933), p. 193.

"hunter-gatherers" even though they get just a third of their livelihood from foraging. The Aché also grow crops, have domesticated animals, and live in or near mission posts, where they receive food from missionaries (Hawkes et al. 1982; Hill et al. 1987).

Throughout the world, foraging survived mainly in environments that posed major obstacles to food production. (Some foragers took refuge in such areas after the rise of food production, the state, colonialism, or the modern world system.) The difficulties of cultivating at the North Pole are obvious. In southern Africa, the Dobe Ju/'hoansi San area studied by Richard Lee is surrounded by a waterless belt 70 to 200 kilometers in breadth. The Dobe area is hard to reach even

today, and there is no archaeological evidence of occupation of this area by food producers before the 20th century (Solway and Lee 1990). However, environmental limits to other adaptive strategies aren't the only reason foragers survived. Their niches have one thing in common: their marginality. Their environments haven't been of immediate interest to groups with other adaptive strategies.

The hunter-gatherer way of life did persist in a few areas that could be cultivated, even after contact with cultivators. Those tenacious foragers, such as indigenous foragers in what is now California, did not turn to food production because they were supporting themselves adequately by hunting and gathering. As the modern world system spreads, the number of foragers continues to decline.

Beyond the *Classroom*

Integrating Archaeological, Ethnographic, and Analytic Subsistence Data: A Case Study from Patagonia, South America

Background Information

STUDENT:

SUPERVISING PROFESSOR:

SCHOOL:

YEAR IN SCHOOL/MAJOR

FUTURE PLANS:

Jennifer A. Kelly

Robert Tykot

University of South Florida

Senior/Archaeology

Graduate school in archaeology

In this account, Jennifer Kelly uses various sources to reconstruct the subsistence strategies and diets of the aboriginal inhabitants of Patagonia, located at South America's southern tip. For her senior thesis, Kelly began by reading historic and ethnographic accounts of the region. Then she turned to archaeological data from sites in coastal and inland areas once occupied by different ethnic groups, such as the Ona, the Yamana, and the Tehuelche. Working with samples of human bone and tooth, she did isotope analysis, which demonstrates how specific dietary resources affect the skeleton. From her analysis she concludes there was more variation in subsistence economies and diets than the ethnographic accounts suggested. Classic ethnographies have a tendency to see human groups as culturally programmed to go after certain foods and to ignore others, which may be used by their neighbors. This account suggests that foragers are more opportunistic. Although there are certainly cultural preferences for certain foods and ways of getting them, humans are malleable, pursuing a range of resources as they become available and are needed.

Ethnohistoric, archaeological, and other scientific methods are integrated here to reconstruct prehistoric subsistence adaptations in Patagonia and Tierra del Fuego.

Ethnohistoric data from the late 19th and early 20th centuries emphasize discrete dietary practices in coastal, inland, and Fuegan Patagonia. More recent archaeological evidence, however, suggests significant variations in subsistence strategies, each tailored to specific local resources.

At the time of European arrival, several indigenous groups inhabited Patagonia and Tierra del Fuego. The Onas (Haush and Selk'nam) lived in the wooded southern part of Tierra del Fuego. Archaeological evidence suggests that the Ona diet was based mainly on the guanaco (a wild grazing animal related to the llama). Other reports indicate that in some places the Onas did intensive shellfish collection and hunted fish in tidal pools. The Yamana lived along the southern and western coasts and island archipelagos of Tierra del Fuego. Early ethnographies report that they relied on marine mammals. Later accounts suggest a diet based on shellfish and seabirds.

Archaeological evidence indicates that the use of marine resources increased after 6000 B.P.,

CORRELATES OF FORAGING

Typologies, such as Cohen's adaptive strategies, are useful because they suggest **correlations**—that is, association or covariation between two or more variables. (Correlated variables are factors that are linked and interrelated, such as food intake and body weight, such that when one increases or decreases, the other tends to change, too.) Ethnographic studies in hundreds of societies have revealed many correlations between the economy and social life. Associated (correlated) with each adaptive strategy is a bundle of particular cultural features. Correlations, however, are rarely perfect. Some foragers lack cultural features usually associated with foraging, and some of those features are found in groups with other adaptive strategies.

What, then, are the usual correlates of foraging? People who subsist by hunting, gathering, and fishing often live in band-organized societies. Their basic social unit, the **band**, is a small group of fewer than a hundred people, all related by kinship or marriage. Band size varies between cultures and often from one season to the next in a given culture. In some foraging societies, band size and suggests non-specialized seasonal procurement of shellfish, fish, and mammals using simple hunting and gathering technology.

Carbon and nitrogen isotope analysis of human skeletal remains can differentiate between diets based on land and marine foods, as well as those based on plant foods that use different photosynthetic pathways. Bone collagen (a protein) and bone apatite (the mineral portion of bone) reveal the average diet over the last several years of an individual's life. Tooth enamel reflects diet only at the time of crown formation. As little as one gram of bone and a few milligrams of tooth enamel are sufficient for analysis. Samples of 40 individuals were obtained from coastal sites along the Straits of Magellan, and from sites located well inland. The sites range in age from 7000 B.P. through the early historic period.

For northern Patagonia, the results indicate that the northern Tehuelches who lived on the coast ate a lot of seafood in addition to guanaco. This conclusion is based on positive carbon and nitrogen isotope ratios in their bone collagen and apatite. Inland samples from this region have isotope ratios that suggest consumption of guanaco, which grazed on certain grasses.

Isotope data for coastal areas near the Straits of Magellan, homeland of the southern Tehuelches, also suggest diets dependent on both guanaco and marine resources, although the latter appear more important than in the north. The slightly enriched carbon isotope ratios of individuals from inland sites in this area may reflect their consumption of marine foods on a seasonal basis. In the Selk'nam area of Isla Grande, however, marine foods were less important than the guanaco, even along the coast, thus corroborating ethnohistoric descriptions of this area.

In the Haush region, however, marine foods of high trophic level (e.g. sea lions) accounted for most of the dietary protein. This finding contradicts ethnohistoric accounts, which describe the Haush as intermediate between the Selk'nam and the Yamana in their dependence on marine resources.

In conclusion, isotope analysis confirms some but not all of the ethnohistoric descriptions of subsistence patterns in Patagonia, while providing evidence of significant variation within each cultural group. A larger number of skeletal samples from dated archaeological contexts, and a better sampling of faunal and floral resources in each area, would allow for fuller understanding of dynamic, prehistoric Patagonian subsistence adaptations.

stays about the same year-round. In others, the band splits up for part of the year. Families leave to gather resources that are better exploited by just a few people. Later, they regroup for cooperative work and ceremonies.

Several examples of seasonal splits and reunions are known from ethnography and archaeology. In southern Africa, some San aggregate around waterholes in the dry season and split up in the wet season, whereas other bands disperse in the dry season (Barnard 1979; Kent 1992). This reflects environmental variation. San who lack permanent water must disperse and forage widely for moisture-filled plants. In ancient Oaxaca, Mexico, before the advent of plant cultivation there around 4,000 years ago, foragers assembled in large bands in summer. They collectively harvested tree pods and cactus fruits. Then, in fall, they split into much smaller family groups to hunt deer and gather grasses and plants that were effectively foraged by small teams.

One typical characteristic of the foraging life is mobility. In many San groups, as among the Mbuti of Congo, people shift band membership several times in a lifetime. One may be born, for example,

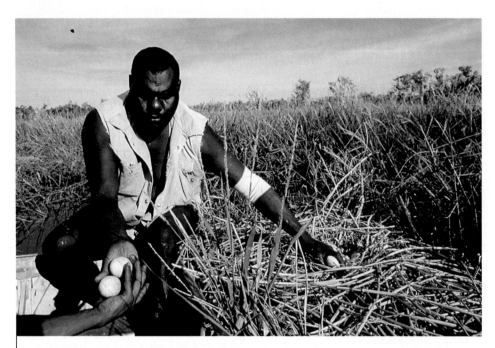

A contemporary forager from Australia's Cape York peninsula collects eggs from the nest of a magpie goose. Such hunter-gatherers are not isolated survivors of the Stone Age, but contemporary people who live in nation-states and have contact with outsiders. In what forms does foraging survive in our own society?

in a band where one's mother has kin. Later, one's family may move to a band where the father has relatives. Because bands are exogamous (people marry outside their own band), one's parents come from two different bands, and one's grandparents may come from four. People may join any band to which they have kinship or marriage links. A couple may live in, or shift between, the husband's band and the wife's band.

One also may affiliate with a band through *fictive kinship*—personal relationships modeled on kinship, such as that between godparents and godchildren. San, for example, have a limited number of personal names. People with the same name have a special relationship; they treat each other like siblings. San expect the same hospitality in bands where they have *namesakes* as they do in a band in which a real sibling lives. Namesakes share a strong identity. They call everyone in a namesake's band by the kin terms the namesake uses. Those people reply as if they were addressing a real relative. Kinship, marriage, and fictive kinship permit San to join several bands, and nomadic (regularly on-the-move) foragers do

change bands often. Band membership therefore can change tremendously from year to year.

Understanding Ourselves How do we use fictive kinship? Although most of us are born in families, most of the people in our lives are nonrelatives. This is a major contrast with a kin-based society, such as that of the San. There is a human tendency to be social, to seek friends, to make alliances, and to convert nonrelatives to whom we are especially close into something more—something like kin. Do you have godparents? Often godparents are close friends of one's parents. Or they may be actual relatives to whom one's parents felt especially close, and so they sought to strengthen the relationship. Adoptive parents and siblings are fictive kin who become legal kin. Fraternities and sororities have fictive kin including "brothers," "sisters," and house "mothers." Priests are addressed as "father"; nuns, as "sister." What other fictive kin can you think of? In our society how is fictive kinship like and unlike the San namesake system?

All human societies have some kind of division of labor based on gender. Among foragers, men typically hunt and fish while women gather and collect, but the specific nature of the work varies among cultures. Sometimes women's work contributes most to the diet. Sometimes male hunting and fishing predominate. Among foragers in tropical and semitropical areas, gathering tends to contribute more to the diet than hunting and fishing do—even though the labor costs of gathering tend to be much higher than those of hunting and fishing.

All foragers make social distinctions based on age. Often old people receive great respect as guardians of myths, legends, stories, and traditions. Younger people value the elders' special knowledge of ritual and practical matters. Most foraging societies are *egalitarian*. This means that contrasts in prestige are minor and are based on age and gender.

When considering issues of "human nature," we should remember that the egalitarian band was a basic form of human social life for most of our history. Food production has existed less than 1 percent of the time *Homo* has spent on earth. However, it has produced huge social differences. We now consider the main economic features of food-producing strategies.

Cultivation

In Cohen's typology, the three adaptive strategies based on food production in nonindustrial societies are horticulture, agriculture, and pastoralism. In non-Western cultures, as is also true in modern nations, people carry out a variety of economic activities. Each adaptive strategy refers to the main economic activity. Pastoralists (herders), for example, consume milk, butter, blood, and meat from their animals as mainstays of their diet. However, they also add grain to the diet by doing some cultivating or by trading with neighbors. Food producers also may hunt or gather to supplement a diet based on domesticated species.

HORTICULTURE

Horticulture and agriculture are two types of cultivation found in nonindustrial societies. Both differ from the farming systems of industrial nations like the United States and Canada, which use large land areas, machinery, and petrochemicals. According to

Cohen, **horticulture** is cultivation that makes intensive use of *none* of the factors of production: land, labor, capital, and machinery. Horticulturalists use simple tools such as hoes and digging sticks to grow their crops. Their fields are not permanently cultivated and lie fallow for varying lengths of time.

Horticulture often involves *slash-and-burn techniques*. Here, horticulturalists clear land by cutting down (slashing) and burning forest or bush or by setting fire to the grass covering the plot. The vegetation is broken down, pests are killed, and the ashes remain to fertilize the soil. Crops are then sown, tended, and harvested. Use of the plot is not continuous. Often it is cultivated for only a year. This depends, however, on soil fertility and weeds, which compete with cultivated plants for nutrients.

In slash-and-burn horticulture, the land is cleared by cutting down (slashing) and burning trees and bush, using simple technology. After such clearing this woman uses a digging stick to plant mountain rice in Madagascar. What might be the environmental effects of slash-and-burn cultivation?

When horticulturalists abandon a plot because of soil exhaustion or a thick weed cover, they clear another piece of land, and the original plot reverts to forest. After several years of fallowing (the duration varies in different societies), the cultivator returns to farm the original plot again. Horticulture is also called *shifting cultivation*. Such shifts from plot to plot do not mean that whole villages must move when plots are abandoned. Horticulture can support large permanent villages. Among the Kuikuru of the South American tropical forest, for example, one village of 150 people remained in the same place for 90 years (Carneiro 1956). Kuikuru houses are large and well made. Because the work involved in building them is great, the Kuikuru would rather walk farther to their fields than construct a new village. They shift their plots rather than their settlements. On the other hand, horticulturalists in the montaña (Andean foothills) of Peru live in small villages of about 30 people (Carneiro 1961/1968). Their houses are small and simple. After a few years in one place, these people build new villages near virgin land. Because their houses are so simple, they prefer rebuilding to walking even a half mile to their fields.

AGRICULTURE

Agriculture is cultivation that requires more labor than horticulture does, because it uses land intensively and continuously. The greater labor demands associated with agriculture reflect its common use of domesticated animals, irrigation, or terracing.

Domesticated Animals Many agriculturalists use animals as means of production—for transport, as cultivating machines, and for their manure. Asian farmers typically incorporate cattle and/or water buffalo into agricultural economies based on rice production. Rice farmers may use cattle to trample pretilled flooded fields, thus mixing soil and water, prior to transplanting. Many agriculturalists attach animals to plows and harrows for field preparation before planting or transplanting. Also, agriculturalists typically collect manure from their animals, using it to fertilize their plots, thus increasing yields. Animals are attached to carts for transport, as well as to implements of cultivation.

Irrigation While horticulturalists must await the rainy season, agriculturalists can schedule their planting in advance, because they control water. Like other irrigation experts in the Philippines, the Ifugao (Figure 16.2) irrigate their fields with canals from rivers, streams, springs, and ponds. Irrigation makes it possible to cultivate a plot year after year. Irrigation enriches the soil because the irrigated field is a unique ecosystem with several species of plants and animals, many of them minute organisms, whose wastes fertilize the land.

An irrigated field is a capital investment that usually increases in value. It takes time for a field to start yielding; it reaches full productivity only after several years of cultivation. The Ifugao, like other irrigators, have farmed the same fields for generations. In some agricultural areas, including the Middle East, however, salts carried in the irrigation water can make fields unusable after 50 or 60 years.

Terracing Terracing is another agricultural technique the Ifugao have mastered. Their homeland has small valleys separated by steep hillsides. Because the population is dense, people need to farm the hills. However, if they simply planted on

Figure 16.2 Location of the Ifugao.

the steep hillsides, fertile soil and crops would be washed away during the rainy season. To prevent this, the Ifugao cut into the hillside and build stage after stage of terraced fields rising above the valley floor. Springs located above the terraces supply their irrigation water. The labor necessary to build and maintain a system of terraces is great. Terrace walls crumble each year and must be partially rebuilt. The canals that bring water down through the terraces also demand attention.

Costs and Benefits of Agriculture Agriculture requires human labor to build and maintain irrigation systems, terraces, and other works. People must feed, water, and care for their animals. Given sufficient labor input and management, agricultural land can yield one or two crops annually for years or even generations. An agricultural field does not necessarily produce a higher single-year yield than does a horticultural plot. The first crop grown by horticulturalists on long-idle land may be larger than that from an agricultural plot of the same size. Furthermore, because agriculturalists work harder than horticulturalists do, agricul-

ture's yield relative to labor is also lower. Agriculture's main advantage is that the long-term yield per area is far greater and more dependable. Because a single field sustains its owners year after year, there is no need to maintain a reserve of uncultivated land as horticulturalists do. This is why agricultural societies tend to be more densely populated than are horticultural ones.

THE CULTIVATION CONTINUUM

Because nonindustrial economies can have features of both horticulture and agriculture, it is useful to discuss cultivators as being arranged along a **cultivation continuum**. Horticultural systems stand at one end—the "low-labor, shifting-plot" end. Agriculturalists are at the other—the "labor-intensive, permanent-plot" end.

We speak of a continuum because there are today intermediate economies, combining horticultural and agricultural features—more intensive than annually shifting horticulture but less intensive than agriculture. These recall the intermediate economies revealed by archaeological sequences

Agriculture requires more labor than horticulture does and uses land intensively and continuously. Labor demands associated with agriculture reflect its use of domesticated animals, irrigation, and terracing. The rice farmers of Luzon in the Philippines, such as the Ifugao, are famous for their irrigated and terraced fields.

leading from horticulture to agriculture in the Middle East, Mexico, and other areas of early food production. Unlike nonintensive horticulturalists, who farm a plot just once before fallowing it, the South American Kuikuru grow two or three crops of *manioc*, or cassava— an edible tuber—before abandoning their plots. Cultivation is even more intense in certain densely populated areas of Papua New Guinea, where plots are planted for two or three years, allowed to rest for three to five, and then recultivated. After several of these cycles, the plots are abandoned for a longer fallow period. Such a pattern is called *sectorial fallowing* (Wolf 1966). Besides Papua New Guinea, such systems occur in places as distant as West Africa and highland Mexico. Sectorial fallowing is associated with denser populations than is simple horticulture. The simpler system is the norm in tropical forests, where weed invasion and delicate soils prevent more intensive cultivation.

The key difference between horticulture and agriculture is that horticulture always uses a fallow period whereas agriculture does not. The earliest cultivators in the Middle East and in Mexico were rainfall-dependent horticulturalists. Until recently, horticulture was the main form of cultivation in several areas, including parts of Africa, Southeast Asia, the Pacific islands, Mexico, Central America, and the South American tropical forest.

INTENSIFICATION: PEOPLE AND THE ENVIRONMENT

The range of environments available for food production has widened as people have increased their control over nature. For example, in arid areas of California, where Native Americans once foraged, modern irrigation technology now sustains rich agricultural estates. Agriculturalists live in many areas that are too arid for nonirrigators or too hilly for nonterracers. Many ancient civilizations in arid lands arose on an agricultural base. Increasing labor intensity and permanent land use have major demographic, social, political, and environmental consequences.

Interpret the World Look at Map 16, Atlas Map 16 "World Land Use: 1500 AD," in your atlas. Map 16 shows prevailing land uses and predominant economies over large areas, primarily types of agriculture. Shown on the map are the kinds of economies that existed throughout the world at the start of the European age of discovery and conquest—250 years before the Industrial Revolution. Note especially the areas of intensive agriculture as you read this discussion of the effects of intensification.

Thus, because of their permanent fields, intensive cultivators are sedentary. People live in larger and more permanent communities located closer to other settlements. Growth in population size and density increases contact between individuals and groups. There is more need to regulate interpersonal relations, including conflicts of interest. Economies that support more people usually require more coordination in the use of land, labor, and other resources.

Intensive agriculture has significant environmental effects. Irrigation ditches and paddies (fields with irrigated rice) become repositories for organic wastes, chemicals (such as salts), and disease microorganisms. Intensive agriculture typically spreads at the expense of trees and forests, which are cut down to be replaced by fields. Accompanying such deforestation is loss of environmental diversity. Agricultural economies grow increasingly specialized—focusing on one or a few caloric staples, such as rice, and on the animals that are raised and tended to aid the agricultural economy. Because tropical horticulturalists typically cultivate dozens of plant species simultaneously, a horticultural plot tends to mirror the botanical diversity that is found in a tropical forest. Agricultural plots, by contrast, reduce ecological diversity by cutting down trees and concentrating on just a few staple foods. Such crop specialization is true of agriculturalists both in the tropics (e.g., Indonesian paddy farmers) and outside the tropics (e.g., Middle Eastern irrigated farmers).

At least in the tropics, the diets of both foragers and horticulturalists are typically more diverse, although under less secure human control, than the diets of agriculturalists. Agriculturists attempt to reduce risk in production by favoring stability in the form of a reliable annual harvest and long-term production. Tropical foragers and horticulturalists, by contrast, attempt to reduce risk by relying on multiple species and benefiting from ecological diversity. The agricultural strategy is to put all one's eggs in one big and very dependable basket.

Of course, even with agriculture, there is a possibility that the single staple crop may fail, and famine may result. The strategy of tropical foragers and horticulturalists is to have several smaller baskets, a few of which may fail without endangering subsistence. The agricultural strategy makes sense when there are lots of children to raise and adults to be fed. Foraging and horticulture, of course, are associated with smaller, sparser, and more mobile populations.

Agricultural economies also pose a series of regulatory problems—which central governments often have arisen to solve. How is water to be managed—along with disputes about access to and distribution of water? With more people living closer together on more valuable land, agriculturalists are more likely to come into conflict than foragers and horticulturalists are. Agriculture paved the way for the origin of the state, and most agriculturalists live in *states*: complex sociopolitical systems that administer a territory and populace with substantial contrasts in occupation, wealth, prestige, and power. In such societies, cultivators play their role as one part of a differentiated, functionally specialized, and tightly integrated sociopolitical system. The social and political implications of food production and intensification are examined more fully in the chapter "Political Systems."

Pastoralists may be nomadic or transhumant, but they don't typically live off their herds alone. They either trade or cultivate. The photo at the top shows female shepherds in Morocco's Drâa Valley. The photo at the bottom shows a male Alpine shepherd in Germany. This man accompanies his flocks to highland meadows each year.

Pastoralism

For more on pastoralism, see the Internet Exercises at your OLC

/kottak

Pastoralists live in North Africa, the Middle East, Europe, Asia, and sub-Saharan Africa. These herders are people whose activities focus on such domesticated animals as cattle, sheep, goats, camels, and yak. East African pastoralists, like many others, live in symbiosis with their herds. (*Symbiosis* is an obligatory interaction between groups—here humans and animals—that is beneficial to each.) Herders attempt to protect their animals and to ensure their reproduction in return for food and other products, such as leather. Herds provide dairy products, meat, and blood. Animals are killed at ceremonies, which occur throughout the year, and so beef is available regularly.

People use livestock in a variety of ways. Natives of North America's Great Plains, for example, didn't eat, but only rode, their horses. (Europeans reintroduced horses to the Western Hemisphere; the native American horse had become extinct thousands of years earlier.) For Plains Indians, horses served as "tools of the trade," means of production used to hunt buffalo, a main target of their economies. So the Plains Indians were not true pastoralists but *hunters* who used horses—as many agriculturalists use animals—as means of production.

Unlike the use of animals merely as productive machines, pastoralists, including the Samis discussed at the beginning of this chapter, typically make direct use of their herds for food. They consume their meat, blood, and milk, from which they make yogurt, butter, and cheese. Although some pastoralists rely on their herds more completely than others do, it is impossible to base subsistence solely on animals. Most pastoralists therefore supplement their diet by hunting, gathering, fishing, cultivating, or trading. To get crops, pastoralists either trade with cultivators or do some cultivating or gathering themselves.

Unlike foraging and cultivation, which existed throughout the world before the Industrial Revolution, pastoralism was almost totally confined to the Old World. Before European conquest, the only pastoralists in the Americas lived in the Andean region of South America. They used their llamas and alpacas for food and wool and in agriculture and transport. Much more recently, Navajo of the southwestern United States developed a pastoral economy based on sheep, which were brought to North America by Europeans. The populous Navajo are now the major pastoral population in the Western Hemisphere.

Two patterns of movement occur with pastoralism: nomadism and transhumance. Both are based on the fact that herds must move to use pasture available in particular places in different seasons. In **pastoral nomadism**, the entire group—women, men, and children—moves with the animals throughout the year. The Middle East and North Africa provide numerous examples of pastoral nomads. In Iran, for example, the Basseri and the Qashqai ethnic groups traditionally followed a nomadic route more than 300 miles (480 kilometers) long. Starting each year near the coast, they took their animals to grazing land 17,000 feet (5,400 meters) above sea level.

With **transhumance**, part of the group moves with the herds, but most people stay in the home village. There are examples from Europe and Africa. In Europe's Alps, it is just the shepherds and goatherds—not the whole village—who accompany the flocks to highland meadows in summer. Among the Turkana of Uganda, men and boys accompany the herds to distant pastures, while much of the village stays put and does some horticultural farming. Villages tend to be located in the best-watered areas, which have the longest pasture season. This permits the village population to stay together during a large chunk of the year.

During their annual trek, pastoral nomads trade for crops and other products with more sedentary people. Transhumants don't have to trade for crops. Because only part of the population accompanies the herds, transhumants can maintain year-round villages and grow their own crops. Table 16.1 summarizes the main features of Cohen's adaptive strategies.

Modes of Production

An **economy** is a system of production, distribution, and consumption of resources; *economics* is the study of such systems. Economists tend to focus on modern nations and capitalist systems, while anthropologists have broadened understanding of economic principles by gathering data on nonindustrial economies. Economic anthropology studies economics in a comparative perspective (see Gudeman 1999; Plattner 1989; Wilk 1996).

A **mode of production** is a way of organizing production—"a set of social relations through which labor is deployed to wrest energy from nature by means of tools, skills, organization, and knowledge" (Wolf 1982, p. 75). In the capitalist mode of production, money buys labor power, and there is a social gap between the people (bosses and workers) involved in the production process. By contrast, in nonindustrial societies, labor is not usually bought but is given as a social obligation. In such a *kin-based* mode of production, mutual aid in production is one among many expressions of a larger web of social relations.

Table 16.1 Yehudi Cohen's Adaptive Strategies (Economic Typology) Summarized

Adaptive Strategy	Also Known as	Key Features/Varieties
Foraging	Hunting-gathering	Mobility, use of nature's resources
Horticulture	Slash-and-burn, shifting cultivation, swiddening, dry farming	Fallow period
Agriculture	Intensive farming	Continuous use of land, intensive use of labor
Pastoralism	Herding	Nomadism and transhumance
Industrialism	Industrial production	Factory production, capitalism, socialist production

See the Interactive Exercises for a quiz on economics

mhhe **com** **/kottak**

Societies representing each of the adaptive strategies just discussed (e.g., foraging) tend to have a similar mode of production. Differences in the mode of production within a given strategy may reflect the differences in environments, target resources, or cultural traditions. Thus, a foraging mode of production may be based on individual hunters or teams, depending on whether the game is a solitary or a herd animal. Gathering is usually more individualistic than hunting, although collecting teams may assemble when abundant resources ripen and must be harvested quickly. Fishing may be done alone (as in ice or spear fishing) or in crews (as with open sea fishing and hunting of sea mammals).

PRODUCTION IN NONINDUSTRIAL SOCIETIES

Although some kind of division of economic labor related to age and gender is a cultural universal, the specific tasks assigned to each sex and to people of different ages vary. Many horticultural societies assign a major productive role to women, but some make men's work primary. Similarly, among pastoralists, men generally tend large animals, but in some cultures women do the milking. Jobs accomplished through teamwork in some cultivating societies are done by smaller groups or individuals working over a longer period of time in others.

The Betsileo of Madagascar have two stages of teamwork in rice cultivation: transplanting and harvesting. Team size varies with the size of the field. Both transplanting and harvesting feature a traditional division of labor by age and gender that is well known to all Betsileo and is repeated across the generations. The first job in transplanting is the trampling of a previously tilled flooded field by young men driving cattle, in order to mix

Women transplant rice in northern Iran in May 2001. Transplanting and weeding are arduous tasks that strain the back especially.

earth and water. They bring cattle to trample the fields just before transplanting. The young men yell at and beat the cattle, striving to drive them into a frenzy so that they will trample the fields properly. Trampling breaks up clumps of earth and mixes irrigation water with soil to form a smooth mud into which women transplant seedlings. Once the tramplers leave the field, older men arrive. With their spades, they break up the clumps that the cattle missed. Meanwhile, the owner and other adults uproot rice seedlings and bring them to the field.

At harvest time, four or five months later, young men cut the rice off the stalks. Young women carry it to the clearing above the field. Older women arrange and stack it. The oldest men and women then stand on the stack, stomping and compacting it. Three days later, young men thresh the rice, beating the stalks against a rock to remove the grain. Older men then attack the stalks with sticks to make sure all the grains have fallen off.

Most of the other tasks in Betsileo rice cultivation are done by individual owners and their immediate families. All household members help weed the rice field. It's a man's job to till the fields with a spade or a plow. Individual men repair the irrigation and drainage systems and the earth walls that separate one plot from the next. Among other agriculturalists, however, repairing the irrigation system is a task involving teamwork and communal labor.

MEANS OF PRODUCTION

In nonindustrial societies, there is a more intimate relationship between the worker and the means of production than there is in industrial nations. **Means, or factors, of production** include land (territory), labor, and technology.

Land Among foragers, ties between people and land are less permanent than they are among food producers. Although many bands have territories, the boundaries are not usually marked, and there is no way they can be enforced. The hunter's stake in an animal that is being stalked or has been hit with a poisoned arrow is more important than where the animal finally dies. A person acquires the rights to use a band's territory by being born in the band or by joining it through a tie of kinship,

marriage, or fictive kinship. In Botswana in southern Africa, Ju/'hoansi San women, whose work provides over half the food, habitually use specific tracts of berry-bearing trees. However, when a woman changes bands, she immediately acquires a new gathering area.

Among food producers, rights to the means of production also come through kinship and marriage. Descent groups (groups whose members claim common ancestry) are common among nonindustrial food producers, and those who descend from the founder share the group's territory and resources. If the adaptive strategy is horticulture, the estate includes garden and fallow land for shifting cultivation. As members of a descent group, pastoralists have access to animals to start their own herds, to grazing land, to garden land, and to other means of production.

Labor, Tools, and Specialization Like land, labor is a means of production. In nonindustrial societies, access to both land and labor comes through social links such as kinship, marriage, and descent. Mutual aid in production is merely one aspect of ongoing social relations that are expressed on many other occasions.

Nonindustrial societies contrast with industrial nations in regard to another means of production: technology. In bands and tribes, manufacturing is often linked to age and gender. Women may weave and men may make pottery or vice versa. Most people of a particular age and gender share the technical knowledge associated with that age and gender. If married women customarily make baskets, all or most married women know how to make baskets. Neither technology nor technical knowledge is as specialized as it is in states.

However, some tribal societies do promote specialization. Among the Yanomami of Venezuela and Brazil (Figure 16.3), for instance, certain villages manufacture clay pots and others make hammocks. They don't specialize, as one might suppose, because certain raw materials happen to be available near particular villages. Clay suitable for pots is widely available. Everyone knows how to make pots, but not everybody does so. Craft specialization reflects the social and political environment rather than the natural environment. Such specialization promotes trade, which is the first step in creating an alliance with enemy villages

Figure 16.3   Location of the Yanomami.

product. The fruits of their labor are their own, rather than someone else's.

In nonindustrial societies, the economic relation between coworkers is just one aspect of a more general social relation. They aren't just coworkers but kin, in-laws, or celebrants in the same ritual. In industrial nations, people don't usually work with relatives and neighbors. If coworkers are friends, the personal relationship usually develops out of their common employment rather than being based on a previous association.

Thus, industrial workers have impersonal relations with their products, coworkers, and employers. People sell their labor for cash, and the economic domain stands apart from ordinary social life. In nonindustrial societies, however, the relations of production, distribution, and consumption are *social relations with economic aspects*. Economy is not a separate entity but is *embedded* in the society.

Economizing and Maximization

Economic anthropologists have been concerned with two main questions:

1. How are production, distribution, and consumption organized in different societies? This question focuses on *systems* of human behavior and their organization.

2. What motivates people in different cultures to produce, distribute or exchange, and consume? Here the focus is not on systems of behavior but on the motives of the *individuals* who participate in those systems.

Anthropologists view both economic systems and motivations in a cross-cultural perspective. Motivation is a concern of psychologists, but it also has been, implicitly or explicitly, a concern of economists and anthropologists. Economists tend to assume that producers and distributors make decisions rationally using the *profit motive*, as do consumers when they shop around for the best value.

(Chagnon 1997). Specialization contributes to keeping the peace, although it has not prevented intervillage warfare.

ALIENATION IN INDUSTRIAL ECONOMIES

There are some significant contrasts between industrial and nonindustrial economies. When factory workers produce for sale and for their employer's profit, rather than for their own use, they may be alienated from the items they make. Such alienation means they don't feel strong pride in or personal identification with their products. They see their product as belonging to someone else, not to the man or woman whose labor actually produced it. In nonindustrial societies, by contrast, people usually see their work through from start to finish and have a sense of accomplishment in the

Not just factory work but agricultural production may be industrialized, so that workers feel alienated from their product. This scene shows not a family farm but the mass production of rice in Thailand. Is alienation an issue in your own work?

Although anthropologists know that the profit motive is not universal, the assumption that individuals try to maximize profits is basic to the capitalist world economy and to much of Western economic theory. In fact, the subject matter of economics is often defined as **economizing**, or the rational allocation of scarce means (or resources) to alternative ends (or uses). What does that mean? Classical economic theory assumes that our wants are infinite and that our means are limited. Since means are limited, people must make choices about how to use their scarce resources: their time, labor, money, and capital. (The "Interesting Issues" on "Scarcity and the Betsileo" disputes the idea that people always make economic choices based on scarcity.) Economists assume that when confronted with choices and decisions, people tend to make the one that maximizes profit. This is assumed to be the most rational (reasonable) choice.

The idea that individuals choose to maximize profits was a basic assumption of the classical economists of the 19th century and one that is held by many contemporary economists. However, certain economists now recognize that individuals in Western cultures, as in others, may be motivated by many other goals. Depending on the society and the situation, people may try to maximize profit, wealth, prestige, pleasure, comfort, or social harmony. Individuals may want to realize their personal or family ambitions or those of another group to which they belong.

Understanding Ourselves What motivates us? Do we have the same motives our parents had? People must choose among alternatives, and economists think such choices are guided mainly by the desire for economic gain. Do you agree? Such an assumption isn't evident among the Betsileo. Is it true of individual Americans? Think about the choices your parents have made. Did they make decisions that maximized their incomes, their life styles, their individual happiness, family benefits, or what? What about you? What factors were involved when you chose to apply to and attend a college? Did you want to stay close to home, to attend college with friends, or to maintain a romantic attachment (all social reasons). Did you seek the lowest tuition and college costs—or get a generous scholarship (economic decisions)? Did you choose prestige, or perhaps the likelihood that one day you would earn more money because of the reputation of your alma mater (maximizing prestige and future wealth)? The profit motive may predominate in contemporary North America, but different individuals, like different cultures, may choose to pursue other goals.

ALTERNATIVE ENDS

To what uses do people in various societies put their scarce resources? Throughout the world, people devote some of their time and energy to building up a *subsistence fund* (Wolf 1966). In other words, they have to work to eat, to replace the calories they use in their daily activity. People also must invest in a *replacement fund*. They must maintain their technology and other items essential to production. If a hoe or plow breaks, they must repair or replace it. They also must obtain and replace items that are essential not to production but to everyday life, such as clothing and shelter.

People also have to invest in a *social fund*. They have to help their friends, relatives, in-laws, and neighbors. It is useful to distinguish between a social fund and a *ceremonial fund*. The latter term refers to expenditures on ceremonies or rituals. To prepare a festival honoring one's ancestors, for example, requires time and the outlay of wealth.

Citizens of nonindustrial states also must allocate scarce resources to a *rent fund*. We think of rent as payment for the use of property. However, rent fund has a wider meaning. It refers to resources that people must render to an individual or agency that is superior politically or economically. Tenant farmers and sharecroppers, for example, either pay rent or give some of their produce to their landlords, as peasants did under feudalism.

Peasants are small-scale agriculturalists who live in nonindustrial states and have rent fund obligations (see Kearney 1996). They produce to feed themselves, to sell their produce, and to pay rent. All peasants have two things in common:

1. They live in state-organized societies.

2. They produce food without the elaborate technology—chemical fertilizers, tractors, airplanes to spray crops, and so on—of modern farming or agribusiness.

In addition to paying rent to landlords, peasants must satisfy government obligations, paying taxes in the form of money, produce, or labor. The rent fund is not simply an *additional* obligation for peasants. Often it becomes their foremost and unavoidable duty. Sometimes, to meet the obligation to pay rent, their own diets suffer. The demands of paying rent may divert resources from subsistence, replacement, social, and ceremonial funds.

Motivations vary from society to society, and people often lack freedom of choice in allocating their resources. Because of obligations to pay rent, peasants may allocate their scarce means toward ends that are not their own but those of government officials. Thus, even in societies where there is a profit motive, people are often prevented from rationally maximizing self-interest by factors beyond their control.

Distribution, Exchange

The economist Karl Polanyi (1968) stimulated the comparative study of exchange, and several anthropologists followed his lead. To study exchange cross-culturally, Polanyi defined three principles orienting exchanges: the market principle, redistribution, and reciprocity. These principles can all be present in the same society, but in that case they govern different kinds of transactions. In any society, one of them usually dominates. The principle of exchange that dominates in a given society is the one that allocates the means of production.

THE MARKET PRINCIPLE

In today's world capitalist economy, the **market principle** dominates. It governs the distribution of the means of production: land, labor, natural resources, technology, and capital. "Market exchange refers to the organizational process of purchase and sale at money price" (Dalton 1967). With market exchange, items are bought and sold, using money, with an eye to maximizing profit, and value is determined by the *law of supply and demand* (things cost more the scarcer they are and the more people want them).

Bargaining is characteristic of market-principle exchanges. The buyer and seller strive to maximize—to get their "money's worth." In bargaining, buyers and sellers don't need to meet personally. But their offers and counteroffers do need to be open for negotiation over a fairly short time period.

From October 1966 through December 1967, my wife and I lived among the Betsileo people of Madagascar, studying their economy and social life (Kottak 1980). Soon after our arrival, we met two well-educated schoolteachers who were interested in our research. The woman's father was a congressman who became a cabinet minister during our stay. Our schoolteacher friends told us that their family came from a historically important and typical Betsileo village called Ivato, which they invited us to visit with them.

We had traveled to many other villages, where we were often displeased with our reception. As we drove up, children would run away screaming. Women would hurry inside. Men would retreat to doorways, where they lurked bashfully. Eventually someone would summon the courage to ask what we wanted. This behavior expressed the Betsileo's great fear of the *mpakafo*. Believed to cut out and devour his victim's heart and liver, the *mpakafo* is the Malagasy vampire. These cannibals are said to have fair skin and to be very tall. Because I have light skin and stand six feet four inches tall, I was a natural suspect. The fact that such creatures were not known to travel with their wives helped convince the Betsileo that I wasn't really a *mpakafo*.

When we visited Ivato, we found that its people were different. They were friendly and hospitable. Our very first day there, we did a brief census and found out who lived in which households. We learned people's names and their relationships to our schoolteacher friends and to each other. We met an excellent informant who knew all about the local history. In a few afternoons, I learned much more than I had in the other villages in several sessions.

Ivatans were willing to talk because I had powerful sponsors, village natives who had made it in the outside world, people the Ivatans knew would protect them. The schoolteachers vouched for us, but even more significant was the cabinet minister, who was like a grandfather and benefactor to everyone in town. The Ivatans had no reason to fear me because their more influential native son had asked them to answer my questions.

Once we moved to Ivato, the elders established a pattern of visiting us every evening. They came to talk, attracted by the inquisitive foreigners but also by the wine, cigarettes, and food we offered. I asked questions about their customs and beliefs. I eventually developed interview schedules about various subjects, including rice production. I mimeographed these forms to use in Ivato and in two other villages I was studying less intensively. Never have I interviewed as easily as I did in Ivato. So enthusiastic were the Ivatans about my questions that even people from neighboring villages came to join the study. Since these people knew nothing about the social scientist's techniques, I couldn't discourage them by saying that they weren't in my sample. Instead, I agreed to visit each village, where I filled out the interview schedule in just one house. Then I told the other villagers that the household head had done such a good job of teaching me about their village, I wouldn't need to ask questions in the other households.

As our stay drew to an end, the elders of Ivato began to lament, saying, "We'll miss you. When you leave, there won't be any more cigarettes, any more wine, or any more questions." They wondered what it would be like for us back in the United States. They knew that I had an automobile and that I regularly purchased things, including the wine, cigarettes, and food I shared with them. I could afford to buy products they would never have. They commented, "When you go back to your country, you'll need a lot of money for things like cars, clothes, and food. We don't need to buy those things. We make almost everything we use. We don't need as much money as you, because we produce for ourselves."

The Betsileo are not unusual among people whom anthropologists have studied. Strange as it may seem to an American consumer, who may believe that he or she can never have enough money, some rice farmers actually believe that *they have all they need*. The lesson from the Betsileo is that scarcity, which economists view as universal, is variable. Although shortages do arise in nonindustrial societies, the concept of scarcity (insufficient means) is much less developed in stable subsistence-oriented societies than in the societies characterized by industrialism, particularly as the reliance on consumer goods increases.

REDISTRIBUTION

Redistribution operates when goods, services, or their equivalent move from the local level to a center. The center may be a capital, a regional collection point, or a storehouse near a chief's residence. Products often move through a hierarchy of officials for storage at the center. Along the way, officials and their dependents may consume some of them, but the exchange principle here is *re*distribution. The flow of goods eventually reverses direction—out from the center, down through the hierarchy, and back to the common people.

One example of a redistributive system comes from the Cherokee, the original owners of the Tennessee Valley. Productive farmers who subsisted on maize, beans, and squash, supplemented by hunting and fishing, the Cherokee had chiefs. Each of their main villages had a central plaza, where meetings of the chief's council took place, and where redistributive feasts were held. According to Cherokee custom, each family farm had an area where the family, if they wished, could set aside a portion of their annual harvest for the chief. This supply of corn was used to feed the needy, as well as travelers

and warriors journeying through friendly territory. This store of food was available to all who needed it, with the understanding that it "belonged" to the chief and was dispersed through his generosity. The chief also hosted the redistributive feasts held in the main settlements (Harris 1978).

RECIPROCITY

Reciprocity is exchange between social equals, who are normally related by kinship, marriage, or another close personal tie. Because it occurs between social equals, it is dominant in the more egalitarian societies—among foragers, cultivators, and pastoralists. There are three degrees of reciprocity: generalized, balanced, and negative (Sahlins 1968, 1972; Service 1966). These may be imagined as areas of a continuum defined by these questions:

1. How closely related are the parties to the exchange?

2. How quickly and unselfishly are gifts reciprocated?

Sharing the fruits of production, a keystone of many nonindustrial societies, also has been a goal of socialist nations, such as China. These workers in Yunnan province strive for an equal distribution of meat.

Generalized reciprocity, the purest form of reciprocity, is characteristic of exchanges between closely related people. In *balanced reciprocity*, social distance increases, as does the need to reciprocate. In *negative reciprocity*, social distance is greatest and reciprocation is most calculated.

With **generalized reciprocity**, someone gives to another person and expects nothing concrete or immediate in return. Such exchanges (including parental gift giving in contemporary North America) are not primarily economic transactions but expressions of personal relationships. Most parents don't keep accounts of every penny they spend on their children. They merely hope that the children will respect their culture's customs involving love, honor, loyalty, and other obligations to parents.

Among foragers, generalized reciprocity tends to govern exchanges. People routinely share with other band members (Bird-David 1992; Kent 1992). A study of the Ju/'hoansi San (Figure 16.4) found that 40 percent of the population contributed little

Figure 16.4
Location of the San, including Ju/'hoansi.

Legend:
Northern San including Ju/'hoansi distribution
Dobe area

to the food supply (Lee 1968/1974). Children, teenagers, and people over 60 depended on other people for their food. Despite the high proportion of dependents, the average worker hunted or gathered less than half as much (12 to 19 hours a week) as the average American works. Nonetheless, there was always food because different people worked on different days.

So strong is the ethic of reciprocal sharing that most foragers lack an expression for "thank you." To offer thanks would be impolite because it would imply that a particular act of sharing, which is the keystone of egalitarian society, was unusual. Among the Semai, foragers of central Malaysia (Dentan 1979), to express gratitude would suggest surprise at the hunter's generosity or success (Harris 1974).

Balanced reciprocity applies to exchanges between people who are more distantly related than are members of the same band or household. In a horticultural society, for example, a man presents a gift to someone in another village. The recipient may be a cousin, a trading partner, or a brother's fictive kinsman. The giver expects something in return. This may not come immediately, but the social relationship will be strained if there is no reciprocation.

Exchanges in nonindustrial societies also may illustrate **negative reciprocity**, mainly in dealing with people outside or on the fringes of their social systems. To people who live in a world of close personal relations, exchanges with outsiders are full of ambiguity and distrust. Exchange is one way of establishing friendly relations with outsiders, but especially when trade begins, the relationship is still tentative. Often, the initial exchange is close to being purely economic; people want to get something back immediately. Just as in market economies, but without using money, they try to get the best possible immediate return for their investment.

See the Virtual Exploration for ways in which redistribution and reciprocity can change over time

Generalized and balanced reciprocity are based on trust and a social tie. But negative reciprocity involves the attempt to get something for as little as possible, even if it means being cagey or deceitful or cheating. Among the most extreme and "negative" examples of negative reciprocity was 19th-century horse thievery by North American Plains

Indians. Men would sneak into camps and villages of neighboring tribes to steal horses. A similar pattern of cattle raiding continues today in East Africa, among tribes like the Kuria (Fleisher 2000). In these cases, the party that starts the raiding can expect reciprocity—a raid on their own village—or worse. The Kuria hunt down cattle thieves and kill them. It's still reciprocity, governed by "Do unto others as they have done unto you."

One way of reducing the tension in situations of potential negative reciprocity is to engage in "silent trade." One example is the silent trade of the Mbuti "pygmy" foragers of the African equatorial forest and their neighboring horticultural villagers. There is no personal contact during their exchanges. A Mbuti hunter leaves game, honey, or another forest product at a customary site. Villagers collect it and leave crops in exchange. Often the parties bargain silently. If one feels the return is insufficient, he or she simply leaves it at the trading site. If the other party wants to continue trade, it will be increased.

COEXISTENCE OF EXCHANGE PRINCIPLES

In today's North America, the market principle governs most exchanges, from the sale of the means of production to the sale of consumer goods. We also have redistribution. Some of our tax money goes to support the government, but some of it also comes back to us in the form of social services, education, health care, and road building. We also have reciprocal exchanges. Generalized reciprocity characterizes the relationship between parents and children. However, even here the dominant market mentality surfaces in comments about the high cost of raising children and in the stereotypical statement of the disappointed parent: "We gave you everything money could buy."

Exchanges of gifts, cards, and invitations exemplify reciprocity, usually balanced. Everyone has heard remarks like "They invited us to their daughter's wedding, so when ours gets married, we'll have to invite them" and "They've been here for dinner three times and haven't invited us yet. I don't think we should ask them back until they do." Such precise balancing of reciprocity would be out of place in a foraging band, where resources are communal (common to all) and daily sharing based on generalized reciprocity is an essential ingredient of social life and survival.

Potlatching

One of the most thoroughly studied cultural practices known to ethnography is the **potlatch**, a festive event within a regional exchange system among tribes of the North Pacific Coast of North America, including the Salish and Kwakiutl of Washington and British Columbia and the Tsimshian of Alaska (Figure 16.5). Some tribes still practice the potlatch, sometimes as a memorial to the dead (Kan 1986, 1989). At each such event, assisted by members of their communities, potlatch sponsors traditionally gave away food, blankets, pieces of copper, or other items. In return for this, they got prestige. To give a potlatch enhanced one's reputation. Prestige increased with the lavishness of the potlatch, the value of the goods given away in it.

The potlatching tribes were foragers, but atypical ones. They were sedentary and had chiefs. And unlike the environments of most other recent foragers, theirs was not marginal. They had access

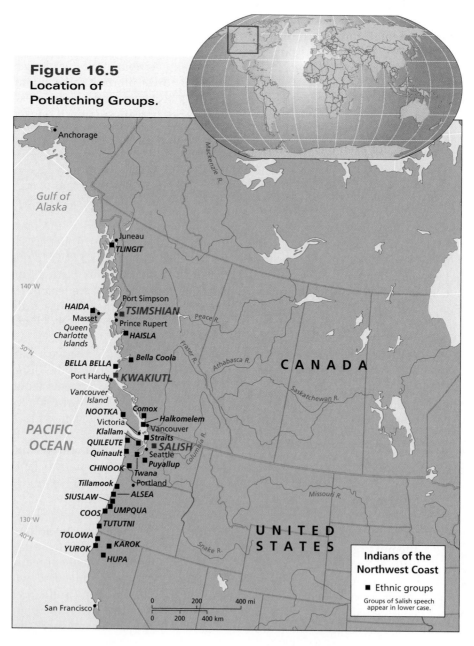

Figure 16.5
Location of Potlatching Groups.

to a wide variety of land and sea resources. Among their most important foods were salmon, herring, candlefish, berries, mountain goats, seals, and porpoises (Piddocke 1969).

If classical economic theory is correct that the profit motive is universal, with the goal of maximizing material benefits, then how does one explain the potlatch, in which wealth is given away? Many scholars once cited the potlatch as a classic case of economically wasteful behavior. In this view, potlatching was based on an economically irrational drive for prestige. This interpretation stressed the lavishness and supposed wastefulness, especially of the Kwakiutl displays, to support the contention that in some societies people strive to maximize prestige at the expense of their material well-being. This interpretation has been challenged.

Ecological anthropology, also known as *cultural ecology*, is a theoretical school in anthropology that attempts to interpret cultural practices, such as the potlatch, in terms of their long-term role in helping humans adapt to their environments. A different interpretation of the potlatch has been offered by the ecological anthropologists Wayne Suttles (1960) and Andrew Vayda (1961/ 1968). These scholars see potlatching not in terms of its apparent wastefulness, but in terms of its long-term role as a cultural adaptive mechanism. This view not only helps us understand potlatching, it also has comparative value because it helps us understand similar patterns of lavish feasting in many other parts of the world. Here is the ecological interpretation: Customs like the potlatch are cultural adaptations to alternating periods of local abundance and shortage.

How does this work? The overall natural environment of the North

See the Internet Exercises at your OLC for feasting among the Hoploi of Papua New Guinea

mhhe
●com
/kottak

Pacific Coast is favorable, but resources fluctuate from year to year and place to place. Salmon and herring aren't equally abundant every year in a given locality. One village can have a good year while another is experiencing a bad one. Later their fortunes reverse. In this context, the potlatch cycle of the Kwakiutl and Salish had adaptive value, and

The historic photo (above) shows Tlingit clan members attending a potlatch at Sitka, Alaska, in 1904. Such ancestral headdresses have been repatriated recently from museums back to Tlingit clans. The photo below shows a modern potlatch, lasting four days, celebrated by Alaska's Tsimshian Indians. The gifts to be distributed are piled at the center of the large room where the event is taking place. Have you ever partaken in anything like a potlatch?

the potlatch was not a competitive display that brought no material benefit.

A village enjoying an especially good year had a surplus of subsistence items, which it could trade for more durable wealth items, like blankets, canoes, or pieces of copper. Wealth, in turn, by being distributed, could be converted into prestige. Members of several villages were invited to any potlatch and got to take home the resources that were given away. In this way, potlatching linked villages together in a regional economy—an exchange system that distributed food and wealth from wealthy to needy communities. In return, the potlatch sponsors and their villages got prestige. The decision to potlatch was determined by the health of the local economy. If there had been subsistence surpluses, and thus a buildup of wealth over several good years, a village could afford a potlatch to convert its food and wealth into prestige.

The long-term adaptive value of intercommunity feasting becomes clear when we consider what happened when a formerly prosperous village had a run of bad luck. Its people started accepting invitations to potlatches in villages that were doing better. The tables were turned as the temporarily rich became temporarily poor and vice versa. The newly needy accepted food and wealth items. They were willing to receive rather than bestow gifts and thus to relinquish some of their stored-up prestige. They hoped their luck would eventually improve so that resources could be recouped and prestige regained.

The potlatch linked local groups along the North Pacific Coast into a regional alliance and exchange network. Potlatching and intervillage exchange had adaptive functions, regardless of the motivations of the individual participants. The anthropologists who stressed rivalry for prestige were not wrong. They were merely emphasizing motivations at the expense of an analysis of economic and ecological systems.

The use of feasts to enhance individual and community reputations and to redistribute wealth is not peculiar to populations of the North Pacific Coast. Competitive feasting is widely characteristic of nonindustrial food producers. But among most foragers, who live, remember, in marginal areas, resources are too meager to support feasting on such a level. In such societies, sharing rather than competition prevails.

Like many other cultural practices that have attracted considerable anthropological attention, the potlatch does not, and did not, exist apart from larger world events. For example, within the spreading world capitalist economy of the 19th century, the potlatching tribes, particularly the Kwakiutl, began to trade with Europeans (fur for blankets, for example). Their wealth increased as a result. Simultaneously, a huge proportion of the Kwakiutl population died from previously unknown diseases brought by the Europeans. As a result, the increased wealth from trade flowed into a drastically reduced population. With many of the traditional sponsors dead (such as chiefs and their families), the Kwakiutl extended the right to give a potlatch to the entire population. This stimulated very intense competition for prestige. Given trade, increased wealth, and a decreased population, the Kwakiutl also started converting wealth into prestige by destroying wealth items such as blankets, pieces of copper, and houses (Vayda 1961/1968). Blankets and houses could be burned, and coppers could be buried at sea. Here, with dramatically increased wealth and a drastically reduced population, Kwakiutl potlatching changed its nature. It became much more destructive than it had been previously and than potlatching continued to be among tribes that were less affected by trade and disease.

In any case, note that potlatching also served to prevent the development of socioeconomic stratification, a system of social classes. Wealth relinquished or destroyed was converted into a nonmaterial item: prestige. Under capitalism, we reinvest our profits (rather than burning our cash), with the hope of making an additional profit. However, the potlatching tribes were content to relinquish their surpluses rather than use them to widen the social distance between themselves and their fellow tribe members.

SUMMARY

1. Cohen's adaptive strategies include foraging (hunting and gathering), horticulture, agriculture, pastoralism, and industrialism. Foraging was the only human adaptive strategy until the advent of food production (farming and herding) 10,000 years ago. Food production eventually replaced foraging in most places. Almost all modern foragers have at least some dependence on food production or food producers.

2. Horticulture and agriculture stand at opposite ends of a continuum based on labor intensity and continuity and land use. Horticulture doesn't use land or labor intensively. Horticulturalists cultivate a plot for one or two years and then abandon it. Further along the continuum, horticulture becomes more intensive, but there is always a fallow period. Agriculturalists farm the same plot of land continuously and use labor intensively. They use one or more of the following: irrigation, terracing, domesticated animals as means of production, and manuring.

3. The pastoral strategy is mixed. Nomadic pastoralists trade with cultivators. Part of a transhumant pastoral population cultivates while another part takes the herds to pasture. Except for some Peruvians and the Navajo, who are recent herders, the New World lacks native pastoralists.

4. Economic anthropology is the cross-cultural study of systems of production, distribution, and consumption. In nonindustrial societies, a kin-based mode of production prevails. One acquires rights to resources and labor through membership in social groups, not impersonally through purchase and sale. Work is just one aspect of social relations expressed in varied contexts.

5. Economics has been defined as the science of allocating scarce means to alternative ends. Western economists assume the notion of scarcity is universal—which it isn't—and that in making choices, people strive to maximize personal profit. In nonindustrial societies, indeed as in our own, people often maximize values other than individual profit. Furthermore, people may lack free choice in allocating their resources.

6. In nonindustrial societies, people invest in subsistence, replacement, social, and ceremonial funds. States add a rent fund: People must share their output with social superiors. In states, the obligation to pay rent often becomes primary.

7. Besides production, economic anthropologists study and compare exchange systems. The three principles of exchange are the market principle, redistribution, and reciprocity. The market principle, based on supply and demand and the profit motive, dominates in states. With redistribution, goods are collected at a central place, but some of them are eventually given back, or redistributed, to the people. Reciprocity governs exchanges between social equals. It is the characteristic mode of exchange among foragers and horticulturists. Reciprocity, redistribution, and the market principle may coexist in a society, but the primary exchange mode is the one that allocates the means of production. Patterns of feasting and exchanges of wealth among villages are common among nonindustrial food producers, as among the potlatching cultures of North America's North Pacific Coast. Such systems help even out the availability of resources over time.

KEY TERMS

agriculture   Nonindustrial systems of plant cultivation characterized by continuous and intensive use of land and labor.

balanced reciprocity   See *generalized reciprocity.*

band   Basic unit of social organization among foragers. A band includes fewer than 100 people; it often splits up seasonally.

correlation   An association between two or more variables such that when one changes (varies), the other(s) also change(s) (covaries); for example, temperature and sweating.

cultivation continuum   A continuum based on the comparative study of nonindustrial cultivating societies in which labor intensity increases and fallowing decreases.

449

economizing   The rational allocation of scarce means (or resources) to alternative ends (or uses); often considered the subject matter of economics.

economy   A population's system of production, distribution, and consumption of resources.

generalized reciprocity   Principle that characterizes exchanges between closely related individuals. As social distance increases, reciprocity becomes balanced and finally negative.

horticulture   Nonindustrial system of plant cultivation in which plots lie fallow for varying lengths of time.

market principle   Profit-oriented principle of exchange that dominates in states, particularly industrial states. Goods and services are bought and sold, and values are determined by supply and demand.

means (or factors) of production   Land, labor, technology, and capital—major productive resources.

mode of production   Way of organizing production—a set of social relations through which labor is deployed to wrest energy from nature by means of tools, skills, and knowledge.

negative reciprocity   See *generalized reciprocity*.

nomadism, pastoral   Movement throughout the year by the whole pastoral group (men, women, and children) with their animals; more generally, such constant movement in pursuit of strategic resources.

pastoralists   People who use a food-producing strategy of adaptation based on care of herds of domesticated animals.

peasant   Small-scale agriculturalist living in a state with rent fund obligations.

potlatch   Competitive feast among Indians on the North Pacific Coast of North America.

reciprocity   One of the three principles of exchange; governs exchange between social equals; major exchange mode in band and tribal societies.

redistribution   Major exchange mode of chiefdoms, many archaic states, and some states with managed economies.

transhumance   One of two variants of pastoralism; part of the population moves seasonally with the herds while the other part remains in home villages.

CRITICAL THINKING QUESTIONS

For more self testing, see the self quizzes

/kottak

1. What are some of the main advantages and disadvantages of living in a foraging society? How about horticulture? Agriculture? Pastoralism? In which one would you want to live, and why?

2. If you had to spend the rest of your life in a foraging society, how would you go about becoming a member of that society?

3. What do you see as the main differences and similarities between ancient and modern hunter-gatherers?

4. What are the benefits and costs, including the environmental costs, of horticulture compared with irrigated agriculture?

5. What are your scarce means? How do you make decisions about allocating them?

6. What do you attempt to maximize? Does that vary depending on the situation?

7. Does anything (or many things) about living in a nonindustrial society strike you as attractive?

8. Give examples from your own exchanges of reciprocity, redistribution, and the market principle.

9. Give examples from your own exchanges of different degrees of reciprocity.

Atlas Questions

Look at Map 16, "World Land Use: 1500 AD."

1. Name three continents with significant herding economies. On which continents was pastoralism absent?

2. How do the various types of agriculture vary among the continents? Which continent had the largest area under intensive cultivation? Which continent or continents had the least amount of intensive cultivation?

3. What were the main uses of land in Europe when the European age of discovery and conquest began?

SUGGESTED ADDITIONAL READINGS

Bates, D. G.

2001   *Human Adaptive Strategies: Ecology, Culture, and Politics*. 2nd ed. Boston: Allyn and Bacon. Recent discussion of the different adaptive strategies and their political correlates.

Chatty, D.

1996   *Mobile Pastoralists: Development Planning and Social Change in Oman*. New York: Columbia University Press. Based on 10 years of research in a nomadic Middle Eastern community, this study examines forces of "modernization," including a shift from herding to cash employment and the changing role of women.

Cohen, Y.

1974   *Man in Adaptation: The Cultural Present*, 2nd ed. Chicago: Aldine. Presents Cohen's economic typology of adaptive strategies and uses it to organize a valuable set of essays on culture and adaptation.

Gudeman, S.

2001   *The Anthropology of Economy: Community, Market, and Culture*. Malden, MA: Blackwell. Economic aspects of globalization in relation to economic anthropology.

Gudeman, S., ed.

1998   *Economic Anthropology*. Northhampton, MA: E. Elgar. Reference essays in economic anthropology.

Ingold, T., D. Riches, and J. Woodburn

1991   *Hunters and Gatherers*. New York: Berg (St. Martin's). Volume I examines history and social change among foragers. Volume II looks at their property, ideology, and power relations. These broad regional surveys illuminate current issues and debates.

Kearney, M.

1996   *Reconceptualizing the Peasantry: Anthropology in Global Perspective*. Boulder, CO: Westview. How peasants live today, in post–Cold War nation-states.

Kent, S.

1996   *Cultural Diversity among Twentieth-Century Foragers: An African Perspective*. New York: Cambridge University Press. Africa's hunter-gatherers, their adaptations, social life, and variety.

Lee, R. B.

2002   *The Dobe Ju/'hoansi*, 3rd ed. Belmont, CA: Wadsworth. Account of well-known San foragers, by one of their principal ethnographers.

Lee, R. B., and R. H. Daly

1999   *The Cambridge Encyclopedia of Hunters and Gatherers*. New York: Cambridge University Press. Indispensable reference work on foragers.

Plattner, S., ed.

1989   *Economic Anthropology*. Stanford, CA: Stanford University Press. Articles on economic features of foraging, tribal, peasant, state, and industrial societies.

Salzman, P. C., and J. G. Galaty, eds.

1990   *Nomads in a Changing World*. Naples: Istituto Universitario Orientale. Pastoral nomads in varied contemporary settings.

Srivastava, J., N. J. H. Smith, and D. A. Forno

1998   *Integrating Biodiversity in Agricultural Intensification: Toward Sound Practices.* Washington, DC: World Bank. Environmentally and socially sustainable agriculture in today's world.

Wilk, E. R.

1996   *Economies and Cultures: An Introduction to Economic Anthropology.* Boulder, CO: Westview. An up-to-date introduction to economic anthropology.

Wilmsen, R.

1989   *Land Filled with Flies: A Political Economy of the Kalahari.* Chicago: University of Chicago Press. A revisionist view of the San, in the context of colonialism and the world system.

Young, W. C.

1996   *The Rashaayada Bedouin: Arab Pastoralists of Eastern Sudan.* Fort Worth: Harcourt Brace. This examination of a pastoral economy also weaves in information on gender and "race."

INTERNET EXERCISES

1. *Reciprocity*: Go to the Living Link's video collection at Emory University's Center for the Advanced Study of Ape and Human Evolution web page, **http://www.emory.edu/LIVING_LINKS/ a/video. html,**and watch the Chimpanzee Food Sharing Movie, **http://www.emory.edu/LIVING_LINKS/ sounds/ram_text/food_sharing28k.ram.**

    a. What is an example in this film of generalized reciprocity?

    b. What is an example of balanced reciprocity?

    c. What is an example of negative reciprocity?

    d. What inferences can be made from the observation that humans and chimpanzees exhibit similar capacities for reciprocity? Even when humans and chimpanzees enact similar behaviors (i.e., generalized reciprocity), are there important differences?

2. *Subsistence and Settlement*: Go to the Ethnographic Atlas Cross-tabulations page, **http:// lucy.ukc.ac.uk/cgi-bin/uncgi/Ethnoatlas/ atlas.vopts.** This site has compiled ethnographic information on many different groups, and you can use the tools provided to cross-tabulate the prevalence of certain traits. Go to the site, under "Select Row Category" choose "subsistence economy," and under "Select Column Category" select "settlement patterns." Press the Submit Query button. The table that appears shows the frequency with which groups of different subsistence systems use certain mobility strategies.

    a. Notice that a high number of groups with agriculture use "Compact and relatively permanent settlements." Is this what you would expect?

    b. What kinds of subsistence strategies are used by groups that are the most mobile (have "Migratory or nomadic," "Seminomadic," or "Semisedentary" settlement patterns)?

    c. Now let's focus on the groups that are exceptional and do not combine subsistence and settlement strategies in the most usual or common way. There is a single group that uses intensive agriculture and is seminomadic. Click on the number at that location. What is the name of that group, and where are they found?

    d. There are a few groups that are in permanent settlements and use hunting, gathering, or fishing. What region of the world are most of these groups from?

    e. Feel free to explore many of the other variables listed in the table. We suggest you check "mean size of local communities," "settlement patterns," and "subsistence economy" against each other. What patterns do you see?

See Chapter 16 at your McGraw-Hill Online Learning Center for additional review and interactive exercises.

17

POLITICAL SYSTEMS

Overview

Some people make a career of politics, also known as "leadership" or "public service." In holding office, our politicians lead and manage affairs of public policy. They make decisions and try to implement them. Anthropologists have wondered whether societies with neither politicans nor permanent political offices can have politics.

Political anthropology is the cross-cultural study of political systems, of formal and informal political institutions. A related field is legal anthropology, the comparative study of legal systems or law. Although not all societies have had law—in the sense of a formal legal code, judiciary, and enforcement—all societies have had some means of social control. Human groups have never lived in total anarchy. Surveying many societies, present and past, we see a range of political systems. Some have informal or temporary leaders with limited authority, exercised only at the local level. Oth-

ers have strong and permanent political institutions that prevail over entire regions.

The terms *band, tribe, chiefdom,* and *state* describe different forms of social and political organization, with different degrees of political authority and power. Bands are small, mobile, kin-based groups with little differential power. Tribes have villages and/or descent groups but lack a formal government. Chiefdoms, intermediate between tribes and states, are kin-based, but they have differential access to resources and a permanent political structure. The state is an autonomous political unit encompassing many communities. Its government has the power to collect taxes, to draft people for work or war, and to decree and enforce laws. The state is defined as a form of political organization based on central government and socioeconomic stratification—a division of society into classes.

Chat Rooms, Bedouin Style

NGNEWS.COM NEWS BRIEF

by Ilene R. Prusher

April 28, 2000

When we think of politics, we think of government, of federal and state institutions, of Washington, Ottawa, or perhaps our state or provincial capital, city hall, or court-house. We hear discussions of public service, political offices, and elections—and maybe the economic and political power that goes along with holding office, or with influencing those who hold office. Binding decisions get made at the top levels of government. There are also informal political institutions, which aren't part of the governmental apparatus, but which substantially influence it. Described in this article are the *diwaniyas* of Kuwait—informal, local-level meeting places where informal discussions can have formal consequences. The author contends that much of Kuwait's decision making, networking, and influence peddling takes place in *diwaniyas*. What do you see as the advantages and disadvantages of the *diwaniya* system. Do we have anything like it in our society?

In the historical fabric of Kuwait, *diwaniyas* have been men-only political salons—a local equivalent of neighborhood pub and town-hall meeting combined. They serve not only as parlors for chit-chats, but governance, too. *Diwaniyas* are so integral to Kuwaiti culture that during election season, candidates don't go door to door, but *diwaniya* to *diwaniya*. This is where business deals are made and marriages arranged. . . .

Traditionally, most men have an open invitation to attend a *diwaniya* on any given night, and wealthy families have a large, long room adjacent to their homes expressly for their *diwaniya*. Some neighborhoods have a common *diwaniya*, much like a community center.

At a typical men-only *diwaniya* . . . the attendees lounge among the partitions of a never-ending couch that follow the contours of the room in one giant U. They usually gather once a week, starting at 8 in the evening and sometimes going past midnight.

As they discuss issues . . . they twirl smoothly polished beads around their fingers and worry aloud whether change has come to Kuwait too fast. The presence of malls and movies, they fret, is breaking down social norms like the taboo against premarital dating. . . .

At the Al-Fanar Center, with its bevy of Body Shops and Benettons, teenage boys say they also have no interest in chattering the night away when they could be flirting. "We like to follow around girls without hijab [veil]," says teenager Abdul Rahman Al-Tarket, roaming the mall with his two friends. . . .

Mixed [male and female] *diwaniyas* are still an anomaly. "For me, the *diwaniya* is a very comfortable place to have people come and see me," says artist Thoraya al-Baqsami, who co-hosts one mixed gathering. "I know many people don't like it, but we are in the 21st century now," she says as she gives a tour of her adjacent gallery. . . .

Many women here say they're happy to leave the *diwaniya* to the domain of men. But more problematic is that it is the *diwaniya* at which much of the country's decision-making and networking takes place. It is also a forum where a constituent can meet his parliamentary representative and consult him about major problems or minor potholes.

The importance of *diwaniyas* to Kuwaiti society cannot be understated. Kuwait's parliament emerged from a 1921 proposal by *diwaniyas*. And Sheik Jaber al-Sabah, who dissolved the assembly in 1986, restored it in 1992 following pressure from *diwaniyas*.

And since that is a male-only world, even liberal-minded youth say they can't see allowing a woman to represent them in office. A bill to give women the right to vote and to run for parliament lost by a narrow vote of 32 to 20 last November.

A Kuwaiti *diwaniya*.

"I was stopped for driving without a license, and a friend of my father's got me released," says one teenager. "If we elected a woman, what would she do? She can't come to the *diwaniya* and she can't have those kinds of contacts, so she can't represent us."

Some here say they wouldn't mind seeing the decline of the *diwaniya*. Says Kuwait University political scientist Shamlan El-Issa: "The positive aspects are that it helps democracy—men meet every day and talk and complain for two or three hours. The negative is that it replaces the family—men go to work and *diwaniya*, and never see their wives."

SOURCE: http://www.ngnews.com/news/2000/04/ 04282000/ kuwait_12448.asp. © 2000 The Christian Science Publishing Society.

Surely the process of deliberation and decision making that goes on within—and then outside—the *diwaniya* system is political. What is "the political" anyway? Anthropologists and political scientists share an interest in political systems and organization, but the anthropological approach is global and comparative. Anthropological studies have revealed substantial variation in power (formal and informal), authority, and legal systems in different societies and communities. (Power is the ability to exercise one's will over others; authority is the socially approved use of power.)

Types and Trends

Decades ago, the anthropologist Elman Service (1962) listed four types, or levels, of political organization: band, tribe, chiefdom, and state. Today, none of these political entities (*polities*) can be studied as a self-contained form of political organization, since all exist within nation-states and are subject to state control. There is archaeological evidence for early bands, tribes, and chiefdoms that existed before the first states appeared. However, since anthropology came into being long after the origin of the state, anthropologists have never been able to observe "in the flesh" a band, tribe, or chiefdom outside the influence of some state. All the bands, tribes, and chiefdoms known to ethnography have been within the borders of a state.

There still may be local political leaders (e.g., village heads) and regional figures (e.g., chiefs) of the sort discussed in this chapter, but all exist and function within the context of state organization.

A *band* refers to a small *kin-based* group (all the members are related to each other by kinship or marriage ties) found among foragers. **Tribes** had economies based on nonintensive food production (horticulture and pastoralism). Living in villages and organized into kin groups based on common descent (clans and lineages), tribes lacked a formal government and had no reliable means of enforcing political decisions. **Chiefdom** refers to a form of sociopolitical organization intermediate between the tribe and the state. In chiefdoms, social relations were based mainly on kinship, marriage, descent, age, generation, and gender—just as they were in bands and tribes. Although chiefdoms were kin-based, they featured differential access to resources (some people had more wealth, prestige, and power than others) and a permanent political structure. The **state** is a form of sociopolitical organization based on a formal government structure and socioeconomic stratification.

The four labels in Service's typology are much too simple to account for the full range of political diversity and complexity known to archaeology and ethnography. We'll see, for instance, that tribes have varied widely in their political systems and institutions. Nevertheless, Service's typology does highlight some significant contrasts in political organization, especially those between states and nonstates. For example, in bands and tribes—unlike states, which have clearly visible governments—political organization did not stand out as separate and distinct from the total social order. In bands and tribes, it was difficult to characterize an act or event as political rather than merely social.

Recognizing that political organization is sometimes just an aspect of social organization, Morton Fried offered this definition:

> Political organization comprises those portions of social organization that specifically relate to the individuals or groups that manage the affairs of public policy or seek to control the appointment or activities of those individuals or groups. (Fried 1967, pp. 20–21, emphasis added)

On April 17, 2002, protesters at the Lincoln Memorial in Washington, D.C., demand that all "grandfathered" power plants meet the clean air regulations of 1978. Protesters and lobbyists are part of the political process.

organization. Service's labels "band," "tribe," "chiefdom," and "state" are categories or types within a sociopolitical typology. These types are correlated with the adaptive strategies (economic typology) discussed in the chapter "Making a Living." Thus, foragers (an economic type) tended to have band organization (a sociopolitical type). Similarly, many horticulturalists and pastoralists lived in tribal societies (or, more simply, tribes). Although most chiefdoms had farming economies, herding was important in some Middle Eastern chiefdoms. Nonindustrial states usually had an agricultural base.

With food production came larger, denser populations and more complex economies than was the case among foragers. These features posed new regulatory problems, which gave rise to more complex relations and linkages. Many sociopolitical trends reflect the increased regulatory demands associated with food production. Archaeologists have studied these trends through time, and cultural anthropologists have observed them among contemporary groups.

Bands and Tribes

This chapter examines a series of societies with different political systems. A common set of questions will be addressed for each one. What kinds of social groups does the society have? How do people affiliate with those groups? How do the groups link up with larger ones? How do the groups represent themselves to each other? How are their internal and external relations regulated? To answer these questions, we begin with bands and tribes and then move on to chiefdoms and states.

FORAGING BANDS

How representative are modern hunter-gatherers of Stone Age peoples, all of whom were foragers? G. P. Murdock (1934) erroneously described living hunter-gatherers as "our primitive contemporaries." This label gave an image of foragers as

This definition certainly fits contemporary North America. Under "individuals or groups that manage the affairs of public policy" come federal, state (provincial), and local (municipal) governments. Those who seek to control the activities of the groups that manage public policy include such interest groups as political parties, unions, corporations, consumers, activists, action committees, religious groups, and nongovernmental organizations (NGOs).

Fried's definition is much less applicable to bands and tribes, where it was often difficult to detect any "public policy." For this reason, I prefer to speak of *socio*political organization in discussing the regulation or management of interrelations among groups and their representatives. In a general sense, regulation is the process that ensures that variables stay within their normal ranges, corrects deviations from the norm, and thus maintains a system's integrity. In the case of political regulation, this includes such things as decision making and conflict resolution. The study of political regulation draws our attention to those who make decisions and resolve conflicts (are there formal leaders?).

Ethnographic and archaeological studies in hundreds of places have revealed many correlations between economy and social and political living fossils—frozen, primitive, unchanging social forms that had managed to hang on in remote areas.

Later, many anthropologists followed the prolific ethnographer Richard Lee (1984) in using the San ("Bushmen") of the Kalahari Desert of southern Africa to represent the hunting-gathering way of life and band organization. But anthropologists increasingly wonder about how much contemporary foragers can tell us about the economic and social relations that characterized humanity before food production. Modern foragers, after all, live in nation-states and in an increasingly interlinked world.

Understanding Ourselves You've seen vivid images of difference, of faraway places with strange-sounding names. Anthropology, the study of human diversity, is sometimes accused of exoticizing, of dwelling on the unusual and exaggerating difference. This charge was truer in the past than it is today. Knowing how rare isolation has become, contemporary anthropologists don't seek out—or even believe in—"lost tribes." The focus of modern anthropology is more on connectedness than on separation. It's the media that do most of the exoticizing. In this respect, *National Geographic* is more sensitive and accurate in its treatment of non-Western peoples than it used to be, but strange and exotic people, theories, and explanations are commonplace on the Discovery Channel. Understanding what anthropology knows about today's world means taking such images and information with more than a grain of salt.

For generations, the pygmies of Congo have shared a social world with their neighbors who are cultivators. They exchange forest products (e.g., honey and meat) for crops (e.g., bananas and manioc). The San speakers of southern Africa have been influenced by Bantu speakers (farmers and herders) for 2,000 years and by Europeans for centuries. All foragers now trade with food producers. Most contemporary hunter-gatherers rely on governments and on missionaries for at least part of what they consume. The Aché of Paraguay get food from missionaries, grow crops, and have domesticated animals (Hawkes et al. 1982; Hill et al. 1987). They spend only a third of their subsistence time foraging.

Anthropologists increasingly reject depictions of foragers as uniform and frozen in time and space. Internal social variation, change, and the influence of contact and globalization are important concerns of contemporary anthropology. The debate about foragers has focused on the San, traditionally viewed as autonomous, culturally distinct foragers—albeit in contact with farmers and herders (Lee 1979; Silberbauer 1981; Tanaka 1980). Traditionally the San have been depicted as an egalitarian band-organized people who until recently were nomadic or seminomadic.

The "revisionist" position insists that the San tell us little about the ancient world in which all humans were foragers. It is argued that the San have been linked to food producers for generations, and that this contact has changed the basis of their culture. For Edwin Wilmsen (1989), the San are far from being isolated survivors of a primitive era. They are a rural underclass in a larger political and economic system dominated by Europeans and Bantu food producers. Many San now tend cattle for wealthier Bantu rather than foraging independently. Wilmsen also argues that many San descend from herders who were pushed into the desert by poverty or oppression.

The isolation and autonomy of foragers also have been questioned for African pygmies (Bailey et al. 1989) and for foragers in the Philippines (Headland and Reid 1989). The Mikea of southwestern Madagascar may have moved into their remote forest habitat to escape from a nearby state. Eventually, the Mikea became an economically specialized group of hunter-gatherers on the fringes of that state. The Tasaday of the Philippines maintain ties with food producers and probably descend from cultivating ancestors. This is true despite the initial "lost tribe" media accounts. The reports that followed the "discovery" of the Tasaday portrayed them as survivors of the Stone Age, hermetically sealed in a pristine world all their own. Many scholars now question the authenticity of the Tasaday as a separate cultural group (Headland 1992).

The debate about foragers raises a larger question: Why do the ethnographic accounts and interpretations vary? The reasons include variation in space and time in the society, and different assumptions by ethnographers. Susan Kent (1992, 1996) notes a tendency to stereotype foragers, to treat them as all alike. Foraging bands used to be

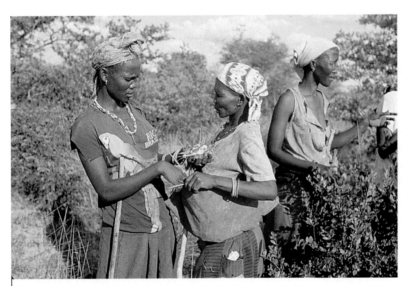

Among tropical foragers, gathering (for example, of edible roots like the ones shown here) typically contributes more to the diet than hunting and fishing do. Women make an important economic contribution through gathering, as is true among the San shown here in Botswana. What evidence do you see in the photo that contemporary foragers participate in the modern world system?

Coke bottle that fell from the sky into a San band in the movie *The Gods Must Be Crazy*—a film filled with many stereotypes.)

The nature of San life has changed appreciably since the 1950s and 1960s, when a series of anthropologists from Harvard University, including Richard Lee, embarked on a systematic study of life in the Kalahari. Lee and others have documented many of the changes in various publications. Such longitudinal research monitors variation in time, while field work in many San areas has revealed variation in space. One of the most important contrasts is between settled (sedentary) and nomadic groups (Kent and Vierich 1989). Sedentism is increasing, but some San groups (along rivers) have been sedentary, or have traded with outsiders, for generations. Others, including Lee's Dobe Ju/'hoansi San and Kent's Kutse San, have been more cut off and have retained more of the hunter-gatherer life style.

Modern foragers are not Stone Age relics, living fossils, lost tribes, or noble savages. Still, to the extent that foraging is the basis of their subsistence, modern hunter-gatherers can illustrate links between a foraging economy and other aspects of society and culture. For example, San groups that are still mobile, or that were so until recently, emphasize social, political, and gender equality. Social relations that stress kinship, reciprocity, and sharing work well in an economy with limited resources and few people. The nomadic pursuit of wild plants and animals tends to discourage permanent settlements, accumulation of wealth, and status distinctions. In this context families and bands are adaptive social units. People have to share meat when they get it; otherwise it rots. Kent (1996) suggests that by studying diversity among the San, we can better understand foraging and how it is influenced by sedentism and other factors.

stereotyped as isolated, primitive survivors of the Stone Age. A new stereotype sees foragers as culturally deprived people forced by states, colonialism, or world events into marginal environments. Although this view is often exaggerated, it is probably more accurate. All modern foragers have links with external systems, including food producers and nation-states. Because of this, they differ substantially from Stone Age hunter-gatherers.

Kent (1996) stresses variation among foragers, focusing on diversity in time and space among the San. The traditionalist–revisionist debate, suggests Kent, is based largely on failure to recognize the extent of diversity among the San. Researchers on both sides may be correct, depending on the group of San being described and the time period of the research. San economic adaptations range from hunting and gathering to fishing, farming, herding, and wage work. Solway and Lee (1990) describe environmental degradation caused by herding and population increase. These factors are depleting game and forcing more and more San to give up foraging. Even traditionalists recognize that all San are being drawn inexorably into the modern world system. (Many of us remember the

For a discussion of relative affluence among foragers, see the Internet Exercises at your OLC

mhhe
.com
/kottak

Such study will enhance our knowledge of past, present, and future small-scale societies.

Given the magnitude of change affecting the societies ethnographers traditionally studied, it's difficult to know whether to use the present or the past tense when discussing bands, tribes, and chiefdoms. Earlier we saw that none of these political systems is totally autonomous, and we've just seen that contemporary "foragers" derive less and less of their subsistence from hunting and gathering and participate in larger sociopolitical systems. Many San have forsaken nomadic bands for settled villages.

Traditionally foragers have been seen as having two kinds of social groups: the nuclear family and the band—nomadic or seminomadic. Bands were impermanent, forming seasonally when component nuclear families got together. The particular combination of families in a band varied from year to year. The main social building blocks were the personal relationships of individuals. Marriage and kinship created ties between members of different bands. Because one's parents and grandparents came from different bands, a person had relatives in several of those groups. Trade and visiting also linked local groups, as did fictive kinship, such as the San namesake system described in the chapter "Making a Living." Similarly, Inuit men traditionally had trade partners, whom they treated almost like brothers, in different bands.

Foraging bands were fairly egalitarian in terms of power and authority, although particular talents did lead to special respect. For example, someone could sing or dance well, was an especially good storyteller, or could go into a trance and communicate with spirits. Band leaders were leaders in name only. They were first among equals. Sometimes they gave advice or made decisions, but they had no way to enforce their decisions.

Foragers lacked formal **law** in the sense of a legal code with trial and enforcement, but they did have methods of social control and dispute settlement. The absence of law did not entail total anarchy. The aboriginal Inuit (Hoebel 1954, 1954/1968) provide a good example of methods of settling disputes in stateless societies. As described by E. A. Hoebel (1954) in a study of Inuit conflict resolution, a sparse population of some 20,000 Inuit spanned 9,500 kilometers (6,000 miles) of the Arctic region (Figure 17.1). The most significant social groups were the nuclear family and the band. Personal relationships linked the families and bands. Some bands had headmen. There were also shamans (part-time religious specialists). However, these positions conferred little power on those who occupied them.

Hunting and fishing by men were the primary Inuit subsistence activities. The diverse and abundant plant foods available in warmer areas, where female labor in gathering is important, were absent in the Arctic. Traveling on land and sea in a bitter environment, Inuit men faced more dangers than women did. The traditional male role took its toll in lives. Adult women would have outnumbered men substantially without occasional female infanticide (killing of a baby), which Inuit culture permitted.

Despite this crude (and to us unthinkable) means of population regulation, there were still more adult women than men. This permitted some men to have two or three wives. The ability to support more than one wife conferred a certain amount of prestige, but it also encouraged envy. (*Prestige* is esteem, respect, or approval for culturally valued acts or qualities.) If a man seemed to be taking additional wives just to enhance his reputation, a rival was likely to steal one of them. Most disputes were between men and originated over women, caused by wife stealing or adultery. If a man discovered that his wife had been having sexual relations without his permission, he considered himself wronged.

Although public opinion would not let the husband ignore the matter, he had several options. He could try to kill the wife stealer. However, if he succeeded, one of his rival's kinsmen would surely try to kill him in retaliation. One dispute could escalate into several deaths as relatives avenged a succession of murders. No government existed to intervene and stop such a blood feud (a murderous feud between families). However, one also could challenge a rival to a song battle. In a public setting, contestants made up insulting songs about each other. At the end of the match, the audience judged one of them the winner. However, if a man whose wife had been stolen won, there was no guarantee she would return. Often she would decide to stay with her abductor.

Several acts of killing that are crimes in contemporary North America were not considered criminal by the Inuit. Infanticide already has been mentioned. Furthermore, people who felt that,

Figure 17.1   Location of the Inuit.

because of age or infirmity, they were no longer useful might kill themselves or ask others to kill them. Old people or invalids who wished to die would ask a close relative, such as a son, to end their lives. It was necessary to ask a close relative to ensure that the kin of the deceased did not take revenge on the killer.

Thefts are common in societies with marked property differentials, like our own, but thefts are uncommon among foragers. Each Inuit had access to the resources needed to sustain life. Every man could hunt, fish, and make the tools necessary for subsistence. Every woman could obtain the materials needed to make clothing,

prepare food, and do domestic work. Inuit men could even hunt and fish in the territories of other local groups. There was no notion of private ownership of territory or animals. However, certain minor personal items were associated with a specific person. In various societies, such items include things such as arrows, a tobacco pouch, clothing, and personal ornaments. One of the most basic Inuit beliefs was that "all natural resources are free or common goods" (Hoebel 1954/1968). Band-organized societies usually lack differential access to strategic resources. If people want something from someone else, they ask for it, and it usually is given.

TRIBAL CULTIVATORS

As is true with foraging bands, there are no totally autonomous tribes in today's world. Still, there are societies, for example, in Papua New Guinea and in South America's tropical forests, in which tribal principles still operate. Tribes typically have a horticultural or pastoral economy and are organized by village life and/or membership in *descent groups* (kin groups whose members trace descent from a common ancestor). Tribes lack socioeconomic stratification (i.e., a class structure) and a formal government of their own. A few tribes still conduct small-scale warfare, in the form of intervillage raiding. Tribes have more effective regulatory mechanisms than foragers do, but tribal societies have no sure means of enforcing political decisions. The main regulatory officials are village heads, "big men," descent-group leaders, village councils, and leaders of pantribal associations. All these figures and groups have limited authority.

Like foragers, horticulturalists tend to be egalitarian, although some have marked gender stratification: an unequal distribution of resources, power, prestige, and personal freedom between men and women. Horticultural villages are usually small, with low population density and open access to strategic resources. Age, gender, and personal traits determine how much respect people receive and how much support they get from others. Egalitarianism diminishes, however, as village size and population density increase. Horticultural villages usually have headmen—rarely, if ever, headwomen.

THE VILLAGE HEAD

The Yanomami (Chagnon 1997) are Native Americans who live in southern Venezuela and the adjacent part of Brazil. Their tribal society has about 20,000 people living in 200 to 250 widely scattered villages, each with a population between 40 and 250. The Yanomami are horticulturalists who also hunt and gather. Their staple crops are bananas and plantains (a banana-like crop). There are more significant social groups among the Yanomami than exist in a foraging society. The Yanomami have nuclear families, villages, and descent groups. Their descent groups, which span more than one village, are patrilineal (ancestry is traced back through males only) and exogamous (people must marry outside their own descent group).

However, local branches of two different descent groups may live in the same village and intermarry.

As has been true in many village-based tribal societies, the only leadership position among the Yanomami is that of **village head** (always a man). His authority, like that of a foraging band's leader, is severely limited. If a headman wants something done, he must lead by example and persuasion. The headman lacks the right to issue orders. He can only persuade, harangue, and try to influence public opinion. For example, if he wants people to clean up the central plaza in preparation for a feast, he must start sweeping it himself, hoping that his covillagers will take the hint and relieve him.

When conflict erupts within the village, the headman may be called on as a mediator who listens to both sides. He will give an opinion and advice. If a disputant is unsatisfied, the headman can do nothing. He has no power to back his decisions and no way to impose punishments. Like the band leader, he is first among equals.

A Yanomami village headman also must lead in generosity. Because he must be more generous than any other villager, he cultivates more land. His garden provides much of the food consumed when his village holds a feast for another village. The headman represents the village in its dealings with outsiders. Sometimes he visits other villages to invite people to a feast. The way a person acts as headman depends on his personal traits and the number of supporters he can muster. One village headman, Kaobawa, intervened in a dispute between a husband and a wife and kept him from killing her (Chagnon 1983/1992). He also guaranteed safety to a delegation from a village with which a covillager of his wanted to start a war. Kaobawa was a particularly effective headman. He had demonstrated his fierceness in battle, but he also knew how to use diplomacy to avoid offending other villagers. No one in the village had a better personality for the headmanship. Nor (because Kaobawa had many brothers) did anyone have more supporters. Among the Yanomami, when a group is dissatisfied with a village headman, its members can leave and found a new village; this is done from time to time.

Yanomami society, with its many villages and descent groups, is more complex than a band-organized society. The Yanomami also face more regulatory problems. A headman sometimes can prevent a specific violent act, but there is no government to maintain order. In fact, intervillage raiding in which men are killed and women are captured has been a feature of some areas of Yanomami territory, particularly those studied by Chagnon (1997).

We also must stress that the Yanomami are not isolated from outside events (although there still may be uncontacted villages). The Yanomami live in two nation-states, Venezuela and Brazil, and external warfare waged by Brazilian ranchers and miners increasingly has threatened them (Chagnon 1997; *Cultural Survival Quarterly* 1989; Ferguson 1995). During a Brazilian gold rush between 1987 and 1991, one Yanomami died each day, on average, from external attacks (including biological warfare—introduced diseases to which the Indians lack resistance). By 1991, there were some 40,000 Brazilian miners in the Yanomami homeland. Some Indians were killed outright. The miners introduced new diseases, and the swollen population ensured that old diseases became epidemic. In 1991, a commission of the American Anthropological Association reported on the plight of the Yanomami (*Anthropology Newsletter*, September 1991). Brazilian Yanomami were dying at a rate of 10 percent annually, and their fertility rate had dropped to zero. Since then, both the Brazilian and the Venezuelan governments have intervened to protect the Yanomami. One Brazilian president declared a huge Yanomami territory off-limits to outsiders. Unfortunately, by mid-1992, local politicians, miners, and ranchers were increasingly evading the ban. The future of the Yanomami remains uncertain.

The "Big Man"

In many areas of the South Pacific, particularly the Melanesian Islands and Papua New Guinea, native cultures had a kind of political leader that we call the big man. The **big man** (almost always a male) was an elaborate version of the village head, but with one significant difference. The village head's leadership is within one village; the big man had supporters in several villages. The big man therefore was a regulator of regional political organization. Here we see the trend toward expansion in the scale of sociopolitical regulation—from village to region.

The Kapauku Papuans live in Irian Jaya, Indonesia (which is on the island of New Guinea)

The "big man" persuades people to organize feasts, which distribute pork and wealth. Shown here is such a regional event, drawing on several villages, in Papua New Guinea. Big men owe their status to their individual personalities rather than to inherited wealth or position. Does our society have equivalents of big men?

(Figure 17.2). Anthropologist Leopold Pospisil (1963) studied the Kapauku (45,000 people), who grow crops (with the sweet potato as their staple) and raise pigs. Their economy is too complex to be described as simple horticulture. The only political figure among the Kapauku was the big man, known as a *tonowi*. A tonowi achieved his status through hard work, amassing wealth in the form of pigs and other native riches. Characteristics that distinguished a big man from his fellows included wealth, generosity, eloquence, physical fitness, bravery, and supernatural powers. Men became big men because they had certain personalities. They had amassed resources during their own lifetimes, as they did not inherit their wealth or position.

A man who was determined enough could become a big man, creating wealth through hard

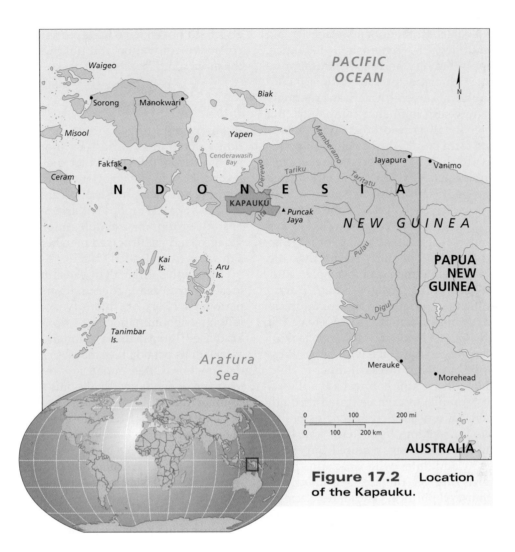

Figure 17.2 Location of the Kapauku.

work and good judgment. Wealth resulted from successful pig breeding and trading. As a man's pig herd and prestige grew, he attracted supporters. He sponsored ceremonial pig feasts in which pigs were slaughtered, and their meat distributed to guests.

Unlike the Yanomami village head, a big man's wealth exceeded that of his fellows. His supporters, recognizing his past favors and anticipating future rewards, recognized him as a leader and accepted his decisions as binding. The big man was an important regulator of regional events in Kapauku life. He helped determine the dates for feasts and markets. He persuaded people to sponsor feasts, which distributed pork and wealth. He initiated economic projects requiring the cooperation of a regional community.

The Kapauku big man again exemplifies a generalization about leadership in tribal societies: If someone achieves wealth and widespread respect and support, he or she must be generous. The big man worked hard not to hoard wealth but to be able to give away the fruits of his labor, to convert wealth into prestige and gratitude. A stingy big man would lose his support, his reputation plummeting. The Kapauku might take even more extreme measures against big men who hoarded wealth. Selfish and greedy men sometimes were murdered by their fellows.

Understanding Ourselves Many factors contribute to political success in a modern nation such as the United States. They include personality, kin connections, and inherited status.

Politically valuable attributes of a Melanesian big man included wealth, generosity, eloquence, physical fitness, bravery, and supernatural powers. How do such characteristics influence contemporary political careers? Americans routinely use their own wealth to finance campaigns. Big men get their loyalists to produce and deliver wealth in the form of pigs, just as modern politicians persuade their supporters to make campaign contributions. And, like big men, successful American politicians try to be generous with their supporters. Payback may take the form of a night in the Lincoln bedroom, an invitation to a strategic dinner, an ambassadorship, or largesse to a place that was particularly supportive. Big men amass wealth and then give away pigs. Successful American politicians give away "pork." As with the big man, eloquence and communication skills contribute to political success (e.g., Bill Clinton and Ronald Reagan), although lack of such skills isn't necessarily fatal (e.g., either President Bush). What about physical fitness? Hair, height, and health are still political advantages. Bravery, for example, as demonstrated through distinguished military service, also helps political careers (e.g., Senators John Kerry and John McCain), but it certainly isn't required. Supernatural powers? Candidates who proclaim themselves atheists are as rare as self-identified witches. Almost all political candidates claim to belong to a mainstream religion. Some even present their candidacies as promoting divine wishes. However, contemporary politics isn't just about personality, as it is in big man systems. We live in a state-organized, stratified society with inherited wealth, power, and privilege, all of which have political implications. As is typical of states, inheritance and kin connections play a role in political success. Just think of Kennedys, Bushes, Clintons, and Gores.

Political figures such as the big man emerge as regulators both of demographic growth and of economic complexity. Kapauku cultivation has used varied techniques for specific kinds of land. Labor-intensive cultivation in valleys involves mutual aid in turning the soil before planting. The digging of long drainage ditches is even more complex. Kapauku plant cultivation supports a larger and denser population than does the simpler horticulture of the Yanomami. Kapauku society could not survive in its current form without collective cultivation and political regulation of the more complex economic tasks.

PANTRIBAL SODALITIES AND AGE GRADES

Big men could forge regional political organization—albeit temporarily—by mobilizing people from different villages. Other social and political mechanisms in tribal societies, such as a belief in common ancestry, kinship, or descent, could be used to link local groups within a region. The same descent group, for example, might span several villages, and its dispersed members might follow a descent group leader.

Principles other than kinship can also link local groups. In a modern nation, a labor union, national sorority or fraternity, political party, or religious denomination may provide such a nonkin-based link. In tribes, nonkin groups called associations or sodalities may serve the same linking function. Often, sodalities are based on common age or gender, with all-male sodalities more common than all-female ones.

Pantribal sodalities (those that extend across the whole tribe, spanning several villages) sometimes arose in areas where two or more different cultures came into regular contact. Such sodalities were especially likely to develop in the presence of warfare between tribes. Drawing their membership from different villages of the same tribe, pantribal sodalities could mobilize men in many local groups for attack or retaliation against another tribe.

In the cross-cultural study of nonkin groups, we must distinguish between those that are confined to a single village and those that span several local groups. Only the latter, the pantribal groups, are important in general military mobilization and regional political organization. Localized men's houses and clubs, limited to particular villages, are found in many horticultural societies in tropical South America, Melanesia, and Papua New Guinea. These groups may organize village activities and even intervillage raiding, but their leaders are similar to village heads and their political scope is mainly local. The following discussion, which continues our examination of the growth in scale of regional sociopolitical organization, concerns pantribal groups.

The best examples of pantribal sodalities come from the Central Plains of North America and from tropical Africa. During the 18th and 19th centuries, native populations of the Great Plains of the United States and Canada experienced a rapid growth of pantribal sodalities. This development reflected an economic change that followed the spread of horses, which had been reintroduced to the Americas by the Spanish, to the states between the Rocky Mountains and the Mississippi River. Many Plains Indian societies changed their adaptive strategies because of the horse. At first, they had been foragers who hunted bison (buffalo) on foot. Later, they adopted a mixed economy based on hunting, gathering, and horticulture. Finally, they changed to a much more specialized economy based on horseback hunting of bison (eventually with rifles).

As the Plains tribes were undergoing these changes, other Indians also adopted horseback hunting and moved into the Plains. Attempting to occupy the same area, groups came into conflict. A pattern of warfare developed in which the members of one tribe raided another, usually for horses. The new economy demanded that people follow the movement of the bison herds. During the winter, when the bison dispersed, a tribe fragmented into small bands and families. In the summer, as huge herds assembled on the Plains, members of the tribe reunited. They camped together for social, political, and religious activities, but mainly for communal bison hunting.

Only two activities in the new adaptive strategy demanded strong leadership: organizing and carrying out raids on enemy camps (to capture horses) and managing the summer bison hunt. All the Plains cultures developed pantribal sodalities, and leadership roles within them, to police the summer hunt. Leaders coordinated hunting efforts, making sure that people did not cause a stampede with an early shot or an ill-advised action. Leaders imposed severe penalties, including seizure of a culprit's wealth, for disobedience.

Natives of the Great Plains of North America originally hunted bison (buffalo) on foot, using the bow and arrow. The introduction of horses and rifles fueled a pattern of horse raiding and warfare. How far had the change gone, as depicted in this painting?

Some of the Plains sodalities were **age sets** of increasing rank. Each set included all the men—from that tribe's component bands—born during a certain time span. Each set had its distinctive dance, songs, possessions, and privileges. Members of each set had to pool their wealth to buy admission to the next higher level as they moved up the age hierarchy. Most Plains societies had pantribal warrior associations whose rituals celebrated militarism. As noted previously, the leaders of these associations organized bison hunting and raiding. They also arbitrated disputes during the summer, when large numbers of people came together.

Many of the tribes that adopted this Plains strategy of adaptation had once been foragers for whom hunting and gathering had been individual or small-group affairs. They had never come together previously as a single social unit. Age and gender were available as social principles that could quickly and efficiently forge unrelated people into pantribal groups.

Raiding of one tribe by another, this time for cattle rather than horses, also was common in eastern and southeastern Africa, where pantribal sodalities, including age sets, also developed. Among the pastoral Masai of Kenya (Figure 17.3), men born during the same four-year period were circumcised together and belonged to the same named group, an age set, throughout their lives. The sets moved through grades, the most important of which was the warrior grade. Members of the set who wished to enter the warrior grade were at first discouraged by its current occupants, who eventually vacated the warrior grade and married. Members of a set felt a strong allegiance to one another and eventually had sexual rights to each other's wives. Masai women lacked comparable set organization, but they also passed through culturally recognized age grades: the initiate, the married woman, and the postmenopausal woman.

To understand the difference between an age set and an age grade, think of a college class, the Class of 2007, for example, and its progress through the university. The age set would be the group of people constituting the Class of 2007, while the first ("freshman"), sophomore, junior, and senior years would represent the age grades.

Not all cultures with age grades also have age sets. When there are no sets, men can enter or leave a particular grade individually or collectively, often by going through a predetermined ritual. The grades most commonly recognized in Africa are these:

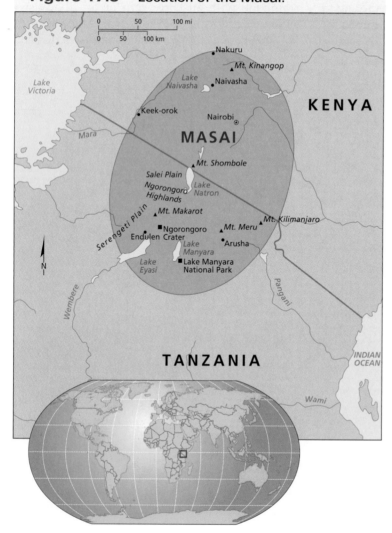

Figure 17.3   Location of the Masai.

1. Recently initiated youths.

2. Warriors.

3. One or more grades of mature men who play important roles in pantribal government.

4. Elders, who may have special ritual responsibilities.

In certain parts of West Africa and Central Africa, the pantribal sodalities are *secret societies*, made up exclusively of men or women. Like our college fraternities and sororities, these associations have secret initiation ceremonies. Among the Mende of Sierra Leone, men's and women's secret societies are very influential. The men's group, the Poro, trains boys in social conduct, ethics, and religion and supervises political and economic activities. Leadership roles in the Poro often overshadow village headship and play an important part in social control, dispute management, and tribal political regulation. Like descent, then, age, gender, and ritual can link members of different local groups into a single social collectivity in tribal society and thus create a sense of ethnic identity, of belonging to the same cultural tradition.

NOMADIC POLITICS

Although many pastoralists, such as the Masai, had tribal sociopolitical organization, a range of demographic and sociopolitical diversity occurs with pastoralism. A comparison of pastoralists shows that as regulatory problems increase, political hierarchies become more complex. Political organization becomes less personal, more formal, and less kinship-oriented. The pastoral strategy of adaptation does not dictate any particular political organization. A range of authority structures manage regulatory problems associated with specific environments. Some pastoralists have traditionally existed as well-defined ethnic groups in nation-states. This reflects pastoralists' need to interact with other populations—a need that is less characteristic of the other adaptive strategies.

The scope of political authority among pastoralists expands considerably as regulatory prob-

Among the Masai of Kenya, men born during the same four-year period were circumcised together. They belonged to the same named group, an age set, throughout their lives. The sets moved through grades, of which the most important was the warrior grade. Here we see the warrior (*ilmurran*) age grade dancing with a group of girls of a lower age grade (*intoyie*). Do we have any equivalents of age sets or grades in our own society?

Beyond the *Classroom*
Perspectives on Group Membership

Background Information

STUDENT: Abigail Dreibelbis
SUPERVISING PROFESSOR: Miriam Chaiken
SCHOOL: Indiana University of Pennsylvania
YEAR IN SCHOOL/MAJOR: Senior/Anthropology
FUTURE PLANS: Seeking positions in resource management and environmental protection
PROJECT TITLE: Delta, Delta, Delta, Can I Help Ya, Help Ya, Help Ya

This research examines reasons why college women do or don't join sororities. Does the achieved status of sorority membership differ significantly from the mainly ascribed group memberships discussed in this chapter? Do you think that men join fraternities for the same reasons women join sororities? What relation do you see between the Greek system on college campuses and politics?

There is a human need for belonging, for affiliation. Identi-fication with a group that has common norms and roles helps fulfill this need for security and creates social bonds that establish and assure companion-ship and personal identification.

This understanding has come from the study I did on members and nonmembers of social sororities at Indiana University of Pennsylvania. Since I started college, I had noticed a dichotomy between these two groups. I wanted to find out the real and perceived differences between them. My hypothesis was that there was a higher level of need for group identity and involvement in sorority members, and conversely more inde-pendence in nonmembers. I formed a survey for both groups, with ques-tions about demographics and activi-ties and I used open-ended questions to elicit their views and followed up with in-depth interviews to get a more personal response.

I found that participation in high school student government had been three times higher for members of sororities. This showed the great importance of social identity for Greeks, as student government members have prestige as a minority segment of the student body. Mem-bership is competitive and based on peer acceptance. Conversely, activ-ity in the arts was twice as high in the independent (nonsorority) group. This is a more aesthetic, personal activity, done for the act itself (singing or performing) rather than to gain the acceptance of peers.

The affinity for group identity is reflected in the expressed reasons for joining a sorority. Members found a "sense of belonging" and "self-

lems increase in densely populated regions. Con-sider two Iranian pastoral nomadic tribes: the Basseri and the Qashqai (Salzman 1974). Starting each year from a plateau near the coast, these groups took their animals to grazing land 5,400 meters (17,000 feet) above sea level. The Basseri and the Qashqai shared this route with one another and with several other ethnic groups (Figure 17.4).

Use of the same pasture land at different times was carefully scheduled. Ethnic-group movements were tightly coordinated. Expressing this schedule is *il-rah*, a concept common to all Iranian nomads. A group's *il-rah* is its customary path in time and space. It is the schedule, different for each group, of when specific areas can be used in the annual trek.

Each tribe had its own leader, known as the *khan* or *il-khan*. The Basseri *khan*, because he dealt with a smaller population, faced fewer problems in coordinating its movements than did the lead-ers of the Qashqai. Correspondingly, his rights, privileges, duties, and authority were weaker. Nevertheless, his authority exceeded that of any political figure we have discussed so far. However, the *khan*'s authority still came from his personal traits rather than from his office. That is, the Basseri followed a particular *khan* not because of a confidence." Independents cited these same as reasons for joining, yet they saw this need as negative, and leading to a "group identity [that] is their identity." They did not like the "controlling" qualities of the sorority. The sorority member acknowledges the search for social and personal identification in a group as well as the resulting gratification in joining.

It has been hypothesized that the eldest child is the most independent. I found that twice as many non-sorority women were the oldest siblings in their family. Independents "just weren't the type" for a sorority. Nonmembers seem to find identity or belonging through other groups (volunteering, sports, honors societies) more for personal interest than

social merit. This statistic seemed to support the idea that women who join sororities have a higher value of social involvement and acceptance for security and identity.

Everyone finds support and identity in groups. Groups provide safety along with a sense of personal worth and common identity with at least a few people in this vast world. Through my research I found that this need varies in degree among individuals. Those with a higher level of need find fulfillment in a social group such as a sorority. Non-Greeks do not value and are less dependent on such a social identity. These personality differences may create a sense of separation between the two groups and result in the dichotomy observed on campus.

It was fulfilling to challenge my hypothesis through questions of my own making and to come to an understanding of how and why people function. By gaining these insights on aspects of personality that underlie culture, I have developed a broader view of the intangible differences that affect our daily interactions.

political position he happened to fill but because of their personal allegiance and loyalty to him as a man. The *khan* relied on the support of the heads of the descent groups into which Basseri society was divided.

In Qashqai society, however, allegiance shifts from the person to the office. The Qashqai had multiple levels of authority and more powerful chiefs or *khans*. Managing 400,000 people required a complex hierarchy. Heading it was the *il-khan*, helped by a deputy, under whom were the heads of constituent tribes, under each of whom were descent-group heads.

A case illustrates just how developed the Qashqai authority structure was. A hailstorm prevented some nomads from joining the annual migration at the appointed time. Although everyone recognized that they were not responsible for their delay, the *il-khan* assigned them less favorable grazing land, for that year only, in place of their usual pasture. The tardy herders and other Qashqai considered the judgment fair and didn't question it. Thus, Qashqai authorities regulated the annual migration. They also adjudicated disputes between people, tribes, and descent groups.

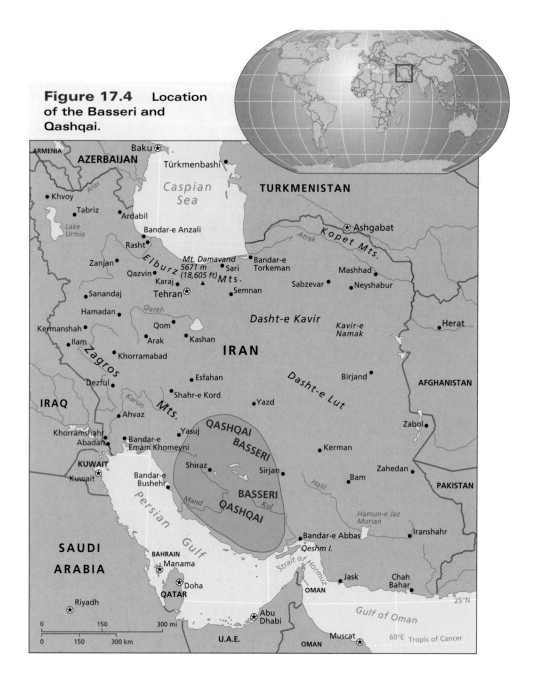

Figure 17.4 Location of the Basseri and Qashqai.

These Iranian cases illustrate the fact that pastoralism is often just one among many specialized economic activities within complex nation-states and regional systems. As part of a larger whole, pastoral tribes are constantly pitted against other ethnic groups. In these nations, the state becomes a final authority, a higher-level regulator that attempts to limit conflict between ethnic groups. State organization arose not just to manage agricultural economies but also to regulate the activities of ethnic groups within expanding social and economic systems.

Chiefdoms

Having looked at bands and tribes, we turn to more complex forms of sociopolitical organization: chiefdoms and states. The first states emerged in the Old

Political organization is well developed among the Qashqai, who share their nomadic route and strategic resources with several other tribes. Here, Qashqai nomads cross a river in Iran's Fars province.

World about 5,500 years ago. The first chiefdoms developed perhaps a thousand years earlier, but few survive today. The chiefdom was a transitional form of organization that emerged during the evolution of tribes into states. State formation began in Mesopotamia (currently Iran and Iraq). It next occurred in Egypt, the Indus Valley of Pakistan and India, and northern China. A few thousand years later, states also arose in two parts of the Western Hemisphere: Mesoamerica (Mexico, Guatemala, Belize) and the central Andes (Peru and Bolivia). Early states are known as *archaic states*, or nonindustrial states, in contrast to modern industrial nation-states. Robert Carneiro defines the state as "an autonomous political unit encompassing many communities within its territory, having a centralized government with the power to collect taxes, draft men for work or war, and decree and enforce laws" (Carneiro 1970, p. 733).

The chiefdom and the state, like many categories used by social scientists, are *ideal types*. That is, they are labels that make social contrasts seem sharper than they really are. In reality, there is a continuum from tribe to chiefdom to state. Some societies have many attributes of chiefdoms but retain tribal features. Some advanced chiefdoms have many attributes of archaic states and thus are difficult to assign to either category. Recognizing this "continuous change" (Johnson and Earle 2000), some anthropologists speak of "complex chiefdoms" (Earle 1987), which are almost states.

POLITICAL AND ECONOMIC SYSTEMS IN CHIEFDOMS

State formation remained incomplete and only chiefdoms emerged in several areas, including the circum-Caribbean (e.g., Caribbean islands, Panama, Colombia), lowland Amazonia, what is now the southeastern United States, and Polynesia. Between the emergence and spread of food production and the expansion of the Roman empire, much of Europe was organized at the chiefdom level, to which it reverted for centuries after the fall of Rome in the fifth century AD. Chiefdoms created the megalithic cultures of Europe, such as the one that built Stonehenge.

For more on prehistoric chiefdoms in the southeastern U.S., see the Internet Exercises at your OLC

mhhe
com
/kottak

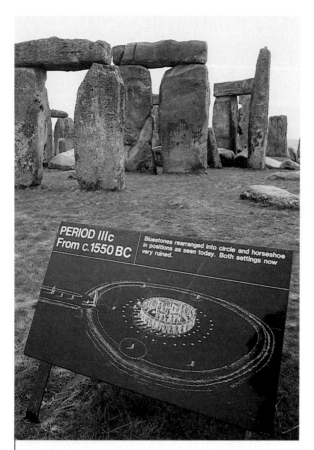

Stonehenge, England, and an educational display designed for tourists and visitors. Chiefdoms created the megalithic cultures of Europe, such as the one that built Stonehenge over 5,000 years ago. Between the emergence and spread of food production and the expansion of the Roman empire, much of Europe was organized at the chiefdom level, to which it reverted after the fall of Rome.

Much of our ethnographic knowledge about chiefdoms comes from Polynesia (Kirch 2000), where they were common at the time of European exploration. In chiefdoms, social relations are mainly based on kinship, marriage, descent, age, generation, and gender—as they are in bands and tribes. This is a basic difference between chiefdoms and states. States bring nonrelatives together and oblige them to pledge allegiance to a government.

Unlike bands and tribes, however, chiefdoms are characterized by *permanent political regulation* of the territory they administer. Chiefdoms might include thousands of people living in many villages and/or hamlets. Regulation was carried out by the chief and his or her assistants, who occupied political offices. An **office** is a permanent position, which must be refilled when it is vacated by death or retirement. Because offices were systematically refilled, the structure of a chiefdom endured across the generations, ensuring permanent political regulation.

In the Polynesian chiefdoms, the chiefs were full-time political specialists in charge of regulating the economy—production, distribution, and consumption. Polynesian chiefs relied on religion to buttress their authority. They regulated production by commanding or prohibiting (using religious taboos) the cultivation of certain lands and crops. Chiefs also regulated distribution and consumption. At certain seasons—often on a ritual occasion such as a first-fruit ceremony—people would offer part of their harvest to the chief through his or her representatives. Products moved up the hierarchy, eventually reaching the chief. Conversely, illustrating obligatory sharing with kin, chiefs sponsored feasts at which they gave back much of what they had received.

Such a flow of resources to and then from a central office is known as *chiefly redistribution.* Redistribution offers economic advantages. If the different areas specialized in particular crops, goods, or services, chiefly redistribution made those products available to the whole society. Chiefly redistribution also played a role in risk management. It stimulated production beyond the immediate subsistence level and provided a central storehouse for goods that might become scarce at times of famine (Earle 1987, 1991). Chiefdoms and archaic states had similar economies, often based on intensive cultivation, and both administered systems of regional trade or exchange.

Social Status in Chiefdoms

Social status in chiefdoms was based on seniority of descent. Because rank, power, prestige, and resources came through kinship and descent, Polynesian chiefs kept extremely long genealogies. Some chiefs (without writing) managed to trace their ancestry back 50 generations. All the people in the chiefdom were thought to be related to each other. Presumably, all were descended from a group of founding ancestors.

The chief (usually a man) had to demonstrate seniority in descent. Degrees of seniority were calculated so intricately on some islands that there were as many ranks as people. For example, the third son would rank below the second, who in turn would rank below the first. The children of an eldest brother, however, would all rank above the children of the next brother, whose children would in turn outrank those of younger brothers. However, even the lowest-ranking person in a chiefdom was still the chief's relative. In such a kin-based context, everyone, even a chief, had to share with his or her relatives.

Because everyone had a slightly different status, it was difficult to draw a line between elites and common people. Although other chiefdoms calculated seniority differently and had shorter genealogies than did those in Polynesia, the concern for genealogy and seniority and the absence of sharp gaps between elites and commoners were features of all chiefdoms.

STATUS SYSTEMS IN CHIEFDOMS AND STATES

The status systems of chiefdoms and states are similar in that both are based on **differential access** to resources. This means that some men and women had privileged access to power, prestige, and wealth. They controlled strategic resources such as land, water, and other means of production. Earle characterizes chiefs as "an incipient aristocracy with advantages in wealth and lifestyle" (1987, p. 290). Nevertheless, differential access in chiefdoms was still very much tied to kinship. The people with privileged access were generally chiefs and their nearest relatives and assistants.

Compared with chiefdoms, archaic states drew a much firmer line between elites and masses, distinguishing at least between nobles and commoners. Kinship ties did not extend from the nobles to the commoners because of *stratum endogamy*—marriage within one's own group. Commoners married commoners; elites married elites.

Such a division of society into socioeconomic strata contrasts strongly with bands and tribes, whose status systems are based on prestige, rather than on differential access to resources. The prestige differentials that do exist in bands reflect special qualities and abilities. Good hunters get respect from their fellows as long as they are generous. So does a skilled curer, dancer, storyteller—or anyone else with a talent or skill that others appreciate.

A French Polynesian chief wears a feather headdress at the Pacific Arts festival. How do chiefs differ from ordinary people? What kind of status do you imagine this chief has today?

In tribes, some prestige goes to descent-group leaders, to village heads, and especially to the big man, a regional figure who commands the loyalty and labor of others. However, all these figures must be generous. If they accumulate more resources—that is, property or food—than others in the village, they must share them with the others. Since strategic resources are available to everyone, social classes based on the possession of unequal amounts of resources can never exist.

In many tribes, particularly those with patrilineal descent, men have much greater prestige and power than women do. The gender contrast in rights could diminish in chiefdoms, where prestige and access to resources were based on seniority of descent, so that some women were senior to some men. Unlike big men, chiefs were exempt from ordinary work and had rights and privileges that were unavailable to the masses. However, like big men, they still gave back much of the wealth they took in.

The status system in chiefdoms, although based on differential access, differed from the status system in states because the privileged few

This employee of the Chirping Chicken fast-food store, shown with her coworkers, just won $22,500,000 in the New York State lottery. Wealth and prestige are not always correlated. Do you imagine the winner's eating habits will change? Will her prestige rise?

were always relatives and assistants of the chief. However, this type of status system didn't last very long. Chiefs would start acting like kings and try to erode the kinship basis of the chiefdom. In Madagascar, they would do this by demoting their more distant relatives to commoner status and banning marriage between nobles and commoners (Kottak 1980). Such moves, *if accepted by the society,* created separate social strata—*unrelated* groups that differ in their access to wealth, prestige, and power. (A *stratum* is one of two or more groups that contrast in regard to social status and access to strategic resources. Each stratum includes people of both sexes and all ages.) The creation of separate social strata is called **stratification**, and its emergence signified the transition from chiefdom to state. *The presence and acceptance of stratification is one of the key distinguishing features of a state.*

The influential sociologist Max Weber (1922/1968) defined three related dimensions of social stratification: (1) Economic status, or **wealth**, encompasses all a person's material assets, including income, land, and other types of property (Schaefer and Lamm 1992). (2) **Power**, the ability to exercise one's will over others—to do what one

Table 17.1 Max Weber's Three Dimensions of Stratification

wealth	=>	economic status
power	=>	political status
prestige	=>	social status

wants—is the basis of political status. (3) **Prestige**—the basis of social status—refers to esteem, respect, or approval for acts, deeds, or qualities considered exemplary. Prestige, or "cultural capital" (Bourdieu 1984), provides people with a sense of worth and respect, which they may often convert into economic and political advantage (Table 17.1).

These Weberian dimensions of stratification were present to varying degrees in chiefdoms. However, chiefdoms lacked the sharp division into classes that characterizes states. Wealth, power, and prestige in chiefdoms were all tied to kinship factors.

In archaic states—for the first time in human evolution—there were contrasts in wealth, power, and prestige between entire groups (social strata) of men and women. Each stratum included people of both sexes and all ages. The **superordinate** (the higher or elite) stratum had privileged access to wealth, power, and other valued resources. Access to resources by members of the **subordinate** (lower or underprivileged) stratum was limited by the privileged group.

Interpret the World
Atlas Map 17

In your atlas, Map 17, "Organized States and Chiefdoms, 1500 A.D.," shows the global distribution of organized states and chiefdoms on the eve of European colonization. Organized states existed then in Mexico, the Andes, Africa, Asia, and Europe. Anywhere else? Besides Polynesia, where were chiefdoms located?

Socioeconomic stratification continues as a defining feature of all states, archaic or industrial. The elites control a significant part of the means of production, for example, land, herds, water, capital, farms, or factories. Those born at the bottom of the hierarchy have reduced chances of social mobility. Because of elite ownership rights, ordinary people lack free access to resources. Only in states do the elites get to keep their differential wealth. Unlike big men and chiefs, they don't have to give it back to the people whose labor has built and increased it.

For a quiz on sociopolitical types, see the Interactive Exercise

States

To see how states are created see the Virtual Exploration

Table 17.2 summarizes the information presented so far on bands, tribes, chiefdoms, and states. States, remember, are autonomous political units with social classes and a formal government, based on law. States tend to be large and populous, as compared to bands, tribes, and chiefdoms. Certain statuses, systems, and subsystems with specialized functions are found in all states. They include the following:

1. *Population control*: fixing of boundaries, establishment of citizenship categories, and the taking of a census.

2. *Judiciary*: laws, legal procedure, and judges.

3. *Enforcement*: permanent military and police forces.

4. *Fiscal*: taxation.

In archaic states, these subsystems were integrated by a ruling system or government composed of civil, military, and religious officials (Fried 1960).

POPULATION CONTROL

To know whom they govern, all states conduct censuses. States demarcate boundaries that separate them from other societies. Customs agents, immigration officers, navies, and coast guards

Table 17.2 Economic Basis of and Political Regulation in Bands, Tribes, Chiefdoms, and States

Sociopolitical Type	Economic Type	Examples	Type of Regulation
Band	Foraging	Inuit, San	Local
Tribe	Horticulture, pastoralism	Yanomami, Kapauku, Masai	Local, temporary regional
Chiefdom	Productive horticulture, pastoral nomadism, agriculture	Qashqai, Polynesia, Cherokee	Permanent regional
State	Agriculture, industrialism	Ancient Mesopotamia, contemporary United States and Canada	Permanent regional

patrol frontiers. Even nonindustrial states have boundary-maintenance forces. In Buganda, an archaic state on the shores of Lake Victoria in Uganda, the king rewarded military officers with estates in outlying provinces. They became his guardians against foreign intrusion.

States also control population through administrative subdivision: provinces, districts, "states," counties, subcounties, and parishes. Lower-level officials manage the populations and territories of the subdivisions.

In nonstates, people work and relax with their relatives, in-laws, fictive kin, and age mates—people with whom they have a personal relationship. Such a personal social life existed throughout most of human history, but food production spelled its eventual decline. After millions of years of human evolution, it took a mere 4,000 years for the population increase and regulatory problems spawned by food production to lead from tribe to chiefdom to state. With state organization, kinship's pervasive role diminished. Descent groups may continue as kin groups within states, but their importance in political organization declines.

States foster geographic mobility and resettlement, severing long-standing ties among people, land, and kin. Population displacements have increased in the modern world. War, famine, and job seeking across national boundaries churn up migratory currents. People in states come to identify themselves by new statuses, both ascribed and achieved, including ethnic background, place of birth or residence, occupation, party, religion, and team or club affiliation, rather than only as members of a descent group or extended family.

States also manage their populations by granting different rights and obligations to citizens and noncitizens. Status distinctions among citizens are also common. Many archaic states granted different rights to nobles, commoners, and slaves. Unequal rights within state-organized societies persist in today's world. In recent American history, before the Emancipation Proclamation, there were different laws for slaves and free people. In European colonies, separate courts judged cases involv-ing only natives and those that involved Europeans. In contemporary America, a military code of justice and court system continue to coexist alongside the civil judiciary.

JUDICIARY

States have *laws* based on precedent and legislative proclamations. Without writing, laws may be preserved in oral tradition, with justices, elders, and other specialists responsible for remembering them. Oral traditions as repositories of legal wisdom have continued in some nations with writing, such as Great Britain. Laws regulate relations between individuals and groups.

Crimes are violations of the legal code, with specified types of punishment. However, a given act, such as killing someone, may be legally defined in different ways (e.g., as manslaughter, justifiable homicide, or first-degree murder). Furthermore, even in contemporary North America, where justice is supposed to be "blind" to social distinctions, the poor are prosecuted more often and more severely than are the rich.

To handle disputes and crimes, all states have courts and judges. Precolonial African states had subcounty, county, and district courts, plus a high court formed by the king or queen and his or her advisers. Most states allow appeals to higher

To handle disputes and crimes, all states, including Bermuda, shown here, have courts and judges. Does this photo say anything about cultural diffusion?

courts, although people are encouraged to solve problems locally.

A striking contrast between states and nonstates is intervention in family affairs. In states, aspects of parenting and marriage enter the domain of public law. Governments step in to halt blood feuds and regulate previously private disputes. States attempt to curb *internal* conflict, but they aren't always successful. About 85 percent of the world's armed conflicts since 1945 have begun within states—in efforts to overthrow a ruling regime or as disputes over tribal, religious, and ethnic minority issues. Only 15 percent have been fights across national borders (Barnaby, 1984). Rebellion, resistance, repression, terrorism, and warfare continue. Indeed, recent states have perpetrated some of history's bloodiest deeds.

ENFORCEMENT

All states have agents to enforce judicial decisions. Confinement requires jailers, and a death penalty calls for executioners. Agents of the state collect fines and confiscate property. These officials wield real power.

A major concern of government is to defend hierarchy, property, and the power of the law. The government suppresses internal disorder (with police) and guards the nation against external threats (with the military). As a relatively new form of sociopolitical organization, states have competed successfully with less-complex societies throughout the world. Military organization helps states subdue neighboring nonstates, but this is not the only reason for the spread of state organization. Although states impose hardships, they also offer advantages. More obviously, they provide protection from outsiders and preserve internal order. They curb the feuding that has plagued tribes such as the Yanomami. By promoting internal peace, states enhance production. Their economies support massive, dense populations, which supply armies and colonists to promote expansion.

FISCAL SYSTEMS

A financial or **fiscal** system is needed in states to support rulers, nobles, officials, judges, military personnel, and thousands of other specialists. As in the chiefdom, the state intervenes in production, distribution, and consumption. The state may decree that a certain area will produce certain things or forbid certain activities in particular places. Although, like chiefdoms, states also have redistribution (through taxation), generosity and sharing are played down. A smaller proportion of what comes in flows back to the people.

In nonstates, people customarily share with relatives, but residents of states face added obligations to bureaucrats and officials. Citizens must turn over a substantial portion of what they produce to the state. Of the resources that the state collects, it reallocates part for the general good and uses another part (often larger) for the elite.

The state does not bring more freedom or leisure to the common people, who usually work harder than do the people in nonstates. They may be called on to build monumental public works. Some of these projects, such as dams and irrigation systems, may be economically necessary. However, people also build temples, palaces, and tombs for the elites.

Monument building began in chiefdoms, where "ceremonies of place" were associated with the creation of a "sacred landscape" through constructions such as the (stone) henges of Europe, the mounds of the southeastern United States, and the temples of Hawaii (Earle 1987, 1991). Like chiefs, state officials may use religion to buttress their authority. Archaeology shows that temples abounded in early states. Even in mature states, rulers may link themselves to godhood through divine right or claim to be deities or their earthly representatives. Rulers convoke peons or slaves to build magnificent castles or tombs, cementing the ruler's place in history or status in the afterlife. Monumental architecture survives as an enduring reminder of the exalted prestige of priests and kings.

Markets and trade are usually under at least some state control, with officials overseeing distribution and exchange, standardizing weights and measures, and collecting taxes on goods passing into or through the state. Taxes support government and the ruling class, which is clearly separated from the common people in regard to activities, privileges, rights, and obligations. Taxes also support the many specialists: administrators, tax collectors, judges, lawmakers, generals, scholars, and priests. As the state matures, the segment of the population freed from direct concern with subsistence grows.

The elites of archaic states reveled in the consumption of *sumptuary goods*: jewelry, exotic food and drink, and stylish clothing reserved for, or affordable only by, the rich. Peasants' diets suffered as they struggled to meet government demands.

Commoners might perish in territorial wars that had little relevance to their own needs. Are any of these observations true of contemporary states?

SUMMARY

1. One sociopolitical typology classifies societies as bands, tribes, chiefdoms, and states. Foragers tended to live in egalitarian band-organized societies. Personal networks linked individuals, families, and bands. Band leaders were first among equals, with no sure way to enforce decisions. Disputes rarely arose over strategic resources, which were open to all. Political authority and power tend to increase along with population and the scale of regulatory problems. More people mean more relations among individuals and groups to regulate. Increasingly complex economies pose further regulatory problems.

2. Heads of horticultural villages are local leaders with limited authority. They lead by example and persuasion. Big men have support and authority beyond a single village. They are regional regulators, but temporary ones. In organizing a feast, they mobilize labor from several villages. Sponsoring such events leaves them with little wealth but with prestige and a reputation for generosity.

3. Age and gender also can be used for regional political integration. Among North America's Plains Indians, men's associations (pantribal sodalities) organized raiding and buffalo hunting. Such men's associations tend to emphasize the warrior grade. They serve for offense and defense when there is intertribal raiding for animals. Among pastoralists, the degree of authority and political organization reflects population size and density, interethnic relations, and pressure on resources.

4. The state is an autonomous political unit that encompasses many communities. Its government collects taxes, drafts people for work and war, and decrees and enforces laws. The state is defined as a form of sociopolitical organization based on central government and social stratification—a division of society into classes. Early states are known as archaic, or nonindustrial, states, in contrast to modern industrial nation-states.

5. Unlike tribes, but like states, chiefdoms had permanent regional regulation and differential access to resources. But chiefdoms lacked stratification. Unlike states, but like bands and tribes, chiefdoms were organized by kinship, descent, and marriage. State formation remained incomplete, and only chiefdoms emerged in several areas, including the circum-Caribbean, lowland Amazonia, the southeastern United States, and Polynesia.

6. Weber's three dimensions of stratification are wealth, power, and prestige. In early states—for the first time in human history—contrasts in wealth, power, and prestige between entire groups of men and women came into being. A socioeconomic stratum includes people of both sexes and all ages. The superordinate—higher or elite—stratum enjoys privileged access to resources.

7. Certain systems are found in all states: population control, judiciary, enforcement, and fiscal. These are integrated by a ruling system or government composed of civil, military, and religious officials. States conduct censuses and demarcate boundaries. Laws are based on precedent and legislative proclamations. Courts and judges handle disputes and crimes. A police force maintains internal order, and a military defends against external threats. A financial or fiscal system supports rulers, officials, judges, and other specialists.

KEY TERMS

age set Group uniting all men or women born during a certain time span; this group controls property and often has political and military functions.

big man Regional figure found among tribal horticulturalists and pastoralists. The big man occupies no office but creates his reputation through entrepreneurship and generosity to others. Neither his wealth nor his position passes to his heirs.

chiefdom Form of sociopolitical organization intermediate between the tribe and the state; kin-based with differential access to resources and a permanent political structure.

differential access Unequal access to resources; basic attribute of chiefdoms and states. Superordinates have favored access to such resources, while the access of subordinates is limited by superordinates.

fiscal Pertaining to finances and taxation.

head, village A local leader in a tribal society who has limited authority, leads by example and persuasion, and must be generous.

law A legal code, including trial and enforcement; characteristic of state-organized societies.

office Permanent political position.

power The ability to exercise one's will over others—to do what one wants; the basis of political status.

prestige Esteem, respect, or approval for acts, deeds, or qualities considered exemplary.

sodality, pantribal A non-kin-based group that exists throughout a tribe, spanning several villages.

state Sociopolitical organization based on central government and socioeconomic stratification—a division of society into classes.

stratification Characteristic of a system with socioeconomic strata—groups that contrast in regard to social status and access to strategic resources. Each stratum includes people of both sexes and all ages.

subordinate The lower, or underprivileged, group in a stratified system.

superordinate The upper, or privileged, group in a stratified system.

tribe Form of sociopolitical organization usually based on horticulture or pastoralism. Socioeconomic stratification and centralized rule are absent in tribes, and there is no means of enforcing political decisions.

wealth All a person's material assets, including income, land, and other types of property; the basis of economic status.

CRITICAL THINKING QUESTIONS

For more self testing, see the self quizzes

mhhe
●com
/kottak

1. What's the rationale for using the term "sociopolitical organization" instead of "political organization"?

2. Classify the Inuit and Yanomami according to Service's sociopolitical typology and according to Cohen's typology of adaptive strategies (see the chapter "Making a Living").

3. What is law? Does the absence of law entail social disorder?

4. What kinds of authority figures exist in bands? Compare them with Yanomami village heads. Do any authority figures in your own society remind you of such people in band and tribal society?

5. How do the political roles of village head and big man differ? Does your own society have figures comparable to big men?

6. What are sodalities? Does your society have them? Do you belong to any?

7. What conclusions do you draw from this chapter about the relationship between population density and political hierarchy?

8. What are the main similarities and differences between chiefdoms and tribes? In which would you like to live and why?

9. What are the main similarities and differences between chiefdoms and states? In which would you prefer to live and why?

10. In your opinion, how does redistribution differ from taxation?

11. Give examples from your own society of the four special-purpose subsystems found in all states.

12. What are the advantages and disadvantages of the state from the ordinary citizen's perspective?

Look at Map 17, "Organized States and Chiefdoms, 1500 A.D."

1. Locate and name the states that existed in the western hemisphere in A.D. 1500. Compare Map 16, "World Land Use: 1500 A.D.," with Map 17. Looking at the western hemisphere, can you detect a correlation between land use (and economy) and the existence of states? What's the nature of that correlation? Does that correlation also characterize other parts of the world?

2. Locate three regions of the world where chiefdoms existed in A.D. 1500. Compare Map 16, "World Land Use: 1500 A.D.," with Map 17. Can you detect a correlation between land use (and economy) and the existence of chiefdoms? What's the nature of that correlation?

3. Some parts of the world lacked either chiefdoms or states in A.D. 1500. What are some of those areas? What kinds of political systems did they probably have?

SUGGESTED ADDITIONAL READINGS

Arnold, B., and B. Gibson, eds.

1995   *Celtic Chiefdom, Celtic State.* New York: Cambridge University Press. This collection of articles examines the structure and development of Europe's prehistoric Celtic societies and debates whether they were chiefdoms or states.

Borneman, J.

1998   *Subversions of International Order: Studies in the Political Anthropology of Culture.* Albany: State University of New York Press. Political culture, international relations, world politics, and national characteristics.

Chagnon, N.

1997   *Yanomamö,* 5th ed. Fort Worth: Harcourt Brace. Most recent revision of a well-known account of the Yanomami, including their social organization, politics, warfare, and cultural change, and the crisis they now confront.

Cheater, A. P., ed.

1999   *The Anthropology of Power: Empowerment and Disempowerment in Changing Structures.* New York: Routledge. Overcoming social marginality through participation and political mobilization in today's world.

Cohen, R., and E. R. Service, eds.

1978   *Origins of the State: The Anthropology of Political Evolution.* Philadelphia: Institute for the Study of Human Issues. Several articles on state formation in many areas.

Earle, T. K.

1997   *How Chiefs Come to Power: The Political Economy in Prehistory.* Stanford, CA: Stanford University Press. Political succession and the economic basis of power in chiefdoms.

Ferguson, R. B.

1995   *Yanomami Warfare: A Political History.* Santa Fe, NM: School of American Research. From village raiding to incursions from nation-states.

2002   *The State, Identity, and Violence: Political Disintegration in the Post–Cold War Era.* New York: Routledge. Political relations, the state, ethnic relations, and violence.

Gledhill, J.

2000   *Power and Its Disguises: Anthropological Perspectives on Politics.* Sterling, VA: Pluto Press. The anthropology of power.

Heider, K. G.

1997   *Grand Valley Dani: Peaceful Warriors,* 3rd ed. Fort Worth: Harcourt Brace. Comprehensive and readable account of a tribal group on the island of New Guinea, now under Indonesian rule.

Johnson, A. W., and T. K. Earle

2000   *The Evolution of Human Societies: From Foraging Group to Agrarian State,* 2nd ed. Stanford, CA: Stanford University Press. Recent revision of important study of human social evolution.

Kelly, R. C.

2000   *Warless Societies and the Origin of War*. Ann Arbor, MI: University of Michigan Press. An anthropologist looks at stateless societies in Papua New Guinea to reconstruct the origins of warfare.

Kirch, P. V.

1984   *The Evolution of the Polynesian Chiefdoms*. Cambridge: Cambridge University Press. Diversity and sociopolitical complexity in native Oceania.

2000   *On the Road of the Winds: An Archaeological History of the Pacific Islands before European Contact*. Berkeley, CA: University of California Press. The settling and development of island societies where chiefdoms arose.

Kurtz, D. V.

2001   *Political Anthropology: Power and Paradigms*. Boulder, CO: Westview. Up-to-date treatment of the field of political anthropology.

Saitoti, T. O.

1988   *The Worlds of a Masai Warrior: An Autobiography*. Berkeley: University of California Press. The autobiography of a former warrior from Kenya.

Vincent, J., ed.

2002   *The Anthropology of Politics: A Reader in Ethnography, Theory, and Critique*. Malden, MA: Blackwell. Basic and classic articles in political anthropology.

Wolf, E. R., with S. Silverman

2001   *Pathways of Power: Building an Anthropology of the Modern World*. Berkeley, CA: University of California Press. Political and social identity and power in the modern world.

INTERNET EXERCISES

1. *Subsistence and Status*: Go to the Ethnographic Atlas Cross-tabulations page, **http://lucy.ukc. ac.uk/cgi-bin/uncgi/Ethnoatlas/atlas.vopts.** This site has compiled ethnographic information on many different groups, and you can use the tools provided to cross-tabulate the prevalence of certain traits. Go to the site; under "Select Row Category" choose "subsistence economy," and under "Select Column Category" select "class stratification, prevailing type." Press the Submit Query button. This table shows the frequency of class stratification among groups with different subsistence strategies.

   a. What kinds of subsistence strategies are most common among groups with "Complex" class stratification? Do any of these groups use hunting, gathering, or fishing as the primary means of feeding themselves?

   b. Is any one subsistence strategy predominant among groups with "Absence among freemen" class stratification (egalitarian)?

   c. Looking at the table, which of the following statements is (are) true: All societies with complex class stratification are agriculturalists. All agriculturalists have complex class stratification. No societies that practice hunting, fishing, and gathering have complex class stratification. All hunting, fishing, and gathering societies have class stratification absent among freemen (egalitarian).

2. Read the Mesa Community College page on "A Look at Bigman: Bougainville," **http://www. mc.maricopa.edu/dept/d10/asb/learning/glues/ bigman/mumi.html** and their "Rules for a Bigman," **http://www.mc.maricopa.edu/dept/d10/ asb/learning/glues/bigman/rules.html**

   a. Where is Bougainville? What is the environment like? What are the main sources of food?

   b. What is a *mumi?* How does one become a *mumi?* What role do feasts play in determining who is a *mumi?* How important are friends and family for an aspiring *mumi?*

   c. What other statuses exist in Bougainville society for men?

   d. After reading the rules for a bigman, does the life of a bigman appear to be a life of leisure or does it involve a lot of work?

3. In the year 2000, the field of anthropology was jolted by the announcement of the publication of a book called *Darkness in El Dorado* by the journalist Patrick Tierney (New York: W. W. Norton, 2000). The book contained accusations of inappropriate, unethical, and perhaps even criminal behavior by scientists who had studied the Yanomami Indians of Brazil and Venezuela since the late 1960s.

a. For a brief account of the controversy, check out **www.salon.com/books/feature/2000/09/28/yanomamo/index.html**.

b. For the author's main arguments and response to his critics, go to the book's official website: **http://darknessineldorado.com**.

c. Now visit various sites that document the history of the controversy, offer critiques of Tierney's account, and rebut the changes in his book: **http://www.anth.uconn.edu/gradstudents/dhume/index.htm**; **http://www.umich.edu/~urel/darkness.html**; **http://www.umich.edu/~idpah/SEP/sepmenu.html**; and **http://www.aaanet.org/press/pr_edtf.htm**.

d. What do you make of the controversy? Is it possible to choose sides from the information you have examined?

e. What are the larger ethical issues raised by the furor surrounding Tierney's book?

See Chapter 17 at your McGraw-Hill Online Learning Center for additional review and interactive exercises.

18

FAMILIES, KINSHIP, AND DESCENT

Overview

Especially in nonindustrial societies, kinship, descent, and marriage are basic social building blocks, linking otherwise separate groups in a common social system. Kin groups, such as families and descent groups, are social units whose members can be identified and whose residence patterns and activities can be observed. A nuclear family, for instance, consists of a married couple and their children, living together. Although nuclear families are widespread among the world's societies, other social forms, such as extended families and descent groups, can complement or even replace the nuclear family.

In the United States and Canada, the nuclear family has long been a basic kin group, especially for the middle class. Among the poor, expanded family households and sharing with extended kin occur more frequently; resources may be pooled to deal with poverty. Also, in contempo-

rary North America, the nuclear family household is declining both in frequency and as a cultural norm. We observe more diversity in family, household, and living arrangements.

Unlike families, descent groups have perpetuity—they last for generations. There are several kinds of descent groups, such as lineages and clans. Some descent groups are patrilineal; they reckon descent through males only. Some are matrilineal; they trace descent exclusively through females.

Kinship terminologies are ways of classifying one's relatives based on perceived differences and similarities. Comparative research has made it clear that the number of systems of kinship terminology is limited. For the parental generation, there are four basic ways of classifying kin. There are six basic ways of classifying relatives in one's own generation, which includes siblings and cousins.

When Are Two Dads Better Than One? When the Women Are in Charge

EAST LONDON NEWS BRIEF

by Patrick Wilson

June 12, 2002

Like race, kinship is socially constructed. Cultures develop their own explanations for biological processes, such as the role of insemination in the creation and growth of a human embryo. Scientifically, we know that fertilization of an ovum by a single sperm is responsible for conception. But the Barí people of Venezuela, as is the case in many societies, have more elaborate accounts of procreation. In some societies it is believed that spirits, rather than men, place babies in women's wombs. In others it is believed that a fetus must be nourished by continuing insemination during pregnancy. In the societies discussed in this article people believe that multiple men can create the same fetus. When the baby is born, the mother names the men she recognizes as fathers, and they assist her in raising the child. The realm of cultural diversity contains much more than contemporary North American notions of marriage and the family. In the United States, having two dads may be the stuff of sitcoms, and the product of divorce, remarriage, and step-parenthood. In the societies discussed here, multiple (partible) paternity is a common and beneficial social fact.

> [Among] the Barí people of Venezuela, . . . multiple paternity is the norm. . . . In such societies, children with more than one official father are more likely to survive to adulthood than those with just one Dad. . . . The findings have . . . been published in a book, *Cultures of Multiple Fathers: The Theory and Practice of Partible Paternity in Lowland South America* [Beckerman and Valentine 2002], that questions accepted theories about social organization, the balance of power between the sexes and human evolution.
>
> [The book] . . . draws on more than two decades of fieldwork among South American tribal peoples. The central theme . . . is the concept of partible paternity—the widespread belief that fertilization is not a one-time event and that more than one father can contribute to the developing embryo. . . .

The authors have discovered a strong correlation between the status of women in the society and the benefits of multiple paternity. . . . Among the Barí, 80% of children with two or more official dads survive to adulthood, compared with 64% with one father.

This contrasts with male-dominated cultures such as the neighboring Curripaco, where children of doubtful parentage are outcast and frequently die young.

Explaining the significance of this discovery, Paul Valentine said: "The conventional view of the male-female bargain is that a man will provide food and shelter for a woman and her children if he can be assured that the children are biologically his. Our research turns this idea on its head . . . In societies where women control marriages and other aspects of social life, both men and women have multiple partners and spread the responsibilities of child rearing." It is of course scientifically impossible to have more than one biological father, but aboriginal peoples in South America, Africa and Australasia [Australia and Asia] believe that it takes more than one act of intercourse to make a baby. In some of these societies, nearly all children have multiple fathers. In

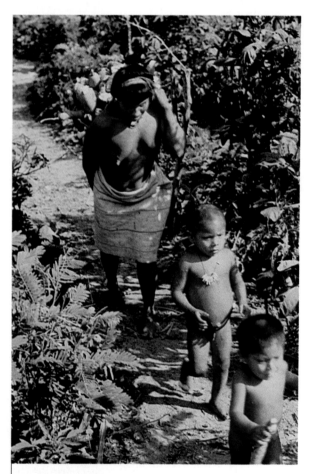

The Barí of Venezuela believe that a child can have multiple fathers.

others, while partible paternity is accepted, socially the child has only one father. However, in the middle are groups where some children do have multiple fathers and some do not. In this case, the children can be compared to see how having more than one father benefits the children—and generational studies show that the children do benefit from the extra care.

When a child is born among the Barí, the mother publicly announces the names of the one or more men she believes to be the fathers, who, if they accept paternity, are expected to provide care for the mother and child. . . . "In small egalitarian societies, women's interests are best served if mate choice is a non-binding, female decision; if a network of multiple females to aid or substitute for a woman in her mothering responsibilities exists; if multiple men support a woman and her children; and if a woman is shielded from the effects of male sexual jealousy."

"In contrast, men's reproductive interests are best served by male control over female sexual behavior. To do this, men must choose the spouses either for themselves or their children, marriage must be for life, female promiscuity is forbidden, and support networks of women for women are disrupted or male support by other than a husband and his family forbidden. It is obvious that neither sex can fully win this contest," says Valentine.

In cultures where women chose their mates, women have broad sexual freedom and partible paternity is accepted, women clearly have the upper hand. In Victorian-style societies where women's sexual activity is controlled by men, marriage is exclusive and male sexual jealousy is a constant threat, men have the upper hand. In between is a full range of combinations and options, all represented in the varying South American cultures . . .

Robert Carneiro, curator at the American Museum of Natural History, said: "Rarely does a book thrust open a door, giving us a striking new view. It has long been known that . . . peoples around the world believe that one act of sexual intercourse is not enough for a child to be born. Now for the first time we have a volume that deals with the consequences and ramifications of this belief, and it does so in exhaustive and fascinating detail." . . .

SOURCE: alphagalileo: the Internet Press Center for European Science and the Arts. http://www.alphagalileo.org/index.cfm?fuseaction =readRelease&Releaseid=9918.

The kinds of societies anthropologists have traditionally studied, such as the Barí and their neighbors, have stimulated a strong interest in families, along with larger systems of kinship, descent, and marriage. Cross-culturally, the social construction of kinship illustrates considerable cultural diversity. And kinship—as vitally important in daily life in nonindustrial societies as work outside the home is in our own—has become an essential part of anthropology because of its importance to the people we study. We are ready to take a closer look at the systems of kinship and descent that have organized human life for much of our history.

Families

Ethnographers quickly recognize social divisions, groups, within any society they study. During field work, they learn about significant groups by observing their activities and composition. People often live in the same village or neighborhood or work, pray, or celebrate together because they are related in some way. To understand the social structure, an ethnographer must investigate such kin ties. For example, the most significant local groups may consist of descendants of the same grandfather. These people may live in neighboring houses, farm adjoining fields, and help each other in everyday tasks. Other sorts of groups, based on other kin links, get together less often.

The nuclear family is one kind of kin group that is widespread in human societies. Other kin groups include extended families (families consisting of three or more generations) and descent groups—lineages and clans. Descent groups, which are composed of people claiming common ancestry, are basic units in the social organization of nonindustrial food producers.

NUCLEAR AND EXTENDED FAMILIES

A nuclear family lasts only as long as the parents and children remain together. Most people belong to at least two nuclear families at different times in their lives. They are born into a family consisting of their parents and siblings. When they reach adulthood, they may marry and establish a nuclear family that includes the spouse and eventually the children. Since most societies permit

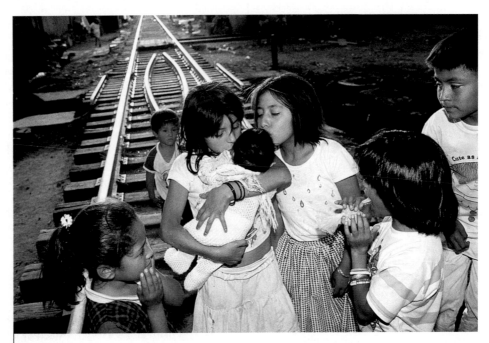

In many cultures siblings play important roles in child rearing, as in this Mexico City slum. Are siblings part of your family of orientation or family of procreation?

divorce, some people establish more than one family through marriage.

Anthropologists distinguish between the **family of orientation** (the family in which one is born and grows up) and the **family of procreation** (formed when one marries and has children). From the individual's point of view, the critical relationships are with parents and siblings in the family of orientation and with spouse and children in the family of procreation.

Nuclear family organization is widespread but not universal. In certain societies, the nuclear family is rare or nonexistent. In other cultures, the nuclear family has no special role in social life. Other social units—most notably descent groups and extended families—can assume most or all of the functions otherwise associated with the nuclear family. In other words, there are many alternatives to nuclear family organization.

Consider an example from the former Yugoslavia. Traditionally, among the Muslims of western Bosnia (Lockwood 1975), nuclear families lacked autonomy. Several such families were embedded in an extended-family household called a *zadruga*. The *zadruga* was headed by a male household head and his wife, the senior woman. It also included married sons and their wives and children, and unmarried sons and daughters. Each nuclear family had a sleeping room, decorated and partly furnished from the bride's trousseau. However, possessions—even clothing items—were freely shared by *zadruga* members. Even trousseau items were appropriated for use elsewhere. Such a residential unit is known as a *patrilocal* extended family, because each couple resides in the husband's father's household after marriage.

The *zadruga* took precedence over its component units. Social interaction was more usual among women, men, or children than between spouses or between parents and children. Larger households ate at three successive settings: for men, women, and children. Traditionally, all children over 12 slept together in boys' or girls' rooms. When a woman wished to visit another village, she sought the permission of the male *zadruga* head. Although men usually felt closer to their own children than to those of their brothers, they were obliged to treat them equally. Children were disciplined by any adult in the household. When a nuclear family broke up, children under seven went with the mother. Older children could choose between their parents. Children were considered part of the household where they were born even if their mother left. One widow who remarried had to leave her five children, all over seven, in their father's *zadruga*, now headed by his brother.

Another example of an alternative to the nuclear family is provided by the Nayars (or Nair), a large and powerful caste on the Malabar Coast of southern India (Figure 18.1). Their traditional kinship system was matrilineal (descent traced only through females). Nayar lived in matrilineal extended family compounds called *tarawads*. The *tarawad* was a residential complex with several buildings, its own temple, granary, water well, orchards, gardens, and land holdings. Headed by a senior woman, assisted by her brother, the *tarawad* housed her siblings, sisters' children, and other matrikin—matrilineal relatives (Gough 1959; Shivaram 1996).

Traditional Nayar marriage seems to have been hardly more than a formality—a kind of coming of age ritual. A young woman would go through a marriage ceremony with a man, after which they might spend a few days together at her *tarawad*. Then the man would return to his own *tarawad*, where he lived with his sisters, aunts, and other matrikin. Nayar men belonged to a warrior class, who left home regularly for military expeditions, returning permanently to their *tarawad* on retirement. Nayar women could have multiple sexual partners. Children became members of the mother's *tarawad*; they were not considered to be relatives of their biological father. Indeed, many Nayar children didn't even know who their genitor was. Child care was the responsibility of the *tarawad*. Nayar society therefore reproduced itself biologically without the nuclear family.

Interpret the World
Atlas Map 18

In your atlas, Map 18, "Household and Family Structures," shows the global distribution of household types and family structure arrangements. Note the areas, including the contemporary United States, Canada,

Figure 18.1
Location of the Nayars in India's Kerala province.

Australia, and western Europe, where nuclear family organization is the norm. Nuclear family organization and neolocality also characterize social organization in Latin America, although extended family relationships tend to be more prominent there than in Anglo America. On the basis of Map 18, what household types and family arrangements are the most common and the least common?

INDUSTRIALISM AND FAMILY ORGANIZATION

For many Americans and Canadians, the nuclear family is the only well-defined kin group. Family isolation arises from geographic mobility, which is associated with industrialism, so that a nuclear family focus is characteristic of many modern nations. Born into a family of orientation, North

Among herders living in the steppe region of the Mongolian People's Republic, patrilocal extended families often span four generations. Is the family shown here more like a *zadruga* or a *tarawad*?

Many married couples live hundreds of miles from their parents. Their jobs have determined where they live. Such a postmarital residence pattern is called **neolocality**: Married couples are expected to establish a new place of residence—a "home of their own." Among middle-class North Americans, neolocal residence is both a cultural preference and a statistical norm. Most middle-class Americans eventually establish households and nuclear families of their own.

Within stratified nations, value systems vary to some extent from class to class, and so does kinship. There are significant differences between middle-class and poorer North Americans. For example, in the lower class the incidence of *expanded family households* (those that include nonnuclear relatives) is greater than it is in the middle class. When an expanded family household includes three or more generations, it is an **extended family**. Another type of expanded family is the *collateral household*, which includes siblings and their spouses and children.

The higher proportion of expanded family households among poorer Americans has been explained as an adaptation to poverty (Stack 1975). Unable to survive economically as nuclear family units, relatives band together in an expanded household and pool their resources. Adaptation to poverty causes kinship values and attitudes to diverge from middle-class norms. Thus, when North Americans raised in poverty achieve financial success, they often feel obligated to provide financial help to a wide circle of less fortunate relatives.

A Tewa extended family. This Native American household consists of three generations living together in Santa Clara Pueblo, New Mexico.

CHANGES IN NORTH AMERICAN KINSHIP

Although the nuclear family remains a cultural ideal for many Americans, Table 18.1 and Figure 18.2 show that nuclear families accounted for just 24 percent of American households in 2000. Other domestic arrangements now outnumber the "traditional" American household more than three to one. There are several reasons for the changing household composition documented in Table 18.1 and Figure 18.2. Women are increasingly joining men in the cash work force. This often removes

Americans leave home for work or college, and the break with parents is underway. Eventually most North Americans marry and start a family of procreation. Because less than 3 percent of the U.S. population now farms, most people aren't tied to the land. Selling our labor on the market, we often move to places where jobs are available.

Table 18.1 Changes in Family and Household Organization in the United States: 1970 versus 2000

	1970	2000
Married couples with children	40%	24%
Number of people per household	3.1	2.6
Family households	81%	69%
Households with five or more people	21%	10%
People living alone	17%	26%
Number of single-mother families	3 million	12 million
Number of single-father families	393,000	2 million
Households that included own children under 18	45%	33%

SOURCE: From data in Fields 2001.

For more on the relation between education and American families, see the Internet Exercises at your OLC

them from their families of orientation while making it economically feasible to delay marriage. Furthermore, job demands compete with romantic attachments. The median age at first marriage for American women jumped from 20 years in 1955 to over 25 in 2000 (Saluter 1996; Fields 2001). The comparable ages for men were 23 and 27 (*World Almanac 1992*, p. 943; Fields 2001).

Also, the U.S. divorce rate has risen, with the number of divorced Americans more than quadrupling from 4.3 million in 1970 to over 19 million in 2000. Single-parent families increased from fewer than 4 million in 1970 to 12 million in 2000. The percentage of children in fatherless households in 2000 was three times the 1960 rate, while the percentage in motherless homes increased fivefold. Only 52 percent of American women and 56 percent of American men were currently married in 2000, versus 60 and 65 percent, respectively, in 1970 (Fields 2001). To be sure, contemporary Americans maintain social lives through work, friendship, sports, clubs, religion, and organized social activities. However, the isolation from kin that these figures suggest is unprecedented in human history.

Table 18.2 documents similar changes in family and household size in the United States and Canada

between 1975 and 2000. Those figures confirm a general trend toward smaller families and living units in North America. This trend is also detectable in Western Europe and other industrial nations.

Our changing household organization has been reflected in the mass media. During the 1950s and early 1960s, such television sitcoms as *Father Knows Best*, *The Adventures of Ozzie and Harriet*, and *Leave It to Beaver* portrayed "traditional" nuclear families.

Table 18.2 Household and Family Size in the United States and Canada, 1975 versus 2000.

	1975	2000
Average family size:		
United States	3.4	3.2
Canada	3.5	3.1
Average household size:		
United States	2.9	2.6
Canada	2.9	2.6

SOURCE: Fields 2001; Census Bureau, Statistical Abstract of the United States, 2000; Statistics Canada, Catalogue no. 91-213, http://www.StatCan.CA/english/Pgdb/People/Famili.htm#fam.

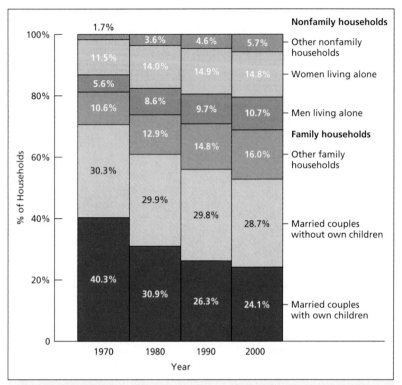

Figure 18.2 Households by Type: Selected Years, 1970–2000

SOURCE: Fields 2001.

In contemporary North America, single-parent families are increasing at a rapid rate. In 1960, 88 percent of American children lived with both parents, compared with 68 percent today. This divorced mom, Valerie Jones, is enjoying a candlelight dinner with her kids. What do you see as the main differences between nuclear families and single-parent families?

The incidence of *blended families* (kin units formed when parents remarry and bring their children into a new household) has risen, as represented in programs such as *The Brady Bunch* (see "Interesting Issues" on pp. 496–497). Three-quarters of divorced Americans remarry. Television programs and other media presentations now routinely feature coresident friends, roommates, unmarried couples, singles, single parents, unrelated retirees or "survivors," nannies, hired male housekeepers, and working mothers.

The idealized middle-class and upper-middle-class TV families of the 1950s and 1960s survived through the 1980s and 1990s, as portrayed on *Family Ties* and *The Cosby Show*. But changes in family dynamics and in the roles of parents and kids have evolved in the media and in "real life." In particular, TV fathers have become much less omniscient. More recently TV has brought us working-class families like that of *Roseanne* (sometimes an expanded family household) and the often dysfunctional families of *Married with Children* and *The Simpsons*. It would be hard to accuse Homer Simpson of knowing best most of the time. Changes in life styles are reflected by the media, which in turn help promote further modifications in our values concerning kinship, marriage, and living arrangements (Kottak 1990a, Kottak and Kozaitis 2003).

The entire range of kin attachments is narrower for North Americans, particularly those in the middle class, than it is for nonindustrial peoples. Although we recognize ties to grandparents, uncles, aunts, and cousins, we have less contact with, and depend less on, those relatives than people in other cultures do. We see this when we answer a few questions: Do we know exactly how we are related to all our cousins? How much do we know about our ancestors, such as their full names and where they lived? How many of the people with whom we associate regularly are our relatives?

Differences in the answers to these questions by people from industrial and those from nonindustrial societies confirm the declining importance of kinship in contemporary nations. Immigrants are often shocked by what they perceive as weak kinship bonds and lack of proper respect for family in contemporary North America. In fact, most of the people whom middle-class North Americans see every day are either nonrelatives or members of the nuclear family. On the other hand, Stack's (1975) study of welfare-dependent families in a ghetto area of a Midwestern city shows that sharing with nonnuclear relatives is an important strategy that the urban poor use to adapt to poverty.

One of the most striking contrasts between the United States and Brazil, the two most populous nations of the Western Hemisphere, is in the meaning and role of the family. Contemporary North American adults usually define their families as consisting of their husbands or wives and their children. However, when middle-class Brazilians talk about their families, they mean their parents, siblings, aunts, uncles, grandparents, and cousins. Later they add their children, but rarely the husband or wife, who has his or her own family. The children are shared by the two families. Because middle-class Americans lack an extended family support system, marriage assumes more importance. The husband–wife relationship is supposed to take precedence over either spouse's relationship with his or her own parents. This places a significant strain on North American marriages.

Living in a less mobile society, Brazilians stay in closer contact with their relatives, including members of the extended family, than North Americans do. Residents of Rio de Janeiro and São Paulo, two of South America's largest cities, are reluctant to leave those urban centers to live away from family and friends. Brazilians find it hard to imagine, and

unpleasant to live in, social worlds without relatives. Contrast this with a characteristic American theme: learning to live with strangers.

Understanding Ourselves   Americans are supposed to love their parents, their siblings, their spouse, and especially their children. Many, perhaps most, of us would agree that "family" is very important, but just how important is kinship in our lives? How might one answer such a question? In nonindustrial societies, people are with their kin *all the time*—at home, at work, at play, in the village, in the fields, with the herds. Contemporary North Americans, by contrast, typically spend our days—weekdays at least—with people we don't love—and may not even like. We have to do balancing acts to be with our families as we also fulfill work demands. How different were TV's leisured Harriet Nelson and Carol Brady from the harried physicians of NBC's medical drama *ER* and all the other TV parents who struggle to maintain family responsibilities even as work demands compete for their time.

How did your parents manage their work/family responsibilities? It's statistically probable that both of your parents worked outside the home at least part of the time you were growing up. It's also likely that your mother, even if she had the

Friends: Ross (David Schwimmer), Joey (Matt LeBlanc), and Chandler (Matthew Perry) during the seventh season of the NBC show. How are family relations depicted on *Friends*?

Interesting *Issues*

Brady Bunch Nirvana

One teaching technique I started using several years ago, taking advantage of students' familiarity with television, is to demonstrate changes in American kinship and marriage patterns by contrasting the TV programs of the 50s with more recent ones. (Students know about the history of sitcom families from syndicated reruns, especially on the cable channel Nickelodeon.) In the 1950s, the usual TV family was a nuclear family consisting of employed dad, homemaker mom, and kids. Examples include *Father Knows Best*, *Ozzie and Harriet*, and *Leave It to Beaver*. These programs, appropriate for the 1950s market, are dramatically out of sync with today's social and economic realities. Only 16 million American women worked outside the home in 1950, compared with three times that number today. Today less than 7 percent of American households fit the former ideal: breadwinner father, homemaker mother, and two children.

Most of my students (even in the 21st century) have watched reruns of the 1960s family series *The Brady Bunch*, whose social organization offers an instructive contrast with 1950s programs. Here a new, blended, family forms when a widow with three daughters marries a widower with three sons. Blended families have been increasing in American society because of more frequent divorce and remarriage. When *The Brady Bunch* first aired, divorce was too controversial to give rise to a prime-time TV family. Widow(er)hood had to be the basis of the blended family, as it was in *The Brady Bunch*.

The Brady husband-father was a successful architect. The Bradys were wealthy enough to employ a housekeeper, Alice. Mirroring American culture when the program was made, the wife's career was part-time and subsidiary. Women lucky enough to find wealthy husbands didn't compete with other women—even professional housekeepers—in the work force.

Each time I begin my kinship lecture using sitcom material, a few people in the class immediately recognize (from reruns) the nuclear families of the 1950s, especially the Beaver Cleaver family. And when I start diagraming the Bradys, students start shouting out their names: "Jan," "Bobby," "Greg," "Cindy," "Marsha," "Peter," "Mike," "Carol," "Alice." As the cast of characters nears completion, my class, filled with TV-enculturated natives, is usually shouting out in unison names made almost as familiar as their parents' through exposure to TV reruns. My students almost seem to find nirvana (a feeling of religious ecstasy) through their collective remembrance of the Bradys and in the ritual-like incantation of their names.

Given its massive penetration of the modern home (at least 98 percent

higher-paying job, spent more time on child care and home care than your father did. Did your family of orientation illustrate the rule, or was it an exception to it? Do you think it will be different in your household if you form a family of procreation? Why or why not?

THE FAMILY AMONG FORAGERS

Populations with foraging economies are far removed from industrial societies in terms of social complexity. Here again, however, the nuclear family is often the most significant kin group, although in no foraging society is the nuclear family the only group based on kinship. The two basic social units of traditional foraging societies are the nuclear family and the band.

Unlike middle-class couples in industrial nations, foragers don't usually reside neolocally. Instead, they join a band in which either the husband or the wife has relatives. However, couples and families may move from one band to another several times. Although nuclear families are ultimately as impermanent among foragers as they are in any other society, they are usually more stable than bands are.

Many foraging societies lacked year-round band organization. The Native American Shoshoni of the Great Basin in Utah and Nevada (Figure 18.3) provide an example. The resources available to the Shoshoni were so meager that for most of the year families traveled alone through the countryside hunting and gathering. In certain seasons families assembled to hunt cooperatively of all households), television's effects on our socialization and enculturation can hardly be trivial. Indeed, the common information and knowledge we acquire by watching the same TV programs is indisputably culture in the anthropological sense. Culture is collective, shared, meaningful. It is transmitted by conscious and unconscious learning experiences acquired by humans, not through their genes but as a result of growing up in a particular society. Of the hundreds of culture bearers who have passed through the Anthropology 101 classroom over the past decade, many have been unable to recall the full names of their parents' first cousins. Some have forgotten their grandmother's maiden name. But most have absolutely no trouble identifying names and relationships in a family that exists only in television land.

How might *The Brady Bunch* have differed if this blended family had been created after divorce, rather than after the deaths of two former spouses?

as a band; after just a few months together they dispersed.

Industrial and foraging economies do have something in common. In neither type are people tied permanently to the land. The mobility and the emphasis on small, economically self-sufficient family units promote the nuclear family as a basic kin group in both types of societies.

Descent

We've seen that the nuclear family is important in industrial nations and among foragers. The analogous group among nonindustrial food producers is the descent group. A **descent group** is a permanent social unit whose members say they have ancestors in common. Descent-group members believe they share, and descend from, those common ancestors. The group endures even though its membership changes, as members are born and die, move in and move out. Often, descent-group membership is determined at birth and is lifelong. In this case, it is an ascribed status.

DESCENT GROUPS

Descent groups frequently are exogamous (members must seek their mates from other descent groups). Two common rules serve to admit certain people as descent-group members while excluding others. With a rule of **matrilineal descent**, people join the mother's group automatically at birth

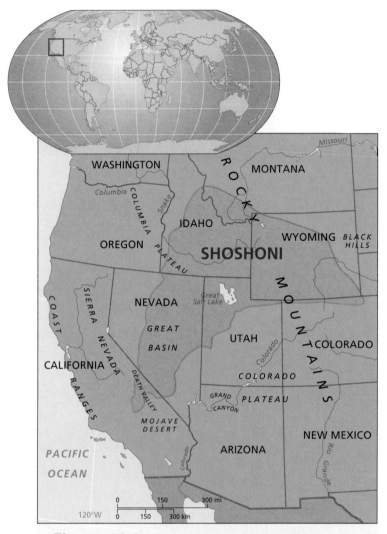

Figure 18.3   Location of the Shoshoni.

(Murdock 1957), about three times as many were found to be patrilineal (247 to 84).

Descent groups may be **lineages** or **clans**. Common to both is the belief that members descend from the same *apical ancestor*. That person stands at the apex, or top, of the common genealogy. For example, Adam and Eve are the apical ancestors of the biblical Jews, and, according to the Bible, of all humanity. Since Eve is said to have come from Adam's rib, Adam stands as the original apical ancestor for the patrilineal genealogy laid out in the Bible.

How do lineages and clans differ? A lineage uses *demonstrated descent*. Members can recite the names of their forebears in each generation from the apical ancestor through the present. (This doesn't mean their recitations are accurate, only that lineage members think they are.) In the Bible the litany of men who "begat" other men is a demonstration of genealogical descent for a large patrilineage that ultimately includes Jews and Arabs (who share Abraham as their last common apical ancestor).

Unlike lineages, clans use *stipulated descent*. Clan members merely say they descend from the apical ancestor. They don't try to trace the actual genealogical links between themselves and that ancestor. The Betsileo of Madagascar have both clans and lineages. Descent may be demonstrated for the most recent 8 to 10 generations, then stipulated for the more remote past—sometimes with mermaids and vaguely defined foreign royalty mentioned among the founders (Kottak 1980). Like the Betsileo, many societies have both lineages and clans. In such a case, clans have more members and cover a larger geographic area than lineages do. Sometimes a clan's apical ancestor is not a human at all but an animal or plant (called a *totem*). Whether human or not, the ancestor symbolizes the social unity and identity of the members, distinguishing them from other groups.

and stay members throughout life. Matrilineal descent groups therefore include only the children of the group's women. With **patrilineal descent**, people automatically have lifetime membership in the father's group. The children of all the group's men join the group, but the children of the female members of that group are excluded. (In Figures 18.4 and 18.5, which show matrilineal and patrilineal descent groups, respectively, the pyramids stand for males and the circles for females.) Matrilineal and patrilineal descent are types of **unilineal descent**. This means the descent rule uses one line only, either the male or the female line. Patrilineal descent is much more common than is matrilineal descent. In a sample of 564 societies

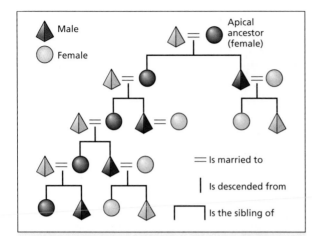

Figure 18.4   A Matrilineage Five Generations Deep.   Matrilineages are based on demonstrated descent from a female ancestor. Only the children of the group's women (blue) belong to the matrilineage. The children of the group's men are excluded; they belong to their mother's matrilineage.

Figure 18.5   A Patrilineage Five Generations Deep.   Lineages are based on demonstrated descent from a common ancestor. With patrilineal descent, children of the group's men (blue) are included as descent-group members. Children of the group's female members are excluded; they belong to their father's patrilineage. Also notice lineage exogamy.

The economic types that usually have descent group organization are horticulture, pastoralism, and agriculture, as discussed in the chapter "Making a Living." Such societies tend to have several descent groups. Any one of them may be confined to a single village, but they usually span more than one village. Any branch of a descent group that lives in one place is a *local descent group*. Two or more local branches of different descent groups may live in the same village. Descent groups in the same village or different villages may establish alliances through frequent intermarriage.

LINEAGES, CLANS, AND RESIDENCE RULES

As we've seen, descent groups, unlike nuclear families, are permanent and enduring units, with new members added in every generation. Members have access to the lineage estate, where some of them must live, in order to benefit from and manage that estate across the generations. To endure, descent groups need to keep at least some of their members at home, on the ancestral estate. An easy way to do this is to have a rule about who belongs to the descent group and where they should live after they get married. Patrilineal and matrilineal descent, and the postmarital residence rules that usually accompany them, ensure that about half the people born in each generation will live out their lives on the ancestral estate. Neolocal residence, which is the rule for most middle-class Americans, isn't very common outside modern North America, Western Europe, and the European-derived cultures of Latin America.

Much more common is **patrilocality**: When a couple marries, it moves to the husband's father's community, so that their children will grow up in their father's village. Patrilocality is associated with patrilineal descent. This makes sense. If the group's male members are expected to exercise their rights in the ancestral estate, it's a good idea to raise them on that estate and to keep them there after they marry. This can be done by having wives move to their husband's village, rather than vice versa.

A less common postmarital residence rule, associated with matrilineal descent, is **matrilocality**: Married couples live in the wife's mother's community, and their children grow up

Most societies have a prevailing opinion about where a couple should live after they marry; this is called a postmarital residence rule. A common rule is patrilocality: the couple lives with the husband's relatives, so that children grow up in their father's community. On the top, a traditional Korean wedding. The residence change takes place via a spousal utility vehicle with four-person drive. On the bottom, in Lendak, Slovakia, women transport part of the bride's dowry to the groom's house.

the male. Besides the unilineal rules, there is another descent rule called nonunilineal or **ambilineal** descent. As in any descent group, membership comes through descent from a common ancestor. However, ambilineal groups differ from unilineal groups in that they do not *automatically* exclude either the children of sons or those of daughters. People can choose the descent group they join (for example, that of their father's father, father's mother, mother's father, or mother's mother). People also can change their descent-group membership, or belong to two or more groups at the same time.

Unilineal descent is a matter of ascribed status; ambilineal descent illustrates achieved status. With unilineal descent, membership is automatic; no choice is permitted. People are born members of their father's group in a patrilineal society or of their mother's group in a matrilineal society. They are members of that group for life. Ambilineal descent permits more flexibility in descent-group affiliation.

Before 1950, descent groups were generally described simply as patrilineal or matrilineal. If the society tended toward patrilineality, the anthropologist classified it as a patrilineal rather than an ambilineal group. The treatment of ambilineal descent as a separate category was a formal recognition that many descent systems are flexible—some more so than others.

in their mother's village. This rule keeps related women together. Together, patrilocality and matrilocality are known as *unilocal* rules of postmarital residence.

AMBILINEAL DESCENT

The descent rules examined so far admit certain people as members while excluding others. A unilineal rule uses one line only, either the female or

Kinship Calculation

In addition to studying kin groups, anthropologists also are interested in **kinship calculation**: the system by which people in a society reckon kin relationships. To study kinship calculation, an ethnographer must first determine the word or words for different types of "relatives" used in a particular language and then ask questions such as, "Who are your relatives?" Kinship, like race and gender (discussed in other chapters), is culturally constructed. This means that some genealogical kin are considered to be relatives whereas others are not. As we saw in the account of the Barí of Venezuela at the beginning of this chapter, even people who aren't genealogical relatives can be constructed socially as kin. The Barí recognize multiple fathers, even though biologically there can be only one actual genitor. Through questioning, the ethnographer discovers the specific genealogical relationships between "relatives" and the person who has named them—the **ego**. *Ego* means *I* (or *me*) in Latin. It's who you, the reader, are in the kin charts that follow. It's your perspective looking out on your kin. By posing the same questions to several local people, the ethnographer learns about the extent and direction of kinship calculation in that society. The ethnographer also begins to understand the relationship between kinship calculation and kin groups: how people use kinship to create and maintain personal ties and to join social groups. In the kinship charts that follow, the black cube labeled "ego" identifies the person whose kinship calculation is being examined.

GENEALOGICAL KIN TYPES AND KIN TERMS

At this point, we may distinguish between *kin terms* (the words used for different relatives in a particular language) and *genealogical kin types*. We designate genealogical kin types with the letters and symbols shown in Figure 18.6. *Genealogical kin type* refers to an actual genealogical relationship (e.g., father's brother) as opposed to a kin term (e.g., *uncle*).

Kin terms reflect the social construction of kinship in a given culture. A kin term may (and usually does) lump together several genealogical relationships. In English, for instance, we use *father* primarily for one kin type: the genealogical father. However, *father* can be extended to an adoptive father or stepfather—and even to a priest. *Grandfather* includes mother's father and father's father. The term *cousin* lumps together several kin types. Even the more specific *first cousin* includes mother's brother's son (MBS), mother's brother's daughter (MBD), mother's sister's son (MZS),

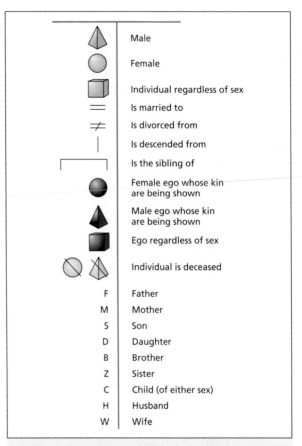

Figure 18.6 Kinship Symbols and Genealogical Kin Type Notation.

mother's sister's daughter (MZD), father's brother's son (FBS), father's brother's daughter (FBD), father's sister's son (FZS), and father's sister's daughter (FZD). *First cousin* thus lumps together at least eight genealogical kin types.

Uncle encompasses mother's and father's brothers, and *aunt* includes mother's and father's sisters. We also used *uncle* and *aunt* for the spouses of our "blood" aunts and uncles. We use the term for mother's brother and father's brother because we perceive them as being the same sort of relative. Calling them *uncles*, we distinguish between them and another kin type, F, whom we call *Father, Dad,* or *Pop*. In many societies, however, it is common to call a father and a father's brother by the same term. Later we'll see why.

In the United States and Canada, the nuclear family continues to be the most important group based on kinship. This is true despite an increased

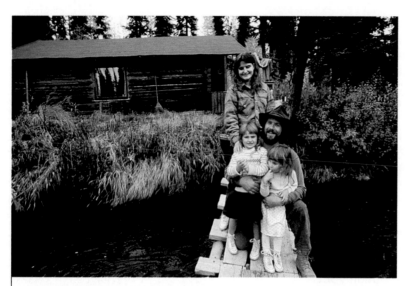

A Canadian nuclear family—Richard and Jenny Dix and their two daughters. The Dixes are one of Canada's westernmost nuclear families. They live in Yukon territory just miles from the Alaska border. Nuclear family organization is associated with geographic mobility.

incidence of single parenthood, divorce, and re-marriage. The nuclear family's relative isolation from other kin groups in modern nations reflects geographic mobility within an industrial economy with sale of labor for cash.

It's reasonable for North Americans to distinguish between relatives who belong to their nuclear families and those who don't. We are more likely to grow up with our parents than with our aunts and uncles. We tend to see our parents more often than we see our uncles and aunts, who may live in different towns and cities. We often inherit from our parents, but our cousins have first claim to inherit from our aunts and uncles. If our marriage is stable, we see our children daily as long as they remain at home. They are our heirs. We feel closer to them than to our nieces and nephews.

American kinship calculation and kin terminology reflect these social features. Thus, the term *uncle* distinguishes between the kin types MB and FB on the one hand and the kin type F on the other. However, this term also lumps kin types together. We use the same term for MB and FB, two different kin types. We do this because American kinship calculation is **bilateral**—traced equally through males and females, for example, father and mother. Both kinds of uncle are brothers of one of our parents. We think of both as roughly the same kind of relative.

"No," you may object, "I'm closer to my mother's brother than to my father's brother." That may be. However, in a representative sample of American students, we would find a split, with some favoring one side and some favoring the other. We'd actually expect a bit of *matrilateral skewing*—a preference for relatives on the mother's side. This occurs for many reasons. When contemporary children are raised by just one parent, it's much more likely to be the mother than the father. Also, even with intact marriages, the wife tends to play a more active role in managing family affairs, including family visits, reunions, holidays, and extended family relations than the husband does. This would tend to reinforce her kin network over his and thus favor matrilateral skewing.

Bilateral kinship means that people tend to perceive kin links through males and females as being similar or equivalent. This bilaterality is expressed in interaction with, living with or near, and rights to inherit from relatives. We don't usually inherit from uncles, but if we do, there's about as much chance that we'll inherit from the father's brother as from the mother's brother. We don't usually live with either aunt, but if we do, the chances are about the same that it will be the father's sister as the mother's sister.

For a review and quiz on kinship terminology, see the Virtual Exploration

mhhe
com
/kottak

Kinship Terminology

People perceive and define kin relations differently in different cultures. In any culture, kinship terminology is a classification system, a taxonomy or typology. It is a *native taxonomy*, developed over generations by the people who live in a particular society. A native classification system is based on how people perceive similarities and differences in the things being classified.

However, anthropologists have discovered that there are a limited number of patterns in which people classify their kin. People who speak very different languages may use exactly the same system of kinship terminology. This section examines the four main ways of classifying kin on the parental generation: lineal, bifurcate merging, generational, and bifurcate collateral. We also consider the social correlates of these classification systems. (Note that each of the systems described here applies to the parental generation. There are also differences in kin terminology on ego's generation. These involve the classification of siblings and cousins. There are six such systems, called Eskimo, Iroquois, Hawaiian, Crow, Omaha, and Sudanese cousin terminology, after societies that traditionally used them. You can see them diagrammed and discussed on our website.)

A **functional explanation** will be offered for each system of kinship terminology, such as lineal, bifurcate merging, and generational terminology. Functional explanations attempt to relate particular customs (such as the use of kin terms) to other features of a society, such as rules of descent and postmarital residence. Certain aspects of a culture are *functions* of others. That is, they are correlated variables, so that when one of them changes, the others inevitably change too. For certain terminologies, the social correlates are very clear.

Kinship terms provide useful information about social patterns. If two relatives are designated by the same term, we can assume that they are perceived as sharing socially significant attributes. Several factors influence the way people interact with, perceive, and classify relatives. For instance, do certain kinds of relatives customarily live together or apart? How far apart? What benefits do they derive from each other, and what are their obligations? Are they members of the same descent group or of different descent groups? With these questions in mind, let's examine systems of kinship terminology.

LINEAL TERMINOLOGY

Our own system of kinship classification is called the *lineal system* (Figure 18.7). The number 3 and the color green stand for the term *uncle*, which we apply both to FB and to MB. **Lineal kinship terminology** is found in societies such as the United States and Canada in which the nuclear family is the most important group based on kinship.

Lineal kinship terminology has absolutely nothing to do with lineages, which are found in

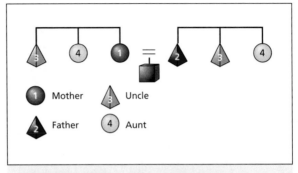

Figure 18.7 Lineal Kinship Terminology.

very different social contexts. (What contexts are those?) Lineal kinship terminology gets its name from the fact that it distinguishes lineal relatives from collateral relatives. What does that mean? A **lineal relative** is an ancestor or descendant, anyone on the direct line of descent that leads to and from ego (Figure 18.8). Thus, lineal relatives are one's parents, grandparents, great-grandparents, and other direct forebears. Lineal relatives also include children, grandchildren, and great-grandchildren. **Collateral relatives** are all other kin. They include siblings, nieces and nephews, aunts and uncles, and cousins (Figure 18.8). **Affinals** are relatives by marriage, whether of lineals (e.g., son's wife) or of collaterals (sister's husband).

BIFURCATE MERGING TERMINOLOGY

Bifurcate merging kinship terminology (Figure 18.9) *bifurcates*, or splits, the mother's side and the father's side. But it also *merges* same-sex siblings of each parent. Thus, mother and mother's sister are merged under the same term (1), while father and father's brother also get a common term (2). There are different terms for mother's brother (3) and father's sister (4).

People use this system in societies with unilineal (patrilineal and matrilineal) descent rules and unilocal (patrilocal and matrilocal) postmarital residence rules. When the society is unilineal and unilocal, the logic of bifurcate merging terminology is fairly clear. In a patrilineal society, for example, father and father's brother belong to the same descent group, gender, and generation. Since patrilineal societies usually have patrilocal residence,

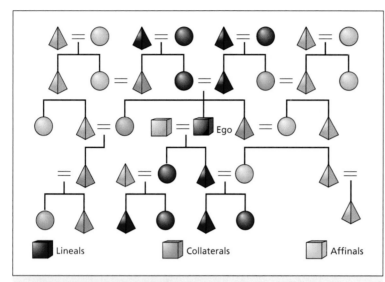

Figure 18.8 The Distinctions among Lineals, Collaterals, and Affinals as Perceived by Ego.

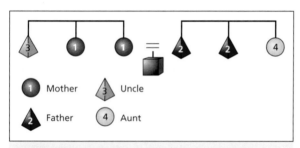

Figure 18.9 Bifurcate Merging Kinship Terminology.

of his mother's clan, the Raven clan. Ego's father is a member of the Wolf clan. His mother and her sister are female Ravens of the same generation. If there is matrilocal residence, as there often is in matrilineal societies, they will live in the same village. Because they are so similar socially, ego calls them by the same kin term—1.

The father's sister, however, belongs to a different group, the Wolves; lives elsewhere; and have a different kin term—4. Ego's father and father's brother are male Wolves of the same generation. If they marry women of the same clan and live in the same village, this creates additional social similarities that reinforce this usage.

GENERATIONAL TERMINOLOGY

Like bifurcate merging kinship terminology, **generational kinship terminology** uses the same term for parents and their siblings, but the lumping is more complete (Figure 18.10). With generational terminology, there are only two terms for the parental *generation*. We may translate them as "father" and "mother," but more accurate translations would be "male member of the parental generation" and "female member of the parental generation."

Generational kinship terminology does not distinguish between the mother's and father's sides. It does not bifurcate, but it certainly does merge. It uses just one term for father, father's brother, and mother's brother. In a unilineal society, these three kin types would never belong to the same descent group. Generational kinship terminology also uses a single term for mother, mother's sister, and father's sister. Nor, in a unilineal society, would these three ever be members of the same group.

Nevertheless, generational terminology suggests closeness between ego and his or her aunts and uncles—much more closeness than exists between Americans and these kin types. How likely would you be to call your uncle "Dad" or your aunt "Mom"? We'd expect to find generational terminology in cultures in which kinship is much more important than it is in our own but in

the father and his brother live in the same local group. Because they share so many attributes that are socially relevant, ego regards them as social equivalents and calls them by the same kinship term—2. However, the mother's brother belongs to a different descent group, lives elsewhere, and has a different kin term—3.

What about mother and mother's sister in a patrilineal society? They belong to the same descent group, the same gender, and the same generation. Often they marry men from the same village and go to live there. These social similarities help explain the use of the same term—1—for both.

Similar observations apply to matrilineal societies. Consider a society with two matrilineal clans, the Ravens and the Wolves. Ego is a member

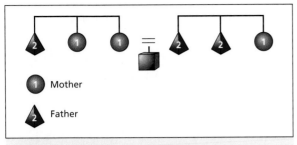

Figure 18.10 Generational Kinship Terminology.

which there is no rigid distinction between the father's side and the mother's side.

It's logical, then, that generational kin terminology is typical of societies with ambilineal descent. In such contexts, descent-group membership is not automatic. People may choose the group they join, change their descent-group membership, or belong to two or more descent groups simultaneously. Generational terminology fits these conditions. The use of intimate kin terms signals that people have close personal relations with all their relatives of the parental generation. People exhibit similar behavior toward their aunts, uncles, and parents. Someday they'll have to choose a descent group to join. Furthermore, in ambilineal societies, postmarital residence is usually ambilocal. This means that the married couple can live with either the husband's or the wife's group.

Understanding Ourselves The nuclear family still dominates in our society, ideologically if not statistically. Imagine a society where someone doesn't know for sure, and doesn't care much about, who his actual mother was. Consider Joseph Rabe, a Betsileo man who was my field assistant in Madagascar. One of the villages where I worked was his village of origin, where Rabe had been raised by his father's sister. How and why did that happen? I asked him. Rabe told me about two sisters, one of whom was his mother and the other was his mother's sister. He knew their names, but he didn't know which was which. Illustrating a pattern of child fosterage and adoption that is common among the Betsileo, Rabe was given to his childless father's sister to raise when he was a toddler. His mother and her sister lived far away and died in his childhood, and so he didn't really know them. But he was very close to his father's sister, for whom he used the term for mother. Indeed, he had to call her that, because the Betsileo have generational kinship terminology. They call mother, mother's sister, and father's sister by the same term, *reny*. The Betsileo live in an ambilineal society (albeit with a patrilineal tilt), and they use generational kin terms, which are associated with ambilineality. Since the Betsileo socially construct kinship, and encourage fosterage (typically by childless relatives), in these ways, the difference between "real" and socially constructed kinship did not matter to Rabe, or to many others like him.

Contrast the Betsileo case with Americans' attitudes about kinship and adoption. On family-oriented radio talk shows, I've heard hosts who are "helping professionals" distinguish between "birth mothers" and adoptive mothers, and between "sperm daddies" and "daddies of the heart." The latter may be adoptive fathers, or stepfathers who have "been like fathers" to someone. American culture tends to promote the view that kinship is, and should be, biological. Americans have some trouble with the social construction of kinship. Less and less are we warned against searching for our birth parents (which was formerly discouraged as disruptive), even if we've had a perfectly satisfactory upbringing with our adoptive parents. One common reason an adopted person might give for trying to track down his or her birth parents is based in biology—to discover family health history, including inherited diseases. The American emphasis on biology for kinship is also seen in the recent proliferation of DNA testing. Understanding ourselves through cross-cultural comparison helps us see that kinship and biology don't always converge, nor do they need to.

Significantly, generational terminology also characterizes certain foraging bands, including Kalahari San groups and several native societies of North America. Use of this terminology reflects certain similarities between foraging bands and ambilineal descent groups. In both societies, people have a choice about their kin-group affiliation. Foragers always live with kin, but they often shift band affiliation and so may be members of several different bands during their lifetimes. Just as in food-producing societies with ambilineal descent, generational terminology among foragers helps

Table 18.3   The Four Systems of Kinship Terminology, with Their Social and Economic Correlates

Kinship Terminology	Kin Group	Residence Rule	Economy
Lineal	Nuclear family	Neolocal	Industrialism, foraging
Bifurcate merging	Unilineal descent group—patrilineal or matrilineal	Unilocal—patrilocal or matrilocal	Horticulture, pastoralism, agriculture
Generational	Ambilineal descent group, band	Ambilocal	Agriculture, horticulture, foraging
Bifurcate collateral	Varies	Varies	Varies

For a quiz on kinship systems, see the Interactive Exercise

mhhe
● **com**
/kottak

maintain close personal relationships with several parental-generation relatives whom ego may eventually use as a point of entry into different groups. Table 18.3 summarizes the types of kin group, the postmarital residence rule, and the economy associated with the four types of kinship terminology.

BIFURCATE COLLATERAL TERMINOLOGY

Of the four kin classification systems, **bifurcate collateral kinship terminology** is the most specific. It has separate terms for each of the six kin types of the parental generation (Figure 18.11). Bifurcate collateral terminology isn't as common as the other types. Many of the societies that use it are in North Africa and the Middle East, and many of them are offshoots of the same ancestral group.

Figure 18.11   **Bifurcate Collateral Kinship Terminology.**

Bifurcate collateral terminology also may be used when a child has parents of different ethnic backgrounds and uses terms for aunts and uncles derived from different languages. Thus, if you have a mother who is Latina and a father who is Anglo, you may call your aunts and uncles on your mother's side "tia" and "tio," while calling those on your father's side "aunt" and "uncle." And your mother and father may be "Mom" and "Pop." That's a modern form of bifurcate collateral kinship terminology.

SUMMARY

1. In nonindustrial societies, kinship, descent, and marriage organize social and political life. In studying kinship, we must distinguish between kin groups, whose composition and activities can be observed, and kinship calculation—how people identify and designate their relatives.

2. One widespread kin group is the nuclear family, consisting of a married couple and their children. There are functional alternatives to the nuclear family. That is, other groups may assume functions usually associated with the nuclear family. Nuclear families tend to be especially important in foraging and industrial societies. Among farmers and herders, other kinds of kin groups often overshadow the nuclear family.

3. In contemporary North America, the nuclear family is the characteristic kin group for the middle class. Expanded households and sharing with extended family kin occur more frequently among the poor, who may pool their resources in dealing with poverty. Today, however, even in the American middle class, nuclear family households are declining as single-person households and other domestic arrangements increase.

4. The descent group is a basic kin group among nonindustrial food producers (farmers and herders). Unlike families, descent groups have perpetuity—they last for generations. Descent-group members share and manage a common estate; land, animals, and other resources. There are several kinds of descent groups. Lineages are based on demonstrated descent; clans, on stipulated descent. Descent rules may be unilineal or ambilineal. Unilineal (patrilineal and matrilineal) descent is associated with unilocal (respectively, patrilocal and matrilocal) postmarital residence.

5. A kinship terminology is a classification of relatives based on perceived differences and similarities. Comparative research has revealed a limited number of ways of classifying kin. Because there are correlations between kinship terminology and other social practices, we often can predict kinship terminology from other aspects of culture. The four basic kinship terminologies for the parental generation are lineal, bifurcate merging, generational, and bifurcate collateral. Many foraging and industrial societies use lineal terminology, which is associated with nuclear family organization. Cultures with unilocal residence and unilineal descent tend to have bifurcate merging terminology. Generational terminology correlates with ambilineal descent and ambilocal residence.

KEY TERMS

affinals Relatives by marriage, whether of lineals (e.g., son's wife) or collaterals (e.g., sister's husband).

ambilineal Principle of descent that does not automatically exclude the children of either sons or daughters.

bifurcate collateral kinship terminology
Kinship terminology employing separate terms for M, F, MB, MZ, FB, and FZ.

bifurcate merging kinship terminology
Kinship terminology in which M and MZ are called by the same term, F and FB are called by the same term, and MB and FZ are called by different terms.

bilateral kinship calculation A system in which kinship ties are calculated equally through both sexes: mother and father, sister and brother, daughter and son, and so on.

clan Unilneal descent group based on stipulated descent.

collateral relative A genealogical relative who is not in ego's direct line, such as B, Z, FB, or MZ.

descent group A permanent social unit whose members claim common ancestry; fundamental to tribal society.

ego Latin for *I*. In kinship charts, the point from which one views an egocentric genealogy.

extended family Expanded household including three or more generations.

family of orientation Nuclear family in which one is born and grows up.

family of procreation Nuclear family established when one marries and has children.

functional explanation Explanation that establishes a correlation or interrelationship between social customs. When customs are functionally interrelated, if one changes, the others also change.

generational kinship terminology
Kinship terminology with only two terms for the parental generation, one designating M, MZ, and FZ and the other designating F, FB, and MB.

kinship calculation The system by which people in a particular society reckon kin relationships.

lineage   Unilineal descent group based on demonstrated descent.

lineal kinship terminology   Parental generation kin terminology with four terms: one for M, one for F, one for FB and MB, and one for MZ and FZ.

lineal relative   Any of ego's ancestors or descendants (e.g., parents, grandparents, children, grandchildren); on the direct line of descent that leads to and from ego.

matrilineal descent   Unilineal descent rule in which people join the mother's group automatically at birth and stay members throughout life.

matrilocality   Customary residence with the wife's relatives after marriage, so that children grow up in their mother's community.

neolocality   Postmarital residence pattern in which a couple establishes a new place of residence rather than living with or near either set of parents.

patrilineal descent   Unilineal descent rule in which people join the father's group automatically at birth and stay members throughout life.

patrilocality   Customary residence with the husband's relatives after marriage, so that children grow up in their father's community.

unilineal descent   Matrilineal or patrilineal descent.

CRITICAL THINKING QUESTIONS

For more self testing, see the self quizzes

mhhe
● **com**
/kottak

1. Why is kinship so important to anthropologists? How might the study of kinship be useful for research in fields of anthropology other than cultural anthropology?
2. To what sorts of family or families do you belong? Have you belonged to other kinds of families? When you were growing up, how did you feel about your family compared with those of your friends?
3. Choose two of your friends who have families of orientation that differ from your own. How do they differ?
4. How might a society reproduce itself biologically without the nuclear family?
5. What residence choices have you made during your lifetime? What factors do you think will determine your future residence choices?
6. Do you belong to any kin group that has lasted or will last for more than one generation?
7. What do "family" and "family values" mean to you?
8. Based on your experience, do you agree with the discussion of changing portrayals of families on North American TV? What other changes have you noticed? Has TV actually caused any of those changes?

9. Besides industrial societies, where else are nuclear families important, and why?
10. How do the kin terms you use compare with the four classification systems discussed in this chapter? What's the strangest use of kin terms you've ever heard (among your friends or acquaintances)?

Atlas Questions

Look at Map 18, "Household and Family Structures."

1. On what continents does the nuclear family predominate? What postmarital residence rule is associated with nuclear family organization?
2. On what continent is the nuclear family least characteristic? What kinds of families/kin groups instead characterize that continent? Are there exceptions to the rule on that continent, and, if so, what are they?
3. How would you describe variation in household and family structures in Asia? Are there dominant forms of family and household there? Are there many exceptions to the dominant form—and if so, where?

Suggested Additional Readings

Buchler, I. R., and H. A. Selby

1968 *Kinship and Social Organization: An Introduction to Theory and Method*. New York: Macmillan. Introduction to comparative social organization; includes several chapters on interpretations of kinship classification systems.

Cigno, A.

1994 *Economics of the Family*. New York: Oxford University Press. How economists explain changes in birth rates and divorce rates and other features of family organization and functioning.

Collier, J. F., and S. J. Yangisako, eds.

1987 *Gender and Kinship: Essays toward a Unified Analysis*. Stanford, CA: Stanford University Press. Consideration of kinship in the context of gender issues.

Finkler, K.

2000 *Experiencing the New Genetics: Family and Kinship on the Medical Frontier*. Philadelphia: University of Pennsylvania Press. Examines some medical and genetic aspects of kinship, along with social dimensions of contemporary medical/genetics debates.

Graburn, N., ed.

1971 *Readings in Kinship and Social Structure*. New York: Harper & Row. Several important articles on kinship terminology.

Hansen, K. V., and A. I. Garey, eds.

1998 *Families in the U.S.: Kinship and Domestic Politics*. Philadelphia: Temple University Press. Families, family policy, and diversity in the contemporary United States.

Netting, R. M. C., R. R. Wilk, and E. J. Arnould, eds.

1984 *Households: Comparative and Historical Studies of the Domestic Groups*. Berkeley, CA: University of California Press. Excellent collection of articles on household research.

Parkin, R.

1997 *Kinship: An Introduction to Basic Concepts*. Cambridge, MA: Blackwell. The basics of kinship study.

Pasternak, B., C. R. Ember, and M. Ember

1997 *Sex, Gender, and Kinship: A Cross-Cultural Perspective*. Upper Saddle River, NJ: Prentice-Hall. Sex roles, kinship, and marriage in comparative perspective.

Radcliffe-Brown, A. R., and D. Forde, eds.

1994 *African Systems of Kinship and Marriage*. New York: Columbia University Press. Reissue of a classic work, indispensable to understand kinship, descent, and marriage.

Scheffler, H. W.

2001 *Filiation and Affiliation*. Boulder, CO: Westview. How does one recognize his or her kin if unilineal descent excludes some very close relatives?

Stacey, J.

1998 *Brave New Families: Stories of Domestic Upheaval in Late Twentieth Century America*. Berkeley, CA: University of California Press. Contemporary family life in the United States, based on field work in California's Silicon Valley.

Stone, L.

2000 *Kinship and Gender: An Introduction*, 2nd ed. Boulder, CO: Westview. Kinship, gender roles, and gender identity.

2001 *New Directions in Anthropological Kinship*. Lanham, MD: Rowman and Littlefield. How contemporary anthropologists think about kinship.

Weston, K.

1991 *Families We Choose: Lesbians, Gays, Kinship*. New York: Columbia University Press. Kinship and family issues affecting gays and lesbians.

Willie, C. V.

2003 *A New Look at Black Families*. Walnut Creek, CA: Altamira. Family experience in relation to socioeconomic status, presented through case studies.

INTERNET EXERCISES

1. *Kinship and Conflict*: Go to the Yanamamo Interactive: Understanding the Ax Fight web page, **http://www.anth.ucsb.edu/projects/axfight/index.html,** and go to the Web version of the CD-ROM, **http://www.anth.ucsb.edu/projects/axfight/prep.html.** View the film of the Ax Fight and read the text entitled "Chagnon's Voice-Over Narration from the 1975 *The Ax Fight.*" The questions below ask you to interpret the fight, and it may be necessary to view the film or read the text more than once to understand it.

   a. What is the cause of the fight?

   b. Who are the aggressors? Who are they attacking?

   c. As the fight escalates, more people join in. What is their relationship to the people who start the fight? Why is that important?

   d. How is kinship important for understanding this conflict? Can you think of examples from your own society where kinship served to escalate or diffuse conflict?

2. *Descent and Subsistence*: Go to the Ethnographic Atlas Cross-tabulations page, **http://lucy.ukc.ac.uk/cgi-bin/uncgi/Ethnoatlas/atlas.vopts.** This site has compiled ethnographic information on many different groups, and you can use the tools provided to cross-tabulate the prevalence of certain traits. Go to the site. Under "Select Row Category" choose "region," and under "Select Column Category" select "descent." Press the Submit Query button. The table that appears shows the frequency of descent patterns from regions around the world.

   a. Look at the total row for descent. Which forms of descent are most common worldwide? What is the *most* common? Is that the system with which you are most familiar in your own society?

   b. Where are most of the patrilineal societies found? Where are most of the bilateral societies found? In the Insular Pacific, is any one descent system predominant?

   c. Now go back to the Ethnographic Atlas Cross-tabulations page and change the "Select Row Category" from "region" to "subsistence economy" and press the Submit Query button. What kind of subsistence economy do most patrilineal societies practice? Are matrilineal societies more likely to use hunting, gathering, or fishing or to use agriculture? Is the pattern as strong as with patrilineal groups? Are there any strong patterns for the type of subsistence economy practiced by bilateral groups?

3. *Kinship Terminologies*: Go to the website created by Professor Brian Schwimmer of the Department of Anthropology at the University of Manitoba, **http://www.umanitoba.ca/faculties/arts/anthropology/kintitle.html.** Click on "Begin Tutorial." Next click on topic 3—Kinship Terminology. Press "Continue" at the bottom left of the next two pages until you reach a page titled "Systematic Kinship Terminologies." Scroll down the page to the diagram labeled "Eskimo Kin Terms."

   a. To what parental generation kin terminology discussed in the book (lineal, bifurcate merging, generational, or bifurcate collateral) do the Eskimo cousin terms correspond?

   b. Answer the same question for Iroquois, Hawaiian, and Sudanese terms.

   c. Do you see any logic in the relation between the terms used on the parental generation (for parents, aunts, and uncles) and those used on ego's own generation (for siblings and cousins)?

   d. How do these associated sets of kin terms fit with particular kinds of kin groups, for example, the nuclear family, a unilineal descent group, an ambilineal descent group?

   e. At the bottom of the web page, can you see how Omaha kin terms might fit with patrilineal descent, and Crow terms with matrilineal descent?

See Chapter 18 at your McGraw-Hill Online Learning Center for additional review and interactive exercises.

19
MARRIAGE

Overview

Marriage, which is usually a form of domestic partnership, is difficult to define. Marriage is an important means of forming alliances beyond one's own kin group. Scholars still debate why all societies have some sort of incest taboo. Does that taboo reflect instinctive horror of incest? Does it express worries about the biological results of inbreeding? Is it an attempt to channel sexual feelings that develop as people grow up in the same household? Does it have an adaptive advantage because it promotes exogamy (outmarriage), thus widening social networks? Those questions illustrate the main arguments proposed to explain why the incest taboo is universal.

Marriage transforms relationships and conveys certain rights. Marriage establishes legal parentage of children. It gives spouses rights to each other's sexuality, labor, and property. And it establishes a social relationship (an affinal relationship, or "affinity") between spouses and each other's relatives.

In societies with descent groups, marriages are relationships between groups as well as between the individual spouses. With the custom of bridewealth, the groom and his relatives transfer wealth to the bride and her relatives. As the value of the bridewealth increases, the divorce rate declines. Bridewealth customs show how marriages create and maintain group alliances. So do replacement marriages, for example, when a man marries the sister of his deceased wife, or a woman marries the brother of her deceased husband.

The ease and frequency of divorce vary among societies. When marriage is a matter of intergroup alliance, as is typically true in societies with descent groups, divorce is less common. A large fund of joint property complicates divorce.

Many societies permit plural marriages. The two kinds of plural marriage (polygamy) are polygyny and polyandry. The former involves multiple wives; the latter, multiple husbands. Polygyny is much more common than polyandry is.

Few Risks Seen to the Children of 1st Cousins

NEW YORK TIMES NEWS BRIEF

by Denise Grady

April 4, 2002

Should first cousins marry? Why or why not? Your answer(s) probably will reveal aspects of the debate among anthropologists about why all societies have some form of incest taboo—a ban on mating and marriage with close relatives. However, societies differ in regard to the kin they include within the incest taboo. All cultures ban marriage between parents and children, and brother–sister marriage is limited to a few instances of royal marriage in ancient states. But many societies permit, and many even require, that people marry their first cousins. First cousins are genetically more similar to each other than they are to nonrelatives, and their offspring are more likely to inherit certain diseases. The research described below did not find the increased genetic risk of marriage between first cousins to be a sufficient reason for banning it. Do you agree?

Contrary to widely held beliefs and longstanding taboos in America, first cousins can have children together without a great risk of birth defects or genetic disease, scientists are reporting today. They say there is no biological reason to discourage cousins from marrying.

First cousins are somewhat more likely than unrelated parents to have a child with a serious birth defect, mental retardation or genetic disease, but their increased risk is nowhere near as large as most people think, the scientists said.

In the general population, the risk that a child will be born with a serious problem like spina bifida or cystic fibrosis is 3 percent to 4 percent; to that background risk, first cousins must add another 1.7 to 2.8 percentage points, the report said.

Although the increase represents a near doubling of the risk, the result is still not considered large enough to discourage cousins from having children, said Dr. Arno Motulsky, . . . the senior author of the report. . . .

The researchers, a panel convened by the National Society of Genetic Counselors, based their conclusions on a review of six major studies conducted from 1965 to August 2000, involving many thousands of births.

Dr. Motulsky said medical geneticists had known for a long time that there was little or no harm in cousins marrying and having children. "Somehow, this hasn't become general knowledge," even among doctors, he said.

Twenty-four states have laws forbidding first cousins from marrying, and seven states have limits like requiring genetic counseling. But no countries in Europe have such prohibitions, and in parts of the Middle East, Africa and Asia, marriages between cousins are considered preferable.

"In some parts of the world," the report says, "20 to 60 percent of all marriages are between close biological relatives." Dr. Motulsky said many immigrants from cultures where cousin marriages are common expect to continue the tradition in the United States. . . .

It is not known how many cousins marry or live together. Estimates of marriages between related people, which include first cousins and more distant ones, range from less than 0.1 percent of the general population to 1.5 percent. In the past, small studies have found much higher rates in some areas. A

Rock 'n' roll legend Jerry Lee Lewis married his third cousin Myra in 1958 when she was thirteen or fourteen years old—and possibly before his divorce from his second wife had become final.

survey in 1942 found 18.7 percent in a small town in Kentucky and a 1980 study found 33 percent in a Mennonite community in Kansas.

The report made a point of saying that the term "incest" should not be applied to cousins but only to sexual relations between siblings or between parents and children. Babies who result from those unions are thought to be at significantly higher risk of genetic problems, the report said, but there is not enough data to be sure.

The new report says that genetic counselors should advise cousins who want to have children together in much the same way they advise everybody else and that no extra genetic tests are required before conception.

The guidelines urge counselors to take a thorough family history and, as they do for all clients, look for any diseases that might run in the family or in the clients' ethnic groups and order tests accordingly. During pregnancy, the woman should have the standard blood tests used to screen for certain neurological problems and other disorders and an ultrasound examination.

Their children should be tested as newborns for deafness and certain rare metabolic diseases—tests already given to all newborns in some parts of the country. These are among the conditions that may be slightly more likely to occur in children whose parents are cousins. Some of the metabolic problems are treatable, and children with hearing losses do better if they get help early in life. . . .

The small increase in risk is thought to occur because related people may be carrying some of the same disease-causing genes, inherited from common ancestors. The problems arise from recessive genes, which have no effect on people who carry single copies, but can cause disease in a person who inherits two copies of the gene, one from each parent. When two carriers of a recessive gene have a child, the child has a one-in-four chance of inheriting two copies of that gene. When that happens, disease can result. Cystic fibrosis and the fatal Tay-Sachs disease, for example, are caused by recessive genes. Unrelated people share fewer genes and so their risk of illness caused by recessive genes is a bit lower. . . .

SOURCE: *New York Times*, April 4, 2002, late edition—final, section A, p. 1, column 3, and www.nytimes.com.

The viability and health of children are important, since children are probably marriage's most important product. "Love and marriage," "marriage and the family": These familiar phrases show how we link the romantic love of two individuals to marriage, and how we link marriage to reproduction and family creation. But marriage is an institution with significant roles and functions in addition to reproduction. What is marriage, anyway?

No definition of marriage is broad enough to apply easily to all societies and situations. A commonly quoted definition comes from *Notes and Queries on Anthropology*:

> Marriage is a union between a man and a woman such that the children born to the woman are recognized as legitimate offspring of both partners. (Royal Anthropological Institute 1951, p. 111)

This definition isn't universally valid for several reasons. For example, some societies recognize same-sex marriages. Also, in many societies, marriages unite more than two spouses. Here we speak of *plural marriages*, as when a woman weds a group of brothers—an arrangement called *fraternal polyandry* that is characteristic of certain Himalayan cultures. In the Brazilian community of Arembepe, people can choose among various forms of marital union. Most people live in long-term "common-law" domestic partnerships that are not legally sanctioned. Some have civil marriages, which are licensed and legalized by a justice of the peace. Still others go through religious ceremonies, so they are united in "holy matrimony," although not legally. And some have both civil and religious ties. The different forms of union permit someone to have multiple spouses (e.g., one common-law, one civil, one religious) without ever getting divorced.

In Sudan, a Nuer woman can marry a woman if her father has only daughters but no male heirs, who are necessary if his patrilineage is to survive. He may ask his daughter to stand as a son in order to take a bride. This daughter will become the socially recognized husband of another woman (the wife). This is a symbolic and social relationship rather than a sexual one. The "wife" has sex with a man or men (whom her female "husband" must approve) until she gets pregnant. The children born to the wife are accepted as the offspring of both the female husband and the wife. Although the female husband is not the actual **genitor**, the biological father, of the children, she is their **pater**, or socially recognized father. What's important in this Nuer case is *social* rather than *biological paternity*. We see again how kinship is socially constructed. The bride's children are considered the legitimate offspring of her female "husband," who is biologically a woman but socially a man, and the descent line continues.

Incest and Exogamy

In many nonindustrial societies, a person's social world includes two main categories: kin and strangers. Strangers are potential or actual enemies. Marriage is one of the primary ways of converting strangers into kin, of creating and maintaining personal and political alliances, relationships of affinity (*affinal* relationships). **Exogamy**, the practice of seeking a husband or wife outside one's own group, has adaptive value because it links people into a wider social network that nurtures, helps, and protects them in times of need.

Incest refers to sexual relations with someone considered to be a close relative. All cultures have taboos against it. However, although the taboo is a cultural universal, cultures define incest differently. As an illustration, consider some implications of the distinction between two kinds of first cousins: cross cousins and parallel cousins.

The children of two brothers or two sisters are **parallel cousins**. The children of a brother and a sister are **cross cousins**. Your mother's sister's children and your father's brother's children are your parallel cousins. Your father's sister's children and your mother's brother's children are your cross cousins.

The American kin term *cousin* doesn't distinguish between cross and parallel cousins, but in many societies, especially those with unilineal descent, the distinction is essential. As an example, consider a community with only two descent groups. This exemplifies what is known as *moiety* organization—from the French *moitié*, which means "half." Descent bifurcates the community so that everyone belongs to one half or the other. Some societies have patrilineal moieties; others have matrilineal moieties.

In Figures 19.1 and 19.2, notice that cross cousins are always members of the opposite moiety and parallel cousins always belong to your (ego's) own moiety. With patrilineal descent (Figure 19.1), people take the father's descent-group

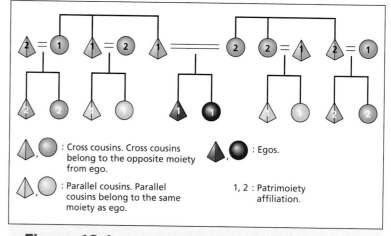

Figure 19.1 Parallel and Cross Cousins and Patrilineal Moiety Organization.

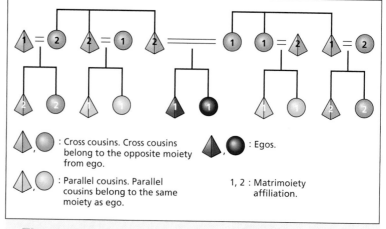

Figure 19.2 Matrilineal Moiety Organization.

affiliation; in a matrilineal society (Figure 19.2), they take the mother's affiliation. You can see from these diagrams that your mother's sister's children (MZC) and your father's brother's children (FBC) always belong to your group. Your cross cousins—that is, FZC and MBC—belong to the other moiety.

Parallel cousins belong to the same generation and the same descent group as ego does, and they are like ego's brothers and sisters. They are called by the same kin terms as brother and sister are. Defined as close relatives, parallel cousins are tabooed as sex or marriage partners. They fall within the incest taboo, but cross cousins don't.

For a quiz on marriage patterns, see the Interactive Exercise

mhhe
com
/kottak

In societies with unilineal moieties, cross cousins always belong to the opposite group. Sex with cross cousins isn't incestuous, because they aren't considered relatives. In fact, in many unilineal societies, people must marry either a cross cousin or someone from the same descent group as a cross cousin. A unilineal descent rule ensures that the cross cousin's descent group is never one's own. With moiety exogamy, spouses must belong to different moieties.

Among the Yanomami of Venezuela and Brazil (Chagnon 1997), men anticipate eventual marriage to a cross cousin by calling her "wife." They call their male cross cousins "brother-in-law." Yanomami women call their male cross cousins "husband" and their female cross cousins "sister-in-law." Among the Yanomami, as in many societies with unilineal descent, sex with cross cousins is proper but sex with parallel cousins is considered incestuous.

A custom that is much rarer than cross-cousin marriage also illustrates that people define their kin, and thus incest, differently in different societies. When unilineal descent is very strongly developed, the parent who does not belong to one's own descent group isn't considered a relative. Thus, with strict patrilineality, the mother is not a relative but a kind of in-law who has married a member of ego's group—ego's father. With strict matrilineality, the father isn't a relative, because he belongs to a different descent group.

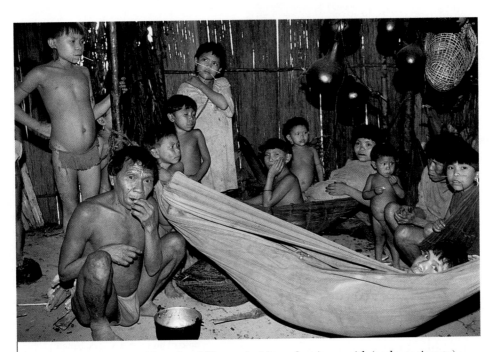

Among the Yanomami of Brazil and Venezuela (shown here), sex with (and marriage to) cross cousins is proper, but sex with parallel cousins is considered incestuous. With unilineal descent, sex with cross cousins isn't incestuous because cross cousins never belong to ego's descent group.

Figure 19.3   Location of the Lakher.

Ego

Incestuous union   Nonincestuous union

🔴 , 🔺 : Ego's patrilineage   🔴 🔺 : Ego's mother's second husband's patrilineage

🔵 : Ego's mother's patrilineage   ⚪ : Ego's father's second wife's patrilineage

≠ : Separation or divorce.
FD by second marriage is a comember of ego's descent group and is included within the incest taboo.
MD by second marriage is not a comember of ego's descent group and is not tabooed.

Figure 19.4   Patrilineal Descent-Group Identity and Incest among the Lakher.

The Lakher of Southeast Asia (Figure 19.3) are strictly patrilineal (Leach 1961). Using the male ego in Figure 19.4, let's suppose that ego's father and mother get divorced. Each remarries and has a daughter by a second marriage. A Lakher always belongs to his or her father's group, all the members of which (one's *agnates*, or patrikin) are considered too closely related to marry because they are members of the same patrilineal descent group. Therefore, ego can't marry his father's daughter by the second marriage, just as in contemporary North America it's illegal for half-siblings to marry.

However, in contrast to our society, where all half-siblings are tabooed, the Lakher permit ego to marry his mother's daughter by a different father. She is not a forbidden relative because she belongs to her own father's descent group rather than ego's. The Lakher illustrate clearly that definitions of forbidden relatives, and therefore of incest, vary from culture to culture.

We can extend these observations to strict matrilineal societies. If a man's parents divorce and his father remarries, ego may marry his paternal half-sister. By contrast, if his mother remarries and has a daughter, the daughter is considered ego's sister, and sex between them is taboo. Cultures therefore have different definitions and expectations of relationships that are biologically or genetically equivalent.

Explaining the Taboo

INSTINCTIVE HORROR

There is no simple or universally accepted explanation for the fact that all cultures ban incest. Do primate studies offer any clues? Research with primates does show that adolescent males (among monkeys) or females (among apes) often move away from the group in which they were born (Rodseth et al. 1991). This emigration helps reduce the frequency of incestuous unions. The human avoidance of mating with close relatives may therefore express a generalized primate tendency.

One argument (Hobhouse 1915; Lowie 1920/1961) is that the incest taboo is universal because incest horror is instinctive: *Homo sapiens* has a genetically programmed disgust toward incest. Because of this feeling, early humans banned it. However, cultural universality doesn't necessarily entail an instinctual basis. Fire making, for example, is a cultural universal, but it certainly is not an ability transmitted by the genes. Furthermore, if people really did have an instinctive horror of mating with blood relatives, a formal incest taboo would be unnecessary. No one would ever do it. However, as social workers, judges, psychiatrists, and psychologists know, incest is not as uncommon as we might suppose.

A final objection to the instinctive horror theory is that it can't explain why in some societies people can marry their cross cousins but not their parallel cousins. Nor does it tell us why the Lakher can marry their maternal, but not their paternal, half-siblings. No known instinct can distinguish between parallel and cross cousins.

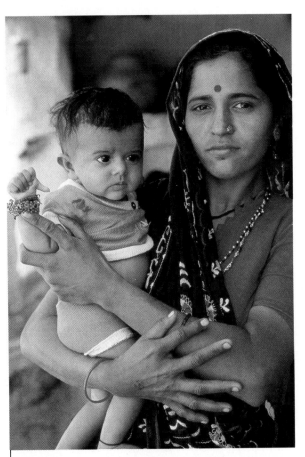

How many fingers do this Indian woman and her child have? Such genetically determined traits as polydactylism (extra fingers) may show up when there is high incidence of endogamy. Despite the biological effects of inbreeding, marriage preferences and prohibitions are based on specific cultural beliefs rather than universal concerns about future biological degeneration.

The specific kin types included within the incest taboo—and the taboo itself—have a cultural rather than a biological basis. Even among nonhuman primates, there is no definite evidence for an instinct against incest. Adolescent dispersal does not prevent—but merely limits the frequency of—incestuous unions. Among humans, cultural traditions determine the specific relatives with whom sex is considered incestuous. They also deal with the people who violate prohibited relationships in different ways. Banishment, imprisonment, death, and threats of supernatural retaliation are some of the punishments imposed.

Biological Degeneration

Another theory is that the taboo emerged because early *Homo* noticed that abnormal offspring were born from incestuous unions (Morgan 1877/1963). To prevent this, our ancestors banned incest. The human stock produced after the taboo originated was so successful that it spread everywhere.

What is the evidence for this theory? Laboratory experiments with animals that reproduce faster than humans do (such as mice and fruit flies) have been used to investigate the effects of inbreeding: A decline in survival and fertility does accompany brother–sister mating across several generations. However, despite the potentially harmful biological results of systematic inbreeding, human marriage patterns are based on specific cultural beliefs rather than universal concerns about biological degeneration several generations in the future. Neither instinctive horror nor fear of biological degeneration explains the very widespread custom of marrying cross cousins. Nor can fears about degeneration explain why breeding with parallel cousins but not cross cousins is so often tabooed. Remember, too, the news story at the beginning of this chapter, which showed that the genetic risk associated with marriage between cousins isn't as great as is commonly thought.

Attempt and Contempt

Sigmund Freud is the most famous advocate of the theory that children have sexual feelings toward their parents, which they eventually repress or resolve. Other scholars have looked to the dynamics of growing up for an explanation of the incest taboo. Bronislaw Malinowski believed that children would naturally seek to express their sexual feelings, particularly as they increased in adolescence, with members of their nuclear family, because of preexisting intimacy and affection. Yet, he thought, sex was too powerful a force to unleash in the family. It would threaten existing family roles and ties; it could destroy the family. Malinowski proposed that the incest taboo originated to direct sexual feeling outside, so as to avoid disruption of existing family structure and relations.

The opposite theory is that children are not likely to be sexually attracted to those with whom they have grown up (Westermarck 1894). This is related to the idea of instinctive horror, but without assuming a biological (instinctual) basis. The notion here is that a lifetime of living together in particular, nonsexual relationships would make the idea of sex with a family member less desirable. The two opposed theories are sometimes characterized as "familiarity breeds attempt" versus "familiarity breeds contempt." One bit of evidence to support the contempt theory comes from Joseph Shepher's (1983) study of Israeli *kibbutzim*. He found that unrelated people who had been raised in the same *kibbutz* (domestic community) avoided intermarriage. They tended to choose their mates from outside—not because they were related, but because their prior residential histories and roles made sex and marriage unappealing. Again, there is no final answer to the question of whether people who grow up together, related or unrelated, are likely to be sexually attracted to one another. Usually they aren't; sometimes they are. Incest is universally tabooed, but it does happen.

Marry Out or Die Out

One of the most accepted explanations for the incest taboo is that it arose in order to ensure exogamy, to force people to marry outside their kin groups (Lévi-Strauss 1949/1969; Tylor 1889; White 1959). In this view, the taboo originated early in human evolution because it was adaptively advantageous. Marrying a close relative, with whom one is already on peaceful terms, would be counterproductive. There is more to gain by extending peaceful relations to a wider network of groups.

This view emphasizes the role of marriage in creating and maintaining alliances. By forcing members to marry out, a group increases its allies. Marriage within the group, by contrast, would isolate that group from its neighbors and their resources and social networks, and might ultimately lead to the group's extinction. Exogamy and the incest taboo that propels it help explain human adaptive success. Besides the sociopolitical function, exogamy ensures genetic mixture between groups and thus maintains a successful human species.

Endogamy

The practice of exogamy pushes social organization outward, establishing and preserving alliances among groups. In contrast, rules of **endogamy** dictate mating or marriage within a group to which one belongs. Formal endogamic rules are less common but are still familiar to anthropologists. Indeed, most societies *are* endogamous units, although they usually do not need a formal rule requiring people to marry someone from their own society. In our own society, classes and ethnic groups are quasi-endogamous groups. Members of an ethnic or religious group often want their children to marry within that group, although many of them do not do so. The outmarriage rate varies among such groups, with some more committed to endogamy than others are.

Homogamy means to marry someone similar, as when members of the same social class intermarry. There's a correlation between socioeconomic status (SES) and education. People with similar SES tend to have similar educational aspirations, to attend similar schools, and to aim at similar careers. For example, people who meet at an elite private university are likely to have similar backgrounds and career prospects. Homogamous marriage may work to concentrate wealth in social classes and to reinforce the system of social stratification. In the United States, for example, the rise in female employment, especially in professional careers, when coupled with homogamy, has dramatically increased household incomes in the upper classes. This pattern has been one factor in sharpening the contrast in household income between the richest and poorest quintiles (top and bottom 20 percent) of Americans.

CASTE

An extreme example of endogamy is India's caste system, which was formally abolished in 1949, although its structure and effects linger. Castes are stratified groups in which membership is ascribed at birth and is lifelong. Indian castes are grouped into five major categories, or *varna*. Each is ranked relative to the other four, and these categories extend throughout India. Each *varna* includes a large number of subcastes (*jati*), each of which includes people within a region who may intermarry. All the *jati* in a single *varna* in a given region are ranked, just as the *varna* themselves are ranked.

Occupational specialization often sets off one caste from another. A community may include castes of agricultural workers, merchants, artisans, priests, and sweepers. The untouchable *varna*, found

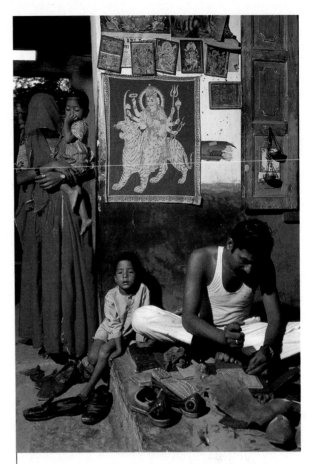

An extreme example of endogamy is India's caste system, which was formally abolished in 1949, although its structure and effects linger. In Gadwada village, cobblers still make shoes in a traditional style. Here, Devi-Lal sits with his child as his wife looks on. In the traditional caste system, such cobblers had a higher status than did sweepers and tanners, whose work is considered so smelly and dirty that they live at the far end of the village.

throughout India, includes subcastes whose ancestry, ritual status, and occupations are considered so impure that higher-caste people consider even casual contact with untouchables to be defiling.

The belief that intercaste sexual unions lead to ritual impurity for the higher-caste partner has been important in maintaining endogamy. A man who has sex with a lower-caste woman can restore his purity with a bath and a prayer. However, a woman who has intercourse with a man of a lower caste has no such recourse. Her defilement cannot be undone. Because the women have the babies, these differences protect the purity of the caste

Beyond the *Classroom*
Human Mate Preference In Matrimonial Advertisements from Gujarat, India

Background Information

STUDENT: **Kim Shah**

SCHOOL: **Rutgers University**

SUPERVISING PROFESSOR: **Lee Kronk**

YEAR IN SCHOOL/MAJOR **Senior/Anthropology**

FUTURE PLANS: **Graduate study of nutritional attitudes anthropology and public health**

This study suggests that Indian marriage customs are changing, and particularly that women may have a stronger role in marital choices than has been thought traditionally (see the section "Bridewealth and Dowry"). It's also true that marriage customs and the roles of men and women vary by region in a country as large and populous as India, which contains considerable cultural diversity. Still, this account also demonstrates that caste still matters and that parents play a significant role in arranging marriages.

Human mate preferences have been studied in many settings, among them newspaper ads, often termed lonely-hearts personal advertisements. In these ads, people describe their own attributes and those they seek in potential mates. The ad might look something like this, "Tall, handsome, intelligent investment banker seeks smart, slim, fun-loving woman."

Most studies of mate preference theory using such advertisements have been done in western settings. My research involved the study of nonwestern advertisements, specifically from the state of Gujarat in India. These ads were taken from the matrimonial section of a Gujarati newspaper. A typical one looked something like this: "For marriage: vaisshnav, vanik (caste designation) man, 34 years old, owns his own home and car, makes 75,000Rs. per year, (seeks) pretty, smart, lady."

The purpose of my project was to test hypotheses of mate preference based on evolutionary theory. I did this by content analysis focusing on the characteristics sought and offered by advertisers. For this task I took advantage of the cultural diversity of my university (Rutgers) and hired international students from Gujarat to help me in this procedure.

A total of 342 advertisements, 20 seeking wives and 122 seeking husbands, were studied. Under "physical attractiveness" I coded for looks, stature/weight, and fairness. I hypothesized that advertisers seeking wives would look for physical attractiveness more than advertisers seeking husbands would. In turn, women seeking husbands would mention their own physical attractiveness more often than men seeking wives would. These hypotheses were confirmed with the data on good looks and stature/weight.

---

line, ensuring the pure ancestry of high-caste children. Although Indian castes are endogamous groups, many of them are internally subdivided into exogamous lineages. Traditionally this meant that Indians had to marry a member of another descent group from the same caste.

ROYAL INCEST

Royal incest is similar to caste endogamy. The best-known examples come from Inca Peru, ancient Egypt, and traditional Hawaii. Those cultures allowed royal brother–sister marriages. In Peru and Hawaii, privileged endogamy, a violation of the incest taboo that applied to commoners in those societies, was a means of differentiating between rulers and subjects.

Manifest and Latent Functions To understand royal brother–sister marriage, it is useful to distinguish between the manifest and latent functions of behavior. The *manifest function* of a custom refers to the reasons natives give for it. Its *latent function* is an effect the custom has on the society that the native people don't mention or may not even recognize.

Royal incest illustrates this distinction. Hawaiians and other Polynesians believed in an impersonal force called *mana*. Mana could exist in things

Yet cultural differences were also apparent. Compared with similar studies done elsewhere, the male preference for good looks was de-emphasized in my results. Only 14% of wife-seeking advertisers requested good looks, significantly fewer than in other studies. An explanation may be that parental involvement in writing and/or answering these ads affects the male request for good looks. Indeed, on re-analysis, I found that 46% of all advertisers sought responses not from the prospective mate himself or herself, but from the parents of the prospective mate. Thus de-emphasis of the male preference for physical attractiveness may reflect the advertisers' awareness of parental involvement.

Male advertisers were on average 4 years older than female advertisers. The content analysis also revealed that advertisers seeking wives offered information about financial resources more than advertisers seeking husbands did. In other words, prospective husbands were more likely to include information about their salary or possessions than prospective wives were. Logically, advertisers seeking husbands made more inquiries about the prospective mate's financial situation.

Throughout this project it was apparent that cultural and social forces played a significant role. Gujarati society displayed strong adherence to maintaining caste integrity. I also learned that the advertisers had above average educations, so I must view the results of my project as representative of this particular group only. I was able to understand many aspects of Gujarati culture, language, and religion because my own family is from the state of Gujarat. I presented this project at the 14th annual meeting of the Human Evolution and Behavior Society in 2002. Future work on this project will include a study of response rates.

or people, in the latter case marking them off from other people and making them divine. The Hawaiians believed that no one had as much mana as the ruler. Mana depended on genealogy. The person whose own mana was exceeded only by the king's was his sibling. The most appropriate wife for a king was his own full sister. Notice that the brother–sister marriage also meant that royal heirs would be as manaful, or divine, as possible. The manifest function of royal incest in ancient Hawaii was part of that culture's beliefs about mana and divinity.

Royal incest also had latent functions—political repercussions. The ruler and his spouse had the same parents. Since mana was believed to be inherited, they were almost equally divine. When the king and his sister married, their children indisputably had the most mana in the land. No one could question their right to rule. However, if the king had taken a wife with less mana than his sister, his sister's children with someone else might eventually cause problems. Both sets of children could assert their divinity and right to rule. Royal sibling marriage therefore limited conflicts about succession because it reduced the number of people with claims to rule. The same result would be true in ancient Egypt and Peru as in ancient Hawaii. Other kingdoms have solved this problem differently. Some succession rules, for instance, specify that only the oldest child (usually the son) of the reigning monarch can succeed; this custom is called *primogeniture.* Commonly, rulers have banished or killed claimants who rival the chosen heir.

Royal incest also had a latent economic function. If the king and his sister had rights to inherit the ancestral estate, their marriage to each other, again by limiting the number of heirs, kept it intact. Power often rests on wealth, and royal incest tended to ensure that royal wealth remained concentrated in the same line.

A lesbian wedding in Berlin, Germany, on August 2, 2001. A 2001 German law allowed gay couples to wed in civil ceremonies and to receive rights such as inheritance and health insurance.

Marital Rights and Same-Sex Marriage

The British anthropologist Edmund Leach (1955) observed that, depending on the society, several different kinds of rights are allocated by institutions classified as marriage. According to Leach, marriage can, but doesn't always, accomplish the following:

1. Establish the legal father of a woman's children and the legal mother of a man's.

2. Give either or both spouses a monopoly in the sexuality of the other.

3. Give either or both spouses rights to the labor of the other.

4. Give either or both spouses rights over the other's property.

5. Establish a joint fund of property—a partnership—for the benefit of the children.

6. Establish a socially significant "relationship of affinity" between spouses and their relatives.

The discussion of same-sex marriage that follows will serve to illustrate the six rights just listed by seeing what happens in their absence. What if same-sex marriages, which by and large are illegal in the United States, were legal? Could a same-sex marriage establish legal parentage of children born to one or both partners after the partnership is

For more on laws affecting same-sex marriage, see the Internet Exercises at your OLC

/kottak

formed? In the case of a different-sex marriage, children born to the wife after the marriage takes place usually are legally defined as her husband's regardless of whether he is the genitor.

Nowadays, of course, DNA testing makes it possible to establish paternity, just as modern reproductive technology makes it possible for a lesbian couple to have one or both partners artificially inseminated. If same-sex marriages were legal, the social construction of kinship could easily make both partners parents (as in the controversial children's book *Heather's Two Mommies,* which pops into the news from time to time as the target of a book banning). If a Nuer woman married to a woman can be the pater of a child she did not father, why can't two lesbians be the **maters** (socially recognized mothers) of a child one of them did not father? And if a married different-sex couple can adopt a child and have it be theirs through the social and legal construction of kinship, the same logic could be applied to a gay male or lesbian couple.

Continuing with Leach's list of the rights transmitted by marriage, same-sex marriage could certainly give each spouse rights to the sexuality of the other. Unable to marry legally, gay men and lesbians use various devices, such as a mock wedding to declare their commitment and desire for a monogamous sexual relationship. In April 2000, Vermont passed a bill allowing same-sex couples to unite legally, with virtually all the benefits of marriage. Same-sex marriages, as forms of monogamous commitment, have been endorsed by representatives of many religions, including Unitarians and Quakers (the Society of Friends). Among Quakers, such issues are decided by local congregations, which have sanctioned thousands of same-sex marriages. In 1993, the General Assembly of the Union of American Hebrew Congregations (reform Jewish synagogues) passed a resolution advocating legal recognition of same-sex unions (Eskridge 1996). According to Eskridge (1996), a 1990 survey of several thousand gay men and lesbians found that 75 percent of the lesbians and 60 percent of the gay men were living in long-term domestic partnerships.

If they were legal, same-sex marriages could easily give each spouse rights to the other spouse's labor and its products. Some societies do allow marriage between members of the same biological sex. Several Native American groups had figures known as *berdaches*. These were biological men who assumed many of the mannerisms, behavior patterns, and tasks of women. Sometimes *berdaches* married men, who shared the products of their labor from hunting and traditional male roles, as the *berdache* fulfilled the traditional wifely role. Also, in some Native American cultures, a marriage of a "manly-hearted women" to another woman brought the traditional male–female division of labor to their household. The manly woman hunted and did other male tasks, while the wife played the traditional female role.

There's no logical reason why same-sex marriage could not give spouses rights over the other's property. But in the United States, the same inheritance rights that apply to male–female couples do not apply to same-sex couples. For instance, even in the absence of a will, property can pass to a widow or a widower without going through probate. The wife or husband pays no inheritance tax. This benefit is not available to gay men and lesbians. Nor, in most cities, can rights to rent-controlled apartments be passed on to a same-sex heir. They can be to a wife or a husband. Many other legal rights that apply to male–female marriages are missing for same-sex partners. What happens when a same-sex partner is in a nursing home, prison, or hospital? The other partner may not have the same visiting rights as would a husband, wife, or biological relative. With same-sex marriage illegal, couples may even find themselves unable in some places to share accommodations that require roommates or housemates to be related by blood or marriage (Weston 1991).

What about Leach's fifth right—to establish a joint fund of property—to benefit the children? Here again, gay and lesbian couples are at a disadvantage. As mentioned previously, same-sex couples cannot count on the inheritance laws that apply to different-sex couples. If there are children, property is separately, rather than jointly, transmitted. Nor, usually, can gay and lesbian couples and their children benefit from family discounts available to traditional families. Some organizations do make staff benefits, such as health and dental insurance, available to same-sex domestic partners. Typically, this requires some official sworn statement that such a partnership exists.

Finally, there is the matter of establishing a socially significant "relationship of affinity" between spouses and their relatives. In many societies, one of the main roles of marriage is to establish an alliance between groups, in addition to the individual bond. As we saw in the chapter "Families, Kinship, and Descent," affinals are relatives through marriage, such as a brother-in-law or mother-in-law. Only married people have these official relationships. I remember a Brazilian man who had lived with the same woman for more than 20 years. Their "marriage" was an unofficial domestic partnership of a sort that is common in the village of Arembepe, Bahia. Although his wife had given birth to 13 of his children, and although they ran a successful business together, he insisted she was his "woman" rather than his "wife." An official marriage requires a license and a service performed by a justice of the peace. They had chosen to have neither. According to Brazilian inheritance law, children receive at least half of any estate, with the legal spouse getting the other half. Neither my informant nor his wife could inherit from each other. Their children, who were officially registered in the names of both parents, could and would inherit from each. Nor could he or she receive a pension from the other. Finally, neither had affinals. He recognized no brothers- or sisters-in-law, mother-in-law, or father-in-law, nor did she. Such arrangements are typical of Arembepe, where estates are generally meager and there is no social pressure to marry formally (Kottak 1999).

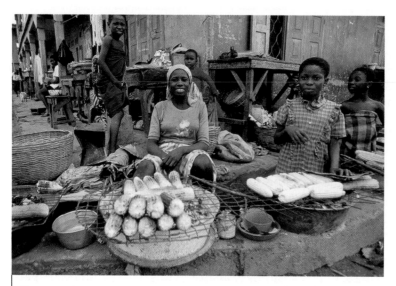

In parts of Nigeria, shown here, prominent market women may take a wife. Such marriage allows wealthy women to strengthen their social status and the economic importance of their households.

For same-sex couples in contemporary North America, affinal relations are problematic. In an unofficial union, terms like "daughter-in-law" and "mother-in-law" may sound strange. Despite the existence of organizations like PFLAG, Parents and Friends of Lesbians and Gays, many parents are suspicious of their children's sexuality and lifestyle choices. As long as same-sex marriage is illegal, parents retain certain rights with respect to their adult children, for example, to make medical decisions that a legal spouse would otherwise make. Consider also the case of a woman who divorces a man for another woman, or whose husband dies, after which she forms a lesbian domestic partnership. There are legal cases in the United States in which custody of her children has been awarded to her former husband's parents, or to her own, rather than to her—because of her lifestyle choice. Ties of "blood" and formal marriage take legal precedence in the United States, as in many countries.

This discussion of same-sex marriage has been intended to illustrate the different kinds of rights that typically accompany marriage, by seeing what may happen when there is a permanent pair bond without legal sanction. In all 50 United States, with the fleeting exception of Hawaii, which flirted with the legalization of same-sex marriage, and Vermont, as mentioned previously,

such unions are illegal. As we have seen, same-sex marriages have been recognized in different historical and cultural settings. In certain African cultures, including the Igbo of Nigeria and the Lovedu of South Africa, women may marry other women. In situations in which women, such as prominent market women in West Africa, are able to amass property and other forms of wealth, they may take a wife. Such marriage allows the prominent woman to strengthen her social status and the economic importance of her household (Amadiume 1987).

One of the most famous examples of same-sex marriage is that of the Azande of Sudan, where male warriors took younger male brides, who served them sexually and by performing domestic duties. The warriors paid "brideprice" (discussed later in this chapter) for their male "brides," which established an affinal relationship with the young man's lineage. When Azande warriors retired from that role, they gave up their male bride and sometimes married the sister of the former male bride. The former male brides, in turn, moved into the warrior grade and took their own younger male brides. The Azande, flexible in their sexuality, had no trouble shifting from homosexual acts to heterosexual acts (see Murray and Roscoe 1998).

Marriage as Group Alliance

For more information about marriage among the Hmong, see the Internet Exercises at your OLC

mhhe ●com /kottak

Outside industrial societies, marriage is often more a relationship between groups than one between individuals. We think of marriage as an individual matter. Although the bride and groom usually seek their parents' approval, the final choice (to live together, to marry, to divorce) lies with the couple. The idea of romantic love symbolizes this individual relationship.

In nonindustrial societies, although there can be romantic love, as we see in "Interesting Issues" (on pages 528–529), marriage is a group concern.

People don't just take a spouse; they assume obligations to a group of in-laws. When residence is patrilocal, for example, a woman often must leave the community where she was born. She faces the prospect of spending the rest of her life in her husband's village, with his relatives. She may even have to transfer her major allegiance from her own group to her husband's.

Understanding Ourselves It's hard to make the transition from the family of orientation to the family of procreation. Unlike people in nonindustrial societies, most of us get a head start by "leaving home" long before we marry. We go off to college or find a job that enables us to support ourselves so that we can live independently, or with roommates. In nonindustrial societies people, especially women, may have to leave home abruptly when they marry. In patrilocal societies a woman must leave her home village and her own kin and move in with her husband and his relatives. This can be an unpleasant and alienating transition. Many women complain about feeling isolated when they first arrive in the husband's village. Later they may be mistreated by their husband or in-laws, including the mother-in-law. However, things will be brighter if women from village or descent group A typically marry men from village or descent group B. If this is the case, a woman can be sure to find some of her own relatives, such as her sister or aunt (father's sister), living as wives in her husband's village, and she will feel more at home.

In contemporary North America, neither women nor men typically have to adjust to in-laws living close at hand. But we do have to learn to live with our spouses. Marriage always raises issues of accommodation and adjustment. Initially the married couple is just that, unless there are children from a previous marriage. If there are, adjustment issues will involve stepparenthood—and a prior spouse—as well as the new marital relationship. Once a couple has its own child, the family-of-procreation mentality takes over. In the United States family loyalty shifts, but not completely, from the family of orientation to the family that includes spouse and child(ren). Given our bilateral kinship system, we maintain relations with our sons and daughters after they marry, and grandchildren theoretically are as close to one set of grandparents as to the other. In a patrilineal society there would be a closer bond with the paternal grandparents. What about in a matrilineal society?

BRIDEWEALTH AND DOWRY

See the Virtual Exploration for bridewealth traditions of the Nenetsi of Siberia

mhhe
●com
/kottak

In societies with descent groups, people enter marriage not alone but with the help of the descent group. Descent-group members often have to contribute to the **bridewealth**, a customary gift before, at, or after the marriage from the husband and his kin to the wife and her kin. Another word for bridewealth is *brideprice*, but this term is inaccurate because people with the custom don't usually regard the exchange as a sale. They don't think of marriage as a commercial relationship between a man and an object that can be bought and sold.

Bridewealth compensates the bride's group for the loss of her companionship and labor. More important, it makes the children born to the woman full members of her husband's descent group. For this reason, the institution is also called **progeny price**. Rather than the woman herself, it is her children, or progeny, who are permanently transferred to the husband's group. Whatever we call it, such a transfer of wealth at marriage is common in patrilineal groups. In matrilineal societies, children are members of the mother's group, and there is no reason to pay a progeny price.

Dowry is a marital exchange in which the wife's group provides substantial gifts to the husband's family. Dowry, best known from India, correlates with low female status. Women are perceived as burdens. When husbands and their families take a wife, they expect to be compensated for the added responsibility.

Although India passed a law in 1961 against compulsory dowry, the practice continues. When the dowry is considered insufficient, the bride may be harassed and abused. Domestic violence can escalate to the point where the husband or his family burn the bride, often by pouring kerosene on her and lighting it, usually killing her. It should be pointed out that dowry doesn't necessarily lead to domestic abuse. In fact, Indian dowry murders seem to be a fairly recent phenomenon. It also has been estimated that the rate of spousal murders in the contemporary United States may rival the incidence of India's dowry murders (Narayan 1997).

Love and marriage, the song says, go together like a horse and carriage. But the link between love and marriage, like the horse–carriage combination, isn't a cultural universal. Described here is a cross-cultural survey, published in the anthropological journal *Ethnology*, which found romantic ardor to be widespread, perhaps universal. Previously anthropologists had tended to ignore evidence for romantic love in other cultures, probably because arranged marriages were so common. Today, diffusion, mainly via the mass media, of Western ideas about the importance of love for marriage appears to be influencing marital decisions in other cultures.

Some influential Western social historians have argued that romance was a product of European medieval culture that spread only recently to other cultures. They dismissed romantic tales from other cultures as representing the behavior of just the elites. Under the sway of this view, Western anthropologists did not even look for romantic love among the peoples they studied. But they are now beginning to think that romantic love is universal . . .

"For decades anthropologists and other scholars have assumed romantic love was unique to the modern West," said Dr. Leonard Plotnicov, an anthropologist at the University of Pittsburgh and editor of the journal *Ethnology*. "Anthropologists came across it in their field work, but they rarely mentioned it because it wasn't supposed to happen."

"Why has something so central to our culture been so ignored by anthropology?" asked Dr. William Jankowiak, an anthropologist at the University of Nevada.

The reason, in the view of Dr. Jankowiak and others, is a scholarly bias throughout the social sciences that viewed romantic love as a luxury in human life, one that could be indulged only by people in Westernized cultures or among the educated elites of other societies. For example it was assumed in societies where life is hard that romantic love has less chance to blossom, because higher economic standards and more leisure time create more opportunity for dalliance. That also contributed to the belief that romance was for the ruling class, not the peasants.

But, said Dr. Jankowiak, "There is romantic love in cultures around the world." Last year Dr. Janko-

wiak, with Dr. Edward Fischer, an anthropologist at Tulane University, published in *Ethnology* the first cross-cultural study, systematically comparing romantic love in many cultures.

In the survey of ethnographies from 166 cultures, they found what they considered clear evidence that romantic love was known in 147 of them—89 percent. And in the other 19 cultures, Dr. Jankowiak said, the absence of conclusive evidence seemed due more to anthropologists' oversight than to a lack of romance.

Some of the evidence came from tales about lovers, or folklore that offered love potions or other advice on making someone fall in love.

Another source was accounts by informants to anthropologists. For example, Nisa, a !Kung woman among the Bushmen of the Kalahari, made a clear distinction between the affection

Sati is the practice through which widows are burned alive, voluntarily or forcibly, on their husband's funeral pyre (Hawley 1993). Although it has become well known, *sati* was mainly practiced in a particular area of northern India by a few small castes. It was banned in 1829, but the practice has recurred. India had to ban *sati* again as recently as 1987 (Kantor 1996). Dowry murders and *sati* are flagrant examples of *patriarchy*, a political system ruled by men in which women have inferior social and political status, including basic human rights.

Bridewealth exists in many more cultures than dowry does, but the nature and quantity of transferred items differ. In many African societies, cattle constitute bridewealth, but the number of cattle given varies from society to society. *As the value of bridewealth increases, marriages become more stable.* Bridewealth is insurance against divorce.

Imagine a patrilineal society in which a marriage requires the transfer of about 25 cattle from the groom's descent group to the bride's. Michael, a member of descent group A, marries Sarah from she felt for her husband, and that she felt for her lovers, which was "passionate and exciting," though fleeting. Of these extramarital affairs, she said: "When two people come together their hearts are on fire and their passion is very great. After a while the fire cools and that's how it stays." . . .

While finding that romantic love appears to be a human universal, Dr. Jankowiak allows that it is still an alien idea in many cultures that such infatuation has anything to do with the choice of a spouse.

"What's new in many cultures is the idea that romantic love should be the reason to marry someone," said Dr. Jankowiak. "Some cultures see being in love as a state to be pitied. One tribe in the mountains of Iran ridicules people who marry for love."

Of course, even in arranged marriages, partners may grow to feel romantic love for each other. For example, among villagers in the Kangra valley of northern India, "people's romantic longings and yearnings ideally would become focused on the person they're matched with by their families," said Dr. Kirin Narayan, an anthropologist at the University of Wisconsin.

But that has begun to change, Dr. Narayan is finding, under the influence of popular songs and movies. "In these villages the elders are worried that the younger men and women are getting a different idea of romantic love, one where you choose a partner yourself," said Dr. Narayan. "There are starting to be elopements, which are absolutely scandalous."

The same trend toward love matches, rather than arranged marriages, is being noted by anthropologists in many other cultures. Among aborigines in Australia's Outback, for example, marriages had for centuries been arranged when children were very young.

That pattern was disrupted earlier in this century by missionaries, who urged that marriage not occur until children reached adolescence. Dr. Victoria Burbank, an anthropologist at the University of California at Davis, said that in pre-missionary days, the average age of a girl at marriage was always before menarche, sometimes as young as 9 years. Today the average age at marriage is 17; girls are more independent by the time their parents try to arrange a marriage for them.

"More and more adolescent girls are breaking away from arranged marriages," said Dr. Burbank. "They prefer to go off into the bush for a 'date' with someone they like, get pregnant, and use that pregnancy to get parental approval for the match."

Even so, parents sometimes are adamant that the young people should not get married. They prefer, instead, that the girls follow the traditional pattern of having their mothers choose a husband for them.

"Traditionally among these people, you can't choose just any son-in-law," said Dr. Burbank. "Ideally, the mother wants to find a boy who is her maternal grandmother's brother's son, a pattern that insures partners are in the proper kin group."

Dr. Burbank added: "These groups have critical ritual functions. A marriage based on romantic love, which ignores what's a proper partner, undermines the system of kinship, ritual, and obligation."

Nevertheless, the rules for marriage are weakening. "In the grandmothers' generation, all marriages were arranged. Romantic love had no place, though there were a few stories of a young man and woman in love running off together. But in the group I studied, in only one recent case did the girl marry the man selected for her. All the rest are love matches." . . .

SOURCE: Daniel Goleman, "Anthropology Goes Looking in All the Old Places," *New York Times*, November 24, 1992, p. B1.

group B. His relatives help him assemble the bridewealth. He gets the most help from his close agnates (patrilineal relatives): his older brother, father, father's brother, and closest patrilineal cousins.

The distribution of the cattle once they reach Sarah's group mirrors the manner in which they were assembled. Sarah's father, or her oldest brother if the father is dead, receives her bridewealth. He keeps most of the cattle to use as bridewealth for his sons' marriages. However, a share also goes to everyone who will be expected to help when Sarah's brothers marry.

When Sarah's brother David gets married, many of the cattle go to a third group: C, which is David's wife's group. Thereafter, they may serve as bridewealth to still other groups. Men constantly use their sisters' bridewealth cattle to acquire their own wives. In a decade, the cattle given when Michael married Sarah will have been exchanged widely.

In such societies, marriage entails an agreement between descent groups. If Sarah and

Gift-giving customs are associated with marriage throughout the world. In this photo, guests bring presents in baskets to a wedding in Wenjiang, China.

Michael try to make their marriage succeed but fail to do so, both groups may conclude that the marriage can't last. Here it becomes especially obvious that such marriages are relationships between groups as well as between individuals. If Sarah has a younger sister or niece (her older brother's daughter, for example), the concerned parties may agree to Sarah's replacement by a kinswoman.

However, incompatibility isn't the main problem that threatens marriage in societies with bridewealth. Infertility is a more important concern. If Sarah has no children, she and her group have not fulfilled their part of the marriage agreement. If the relationship is to endure, Sarah's group must furnish another woman, perhaps her younger sister, who can have children. If this happens, Sarah may choose to stay with her husband. Perhaps she will someday have a child. If she does stay on, her husband will have established a plural marriage.

Most nonindustrial food-producing societies, unlike most foraging societies and industrial nations, allow **plural marriages**, or *polygamy*.

There are two varieties; one is common, and the other is very rare. The more common variant is **polygyny**, in which a man has more than one wife. The rare variant is **polyandry**, in which a woman has more than one husband. If the infertile wife remains married to her husband after he has taken a substitute wife provided by her descent group, this is polygyny. Reasons for polygyny other than infertility will be discussed shortly.

DURABLE ALLIANCES

It is possible to exemplify the group-alliance nature of marriage by examining still another common practice: continuation of marital alliances when one spouse dies.

Sororate What happens if Sarah dies young? Michael's group will ask Sarah's group for a substitute, often her sister. This custom is known as the **sororate** (Figure 19.5). If Sarah has no sister or if all her sisters are already married, another woman from her group may be available. Michael marries her, there is no need to return the

In this photo of an elaborate royal wedding, plates of money are presented at the marriage of an Indian maharajah. How does marriage vary with social status in your society?

Levirate What happens if the husband dies? In many societies, the widow may marry his brother. This custom is known as the **levirate** (Figure 19.5). Like the sororate, it is a continuation marriage that maintains the alliance between descent groups, in this case by replacing the husband with another member of his group. The implications of the levirate vary with age. A recent study found that in African societies, the levirate, though widely permitted, rarely involves cohabitation of the widow and her new husband. Furthermore, widows don't automatically marry the husband's brother just because they are allowed to. Often, they prefer to make other arrangements (Potash 1986).

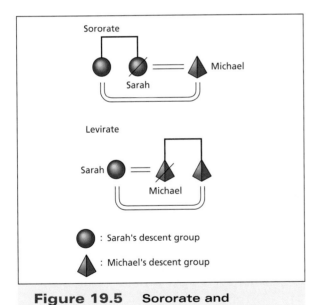

Figure 19.5 **Sororate and Levirate.**

bridewealth, and the alliance continues. The sororate exists in both matrilineal and patrilineal societies. In a matrilineal society with matrilocal postmarital residence, a widower may remain with his wife's group by marrying her sister or another female member of her matrilineage (Figure 19.5).

Divorce

Ease of divorce varies across cultures. What factors work for and against divorce? As we've seen, marriages that are political alliances between groups are more difficult to dissolve than are marriages that are more individual affairs, of concern mainly to the married couple and their children. We've seen that substantial bridewealth may decrease the divorce rate for individuals and that replacement marriages (levirate and sororate) also work to preserve group alliances. Divorce tends to be more common in matrilineal than in patrilineal societies. When residence is matrilocal (in the wife's place), the wife may simply send off a man with whom she's incompatible. Divorce is harder in a patrilineal society, especially when substantial bridewealth would have to be reassembled and repaid if the marriage failed. A woman residing patrilocally (in her husband's household and community) might be reluctant to leave him. Their children, after all, would need to stay with their father, as members of his patrilineage.

Political and economic factors complicate the divorce process. Among foragers, different factors tend to favor and oppose divorce. What factors work against durable marriages? Since foragers tend to lack descent groups, the political alliance functions of marriage are less important to them than they are to food producers. Foragers also tend to have minimal material possessions. The process of dissolving a joint fund of property is less complicated when spouses do not hold substantial resources in common. What factors favor marital stability among foragers? In societies where the family is an important year-round unit with a gender-based division of labor, ties between spouses tend to be durable. Also, sparse populations mean few alternative spouses if a marriage doesn't work out. But in band-organized societies, foragers can always find a band to join or rejoin if a marriage doesn't work. And food producers can always draw on their descent-group estate if a marriage fails. With patriliny, a woman often can return home, albeit without her children, and with matriliny, a man can do the same. Descent-group estates are not transferred through marriages, although movable resources such as bridewealth cattle certainly are.

Understanding Ourselves In our own society, the more substantial the joint property, the more complicated the divorce process. The divorce squabbles of the rich and famous routinely make the news. The increasing prominence of prenuptial agreements in today's North America shows that in our own society some aspects of marriage involve more than romantic love, especially when the financial/material stakes are high. And, of course, we have divorce specialists, lawyers (match breakers), who are absent in nonindustrial societies. In those settings, the specialist, the matchmaker, comes before the marriage, rather than at its end. It's up to the matchmakers who arrange marriages to do as good a job as possible so that the union doesn't end in divorce.

In contemporary Western societies, we do stress the idea that romantic love is necessary for a good marriage (see "Interesting Issues," pages 528–529). When romance fails, so may the marriage. Or it may not fail, if the other rights associated with marriage, as discussed previously in this chapter, are compelling. Economic ties and obligations to kids, along with other factors, such as concern about public opinion, or simple inertia, may keep marriages intact after sex, romance, and/or companionship

fade. Also, even in modern societies, royalty, leaders, and other elites may have political marriages similar to the arranged marriages of nonindustrial societies.

Divorce is more common now than it was a generation ago or a century ago. In the United States, divorce figures have been kept since 1860, with a fairly steady increase since then in the divorce rate. Divorces tend to increase after wars and to decrease when times are bad economically. But with more women working outside the home, economic dependence on the husband as breadwinner is weaker, which no doubt facilitates a decision to divorce when a marriage has major problems.

Table 19.1 is based on two measures of the divorce rate (Hughes 1996). The left column shows the rate per 1,000 people per year in the overall population. The right column shows the annual rate per 1,000 married women over the age of 15, which is the best measure of divorce. In either case, comparing 2000 with 1960, the divorce rate more than doubled. Note that the rate rose slightly after World War II (1950), then declined a decade later (1960). The most notable rate rise occurred between 1960 and 1980. The rate actually has been falling since 1980.

Table 19.1 Changing Divorce Rates (Number per Year) in the United States, 1940 through 2000

Year	Divorce Rate per 1,000 Population	Divorce Rate per 1,000 Women Aged 15 and Older
1940	2.0	8.8
1950	2.6	10.3
1960	2.2	9.2
1970	3.5	14.9
1980	5.2	22.6
1990	4.7	20.9
2000	4.2	19.5

SOURCES: Clarke 1995; Hughes 1996; National Vital Statistics Reports, vol. 46, no. 6, 2001.

The United States has one of the world's highest divorce rates. There are several probable causes: economic, cultural, and religious among them. Economically, the United States has a larger percentage of gainfully employed women than most nations. Work outside the home provides a cash basis for independence, as it also places strains on marriage and social life for both partners. Culturally, Americans tend to value independence and its modern form, self-actualization. Also, Protestantism (in its various guises) is the most common form of religion in the United States. Of the two major religions in the United States and Canada (where Catholicism predominates), Protestantism has been less stringent in denouncing divorce than has Catholicism. Also, notions of salvation in traditional Protestantism focus more on the individual than on the household or family (Weber 1904/1958).

Cherlin (1992) has done a study of changing patterns of American marriage, divorce, and remarriage, using four generations of American women, the first born 1908–1912, the last born in 1970. Although there was little change in the first marriage rate across the generations, the likelihood of divorce changed strikingly. Likelihood for the first generation was 22 percent, versus its double, 44 percent, for women born in 1970. The chance of remarriage and redivorce also increased across the generations. The likelihood of a second divorce was 2 percent for the oldest generation, versus 16 percent for women born in 1970. The changing rate of divorce has obvious implications for family life and child care, some of which were discussed in the last chapter.

Plural Marriages

In contemporary North America, where divorce is fairly easy and common, polygamy (marriage to more than one spouse at the same time) is against the law. Marriage in industrial nations joins individuals, and relationships between individuals can be severed more easily than can those between groups. As divorce grows more common, North Americans practice *serial monogamy*: Individuals have more than one spouse but never, legally, more than one at the same time. As stated earlier, the two forms of polygamy are polygyny and polyandry. Polyandry is practiced in only a few cultures, notably among certain groups in Tibet, Nepal, and India. Polygyny is much more common.

POLYGYNY

We must distinguish between the social approval of plural marriage and its actual frequency in a particular society. Many cultures approve of a man having more than one wife. However, even when polygyny is encouraged, most men are monogamous, and polygyny characterizes only a fraction of the marriages. Why is this true?

One reason is equal sex ratios. In the United States, about 105 males are born for every 100 females. In adulthood, the ratio of men to women equalizes, and eventually it reverses. The average North American woman outlives the average man. In many nonindustrial societies as well, the male-biased sex ratio among children reverses in adulthood.

The custom of men marrying later than women promotes polygyny. Among the Kanuri people of Bornu, Nigeria (Figure 19.6), men get

In Cameroon, a man (front left) with five of his six wives and 20 of his 36 children. Why do people marry polygynously?

married between the ages of 18 and 30; women, between 12 and 14 (Cohen 1967). The age difference between spouses means that there are more widows than widowers. Most of the widows remarry, some in polygynous unions. Among the Kanuri of Bornu and in other polygynous societies, widows make up a large number of the women involved in plural marriages (Hart, Pilling, and Goodale 1988). In many societies, including the Kanuri, the number of wives is an indicator of a man's household productivity, prestige, and social position. The more wives, the more workers. Increased productivity means more wealth. This wealth in turn attracts additional wives to the household. Wealth and wives bring greater prestige to the household and head.

If a plural marriage is to work, there needs to be some agreement among the existing spouses when another one is to be added, especially if they are to share the same household. In certain societies, the first wife requests a second wife to help

with household chores. The second wife's status is lower than that of the first; they are senior and junior wives. The senior wife sometimes chooses the junior one from among her close kinswomen. Among the Betsileo of Madagascar, the different wives always lived in different villages. A man's first and senior wife, called "Big Wife," lived in the village where he cultivated his best rice field and spent most of his time. High-status men with several rice fields and multiple wives had households near each field. They spent most of their time with the senior wife but visited the others throughout the year.

Plural wives can play important political roles in nonindustrial states. The king of the Merina, a society with more than one million people in the highlands of Madagascar, had palaces for each of his 12 wives in different provinces. He stayed with

Figure 19.6 Location of Bornu, home of the Kanuri, in Nigeria.

On August 25, 2001 Utah polygamist Tom Green was sentenced to five years in prison on felony bigamy charges, while his five wives and some of his 30 children wept in the courtroom. Shown here, Green holds his daughter's hand as his family follows him out of the courthouse.

them when he traveled through the kingdom. They were his local agents, overseeing and reporting on provincial matters. The king of Buganda, the major precolonial state of Uganda, took hundreds of wives, representing all the clans in his nation. Everyone in the kingdom became the king's in-law, and all the clans had a chance to provide the next ruler. This was a way of giving the common people a stake in the government.

These examples show that there is no single explanation for polygyny. Its context and function vary from society to society and even within the same society. Some men are polygynous because they have inherited a widow from a brother (the levirate). Others have plural wives because they seek prestige or want to increase household productivity. Still others use marriage as a political tool or a means of economic advancement. Men and women with political and economic ambitions cultivate marital alliances that serve their aims. In many societies, including the Betsileo of Madagascar and the Igbo of Nigeria, women arrange the marriages.

POLYANDRY

Polyandry is rare and is practiced under very specific conditions. Most of the world's polyandrous peoples live in South Asia: Tibet, Nepal, India, and

Sri Lanka. India's polyandrous groups inhabit the lower ranges of the Himalayas, in northern India. They are known as Paharis, which means "people of the mountains." Gerald Berreman (1962, 1975) did a comparative study of two Pahari groups, one in the foothills of the western Himalayas and the other in the central foothills (Figure 19.7).

Interpret the World In your
Atlas Map 19 atlas,
Map 19, "Systems of Marriage Relationships," shows the distribution of plural, arranged, and cousin marriages. Notice that polyandry has a much more limited distribution than polygyny does. Understand, too, that, increasingly, modern nations are restricting the legality of plural marriages. This means that some of the information shown on Map 19 reflects what has been allowed rather than what is valued or common today. As we have seen, nation-states limit their citizens' choices about marriage and domestic partnerships. Cousin marriage is legal in some countries (and states in the United States), but not in others. Can you locate three countries in which arranged marriage is the norm?

The western and central Paharis are historically and genetically related to each other and speak dialects of the same language. Polyandry exists among the western, but not the central, Paharis. Because there are so many other cultural and social similarities between the western and central Paharis, including caste stratification and patrilineal clans, Berreman wondered why one group practiced polyandry and the other did not.

Pahari marriage customs turned out to correlate with demographic contrasts. Sex ratios were different in the two areas. In the polyandrous west, there was a shortage of females (789 per 1,000 males). Although female infanticide was not documented in the area, neglect of girls (*covert* female infanticide) helped explain the shortage of women (Levine 1988). In some parts of the Himalayas, the practice of sending girls to Buddhist nunneries also contributes to a shortage of marriageable

Figure 19.7   Location of the Paharis.

women. Among the western Paharis, the polyandry was always *fraternal*: Husbands were brothers. The oldest brother arranged the marriage, which made all the brothers legal husbands of the wife. Subsequently, they could marry additional women. All these women were joint wives and sexual partners of the brothers. Children born to any wife called all the brothers "father."

Nevertheless, there was considerable variation in the actual marriage arrangements in western Pahari households (Berreman 1975). In one village, only 9 percent of the households were polyandrous, 25 percent were polygynous, and 34 percent were monogamous. The others had mixed marriage types, such as polyandrous-polygynous (see below). Variation in the marriage type and household composition reflected household wealth, the age of the brothers, and divorce. Household composition went through a developmental cycle. For example, one group of three brothers took their first wife in 1910. In 1915, they added a second wife. This changed simple fraternal polyandry into a polyandrous-polygynous household. A few years later, they added a third wife, and later they added a fourth. By a decade later, one of the brothers had died and two of the wives had divorced and remarried elsewhere. By 1955, the household had become monogamous, as only one husband and one wife survived.

Polyandry in northwest Nepal. The seated young woman is Terribal, age 15. She holds her youngest husband, age five. Left of Terribal is another husband, age 12. Standing directly behind her is her third husband, age nine. The two older standing men are brothers who are married to the same woman, standing to the right. These are Terribal's "fathers" and mother.

This flexible marriage system was adaptive because it allowed the western Paharis to spread people and labor out over the land. The number of working adults in a western Pahari household was proportional to the amount of farmland it owned. Because women did as much agricultural work as men, given the same amount of land, two brothers might require and support three or four wives whereas three or four brothers might have only one or two. Plural marriages were uncommon in landless households, whose resources and labor needs were lowest. Landless people were more monogamous (43 percent) than were landowners (26 percent).

Among the nonpolyandrous central Paharis, by contrast, there were more women than men. Most (85 percent) marriages were monogamous. Only 15 percent were plural—polygynous. Despite the absence of a formal polyandry here, it was customary for brothers to contribute to each other's bridewealth, and they could have sex with each other's wives. The major difference was that central Pahari children recognized only one father. However, because brothers had common sexual rights, socially recognized fathers were not necessarily the true genitors.

Polyandry in other parts of South Asia seems to be a cultural adaptation to mobility associated with customary male travel for trade, commerce, and military operations. Polyandry ensures that there will be at least one man at home to accomplish male activities within a gender-based division of labor. Fraternal polyandry is also an effective strategy when resources are scarce. Brothers with limited resources (in land) pool their resources in expanded (polyandrous) households. They take just one wife. Polyandry restricts the number of wives and heirs. Less competition among heirs means that land can be transmitted with minimal fragmentation.

SUMMARY

1. Marriage, which is usually a form of domestic partnership, is hard to define. All societies have some kind of incest taboo. The following are some of the explanations that have been offered for this universal taboo: (1) It codifies instinctive horror of incest, (2) it expresses concern about the biological effects of incestuous unions, (3) it reflects feelings of attraction or aversion that develop as one grows up in a household, and (4) it has an adaptive advantage because it promotes exogamy, thereby increasing networks of friends and allies.

2. Exogamy extends social and political ties outward. This is confirmed by a consideration of endogamy—marriage within the group. Endogamic rules are common in stratified societies. One extreme example is India, where castes are the endogamous units. Castes are subdivided into exogamous descent groups. The same culture can therefore have both endogamic and exogamic rules. Certain ancient kingdoms encouraged royal incest while condemning incest by commoners.

3. The discussion of same-sex marriage, which, by and large, is illegal in contemporary North America, illustrates the various rights that go along with different-sex marriages. Marriage establishes the legal parents of children. It gives spouses rights to the sexuality, labor, and property of the other. And it establishes a socially significant "relationship of affinity" between spouses and each other's relatives. Some of these rights may be established by same-sex domestic partnerships.

4. In societies with descent groups, marriages are relationships between groups as well as between spouses. With the custom of bridewealth, the groom and his relatives transfer wealth to the bride and her relatives. As the bridewealth's value increases, the divorce rate declines. Bridewealth customs show that marriages among nonindustrial food producers create and maintain group alliances. So do the sororate, by which a man marries the sister of his deceased wife, and the levirate, by which a woman marries the brother of her deceased husband.

5. The ease and frequency of divorce vary across cultures. Political, economic, social, cultural, and religious factors affect the divorce rate. When marriage is a matter of intergroup alliance, as is typically true in societies with descent groups, divorce is less common. A large fund of joint property also complicates divorce.

6. Many societies permit plural marriages. The two kinds of polygamy are polygyny and polyandry. The former involves multiple wives; the latter, multiple husbands. Polygyny is much more common than is polyandry.

KEY TERMS

See the flash cards

mhhe
●com
/kottak

bridewealth   See progeny price.

cross cousins   Children of a brother and a sister.

dowry   A marital exchange in which the wife's group provides substantial gifts to the husband's family.

endogamy   Rule or practice of marriage between people of the same social group.

exogamy   Rule requiring people to marry outside their own group.

genitor   Biological father of a child.

incest   Forbidden sexual relations with a close relative.

levirate   Custom by which a widow marries the brother of her deceased husband.

mater   Socially recognized mother of a child.

parallel cousins   Children of two brothers or two sisters.

pater   Socially recognized father of a child; not necessarily the genitor.

plural marriage   Any marriage with more than two spouses, a.k.a. polygamy.

polyandry   Variety of plural marriage in which a woman has more than one husband.

polygyny   Variety of plural marriage in which a man has more than one wife.

progeny price   A gift from the husband and his kin to the wife and her kin before, at, or after marriage; legitimizes children born to the woman as members of the husband's descent group.

sororate   Custom by which a widower marries the sister of the deceased wife.

CRITICAL THINKING QUESTIONS

For more self testing, see the self quizzes

1. Try to come up with a definition of marriage that fits all the cases examined in this chapter. What problems do you encounter in doing this?

2. What explanations have been offered for the universality of the incest taboo? Which do you prefer, and why? What, if any, are the problems with the explanation you prefer?

3. When advocates argue for same-sex marriage, are they asking for special rights?

4. What are your views about traditional marriage in India after reading this chapter? Is that an ethnocentric opinion? Review the discussions of ethnocentrism and human rights in the chapter "Culture."

5. What is bridewealth? What else is it called, and why? Do we have anything like it in our own society? Why or why not?

6. What is the difference between sororate and levirate? What do they have in common? Do these customs make sense to you?

7. How would you explain the high rate of divorce in contemporary North America?

8. If you had to live in a society with plural marriage, would you prefer polygyny or polyandry? Why?

9. What general conclusions do you draw about the differences between marriage in your society and marriage in nonindustrial societies?

Atlas Questions

Look at Map 19, "Systems of Marriage Relationships."

1. Which is the most widespread—cousin marriage, arranged marriage, or polygyny? Name three countries in which each is practiced.

2. Is there one continent on which arranged marriages are most typical? Do you know personally of anyone in an arranged marriage? If so, does that tell you something about their cultural background?

3. How would you describe marital relationships in Asia? Is there more diversity there in terms of arranged, plural, and cousin marriages than there in South America? If so, how might one explain this contrast?

SUGGESTED ADDITIONAL READINGS

Chagnon, N.
1997   *Yanomamö*, 5th ed. Fort Worth: Harcourt Brace. Latest edition of well-known case study of marital alliances and politics in a nonindustrial society—now in the context of genocide and habitat destruction.

Collier, J. F., ed.
1988   *Marriage and Inequality in Classless Societies.* Stanford, CA: Stanford University Press. Marriage and issues of gender stratification in bands and tribes.

Fox, R.

1985   *Kinship and Marriage*. New York: Viking Penguin. Well-written survey of kinship and marriage systems and theories about them.

Goody, J., and S. T. Tambiah

1973   *Bridewealth and Dowry*. Cambridge, England: Cambridge University Press. Marital exchanges in comparative perspective.

Hart, C. W. M., A. R. Pilling, and J. C. Goodale

1988   *The Tiwi of North Australia*, 3rd ed. Fort Worth: Harcourt Brace. Latest edition of classic case study of Tiwi marriage arrangements, including polygyny, and social change over 60 years of anthropological study.

Hawley, J. S., ed.

1993   *Sati, the Blessing and the Curse: The Burning of Wives in India*. New York: Oxford University Press. A collection of essays on sati and a celebrated case from India.

Ingraham, C.

1999   *White Weddings: Romancing Heterosexuality in Popular Culture*. New York: Routledge. Love and marriage, including the ceremony, in today's United States.

Levine, N. E.

1988   *The Dynamics of Polyandry: Kinship, Domesticity, and Population in the Tibetan Border*. Chicago: University of Chicago Press. Case study of fraternal polyandry and household organization in northwestern Nepal.

Malinowski, B.

1985   (orig. 1927) *Sex and Repression in Savage Society*. Chicago: University of Chicago Press. Classic study of sex, marriage, and kinship among the matrilineal Trobrianders.

Murray, S. O., and W. Roscoe, eds.

1998   *Boy-Wives and Female Husbands: Studies in African Homosexualities*. New York: St. Martin's. Same-sex sex and marriage in Africa.

Radcliffe-Brown, A. R., and D. Forde, eds.

1994   *African Systems of Kinship and Marriage*. New York: Columbia University Press. Reissue of a classic work, indispensable to understand kinship, descent, and marriage.

Shepher, J.

1983   *Incest, a Biosocial View*. New York: Academic Press. A view from Israel, based on a case study in the kibbutz.

Shostak, M.

1981   *Nisa, the Life and Words of a !Kung Woman*. New York: Vintage Books. An insider's account of social life, including marriage, love, and sex, from a Ju/'hoansi San woman.

2000   *Return to Nisa*. Cambridge, MA: Harvard University Press. A revisit to the !Kung woman immortalized in Shostak's earlier book, *Nisa*.

Simpson, B.

1998   *Changing Families: An Ethnographic Approach to Divorce and Separation*. New York: Berg. Current marriage and divorce trends in Great Britain.

INTERNET EXERCISES

1. Weddings: Here are some websites that sell wedding supplies for couples from different nationalities and traditions. Pick three of these websites and answer the questions below: Indian, **www.weddingsutra.com/**; Jewish, **http://www.mazornet.com/jewishcl/jewishwd.htm**; African-American, **http://melanet.com/awg/**; Mormon, **http://www.ldsweddings.com/**; Eastern Orthodox, **http://www.askginka.com/religions/eastern_orthodox.htm**.

   a. What kind of clothes are worn by the bride and the groom? To what degree are the clothes dictated by tradition or modern style? How much choice do the wedding planners have in the clothing that is worn?

   b. What kind of locations are popular for the weddings?

   c. What aspects of each of these weddings is most different from your own? What aspects are similar?

   d. Why do you think wedding traditions vary so much by culture and religion?

2. *Descent and Postmarital Residence Rules*: Go to the Ethnographic Atlas Cross-tabulations page, **http://lucy.ukc.ac.uk/cgi-bin/uncgi/Ethnoatlas/atlas.vopts**. This site has compiled ethnographic information on many different groups, and you can use the tools provided to cross-tabulate the prevalence of certain traits. Go to the site; under "Select Row Category" choose "descent," and under "Select Column Category" select "transfer of residence at marriage: prevalent form." Press the Submit Query button. The table that appears shows the frequency of postmarital residence rules for groups with different descent systems.

   a. What postmarital residence rules are most common for patrilineal groups? For matrilineal groups? Is this what you would expect?

   b. Based on your observations in section a, what postmarital residence practice would you least expect to find in patrilineal societies? How many groups in this chart practice such a pattern? Click on the number at that location to find out which groups those are and where they are located. What postmarital residence pattern would you least expect to find in matrilineal societies? Which groups practice that pattern?

   c. What is the most common form of descent for groups with an "Optional for couple" (ambilocal) postmarital residence pattern? Does this make sense?

See Chapter 19 at your McGraw-Hill Online Learning Center for additional review and interactive exercises.

20

GENDER

Overview

Gender refers to the cultural construction of sexual difference. Male and female are biological sexes that differ in their X and Y chromosomes. Although there are cross-cultural generalities in the gender-based division of labor, culture takes biological differences and associates them with certain activities, behavior, and ideas. Some cultures recognize more than two genders.

Gender roles are the activities a culture assigns to each sex. Gender stratification describes an unequal distribution of rights and resources between men and women. Although, cross-culturally, women and men expend about the same amount of time and effort on subsistence activities, women do most of the domestic work. Sometimes a distinction between women's domestic work and men's extradomestic "productive" labor can reinforce a contrast between men as public and valuable and women as domestic and less valuable. Gender stratification varies with the economy, political system, rule of descent, and postmarital residence pattern. Matrilineal and bilateral societies tend to have less gender stratifica-

tion than patrilineal-patrilocal societies do.

Anthropological evidence casts some doubt on the idea that sexual orientation is fixed. To some extent at least, erotic expression is learned and malleable. Despite individual variation in sexual orientation within a society, culture always plays a role in molding individual sexual urges toward a collective norm. Sexual norms vary widely from culture to culture.

Patriarchy describes a political system in which women have inferior social and political status, including basic human rights. Although anthropologists know of no society in which women as a group dominate men as a group, women in many societies wield power and serve as leaders.

Economic forces have contributed to recent changes in gender roles and stratification. In North America, female cash labor has increased, promoting greater economic and social autonomy for many women. But also increasing, globally, is the feminization of poverty, the rise in the percentages of female-headed households and of poor families headed by women.

543

Indonesia's Matriarchal Minangkabau Offer an Alternative Social System

EUREKALERT NEWS BRIEF

by Pam Kosty

May 9, 2002

If a patriarchy is a political system ruled by men, what would a matriarchy be? Would a matriarchy be a political system ruled by women, or a political system in which women play a much more prominent role than men do in social and political organization? As you read this account, pay attention to the centrality of Minangkabau women in social, economic, and ceremonial life and as key symbols. Matriliny or matrilineality (reckoning of kinship through females only) is uncommon as an organizing principle in nation-states, such as Indonesia, where the Minangkabau live. But political systems operate at different levels. We see here that matriliny and matriarchy are expressed locally, at the village level, and regionally, where seniority of matrilineal descent serves as a way to rank villages. This news account also illustrates the idea that contemporary non-Western societies should not be seen as isolated and pristine social and political systems, but as blends in which different religious, philosophical, and political principles may coexist.

> For the last century, . . . scholars have searched both human history and the continents to find a matriarchy—a society where the power was in the hands of women, not men. Most have concluded that a genuine matriarchy does not exist, perhaps may never have existed.
>
> Anthropologist Peggy Reeves Sanday, Consulting Curator, University of Pennsylvania Museum of Archaeology and Anthropology, disagrees. After years of research among the Minangkabau people of West Sumatra, Indonesia, she has accepted that group's own self-labeling, as a "matriarchate," or matriarchy. The problem, she asserts, lies in Western cultural notions of what a matriarchy "should" look like—patriarchy's female-twin.
>
> "Too many anthropologists have been looking for a society where women rule the affairs of everyday life, including government," she said. "That template—and a singular, Western perspective on power—doesn't fit very well when you're looking at non-Western cultures like the Minangkabau of West Sumatra, Indonesia, where males and females are

partners for the common good rather than competitors ruled by self-interest. Social prestige accrues to those who promote good relations by following the dictates of custom and religion."

The four million Minangkabau, one of Indonesia's largest ethnic groups, live in the highlands of the province of West Sumatra. Their society is founded on the coexistence of matrilineal custom and a nature-based philosophy called adat. More recently, Islam has been incorporated into the foundation. . . .

The key to Minangkabau matriarchy, according to Sanday, is found in the ever-present adat idea [that] "One must nurture growth in humans, animals, and plants so that society will be strong." . . .

The emphasis on nurturing growth yields a unique emphasis on the maternal in daily life. The Minangkabau glorify their mythical Queen Mother and cooperation. In village social relations senior

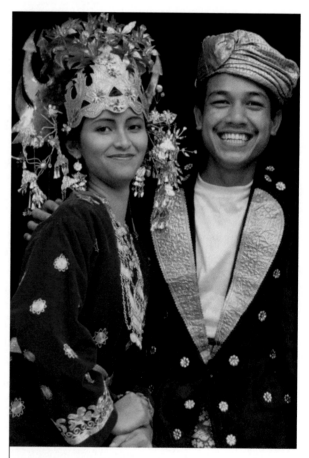

A Minangkabau bride and groom in West Sumatra, Indonesia, where anthropologist Peggy Reeves Sanday has conducted several years of ethnographic field work.

women are associated with the central pillar of the traditional house, which is the oldest pillar because it is the first erected. The oldest village in a group of villages is referred to as the "mother village." When they stage ceremonies in their full ceremonial regalia, women are addressed by the same term reserved for the mythical Queen. Such practices suggest that matriarchy in this society is about making the maternal the center, origin, and foundation, not just of life but of the social order as well.

The power of Minangkabau women extends to the economic and social realms. Women control land inheritance, and husbands move into the households of their wives. . . . During the wedding ceremony the wife collects her husband from his household and, with her female relatives, brings him back to her household to live. In the event of a divorce the husband collects his clothes and leaves. Yet, despite the special position women are accorded in the society, the Minangkabau matriarchy is not the equivalent of female rule.

"Neither male nor female rule is possible because of the Minangkabau belief that decision-making should be by consensus," Dr. Sanday said. "In answer to my persistent questions about 'who rules,' I was often told that I was asking the wrong question. Neither sex rules, it was explained to me, because males and females complement one another."

Today, according to Dr. Sanday, while the Minangkabau matriarchy is based largely on adat, Islam also plays a role. Islam arrived in West Sumatra sometime in the 16th century, long after adat customs and philosophy had been established. At first there was an uneasy relationship between adat and Islam and, in the 19th century, a war between adherents of adat customs and fundamentalist beliefs imported from Mecca. The conflict was resolved by both sides making accommodations. Today, matrilineal adat and Islam are accepted as equally sacred and inviolate.

Resurgent Islamic fundamentalism, nationalism, and expanding capitalism may erode the Minangkabau's nature-based matriarchal culture and the adat that infuses meaning into their lives. [Sanday] remains optimistic that their culture has the innate flexibility to adapt to a changing world. "Had the Minangkabau chosen to fight rather than to accommodate the numerous influences that impinged on their world over the centuries, had they chosen to assert cultural purity, no doubt their 'adat' would have long ago succumbed. The moral of the Minangkabau story is that accommodating differences can preserve a world."

Source: http://www.eurekalert.org/pub_releases/2002-05/uop-imm050902.php.

Peggy Sanday (2002) thus argues that *matriarchies* exist, but not as mirror images of *patriarchies*, political systems ruled by men. The superior power that men typically have in a patriarchy isn't matched by women's equally disproportionate power in a matriarchy. Many societies, like the Minangkabau, lack the substantial power differentials that typify nation-states. Cross-culturally there is tremendous variation in the roles of men and women, and the power differentials between them. How do we explain this variation?

Because anthropologists study biology, society, and culture, they are in a unique position to comment on nature (biological predispositions) and nurture (environment) as determinants of human behavior. Human attitudes, values, and behavior are limited not only by our genetic predispositions—which are often difficult to identify—but also by our experiences during enculturation. Our attributes as adults are determined both by our genes and by our environment during growth and development.

Questions about nature and nurture emerge in the discussion of human sex-gender roles and sexuality. Men and women differ genetically. Women have two X chromosomes, and men have an X and a Y. The father determines a baby's sex because only he has the Y chromosome to transmit. The mother always provides an X chromosome.

The chromosomal difference is expressed in hormonal and physiological contrasts. Humans are sexually dimorphic, more so than some primates, such as gibbons (small tree-living Asiatic apes) and less so than others, such as gorillas and orangutans. **Sexual dimorphism** refers to differences in male and female biology besides the contrasts in breasts and genitals. Women and men differ not just in primary (genitalia and reproductive organs) and secondary (breasts, voice, hair distribution) sexual characteristics but in average weight, height, strength, and longevity. Women tend to live longer than men and have excellent endurance capabilities. In a given population, men tend to be taller and to weigh more than women do. Of course, there is a considerable overlap between the sexes in terms of height, weight, and physical strength, and there has been a pronounced reduction in sexual dimorphism during human biological evolution.

Just how far, however, do such genetically and physiologically determined differences go? What effects do they have on the way men and women act and are treated in different societies? Anthropologists have discovered both similarities and differences in the roles of men and women in different cultures. The predominant anthropological position on sex-gender roles and biology may be stated as follows:

> The biological nature of men and women [should be seen] not as a narrow enclosure limiting the human organism, but rather as a broad base upon which a variety of structures can be built. (Friedl 1975, p. 6)

Although in most societies men tend to be somewhat more aggressive than women are, many of the behavioral and attitudinal differences between the sexes emerge from culture rather than

biology. Sex differences are biological, but gender encompasses all the traits that a culture assigns to and inculcates in males and females. "Gender," in other words, refers to the cultural construction of male and female characteristics (Rosaldo 1980*b*).

Given the "rich and various constructions of gender" within the realm of cultural diversity, Susan Bourque and Kay Warren (1987) note that the same images of masculinity and femininity do not always apply. Margaret Mead did an early ethnographic study of variation in gender roles. Her book *Sex and Temperament in Three Primitive Societies* (1935/1950) was based on field work in three societies in Papua New Guinea: the Arapesh, Mundugumor, and Tchambuli. The extent of personality variation in men and women in those three societies on the same island amazed Mead. She found that Arapesh men and women both acted as Americans have traditionally expected women to act: in a mild, parental, responsive way. Mundugumor men and women both, in contrast, acted as she believed we expect men to act: fiercely

For information on multiple genders among Native Americans, see the Internet Exercises at your OLC

mhhe
com
/kottak

The realm of cultural diversity contains richly different social constructions and expressions of gender roles, as is illustrated by these Bororo male dancers. For what reasons do men decorate their bodies in our society?

and aggressively. Tchambuli men were "catty," wore curls, and went shopping, but Tchambuli women were energetic and managerial and placed less emphasis on personal adornment than did the men. [Drawing on their recent case study of the Tchambuli, whom they call the Chambri, Errington and Gewertz (1987), while recognizing gender malleability, have disputed the specifics of Mead's account.]

There is a well-established field of feminist scholarship within anthropology (di Leonardo 1991; Nash and Safa 1986; Rosaldo 1980b; Strathern 1988). Anthropologists have gathered systematic ethnographic data about similarities and differences involving gender in many cultural settings (Bonvillain 2001; Gilmore 2001; Morgen 1989; Mukhopadhyay and Higgins 1988; Peplau 1999; Ward 2003). Anthropologists can detect recurrent themes and patterns involving gender differences. They also can observe that gender roles vary with environment, economy, adaptive strategy, and type of political system. Before we examine the cross-cultural data, some definitions are in order.

Figure 20.1 Location of Ilongots in the Philippines.

Gender roles are the tasks and activities a culture assigns to the sexes. Related to gender roles are **gender stereotypes**, which are oversimplified but strongly held ideas about the characteristics of males and females. **Gender stratification** describes an unequal distribution of rewards (socially valued resources, power, prestige, human rights, and personal freedom) between men and women, reflecting their different positions in a social hierarchy. According to Ann Stoler (1977), the "economic determinants of female status" include freedom or autonomy (in disposing of one's labor and its fruits) and social power (control over the lives, labor, and produce of others).

In stateless societies, gender stratification is often more obvious in regard to prestige than it is in regard to wealth. In her study of the Ilongots of northern Luzon in the Philippines (Figure 20.1),

Michelle Rosaldo (1980a) *described gender differences related to the positive cultural v*alue placed on adventure, travel, and knowledge of the external world. More often than women, Ilongot men, as headhunters, visited distant places. They acquired knowledge of the external world, amassed experiences there, and returned to express their knowledge, adventures, and feelings in public oratory. They received acclaim as a result. Ilongot women had inferior prestige because they lacked external experiences on which to base knowledge and dramatic expression. On the basis of Rosaldo's study and findings in other stateless societies, Ong (1989) argues that we must distinguish between prestige systems and actual power in a given society. High male prestige may not entail economic or political power held by men over their families.

Recurrent Gender Patterns

Remember from previous chapters that ethnologists compare ethnographic data from several cultures (i.e., cross-cultural data) to discover and explain differences and similarities. Data relevant to the cross-cultural study of gender can be drawn from the domains of economics, politics, domestic activity, kinship, and marriage. Table 20.1 shows cross-cultural data from 185 randomly-selected societies on the division of labor by gender.

Table 20.1 Generalities in the Division of Labor by Gender, Based on Data from 185 Societies

Generally Male Activities	Swing (Male or Female) Activities	Generally Female Activities
Hunting of large aquatic animals (e.g., whales, walrus)	Making fire	Gathering fuel (e.g., firewood)
Smelting of ores	Body mutilation	Making drinks
Metalworking	Preparing skins	Gathering wild vegetal foods
Lumbering	Gathering small land animals	Dairy production (e.g., churning)
Hunting large land animals	Planting crops	Spinning
Working wood	Making leather products	Doing the laundry
Hunting fowl	Harvesting	Fetching water
Making musical instruments	Tending crops	Cooking
Trapping	Milking	Preparing vegetal food (e.g., processing cereal grains)
Building boats	Making baskets	
Working stone	Carrying burdens	
Working bone, horn, and shell	Making mats	
Mining and quarrying	Caring for small animals	
Setting bones	Preserving meat and fish	
Butchering*	Loom weaving	
Collecting wild honey	Gathering small aquatic animals	
Clearing land	Clothing manufacture	
Fishing	Making pottery	
Tending large herd animals		
Building houses		
Preparing the soil		
Making nets		
Making rope		

*All the activities above "butchering" are almost always done by men; those from "butchering" through "making rope" usually are done by men.
Source: Murdock and Provost 1973.

Remembering the discussion, in the chapter "Culture," of universals, generalities, and particularities, the findings in Table 20.1 about the division of labor by gender illustrate generalities rather than universals. That is, among the societies known to ethnography, there is a very strong tendency for men to build boats, but there are exceptions. One was the Hidatsa, a Native American group in which the women made the boats used to cross the Missouri River. (Traditionally, the Hidatsa were village farmers and bison hunters on the North American Plains; they now live in North Dakota). Another exception: Pawnee women worked wood; this is the only Native American group that assigned this activity to women. (The Pawnee, also traditionally Plains farmers and bison hunters, originally lived in what is now central Nebraska and central Kansas; they now live on a reservation in north central Oklahoma.) Among the Mbuti "pygmies" of Africa's Ituri forest, women hunt by catching small, slow animals, using their hands or a net (Murdock and Provost 1973).

Exceptions to cross-cultural generalizations may involve societies or individuals. That is, a society like the Hidatsa can contradict the cross-cultural generalization that men build boats by assigning that task to women. Or, in a society where the cultural expectation is that only men build boats, a particular woman or women can contradict that expectation by doing the male activity. Table 20.1 shows that in a sample of 185 societies, certain activities ("swing actvities") are assigned to either or both men and women. Among the most important of such activities are planting, tending, and harvesting crops. We'll see below that some societies customarily assign more farming chores to women, whereas others call on men to be the main farm laborers. Among the tasks almost always assigned to men (Table 20.1), some (e.g., hunting large animals on land and sea) seem clearly related to the greater average size and strength of males. Others, such as working wood and making musical instruments, seem more culturally arbitrary. And women, of course, are not exempt from arduous and time-consuming physical labor, such as gathering firewood and fetching water. In Arembepe, Bahia, Brazil, women routinely transport water in five-gallon tins, balanced on their heads, from wells and lagoons located at long distances from their homes.

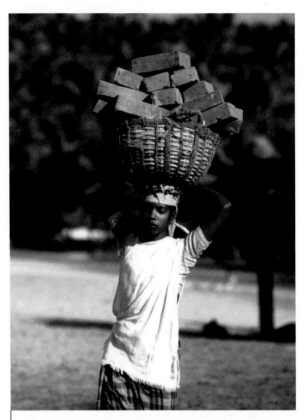

In some societies women routinely do hard physical labor, as is illustrated by this female construction worker in India. Anthropologists have described both commonalities and differences in gender roles and activities among the world's societies.

Understanding Ourselves What's missing from Table 20.1? Notice that there's no mention of trade and market activity, in which either or both men and women are active. Is Table 20.1 somewhat ethnocentric in detailing more tasks for men than for women? More than men, women do child care, but the study on which Table 20.1 is based (Murdock and Provost 1973) does not break down domestic activities to the same extent that it details extradomestic activities.

Both women and men have to fit their activities into 24-hour days. Based on cross-cultural data, Table 20.2 shows that the time and effort spent in subsistence activities by men and women tend to be about equal. If anything, men do slightly less subsistence work than women do. Think about how female domestic activities could have been specified in greater detail in Table 20.1. The original coding of the data in Table 20.1 probably illustrates a male bias in that extradomestic activities received much more prominence than domestic activities did. For example, is collecting wild honey (listed in Table 20.1) more necessary and/or time-consuming than cleaning a baby's bottom (absent from Table 20.1)? Think about the tasks listed in Table 20.1 in terms of today's home and job roles and with respect to the activities done by contemporary women and men. Men still do most of the hunting; either gender can collect the honey from a supermarket, even as most baby bottom wiping continues to be in female hands.

Cross-culturally the subsistence contributions of men and women are roughly equal (Table 20.2). But in domestic activities and child care, female labor predominates, as we see in Tables 20.3 and 20.4. Table 20.3 shows that in about half the societies studied, men did virtually no domestic work. Even in societies where men did some domestic chores, the bulk of such work was done by women. Adding together their subsistence activities and their domestic work, women tend to work more hours than men do. Has this changed in the contemporary world?

What about child care? Women tend to be the main caregivers in most societies, but men often play a role. Again there are exceptions, both within and between societies. Table 20.4 uses cross-cultural data to answer the question "Who—men or women—have final authority over the care, handling, and discipline of children younger than four years?" Although women have primary authority over infants in two-thirds of the societies, there are still societies (18 percent of the total) in which men have the major say. In the United States and Canada today, some men are primary child caregivers despite the cultural fact that the female role in child care remains more prominent in both countries. Given the critical role of breast-feeding in ensuring infant survival, it makes sense, for infants especially, for the mother to be the primary caregiver.

There are differences in male and female reproductive strategies. Women give birth, breast-feed, and assume primary responsibility for infant care. Women ensure that their progeny will survive by establishing a close bond with each baby. It's also advantageous for a woman to have a reliable mate to ease the child-rearing process and ensure the survival of her children. (Again, there are exceptions, for example, the matrilineal Nayars discussed in the chapter "Families, Kinship, and Descent.") Women can have only so many babies during the course of their reproductive years, which begin after menarche (the advent of first menstruation) and end with menopause (cessation of menstruation). Men, in contrast, have a longer reproductive period, which can last into the elder

Table 20.2   Time and Effort Expended on Subsistence Activities by Men and Women*

More by men	16
Roughly equal	61
More by women	23

*Percentage of 88 randomly selected societies for which information was available on this variable.

Source: Whyte 1978.

Table 20.3   Who Does the Domestic Work?*

Males do virtually none	51
Males do some, but mostly done by females	49

*Percentage of 92 randomly selected societies for which information was available on this variable.

Source: Whyte 1978.

Table 20.4   Who Has Final Authority over the Care, Handling, and Discipline of Infant Children (under Four Years Old)?*

Males have more say	18
Roughly equal	16
Females have more say	66

*Percentage of 67 randomly selected societies for which information was available on this variable.

Source: Whyte 1978).

Table 20.5 Does the Society Allow Multiple Spouses?*

Only for males	77
For both, but more commonly for males	4
For neither	16
For both, but more commonly for females	2

*Percentage of 92 randomly selected societies.
SOURCE: Whyte 1978.

Table 20.7 Is There a Double Standard with Respect to EXTRAMARITAL Sex*

Yes—females are more restricted	43
Equal restrictions on males and females	55
Males punished more severely for transgression	3

*Percentage of 75 randomly selected societies for which information was available on this variable.
SOURCE: Whyte 1978.

Table 20.6 Is There a Double Standard with Respect to PREMARITAL Sex*

Yes—females are more restricted	44
No—equal restrictions on males and females	56

*Percentage of 73 randomly selected societies for which information was available on this variable.
SOURCE: Whyte 1978.

years. If they choose to do so, men can enhance their reproductive success by impregnating several women over a longer time period. Although men do not always have multiple mates, they do have a greater tendency to do so than women do (see Tables 20.5, 20.6, and 20.7). Among the societies known to ethnography, polygyny is much more common than polyandry is (see Table 20.5).

Men mate, within and outside marriage, more than women do. Table 20.6 shows cross-cultural data on premarital sex, and Table 20.7 summarizes the data on extramarital sex. In both cases men are less restricted than women are, although the restrictions are equal in about half the societies studied.

Double standards that restrict women more than men illustrate gender stratification. Several studies have shown that economic roles affect gender stratification. In one cross-cultural study, Sanday (1974) found that gender stratification decreased when men and women made roughly equal contributions to subsistence. She found that gender stratification was greatest when the women contributed either much more or much less than the men did.

Gender Among Foragers

Sanday's finding applied mainly to food producers, not to foragers. In foraging societies, gender stratification was most marked when men contributed much more to the diet than women did. This was true among the Inuit and other northern hunters and fishers. Among tropical and semitropical foragers, by contrast, gathering usually supplies more food than hunting and fishing do. Gathering is generally women's work. Men usually hunt and fish, but women also do some fishing and may hunt small animals. When gathering is prominent, gender status tends to be more equal than it is when hunting and fishing are the main subsistence activities.

Gender status is also more equal when the domestic and public spheres aren't sharply separated. (*Domestic* means within or pertaining to the home.) Strong differentiation between the home and the outside world is called the **domestic–public dichotomy** or the *private–public contrast*. The outside world can include politics, trade, warfare, or work. Often when domestic and public spheres are clearly separated, public activities have greater prestige than domestic ones do. This can promote gender stratification, because men are more likely to be

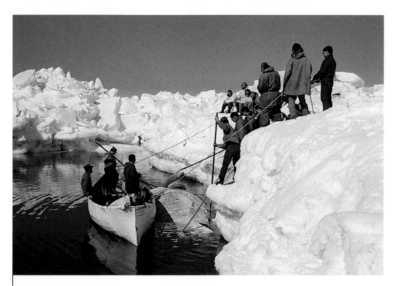

Among foragers, gender stratification tends to increase when men contribute much more to the diet than women do—as has been true among the Inuit and other northern hunters and fishers. Shown here, unable to bring a whale ashore for butchering, these Inuit are taking its muktuk (skin and blubber).

active in the public domain than women are. Cross-culturally, women's activities tend to be closer to home than men's are. Thus, another reason hunter-gatherers have less gender stratification than food producers do is that the domestic–public dichotomy is more developed among food producers.

We've seen that certain gender roles are more sex-linked than others. Men are the usual hunters and warriors. Given such tools and weapons as spears, knives, and bows, men make better hunters and fighters because they are bigger and stronger on the average than are women in the same population (Divale and Harris 1976). The male hunter-fighter role also reflects a tendency toward greater male mobility.

In foraging societies, women are either pregnant or lactating during most of their childbearing period. Late in pregnancy and after childbirth, carrying a baby limits a woman's movements, even her gathering. However, among the Agta of the Philippines (Griffin and Estioko-Griffin, eds. 1985) women not only gather, they also hunt with dogs while carrying their babies with them. Still, given the effects of pregnancy and breast-feeding on mobility, it is rarely feasible for women to be the primary hunters (Friedl 1975). Warfare, which also requires mobility, is not found in most foraging

societies, nor is interregional trade well developed. Warfare and trade are two public arenas that can contribute to status inequality of males and females among food producers.

The Ju/'hoansi San illustrate the extent to which the activities and spheres of influence of men and women may overlap among foragers (Draper 1975). Traditional Ju/'hoansi gender roles were interdependent. During gathering, women discovered information about game animals, which they passed on to the men. Men and women spent about the same amount of time away from the camp, but neither worked more than three days a week. Between one-third and one-half of the band stayed home while the others worked.

The Ju/'hoansi saw nothing wrong in doing the work of the other gender. Men often gathered food and collected water. A general sharing ethos dictated that men distribute meat and that women share the fruits of gathering. Boys and girls of all ages played together. Fathers took an active role in raising children. Resources were adequate, and competition and aggression were discouraged. Exchangeability and interdependence of roles are adaptive in small groups.

Patricia Draper's field work among the Ju/'hoansi is especially useful in showing the relationships between economy, gender roles, and stratification because she studied both foragers and a group of former foragers who had become sedentary. Just a few thousand Ju/'hoansi continue their culture's traditional foraging pattern. Most are now sedentary, living near food producers or ranchers (see Kent 1992; Solway and Lee 1990; Wilmsen 1989).

Draper studied sedentary Ju/'hoansi at Mahopa, a village where they herded, grew crops, worked for wages, and did a small amount of gathering. Their gender roles were becoming more rigidly defined. A domestic–public dichotomy was developing as men traveled farther than women did. With less gathering, women were confined more to the home. Boys could gain mobility through herding, but girls' movements were more limited. The equal and communal world of the

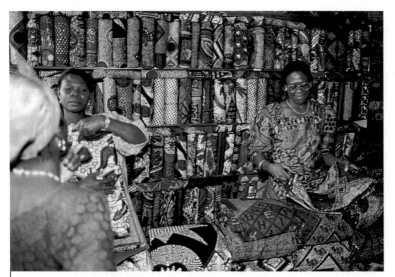

Many jobs that men do in some societies are done by women in others, and vice versa. In West Africa, women play a prominent role in trade and marketing. In Togo, shown here, women dominate textile sales. Is there a textile shop near you? Who runs it?

and the rights, activities, and spheres of influence of men and women overlap the most. Our ancestors lived entirely by foraging until 10,000 years ago. If there is any most "natural" form of human society, it is best, although imperfectly, represented by foragers. Despite the popular stereotype of the club-wielding caveman dragging his mate by the hair, relative gender equality is a much more likely ancestral pattern.

Gender among Horticulturalists

Gender roles and stratification among cultivators vary widely, depending on specific features of the economy and social structure. Demonstrating this, Martin and Voorhies (1975) studied a sample of 515 horticultural societies, representing all parts of the world. They looked at several variables, including descent and postmarital residence, the percentage of the diet derived from cultivation, and the productivity of men and women.

Women were found to be the main producers in horticultural societies. In 50 percent of those societies, women did most of the cultivating. In 33 percent, contributions to cultivation by men and women were equal. In only 17 percent did men do most of the work. Women tended to do a bit more cultivating in matrilineal compared with patrilineal societies. They dominated horticulture in 64 percent of the matrilineal societies versus 50 percent of the patrilineal ones.

REDUCED GENDER STRATIFICATION— MATRILINEAL, MATRILOCAL SOCIETIES

Cross-cultural variation in gender status is related to rules of descent and postmarital residence (Friedl 1975; Martin and Voorhies 1975). Among horticulturalists with matrilineal descent and *matrilocality* (residence after marriage with the wife's relatives, so that children grow up in their mother's village), female status tends to be high (see Blackwood 2000). Matriliny and matrilocality disperse related males, rather than consolidating

bush was yielding to the social features of sedentary life. A differential ranking of men according to their herds, houses, and sons began to replace sharing. Males came to be seen as the most valuable producers.

See the Virtual Exploration for more on how gender roles can change

/kottak

If there is some degree of male dominance in virtually every contemporary society, it may be because of changes such as those that have drawn the Ju/'hoansi into wage work, market sales, and thus the world capitalist economy. A historical interplay between local, national, and international forces influences systems of gender stratification (Ong 1989). In traditional foraging cultures, however, egalitarianism extended to the relations between the sexes. The social spheres, activities, rights, and obligations of men and women overlapped. Foragers' kinship systems tend to be bilateral (calculated equally through males and females) rather than favoring either the mother's side or the father's side. Foragers may live with either the husband's or the wife's kin and often shift between one group and the other.

One last observation about foragers: It is among them that the public and private spheres are least separate, hierarchy is least marked, aggression and competition are most discouraged,

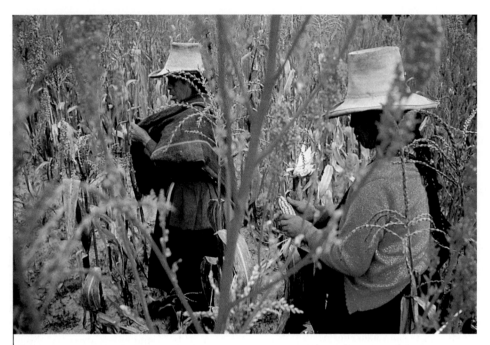

Women are the main producers in horticultural societies. Women like these South American corn farmers do most of the cultivating in such societies. What kinds of roles do women play in contemporary North American farming?

them. By contrast, patriliny and *patrilocality* (residence after marriage with the husband's kin) keep male relatives together, an advantage given warfare. Matrilineal-matrilocal systems tend to occur in societies where population pressure on strategic resources is minimal and warfare is infrequent.

As we saw in the news story that opened this chapter, women tend to have high status in matrilineal, matrilocal societies for several reasons. Descent-group membership, succession to political positions, allocation of land, and overall social identity all come through female links. In Negeri Sembilan, Malaysia (Peletz 1988), matriliny gave women sole inheritance of ancestral rice fields. Matrilocality created solidarity clusters of female kin. Women had considerable influence beyond the household (Swift 1963). In such matrilineal contexts, women are the basis of the entire social structure. Although public authority may be (or may appear to be) assigned to the men, much of the power and decision making may actually belong to the senior women. Some matrilineal societies, including the *Iroquois* (Brown 1975), a confederation of tribes in aboriginal New York,

show that women's economic, political, and ritual influence can rival that of the men (Figure 20.2).

Iroquois women played a major subsistence role, while men left home for long periods to wage war. As is usual in matrilineal societies, *internal* warfare was uncommon. Iroquois men waged war only on distant groups; this could keep them away for years.

Iroquois men hunted and fished, but women controlled the local economy. Women did some fishing and occasional hunting, but their major productive role was in horticulture. Women owned the land, which they inherited from matrilineal kinswomen. Women controlled the production and distribution of food.

Iroquois women lived with their husbands and children in the family compartments of a communal longhouse. Women born in a longhouse remained there for life. Senior women, or *matrons*, decided which men could join the longhouse as husbands, and they could evict incompatible men. Women therefore controlled alliances between descent groups, an important political job in tribal society.

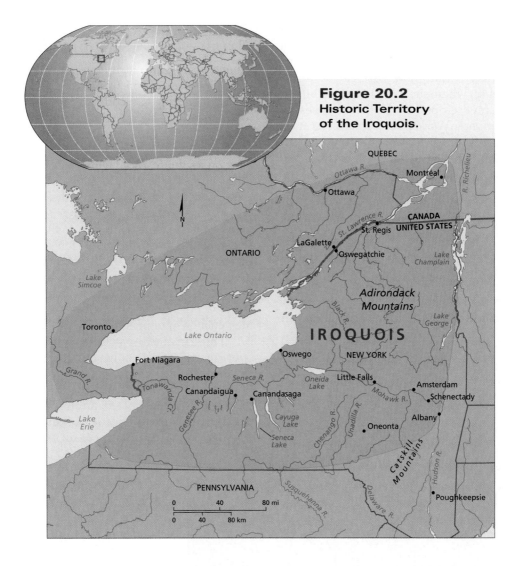

Figure 20.2
Historic Territory of the Iroquois.

Iroquois women thus managed production and distribution. Social identity, succession to office and titles, and property all came through the female line, and women were prominent in ritual and politics. Related tribes made up a confederacy, the League of the Iroquois, with chiefs and councils.

A council of male chiefs managed military operations, but chiefly succession was matrilineal. That is, succession went from a man to his brother, his sister's son, or another matrilineal relative. The matrons of each longhouse nominated a man as their representative. If the council rejected their first nominee, the women proposed others until one was accepted. Matrons constantly monitored the chiefs and could impeach them. Women could veto war declarations, withhold provisions for war, and initiate peace efforts. In religion, too,

women shared power. Half the tribe's religious practitioners were women, and the matrons helped select the others.

REDUCED GENDER STRATIFICATION— MATRIFOCAL SOCIETIES

Nancy Tanner (1974) also found that the combination of male travel and a prominent female economic role, as was true among the Iroquois, reduced gender stratification and promoted high female status. She based this finding on a survey of the **matrifocal** (mother-centered, often with no resident husband-father) organization of certain societies in Indonesia, West Africa, and the Caribbean. Matrifocal societies are not necessarily matrilineal. A few are even patrilineal.

For example, Tanner (1974) found matrifocality among the Igbo (Figure 20.3) of eastern Nigeria, who are patrilineal, patrilocal, and polygynous (men have multiple wives). Each wife had her own house, where she lived with her children. Women planted crops next to their houses and traded surpluses. Women's associations ran the local markets, while men did the long-distance trading.

In a case study of the Igbo, Ifi Amadiume (1987) noted that either sex could fill male gender roles. Before Christian influence, successful Igbo women and men used wealth to take titles and acquire wives. Wives freed husbands (male and female) from domestic work and helped them accumulate wealth. Female husbands were not considered masculine but preserved their femininity. Igbo women asserted themselves in women's groups, including those of lineage daughters, lineage wives, and a community-wide women's council led by titled women. The high status and influence of Igbo women rested on the separation of males from local subsistence and on a marketing system that encouraged women to leave home and gain prominence in distribution and—through these accomplishments—in politics.

A significant number of female-centered, or matrifocal, households characterize many Caribbean societies, such as the Bahamas, shown here. As men travel, women pursue such economic activities as handicraft production and sales. This Cat Island beach scene shows a female-run basketry shop.

INCREASED GENDER STRATIFICATION— PATRILINEAL-PATRILOCAL SOCIETIES

The Igbo are unusual among patrilineal-patrilocal societies, many of which have marked gender stratification. Martin and Voorhies (1975) link the decline of matriliny and the spread of the **patrilineal-patrilocal complex** (consisting of patrilineality, patrilocality, warfare, and male supremacy) to pressure on resources. Faced with scarce resources, patrilineal-patrilocal cultivators such as the Yanomami often wage warfare against other villages. This favors patrilocality and patriliny, customs that keep related men together in the same village, where they make strong allies in battle. Such societies tend to have a sharp domestic–public dichotomy, and men tend to dominate the prestige hierarchy. Men may use their public roles in warfare and trade and their greater prestige to symbolize and reinforce the devaluation or oppression of women.

The patrilineal-patrilocal complex characterizes many societies in highland Papua New Guinea. Women work hard growing and processing subsistence crops, raising and tending pigs (the main domesticated animal and a favorite food), and doing domestic cooking, but they are isolated from the public domain, which men control. Men grow and distribute prestige crops, prepare food for feasts, and arrange marriages. The men even get to trade the pigs and control their use in ritual.

In densely populated areas of the Papua New Guinea highlands, male–female avoidance is associated with strong pressure on resources (Lindenbaum 1972). Men fear all female contacts, including sex. They think that sexual contact with women will weaken them. Indeed, men see everything female as dangerous and polluting. They segregate themselves in men's houses and hide their precious ritual objects from women. They delay marriage, and some never marry.

By contrast, the sparsely populated areas of Papua New Guinea, such as recently settled areas, lack taboos on male–female contacts. The image of woman as polluter

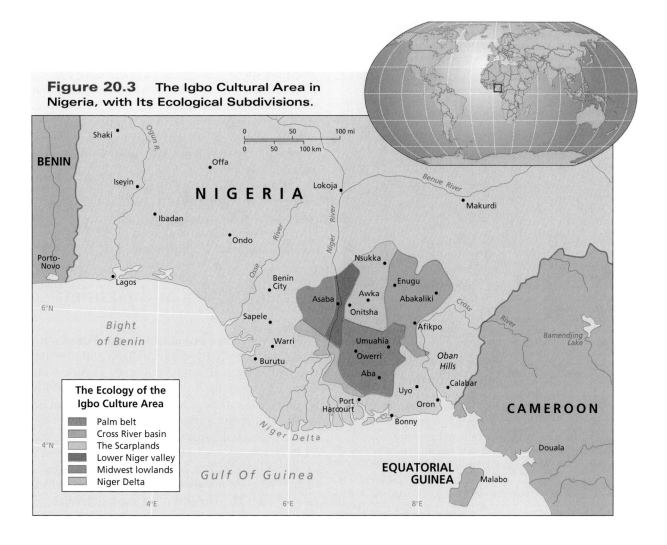

Figure 20.3 The Igbo Cultural Area in Nigeria, with Its Ecological Subdivisions.

The Ecology of the Igbo Culture Area
- Palm belt
- Cross River basin
- The Scarplands
- Lower Niger valley
- Midwest lowlands
- Niger Delta

fades, heterosexual intercourse is valued, men and women live together, and reproductive rates are high.

HOMOSEXUAL BEHAVIOR AMONG THE ETORO

One of the most extreme examples of male–female sexual antagonism in Papua New Guinea comes from the *Etoro* (Kelly 1976), a group of 400 people who subsist by hunting and horticulture in the Trans-Fly region (Figure 20.4). The Etoro also illustrate the power of culture in molding human sexuality. The following account applies only to Etoro males and their beliefs. Etoro cultural norms prevented the male anthropologist who studied them from gathering comparable information about female attitudes. Etoro opinions about sexuality are linked to their beliefs about the cycle of birth, physical growth, maturity, old age, and death.

Etoro men believe that semen is necessary to give life force to a fetus, which is said to be placed within a woman by an ancestral spirit. Because men are believed to have a limited supply of semen, sexuality saps male vitality. The birth of children, nurtured by semen, symbolizes a necessary (and unpleasant) sacrifice that will lead to the husband's eventual death. Heterosexual intercourse, which is required only for reproduction, is discouraged. Women who want too much sex are viewed as witches, hazardous to their husbands' health. Etoro culture permits heterosexual intercourse only about 100 days a year. The rest of the time it is tabooed. Seasonal birth clustering shows that the taboo is respected.

In some parts of Papua New Guinea, the patrilineal-patrilocal complex has extreme social repercussions. Regarding females as dangerous and polluting, men may segregate themselves in men's houses (such as this one, located near the Sepik River), where they hide their precious ritual objects from women. Are there places like this in your society?

So objectionable is heterosexuality that it is removed from community life. It can occur neither in sleeping quarters nor in the fields. Coitus can happen only in the woods, where it is risky because poisonous snakes, the Etoro say, are attracted by the sounds and smells of sex.

Although coitus is discouraged, homosexual acts are viewed as essential. Etoro believe that boys cannot produce semen on their own. To grow into men and eventually give life force to their children, boys must acquire semen orally from older men. From the age of 10 until adulthood, boys are inseminated by older men. No taboos are attached to this. Homosexual activity can go on in the sleeping area or garden. Every three years, a group of boys around the age of 20 are formally initiated into manhood. They go to a secluded mountain lodge, where they are visited and inseminated by several older men.

Etoro homosexuality is governed by a code of propriety. Although homosexual relations between older and younger males are considered culturally essential, those between boys of the same age are discouraged. A boy who gets semen from other youths is believed to be sapping their life force and stunting their growth. When a boy develops very rapidly, this suggests that he is ingesting semen from other boys. Like a sex-hungry wife, he is shunned as a witch.

Etoro homosexuality rests not on hormones or genes but on cultural traditions. The Etoro represent one extreme of a male–female avoidance pattern that is widespread in Papua New Guinea and in patrilineal-patrilocal societies.

Sexualities and Gender

The Etoro share a pattern, which Gilbert Herdt (1984) has characterized as ritualized homosexuality, with about 50 other tribes in Papua New Guinea, especially in that country's Trans-Fly region. These tribes demonstrate the extent to which culture can influence basic biological forces, such as sexual urges. Etoro culture regards male–female sex as unpleasant, although necessary for reproduction. The taboos that apply to heterosexual coitus do not apply to male–male sex, which also is seen as necessary for reproduction, but which is viewed much more positively. For cultural reasons, Etoro men are freer to enjoy the sex they have with other men than they are to enjoy the sex they have with their wives.

Understanding Ourselves Do the taboos that have surrounded homosexuality in our own society remind you of Etoro taboos? Homosexual activity has been stigmatized in Western industrial societies. Indeed, sodomy laws continue to make it illegal in many U.S. states. Among the Etoro, male–female sex is banned from the social center and moved to the fringes or margins of society (the woods, filled with dangerous snakes). In our own society, homosexual activity has traditionally been hidden, furtive, and secretive—also moved to the margins of society rather than its valued center. Imagine what our own sex lives would be like if we had been raised with Etoro beliefs and taboos.

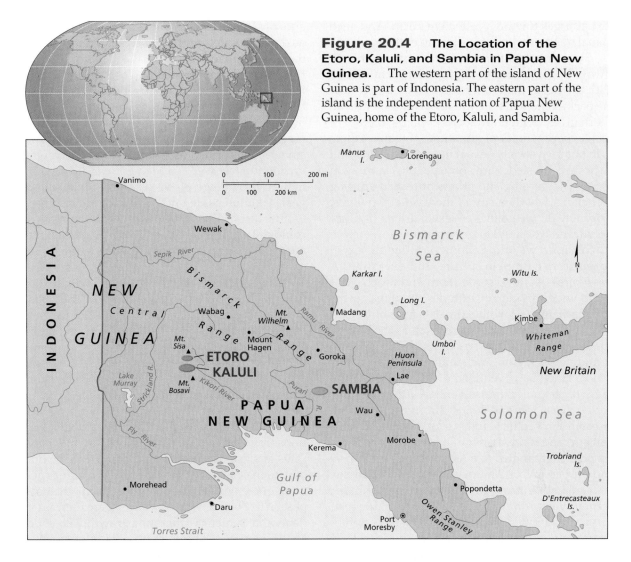

Figure 20.4   The Location of the Etoro, Kaluli, and Sambia in Papua New Guinea. The western part of the island of New Guinea is part of Indonesia. The eastern part of the island is the independent nation of Papua New Guinea, home of the Etoro, Kaluli, and Sambia.

Recently in the United States, there has been a tendency to see sexual orientation as fixed and probably biologically based. There is not enough information at this time to say for sure that sexual orientation is based on biology. What we can say is that to some extent at least, all human activities and preferences, including erotic expression, are learned and malleable. **Sexual orientation** stands for a person's habitual sexual attraction to, and activities with: persons of the opposite sex, *heterosexuality*; the same sex, *homosexuality*; or both sexes, *bisexuality*. *Asexuality*, indifference toward, or lack of attraction to, either sex, is also a sexual orientation. All four of these forms are found in contemporary North America, and throughout the world (see Blackwood and Wieringa, eds. 1999; Rathus, Nevid, and Fichner-Rathus 2000). But each type of desire and experience holds different meanings for individuals and groups. For example, an asexual disposition may be acceptable in some places but may be perceived as a character flaw in others. Bisexuality may be a private orientation in Mexico, rather than socially sanctioned and encouraged as among the Sambia of Papua New Guinea (see Kottak and Kozaitis 2003, Chapter 10).

In any society, individuals will differ in the nature, range, and intensity of their sexual interests and urges. No one knows for sure why such individual sexual differences exist. Part of the answer is probably biological, reflecting genes or hormones. Another part probably has to do with experiences during growth and development. But whatever the reasons for individual variation, culture always plays a role in molding individual sexual urges toward a collective norm. And such sexual norms vary from culture to culture.

Since people differ within any culture, there'll always be some people who are more comfortable with the norm than others are. Some will follow the pack; some will trail, resist, or experiment with alternatives. Sometimes society will be tolerant of such experimentation; sometimes it won't. Often, as in our own society, sexual norms and mores will be hotly contested, with some people claiming to know what's right, and others bitterly disputing that claim. Sex then enters the world of politics. (For more on the politics of sexual orientation, see Kottak and Kozaitis 2003, Chapter 10.)

What do we know about variation in sexual norms from culture to culture, and over time? A classic cross-cultural study (Ford and Beach 1951) found wide variation in attitudes about masturbation, bestiality (sex with animals), and homosexuality. Even in a single culture, such as the United States, attitudes about sex differ with socioeconomic status, region, and rural versus urban residence. However, even in the 1950s, prior to the "age of sexual permissiveness" (the pre-HIV period from the mid-1960s through the 1970s), research showed that almost all American men (92 percent) and more than half of American women (54 percent) admitted to masturbation. Between 40 and 50 percent of American farm boys had sex with animals. In the famous Kinsey report (Kinsey, Pomeroy, and Martin 1948), 37 percent of the men surveyed admitted having had at least one homosexual experience leading to orgasm. In a later study of 1,200 unmarried women, 26 percent reported same-sex sexual activities.

Attitudes toward homosexuality, masturbation, and bestiality in other cultures differ strikingly, as I find when I contrast the cultures I know best: the United States, urban and rural Brazil, and Madagascar. During my first stay in Arembepe, Brazil, when I was 19 years old and unmarried, young men told me details of their experience with prostitutes in the city. In Arembepe, a rural community, sex with animals was common. Targets of the male sex drive included cattle, horses, sheep, goats, and turkeys. Arembepe's women were also more open about their sex lives than North American women were at that time.

Arembepeiros talked about sex so willingly that I wasn't prepared for the silence and avoid-ance of sexual subjects that I encountered in Madagascar. My wife's and my discreet attempts to get the Betsileo to tell us at least the basics of their culture's sexual practices led nowhere. I did discover from city folk that, as in many non-Western cultures, traditional ceremonies were times of ritual license, when normal taboos lapsed and Betsileo men and women engaged in what Christian missionaries described as "wanton" sexuality. Only during my last week in Madagascar did a young man in the village of Ivato, where I had spent a year, take me aside and offer to write down the words for genitals and sexual intercourse. He could not say these tabooed words, but he wanted me to know them so that my knowledge of Betsileo culture would be as complete as possible.

I have never worked in a culture with institutionalized homosexuality of the sort that exists among several tribes in Papua New Guinea, such as Etoro, Kaluli (Schieffelin 1976), or Sambia (Herdt 1981, 1986). The Kaluli believe that semen has a magical quality that promotes knowledge and growth. Before traveling into alien territory, boys must eat a mixture of semen, ginger, and salt to enhance their ability to learn a foreign language. At age 11 or 12, a Kaluli boy forms a sexual relationship with an older man chosen by his father. (This man cannot be a relative, because that would violate their incest taboo.) The older man has anal intercourse with the boy. The Kaluli cite the boy's peach-fuzz beard, which appears thereafter, as evidence that semen is promoting growth. The young Kaluli men also have homosexual intercourse at the hunting lodges, where they spend an extended period learning the lore of the forest and the hunt from older bachelors.

Homosexual activities were absent, rare, or secret in only 37 percent of 76 societies for which data were available (Ford and Beach 1951). In the others, various forms of homosexuality were considered normal and acceptable. Sometimes sexual relations between people of the same sex involved transvestism on the part of one of the partners, like the *berdaches* discussed in the chapter "Marriage." See "Interesting Issues" (pages 562–563) for more on transvestism and men who have sex with men.

Transvestism did not characterize male–male sex among the Sudanese Azande, who valued the warrior role (Evans-Pritchard 1970). Prospective warriors—boys aged 12 to 20—left their families and shared quarters with adult fighting men, who paid bridewealth for, and had sex with, them. During this apprenticeship, the young men did the domestic duties of women. Upon reaching warrior status, those young men took their own younger male brides. Later, retiring from the warrior role, Azande men married women. Flexible in their sexual expression, Azande males had no difficulty shifting from sex with older men (as male brides), to sex with younger men (as warriors), to sex with women (as husbands).

There appears to be greater cross-cultural acceptance of homosexuality than of bestiality or masturbation. Most societies in the Ford and Beach (1951) study discouraged masturbation. Only five allowed human–animal sex. However, these figures measure only the social approval of sexual practices, not their actual frequency. As in our own society, socially disapproved sex acts are more widespread than people admit.

Flexibility in human sexual expression seems to be an aspect of our primate heritage. Both masturbation and homosexual behavior exist among chimpanzees and other primates. Male bonobos (pygmy chimps) regularly engage in a form of mutual masturbation known as "penis fencing." Female bonobos get sexual pleasure from rubbing their genitals against those of other females (De Waal 1997). Our primate sexual potential is molded by culture, the environment, and reproductive necessity. Heterosexuality is practiced in all human societies—which, after all, must reproduce themselves—but alternatives are also widespread (Davis and Whitten 1987; Rathus, Nevid, and Fichner-Rathus 2000). The sexual component of human personality—just how we express our "natural" sexual urges—is a matter that culture and environment determine and limit.

Gender among Agriculturalists

As horticulture developed into agriculture, women lost their role as primary cultivators. Certain agricultural techniques, particularly plowing, were assigned to men because of their greater average size and strength (Martin and Voorhies 1975). Except when irrigation was used, plowing eliminated the need for constant weeding, an activity usually done by women.

Cross-cultural data illustrate these changes in productive roles. Women were the main workers in 50 percent of the horticultural societies surveyed but in only 15 percent of the agricultural groups. Male subsistence labor dominated 81 percent of the agricultural societies but only 17 percent of the horticultural ones (Martin and Voorhies 1975) (see Table 20.8).

With agriculture, women were cut off from production for the first time in human history. Perhaps this reflected the need for women to stay closer to home to care for the larger numbers of children that typify agriculture, compared with less labor-intensive economies. Belief systems started contrasting men's valuable extradomestic labor with women's domestic role, now viewed as inferior. (**Extradomestic** means outside the home; within or pertaining to the public domain.) Changes in kinship and postmarital residence patterns also hurt women. Descent groups and polygyny declined with agriculture, and the nuclear family became more common. Living with her husband and children, a woman was isolated from her kinswomen and cowives. Female sexuality is

Table 20.8	Male and Female Contributions to Production in Cultivating Societies
	Horticulture (Percentage of 104 Societies)	Agriculture (Percentage of 93 Societies)
Women are primary cultivators	50	15
Men are primary cultivators	17	81
Equal contributions to cultivation	33	3

SOURCE: Martin and Voorhies 1975, p. 283.

For several years, one of Brazil's top sex symbols was Roberta Close, whom I first saw in a furniture commercial. Roberta, whose looks reminded me of those of the young Natalie Wood, ended her pitch with an admonition to prospective furniture buyers to accept no substitute for the advertised product. "Things," she warned, "are not always what they seem."

Nor was Roberta. This petite and incredibly feminine creature was actually a man. Nevertheless, despite the fact that he—or she (speaking as Brazilians do)—is a man posing as a woman, Roberta has won a secure place in Brazilian mass culture. Her photos have decorated magazines. She has been a panelist on a TV variety show and has starred in a stage play in Rio with an actor known for his supermacho image. Roberta even inspired a well-known, and apparently heterosexual, pop singer to make a "video" honoring her. In it, she pranced around Rio's Ipanema Beach in a bikini, showing off her ample hips and buttocks.

The video depicted the widespread male appreciation of Roberta's beauty. As confirmation, one heterosexual man told me that he had recently been on the same plane as Roberta and had been struck by her looks. Another man said he wanted to have sex with her. These comments, it seemed to me, illustrated striking cultural contrasts about gender and sexuality. In Brazil, a Latin American country noted for its machismo, heterosexual men do not feel that attraction toward a transvestite blemishes their masculine identities.

Roberta Close exists in relation to a gender-identity scale that jumps from extreme femininity to extreme masculinity, with little in between. Masculinity is stereotyped as active and public, femininity as passive and domestic. The male–female contrast in rights and behavior is much stronger in Brazil than it is in North America. Brazilians confront a more rigidly defined masculine role than North Americans do.

The active–passive dichotomy also provides a stereotypical model for male–male sexual relations. One man is supposed to be the active, masculine (inserting) partner, whereas the other is the passive, effeminate one. The latter man is derided as a *bicha* (intestinal worm), but little stigma attaches to the inserter. Indeed, many "active" (and married) Brazilian men like to have sex with transvestite prostitutes, who are biological males.

If a Brazilian man is unhappy pursuing either active masculinity or passive effeminacy, there is one other choice—active femininity. For Roberta Close and others like her, the cultural demand of ultramasculinity has yielded to a performance of ultrafemininity. These men-women form a third gender in relation to Brazil's polarized male–female identity scale.

Transvestites like Roberta are particularly prominent in Rio de Janeiro's annual Carnaval, when an ambience of inversion rules the city. In the culturally accurate words of the American popular novelist Gregory McDonald, who sets one of his books in Brazil at Carnaval time:

carefully supervised in agricultural economies; men have easier access to divorce and extramarital sex, reflecting a "double standard."

Still, female status in agricultural societies is not inevitably bleak. Gender stratification is associated with plow agriculture rather than with intensive cultivation per se. Studies of peasant gender roles and stratification in France and Spain (Harding 1975; Reiter 1975), which have plow agriculture, show that people think of the house as the female sphere and the fields as the male domain. However, such a dichotomy is not inevitable, as my own research among Betsileo agriculturalists in Madagascar shows.

Betsileo women play a prominent role in agriculture, contributing a third of the hours invested in rice production. They have their customary tasks in the division of labor, but their work is more seasonal than men's is.

No one has much to do during the ceremonial season, between mid-June and mid-September. Men work in the rice fields almost daily the rest of the year. Women's cooperative work occurs during transplanting (mid-September through November) and harvesting (mid-March through early May). Along with other members of the household, women do daily weeding in December and January. After the harvest, all family members

Roberta Close, in her prime.

Everything goes topsy-turvy . . . Men become women; women become men; grown-ups become children; rich people pretend they're poor; poor people, rich; sober people become drunkards; thieves become generous. Very topsy-turvy. (McDonald 1984, p. 154)

Most notable in this costumed inversion (DaMatta 1991), men dress as women. Carnaval reveals and expresses normally hidden tensions and conflicts as social life is turned upside down. Reality is illuminated through a dramatic presentation of its opposite.

This is the final key to Roberta's cultural meaning. She emerged in a setting in which male–female inversion is part of the year's most popular festival. Transvestites are the pièces de résistance at Rio's Carnaval balls, where they dress as scantily as the real women do. They wear postage-stamp bikinis, sometimes with no tops. Photos of real women and transformed ones vie for space in the magazines. It is often impossible to tell the born women from the hidden men. Roberta Close is a permanent incarnation of Carnaval—a year-round reminder of the spirit of Carnavals past, present, and yet to come.

Roberta emerges from a Latin culture whose gender roles contrast strongly with those of the United States. From small village to mas-sive city, Brazilian males are public and Brazilian females are private creatures. Streets, beaches, and bars belong to the men. Although bikinis adorn Rio's beaches on weekends and holidays, there are many more men than women there on weekdays. The men revel in their ostentatiously sexual displays. As they sun themselves and play soccer and volleyball, they regularly stroke their genitals to keep them firm. They are living publicly, assertively, and sexually in a world of men.

Brazilian men must work hard at this public image, constantly acting out their culture's definition of masculine behavior. Public life is a play whose strong roles go to men. Roberta Close, of course, is a public figure. Given that Brazilian culture defines the public world as male, we can perhaps better understand now why the nation's number one sex symbol has been a man who excels at performing in public as a woman.

---

work together winnowing the rice and then transporting it to the granary.

If we consider the strenuous daily task of husking rice by pounding (a part of food preparation rather than production per se), women actually contribute slightly more than 50 percent of the labor devoted to producing and preparing rice before cooking.

Not just women's prominent economic role but traditional social organization enhances female status among the Betsileo. Although postmarital residence is mainly patrilocal, descent rules permit married women to keep membership in and a strong allegiance to their own descent groups. Kinship is broadly and bilaterally calculated (on both sides—as in contemporary North America). The Betsileo exemplify Aihwa Ong's (1989) generalization that bilateral (and matrilineal) kinship systems, combined with subsistence economies in which the sexes have complementary roles in food production and distribution, are characterized by reduced gender stratification. Such societies are common among South Asian peasants (Ong 1989).

Betsileo men do not have exclusive control over the means of production. Women can inherit rice fields, but most women, on marrying, relinquish their shares to their brothers. Sometimes a woman and her husband cultivate her field, eventually passing it on to their children.

Traditionally, Betsileo men participate more in politics, but the women also hold political office. Women sell their produce and products in markets, invest in cattle, sponsor ceremonials, and are mentioned during offerings to ancestors. Arranging marriages, an important extradomestic activity, is more women's concern than men's. Sometimes Betsileo women seek their own kinswomen as wives for their sons, reinforcing their own prominence in village life and continuing kin-based female solidarity in the village.

The Betsileo illustrate the idea that intensive cultivation does not necessarily entail sharp gender stratification. We can see that gender roles and stratification reflect not just the type of adaptive strategy but also specific environmental variables and cultural attributes. Betsileo women continue to play a significant role in their society's major economic activity, rice production.

We have seen that patrilocality is usually associated with gender stratification. However, some cultures with these institutions, including the Betsileo and the matrifocal Igbo of eastern Nigeria, offer contrasts to the generalization. The Igbo and Betsileo are not alone in having female traders. Many patrilineal, polygynous societies in West Africa also include women with careers in commerce. Polygyny may even help an aspiring woman trader, who can leave her children with her cowives while she pursues a business career. She repays them with cash and other forms of assistance.

Bilateral kinship systems, combined with subsistence economies in which the sexes have complementary roles in food production and distribution, have reduced gender stratification. Such features are common among Asian rice cultivators, such as the Ifugao of the Philippines (shown here).

Patriarchy and Violence

In the chapter "Marriage," dowry murders and sati (widow burning) in India were cited as blatant examples of **patriarchy**. This term describes a political system ruled by men in which women have inferior social and political status, including

basic human rights. Barbara Miller (1997), in a study of systematic neglect of females, describes women in rural northern India as "the endangered sex." Societies that feature a full-fledged patrilineal-patrilocal complex, replete with warfare and intervillage raiding, also typify patriarchy. Chagnon (1968) has described Yanomami males as "fierce" warriors, who exalt the male role in warfare and devalue females in relation to males. In such settings, women may be captured, raped, or murdered in intervillage raiding. Since such societies value the male war role, they tend to prefer sons over daughters. This may be expressed in female infanticide. For example, if a first child is a girl, she may be killed. But a first-born son is allowed to survive. Such practices as dowry murders, *sati*, and female infanticide illustrate patriarchy, which extends from tribal societies like the Yanomami to state societies like India, Pakistan, and even contemporary Western societies.

Although more prevalent in certain social settings than in others, family violence and domestic abuse of women are worldwide problems. We've seen that gender stratification is typically reduced in matrilineal, matrifocal, and bilateral societies in which women have prominent roles in the economy and social life. When a woman lives in her own village, she has kin nearby to look after and protect her interests. Even in patrilocal polygynous settings, women often count on the support of their cowives and sons in disputes with potentially abusive husbands. However, such settings, which tend to provide a safe haven for women, are retracting rather than expanding in today's world. Isolated families and patrilineal social forms have spread at the expense of matrilineality. Many nations have declared polygyny illegal. More and more women, and men, find themselves cut off from extended kin and families of orientation.

Domestic violence is often associated with a woman's isolation from supportive kin ties. This happens in patrilineal-patrilocal settings ranging from the Yanomami to India, Pakistan, Afghanistan, and substantial chunks of Central Asia and North Africa. In Pakistan, for example, 50 percent of all murders are those of a woman by her husband (Kantor 1996). Domestic violence also occurs in neolocal–nuclear family settings, such as Canada and the United States. In Canada, 62 percent of murdered women are killed by their husband or domestic partner (Kantor 1996). Cities, with their impersonality and isolation from extended kin networks, are breeding groups for domestic violence.

Domestic violence is one of a series of often-interconnected manifestations of patriarchy. It is in patrilineal-patrilocal societies that anthropologists most typically find forced female (and male) genital operations, intervillage raiding, preference for males, female infanticide, dowry, and oppression of women by their in-laws. With the spread of the women's rights movement and the human rights movement, attention to domestic violence and abuse of women has increased. Laws have been passed; and mediating institutions established. Brazil's female-run police stations for battered women provide an example, as do shelters for victims of domestic abuse in the United States and Canada. But patriarchal institutions clearly do persist in what should be a more enlightened world.

Gender and Industrialism

The domestic–public dichotomy, which is developed most fully among patrilineal-patrilocal food producers and plow agriculturalists, also has affected gender stratification in industrial societies, including the United States and Canada. However, gender roles have been changing rapidly in North America. The "traditional" idea that "a woman's place is in the home" developed among middle- and upper-class Americans as industrialism spread after 1900. Earlier, pioneer women in the Midwest and West had been recognized as fully productive workers in farming and home industry. Under industrialism, attitudes about gendered work came to vary with class and region. In early industrial Europe, men, women, and children had flocked to factories as wage laborers. Enslaved Americans of both sexes had done grueling work in cotton fields. After abolition, southern African-American women continued working as field hands and domestics. Poor white women labored in the South's early cotton mills. In the 1890s, more than one million American women held menial, repetitious, and unskilled factory positions (Margolis 1984, 2000; Martin and Voorhies 1975). Poor, immigrant, and African-American women continued to work throughout the 20th century.

After 1900, European immigration produced a male labor force willing to work for wages lower than those of American-born men. Those immigrant men moved into factory jobs that previously had gone to women. As machine tools and mass production further reduced the need for female labor, the notion that women were biologically unfit for factory work began to gain ground (Martin and Voorhies 1975).

Maxine Margolis (1984, 2000) has shown how gendered work, attitudes, and beliefs have varied in response to American economic needs. For example, wartime shortages of men have promoted the idea that work outside the home is women's patriotic duty. During the world wars, the notion that women are biologically unfit for hard physical labor faded. Inflation and the culture of consumption have also spurred female employment. When prices and/or demand rises, multiple paychecks help maintain family living standards.

The steady increase in female paid employment since World War II also reflects the baby boom and industrial expansion. American culture has traditionally defined clerical work, teaching, and nursing as female occupations. With rapid population growth and business expansion after World War II, the demand for women to fill such

During the world wars, the notion that women were biologically unfit for hard physical labor faded. Shown here is World War II's famous Rosie the Riveter. Is there a comparable poster woman today? What does her image say about modern gender roles?

including the goal of equal pay for equal work. Between 1970 and 2000, the female percentage of the American work force rose from 38 to more than 47 percent. In other words, almost half of all Americans who work outside the home are women. Almost 66 million women now have paid jobs, compared with 75 million men. Women now fill more than half (54 percent) of all professional jobs (*Statistical Abstract of the United States 1999*, pp. 411, 424). And it's not mainly single women working, as once was the case. Table 20.9 presents figures on the ever-increasing cash employment of American wives and mothers.

Note in Table 20.9 that the cash employment of American married men has been falling while that of American married women has been rising. There has been a dramatic change in behavior and attitudes since 1960, when 89 percent of all married men worked, compared with just 32 percent of married women. The comparable figures in 2000 were 77 percent and 61 percent. Ideas about the gender roles of males and females have changed. Compare your grandparents and your parents. Chances are you have a working mother, but your grandmother was more likely a stay-home mom. Your grandfather is more likely than your father to have worked in manufacturing and to have belonged to a union. Your father is more likely than your grandfather to have shared child care and domestic responsibilities. Age at marriage has been delayed for both men and women. College educations and professional degrees have increased. What other changes do you associate with the increase in female employment outside the home?

jobs grew steadily. Employers also found that they could increase their profits by paying women lower wages than they would have to pay returning male war veterans.

Woman's role in the home has been stressed during periods of high unemployment, although when wages fall or inflation occurs simultaneously, female employment may still be accepted. Margolis (1984, 2000) contends that changes in the economy lead to changes in attitudes toward and about women. Economic changes paved the way for the contemporary woman's movement, which also was spurred by the publication of Betty Friedan's book *The Feminine Mystique* in 1963 and the founding of NOW, the National Organization of Women, in 1966. The movement in turn promoted expanded work opportunities for women,

Understanding Ourselves Sure, ideas about gender are changing along with the employment patterns of men and women. We see this in the media, as shows like *Sex and the City* and *Queer as Folk*, featuring characters who display nontraditional gender behavior and sexual behavior, attract significant audiences. But old beliefs, cultural expectations, and gender stereotypes linger. Thus, American culture expects women to be meeker than men. This poses a challenge for women, since our culture also values decisiveness and "standing up for your beliefs." When American men and women display certain behavior—speaking up for their ideas, for example—they are

Table 20.9 Cash Employment of American Mothers, Wives, and Husbands, 1960–2000*

Year	Percentage of Married Women, Husband Present with Children under 6	Percentage of All Married Women[a]	Percentage of All Married Men[b]
1960	19	32	89
1970	30	40	86
1980	45	50	81
1990	59	58	79
2000	63	61	77

*Civilian population 16 years of age and older.
[a]Husband present.
[b]Wife present.
SOURCE: *Statistical Abstract of the United States* 2001, pp. 577, p. 373; Table 575, p. 372.

judged differently. A man's assertive behavior may be admired and rewarded, but a women's similar behavior may be labeled "aggressive"—or worse. Women must constantly negotiate this conundrum.

Both men and women are constrained by their cultural training, stereotypes, and expectations. For example, American culture stigmatizes male crying. It's okay for little boys to cry, but becoming a man discourages this natural expression of joy and sadness. Why shouldn't men cry when they feel emotions? The movie entitled *Boys Don't Cry* tells the story of a female who dressed, acted, and for a time passed as a man; she was murdered for her transgression of gender norms. American men are trained to make decisions and stick to them. Politicians routinely criticize their opponents for being indecisive, for waffling or flip-flopping on issues. What a strange idea—that people shouldn't change their positions if they've discovered there's a better way. Cultural biases against flexibility probably have caused many wars. Males, females, and humanity may be equally victimized by aspects of cultural training.

Table 20.10 details employment in the United States in 2000 by gender, income, and job type. Notice that the income gap between women and men was widest in sales, where women averaged 60 percent the male salary. Overall, the ratio rose from 68 percent in 1989 to 76 percent in 2000.

Today's jobs aren't especially demanding in terms of physical labor. With machines to do the heavy work, the smaller average body size and lesser average strength of women are no longer impediments to blue-collar employment. The main reason we don't see more modern-day Rosies working alongside male riveters is that the U.S. work force itself is abandoning heavy-goods manufacture. In the 1950s, two-thirds of American jobs were blue-collar, compared with less than 15 percent today. The location of those jobs has shifted within the world capitalist economy. Third World countries with cheaper labor produce steel, automobiles, and other heavy goods less expensively than the United States can, but the United States excels at services. The American mass education system has many inadequacies, but it does train millions of people for service- and information-oriented jobs, from sales clerks to computer operators.

THE FEMINIZATION OF POVERTY

For more on gender differences and poverty, see the Internet Exercises at your OLC

mhhe ● com /kottak

Alongside the economic gains of many American women stands an opposite extreme: the feminization of poverty. This refers to the increasing representation of women (and their children) among America's poorest people. Women head over half of

Table 20.10 Earnings in the United States by Gender and Job Type for Year-Round Full-Time Workers, 2000*

| | Median Annual Salary | | Ratio of Earnings Female/Male | |
	Women	Men	2000	1989
Median earnings	$25,532	$33,592	76	68
By Job Type				
Executive/administrative/ managerial	$35,672	$52,728	68	61
Professional	37,700	50,804	74	71
Sales	21,164	35,568	60	54
Service	16,432	21,528	76	62

*By occupation of longest job held.

SOURCE: Based on data in *Statistical Abstract of the United States* 2001, Table 621, p. 403.

U.S. households with incomes below the poverty line. Feminine poverty has been a trend in the United States since World War II, but it has accelerated recently. In 1959, female-headed households accounted for just one-fourth of the American poor. Since then, that figure has more than doubled. About half the female poor are "in transition." These are women who are confronting a temporary economic crisis caused by the departure, disability, or death of a husband. The other half are more permanently dependent on the welfare system or on friends or relatives who live nearby (Schaefer and Lamm 1994). The feminization of poverty and its consequences in regard to living standards and health are widespread even among wage earners. Many American women continue to work part time for low wages and meager benefits.

Married couples are much more secure economically than single mothers are. The data in Table 20.11 demonstrate that the average income for married-couple families is more than twice that of families maintained by a woman. The average one-earner family maintained by a woman had an annual income of $26,164 in 1998. This was less than one-half the mean income ($56,827) of a married-couple household.

The feminization of poverty isn't just a North American trend. The percentage of female-headed households has been increasing worldwide. In Western Europe, for example, it rose from 24 percent in 1980 to 30 percent in 2000. The figure ranges from below 20 percent in certain South Asian and Southeast Asian countries to almost 50 percent in certain African countries and the Caribbean (Buvinic 1995).

Interpret the World In your atlas, Map 20, "Female/Male Inequality in Education and Employment," shows inequalities in cash employment and secondary education, by country, for 1999. Despite the continuing inequalities documented in this chapter, the United States, Canada, Western Europe, and Australia have less gender-based inequality in education and employment than most Third World countries do. In what regions is the gender gap most evident on Map 20?

Why must so many women be solo household heads? Where are the men going, and why are they leaving? Among the causes are male migration,

Table 20.11   Median Annual Income of U.S. Households, by Household Type, 1999

	Number Households (1000s)	Median Annual Income (Dollars)	Percentage of Median Earnings Compared with Married-Couple Households
All households	104,705	$40,816	72
Family households	72,025	49,940	88
Married-couple households	55,311	56,827	100
Male earner, no wife	4,028	41,838	74
Female earner, no husband	12,687	26,164	46
Nonfamily households	32,680	24,566	43
Single male	14,641	30,753	54
Single female	18,039	19,919	35

civil strife (men off fighting), divorce, abandonment, widowhood, unwed adolescent parenthood, and, more generally, the idea that children are women's responsibility.

Globally, households headed by women tend to be poorer than are those headed by men. In one study, the percentage of single-parent families considered poor was 18 percent in Britain, 20 percent in Italy, 25 percent in Switzerland, 40 percent in Ireland, 52 percent in Canada, and 63 percent in the United States. Poverty, of course, has health consequences. Studies in Brazil, Zambia, and the Philippines show the survival rates of children from female-headed households to be inferior to those of other children (Buvinic 1995).

In the United States, the feminization of poverty is a concern of the National Organization of Women. NOW still exists, alongside many newer women's organizations. The women's movement has become international in scope and membership. And its priorities have shifted from mainly job-oriented to more broadly social issues. These include poverty, homelessness, women's health care, day care, domestic violence, sexual assault, and reproductive rights (Calhoun, Light,

and Keller 1997). These issues and others that particularly affect women in the developing countries were addressed at the United Nations' Fourth World Conference on Women held in 1995 in Beijing. In attendance were women's groups from all over the world. Many of these were national and international NGOs (nongovernmental organizations), which work with women at the local level to augment productivity and improve access to credit.

It is widely believed that one way to improve the situation of poor women is to encourage them to organize. New women's groups can in some cases revive or replace traditional forms of social organization that have been disrupted. Membership in a group can help women to mobilize resources, to rationalize production, and to reduce the risks and costs associated with credit. Organization also allows women to develop self-confidence and to decrease dependence on others. Through such organization, poor women throughout the world are working to determine their own needs and priorities, and to change things so as to improve their social and economic situation (Buvinic 1995).

SUMMARY

1. *Gender roles* are the tasks and activities that a culture assigns to each sex. *Gender stereotypes* are oversimplified ideas about attributes of males and females. *Gender stratification* describes an unequal distribution of rewards by gender, reflecting different positions in a social hierarchy. Cross-cultural comparison reveals some recurrent patterns involving the division of labor by gender and gender-based differences in reproductive strategies. Gender roles and gender stratification also vary with environment, economy, adaptive strategy, level of social complexity, and degree of participation in the world economy.

2. When gathering is prominent, gender status is more equal than it is when hunting or fishing dominates the foraging economy. Gender status is more equal when the domestic and public spheres aren't sharply separated. Foragers lack two public arenas that contribute to higher male status among food producers: warfare and organized interregional trade.

3. Gender stratification also is linked to descent and residence. Women's status in matrilineal societies tends to be high because descent-group membership, political succession, land allocation, and overall social identity come through female links. Although there are no matriarchies, women in many societies wield power and make decisions. Scarcity of resources promotes intervillage warfare, patriliny, and patrilocality. The localization of related males is adaptive for military solidarity. Men may use their warrior role to symbolize and reinforce the social devaluation and oppression of women.

4. There has been a recent tendency to see sexual orientation as fixed and biologically based. But to some extent, at least, all human activities and preferences, including erotic expression, are influenced by culture. Sexual orientation stands for a person's habitual sexual attraction to, and activities with, persons of the opposite sex, *heterosexuality;* the same sex, *homosexuality;* or both sexes, *bisexuality.* Sexual norms vary widely from culture to culture.

5. With the advent of plow agriculture, women were removed from production. The distinction between women's domestic work and men's "productive" labor reinforced the contrast between men as public and valuable and women as homebound and inferior. Patriarchy describes a political system ruled by men in which women have inferior social and political status, including basic human rights. Some expressions of patriarchy include female infanticide, dowry murders, widow burning, domestic abuse, and forced genital operations.

6. Americans' attitudes toward gender vary with class and region. When the need for female labor declines, the idea that women are unfit for many jobs increases, and vice versa. Factors such as war, falling wages, and inflation help explain female cash employment and Americans' attitudes toward it. Countering the economic gains of many American women is the feminization of poverty. This has become a global phenomenon, as impoverished female-headed households have increased worldwide.

KEY TERMS

domestic–public dichotomy Contrast between women's role in the home and men's role in public life, with a corresponding social devaluation of women's work and worth.

extradomestic Outside the home; within or pertaining to the public domain.

gender roles The tasks and activities that a culture assigns to each sex.

gender stereotypes Oversimplified but strongly held ideas about the characteristics of males and females.

gender stratification Unequal distribution of rewards (socially valued resources, power, prestige, and personal freedom) between men and women, reflecting their different positions in a social hierarchy.

matrifocal   Mother-centered; often refers to a household with no resident husband-father.

patriarchy   Political system ruled by men in which women have inferior social and political status, including basic human rights.

patrilineal-patrilocal complex   An interrelated constellation of patrilineality, patrilocality, warfare, and male supremacy.

sexual dimorphism   Marked differences in male and female biology besides the contrasts in breasts and genitals.

sexual orientation   A person's habitual sexual attraction to, and activities with, persons of the opposite sex, heterosexuality; the same sex, homosexuality; or both sexes, bisexuality.

CRITICAL THINKING QUESTIONS

For more self testing, see the self quizzes

mhhe
●**com**
/kottak

1. Is anatomy destiny? What characteristics of men and women do you see as most directly linked to biological differences between the sexes? What kinds of characteristics are most influenced by culture?

2. Using your own society, give an example of a gender role, a gender stereotype, and gender stratification.

3. How do gender roles among northern foragers compare with those in U.S. or Canadian society?

4. Would you prefer to live in a society that is matrilineal and matrilocal or in one that is patrilineal and patrilocal? Why?

5. What lessons about human sexuality do you draw from the Etoro? How fixed is human sexual orientation, in your opinion?

6. Would you rather live in an agricultural or a horticultural society? Why?

7. What do you see as the main factor that has changed North American gender roles since

World War II? How do you expect gender roles to change in the next generation?

8. If you had to pick three factors that play a role in determining cross-cultural variation in gender roles, what would they be?

Atlas Questions

Look at Map 20, "Female/Male Inequality in Education and Employment."

1. Locate and name three Third World countries with the same degree of gender-based inequality as the United States and Canada.

2. Two of the world's largest developing nations are coded as having "less inequality." What are they?

3. Most European countries are coded as having "least inequality." Which western European countries are exceptions?

SUGGESTED ADDITIONAL READINGS

Behar, R., and D. A. Gordon, eds.
1995   *Women Writing Culture.* Berkeley: University of California Press. Feminist scholars reflect on identity and difference.

Blackwood, E.
2000   *Webs of Power: Women, Kin, and Community in a Sumatran Village.* Lanham, MD: Rowman and Littlefield. Women, sex-gender roles, and social conditions in a matrilineal society: the Minangkabau.

Blackwood, E., and S. Wieringa, eds.

1999   *Female Desires: Same-Sex Relations and Transgender Practices across Cultures*. New York: Columbia University Press. Lesbianism and male homosexuality in cross-cultural perspective.

Bonvillain, N.

2001   *Women and Men: Cultural Constructions of Gender*, 3rd ed. Upper Saddle River, NJ: Prentice-Hall. A cross-cultural study of gender roles and relationships, from bands to industrial societies.

Carver, T.

1996   *Gender Is Not a Synonym for Women*. Boulder, CO: Lynne Reinner. Gender in relation to class, race, ethnicity, sex, and sexuality.

Connell, R. W.

1995   *Masculinities*. Berkeley: University of California Press. Changing notions of masculinity in the context of a global economy.

2002   *Gender*. Malden, MA: Blackwell. Sex-gender roles, gender identity, and sexuality.

Dahlberg, F., ed.

1981   *Woman the Gatherer*. New Haven, CT: Yale University Press. Female roles and activities among prehistoric and contemporary foragers.

Gilchrist, R.

1999   *Gender and Archaeology: Contesting the Past*. New York: Routledge. Feminist perspectives in archaeology.

Gilmore, D.

1991   *Manhood in the Making: Cultural Concepts of Masculinity*. New Haven, CT: Yale University Press. Cross-cultural study of manhood as an achieved status.

2001   *Misogyny: The Male Malady*. Philadelphia: University of Pennsylvania Press. Why men devalue women.

Kimmel, M. S., and M. A. Messner, eds.

2001   *Men's Lives*, 5th ed. Boston: Allyn & Bacon. The study of men in society and concepts of masculinity in the United States.

Lamphere, L., H. Ragone, and P. Zavella, eds.

1997   *Situated Lives: Gender and Culture in Everyday Life*. New York: Routledge. Essays on gender and culture as illustrated by everyday social interaction.

Lancaster, R. N., and M. Di Leonardo, eds.

1997   *The Gender/Sexuality Reader: Culture, History, Political Economy*. New York: Routledge. Gender and sexuality in history and in the modern social context.

Miller, B. D., ed.

1993   *Sex and Gender Hierarchies*. New York: Cambridge University Press. A series of articles, including several essays on human gender hierarchies, as well as those of nonhuman primates.

Nelson, S. N., and M. Rosen-Ayalon, eds.

2002   *In Pursuit of Gender: Worldwide Archaeological Approaches*. Social archaeology, history of gender roles, and women in prehistory.

Peplau, L. A., ed.

1999   *Gender, Culture, and Ethnicity: Current Research about Women and Men*. Mountain View, CA: Mayfield. Gender in relation to ethnic issues.

Pollard, T. M., and S. B. Hyatt

1999   *Sex, Gender, and Health*. New York: Cambridge University Press. This study in medical anthropology relates health conditions and gender cross-culturally.

Rathus, S. A., J. S. Nevid, and J. Fichner-Rathus

2000   *Human Sexuality in a World of Diversity*, 4th ed. Boston: Allyn & Bacon. Multicultural and ethnic perspectives.

Reiter, R., ed.

1975   *Toward an Anthropology of Women*. New York: Monthly Review Press. Classic anthology, with a particular focus on peasant societies.

Rosaldo, M. Z., and L. Lamphere, eds.

1974   *Woman, Culture, and Society*. Stanford, CA: Stanford University Press. Another classic anthology, covering many areas of the world.

Ward, M. C.

2003   *A World Full of Women*. 3rd ed. Boston: Allyn & Bacon. A global and comparative approach to the study of women.

INTERNET EXERCISES

1. *Gender in the Classroom*: Read the article "Student Ratings of Professors Are Not Gender Blind" by Susan Basow, **http://eserver.org/feminism/workplace/fces-not-gender-blind.txt**.

   a. How much difference is there between male and female students who are rating a male professor? How much difference is there between male and female students in rating a female professor?

   b. What are the added expectations students have for female professors? What do you think is the source of those expectations? Do you think the expectations discussed in this article hold true for female teachers all over the world?

   c. Do you think the findings of this study are consistent with the way you and your friends rate professors?

2. *Gender on the Internet*: Read the paper by Amy Bruckman entitled "Gender Swapping on the Internet," **www.inform.umd.edu/EdRes/Topic/WomensStudies/Computing/Articles+Research Papers/gender-swapping**.

   a. Do gender roles exist on the Internet, such as in the MUDs described in this article, or in chat rooms, or e-mail? Do gender roles belong on the Internet? Would it be possible for people to remain gender-neutral on the Internet indefinitely?

   b. Imagine you are using a MUD. You encounter a character with a gender-neutral name (like Pat) and description. What clues would you use to identify the gender of Pat and Pat's user? Do you think this detective work would be more or less difficult if Pat's user was also from a different culture than your own?

   c. Do the cases described in this paper say more about the person swapping genders or about the other users?

   See Chapter 20 at your McGraw-Hill Online Learning Center for additional review and interactive exercises.

BRINGING IT ALL TOGETHER

The Basques

The Basque people of Spain and France, and their diaspora, including their migration to the United States, have attracted the attention of anthropology's four subfields. Having maintained a strong ethnic identity, perhaps for millennia, the Basques are linguistically unique in that their language is unrelated to any other known language. Genetic differences also set them off from neighboring European populations.

Their homeland lies in the western Pyrenees mountains, straddling the French-Spanish border. Seven traditional provinces within Basque country (three in France and four in Spain) are distinguished by dialect differences. Basques refer to their homeland as Euskal-Herria ("Land of the Basques") or Euskadi ("Country of the Basques"). Although their seven regions have not been unified politically for nearly a millennium, the Basques remain one of Europe's most distinctive ethnic groups.

Romans, Goths, Franks, and Moors all controlled parts of Basque country without ever totally subduing it. For the last thousand years the Basque territory has been influenced by European polities. Yet for much of this time the Basques have managed to retain significant autonomy in their affairs.

The French Revolution of 1789 ended the political autonomy of the three Basque provinces in France. During the 19th century in Spain the Basques fought on the losing side in two internal wars, yielding much of their political autonomy in defeat. When the Spanish Civil War broke out in 1936, the Basques remained loyal to the republic, opposing the eventual Spanish dictator, Francisco Franco, who eventually defeated them. Under Franco's rule (1936–1975), Basques were executed, imprisoned, and exiled, and Basque culture was systematically repressed.

In the late 1950s disaffected Basque youths founded ETA (Euskadi Ta Azkatasuna, or "Basque Country and Freedom"). Its goal was complete independence from Spain. Its opposition to Franco escalated into violence, which continues today among ETA members who seek full independence (see Zulaika 1988). Franco's death in 1975 ushered in an era of democracy in Spain. Mainline Basque nationalists collaborated in framing a new constitution which gave considerable autonomy to the Basque regions (Trask 1996).

Since 1979 the three Spanish Basque provinces of Vizcaya, Guipuzcoa, and Alava have been united as the Basque Autonomous Region, which governs the Basque homeland. The Basque language is co-official with Spanish in this territory. Spain's fourth Basque province, Navarra, formed its own autonomous region, where the Basque language has a degree of official standing. In France, like other regional languages, Basque has been victimized for centuries by laws hostile to languages other than French (Trask 1996).

The ancestral form of the Basque language reached Western Europe thousands—perhaps even tens of thousands—of years ago—from where we

The prolific Spanish painter Pablo Picasso portrayed the destruction of a Basque town in his famous painting *Guernica* (1937).

Location of the Basque homeland.

Lapurdi
Vizcaya
Guipuzcoa
Benaparre
Zuberoa
Alava
Navarra
La Rioja

Basque Autonomous Region

ATLANTIC OCEAN

FRANCE
PORTUGAL
SPAIN

0   100   200 mi
0   100   200 km

tion, publishing, and broadcasting now proceeds in Basque in the Autonomous Region. Still, Basque faces the same pressures that all other minority languages do: Knowledge of the national language (Spanish or French) is essential, and most education, publishing, and broadcasting is in the national language (Trask 1996).

How long have the Basques been in their homeland? Some scholars believe the Basques may be direct descendants of the Upper Paleolithic cave painters active in southwestern Europe 15,000 years ago. Archaeological evidence suggests that a single group of people lived in the Basque country continuously from late Paleolithic times through the Bronze Age (about 3,000 years ago). There is no evidence to suggest that any new population entered the area after that. However, such an intrusion cannot be ruled out (La Fraugh n.d.).

We've seen that linguistically the Basques are absolutely distinct. To an extent, they also contrast biologically with other Europeans. For example, Basques have the highest proportion of RH-negative blood in Europe (25 percent), and one of the highest percentages of type O blood (55 percent). The geneticist Luigi Cavalli-Sforza (2000), who developed a gene map of Europe, found the Basques to be strikingly different from their neighbors.

However, a recent genetic study involving the Y chromosome, which is passed exclusively from father to son, establishes links between the Basques and the Celts of Wales and Ireland. In terms of the Y chromosome, the researchers found Celts and Basques to be statistically indistinguishable (Wade 2001).

Historically the Basques have been herders, fishers, and farmers. (Today most of them work in business and industry.) Through the Middle Ages they were mainly herders. As Europe's earliest and most efficient whalers, Basques may have reached North America before Columbus did. There is documentation of Basque whaling and cod fishing along Canada's Labrador coast by 1500. Some Atlantic coastal Native American languages in Canada have Basque loan words. Canadian archivists and archeologists have discovered a 16th-century Basque whaling station (used seasonally) and a sunken whaling ship at Red Bay, Labrador. Basque activity in Canadian coastal waters lasted into the 19th century (Douglass 1992).

The Basque homeland contains major cities, along with coastal fishing communities and farming

cannot say. All the other modern languages of Western Europe arrived much later. Spreading across Europe from the east, the Indo-European languages, such as Latin, Germanic, and Celtic, gradually displaced all but one of the indigenous languages. When the Romans invaded Gaul (France), an early form of Basque, known as Aquitanian, was the only non-Indo-European language that survived there. In Spain, several pre-Indo-European languages were still spoken, including Aquitanian and Iberian. Latin replaced them all, with the sole exception of Aquitanian (ancestral Basque) (Trask 1996).

After generations of decline, the number of Basque speakers is increasing today. Much educa-

Women unload the catch in Bermeo, a Basque fishing village in Spain. Fishing, farming, and herding are mainstays of the Basque economy.

Basque Americans

Basque immigrants originally entered North America as either Spanish or French nationals. Basque Americans, numbering some 50,000, now invoke Basqueness as their primary ethnic identity. They are concentrated in California, Idaho, and Nevada. First-generation immigrants are usually fluent in Basque. They are more likely to be bilingual in Basque and English than to have their parents' fluency in Spanish or French (Douglass 1992).

Building on a traditional occupation in Basque country, Basques in the United States are notable for their identification with sheep herding (see Ott 1981). Most of them settled and worked in the open-range livestock districts of the 13 states of the American West. Basques first entered the western United States as agents of Spanish colonialism. They numbered among the Spanish soldiers, explorers, missionaries, and administrators in the American Southwest and Spanish California. More Basques came during the California gold rush, many from southern South America, where they were established sheep herders. In the 1870s Basque shepherds spread throughout California's central valleys and expanded into Arizona, New Mexico, and western Nevada (Douglass 1992).

Restrictive immigration laws enacted in the 1920s, which had an anti–southern European bias, limited Basque immigration to the United States. During World War II, with the country in need of shepherds, the U.S. government exempted Basque herders from immigration quotas. Between 1950 and 1975, several thousand Basques entered the United States on three-year contracts. Later, the decline of the U.S. sheep industry would slow Basque immigration dramatically (Douglass 1992).

With that decline, many Basque herders returned to Europe; others converted sheep ranches to cattle. Many more moved to nearby small towns where they did construction work or established small businesses (bars, bakeries, motels, gasoline stations). Wherever jai alai (words which mean "happy festival" in Basque) is legal, Basque players are recruited from Europe. They play part of the year in Basque country and the rest in the United States (Douglass 1992).

Catering to Basque sheep herders, most western towns in the open-range country had one or more Basque boardinghouses. The typical one had

(peasant) villages. The typical peasant village includes a river valley, where the village is seated, and the surrounding hillsides, which have *baserriak*, or farmsteads. These houses are large stone structures, often three stories tall. The ground floor is for animal stables; the second floor is living space, while the third is used to store hay and other crops (Douglass 1992).

The Basque *basseria* (family farm) once thrived as a mixed-farming unit emphasizing self-sufficiency. The farm family grew wheat, corn, vegetables, fruits, and nuts and raised poultry, rabbits, pigs, cows, and sheep. Subsistence pursuits have become increasingly commercialized, with the production of vegetables, dairy products, and fish aimed at urban markets (Greenwood 1976).

On the family farm, the stem family was the basic social unit. This included an older couple, their heir (usually male), and his wife and children. Unmarried siblings of the heir could reside in their natal households until death, but they had to respect the authority of the male and female heads. The household had to approve the selection of the spouse of the designated heir. Ownership of the farm was transferred to the newlyweds as part of the marital arrangements—to a single heir(ess) in each generation. By custom, male primogeniture was preferred. Siblings who married and moved away received dowries. Because only one child was socialized into the role of the heir(ess), his or her siblings were raised anticipating that they would leave. This system has made the rural Basque country a font of emigration (Douglass 1975, 1992).

a bar and a dining room, where meals were served family-style at long tables. A second floor of sleeping rooms was reserved for permanent boarders. Also lodged were herders in town for a brief visit, vacation, or employment layoff or in transit to an employer (Echeverria 1999).

Both traditionally and in the United States, Basque culture has promoted a degree of equality between men and women. In farming, women and men have shared many tasks, including working together in the fields. In Basque cities, where women are increasingly employed in industry and services, there is a income gender gap comparable to the one that exists in the United States. Although domestic tasks remain largely the domain of women, they are not regarded as demeaning for men, including sheep herders. Also, whether running a ranching operation, a boardinghouse, or a town business, Basque-American women work alongside men and perform virtually any task (Douglass 1992).

Ths social glue that holds Basque Americans together includes extended bilateral kinship and affinal ties. Basque men recruited their brothers and cousins to herd sheep in the American West. Basque-American colonies often included family clusters, with local endogamy increasing the degree of interrelatedness. Even today, extended Basque-American families maintain close ties, as they gather for baptisms, graduations, weddings, and funerals (Douglass 1992).

Initially, few Basques came to the United States intending to stay. Most early immigrants were young, unmarried men. The transhumant sheep herding pattern, with solitary summers in the mountains, did not fit well with family life. Eventually, Basque men came with the intent to stay. They either sent back or went back to Europe for brides (few married non-Basques). Many brides, of the "mail order" sort, were sisters or cousins of an acquaintance made in the United States. Basque boardinghouses also became a source of spouses. The boardinghouse owners sent back to Europe for women willing to come to America as domestics. Few remained single for long (Douglass 1992). In these ways Basque Americans drew on their homeland society and culture in establishing the basis of their family and community life in North America.

Among the homeland patterns that the Basques transferred from the Old World to the New were transhumant herding, a blurred division of labor by gender in farming and industry, ethnic endogamy,

and strong family ties. Yet another is the role of unrelated neighbors, who traditionally played an important role in rural Basque society (Douglass 1992). After the family, the most important social institution for Basque Americans has been the boardinghouse, where Basques could again draw on the support of their neighbors. The boardinghouse was a multifunctional institution that served as a town address, a bank, an employment agency, an ethnic haven, a source of help and advice, a place to leave one's possessions, a possible source of a bride, and a potential retirement home. For the Basque American, it was a place to recharge ethnic batteries, practice one's rusty Basque, learn something about traditional culture, dance to Basque music, eat Basque cuisine, hire help, and hold baptisms, weddings, and wakes (Douglass 1992; Echeverria 1999).

Basques have not escaped discrimination in the United States. In the American West, sheep herding is an occupation that carries some stigma. Mobile sheep herders competed with settled livestock interests for access to the range. These were some of the sources of anti-Basque sentiment and even legislation. More recently, newspaper coverage of enduring conflict in the Basque country, particularly the activities of the ETA, has made Basque Americans sensitive to the possible charge of being terrorist sympathizers (Douglass 1992; see also Zulaika 1988).

The herding of sheep, shown here in the Basque homeland (Pyrenees), remained a primary occupation of Basque men who started migrating to the American West in the 19th century.

21
RELIGION

Overview

Religion is a cultural universal. It consists of beliefs and behavior concerned with supernatural beings, powers, and forces. Cross-cultural studies have revealed many expressions and functions of religion. These include explanatory, emotional, social, and ecological functions.

People may use magic to try to influence outcomes over which they have no technical or rational control. Religion can provide comfort and psychological security at times of crisis. But rites also can create anxiety. Rituals are formal, invariant, earnest acts that require people to join actively in a social collectivity. Rites of passage may mark any change in social status, age, place, or social condition. Collective rituals often are cemented by communitas, a feeling of intense fellowship and solidarity.

Religion establishes and maintains social control. It does this through a series of moral and ethical beliefs, along with real and imagined rewards and punishments, internalized in individuals. Religion also achieves social control by mobilizing its members for collective action. Although it maintains social order, religion also can promote change. Religious movements aimed at the revitalization of society have helped people cope with changing conditions.

Contemporary religious trends include both rising secularism and a resurgence of religious fundamentalism. Some of today's new religions are inspired by science and technology; others, by spiritualism. Rituals can be secular as well as religious.

Rising Muslim Power in Africa Causes Unrest in Nigeria and Elsewhere

NEW YORK TIMES NEWS BRIEF

by Norimitsu Onishi

November 1, 2001

In today's world, local religious practices aren't separate, discrete, and self-sustaining; they depend on external support. World religions go on battling—and paying—for the hearts, minds, and souls of local people. Religious expressions in Nigeria are financed, at least partly, by outsiders. Saudi Arabia funds Islamic projects in Nigeria. Donations in North American churches also find their way to African countries, but this article suggests that Islam, which is spreading more rapidly than Christianity is, has more reliable external funding. How does and should religion fit into nation-states? Should religious principles and beliefs be the basis of the legal code? Can laws based on religion work in nation-states that contain strong religious differences?

KANO, Nigeria— . . . Islam in sub-Saharan Africa, an often overlooked member of the world's Muslim community, is growing in size and influence . . . Most experts agree that Islam is spreading faster than any other faith in East and West Africa. In Africa it is not difficult to see why. Islamic values have much in common with traditional African life: its emphasis on communal living, its clear roles for men and women, its tolerance of polygamy. Christianity, Muslims argue, was alien to most Africans. Today, while Islam embraces the poor, they add, Christian churches are more interested in making money—a criticism that is widely shared by many African Christians. . . .

Islam came to sub-Saharan Africa on camel caravans that crossed the Sahara and boats that crossed the Indian Ocean; Christianity arrived from Europe on the coasts of West Africa and in much of central and southern Africa. Today, northern Africa is predominantly Muslim and the south is Christian. In between, the two religions rub shoulders uneasily.

In East Africa, in Kenya and Tanzania, where American embassies were bombed in 1998, Muslims have long been shut out of power. That has given rise there, as well as in Uganda, to the emergence of radical Islam.

Radicals have organized themselves politically and some have received military help from the Islamist government of Sudan.

In turn, the governments of Kenya and Uganda have supported rebels opposed to the Sudanese government. In the Horn of Africa, governmental collapse in Somalia in the last decade led to a rigid application of Islamic law. In Sudan and Chad, Muslim northerners have long dominated Christians in the south, and new oil wealth is likely to tip the balance more in their favor. Sudan's Islamic government has sharpened its war against the Christians in the last year; Chad's Islamic government is likely to face opposition once it starts pumping oil in the Christian south in a few years.

In West Africa, Ivory Coast has seen its Muslim population grow politically unified. In a country that was once a model of tolerance, successive Christian leaders in the last decade have sidelined Muslims, who have come to identify themselves as Muslims, first, Ivorians, second. Even in countries with near-total Muslim populations, like Mali or Niger, Islamic clerics have begun agitating and challenging their governments. But it is in Nigeria, Africa's most populated country, that the rise of Islam as a political force has been most explosive and violent. It began shortly after the country emerged [in 1999] from nearly 16 years of ruinous military rule. The 120 million inhabitants were living in a society where

Muslims before an Islamic mosque in Kano, northern Nigeria.

almost everything had collapsed. Their leaders were above laws and preyed on ordinary people.

Perhaps sensing this void, the leaders of a small northern state called Zamfara introduced Islamic law, or Shariah, in late 1999. The move proved wildly popular.

Crime has reportedly dropped in some of the states with Shariah, with all of them banning alcohol and prostitution. Women are pressed to cover their hair; girls are separated from boys at school, if they are schooled at all.

Cow thieves have had their hands cut off. A teenage girl was given 100 cane strokes for premarital sex; another woman has just been sentenced to death by stoning for adultery . . .

When Shariah was introduced last year in the northern city of Kano, Nigeria's biggest Muslim city, hundreds of thousands celebrated downtown. No one had ever seen such a crowd. Kano has been a center of a new generation of radical Islamic preachers who have been spreading anti-Western messages here and pressing the government to impose Shariah. . . .

Asked to explain the emergence of Islam in politics, Dr. Ibrahim D. Ahmad . . . said: "It is the failure of every system we have known. We had colonialism, which was exploitative. We had a brief period of happiness after independence, then the military came in, and everything has been going downward since then. But before all this, we had a system that worked. We had Shariah. We are Muslims. Why don't we return to ourselves?"

Islam came centuries ago to the Hausa ethnic group who dominate northern Nigeria. Two hundred years ago a famous jihad was started to spread Islam as far south as possible. The jihad reached the center of the country, now known as the Middlebelt, where the Hausa converted the natives to Islam. But the campaign stopped at Jos, the capital of Plateau state, about 200 miles south of here. The effects of the jihad linger still, especially in areas inhabited by Hausa settlers and natives who resisted Islam, eventually becoming Christian or remaining animist. . . .

To Christians in Jos, Muslims are more aggressive and are getting strong support from the Arab world. By contrast, African Christians can no longer rely on the backing of a secular West.

"We have been abandoned by the West—the West no longer believes in God," Bishop Kwashi said on Sunday . . . in Jos. "If a church here goes to America for assistance, it might get $10,000, $15,000 a year. But when the Saudis fund a project, they will fund it from start to finish." . . .

SOURCE: Norimitsu Onishi, "Rising Muslim Power in Africa Causes Unrest in Nigeria and Elsewhere," *New York Times*, November 1, 2001, late edition—final, section A, p. 14, column 1.

The anthropologist Anthony F. C. Wallace has defined **religion** as "belief and ritual concerned with supernatural beings, powers, and forces" (1966, p. 5). Like ethnicity or language, religion may be associated with social divisions within and between societies and nations, such as Nigeria. Religious behavior and beliefs both unite and divide. Participation in common rites may affirm, and thus maintain, the social solidarity of a religion's adherents. However, religious differences may be associated with bitter enmity, again as in Nigeria, where the divide between Christians and Muslims has fueled rioting and killing.

In studying religion cross-culturally, anthropologists pay attention not only to the social roles of religion but also to the content and nature of religious acts, events, processes, settings, practitioners, and organizations. We also consider such verbal manifestations of religious beliefs as prayers, chants, myths, texts, and statements about ethics and morality.

The supernatural is the extraordinary realm outside (but believed to impinge on) the observable world. It is nonempirical, mysterious, and inexplicable in ordinary terms. It must be accepted "on faith." Supernatural beings—gods and goddesses, ghosts, and souls—are not of the material world. Nor are supernatural forces, some of which are wielded by beings. Other sacred forces are impersonal; they simply exist. In many societies, however, people believe they can benefit from, become imbued with, or manipulate supernatural forces.

Religion, as defined here, exists in all human societies. It is a cultural universal. However, we'll see that it isn't always easy to distinguish the supernatural from the natural and that different cultures conceptualize supernatural entities very differently.

Origins, Functions, and Expressions of Religion

When did religion begin? No one knows for sure. There are suggestions of religion in Neandertal burials and on European cave walls, where painted stick figures may represent shamans, early religious specialists. Nevertheless, any statement about when, where, why, and how religion arose, or any description of its original nature, can only be speculative. However, although such speculations are inconclusive, many have revealed important functions and effects of religious behavior. Several theories will be examined now.

ANIMISM

The founder of the anthropology of religion was the Englishman Sir Edward Burnett Tylor (1871/1958). Religion was born, Tylor thought, as people tried to understand conditions and events they could not explain by reference to daily experience. Tylor believed that our ancestors—and contemporary nonindustrial peoples—were particularly intrigued with death, dreaming, and trance.

Ancient Greek polytheism is illustrated by this image of Apollo, with a lyre, and Artemis, sacrificing over an altar fire. The red-figured terra-cotta vessel dates to 490–480 BCE.

In dreams and trances, people see images they may remember when they wake up or come out of the trance state.

Tylor concluded that attempts to explain dreams and trances led early humans to believe that two entities inhabit the body: one active during the day and the other—a double or soul—active during sleep and trance states. Although they never meet, they are vital to each other. When the double permanently leaves the body, the person dies. Death is departure of the soul. From the Latin for soul, *anima*, Tylor named this belief animism. The soul was one sort of spiritual entity; people remembered various images from their dreams and trances—other spirits. For Tylor, **animism**, the earliest form of religion, was a belief in spiritual beings.

Tylor proposed that religion evolved through stages, beginning with animism. *Polytheism* (the belief in multiple gods) and then *monotheism* (the belief in a single, all-powerful deity) developed later. Because religion originated to explain things people didn't understand, Tylor thought it would decline as science offered better explanations. To an extent, he was right. We now have scientific explanations for many things that religion once elucidated. Nevertheless, because religion persists, it must do something more than explain the mysterious. It must, and does, have other functions and meanings.

MANA AND TABOO

Besides animism—and sometimes coexisting with it in the same society—is a view of the supernatural as a domain of raw impersonal power, or *force*, that people can control under certain conditions. (You'd be right to think of *Star Wars*.) Such a conception of the supernatural is particularly prominent in Melanesia, the area of the South Pacific that includes Papua New Guinea and adjacent islands. Melanesians believed in mana, a sacred impersonal force existing in the universe. Mana can reside in people, animals, plants, and objects.

Melanesian mana was similar to our notion of efficacy or luck. Melanesians attributed success to mana,

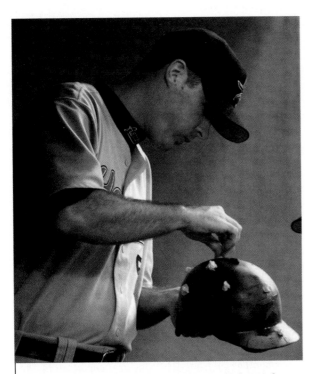

Mana is a supernatural force or power, which people may manipulate for their own ends. Mana can reside in people, animals, plants, and objects—even bubble gum. Illustrating baseball magic, Houston Astros pitcher Scott Elarton covers the helmet of teammate Craig Biggio with wads of lucky gum during a game against Detroit on July 14, 2000. Do you own anything that contains mana? Do you need mana to beat the Detroit Tigers?

which people could acquire or manipulate in different ways, such as through magic. Objects with mana could change someone's luck. For example, a charm or amulet belonging to a successful hunter might transmit the hunter's mana to the next person who held or wore it. A woman might put a rock in her garden, see her yields improve dramatically, and attribute the change to the force contained in the rock.

Beliefs in manalike forces are widespread, although the specifics of the religious doctrines vary. Consider the contrast between mana in Melanesia and Polynesia (the islands included in a triangular area marked by Hawaii to the north, Easter Island to the east, and New Zealand to the southwest). In Melanesia, one could acquire mana by chance, or by working hard to get it. In Polynesia, however, mana wasn't potentially available to everyone but was attached to political offices.

Chiefs and nobles had more mana than ordinary people did.

So charged with mana were the highest chiefs that contact with them was dangerous to the commoners. The mana of chiefs flowed out of their bodies wherever they went. It could infect the ground, making it dangerous for others to walk in the chief's footsteps. It could permeate the containers and utensils chiefs used in eating. Contact between chief and commoners was dangerous because mana could have an effect like an electric shock. Because high chiefs had so much mana, their bodies and possessions were taboo (set apart as sacred and off-limits to ordinary people). Contact between a high chief and commoners was forbidden. Because ordinary people couldn't bear as much sacred current as royalty could, when commoners were accidentally exposed, purification rites were necessary.

One role of religion is to explain (see Horton 1993). A belief in souls explains what happens in sleep, trance, and death. Melanesian mana explains differential success that people can't understand in ordinary, natural terms. People fail at hunting, war, or gardening not because they are lazy, stupid, or inept but because success comes—or doesn't come—from the supernatural world.

The beliefs in spiritual beings (e.g., animism) and supernatural forces (e.g., mana) fit within the definition of religion given at the beginning of this chapter. Most religions include both spirits and impersonal forces. Likewise, the supernatural beliefs of contemporary North Americans include beings (gods, saints, souls, demons) and forces (charms, talismans, crystals, and sacred objects).

MAGIC AND RELIGION

Magic refers to supernatural techniques intended to accomplish specific aims. These techniques include spells, formulas, and incantations used with deities or with impersonal forces. Magicians use *imitative magic* to produce a desired effect by imitating it. If magicians wish to injure or kill someone, they may imitate that effect on an image of the victim. Sticking pins in "voodoo dolls" is an example. With *contagious magic,* whatever is done to an object is believed to affect a person who once had contact with it. Sometimes practitioners of contagious magic use body products from prospective victims—their nails or hair, for example. The spell performed on the body product is believed to reach the person eventually and work the desired result.

We find magic in cultures with diverse religious beliefs. It can be associated with animism, mana, polytheism, or monotheism. Magic is neither simpler nor more primitive than animism or the belief in mana.

ANXIETY, CONTROL, SOLACE

Religion and magic don't just explain things and help people accomplish goals. They also enter the realm of human feelings. In other words, they serve emotional needs as well as cognitive (e.g., explanatory) ones. For example, supernatural beliefs and practices can help reduce anxiety. Magical techniques can dispel doubts that arise when outcomes are beyond human control. Similarly, religion helps people face death and endure life crises.

Although all societies have techniques to deal with everyday matters, there are certain aspects of people's lives over which they lack control. When people face uncertainty and danger, according to Malinowski, they turn to magic.

> [H]owever much knowledge and science help man in allowing him to obtain what he wants, they are unable completely to control chance, to eliminate accidents, to foresee the unexpected turn of natural events, or to make human handiwork reliable and adequate to all practical requirements. (Malinowski 1931/1978, p. 39)

Malinowski found that the Trobriand Islanders used magic when sailing, a hazardous activity. He proposed that because people can't control matters such as wind, weather, and the fish supply, they turn to magic. People may call on magic when they come to a gap in their knowledge or powers of practical control yet have to continue in a pursuit (Malinowski 1931/1978).

For information on Ecuadorian curers, see the Internet Exercises at your OLC

According to Malinowski, magic is used to establish control, but religion "is born out of . . . the real tragedies of human life" (1931/1978, p. 45). Religion offers emotional comfort, particularly when people face a crisis. Malinowski saw tribal religions as concerned mainly with organizing, commemorating, and helping

people get through such life events as birth, puberty, marriage, and death.

RITUALS

Several features distinguish rituals from other kinds of behavior (Rappaport 1974). Rituals are formal—stylized, repetitive, and stereotyped. People perform them in special (sacred) places and at set times. Rituals include *liturgical orders*—sequences of words and actions invented prior to the current performance of the ritual in which they occur.

These features link rituals to plays, but there are important differences. Plays have audiences rather than participants. Actors merely *portray* something, but ritual performers—who make up congregations—are in earnest. Rituals convey information about the participants and their traditions. Repeated year after year, generation after generation, rituals translate enduring messages, values, and sentiments into action.

For information on spiritual beliefs among Native Australians, see the Internet Exercises at your OLC

Rituals are *social* acts. Inevitably, some participants are more committed than others are to the beliefs that lie behind the rites. However, just by taking part in a joint public act, the performers signal that they accept a common social and moral order, one that transcends their status as individuals.

RITES OF PASSAGE

Magic and religion, as Malinowski noted, can reduce anxiety and allay fears. Ironically, beliefs and rituals also can *create* anxiety and a sense of insecurity and danger (Radcliffe-Brown 1962/1965). Anxiety may arise *because* a rite exists. Indeed, participation in a collective ritual may build up stress, whose common reduction, through the completion of the ritual, enhances the solidarity of the participants.

Rites of passage, for example, the collective circumcision of teenagers, can be very stressful. The traditional vision quests of Native Americans, particularly the Plains Indians, illustrate **rites of passage** (customs associated with the transition from one place or stage of life to another), which are found throughout the world. Among the Plains Indians, to move from boyhood to manhood, a youth temporarily separated from his community.

Trobriand Islanders prepare a traditional trading canoe for use in the Kula, which is a regional exchange system. The woman's basket contains trade goods, while the men prepare the long canoe to set sail. Magic is often associated with uncertainty, such as sailing in unpredictable waters.

After a period of isolation in the wilderness, often featuring fasting and drug consumption, the young man would see a vision, which would become his guardian spirit. He would then return to his community as an adult.

The rites of passage of contemporary cultures include confirmations, baptisms, bar and bat mitzvah, and fraternity hazing. Passage rites involve changes in social status, such as from boyhood to manhood and from nonmember to sorority sister. There are also rites and rituals in our business and corporate lives. Examples include promotion and retirement parties. More generally, a rite of passage may mark any change in place, condition, social position, or age.

All rites of passage have three phases: separation, liminality, and incorporation. In the first phase, people withdraw from the group and begin moving from one place or status to another. In the third phase, they reenter society, having completed the rite. The *liminal* phase is the most interesting. It is the period between states, the limbo during which people have left one place or state but haven't yet entered or joined the next (Turner 1974).

Liminality always has certain characteristics. Liminal people occupy ambiguous social positions. They exist apart from ordinary distinctions and expectations, living in a time out of time. They are cut off from normal social contacts. A variety of contrasts may demarcate liminality from regular social life. For example, among the Ndembu of Zambia, a chief underwent a rite of passage before taking office. During the liminal period, his past and future positions in society were ignored, even reversed. He was subjected to a variety of insults, orders, and humiliations.

Unlike the vision quest and the Ndembu initiation, which are individual experiences, passage rites are often collective. Several individuals—boys being circumcised, fraternity or sorority initiates, men at military boot camps, football players in summer training camps, women becoming nuns—pass through the rites together as a group. Table 21.1 summarizes the contrasts or oppositions between liminality and normal social life.

Most notable is a social aspect of *collective liminality* called **communitas** (Turner 1969), an

Table 21.1 Oppositions between Liminality and Normal Social Life

Liminality	Normal Social Structure
Transition	State
Homogeneity	Heterogeneity
Communitas	Structure
Equality	Inequality
Anonymity	Names
Absence of property	Property
Absence of status	Status
Nakedness or uniform dress	Dress distinctions
Sexual continence or excess	Sexuality
Minimization of sex distinctions	Maximization of sex distinctions
Absence of rank	Rank
Humility	Pride
Disregard of personal appearance	Care for personal appearance
Unselfishness	Selfishness
Total obedience	Obedience only to superior rank
Sacredness	Secularity
Sacred instruction	Technical knowledge
Silence	Speech
Simplicity	Complexity
Acceptance of pain and suffering	Avoidance of pain and suffering

SOURCE: Adapted from Victor W. Turner, *The Ritual Process.* Copyright © 1969 by Victor W. Turner. By permission of Aldine de Gruyter, New York.

intense community spirit, a feeling of great social solidarity, equality, and togetherness. People experiencing liminality together form a community of equals. The social distinctions that have existed before or will exist afterward are temporarily forgotten. Liminal people experience the same treatment and conditions and must act alike. Liminality may be marked ritually and symbolically by reversals of ordinary behavior. For example, sexual taboos may be intensified, or, conversely, sexual excess may be encouraged.

Liminality is a basic part of every passage rite. Furthermore, in certain societies, including our own, liminal symbols may be used to set off one (religious) group from another, and from society as a whole. Such "permanent liminal groups" (e.g., sects, brotherhoods, and cults) are found most characteristically in complex societies—nation-states. Liminal features such as humility, poverty, equality, obedience, sexual abstinence, and silence may be required for all sect or cult members. Those who join such a

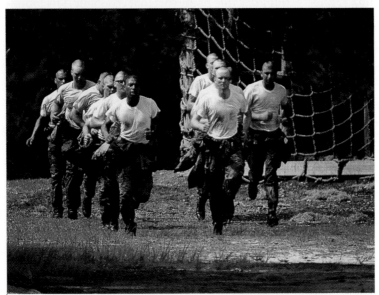

Passage rites are often collective. A group—such as these initiates in Togo or these Marine recruits in South Carolina—passes through the rites as a unit. Such liminal people experience the same treatment and conditions and must act alike. They share communitas, an intense community spirit, a feeling of great social solidarity or togetherness.

In a variety of contexts, liminal features signal the sacredness or distinctiveness of groups, persons, settings, and events. Liminal symbols mark entities and circumstances as extraordinary—outside and beyond ordinary social space and routine social events. In the case of cults, group identity typically is expected to transcend individuality. Cult members often wear uniform clothing. They may try to reduce distinctions based on age and gender by using a common hairstyle (shaved head, short hair, or long hair). The Heaven's Gate cult, whose mass suicide garnered headlines in 1997, even used castration to increase androgyny (similarity between males and females). In such cults, the individual, so important in American culture, is submerged in the collective. This is one reason Americans are so fearful and suspicious of "cults."

TOTEMISM

Rituals serve the social function of creating temporary or permanent solidarity among people—forming a social community. We see this also in practices known as totemism. Totemism has been important in the religions of Native Australians. *Totems* can be animals, plants, or geographic features. In each tribe, groups of people have particular totems. Members of each totemic group believe themselves to be descendants of their totem. Traditionally they customarily neither killed nor ate a totemic animal, but this taboo was lifted once a year, when people assembled for ceremonies dedicated to the totem. These annual rites were believed to be necessary for the totem's survival and reproduction.

Totemism uses nature as a model for society. The totems are usually animals and plants, which are part of nature. People relate to nature through their totemic association with natural species.

group agree to abide by its rules. As if they were undergoing a passage rite—but in this case a never-ending one—they may rid themselves of their previous possessions and cut themselves off from former social links, including those with family members.

Origins, Functions, and Expressions of Religion　　**587**

Because each group has a different totem, social differences mirror natural contrasts. Diversity in the natural order becomes a model for diversity in the social order. However, although totemic plants and animals occupy different niches in nature, on another level they are united because they all are part of nature. The unity of the human social order is enhanced by symbolic association with and imitation of the natural order (Durkheim 1912/1961; Lévi-Strauss 1963; Radcliffe-Brown 1962/1965).

One role of religious rites and beliefs is to affirm, and thus maintain, the solidarity of a religion's adherents. Totems are sacred emblems symbolizing common identity. This is true not just among Native Australians, but also among Native American groups of the North Pacific coast of North America, whose totem poles are well known. Their totemic carvings, which commemorate, and tell visual stories about, ancestors, animals, and spirits, also are associated with ceremonies. In totemic rites, people gather together to honor their totem. In so doing, they use ritual to maintain the social oneness that the totem symbolizes.

Religion and Cultural Ecology

Another domain in which religion plays a prominent role is cultural ecology. Behavior motivated by beliefs in supernatural beings, powers, and forces may help people survive in their material environment. In this section, we will see how beliefs and rituals may function as part of a group's cultural adaptation to its environment.

SACRED CATTLE IN INDIA

The people of India worship zebu cattle, which are protected by the Hindu doctrine of *ahimsa,* a principle of nonviolence that forbids the killing of animals generally. Western economic development experts occasionally (and erroneously) cite the Hindu cattle taboo to illustrate the idea that religious beliefs can stand

in the way of rational economic decisions. Hindus seem to be irrationally ignoring a valuable food (beef) because of their cultural or religious traditions. The economic developers also comment that Indians don't know how to raise proper cattle. They point to the scraggly zebus that wander about town and country. Western techniques of animal husbandry grow bigger cattle that produce more beef and milk. Western planners lament that Hindus are set in their ways. Bound by culture and tradition, they refuse to develop rationally.

However, these assumptions are both ethnocentric and wrong. Sacred cattle actually play an important adaptive role in an Indian ecosystem that has evolved over thousands of years (Harris 1974, 1978). Peasants' use of cattle to pull plows and carts is part of the technology of Indian agriculture. Indian peasants have no need for large, hungry cattle of the sort that economic developers, beef marketers, and North American cattle ranchers prefer. Scrawny animals pull plows and carts well enough but don't eat their owners out of house and home. How could peasants with limited land and marginal diets feed supersteers without taking food away from themselves?

India's zebu cattle are protected by the doctrine of ahimsa, a principle of nonviolence that forbids the killing of animals generally. This Hindu doctrine puts the full power of organized religion behind the command not to destroy a valuable resource even in times of extreme need. What kinds of animal avoidance taboos do you observe? Is their origin religious or secular?

Indians use cattle manure to fertilize their fields. Not all the manure is collected, because peasants don't spend much time watching their cattle, which wander and graze at will during certain seasons. In the rainy season, some of the manure that cattle deposit on the hillsides washes down to the fields. In this way, cattle also fertilize the fields indirectly. Furthermore, in a country where fossil fuels are scarce, dry cattle dung, which burns slowly and evenly, is a basic cooking fuel.

Far from being useless, as the development experts contend, sacred cattle are essential to Indian cultural adaptation. Biologically adapted to poor pasture land and a marginal environment, the scraggly zebu provides fertilizer and fuel, is indispensable in farming, and is affordable for peasants. The Hindu doctrine of *ahimsa* puts the full power of organized religion behind the command not to destroy a valuable resource even in times of extreme need.

Social Control

Religion has meaning for people. It influences their use of various resources. It helps men and women cope with adversity and tragedy. It offers hope that things will get better. Lives can be transformed through spiritual healing or rebirth. Sinners can repent and be saved—or they can go on sinning and be damned. If the faithful truly internalize a system of religious rewards and punishments, their religion becomes a powerful means of controlling their beliefs, their behavior, and what they teach their children.

Many people engage in religious activity because it seems to work. Prayers get answered. Faith healers heal. Sometimes it doesn't take much to convince the faithful that religious actions are efficacious. Many American Indian people in southwestern Oklahoma use faith healers at high monetary costs, not just because it makes them feel better about the uncertain but because it works (Lassiter 1998). Each year legions of Brazilians visit a church, Nosso Senhor do Bomfim, in the city of Salvador, Bahia. They vow to repay "Our Lord" (Nosso Senhor) if healing happens. Showing that the vows work, and are repaid, are the thousands of ex votos, plastic impressions of every conceivable body part, that

adorn the church, along with photos of people who have been cured.

Religion can work by getting inside people and mobilizing their emotions—their joy, their wrath, their righteousness. Emile Durkheim (1912/1961), a prominent French social theorist and scholar of religion, described the collective "effervescence" that can develop in religious contexts. Intense emotion bubbles up. People feel a deep sense of shared joy, meaning, experience, communion, belonging, and commitment to their religion.

The power of religion affects action. When religions meet, they can coexist peacefully, or their differences can be a basis for enmity and disharmony, even battle. Religious fervor has inspired Christians on crusades against the infidel and has led Muslims to wage jihads, holy wars against non-Islamic peoples. Throughout history, political leaders have used religion to promote and justify their views and policies.

By late September 1996, the Taliban movement had firmly imposed an extreme form of social control in the name of religion on Afghanistan (Figure 21.1) and its people. Led by Muslim clerics, the Taliban attempted to create their version of an Islamic society modeled on the teachings of the Koran (Burns 1997). Various repressive measures were instituted. The Taliban barred women from work and girls from school. Females past puberty were prohibited from talking to unrelated men. Women needed an approved reason, such as shopping for food, to leave their homes. Men, who were required to grow bushy beards, also faced an array of bans—against playing cards, listening to music, keeping pigeons, and flying kites.

To enforce their decrees, the Taliban sent armed enforcers throughout the country. Those agents took charge of "beard checks" and other forms of scrutiny on behalf of a religious police force known as the General Department for the Preservation of Virtue and the Elimination of Vice (Burns 1997). By late fall 2001 the Taliban had been overthrown, with a new interim government established in Kabul, the Afghani capital, on December 22. The collapse of the Taliban followed American bombing of Afghanistan in response to the September 11, 2001, attacks on New York's World Trade Center and Washington's Pentagon. As the Taliban yielded Kabul to victorious Northern Alliance forces, local men flocked to barbershops to have their beards

Figure 21.1 Location of Afghanistan.

trimmed or shaved. They were using a key Taliban symbol to celebrate the end of repression in religion's name.

How may religious leaders mobilize communities and, in so doing, gain support for their own policies? One way is by persuasion; another is by instilling hatred or fear. Consider witchcraft accusations. Witch hunts can be powerful means of social control by creating a climate of danger and insecurity that affects everyone, not just the people who are likely targets. No one wants to seem

deviant, to be accused of being a witch. In state societies, witch hunts often take aim at people who can be accused and punished with the least chance of retaliation. During the great European witch craze in the 15th, 16th, and 17th centuries (Harris 1974), most accusations and convictions were against poor women who had little social support.

Witchcraft accusations often are directed at socially marginal or anomalous individuals. Among the Betsileo of Madagascar, for example, who prefer patrilocal postmarital residence, men

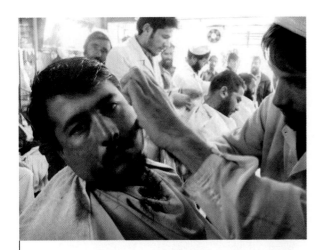

Syed Mohammed has his beard shaved off in a Kabul barbershop on November 14, 2001. Mohammed said he felt "free" without his beard. Afghans like Mohammed were using a key Taliban symbol to celebrate the end of repression in religion's name.

living in the wife's or the mother's village violate a cultural norm. Linked to their anomalous social position, just a bit of unusual behavior (e.g., staying up late at night) on their part is sufficient for them to be called witches and avoided as a result. In tribes and peasant communities, people who stand out economically, especially if they seem to be benefiting at the expense of others, often face accusations of witchcraft, leading to social ostracism or punishment. In this case witchcraft accusation becomes a **leveling mechanism,** a custom or social action that operates to reduce differences in wealth and thus to bring standouts in line with community norms—another form of social control.

To ensure proper behavior, religions offer rewards, such as the fellowship of the religious community, and punishments, such as the threat of being cast out or excommunicated. "The Lord giveth and the Lord taketh away." Many religions promise rewards for the good life and punishment for the bad. Your physical, mental, moral, and spiritual health, now and forever, may depend on your beliefs and behavior. For example, if you don't pay enough attention to the ancestors, they may snatch your kids from you.

Religions, especially the formal organized ones typically found in state societies, often prescribe a code of ethics and morality to guide behavior. The Judaic Ten Commandments lay down a set of prohibitions against killing, stealing, adultery, and other misdeeds. Crimes are breaches of secular laws, just as sins are breaches of religious strictures. Some rules (e.g., the Ten Commandments) proscribe or prohibit behavior; others prescribe behavior. The Golden Rule, for instance, is a religious guide to do unto others as you would have them do unto you. Moral codes are ways of maintaining order and stability. Codes of morality and ethics are repeated constantly in religious sermons, catechisms, and the like. They become internalized psychologically. They guide behavior and produce regret, guilt, shame, and the need for forgiveness, expiation, and absolution when they are not followed.

Religions also maintain social control by stressing the temporary and fleeting nature of this life. They promise rewards (and/or punishment) in an afterlife (Christianity) or reincarnation (Hinduism and Buddhism). Such beliefs serve to reinforce the status quo. People accept what they have now, knowing they can expect something better in the afterlife or the next life if they follow religious guidelines. Under slavery in the American South, the masters taught portions of the Bible, such as the story of Job, that stressed compliance. The slaves, however, seized on the story of Moses, the promised land, and deliverance.

Kinds of Religion

Religion is a cultural universal. But religions are parts of particular cultures, and cultural differences show up systematically in religious beliefs and practices. For example, the religions of stratified, state societies differ from those of cultures with less marked social contrasts and power differentials.

Considering several cultures, Wallace (1966) identified four types of religion: shamanic, communal, Olympian, and monotheistic (Table 21.2).

For more on shamans, see the Virtual Exploration

**mhhe
●com
/kottak**

Unlike priests, the shamans of a shamanic religion aren't full-time religious officials but part-time religious figures who mediate between people and supernatural beings and forces. All cultures have medico-magico-religious specialists. *Shaman* is the general term encompassing curers ("witch doctors"), mediums, spiritualists, astrologers, palm readers, and other diviners. Wallace found shamanic religions to be most characteristic of foraging societies, particularly those found in the northern latitudes, such as the Inuit and the native peoples of Siberia.

Although they are only part-time specialists, shamans often set themselves off symbolically from ordinary people by assuming a different or ambiguous sex or gender role. (In nation-states, priests, nuns, and vestal virgins do something similar by taking vows of celibacy and chastity.) Transvestism is one way of being sexually ambiguous. Among the Chukchee of Siberia (Bogoras 1904), where coastal populations fished and interior groups hunted, male shamans copied the dress, speech, hair arrangements, and life styles of women (Figure 21.2). These shamans took other men as husbands and sex partners and received respect for their supernatural and curative expertise. Female shamans could join a fourth gender, copying men and taking wives.

Among the Crow of the North American Plains, certain ritual duties were reserved for *berdaches*, men who rejected the male role of bison hunter, raider, and warrior and joined a third gender. The fact that certain key rituals could be conducted only by *berdaches* indicates their regular and normal place in Crow social life (Lowie 1935).

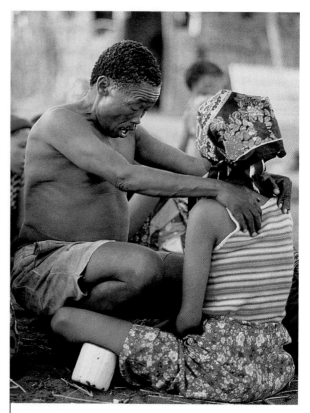

What are the world's oldest professions? Shaman is one. Shamanic religions are typically found among foragers, such as the San (shown here). This San shaman (left) falls into a trance as he heals.

mhhe.com
/kottak

For a quiz on types of religion, see the Interactive Exercise

Table 21.2   Anthony F. C. Wallace's Typology of Religions

Type of Religion (Wallace)	Type of Practitioner	Conception of Supernatural	Type of Society
Monotheistic	Priests, ministers, etc.	Supreme being	States
Olympian	Priesthood	Hierarchical pantheon with powerful deities	Chiefdoms and archaic states
Communal	Part-time specialists; occasional community-sponsored events, including rites of passage	Several deities with some control over nature	Food-producing tribes
Shamanic	Shaman = part-time practitioner	Zoomorphic (plants and animals)	Foraging bands

Figure 21.2 Location of Chukchee in Siberia.

Communal religions have, in addition to shamans, community rituals such as harvest ceremonies and rites of passage. Although communal religions lack *full-time* religious specialists, they believe in several deities (**polytheism**) who control aspects of nature. Although some hunter-gatherers, including Australian totemites, have communal religions, these religions are more typical of farming societies.

Olympian religions, which arose with state organization and marked social stratification, add full-time religious specialists—professional *priesthoods*. Like the state itself, the priesthood is hierarchically and bureaucratically organized. The term *Olympian* comes from Mount Olympus, home of the classical Greek gods. Olympian religions are polytheistic. They include powerful anthropomorphic gods with specialized functions, for example, gods of love, war, the sea, and death. Olympian *pantheons* (collections of supernatural beings) were prominent in the religions of many nonindustrial

nation-states, including the Aztecs of Mexico, several African and Asian kingdoms, and classical Greece and Rome. Wallace's fourth type—**monotheism**—also has priesthoods and notions of divine power, but it views the supernatural differently. In monotheism, all supernatural phenomena are manifestations of, or are under the control of, a single eternal, omniscient, omnipotent, and omnipresent supreme being.

Religion in States

Robert Bellah (1978) coined the term "world-rejecting religion" to describe most forms of Christianity, including Protestantism. The first world-rejecting religions arose in ancient civilizations, along with literacy and a specialized priesthood. These religions are so named because of their tendency to reject the natural (mundane, ordinary, material, secular) world and to focus instead on a higher (sacred, transcendent) realm of reality. The divine is a domain of exalted morality to which humans can only aspire. Salvation through fusion with the supernatural is the main goal of such religions.

CHRISTIAN VALUES

Notions of salvation and the afterlife dominate Christian ideologies. However, most varieties of Protestantism lack the hierarchical structure of earlier monotheistic religions, including Roman Catholicism. With a diminished role for the priest (minister), salvation is directly available to individuals. Regardless of their social status, Protestants have unmediated access to the supernatural. The individualistic focus of Protestantism offers a close fit with capitalism and with American culture.

In his influential book *The Protestant Ethic and the Spirit of Capitalism* (1904/1958), the social theorist Max Weber linked the spread of capitalism to the values preached by early Protestant leaders. Weber saw European Protestants (and eventually their American descendants) as more successful financially than Catholics. He attributed this difference to the values stressed by their religions. Weber saw Catholics as more concerned with immediate happiness and security. Protestants were more ascetic, entrepreneurial, and future-oriented, he thought.

Capitalism, said Weber, required that the traditional attitudes of Catholic peasants be replaced by values fitting an industrial economy based on capital accumulation. Protestantism placed a premium on hard work, an ascetic life, and profit seeking. Early Protestants saw success on earth as a sign of divine favor and probable salvation. According to some Protestant credos, individuals could gain favor with God through good works. Other sects stressed predestination, the idea that only a few mortals have been selected for eternal life and that people could not change their fates. However, material success, achieved through hard work, could be a strong clue that someone is predestined to be saved.

Weber also argued that rational business organization required the removal of industrial production from the home, its setting in peasant societies. Protestantism made such a separation possible by emphasizing individualism: individuals, not families or households, would be saved or not. Interestingly, given the connection that is usually made

with morality and religion in contemporary American discourse about family values, the family was a secondary matter for Weber's early Protestants. God and the individual reigned supreme.

Today, of course, in North America as throughout the world, people of many religions and with diverse worldviews are successful capitalists. Furthermore, the old Protestant emphasis on honesty and hard work often has little to do with today's economic maneuvering. Still, there is no denying that the individualistic focus of Protestantism was compatible with the severance of ties to land and kin that industrialism demanded. These values remain prominent in the religious background of many of the people of the United States.

World Religions

Information about the world's major religions is provided in Table 21.3 and on Map 21 in your atlas. Based on people's claimed religions, Christianity is the world's largest, with some 2 billion members. Islam, with 1.2 billion to 1.3 billion practitioners, is next, followed by Hinduism, Buddhism, and Chinese traditional religion, also known as Chinese folk religion and Confucianism. More than a billion people in the world either claim no religion or say they are atheists. Worldwide, Islam is growing faster than Christianity, about 2.9 percent annually versus 2.3 percent for Christianity, whose growth rate is the same as the rate of world population increase (Ontario Consultants 2001; Adherents.com 2001).

Interpret the World On Map 21 note the
Atlas Map 21   extent to which Roman Catholicism and Protestantism dominate in the Western Hemisphere. On the map, the religions of Canada are coded as "Mixed Sects," with Roman Catholicism dominating in French-speaking Canada. Actually, as you can see in Table 21.5 (on page 599), there are significantly more Catholics than Protestants in Canada as a whole. Catholicism also predominates in much of Europe. Map 21 differentiates the two major variants of Islam, Sunni and Shi'a, with the former being much more widespread than the latter. Note the wide distribution of the Sunni variant of Islam in Africa. Map 21 will help you interpret the news story that opened this chapter.

Table 21.3 Religions of the World

Religion	Date Founded	Sacred Texts	Members (millions)	Percent of the World
Christianity	30 CE	Bible	2,015	33 (dropping)
Islam	622 CE	Qur'an and Hadith	1,215	20 (growing)
No religion*	No date	None	925	15 (dropping)
Hinduism	1500 BCE	Veda	786	13 (stable)
Buddhism	523 BCE	Tripitaka	362	6 (stable)
Atheists	No date	None	211	4
Chinese folk religion	270 BCE	None	188	4
New Asian religion	Various	Various	106	2
Tribal religions	Prehistory	Oral tradition	91	2
Other	Various	Various	19	<1
Judaism	No consensus	Torah, Talmud	18	<1
Sikhism	1500 CE	Guru Granth Sahib	16	<1
Shamanists	Prehistory	Oral tradition	12	<1
Spiritism			7	<1
Confucianism	520 BCE	Lun Yu	5	<1
Baha'i faith	1863 CE	Mostly Holy Book	4	<1
Jainism	570 BCE	Siddhanta, Pakrit	3	<1
Shinto	500 CE	Kojiki, Nohon Shoki	3	<1
Zoroastrianism	No consensus	Avesta	0.2	<1

*Persons with no religions, agnostics, freethinkers, humanists, secularists, etc.
SOURCE: http://religioustolerance.org/worldrel.htm. Reprinted by permission of Ontario Consultants on Religious Tolerance.

Within Christianity, there is variation in the growth rate. There were an estimated 680 million "born-again" Christians (e.g., Pentecostals and Evangelicals) in the world in 2001, with an annual worldwide growth rate of 7 percent, versus just 2.3 percent for Christianity overall. The global growth rate of Roman Catholics and other non-Protestant Christians is estimated at only 1.3 percent, compared with a Protestant growth rate of 3.3 percent per year (Winter 2001).

The website Adherents.com (2001) classifies 11 world religions according to their degree of inter-nal unity and diversity. Listed first in Table 21.4 are the most cohesive/unified groups. Listed last are the religions with the most internal diversity. The list is based mainly on the degree of doctrinal similarity among the various subgroups. To a lesser extent it reflects diversity in practice, ritual, and organization. (The list includes the majority manifestations of each religion, as well as subgroups that the larger branches may label "heterodox.") How would you decide whether a value judgment is implied by this list? Is it better for a religion to be highly unified, cohesive, monolithic, and lacking in

Table 21.4   **Classical World Religions Ranked by Internal Religious Similarity**

Most unified
Baha'i
Zoroastrianism
Sikhism
Islam
Jainism
Judaism
Taoism
Shinto
Christianity
Buddhism
Hinduism
Most diverse

SOURCE: Adherents.com 2001.

internal diversity, or to be fragmented, schismatic, multifaceted, and abounding in variations on the same theme? Over time such diversity can give birth to new religions; for example Christianity arose from Judaism, Buddhism from Hinduism, Baha'i from Islam, and Sikhism from Hinduism. Within Christianity, Protestantism developed out of Roman Catholicism.

Religion and Change

Fundamentalists seek order based on strict adherence to purportedly traditional standards, beliefs, rules, and customs. Christian and Islamic fundamentalists recognize, decry, and attempt to redress change, yet they also contribute to change. In a worldwide process, new religions challenge established churches. In the United States, conservative Christian TV hosts have become influential broadcasters and opinion shapers. In Latin America, evangelical Protestantism is winning millions of converts from Roman Catholicism.

Religion helps maintain social order, but it also can be an instrument not just of change, but also of revolution. As a response to conquest or foreign domination, for example, religious leaders often undertake to alter or revitalize a society. In an "Islamic Revolution," Iranian ayatollahs marshaled religious fervor to create national solidarity and radical change. We call such movements nativistic movements (Linton 1943) or revitalization movements (Wallace 1956).

REVITALIZATION MOVEMENTS

Revitalization movements are social movements that occur in times of change, in which religious leaders emerge and undertake to alter or revitalize a society. Christianity originated as a revitalization movement. Jesus was one of several prophets who preached new religious doctrines while the Middle East was under Roman rule. It was a time of social unrest, when a foreign power ruled the land. Jesus inspired a new, enduring, and major religion. His contemporaries were not so successful.

The Handsome Lake religion arose around 1800 among the Iroquois of New York State (Wallace 1970). Handsome Lake, the founder of this revitalization movement, was a leader of one of the Iroquois tribes. The Iroquois had suffered because of their support of the British against the American colonials (and for other reasons). After the colonial victory and a wave of immigration to their homeland, the Iroquois were dispersed on small reservations. Unable to pursue traditional horticulture and hunting in their homeland, they became heavy drinkers and quarreled among themselves.

Handsome Lake was a heavy drinker who started having visions from heavenly messengers. The spirits warned him that unless the Iroquois changed their ways, they would be destroyed. His visions offered a plan for coping with the new order. Witchcraft, quarreling, and drinking would end. The Iroquois would copy European farming techniques, which, unlike traditional Iroquois horticulture, stressed male rather than female labor. Handsome Lake preached that the Iroquois should also abandon their communal long houses and matrilineal descent groups for more permanent marriages and individual family households. The teachings of Handsome Lake produced a new church and religion, one that still has members in New York and Ontario. This revitalization movement helped the Iroquois adapt to and survive in a modified environment. They eventually gained a reputation among their non-Indian neighbors as sober family farmers.

SYNCRETISMS

Especially in today's world, religious expressions emerge from the interplay of local, regional, national, and international cultural forces. **Syncretisms** are cultural mixes, including religious blends, that emerge from acculturation—the exchange of cultural features when cultures come into continuous firsthand contact. One example of religious syncretism is the mixture of African, Native American, and Roman Catholic saints and deities in Caribbean vodun, or "voodoo," cults. This blend also is present in Cuban santeria and in candomblé, an "Afro-Brazilian" cult. Another syncretism is the blend of Melanesian and Christian beliefs in cargo cults.

Like the Handsome Lake religion just discussed, cargo cults are revitalization movements. Such movements may emerge when natives have regular contact with industrial societies but lack their wealth, technology, and living standards. Some such movements attempt to explain European domination and wealth and to achieve similar success magically by mimicking European behavior and manipulating symbols of the desired life style. The syncretic **cargo cults** of Melanesia and Papua New Guinea weave Christian doctrine with aboriginal beliefs (Figure 21.3). They take their name from their focus on cargo: European goods of the sort natives have seen unloaded from the cargo holds of ships and airplanes.

In one early cult, members believed that the spirits of the dead would arrive in a ship. These ghosts would bring manufactured goods for the natives and would kill all the whites. More recent cults replaced ships with airplanes (Worsley 1959/1985). Many cults have used elements of European culture as sacred objects. The rationale is that Europeans use these objects, have wealth,

Figure 21.3   Location of Melanesia.

and therefore must know the "secret of cargo." By mimicking how Europeans use or treat objects, natives hope also to come upon the secret knowledge needed to gain cargo.

For example, having seen Europeans' reverent treatment of flags and flagpoles, the members of one cult began to worship flagpoles. They believed the flagpoles were sacred towers that could transmit messages between the living and the dead. Other natives built airstrips to entice planes bearing canned goods, portable radios, clothing, wristwatches, and motorcycles. Near the airstrips they made effigies of towers, airplanes, and radios. They talked into the cans in a magical attempt to establish radio contact with the gods.

Some cargo cult prophets proclaimed that success would come through a reversal of European domination and native subjugation. The day was near, they preached, when natives, aided by God, Jesus, or native ancestors, would turn the tables. Native skins would turn white, and those of Europeans would turn brown; Europeans would die or be killed.

As syncretisms, cargo cults blend aboriginal and Christian beliefs. Melanesian myths told of ancestors shedding their skins and changing into

powerful beings and of dead people returning to life. Christian missionaries, who had been in Melanesia since the late 19th century, also spoke of resurrection. The cults' preoccupation with cargo is related to traditional Melanesian big-man systems. In the chapter "Political Systems," we saw that a Melanesian big man had to be generous. People worked for the big man, helping him amass wealth, but eventually he had to give a feast and give away all that wealth.

Because of their experience with big-man systems, Melanesians believed that all wealthy people eventually had to give their wealth away. For decades, they had attended Christian missions and worked on plantations. All the while they expected Europeans to return the fruits of their labor as their own big men did. When the Europeans refused to distribute the wealth or even to let natives know the secret of its production and distribution, cargo cults developed.

Like arrogant big men, Europeans would be leveled, by death if necessary. However, natives lacked the physical means of doing what their traditions said they should do. Thwarted by well-armed colonial forces, natives resorted to magical leveling. They called on supernatural beings to

A cargo cult in Vanuatu. Boys and men march with spears, imitating British colonial soldiers. Does anything in your own society remind you of a cargo cult?

intercede, to kill or otherwise deflate the European big men and redistribute their wealth.

Cargo cults are religious responses to the expansion of the world capitalist economy. However, this religious mobilization had political and economic results. Cult participation gave Melanesians a basis for common interests and activities and thus helped pave the way for political parties and economic interest organizations. Previously separated by geography, language, and customs, Melanesians started forming larger groups as members of the same cults and followers of the same prophets. The cargo cults paved the way for political action through which the indigenous peoples eventually regained their autonomy.

A NEW AGE

Among the changes involving religion in contemporary North America is a certain decline in formal organized religions and a rise of secularism. Between 1967 and 2000, the number of Americans giving no religious preference grew from 2 to 8 percent. The comparable Canadian figure was a rise from 7 to 12 percent between 1981 and 1991 (Table 21.5). Atheists and "secular humanists" are not just bugaboos for religious conservatives. They really do exist, and they, too, are organized. Like members of religious groups, they use varied media, including print and the Internet, to communicate among themselves. Just as Buddhists can peruse *Tricycle: The Buddhist Review*, secular humanists can find their views validated in *Free Inquiry*, a quarterly identifying itself as "the international secular humanist magazine." Secular humanists speak out against organized religion and its "dogmatic pronouncements" and "supernatural or spiritual agendas" and the "obscurantist views" of religious leaders who presume "to inform us of God's views" by appealing to sacred texts (Steinfels 1997).

Even as our society appears to be growing more secular, some middle-class people have also turned to spiritualism, in search of the meaning of life. Spiritual orientations serve as the basis of new social movements. Some white people have appropriated the symbols, settings, and purported religious practices of Native Americans and, in Australia, of Native Australians, for New Age religions. Many natives have strongly protested the use of their sacred property and places by such groups.

New religious movements have varied origins. Some have been influenced by Christianity, others by Eastern (Asian) religions, still others by mysticism and spiritualism. Religion also evolves in tandem with science and technology. For example, the Raelian Movement, a religious group centered in Switzerland and Montreal, promotes cloning as a way of achieving "eternal life." Raelians believe that extraterrestrials called "Elohim" artificially created all life on earth. The group has established a company called Valiant Venture Ltd., which offers infertile and homosexual couples the opportunity to have a child cloned from one of the spouses (Ontario Consultants on Religious Tolerance 1996).

Table 21.5 Religious Composition (in Percentages) of the Populations of the United States, 1967 and 2000, and Canada, 1981 and 1991

	United States		Canada	
	1967	2000	1981	1991
Protestant	67%	56%	41%	36%
Catholic	25	27	47	46
Jewish	3	2	1	1
Other	3	7	3	4
None given	2	8	7	12

SOURCE: *Statistical Abstract of the United States 2001*, p. 56, Table 66. 1991, and Census of Canada, http://www.StatCan.ca.

In the United States, the official recognition of a religion entitles it to a modicum of respect, and certain benefits, such as exemption from taxation on its income and property (as long as it does not engage in political activity). Not all would-be religions receive official recognition. For example, Scientology is recognized as a church in the United States but not in Germany. In 1997, United States government officials spoke out against Germany's persecution of Scientologists as a form of "human rights abuse." Germans protested vehemently, calling Scientology a dangerous nonreligious political movement, with between 30,000 and 70,000 German members.

Secular Rituals

In concluding this discussion of religion, we may recognize some problems with the definition of religion given at the beginning of this chapter. The first problem: If we define religion with reference to supernatural beings, powers, and forces, how do we classify ritual-like behavior that occurs in secular contexts? Some anthropologists believe there are both sacred and secular rituals. Secular rituals include formal, invariant, stereotyped, earnest, repetitive behavior and rites of passage that take place in nonreligious settings.

A second problem: If the distinction between the supernatural and the natural is not consistently made in a society, how can we tell what is religion and what isn't? The Betsileo of Madagascar, for example, view witches and dead ancestors as real people who play roles in ordinary life. However, their occult powers are not empirically demonstrable.

A third problem: The behavior considered appropriate for religious occasions varies tremendously from culture to culture. One society may consider drunken frenzy the surest sign of faith, whereas another may inculcate quiet reverence. Who is to say which is "more religious"?

A PILGRIMAGE TO WALT DISNEY WORLD

This final section will illustrate some of the approaches that anthropologists use to analyze and interpret religious behavior, with reference to a familiar and apparently nonreligious example. Secular behavior may exhibit clear parallels to religious behavior. We can see this by considering how a visit to Walt Disney World takes on some of the attributes of a religious pilgrimage. Florida's Walt Disney World, along with California's Disneyland, is one of two Disney "shrines" in the United States. These centers of mass visitation owe their success not just to the amusement they offer but to years of preprogramming that have influenced Americans for well over half a century. Disney's creations—movies, television programs, cable TV channels, Broadway musicals, cartoons, comics, toys, stores, and theme parks—are important forces in American enculturation.

The religions of many cultures focus on sacred sites and shrines. Infertile women in Madagascar seek fecundity by spilling the blood of a rooster in front of phallic stones. Australian totems are associated with holy sites where, in mythology, totemic beings first emerged from the ground. Sacred groves provide symbolic unity for dispersed clans among the Jie of Uganda (Gulliver 1965/1974). Pilgrims seek miraculous cures at shrines such as Lourdes, in France, and Fátima, in Portugal, which are associated with Roman Catholicism. In the arid sertão of northeastern Brazil, thousands of pilgrims journey each August 6 to fulfill their vows to a wooden statue in a cave—Bom Jesus de Lapa. Similarly, but virtually every day of the year, thousands of American families travel long distances and invest significant amounts of time, effort, and money to experience Disneyland and Walt Disney World (Figure 21.4).

A conversation with the anthropologist Alexander Moore, now of the University of Southern California, then of the University of Florida, first prompted me to think of Walt Disney World as analogous to religious pilgrimage centers. Moore pointed out that like other shrines, Walt Disney World has an inner, sacred center and an outer, more secular domain. At Walt Disney World, appropriately enough, the inner, sacred area is known as "the Magic Kingdom."

Motels, restaurants, and campgrounds dot the approach to Walt Disney World, becoming increasingly concentrated near the resort. You enter Walt Disney World on "World Drive." You can choose between the Magic Kingdom and turnoffs to Epcot, Disney's Animal Kingdom Theme Park, or the Disney–MGM Studios. The following analysis applies only to the Magic Kingdom.

Travelers enter a mammoth parking lot by driving through a structure like a turnpike toll booth. Sections of the parking lot have totemlike designations—Minnie, Goofy, Pluto, and Chip 'n' Dale—each with numbered rows. Uniformed attendants direct motorists to parking places, making sure every space is filled in order. As visitors emerge from their cars, they are directed to open-air trams. Lest they forget where their cars are parked, they are told as they board the tram to "remember" Minnie, Pluto, or whichever mythological figure has become the temporary guardian of their vehicle. Many travelers spend the first minute of the tram ride reciting "Minnie 30, Minnie 30," memorizing the automobile's row number. Leaving the tram, visitors hurry to booths where they purchase entrance to the Magic Kingdom and its attractions ("adventures"). They then pass through turnstiles behind the ticket sales booths and prepare to be transported, usually by "express" monorail, to the Magic Kingdom itself.

On that monorail, which bridges the opposition between the outer, secular, areas and the Magic Kingdom, similarities between Disney pilgrims and participants in rites of passage are especially obvious. (Rites of passage may be transitions in space, age, or social status.) Disney pilgrims on the monorail exhibit, as one might expect in a transition from secular to sacred space (a magic kingdom), many liminal attributes. Like liminal periods in other passage rites, aboard the monorail all prohibitions that apply everywhere else in Walt Disney World are intensified. In the outer, secular, areas and in the Magic Kingdom itself, people may smoke and eat, and in the secular areas they can consume alcohol and go shoeless, but all these things are taboo on the monorail. Like ritual passengers, monorail riders temporarily relinquish control over their destinies. Herded like cattle into the monorail, passengers move out of ordinary space and into a time out of time. Social distinctions disappear; everyone is reduced to a common level. As the monorail departs, a disembodied voice prepares the pilgrims for what is to come, enculturating them in the lore and standards of Walt Disney World.

Symbols of rebirth at the end of liminality are typical of liminal periods. Rebirth symbolism is an aspect of the monorail ride. As the monorail speeds through Disney's Contemporary Resort Hotel, travelers facing forward observe and pass through an enormous tiled mural that covers an entire wall. Just before the monorail reaches the hotel, but much more clearly after it emerges, travelers see Walt Disney World's primary symbol: Cinderella Castle. The sudden emergence from the mural into full view of the Magic Kingdom can be seen as a simulation of rebirth.

Figure 21.4   Location of Walt Disney World.

WITHIN THE MAGIC KINGDOM

Once the monorail pulls into the Magic Kingdom station, the transition is complete. Passengers are now on their own. Soon they are in the Magic Kingdom, walking down "Main Street, U.S.A." The Magic Kingdom itself invites comparison with shrines and rites. Pilgrims agree implicitly to constitute a temporary community, to spend a few hours or days observing the same rules, sharing experiences, and behaving alike. They share a common social status as pilgrims, waiting for hours in line and partaking in the same "adventures." As we have seen, several anthropologists contend that a major social function of rituals is to reaffirm, and thus to maintain, solidarity among members of a congregation. Victor Turner (1974) suggested that certain rituals among the Ndembu of Zambia serve a mnemonic function (they make people remember). Women's belief that they can be made ill by the spirits of their deceased matrilineal kinswomen leads them to take part in rites that remind them of their ancestors.

Similar observations can be made about Walt Disney World: Frontierland; Liberty Square; Main Street, U.S.A.; Tomorrowland; Fantasyland; and Mickey's Toontown Fair—the major sections of the Magic Kingdom—make us remember departed presidents (our national ancestors) and American history. They also juxtapose and link together the past, present, and future; childhood and adulthood; the real and the unreal. Many of the adventures, or rides, particularly the roller coasters, can be compared to anxiety-producing rites. Anxiety is dispelled when the pilgrims realize they have survived simulated speeds of 90 miles an hour.

One might wonder how a visitor from a nonindustrial society would view Walt Disney World adventures, particularly those based on fantasy. In many nonindustrial societies, witches are actual people—part of reality rather than fantasy. Peasants in many countries believe in witches, werewolves, and nefarious creatures of the night. Such a visitor might find it hard to understand why Americans voluntarily take rides designed to produce uncertainty and fright.

The structure and attractions of the Magic Kingdom are meant to represent, recall, and reaffirm a set of American memories and values. In Liberty Square's Hall of Presidents, pilgrims silently and reverently view moving, talking, lifelike dummies. Like Tanzanian rites, the Magic Kingdom makes us remember not just presidents and history but characters in children's literature, such as Tom Sawyer. And, of course, we meet the cartoon characters who, in the person of costumed humans, walk around the Magic Kingdom, posing for photographs with children.

The juxtaposition of past, present, future, and fantasy symbolizes eternity. It argues that our nation, our people, our technological expertise, our beliefs, myths, and values will endure. Disney propaganda uses Walt Disney World itself to illustrate what American creativity joined with technical know-how can accomplish. Students in American history are told how our ancestors carved a new land out of wilderness. Similarly, Walt Disney is presented as a mythic figure, creator of cosmos out of chaos—a structured world from the undeveloped chaos of Florida's central interior.

A few other links between Walt Disney World and religious and quasi-religious symbols and shrines should be examined. Walt Disney World's most potent symbol is Cinderella Castle, complete with a moat where pilgrims throw coins and make

At Florida's Walt Disney World Resort, what is the role and function of Cinderella Castle? Have you ever visited such a place? Do you think of your journey there as a pilgrimage?

wishes. On my first visit, I was surprised to discover that the castle has a largely symbolic function as a trademark or logo for Walt Disney World. The castle has little utilitarian value. A few shops on the ground floor and a restaurant on the second floor were open to the public, but the rest of the building was off limits. In interpreting Cinderella Castle, I recalled a lecture given in 1976 by British anthropologist Sir Edmund Leach. In describing the ritual surrounding his dubbing as a knight, Leach noted that Queen Elizabeth stood in front of the British throne and did not, in accordance with our stereotype of monarchs, sit on it. Leach surmised that the primary value of the throne is to represent, to make concrete, something enduring but abstract—the British sovereign's right to rule. Similarly, the most important thing about Cinderella Castle is its symbolism. It offers concrete testimony to the eternal aspects of Disney creations.

RECOGNIZING RELIGION

Some anthropologists think that rituals are distinguished from other behavior by special emotions, nonutilitarian intentions, and supernatural entities. However, other anthropologists define ritual more broadly. Writing about football, W. Arens (1981) pointed out that behavior can simultaneously have sacred and secular aspects. On one level, football is "simply a sport"; on another, it is a public ritual. Similarly, Walt Disney World, an amusement park, is on one level a mundane, secular place, but, on another, it assumes some of the attributes of a sacred place.

In the context of comparative religion, this isn't surprising. The French sociologist/anthropologist Émile Durkheim (1912/1961) pointed out long ago that almost everything from the sublime to the ridiculous has in some societies been treated as sacred. The distinction between sacred and profane doesn't depend on the intrinsic qualities of the sacred symbol. In Australian totemism, for example, sacred beings include such humble creatures as ducks, frogs, rabbits, and grubs, whose inherent qualities could hardly have given rise to the religious sentiment they inspire. If frogs and grubs can be elevated to a sacred level, why not the products of popular and commercial culture?

Many Americans believe that recreation and religion are separate domains. From my field work in Brazil and Madagascar and my reading about other societies, I believe that this separation is both ethnocentric and false. Madagascar's tomb-centered ceremonies are times when the living and the dead are joyously reunited, when people get drunk, gorge themselves, and enjoy sexual license. Perhaps the gray, sober, ascetic, and moralistic aspects of many religious events in the United States, in taking the "fun" out of religion, force us to find our religion in fun. Many Americans seek in such apparently secular contexts as amusement parks, rock concerts, and sporting events what other people find in religious rites, beliefs, and ceremonies.

SUMMARY

1. Religion, a cultural universal, consists of belief and behavior concerned with supernatural beings, powers, and forces. Religion also encompasses the feelings and meanings associated with such beliefs and behavior. Anthropological studies have revealed many aspects and functions of religion.

2. Tylor considered animism—the belief in spirits or souls—to be religion's earliest and most basic form. He focused on religion's explanatory role, arguing that religion would eventually disappear as science provided better explanations. Besides animism, yet another view of the supernatural also occurs in nonindustrial societies. This sees the supernatural as a domain of raw, impersonal power or force (called mana in Polynesia and Melanesia). People can manipulate and control mana under certain conditions.

3. When ordinary technical and rational means of doing things fail, people may turn to magic. Often they use magic when they lack control over outcomes. Religion offers comfort and psychological security at times of crisis. However, rites also can create anxiety. Rituals are formal, invariant, stylized, earnest acts in which people subordinate their particular beliefs to a social collectivity. Rites of passage have three stages: separation, liminality, and incorporation. Such

rites can mark any change in social status, age, place, or social condition. Collective rites often are cemented by communitas, a feeling of intense solidarity.

4. Besides their psychological and social functions, religious beliefs and practices play a role in the adaptation of human populations to their environments. The Hindu doctrine of ahimsa, which prohibits harm to living things, makes cattle sacred and beef a tabooed food. The taboo's force stops peasants from killing their draft cattle even in times of extreme need.

5. Religion establishes and maintains social control through a series of moral and ethical beliefs, and real and imagined rewards and punishments, internalized in individuals. Religion also achieves social control by mobilizing its members for collective action.

6. Wallace defines four types of religion: shamanic, communal, Olympian, and monotheistic. Each has its characteristic ceremonies and practitioners. Religion helps maintain social order, but it also can promote change. Revitalization movements blend old and new beliefs and have helped people adapt to changing conditions.

7. Protestant values have been important in the United States, as they were in the rise and spread of capitalism in Europe. The world's major religions vary in their growth rates, with Islam expanding more rapidly than Christianity. There is growing religious diversity in the United States and Canada. Religious trends in contemporary North America include rising secularism and new religions, some inspired by science and technology, some by spiritism. There are secular as well as religious rituals.

KEY TERMS

See the flash cards

mhhe
●**com**
/kottak

animism Belief in souls or doubles.

cargo cults Postcolonial, acculturative religious movements, common in Melanesia, that attempt to explain European domination and wealth and to achieve similar success magically by mimicking European behavior.

communal religions In Wallace's typology, these religions have, in addition to shamanic cults, communal cults in which people organize community rituals such as harvest ceremonies and rites of passage.

communitas Intense community spirit, a feeling of great social solidarity, equality, and togetherness; characteristic of people experiencing liminality together.

leveling mechanism A custom or social action that operates to reduce differences in wealth and thus to bring standouts in line with community norms.

liminality The critically important marginal or in-between phase of a rite of passage.

magic Use of supernatural techniques to accomplish specific aims.

mana Sacred impersonal force in Melanesian and Polynesian religions.

monotheism Worship of an eternal, omniscient, omnipotent, and omnipresent supreme being.

Olympian religions In Wallace's typology, develop with state organization; have full-time religious specialists—professional priesthoods.

polytheism Belief in several deities who control aspects of nature.

religion Belief and ritual concerned with supernatural beings, powers, and forces.

revitalization movements Movements that occur in times of change, in which religious leaders emerge and undertake to alter or revitalize a society.

rites of passage Culturally defined activities associated with the transition from one place or stage of life to another.

ritual Behavior that is formal, stylized, repetitive, and stereotyped, performed earnestly as a social act; rituals are held at set times and places and have liturgical orders.

shaman A part-time religious practitioner who mediates between ordinary people and supernatural beings and forces.

syncretisms Cultural mixes, including religious blends, that emerge from acculturation—the exchange of cultural features when cultures come into continuous firsthand contact.

taboo Set apart as sacred and off-limits to ordinary people; prohibition backed by supernatural sanctions.

CRITICAL THINKING QUESTIONS

For more self testing, see the self quizzes

1. What are the problems with the definition of religion given at the beginning of this chapter?
2. What are some of the explanatory, emotional, and social functions of religion? Do you see any problem in talking about religion in terms of its functions?
3. What's an example of a religious ritual in which you've engaged? How about a nonreligious ritual?
4. Describe a rite of passage you, or a friend, have been through. How did it fit the three-stage model given in the text?
5. Name three rites of passage that take place in your own society.
6. Can you think of additional ways in which religion has ecological functions?
7. What are two ways in which religion establishes and maintains social control?
8. From the news or your own knowledge, can you provide additional examples of revitalization movements, new religions, or liminal cults?
9. How are shamans similar to and different from priests? Are there shamans in your society? Who are they?
10. Have you participated in a secular ritual of the sort described at the end of the chapter?

Atlas Questions

Look at Map 21, "World Religions."

1. Which continent has the most diversity with respect to the major religions?
2. Which continent is most Protestant? Why do you think that is the case?
3. Where in the world are "tribal" religions still practiced?

SUGGESTED ADDITIONAL READINGS

Brown, K. M.
2001   *Mama Lola: A Vodou Priestess in Brooklyn,* rev. ed. Berkeley: University of California Press. Ethnographic study of a religious community and its leader.

Child, A. B., and I. L. Child
1993   *Religion and Magic in the Lives of Traditional Peoples.* Englewood Cliffs, NJ: Prentice Hall. A cross-cultural study.

Harris, M.
1974   *Cows, Pigs, Wars, and Witches: The Riddles of Culture.* New York: Vintage. The cultural ecology of religion, taboos, and witchcraft.

Hicks, D., ed.
2001   *Ritual and Belief: Readings in the Anthropology of Religion,* 2nd ed. Boston: McGraw-Hill. Up-to-date reader, with useful annotation.

Horton, R.

1993   *Patterns of Thought in Africa and the West: Essays on Magic, Religion and Science.* New York: Cambridge University Press. Essays address issues involving religion and explanation.

Klass, M.

1995   *Ordered Universes: Approaches to the Anthropology of Religion.* Boulder, CO: Westview. Wide-ranging overview of key issues in the anthropology of religion.

Klass, M., and M. Weisgrau, eds.

1999   *Across the Boundaries of Belief: Contemporary Issues in the Anthropology of Religion.* Boulder CO: Westview. Up-to-date collection of articles.

Lehmann, A. C., and J. E. Meyers, eds.

2001   *Magic, Witchcraft, and Religion: An Anthropological Study of the Supernatural,* 5th ed. Boston: McGraw-Hill. A comparative reader covering Western and non-Western cultures.

Lessa, W. A., and E. Z. Vogt, eds.

1979   *Reader in Comparative Religion: An Anthropological Approach,* 4th ed. New York: Harper & Row. Excellent collection of major articles on the origins, functions, and expressions of religion in comparative perspective.

Rappaport, R. A.

1999   *Holiness and Humanity: Ritual in the Making of Religious Life.* New York: Cambridge University Press. The nature, meaning, and functions of ritual in religion.

Turner, V. W.

1995   (orig. 1969) *The Ritual Process.* Hawthorne, NY: Aldine de Gruyter. Liminality among the Ndembu discussed in a comparative perspective.

Wallace, A. F. C.

1966   *Religion: An Anthropological View.* New York: Random House. Survey of anthropological approaches to religion.

1970   *The Death and Rebirth of the Seneca.* New York: Knopf. The story of the Handsome Lake religion.

INTERNET EXERCISES

1. Boot Camp: Go to the Parris Island home page of the U.S. Marines and read the page on "The Transformation Process" in basic training, **http://www.parrisisland.com/transfor.htm.**

   a. In your textbook, basic training is presented as an example of a communal rite of passage. After reading this page, do you agree?

   b. If this is a rite of passage, we should be able to identify the phases: separation, liminality, and incorporation. Can you do so?

   c. Do recruits experience communitas while at Parris Island?

   d. Can you think of a rite of passage that you have experienced? For instance, joining a club or a team, being confirmed in the Catholic Church, celebrating your bar/bat mitzvah? In what ways are these experiences similar to basic training? In what ways are they different?

2. Read the article by Robert Hefner entitled "September 11 and the Struggle for Islam," **http://www.ssrc.org/sept11/essays/hefner.htm.**

   a. How might the rise of "hardline" Islam be viewed as a revitalization movement? How is it different?

   b. Where is the "real struggle," according to this author? Do you agree? Why or why not?

   c. How can anthropology contribute to an understanding of September 11 and its aftermath? What questions should anthropologists now look at to achieve this understanding?

See Chapter 21 at your McGraw-Hill Online Learning Center for additional review and interactive exercises.

22

THE ARTS

Overview

Is art, like religion, a cultural universal? People in all cultures do seem to associate an aesthetic experience with certain objects and events. Experiencing art involves feelings as well as appreciation of form. The arts, sometimes called "expressive culture," include the visual arts, literature, music, and theater arts.

Students of non-Western art have been criticized for ignoring individual artists, and for focusing too much on the social nature and context of art. Many non-Western societies do recognize the achievements of individual artists. Community standards judge the completeness and mastery displayed in a work of art. Standards may be maintained informally in society, or by specialists, such as art critics.

Folk art, music, and lore refer to the expressive culture of ordinary, usually rural, people. The arts are part of culture, and aesthetic judgments depend, at least to an extent, on cultural background. Growing acceptance of the anthropological definition of culture has helped broaden the study of the humanities from fine art and elite art to popular and folk art and the creative expressions of the masses and of many peoples. Myths, legends, tales, and storytelling play important roles in transmitting culture and preserving traditions.

The arts go on changing, although certain art forms have survived for thousands of years. In today's world, a huge "arts and leisure" industry links Western and non-Western art forms in an international network with both aesthetic and commercial dimensions.

Is There a Music Gene? Scholars Mull Music's Roots

FOXNEWS.COM NEWS BRIEFS

by Matt Crenson

July 17, 2000

This article argues that there may be a gene that leads humans to respond to music. Music is thus a cultural universal with possible biological roots. How, according to the article, might music have conferred a selective advantage? That is, how might it have helped early humans survive and reproduce? Do musical abilities run in families? What about artistic abilities? The article calls music a group phenomenon. Do you agree?

NEW YORK— . . . Some scientists have recently proposed that music may have been an evolutionary adaptation, like upright walking or spoken language, that arose early in human history and helped the species survive.

"Of course it's utter speculation," says David Huron, a professor of music at The Ohio State University in Columbus.

Most experts still assume music was a cultural invention, like cave painting or writing, that humans invented to make their lives easier or more pleasant.

Yet Huron and many of his colleagues wonder if music might have biological roots. The "music gene" would have arisen tens or hundreds of thousands of years ago, and conferred an evolutionary advantage on those who possessed it. Natural selection would have nurtured the gift of music, favoring those who possessed it with more offspring who were themselves more likely to reproduce. . . .

That music is everywhere suggests it arose early in the history of the species, before humans scattered across the globe and developed manifold cultures. In fact, concrete evidence of music's antiquity exists in the form of a carved bone flute found recently in a cave in Slovenia. The "Divje babe flute," as musicologists call it, is the oldest known musical instrument. It dates back 40,000 years, to a time when Europe and much of North America were mantled in ice, and humans lived side by side with Neanderthals. . . .

Sandra Trehub of the University of Toronto . . . travels the globe, studying mothers as they sing to their children. No matter where she goes, people sing to their infants the same way, at a high pitch, in a slow tempo and in a distinctive tone. Every culture has lullabies. They are so similar that you could never mistake them for anything else. . . .

Music would have been adaptive because mothers who were better musicians had an easier time calming their babies, Trehub suggests. A happy baby who fell asleep easily and rarely made a fuss was much more likely to survive to adulthood, especially in primitive societies. Their cries would not attract predators; they and their mothers would get more rest; they would be less likely to be mistreated.

So if a genetic predisposition to music appeared early in human history, those who had it would have produced more healthy offspring who themselves reproduced. The most musical of those children would have the same advantage, and they would pass the music genes to their children, and so on, each generation benefitting from the gift of music. . . .

Perhaps music is something that pulls us together into groups. As individuals we are slow, clawless and hairless—easy prey for all manner of vicious beasts. But in groups, *Homo sapiens* has conquered the globe.

These five siblings living in New York City—all master pianists—would certainly seem to share a music gene.

Music is all about groups—choirs, symphonies, ensembles, and bands. Maybe people with a biological penchant for music lived more effectively in societies. . . .

SOURCE: http://www.foxnews.com/science/071700/ music.sml.

What Is Art?

For cross-cultural meanings of art, see the Virtual Exploration

/kottak

As the article contends, music is among the most social of the **arts,** which also include theater arts, visual arts, and storytelling and literature (oral and written). These manifestations of human creativity are sometimes called **expressive culture.** People express themselves creatively in dance, music, song, painting, sculpture, pottery, cloth, storytelling, verse, prose, drama, and comedy.

Many cultures lack terms that can be translated easily as "art" or "the arts." Yet even without a word for art, people everywhere do associate an aesthetic experience—a sense of beauty, appreciation, harmony, pleasure—with sounds, patterns, objects, and events that have certain qualities. The Bamana people of Mali have a word (like "art") for something that attracts your attention and directs your thoughts (Ezra 1986). Among the Yoruba of Nigeria, the word for art, *ona,* encompasses the designs made on objects, the art objects themselves, and the profession of the creators of such patterns and works. For two Yoruba lineages of leather workers, Otunisona and Osiisona, the suffix *-ona* in their names denotes art (Adepegba 1991).

A dictionary defines **art** as "the quality, production, expression, or realm of what is beautiful or of more than ordinary significance; the class of objects subject to aesthetic criteria" (*The Random House College Dictionary* 1982, p. 76). Drawing on the same dictionary, **aesthetics** involves "the qualities perceived in works of art . . . ; the . . . mind and emotions in relation to the sense of beauty" (p. 22). However, it is possible for a work of art to attract our attention, direct our thoughts, and have more than ordinary significance without being judged as beautiful by most people who experience that work. Pablo Picasso's Guernica, a famous painting of the Spanish Civil War (see page 574), comes to mind as a scene that, while not beautiful, is indisputably moving, and thus is a work of art.

George Mills (1971) notes that in many cultures, the role of art lover lacks definition because art isn't viewed as a separate activity. But this doesn't stop individuals from being moved by sounds, patterns, objects, and events in a way that we would call aesthetic. Our own society does provide a fairly well-defined role for the connoisseur of the arts, as well as sanctuaries—concert halls, theaters, museums—where people can retreat to be aesthetically pleased and emotionally moved by objects and performances.

This chapter will not attempt to do a systematic survey of all the arts, or even their major subdivisions. Rather, the approach will be to examine topics and issues that apply to expressive culture generally. "Art" will be used to encompass all the arts, not just the visual ones. In other words, the observations to be made about "art" are generally intended to apply to music, theater, stories, and lore, as well as to painting and sculpture.

That which is aesthetically pleasing is perceived with the senses. Usually, when we think of art, we have in mind something that can be seen or heard. But others might define art more broadly to include things that can be smelled (scents, fragrances), tasted (recipes), or touched (cloth textures). How enduring must art be? Visual works and written works, including musical compositions, may last for centuries. Can a single noteworthy event, such as a feast, which is not in the least eternal, except in memory, be a work of art?

ART AND RELIGION

Some of the issues raised in the discussion of religion also apply to art. Definitions of both art and religion mention the "more than ordinary" or the "extraordinary." Religious scholars may distinguish between the sacred (religious) and the profane (secular). Similarly, art scholars may distinguish between the artistic and the ordinary.

If we adopt a special attitude or demeanor when confronting a sacred object, do we display something similar when experiencing a work of art? According to the anthropologist Jacques Maquet (1986), an artwork is something that stimulates and sustains contemplation. It compels attention and reflection. Maquet stresses the importance of the

Art serving religion. This photo was taken in Phnom Penh, Cambodia, in 1988. On the grounds of a Buddhist temple, artisans make religious artifacts. We see a young man carving a Buddha, along with several completed Buddha statues.

object's form in producing such artistic contemplation. But other scholars stress feeling and meaning in addition to form. The experience of art involves feeling, such as being moved, as well as appreciation of form, such as balance or harmony.

Such an artistic attitude can be combined with and used to bolster a religious attitude. Much art has been done in association with religion. Many of the high points of Western art and music had religious inspiration, or were done in the service of religion, as a visit to a church or a large museum will surely illustrate. Bach and Handel are as well known for their church music as Michelangelo is for his religious painting and sculpture. The buildings (churches and cathedrals) in which religious music is played and in which visual art is displayed may themselves be works of art. Some of the major architectural achievements of Western art are religious structures. Examples include the Amiens, Chartres, and Notre Dame cathedrals in France.

Art may be created, performed, or displayed outdoors in public, or in special indoor settings, such as a theater, concert hall, or museum. Just as churches demarcate religion, museums and the-aters set art off from the ordinary world, making it special, while inviting spectators in. Buildings dedicated to the arts help create the artistic atmosphere. Architecture may accentuate the setting as a place for works of art to be presented.

The settings of rites and ceremonies, and of art, may be temporary or permanent. State societies have permanent religious structures: churches and temples. So, too, may state societies have buildings and structures dedicated to the arts. Nonstate societies tend to lack such permanently demarcated settings. Both art and religion are more "out there" in society. Still, in bands and tribes, religious settings can be created without churches. Similarly, an artistic atmosphere can be created without museums. At particular times of the year, ordinary space can be set aside for a visual art display or a musical performance. Such special occasions parallel the times set aside for religious ceremonies. In fact, in tribal performances, the arts and religion often mix. For example, masked and costumed performers may imitate spirits. Rites of passage often feature special music, dance, song, bodily adornment, and other manifestations of expressive culture.

In the chapter "Making a Living," we looked at the potlatching tribes of the North Pacific Coast of North America. Erna Gunther (1971) shows how various art forms combined among those tribes to create the visual aspects of ceremonialism. During the winter, spirits were believed to pervade the atmosphere. Masked and costumed dancers represented the spirits. They dramatically reenacted spirit encounters with human beings, which are part of the origin myths of villages, clans, and lineages. In some areas, dancers devised intricate patterns of choreography. Their esteem was measured by the number of people who followed them when they danced.

In any society, art is produced for its aesthetic value as well as for religious purposes. According to Schildkrout and Keim (1990), non-Western art is usually, but wrongly, assumed to have some kind of connection to ritual. Non-Western art may be, but isn't always, linked with religion. Westerners have trouble accepting the idea that non-Western societies have art for art's sake just as Western societies do. There has been a tendency for Westerners to ignore the individuality of non-Western artists and their interest in creative expression. According to Isidore Okpewho (1977), an oral literature specialist, scholars have tended to see religion in all traditional African arts. Even when acting in the service of religion, there is room for individual creative expression. In the oral arts, for example, the audience is much more interested in the delivery and performance of the artist than in the particular god for whom the performer may be speaking.

LOCATING ART

Aesthetic value is one way of distinguishing art. Another way is to consider placement. The special places where we find art include museums, concert halls, opera houses, and theaters. If something is displayed in a museum, or in another socially accepted artistic setting, someone at least must think it's art. But decisions about what to admit as a work of art may be political and controversial. In our own society, museums often have to balance concern over community standards with a wish to be as creative and innovative as the artists and works they display. Although tribal societies typically lack museums, they may maintain special areas where artistic expression takes place. One example, discussed below, is the separate space in which ornamental burial poles are manufactured among the Tiwi of North Australia.

Will we know art if we see it? Art has been defined as involving that which is beautiful and of more than ordinary significance. But isn't beauty in the eye of the beholder? Don't reactions to art differ among spectators? And, if there can be secular ritual, can there also be ordinary art? The boundary between what's art and what's not is blurred. The American artist Andy Warhol is famous for transforming Campbell's soup cans, Brillo pads, and images of Marilyn Monroe into art. Many recent artists, such as Christo (see the photo on page 614) have tried to erase the distinction between art and ordinary life by converting the everyday into a work of art.

If something is mass produced or industrially modified, can it be art? Prints made as part of a series may certainly be considered art. Sculptures that are created in clay, then fired with molten metal, such as bronze, at a foundry, are also art. But how does one know if a film is art? Is *Star Wars* art? How about *Citizen Kane?* When a book wins a National Book Award, is it immediately elevated to the status of art? What kinds of prizes make art? Objects never intended as art, such as an Olivetti typewriter, may be transformed into art by being placed in a museum, such as New York's Museum of Modern Art. Jacques Maquet (1986) distinguishes such "art by transformation" from art created and intended to be art, which he calls "art by destination."

In state societies, we have come to rely on critics, judges, and experts to tell us what's art and what isn't. A recent play titled *Art* is about conflict that arises among three friends when one of them buys an all-white painting. They disagree, as people often do, about the definition and value of a work of art. Such variation in art appreciation is especially common in contemporary society, with its professional artists and critics and great cultural diversity. We'd expect more uniform standards and agreement in less-diverse, less-stratified societies.

To be culturally relativistic, we need to avoid applying our own standards about what art is to the products of other cultures. Sculpture is art, right? Not necessarily. Previously, we challenged the view that non-Western art always has some kind of connection to religion. The Kalabari case to be discussed now makes the opposite point: that religious sculpture is not always art.

This photo, taken in Berlin, Germany, illustrates art within art. In the background, the experimental artist Christo has wrapped the Reichstag, a German parliament building. In the foreground, visitors pose for souvenir photos. One man has wrapped himself in gold and stands on a box wrapped in green. The man and Christo's wrapped Reichstag are being incorporated as new art in the photo being taken. Do you think this is art?

Among the Kalabari of southern Nigeria (Figure 22.1), wooden sculptures are not carved for aesthetic reasons, but to serve as "houses" for spirits (Horton 1963). These sculptures are used to control the spirits of Kalabari religion. The Kalabari place such a carving, and thus localize a spirit, in a cult house into which the spirit is invited. Here, sculpture is done not for art's sake but as a means of manipulating spiritual forces. The Kalabari do have standards for the carvings, but beauty isn't one of them. A sculpture must be sufficiently complete to represent its spirit. Carvings judged too crude are rejected by cult members. Also, carvers must base their work on past models. Particular spirits have particular images associated with them. It's considered dangerous to produce a carving that deviates too much from a previous image of the spirit or that resembles another spirit. Offended spirits may retaliate. As long as they observe these standards of completeness and established images, carvers are free to express themselves.

See the Internet Exercises at your OLC for Kalabari masks

But these images are considered repulsive rather than beautiful. And they are not manufactured for artistic but for religious reasons. For these reasons, they probably should not be classified as art.

ART AND INDIVIDUALITY

Those who work with non-Western art have been criticized for ignoring the individual and focusing too much on the social nature and context of art. When art objects from Africa or Papua New Guinea are displayed in museums, generally only the name of the tribe and of the Western donor are given, rather than that of the individual artist. It's as though skilled individuals don't exist in non-Western societies. The impression is that art is collectively produced. Sometimes it is; sometimes it isn't.

To some extent, there is more collective production in non-Western societies than in the United States and Canada. According to Hackett (1996), African artworks (sculpted figures, textiles, paintings, or pots) are generally enjoyed, critiqued, and used by communities or groups, rather

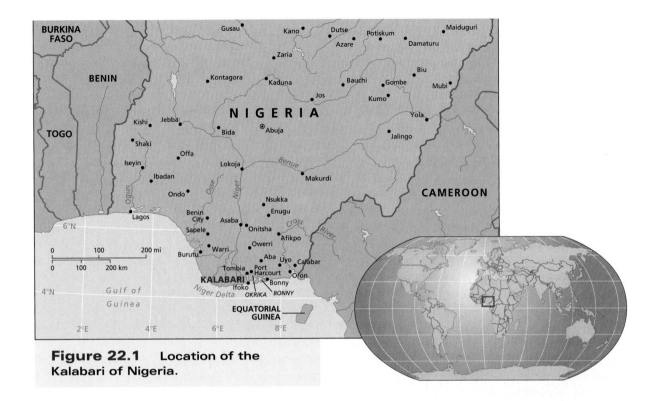

Figure 22.1 Location of the Kalabari of Nigeria.

than being the prerogative of the individual alone. The artist may receive more feedback during the creative process than the individual artist typically encounters in our own society. Here, the feedback often comes too late, after the product is complete, rather than during production, when it can still be changed.

During his field work among Nigeria's Tiv people, Paul Bohannan (1971) concluded that the proper study of art there should pay less attention to artists and more attention to art critics and products. There were few skilled Tiv artists, and such people avoided doing their art publicly. However, mediocre artists would work in public, where they routinely got comments from onlookers (critics). Based on critical suggestions, an artist often changed a design, such as a carving, in progress. There was yet another way in which Tiv artists worked socially rather than individually. Sometimes, when an artist put his work aside, someone else would pick it up and start working on it. The Tiv clearly didn't recognize the same kind of connection between individuals and their art that we do. According to Bohannan, every Tiv was free to know what he liked and to try to make it if he could. If not, one or more of his fellows might help him out.

In Western societies, artists of many sorts (e.g., painters, sculptors, actors, classical and rock musicians) have reputations for being iconoclastic and antisocial. Social acceptance may be more important in the societies anthropologists have traditionally studied. Still, there are well-known individual artists in non-Western societies. They are recognized as such by other community members and perhaps by outsiders as well. Their artistic labor may even be conscripted for special displays and performances, including ceremonies, or palace arts and events.

To what extent can a work of art stand apart from its artist? Philosophers of art commonly regard works of art as autonomous entities, independent of their creators (Haapala 1998). Haapala argues the contrary, that artists and their works are inseparable. "By creating works of art a person creates an artistic identity for himself. He creates himself quite literally into the pieces he puts into his art. He exists in the works he has created." In this view, Picasso created many Picassos, and exists in and through those works of art.

Sometimes little is known or recognized about the individual artist responsible for an enduring art work. We are more likely to know the name of the recording artist than of the writer of the songs we most commonly remember and perhaps sing. Sometimes we fail to acknowledge art individually because the artwork was collectively created. To whom should we attribute a pyramid or a cathedral? Should it be the architect, the ruler or leader who commissioned the work, or the master builder who implemented the design? A thing of beauty may be a joy forever even if and when we do not credit its creator(s).

THE WORK OF ART

Some may see art as a form of expressive freedom, as giving free range to the imagination and the human need to create or to be playful. But consider the word *opera*. It is the plural of *opus*, which means a work. For the artist, at least, art is work, albeit creative work. In nonstate societies, artists may have to hunt, gather, herd, fish, or farm in order to eat, but they still manage to find time to work on their art. In state societies, at least, artists have been defined as specialists—professionals who have chosen careers as artists, musicians, writers, or actors. If they manage to support themselves from their art, they may be full-time professionals. If not, they do their art part time, while earning a living from another activity. Sometimes artists associate in professional groups such as medieval guilds or contemporary unions. Actors Equity in New York, a labor union, is a modern guild, designed to protect the interests of its artist members.

Just how much work is needed to make a work of art? In the early days of French impressionism, many experts viewed the paintings of Claude Monet and his colleagues as too sketchy and spontaneous to be true art. Established artists and critics were accustomed to more formal and classic studio styles. The French impressionists got their name from their sketches—*impressions*—of natural and social settings. They took advantage of technological innovations, particularly the availability of oil paints in tubes, to take their palettes, easels, and canvases into the field. There they captured the images of changing light and color that hang today in so many museums, where they are now fully recognized as art. But before impressionism became an officially recognized "school" of art, its works were perceived by its critics as crude and unfinished. In terms of community standards, the first impressionist paintings were evaluated as harshly

as were the overly crude and incomplete Kalibari wood carvings of spirits, as discussed previously.

To what extent does the artist—or society—make the decision about completeness? For familiar genres, such as painting or music, societies tend to have standards by which they judge whether an art work is complete or fully realized. Most people would doubt, for instance, that an all-white painting could be a work of art. Standards may be maintained informally in society, or by specialists, such as art critics. It may be difficult for unorthodox or renegade artists to innovate. But, like the impressionists, they may eventually succeed. Some societies tend to reward conformity, an artist's skill with traditional models and techniques. Others encourage breaks with the past, innovation.

Art, Society, and Culture

More than 70,000 years ago, some of the world's first artists occupied Blombos Cave, located in a high cliff facing the Indian Ocean at the tip of what is now South Africa. They hunted game and ate fish from the waters below them. In terms of body and brain size, these ancient Africans were anatomically modern humans. They also were turning animal bones into finely worked tools and weapon points. Furthermore, they were engraving artifacts with symbolic marks—manifestations of abstract and creative thought and, presumably, communication through language (Wilford 2002).

A group led by Christopher Henshilwood of South Africa has analyzed 28 bone tools and other artifacts from Blombos Cave, along with the mineral ocher, which may have been used for body painting. The most impressive bone tools are three sharp instruments. The bone appears first to have been shaped with a stone blade, then finished into a symmetrical shape and polished for hours. According to Henshilwood (quoted in Wilford 2002), "It's actually unnecessary for projectile points to be so carefully made. It suggests to us that this is an expression of symbolic thinking. The people said, `Let's make a really beautiful object . . . ' Symbolic thinking means that people are using something to mean something else. The tools do not have to have only a practical purpose. And the ocher might be used to decorate their equipment, perhaps themselves."

In Europe, art goes back at least 30,000 years, to the Upper Paleolithic period in Western Europe (see Conkey et al. 1997). As reported at the beginning of this chapter, the first musical instrument, the "Divje babe flute," was made some 40,000 years ago. Cave paintings, the best-known examples of Upper Paleolithic art, were separated from ordinary life and everyday social space. Those images were painted in true caves, located deep in the bowels of the earth. They may have been painted as part of some kind of rite of passage involving retreat from society. Portable art objects carved in bone and ivory, along with musical whistles and flutes, also confirm artistic expression throughout the Upper Paleolithic.

Interpret the World   Map 22 in your atlas
Atlas Map 22   shows the worldwide distribution of sites of rock art (megaliths, petroglyphs, and cave paintings). What continents have several of those sites? Look at the image on page 608. Based on that image and on what you've read in this book, what kinds of economies do you think are associated with the production of rock art?

Art is usually more public than the cave paintings. Typically, it is exhibited, evaluated, performed, and appreciated in society. It has spectators or audiences. It isn't just for the artist.

Ethnomusicology is the comparative study of the musics of the world and of music as an aspect of culture and society. The field of ethnomusicology thus unites music and anthropology. The music side involves the study and analysis of the music itself and the instruments used to create it. The anthropology side views music as a way to explore a culture, to determine the role—historic and contemporary—that music plays in that society, and the specific social and cultural features that influence how music is created and performed.

Ethnomusicology studies non-Western music, traditional and folk music, even contemporary popular music from a cultural perspective. To do this there has to be field work—firsthand study of particular forms of music, their social functions and cultural meanings, within particular societies. Ethnomusicologists talk with local musicians, make recordings in the field, and learn about the place of musical instruments, performances, and performers in a given society (Kirman 1997).

Nowadays, given globalization, diverse cultures and musical styles easily meet and mix. Music that draws on a wide range of cultural instruments and styles is called World Fusion, World Beat, or World Music—another topic within contemporary ethnomusicology

Music, which is often performed in groups, would seem to be among the most social of the arts. Even master pianists and violinists are frequently accompanied by orchestras or singers. Alan Merriam (1971) describes how the Basongye people of the Kasai province of Congo (Figure 22.2) use three features to distinguish between music and other sounds, which are classified as "noise." First, music always involves humans. Sounds emanating from nonhuman creatures, such as birds and animals, are not music. Second, musical sounds must be organized. A single tap on the drum isn't music, but drummers playing together in a pattern is. Third, music must continue. Even if several drums are struck together simultaneously, it isn't music. They must go on playing to establish some kind of sound pattern. For the Basongye, then, music is inherently cultural (distinctly human) and social (dependent on cooperation).

Originally coined for European peasants, **"folk"** art, music, and lore refer to the expressive culture of ordinary people, as contrasted with the "high" art or "classic" art of the European elites. When European folk music is performed (see top photo on page 619), the combination of costumes, music, and often song and dance is supposed to say something about local culture and about tradition. Tourists and other outsiders often perceive rural and "folk" life mainly in terms of such performances. And community residents themselves often use such performances to display and enact their local culture and traditions for outsiders.

Art says something about continuity and change. Art can stand for tradition, even when traditional art is removed from its original (rural) context. As will be seen in the chapter "Cultural Exchange and Survival," the creative products and images of folk, rural, and non-Western cultures are increasingly spread—and commercialized—by the media and tourism. A result is that many Westerners have come to think of "culture" in terms of colorful customs, music, dancing, and adornments—clothing, jewelry, and hairstyles.

A bias toward the arts and religion, rather than more mundane, less photogenic, economic and

Figure 22.2 Location of the Basongye of the Democratic Republic of the Congo.

social tasks, shows up on TV's Discovery Channel, and even in many anthropological films. Many ethnographic films start off with music, often drum beats: "Bonga, bonga, bonga, bonga. Here in (supply place name), the people are very religious." We see in such presentations the previously critiqued assumption that the arts of nonindustrial societies usually have a link with religion. The (usually unintended) message is that non-Western peoples spend much of their time wearing colorful clothes, singing, dancing, and practicing religious rituals. Taken to an extreme, such images portray culture as recreational and ultimately unserious, rather than as something that ordinary people live every day of their lives—not just when they have festivals.

Art also functions in society as a form of communication between artist and community or audience. Sometimes, however, there are intermediaries between the artist and the audience. Actors, for example, are artists who translate the works and ideas of other artists (writers and directors) into the performances that audiences see and appreciate. Musicians play compositions of other people along with music they themselves have composed. Using music written by others, choreographers plan and direct patterns of dance, which dancers then execute for audiences.

Musicians in folk outfits play violins in a town square in Ljubljana, Slovenia. For whose pleasure do you suppose this performance is being given? Nowadays, such performances attract tourists as well as local people.

When it creates a significant national following, music can play a role in nation building. Nigeria's immensely popular singer Fela Kuti is shown here with three of his many wives, and fans in Lagos. What kind of music helps define your society?

How does art communicate? We need to know what the artist intends to communicate and how the audience reacts. Often, the audience communicates right back to the artist. Live performers, for instance, get immediate feedback, as may writers and directors by viewing a performance of their own work. Artists expect at least some variation in reception. In contemporary societies, with increasing diversity in the audience, uniform reactions are rare. Contemporary artists, like businesspeople, are well aware that they have target audiences. Certain segments of the population are more likely to appreciate certain forms of art than other segments are.

Understanding Ourselves One key development in North American culture since the 1970s, especially evident in the media, is a general shift from "massification" to "segmental appeal." An increasingly differentiated nation celebrates diversity. The mass media—print and electronic—join the trend, measuring various "demographics." The media aim their products and messages at particular segments—*target audiences*—rather than at an undifferentiated mass audience. Television, films, radio, music, magazines, and Internet forums all gear their topics, formats, and styles toward particular homogeneous segments of the population. In particular, cable and satellite TV, along with VCR and DVD players, have helped direct television, the most important mass medium, away from the networks' cherished mass audiences of the 1950s and 1960s and toward particular viewing segments. Special interest audiences can now choose from a multiplicity of targeted channels. Those channels specialize in music (country, pop, rock, Latin, or Black Entertainment), sports, news (financial, weather, headline), comedy, science fiction, gossip, movies (commercial, foreign, "art," "classic"), cartoons, old TV sitcoms, Spanish language, nature, travel, adventure, history, biography, and home shopping. The Super Bowl, Academy Awards, and Olympics still manage to capture large national and international audiences. But in 1998, the final episode of *Seinfeld,* though hugely popular, could not rival the mass audience shares of *Roots,* Lucy Ricardo's childbirth, or the final episode of *M*A*S*H.*

This photo, taken on October 13, 1996, shows the Names Project Memorial AIDS Quilt display, in Washington, D.C. Quilts with the names of AIDS victims are displayed on Washington Mall. What functions of art are illustrated in this photo?

Art can transmit several kinds of messages. It can convey a moral lesson or tell a cautionary tale. It can teach lessons the artist, or society, wants told. Like the rites that induce, then dispel, anxiety, the tension and resolution of drama can lead to **catharsis,** intense emotional release, in the audience. Art can move emotions, make us laugh, cry, feel up or down. Art appeals to the intellect as well as to the emotions. We may delight in a well-constructed, nicely balanced, well-realized work of art.

Art can be self-consciously prosocial. It can express community sentiment, with political goals, used to call attention to social issues. Often, art is meant to commemorate and to last. Like a ceremony, art may serve a mnemonic function, making people remember. Art, such as the quilt display shown in the photo on page 620, may be designed to make people remember either individuals or events, such as the AIDS epidemic that has proved so lethal in many world areas.

What is art's social role? To what extent should art serve society? Should the arts reflect, or question, community standards? We've seen that art has entered the political arena. Today, no museum director can mount an exhibit without worrying that it will offend some politically organized segment of society. The United States has an ongoing battle between liberals and conservatives involving the National Endowment for the Arts. Artists have been criticized as aloof from society, as creating only for themselves and for elites, as out of touch with conventional and traditional aesthetic values, even as mocking the values of ordinary people.

THE CULTURAL TRANSMISSION OF THE ARTS

For art on the Web, see the Internet Exercises at your OLC

mhhe
●com
/kottak

Because art is part of culture, appreciation of the arts depends on cultural background. Watch Japanese tourists in a Western art museum trying to interpret what they are seeing. Conversely, the form and meaning of a Japanese tea ceremony, or a demonstration of origami (Japanese paper folding), will be alien to a foreign observer. Appreciation for the arts must be learned. It is part of enculturation, as well as of more formal education. Robert Layton (1991) suggests that whatever universal principles

Appreciation for the arts must be learned. Here, three American boys seem intrigued by the painting "Paris on a Rainy Day" at the Chicago Art Institute. How does the placement of art in museums affect art appreciation?

Figure 22.3   Location of the Navajo.

of artistic expression may exist, they have been put into effect in a diversity of ways in different cultures.

What is aesthetically pleasing depends to some extent on culture. Based on familiarity, music with certain tonalities and rhythm patterns will please some people and alienate others. In a study of Navajo music, McAllester (1954) found that it reflected the overall culture of that time in three main ways: First, individualism is a key Navajo cultural value. Thus, it's up to the individual to decide what to do with his or her property—whether it be physical property, knowledge, ideas, or songs. Second, McAllester found that a general Navajo conservatism also extended to music. The Navajo saw foreign music as dangerous and rejected it as not part of their culture. (This second point is no longer true; there are now Navajo rock bands.) Third, a general stress on proper form applied to music. There is, in Navajo belief, a right way to sing every kind of song (see Figure 22.3 for the location of the Navajo).

People learn to listen to certain kinds of music and to appreciate particular art forms, just as they learn to hear and decipher a foreign language. Unlike Londoners and New Yorkers, Parisians don't flock to musicals. Despite its multiple French origins, even the musical *Les Miserables*, a huge hit in London, New York, and dozens of cities worldwide, bombed in Paris. Humor, too, a form of verbal art, depends on cultural background and setting. What's funny in one culture may not translate as funny in another. When a joke doesn't work, an American may say, "Well, you had to be there at the time." Jokes, like aesthetic judgments, depend on context.

At a smaller level of culture, certain artistic traditions may be transmitted in families. In Bali, for example, there are families of carvers, musicians, dancers, and mask makers. Among the Yoruba of Nigeria, two lineages of leather workers are entrusted with important bead embroidery works,

This photo was taken on St. Paul Island, on the Bering Sea coast of Alaska. A traditional Aleut storyteller uses a drum to tell his tale to young Aleut people. Who are the storytellers of your society? How do their narrative techniques and styles differ from the one shown here?

such as for the king's crown and the bags and bracelets of priests. The arts, like other professions, often "run" in families. The Bachs, for example, produced not only Johann Sebastian, but several other noted composers and musicians.

In Chapter 1, anthropology's approach to the arts was contrasted with a traditional humanities focus on "fine arts" and elite expressions. Anthropology has extended the definition of "cultured" well beyond the elitist meaning of "high" art and culture. For anthropologists, everyone acquires culture through enculturation. In academia, growing acceptance of the anthropological definition of culture has helped broaden the study of the humanities from fine art and elite art to popular and folk art and the creative expressions of the masses and of many cultures.

In many societies, myths, legends, tales, and the art of storytelling play important roles in the transmission of culture and the preservation of tradition. In the absence of writing, oral traditions may preserve details of history and genealogy, as in many parts of West Africa. Art forms often go together. For example, music and storytelling may be combined for drama and empha-sis (see the photo above), much as they are in films and theater.

At what age do children start learning the arts? In some cultures, they start early. Contrast the photo of the Korean violin class on page 627 with the photo of the Native Australian man playing the didgeridoo. The Korean scene shows formal instruction. The teachers take the lead in showing the kids how to play the violin. The Australian photo shows a more informal local scene in which children are observing, rather than being taught, about performing. Presumably, the Korean children are learning the arts because their parents want them to, not necessarily because they have an artistic temperament that they need or wish to express. Sometimes children's participation in arts or performance, including sports, exemplifies forced enculturation. It may be pushed by parents rather than by kids themselves. In the United States, performance, usually associated with schools, has a strong social, and usually competitive, component. Kids perform with their peers. In the process, they learn to compete, whether for a first place finish in a sports event or a first chair in the school orchestra or band.

Techniques that anthropologists have used to analyze myths and tales can be extended to two fantasy films that most of you have seen. *The Wizard of Oz* has been telecast annually for decades. The original *Star Wars* remains one of the most popular films of all time. Both are familiar and significant cultural products with obvious mythic qualities. The contributions of the French structuralist anthropologist Claude Lévi-Strauss (1967) and the neo-Freudian psychoanalyst Bruno Bettelheim (1975) to the study of myths and fairy tales permit the following analysis of visual fairy tales that contemporary Americans know well.

Examining the myths and tales of different cultures, Lévi-Strauss determined that one tale could be converted into another through a series of simple operations, for example, by doing the following:

1. Converting the positive element of a myth into its negative.
2. Reversing the order of the elements.
3. Replacing a male hero with a female hero.
4. Preserving or repeating certain key elements.

Through such operations, two apparently dissimilar myths can be shown to be variations on a common structure, that is, to be transformations of each other.

We'll see now that *Star Wars* is a systematic structural transformation of *The Wizard of Oz*. We may speculate about how many of the resemblances were conscious and how many simply reflect a process of enculturation that *Star Wars* writer and director George Lucas shares with other Americans.

The Wizard of Oz and *Star Wars* both begin in arid country, the first in Kansas and the second on the desert planet Tatooine (Table 22.1). *Star Wars* converts *The Wizard's* female hero into a boy, Luke Skywalker. Fairy-tale heroes usually have short, common first names and second names that describe their origin or activity. Thus Luke, who travels aboard spaceships, is a Skywalker, while Dorothy Gale is swept off to Oz by a cyclone (a gale of wind). Dorothy leaves home with her dog, Toto, who is pursued by and has managed to escape from a woman who in Oz becomes the Wicked Witch of the West. Luke follows his "Two-Two" (R2D2), who is fleeing Darth Vader, the witch's structural equivalent.

Dorothy and Luke each start out living with an uncle and an aunt. However, because of the gender change of the hero, the primary relationship is reversed and inverted. Thus, Dorothy's relationship with her aunt is primary, warm, and loving, whereas Luke's relationship with his uncle, though primary, is strained and distant. Aunt and uncle are in the tales for the same reason. They represent home (the nuclear family of orientation), which children (according to American culture norms) must eventually leave to make it on their own. As Bettelheim (1975) points out, fairy tales often disguise parents as uncle and aunt, and this establishes social distance. The child can deal with the hero's separation (in *The Wizard of Oz*) or the aunt's and uncle's deaths (in *Star Wars*) more easily than with the death of or separation from real parents. Furthermore, this permits the child's strong feelings toward his or her real parents to be represented in different, more central characters, such as the Wicked Witch of the West and Darth Vader.

Both films focus on the child's relationship with the parent of the same sex, dividing that parent into three parts. In *The Wizard,* the mother is split into two parts bad and one part good. They are the Wicked Witch of the East, dead at the beginning of the movie; the Wicked Witch of the West, dead at the end; and Glinda, the good mother, who survives. The original *Star Wars* reversed the proportion of good and bad, giving Luke a good father (his own), the Jedi knight who is proclaimed dead at the film's beginning. There is another good father, Ben Kenobi, who is ambiguously dead when the movie ends. Third is the evil father figure, Darth Vader. As the good-mother third survives *The Wizard of Oz*, the bad-father third lives on after *Star Wars*, to strike back in the sequel.

The child's relationship with the parent of the opposite sex also is represented in the two films. Dorothy's father figure is the Wizard of Oz, an initially terrifying figure who later is proved to be a fake. Bettelheim notes that the typical fairy-tale father is disguised as a monster or giant. Or else, when preserved as a human, he is weak, distant, or ineffective. Dorothy counts on the wizard to save her but finds that he makes seemingly impossible demands and in the end is just an ordinary man. She succeeds on her own, no longer relying on a father who offers no more than she herself possesses.

In *Star Wars* (although emphatically not in the later films), Luke's mother figure is Princess Leia. Bettelheim notes that boys commonly fantasize their mothers to be unwilling captives of their fathers. Fairy tales often disguise mothers as princesses whose freedom the boy-hero must obtain. In graphic Freudian imagery, Darth Vader threatens Princess Leia with a needle the size of the witch's broomstick. By the end of the film, Luke has freed Leia and defeated Vader.

(continued on next page)

Table 22.1   *Star Wars* **as a Structural Transformation of** *The Wizard of Oz*

Star Wars	The Wizard of Oz
Male hero (Luke Skywalker)	Female hero (Dorothy Gale)
Arid Tatooine	Arid Kansas

Luke follows R2D2:
  R2D2 flees Vader
	Dorothy follows Toto:
	  Toto flees witch

Luke lives with uncle and aunt:
  Primary relationship with uncle
   (same sex as hero)
  Strained, distant relationship with uncle
	Dorothy lives with uncle and aunt:
	  Primary relationship with aunt
	   (same sex as hero)
	  Warm, close relationship with aunt

Tripartite division of same-sex parent:
  2 parts good, 1 part bad father
  Good father dead at beginning
  Good father dead (?) at end
  Bad father survives
	Tripartite division of same-sex parent:
	  2 parts bad, 1 part good mother
	  Bad mother dead at beginning
	  Bad mother dead at end
	  Good mother survives

Relationship with parent of opposite sex
   (Princess Leia Organa):
  Princess is unwilling captive
  Needle
  Princess is freed
	Relationship with parent of opposite sex
	   (Wizard of Oz):
	  Wizard makes impossible demands
	  Broomstick
	  Wizard turns out to be sham

Trio of companions:
  Han Solo, C3PO, Chewbacca
	Trio of companions:
	  Scarecrow, Tin Woodman, Cowardly Lion

Minor characters:
  Jawas
  Sand People
  Stormtroopers
	Minor characters:
	  Munchkins
	  Apple Trees
	  Flying Monkeys

Settings:
  Death Star
  Verdant Tikal (rebel base)
	Settings:
	  Witch's castle
	  Emerald City

Conclusion:
  Luke uses magic to accomplish goal
   (destroy Death Star)
	Conclusion:
	  Dorothy uses magic to accomplish goal
	   (return to Kansas)

There are other striking parallels in the structure of the two films. Fairy-tale heroes often are accompanied on their adventures by secondary characters who personify the virtues needed in a successful quest. Such characters often come in threes. Dorothy takes along wisdom (the Scarecrow), love (the Tin Woodman), and courage (the Lion). *Star Wars* includes a structurally equivalent trio—Han Solo, C3PO, and Chewbacca—but their association with particular qualities isn't as precise. The minor characters are also structurally parallel: Munchkins and Jawas, Apple Trees and Sand People, Flying Monkeys and Stormtroopers. And compare settings—the witch's castle and the Death Star, the Emerald City and the rebel base. The endings are also parallel. Luke accomplishes his objective on his own, using the Force (mana, magical power). Dorothy's goal is to return to Kansas. She does that by tapping her shoes together and drawing on the Force in her ruby slippers.

All successful cultural products blend old and new, drawing on familiar themes. They may rearrange them in novel ways and thus win a lasting place in the imaginations of the culture that creates or accepts them. *Star Wars* successfully used old cultural themes in novel ways. It did that by drawing on *the* American fairy tale, one that had been available in book form since the turn of the 20th century.

THE ARTISTIC CAREER

In nonindustrial societies, artists tend to be part-time specialists. In states, there are more ways for artists to practice their craft full time. The number of positions in "arts and leisure" has mushroomed in contemporary societies, especially in North America. Many non-Western societies also offer career tracks in the arts: For example, a child born into a particular family or lineage may discover that he or she is destined for a career in leather working or weaving. Some societies are noted for particular arts, such as dance, wood carving, or weaving.

An artistic career also may involve some kind of a calling. Individuals may discover they have a particular talent and find an environment in which that talent is nourished. Separate career paths for artists usually involve special training and apprenticeship. Such paths are more likely in a complex society, where there are many separate career tracks, than in band or tribal societies, where expressive culture is less formally separated from daily life.

Artists need support if they are to devote full time to creative activity. They find support in their families or lineages if there is specialization in the arts involving kin groups. State societies often have patrons of the arts. Usually members of the elite class, patrons offer various kinds of support to aspiring and talented artists, such as court and palace painters, musicians, or sculptors. In some cases, an artistic career may entail a lifetime of dedication to religious art.

Goodal and Koss (1971) describe the manufacture of ornamental burial poles among the Tiwi of North Australia. Temporary separation and detachment from other social roles allowed burial pole artists to devote themselves to their work. The pole artists were ceremonially commissioned as such after a death. They were granted temporary freedom from the daily food quest. Other community members agreed to serve as their patrons. They supplied the artists with hard-to-get materials needed for their work. The burial pole artists were sequestered in a work area near the grave. That area was taboo to everyone else.

The arts are usually defined as neither practical nor ordinary. They rely on talent, which is individual, but which must be channeled and shaped in socially approved directions. Inevitably, artistic talent and production pull the artist away from the practical need to make a living. The issue of how to support artists and the arts arises again and again. We've all heard the phrase "struggling

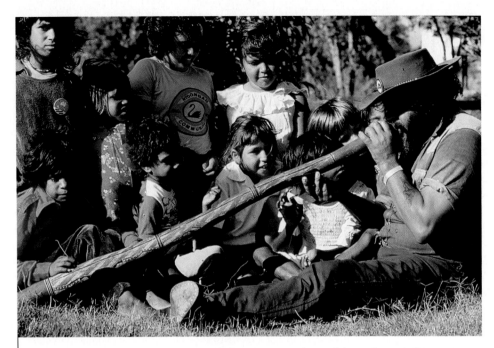

A Native Australian man blows into a didgeridoo, a traditional Australian wind instrument, as several children look on. This musical art is not set off from society. Making and playing the instrument are traditional skills.

A violin class for a large group of four-year-old children at a Korean music school.

Background Information

STUDENT:	Anne Haggerson
SUPERVISING PROFESSOR:	Rudi Colloredo-Mansfeld
SCHOOL:	University of Iowa
YEAR IN SCHOOL/MAJOR:	Senior/Anthropology and Spanish
FUTURE PLANS:	Internship in Washington, D.C.; Ph.D.
PROJECT TITLE:	Capoeira: The Afro-Brazilian Art of Unity and Survival

Which of the features and functions of art are illustrated by this account? Can you think of parallels to capoeira in form and/or function in your own society?

For two months, I lived in a small, concrete apartment in Mangueira, an inner-city shantytown constructed over trash and swamps in Salvador, Bahia. I was doing a fieldwork project for my senior thesis while working as an English teacher for GRUCON (Grupo de União e Consciência Negra), the local black consciousness movement that had been actively involved in community mobilization and youth-based consciousness raising projects for 30 years. My research focused on institutions that helped children and families overcome the forces of poverty, unemployment, racism, and failing schools. Thus, I set out to investigate capoeira, an Afro-Brazilian martial art that assumes metaphors of slavery, liberation, and survival. The capoeira academy in the neighborhood was a subset of GRUCON and was grounded in a shared historical identity, fighting against economic oppression and political exclusion through music, dance, and African pride.

To prepare for this work, I researched problems of street children, took advanced Portuguese language courses, and worked out a research design that included interviews and participant observation. I trained formally with a local capoeira group for five months before going to Brazil, familiarizing myself with the key movements and game etiquette. Joining a capoeira academy in Brazil was one of the most challenging aspects of my research since I was a white, American woman participating in an activity dominated by Afro-Brazilian men. However, my active participation in the art was a crucial part of my fieldwork, allowing me to enter into the physical and psychological space of my informants, experience the power of symbolic movement, and access the sense of friendship, unity, and commitment among the players.

The practices were held in a small, humble concrete room and

artist." But how should society support the arts? If there is state or religious support, something is typically expected in return. There is inevitably some limitation of the artist's "free" expression. Patronage and sponsorship also may result in the creation of art works that are removed from public display. Art commissioned for elites is often displayed only in their homes, perhaps finding its way into museums after their deaths. Church-commissioned art may be closer to the people. Artistic expressions of popular culture, intended for public rather than elite consumption, are discussed further in the chapter "Cultural Exchange and Survival."

CONTINUITY AND CHANGE

The arts go on changing, although certain art forms have survived for thousands of years. The Upper Paleolithic cave art that has survived 30,000 years was itself a highly developed manifestation of human creativity and symbolism, with an undoubtedly long evolutionary history. Monumental architecture along with sculpture, reliefs, ornamental pottery, and written music, literature, and drama have survived from early civilizations.

Countries and cultures are known for particular contributions, including art. The Balinese are known for dance; the Navajo for sand paintings, jewelry, and weaving; and the French for making cuisine an interviewed participants. I witnessed a spectacular annual community event called a batizado or baptism, where the students graduate to a higher-level capoeira belt. By observing and photographing this yearly initiation, it became clear that capoeira was much more than a pastime; it was a survival strategy, an educational tool, and a microcosmic social hierarchy that was maintained by a complex web of community political leaders and organizers.

Associated with rich memories of embarrassment and accomplishment, I proudly wear the capoeira warrior name the mestre gave me, "Serpente" or Snake, which, to me, is a symbolic tattoo that represents the dynamic beauty of doing anthropological fieldwork at the base level of urban society and thereby unleashing important insight on the resilient spirit of a vital civil society and the importance of building robust community institutions that spark political change and cultural solidarity.

were administered with a high level of discipline and seriousness. The mestre served as the teacher, role model, and mediator of the 40 team members and created meaning and stability in their lives, encouraging them to pass physical limits, harness leadership roles on the team, proudly display their skills in the roda or performance circle, and research the history of capoeira in their free time.

Beyond participant observation, I also recorded important events and

art form. We still read Greek tragedies and comedies in college, as we also read Shakespeare and Milton, and view the works of Michelangelo. Greek theater is among the most enduring of the arts. The words of Aeschylus, Sophocles, Euripides, and Aristophanes have been captured in writing and live on. Who knows how many great preliterate creations and performances have been lost?

Classic Greek theater survives throughout the world. It is read in college courses, seen in the movies, and performed live on stages from Athens to New York. In today's world, the dramatic arts are part of a huge "arts and leisure" industry, which links Western and non-Western art forms in an international network that has both aesthetic and commercial dimensions (see Marcus and Myers 1995; Root 1996). For example, non-Western musical traditions and instruments, including the Australian didgeridoo shown in the photo on page 627, don't function apart from the modern world system. We've seen that local musicians perform for outsiders, including tourists who increasingly visit their villages. And "tribal" instruments such as didgeridoos are now exported worldwide. At least one store in Amsterdam, the Netherlands, specializes in didgeridoos, the only item it carries. Dozens of stores in any world capital hawk "traditional" arts, including musical instruments, from a

Art, Society, and Culture   **629**

In Athens, Greece, ancient Greek theater is being staged for a contemporary audience. Theater is typically a multimedia experience, with visual, aural, and often musical attributes.

A synthesis of new and old theater techniques, including puppetry, is used in the Broadway production of Disney's *The Lion King*. What artistic influences have inspired the images shown in this photo?

hundred Third World countries. The commodification of non-Western art and the contemporary use of the arts to forge and redefine group identities are discussed further in the chapter "Cultural Exchange and Survival."

We've seen that the arts typically draw in multiple media. Given the richness of today's media world, multimedia are even more marked. As ingredients and flavors from all over the world are combined in modern cuisine, so, too, are elements from many cultures and epochs woven into contemporary art and performance.

Our culture values change, experimentation, innovation, and novelty. But creativity also may be based on tradition. The Navajo, remember, can be at once individualistic, conservative, and attentive to proper form. In some cases and cultures, it's not necessary for artists to be innovative as they are being creative. Creativity can be expressed in variations on a traditional form. We see an example of this in "Interesting Issues" on pages 624–626, in which *Star Wars,* despite its specific story and innovative special effects, is shown to share its narrative structure with a previous film and fairy tale. It isn't always necessary for artists, in their work, to make a statement separating themselves from the past. Often, artists pay fealty to the past, associating with and building on, rather than rejecting, the work of their predecessors.

SUMMARY

1. Even if they lack a word for "art," people everywhere do associate an aesthetic experience with objects and events having certain qualities. The arts, sometimes called "expressive culture," include the visual arts, literature (written and oral), music, and theater arts. Some issues raised about religion also apply to art. If we adopt a special attitude or demeanor when confronting a sacred object, do we display something similar with art? Much art has been done in association with religion. In tribal performances, the arts and religion often mix. But non-Western art isn't always linked to religion.

2. The special places where we find art include museums, concert halls, opera houses, and theaters. However, the boundary between what's art and what's not may be blurred. Variation in art appreciation is especially common in contemporary society, with its professional artists and critics and great cultural diversity.

3. Those who work with non-Western art have been criticized for ignoring individual artists and for focusing too much on the social context and collective artistic production. Art is work, albeit creative work. In state societies, some people manage to support themselves as full-time artists. In nonstates artists are normally part time. Community standards judge the mastery and completion displayed in a work of art. Typically, the arts are exhibited, evaluated, performed, and appreciated in society. Music, which is often performed in groups, is among the most social of the arts. "Folk" art, music, and lore refer to the expressive culture of ordinary, usually rural, people.

4. Art can stand for tradition, even when traditional art is removed from its original context. Art can express community sentiment, with political goals, used to call attention to social issues. Often, art is meant to commemorate and to last. Growing acceptance of the anthropological definition of culture has guided the humanities beyond fine art, elite art, and Western art to the creative expressions of the masses and of many cultures. Myths, legends, tales, and the art of storytelling often play important roles in the transmission of culture. Many societies offer career tracks in the arts; a child born into a particular family or lineage may discover that he or she is destined for a career in leather working or weaving.

5. The arts go on changing, although certain art forms have survived for thousands of years. Countries and cultures are known for particular contributions. Today, a huge "arts and leisure" industry links Western and non-Western art forms in an international network with both aesthetic and commercial dimensions.

KEY TERMS

See the flash cards

aesthetics Appreciation of the qualities perceived in works of art; the mind and emotions in relation to a sense of beauty.

art An object or event that evokes an aesthetic reaction—a sense of beauty, appreciation, harmony, and/or pleasure; the quality, production, expression, or realm of what is beautiful or of more than ordinary significance; the class of objects subject to aesthetic criteria.

arts The arts include the visual arts, literature (written and oral), music, and theater arts.

catharsis Intense emotional release.

ethnomusicology The comparative study of the musics of the world and of music as an aspect of culture and society.

expressive culture The arts; people express themselves creatively in dance, music, song, painting, sculpture, pottery, cloth, storytelling, verse, prose, drama, and comedy.

folk Of the people; originally coined for European peasants; refers to the art, music, and lore of ordinary people, as contrasted with the "high" art or "classic" art of the European elites.

CRITICAL THINKING QUESTIONS

For more self testing, see the self quizzes

1. Think of something visual that you consider to be art, but whose status as art is debatable. How would you convince someone else that it is art? What kinds of arguments against your position would you expect to hear?

2. Think of a musical composition or performance you consider to be art, but whose status as such is debatable. How would you convince someone else that it is art? What kinds of arguments against your position would you expect to hear?

3. Where did you last witness art? In what kind of a setting was it? Did people go there to appreciate the arts, or for some other reason?

4. Is *Star Wars* art? If so, what kind of art? How would you analyze it as art?

5. Based on your own experience, how may the arts be used to buttress religion?

6. Can you think of a political dispute involving art or the arts? What were the different positions being debated?

7. Should society support the arts? Why or why not? If so, how?

Atlas Questions

Look at Map 22, "Megaliths, Petroglyphs, and Cave Paintings."

1. Is rock art (i.e., megaliths, petroglyphs, and cave paintings) found on all continents? Which continent has the fewest rock art sites? Why is that, do you think?

2. Compare Maps 16 and 22 and consider how the production of rock art may be related to the type of economy.

Suggested Additional Readings

Anderson, R.

1989   *Art in Small-Scale Societies.* Upper Saddle River, NJ: Prentice-Hall. Introduction to non-Western art, with a focus on the visual arts.

1990   *Calliope's Sisters: A Comparative Study of Philosophies of Art.* Upper Saddle River, NJ: Prentice-Hall. A comparative study of aesthetics in 10 cultures.

2000   *American Muse: Anthropological Excursions into Art and Aesthetics.* Upper Saddle River, NJ: Prentice-Hall. Bringing an anthropological perspective to bear on arts in America.

Anderson, R., and K. Field, eds.

1993   *Art in Small-Scale Societies: Contemporary Readings.* Upper Saddle River, NJ: Prentice-Hall. An anthology of studies of non-Western art, with a focus on the visual arts.

Conkey, M., O. Soffer, D. Stratmann, and N. Jablonski

1997   *Beyond Art: Pleistocene Image and Symbol.* San Francisco: Memoirs of the California Academy of Sciences, no. 23. A consideration of the symbolic basis and nature of prehistoric art.

Coote, J., and A. Shelton, eds.

1992   *Anthropology, Art, and Aesthetics.* New York: Oxford University Press. Useful collection of essays.

Hatcher, E. P.

1999   *Art as Culture: An Introduction to the Anthropology of Art,* 2nd ed. Westport, CT: Bergin & Garvey. Up-to-date introduction.

Layton, R.

1991   *The Anthropology of Art,* 2nd ed. New York: Cambridge University Press. Survey of the major issues, with a focus on visual art.

Marcus, G. E., and F. R. Myers, eds.

1995   *The Traffic in Culture: Refiguring Art and Anthropology.* Berkeley: University of California Press. Art, society, and the marketing of culture in global perspective.

Mirzoeff, N.

1999   *An Introduction to Visual Culture.* New York: Routledge. Popular culture, art, and society.

Myers, F. R.

2002   *Painting Culture: The Making of an Aboriginal High Art.* Durham, NC: Duke University Press. Artistic transformation in Australia's western desert.

Napier, A. D.

1992   *Foreign Bodies: Performance, Art, and Symbolic Anthropology.* Berkeley: University of California Press. Focuses on the performing arts and symbols of society.

Otten, C. M., ed.

1971   *Anthropology and Art: Readings in Cross-Cultural Aesthetics.* Garden City, NY: American Museum of Natural History. Classic anthology.

Root, D.

1996   *Cannibal Culture: Art, Appropriation, and the Commodification of Difference.* Boulder, CO: Westview. How Western art and commerce classify, co-opt, and commodify "native" experiences, creations, and products.

Rushing, W. Jackson, ed.

1999   *Native American Art in the Twentieth Century.* New York: Routledge. Themes, motifs, and collections of Indian art.

Internet Exercises

1. *Body Art:* Visit the National Museum of Natural History's online exhibit of "Canela body adornment," **http://www.nmnh.si.edu/naa/canela/canela1.htm.** Read all three pages of the exhibit and answer the questions below:

   a. In this example, how interrelated are art and worldview? How is art being used by the Canela?

   b. What individuals among the Canela get their ears pierced, and what does it signify? Who participates in the piercing? How does this practice compare to ear piercing in Western society?

   c. Cultures can change through time. What kinds of changes have occurred in the Canela practices of ear piercing since the 1950s? In the same way, what kinds of changes have occurred in ear piercing practices in Western society? What do these changes signify?

2. Comparing Art: Go to the Metropolitan Museum of Art's Collection page, **http://www.metmuseum.org/collections/index.asp** and browse their collections of Egyptian Art, **http://www.metmuseum.org/collections/department.asp?dep=10,** European Paintings, **http://www.metmuseum.org/collections/department.asp?dep=11,** and Modern Art, **http://www.metmuseum.org/collections/department.asp?dep=21. ,** For each of these collections, address the following questions:

   a. By whom is this art produced, and for whom is it produced?

   b. For what purpose is this art being produced (e.g., religious, aesthetic, political, monetary)?

   c. What themes and subjects are portrayed in the art?

   d. By just looking at the art, what can you learn about the culture that produced it?

See Chapter 22 at your McGraw-Hill Online Learning Center for additional review and interactive exercises.

Part Four

The Changing World

Part 4 focuses on our changing world. What is the anthropological relevance of the global changes that have occurred over the last several centuries, since the start of the European "Age of Discovery." The chapter entitled "The Modern World System" examines the formation of the world capitalist economy, the rise of industrialization in Europe, the expansion of industrialization and its impact on the rest of the world. Also considered are the new systems of stratification created by industrialism, in Europe and beyond, from the 18th century through the present time. Next, the chapter "Colonialism and Development" begins with a discussion of colonialism and imperialism. We examine the intervention philosophies (justifications for interfering in the affairs of others) that accompanied these forms of political domination. We also examine the effects of colonialism on the peoples and societies that anthropologists traditionally have studied. The second part of this chapter considers the role of anthropology in economic development—a more recent form of intervention by First World nations, with its own goals and intervention philosophy. Various fallacies of development are discussed, along with the

relation between local people and the development schemes that affect them. "Cultural Resistance and Survival," the last chapter, considers how local people throughout the world have experienced and dealt with the expansion of the world system and with various forms of domination—political, economic, cultural, and religious. Forms of compliance and resistance are discussed in relation to cultural change and the survival of native forms and indigenous peoples. The book concludes by recognizing that anthropology has a crucial role to play in promoting a more humanistic vision of social change, one that respects the value of human biological and cultural diversity.

23

THE MODERN WORLD SYSTEM

Overview

Local societies increasingly participate in wider systems, which are regional, national, and global in scale. The modern world system refers to a global system in which nations are economically and politically interdependent.

The world economy is based on production for sale, guided by the profit motive. This capitalist world economy has political and economic specialization based on three positions: core, semiperiphery, and periphery. These positions have existed since the 16th century, although the particular countries filling them have changed.

After 1760, industrialization increased production in farming and manufacturing. The work force moved from homes to factories, from rural areas to industrial cities. Today's world system

maintains the distinction between those who own the means of production and those who don't. But the division is now worldwide. And a middle class of skilled and professional workers has been added to the class structure.

There is a marked contrast between capitalists and workers in the core nations and workers on the periphery. Several forces have worked to remove people from the land, as even peripheral nations have begun to industrialize. One effect of industrialization has been the destruction of indigenous economies, ecologies, cultures, and peoples. For the past 500 years, the main forces influencing cultural interaction have been commercial expansion, industrial capitalism, and the differential power of core nations.

Bones Reveal Some Truth in "Noble Savage Myth"

WASHINGTON POST NEWS BRIEFS

by Jack Lucentini

April 15, 2002

This news brief brings into focus an anthropological debate about the origin and nature of warfare and the role of European contact in fostering violence among indigenous peoples. The study shows that violence among indigenous peoples in North and Central America increased after contact. As the article begins, it suggests, mistakenly, that Native Americans lived in prehistory and lacked "civilization." In fact, Native Americans developed states and "civilizations" (e.g., Aztec, Maya, Inca) comparable to those of the Old World (e.g., ancient Mesopotamia and Egypt). Native Americans, most notably the Maya, also developed writing, which they used to record their history—rendering the label *prehistory* inaccurate. As you read, to understand why violence increased after contact, pay attention to the role of trade, disease, and slave raiding. Does one side of the debate described here strike you as more plausible than the other?

The encounter between Hernán Cortés (1485–1547) and Montezuma II (1466–1520) was the subject of this 1820 painting by Gallo Gallina of Milan, Italy. Cortés went on to conquer Montezuma's Aztec empire.

A romantic-sounding notion dating back more than 200 years has it that people in prehistory, such as Native Americans, lived in peace and harmony.

Then "civilization" showed up, sowing violence and discord. Some see this claim as naive. It even has a derisive nickname, the "noble savage myth." But new research seems to suggest the "myth" contains at least some truth. Researchers examined thousands of Native American skeletons and found that those from after Christopher Columbus landed in the New World showed a rate of traumatic injuries more than 50 percent higher than those from before the Europeans arrived.

"Traumatic injuries do increase really significantly," said Philip L. Walker, an anthropology professor at the University of California at Santa Barbara, who conducted the study with Richard H. Steckel of Ohio State University.

The findings suggest "Native Americans were involved in more violence after the Europeans arrived than before," Walker said. But he emphasized there was also widespread violence before the Europeans came. Nevertheless, he said, "probably we're just seeing the tip of the iceberg" as far as the difference between violence levels before and after.

That's because as many as half of bullet wounds miss the skeleton. Thus, the study couldn't detect much firearm violence, though some tribes wiped each other out using European-supplied guns.

The findings shed light on a controversy that has stirred not only living room discussions, but also an intense, sometimes ugly debate among anthropologists.

It involves two opposing views of human nature: Are we hard-wired for violence, or pushed into it?

Anthropologists who believe the latter seized on the findings as evidence for their view. "What it all says to me is that humans aren't demonic. Human males don't have an ingrained propensity for war. . . . They can learn to be very peaceful, or terribly violent," said R. Brian Ferguson, a professor of anthropology at Rutgers University in Newark. Ferguson contends that before about 10,000 years ago, war was virtually nonexistent. But experts on the opposing side also said the findings fit their views.

"A 50 percent increase is the equivalent of moving from a suburb to the city, in terms of violence," said Charles Stanish, a professor of anthropology at the University of California at Los Angeles. "This shows the Native Americans were like us. Under stress, they fought more." Both sides called the study, which was presented Friday at the annual meeting of the American Association of Physical Anthropologists in Buffalo, a valuable contribution. . . .

Walker and colleagues examined the skeletons of 3,375 pre-Columbian and 1,165 post-Columbian Native Americans, from archaeological sites throughout North and Central America.

The North Americans came mostly from the coasts and the Great Lakes region, Walker said.

Pre-Columbian skeletons showed an 11 percent incidence of traumatic injuries, he said, compared with almost 17 percent for the post-Columbians.

Walker said his findings surprised him. "I wasn't really expecting it," he said. Yet it undeniably suggests violence, he added. Most of the increase consisted of head injuries in young males, "which conforms pretty closely to the pattern you see today in homicides."

The researchers defined "traumatic injury" as anything leaving a mark on the skeleton, such as a skull fracture, a healed broken arm, or an embedded arrow point or bullet.

Walker said that although part of the increased injury rate doubtless stems from violence by whites themselves, it probably reflects mostly native-on-native violence. "In a lot of cases, such as in California, there weren't that many Europeans around—just a few priests, and thousands of Indians," he said.

Walker said the higher injury rate could have many explanations. Increased violence is normally associated with more densely populated, settled life, which Native Americans experienced in modernity, he said. Disease could also touch off war, he said.

"Here in California, there was a lot of inter-village warfare associated with the introduction of European diseases. People would attribute the disease to evil shamanic activity in another village," he said. Ferguson cited other factors. The Europeans often drew natives into their imperial wars, he said.

"Sometimes, the Europeans would enable someone to pursue a preexisting fight more aggressively, by backing one side," he added. Other times, he said, Europeans got natives to conduct slave raids on one another. Natives also fought over control of areas around trading outposts, to become middlemen, he said. "Sometimes that was a life-or-death matter, since it meant the difference between who would get guns or not." Stanish agreed. "Obviously, having an expanding imperial power coming at you is going to

exacerbate tensions," he said . . . They're going to push you somewhere—into other groups."

"You're also going to get competition over access to the Europeans, who are a form of wealth," he added. Native Americans fought over areas rich in fur, which the whites would buy.

Yet Native American warfare was widespread long before that, Stanish said. . . .

Keith F. Otterbein, an anthropology professor at the State University of New York at Buffalo, said the skeleton findings contribute to a balanced, middle-of-the-road view.

"The folks who are saying there was no early warfare—they're wrong, too. There is, in fact, a myth of the peaceful savage," he said. Otterbein said the controversy won't end here; both sides are too ideologically entrenched.

"Underlying the 'noble savage' myth," Stanish said, "is a political agenda by both the far right and far left. The right tries to turn the 'savages' into our little brown brothers, who need to be pulled up. . . . On the left, they have another agenda, that the Western world is bad."

Source: http://www.washingtonpost.com/ac2/wp-dyn?pagename=article &node=&contentId=A48 202-2002Apr14; in newspaper on p. A09.

Travel, trade, and murder may be as old as humanity. However, there is no doubt, as the study you just read confirms, that contact with Europe increased the scale of trade, interethnic contact, and violence in the Americas—and throughout the world. These trends continue today. Thus, although field work in small communities is anthropology's hallmark, isolated groups are impossible to find today and probably have never existed. For thousands of years, human groups have been in contact with one another. Local societies have always participated in a larger system, which today has global dimensions. We call it the modern world system, by which we mean a world in which nations are economically and politically interdependent.

City, nation, and world increasingly invade local communities. Today, if anthropologists want to study a fairly isolated society, they must journey to the highlands of Papua New Guinea or the tropical forests of South America. Even in those places, they probably will encounter missionaries, prospectors, and tourists. In contemporary Australia, sheep owned by people who speak English graze where totemic ceremonies once were held. Farther in the outback, some descendants of those totemites may be working for a TV crew making the latest version of a *Crocodile Dundee* movie or a *Survivor* telecast. A Hilton hotel stands in the capital of faraway Madagascar, and a paved highway now has an exit for Arembepe, the Brazilian fishing village I have been studying since 1962. When and how did the modern world system begin?

The world system and the relations among the countries within that system are shaped by the world capitalist economy. World-system theory can be traced to the French social historian Fernand Braudel. In his three-volume work *Civilization and Capitalism, 15th–18th Century* (1981, 1982, 1992), Braudel argued that society consists of parts assembled into an interrelated system. Societies are subsystems of bigger systems, with the world system as the largest.

The modern world system rests on the world capitalist economy. Shown here is a Honda motorcycle plant, the world's largest such plant, in Bangkok, Thailand. Is Honda a Thai firm? Where do you imagine such motorcycles are sold?

The Emergence of the World System

As Europeans took to ships, developing a transoceanic trade-oriented economy, people throughout the world entered Europe's sphere of influence. In the 15th century, Europe established regular contact with Asia, Africa, and eventually the New World (the Caribbean and the Americas). Christopher Columbus's first voyage from Spain to the Bahamas and the Caribbean in 1492 was soon followed by additional voyages. These journeys opened the way for a major exchange of people, resources, diseases, and ideas, as the Old and New Worlds were forever linked (Crosby 1972, 1986; Diamond 1997; Viola and Margolis 1991). Led by Spain and Portugal, Europeans extracted silver and gold, conquered the natives (taking some as slaves), and colonized their lands.

Previously in Europe as throughout the world, rural people had produced mainly for their own needs, growing their own food and making clothing, furniture, and tools from local products. Production beyond immediate needs was undertaken to pay taxes and purchase trade items such as salt and iron. As late as 1650, the English diet, like diets in most of the world today, was based on locally grown starches (Mintz 1985). However, in the 200 years that followed, the English became extraordinary consumers of imported goods. One of the earliest and most popular of those goods was sugar (Mintz 1985).

Sugarcane was originally domesticated in Papua New Guinea, and sugar was first processed in India. Reaching Europe via the Middle East and the eastern Mediterranean, it was carried to the New World by Columbus (Mintz 1985). The climate of Brazil and the Caribbean proved ideal for growing sugarcane, and Europeans built plantations there to supply the growing demand for sugar. This led to the development in the 17th century of a plantation economy based on a single cash crop—a system known as monocrop production.

The demand for sugar in a growing international market spurred the development of the

From producer to consumer, in the modern world system. The top photo, taken in the Caribbean nation of Dominica, shows the hard labor required to extract sugar using a manual press. In the bottom photo, an English middle-class family enjoys afternoon tea, sweetened with imported sugar. Which of the ingredients in your breakfast today were imported?

transatlantic slave trade and New World plantation economies based on slave labor. By the 18th century, an increased English demand for raw cotton led to rapid settlement of what is now the southeastern United States and the emergence there of another slave-based monocrop production system. Like sugar, cotton was a key trade item that fueled the growth of the world system.

The increasing dominance of trade led to the **capitalist world economy** (Wallerstein 1982), a single world system committed to production for sale or exchange, with the object of maximizing profits rather than supplying domestic needs. **Capital** refers to wealth or resources invested in business, with the intent of producing a profit; the defining attribute of capitalism is economic orientation to the world market for profit.

The key claim of world-system theory is that an identifiable social system, based on wealth and power differentials, extends beyond individual states and nations. That system is formed by a set of economic and political relations that have characterized much of the globe since the 16th century, when the Old World established regular contact with the New World.

According to Wallerstein (1982), the nations within the world system occupy three different positions of economic and political power: core, periphery, and semiperiphery. There is a geographic center or **core,** the dominant position in the world system, consisting of the strongest and most powerful nations. In core nations, "the complexity of economic activities and the level of capital accumulation is [sic] the greatest" (Thompson 1983, p. 12). With its sophisticated technologies and mechanized means of production, the core produces capital-intensive high-technology goods. Most of those products flow to other core nations, but some also go to the periphery and semiperiphery. According to Arrighi (1994), the core monopolizes the most profitable activities, especially the control of world finance.

Semiperiphery and **periphery** nations, which roughly correspond to what is usually called the Third World, have less power, wealth, and influence. The semiperiphery is intermediate between the core and the periphery. Contemporary nations of the semiperiphery are industrialized. Like core nations, they export both industrial goods and commodities, but they lack the power and economic dominance of core nations. Thus Brazil, a semiperiphery nation, exports automobiles to Nigeria and auto engines, orange juice extract, and coffee to the United States.

Economic activities in the periphery are less mechanized and use human labor more intensively than do those in the semiperiphery. The periphery produces raw materials, agricultural commodities, and, increasingly, human labor for export to the core and the semiperiphery. In the modern world, industrialization has reached even peripheral nations. The relationship between the core and the periphery is fundamentally exploitative. Trade and other forms of economic relations between core and periphery disporportionately benefit capitalists in the core (Shannon 1996).

Thus, in the United States and Western Europe today, migrants, legal and illegal, supply cheap labor for agriculture in core countries. U.S. states as distant as California, Michigan, and South Carolina make significant use of farm labor from Mexico. The availability of relatively cheap workers from noncore nations such as Mexico (in the United States) and Turkey (in Germany) benefits farmers and business owners in core countries, while also supplying remittances to families in the semiperiphery and periphery.

Industrialization

By the 18th century, the stage had been set for the **Industrial Revolution**—the historic transformation (in Europe, after 1750) of "traditional" into "modern" societies through industrialization of the economy. Industrialization required capital for investment. The established system of transoceanic trade and commerce supplied this capital from the enormous profits it generated. Wealthy people sought investment opportunities and eventually found them in machines and engines to drive machines. Industrialization increased production in both farming and manufacturing, as capital and scientific innovation fueled invention.

European industrialization developed from (and eventually replaced) the domestic system (cottage industry or home-handicraft system) of manufacture. In this system, an organizer-entrepreneur supplied the raw materials to workers in their homes and collected the finished products from them. The entrepreneur, whose sphere of operations might span several villages, owned the materials, paid for the work, and arranged the marketing.

CAUSES OF THE INDUSTRIAL REVOLUTION

The Industrial Revolution began in the cotton products, iron, and pottery trades. These were widely used goods whose manufacture could be broken down into simple routine motions that machines could perform. When manufacturing moved from home to factory, where machinery replaced handwork, agrarian societies evolved into industrial ones. As factories produced cheap staple goods, the Industrial Revolution led to a dramatic increase in production. Industrialization fueled urban growth and created a new kind of city, with factories crowded together in places where coal and labor were cheap.

The Industrial Revolution began in England rather than in France (Figure 23.1). Why? Unlike the English, the French didn't have to transform

Figure 23.1   **Location of England (United Kingdom) and France.**

their domestic manufacturing system by industrializing. Faced with an increased need for products, with a late-18th-century population twice that of Great Britain, France could simply extend its domestic system of production by drawing in new homes. The French were able to increase production without innovating—they could enlarge the existing system rather than adopt a new one. However, to meet mounting demand for staples—at home and in its colonies—England, with fewer workers, had to industrialize.

Britain's population doubled during the 18th century (particularly after 1750) and did so again between 1800 and 1850. This demographic explosion fueled consumption, but British entrepreneurs couldn't meet the increased demand with the traditional production methods. This spurred experimentation, innovation, and rapid technological change.

English industrialization drew on national advantages in natural resources. Great Britain was rich in coal and iron ore and had navigable waterways and easily negotiated coasts. It was a seafaring island-nation located at the crossroads of international trade. These features gave Britain a favored position for importing raw materials and exporting manufactured goods. Another factor in England's industrial growth was the fact that much of its 18th-century colonial empire was occupied by English settler families who looked to the mother country as they tried to replicate European civilization in the New World. These colonies bought large quantities of English staples.

It also has been argued that particular cultural values and religion contributed to industrialization. Thus, many members of the emerging English middle class were Protestant nonconformists. Their beliefs and values encouraged industry, thrift, the dissemination of new knowledge, inventiveness, and willingness to accept change (Weber 1904/1958). Weber's ideas about Protestant values and capitalism were discussed in the chapter "Religion."

In the home-handicraft, or domestic, system of production, an organizer supplied raw materials to workers in their homes and collected their products. Family life and work were intertwined, as in this English scene. Is there a modern equivalent to the domestic system of production?

Stratification

The socioeconomic effects of industrialization were mixed. English national income tripled between 1700 and 1815 and increased 30 times more by 1939. Standards of comfort rose, but prosperity was uneven. At first, factory workers got wages higher than those available in the domestic system. Later, owners started recruiting labor in places where living standards were low and labor (including that of women and children) was cheap.

Social ills increased with the growth of factory towns and industrial cities, with conditions like those Charles Dickens described in *Hard Times*. Filth and smoke polluted the 19th-century cities. Housing was crowded and unsanitary, with insufficient water and sewage disposal facilities and rising disease and death rates. This was the world of Ebenezer Scrooge, Bob Cratchit, Tiny Tim—and Karl Marx.

INDUSTRIAL STRATIFICATION

The social theorists Karl Marx and Max Weber focused on the stratification systems associated with industrialization. From his observations in England

Karl Marx (1818–1883), shown in 1860.

working class, or proletariat, was made up of people who had to sell their labor to survive. With the decline of subsistence production and with the rise of urban migration and the possibility of unemployment, the bourgeoisie came to stand between workers and the means of production.

Industrialization hastened the process of *proletarianization*—the separation of workers from the means of production. The bourgeoisie also came to dominate the means of communication, the schools, and other key institutions. Marx viewed the nation-state as an instrument of oppression and religion as a method of diverting and controlling the masses.

Class consciousness (recognition of collective interests and personal identification with one's economic group) was a vital part of Marx's view of class. He saw bourgeoisie and proletariat as socioeconomic divisions with radically opposed interests. Marx viewed classes as powerful collective forces that could mobilize human energies to influence the course of history. Finding strength through common experience, workers would develop organizations to protect their interests and increase their share of industrial profits.

And so they did. During the 19th century, trade unions and socialist parties emerged to express a rising anticapitalist spirit. The concerns of the English labor movement were to remove young children from factories and limit the hours during which women and children could work. The profile of stratification in industrial core nations gradually took shape. Capitalists controlled production, but labor was organizing for better wages and working conditions. By 1900, many governments had factory legislation and social-welfare programs. Mass living standards in core nations rose as population grew.

The modern capitalist world system maintains the distinction between those who own the means of production and those who don't. The class division into capitalists and propertyless workers is now worldwide. Nevertheless, modern stratification systems aren't simple and dichotomous. They include (particularly in core and semiperiphery nations) a middle class of skilled and professional workers. Gerhard Lenski (1966) argues that social equality tends to increase in advanced industrial societies. The masses improve their access to economic benefits and political power. In Lenski's scheme, the shift of political power to the masses

and his analysis of 19th-century industrial capitalism, Marx (Marx and Engels 1848/1976) saw socioeconomic stratification as a sharp and simple division between two opposed classes: the bourgeoisie (capitalists) and the proletariat (propertyless workers). The bourgeoisie traced its origins to overseas ventures and the world capitalist economy, which had transformed the social structure of northwestern Europe, creating a wealthy commercial class.

Industrialization shifted production from farms and cottages to mills and factories, where mechanical power was available and where workers could be assembled to operate heavy machinery. The **bourgeoisie** were the owners of the factories, mines, large farms, and other means of production. The

Max Weber (1864–1920). Did Weber improve on Marx's view of stratification?

reflects the growth of the middle class, which reduces the polarization between owning and working classes. The proliferation of middle-class occupations creates opportunities for social mobility. The stratification system grows more complex (Giddens 1973).

Faulting Marx for an overly simple and exclusively economic view of stratification, Weber (1922/1968) defined three dimensions of social stratification: wealth (economic status), power (political status), and prestige (social status). Although, as Weber showed, wealth, power, and prestige are separate components of social ranking, they do tend to be correlated. Weber also believed that social identities based on ethnicity, religion, race, nationality, and other attributes could take priority over class (social identity based on economic status). In addition to class contrasts, the modern world system is cross-cut by status groups, such as ethnic and religious groups and nations (Shannon 1996). Class conflicts tend to occur within nations, and nationalism has prevented global class solidarity, particularly of proletarians.

Although the capitalist class dominates politically in most countries, the leaders of core nations have found it to be in their interest to allow proletarians to organize and make demands. Growing wealth has made it easier for core nations to grant higher wages to their own citizens (Hopkins and Wallerstein 1982). However, the improvement in core workers' living standards wouldn't have occurred without the world system. The added surplus and cheaper labor that come from the semiperiphery and the periphery allow core capitalists to maintain their profits while satisfying the demands of core workers. In the periphery, wages and living standards are much lower. The current *world stratification system* features a substantial contrast between both capitalists and workers in the core nations and workers on the periphery.

POVERTY ON THE PERIPHERY

With the expansion of the world capitalist economy, people on the periphery have been removed from the land by large landowners and agribusiness interests. One result is increased poverty, including food shortages. Displaced people can't earn enough to buy the food they can no longer grow.

Bangladesh illustrates some of the causes of Third World poverty and food shortages. Climate, soils, and water availability in Bangladesh are favorable for a productive agriculture. Indeed, before the arrival of the British in the 18th century, Bangladesh (then called Bengal; see Figure 23.2) had a prosperous local cotton industry. There was some stratification, but peasants had enough land to provide an adequate diet. Land was neither privately owned nor part of the market economy. Things changed under British colonial rule. The British encouraged cash-crop farming for export and converted land into a commodity that could be bought and sold.

Increased stratification was a result of colonialism and tighter linkage with the world capitalist economy. The peasantry of Bangladesh gradually lost its land. A study done in 1977 (Bodley 2000) showed that a small group of wealthy people owned most of the land. One-third of the households owned no land at all. Poverty was expressed in food shortages. Many landless people worked as sharecroppers, with landowners claiming at least half the crop. The peasants were underpaid for their crops and overcharged for the commodities they needed.

MALAYSIAN FACTORY WOMEN

Successive waves of integration into the world system have washed Malaysia, another former British colony (Figure 23.2). The Malays have

Figure 23.2 Location of Bangladesh, Malaysia, and Vietnam.

witnessed sea trade, conquest, the influx of British and Chinese capital, and immigration from China and India. For centuries, Malaysia has been part of the world system. Recently, the Malaysian government has promoted export-oriented industry to bring rural Malays into the capitalist system. This has been done in response to rural discontent over poverty and landlessness as some 10,000 families per year are pushed off the land. Transnational companies have been installing labor-intensive manufacturing operations in rural Malaysia.

The industrialization of Malaysia is part of a global strategy. To escape the mounting labor costs in the core, corporations headquartered in Japan, Western Europe, and the United States have been moving labor-intensive factories to the periphery. Malaysia now has hundreds of Japanese and American subsidiaries, which mainly produce garments, foodstuffs, and electronics components. In electronics plants in rural Malaysia, thousands of young women from peasant families now assemble microchips and microcomponents for transistors and capacitors. Aihwa Ong (1987) did a study of electronics assembly workers in an area where 85 percent of the workers were young unmarried females from nearby villages.

Ong found that factory discipline and social relations contrasted strongly with traditional community life. Previously, agricultural cycles and daily Islamic prayers, rather than production quotas and work shifts, had framed the rural economy and social life. Villagers had planned and done their own work, without bosses. In factories, however, village women had to cope with a rigid work routine and constant supervision by men.

Factory relations of production featured a hierarchy, pay scale, and division of labor based on ethnicity and gender. Japanese men filled top management, while Chinese men were the engineers and production supervisors. The Malay men also worked as supervisors of the factory work force, which consisted of nonunion female semiskilled workers from poor Malay peasant families.

The Japanese firms in rural Malaysia were paternalistic. Managers assured village parents that they would care for their daughters as though they were their own. Unlike the American firms, the Japanese subsidiaries worked hard at maintaining good relations with rural elders. Management gave money for village events, visited workers' home communities, and invited parents to the plant for receptions. In return, village elders accorded high status to the Japanese managers. The elders colluded with the managers to urge young women to accept and stay with factory work.

The discipline, diligence, and obedience that factories value is learned in local schools, where uniforms help prepare girls for the factory dress code. Peasant women wear loose, flowing tunics, sarongs, and sandals, but factory workers must don tight overalls and heavy rubber gloves, in which they feel constrained and controlled.

Assembling electronics components requires precise, concentrated labor. Demanding, exhausting, depleting, and dehumanizing, labor in these factories illustrates the separation of intellectual and manual activity that Marx considered the defining feature of industrial work. One woman said about her bosses, "They exhaust us very much, as if they do not think that we too are human beings" (Ong 1987, p. 202). Nor does factory work bring women a substantial financial reward, given low wages, job uncertainty, and family claims on wages. Young women typically work just a few years. Production quotas, three daily shifts, overtime, and surveillance take their toll in mental and physical exhaustion.

One response to factory discipline and relations of production is spirit possession, which Ong interprets as an unconscious protest against labor discipline and male control of the industrial setting. Sometimes possession takes the form of mass hysteria. The spirits have simultaneously invaded as many as 120 factory workers. Weretigers (the Malay equivalent of the werewolf) arrive to avenge the construction of a factory on local burial grounds. Disturbed earth and grave spirits swarm on the shop floor. First the women see the spirits, then their bodies are invaded. The women become violent and scream abuses. The vengeful weretigers send the women into sobbing, laughing, and shrieking fits. To deal with possession, factories employ local medicine men, who sacrifice chickens and goats to fend off the spirits. This solution works only some of the time; possession still goes on. Factory women continue to act as vehicles to express the anger of avenging ghosts and their own frustrations.

India's rural division of labor is based on caste and gender. This northern Indian woman is piling up cow dung cakes, to be burned for cooking. At every caste level, Indian women tend to do more menial labor than men of the same caste. The word for caste, *jati*, means kind or sort. Many Indians say there are only two *jati*: men and women. They recognize that gender stratification exists alongside caste stratification.

Ong argues that spirit possession expresses anguish caused by, and resistance to, capitalist relations of production. However, she also notes that by engaging in this form of rebellion, factory women avoid a direct confrontation with the source of their distress. Ong concludes that spirit possession, while expressing repressed resentment, doesn't do much to modify factory conditions. (Other tactics, such as unionization, would do more—see "Interesting Issues: Troubles in Swooshland.") Spirit possession may even help maintain the current conditions of inequality and dehumanization by operating as a safety valve for accumulated tensions.

OPEN AND CLOSED CLASS SYSTEMS

Inequalities, which are built into the structure of state societies, tend to persist across the generations. The extent to which they do or don't is a measure of the openness of the stratification system, the ease of social mobility it permits. Within the world capitalist economy, stratification has taken many forms, including caste, slavery, and class systems.

Caste systems are closed, hereditary systems of stratification that often are dictated by religion. Hierarchical social status is ascribed at birth, so that people are locked into their parents' social position. Caste lines are clearly defined, and legal and religious sanctions are applied against those who seek to cross them.

The world's best-known caste system is associated with Hinduism in traditional India. As described by Gargan (1992), despite the formal abolition of the caste system in 1949, caste-based stratification remains important in modern India. An estimated 5 million adults and 10 million children are bonded laborers. These people live in complete servitude, working to repay real or imagined debts. Most of them are untouchables, impoverished and powerless people at the bottom of the caste hierarchy. Some families have been bonded for generations; people are born into servitude because their parents or grandparents were sold previously. Bonded workers toil unpaid in stone quarries, brick kilns, and rice paddies.

Once indentured, it is difficult to escape. Bonded labor is against Indian law, but it persists despite court rulings and efforts to stop it. Social workers obtain court orders to release bonded workers, but local officials and police often ignore them. Agents for quarries and kilns continue to entice

Slavery is the most extreme, coercive, and abusive form of legalized inequality. Although proletarians, such as these "white slaves of England," also lacked control over the means of production, they did have some control over where they worked. In what other ways do proletarians differ from slaves?

untouchables into bonded labor with deceptive promises. Others enter bondage seeking to repay loans that can never be fully repaid. In this way, the caste system continues to form a highly restrictive system of social and economic stratification in India.

Another castelike system, *apartheid*, existed until recently in South Africa (see Beyond the Classroom). In that legally maintained hierarchy, blacks, whites, and Asians had their own separate (and unequal) neighborhoods, schools, laws, and punishments.

In **slavery,** the most inhumane and degrading form of stratification, people are treated as property.

Famous for its Swoosh, Nike is the world's leading manufacturer of athletic shoes. Asian labor plays a prominent role in shoe making, which Nike subcontracts to factories in Vietnam, Indonesia, China, Thailand, and Pakistan. Most of the 530,000 workers in these factories are women between the ages of 15 and 28.

In 1996, the CBS program *48 Hours* ran a segment critical of work conditions at Nike factories in Vietnam (Figure 23.2 and 23.3). The practices of Nike's Asian subcontractors, and of Nike itself, were questioned by international media, labor, and human rights groups. Publicity centered on the fact that the shoes were being produced by very cheap Asian labor, then being sold in North America for up to $100 a pair. Nike also was faulted for celebrity endorsements featuring such highly paid sports figures as Michael Jordan and Tiger Woods, when Asian workers were making less than $2.00 a day. Disturbed by the CBS report, a group of Vietnamese Americans organized to form a new NGO, Vietnam Labor Watch. With the company's cooperation, this group carried out a study of Nike's Vietnamese operations.

They confirmed that wages and working conditions were problematic. Across Asia, the wages paid to Nike workers averaged $1.84 per day. In Vietnam's Ho Chi Minh City, where the cost of three simple meals was $2.10 per day, Nike factory workers made only $1.60 per day.

Health was also a concern, as was factory safety. Salaries were too low to ensure adequate nutrition. According to law, factory doors must be kept open during operating hours, a precaution against fire. In fact, doors were often closed. Workers also had to endure overheated factories with bad air, filled with chemical smells of paint and glue.

Nike's young female workers, like those in the Malaysian electronics factories described in the text, had to wear uniforms. Adding to their regimentation was a military boot camp atmosphere. Workers were bullied, insulted, and subjected to harsh discipline. Workers were allowed only one toilet break and two chances to drink per eight hours. There were complaints of physical abuse and sexual harassment by male supervisors and insults by foreign supervisors (Koreans).

Prior to 1996, Nike already had a Code of Conduct, but the company had no effective way of ensuring that its contractors would abide by the code. In theory, the Vietnamese workers should have been protected both by Nike's Code of Conduct and by Vietnam's labor standards and laws. But the study by Vietnam Labor Watch (1997) found that many labor laws were being broken. Some women were working 11 hours a day, six days a week, sometimes also on Sunday. By law, but not consistently in practice, overtime work should have a higher rate of compensation. Nor

should workers have to work more than 200 overtime hours annually. In fact, the Nike workers in Ho Chi Minh City weren't receiving proper overtime pay, and many were working well over the 200-hour limit. Workers were threatened with punishment or firing if they refused requests to work overtime. The factory needed to keep working to meet production quotas.

After more than a year of negative publicity and accusations by human rights and labor groups, Nike announced a new policy on May 12, 1998. Nike chairman and CEO Philip Knight proposed "major changes" to Nike's overseas operations. The new policy would institute a minimum age of 18 for shoe workers and 16 for workers in Nike's apparel and athletic equipment (e.g., soccer ball) factories. The previous minimum age for shoes had been 16, but younger women had sometimes been hired.

The new policy also would improve factory safety by implementing U.S. standards. Nike committed to "adopting U.S. Occupational Safety and Health Administration (OSHA) indoor air quality standards for all footwear factories" (http://www. corpwatch.org/trac/nike/announce/ clr.html).

In addition, Nike committed to "expanding its current independent monitoring programs to include nongovernmental organizations (NGOs), foundations and educational institutions and making summaries of

Figure 23.3 **Location of Vietnam.**

the findings public" (http://www.corpwatch.org/trac/nike/announce/clr.html).

The Campaign for Labor Rights, a labor NGO, immediately countered that NGOs should not just participate in monitoring; they should lead monitoring. Nike had previously used accounting and consulting firms to audit its labor practices. The NGOs claimed (correctly) that such firms lack the language skills, impartiality, and social sensitivity to objectively monitor workers, work conditions, and progress. NGOs and labor organizations suggested that Nike form an independent monitoring board, consisting of representatives from neutral parties, including government labor officials, NGOs, and labor unions.

The Malaysian factory women described in the text used spirit possession to vent their frustration over working conditions. The Vietnamese Nike workers did something more effective. They employed labor union tactics, including strikes and frequent work stoppages and slowdowns. These practices were in response to disputes about overtime pay, arbitrary firings, and abusive treatment. The Vietnamese workers also enlisted the support of NGOs, international labor organizations, and concerned Vietnamese Americans. Some of their efforts have already paid off.

Background Information

STUDENT: **Chanelle Mac Nab**
SUPERVISING PROFESSOR: **Les Field**
SCHOOL: **University of New Mexico**
YEAR IN SCHOOL/MAJOR: **Senior/Anthropology (Ethnology)**
FUTURE PLANS: **Graduate or medical school**
PROJECT TITLE: **The Residue of Apartheid in Southern Africa**

Pay attention to the author's use of a personal perspective and personal vignettes in describing an experience abroad. How would you react in the author's situation? Are you surprised that the legacy of apartheid lingers in Southern Africa?

In 1997 I spent six months in Botswana, Africa, on an international youth exchange program. I lived in six different villages and gained insight into the rural life of these pastoral people. During this time, I traveled to South Africa, Namibia, and Zimbabwe and witnessed varying degrees of racism. The color of my skin as a Caucasian allowed me to review both the white and black perspectives on racism.

Apartheid, which is an Afrikaans word that literally means "separateness," was a policy of racial segregation that was implemented in South Africa in 1948 when the Nationalist Party came to power. Apartheid resulted in one of the most unabashed forms of racism in the world.

Prior to going to southern Africa, like most of my American counterparts, I could see little good in the Afrikaners because of all the hate and violence they have bred. However, once I had lived in southern Africa, I realized that I too was passing judgment. In my own personal experience with Afrikaners, I found them to be quite opposite than their stereotypes had described them. To me they were a kindly and humane people, often giving me a ride, a meal, and a free place to stay. It is unfortunate that their view on race has separated them from the world. I had to stop blaming the whites for one moment and realize that the whites, like the blacks, are a product of their own cultural conditioning. They are victims of their own cultural constructions. Yes, the whites are capable of taking a new stance on racism. South Africa must move beyond their issues of race and strive for cohesion if they wish to build an equitable future for both whites and blacks in all of Africa.

Why did the supposed nonracial governments of the neighboring South African countries such as Botswana and Namibia also allow whites to come in and implement their racist laws? This answer lies in the history of Africa. Colonial powers drew lines across the African continent and divided it into pieces. With colonial rule controlling Africa

---

In the Atlantic slave trade, millions of human beings were treated as commodities. The plantation systems of the Caribbean, the southeastern United States, and Brazil were based on forced slave labor. Slaves lacked control over the means of production. They were like proletarians in this respect. But proletarians at least are legally free. Unlike slaves, they have some control over where they work, how much they work, for whom they work, and what they do with their wages. Slaves, in contrast, were forced to live and work at their master's whim. Defined as lesser human beings, slaves lacked legal rights. They could be sold and resold; their families, split apart. Slaves had nothing to sell—not even their own labor (Mintz 1985). Slavery is the most extreme, coercive, and abusive form of legalized inequality.

Vertical mobility is an upward or downward change in a person's social status. A truly **open class system** would facilitate mobility. Individual achievement and personal merit would determine social rank. Hierarchical social statuses would be achieved on the basis of people's efforts. Ascribed statuses (family background, ethnicity, gender, religion) would be less important. Open class systems would have blurred class lines and a wide range of status positions.

throughout most of the 20th century, I assume that racism was adopted and implemented in all countries where whites were the minority in an effort to maintain power.

The greatest obstacle during my stay in Africa was overcoming the numerous confrontations I had with the whites in regards to race. Every day my own beliefs and cultural norms were being challenged by this unfamiliar culture. I had extensive conversations with whites and blacks about race. Here is a brief description of one of my journal entries.

August 14—Tonight I went with Rey (the Afrikaner who drove me from Namibia to Botswana) to the opening of the annual Agricultural Trade Fair . . . I am aware that apartheid ended only three years ago, and that, although apartheid is physically gone, it is latently present, but never did those words seem more real than tonight . . . As we drove into the fair grounds, I could see the silhouettes of hundreds of black people dancing against the dimness of the lantern lights. The loud African music was familiar to me . . . [I]nstead of continuing forward to where the blacks were, we took a sharp left turn to the white sector of the fair. The whites were standing around a fire drinking while their black servants stoked the fire and prepared the food. I was stunned to be standing on segregated soil. I could not believe that I was in Botswana and not in South Africa. I could not believe that less than 10 years ago, blacks were not allowed to attend this very same trade fair. Every moment that I was with the whites I felt uncomfortable . . . I could not identify with these people . . . I was furious underneath my skin because they did not know who I was on the inside. Yes, I was white but I was not one of them . . . I felt guilty, as if I were betraying all of my black friends and my black host family . . . As hard as it was, I kept my calm and I told Rey I would never be able to see it the way he does because of my different upbringing. Rey admitted that perhaps his children's children would one day see it the way I do.

As Rey and I left the party to go home, I dared him to go with me to the "other side" so that we could dance. He responded with two words: "I cannot." Our conversation ended and we drove home in silence.

Today, the ideology of racism has seeped across borders and across imaginary lines like an oil spill and is ever present throughout the world's social, political, and economic systems. It is important to understand that apartheid is not isolated in South Africa. Apartheid has permeated all of the borders of southern Africa. Hence, racism is not exclusively a South African problem.

This research has attempted to shed light on the serious issue of racism, with its emphasis on the continuing effects of the apartheid regime in southern Africa. I hope that more people will come to understand apartheid and use this knowledge to understand why racism denies and oppresses people all around the world.

Compared with nonindustrial states and contemporary peripheral and semiperipheral nations, core industrial nations tend to have more open class systems. Under industrialism, wealth is based to some extent on **income**—earnings from wages and salaries. Economists contrast such a return on labor with interest, dividends, rent, and profits, which are *returns on property* or capital.

Understanding Ourselves Most Americans think they belong to, and claim identity with, the middle class, which they tend to perceive as a vast undifferentiated group. However, the American class system isn't as open or undifferentiated as most Americans assume it to be. There are substantial differences in income and wealth between the richest and the poorest Americans, and the gap is widening. According to U.S. Census data, from 1967 to 2000 the top (richest) fifth, or quintile, of American households increased their share of national income by 13.5 percent, while the shares of all the other quintiles fell. The percentage share of the lowest fifth fell most dramatically—17.6 percent. In 2000 the highest fifth of American households got about 50 percent of all national income, while the share of the lowest fifth was less than

4 percent. The 2000 ratio was 14 to 1, versus 11 to 1 in 1967. In other words, the richest fifth of American households, with a mean annual income of $141,621, is now 14 times wealthier than the poorest fifth, with a mean annual income of $10,188 (U.S. Census 2000). When we consider wealth (investments, property, possessions, etc.) rather than income, the contrast is even more striking: 1 percent of American families hold one-third of the nation's wealth (Calhoun, Light, and Keller 1997). Understanding ourselves means recognizing that our ideology about class doesn't accord with socioeconomic reality.

The World System Today

We will see in "Interesting Issues: The American Periphery" (pp. 657–658) that the world economy also can create peripheral regions within core nations, such as rural areas of the American South. World-system theory stresses the existence of a global culture. It emphasizes historic contacts, linkages, and power differentials between local people and international forces. The major forces influencing cultural interaction during the past 500 years have been commercial expansion, industrial capitalism, and the differential power of colonial and core nations (Wallerstein 1982, 2000; Wolf 1982). As state formation had done previously, industrialization accelerated local participation in larger networks. According to Bodley (2000), perpetual expansion (whether in population or consumption) is the distinguishing feature of industrial economic systems. Bands and tribes are small, self-sufficient, subsistence-based systems. Industrial economies,

by contrast, are large, highly specialized systems in which local areas don't consume the products they produce and in which market exchanges occur with profit as the primary motive (Bodley 2000).

See your OLC Internet Exercises

mhhe com /kottak

After 1870, European business initiated a concerted search for more secure markets in Asia, Africa, and other less-developed areas. This process led to European imperialism in Africa, Asia, and Oceania. **Imperialism** (*colonialism* is a near synonym) refers to a policy of extending the rule of a nation or empire, such as the British empire, over foreign nations and of taking and holding foreign colonies. *Colonialism* refers to the political, social, economic, and cultural domination of a territory and its people by a foreign power for an extended time. European imperial expansion was aided by improved transportation, which brought huge new areas within easy reach. Europeans also colonized vast areas of previously unsettled or sparsely settled lands in the interior of North and South America and Australia. The new colonies purchased masses of goods from the industrial centers and shipped back wheat, cotton, wool, mutton, beef, and leather. Thus began the second phase of colonialism (the first had been in the New World after Columbus) as European nations competed for colonies between 1875 and 1914, a process that helped cause World War I.

Industrialization spread to many other nations in a process that continues today (Table 23.1). By 1900, the United States had become a core nation within the world system. It had overtaken Great Britain in iron, coal, and cotton production. In a

Table 23.1	Ascent and Decline of Nations within the World System	
Periphery to Semiperiphery	**Semiperiphery to Core**	**Core to Semiperiphery**
United States (1800–1860)	United States (1860–1900)	Spain (1620–1700)
Japan (1868–1900)	Japan (1945–1970)	
Taiwan (1949–1980)	Germany (1870–1900)	
S. Korea (1953–1980)		

SOURCE: Reprinted by permission of Westview Press from *An Introduction to the World-System Perspective* by Thomas Richard Shannon. Copyright Westview Press 1989, Boulder, Colorado.

The effects of the world economy also can create peripheral regions within core nations, such as areas of the rural South in the United States. In a comparative study of two counties at opposite ends of Tennessee (Figure 23.4), Thomas Collins (1989) reviews the effects of industrialization on poverty and unemployment. Hill County, with an Appalachian white population, is on the Cumberland Plateau in eastern Tennessee. Delta County, which is predominantly African-American, is 60 miles from Memphis in western Tennessee's lower Mississippi region. Both counties once had economies based on agriculture and timber, but jobs in those sectors declined sharply with the advent of mechanization. Both counties have unemployment rates more than twice that of Tennessee as a whole. More than a third of the people in each county live below the poverty level. Such poverty pockets represent a slice of the world periphery within modern America. Given very restricted job opportunities, the best-educated local youths have migrated to northern cities for three generations.

To increase jobs, local officials and business leaders have tried to attract industries from outside. Their efforts exemplify a more general rural southern strategy, which began during the 1950s, of courting industry by advertising "a good business climate"—which means low rents, cheap utilities, and a nonunion labor pool. However, few firms are attracted to an impoverished and poorly educated work force. All the industries

(continued on next page)

Figure 23.4   Location of Cumberland Plateau and Memphis vicinity (Delta county) in Tennessee.

that have come to such areas have very limited market power and a narrow profit margin. Such firms survive by offering low wages and minimal benefits, with frequent layoffs. These industries tend to emphasize traditional female skills such as sewing and mostly attract women.

The garment industry, which is highly mobile, is Hill County's main employer. The knowledge that a garment plant can be moved to another locale very rapidly tends to reduce employee demands. Management can be as arbitrary and authoritarian as it wishes. The unemployment rate and low educational level ensure that many women will accept sewing jobs for a bit more than the minimum wage.

In neither county has new industry brought many jobs for men, who have a higher unemployment rate than do women (as do blacks, compared with whites). Collins found that many men in Hill County had never been permanently employed; they had just done temporary jobs, always for cash.

The effects of industrialization in Delta County have been similar. That county's recruitment efforts also have drawn only marginal industries. The largest is a bicycle seat and toy manufacturer, which employs 60 percent women. Three other large plants, which make clothing and auto seat covers, employ 95 percent women. Egg production was once significant in Delta County but folded when the market for eggs fell in response to rising national concern over the effects of cholesterol.

In both counties, the men, ignored by industrialization, maintain an informal economy. They sell and trade used goods through personal networks. They take casual jobs, such as operating farm equipment on a daily or seasonal basis. Collins found that maintaining an automobile was the most important and prestigious contribution these men made to their families. Neither county has public transportation; Hill County even lacks school buses. Families need cars to get women to work and kids to

school. Men who keep an old car running longest get special respect.

Reduced opportunities for men to do well at work—to which American culture attributes great importance—lead to a feeling of lowered self-worth, which is expressed in physical violence. The rate of domestic violence in Hill County exceeds the state average. Spousal abuse arises from men's demands to control women's paychecks. (Men regard the cash they earn themselves as their own, to spend on male activities.)

One important difference between the two counties involves unionization. In Delta County, organizers have waged successful campaigns for unionization. Attitudes toward workers' rights in Tennessee correlate with race. Rural southern whites usually don't vote for unions when they have a chance to do so, whereas African Americans are more likely to challenge management about pay and work rules. Local blacks view their work situation in terms of black against white

few decades (1868–1900), Japan changed from a medieval handicraft country to an industrial one, joining the semiperiphery by 1900 and moving to the core between 1945 and 1970. Figure 23.5 is a map showing the modern world system.

Twentieth-century industrialization added hundreds of new industries and millions of new jobs. Production increased, often beyond immediate demand. This spurred strategies such as advertising to sell everything that industry could churn out. Mass production gave rise to a culture of overconsumption, which valued acquisitiveness and conspicuous consumption (Veblen 1934). Bodley defines overconsumption as "consumption in a

given area that exceeds the rates at which natural resources are produced by natural processes, to such an extent that the longrun stability of the culture involved is threatened" (1985, p. 39).

Interpret the World
Atlas Map 23

Industrialization entailed a shift from reliance on renewable resources to the use of fossil fuels, such as oil. Energy from fossil fuels, which have been stored over millions of years, is being depleted rapidly to support a previously unknown and probably unsustainable level of consumption (Bodley 2000). Map 23 in your atlas shows the annual consump-

Rural poverty is part of the American periphery. This Appalachian family represents the bottom fifth of families in terms of income. How much does the top fifth get compared with the bottom fifth? The answer is in the text.

rather than from a position of working-class solidarity. They are attracted to unions because they see only whites in managerial positions and resent differential advancement of white factory workers. One manager expressed to Collins that "once the work force of a plant becomes more than one-third black, you can expect to have union representation within a year" (Collins 1989, p. 10). Responding to this probability of unionization, core capitalists from Japan don't build plants in the primarily African American counties of the lower Mississippi. The state's Japanese factories cluster in eastern and central Tennessee.

Poverty pockets of the rural South (and other regions) represent a slice of the world periphery within modern America. Through mechanization, industrialization, and the other changes promoted by larger systems, local people have been deprived of land and jobs. After years of industrial development, a third of the people of Hill and Delta counties remain below the poverty level. Emigration of educated and talented locals continues as the opportunities shrink. Collins concluded that rural poverty would not be reduced by attracting additional peripheral industries because these firms lack the market power to improve wages and benefits. Different development schemes are needed for these counties and the rural South generally.

tion of commercial energy per capita by country, measured with reference to kilograms of oil. Note that the United States, Canada, and Australia have the highest consumption rates. Nations on the periphery tend to have the lowest rates, with semi-periphery being intermediate. Consumption rates are also high in certain oil-producing countries, such as Venezuela and Saudi Arabia.

Table 23.3 compares energy consumption in various types of cultures. Americans are the world's foremost consumers of nonrenewable resources. In energy terms, the average American, drawing on 275,000 calories of energy each day (Table 23.2), is about 35 times more expensive than is the average forager or tribesperson, averaging just 8,000 daily calories. Since 1900, the United States has tripled its per capita energy use. It also has increased its total energy consumption 30-fold.

INDUSTRIAL DEGRADATION

Today's industrialization extends to the Third World. Factory labor now characterizes many countries in Latin America, Africa, the Pacific, and Asia. One effect of the spread of industrialization has been the destruction of indigenous economies, ecologies, and populations.

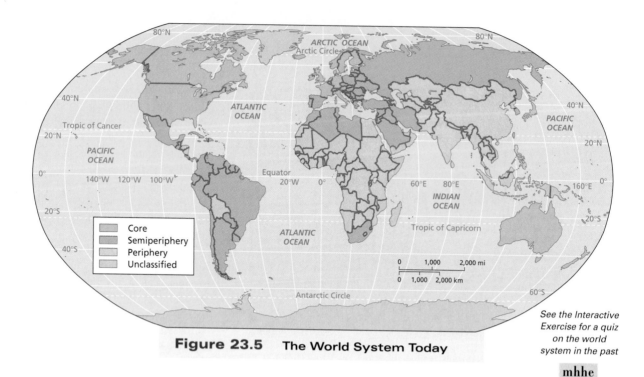

Figure 23.5   The World System Today

See the Interactive
Exercise for a quiz
on the world
system in the past

mhhe
.com
/kottak

Two centuries ago, as industrialization was developing, 50 million people still lived beyond the periphery in politically independent bands, tribes, and chiefdoms. Occupying vast areas, those non-state societies, although not totally isolated, were only marginally affected by nation-states and the world capitalist economy. In 1800, bands, tribes, and chiefdoms controlled half the globe and 20 percent of its population (Bodley 1988). Industrializa-tion then tipped the balance in favor of states.

Industrialization is "a global process that has destroyed or transformed all previous cultural adaptations and has given humanity the power not only to bring about its own extinction as a species, but also to speed the extinction of many other species and to alter biological and geological processes as well" (Bodley 1985, p. 4). The negative effects of an expanding industrial world system include genocide, ethnocide, and ecocide. *Genocide* is the physical destruction of ethnic groups by murder, warfare, and introduced diseases. When ethnic groups survive but lose or severely modify their ancestral cultures, we speak of *ethnocide*. The term for the destruction of local ecosystems is *ecocide*.

As industrial states have conquered, annexed, and "developed" nonstates, there has been geno-cide on a grand scale. Bodley (1988) estimates that an average of 250,000 indigenous people perished annually between 1800 and 1950. The causes included foreign diseases (to which natives had no resistance), warfare, slavery, land grabbing, and other forms of dispossession and impoverishment.

Native groups have been incorporated with-in nation-states, where they have become ethnic minorities. Some such groups have been able to

Table 23.2   Energy Consumption in Various Contexts

Type of Society	Daily Kilocalories per Person
Bands and tribes	4,000–12,000
Preindustrial states	26,000 (maximum)
Early industrial states	70,000
Americans in 1970	230,000
Americans in 1990	275,000

SOURCE: From John H. Bodley, *Anthropology and Contemporary Human Problems*, 1985. Reprinted by permission of Mayfield Publishing, Mountain View, CA.

Copsa Mica, Romania, may well be the world's most polluted city. A factory belches out smoke that leaves its mark on these boys' faces, food, and lungs. What's the term for such environmental devastation?

Only a handful of autonomous tribal nations survive. At the dawn of food production 10,000 years ago, the world's human population is estimated to have been 75 million. Those people belonged to perhaps 150,000 independent bands and tribes (Bodley 1988). Today, many descendants of tribespeople live on as culturally distinct and self-conscious colonized peoples, many of whom aspire to autonomy. As the original inhabitants of their territories, they are called **indigenous peoples.** Bodley (1988) argues that such groups typically resist integration into nation-states. They fear that such integration, which is usually into the impoverished classes, will lead to a decline in their quality of life.

Many contemporary nations are repeating—at an accelerated rate—the process of resource depletion that occurred in Europe and the United States during the Industrial Revolution. Fortunately, however, today's world has some environmental watchdogs that were absent during the first centuries of the Industrial Revolution. Given national and international cooperation and sanctions, the modern world may benefit from the lessons of the past.

See your OLC Internet Exercises for more on indigenous peoples

mhhe
●com
/kottak

recoup their population. Many indigenous peoples survive and maintain their ethnic identity despite having lost their ancestral cultures to varying degrees (partial ethnocide).

Today's world contains around 200 million tribespeople, most of whom belong to conquered tribes.

SUMMARY

1. Local societies increasingly participate in wider systems—regional, national, and global. Columbus's voyages opened the way for a major and continuing exchange between the Old and New Worlds. Seventeenth-century plantation economies in the Caribbean and Brazil were based on sugar. In the 18th century, plantation economies based on cotton arose in the southeastern United States.

2. The capitalist world economy is based on production for sale, with the goal of maximizing profits. World capitalism has political and economic specialization based on three positions. Core, semiperiphery, and periphery have existed since the 16th century, although the particular countries filling these niches have changed.

3. The Industrial Revolution began around 1750. Transoceanic trade and commerce supplied capital for industrial investment. Industrialism began in England rather than in France because French industry could grow through expansion of the domestic system. England, with fewer people, had to industrialize.

4. Industrialization hastened the separation of workers from the means of production. Marx saw stratification as a sharp division between the bourgeoisie (capitalists) and the proletariat (propertyless workers). Class consciousness was a key part of Marx's view of class. Weber believed that social solidarity based on ethnicity, religion, race, or nationality could take priority

over class. Today's capitalist world system maintains the contrast between those who own the means of production and those who don't, but the division is now worldwide. Modern stratification systems also include a middle class of skilled and professional workers.

5. Nationalism has prevented global class solidarity. There is a substantial contrast between capitalists and workers in the core nations and workers on the periphery. The extent to which inequalities persist across the generations is a measure of the openness of the class system, the ease of social mobility it permits. Under world capitalism, stratification has taken many forms, including caste, slavery, and class systems.

6. The major forces influencing cultural interaction during the past 500 years have been commercial expansion and industrial capitalism. In the 19th century, industrialization spread to Belgium, France, Germany, and the United States. After 1870, businesses began a concerted search for more secure markets. This process led to European imperialism in Africa, Asia, and Oceania. By 1900 the United States had become a core nation. Mass production gave rise to a culture that valued acquisitiveness and conspicuous consumption. One effect of industrialization has been the destruction of indigenous economies, ecologies, and populations. Two centuries ago, 50 million people lived in independent bands, tribes, and chiefdoms. Industrialization tipped the balance in favor of states.

KEY TERMS

See the flash cards

mhhe
●com
/kottak

bourgeoisie   One of Marx's opposed classes; owners of the means of production (factories, mines, large farms, and other sources of subsistence).

capital   Wealth or resources invested in business, with the intent of producing a profit.

capitalist world economy   The single world system, which emerged in the 16th century, committed to production for sale, with the object of maximizing profits rather than supplying domestic needs.

caste system   Closed, hereditary system of stratification, often dictated by religion; hierarchical social status is ascribed at birth, so that people are locked into their parents' social position.

core   Dominant structural position in the world system; consists of the strongest and most powerful states with advanced systems of production.

imperialism   A policy of extending the rule of a nation or empire over foreign nations or of taking and holding foreign colonies.

income   Earnings from wages and salaries.

indigenous peoples   The original inhabitants of particular territories; often descendants of tribespeople who live on as culturally distinct colonized peoples, many of whom aspire to autonomy.

Industrial Revolution   The historic transformation (in Europe, after 1750) of "traditional" into "modern" societies through industrialization of the economy.

open class system   Stratification system that facilitates social mobility, with individual achievement and personal merit determining social rank.

periphery   Weakest structural position in the world system.

semiperiphery   Structural position in the world system intermediate between core and periphery.

slavery   The most extreme, coercive, abusive, and inhumane form of legalized inequality; people are treated as property.

vertical mobility   Upward or downward change in a person's social status.

working class   Or proletariat; those who must sell their labor to survive; the antithesis of the bourgeoisie in Marx's class analysis.

CRITICAL THINKING QUESTIONS

For more self testing, see the self quizzes

mhhe
●com
/kottak

1. According to world-system theory, societies are subsystems of bigger systems, with the world system as the largest. What are the various systems, at different levels, in which you participate?

2. What is the capitalist world economy? Does it have political as well as economic dimensions? What are they?

3. Give two examples each of core, semiperiphery, and periphery nations. Does any nation seem poised to move from one slot to another, such as semiperiphery to core, or vice versa? What's the last nation to make such a move?

4. How has social stratification in industrial societies changed over time? Think of comparing London of the 1850s (the era of Dickens and Marx) and today. Or compare the class structure of the United States in the 1930s with contemporary socioeconomic stratification.

5. Name three causes of the Industrial Revolution. Are they being repeated anywhere today?

6. How did proletarianization change human work? Is any of your work proletarianized?

7. How did the views of Marx and Weber on stratification differ? Which approach makes the most sense to you? Why?

8. How open is the class system of your society? Describe what's open and what's closed about it.

9. How would our class system differ if the Third World didn't exist?

10. Evaluate the positive and negative effects of industrialization, giving five examples of each.

Atlas Questions

Look at Map 23, "Energy Consumption Per Capita."

1. Compare energy consumption in Europe and North America.

2. What are some exceptions to the generalization that the highest rates of energy consumption are in core countries, with the lowest rates on the periphery.

3. Compare rates of energy consumption with the rates of population growth shown on Map 2. Do the nations with the fastest-growing populations use the most energy, or vice versa.

SUGGESTED ADDITIONAL READINGS

Abu-Lughod, J. L.
1989 *Before European Hegemony : The World System A. D. 1250–1350.* New York: Oxford University Press. Regional economies and politics before the age of European exploration and the capitalist world economy.

Arrighi, G.
1994 *The Long Twentieth Century: Money, Power, and the Origins of Our Times.* New York: Verso. How core nations control finance and power in the modern world system.

Braudel, F.
1973 *Capitalism and Material Life: 1400–1800.* London: Fontana. The role of the masses in the history of capitalism.

1982 *Civilization and Capitalism, 15th–18th Century.* Volume II: The Wheels of Commerce. New York: HarperCollins. On the history of capitalism and the role of trade from precapitalist mercantilism to the present.

1992   *Civilization and Capitalism, 15th–18th Century.* Volume III: The Perspective of the World. Berkeley, CA: University of California Press. On the emergence of the world capitalist economy; case histories of European countries and various areas of the rest of the world.

Crosby, A. W., Jr.

1972   *The Columbian Exchange: Biological and Cultural Consequences of 1492.* Westport, CT: Greenwood Press. Describes how Columbus's voyages opened the way for a major exchange of people, resources, and ideas as the Old and New Worlds were forever joined together.

Diamond, J. M.

1997   *Guns, Germs, and Steel: The Fates of Human Societies.* New York: W. W. Norton. An ecological approach to expansion and conquest in world history.

Fagan, B. M.

1998   *Clash of Cultures.* 2nd ed. Walnut Creek, CA: AltaMira. Culture conflicts during European territorial expansion.

Hall, T. D., ed.

1999   *A World-System Reader: New Perspectives on Gender, Urbanism, Cultures, Indigenous Peoples, and Ecology.* Lanham, MD: Rowman and Littlefield. Urbanization, globalization, and indigenous peoples.

Kardulias, P. N.

1999   *World-Systems Theory in Practice: Leadership, Production, and Exchange.* Lanham, MD: Rowman and Littlefield. Social systems, social change, and economic history in the context of world-system theory.

Kearney, M.

1996   *Reconceptualizing the Peasantry: Anthropology in Global Perspective.* Boulder, CO: Westview. The nature of peasant life styles and subsistence patterns within the modern world system.

Mintz, S.

1985   *Sweetness and Power: The Place of Sugar in Modern History.* New York: Viking Penguin. The place of sugar in the formation of the modern world system.

Shannon, T. R.

1996   *An Introduction to the World-System Perspective,* 2nd ed. Boulder, CO: Westview Press. Useful review of world-system theory and developments.

Wallerstein, I. M.

1974   *The Modern World-System: Capitalist Agriculture and the Origins of the European World-Economy in the Sixteenth Century.* New York: Academic Press. The origins of the capitalist world economy; a classic work.

1980   *The Modern World-System II: Mercantilism and the Consolidation of the European World Economy, 1600–1750.* New York: Academic Press. Further development of the world system and the underpinnings of industrialization.

2000   *The Essential Wallerstein.* New York: New Press, W. W. Norton. The father of world-system theory offers the basics of his influential theory.

Wolf, E. R.

1982   *Europe and the People without History.* Berkeley: University of California Press. An anthropologist examines the effects of European expansion on tribal peoples and sets forth a world-system approach to anthropology.

Wolf, E. R., with S. Silverman

2001   *Pathways of Power: Building an Anthropology of the Modern World.* Berkeley: University of California Press. Political anthropology for the modern world, a comparative approach.

INTERNET EXERCISES

1. Read the page entitled "Life of the Industrial Workers in Nineteenth-Century Britain" by Laura Del Col (**http://65.107.211.206/history/workers1.htm**). The page contains excerpts from a report generated by a parliamentary panel charged with investigating conditions in British factories.

   a. What were conditions like for workers? What were their lives like? Their work? What are their expectations?

   b. What are the conditions like for children?

   c. In what way are these life stories different from those which might have been told 100 or 200 years earlier in preindustrial Britain?

   d. How are these conditions different from today's Britain? Are there areas of the world where workers might identify with these accounts?

2. Go to the U.S. Census Bureau's Factfinder service at **http://factfinder.census.gov**. Choose to make a map. Under "Show me," choose "Income"; under "for," choose "State by County" and then pick a state in which you are interested. Press Go to view a map of income distributions in your state. Study the map and try to determine the overall patterns. Try to identify the locations with a high income and the locations with low average incomes. Do these patterns make sense? What explains them? Now go back to the Factfinder, and under "Show me" choose "Education" and view and study that map. Finally, make a map of "Poverty."

   a. What are the similarities between the three maps? What are the major differences?

   b. Based on these maps, what is the relationship between poverty, income, and education in a state of your choice?

   c. How do you explain the relationships you see between poverty, education, and income?

See Chapter 23 at your McGraw-Hill Online Learning Center for additional review and interactive exercises.

24

COLONIALISM AND
DEVELOPMENT

Overview

Imperialism is the policy of extending the rule of a nation or empire over other nations. Colonialism is the long-term domination of a territory and its people by a foreign power.

European colonialism had two broad phases. The first spanned the period from 1492 to 1825. For Britain, this phase ended with the American Revolution. For Spain, it ended with the independence of most of its Latin American colonies. The second, more imperialistic, phase ran from 1850 to just after the end of World War II. The British and French colonial empires reached their height around 1914.

Economic development and colonialism are related because, like colonialism, economic development usually has an intervention philosophy—an ideological justification for outsiders, who often are former

colonial powers, to guide native peoples toward particular goals. Development is often justified by the idea that industrialization and westernization are desirable advances. But many problems faced by Third World peoples reflect their increasing dependence on cash.

Development anthropology focuses on social issues in, and the cultural dimension of, economic development. Culturally compatible development projects tend to be more successful than incompatible ones are. Compatible and successful projects try to change just enough, not too much. Motives to change come from people's traditional culture and the small concerns of everyday life. The most productive strategy for change is to base the social design for innovation on traditional social forms in each affected area.

Britain in Africa: Colonialism's Legacy Becomes a Burden

Nytimes.com News Brief

by Alan Cowell

June 10, 2000

This report contrasts attitudes toward Great Britain in the former British colonies of Sierra Leone and Zimbabwe. On the one hand, Sierra Leone's president pleaded for (and received) British aid aimed at quashing a rebellion. On the other hand, Zimbabwe's president, Robert Mugabe, lambasted his country's legacy of British colonialism, still evident in the distribution of national wealth, including land holding. Mugabe's party lost the parliamentary elections mentioned in this account in June 2002, but Mugabe won reelection as president in March 2002. His presidential campaign portrayed his opponent as an apologist for colonialism, and for British and white interests. As of this writing (December 2002), fighting continues in Sierra Leone, with a token presence of at least 200 British troops. And in Zimbabwe, by decree and at Mugabe's urging, large farms held by whites are being seized by the government and turned over to black Africans. Great Britain has led the international opposition to this policy. The legacy of colonialism continues.

LONDON—In recent weeks, Britons have been treated to two conflicting, almost puzzling, sets of images. In Sierra Leone, an African leader pleads with British troops to stay on, after they arrive there to protect the capital from rebel forces who had kidnapped hundreds of United Nations peacekeepers. Across the continent in Zimbabwe, another African president reviles just about everything that smacks of the British and tells them to be gone.

Binding the two images is Britain's colonial past and, with it, a message that has some resonance for the United States in its own new imperial age: Once power is extended, it creates a stubborn, messy and enduring legacy. And even when influence recedes, the tangle of obligation, expectation and resentment survives. . . .

In Sierra Leone, a chaotic assemblage of rebel and pro-government forces has turned the nation into a patchwork of armed fiefs competing, essentially, for the country's diamond riches. A United Nations mission to achieve and preserve a peace had collapsed, leaving a dangerous vacuum. This threatened to propel the war-weary nation into further mayhem. . . .

In Zimbabwe the fight is different: After 20 unchallenged years in power, [President Robert] Mugabe is facing elections this month that he is afraid of losing. And he has seized on the emotional issue of racial discrimination left over from colonial days—in this case, unfair patterns of land distribution—as a pretext to order a campaign of bloody intimidation of his principal opponents. These include white farmers and workers on the farmers' land.

Hundreds of white-owned farms have been occupied by so-called veterans of Zimbabwe's liberation war in the 1970s, and at least 25 people have died.

In other words, Mr. Mugabe is assailing the very legacy that Britons feel links them to the land. And Britain's choices are circumscribed, illuminating both the ambiguities of its colonial history and the limits on its modern influence.

While Sierra Leone was established in 1787 as a coastal settlement for freed black slaves, white British settlers were encouraged to migrate to Rhodesia—as Zimbabwe was then known—in the late 19th and early 20th centuries, simply seizing vast tracts of land from the indigenous people.

When British officials started to protest Mr. Mugabe's behavior, that inescapable history clouded

A Zimbabwe scene: whites and blacks separated by an electrified fence.

the moral issue and gave Mr. Mugabe the ammunition to defy the onetime colonial ruler. The collision left Britain's standing in Zimbabwe at its lowest in decades, even as its star rose ever higher in Sierra Leone. . . .

The deeper reality in both Zimbabwe and Sierra Leone is that colonialism does not have an easy cut-off point, or a simple close-of-sale date. When the flags are furled, the colonial power maintains a vast array of commercial and other involvements. Just as colonialism itself was propelled by the economics of Europe's industrial revolution with its need for raw materials and markets, so the post-colonial era has been driven by Lord Palmerston's 19th-century dictum that nations do not have eternal allies, but they do have eternal interests.

In Zimbabwe, for instance, by insisting that this month's elections be free and fair and by offering increased financial aid for land redistribution, Britain is signaling its broader interest in the stability of a region that encompasses vast British investment, particularly in South Africa.

Source: http://www.nytimes.com. Copyright 2000 The New York Times Company.

Colonialism

In the last chapter, we saw that after 1870, Europe began a concerted search for markets in Asia and Africa. That process led to European imperialism in Africa, Asia, and Oceania. Imperialism (colonialism is a near synonym) refers to a policy of extending the rule of a nation or empire, such as the British empire, over foreign nations and of taking and holding foreign colonies. **Colonialism** refers to the political, social, economic, and cultural domination of a territory and its people by a foreign power for an extended period of time. And as is clear in the news account you just read, the influence of colonialism doesn't disappear just because formal independence has been granted.

IMPERIALISM

Imperialism goes back to early states, including Egypt in the Old World and the Incas in the New. A Greek empire was forged by Alexander the

Great, and Julius Caesar and his successors spread the Roman empire. The term also has been used for more recent examples, including the British, French, and Soviet empires (Scheinman 1980).

For a quiz on colonies throughout history, see the Interactive Exercise

If imperialism is almost as old as the state itself, colonialism can be traced back to the ancient Phoenicians, who established colonies along the eastern Mediterranean by 3,000 years ago. The ancient Greeks and Romans were avid colonizers, as well as empire builders. Modern colonialism began with the European "Age of Discovery"—of the Americas and of a sea route to the Far East. After 1492, European states started founding colonies abroad. In South America, Portugal gained rule over Brazil. The Spanish, the original conquerors of the Aztecs and the Incas, explored the New World widely. They looked to the Caribbean, Mexico, and the southern portions of what was to become the United States, as well as colonizing in Central and South America. In what is now Latin America, especially in areas that had indigenous chiefdoms (e.g., Colombia and Venezuela) and states (e.g., Mexico, Guatemala, Peru, and Bolivia), native populations were large and dense. Today's Latin American population still reflects the intermingling of peoples and cultures during the first phase of colonialism. North of Mexico, indigenous populations were smaller and sparser. Such intermingling is less marked in the United States and Canada than in Latin America.

Rebellions and wars aimed at independence for American nations ended the first phase of European colonialism by the early 19th century. Brazil's independence from Portugal was declared in 1822. By 1825, most of Spain's colonies were politically independent. Spain held on to Cuba and the Philippines until 1898, but otherwise withdrew from the colonial field.

BRITISH COLONIALISM

The British empire grew through the search for resources and markets. At its peak around 1914, the British empire covered a fifth of the world's land surface and ruled a fourth of its population (see Figure 24.1). Like several other European nations, Britain had two stages of colonialism. The first began with the Elizabethan voyages of

Figure 24.1   Map of the British Empire in 1914.

the 16th century. During the 17th century, Britain acquired most of the eastern coast of North America, Canada's St. Lawrence basin, islands in the Caribbean, slave stations in Africa, and interests in India. The British shared the exploration of the New World with the Spanish, Portuguese, French, and Dutch. The British by and large left Mexico, along with Central and South America, to the Spanish and the Portuguese. The end of the Seven Years War in 1763 forced a French retreat from most of Canada and India, where France had previously competed with Britain (Cody 1998; Farr 1980).

See your OLC Internet Exercises for more on the British colonization of the Americas

**mhhe
●com
/kottak**

The American revolution ended the first stage of British colonialism. A second colonial empire, on which the "sun never set," rose from the ashes of the first. Beginning in 1788, but intensifying after 1815, was the British settlement of Australia. Britain had acquired Dutch South Africa by 1815. The establishment of Singapore in 1819 provided a base for a British trade network that extended to much of South Asia and along the coast of China. By this time, the empires of Britain's traditional rivals, particularly Spain, had been severely diminished in size. Britain's position as an

imperial power and the world's leading industrial nation was unchallenged. Much of the world was dominated by British commercial, financial, and naval power (Cody 1998; Farr 1980).

By the mid-19th century, Britain controlled virtually all of India, which was governed by a British viceroy from 1858. The Dutch exerted similar control over Indonesia, then known as the Dutch East Indies. By 1893, French rule was established in Indochina (Laos, Cambodia, and Vietnam). In 1885, the Conference of Berlin divided Africa among several European nations (see Figure 24.2). The British received most of eastern and southern Africa, along with substantial portions of West Africa. French Equatorial Africa stretched across the continent, with the French also controlling Madagascar and most of northern Africa. Belgium was awarded the Congo. Germany received territory on the Atlantic and Indian Ocean coasts. Portugal extended its control from the coasts to the interiors of Angola and Mozambique (Scheinman 1980).

During the Victorian Era (1837–1901), Britain's acquisition of territory and of further trading concessions continued. Victoria's prime minister, Benjamin Disraeli, implemented a foreign policy justified by a view of imperialism as reflecting "the white man's burden"—a term coined by the poet Rudyard

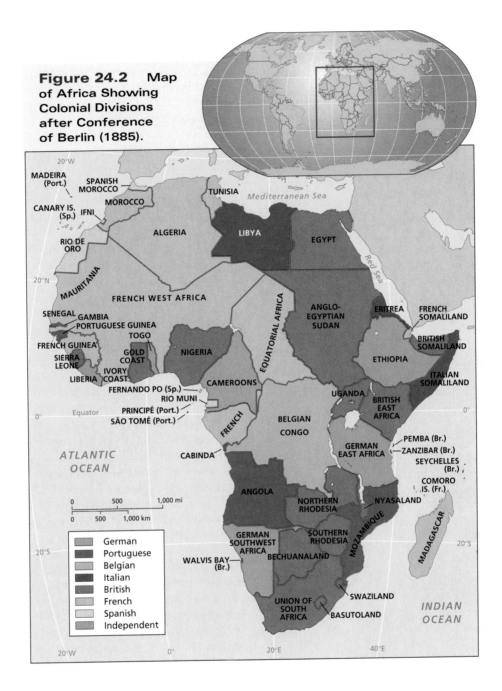

Figure 24.2 Map of Africa Showing Colonial Divisions after Conference of Berlin (1885).

Kipling. People in the empire were seen as unable to govern themselves, so that British guidance was needed to civilize and Christianize them. This paternalistic and racist intervention philosophy served to legitimize Britain's acquisition and control of parts of Central Africa and Asia (Cody 1998).

At the height of the British empire in 1914, nationalist movements had already emerged in various colonies. But immediately after World War

I (1914–1918), the British empire actually increased in size. Britain became the "trustee" of former German and Turkish territories in Africa and the Middle East. In 1931, Britain, along with its self-governing dominions—Canada, Australia, New Zealand, South Africa, and the Irish Free State—formed the "Commonwealth of Nations." Its *dominions* were autonomous units with status equal to Britain's.

After World War II, the British empire fell apart, with nationalist movements for independence. India became independent in 1947, as did Ireland in 1949. Decolonization in Africa and Asia accelerated during the late 1950s. Today, the ties that remain between Britain and its former colonies are linguistic, cultural, and sometimes still political, as we saw in the news story at the beginning of this chapter.

FRENCH COLONIALISM

French colonialism also had two phases. The first began in the early 1600s. The second came late in the 19th century. This was the French manifestation of a more general European imperialism that followed the spread of industrialization and the search for new markets, raw materials, and cheap labor. However, compared with Great Britain, where the drive for profit led expansion, French colonialism was spurred more by the state, church, and armed forces than by business interests. Prior to the French Revolution, in 1789, missionaries, explorers, and traders had led French expansion. They carved niches for France in Canada, the Louisiana territory, and several Caribbean islands, along with parts of India, which were lost, along with Canada (New France), to Great Britain in 1763. By 1815, only West Indian sugar islands and scattered African and Asian posts remained under French control (Harvey 1980).

The foundations of the second French empire were established between 1830 and 1870. France acquired Algeria and part of what eventually became Indochina. Like Britain, France rode a post-1870 wave of new imperialism. By 1914, the French empire covered 4 million square miles and included some 60 million people (see Figure 24.3). By 1893, French rule had been fully established in Indochina, and Tunisia and Morocco became French protectorates (Harvey 1980).

To be sure, the French, like the British, had substantial business interests in their colonies. But they also sought, again like the British, international glory and prestige. The French intervention philosophy was that of a *mission civilisatrice*, their equivalent of Britain's "white man's burden." The goal was to implant French culture, language, and religion—in the form of Roman Catholicism—throughout the colonies (Harvey 1980).

The French used two forms of colonial rule. They used *indirect rule,* governing through native leaders and established political structures, in areas with long histories of state organization, such as Morocco and Tunisia. They brought *direct rule* by French officials to many areas of Africa. Here, the French imposed new government structures to control diverse tribes and cultures, many of them previously stateless. Like the British empire, the French empire began to disintegrate after World War II. France fought long—and ultimately futile—wars to keep its empire intact in Indochina and Algeria (Harvey 1980).

Indochina fell fully under French colonial control in 1893. In this historical photo, from the 1920s, a Frenchman sits in a rickshaw (*pousse-pousse*). What does this mode of transit say to you about colonialism?

See your OLC Internet Exercises for information on Columbus's efforts at colonialism

mhhe com /kottak

COLONIALISM AND IDENTITY

Many political and social labels heard in the news today had no equivalent meaning before colonialism. Whole countries, along with social groups and divisions within them, were colonial inventions. In

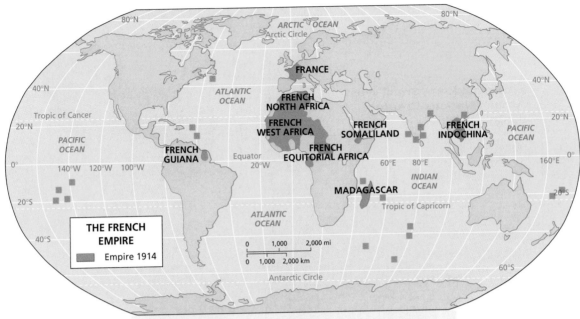

Figure 24.3 Map of the French Empire at Its Height around 1914.

West Africa, for example, by geographic logic, several adjacent countries could be one (Togo, Ghana, Côte d'Ivoire, Guinea, Guinea-Bissau, Sierra Leone, Liberia) (Figure 24.4). Instead, they are separated by linguistic, political, and economic contrasts promoted under colonialism.

In Madagascar, the French colonial census crystallized a series of ethnic groups (*ethnies*) that had been less distinct previously. Prior to French rule, the indigenous Merina state had conquered most of the island, establishing its own empire. The Merina, too, created ethnic identities where previously they did not exist. Betsileo, which means "too many to be counted," was coined to refer to the large population living south of a certain river. After 1820, reinforced by the census and by official documents, "Betsileo" gradually acquired an ethnic meaning.

Hundreds of ethnic groups and "tribes" are colonial constructions (see Ranger 1996). The Sukuma of Tanzania, for instance, were first registered as a single tribe by the colonial administration. Then missionaries standardized a series of dialects into a single Sukuma language as they translated the Bible and other religious texts. Thereafter, those texts were taught in missionary schools, and to European foreigners and other non-

Sukuma speakers. Over time, this standardized the Sukuma language and ethnicity (Finnstrom 1997).

As in much of East Africa, in Rwanda and Burundi, farmers and herders live in the same areas and speak the same language. Historically, they have shared the same social world, although their social organization is "extremely hierarchical," almost "castelike" (Malkki 1995:24). There has been a tendency to see the pastoral Tutsis as superior to the agricultural Hutus. Tutsis have been presented as nobles, Hutus as commoners. Yet when distributing identity cards in Rwanda, the Belgian colonizers simply identified all people with more than 10 heads of cattle as Tutsi. Owners of fewer cattle were registered as Hutus (Bjuremalm 1997). Years later, these arbitrary colonial registers were used systematically for "ethnic" identification during the mass killings that took place in Rwanda in 1994.

POSTCOLONIAL STUDIES

In anthropology, history, and literature, the field of postcolonial studies has gained prominence since the 1970s (see Ashcroft, Griffiths, and Tiffin 1989; Cooper and Stoler 1997). **Postcolonial** refers to the study of the interactions between European

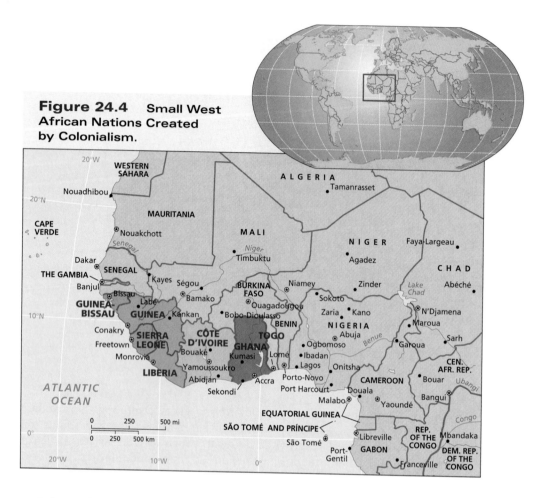

Figure 24.4 Small West African Nations Created by Colonialism.

nations and the societies they colonized (mainly after 1800). In 1914, European empires, which broke up after World War II, ruled more than 85 percent of the world (Petraglia-Bahri 1996). The term "postcolonial" also has been used to describe the second half of the 20th century in general, the period succeeding colonialism. Even more generically, "postcolonial" may be used to signify a position against imperialism and Eurocentrism (Petraglia-Bahri 1996).

The former colonies (*postcolonies*) can be divided into settler, nonsettler, and mixed (Petraglia-Bahri 1996). The settler countries, with large numbers of European colonists and sparser native populations, include Australia and Canada. Examples of nonsettler countries include India, Pakistan, Bangladash, Sri Lanka, Malaysia, Indonesia, Nigeria, Senegal, Madagascar, and Jamaica. All these had substantial native populations and relatively few European settlers. Mixed countries include South Africa, Zimbabwe, Kenya

(photo on page 675), and Algeria. Such countries had significant European settlement despite having sizable native populations.

Given the varied experiences of such countries, "postcolonial" has to be a loose term. The United States, for instance, was colonized by Europeans and fought a war for independence from Britain. Is the United States a postcolony? It isn't usually perceived as such, given its current world power position, its treatment of native Americans (sometimes called internal colonization), and its annexation of other parts of the world (Petraglia-Bahri 1996). Research in postcolonial studies is growing, permitting a wide-ranging investigation of power relations in varied contexts. Broad topics in the field include the formation of an empire, the impact of colonization, and the state of the post-colony today (Petraglia-Bahri 1996).

Here are some common questions addressed in postcolonial studies: How did colonization affect colonized people—and their colonizers?

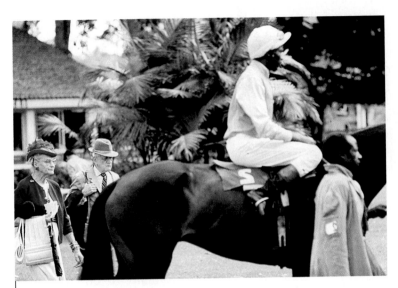

What traces of colonialism do you detect in this photo, taken recently at the Jockey Club in Nairobi, Kenya? What story is the photo telling you?

How did colonial powers manage to subjugate so much of the world? How did people in the colonies resist colonial control? How have cultures and identities been affected by colonization? How do gender, race, and class function in colonial and postcolonial settings? How have colonial education systems influenced the postcolonies? With regard to literature, should postcolonial writers use a colonial language, like English or French, to reach a wider audience? Or should they write in their native language, to reach others in the postcolony? Finally, are new forms of imperialism, such as development and globalization, replacing old ones? (Petraglia-Bahri 1996).

Development

For more on development efforts, see the Virtual Exploration

/kottak

During the Industrial Revolution, a strong current of thought viewed industrialization as a beneficial process of organic development and progress. Many economists still assume that industrialization increases production and income. They seek to create in Third World ("developing") countries a process—*economic development*—like the one that first occurred spontaneously in 18th-century Great Britain. Economic development generally aims at getting people to convert from subsistence to cash economies and thus to increase local participation in the world capitalist economy.

We just saw that Great Britain used the "white man's burden" to justify its imperialist expansion. Similarly, France claimed to be involved in a *mission civilisatrice*, a civilizing mission, in its colonies. Both these ideas illustrate an **intervention philosophy,** an ideological justification for outsiders to guide native peoples in specific directions. Economic development plans also have intervention philosophies. John Bodley (1988) argues that the basic belief behind interventions—whether by colonialists, missionaries, governments, or development planners—has been the same for more than 100 years. This belief is that industrialization, modernization, westernization, and individualism are desirable evolutionary advances and that development schemes that promote them will bring long-term benefits to natives. In a more extreme form, intervention philosophy may pit the assumed wisdom of enlightened colonial or other First World planners against the purported conservatism, ignorance, or "obsolescence" of "inferior" natives.

Anthropologists dispute such views. We know that for thousands of years, bands and tribes have done "a reasonable job of taking care of themselves" (Bodley 1988, p. 93). Indeed, because of their low energy needs, they usually managed their resources better than we manage our own. Many problems that people face today are due to their position within nation-states and their increasing dependence on the world cash economy.

Sometimes when natives are reluctant to change, it isn't because they have unduly conservative attitudes but because powerful interest groups oppose reform. Many Third World governments are reluctant to tamper with existing socioeconomic conditions in their countries (Manners 1956/1973). The attempt to bring the "green revolution" to Java that is analyzed below illustrates this situation. Resistance by elites to land reform is a reality throughout the Third World. Millions of people in colonies and underdeveloped nations have learned from bitter experience that if they increase their incomes, their taxes and rents also rise.

An anthropological study of an irrigated rice project in Madagascar found several reasons why it failed. If there are no machines to do the work, there have to be people around to do it— like these Betsileo women who are transplanting rice in the traditional manner.

exclusively on economic measures, such as per capita income and gross national product. Rather, it includes demographic statistics (e.g., literacy, years of schooling) as well as economic data. This measurement is called the human development index. Countries with the lowest quality of life tend to be in Africa and southern Asia. On the whole the Western Hemisphere does better than the Old World does. How does Europe compare with North America in terms of levels of human development?

Today, many government agencies, international groups, NGOs, and private foundations encourage attention to local-level social factors and the cultural dimension of economic development. Anthropological expertise in economic development planning is important because social problems can doom even potentially beneficial projects to failure. A study of 50 economic development projects (Lance and McKenna 1975) judged only 21 to be successes. Social and cultural incompatibilities had doomed most of the failed projects.

For example, a 1981 anthropological study of a multimillion-dollar development project in Madagascar uncovered several reasons for its failure. The project had been planned and funded by the World Bank in the late 1960s. The planners (no anthropologists among them) anticipated none of the problems that emerged. The project was aimed at draining and irrigating a large plain to increase rice production. Its goal was to raise production through machinery and double cropping—growing two crops annually on the same plot. However, the planners disregarded several things, including the unavailability of spare parts and fuel for the machines. The designers also ignored the fact, well known to anthropologists, that cross-culturally, intensive cultivation is associated with dense populations. If there are no machines to do the work, there have to be people around to do it. However, population densities in the project area (15 people per square kilometer) were much too low to support intensive cultivation without modern machinery.

Conflicts between governments and natives often arise when outside interests exploit resources on tribal lands. Driven by deficits and debts, governments seek to wrest as much wealth as possible from the territory they administer. This goal helps explain the worldwide intrusion on indigenous peoples and their local ecosystems by such forms of economic development as highway construction, mining, hydroelectric projects, ranching, lumbering, agribusiness, and planned colonization.

Studying people at the local level, ethnographers have a unique view of the impact of national and international development planning on intended "beneficiaries." Local-level research often reveals inadequacies in the measures that economists use to assess development and a nation's economic health. For example, per capita income and gross national product don't measure the distribution of wealth. Because the first is an average and the second is a total, they may rise as the rich get richer and the poor get poorer.

Interpret the World
Atlas Map 24

Map 24 in your atlas, "The Quality of Life: The Human Development Index," represents an attempt to assess and display the quality of life by country. It is not based

The planners should have known that labor and machinery for the project were unavailable. Furthermore, many local people were understandably hostile toward the project because it gave their ancestral land away to outsiders. (Unfortunately, this is a common occurrence in development projects.) Many land-grant recipients were members of regional and national elites. They used their influence to get fields that were intended for poor farmers. The project also suffered from technical problems. The foreign firm hired to dig the irrigation canals dug them lower than the land they had to irrigate. The water couldn't flow up into the fields.

Millions of development dollars could have been spent more wisely if anthropologists, consulting with local farmers, had helped plan, implement, and monitor the project. It stands to reason that experts, such as anthropologists, who are familiar with the language and customs of a country can better evaluate prospects of project success than can those who are not. Accordingly, anthropologists increasingly work in organizations that promote, manage, and assess programs that influence human life in the United States and abroad.

Applied anthropology, already examined in Chapter 2, refers to the application of anthropological perspectives, theory, methods, and data to identify, assess, and solve social problems. **Development anthropology** is the branch of applied anthropology that focuses on social issues in, and the cultural dimension of, economic development. Development anthropologists do not just carry out development policies planned by others; they also plan and guide policy. (For more detailed discussions of issues in development anthropology, see Escobar [1995], Ferguson [1994], and Robertson [1995].)

However, ethical dilemmas often confront development anthropologists (Escobar 1991, 1995). Our respect for cultural diversity is often offended because efforts to extend industry and technology may entail profound cultural changes. Foreign aid doesn't usually go where need and suffering are greatest. It is spent on political, economic, and strategic priorities as political leaders and powerful interest groups perceive them. Planners' interests don't always coincide with the best interests of the local people. Although the aim of most development projects is to enhance the quality of life, living standards often decline in the target area (Bodley 1988).

THE BRAZILIAN SISAL SCHEME

A well-studied case in which development harmed the intended beneficiaries occurred in an arid area of Brazil's northeastern interior called the *sertão.* Here development increased dependence on the world economy, ruined the local subsistence economy, and worsened local health and income distribution. Until the 1950s, the *sertão's* economy was based on corn, beans, manioc, and other subsistence crops. The *sertão* was also a grazing region for cattle, sheep, and goats. Most years, peasants subsisted on their crops. However, about once every decade, a major drought drastically reduced yields and forced people to migrate to the coast to seek jobs. To develop the northeast and dampen the effects of drought, the Brazilian government began encouraging peasants to plant sisal, a fibrous plant used to make rope, as a cash crop.

To ready sisal for export, preparation in the field was necessary. Throughout the sertão, there arose local centers with decorticating machines, devices that strip water and residue from sisal leaf, leaving only the fiber. These machines were expensive. Small-scale farmers couldn't afford them and had to use machines owned by the elite.

Small teams of workers were in charge of decorticating. Two jobs were especially hard, both done by adult men. One was that of disfiberer, the person who fed the sisal leaf into the machine. This was a demanding and dangerous job. The machine exerted a strong pull, making it possible for the disfiberers to get their fingers caught in the press. The other job was that of residue man, who shoveled away the residue that fell under the machine and brought new leaves to the disfiberer.

Anthropologist Daniel Gross (1971) studied the effects of sisal on the people of the sertão. Most sisal growers were people who had converted their land to the cash crop, completely abandoning subsistence cultivation. Because sisal takes four years to mature, peasants had to seek wage work until they could harvest their crop. When they did harvest, they often found that the price of sisal on the world market was less than it had been when they planted the crop. Moreover, once sisal was planted, its strong root system made it almost impossible for the peasants to return to other

To develop its impoverished northeast and to dampen the effects of drought, the Brazilian government encouraged farmers to plant sisal, a fibrous plant, as a cash crop. Have you ever seen sisal? For what might you use it?

Gross then examined the diets of the households headed by each man. The disfiberer earned the equivalent of $3.65 per week, whereas the residue man made less—about $3.25. The disfiberer's household included just himself and his wife. The residue man had a pregnant wife and four children, aged three, five, six, and eight. By spending most of his income on food, the disfiberer was getting at least 7,100 calories a day for himself and his wife. This was ample to supply his daily needs of 4,400 calories. It also left his wife a comfortable 2,700 calories.

However, the residue man's household was less fortunate. With more than 95 percent of his tiny income going for food, he could provide himself, his wife, and his four children with only 9,400 calories per day. Of this, he consumed 3,600 calories—enough to go on working. His wife ate 2,200 calories. His children, however, suffered nutritionally. Table 24.1 compares the minimum daily requirements for his children with their actual intake.

Long-term malnutrition has results that are reflected in body weight. Table 24.1 shows that the weights of the residue man's malnourished children compared poorly with the standard weights for their ages. The longer malnutrition continues, the greater is the gap between children with poor diets and those with normal diets. The residue

crops. The land and people of the *sertão* became hooked on sisal.

A nutritionist, Barbara Underwood, collaborated with Gross in studying the new economy's effects on nutrition. For people to subsist, they must consume sufficient calories to replace those they expend in daily activity. Gross calculated the energy expended in two of the jobs on the decorticating team: disfiberer and residue man. The former expended an average of 4,400 calories per day; the latter, 3,600 calories.

Table 24.1	Malnutrition among the Children of a Brazilian Sisal Residue Man		
	CALORIES		
Age of Child	Minimum Daily Requirement	Actual Daily Allotment	Percentage of Standard Body Weight
8 (M)	2,100	1,100	62
6 (F)	1,700	900	70
5 (M)	1,700	900	85
3 (M)	1,300	700	90

SOURCE: Gross and Underwood 1971, p. 733.

man's oldest children had been malnourished longest. They compared least favorably with the standard body weight.

The children of sisal workers were being malnourished to enable their fathers to go on working for wages that were too low to feed them. However, the children of businesspeople and owners of decorticating machines were doing better; malnutrition was much less severe among them. Finally, the nutrition of sisal workers was also worse than that of traditional cultivators in the sertão. People who had reached adulthood before sisal cultivation began had more normal weights than did those who grew up after the shift.

This study is important for understanding problems that beset many people today. A shift from a subsistence economy to a cash economy led neither to a better diet nor to more leisure time for most people. The rich merely got richer and the poor got poorer. Badly planned and socially insensitive economic development projects often have such unforeseen consequences.

THE GREENING OF JAVA

Like Gross in Brazil, anthropologist Richard Franke (1977) conducted an independent study of discrepancies between goals and results in a scheme to promote social and economic change in Java, Indonesia (Figure 24.5). Experts and planners of the 1960s and 1970s assumed that as small-scale farmers got modern technology and more productive crop varieties, their lives would improve. The media publicized new, high-yielding varieties of wheat, maize, and rice. These new crops, along with chemical fertilizers, pesticides, and new cultivation techniques, were hailed as the basis of a **green revolution.** This "revolution" was expected to increase the world's food supply and thus improve the diets and living conditions of victims of poverty, particularly in land-scarce, overcrowded regions.

The green revolution was an economic success. It did increase the global food supply. New strains of wheat and rice doubled or tripled farm supplies in many Third World countries. Thanks to the **green revolution,** world food prices declined by more than 20 percent during the 1980s (Stevens 1992). But its social effects were not what its advocates had intended, as we learn from Javanese experience.

Java received a genetic cross between rice strains from Taiwan and Indonesia—a high-yielding "miracle" rice known as IR-8. This hybrid could raise the productivity of a given plot by at least half. Governments throughout southern Asia, including Indonesia, encouraged the cultivation of IR-8, along with the use of chemical fertilizers and pesticides.

The Indonesian island of Java, one of the most densely populated places in the world (over 2,000 people per square mile), was a prime target for the green revolution. Java's total crop was insufficient to supply its people with minimal daily requirements of calories (2,150) and protein (55 grams). In 1960, Javanese agriculture supplied 1,950 calories and 38 grams of protein per capita. By 1967, these already inadequate figures had fallen to 1,750 calories and 33 grams. Could miracle rice, by increasing crop yields 50 percent, reverse the trend?

Figure 24.5 Location of Java (yellow) in Indonesia (orange).

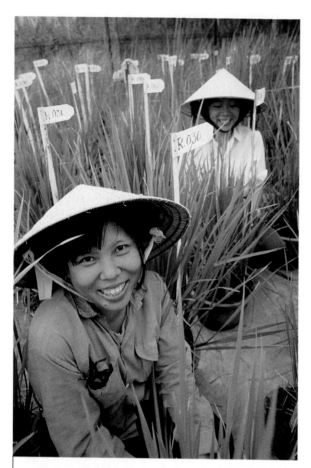

Many Asian governments have promoted the cultivation of new rice varieties, along with the use of chemical fertilizers and pesticides. What costs and benefits may accompany such changes? Shown here is Vietnam's Can Tho Rice Research Institute.

Java shares with many other underdeveloped nations a history of socioeconomic stratification and colonialism. Indigenous contrasts in wealth and power were intensified by Dutch colonialism. Although Indonesia gained political independence from the Netherlands in 1949, internal stratification continued. Today, contrasts between the wealthy (government employees, businesspeople, large landowners) and the poor (small-scale peasants) exist even in small farming communities. Stratification led to problems during Java's green revolution.

In 1963, the University of Indonesia's College of Agriculture launched a program in which students went to live in villages. They worked with peasants in the fields and shared their knowledge of new agricultural techniques while learning from the peasants. The program was a success. Yields in the affected villages increased by half. The program, directed by the Department of Agriculture, was expanded in 1964; nine universities and 400 students joined. These intervention programs succeeded where others had failed because the outside agents recognized that economic development rests not only on technological change but on political change as well. Students could observe firsthand how interest groups resisted attempts by peasants to improve their lot. Once, when local officials stole fertilizer destined for peasant fields, students got it back by threatening in a letter to turn evidence of the crime over to higher-level officials.

The combination of new work patterns and political action was achieving promising results when, in 1965–1966, there was an insurrection against the government. In the eventual military takeover, Indonesia's President Sukarno was ousted and replaced by President Suharto, who ruled Indonesia until 1998. Efforts to increase agricultural production resumed soon after Suharto took control. However, the new government assigned the task to multinational corporations based in Japan, West Germany, and Switzerland rather than to students and peasants. These industrial firms were to supply miracle rice and other high-yielding seeds, fertilizers, and pesticides. Peasants adopting the whole green revolution kit were eligible for loans that would allow them to buy food and other essentials in the lean period just before harvesting.

Java's green revolution soon encountered problems. One pesticide, which had never been tested in Java, killed the fish in the irrigation canals and thus destroyed an important protein resource. Java's green revolution also encountered problems at the village level because of entrenched interests. Traditionally, peasants had fed their families by taking temporary jobs, or borrowing, from wealthier villagers before the harvest. However, having accepted loans, the peasants were obliged to work for wages lower than those paid on the open market. Low-interest loans would have made peasants less dependent on wealthy villagers, thus depriving local patrons of cheap labor.

Local officials were put in charge of spreading information about how the program worked. Instead, they limited peasant participation by withholding information. Wealthy villagers also discouraged peasant participation more subtly: They raised doubts about the effectiveness of the new techniques and about the wisdom of taking government loans when familiar patrons were nearby. Faced with the thought that starvation might follow if innovation failed, peasants were reluctant to take risks—an understandable reaction.

Production increased, but wealthy villagers rather than small-scale farmers reaped the benefits of the green revolution. Just 20 percent of one village's 151 households participated in the program. However, because they were the wealthiest households, headed by people who owned the most land, 40 percent of the land was being cultivated by means of the new system. Some large-scale landowners used their green revolution profits at the peasants' expense. They bought up peasants' small plots and purchased labor-saving machinery, including rice-milling machines and tractors. As a result, the poorest peasants lost both their means of subsistence—land—and local work opportunities. Their only recourse was to move to cities, where a growing pool of unskilled laborers depressed already low wages.

In a complementary view of the green revolution's social effects, Ann Stoler (1977) focused on gender and stratification. She took issue with Esther Boserup's (1970) contention that colonialism and development inevitably hurt Third World women more than men by favoring commercial agriculture and excluding women from farming. Stoler found that the green revolution had permitted some women to gain power over other women and men. Javanese women were not a homogeneous group but varied by class. Stoler found that whether the green revolution helped or harmed Javanese women depended on their position in the class structure. The status of landholding women rose as they gained control over more land and the labor of more poor women. The new economy offered wealthier women higher profits, which they used in trading. However, poor women suffered along with poor men as traditional economic opportunities declined. Nevertheless, the poor women fared better than did the poor men, who had no access at all to off-farm work.

Like Gross's analysis of the Brazilian sisal scheme, these studies of the local effects of the green revolution reveal results different from those foreseen by policy makers, planners, and the media. Again, we see the unintended and undesirable effects of development programs that ignore traditional social, political, and economic divisions. New technology, no matter how promising, does not inevitably help the intended beneficiaries. It may very well hurt them if vested interests interfere. The Javanese student–peasant projects of the 1960s worked because peasants need not just technology but also political clout. Two ambitious development programs in Brazil and Java, although designed to alleviate poverty, actually increased it. Peasants stopped relying on their own subsistence production and started depending on a more volatile pursuit—cash sale of labor. Agricultural production became profit-oriented, machine-based, and chemical-dependent. Local autonomy diminished as linkages with the world system increased. Production rose, as the rich got richer and poverty increased.

EQUITY

A commonly stated goal of development policy today is to promote equity. **Increased equity** means reduced poverty and a more even distribution of wealth. However, if projects are to increase equity, they must have the support of reform-minded governments. Wealthy and powerful people typically resist projects that threaten their vested interests.

Some types of development projects, particularly irrigation schemes, are more likely than others to widen wealth disparities, that is, to have a negative equity impact. An initial uneven distribution of resources (particularly land) often becomes the basis for greater skewing after the project. The social impact of new technology tends to be more severe, contributing negatively to quality of life and to equity, when inputs are channeled to or through the rich, as in Java's green revolution.

Many fisheries projects also have had negative equity results. In Bahia, Brazil (Kottak 1999), sailboat owners (but not nonowners) got loans to buy motors for their boats. To repay the loans, the owners increased the percentage of the catch they took from the men who fished in their boats. Over the years, they used their rising profits to buy larger and more expensive boats. The result was stratification—the creation of a group of wealthy people within a formerly egalitarian community. These events hampered individual initiative and interfered with further development of the fishing

A mix of boats harbored at Dai-Lanh fishing village in Vietnam. A boat owner gets a loan to buy a motor. To repay it, he increases the share of the catch he takes from his crew. Later, he uses his rising profits to buy a more expensive boat, and takes even more from his crew. Can a more equitable solution be found?

Batalla also criticized the multiple causation theory, which assumes that any social event has countless small and diverse causes. Such a theory does not perceive major social and economic inequities as targets for attack. Batalla also faulted certain anthropologists for seeing communities as isolated units, because local-level changes are always accepted or opposed in a larger context. He argued that applied anthropologists should pay more attention to regional, national, and international contexts. Finally, Batalla criticized anthropologists for thinking that diffusion, usually of technical skills and equipment from the First World, is the most significant process involved in change.

Batalla didn't argue that all applied anthropology suffered from these faults. However, many of his criticisms were valid, and other Third World social scientists agreed with him. Those scholars also criticized American anthropology for links between some anthropologists and government agencies that did not promote the best interests of the people.

Partly in response to critics like Batalla, partly out of concern with collaboration by a few anthropologists with the CIA (U.S. Central Intelligence Agency) during the Vietnam War, the American Anthropological Association (AAA) in 1971 adopted a code of ethics entitled "AAA: Principles of Professional Responsibility." In the most recent (1997) revision of that code, as we saw in previous chapters, the AAA notes that anthropologists have obligations to their scholarly field, to the wider society and culture, and to the human species, other species, and the environment. The code's aim is to offer guidelines and to promote education and discussion of socially responsible anthropology, whether academic or applied.

industry. With new boats so expensive, ambitious young men who once would have sought careers in fishing no longer had any way to obtain their own boats. They sought wage labor on land instead. To avoid such results, credit-granting agencies must seek out enterprising young fishers rather than giving loans only to owners and established businesspeople.

THE THIRD WORLD TALKS BACK

In the postcolonial world, anthropologists from industrial nations have heeded criticisms leveled against them by Third World colleagues. For example, the late Mexican anthropologist Guillermo Batalla (1966) decried certain "conservative and essentially ethnocentric assumptions" of applied anthropology of the 1950s and 1960s in Latin America. He criticized the heavy psychological emphasis of many studies. These studies, he argued, focused too much on attitudes and beliefs about health and nutrition and not enough on the material causes of poor health and malnutrition. Another problem he mentioned was the misuse of cultural relativism by certain anthropologists. Batalla faulted those researchers for refusing to interfere in existing social situations because they considered it inappropriate to judge and to promote change.

Strategies for Innovation

Development anthropologists, who are concerned with social issues in, and the cultural dimension of, economic development, must work closely with local people to assess and help real-ize their own wishes and needs for change. Too many true local needs cry out for a solution to waste money funding development projects that are inappropriate in area A but needed in area B, or unnecessary anywhere. Development anthropol-ogy can help sort out the A's and B's and fit projects accordingly. Projects that put people first by consulting with them, and responding to their expressed needs, must be identified (Cernea 1991). Thereafter, develop-ment anthropologists can work to ensure socially compatible ways of implementing the project.

In a comparative study of 68 rural development projects from all around the world, I found the *cul-turally compatible* economic develop-ment projects to be twice as success-ful financially as the incompatible ones (Kottak 1990*b*, 1991). This finding shows that using applied anthropological expertise in plan-ning, to ensure cultural compatibility, is cost-effec-tive. To maximize social and economic benefits, projects must (1) be culturally compatible, (2) respond to locally perceived needs, (3) involve men and women in planning and carrying out the changes that affect them, (4) harness traditional organizations, and (5) be flexible.

To maximize benefits, development projects should be culturally compatible and respond to locally perceived needs for change. What else should they do? This Zambian farm club, which draws on traditional social organization, plants cabbages.

OVERINNOVATION

In my comparative study, the compatible and suc-cessful projects avoided the fallacy of **overinnova-tion** (too much change). We would expect people to resist development projects that require major changes in their daily lives, especially ones that interfere with subsistence pursuits. People usually want to change just enough to keep what they have. Motives for modifying behavior come from the tra-ditional culture and the small concerns of ordinary life. Peasants' values are not such abstract ones as "learning a better way," "progressing," "increasing technical know-how," "improving efficiency," or "adopting modern techniques." (Those phrases exemplify intervention philosophy.) Instead, their objectives are down-to-earth and specific ones. Peo-ple want to improve yields in a rice field, amass

resources for a ceremony, get a child through school, or have enough cash to pay the tax bill on time. The goals and values of subsistence produc-ers differ from those of people who produce for cash, just as they differ from the intervention philosophies of development planners. Different value systems must be considered during planning.

In the comparative study, the projects that failed were usually both economically and cultur-ally incompatible. For example, one South Asian project promoted the cultivation of onions and pep-pers, expecting this practice to fit into a preexisting labor-intensive system of rice-growing. Cultivation of these cash crops wasn't traditional in the area. It conflicted with existing crop priorities and other interests of farmers. Also, the labor peaks for pep-per and onion production coincided with those for rice, to which the farmers naturally gave priority.

Throughout the world, project problems have arisen from inadequate attention to, and conse-quent lack of fit with, local culture. Another naive and incompatible project was an overinnovative scheme in Ethiopia. Its major fallacy was to try to convert nomadic herders into sedentary cultivators. It ignored traditional land rights. Outsiders—com-mercial farmers—were to get much of the herders' territory. The pastoralists were expected to settle down and start farming. This project helped wealthy outsiders instead of the natives. The planners naively expected free-ranging herders to give up a generations-old way of life to work three times harder growing rice and picking cotton. "Interesting Issues" describes an extreme—and ongoing—example of a centrally planned, culturally incompatible project. Planning for the world's largest dam involved no consultation with local people and no attention to their needs and wishes. Strong resistance can be expected to continue.

Understanding Ourselves   Change, we think, is good. Leaders are expected to offer "visions" of change. Few politicians get elected by promising, "I'm going to keep things just as they are." The assumption usually is that change is better—but what kind of change? From this discussion of the fallacy of overinnovation there are lessons to be learned and applied in our own lives.

Like most people, contemporary North Americans generally seek changes that will enable them to maintain or improve their life styles—not to revise them radically. Imagine someone chosen to lead an organization, someone from outside who is unfamiliar with the culture of that organization. He or she should follow the anthropologist's example and study the local culture before trying to change it. The leader should try to determine what works and what doesn't and what the natives (i.e., the men and women within the organization) want and really need. After local perceptions and needs have been assessed, if change seems in order, the leader must determine how to plan and implement change in the least disruptive way. Again, he or she should follow the applied anthropologist's strategy of consulting with and enlisting the help and support of local people throughout the process of change. To be an effective "change agent" requires listening and trying to tailor innovation to fit the local culture.

This process of study and collaboration illustrates participatory change—change from the "bottom up." By contrast, top-down change is often problematic. A top-down leader typically draws on an organizational blueprint—perhaps one he or she has brought from a former organization. Unmodified blueprints usually don't work. Just as the linguistic blueprint in our brain is modified to fit a particular language, an organizational blueprint must be flexible enough to be modified to fit a specific organization. If it is not, that blueprint should be discarded. The fallacies of blueprint planning and overinnovation aren't just obscure lessons from failed development projects. They are vital considerations for any leader who wishes to run, or change, an organization.

UNDERDIFFERENTIATION

The fallacy of **underdifferentiation** is the tendency to view "the less-developed countries" as more alike than they are. Development agencies often have ignored cultural diversity (e.g., between Brazil and Burundi) and adopted a uniform approach to deal with very different sets of people. Neglecting cultural diversity, many projects also have tried to impose incompatible property notions and social units. Most often, the faulty social design assumes either (1) individualistic productive units that are privately owned by an individual or couple and worked by a nuclear family or (2) cooperatives that are at least partially based on models from the former Eastern bloc and socialist countries.

Often, development aims at generating *individual* cash wealth through exports. This goal contrasts with the tendency of bands and tribes to share resources and to depend on local ecosystems and renewable resources (Bodley 1988). Development planners commonly emphasize benefits that will accrue to individuals. More concern with the effects on communities is needed (Bodley 1988).

One example of faulty Euro-American models (the individual and the nuclear family) was a West African project designed for an area where the extended family was the basic social unit. The project succeeded despite its faulty social design because the participants used their traditional extended family networks to attract additional settlers. Eventually, twice as many people as planned benefited as extended family members flocked to the project area. Here, settlers modified the project design that had been imposed on them by following the principles of their traditional society.

The second dubious foreign social model that is common in development strategy is the cooperative. In the comparative study of rural development projects, new cooperatives fared badly. Cooperatives succeeded only when they harnessed preexisting local-level communal institutions. This is a corollary of a more general rule: Participants'

Interesting *Issues*
People Be Dammed

The relocation of at least 1.2 million people to make way for the Three Gorges Dam in central China is off to a poor start . . . a Chinese social scientist who toured five of the most heavily affected counties in January says.

Interviews with local officials and people affected by the giant project to tame the Yangtze River suggested that the resettlement program . . . has been plagued by inadequate compensation and a shortage of new jobs and farmland for people being relocated, official corruption and false reports of progress by local officials to national leaders.

In November 1997, to nationalistic fanfare, China diverted the Yangtze around the construction site and began building the dam, which will be the world's largest. . . . The Government signed contracts with Western companies for turbines and other equipment. . . .

Government officials say the dam will provide huge benefits by controlling floods, providing clean energy and opening the interior to shipping. Critics say that the benefits are exaggerated and that the dam will destroy the Yangtze ecosystem, bury priceless cultural relics and cause suffering for hundreds of thousands.

Because of these concerns, the World Bank and United States Export-Import Bank have not lent money to the project, and opponents hope to curb European export credits.

The author of the new report on resettlement, an experienced field researcher, has concealed his identity to protect his career. His report [was] distributed by the International Rivers Network and Human Rights in

Viewing the construction of China's Three Gorges Dam.

China, two American-based groups that oppose the dam on environmental and human rights grounds.

By 2003, when the dam is built and the reservoir of water behind it is filled to its initial level, at least 500,000 people must be moved from cities, towns and villages of Sichuan and Hubei Provinces. By 2009, when the reservoir is filled still higher, the Government says a total of 1.2 million people will have to be moved. . . .

But some people are resisting.

"Foot-dragging opposition to resettlement is widespread, presaging a major crisis if the dam project continues as planned," wrote the Chinese researcher, estimating that the number of people moved to date may be little more than half of the official total. Given the slow pace, he wrote, officials in one county said no official would want to be in charge of resettlement . . . because so many people will have to be moved within

such a short time, raising a specter of unrest. . . .

To improve the prospects for displaced people, the Government has offered incentives for companies to locate in the region. But the current effort to shed excess workers in ailing state industries has instead meant rising unemployment. One county official in Sichuan reportedly said, "There is no way to find industrial jobs for rural settlers."

The researcher met with several "model resettlers," families who were happy with their new lives and are showcased by officials as success stories. But the small number who have been officially designated as models have received four times the average compensation for relocation, the report says.

SOURCE: "Relocations for China Dam Are Found to Lag," by Erik Eckholm, March 12, 1998, www.nytimes.com.

groups are most effective when they are based on traditional social organization or on a socioeconomic similarity among members.

Neither foreign social model—the nuclear family farm nor the cooperative—has an unblemished record in development. An alternative is needed: greater use of Third World social models for Third World development. These are traditional social units, such as the clans, lineages, and other extended kinship groups of Africa, Oceania, and many other nations, with their communally held estates and resources. The most humane and productive strategy for change is to base the social design for innovation on traditional social forms in each target area.

THIRD WORLD MODELS

Many governments are not genuinely, or realistically, committed to improving the lives of their citizens. Interference by major powers also has kept governments from enacting needed reforms. In highly stratified societies, the class structure is very rigid. Movement of individuals into the middle class is difficult. It is equally hard to raise the living standards of the lower class as a whole. Many nations have a long history of government control by antidemocratic leaders and powerful interest groups, which tend to oppose reform. (Such governments often have been supported by the United States, especially during the Cold War.)

In some nations, however, the government acts more as an agent of the people. Madagascar provides an example. As in many areas of Africa, precolonial states had developed in Madagascar before its conquest by the French in 1895. The people of Madagascar, the Malagasy, had been organized into descent groups before the origin of the state. The Merina, creators of the major precolonial state of Madagascar, wove descent groups into its structure, making members of important groups advisers to the king and thus giving them authority in government. The Merina state made provisions for the people it ruled. It collected taxes and organized labor for public works projects. In return, it redistributed resources to peasants in need. It also granted them some protection against war and slave raids and allowed them to cultivate their rice fields in peace. The government maintained the water works for rice cultivation. It opened to ambitious peasant boys the chance of becoming, through hard work and study, state bureaucrats.

Throughout the history of the Merina state—and continuing in modern Madagascar—there have been strong relationships between the individual, the descent group, and the state. Local Malagasy communities, where residence is based on descent, are more cohesive and homogeneous than are communities in Java or Latin America. Madagascar gained political independence from France in 1960. Although it was still economically dependent on France when I first did research there in 1966–1967, the new government was committed to a form of economic development designed to increase the ability of the Malagasy to feed themselves. Government policy emphasized increased production of rice, a subsistence crop, rather than cash crops. Furthermore, local communities, with their traditional cooperative patterns and solidarity based on kinship and descent, were treated as partners in, not obstacles to, the development process.

In Bangladesh, women count money at a weekly meeting where loans from the female-run Grameen Credit Bank are repaid. Groups promoting development can be particularly effective when they are based on traditional social organization or on a socioeconomic similarity among members.

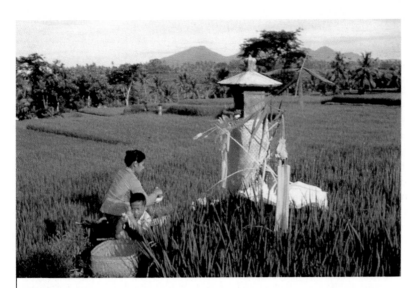

An effective social design for innovation may incorporate existing groups and institutions, such as descent groups in Africa and Oceania. Here, in Bali, Indonesia, a traditional system of planning and management by Hindu temples and priests has been harnessed for culturally appropriate agricultural development (see Lansing 1991).

Malagasy administrations appear generally to have shared a commitment to democratic economic development. Perhaps this is because government officials are of the peasantry or have strong personal ties to it. By contrast, in Latin American countries, the elites and the lower class typically have different origins and no strong connections through kinship, descent, or marriage.

Furthermore, societies with descent-group organization contradict an assumption that many social scientists and economists seem to make. It is not inevitable that as nations become more tied to the world capitalist economy, native forms of social organization will break down into nuclear family organization, impersonality, and alienation. Descent groups, with their traditional communalism and corporate solidarity, have important roles to play in economic development.

Realistic development promotes change but not overinnovation. Many changes are possible if the aim is to preserve local systems while making them work better. Successful economic development projects respect, or at least don't attack, local cultural patterns. Effective development draws on indigenous cultural practices and social structures.

In a sense, the descent group is preadapted to equitable national development. In Madagascar, members of local descent groups have customarily pooled their resources to educate their ambitious members. Once educated, these men and women gain economically secure positions in the nation. They then share the advantages of their new positions with their kin. For example, they give room and board to rural cousins attending school and help them find jobs.

SUMMARY

1. Imperialism is the policy of extending the rule of a nation or empire over other nations and of taking and holding foreign colonies. Colonialism is the domination of a territory and its people by a foreign power for an extended time. European colonialism has had two main phases. The first started in 1492 and lasted through 1825. For Britain this phase ended with the American Revolution. For France it ended when Britain won the Seven Years War, forcing the French to abandon Canada and India. For Spain, it ended with Latin American independence. The second phase of European colonialism extended approximately from 1850 to 1950. The British and French empires were at their height around 1914, when European empires controlled 85 percent of the world. Britain and France had colonies in Africa, Asia, Oceania, and the New World.

2. Political, ethnic, and tribal labels and identities were created under colonialism. Postcolonial studies is a growing academic field. It studies the interactions between European nations and the societies they colonized (mainly after 1800). Its topics include the impact of colonization and the state of postcolonies today.

3. Like colonialism, economic development has an intervention philosophy. This provides a justification for outsiders to guide native peoples toward particular goals. Development is usually justified by the idea that industrialization and modernization are desirable evolutionary advances. Yet many problems faced by Third World peoples have been caused by their incorporation in the world cash economy. Roads, mining, hydroelectric projects, ranching, lumbering, and agribusiness threaten indigenous peoples and their ecosystems.

4. Development anthropology focuses on social issues in, and the cultural dimension of, economic development. Development projects typically promote cash employment and new technology at the expense of subsistence economies.

Following a shift to cash cropping in northeastern Brazil, the local diet and poverty worsened. Research in Java found that the green revolution was failing. The reason: It promoted only new technology, rather than a combination of technology and peasant political organization.

5. Not all governments seek to increase equality and end poverty. Resistance by elites to reform is typical—and hard to combat. Local people rarely cooperate with projects requiring major changes in their daily lives, especially ones that interfere with customary subsistence pursuits. Many projects seek to impose inappropriate property notions and incompatible social units on their intended beneficiaries. The best strategy for change is to base the social design for innovation on traditional social forms in each target area.

KEY TERMS

See the flash cards

mhhe
●com
/kottak

colonialism   The political, social, economic, and cultural domination of a territory and its people by a foreign power for an extended time.

development anthropology   The branch of applied anthropology that focuses on social issues in, and the cultural dimension of, economic development.

equity, increased   A reduction in absolute poverty and a fairer (more even) distribution of wealth.

green revolution   Agricultural development based on chemical fertilizers, pesticides, 20th-century cultivation techniques, and new crop varieties such as IR-8 ("miracle rice").

intervention philosophy   Guiding principle of colonialism, conquest, missionization, or development; an ideological justification for outsiders to guide native peoples in specific directions.

overinnovation   Characteristic of projects that require major changes in natives' daily lives, especially ones that interfere with customary subsistence pursuits.

postcolonial   Referring to interactions between European nations and the societies they colonized (mainly after 1800); more generally, "postcolonial" may be used to signify a position against imperialism and Eurocentrism.

underdifferentiation   Planning fallacy of viewing less-developed countries as an undifferentiated group; ignoring cultural diversity and adopting a uniform approach (often ethnocentric) for very different types of project beneficiaries.

CRITICAL THINKING QUESTIONS

For more self testing, see the self quizzes

mhhe com /kottak

1. How is the diversity you see in your classroom related to the colonies and empires discussed in this chapter?

2. Have you read a postcolonial novel? What was the last one you read? What made it postcolonial?

3. Defend the proposition: The United States and Canada are both postcolonies.

4. Think of a recent case in which a core nation, such as the United States, has intervened in the affairs of another nation. What was the intervention philosophy used to justify the action?

5. Broadly describe the equity results of the Brazilian sisal scheme and the green revolution in Java. Do you think that most economic development schemes have similar results? Does this description of Java's green revolution fit what you have previously heard about the green revolution?

6. Devise a plan to equalize the distribution of computers in your public school system. What kind of opposition would you expect? Who would your supporters be?

7. Can you think of some good reasons to get herders to start farming? How would you try to implement such a change? Do you think you'd be successful? Is there an intervention philosophy behind your thinking?

8. Think about ways in which economic development might differently affect men and women.

9. Thinking of your own society and recent history, give an example of a proposal or policy that failed because it was overinnovative.

10. Thinking of your own society and recent history, give an example of a proposal or policy that failed because it did not differentiate sufficiently.

11. Think of a change you'd like to see happen. What groups would you enlist to make it happen? What would their roles be, from start to finish?

Atlas Questions

Look at Map 24, "The Quality of Life: The Human Development Index."

1. What countries in the Western Hemisphere have Human Development Index (HDI) scores comparable to those of some European nations? Does this surprise you?

2. Given that Brazil has one of the world's top 10 economies, does its HDI score surprise you? How do Brazil, Mexico, and Venezuela compare in terms of the HDI?

3. Do you notice a correlation between deforestation (Map 3) and quality of life? Does India fit this correlation?

SUGGESTED ADDITIONAL READINGS

Arce, A., and N. Long, eds.

2000   *Anthropology, Development, and Modernities: Exploring Discourses, Counter-tendencies, and Violence.* New York: Routledge. Applied anthropology, rural development, social change, violence, and social and economic policy in developing countries.

Barlett, P. F., ed.

1980   *Agricultural Decision Making: Anthropological Contribution to Rural Development.* New York: Academic Press. How farmers choose what to plant and decide how to plant it in various cultures.

Bodley, J. H.

2001   *Anthropology and Contemporary Human Problems,* 4th ed. Boston: McGraw-Hill. Overview of major problems of today's industrial world: overconsumption, the environment, resource depletion, hunger, overpopulation, violence, and war.

Bodley, J. H., ed.

1988   *Tribal Peoples and Development Issues: A Global Overview.* Mountain View, CA: Mayfield. An overview of case studies, policies, assessments, and recommendations concerning tribal peoples and development.

Cernea, M., ed.

1991   *Putting People First: Sociological Variables in Rural Development,* 2nd ed. New York: Oxford University Press (published for the World Bank). First collection of articles by social scientists based on World Bank files and project experiences. Examines development successes and failures and the social and cultural reasons for them.

Cernea, M. and C. McDowell, eds.

2000   *Risks and Reconstruction: Experiences of Resettlers and Refugees.* Washington, DC: World Bank. Economic development, environmental and population disruption, and forced relocation.

Cooper, F., and A. L. Stoler, eds.

1997   *Tensions of Empire: Colonial Cultures in a Bourgeois World.* Berkeley, CA: University of California Press. The social complexity of colonial encounters is explored in several articles.

Escobar, A.

1995   *Encountering Development: The Making and Unmaking of the Third World.* Princeton, NJ: Princeton University Press. A critique of economic development and development anthropology.

Lansing, J. S.

1991   *Priests and Programmers: Technologies of Power in the Engineered Landscape of Bali.* Princeton, NJ: Princeton University Press. The role of a traditional priesthood in managing irrigation and culturally appropriate economic development in Bali, Indonesia.

Nussbaum, M. C.

2000   *Women and Human Development: The Capabilities Approach.* New York: Cambridge University Press. The untapped power of women in developing countries.

Nussbaum, M. C., and J. Glover, eds.

1995   *Women, Culture, and Development: A Study of Human Capabilities.* New York: Oxford University Press. How to overcome generalized inequities between men and women in the less-developed countries.

Van Bremen, J., and A. Shimizu, eds.

1999   *Anthropology and Colonialism in Asia and Oceania.* London: Curzon. One in a series on the anthropology of Asia.

INTERNET EXERCISES

1. Colonialism in California: Go to the Original Voices website, **http://originalvoices.org/,** and read the chapters on Precontact Culture and Economy, **http://originalvoices.org/PreContactOne. htm;** Human Price of Gold Rush, **http://origi-nalvoices.org/PriceOfGoldOne.htm;** and U.S. Government Roles, **http://originalvoices.org/ USGovtRolesOne.htm.**

   a. What cultures lived in Northern California before the gold rush? What were their life styles like?

   b. What were the gold miners' attitudes toward the indigenous people? What actions did they take that reflected those attitudes? Would you characterize these actions as ethnocide or genocide?

   c. What role did the U.S. government play in the gold rush? Did it just tolerate the actions of the miners or did it encourage them?

   d. Some names of professional sports teams have been in the news recently because some Native Americans consider them offensive (e.g., Washington Redskins, Atlanta Braves, Cleveland Indians). After reading this page, what do you think native groups from Northern California might feel about the name of the San Francisco 49ers (named after the gold rushers of 1849)?

2. Human Rights: Read the preamble and skim the articles of the United Nations Universal Declaration of Human Rights, **http://www.un.org/ Overview/rights.html.**

   a. What are the central points of the declaration?

   b. Do you agree with them? Do you find them all reasonable? Is anything missing?

   c. How do colonial strategies and development projects threaten human rights as spelled out in this declaration?

   d. How would you suggest the U.N. enforce these rights?

See Chapter 24 at your McGraw-Hill Online Learning Center for additional review and interactive exercises.

25

CULTURAL EXCHANGE AND SURVIVAL

Overview

People travel more than ever. But they also maintain ties with home, thus living multilocally. In this world in flux, new identities and political and ethnic units emerge as others disappear. In worse cases, a culture may collapse or be absorbed (ethnocide). Its people may die off or be exterminated (genocide). Systems of domination have private, "offstage" aspects along with their evident, public dimensions. A critique of power usually goes on out of sight of the power holders. Resistance can be individual and disguised, or collective and defiant.

Cultural imperialism refers to the spread of one culture at the expense of others. A text, such as a media-born image, is interpreted by each person exposed to it. People may accept, resist, or oppose a text's established meaning. People manufacture their own meanings for texts. When outside forces enter new settings, they are typically modified to fit the local culture. Mass media can diffuse the culture of a country within its borders, thus enhancing national identity. The mass media also play a role in preserving ethnic identities among people who lead transnational lives.

Today's global culture is driven by flows of people, technology, finance, and information. Business and the media have stoked a craving for commodities and images worldwide. This has created a global culture of consumption.

A Museum to Right Past Wrongs

ARCHAEOLOGY.ORG NEWS BRIEF

by Ellen Herscher

December 6, 1999

The last chapter, "Colonialism and Development," examined the intervention philosophies, policies, and practices associated with colonialism and development. Today concern is voiced about cultural colonialism, the spread of one culture, usually American or "Western," at the expense of others. Confronting this process, nations as different as France and Iran, as well as indigenous peoples such as the Native Americans described in this account, have taken steps to preserve their own language and culture. Do you see cultural colonialism at work? Whose culture is being spread? What cultures are most endangered? Can you suggest solutions?

In a vivid and moving ceremony punctuated by whoops and insistent drumming, ancient incantations called upon Mother Earth to lend a small piece of her bosom to hold a new museum, the National Museum of the American Indian. Thus on an overcast day in late September [1999], Native Americans returned in triumph to the National Mall in Washington, D.C., to begin the construction of a living monument to their history and culture. The museum, scheduled to open in 2004 and part of the revered Smithsonian Institution, now rises in the shadow of the U.S. Capitol, where 170 years ago Congress passed the Indian Removal Act to push tribes westward . . .

The new museum will display the world's finest and largest collection of Native American objects. . . . There the 800,000 catalogued items will not simply be stored and conserved, but will be placed according to tribal wishes and readily accessible to native groups. . . . Former Smithsonian Secretary Robert Adams, in his remarks at the groundbreaking, succinctly stated the unique perspective of the new institution, that "relics do not float in a timeless void, but have living meaning tied to the past and continually made relevant to the present." . . .

It will be the Smithsonian's sixteenth museum and the tenth located on the prestigious National Mall, where it will fill the last available site. But with its independent board of trustees and largely native staff, it will maintain its unique identity. Even its cafeteria will be different, serving only cuisine of

U.S. Senator Ben Nighthorse Campbell speaking at the groundbreaking ceremony for the National Museum of the American Indian on August 28, 1999.

native foods. . . . Here the Indians will tell their own story in their own way. . . .

A large central rotunda space will be used for performances and demonstrations, as will a planned outdoor space. Three-quarters of the 4.25-acre site will be devoted to reconstructed indigenous natural habitats: hardwood forest, freshwater wetlands, and meadows. Part of the site will be used to grow crops, including ancient corn. . . . Collaboration, consultation, and cooperation with the peoples whose history will be celebrated here have marked the gestation of the building and the plans for the programs and exhibits which it will house. The recent groundbreaking ceremony paid homage to the way this new kind of institution came into being and embodied its hopes for the future. Washington suits and traditional native dress mingled in the audience while the blessings from the four cardinal directions were pronounced, invoking the native peoples' ties to the land. . . .

The NMAI will not just house objects, but will protect and support the development and continuation of Native culture and community, sustaining the Indian view that cultural objects form a metaphysical chain linking the ancestors with the living people of the tribe.

In the past decade the repatriation issue has engaged the energies of most American museums with Native collections, as they struggled to reconcile the claims of tribes who wished to recover funerary remains with institutions' traditional duty to preserve their collections. The National Museum of the American Indian is pointing a new direction for the future: by honoring the wishes of Native peoples for the care and protection of the collection, it hopes to create a place where Indians will want to leave their traditional artifacts while providing the general public with a new understanding of these ancient cultures.

How has cultural diversity survived in the context of the increasing participation by local societies in wider systems: regional, national, colonial, and global? Museums such as the National Museum of the American Indian (NMAI), part of Washington, DC's, Smithsonian Institution, provide sites for cultural activities and preservation. NMAI's mission is "helping to foster, protect, and promote understanding of Native American cultures by collaborating with indigenous peoples across the Western Hemisphere" (http://www.nmai.si.edu). The media, especially the Internet and audio and video recording, also play an increasingly prominent role in cultural preservation. Throughout the world, governments, along with local communities and nongovernmental organizations (NGOs), are taking steps to preserve, revive, and even intensify the scale of "traditional" ceremonies, performances, and other local and indigenous cultural productions—even as the world system spreads.

Since at least the 1920s anthropologists have investigated the changes—on both sides—that arise from contact between industrial and nonindustrial societies. Studies of "social change" and "acculturation" are abundant. British and American ethnographers, respectively, have used these terms to describe the same process. *Acculturation* refers to changes that result when groups come into continuous firsthand contact—changes in the cultural patterns of either or both groups (Redfield, Linton, and Herskovits 1936, p. 149).

Contact and Domination

Acculturation differs from diffusion, or cultural borrowing, which can occur without firsthand contact. For example, most North Americans who eat hot dogs ("frankfurters") have never been to Frankfurt, Germany, nor have most North American Toyota owners or sushi eaters ever visited Japan. Although *acculturation* can be applied to any case of cultural contact and change, the term most often has described **westernization**—the influence of Western expansion on indigenous peoples and their cultures. Thus, local people who wear store-bought clothes, learn Indo-European languages, and otherwise adopt Western customs are called acculturated. Acculturation may be voluntary or forced, and there may be considerable resistance to the process.

In the chapter "Ethnicity," we saw that sometimes a dominant group may try to destroy the cultures of certain ethnic groups (*ethnocide*) or force them to adopt the dominant culture (*forced assimilation*). Sometimes this involves a ban on, or penalties against, religious practices or the use of a minority language.

Different degrees of destruction, domination, resistance, survival, adaptation, and modification of native cultures may follow interethnic contact. In the most destructive encounters, native and subordinate cultures face obliteration. In cases where contact between the indigenous societies and more powerful outsiders leads to destruction—a situation that is particularly characteristic of colonialist and expansionist eras—a "shock phase" often follows the initial encounter (Bodley 1988). Outsiders may attack or exploit the native people. Such exploitation may increase mortality, disrupt subsistence, fragment kin groups, damage social support systems, and inspire new religious movements, such as the cargo cults examined in the chapter "Religion" (Bodley 1988). During the shock phase, there may be civil repression backed by military force. Such factors may lead to the group's cultural collapse (*ethnocide*) or physical extinction (*genocide*).

This photo, taken on April 16, 1945, shows Holocaust survivors at the Buchenwald (Germany) Concentration Camp, which had just been liberated by U.S. troops. Genocidal policies, such as the Nazis' campaign against the Jews, aim at the physical extinction of a people.

Outsiders often attempt to remake native landscapes and cultures in their own image. Political and economic colonialists have tried to redesign conquered and dependent lands, peoples, and cultures, imposing their cultural standards on others. The aim of many agricultural development projects, for example, seems to have been to make the world as much like Iowa as possible, complete with mechanized farming and nuclear family ownership—despite the fact that these models may be inappropriate for settings outside the North American heartland.

DEVELOPMENT AND ENVIRONMENTALISM

Today it is often multinational corporations, usually based in core nations, rather than the governments of those nations, that are changing the nature of Third World economies. However, nations do tend to support the predatory enterprises that seek cheap labor and raw materials in countries outside the core, such as Brazil, where economic development has contributed to ecological devastation.

Simultaneously, environmentalists from core nations increasingly state their case, promoting conservation, to the rest of the world. The ecological devastation of the Amazon has become a focus of international environmentalist attention. Yet many Brazilians complain that northerners talk about global needs and saving the Amazon after having destroyed their own forests for First World economic growth. Akbar Ahmed (1992) concludes that non-Westerners tend to be cynical about Western ecological morality, seeing it as yet another imperialist message. "The Chinese have cause to snigger at the Western suggestion that they forgo the convenience of the fridge to save the ozone layer" (Ahmed 1992, p. 120).

In the last chapter, we saw that development projects usually fail if they try to replace native forms with culturally alien property concepts and productive units. A strategy that incorporates the native forms is more effective than the fallacies of overinnovation and underdifferentiation. The same caveats would seem to apply to an intervention philosophy that seeks to impose global ecological morality without due attention to cultural variation and autonomy. Countries and cultures may resist interventionist philosophies aimed at either development or globally justified environmentalism.

A clash of cultures related to environmental change may occur when *development threatens indigenous peoples and their environments.* Hundreds of native groups throughout the world, including the Kayapó Indians of Brazil (Turner 1993) and the Kaluli of Papua New Guinea (see "Interesting Issues" on pages 698–699), have been threatened by plans and forces, such as dam construction or commercially driven deforestation, that would destroy their homelands.

For information on Sarawak cultural survival see your OLC Internet Exercises

mhhe
●com
/kottak

A second clash of cultures related to environmental change occurs when *external regulation threatens indigenous peoples.* Native groups may actually be threatened by environmental plans that seek to *save* their homelands. Sometimes outsiders expect local people to give up many of their customary economic and cultural activities without clear substitutes, alternatives, or incentives in order to conserve endangered species. The traditional approach to conservation has been to restrict access to protected areas, hire guards, and punish violators.

Problems often arise when external regulation replaces the native system. Like development projects, conservation schemes may ask people to change the way they have been doing things for generations to satisfy planners' goals rather than

At a mall in Poodong district, China, consumers can shop in one of Asia's biggest supermarkets. What would be the environmental effects if China had a level of consumption paralleling that of the United States?

local goals. Ironically, well-meaning conservation efforts can be as insensitive as development schemes that promote radical changes without involving local people in planning and carrying out the policies that affect them. When people are asked to give up the basis of their livelihood, they usually resist.

Consider the case of a Tanosy man who lives on the edge of the Andohahela forest reserve of southeastern Madagascar. For years he has relied on rice fields and grazing land inside that reserve. Now external agencies are trying to get him to abandon this land for the sake of conservation. This man is a wealthy *ombiasa* (traditional sorcerer-healer). With four wives, a dozen children, and 20 head of cattle, he is an ambitious, hard-working, and productive peasant. With money, social support, and supernatural authority, he is mounting effective resistance against the park ranger who has been trying to get him to abandon his fields. The *ombiasa* claims he has already relinquished some of his land, but he is waiting for compensatory fields. His most effective resistance has been supernatural. The death of the ranger's son was attributed to the *ombiasa's* magical power.

Since then, the ranger has been less vigilant in his enforcement efforts.

Given the threat that deforestation poses to global biodiversity, it is vitally important to devise conservation strategies that will work. Laws and enforcement may help stem the tide of commercially driven deforestation, which takes the form of burning and clear cutting. However, local people also use and abuse forested lands. A challenge for the environmentally oriented applied anthropologist is to make forest preservation attractive to people like the Tanosy of Madagascar. Like development plans, effective conservation strategies must pay attention to the customs, needs, and incentives of the people living in the affected area. Conservation depends on local cooperation. In the Tanosy case, the guardians of the reserve must do more to satisfy the *ombiasa* and other affected people, through boundary adjustments, negotiation, and compensation. For effective conservation (as for development), the task is to devise culturally appropriate strategies. Neither development agencies nor NGOs will succeed if they try to impose their goals without considering the practices, customs, rules, laws, beliefs, and values of the people to be affected (see Reed 1997).

The government of Papua New Guinea has approved oil exploration by American, British, Australian, and Japanese companies in the rainforest habitat of the Kaluli (Figure 25.1) and other indigenous peoples. The forest degradation that usually accompanies logging, ranching, road building, and drilling endangers plants, animals, peoples, and cultures. Lost along with trees are songs, myths, words, ideas, artifacts, and techniques—the cultural knowledge and practices of rainforest people like the Kaluli, whom the anthropologist and ethnomusicologist Steven Feld has been studying for more than 20 years.

Feld teamed up with Mickey Hart of the Grateful Dead in a project designed to promote the cultural survival of the Kaluli through their music. For years, Hart has worked to preserve musical diversity through educational funding, concert promotion, and recording, including a successful series called "The World" on the Rykodisc label. *Voices of the Rainforest* was the first CD completely devoted to indigenous music from Papua New Guinea. In 1 hour, it encapsulates 24 hours of a day in Kaluli life in Bosavi village. The recording permits a form of cultural survival and diffusion in a high-quality commercial product. Bosavi is presented as a "soundscape" of blended music and natural environmental sounds. Kaluli weave the natural sounds of birds, frogs, rivers, and streams into their texts, melodies, and rhythms. They sing and whistle with birds and water-

Figure 25.1 **Location of the Kaluli in Papua New Guinea.**

falls. They compose instrumental duets with birds and cicadas.

The Kaluli project was launched on Earth Day 1991 at Star Wars creator George Lucas's Skywalker Ranch. There, Randy Hayes, the executive director of the Rainforest Action Network, and musician Mickey Hart spoke about the linked issues of rainforest destruction and musical survival. Next came a San Francisco benefit dinner for the Bosavi People's Fund. This is the trust established to receive royalties

A teacher shows Kaluli children Steven Feld's *Voices of the Rainforest*.

from the Kaluli recording—a financial prong in Steven Feld's strategy to foster Kaluli cultural survival.

Voices of the Rainforest has been marketed as "world music." This term is intended to point up musical diversity, the fact that musics originate from all world regions and all cultures. "Tribal" music joins Western music as a form of artistic expression worth performing, hearing, and preserving. Hart's series offers musics of non-Western origin as well as those of ethnically dominated groups of the Western world.

Hart's record series aims at preserving "endangered music" against the artistic loss suffered by indigenous peoples. Its intent is to give a "world voice" to people who are being silenced by the dominant world system. In 1993, Hart launched a new

series, the Library of Congress Endangered Music Project, which includes digitally remastered field recordings collected by the American Folklife Center. The first of this series, *The Spirit Cries*, concentrated on music from a broad range of cultures in South and Central America and the Caribbean. Proceeds from this project were used to support the performers and their cultural traditions.

In *Voices of the Rainforest*, Feld and Hart excised all "modern" and "dominant" sounds from their recording. Gone are the world-system sounds that Kaluli villagers now hear every day. The recording temporarily silences the "machine voices": the tractor that cuts the grass on the local airstrip, the gas generator, the sawmill, the helicopters, and light planes buzzing to

and from the oil-drilling areas. Gone, too, are the village church bells, Bible readings, evangelical prayers and hymns, and the voices of teachers and students at an English-only school.

Initially, Feld anticipated criticism for attempting to create an idealized Kaluli "soundscape" insulated from invasive forces and sounds. Among the Kaluli, he expected varied opinions about the value of his project:

> It is a soundscape world that some Kaluli care little about, a world that other Kaluli momentarily choose to forget, a world that some Kaluli are increasingly nostalgic and uneasy about, a world that other Kaluli are still living and creating and listening to. It is a sound world that increasingly fewer Kaluli will actively know about and value, but one that increasingly more Kaluli will only hear on cassette and sentimentally wonder about. (Feld 1991, p. 137)

Despite these concerns, Feld was met with an overwhelmingly positive response when he returned to Papua New Guinea in 1992 armed with a boombox and the recording. The people of Bosavi reacted very favorably. Not only did they appreciate the recording, they also have been able to build a much-needed community school with the Voices of the Rainforest royalties that have been donated to the Bosavi People's Fund.

SOURCE: Based on Steven Feld, "Voices of the Rainforest," *Public Culture* 4(1): 131–140 (1991).

RELIGIOUS CHANGE

In the movie *Raiders of the Lost Ark*, Indiana Jones, anthropologist extraordinaire, faces an assassin armed with a scimitar. The Middle Easterner displays an elaborate series of moves showing his skills in traditional weaponry. Impressed by the demonstration, as the audience appreciates the threat, Jones takes out a pistol and shoots the man dead.

This sequence makes a point about dominance and cultural diversity, interethnic encounters, the world system, resistance, and survival. The scimitar-wielding Mid-Easterner can be seen as symbolizing traditional culture against the world system. We should not forget that anthropologists, too, are agents of the world system. A century ago, the anthropologist tended to arrive after the traders (the economic proselytizers), but around the same time, and often competing with, the missionaries (the religious proselytizers). The Christians came to "save souls." The anthropologists were there to salvage cultures. But all were Western presences among the natives.

Religious proselytizing can promote ethnocide, as native beliefs and practices are replaced by Western ones. Sometimes a religion and associated customs are replaced by ideology and behavior more compatible with Western culture. One example is the Handsome Lake religion (as described in the chapter on religion), which led the Iroquois to copy European farming techniques, stressing male rather than female labor. The Iroquois also gave up their communal longhouses and matrilineal descent groups for nuclear family households. The teachings of Handsome Lake led to a new church and religion. This revitalization movement helped the Iroquois survive in a drastically modified environment, but much ethnocide was involved.

Handsome Lake was a native who created a new religion, drawing on Western models. More commonly, missionaries and proselytizers representing the major world religions, especially Christianity and Islam, are the proponents of religious change. Protestant and Catholic missionization continues even in remote corners of the world. Evangelical Protestantism, for example, is advancing in Peru, Brazil, and other parts of Latin America. It challenges an often jaded Catholicism that has too few priests and that is sometimes seen mainly as women's religion.

Sometimes the political ideology of a nation-state is pitted against traditional religion. Officials of the former Soviet empire discouraged Catholicism, Judaism, and Islam. In Central Asia, Soviet dominators destroyed Muslim mosques and discouraged religious practice. On the other hand, governments often use their power to advance a religion, such as Islam in Iran or Sudan (see Figure 25.2).

A military government seized power in Sudan in 1989. It immediately launched a campaign to change that country of more than 35 million people, where one-quarter were not Muslims, into an Islamic nation. Sudan adopted a policy of religious, linguistic, and cultural imperialism. The government sought to extend Islam and the Arabic language to the non-Muslim south. This was an area of Christianity and tribal religions that had resisted the central government for a decade. The new government declared a jihad (holy war) against non-Muslims. It persecuted Catholic lead-

Figure 25.2   Location of Sudan.

ers and purged the military, the civil service, the judiciary, and the educational system of non-Muslims. Students in the south were forced to take their exams in Arabic, for them a foreign language (Hedges 1992a).

Resistance and Survival

Systems of domination—whether political, economic, cultural, or religious—have their more muted aspects along with their public dimensions. In studying systems of domination, we must pay attention to what lies beneath the surface of evident, public behavior. In public, the oppressed may seem to accept their own domination, even as they question it offstage in private. James Scott (1990) uses **"public transcript"** to describe the open, public interactions between dominators and oppressed—the outer shell of power relations. He uses **"hidden transcript"** to describe the critique of power that goes on offstage, where the power holders can't see it.

In public, the elites and the oppressed observe the etiquette of power relations. The dominants act like haughty masters while their subordinates show humility and defer. Antonio Gramsci (1971) developed the concept of **hegemony** for a stratified social order in which subordinates comply with domination by internalizing their rulers' values and accepting the "naturalness" of domination (this is the way things were meant to be). According to Pierre Bourdieu (1977, p. 164), every social order tries to make its own arbitrariness (including its oppression) seem natural. All hegemonic ideologies offer explanations about why the existing order is in everyone's interest. Often promises are made (things will get better if you're patient). Gramsci and others use the idea of hegemony to explain why people conform even without coercion.

Both Bourdieu (1977) and Michel Foucault (1979) argue that it is much easier and more effective to dominate people in their minds than to try to control their bodies. Besides, and often replacing, gross physical violence, industrial societies have devised more insidious forms of social control. These include various techniques of persuading and managing people and of monitoring and recording their beliefs, activities, and contacts. Can you think of some contemporary examples?

Hegemony, the internalization of a dominant ideology, is one way to curb resistance. Another way is to let subordinates know they will eventually gain power—as young people usually foresee when they let their elders dominate them. Another way of curbing resistance is to separate or isolate subordinates while supervising them closely, as in prisons. According to Foucault (1979), describing control over prisoners, solitary confinement is one effective way to get them to submit to authority.

For more on strategies of cultural survival, see your OLC Internet Exercises

/kottak

WEAPONS OF THE WEAK

Often, situations that seem to be hegemonic do have active resistance, but it is individual and disguised rather than collective and defiant. James Scott (1985) uses Malay peasants, among whom he did field work, to illustrate small-scale acts of resistance—which he calls "weapons of the weak." The Malay peasants used an indirect strategy to resist an Islamic tithe (religious tax). Peasants were expected to pay the tithe, usually in the form of rice, which was sent to the provincial capital. In theory, the tithe would come back as charity, but it never did. Peasants didn't resist the tithe by rioting, demonstrating, or protesting. Instead they used a "nibbling" strategy, based on small acts of resistance. For example, they failed to declare their land or lied about the amount they farmed. They underpaid or delivered rice contaminated with water, rocks, or mud, to add weight. Because of this resistance, only 15 percent of what was due was actually paid (Scott 1990, p. 89).

Subordinates also use various strategies to resist *publicly*, but, again, usually in disguised form. Discontent may be expressed in public rituals and language, including metaphors, euphemisms, and folk tales. For example, trickster tales (like the Brer Rabbit stories told by slaves in the southern United States) celebrate the wiles of the weak as they triumph over the strong.

Resistance is most likely to be expressed openly when the oppressed are allowed to assemble. The hidden transcript may be publicly revealed on such occasions. People see their dreams and anger shared by others with whom they haven't been in direct contact. The oppressed may draw courage from the crowd, from its visual and emotional impact and its

Because of its costumed anonymity, *Carnaval* is an excellent arena for expressing normally suppressed speech. This is vividly symbolized by these *Carnaval* headdresses in Trinidad. Is there anything like *Carnaval* in your society?

excellent arena for expressing normally suppressed speech and aggression—antihegemonic discourse. (*Discourse* includes talk, speeches, gestures, and actions.) *Carnavals* celebrate freedom through immodesty, dancing, gluttony, and sexuality (DaMatta 1991). *Carnaval* may begin as a playful outlet for frustrations built up during the year. Over time, it may evolve into a powerful annual critique of domination and a threat to the established order (Gilmore 1987). (Recognizing that ceremonial license could turn into political defiance, the Spanish dictator Francisco Franco outlawed *Carnaval*.)

In medieval Europe, according to Mikhail Bakhtin (1984), the market was the main place where the dominant ideology was questioned. The anonymity of the crowd and of commerce put people on an equal footing. The rituals and deference used with lords and clergy didn't apply to the marketplace. Later in Europe, the hidden transcript also went public in pubs, taverns, inns, cabarets, beer cellars, and gin mills. These places fostered a popular culture—in games, songs, gambling, blasphemy, and disorder—that was at odds with the official culture. People met in an atmosphere of freedom encouraged by alcohol. Church and state alike condemned these activities as subversive.

anonymity. Sensing danger, the elites discourage such public gatherings. They try to limit and control holidays, funerals, dances, festivals, and other occasions that might unite the oppressed. Thus, in the pre–Civil War era southern United States, gatherings of five or more slaves were forbidden unless a white person was present.

Factors that interfere with community formation—such as geographic, linguistic, and ethnic separation—also work to curb resistance. Consequently, southern U.S. plantation owners sought slaves with diverse cultural and linguistic backgrounds. Despite the measures used to divide them, the slaves resisted, developing their own popular culture, linguistic codes, and religious vision. The masters taught portions of the Bible that stressed compliance, but the slaves seized on the story of Moses, the promised land, and deliverance. The cornerstone of slave religion became the idea of a reversal in the conditions of whites and blacks. Slaves also resisted directly, through sabotage and flight. In many New World areas, slaves managed to establish free communities in the hills and other isolated areas (Price 1973).

Hidden transcripts tend to be publicly expressed at certain times (festivals and *Carnavals*) and in certain places (for example, markets). Because of its costumed anonymity, *Carnaval* is an

CULTURAL IMPERIALISM

Cultural imperialism refers to the spread or advance of one culture at the expense of others, or its imposition on other cultures, which it modifies, replaces, or destroys—usually because of differential economic or political influence. The chapter "Ethnicity" described a cultural imperialist campaign waged by the Spanish dictator Francisco Franco, designed to eradicate Basque culture, language, and religion. In this chapter, in the section "Religious Change," we examined Sudan's policy of religious, linguistic, and cultural imperialism against non-Muslims. In both cases, there was armed resistance to cultural imperialism.

Some forms of cultural imperialism are more subtle, involving long-term indoctrination. Children in the French colonial empire learned French history, language, and culture from standard textbooks also used in France. Tahitians, Malagasy, Vietnamese, and Senegalese learned the French language by reciting from books about "our ancestors the Gauls."

To what extent is modern technology, especially the mass media, an agent of cultural imperialism? Some commentators see modern technology as erasing cultural differences, as homogeneous products reach more people worldwide. But others see a role for modern technology in allowing social groups (local cultures) to express themselves and to survive (Marcus and Fischer 1999) (see "Interesting Issues" on p. 704). Modern radio and TV, for example, constantly bring local happenings (for example, a "chicken festival" in Iowa) to the attention of a larger public. The North American media play a role in stimulating local activities of many sorts. Similarly, in Brazil, local practices, celebrations, and performances are changing in the context of outside forces, including the mass media and tourism.

In the town of Arembepe Brazil (Kottak 1999), TV coverage has stimulated participation in a traditional annual performance, the *Chegança*. This is a fishermen's danceplay that reenacts the Portuguese discovery of Brazil. Arembepeiros have traveled to the state capital to perform the *Chegança* before television cameras, for a TV program featuring traditional performances from many rural communities.

One national Brazilian Sundaynight variety program (*Fantástico*) is especially popular in rural areas because it shows such local events. In several towns along the Amazon River, annual folk ceremonies are now staged more lavishly for TV cameras. In the Amazon town of Parantíns, for example, boatloads of tourists arriving any time of year are shown a videotape of the town's annual Bumba Meu Boi festival. This is a costumed performance mimicking bullfighting, parts of which have been shown on *Fantástico*. This pattern, in which local communities preserve, revive, and intensify the scale of traditional ceremonies to perform for TV and tourists, is expanding.

However, Brazilian television also has played a "topdown" role, by spreading the popularity of holidays like *Carnaval* and Christmas (Kottak 1990a). TV has aided the national spread of *Carnaval* beyond its traditional urban centers. Still, local reactions to the nationwide broadcasting of *Carnaval* and its trappings (elaborate parades, costumes, and frenzied dancing) are not simple or uniform responses to external stimuli.

Rather than direct adoption of *Carnaval*, local Brazilians respond in various ways. Often they don't take up *Carnaval* itself but modify their local festivities to fit *Carnaval* images. Others actively spurn *Carnaval*. One example is Arembepe, where Carnaval has never been important, probably because of its calendrical closeness to the main local festival, which is held in February to honor Saint Francis of Assisi. In the past, villagers couldn't afford to celebrate both occasions. Now, not only do the people of Arembepe reject *Carnaval*, they are also increasingly hostile to their own main festival. Arembepeiros resent the fact that Saint Francis has become "an outsiders' event," because it draws thousands of tourists to Arembepe each February. The villagers think that commercial interests and outsiders have appropriated Saint Francis.

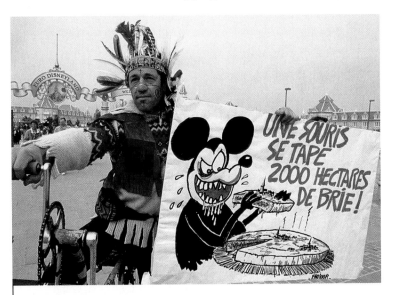

Native children throughout the French colonial empire learned the French language by reciting from books about "our ancestors the Gauls." More recently, French citizens have criticized or resisted what they see as American "cultural imperialism"—one prominent symbol of which has been Euro Disneyland. Has there also been resistance to the expansion of Disney enterprises in the United States?

Although some see modern technology as a threat to cultural diversity, others see a role for this technology in allowing social groups to express themselves. The anthropologist H. Russell Bernard has been a pioneer in teaching speakers of endangered languages how to write their language using a computer. Bernard's work permits the preservation of languages and cultural memories. Native peoples from Mexico to Cameroon are using their mother tongue to express themselves as individuals and to provide insiders' accounts of different cultures.

Jesús Salinas Pedraza, a rural schoolteacher in the Mexican state of Hidalgo, sat down to a word processor a few years back and produced a monumental book, a 250,000-word description of his own Indian culture written in the Ñähñu language. Nothing seems to be left out: folktales and traditional religious beliefs, the practical uses of plants and minerals and the daily flow of life in field and village . . .

Mr. Salinas is neither a professional anthropologist nor a literary stylist. He is, though, the first person to write a book in Ñähñu (NYAW-hnyu), the native tongue of several hundred thousand Indians but a previously unwritten language.

Such a use of microcomputers and desktop publishing for languages with no literary tradition is now being encouraged by anthropologists for recording ethnographies from an insider's perspective. They see this as a means of preserving cultural diversity and a wealth of human knowledge. With even greater urgency, linguists are promoting the techniques as a way of saving some of the world's languages from imminent extinction.

Half of the world's 6,000 languages are considered by linguists to be endangered. These are the languages spoken by small societies that are dwindling with the encroachment of larger, more dynamic cultures. Young people feel economic pressure to learn only the language of the dominant culture, and as the older people die, the non-written language vanishes, unlike languages with a history of writing, like Latin.

Dr. H. Russell Bernard, the anthropologist at the University of Florida at Gainesville who taught Mr. Salinas to read and write his native language, said: "Languages have always come and gone . . . But languages seem to be disappearing faster than ever before.". . .

Dr. Michael E. Krauss, the director of the Alaska Native Language Center at the University of Alaska in Fairbanks, estimates that 300 of the 900 indigenous languages in the Americas are moribund. That is, they are no longer being spoken by children, and so could disappear in a generation or two. Only two of the 20 native languages in Alaska are still being learned by children . . .

In an effort to preserve language diversity in Mexico, Dr. Bernard and Mr. Salinas decided in 1987 on a plan to teach the Indian people to read and write their own language using microcomputers. They established a native literacy center in Oaxaca, Mexico, where others could follow in the footsteps of Mr. Salinas and write books in other Indian languages.

The Oaxaca center goes beyond most bilingual education programs, which concentrate on teaching people to speak and read their native languages. Instead, it operates on the premise that, as Dr. Bernard decided, what most native languages lack is native authors who write books in their own languages. . . .

The Oaxaca project's influence is spreading. Impressed by the work of Mr. Salinas and others, Dr. Norman Whitten, an anthropologist at the University of Illinois, arranged for schoolteachers from Ecuador to visit Oaxaca and learn the techniques.

Now Ecuadorian Indians have begun writing about their cultures in the Quechua and Shwara languages. Others from Bolivia and Peru are learning to use the computers to write their languages, including Quecha, the tongue of the ancient Incas, still spoken by about 12 million Andean Indians. . . .

Dr. Bernard emphasized that these native literacy programs are not intended to discourage people from learning the dominant language of their country as well. "I see nothing useful or charming about remaining monolingual in any Indian language if that results in being shut out of the national economy," he said.

In opposition to these trends, many Arembepeiros now say they like and participate more in the traditional June festivals honoring Saint John, Saint Peter, and Saint Anthony. In the past, these were observed on a much smaller scale than was the festival honoring Saint Francis. Arembepeiros celebrate them now with a new vigor and enthusiasm, as they react to outsiders and their celebrations, real and televised.

Making and Remaking Culture

Any media-borne image, such as that of *Carnaval,* can be analyzed in terms of its nature and effects. It also can be analyzed as a **text.** We usually think of a text as a textbook, like this one. But the term has a more general meaning. Anthropologists use text to refer to anything that may be "read," interpreted, and assigned meaning by anyone exposed to it. In this sense, a text doesn't have to be written. The term may refer to a film, an image, or an event, such as *Carnaval.* As Brazilians participate in *Carnaval,* they "read" it as a text. These "readers" derive their own meanings and feelings from *Carnaval* events, images, and activities. Such meanings may be very different from what the creators of the text, such as official sponsors, imagined. (The "reading" or meaning that the creators intended—or the one that the elites consider to be the intended or correct meaning—can be called the *hegemonic reading.*)

"Readers" of media messages constantly produce their own meanings. They may resist or oppose the hegemonic meanings of a text, or they may seize on the antihegemonic aspects of a text. We saw this process when American slaves preferred the biblical story of Moses and deliverance to the hegemonic lessons of acceptance and obedience that their masters taught.

POPULAR CULTURE

In his book *Understanding Popular Culture* (1989), John Fiske views each individual's use of popular culture as a creative act (an original "reading" of a text). (For example, Madonna, the Grateful Dead, or *Star Wars* means something different to each of its fans.) As Fiske puts it, "the meanings I make

from a text are pleasurable when I feel that they are *my* meanings and that they relate to *my* everyday life in a practical, direct way" (1989, p. 57). All of us can creatively "read" magazines, books, music, television, films, celebrities, and other popular culture products.

Individuals also draw on popular culture to express resistance. Through their use of popular culture, people can symbolically resist the unequal power relations they face each day—in the family, at work, and in the classroom. Popular culture (from hip-hop music to comedy) can be used to express discontent and resistance by groups that are or feel powerless or oppressed.

INDIGENIZING POPULAR CULTURE

To understand culture change, it is important to recognize that meaning may be locally manufactured. People assign their own meanings and value to the texts, messages, and products they receive. Those meanings reflect their cultural backgrounds and experiences. When forces from world centers enter new societies, they are **indigenized**—modified to fit the local culture. This is true of cultural forces as different as fast food, music, housing styles, science, terrorism, celebrations, and political ideas and institutions (Appadurai 1990).

Consider the reception of the movie *Rambo* in Australia as an example of how popular culture may be indigenized. Michaels (1986) found *Rambo* to be very popular among aborigines in the deserts of central Australia, who had manufactured their own meanings from the film. Their "reading" was very different from the one imagined by the movie's creators, and by most North Americans. The Native Australians saw Rambo as a representative of the Third World who was engaged in a battle with the white officer class. This reading expressed their negative feelings about white paternalism and about existing race relations. The Native Australians also imagined that there were tribal ties and kin links between Rambo and the prisoners he was rescuing. All this made sense, based on their experience. Native Australians are disproportionately represented in Australian jails. Their most likely liberator would be someone with a personal link to them. These readings of *Rambo* were relevant meanings produced *from* the text, not *by* it (Fiske 1989).

When products and images enter new settings, they are typically indigenized—modified to fit the local culture. Jeans Street, in Bandung, Indonesia, is a strip of stores, vendors, and restaurants catering to young people interested in Western pop culture. How is the poster of *Batman and Robin* indigenized?

A WORLD SYSTEM OF IMAGES

All cultures express imagination—in dreams, fantasies, songs, myths, and stories. Today, however, more people in many more places imagine "a wider set of 'possible' lives than they ever did before. One important source of this change is the mass media, which present a rich, ever-changing store of possible lives . . ." (Appadurai 1991, p. 197). The United States as a media center has been joined by Canada, Japan, Western Europe, Brazil, Mexico, Nigeria, Egypt, India, and Hong Kong.

As print has done for centuries (Anderson 1991), the electronic mass media also can spread, even help create, national and ethnic identities. Like print, television and radio can diffuse the cultures of different countries within their own boundaries, thus enhancing national cultural identity. For example, millions of Brazilians who were formerly cut off (by geographic isolation or illiteracy) from urban and national events and information now participate in a national communication system, through TV networks (Kottak 1990a).

Cross-cultural studies of television contradict a belief Americans ethnocentrically hold about televiewing in other countries. This misconception is that American programs inevitably triumph over local products. This doesn't happen when there is appealing local competition. In Brazil, for example, the most popular network (TV Globo) relies heavily on native productions. TV Globo's most popular programs are *telenovelas,* locally made serials that are similar to American soap operas. Globo plays each night to the world's largest and most devoted audience (60 to 80 million viewers throughout the nation). The programs that attract this horde are made by Brazilians, for Brazilians. Thus, it is not North American culture but a new pan-Brazilian national culture that Brazilian TV is propagating. Brazilian productions also compete internationally. They are exported to over 100 countries, spanning Latin America, Europe, Asia, and Africa.

We may generalize that programming that is culturally alien won't do very well anywhere when a quality local choice is available. Confirmation comes from many countries. National productions are highly popular in Japan, Mexico, India, Egypt, and Nigeria. In a survey during the mid-1980s, 75 percent of Nigerian viewers preferred local productions. Only 10 percent favored imports, and the remaining 15 percent liked the two options equally. Local productions are successful in Nigeria because "they are filled with everyday moments that audiences can identify with. These shows are locally produced by Nigerians" (Gray 1986). Thirty million people watched one of the most popular series, *The Village Headmaster,* each week. That program brought rural values to the screens of urbanites who had lost touch with their rural roots (Gray 1986).

The mass media also can play a role in maintaining ethnic and national identities among people who lead transnational lives. Arabic-speaking Muslims, including migrants, in several countries follow the TV network Al Jazeera, based in Qatar, which helps reinforce ethnic and religious identities. As groups move, they can stay linked to each other and to their homeland through the media. Diasporas (people who have spread out from an original, ancestral homeland) have enlarged the markets for media, communication, and travel services targeted at specific ethnic, national, or religious audiences. For a fee, a PBS station in Fairfax, Virginia, offers more than 30 hours a week to immigrant groups in the D.C. area, to make programs in their own languages. *Somali Television*, for instance, is a half-hour program with more than 5,000 Somali viewers, who can see their flag and hear their language on TV each week. Starting the program is a reading from the Koran, with clips of mosques from around the world (thus contributing, too, to a transnational Islamic identity). Formerly, an entertainment segment featured folk dances and Somali music. In 1992, as Somalia's civil war dragged on, the entertainment segment was replaced by images of hungry children and parched countryside. *Somali Television* also features obituaries, rallies, and a segment called "Somalia Today," which has interviews with diplomats, immigration lawyers, and travel agents discussing air fares. Guests represent various tribes and subclans. *Somali Television* became a vital link between emigrant Somalis and their homeland (*New York Times*, December 18, 1992).

A TRANSNATIONAL CULTURE OF CONSUMPTION

Besides the electronic media, another key transnational force is finance. Multinational corporations and other business interests look beyond national boundaries for places to invest and draw profits. As Arjun Appadurai (1991, p. 194) puts it, "money, commodities, and persons unendingly chase each other around the world." Residents of many Latin American communities now depend on outside cash, remitted from international labor migration. Also, the economy of the United States is increasingly influenced by foreign investment, especially from Britain, Canada, Germany, the Netherlands, and Japan (Rouse 1991). The American economy also has increased its dependence on foreign labor—through both the immigration of laborers and the export of jobs.

Business and the media have increased the craving for products throughout the world. Here, exiting a shopping mall, a German man takes home a Barbie playset.

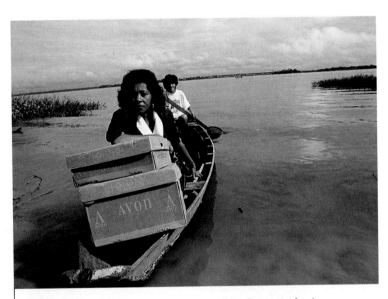

Maria Gomes on Brazil's Tapajos River. Ms. Gomes is the Avon zone manager for 970 representatives in the Amazon rain forest.

Contemporary global culture is driven by flows of people, technology, finance, information, images, and ideology (Appadurai 1990). Business, technology, and the media have increased the craving for commodities and images throughout the world (Gottdiener 2000). This has forced nation-states, including "Iron Curtains," to open to a global culture of consumption. Almost everyone today participates in this culture. Few people have never seen a T-shirt advertising a Western product. American and English rock stars' recordings blast through the streets of Rio de Janeiro, while taxi drivers from Toronto to Madagascar play Brazilian *lambada* tapes. Peasants and tribal people participate in the modern world system not only because they have been hooked on cash, but also because their products and images are appropriated by world capitalism (Root 1996). They are commercialized by others (like the San in the movie *The Gods Must Be Crazy*). Furthermore, indigenous peoples also market their own images and products, through outlets like Cultural Survival (see Mathews 2000).

Linkages

The linkages in the modern world system have both enlarged and erased old boundaries and distinctions. Arjun Appadurai (1990, p. 1) characterizes today's world as a "translocal" "interactive system" that is "strikingly new." Whether as refugees, migrants, tourists, pilgrims, proselytizers, laborers, businesspeople, development workers, employees of nongovernmental organizations, politicians, terrorists, soldiers, sports figures, or media-borne images, people appear to travel more than ever.

In previous chapters, we saw that foragers and herders are typically seminomadic or nomadic. Today, however, the scale of human movement has expanded dramatically. So important is transnational migration that many Mexican villagers find "their most important kin and friends are as likely to be living hundreds or thousands of miles away as immediately around them" (Rouse 1991). Most migrants maintain their ties with their native land (phoning, e-mailing, visiting, sending money, watching "ethnic TV"). In a sense, they live multi-locally—in different places at once. Dominicans in New York City, for example, have been characterized as living "between two islands": Manhattan and the Dominican Republic (Grasmuck and Pessar 1991). Many Dominicans—like migrants from other countries—migrate to the United States temporarily, seeking cash to transform their life styles when they return to the Caribbean.

With so many people on the move, the unit of anthropological study has expanded from the local community to the diaspora. This refers to the offspring of an area (e.g., Africa) who have spread to many lands, such as these Afro-Caribbean pub owners in West Broomwich, England. Do you belong to a diaspora?

PEOPLE IN MOTION

With so many people "in motion," the unit of anthropological study expands from the local community to the **diaspora**—the offspring of an area who have spread to many lands. Anthropologists increasingly follow descendants of the villages we have studied as they move from rural to urban areas and across national boundaries. For the 1991 annual meeting of the American Anthropological Association in Chicago, the anthropologist Robert Kemper organized a session of presentations about long-term ethnographic field work. Kemper's own longtime research focus has been the Mexican village of Tzintzuntzan, which, with his mentor George Foster, he has studied for decades. However, their database now includes not just Tzintzuntzan, but its descendants all over the world (Figure 25.3). Given the Tzintzuntzan diaspora, Kemper was even able to use some of his time in Chicago to visit people from Tzintzuntzan

who had established a colony there. In today's world, as people move, they take their traditions and their anthropologists along with them.

Postmodernity describes our time and situation: today's world in flux, these people on the move who have learned to manage multiple identities depending on place and context. In its most general sense, **postmodern** refers to the blurring and breakdown of established canons (rules or standards), categories, distinctions, and boundaries. The word is taken from **postmodernism**—a style and movement in architecture that succeeded modernism, beginning in the 1970s. Postmodern architecture rejected the rules, geometric order, and austerity of modernism. Modernist buildings were expected to have a clear and functional design. Postmodern design is "messier" and more playful. It draws on a diversity of styles from different times and places—including popular, ethnic, and non-Western cultures. Postmodernism extends

Figure 25.3   Location of Tzintzuntzan in Mexico.

"value" well beyond classic, elite, and Western cultural forms. *Postmodern* is now used to describe comparable developments in music, literature, and visual art. From this origin, *postmodernity* describes a world in which traditional standards, contrasts, groups, boundaries, and identities are opening up, reaching out, and breaking down.

Globalization promotes intercultural communication, including travel and migration, which bring people from different societies into direct contact. The world is more integrated than ever. Yet *dis*integration also surrounds us. Nations dissolve (Yugoslavia, the Soviet Union), as do political blocs (the Warsaw Pact nations) and ideologies ("Communism"). The notion of a "Free World" collapses because it existed mainly in opposition to a group of "Captive Nations"—a label once applied by the United States and its allies to the former Soviet empire that has lost much of its meaning today.

Simultaneously, new kinds of political and ethnic units are emerging. In some cases, cultures and ethnic groups have banded together in larger associations. There is a growing pan-Indian identity (Nagel 1996) and an international pantribal movement as well. Thus, in June 1992, the World Conference of Indigenous Peoples met in Rio de Janeiro concurrently with UNCED (the United Nations Conference on the Environment and Development). Along with diplomats, journalists, and environmentalists came 300 representatives of the tribal diversity that survives in the modern world—from Lapland to Mali (Brooke 1992; see also Maybury-Lewis 2002).

Interpret the World Compare Map 25, Atlas Map 25 "Indigenous People of the World, 2000," in your atlas with Figure 16.1, "Worldwide Distribution of Recent Hunter-Gatherers" in the chapter "Making a Living." Note that three continents (North and South America and Australia) have most of the "recent hunter-gatherers," while Asia and Europe have the fewest. Map 25 has more groups than Figure 16.1 does, because it includes people with adaptive strategies other than foraging. In other words, herders such as the Samis (Lapps) and horticulturalists such as the Yanomami have been added on Map 25. Europe and Asia still have the fewest indigenous peoples because industry and agriculture cover most of those continents. French or Chinese peasants and city dwellers usually are not classified as "indigenous peoples'—no matter how long their families have occupied the space they now live in. The matter of which groups are and are not "indigenous peoples" has become a political issue in an international arena. The specific groups attending the UNCED conference in Rio de Janeiro, Brazil, in 1992, a few of which are shown in the photo on page 711, claimed the status of indigenous peoples. Many others who might have done so did not, but they may eventually assume this identity for future political action.

POSTMODERN MOMENTS

Increasingly, anthropologists experience what might be called "postmodern moments in the world system." Some of my own most vivid ones can be traced back to Ambalavao, Madagascar. In 1966–67, my wife and I rented a house in that town in southern Betsileo country. We spent weekends there when we came in from the rural villages where our field work was based.

By 1966, Madagascar was independent from France, but its towns still had foreigners to remind them of colonialism. In addition to us, Ambalavao had at least a dozen world-system agents, including an Indian cloth merchant, Chinese grocers, and a few French people. A French consultant was there to help develop the tobacco industry. Two young men in the French equivalent of the Peace Corps were there teaching school.

One of them, Noel, served as principal of the junior high school. He lived across the street from a prominent local family (who served as our sponsors in a rural village, their ancestral community, we were studying). Since Noel often spoke disparagingly of the Malagasy, I was surprised to see him courting a young woman from this family. She was Lenore, the sister of Leon, a schoolteacher who became one of my best friends. My wife and I left Ambalavao in December 1967. Noel and the other world-system agents stayed on.

Each of my revisits to Madagascar has brought postmodern moments—encounters with people and products on the move, in multilocal and unexpected contexts. After 1967, my next trip to Madagascar was a brief visit in February 1981. I had to spend a few days in Antananarivo, the capital.

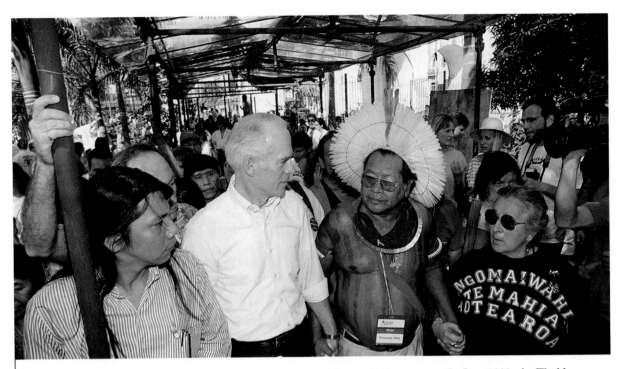

Working to promote cultural survival is a growing international pantribal movement. In June 1992, the World Conference of Indigenous Peoples met in Rio de Janeiro. Along with diplomats, journalists, and environmentalists came 300 representatives of the tribal diversity that survives in the modern world.

There I was confined each evening to the newly built Hilton hotel by a curfew imposed after a civil insurrection. I shared the hotel with a group of Russian MIG pilots (and their wives), there to teach the Malagasy to defend their island, strategically placed in the Indian Ocean, against imagined enemies. Later, I went down to Betsileo country to visit Leon, my schoolteacher friend from Ambalavao, who had become a prominent politician. Unfortunately for me, he was in Moscow, participating in a three-month Soviet exchange program.

My next visit to Madagascar was in summer 1990. This time, a postmodern moment occurred when I met Emily, the 22-year-old daughter of Noel and Lenore, whose courtship I had witnessed in 1967. One of her aunts brought Emily to meet me at my hotel in Antananarivo. Emily was about to visit several cities in the United States, where she planned to study marketing. I met her again just a few months later in Gainesville, Florida, where she was taking a course at Santa Fe Community College. As we lunched in a Mexican restaurant, Emily sold me some woodwork she

had brought from Madagascar. She asked my wife and me to help her market her Malagasy crafts. Finally, she asked us about her father, whom she had never met. She told us she had sent several letters to France, but Noel had never responded.

Descendants of Ambalavao (and thus of rural Betsileo villages) now live all over the world. Emily, a child of colonialism, has two aunts in France (married to French men) and another in Germany (working as a diplomat). Members of her family, which is not especially wealthy, although regionally prominent, have traveled to Russia, Canada, the United States, France, Germany, and West Africa. How many of your classmates, including perhaps you, yourself, are members of such diasporas?

Understanding Ourselves   There's a difference between being a member of a diaspora and having a diasporic identity, such as a pan-Indian or pan-African identity. Diasporic identities, which have been abetted by the media and by various political and cultural organizations devoted to spreading or reinforcing such identities, are increasingly important in today's world. As for being a member of some diaspora, all humans are. All Americans, including Native Americans, originated somewhere else. Several groups, including English, French, Spanish, Portuguese, Dutch, Italians, Poles, Jews, Muslims, Lebanese, Africans, and Chinese, have migrated widely and settled in many countries. But there were older migrations, such as the one the led to the settling of the Polynesian islands—the Polynesian diaspora—starting around 3,000 years ago. Diasporas of ancestral Native Americans spread throughout North and South America. Australia was first settled, probably from Indonesia, between 50,000 and 60,000 years ago, and was "resettled" much later as part of the British colonial diaspora.

Once hunting was incorporated into the human adaptive strategy, *Homo erectus* extended the human range out of Africa and into Eurasia and beyond. Migrating bands of *Homo erectus* were part of a highly significant diaspora, but they certainly lacked a diasporic identity. There would be later diasporas out of Africa, including the migration that took ancient anatomically modern humans to Europe, Asia, and eventually the Americas. The forced migration out of Africa that occurred under slavery was responsible for a more recent African diaspora, contributing to the settlement of the United States, the Caribbean, Brazil, and many other countries in the Western Hemisphere. Although many of us lack any conscious diasporic identity, exposure to anthropology should certainly convince us that we all have the right to such an identity. Few, if any, of us can claim to belong to a lineage that has lived eternally in its homeland.

The Continuance of Diversity

Anthropology has a crucial role to play in promoting a more humanistic vision of social change, one that respects the value of human biological and cultural diversity. The existence of anthropology is itself a tribute to the continuing need to understand similarities and differences among human beings throughout the world. Anthropology teaches us that the adaptive responses of humans can be more flexible than can those of other species because our main adaptive means are sociocultural. However, the cultural forms, institutions, values, and customs of the past always influence subsequent adaptation, producing continued diversity and giving a certain uniqueness to the actions and reactions of different groups. With our knowledge and our awareness of our professional responsibilities, let us work to keep anthropology, the study of humankind, the most humanistic of all the sciences.

SUMMARY

1. Different degrees of destruction, domination, resistance, survival, and modification of native cultures may follow interethnic contact. This may lead to the tribe's cultural collapse (ethnocide) or its physical extinction (genocide). Multinational corporations have fueled economic development and ecological devastation. Either development or external regulation may pose a threat to indigenous peoples, their cultures, or their environments. The most effective conservation strategies pay attention to the needs, incentives, and customs of people living in the affected area.

2. "Public transcript" refers to the open, public interactions between the dominators and the oppressed. "Hidden transcript" describes the critique of power that goes on offstage, where the power holders can't see it. Discontent also may be expressed in public rituals and language. *Hegemony* describes a stratified social order in which subordinates comply with domination by internalizing its values and accepting its "naturalness." Often, situations that appear hegemonic have resistance that is individual and disguised rather than collective and defiant.

3. *Cultural imperialism* refers to the spread of one culture and its imposition on other cultures, which it modifies, replaces, or destroys—usually because of differential economic or political influence. Some worry that modern technology, including the mass media, is destroying traditional cultures. But others see an important role for new technology in allowing local cultures to express themselves.

4. The term *text* is used here to describe anything that can be creatively "read," interpreted, and assigned meaning by someone who receives it. People may resist the hegemonic meaning of a text. Or they may seize on its antihegemonic aspects. When forces from world centers enter new societies, they are *indigenized.* Like print, the electronic mass media can help diffuse a national culture within its own boundaries. The media also play a role in preserving ethnic and national identities among people who lead transnational lives. Business, technology, and the media have increased the craving for commodities and images throughout the world, creating a global culture of consumption.

5. People travel more than ever. But migrants also maintain ties with home, so they live multilocally. With so many people "in motion," the unit of anthropological study expands from the local community to the diaspora. *Postmodernity* describes this world in flux, such people on the move who manage multiple social identities depending on place and context. New kinds of political and ethnic units are emerging as others break down or disappear.

KEY TERMS

cultural imperialism The rapid spread or advance of one culture at the expense of others, or its imposition on other cultures, which it modifies, replaces, or destroys—usually because of differential economic or political influence.

diaspora The offspring of an area who have spread to many lands.

hegemony As used by Antonio Gramsci, a stratified social order in which subordinates comply with domination by internalizing its values and accepting its "naturalness."

hidden transcript As used by James Scott, the critique of power by the oppressed that goes on offstage—in private—where the power holders can't see it.

indigenized Modified to fit the local culture.

postmodern In its most general sense, describes the blurring and breakdown of established canons (rules, standards), categories, distinctions, and boundaries.

postmodernism A style and movement in architecture that succeeded modernism. Compared with modernism, postmodernism is less geometric, less functional, less austere, more playful, and more willing to include elements from diverse times and cultures; postmodern now describes comparable developments in music, literature, visual art, and anthropology.

postmodernity Condition of a world in flux, with people on the move, in which established groups, boundaries, identities, contrasts, and standards are reaching out and breaking down.

public transcript As used by James Scott, the open, public interactions between dominators and oppressed—the outer shell of power relations.

text Something that is creatively "read," interpreted, and assigned meaning by each person who receives it; includes any media-borne image, such as Carnaval.

westernization The acculturative influence of Western expansion on native cultures.

CRITICAL THINKING
QUESTIONS

For more self
testing, see the
self quizzes

mhhe
● **com**
/kottak

1. Have you personally observed or experienced a situation involving acculturation?

2. Can you apply some of the observations made in the text about environmentalist strategy to events in your own society?

3. Use your interaction with your parents or teachers to illustrate the difference between hidden and public transcripts.

4. If you were going to resist publicly, how would you choose to do it, and why?

5. Do you consider the mass media to be instruments of cultural imperialism? How about the Internet? How so?

6. How do you participate in a world system of images? Are the images to which you relate mainly national, or foreign/international as well?

7. How do you use the media? Is there a program or group that has special meaning for you? How does that meaning differ from someone else's, with respect to the same program or group? Are you personally irritated when someone questions your meaning?

8. Among the contemporary global flows—people, technology, finance, information, and ideology— which do you consider most important, and why?

9. Name three significant forms of linkages in today's world. How do they apply to you?

10. Do you now live, or have you ever lived, multi-locally? How so?

11. What's the difference between postmodernity and postmodernism? Have you had postmodern moments, as discussed in the text?

Atlas Questions

Look at Map 25, "Indigenous Peoples of the World, 2000."

1. Which two continents have the largest number of named indigenous societies? How might this distribution be explained? Could it be a matter both of actual survival and of political choices leading to a claimed identity? What factors would have favored actual survival? What factors would have promoted political mobilization?

2. Which two continents have the smallest number of specific indigenous societies? How might this scarcity be explained? What factors might explain the disappearance or destruction of indigenous societies and their identities?

3. Which continent has not yet been named in this set of questions? How would you explain this intermediate position with respect to the survival and self-identification of indigenous peoples?

SUGGESTED ADDITIONAL
READINGS

Ahmed, A. S.
1992   *Postmodernism and Islam: Predicament and Promise.* New York: Routledge. Clear presentation of postmodernism, in relation to the media and to images of Islam.

Balick, M. J., E. Elisabetsky, and S. A. Laird
1995   *Medicinal Resources of the Tropical Forest: Biodiversity and Its Importance to Human Health.* New York: Columbia University Press. The medicinal and health implications of deforestation at the local, regional, national, and global levels.

Bodley, J. H.

1999   *Victims of Progress,* 4th ed. Mountain View, CA: Mayfield. Social change, acculturation, and culture conflict involving indigenous peoples.

2001   *Anthropology and Contemporary Human Problems,* 4th ed. Mountain View, CA: Mayfield. Overview of major problems of today's industrial world: overconsumption, the environment, resource depletion, hunger, overpopulation, violence, and war.

Cultural Survival Inc.

1992   *At the Threshold.* Cambridge, MA: Cultural Survival. Originally published as the Spring 1992 issue of *Cultural Survival Quarterly.* Manual for the promotion of the rights of indigenous peoples. Highlights activist successes, gives instructions for affecting policy, working in schools and communities, directly helping native societies, and using the media as a human rights ally.

DaMatta, R.

1991   *Carnivals, Rogues, and Heroes: An Interpretation of the Brazilian Dilemma.* Translated from the Portuguese by John Drury. Notre Dame, IN: University of Notre Dame Press. Classic study of Brazilian *Carnaval* in relation to Brazilian national culture.

Feld, S.

1990   *Sound and Sentiment: Birds, Weeping, Poetics, and Song in Kaluli Expression,* 2nd ed. Philadelphia: University of Pennsylvania Press. Ethnographic study of sound as a cultural system among the Kaluli people of Papua New Guinea.

Fiske, J.

1989   *Understanding Popular Culture.* Boston: Unwin Hyman. The role of the individual in using popular culture, constructing meaning, and resisting everyday power relations.

Gottdiener, M., ed.

2000   *New Forms of Consumption: Consumers, Culture, and Commodification.* Lanham, MD: Rowman and Littlefield. Cultural consumption, diversity, and market segmentation in today's global economy.

Lutz, C., and J. L. Collins

1993   *Reading National Geographic.* Chicago: University of Chicago Press. How the cultural narratives of the magazine are received and interpreted; the relation between images of other peoples, cultures, and life styles and middle-class North American values.

Marcus, G. E., and M. M. J. Fischer

1999   *Anthropology as Cultural Critique: An Experimental Moment in the Human Sciences,* 2nd ed. Chicago: University of Chicago Press. New edition of an influential book on modern and postmodern anthropology.

Mathews, G.

2000   *Global Culture/Individual Identity: Searching for Home in the Cultural Supermarket.* New York: Routledge. National characteristics, relations, identity, and culture under globalization.

Maybury-Lewis, D.

2002   *Indigenous Peoples, Ethnic Groups, and the State,* 2nd ed. Boston: Allyn & Bacon. Indigenous peoples and ethnicity in the contemporary world.

Nagel, J.

1996   *American Indian Ethnic Renewal: Red Power and the Resurgence of Identity and Culture.* New York: Oxford University Press. The meaning of activism for Native American individual ethnic identification; the role of federal, tribal, and personal politics in the growth of American Indian identity.

Reed, R.

1997   *Forest Dwellers, Forest Protectors: Indigenous Models for International Development.* Boston: Allyn & Bacon. Applying indigenous knowledge and practices to economic development.

Robbins, R.

2002   *Global Problems and the Culture of Capitalism,* 2nd ed. Boston: Allyn & Bacon. Examines issues of domination, resistance, and social and economic problems in today's world.

Root, D.

1996   *Cannibal Culture: Art, Appropriation, and the Commodification of Difference.* Boulder, CO: Westview. How Western art and commerce classify, co-opt, and commodify "native" experiences, creations, and products.

Scott, J. C.

1990   *Domination and the Arts of Resistance.* New Haven, CT: Yale University Press. A study of institutionalized forms of domination, such as colonialism, slavery, serfdom, racism, caste, concentration camps, prisons, and old-age homes—and the forms of resistance that oppose them.

1998   *Seeing Like a State: How Certain Schemes to Improve the Human Condition Have Failed.* New Haven, CT: Yale University Press. Reflections on contemporary lives, social engineering, and authoritarianism.

INTERNET EXERCISES

1. *Peacemaking among the Nuer and Dinka:* Refer back to the discussion of the Nuer in the chapter "Political Systems" to read about the Nuer and their neighbors the Dinka and their segmentary lineage organization. Then read the *Washington Post* article about the recent history of these groups, **http://www.washingtonpost.com/wp-srv/inatl/daily/july99/sudan7.htm**.

   a. Anthropologists in the middle of the 20th century recorded conflict between the Nuer and the Dinka. In this article, they became allies against what opponent? How did conflict reemerge between the Nuer and the Dinka?

   b. What were the traditional views of warfare and death among the Nuer and the Dinka? How did these change with the introduction of modern machine guns?

   c. What impact did these new views have on the recent Nuer/Dinka conflicts?

   d. Despite the cultural changes brought about by the pressures of modern nations and the introduction of machine guns, the Nuer and the Dinka used traditional cultural symbols to help bring about peace. What are some examples?

   e. Do you think this peace will be short-lived? What needs to take place in order to maintain peace?

2. *Ishi, Cultural Survival, and Anthropology:* Read B. Bower's article in *Science News* entitled "Ishi's Long Road Home," **http://www.sciencenews.org/20000108/bob1.asp**.

   a. Who was Ishi? To what tribe did he belong, and what happened to them?

   b. In what way was Ishi successful in preserving native culture and educating people about it?

   c. What attitudes on the part of white Americans led to the demise of Ishi's family? What attitudes on the part of white Americans led to his immense popularity while at the museum in San Francisco? How can you account for the paradox of these seemingly contradictory views of Native Americans among white Americans?

   d. In the past, anthropologists seemed to have cared more about documenting vanishing cultures than about working for the needs of those cultures' living representatives. In what way does the story of Ishi illustrate those conflicts? What role should anthropology play in the future?

See Chapter 25 at your McGraw-Hill Online Learning Center for additional review and interactive exercises.

BRINGING IT ALL TOGETHER

See your OLC Bringing It All Together links

mhhe.com /kottak

The Biology and Culture of Overconsumption

In the chapter "The Modern World System," we learned that Americans are the world's foremost consumers. Using some 275,000 calories of energy per day, the average American is 35 times more expensive than the average forager or tribesperson, who uses just 8,000 calories. Since 1900, the United States has increased its total energy consumption 30-fold. And in the last two decades, Americans have increased their *food* consumption by an average of 200 calories per day. American agribusiness now produces 500 food calories more per person per day than it did 30 years ago, which is about 1,000 more calories per day than most people need (Pollan 2003). This provides a dramatic contrast with the food scarcity that accompanies poverty in the less-developed countries. In the chapter "Colonialism and Development," for example, we saw that in Java, daily food calories available per capita had dropped from 1,950 to 1,750, less than half the current American figure of 3,800 (Pollan 2003).

In his book *Fat Land: Supersizing America* (2003), Greg Critser examines how Americans rapidly are becoming the fattest people on earth. Sixty percent of all Americans, and 25 percent of American children, are now overweight. Since 1970, the percentage of American children who are overweight has doubled. Food companies have fueled this epidemic of obesity as they have attempted to maintain their profitability—by getting people to eat more—at a time when the American food supply has been growing much faster than the American population has. A key ingredient in the fattening of America has been the rise and spread of "supersizing."

Critser (2003) traces how David Wallerstein—currently an executive at McDonald's—invented supersizing. In the 1960s, Wallerstein, then working for a movie theater chain, was looking for ways to expand sales of soda pop and popcorn. He discovered that although the typical moviegoer was reluctant to buy more than one drink or bag of popcorn, people would consume more drink and popcorn if they came in a single large serving. Such supersizing is an effective business strategy because the raw materials for soda, popcorn, fries, and burgers make up only a small fraction of their price-compared with the costs of labor, packaging, and advertising. Expanding the size of portions allowed businesses to raise prices and increase sales without adding much to costs.

Ray Kroc, the founder of McDonald's, adopted Wallerstein's strategy of supersizing. In McDonald's advertising, Big Macs and large fries replaced "regular" (i.e., small) hamburgers and fries. Dave Thomas offered "biggie" fries and drinks at Wendy's. All the fast-food chains started hawking combos (for breakfast, lunch, or later). This greatly enhanced the American (and worldwide) consumption of that old Peruvian domesticate, the "Irish" potato, in the form of "French" fries. (Talk about a world system!)

When people are offered larger portions, studies show they will eat up to 30 percent more than they otherwise would. (Think about our holiday feasts.) For human hunger to be elastic like this

Supersizing affects appetites and bodies.

makes evolutionary sense. By feasting whenever they had the chance, our hunter-gatherer ancestors could store fat to use later when they were confronted with food scarcity or famine. We've seen that in Papua New Guinea and Melanesia, "big men" and their followers work hard to organize feasts at which pigs are killed and cooked and pork is widely distributed and eaten. In those societies it's a rare and welcome treat to "pig out." In the contemporary United States it's easy to "pig out" any day of the year. If a "thrifty gene" facilitating fat storage was adaptive for our hunter-gatherer ancestors, it has become maladaptive today given the food surplus just described (see Brown and Bentley-Condit 1996; Farb and Armelagos 1980).

The American epidemic of obesity is a consequence of cheap and abundant food. As applied anthropologists know, changes take place as part of systems: One change leads to other changes, which are related and compensatory. Thus, as Critser (2003) notes, to accommodate fatter customers, restaurants have increased the size of their seats. American government agencies have relaxed their weight, fitness, and dietary guidelines. Named diets and fitness centers have proliferated, and clothing sizes have been recalibrated to make fatter people feel thinner. "It runs large" and "it runs small" are common phrases in the linguistic strategies of garment salespeople.

Overeating has clear health consequences. The new American diet has ushered in an epidemic of type 2 diabetes, formerly known as "adult-onset diabetes," which, however, now afflicts millions of children. The cost of overconsumption to the American health system runs to billions of dollars annually. According to Pollan (2003), the fattening of America may be emerging as a political issue. A grassroots parents' movement seeks to remove fast food and vending machines from schools. Obese customers have filed lawsuits against fast-food chains, seeking to hold those companies liable for health problems, as tobacco companies have been held liable through legal action. Questions have been raised about the ethics of marketing unhealthy products to children.

We've seen how the business strategy of supersizing fueled the expansion of fast food and overeating. An anthropological perspective can reveal more subtle cultural factors within the culture of overconsumption, which characterizes not only the United States but also the consuming (middle and upper) classes of nations around the world.

The sun, it was said, never set on the British empire. We could make the same observation about the global presence of McDonald's in the 21st century. The number of McDonald's outlets today far surpasses the total number of fast-food restaurants in the United States in 1945. McDonald's has grown from a single hamburger stand in San Bernardino, California, into today's international web of thousands of outlets.

The success of McDonald's is founded on modern technology, particularly automobiles, television, work away from home, and the short lunch break (see Brown and Krick 2001). Several years ago, I began to notice certain ritual-like aspects of Americans' behavior at fast-food restaurants, especially at McDonald's. Tell your fellow Americans that going to a fast-food restaurant is similar in some ways to going to church and their bias as natives will reveal itself in laughter, denial, or questions about your sanity. McDonald's, for natives, is just a place to eat. However, an analysis of what natives do there will reveal a very high degree of formal, uniform behavior by staff members and customers alike. It is particularly interesting that this invariance in word and deed has developed without any theological doctrine. It is striking that a commercial organization should be so successful in producing behavioral invariance. Factors other than low cost, fast service, and the taste of the food—all of which are approximated by other chains—have contributed to our acceptance of McDonald's and adherence to its rules.

A family meal at a Chicago area McDonalds.

Remarkably, when Americans travel abroad, even in countries noted for good food, many go to the local McDonald's outlet. The same factors that lead us to visit McDonald's at home are responsible. Because Americans are thoroughly familiar with how to eat and more or less what they will pay at McDonald's, in its outlets overseas they have a home away from home. In Paris, whose people aren't known for making tourists, particularly Americans, feel at home, McDonald's offers sanctuary (along with relatively clean, free rest rooms). It is, after all, an originally American institution where natives, programmed by years of prior experience, can feel completely at home.

This devotion to McDonald's rests in part on uniformities associated with its outlets: food, setting, architecture, ambience, acts, and utterances. The McDonald's symbol, the golden arches, is an almost universal symbol, as familiar to Americans as Mickey Mouse, Oprah, and the flag. A McDonald's (now closed) near my university was a brick structure whose stained-glass windows had golden arches as their central theme. Sunlight flooded in through a skylight that was like the clerestory of a church.

Americans enter a McDonald's restaurant for an ordinary, secular act—eating. However, the surroundings tell us we are somehow apart from the variability of the world outside. We know what we are going to see, what we are going to say, and what will be said to us. We know what we will eat, how it will taste, and how much it will cost. Behind the counter, agents wear similar attire. Permissible utterances by customer and worker are written above the counter. Throughout the United States, with only minor variations, the menu is in the same place, contains the same items, and has the same prices. The food, again with only minor variation, is prepared according to plan and varies little in taste. Obviously, customers are limited in what they can choose. Less obviously, they are limited—linguistically—in terms of what they can say. Each item has its appropriate designation: "large fry," "quarter pounder with cheese." The novice who innocently asks, "What kind of hamburgers do you have?" or "What's a Big Mac?" is out of place.

A linguistic anthropologist would notice that other ritual phrases are uttered by the person behind the counter. After the customer has completed an order, if no potatoes are requested, the agent ritually asks, "You want the combo?" Once food is presented and picked up, the agent conventionally says, "Have a nice day." (McDonald's has surely played a strong role in the diffusion of this linguistic cliché into every corner of contemporary American life.)

Understandably, as the world's number one fast-food chain, McDonald's evokes hostility. The Ann Arbor campus McDonald's once was the scene of a ritual rebellion—desecration by the Radical Vegetarian League, which held a "puke-in." Standing on the second-story balcony just below the clerestory, a dozen vegetarians gorged themselves on mustard and water and vomited down on the customer waiting area. McDonald's, defiled, lost many customers that day. Worldwide, McDonald's has become one of the most potent symbols of globalization and perceived American

On April 18, 2002, students hold a sit-in at a McDonalds outlet in Beirut, Lebanon, as part of a campaign to boycott American products. McDonalds' international success has made it a target of protests against perceived American cultural imperialism.

cultural and economic imperialism. McDonald's has felt the brunt of cultural, including religious, opposition to its meals, meats, and mission.

Eating at McDonald's and religious feasts are in complementary distribution in American life. That is, when one occurs, the other doesn't. Most Americans would consider it inappropriate to eat at a fast-food restaurant on Christmas, Thanksgiving, Easter, or Passover. Our culture regards these as family days, occasions when relatives and close friends get together. However, although Americans neglect McDonald's on holidays, television reminds us that McDonald's still endures, that it will welcome us back once our holiday is over. The television presence of McDonald's is particularly evident on such occasions—whether through a float in the Macy's Thanksgiving Day parade or through sponsorship of special programs, particularly "family entertainment."

Although Burger King, Wendy's, and Arby's compete with McDonald's for the fast-food business, none has equaled the success of McDonald's. The explanation may lie in the particularly skillful ways in which McDonald's advertising plays up the features just discussed. On Saturday morning television, with its steady stream of cartoons, McDonald's has been a ubiquitous sponsor. Breakfast at McDonald's has been promoted by a fresh-faced, sincere, happy, clean-cut young woman. Actors gambol on ski slopes or in mountain pastures. The single theme that for years has run through the commercials is personalism. McDonald's, the commercials drone on, is something other than a fast-food restaurant. It's a warm, friendly place where you are graciously welcomed and feel at home, where your children won't get into trouble. McDonald's commercials tell you that you aren't simply an anonymous face in an amorphous crowd. You find respite from a hectic and impersonal society, the break you deserve. Your individuality and dignity are respected at McDonald's.

McDonald's advertising tries to deemphasize the fact that the chain is a commercial organization. One jingle proclaimed, "You, you're the one; we're fixin' breakfast for ya"—not "We're making millions off ya." "Family" television entertainment often is "brought to you by McDonald's." McDonald's commercials regularly tell us that it supports and works to maintain the values of American family life.

I am not arguing here that McDonald's has become a religion. I merely am suggesting that specific ways in which Americans participate in McDonald's bear analogies to religious systems involving myth, symbol, and ritual. Just as in rituals, participation in McDonald's requires temporary subordination of individual differences in a social and cultural collectivity. In a land of ethnic, social, economic, and religious diversity, we demonstrate that we share something with millions of others. Furthermore, as in rituals, participation in McDonald's is linked to a cultural system that transcends the chain itself. By eating there, we say something about ourselves as Americans, about our acceptance of certain collective values, customs, and ways of living.

Such widespread learned behavior patterns, fueled in this case by a savvy business model, also have biological—weight and health—consequences, as we saw at the beginning of this essay. Consider finally the explosion of paper, plastic, and Styrofoam associated with the fast-food industry. Such material remains, along with distinctive arches and architecture, offer evidence that contemporary garbologists, or future archaeologists, might use to reconstruct the culture of consumption in the early 21st century.

AMERICAN POPULAR CULTURE

Culture is shared. But all cultures have divisive as well as unifying forces. Tribes are divided by residence in different villages and membership in different descent groups. Nations, though united by government, are divided by class, region, ethnicity, religion, and political party. Unifying forces in tribal cultures include marriage, trade, and a belief in common descent. In any society, of course, a common cultural tradition also may provide a basis for uniformity.

Whatever unity contemporary American culture has doesn't rest on a particularly strong central government. Nor is national unity based on a belief in common descent or marital exchange networks. In fact, many of the commonalities of experience, belief, behavior, and activity that enable us to speak of "contemporary American culture" are relatively new. Like the globalizing forces discussed in the chapter "Cultural Exchange and Survival," they are founded on and perpetuated by recent developments, particularly in business, transportation, and the mass media.

Appendix Outline

Anthropologists and American Culture

Football

Star Trek

Anthropology and "Pop" Culture

Anthropologists and American Culture

When anthropologists study urban ethnic groups or relationships between class and household organization, they focus on variation, a very important topic. When we look at the creative use that each individual makes of popular culture, as we did in the chapter "Cultural Exchange and Survival," we are also considering variation. However, anthropology traditionally has been concerned as much with uniformity as with variation.

"National character" studies of the 1940s and 1950s foreshadowed anthropology's interest in unifying themes in modern nations. Unfortunately, those studies, of such countries as Japan and Russia, focused too much on the psychological characteristics of individuals.

Contemporary anthropologists interested in national culture realize that culture is an attribute of groups. Despite increasing ethnic diversity, we can still talk about an "American national culture." Through common experiences in their enculturation, especially through the media, most Americans do come to share certain knowledge, beliefs, values, and ways of thinking and acting (as was discussed in the chapter "Culture"). The shared aspects of national culture override differences among individuals, genders, regions, or ethnic groups.

The chapter "Cultural Exchange and Survival" examined the creative use that individuals and cultures make of introduced cultural forces, including media images. That chapter discussed how, through different "readings" of the same media "text," individuals and cultures constantly make and remake popular culture. Here we take a different approach. We focus on a few "texts" that have diffused most successfully in a given national (i.e., American) culture. Other such texts examined in previous chapters include Disney amusement parks, *Star Wars*, and *The Wizard of Oz*. These "texts" have spread because they are culturally appropriate. For various reasons, they are able to carry some sort of meaning to millions of people. Previous chapters focused on variation and diversity, but this appendix stresses unifying factors: common experiences, actions, and beliefs in American culture.

Anthropologists *should* study American society and culture. Anthropology, after all, deals with universals, generalities, and uniqueness. A national culture is a particular cultural variant, as interesting as any other. Although survey research traditionally is used to study modern nations, techniques developed to interpret and analyze smaller-scale societies, where sociocultural uniformity is more marked, also can contribute to an understanding of American life.

Native anthropologists are those who study their own cultures, for example, American anthropologists working in the United States, Canadian anthropologists working in Canada, or Nigerians working in Nigeria. Anthropological training and field work abroad provide an anthropologist with a certain degree of detachment and objectivity that most natives lack. However, life experience as a native gives an advantage to anthropologists who wish to study their own cultures. Nevertheless, more than when working abroad, the native anthropologist is both participant and observer, often emotionally and intellectually involved in the events and beliefs being studied. Native anthropologists must be particularly careful to resist their own biases and prejudices as natives. They must strive to be as objective in describing their own cultures as they are in analyzing others.

Natives often see and explain their behavior very differently than anthropologists do. For example, most Americans have probably never considered the possibility that apparently secular, commercial, and recreational institutions such as sports, movies, and fast-food restaurants have things in common with myths, religious beliefs, symbols, and behavior. However, these similarities do exist. A key theme of this book has been that *anthropology helps us understand ourselves*. By studying other cultures, we learn both to appreciate and to question aspects of our own culture. Furthermore, the same techniques that anthropologists use in describing and analyzing other cultures can be applied to American culture.

American readers may not find the analyses that follow convincing. In part, this is because you are natives, who know much more about your own culture than you do about any other. Also, as we saw in the chapter "Cultural Exchange and Survival," people in a culture may "read" that culture differently. Furthermore, American culture assigns a high value to differences in individual opinion—and to the belief that one opinion is as good as another. Here I am trying to extract *culture* (widely shared aspects of behavior) from diverse *individual* opinions, actions, and experiences.

The following analyses depart from areas that can be easily quantified, such as demography and economics. We are entering a more impressionistic domain, where cultural analysis sometimes seems much more like literary analysis than like science. You will be right in questioning some of the conclusions that follow. Some are surely debatable; some may be plain wrong. However, if they illustrate how anthropology can be used to shed light on aspects of your own life and experience and to revise and broaden your understanding of your own culture, they will have served a worthwhile function.

A reminder (from the chapter "Culture") about culture, ethnocentrism, and native anthropologists is needed here. For anthropologists, *culture* means much more than refinement, cultivation, education, and appreciation of "classics" and "fine arts"—its popular usage. Curiously, however, when some anthropologists confront their own culture, they seem to forget this. Like other academics and intellectuals, they may regard American "pop" culture as trivial and unworthy of serious study. In doing so, they demonstrate ethnocentrism and reveal a bias that comes with being members of an academic-intellectual subculture.

In examining American culture, native anthropologists must be careful to overcome the bias associated with the academic subculture. Although some academics discourage their children from watching television, the fact that TVs outnumber toilets in American households is a significant cultural datum that anthropologists can't afford to ignore. My own research on Michigan college students may be generalizable to other young Americans. They visit fast-food restaurants more often than they visit houses of worship. I found that almost all had seen a Walt Disney movie and had attended rock concerts or football games. Such shared experiences are major features of American enculturation patterns. As we saw in the last "Bringing It All Together" essay, they affect our bodies as well as our minds. Certainly, any extraterrestrial anthropologist doing field work in the United States would stress such aspects of mass culture. Within the United States, the mass media and the culture of consumption have created major themes in contemporary national culture. These themes merit study.

From the popular domains of sports, TV, and movies I have chosen certain very popular "texts" to discuss here. (Other features of popular culture, such as fast food, have been discussed previously.)I could have used other texts (for example, blue jeans, baseball, or pizza) to make the same points: that there are powerful shared aspects of contemporary American national culture and that anthropological techniques can be used to interpret them.

Football

Football, we say, is only a game, yet it has become a popular spectator sport. On fall Saturdays, millions of people travel to and from college football games. Smaller congregations meet in high school stadiums. Millions of Americans watch televised football. Indeed, nearly half the adult population of the United States watches the Super Bowl. Because football is of general interest to Americans, it is a unifying cultural institution that merits attention. Our most popular sports manage to attract fans of diverse ethnic backgrounds, regions, religions, political parties, jobs, social statuses, levels of wealth, and even genders.

The popularity of football, particularly professional football, depends directly on the mass media, especially television. Is football, with its territorial incursion, hard hitting, and violence—occasionally resulting in injury—popular because Americans are violent people? Are football spectators vicariously realizing their own hostile and aggressive tendencies? The anthropologist W. Arens (1981) discounts this interpretation. He points out that football is a peculiarly American pastime. Although a similar game is played in Canada, it is less popular there. Baseball has become a popular sport in the Caribbean, parts of Latin America, and Japan. Basketball and volleyball also are spreading. However, throughout most of the world, soccer is the most popular sport. Arens argues that if football were a particularly effective channel for expressing aggression, it would have spread (like soccer and baseball) to many other countries, where people have as many aggressive tendencies and hostile feelings as Americans do. Furthermore, he suggests that if a sport's popularity rested simply on a bloodthirsty temperament, boxing, a far bloodier sport, would be America's national pastime. Arens concludes that the explanation for the sport's popularity lies elsewhere, and I agree.

He contends that football is popular because it symbolizes certain key features of American life. In particular, it is characterized by teamwork based on specialization and division of labor, which are pervasive features of modern life. Susan Montague and Robert Morais (1981) take the analysis a step further. They argue that Americans appreciate football because it presents a miniaturized and simplified version of modern organizations. People have trouble understanding organizational bureaucracies, whether in business, universities, or government. Football, the anthropologists argue, helps us understand how decisions are made and rewards are allocated in organizations.

Montague and Morais link football's values, particularly teamwork, to those associated with business. Like corporate workers, the ideal players are diligent and dedicated to the team. Within corporations, however, decision making is complicated, and workers aren't always rewarded for their dedication and good job performance. Decisions are simpler and rewards are more consistent in football, these anthropologists contend, and this helps explain its popularity. Even if we can't figure out how General Motors and Microsoft run, any fan can become an expert on football's rules, teams, scores, statistics, and patterns of play. Even more important, football suggests that the values stressed by business really do pay off. Teams whose members work the hardest, show the most spirit, and best develop and coordinate their talents can be expected to win more often than other teams do.

Star Trek*

Star Trek, a familiar, powerful, and enduring force in American popular culture, can be used to illustrate the idea that popular media content often is derived from prominent values expressed in many other domains of culture. Americans first encountered the Starship *Enterprise* on NBC in 1966. *Star Trek* was shown in prime time for just three seasons. However, the series not only survives but thrives today in syndication, reruns, books, websites, cassettes, and theatrical films. Revived as a regular weekly series with an entirely new cast in 1987, *Star Trek: The Next Generation* became the third most popular syndicated program in the United States (after *Wheel of Fortune* and *Jeopardy*). *Deep Space Nine, Voyager,* and *Enterprise* have been somewhat less popular successors in the *Star Trek* family.

What does the enduring mass appeal of *Star Trek* tell us about American culture? I believe the answer to be this: *Star Trek* is a transformation of a fundamental American origin myth. The same myth shows up in the image and celebration of Thanksgiving, a distinctively American holiday. Thanksgiving sets the myth in the past, and *Star Trek* sets it in the future.

The myths of contemporary America are drawn from a variety of sources, including such popular-culture fantasies as *Star Wars, The Wizard of Oz* (see the chapter on the arts), and *Star Trek*. Our myths also include real people, particularly national ancestors, whose lives have been reinterpreted and endowed with special meaning over the generations. The media, schools, churches,

*This section is adapted from *Prime-Time Society: An Anthropological Analysis of Television and Culture* by Conrad Phillip Kottak. © 1990 by Wadsworth, Inc. Used by permission of the publisher.

communities, and parents teach the national origin myths to American children. The story of Thanksgiving, for example, continues to be important. It recounts the origin of a national holiday celebrated by Protestants, Catholics, and Jews. All those denominations share a belief in the Old Testament God, and they find it appropriate to thank God for their blessings.

Again and again, Americans have heard idealized retellings of that epochal early harvest. We have learned how Indians taught the Pilgrims to farm in the New World. Grateful Pilgrims then invited the Indians to share their first Thanksgiving. Native American and European labor, techniques, and customs thus blended in that initial biethnic celebration. Annually reenacting the origin myth, the American public schools commemorate "the first Thanksgiving" as children dress up as Pilgrims, Indians, and pumpkins.

More rapidly and pervasively as the mass media grow, each generation of Americans writes its own revisionist history. Our culture constantly reinterprets the origin, nature, and meaning of national holidays. The collective consciousness of contemporary Americans includes TV-saturated memories of "the first Thanksgiving" and "the first Christmas." Our mass culture has instilled the widely shared images of a *Peanuts*-peopled Pilgrim-and-Indian "love-in."

We also conjure up a fictionalized Nativity with Mary, Joseph, Jesus, manger animals, shepherds, three eastern kings, a little drummer boy, and, in some versions, Rudolph the Red-Nosed Reindeer. Note that the interpretation of the Nativity that American culture perpetuates is yet another variation on the same dominant myth. We remember the Nativity as a Thanksgiving involving interethnic contacts (e.g., the three kings) and gift giving. It is set in Bethlehem rather than Massachusetts.

We impose our present on the past as we reinterpret quasi-historic and actual events. For the future, we do it in our science-fiction and fantasy creations. *Star Trek* places in the future what the Thanksgiving story locates in the past: *the myth of the assimilationist, incorporating, melting-pot society.* The myth says that America is distinctive not just because it is assimilationist but because it is *founded* on unity in diversity. (Our *origin* is unity in diversity. After all, we call ourselves "the United States.") Thanksgiving and *Star Trek* illustrate the credo that unity through diversity is essential for survival (whether of a harsh winter or of the perils of outer space). Americans survive by sharing the fruits of specialization.

Star Trek proclaims that the sacred principles that validate American society, because they lie at its foundation, will endure across the generations and even the centuries. The Starship *Enterprise* crew is a melting pot. Captain James Tiberius Kirk is symbolic of real history. His clearest historic prototype is Captain James Cook, whose ship, the *Endeavor,* also sought out new life and civilizations. Kirk's infrequently mentioned middle name, from the Roman general and eventual emperor, links the captain to the earth's imperial history. Kirk is also symbolic of the original Anglo-American. He runs the *Enterprise* (America is founded on free enterprise), just as laws, values, and institutions derived from England continue to guide the United States.

McCoy's Irish (or at least Gaelic) name represents the next wave, the established immigrant. Sulu is the successfully assimilated Asian-American. The African-American female character Uhura, "whose name means freedom," indicates that blacks will become full partners with all other Americans. However, Uhura was the only major female character in the original crew. Female extra-domestic employment was less characteristic of American society in 1966 than it is now.

One of *Star Trek*'s constant messages is that strangers, even enemies, can become friends. Less obviously, this message is about cultural imperialism, the assumed irresistibility of American culture and institutions. Russian nationals (Chekhov) could be seduced and captured by an expansive American culture. Spock, although from Vulcan, is half human, with human qualities. We learn, therefore, that our assimilationist values eventually will not just rule the earth but extend to other planets as well. By "the next generation," Klingons, even more alien than Vulcans, and personified by Bridge Officer Worf, have joined the melting pot.

Even God was harnessed to serve American culture, in the person of Scotty. His role was that of the ancient Greek *deus ex machina.* He was a stage controller who "beamed" people up and down, back and forth, from earth to the heavens. Scotty, who kept society going, was also a servant-employee who did his engineering for management—illustrating loyalty and technical skill.

The Next Generation contained many analogues of the original characters. Several "partial people" were single-character personifications of particular human qualities represented in more complex form by the original *Star Trek* crew members. Kirk, Spock, and McCoy were split into multiple characters. Captain Jean-Luc Picard possessed the intellectual and managerial attributes of James T. Kirk. With his English accent and French name, Picard, like Kirk, drew his legitimacy from symbolic association with historic Western European empires. First Officer Riker replaced Kirk as a romantic man of action.

Spock, an alien (strange ears) who represented science, reason, and intellect, was split in two. One half was Worf, a Klingon bridge officer whose cranial protuberances were analogous to Spock's ears. The other was Data, an android whose brain contained the sum of human knowledge. Two female characters, an empath and the ship's doctor, replaced Dr. McCoy as the repository of healing, emotion, and feeling.

Mirroring contemporaneous American culture, *The Next Generation* featured prominent black, female, and physically challenged characters. An African-American actor played the Klingon Mr. Worf. Another, LeVar Burton, appeared as Geordi La Forge. Although blind, Geordi managed, through a vision-enhancing visor, to see things that other people could not. His mechanical vision expressed the characteristic and enduring American faith in technology. So did the android, Data.

During its first year, *The Next Generation* had three prominent female characters. One was the ship's doctor, a working professional with a teenage son. Another was an empath, the ultimate "helping professional." The third was the ship's security officer.

America had become more specialized, differentiated, and professional than it was in the 1960s. The greater role specificity and diversity of *Next Generation* characters reflected this. Nevertheless, both series convey the central *Star Trek* message, one that dominates the culture that created them: Americans are diverse. Individual qualities, talents, and specialties divide us. However, we make our livings and survive as members of cohesive, efficient groups. We explore and advance as members of a crew, a team, an enterprise, or, most generally, a society. Our nation is founded on and endures through assimilation—effective subordination of individual differences within a smoothly functioning multiethnic team. The team is American culture. It worked in the past. It works today.

It will go on working across the generations. Orderly and progressive democracy based on mutual respect is best. Inevitably, American culture will triumph over all others—by convincing and assimilating rather than conquering them. Unity in diversity guarantees human survival.

Anthropology and "Pop" Culture

The examples of mass or popular culture considered in this appendix and elsewhere in this book are shared cultural forms that have appeared and spread rapidly because of major changes in the material conditions of American life—particularly work organization, communication, and transportation. Most contemporary Americans deem at least one automobile a necessity. Televisions outnumber toilets in our households. Through the mass media, institutions such as sports, movies, TV shows, amusement parks, and fast-food restaurants have become powerful elements of national culture. They provide a framework of common expectations, experiences, and behavior overriding differences in region, class, formal religious affiliation, political sentiments, gender, ethnic group, and place of residence. Although some of us may not like these changes, it's difficult to deny their significance.

The rise of these institutions is linked not just to the mass media but also to decreasing American participation in traditional religion and the weakening of ties based on kinship, marriage, and community within industrial society. Neither a single church, a strong central government, nor a belief in common descent unites most Americans.

These dimensions of contemporary culture are dismissed as passing, trivial, or "pop" by some. However, because millions of people share them, they deserve and are receiving scholarly attention. Such studies help fulfill the promise that by studying anthropology, we can better understand ourselves.

BIBLIOGRAPHY

Abelmann, N., and J. Lie
1995   *Blue Dreams: Korean Americans and the Los Angeles Riots.* Cambridge, MA: Harvard University Press.

Abiodun, R.
1996   Foreword. In *Art and Religion in Africa,* by R. I. J. Hackett, pp. viii–ix. London: Cassell.

Abu-Lughod, J. L.
1989   *Before European Hegemony: The World System A.D. 1250–1350.* New York: Oxford University Press.

Adams, R. M.
1981   *Heartland of Cities.* Chicago: Aldine.

Adepegba, C. O.
1991   The Yoruba Concept of Art and Its Significance in the Holistic View of Art as Applied to African Art. *African Notes* 15: 1–6.

Agar, M. H.
1980   *The Professional Stranger: An Informal Introduction to Ethnography.* New York: Academic Press.

Ahmed, A. S.
1992   *Postmodernism and Islam: Predicament and Promise.* New York: Routledge.

Akazawa, T.
1980   *The Japanese Paleolithic: A Techno-Typological Study.* Tokyo: Rippo Shobo.

Akazawa, T., and C. M. Aikens, eds.
1986   *Prehistoric Hunter-Gatherers in Japan: New Research Methods.* Tokyo: University of Tokyo Press.

Albert, B.
1989   Yanomami "Violence": Inclusive Fitness or Ethnographer's Representation? *Current Anthropology* 30: 637–640.

Amadiume, I.
1987   *Male Daughters, Female Husbands.* Atlantic Highlands, NJ: Zed.

1997   *Reinventing Africa: Matriarchy, Religion, and Culture.* New York: Zed.

American Almanac 1994–1995
1994   *Statistical Abstract of the United States,* 114th ed. Austin, TX: Reference Press.

American Almanac 1996–1997
1996   *Statistical Abstract of the United States,* 116th ed. Austin, TX: Reference Press.

American Anthropological Association
AAA Guide: A Guide to Departments, a Directory of Members. (Formerly *Guide to Departments of Anthropology.*) Published annually by the American Anthropological Association, Washington, DC.

Anthropology Newsletter. Published nine times annually by the American Anthropological Association, Washington, DC.

General Anthropology: Bulletin of the Council for General Anthropology.

Amick III, B., S. Levine, A. R. Tarlov, and D. C. Walsh, eds.
1995   *Society and Health.* New York: Oxford University Press.

Anderson, B.
1991   *Imagined Communities: Reflections on the Origin and Spread of Nationalism,* rev. ed. London: Verso.

1998   *The Spectre of Comparisons: Nationalism, Southeast Asia, and the World.* New York: Verso.

Anderson, R.
1989   *Art in Small Scale Societies.* Upper Saddle River, NJ: Prentice-Hall.

1990   *Calliope's Sisters: A Comparative Study of Philosophy of Art.* Upper Saddle River, NJ: Prentice-Hall.

2000   *American Muse: Anthropological Excursions into Art and Aesthetics.* Upper Saddle River, NJ: Prentice-Hall.

Anderson, R., and K. Field, eds.

1993   *Art in Small-Scale Societies: Contemporary Readings.* Upper Saddle River, NJ: Prentice-Hall.

1996   *Magic, Science, and Health: The Aims and Achievements of Medical Anthropology.* Fort Worth: Harcourt Brace.

Angier, N.

1998   When Nature Discovers the Same Design Over and Over, Lookalike Creatures Spark Evolutionary Debate. *New York Times,* December 15, pp. D1, D6.

2002   Why We're So Nice: We're Wired to Cooperate. *New York Times,* July 23. http://www.nytimes.com/2002/07/23/health/psychology/23COOP.html.

Angrosino, M. V., ed.

2002   *Doing Cultural Anthropology: Projects for Ethnographic Data Collection.* Prospect Heights, IL: Waveland.

Annenberg/CPB Exhibits

2000   "Collapse, Why Do Civilizations Fall?" http://www.learner.org/exhibits/collapse/.

Aoki, M. Y., and M. B. Dardess, eds.

1981   *As the Japanese See It: Past and Present.* Honolulu: University Press of Hawaii.

Appadurai, A.

1990   Disjuncture and Difference in the Global Cultural Economy. *Public Culture* 2(2): 1–24.

1991   Global Ethnoscapes: Notes and Queries for a Transnational Anthropology. In *Recapturing Anthropology: Working in the Present,* ed. R. G. Fox, pp. 191–210. Santa Fe: School of American Research Advanced Seminar Series.

Appel, R., and P. Muysken

1987   *Language Contact and Bilingualism.* London: Edward Arnold.

Appell, G. N.

1978   *Ethical Dilemmas in Anthropological Inquiry: A Case Book.* Waltham, MA: Crossroads Press.

Appiah, K. A.

1990   Racisms. In *Anatomy of Racism,* ed. David Theo Goldberg, pp. 3–17. Minneapolis: University of Minnesota Press.

Applebome, P.

1996   English Unique to Blacks Is Officially Recognized. *New York Times,* December 20. www.nytimes.com.

1997   Dispute over Ebonics Reflects a Volatile Mix. *New York Times,* March 1. www.nytimes.com.

Arce, A., and N. Long, eds.

2000   *Anthropology, Development, and Modernities: Exploring Discourses, Counter-Tendencies, and Violence.* New York: Routledge.

Archer, M. S.

1996   *Culture and Agency: The Place of Culture in Social Theory,* rev ed. Cambridge: Cambridge University Press.

Arens, W.

1981   Professional Football: An American Symbol and Ritual. In *The American Dimension: Cultural Myths and Social Realities,* 2nd ed., ed. W. Arens and S. P. Montague, pp. 1–10. Sherman Oaks, CA: Alfred.

Arens, W., and S. P. Montague

1981   *The American Dimension: Cultural Myths and Social Realities,* 2nd ed. Sherman Oaks, CA: Alfred.

Arensberg, C.

1987   Theoretical Contributions of Industrial and Development Studies. In *Applied Anthropology in America,* ed. E. M. Eddy and W. L. Partridge. New York: Columbia University Press.

Arnold, B., and B. Gibson, eds.

1995   *Celtic Chiefdom, Celtic State.* New York: Cambridge University Press.

Arrighi, G.

1994   *The Long Twentieth Century: Money, Power, and the Origins of Our Times.* New York: Verso.

Asfaw, B., T. White, and O. Lovejoy

1999   *Australopithecus garhi:* A New Species of Early Hominid from Ethiopia. *Science* 284: 629.

Ashcroft, B., G. Griffiths, and H. Tiffin

1989   *The Empire Writes Back: Theory and Practice in Post-colonial Literatures.* New York: Routledge.

Ashmore, W., and R. Sharer

2000   *Discovering Our Past: A Brief Introduction to Archaeology,* 3rd ed. Boston: McGraw-Hill.

Bailey, E. J.
2000   *Medical Anthropology and African American Health.* Westport, CT: Bergin and Garvey.

Bailey, R. C.
1990   *The Behavioral Ecology of Efe Pygmy Men in the Ituri Forest, Zaire.* Ann Arbor: Anthropological Papers, Museum of Anthropology, University of Michigan, no. 86.

Bailey, R. C., G. Head, M. Jenike, B. Owen, R. Rechtman, and E. Zechenter
1989   Hunting and Gathering in Tropical Rain Forests: Is It Possible? *American Anthropologist* 91: 59–82.

Baker, P. T.
1978   *The Biology of High Altitude Peoples.* New York: Cambridge University Press.

Baker, P. T., and J. S. Weiner, eds.
1966   *The Biology of Human Adaptability.* Oxford: Oxford University Press.

Bakhtin, M.
1984   *Rabelais and His World.* Translated by Helen Iswolksy. Bloomington: Indiana University Press.

Balick, M. J., and P. A. Cox
1996   *Plants, People, and Culture: The Science of Ethnobotany.* New York: Scientific American Library.

Balick, M. J., E. Elisabetsky, and S. A. Laird
1995   *Medicinal Resources of the Tropical Forest: Biodiversity and Its Importance to Human Health.* New York: Columbia University Press.

Banton, M.
1957   *West African City: A Study in Tribal Life in Freetown.* London: Oxford University Press.

Bar-Yosef, O.
1987   Pleistocene Connections between Africa and Southwest Asia: An Archaeological Perspective. *African Archaeological Review* 5: 29–38.

Barash, D. P.
1982   *Sociobiology and Behavior,* 2nd ed. Amsterdam: Elsevier.

Barlett, P. F., ed.
1980   *Agricultural Decision Making: Anthropological Contribution to Rural Development.* New York: Academic Press.

Barnaby, F., ed.
1984   *Future War: Armed Conflict in the Next Decade.* London: M. Joseph.

Barnard, A.
1979   Kalahari Settlement Patterns. In *Social and Ecological Systems,* ed. P. Burnham and R. Ellen, pp. 131–144. New York: Academic Press.

Barnouw, V.
1985   *Culture and Personality,* 4th ed. Belmont, CA: Wadsworth.

Baron, D.
1986   *Grammar and Gender.* New Haven, CT: Yale University Press.

Barringer, F.
1989   32 Million Lived in Poverty in '88, a Figure Unchanged. *New York Times,* October 19, p. 18.

1992   New Census Data Show More Children Living in Poverty. *New York Times,* May 29, pp. A1, A12, A13.

Barry, H., M. K. Bacon, and I. L. Child
1959   Relation of Child Training to Subsistence Economy. *American Anthropologist* 61: 51–63.

Barth, F.
1964   *Nomads of South Persia: The Basseri Tribe of the Khamseh Confederacy.* London: Allen & Unwin.

1968   (orig. 1958). Ecologic Relations of Ethnic Groups in Swat, North Pakistan. In *Man in Adaptation: The Cultural Present,* ed. Yehudi Cohen, pp. 324–331. Chicago: Aldine.

1969   *Ethnic Groups and Boundaries: The Social Organization of Cultural Difference.* London: Allen and Unwin.

Batalla, G. B.
1966   Conservative Thought in Applied Anthropology: A Critique. *Human Organization* 25: 89–92.

Bates, D. G.
2001   *Human Adaptive Strategies: Ecology, Culture, and Politics,* 2nd ed. Boston: Allyn & Bacon.

Bateson, M. C.
1984   *With a Daughter's Eye: A Memoir of Margaret Mead and Gregory Bateson.* New York: William Morrow.

Beckerman, S., and P. Valentine
2002   *Cultures of Multiple Fathers: The Theory and Practice of Partible Paternity in Lowland South America.* Gainesville, FL: University Press of Florida.

Beeman, W.

1986   *Language, Status, and Power in Iran.* Bloomington: Indiana University Press.

Begun, D. R., C. V. Ward, and M. D. Rose

1997   *Description: Function, Phylogeny, and Fossils: Miocene Hominoid Evolution and Adaptations.* New York: Plenum.

Behar, R.

1993   *Translated Woman: Crossing the Border with Esperanza's Story.* Boston: Beacon.

Behar, R., and D. A. Gordon, eds.

1995   *Women Writing Culture.* Berkeley: University of California Press.

Bell, W.

1981   Neocolonialism. In *Encyclopedia of Sociology,* p. 193. Guilford, CT: DPG Publishing.

Bellah, R. N.

1978   Religious Evolution. In *Reader in Comparative Religion: An Anthropological Approach,* 4th ed., ed. W. A. Lessa and E. Z. Vogt, pp. 36–50. New York: Harper & Row.

Benedict, B.

1970   Pluralism and Stratification. In *Essays in Comparative Social Stratification,* ed. L. Plotnicov and A. Tuden, pp. 29–41. Pittsburgh: University of Pittsburgh Press.

Benedict, R.

1940   *Race, Science and Politics.* New York: Modern Age Books.

1946   *The Chrysanthemum and the Sword.* Boston: Houghton Mifflin.

1959   (orig. 1934). *Patterns of Culture.* New York: New American Library.

Bennett, J. W.

1969   *Northern Plainsmen: Adaptive Strategy and Agrarian Life.* Chicago: Aldine.

Bennett, J. W., and J. R. Bowen, eds.

1988   *Production and Autonomy: Anthropological Studies and Critiques of Development.* Monographs in Economic Anthropology, no. 5, Society for Economic Anthropology. New York: University Press of America.

Berg, B. L.

1997   *Qualitative Research Methods for the Social Sciences,* 3rd ed. Boston: Allyn & Bacon.

Berkeleyan

1999   Berkeley Researchers Head Team That Discovers New Species of Human Ancestor: Earliest Evidence of Meat-Eating, Early Beings Has Been Unearthed in Ethiopia. April 28–May 4, pp. 27,32. http://www.berkeley.edu/news/berkeleyan/1999/0428/species.html.

Berlin, B. D., E. Breedlove, and P. H. Raven

1974   *Principles of Tzeltal Plant Classification: An Introduction to the Botanical Ethnography of a Mayan-Speaking People of Highland Chiapas.* New York: Academic Press.

Berlin, B. D., and P. Kay

1969   *Basic Color Terms: Their Universality and Evolution.* Berkeley: University of California Press.

1991   *Basic Color Terms: Their Universality and Evolution.* Berkeley, CA: University of California Press.

1992   *Basic Color Terms: Their Universality and Evolution,* 2nd ed. Berkeley: University of California Press.

1999   *Basic Color Terms: Their Universality and Evolution.* Stanford, CA: Center for the Study of Language and Information.

Bernard, H. R.

1994   *Research Methods in Cultural Anthropology,* 2nd ed. Thousand Oaks, CA: Sage.

2002   *Research Methods in Anthropology: Qualitative and Quantitative Methods,* 3rd ed. Walnut Creek, CA: AltaMira.

Bernard, H. R., ed.

1998   *Handbook of Methods in Cultural Anthropology.* Walnut Creek, CA: Altamira.

Berreman, G. D.

1962   Pahari Polyandry: A Comparison. *American Anthropologist* 64: 60–75.

1975   Himalayan Polyandry and the Domestic Cycle. *American Ethnologist* 2: 127–138.

Bettelheim, B.

1975   *The Uses of Enchantment: The Meaning and Importance of Fairy Tales.* New York: Vintage.

Binford, L. R.

1968   Post-Pleistocene Adaptations. In *New Perspectives in Archeology,* ed. S. R. Binford and L. R. Binford, pp. 313–341. Chicago: Aldine.

1981   *Bones: Ancient Men and Modern Myths.* New York: Academic Press.

Binford, L. R., and S. R. Binford
1979   Stone Tools and Human Behavior. In *Human Ancestors, Readings from Scientific American,* ed. G. L. Isaac and R. E. F. Leakey, pp. 92–101. San Francisco: W. H. Freeman.

Bird-David, N.
1992   Beyond "The Original Affluent Society": A Culturalist Reformulation. *Current Anthropology* 33(1): 25–47.

Birdsell, J. B.
1981   *Human Evolution: An Introduction to the New Physical Anthropology,* 3rd ed. Boston: HarperCollins.

Bjuremalm, H.
1997   Rättvisa kan skipas i Rwanda: Folkmordet 1994 går att förklara och analysera på samma sätt som förintelsen av judarna. *Dagens Nyheter* [06-03-1997, p. B3].

Blackwood, E.
2000   *Webs of Power: Women, Kin, and Community in a Sumatran Village.* Lanham, MD: Rowman and Littlefield.

Blackwood, E., and S. Wieringa, eds.
1999   *Female Desires: Same-Sex Relations and Transgender Practices across Cultures.* New York: Columbia University Press.

Blanton, R. E.
1999   *Ancient Oaxaca: The Monte Alban State.* New York: Cambridge University Press.

Blanton, R. E., S. A. Kowalewski, G. M. Feinman, and L. M. Finsten, eds.
1993   *Ancient Mesoamerica: A Comparison of Change in Three Regions,* 2nd ed. New York: Cambridge University Press.

Bloch, M., ed.
1975   *Political Language and Oratory in Traditional Societies.* London: Academic.

Blum, H. F.
1961   Does the Melanin Pigment of Human Skin Have Adaptive Value? *Quarterly Review of Biology* 36: 50–63.

Boas, F.
1966   (orig. 1940). *Race, Language, and Culture.* New York: Free Press.

Boaz, N. T.
1993   *Quarry: Closing In on the Missing Link.* New York: Free Press.

1997   *Eco Homo: How the Human Being Emerged from the Cataclysmic History of the Earth.* New York: Basic Books.

1999   *Essentials of Biological Anthropology.* Upper Saddle River, N.J.: Prentice-Hall.

Bock, P. K.
1980   *Continuities in Psychological Anthropology.* San Francisco: W. H. Freeman.

Bodley, J. H.
1985   *Anthropology and Contemporary Human Problems,* 2nd ed. Mountain View, CA: Mayfield.

1995   *Anthropology and Contemporary Human Problems,* 3rd ed. Mountain View, CA: Mayfield.

1999   *Victims of Progress,* 4th ed. Mountain View, CA: Mayfield.

2001   *Anthropology and Contemporary Human Problems,* 4th ed. Boston: McGraw-Hill.

Bodley, J. H., ed.
1988   *Tribal Peoples and Development Issues: A Global Overview.* Mountain View, CA: Mayfield.

Bogin, B.
1999   *Patterns of Human Growth,* 2nd ed. New York: Cambridge University Press.

2001   *The Growth of Humanity.* New York: Wiley-Liss.

Bogoras, W.
1904   The Chukchee. In *The Jesup North Pacific Expedition,* ed. F. Boas. New York: Memoir of the American Museum of Natural History.

Bogucki, P. I.
1988   *Forest Farmers and Stockherders: Early Agriculture and Its Consequences in North-Central Europe.* New York: Cambridge University Press.

Bohannan, P.
1955   Some Principles of Exchange and Investment among the Tiv. *American Anthropologist* 57: 60–70.

1971   Artist and Critic in an African Society. In *Anthropology and Art: Readings in Cross-Cultural Aesthetics,* ed. C. Otten, pp. 172–181. Austin: University of Texas Press.

1995   *How Culture Works.* New York: Free Press.

Bohannan, P., and J. Middleton, eds.
1968   *Marriage, Family, and Residence.* Garden City, NY: Natural History Press.

Bolton, R.
1981   Susto, Hostility, and Hypoglycemia. *Ethnology* 20(4): 227–258.

Bond, G. C., J. Kreniske, I. Susser, and J. Vincent, eds.
1996   *AIDS in Africa and the Caribbean.* Boulder, CO: Westview.

Bonvillain, N.
2001   *Women and Men: Cultural Constructions of Gender,* 3rd ed. Upper Saddle River, NJ: Prentice-Hall.

2003   *Language, Culture, and Communication: The Meaning of Messages,* 4th ed. Upper Saddle River, NJ: Prentice-Hall.

Borneman, J.
1998   *Subversions of International Order: Studies in the Political Anthropology of Culture.* Albany: State University of New York Press.

Boserup, E.
1965   *The Conditions of Agricultural Growth.* Chicago: Aldine.

1970   *Women's Role in Economic Development.* London: Allen and Unwin.

Bourdieu, P.
1977   *Outline of a Theory of Practice.* Translated by Richard Nice. Cambridge: Cambridge University Press.

1982   *Ce Que Parler Veut Dire.* Paris: Fayard.

1984   *Distinction: A Social Critique of the Judgment of Taste.* Translated by R. Nice. Cambridge, MA: Harvard University Press.

Bourguignon, E.
1979   *Psychological Anthropology: An Introduction to Human Nature and Cultural Differences.* New York: Harcourt Brace Jovanovich.

Bourque, S. C., and K. B. Warren
1981   *Women of the Andes: Patriarchy and Social Change in Two Peruvian Villages.* Ann Arbor: University of Michigan Press.

1987   Technology, Gender and Development. *Daedalus* 116(4): 173–197.

Bower, J., and D. Lubell, eds.
1988   *Prehistoric Cultures and Environments in the Late Quaternary of Africa.* Cambridge Monographs in African Archaeology, 26. Oxford, England: B.A.R.

Brace, C. L.
1964   A Nonracial Approach towards the Understanding of Human Diversity. In *The Concept of Race,* ed. A. Montagu, pp. 103–152. New York: Free Press.

1995   *The Stages of Human Evolution,* 5th ed. Englewood Cliffs, NJ: Prentice-Hall.

2000   *Evolution in an Anthropological View.* Walnut Creek, CA: AltaMira.

Brace, C. L., and F. B. Livingstone
1971   On Creeping Jensenism. In *Race and Intelligence,* ed. C. L. Brace, G. R. Gamble, and J. T. Bond, pp. 64–75. Anthropological Studies, no. 8. Washington, DC: American Anthropological Association.

Bradley, C., C. Moore, M. Burton, and D. White
1990   A Cross-Cultural Historical Analysis of Subsistence Change. *American Anthropologist* 92(2): 447–457.

Brady, I., ed.
1983   Special Section: Speaking in the Name of the Real: Freeman and Mead on Samoa. *American Anthropologist* 85: 908–947.

Braidwood, R. J.
1975   *Prehistoric Men,* 8th ed. Glenview, IL: Scott, Foresman.

Braudel, F.
1973   *Capitalism and Material Life: 1400–1800.* Translated by M. Kochan. London: Weidenfeld and Nicolson.

1981   *Civilization and Capitalism, 15th–18th Century.* Volume I: *The Structure of Everyday Life: The Limits.* Translated by S. Reynolds. New York: Harper & Row.

1982   *Civilization and Capitalism, 15th–18th Century.* Volume II: *The Wheels of Commerce.* New York: HarperCollins.

1984   *Civilization and Capitalism, 15th–18th Century.* Volume III: *The Perspective of the World.* New York: HarperCollins.

1992   *Civilization and Capitalism, 15th–18th Century.* Volume III: *The Perspective of the World.* Berkeley, CA: University of California Press.

Brenneis, D.

1988 Language and Disputing. *Annual Review of Anthropology* 17: 221–237.

Brim, J. A., and D. H. Spain

1974 *Research Design in Anthropology.* New York: Harcourt Brace Jovanovich.

Brogger, J.

1992 *Nazaré: Women and Men in a Prebureaucratic Portuguese Fishing Village.* Fort Worth: Harcourt Brace.

Bronfenbrenner, U.

1975 Nature with Nurture: A Reinterpretation of the Evidence. In *Race and IQ,* ed. A. Montagu, pp. 114–144. New York: Oxford University Press.

Brooke, J.

1992 Rio's New Day in Sun Leaves Laplander Limp. *New York Times,* June 1, p. A7.

Brown, D.

1991 *Human Universals.* New York: McGraw-Hill.

Brown, J. K.

1975 Iroquois Women: An Ethnohistoric Note. In *Toward an Anthropology of Women,* ed. R. Reiter, pp. 235–251. New York: Monthly Review Press.

Brown, K. M.

2001 *Mama Lola: A Vodou Priestess in Brooklyn,* rev. ed. Berkeley: University of California Press.

Brown, P. J.

1998 *Understanding and Applying Medical Anthropology.* Boston: McGraw-Hill.

Brown, P. J., and V. Bentley-Condit

1996 Culture, Evolution, and Obesity. In *Obesity: Its Causes and Management,* eds. A. J. Stunkard and T. Wadden. New York: Raven Press.

Brown, P. J., and S. V. Krick

2001 Culture and Economy in the Etiology of Obesity: Diet, Television and the Illusions of Personal Choice. Atlanta, GA: Emory University MARIAL Center, Working Paper 003-01.

Brown, R. W.

1958 *Words and Things.* Glencoe, IL: Free Press.

Brumfiel, E. M.

1980 Specialization, Market Exchange, and the Aztec State: A View from Huexotla. *Current Anthropology* 21(4): 459–478.

Bryant, B., and P. Mohai

1991 Race, Class, and Environmental Quality in the Detroit Area. In *Environmental Racism: Issues and Dilemmas,* ed. B. P. Bryant and Mohai. Ann Arbor: University of Michigan Office of Minority Affairs.

Bryson, K.

1996 Household and Family Characteristics: March 1995, P20-488, November 26, 1996. United States Department of Commerce, Bureau of Census, Public Information Office, CB96-195.

Buchler, I. R., and H. A. Selby

1968 *Kinship and Social Organization: An Introduction to Theory and Method.* New York: Macmillan.

Burke, P., and R. Porter

1987 *The Social History of Language.* Cambridge: Cambridge University Press.

Burley, D. V., and W. R. Dickinson

2001 Origin and Significance of a Founding Settlement in Polynesia. *Proceedings of the National Academy of Sciences* 98: 11829–11831.

Burling, R.

1970 *Man's Many Voices: Language in Its Cultural Context.* New York: Harcourt Brace Jovanovich.

Burns, J. F.

1992a Bosnian Strife Cuts Old Bridges of Trust. *New York Times,* May 22, pp. A1, A6.

1992b A Serb, Fighting Serbs, Defends Sarajevo. *New York Times,* July 12, section 4, p. E3.

Burton, F. D., and M. Eaton

1995a *The Multimedia Guide to Non-Human Primates.* Upper Saddle River, NJ: Prentice-Hall. A CD-ROM combining photos, illustrations, video, sound, and text—presenting over 200 species of nonhuman primates.

1995b *The Guide to Non-Human Primates.* Englewood Cliffs, NJ: Prentice-Hall. The print version of the above.

Buvinic, M.

1995 The Feminization of Poverty? Research and Policy Needs. In *Reducing Poverty through Labour Market Policies.* Geneva: International Institute for Labour Studies.

Caldeira, T. P. R.

1996 Fortified Enclaves: The New Urban Segregation. *Public Culture* 8(2): 303–328.

Calhoun, C., D. Light, and S. Keller
1997   *Sociology,* 7th ed. New York: McGraw-Hill.

Campbell, B. G.
1998   *Human Evolution: An Introduction to Man's Adaptations,* 4th ed. New York: Aldine de Gruyter.

Campbell, B. G., and J. D. Loy, eds.
2000   *Humankind Emerging,* 8th ed. New York: Longman.

Cann, R. L., M. Stoneking, and A. C. Wilson
1987   Mitochondrial DNA and Human Evolution. *Nature* 325: 31–36.

Carneiro, R. L.
1956   Slash-and-Burn Agriculture: A Closer Look at Its Implications for Settlement Patterns. In *Men and Cultures,* Selected Papers of the Fifth International Congress of Anthropological and Ethnological Sciences, pp. 229–234. Philadelphia: University of Pennsylvania Press.

1968   (orig. 1961). Slash-and-Burn Cultivation among the Kuikuru and Its Implications for Cultural Development in the Amazon Basin. In *Man in Adaptation: The Cultural Present,* ed. Y. A. Cohen, pp. 131–145. Chicago: Aldine.

1970   A Theory of the Origin of the State. *Science* 69: 733–738.

1990   Chiefdom-Level Warfare as Exemplified in Fiji and the Cauca Valley. In *The Anthropology of War,* ed. J. Haas, pp. 190–211. Cambridge: Cambridge University Press.

1991   The Nature of the Chiefdom as Revealed by Evidence from the Cauca Valley of Colombia. In *Profiles in Cultural Evolution,* ed. A. T. Rambo and K. Gillogly, *Anthropological Papers* 85, pp. 167–190. Ann Arbor: University of Michigan Museum of Anthropology.

Carrier, J.
1995   *De Los Otros: Intimacy and Homosexuality among Mexican Men: Hidden in the Blood.* New York: Columbia University Press.

Carter, J.
1988   Freed from Keepers and Cages, Chimps Come of Age on Baboon Island. *Smithsonian,* June, pp. 36–48.

Cartmill, M.
1974   Rethinking Primate Origins. *Science* (April 26): 436–437.

1992   New Views on Primate Origins. *Evolutionary Anthropology* 1: 105–111.

Carver, T.
1996   *Gender Is Not a Synonym for Women.* Boulder, CO: Lynne Reinner.

Casper, L., and K. Bryson
1998   Growth in Single Fathers Outpaces Growth in Single Mothers, Census Bureau Reports. http://www.census.gov/Press-Release/cb98-228.html.

Casson, R.
1983   Schemata in Cognitive Anthropology. *Annual Review of Anthropology* 12: 429–462.

Cavalli-Sforza, L. L.
1977   *Elements of Human Genetics,* 2nd ed. Menlo Park, CA: W. A. Benjamin.

2000   *Genes, Peoples, and Languages.* Translated from the Italian by M. Seielstad. New York: North Point.

Cavalli-Sforza, L. L., P. Menozzi, and A. Piazza
1994   *The History and Geography of Human Genes.* Princeton, NJ: Princeton University Press.

Cernea, M., ed.
1991   *Putting People First: Sociological Variables in Rural Development,* 2nd ed. New York: Oxford University Press (published for the World Bank).

Cernea, M., and C. McDowell, eds.
2000   *Risks and Reconstruction: Experiences of Resettlers and Refugees.* Washington, DC: World Bank.

Chagnon, N. A.
1968   *Yanomamo: The Fierce People.* New York: Holt, Rinehart, and Winston.

1992   (orig. 1983) *Yanomamo: The Fierce People,* 4th ed. New York: Harcourt Brace.

1997   *Yanomamö,* 5th ed. Fort Worth: Harcourt Brace.

Chagnon, N. A., and W. Irons, eds.
1979   *Evolutionary Biology and Human Social Behavior: An Anthropological Perspective.* North Scituate, MA: Duxbury.

Chambers, E.
1985   *Applied Anthropology: A Practical Guide.* Englewood Cliffs, NJ: Prentice-Hall.

1987   Applied Anthropology in the Post-Vietnam Era: Anticipations and Ironies. *Annual Review of Anthropology* 16: 309–337.

2000   *Native Tours: The Anthropology of Travel and Tourism.* Prospect Heights, IL: Waveland.

Chambers, E., ed.
1997   *Tourism and Culture: An Applied Perspective.* Albany: State University of New York Press.

Champion, T., and C. Gamble, eds.
1984   *Prehistoric Europe.* New York: Academic Press.

Chang, K. C.
1977   *The Archaeology of Ancient China.* New Haven, CT: Yale University Press.

Chatty, D.
1996   *Mobile Pastoralists: Development Planning and Social Change in Oman.* New York: Columbia University Press.

Cheater, A. P., ed.
1999   *The Anthropology of Power: Empowerment and Disempowerment in Changing Structures.* New York: Routledge.

Cheney, D. L., and R. M. Seyfarth
1990   In the Minds of Monkeys: What Do They Know and How Do They Know It? *Natural History,* September, pp. 38–46.

Cheney, D. L., R. M. Seyfarth, B. B. Smuts, and R. W. Wrangham
1987   The Study of Primate Societies. In *Primate Societies,* ed. B. B. Smuts, D. L. Cheney, R. M. Seyfarth, R. W. Wrangham, and T. T. Struhsaker, pp. 1–8. Chicago: University of Chicago Press.

Cherlin, A. J.
1992   *Marriage, Divorce, Remarriage.* Cambridge, MA: Harvard University Press.

Child, A. B., and I. L. Child
1993   *Religion and Magic in the Lives of Traditional Peoples.* Englewood Cliffs, NJ: Prentice-Hall.

Childe, V. G.
1951   *Man Makes Himself.* New York: New American Library.

Chiseri-Strater, E., and B. S. Sunstein
2002   *Fieldworking: Reading and Writing Research,* 2nd ed. Upper Saddle River, NJ: Prentice-Hall.

Chomsky, N.
1955   *Syntactic Structures.* The Hague: Mouton.

Cigno, A.
1994   *Economics of the Family.* New York: Oxford University Press.

Ciochon, R. L.
1983   Hominoid Cladistics and the Ancestry of Modern Apes and Humans. In *New Interpretations of Ape and Human Ancestry,* ed. R. L. Ciochon and R. S. Corruccini, pp. 783–843. New York: Plenum.

Ciochon, R. L., J. Olsen, and J. James
1990   *Other Origins: The Search for the Giant Ape in Human Prehistory.* New York: Bantam Books.

Clammer, J., ed.
1976   *The New Economic Anthropology.* New York: St. Martin's.

Clark, J. D., and S. A. Brandt
1984   *From Hunters to Farmers: The Causes and Consequences of Food Production in Africa.* Berkeley: University of California Press.

Clarke, S. C.
1995   Advance Report of Final Divorce Statistics, 1989 and 1990. *Monthly Vital Statistics Report,* v. 43, nos. 8, 9. Hyattsville, MD: National Center for Health Statistics.

Clifford, J.
1982   *Person and Myth: Maurice Leenhardt in the Melanesian World.* Berkeley: University of California Press.

1988   *The Predicament of Culture: Twentieth-Century Ethnography, Literature, and Art.* Cambridge, MA: Harvard University Press.

Clifton, J. A.
1970   *Applied Anthropology: Readings in the Uses of the Science of Man.* Boston: Houghton Mifflin.

Coates, J.
1986   *Women, Men, and Language.* London: Longman.

Cody, D.
1998   British Empire. http://www.stg.brown.edu/ projects/hypertext/landow/victorian/history/ Empire.htm1, May 18.

Coe, M. D., and K. Flannery
1964   Microenvironments and Mesoamerican Prehistory. *Science* 143: 650–654.

Cohen, M.
1998   *Culture of Intolerance: Chauvinism, Class, and Racism.* New Haven, CT: Yale University Press.

Cohen, M. N., and G. J. Armelagos, eds.
1984   *Paleopathology at the Origins of Agriculture.* New York: Academic Press.

Cohen, Roger

1995   Serbs Shift Opens a Chance for Peace, a U.S. Envoy Says. *New York Times*, September 1, pp. A1, A6.

Cohen, Ronald

1967   *The Kanuri of Bornu.* New York: Harcourt Brace Jovanovich.

Cohen, Ronald, and E. R. Service, eds.

1978   *Origins of the State: The Anthropology of Political Evolution.* Philadelphia: Institute for the Study of Human Issues.

Cohen, Y. A.

1974*a*   *Man in Adaptation: The Cultural Present,* 2nd ed. Chicago: Aldine.

1974*b*   Culture as Adaptation. In *Man in Adaptation: The Cultural Present,* 2nd ed., ed. Y. A. Cohen, pp. 45–68. Chicago: Aldine.

Cole, S.

1975   *Leakey's Luck: The Life of Louis Bazett Leakey, 1903–1972.* New York: Harcourt Brace Jovanovich.

Collier, J. F.

1997   *From Duty to Desire: Remaking Families in a Spanish Village.* Princeton, NJ: Princeton University Press.

Collier, J. F., ed.

1988   *Marriage and Inequality in Classless Societies.* Stanford, CA: Stanford University Press.

Collier, J. F., and S. J. Yanagisako, eds.

1987   *Gender and Kinship: Essays toward a Unified Analysis.* Stanford, CA: Stanford University Press.

Collins, T. W.

1989   Rural Economic Development in Two Tennessee Counties: A Racial Dimension. Paper presented at the annual meetings of the American Anthropological Association, Washington, DC.

Colson, E.

1971   *The Social Consequences of Resettlement: The Impact of the Kariba Resettlement on the Gwembe Tonga.* Manchester, England: Manchester University Press.

Colson, E., and T. Scudder

1975   New Economic Relationships between the Gwembe Valley and the Line of Rail. In *Town and Country in Central and Eastern Africa,* ed.

David Parkin, pp. 190–210. London: Oxford University Press.

1988   *For Prayer and Profit: The Ritual, Economic, and Social Importance of Beer in Gwembe District, Zambia, 1950–1982.* Stanford, CA: Stanford University Press.

Comaroff, J.

1982   Dialectical Systems, History and Anthropology: Units of Study and Questions of Theory. *Journal of Southern African Studies* 8: 143–172.

Combs-Schilling, E.

1989   *Sacred Performances: Islam, Sexuality, and Sacrifice.* New York: Columbia University Press.

Conkey, M., O. Soffer, D. Stratmann, and N. Jablonski

1997   *Beyond Art: Pleistocene Image and Symbol.* San Francisco: Memoirs of the California Academy of Sciences, no. 23.

Conklin, H. C.

1954   *The Relation of Hanunóo Culture to the Plant World.* Unpublished Ph.D. dissertation, Yale University.

Connah, G.

1987   *African Civilizations.* New York: Cambridge University Press.

Connell, R. W.

1995   *Masculinities.* Berkeley: University of California Press.

2002   *Gender.* Malden, MA: Blackwell.

Connor, W.

1972   Nation-Building or Nation Destroying. *World Politics* 24(3): 319–355.

Cook-Gumperz, J.

1986   *The Social Construction of Literacy.* Cambridge: Cambridge University Press.

Cooper, F., and A. L. Stoler

1989   Introduction, Tensions of Empire: Colonial Control and Visions of Rule. *American Ethnologist* 16: 609–621.

Cooper, F., and A. L. Stoler, eds.

1997   *Tensions of Empire: Colonial Cultures in a Bourgeois World.* Berkeley: University of California Press.

Coote, J., and A. Shelton, eds.

1992   *Anthropology, Art, and Aesthetics.* New York: Oxford University Press.

Crane, J. G., and M. V. Angrosino
1992   *Field Projects in Anthropology: A Student Handbook*, 3rd ed. Prospect Heights, IL: Waveland.

Crick, F. H. C.
1968   (orig. 1962). The Genetic Code. In *The Molecular Basis of Life: An Introduction to Molecular Biology, Readings from Scientific American*, pp. 198–205. San Francisco: W. H. Freeman.

Critser, G.
2003   *Fat Land: How Americans Became the Fattest People in the World.* Boston: Houghton Mifflin.

Crosby, A. W., Jr.
1972   *The Columbian Exchange: Biological and Cultural Consequences of 1492.* Westport, CT: Greenwood Press.

1986   *Ecological Imperialism: The Biological Expansion of Europe, 900–1900.* New York: Cambridge University Press.

1994   *Germs, Seeds & Animals: Studies in Ecological History.* Armonk, NY: M.E. Sharpe.

Cultural Survival Inc.
1992   *At the Threshold.* Cambridge, MA: Cultural Survival. Originally published as the Spring 1992 issue of *Cultural Survival Quarterly.*

Cultural Survival Quarterly
        Quarterly journal. Cambridge, MA: Cultural Survival.

Cunliffe, B., ed.
1998   *Prehistoric Europe: An Illustrated History.* New York: Oxford University Press.

Dahlberg, F., ed.
1981   *Woman the Gatherer.* New Haven, CT: Yale University Press.

Dalton, G., ed.
1967   *Tribal and Peasant Economies.* Garden City, NY: Natural History Press.

DaMatta, R.
1991   *Carnivals, Rogues, and Heroes: An Interpretation of the Brazilian Dilemma.* Translated from the Portuguese by John Drury. Notre Dame, IN: University of Notre Dame Press.

D'Andrade, R.
1984   Cultural Meaning Systems. In *Culture Theory: Essays on Mind, Self, and Emotion,* ed. R. A. Shweder and R. A. Levine, pp. 88–119. Cambridge: Cambridge University Press.

1995   *The Development of Cognitive Anthropology.* New York: Cambridge University Press.

Darwin, C.
1958   (orig. 1859). *On the Origin of Species.* New York: Dutton.

Darwin, E.
1796   (orig. 1794). *Zoonomia, Or the Laws of Organic Life,* 2nd ed. London: J. Johnson.

Das, V.
1995   *Critical Events: An Anthropological Perspective on Contemporary India.* New York: Oxford University Press.

Davis, D. L., and R. G. Whitten
1987   The Cross-Cultural Study of Human Sexuality. *Annual Review of Anthropology* 16: 69–98.

Degler, C.
1970   *Neither Black nor White: Slavery and Race Relations in Brazil and the United States.* New York: Macmillan.

Delamont, S.
1995   *Appetites and Identities: An Introduction to the Social Anthropology of Western Europe.* London: Routledge.

Delson, E., ed.
1985   *Ancestors: The Hard Evidence.* New York: Alan R. Liss.

DeLumley, H.
1976   (orig. 1969). A Paleolithic Camp at Nice. In *Avenues to Antiquity, Readings from Scientific American,* ed. B. M. Fagan, pp. 36–44. San Francisco: W. H. Freeman.

DeMarco, E.
1997   New Dig at 9,000-Year-Old City Is Changing Views on Ancient Life. www.nytimes.com, November 11.

Dentan, R. K.
1979   *The Semai: A Nonviolent People of Malaya,* fieldwork edition. New York: Harcourt Brace.

Desjarlais, R., L. Eisenberg, B. Good, and A. Kleinman, eds.
1995   *World Mental Health: Problems and Priorities in Low-Income Countries.* New York: Oxford University Press.

Despres, L., ed.
1975   *Ethnicity and Resource Competition.* The Hague: Mouton.

DeVita, P. R., and J. D. Armstrong, eds.
2002   *Distant Mirrors: America as a Foreign Culture,*
        3rd ed. Belmont, CA: Wadsworth.

De Vos, G. A.
1971   *Japan's Outcastes: The Problem of the Burakumin.*
        London: Minority Rights Group.

De Vos, G. A., and H. Wagatsuma
1966   *Japan's Invisible Race: Caste in Culture and
        Personality.* Berkeley: University of California
        Press.

**De Vos, G. A., W. O. Wetherall,
and K. Stearman**
1983   *Japan's Minorities: Burakumin, Koreans, Ainu and
        Okinawans.* Report no. 3. London: Minority
        Rights Group.

De Waal, F. B. M.
1995   Bonobo Sex and Society: The Behavior of a
        Close Relative Challenges Assumptions about
        Male Supremacy in Human Evolution.
        Scientific American, March, pp. 82–88.

1997   *Bonobo: The Forgotten Ape.* Berkeley: University
        of California Press.

1999   *Chimpanzee Politics: Power and Sex among
        Apes,* rev. ed. Baltimore: Johns Hopkins
        University Press.

Diamond, J. M.
1989   Blood, Genes, and Malaria. *Natural History,*
        February, pp. 8–18.

1990   A Pox upon Our Genes. *Natural History,*
        February, pp. 26–30.

1997   *Guns, Germs, and Steel: The Fates of Human
        Societies.* New York: W.W. Norton.

**Dibble, H. L., S. P. McPherron,
and B. J. Roth**
1999   *Virtual Dig: A Simulated Archaeological
        Excavation of a Middle Paleolithic Site in France.*
        Boston: McGraw-Hill.

Di Leonardo, M., ed.
1991   *Gender at the Crossroads of Knowledge: Feminist
        Anthropology in the Postmodern Era.* Berkeley:
        University of California Press.

Divale, W. T., and M. Harris
1976   Population, Warfare, and the Male Supremacist
        Complex. *American Anthropologist* 78: 521–538.

**Dobzhansky, T., F. J. Ayala,
G. L. Stebbins, and J. W. Valentine**
1977   *Evolution.* San Francisco: W. H. Freeman.

Dolhinow, P., and A. Fuentes, eds.
1999   *The Nonhuman Primates.* Mountain View, CA:
        Mayfield.

Douglass, W. A.
1969   *Death in Murelaga: Funerary Ritual in a Spanish
        Basque Village.* Seattle: University of
        Washington Press.

1975   *Echalar and Murelaga: Opportunity and Rural
        Exodus in Two Spanish Basque Villages.* London:
        C. Hurst

1992   Basques. *Encyclopedia of World Cultures,*
        ed. L. Bennett, vol. 4. Boston: GK Hall.
        http://ets.umdl.umich.edu/cgi/e/ehraf/
        ehraf-idx?c=ehrafe&view=owc&owc=EX08.

Downes, W.
1998   *Language and Society,* 2nd ed. New York:
        Cambridge University Press.

Draper, P.
1975   !Kung Women: Contrasts in Sexual
        Egalitarianism in Foraging and Sedentary
        Contexts. In *Toward an Anthropology of Women,*
        ed. R. Reiter, pp. 77–109. New York: Monthly
        Review Press.

Drennan, R. D., and C. A. Uribe, eds.
1987   *Chiefdoms in the Americas.* Landon, MD:
        University Press of America.

Dunn, J. S.
2000   *The Impact of Media on Reproductive Behavior
        in Northeastern Brazil.* Ph.D. dissertation,
        Department of Anthropology, University
        of Michigan, Ann Arbor.

Durkheim, E.
1951   (orig. 1897). *Suicide: A Study in Sociology.*
        Glencoe, IL: Free Press.

1961   (orig. 1912). *The Elementary Forms of the
        Religious Life.* New York: Collier Books.

Dwyer, K.
1982   *Moroccan Dialogues: Anthropology in Question.*
        Baltimore: Johns Hopkins University Press.

Eagleton, T.
1983   *Literary Theory: An Introduction.* Minneapolis:
        University of Minnesota Press.

Earle, T. K.
1987   Chiefdoms in Archaeological and
        Ethnohistorical Perspective. *Annual Review of
        Anthropology* 16: 279–308.

1991   *Chiefdoms: Power, Economy, and Ideology.* New York: Cambridge University Press.

1997   *How Chiefs Come to Power: The Political Economy in Prehistory.* Stanford, CA: Stanford University Press.

Eastman, C. M.
1975   *Aspects of Language and Culture.* San Francisco: Chandler and Sharp.

Echeverria, J.
1999   *Home away from Home: A History of Basque Boardinghouses.* Reno: University of Nevada Press.

Eckert, P.
1989   *Jocks and Burnouts: Social Categories and Identity in the High School.* New York: Teachers College Press, Columbia University.

2000   *Linguistic Variation as Social Practice: The Linguistic Construction of Identity in Belten High.* Malden, MA: Blackwell.

Eckert, P., and S. McConnell-Ginet
2003   *Language and Gender.* New York: Cambridge University Press.

Eckert, P., and J. R. Rickford, eds.
2001   *Style and Sociolinguistic Variation.* New York: Cambridge University Press.

Eddy, E. M., and W. L. Partridge, eds.
1987   *Applied Anthropology in America,* 2nd ed. New York: Columbia University Press.

Eder, J.
1987   *On the Road to Tribal Extinction: Depopulation, Deculturation, and Adaptive Well-Being among the Batak of the Philippines.* Berkeley: University of California Press.

Edgerton, R.
1965   "Cultural" versus "Ecological" Factors in the Expression of Values, Attitudes and Personality Characteristics. *American Anthropologist* 67: 442–447.

Eggert, K.
1988   Malafaly as Misnomer. In *Madagascar: Society and History,* ed. C. P. Kottak, J. A. Rakotoarisoa, A. Southall, and P. Verin, pp. 321–336. Durham, NC: Carolina Academic Press.

Eiseley, L.
1961   *Darwin's Century.* Garden City, NY: Doubleday, Anchor Books.

Eldredge, N.
1985   *Time Frames: The Rethinking of Darwinian Evolution and the Theory of Punctuated Equilibria.* New York: Simon & Schuster.

1997   *Fossils: The Evolution and Extinction of Species.* Princeton, NJ: Princeton University Press.

Ember, M., and C. R. Ember
1997   Science in Anthropology. In *The Teaching of Anthropology: Problems, Issues, and Decisions,* eds. C. P. Kottak, J. J. White, R. H. Furlow, and P. C. Rice, pp. 29–33. Mountain View, CA: Mayfield.

Erlanger, S.
1992   An Islamic Awakening in Central Asian Lands. *New York Times,* June 9, pp. A1, A7.

Errington, F., and D. Gewertz
1987   *Cultural Alternatives and a Feminist Anthropology: An Analysis of Culturally Constructed Gender Interests in Papua New Guinea.* New York: Cambridge University Press.

Escobar, A.
1991   Anthropology and the Development Encounter: The Making and Marketing of Development Anthropology. *American Ethnologist* 18: 658–682.

1994   Welcome to Cyberia: Notes on the Anthropology of Cyberculture. *Current Anthropology* 35(3): 211–231.

1995   *Encountering Development: The Making and Unmaking of the Third World.* Princeton, NJ: Princeton University Press.

Eskridge, W. N., Jr.
1996   *The Case for Same-Sex Marriage: From Sexual Liberty to Civilized Commitment.* New York: Free Press.

Evans-Pritchard, E. E.
1940   *The Nuer: A Description of the Modes of Livelihood and Political Institutions of a Nilotic People.* Oxford: Clarendon Press.

1970   Sexual Inversion among the Azande. *American Anthropologist* 72: 1428–1433.

Ezra, K.
1986   *A Human Ideal in African Art: Bamana Figurative Sculpture.* Washington, DC: Smithsonian Institution Press for the National Museum of African Art.

Fagan, B. M.

1987 *The Great Journey: The Peopling of Ancient America.* London: Thames and Hudson.

1996 *World Prehistory: A Brief Introduction.* New York: HarperCollins.

1998 *Clash of Cultures,* 2nd ed. Walnut Creek, CA: AltaMira.

2000 *Ancient Lives: An Introduction to Method and Theory in Archaeology.* Upper Saddle River, NJ: Prentice-Hall.

2001 *People of the Earth: A Brief Introduction to World Prehistory,* 11th ed. Upper Saddle River, NJ: Prentice-Hall.

2002 *Archaeology: A Brief Introduction,* 8th ed. Upper Saddle River, NJ: Prentice-Hall.

2002 *World Prehistory: A Brief Introduction,* 5th ed. Upper Saddle River, NJ: Prentice-Hall.

Falk, D.

2000 *Primate Diversity.* New York: W. W. Norton.

Farb, P., and G. Armelagos.

1980 *Consuming Passions: The Anthropology of Eating.* Boston: Literary Guild.

Farnsworth, C. H.

1992 Canada to Divide Its Northern Land. *New York Times,* May 6, p. A7.

Farooq, M.

1966 Importance of Determining Transmission Sites in Planning Bilharziasis Control: Field Observations from the Egypt-49 Project Area. *American Journal of Epidemiology* 83: 603–612.

Farr, D. M. L.

1980 British Empire. *Academic American Encyclopedia,* vol. 3, pp. 495–496. Princeton, NJ: Arete.

Fasold, R. W.

1990 *The Sociolinguistics of Language.* Oxford: Basil Blackwell.

Fedigan, L. M.

1992 *Primate Paradigms: Sex Roles and Social Bonds.* Chicago: University of Chicago Press.

Feinman, G. M., and T. D. Price

2001 *Archaeology at the Millennium: A Sourcebook.* New York: Kluwer Academic/Plenum.

Feld, S.

1990 *Sound and Sentiment: Birds, Weeping, Poetics, and Song in Kaluli Expression,* 2nd ed. Philadelphia: University of Pennsylvania Press.

1991 Voices of the Rainforest. *Public Culture* 4(1): 131–140.

Fenlason, L.

1990 Wolpoff Questions "Eve's" Origin Date, Says It Ignores Contradictory Fossil Data. *University Record* (University of Michigan, Ann Arbor) 45(21): 12.

Ferguson, J.

1994 *The Anti-Politics Machine: "Development," Depoliticization, and Bureaucratic Power in Lesotho.* Minneapolis: University of Minnesota Press.

Ferguson, R. B.

1995 *Yanomami Warfare: A Political History.* Santa Fe, NM: School of American Research.

2002 *The State, Identity, and Violence: Political Disintegration in the Post-Cold War Era.* New York: Routledge.

Ferguson, R. B., and N. L. Whitehead

1991 *War in the Tribal Zone: Expanding States and Indigenous Warfare.* Santa Fe, NM: School of American Research Press.

Ferraro, G. P.

2002 *The Cultural Dimension of International Business,* 4th ed. Upper Saddle River, NJ: Prentice-Hall.

Finkler, K.

1985 *Spiritualist Healers in Mexico: Successes and Failures of Alternative Therapeutics.* South Hadley, MA: Bergin and Garvey.

2000 *Experiencing the New Genetics: Family and Kinship on the Medical Frontier.* Philadelphia: University of Pennsylvania Press.

Finnstrom, S.

1997 Postcoloniality and the Postcolony: Theories of the Global and the Local. http://www.stg.brown.edu/projects/hypertext/landow/post/poldiscourse/finnstrom/finnstrom1.html.

Fisher, A.

1988a The More Things Change. *MOSAIC* 19(1): 22–33.

1988b On the Emergence of Humanness. *MOSAIC* 19(1): 34–45.

Fiske, J.

1989 *Understanding Popular Culture.* Boston: Unwin Hyman.

Flannery, K. V.

1969 Origins and Ecological Effects of Early Domestication in Iran and the Near East. In *The Domestication and Exploitation of Plants and Animals,* ed. P. J. Ucko and G. W. Dimbleby, pp. 73–100. Chicago: Aldine.

1972 The Cultural Evolution of Civilizations. *Annual Review of Ecology and Systematics* 3: 399–426.

1973 The Origins of Agriculture. *Annual Review of Anthropology* 2: 271–310.

1995 Prehistoric Social Evolution. In *Research Frontiers in Anthropology,* eds. C. R. Ember and M. Ember, pp. 1–26. Englewood Cliffs, NJ: Prentice-Hall.

1999 Chiefdoms in the Early Near East: Why It's So Hard to Identify Them. In *The Iranian World: Essays on Iranian Art and Archaeology,* eds. A. Alizadeh, Y. Majidzadeh, and S. M. Shahmirzadi. Tehran: Iran University Press.

Flannery, K. V., ed.

1986 *Guila Naquitz: Archaic Foraging and Early Agriculture in Oaxaca, Mexico.* Orlando, FL: Academic Press.

Flannery, K. V., and J. Marcus

2000 Formative Mexican Chiefdoms and the Myth of the "Mother Culture." *Journal of Anthropological Archaeology* 19: 1–37.

Flannery, K. V., J. Marcus, and R. G. Reynolds

1989 *The Flocks of the Wamani: A Study of Llama Herders on the Punas of Ayacucho, Peru.* San Diego: Academic Press.

Fleagle, J. G.

1999 *Primate Adaptation and Evolution,* 2nd ed. San Diego: Academic Press.

Fleagle, J. G., C. H. Janson, and K. E. Reed, eds.

1999 *Primate Communities.* New York: Cambridge University Press.

Fleisher, M. L.

1998 Cattle Raiding and Its Correlates: The Cultural-Ecological Consequences of Market-Oriented Cattle Raiding among the Kuria of Tanzania. *Human Ecology* 26(4): 547–572.

2000 *Kuria Cattle Raiders: Violence and Vigilantism on the Tanzania/Kenya Frontier.* Ann Arbor: University of Michigan Press.

Foley, W. A.

1997 *Anthropological Linguistics: An Introduction.* Cambridge, MA: Blackwell.

Ford, C. S., and F. A. Beach

1951 *Patterns of Sexual Behavior.* New York: Harper Torchbooks.

Forman, S., ed.

1994 *Diagnosing America: Anthropology and Public Engagement.* Ann Arbor: University of Michigan Press.

Fossey, D.

1981 The Imperiled Mountain Gorilla. *National Geographic* 159: 501–523.

1983 *Gorillas in the Mist.* Boston: Houghton Mifflin.

Foster, G. M.

1965 Peasant Society and the Image of Limited Good. *American Anthropologist* 67: 293–315.

Foster, G. M., and B. G. Anderson

1978 *Medical Anthropology.* New York: McGraw-Hill.

Foucault, M.

1979 *Discipline and Punish: The Birth of the Prison.* Translated by Alan Sheridan. New York: Vintage Books, University Press.

Fountain, H.

2002 Iceman's Last Meal. *New York Times,* September 17. http://www.nytimes.com/2002/09/17/science/17OBSE.html.

Fouts, R.

1997 *Next of Kin: What Chimpanzees Have Taught Me about Who We Are.* New York: William Morrow.

Fouts, R. S., D. H. Fouts, and T. E. Van Cantfort

1989 The Infant Loulis Learns Signs from Cross-Fostered Chimpanzees. In *Teaching Sign Language to Chimpanzees,* ed. R. A. Gardner, B. T. Gardner, and T. E. Van Cantfort, pp. 280–292. Albany: State University of New York Press.

Fox, J. W.

1987 *Maya Postclassic State Formation.* Cambridge: Cambridge University Press.

Fox, Richard. G., ed.

1990   Nationalist Ideologies and the Production of National Cultures. American Ethnological Society Monograph Series, no. 2. Washington, DC: American Anthropological Association.

Fox, Robin

1985   *Kinship and Marriage.* New York: Viking Penguin.

Frake, C. O.

1961   The Diagnosis of Disease among the Subanun of Mindanao. *American Anthropologist* 63: 113–132.

Franke, R.

1977   Miracle Seeds and Shattered Dreams in Java. In *Readings in Anthropology,* pp. 197–201. Guilford, CT: Dushkin.

Freeman, D.

1983   *Margaret Mead and Samoa: The Making and Unmaking of an Anthropological Myth.* Cambridge, MA: Harvard University Press.

Freilich, M., D. Raybeck, and J. Savishinsky

1991   *Deviance: Anthropological Perspectives.* Westport, CT: Bergin and Garvey.

French, H. W.

1992   Unending Exodus from the Caribbean, with the U.S. a Constant Magnet. *New York Times,* May 6, pp. A1, A8.

2002   Whistling Past the Global Graveyard. *New York Times,* July 14. http://www.nytimes.com/2002/07/14/weekinreview/14FREN.html.

Freud, S.

1950   (orig. 1918). *Totem and Taboo.* Translated by J. Strachey. New York: W. W. Norton.

Fricke, T.

1994   *Himalayan Households: Tamang Demography and Domestic Processes,* 2nd ed. New York: Columbia University Press.

Fried, M. H.

1960   On the Evolution of Social Stratification and the State. In *Culture in History,* ed. S. Diamond, pp. 713–731. New York: Columbia University Press.

1967   *The Evolution of Political Society: An Essay in Political Anthropology.* New York: McGraw-Hill.

Friedan, B.

1963   *The Feminine Mystique.* New York: Norton.

Friedl, E.

1975   *Women and Men: An Anthropologist's View.* New York: Harcourt Brace Jovanovich.

Friedman, J.

1994   *Cultural Identity and Global Process.* Thousand Oaks, CA: Sage.

Friedman, J., ed.

2002   *Globalization, the State, and Violence.* Walnut Creek, CA: Altamira.

Friedman, J., and M. J. Rowlands, eds.

1978   *The Evolution of Social Systems.* Pittsburgh: University of Pittsburgh Press.

Frisancho, A. R.

1975   Functional Adaptation to High Altitude Hypoxia. *Science* 187: 313–319.

1990   *Anthropometric Standards for the Evaluation of Growth and Nutritional Status.* Ann Arbor: University of Michigan Press.

1993   *Human Adaptation and Accommodation.* Ann Arbor: University of Michigan Press.

Futuyma, D. J.

1995   *Science on Trial,* updated ed. New York: Pantheon.

1998   *Evolutionary Biology.* Sunderland, MA: Sinauer Associates.

Gal, S.

1989   Language and Political Economy. *Annual Review of Anthropology* 18: 345–367.

Gamble, C.

1999   *The Palaeolithic Societies of Europe.* New York: Cambridge University Press.

2000   *Archaeology, the Basics.* New York: Routledge.

Garbarino, M. S., and R. F. Sasso

1994   *Native American Heritage,* 3rd ed. Prospect Heights, IL: Waveland.

Gardner, R. A., B. T. Gardner, and T. E. Van Cantfort, eds.

1989   *Teaching Sign Language to Chimpanzees.* Albany: State University of New York Press.

Gargan, E. A.

1992   A Single-Minded Man Battles to Free Slaves. *New York Times,* June 4, p. A7.

Geertz, C.

1973   *The Interpretation of Cultures.* New York: Basic Books.

1980   Blurred Genres: The Refiguration of Social Thought. *American Scholar* 29(2): 165–179.

1983   *Local Knowledge.* New York: Basic Books.

1995   *After the Fact: Two Countries, Four Decades, One Anthropologist.* Cambridge, MA: Harvard University Press.

Geis, M. L.
1987   *The Language of Politics.* New York: Springer-Verlag.

Gellner, E.
1983   *Nations and Nationalism.* Ithaca, NY: Cornell University Press.

1997   *Nationalism.* New York: New York University Press.

General Anthropology: Bulletin of the Council for General Anthropology

Gibbons, A.
2001   The Peopling of the Pacific. *Science* 291: 1735. http://www.eva.mpg.de/genetics/ Gibbons_Science2001.pdf.

Gibbs, N.
1989   How America Has Run Out of Time. *Time,* April 24, pp. 59–67.

Giddens, A.
1973   *The Class Structure of the Advanced Societies.* New York: Cambridge University Press.

Gilchrist, R.
1999   *Gender and Archaeology: Contesting the Past.* New York: Routledge.

Gillespie, J. H.
1998   *Population Genetics: A Concise Guide.* Baltimore: Johns Hopkins University Press.

Gilmore, D. D.
1987   *Aggression and Community: Paradoxes of Andalusian Culture.* New Haven, CT: Yale University Press.

1991   *Manhood in the Making: Cultural Concepts of Masculinity.* New Haven, CT: Yale University Press.

2001   *Misogyny: The Male Malady* Philadelphia: University of Pennsylvania Press.

Gilmore-Lehne, W. J.
2000   Pre-Sumerian Cultures: Natufian through Ubaid Eras: 10,500–3500 B.C.E. http://www.stockton.edu/~gilbmorew/ consorti/1bnear.htm.

Gledhill, J.
2000   *Power and Its Disguises: Anthropological Perspectives on Politics.* Sterling, VA: Pluto Press.

Glick-Schiller, N., and G. Fouron
1990   "Everywhere We Go, We Are in Danger": Ti Manno and the Emergence of Haitian Transnational Identity. *American Ethnologist* 17(2): 327–347.

Goldberg, D. T.
1997   *Racial Subjects: Writing on Race in America.* New York: Routledge.

Goldberg, D. T., ed.
1990   *Anatomy of Racism.* Minneapolis: University of Minnesota Press.

Golden, T.
1997   Oakland Revamps Plan to Teach Black English. *New York Times,* January 14. www.nytimes.com.

Goldschmidt, W.
1965   Theory and Strategy in the Study of Cultural Adaptability. *American Anthropologist* 67: 402–407.

Goodale, J., and J. D. Koss
1971   The Cultural Context of Creativity among Tiwi. In *Anthropology and Art: Readings in Cross-Cultural Aesthetics,* ed. C. Otten, pp.182–203. Austin, TX: University of Texas Press.

Goodall, J.
1968a   A Preliminary Report on Expressive Movements and Communication in Gombe Stream Chimpanzees. In *Primates: Studies in Adaptation and Variability,* ed. P. C. Jay, pp. 313–374. New York: Harcourt Brace Jovanovich.

1968b   The Behavior of Free Living Chimpanzees in the Gombe Stream Reserve. *Animal Behavior Monographs* 1: 161–311.

1986   *The Chimpanzees of Gombe: Patterns of Behavior.* Cambridge, MA: Belknap Press of Harvard University Press.

1988   *In the Shadow of Man,* rev. ed. Boston: Houghton Mifflin.

1996   *My Life with the Chimpanzees.* New York: Pocket Books.

Goodenough, W. H.
1953   *Native Astronomy in the Central Carolines.* Philadelphia: University of Pennsylvania Press.

Goodman, J., P. E. Lovejoy, and A. Sherratt
1995 *Consuming Habits: Drugs in History and Anthropology.* London: Routledge.

Goodman, M., M. L. Baba, and L. L. Darga
1983 The Bearings of Molecular Data on the Cladograms and Times of Divergence of Hominoid Lineages. In *New Interpretations of Ape and Human Ancestry,* ed. R. L. Ciochon and R. S. Corruccini, pp. 67–87. New York: Plenum.

Goody, J.
1977 *Production and Reproduction: A Comparative Study of the Domestic Domain.* New York: Cambridge University Press.

Goody, J., and S. T. Tambiah
1973 *Bridewealth and Dowry.* Cambridge: Cambridge University Press.

Gordon, A. A.
1996 *Transforming Capitalism and Patriarchy: Gender and Development in Africa.* Boulder, CO: Lynne Reinner.

Gorer, G.
1943 Themes in Japanese Culture. *Transactions of the New York Academy of Sciences* (Series II) 5: 106–124.

Gorman, C. F.
1969 Hoabinhian: A Pebble-Tool Complex with Early Plant Associations in Southeast Asia. *Science* 163: 671–673.

Gottdiener, M., ed.
2000 *New Forms of Consumption: Consumers, Culture, and Commodification.* Lanham, MD: Rowman and Littlefield.

Gough, E. K.
1959 The Nayars and the Definition of Marriage. *Journal of Royal Anthropological Institute* 89: 23–34.

Gould, S. J.
1996 *The Mismeasure of Man.* New York: Norton.

1999 *Rock of Ages: Science and Religion in the Fullness of Life.* New York: Ballantine Books.

Gowlett, J. A. J.
1993 *Ascent to Civilization: The Archaeology of Early Humans.* New York: McGraw-Hill.

Graburn, N.
1976 *Ethnic and Tourist Arts: Cultural Expressions from the Fourth World.* Berkeley: University of California Press.

Graburn, N., ed.
1971 *Readings in Kinship and Social Structure.* New York: Harper & Row.

Gramsci, A.
1971 *Selections from the Prison Notebooks.* Edited and translated by Quenten Hoare and Geoffrey Nowell Smith. London: Wishart.

Grasmuck, S., and P. Pessar
1991 *Between Two Islands: Dominican International Migration.* Berkeley: University of California Press.

Grassmuck, K.
1985 Local Educators Join Push for "a Computer in Every Classroom." *Ann Arbor News,* February 10, p. A11. (Quotes testimony of Linda Tarr-Whelan of the National Education Association to the House Committee on Science, Research and Technology.)

Gray, J.
1986 With a Few Exceptions, Television in Africa Fails to Educate and Enlighten. *Ann Arbor News,* December 8.

Gray, J. P.
1985 *Primate Sociobiology.* New Haven, CT: HRAF Press.

Greaves, T. C.
1995 Problems Facing Anthropologists: Cultural Rights and Ethnography. *General Anthropology* 1(2): 1, 3–6.

Green, E. C.
1992 (orig. 1987). The Integration of Modern and Traditional Health Sectors in Swaziland. In *Applying Anthropology,* ed. A. Podolefsky and P. J. Brown, pp. 246–251. Mountain View, CA: Mayfield.

Green, G. M., and R. W. Sussman
1990 Deforestation History of the Eastern Rain Forests of Madagascar from Satellite Images. *Science* 248: 212–215.

Greenwood, Davydd J.
1976 *Unrewarding Wealth: The Commercialization and Collapse of Agriculture in a Spanish Basque Town.* Cambridge, UK: Cambridge University Press.

Griffin, P. B., and A. Estioko-Griffin, eds.
1985   *The Agta of Northeastern Luzon: Recent Studies.* Cebu City, Philippines: University of San Carlos.

Gross, D.
1971   The Great Sisal Scheme. *Natural History,* March, pp. 49–55.

Gross, D., and B. Underwood
1971   Technological Change and Caloric Costs: Sisal Agriculture in Northeastern Brazil. *American Anthropologist* 73: 725–740.

Gudeman, S.
2001   *The Anthropology of Economy: Community, Market, and Culture.* Malden, MA: Blackwell.

Gudeman, S., ed.
1998   *Economic Anthropology.* Northhampton, MA: E. Elgar.

Gugliotta, G.
2002   Earliest Human Ancestor? Skull Dates to When Apes, Humans Split. *Washington Post,* July 11, p. A01.

Gulliver, P. H.
1974   (orig. 1965). The Jie of Uganda. In *Man in Adaptation: The Cultural Present,* 2nd ed., ed. Y. A. Cohen, pp. 323–345. Chicago: Aldine.

Gumperz, J. J.
1982   *Language and Social Identity.* Cambridge: Cambridge University Press.

Gumperz, J. J., and S. C. Levinson, eds.
1996   *Rethinking Linguistic Relativity.* New York: Cambridge University Press.

Gunther, E.
1971   Northwest Coast Indian Art. In *Anthropology and Art: Readings in Cross-Cultural Aesthetics,* ed. C. Otten, 318–340. Austin: University of Texas Press.

Guthrie, S.
1995   *Faces in the Clouds: A New Theory of Religion.* New York: Oxford University Press.

Gwynne, M. A.
2003   *Applied Anthropology: A Career-Oriented Approach.* Boston: Allyn & Bacon.

Haapala, A.
1998   Literature: Invention of the Self. *Canadian Aesthetics Journal* 2, http://tornade.ere.umontreal.ca/~guedon/AE/vol_2/haapala.html.

Hackett, R. I. J.
1996   *Art and Religion in Africa.* London: Cassell.

Hall, E. T.
1990   *Understanding Cultural Differences.* Yarmouth, ME: Intercultural Press.

1992   *An Anthropology of Everyday Life: An Autobiography.* New York: Doubleday.

Hall, T. D., ed.
1999   *A World-System Reader: New Perspectives on Gender, Urbanism, Cultures, Indigenous Peoples, and Ecology.* Lanham, MD: Rowman and Littlefield.

Hamburg, D. A., and E. R. McCown, eds.
1979   *The Great Apes.* Menlo Park, CA: Benjamin Cummings.

Hamilton, M. B.
1995   *The Sociology of Religion: Theoretical and Comparative Perspectives.* London: Routledge.

Hanks, W. F.
1995   *Language and Communicative Practices.* Boulder, CO: Westview.

Hansen, K. V., and A. I. Garey, eds.
1998   *Families in the U.S.: Kinship and Domestic Politics.* Philadelphia: Temple University Press.

Harcourt, A. H., D. Fossey, and J. Sabater-Pi
1981   Demography of *Gorilla gorilla. Journal of Zoology* 195: 215–233.

Harding, S.
1975   Women and Words in a Spanish Village. In *Toward an Anthropology of Women,* ed. R. Reiter, pp. 283–308. New York: Monthly Review Press.

Hargrove, E. C.
1986   *Religion and Environmental Crisis.* Athens, GA: University of Georgia Press.

Harlan, J. R., and D. Zohary
1966   Distribution of Wild Wheats and Barley. *Science* 153: 1074–1080.

Harlow, H.
1966   Development of Patterns of Affection in Macaques. *Yearbook of Physical Anthropology* 14: 1–7.

Harris, M.
1964   *Patterns of Race in the Americas.* New York: Walker.

1968   *The Rise of Anthropological Theory*. New York: Crowell.

1970   Referential Ambiguity in the Calculus of Brazilian Racial Identity. *Southwestern Journal of Anthropology* 26(1): 1–14.

1974   *Cows, Pigs, Wars, and Witches: The Riddles of Culture*. New York: Random House.

1978   *Cannibals and Kings*. New York: Vintage.

1989   *Our Kind: Who We Are, Where We Came from, Where We Are Going*. New York: Harper & Row.

Harris, M., and C. P. Kottak
1963   The Structural Significance of Brazilian Racial Categories. *Sociologia* 25: 203–209.

Harris, N. M., and G. Hillman
1989   *Foraging and Farming: The Evolution of Plant Exploitation*. London: Unwin Hyman.

Harrison, G. G., W. L. Rathje, and W. W. Hughes
1994   Food Waste Behavior in an Urban Population. In *Applying Anthropology: An Introductory Reader*, 3rd ed., ed. A. Podolefsky and P. J. Brown, pp. 107–112. Mountain View, CA: Mayfield.

Hart, C. W. M., A. R. Pilling, and J. C. Goodale
1988   *The Tiwi of North Australia*, 3rd ed. Fort Worth: Harcourt Brace.

Hartl, D. L.
1997   *Principles of Population Genetics*, 3rd ed. Sunderland, MA: Sinaeur.

2000   *A Primer of Population Genetics*, 3rd ed. Sunderland, MA: Sinauer Associates.

Hartl, D. L., and E. W. Jones
2002   *Essential Genetics*, 3rd ed. Sudbury, MA: Jones and Bartlett.

Harvey, D. J.
1980   French Empire. *Academic American Encyclopedia*, vol. 8, pp. 309–310. Princeton, NJ: Arete.

Harvey, K.
1996   Online for the Ancestors: The Importance of Anthropological Sensibility in Information Superhighway Design. *Social Science Computing Review* 14(1): 65–68.

Hassig, R.
1985   *Trade, Tribute, and Transportation: The Sixteenth-Century Political Economy of the Valley of Mexico*. Norman: University of Oklahoma Press.

Hastings, A.
1997   *The Construction of Nationhood: Ethnicity, Religion, and Nationalism*. New York: Cambridge University Press.

Hatcher, E. P.
1999   *Art as Culture: An Introduction to the Anthropology of Art*, 2nd ed. Westport, CT: Bergin & Garvey.

Hatfield, E., and R. L. Rapson
1996   *Love and Sex: Cross-Cultural Perspectives*. Needham Heights, MA: Allyn & Bacon.

Hausfater, G., and S. Hrdy, eds.
1984   *Infanticide: Comparative and Evolutionary Perspectives*. Hawthorne, NY: Aldine.

Hawkes, K., J. O'Connell, and K. Hill
1982   Why Hunters Gather: Optimal Foraging and the Aché of Eastern Paraguay. *American Ethnologist* 9: 379–398.

Hawley, J. S,. ed.
1993   *Sati, the Blessing and the Curse: The Burning of Wives in India*. New York: Oxford University Press.

Hayden, B.
1981   Subsistence and Ecological Adaptations of Modern Hunter/Gatherers. In *Omnivorous Primates: Gathering and Hunting in Human Evolution*, ed. R. S. Harding and G. Teleki, pp. 344–421. New York: Columbia University Press.

Headland, T. N., ed.
1992   *The Tasaday Controversy: Assessing the Evidence*. Washington, DC: American Anthropological Association.

Headland, T. N., and L. A. Reid
1989   Hunter-Gatherers and Their Neighbors from Prehistory to the Present. *Current Anthropology* 30: 43–66.

Heath, D. B., ed.
1995   *International Handbook on Alcohol and Culture*. Westport, CT: Greenwood Press.

Hedges, C.
1992*a*   Sudan Presses Its Campaign to Impose Islamic Law on Non-Muslims. *New York Times*, June 1, p. A7.

1992*b*   Sudan Gives Its Refugees a Desert to Contemplate. *New York Times*, June 3, p. A4.

Heider, K. G.

1988 The Rashomon Effect: When Ethnographers Disagree. *American Anthropologist* 90: 73–81.

1991 *Grand Valley Dani: Peaceful Warriors,* 2nd ed. Fort Worth: Harcourt Brace.

Heller, M.

1988 *Codeswitching: Anthropological and Sociolinguistic Perspectives.* Berlin: Mouton de Gruyter.

Helman, C.

2001 *Culture, Health, and Illness: An Introduction for Health Professionals,* 4th ed. Boston: Butterworth-Heinemann.

Henry, D. O.

1989 *From Foraging to Agriculture: The Levant at the End of the Ice Age.* Philadelphia: University of Pennsylvania Press.

1995 *Prehistoric Cultural Ecology and Evolution: Insights from Southern Jordan.* New York: Plenum Press.

Henry, J.

1955 Docility, or Giving Teacher What She Wants. *Journal of Social Issues* 2: 33–41.

Herdt, G.

1981 *Guardians of the Flutes.* New York: McGraw-Hill.

1986 *The Sambia: Ritual and Gender in New Guinea.* Fort Worth: Harcourt Brace.

Herdt, G. H., ed.

1984 *Ritualized Homosexuality in Melanesia.* Berkeley: University of California Press.

Herrnstein, R. J.

1971 I.Q. *Atlantic* 228(3): 43–64.

Herrnstein, R. J., and C. Murray

1994 *The Bell Curve: Intelligence and Class Structure in American Life.* New York: Free Press.

Hess, D. J.

1995 A Democratic Research Agenda in the Social Studies of the National Information Infrastructure. Paper prepared for the National Science Foundation Workshop on Culture, Society, and Advanced Information Technology. Washington, DC: May 31–June 1, 1995.

Hess, D. J., and R. A. DaMatta, eds.

1995 *The Brazilian Puzzle: Culture on the Borderlands of the Western World.* New York: Columbia University Press.

Hewitt, R.

1986 *White Talk, Black Talk.* Cambridge: Cambridge University Press.

Heyerdahl, T.

1971 *The Ra Expeditions.* Translated by P. Crampton. Garden City, NY: Doubleday.

Heyneman, D.

1984 Development and Disease: A Dual Dilemma. *Journal of Parasitology* 70: 3–17.

Hicks, D., ed.

2001 *Ritual and Belief: Readings in the Anthropology of Religion,* 2nd ed. Boston: McGraw-Hill.

Hill, C. E., ed.

1986 Current Health Policy Issues and Alternatives: An Applied Social Science Perspective. *Southern Anthropological Society Proceedings.* Athens, GA: University of Georgia Press.

Hill, J. H.

1978 Apes and Language. *Annual Review of Anthropology* 7: 89–112.

Hill, K., H. Kaplan, K. Hawkes, and A. Hurtado

1987 Foraging Decisions among Aché Hunter-Gatherers: New Data and Implications for Optimal Foraging Models. *Ethology and Sociobiology* 8: 1–36.

Hill-Burnett, J.

1978 Developing Anthropological Knowledge through Application. In *Applied Anthropology in America,* ed. E. M. Eddy and W. L. Partridge, pp. 112–128. New York: Columbia University Press.

Hinde, R. A.

1983 *Primate Social Relationships: An Integrated Approach.* Sunderland, MA: Sinaeur.

Hobhouse, L. T.

1915 *Morals in Evolution,* rev. ed. New York: Holt.

Hobsbawm, E. J.

1992 *Nations and Nationalism since 1780: Programme, Myth, Reality,* 2nd ed. New York: Cambridge University Press.

Hoebel, E. A.

1954 *The Law of Primitive Man.* Cambridge, MA: Harvard University Press.

1968 (orig. 1954). The Eskimo: Rudimentary Law in a Primitive Anarchy. In *Studies in Social and Cultural Anthropology,* ed. J. Middleton, pp. 93–127. New York: Crowell.

Hole, F., K. V. Flannery, and J. A. Neely
1969   *The Prehistory and Human Ecology of the Deh Luran Plain.* Memoir no. 1. Ann Arbor: University of Michigan Museum of Anthropology.

Holland, D., and N. Quinn, eds.
1987   *Cultural Models in Language and Thought.* Cambridge: Cambridge University Press.

Holloway, R. L.
1975   (orig. 1974). The Casts of Fossil Hominid Brains. In *Biological Anthropology, Readings from Scientific American,* ed. S. H. Katz, pp. 69–78. San Francisco: W. H. Freeman.

Holmes, L. D.
1987   *Quest for the Real Samoa: The Mead/Freeman Controversy and Beyond.* South Hadley, MA: Bergin and Garvey.

Holtzman, J.
2000   *Nuer Journeys, Nuer Lives.* Boston: Allyn & Bacon.

Hopkins, T. K.
1996   *The Age of Transition: Trajectory of the World-System 1945–2025.* Atlantic Highlands, NJ: Zed.

Hopkins, T., and I. Wallerstein
1982   Patterns of Development of the Modern World System. In *World System Analysis: Theory and Methodology,* by T. Hopkins, I. Wallerstein, R. Bach, C. Chase-Dunn, and R. Mukherjee, pp. 121–141. Thousand Oaks, CA: Sage.

Horton, R.
1963   The Kalabari Ekine Society: A Borderland of Religion and Art. *Africa* 33: 94–113.

1993   *Patterns of Thought in Africa and the West: Essays on Magic, Religion, and Science.* New York: Cambridge University Press.

Hostetler, J., and G. E. Huntington
1992   *Amish Children: Education in the Family,* 2nd ed. Fort Worth: Harcourt Brace.

1996   *The Hutterites in North America,* 3rd ed. Fort Worth: Harcourt Brace.

Howells, W. W.
1976   Explaining Modern Man: Evolutionists versus Migrationists. *Journal of Human Evolution* 5: 477–496.

Hughes, R., Jr.
1996   Demographics of Divorce. http://www.hec.ohio-state.edu/famlife/divorce/demo.htm.

Human Organization
        Quarterly journal. Oklahoma City: Society for Applied Anthropology.

Hutchinson, S.E.
1996   *Nuer Dilemmas: Coping with Money, War, and the State.* Berkeley: University of California Press.

Ingold, T., D. Riches, and J. Woodburn
1991   *Hunters and Gatherers.* New York: Berg (St. Martin's).

Ingraham, C.
1999   *White Weddings: Romancing Heterosexuality in Popular Culture.* New York: Routledge.

Inhorn, M. C., and P. J. Brown
1990   The Anthropology of Infectious Disease. *Annual Review of Anthropology* 19: 89–117.

Irving, W. N.
1985   Context and Chronology of Early Man in the Americas. *Annual Review of Anthropology* 14: 529–555.

Isaac, G. L.
1972   Early Phases of Human Behavior: Models in Lower Paleolithic Archaeology. In *Models in Archaeology,* ed. D. L. Clarke, pp. 167–199. London: Methuen.

1978   Food Sharing and Human Evolution: Archaeological Evidence from the Plio-Pleistocene of East Africa. *Journal of Anthropological Research* 34: 311–325.

Ives, E. D.
1995   *The Tape-Recorded Interview: A Manual for Fieldworkers in Folklore and Oral History,* 2nd. ed. Knoxville: University of Tennessee Press.

Jackson, B.
1987   *Fieldwork.* Champaign-Urbana: University of Illinois Press.

Jacoby, R., and N. Glauberman, eds.
1995   *The Bell Curve Debate: History, Documents, Opinions.* New York: Free Press. New York: Random House Times Books.

Jameson, F.
1984   Postmodernism, or the Cultural Logic of Late Capitalism. *New Left Review* 146: 53–93.

1988   *The Ideologies of Theory: Essays 1971–1986.* Minneapolis: University of Minnesota Press.

Jankowiak, W. R., and E. F. Fischer
1992   A Cross-Cultural Perspective on Romantic Love. *Ethnology* 31(2): 149–156.

Janson, C. H.

1986   Capuchin Counterpoint: Divergent Mating and Feeding Habits Distinguish Two Closely Related Monkey Species of the Peruvian Forest. *Natural History* 95: 44–52.

Jasim, S. A.

1985   The Ubaid Period in Iraq: Recent Excavations in the Hamrin Region. *BAR International Series* 267 (Oxford).

Jensen, A.

1969   How Much Can We Boost I.Q. and Scholastic Achievement? *Harvard Educational Review* 29: 1–123.

Jodelet, D.

1991   *Madness and Social Representations: Living with the Mad in One French Community.* Translated from the French by Gerard Duveen. Berkeley: University of California Press.

Johanson, D. C., and M. Edey

1981   *Lucy: The Origins of Humankind.* New York: Simon & Schuster.

Johanson, D. C., and B. Edgar

1996   *From Lucy to Language.* New York: Simon & Schuster.

Johanson, D. C., and T. D. White

1979   A Systematic Assessment of Early African Hominids. *Science* 203: 321–330.

Johnson, A. W.

1978   *Quantification in Cultural Anthropology: An Introduction to Research Design.* Stanford, CA: Stanford University Press.

Johnson, A. W., and T. Earle, eds.

1987   *The Evolution of Human Societies: From Foraging Group to Agrarian State.* Stanford, CA: Stanford University Press.

2000   *The Evolution of Human Societies: From Foraging Group to Agrarian State,* 2nd ed. Stanford, CA: Stanford University Press.

Johnson, G. A.

1987   The Changing Organization of Uruk Administration in the Susiana Plain. In *The Archaeology of Western Iran,* ed. F. Hole, pp. 107–139. Washington, DC: Smithsonian Institution Press.

Johnson, T. J., and C. F. Sargent, eds.

1990   *Medical Anthropology: A Handbook of Theory and Method.* New York: Greenwood.

Johnston, F. E., and S. Low

1994   *Children of the Urban Poor: The Sociocultural Environment of Growth, Development, and Malnutrition in Guatemala City.* Boulder, CO: Westview.

Jolly, A.

1985   *The Evolution of Primate Behavior,* 2nd ed. New York: Macmillan.

Jolly, C. J., and F. Plog

1986   *Physical Anthropology and Archaeology,* 4th ed. New York: McGraw-Hill.

Jolly, C. J., and R. White

1995   *Physical Anthropology and Archaeology,* 5th ed. New York: McGraw-Hill.

Jones, D.

1999   Hot Asset in Corporate: Anthropology Degrees. *USA Today,* February 18, p. B1.

Jones, G., and R. Krautz

1981   *The Transition to Statehood in the New World.* Cambridge: Cambridge University Press.

Joralemon, D.

1999   *Exploring Medical Anthropology.* Boston: Allyn & Bacon.

Joyce, R. A.

2000   *Gender and Power in Prehispanic Mesoamerica.* Austin, TX: University of Texas Press.

Jurmain, R.

1997   *Introduction to Physical Anthropology,* 7th ed. Belmont, CA: Wadsworth.

Kan, S.

1986   The 19th-Century Tlingit Potlatch: A New Perspective. *American Ethnologist* 13: 191–212.

1989   *Symbolic Immortality: The Tlingit Potlatch of the Nineteenth Century.* Washington, DC: Smithsonian Institution Press.

Kantor, P.

1996   Domestic Violence against Women: A Global Issue. http://metalab.unc.edu/ucis/pubs/Carolina_Papers/Abuse/figure1.html.

Kaplan, R. D.

1994   The Coming Anarchy: How Scarcity, Crime, Overpopulation, and Disease Are Rapidly Destroying the Social Fabric of Our Planet. *Atlantic Monthly,* February, pp. 44–76.

Kardiner, A., ed.

1939   *The Individual and His Society.* New York: Columbia University Press.

Kardulias, P. N.

1999   *World-Systems Theory in Practice: Leadership, Production, and Exchange.* Lanham, MD: Rowman and Littlefield.

Katzenberg, M.A., and S. R. Saunders, eds.

2000   *Biological Anthropology of the Human Skeleton.* New York: Wiley.

Kearney, M.

1996   *Reconceptualizing the Peasantry: Anthropology in Global Perspective.* Boulder, CO: Westview.

Kehoe, A. B.

1989   *The Ghost Dance Religion: Ethnohistory and Revitalization.* Fort Worth: Harcourt Brace.

Keiser, L.

1991   *Friend by Day, Enemy by Night: Organized Vengeance in a Kohistani Community.* Fort Worth: Harcourt Brace.

Kelly, R. C.

1976   Witchcraft and Sexual Relations: An Exploration in the Social and Semantic Implications of the Structure of Belief. In *Man and Woman in the New Guinea Highlands,* ed. P. Brown and G. Buchbinder, pp. 36–53. Special Publication, no. 8. Washington, DC: American Anthropological Association.

1985   *The Nuer Conquest: The Structure and Development of an Expansionist System.* Ann Arbor: University of Michigan Press.

2000   *Warless Societies and the Origin of War.* Ann Arbor: University of Michigan Press.

Kemp, T. S.

1999   *Fossils and Evolution.* New York: Oxford University Press.

Kennedy, R. G.

1994   *Hidden Cities: The Discovery and Loss of Ancient North American Civilization.* New York: Free Press.

Kent, S.

1992   The Current Forager Controversy: Real versus Ideal Views of Hunter-Gatherers. *Man 27:* 45–70.

1996   *Cultural Diversity among Twentieth-Century Foragers: An African Perspective.* New York: Cambridge University Press.

1998   *Gender in African Prehistory.* Walnut Creek, CA: AltaMira Press.

Kent, S., and H. Vierich

1989   The Myth of Ecological Determinism: Anticipated Mobility and Site Organization of Space. In *Farmers as Hunters: The Implications of Sedentism,* ed. S. Kent, pp. 96–130. New York: Cambridge University Press.

Kerr, R. A.

1998   Sea-Floor Dust Shows Drought Felled Akkadian Empire. *Science* 279 (5349—January 16: 325–326.

Kimmel, M. S., and M. A. Messner, eds.

1998   *Men's Lives,* 4th ed. Boston: Allyn & Bacon.

King, B. J., ed.

1994   *The Information Continuum: Evolution of Social Information Transfer in Monkeys, Apes, and Hominids.* Santa Fe: School of American Research Press.

Kinsey, A. C., W. B. Pomeroy, and C. E. Martin

1948   *Sexual Behavior in the Human Male.* Philadelphia: W. B. Saunders.

Kinzer, S.

2002   Museums and Tribes: A Tricky Truce. *New York Times,* December 24, late Edition—final, section 2, p. 1, column 1. www.nytimes.com.

Kirch, P. V.

1984   *The Evolution of the Polynesian Chiefdoms.* Cambridge: Cambridge University Press.

2000   *On the Road of the Winds: An Archaeological History of the Pacific Islands before European Contact.* Berkeley: University of California Press.

Kirman, P.

1997   An Introduction to Ethnomusicology. http://worldmusic.about.com/musicperform/worldmusic/library/weekly/aa101797.htm and http://worldmusic.about.com/music-perform/worldmusic/library/b11011b.htm.

Klass, M.

1995   *Ordered Universes: Approaches to the Anthropology of Religion.* Boulder, CO: Westview.

Klass, M., and M. Weisgrau, eds.

1999   *Across the Boundaries of Belief: Contemporary Issues in the Anthropology of Religion.* Boulder, CO: Westview.

Klein, R. G.

1999   *The Human Career: Human Biological and Cultural Origins,* 2nd ed. Chicago: University of Chicago Press.

Klein, R. G., with B. Edgar
2002   *The Dawn of Human Culture.* New York: Wiley.

Kleinfeld, J.
1975   Positive Stereotyping: The Cultural Relativist in the Classroom. *Human Organization* 34: 269–274.

Kleymeyer, C. D., ed.
1994   *Cultural Expression and Grassroots Development: Cases from Latin America and the Caribbean.* Boulder, CO: Lynne Rienner.

Klineberg, O.
1951   Race and Psychology. In *The Race Question in Modern Science.* Paris: UNESCO.

Kling, R.
1996   Synergies and Competition between Life in Cyberspace and Face-to-Face Communities. *Social Science Computing Review* 14(1): 50–54.

Kluckhohn, C.
1994   *Mirror for Man: A Survey of Human Behavior and Social Attitudes.* Greenwich, CT: Fawcett.

Kluge, A. G.
1983   Cladistics and the Classification of the Great Apes. In *New Interpretations of Ape and Human Ancestry,* ed. R. L. Ciochon and R. S. Corruccini, pp. 151–177. New York: Plenum.

Knecht, H., A. Pike-Tay, and R. White, eds.
1993   *Before Lascaux: The Complex Record of the Early Upper Paleolithic.* Boca Raton, FL: CRC Press.

Kohler, M., and S. Moya-Sola
1997   Ape-Like or Hominid-Like? The Positional Behavior of *Oreopithecus bambolii* Reconsidered. *Proceedings of the National Academy of Sciences* 94 (October 14):11, 747.

Kopytoff, V. G.
1995   Meat Viewed as Staple of Chimp Diet and Mores. *New York Times,* June 27, pp. B5–B6.

Korten, D. C.
1980   Community Organization and Rural Development: A Learning Process Approach. *Public Administration Review,* September–October, pp. 480–512.

Kosty, P.
2002   Indonesia's Matriarchal Minangkabau Offer an Alternative Social System, EurekAlert.org May 9. http://www.eurekalert.org/pub_releases/2002-05/uop-imm050902.php.

Kottak, C. P.
1980   *The Past in the Present: History, Ecology, and Social Organization in Highland Madagascar.* Ann Arbor: University of Michigan Press.

1990a   *Prime-Time Society: An Anthropological Analysis of Television and Culture.* Belmont, CA: Wadsworth.

1990b   Culture and Economic Development. *American Anthropologist* 92(3): 723–731.

1991   When People Don't Come First: Some Lessons from Completed Projects. In *Putting People First: Sociological Variables in Rural Development,* 2nd ed., ed. M. Cernea, pp. 429–464. New York: Oxford University Press.

1992   *Assault on Paradise: Social Change in a Brazilian Village,* 2nd ed. New York:McGraw-Hill.

1999a   *Assault on Paradise: Social Change in a Brazilian Village,* 3rd ed. New York:McGraw-Hill.

1999b   The New Ecological Anthropology. *American Anthropologist* 101(1): 23–35.

Kottak, C. P., ed.
1982   *Researching American Culture: A Guide for Student Anthropologists.* Ann Arbor: University of Michigan Press.

Kottak, C. P., L. L. Gezon, and G. Green
1994   Deforestation and Biodiversity Preservation in Madagascar: The View from Above and Below. CIESIN Human Dimensions Kiosk. http://www.ciesin.com.

Kottak, C. P., and K. A. Kozaitis
2003   *On Being Different: Diversity and Multiculturalism in the North American Mainstream,* 2nd ed. Boston: McGraw-Hill.

Kramarae, R., M. Shulz, and M. O'Barr, eds.
1984   *Language and Power.* Thousand Oaks, CA: Sage.

Kretchmer, N.
1975   (orig. 1972). Lactose and Lactase. In *Biological Anthropology, Readings from Scientific American,* ed. S. H. Katz, pp. 310–318. San Francisco: W. H. Freeman.

Kroeber, A. L., and C. Kluckhohn
1963   *Culture: A Critical Review of Concepts and Definitions.* New York: Vintage.

Kuhn, S. L., M. C. Stiner, and D. S. Reese

2001   Ornaments of the Earliest Upper Paleolithic: New Insights from the Levant. *Proceedings of the National Academy of Sciences of the United States of America* 98(13): 7641–7646.

Kulick, D.

1998   *Travesti: Sex, Gender, and Culture among Brazilian Transgendered Prostitutes.* Chicago: University of Chicago Press.

Kunitz, S. J.

1994   *Disease and Social Diversity: The European Impact on the Health of Non-Europeans.* New York: Oxford University Press.

Kurtz, D. V.

2001   *Political Anthropology: Power and Paradigms.* Boulder, CO: Westview.

Kutsche, P.

1998   *Field Ethnography: A Manual for Doing Cultural Anthropology.* Upper Saddle River, NJ: Prentice-Hall.

LaBarre, W.

1945   Some Observations of Character Structure in the Orient: The Japanese. *Psychiatry* 8: 326–342.

Labov, W.

1972a   *Language in the Inner City: Studies in the Black English Vernacular.* Philadelphia: University of Pennsylvania Press.

1972b   *Sociolinguistic Patterns.* Philadelphia: University of Pennsylvania Press.

La Fraugh, R. J.

n.d.   Euskara: The History, a True Mystery. The La Fraugh Name History. http://planetrjl.tripod.com/LaFraughName/id5.html.

Laguerre, M. S.

1984   *American Odyssey: Haitians in New York.* Ithaca, NY: Cornell University Press.

1998   *Diasporic Citizenship: Haitian Americans in Transnational America.* New York: St. Martin's Press.

1999   *The Global Ethnopolis: Chinatown, Japantown, and Manilatown in American Society.* New York: St. Martin's.

Lakoff, R. T.

1975   *Language and Woman's Place.* New York: Harper & Row.

2000   *Language War.* Berkeley: University of California Press.

Lamberg-Karlovsky, C. C., and J. A. Sabloff

1995   *Ancient Civilizations: The Near East and Mesoamerica.* Prospect Heights, IL: Waveland.

Lamphere, L., H. Ragone, and P. Zavella, eds.

1997   *Situated Lives: Gender and Culture in Everyday Life.* New York: Routledge.

Lancaster, R. N., and M. Di Leonardo, eds.

1997   *The Gender/Sexuality Reader: Culture, History, Political Economy.* New York: Routledge.

Lance, L. M., and E. E. McKenna

1975   Analysis of Cases Pertaining to the Impact of Western Technology on the Non-Western World. *Human Organization* 34: 87–94.

Lansing, J. S.

1991   *Priests and Programmers: Technologies of Power in the Engineered Landscape of Bali.* Princeton, NJ: Princeton University Press.

Larsen, C. S.

2000   *Skeletons in Our Closet: Revealing Our Past through Bioarchaeology.* Princeton, NJ: Princeton University Press.

Larson, A.

1989   Social Context of Human Immunodeficiency Virus Transmission in Africa: Historical and Cultural Bases of East and Central African Sexual Relations. *Review of Infectious Diseases* 11: 716–731.

Lassiter, L. E.

1998   *The Power of Kiowa Song: A Collaborative Ethnography.* Tucson: University of Arizona Press.

Layton, R.

1991   *The Anthropology of Art,* 2nd ed. New York: Cambridge University Press.

Leach, E. R.

1955   Polyandry, Inheritance and the Definition of Marriage. *Man* 55: 182–186.

1961   *Rethinking Anthropology.* London: Athlone Press.

1985   *Social Anthropology.* New York: Oxford University Press.

Leakey, R. E., M. G. Leakey, and A. C. Walker

1988   Morphology of *Afropithecus turkanensis* from Kenya. *American Journal of Physical Anthropology* 76: 289–307.

LeClair, E. E., and H. K. Schneider, eds.
1968   (orig. 1961). *Economic Anthropology: Readings in Theory and Analysis.* New York: Holt, Rinehart and Winston.

Lee, R. B.
1974   (orig. 1968). What Hunters Do for a Living, or, How to Make Out on Scarce Resources. In *Man in Adaptation: The Cultural Present,* 2nd ed., ed. Y. A. Cohen, pp. 87–100. Chicago: Aldine.

1979   *The !Kung San: Men, Women, and Work in a Foraging Society.* New York: Cambridge University Press.

1984   *The Dobe !Kung.* New York: Holt, Rinehart and Winston.

2002   *The Dobe Ju/'hoansi,* 3rd ed. Belmont, CA: Wadsworth.

Lee, R. B., and R. H. Daly
1999   *The Cambridge Encyclopedia of Hunters and Gatherers.* New York: Cambridge University Press.

Lee, R. B., and I. DeVore, eds.
1977   *Kalahari Hunter-Gatherers: Studies of the !Kung San and Their Neighbors.* Cambridge, MA: Harvard University Press.

Lehmann, A. C., and J. E. Meyers, eds.
1997   *Magic, Witchcraft, and Religion: An Anthropological Study of the Supernatural,* 4th ed. Mountain View, CA: Mayfield.

Leman, J.
2001   *The Dynamics of Emerging Ethnicities: Immigrant and Indigenous Ethnogenesis in Confrontation.* New York: Peter Lang.

Lemonick, M. D., and A. Dorfman
1999   Up from the Apes: Remarkable New Evidence Is Filling in the Story of How We Became Human. *Time* 154(8): 5–58.

Lenski, G.
1966   *Power and Privilege: A Theory of Social Stratification.* New York: McGraw-Hill.

Lessa, W. A., and E. Z. Vogt, eds.
1979   *Reader in Comparative Religion: An Anthropological Approach,* 4th ed. New York: Harper & Row.

Lévi-Strauss, C.
1963   *Totemism.* Translated by R. Needham. Boston: Beacon Press.

1967   *Structural Anthropology.* New York: Doubleday.

1969   (orig. 1949). *The Elementary Structures of Kinship.* Boston: Beacon Press.

Levine, L., ed.
1995   *Genetics of Natural Populations: The Continuing Importance of Theodosius Dobzhansky.* New York: Columbia University Press.

Levine, N.
1988   *The Dynamics of Polyandry: Kinship, Domesticity, and Population on the Tibetan Border.* Chicago: University of Chicago Press.

Levine, R. A.
1982   *Culture, Behavior, and Personality: An Introduction to the Comparative Study of Psychosocial Adaptation,* 2nd ed. Chicago: Aldine.

Levine, R. A., ed.
1974   *Culture and Personality: Contemporary Readings.* Chicago: Aldine.

Lewin, R.
1998   *Principles of Human Evolution: A Core Textbook.* Malden, MA: Blackwell Science.

1999   *Human Evolution: An Illustrated Introduction,* 4th ed. Malden, MA: Blackwell Science.

Lewis, H. S.
1989   *After the Eagles Landed: The Yemenites of Israel.* Boulder, CO: Westview.

Lewis, O.
1959   *Five Families.* New York: Basic Books.

Lewis, P.
1992   U.N. Sees a Crisis in Overpopulation. *New York Times,* April 30, p. A6.

Lewontin, R.
2000   *It Ain't Necessarily So: The Dream of the Human Genome and Other Illusions.* New York: New York Review of Books.

Lieban, R. W.
1977   The Field of Medical Anthropology. In *Culture, Disease, and Healing: Studies in Medical Anthropology,* ed. D. Landy, pp. 13–31. New York: Macmillan.

Lieberman, P.
1998   *Eve Spoke: Human Language and Human Evolution.* New York: W. W. Norton.

Light, D., S. Keller, and C. Calhoun
1994   *Sociology,* 6th ed. New York: McGraw-Hill.

Linden, E.
1986   *Silent Partners: The Legacy of the Ape Language Experiments.* New York: Times Books.

Lindenbaum, S.
1972   Sorcerers, Ghosts, and Polluting Women: An Analysis of Religious Belief and Population Control. *Ethnology* 11: 241–253.

Lindholm, C.
2001   *Culture and Identity: The History, Theory, and Practice of Psychological Anthropology.* Boston: McGraw-Hill.

Linton, R.
1927   Report on Work of Field Museum Expedition in Madagascar. *American Anthropologist* 29: 292–307.

1943   Nativistic Movements. *American Anthropologist* 45: 230–240.

Lipke, D. J.
2000   Dead End Ahead? Income May Be the Real Barrier to the Internet On-Ramp. *American Demographics,* August. http://www.demographics.com/publications/ad/00_ad/ad000805c.htm.

Little, K.
1965   *West African Urbanization: A Study of Voluntary Associations in Social Change.* Cambridge: Cambridge University Press.

1971   *Some Aspects of African Urbanization South of the Sahara. McCaleb Modules in Anthropology.* Reading, MA: Addison-Wesley.

Livingstone, F. B.
1958   Anthropological Implications of Sickle Cell Gene Distribution in West Africa. *American Anthropologist* 60: 533–562.

1969   Gene Frequency Clines of the *b* Hemoglobin Locus in Various Human Populations and Their Similarities by Models Involving Differential Selection. *Human Biology* 41: 223–236.

Lizot, J.
1985   *Tales of the Yanomami: Daily Life in the Venezuelan Forest.* New York: Cambridge University Press.

Lockwood, W. G.
1975   *European Moslems: Economy and Ethnicity in Western Bosnia.* New York: Academic Press.

Loomis, W. F.
1967   Skin-Pigmented Regulation of Vitamin-D Biosynthesis in Man. *Science* 157: 501–506.

Lowie, R. H.
1935   *The Crow Indians.* New York: Farrar and Rinehart.

1961   (orig. 1920). *Primitive Society.* New York: Harper & Brothers.

Lugaila, T.
1998a   Numbers of Divorced and Never-Married Adults Increasing, Says Census Bureau Report. http://www.census.gov/Press-Release/cb98-56.html.

1998b   Marital Status and Living Arrangements, March 1998 (Update). http://www.census.gov/prod/99pubs/p20-514.pdf.

1999   Married Adults Still in the Majority, Census Bureau Reports. http://www.census.gov/Press-Release/www/1999/cb99-03.html.

Lutz, C., and J. L. Collins
1993   *Reading National Geographic.* Chicago: University of Chicago Press.

Lyell, C.
1969   (orig. 1830–37). *Principles of Geology.* New York: Johnson.

MacKinnon, J.
1974   *In Search of the Red Ape.* New York: Ballantine.

Maher, J. C., and G. MacDonald, eds.
1995   *Diversity and Language in Japanese Culture.* New York: Columbia University Press.

Mair, L.
1969   *Witchcraft.* New York: McGraw-Hill.

Malinowski, B.
1927   *Sex and Repression in Savage Society.* London and New York: International Library of Psychology, Philosophy and Scientific Method.

1929a   Practical Anthropology. *Africa* 2: 23–38.

1929b   *The Sexual Life of Savages in North-Western Melanesia.* New York: Harcourt, Brace, and World.

1961   (orig. 1922). *Argonauts of the Western Pacific.* New York: Dutton.

1978   (orig. 1931). The Role of Magic and Religion. In *Reader in Comparative Religion: An Anthropological Approach,* 4th ed., ed. W. A. Lessa and E. Z. Vogt, pp. 37–46. New York: Harper & Row.

1985   (orig. 1927). *Sex and Repression in Savage Society.* Chicago: University of Chicago Press.

Malkki, L. H.

1995   *Purity and Exile: Violence, Memory, and National Cosmology among Hutu Refugees in Tanzania.* Chicago: University of Chicago Press.

Mann, A.

1975   *Paleodemographic Aspects of the South African Australopithecines.* Publications in Anthropology, no. 1. Philadelphia: University of Pennsylvania.

Manners, R.

1973   (orig. 1956). Functionalism, Realpolitik and Anthropology in Underdeveloped Areas. *America Indigena* 16. Also in *To See Ourselves: Anthropology and Modern Social Issues,* gen. ed. T. Weaver, pp. 113–126. Glenview, IL: Scott, Foresman.

Maquet, J.

1964   Objectivity in Anthropology. *Current Anthropology* 5: 47–55 (also in Clifton, ed., 1970).

1986   *The Aesthetic Experience: An Anthropologist Looks at the Visual Arts.* New Haven, CT: Yale University Press.

Mar, M. E.

1997   Secondary Colors: The Multiracial Option. *Harvard Magazine,* May–June 1997, pp. 19–20.

Marcus, G. E., and D. Cushman

1982   Ethnographies as Texts. *Annual Review of Anthropology* 11: 25–69.

Marcus, G. E., and M. M. J. Fischer

1986   *Anthropology as Cultural Critique: An Experimental Moment in the Human Sciences.* Chicago: University of Chicago Press.

1999   *Anthropology as Cultural Critique: An Experimental Moment in the Human Sciences,* 2nd ed. Chicago: University of Chicago Press.

Marcus, G. E., and F. R. Myers, eds.

1995   *The Traffic in Culture: Refiguring Art and Anthropology.* Berkeley: University of California Press.

Marcus, J.

1992   *Mesoamerican Writing Systems: Propaganda, Myth, and History in Four Ancient Civilizations.* Princeton, NJ: Princeton University Press.

Marcus, J., and K. V. Flannery

1996   *Zapotec Civilization: How Urban Society Evolved in Mexico's Oaxaca Valley.* New York: Thames and Hudson.

Margolis, M.

1984   *Mothers and Such: American Views of Women and How They Changed.* Berkeley: University of California Press.

1994   *Little Brazil: An Ethnography of Brazilian Immigrants in New York City.* Princeton, NJ: Princeton University Press.

2000   *True to Her Nature: Changing Advice to American Women.* Prospect Heights, IL: Waveland.

Marks, J.

1995   *Human Biodiversity: Genes, Race, and History.* New York: Aldine de Gruyter.

Marshack, A.

1972   *Roots of Civilization.* New York: McGraw-Hill.

Martin, E.

1987   *The Woman in the Body: A Cultural Analysis of Reproduction.* Boston: Beacon Press.

Martin, J.

1992   *Cultures in Organizations: Three Perspectives.* New York: Oxford University Press.

Martin, K., and B. Voorhies

1975   *Female of the Species.* New York: Columbia University Press.

Martin, P., and E. Midgley

1994   Immigration to the United States: Journey to an Uncertain Destination. *Population Bulletin* 49(3): 1–47.

Marx, K., and F. Engels

1976   (orig. 1848). *Communist Manifesto.* New York: Pantheon.

Mathews, G.

2000   *Global Culture/Individual Identity: Searching for Home in the Cultural Supermarket.* New York: Routledge.

Maybury-Lewis, D.

2002   *Indigenous Peoples, Ethnic Groups, and the State,* 2nd ed. Boston: Allyn & Bacon.

Mayr, E.

1970   *Population, Species, and Evolution.* Cambridge, MA: Harvard University Press.

2001   *What Evolution Is.* New York: Basic Books.

McAllester, D. P.

1954   *Enemy Way Music: A Study of Social and Esthetic Values as Seen in Navaho Music.* Cambridge, MA: Peabody Museum of American Archaeology and Ethnology, Papers 41(3).

McBrearty, S., and Brooks, A. S.
2000   The Revolution That Wasn't: A New Interpretation of the Origin of Modern Human Behavior. *Journal of Human Evolution* 39: 453–563.

McCaskie, T. C.
1995   *State and Society in Pre-Colonial Asante.* New York: Cambridge University Press.

McDonald, G.
1984   *Carioca Fletch.* New York: Warner Books.

McDonald, J. H., ed.
2002   *The Applied Anthropology Reader.* Boston: Allyn & Bacon.

McElroy, A., and P. K. Townsend
1996   *Medical Anthropology in Ecological Perspective,* 3rd ed. Boulder, CO: Westview.

McGraw, T. K., ed.
1986   *America versus Japan.* Boston: Harvard Business School Press.

McGrew, W. C.
1979   Evolutionary Implications of Sex Differences in Chimpanzee Predation and Tool Use. In D. A. Hamburg and E. R. McCown, eds. *The Great Apes,* pp. 441–463. Menlo Park, CA: Benjamin Cummings.

McGrew, W., L. Marchant, and T. Nishida
1996   *Great Ape Societies.* Cambridge: Cambridge University Press.

McKinley, J.
1996   Board's Decision on Black English Stirs Debate. *New York Times,* December 21. www.nytimes.com.

McKusick, V.
1966   *Mendelian Inheritance in Man.* Baltimore: Johns Hopkins University Press.

1990   *Mendelian Inheritance in Man: Catalogs of Autosomal Dominant, Autosomal Recessive, and X-Linked Phenotypes,* 9th ed. Baltimore: Johns Hopkins University Press.

Mead, M.
1930   *Growing Up in New Guinea.* New York: Blue Ribbon.

1950   (orig. 1935). *Sex and Temperament in Three Primitive Societies.* New York: New American Library.

1961   (orig. 1928). *Coming of Age in Samoa.* New York: Morrow Quill.

1972   *Blackberry Winter: My Earlier Years.* New York: Simon and Schuster.

Meadow, R., ed.
1991   *Harappa Excavations 1986–1990: A Multi-disciplinary Approach to Third Millennium Urbanism.* Monographs in World Archeology, no. 3. Madison, WI: Prehistory Press.

Meadow, R. H., and J. M. Kenoyer
2000   The Indus Valley Mystery: One of the World's First Great Civilizations Is Still a Puzzle. *Discovering Archaeology,* March/April 2000. http://www.discoveringarchaeology.com/0800toc/8feature1-indus.shtml.

Merriam, A.
1971   The Arts and Anthropology. In *Anthropology and Art: Readings in Cross-Cultural Aesthetics,* ed. C. Otten, pp. 93–105. Austin: University of Texas Press.

Michaels, E.
1986   Aboriginal Content. Paper presented at the meeting of the Australian Screen Studies Association, December, Sydney.

Michaelson, K.
1996   Information, Community, and Access. *Social Science Computing Review* 14(1): 57–59.

Michrina, B. P., and C. Richards
1996   *Person to Person: Fieldwork, Dialogue, and the Hermeneutic Method.* Albany: State University of New York Press.

Middleton, J.
1967   Introduction. In *Myth and Cosmos: Readings in Mythology and Symbolism,* ed. John Middleton, pp. ix–xi. Garden City, NY: Natural History Press.

1993   *The Lugbara of Uganda,* 2nd ed. Fort Worth: Harcourt Brace.

Middleton, J., ed.
1967   *Gods and Rituals.* Garden City, NY: Natural History Press.

Miles, H. L.
1983   Apes and Language: The Search for Communicative Competence. In *Language in Primates,* ed. J. de Luce and H. T. Wilder, pp. 43–62. New York: Springer Verlag.

Miller, B. D.

1997   *The Endangered Sex: Neglect of Female Children in Rural North India.* New York: Oxford University Press.

Miller, B. D., ed.

1993   *Sex and Gender Hierarchies.* New York: Cambridge University Press.

Miller, N., and R. C. Rockwell, eds.

1988   *AIDS in Africa: The Social and Policy Impact.* Lewiston: Edwin Mellen.

Mills, G.

1971   Art: An Introduction to Qualitative Anthropology. In *Anthropology and Art: Readings in Cross-Cultural Aesthetics,* ed. C. Otten, pp. 66–92. Austin: University of Texas Press.

Mintz, S.

1985   *Sweetness and Power: The Place of Sugar in Modern History.* New York: Viking Penguin.

Mirzoeff, N.

1999   *An Introduction to Visual Culture.* New York: Routledge.

Mishler, E. G.

1991   *Research Interviewing: Context and Narrative.* Cambridge, MA: Harvard University Press.

Mitani, J. C., and D. P. Watts

1999   Demographic Influences on the Hunting Behavior of Chimpanzees. *American Journal of Physical Anthropology* 109: 439–454.

Mitchell, J. C.

1966   Theoretical Orientations in African Urban Studies. In *The Social Anthropology of Complex Societies,* ed. M. Banton, pp. 37–68. London: Tavistock.

Moerman, M.

1965   Ethnic Identification in a Complex Civilization: Who Are the Lue? *American Anthropologist* 67(5 Part I): 1215–1230.

Molnar, S.

2001   *Human Variation: Races, Types, and Ethnic Groups,* 5th ed. Upper Saddle River, NJ: Prentice-Hall.

Moncure, S.

1998   Anthropologist Assists in Police Investigations. *University of Delaware Update* 17, no. 39, August 20. http://www.udel.edu/PR/UpDate/98/39/anthrop.html.

Montagu, A.

1975   *The Nature of Human Aggression.* New York: Oxford University Press.

1981   *Statement on Race: An Annotated Elaboration and Exposition of the Four Statements on Race Issued by the United Nations Educational, Scientific, and Cultural Organization.* Westport, CT: Greenwood.

Montagu, A., ed.

1996   *Race and IQ,* expanded ed. New York: Oxford University Press.

1997   *Man's Most Dangerous Myth: The Fallacy of Race,* 6th ed. Walnut Creek, CA: AltaMira.

1999   *Race and IQ,* expanded ed. New York: Oxford University Press.

Montague, S., and R. Morais

1981   Football Games and Rock Concerts: The Ritual Enactment. In *The American Dimension: Cultural Myths and Social Realities,* 2nd ed., ed. W. Arens and S. B. Montague, pp. 33–52. Sherman Oaks, CA: Alfred.

Montgomery, S.

1991   *Walking with the Great Apes: Jane Goodall, Dian Fossey, Biruté Galdikas.* Boston: Houghton Mifflin.

Moore, A. D.

1985   *The Development of Neolithic Societies in the Near East. Advances in World Archaeology* 4:1–69.

Moore, S. F.

1986   *Social Facts and Fabrications.* Cambridge: Cambridge University Press.

Moran, E. F.

1982   *Human Adaptability: An Introduction to Ecological Anthropology.* Boulder, CO: Westview.

Morbeck, M. E., A. Galloway, and A. L. Zihlman, eds.

1997   *The Evolving Female: A Life-History Perspective.* Princeton, NJ: Princeton University Press.

Morgan, L. H.

1963   (orig. 1877). *Ancient Society.* Cleveland: World Publishing.

Morgen, S., ed.

1989   *Gender and Anthropology: Critical Reviews for Research and Teaching.* Washington, DC: American Anthropological Association.

Morris, B.
1987   *Anthropological Studies of Religion: An Introductory Text.* New York: Cambridge University Press.

Mowat, F.
1987   *Woman in the Mists: The Story of Dian Fossey and the Mountain Gorillas of Africa.* New York: Warner Books.

Muhlhausler, P.
1986   *Pidgin and Creole Linguistics.* London: Basil Blackwell.

Mukhopadhyay, C., and P. Higgins
1988   Anthropological Studies of Women's Status Revisited: 1977–1987. *Annual Review of Anthropology* 17: 461–495.

Mullings, L., ed.
1987   *Cities of the United States: Studies in Urban Anthropology.* New York: Columbia University Press.

Murdock, G. P.
1934   *Our Primitive Contemporaries.* New York: Macmillan.

1957   World Ethnographic Sample. *American Anthropologist* 59: 664–687.

Murdock, G. P., and C. Provost
1973   Factors in the Division of Labor by Sex: A Cross-Cultural Analysis. *Ethnology* XII(2): 203–225.

Murphy, R. F.
1990   *The Body Silent.* New York: W. W. Norton.

Murphy, R. F., and L. Kasdan
1959   The Structure of Parallel Cousin Marriage. *American Anthropologist* 61: 17–29.

Murray, S. O., and W. Roscoe, eds.
1998   *Boy-Wives and Female Husbands: Studies in African Homosexualities.* New York: St. Martin's.

Mydans, S.
1992*a*   Criticism Grows over Aliens Seized during Riots. *New York Times*, May 29, p. A8.

1992*b*   Judge Dismisses Case in Shooting by Officer. *New York Times*, June 4, p. A8.

Myers, F. R.
2002   *Painting Culture: The Making of an Aboriginal High Art.* Durham, NC: Duke University Press.

Nafte, M.
2000   *Flesh and Bone: An Introduction to Forensic Anthropology.* Durham, NC: Carolina Academic Press.

Nagel, J.
1996   *American Indian Ethnic Renewal: Red Power and the Resurgence of Identity and Culture.* New York: Oxford University Press.

Napier, A. D.
1992   *Foreign Bodies: Performance, Art, and Symbolic Anthropology.* Berkeley: University of California Press.

Napier, J. R., and P. H. Napier
1985   *The Natural History of Primates.* Cambridge, MA: MIT Press.

Narayan, U.
1997   *Dislocating Cultures: Identities, Traditions, and Third World Feminisms.* New York: Routledge.

Nash, D.
1999   *A Little Anthropology,* 3rd ed. Upper Saddle River, NJ: Prentice-Hall.

Nash, J., and H. Safa, eds.
1986   *Women and Change in Latin America.* South Hadley, MA: Bergin and Garvey.

National Association for the Practice of Anthropology
1991   *NAPA Directory of Practicing Anthropologists.* Washington, DC: American Anthropological Association.

National Vital Statistics Reports
2000   Births, Marriages, Divorces, and Deaths: Provisional Data for November 1999. October 31, 2000. Hyattsville, MD: U.S. Department of Health and Human Services, Center for Disease Control and Prevention, National Center for Health Statistics.

2001   *National Vital Statistics Reports,* vol. 46, no. 6. http://www.cdc.gov/nchs/data/nvsr/nvsr49/nvsr49_06.pdf.

Naylor, L. L.
1996   *Culture and Change: An Introduction.* Westport, CT: Bergin and Garvey.

Nelson, H., and R. Jurmain
1991   *Introduction to Physical Anthropology,* 5th ed. St. Paul, MN: West.

Nelson, S. N., and M. Rosen-Ayalon, eds.
2002   *In Pursuit of Gender: Worldwide Archaeological Approaches.* Walnut Creek, CA: AltaMira.

Netting, R. M. C., R. R. Wilk, and E. J. Arnould, eds.

1984   *Households: Comparative and Historical Studies of the Domestic Group.* Berkeley: University of California Press.

Nevid, J. S., and Rathus, S. A.

1995   *Human Sexuality in a World of Diversity,* 2nd ed. Needham Heights, MA: Allyn & Bacon.

New York Times

1990   Tropical Diseases on March, Hitting 1 in 10. March 28, p. A3.

1992*a*   Alexandria Journal: TV Program for Somalis Is a Rare Unifying Force. December 18.

1992*b*   Married with Children: The Waning Icon. August 23, p. E2.

Newman, M.

1992   Riots Bring Attention to Growing Hispanic Presence in South-Central Area. *New York Times,* May 11, p. A10.

Nielsson, G. P.

1985   States and Nation-Groups: A Global Taxonomy. In *New Nationalisms of the Developed World,* ed. E. A. Tiryakian and R. Rogowski, pp. 27–56. Boston: Allen and Unwin.

Nowak, R. M.

1999   *Walker's Primates of the World.* Baltimore: Johns Hopkins University Press.

Nussbaum, M. C.

2000   *Women and Human Development: The Capabilities Approach.* New York: Cambridge University Press.

Nussbaum, M., and J. Glover, eds.

1995   *Women, Culture, and Development: A Study of Human Capabilities.* New York: Oxford University Press.

Oakley, K. P.

1976   *Man the Tool-Maker,* 6th ed. Chicago: University of Chicago Press.

O'Leary, C. M.

2002   *Class Formation, Diet and Economic Transformation in Two Brazilian Fishing Communities.* Ph.D. Dissertation, Department of Anthropology, University of Michigan, Ann Arbor.

Okpewho, I.

1977   Principles of Traditional African Art. *The Journal of Aesthetics and Art Criticism* 35(3): 301–314.

Ong, A.

1987   *Spirits of Resistance and Capitalist Discipline: Factory Women in Malaysia.* Albany: State University of New York Press.

1989   Center, Periphery, and Hierarchy: Gender in Southeast Asia. In *Gender and Anthropology: Critical Reviews for Research and Teaching,* ed. S. Morgen, pp. 294–312. Washington, DC: American Anthropological Association.

Ong, A., and M. G. Peletz, eds.

1995   *Bewitching Women, Pious Men: Gender and Body Politics in Southeast Asia.* Berkeley: University of California Press.

Ontario Consultants on Religious Tolerance

1996   Religious Access Dispute Resolved. Internet Mailing List, April 12. http://www.religious-tolerance.org/news_694.htm.

1997   Swiss Cult Promotes Cloning. http://www.religious-tolerance.org/news_697.htm.

Ott, S.

1981   *The Circle of Mountains: A Basque Shepherding Community.* Oxford, UK: Clarendon Press.

Otten, C. M., ed.

1971   *Anthropology and Art; Readings in Cross-Cultural Aesthetics.* Garden City, NY: American Museum of Natural History.

Otterbein, K. F.

1968   (orig. 1963). Marquesan Polyandry. In *Marriage, Family and Residence,* ed. P. Bohannan and J. Middleton, pp. 287–296. Garden City, NY: Natural History Press.

Park, M. A.

2002   *Biological Anthropology,* 3rd ed. Boston: McGraw-Hill.

Parker, S., and R. Kleiner

1970   The Culture of Poverty: An Adjustive Dimension. *American Anthropologist* 72: 516–527.

Parkin, R.

1997   *Kinship: An Introduction to Basic Concepts.* Cambridge, MA: Blackwell.

Parsons, J. R.

1974   The Development of a Prehistoric Complex Society: A Regional Perspective from the Valley of Mexico. *Journal of Field Archaeology* 1: 81–108.

1976   The Role of Chinampa Agriculture in the Food Supply of Aztec Tenochtitlan. In *Cultural Change and Continuity: Essays in Honor of James Bennett Griffin,* ed. C. E. Cleland, pp. 233–262. New York: Academic Press.

Pasternak, B., C. R. Ember, and M. Ember
1997   *Sex, Gender, and Kinship: A Cross-Cultural Perspective.* Upper Saddle River, NJ: Prentice-Hall.

Patterson, F.
1978   Conversations with a Gorilla. *National Geographic,* October, pp. 438–465.

Patterson, T. C.
1993   *Archaeology: The Historical Development of Civilizations,* 2nd ed. Englewood Cliffs, NJ: Prentice-Hall.

Paul, R.
1989   Psychoanalytic Anthropology. *Annual Review of Anthropology* 18: 177–202.

Pear, R.
1992   Ranks of U.S. Poor Reach 35.7 Million, the Most since '64. *New York Times,* September 3, pp. A1, A12.

Peletz, M.
1988   *A Share of the Harvest: Kinship, Property, and Social History among the Malays of Rembau.* Berkeley: University of California Press.

Pelto, P.
1973   *The Snowmobile Revolution: Technology and Social Change in the Arctic.* Menlo Park, CA: Cummings.

Pelto, P. J., and G. H. Pelto
1978   *Anthropological Research: The Structure of Inquiry,* 2nd ed. New York: Cambridge University Press.

Peplau, L. A., ed.
1999   *Gender, Culture, and Ethnicity: Current Research about Women and Men.* Mountain View, CA: Mayfield.

Petraglia-Bahri, D.
1996   Introduction to Postcolonial Studies. http://www.emory.edu/ENGLISH/Bahri/.

Pettifor, E.
1995   From the Teeth of the Dragon—*Gigantopithecus blacki.* http://www.wynja.com/arch/gigantopithecus.html.

Pfeiffer, J.
1985   *The Emergence of Humankind,* 4th ed. New York: HarperCollins.

Phillipson, D. W.
1993   *African Archaeology,* 2nd ed. New York: Cambridge University Press.

Piddington, R.
1970   Action Anthropology. In *Applied Anthropology: Readings in the Uses of the Science of Man,* ed. James Clifton, pp. 127–143. Boston: Houghton Mifflin.

Piddocke, S.
1969   The Potlatch System of the Southern Kwakiutl: A New Perspective. In *Environment and Cultural Behavior,* ed. A. P. Vayda, pp. 130–156. Garden City, NY: Natural History Press.

Plattner, S., ed.
1989   *Economic Anthropology.* Stanford, CA: Stanford University Press.

Podolefsky, A.
1992   *Simbu Law: Conflict Management in the New Guinea Highlands.* Fort Worth: Harcourt Brace.

Podolefsky, A., and P. J. Brown, eds.
1992   *Applying Anthropology: An Introductory Reader,* 2nd ed. Mountain View, CA: Mayfield.

2002   *Applying Anthropology: An Introductory Reader,* 7th ed. Boston: McGraw-Hill.

Poirier, F. E., and J. K. Mckee
1998   *Understanding Human Evolution,* 4th ed. Upper Saddle River, NJ: Prentice-Hall.

Polanyi, K.
1968   *Primitive, Archaic and Modern Economies: Essays of Karl Polanyi.* Edited by G. Dalton. Garden City, NY: Anchor Books.

Pollan, M.
2003   You Want Fries with That? *New York Times Book Review,* January 12, p. 6.

Pollard, T. M., and S. B. Hyatt
1999   *Sex, Gender, and Health.* New York: Cambridge University Press.

Pollock, S.
1999   *Ancient Mesopotamia: The Eden That Never Was.* Cambridge: Cambridge University Press.

Pospisil, L.
1963   *The Kapauku Papuans of West New Guinea.* New York: Harcourt Brace Jovanovich.

Potash, B., ed.

1986   *Widows in African Societies: Choices and Constraints.* Stanford, CA: Stanford University Press.

Potts, D. T.

1997   *Mesopotamian Civilization: The Material Foundations.* Ithaca, NY: Cornell University Press.

Prag, J., and R. Neave

1997   *Making Faces: Using Forensic and Archaeological Evidence.* College Station: Texas A&M University Press.

Price, R., ed.

1973   *Maroon Societies.* New York: Anchor Press, Doubleday.

Price, T. D., ed.

2000   *Europe's First Farmers.* New York: Cambridge University Press.

Price, T. D., and G. M. Feinman

2001   *Images of the Past*, 3rd ed. Boston: McGraw-Hill.

Price, T. D. and A. B. Gebauer, eds.

1995   *Last Hunters, First Farmers: New Perspectives on the Prehistoric Transition to Agriculture.* Santa Fe, NM: School of American Research Press.

Public Culture

        Journal published by the University of Chicago.

Punch, M.

1985   *The Politics and Ethics of Fieldwork.* Beverly Hills, CA: Sage.

Quiatt, D., and V. Reynolds

1995   *Primate Behavior: Information, Social Knowledge, and the Evolution of Culture.* New York: Cambridge University Press.

Quinn, N., and C. Strauss

1989   A Cognitive Cultural Anthropology. Paper presented at the Invited Session "Assessing Developments in Anthropology," American Anthropological Association 88th Annual Meeting, November 15–19, 1989, Washington, DC.

1994   A Cognitive Cultural Anthropology. *In Assessing Cultural Anthropology,* ed. R. Borofsky. New York: McGraw-Hill.

Radcliffe-Brown, A. R.

1965   (orig. 1962). *Structure and Function in Primitive Society.* New York: Free Press.

Radcliffe-Brown, A. R., and D. Forde, eds.

1994   *African Systems of Kinship and Marriage.* New York: Columbia University Press.

Rak, Y.

1986   The Neandertal: A New Look at an Old Face. *Journal of Human Evolution* 15(3): 151–164.

Random House College Dictionary

1982   Revised ed. New York: Random House.

Ranger, T. O.

1996   Postscript. In *Postcolonial Identities,* ed. R. Werbner and T. O. Ranger. London: Zed.

Rappaport, R. A.

1974   Obvious Aspects of Ritual. *Cambridge Anthropology* 2: 2–60.

1979   *Ecology, Meaning, and Religion.* Richmond, CA: North Atlantic Books.

1999   *Holiness and Humanity: Ritual in the Making of Religious Life.* New York: Cambridge University Press.

Rathus, S. A., J. S. Nevid, and J. Fichner-Rathus

1997   *Human Sexuality in a World of Diversity,* 3rd ed. Boston: Allyn & Bacon.

2000   *Human Sexuality in a World of Diversity,* 4th ed. Boston: Allyn & Bacon.

Read-Martin, C. E., and D. W. Read

1975   Australopithecine Scavenging and Human Evolution: An Approach from Faunal Analysis. *Current Anthropology* 16: 359–368.

Reade, J.

1991   *Mesopotamia.* Cambridge, MA: Harvard University Press.

Redfield, R.

1941   *The Folk Culture of Yucatan.* Chicago: University of Chicago Press.

Redfield, R., R. Linton, and M. Herskovits

1936   Memorandum on the Study of Acculturation. *American Anthropologist* 38: 149–152.

Redmond, E. M.

1994   Tribal and Chiefly Warfare in South America. *Museum of Anthropology Memoir* 28, University of Michigan (Ann Arbor).

Redmond, E. M., ed.

1998   *Chiefdoms and Chieftaincy in the Americas.* Gainesville, FL: University Press of Florida Press.

Reed, R.

1997   *Forest Dwellers, Forest Protectors: Indigenous Models for International Development*. Boston: Allyn & Bacon.

Reiter, R.

1975   Men and Women in the South of France: Public and Private Domains. In *Toward an Anthropology of Women*, ed. R. Reiter, pp. 252–282. New York: Monthly Review Press.

Reiter, R., ed.

1975   *Toward an Anthropology of Women*. New York: Monthly Review Press.

Relethford, J. H.

2000   *The Human Species: An Introduction to Biological Anthropology*, 4th ed. Boston: McGraw-Hill.

Renfrew, C., and P. Bahn

1996   *Archaeology: Theories, Methods, and Practice*, 2nd ed. London: Thames and Hudson.

2000   *Archaeology: Theories, Methods, and Practices*, 3rd ed. New York: Thames and Hudson.

Reynolds, V.

1971   *The Apes*. New York: Harper Colophon.

Rice, P.

2002   Paleoanthropology 2001—Part II. *General Anthropology*. 8(2): 11–14.

Richards, D.

1994   *Masks of Difference: Cultural Representations in Literature, Anthropology, and Art*. New York: Cambridge University Press.

Richards, P.

1973   The Tropical Rain Forest. *Scientific American* 229(6): 58–67.

Rickford, J. R.

1997   Suite for Ebony and Phonics. http://www.stanford.edu/~rickford/papers/SuiteForEbonyandPhonics.html (also published in *Discover*, December 1997).

1999   *African American Vernacular English: Features, Evolution, Educational Implications*. Malden, MA: Blackwell.

Rickford, J. R., and Rickford, R. J.

2000   *Spoken Soul: The Story of Black English*. New York: Wiley.

Ricoeur, P.

1971   The Model of the Text: Meaningful Action Considered as a Text. *Social Research* 38: 529–562.

Rightmire, G. P.

1990   *The Evolution of* Homo erectus: *Comparative Anatomical Studies of an Extinct Human Species*. New York: Cambridge University Press.

Rilling, J. K., D. A. Gutman, T. R. Zeh, G. Pagnoni, G. S. Berns, and C.D. Kilts

2002   A Neural Basis for Social Cooperation. *Neuron* 35: 395–405.

Robbins, R.

2002   *Global Problems and the Culture of Capitalism* 2nd ed. Boston: Allyn & Bacon.

Roberts, D. F.

1953   Body Weight, Race and Climate. *American Journal of Physical Anthropology* 11: 533–558.

1986   *Genetic Variation and Its Maintenance: With Particular Reference to Tropical Populations*. New York: Cambridge University Press.

Roberts, J. L.

1995   *Dian Fossey*. San Diego, CA: Lucent Books.

Roberts, S.

1979   *Order and Dispute: An Introduction to Legal Anthropology*. New York: Penguin Books.

Robertson, A. F.

1995   *The Big Catch: A Practical Introduction to Development*. Boulder, CO: Westview.

Robertson, J.

1992   Koreans in Japan. Paper presented at the University of Michigan Department of Anthropology, Martin Luther King Jr. Day Panel, January 1992. Ann Arbor: University of Michigan Department of Anthropology (unpublished).

Rodseth, L., R. W. Wrangham, A. M. Harrigan, and B. Smuts

1991   The Human Community as a Primate Society. *Current Anthropology* 32: 221–254.

Romaine, S.

1994   *Language in Society: An Introduction to Sociolinguistics*. New York: Oxford University Press.

1999   *Communicating Gender*. Mahwah, NJ: L. Erlbaum Associates.

Romer, A. S.

1960   *Man and the Vertebrates*, 3rd ed., Vol. 1. Harmondsworth, England: Penguin.

Root, D.

1996   *Cannibal Culture: Art, Appropriation, and the Commodification of Difference*. Boulder, CO: Westview.

Rosaldo, M. Z.

1980a   *Knowledge and Passion: Notions of Self and Social Life*. Stanford, CA: Stanford University Press.

1980b   The Use and Abuse of Anthropology: Reflections on Feminism and Cross-Cultural Understanding. *Signs* 5(3): 389–417.

Rosaldo, M. Z., and L. Lamphere, eds.

1974   *Woman, Culture, and Society*. Stanford, CA: Stanford University Press.

Rose, M.

1997   Neandertal DNA. Newsbriefs. *Archaeology* 50 (September/October): 5, http://www.archaeology.org/9709/newsbriefs/dna.html.

Roseberry, W.

1988   Political Economy. *Annual Review of Anthropology* 17: 161–185.

Rosenberg, K.R., and W.R. Trevathan

2001   The Evolution of Human Birth. *Scientific American* 285(5): 60–65.

Rouse, R.

1991   Mexican Migration and the Social Space of Postmodernism. *Diaspora* 1(1): 8–23.

Royal Anthropological Institute

1951   *Notes and Queries on Anthropology*, 6th ed. London: Routledge and Kegan Paul.

Rushing, W. A.

1995   *The AIDS Epidemic: Social Dimension of an Infectious Disease*. Boulder, CO: Westview.

Rushing, W. Jackson, ed.

1999   *Native American Art in the Twentieth Century*. New York: Routledge.

Russon, A. E., K. A. Bard, and S. Taylor Parker, eds.

1996   *Reaching into Thought: The Minds of the Great Apes*. New York: Cambridge University Press.

Ryan, S.

1990   *Ethnic Conflict and International Relations*. Brookfield, MA: Dartmouth.

1995   *Ethnic Conflict and International Relations*, 2nd ed. Brookfield, MA: Dartmouth.

Sachs, C. E.

1996   *Gendered Fields: Rural Women, Agriculture, and Environment*. Boulder, CO: Westview.

Sade, D.

1972   A Longitudinal Study of Social Behavior of Rhesus Monkeys. In *The Functional and Evolutionary Biology of Primates*, ed. R. Tuttle, pp. 378–398. Chicago: University of Chicago Press.

Saggs, H.

1989   *Civilization before Greece and Rome*. New Haven, CT: Yale University Press.

Sahlins, M. D.

1961   The Segmentary Lineage: An Organization of Predatory Expansion. *American Anthropologist* 63: 322–345.

1968   *Tribesmen*. Englewood Cliffs, NJ: Prentice-Hall.

1972   *Stone Age Economics*. Chicago: Aldine.

1981   *Historical Metaphors and Mythical Realities: Structure in the Early History of the Sandwich Islands Kingdom*. Ann Arbor, MI: University of Michigan Press.

Saitoti, T. O.

1988   *The Worlds of a Maasai Warrior: An Autobiography*. Berkeley: University of California Press.

Saluter, A.

1995   Household and Family Characteristics: March 1994, P20-483, Press release, October 16, CB95-186, Single-Parent Growth Rate Stabilized; 2-parent Family Growth Renewed, Census Bureau Reports. United States Department of Commerce, Bureau of Census, Public Information Office.

1996   Marital Status and Living Arrangements: March 1994, P20-484, U.S. Census Bureau, Press release, March 13, 1996, CB96-33. United States Department of Commerce, Bureau of Census, Public Information Office, http://www.census.gov/prod/www/titles.html#popspec.

Salzman, P. C.

1974   Political Organization among Nomadic Peoples. In *Man in Adaptation: The Cultural Present*, 2nd ed., ed. Y. A. Cohen, pp. 267–284. Chicago: Aldine.

Salzman, P. C., and J. G. Galaty, eds.

1990   *Nomads in a Changing World*. Naples: Istituto Universitario Orientale.

Salzmann, Z.

1993   *Language, Culture, and Society: An Introduction to Linguistic Anthropology*. Boulder, CO: Westview.

Sanday, P. R.

1974   Female Status in the Public Domain. In *Woman, Culture, and Society,* ed. M. Z. Rosaldo and L. Lamphere, pp. 189–206. Stanford, CA: Stanford University Press.

2002   *Women at the Center: Life in a Modern Matriarchy.* Ithaca, NY: Cornell University Press.

Sanders, W. T.

1972   Population, Agricultural History, and Societal Evolution in Mesoamerica. In *Population Growth: Anthropological Implications,* ed. B. Spooner, pp. 101–153. Cambridge, MA: MIT Press.

1973   The Cultural Ecology of the Lowland Maya: A Reevaluation. In *The Classic Maya Collapse,* ed. T. P. Culbert, pp. 325–366. Albuquerque, NM: University of New Mexico Press.

Sanders, W. T., J. R. Parsons, and R. S. Santley

1979   *The Basin of Mexico: Ecological Processes in the Evolution of a Civilization.* New York: Academic Press.

Sankoff, G.

1980   *The Social Life of Language.* Philadelphia: University of Pennsylvania Press.

Santino, J.

1983   Night of the Wandering Souls. *Natural History* 92(10): 42.

Santley, R. S.

1984   Obsidian Exchange, Economic Stratification, and the Evolution of Complex Society in the Basin of Mexico. In *Trade and Exchange in Early Mesoamerica,* ed. K. G. Hirth, pp. 43–86. Albuquerque, NM: University of New Mexico Press.

1985   The Political Economy of the Aztec Empire. *Journal of Anthropological Research* 41(3): 327–337.

Sapir, E.

1931   Conceptual Categories in Primitive Languages. *Science* 74: 578–584.

Sargent, C. F., and C. B. Brettell

1996   *Gender and Health: An International Perspective.* Upper Saddle River, NJ: Prentice-Hall.

Sargent, C. F., and T. J. Johnson, eds.

1996   *Medical Anthropology: A Handbook of Theory and Method,* rev. ed. Westport, CT: Praeger Press.

Schaefer, R.

1989   *Sociology,* 3rd ed. New York: McGraw-Hill.

Schaefer, R., and R. P. Lamm

1994   *Sociology.* New York: McGraw-Hill.

1997   *Sociology,* 2nd ed. New York: McGraw-Hill.

Schaller, G.

1963   *The Mountain Gorilla: Ecology and Behavior.* Chicago: University of Chicago Press.

Scheffler, H. W.

2001   *Filiation and Affiliation.* Boulder, CO: Westview.

Scheinman, M.

1980   Imperialism. *Academic American Encyclopedia,* vol. 11, pp. 61–62. Princeton, NJ: Arete.

Scheper-Hughes, N.

1987   Culture, Scarcity, and Maternal Thinking: Mother Love and Child Death in Northeast Brazil. In *Child Survival,* ed. N. Scheper-Hughes, pp. 187–208. Boston: D. Reidel.

1992   *Death without Weeping: The Violence of Everyday Life in Brazil.* Berkeley: University of California Press.

Schieffelin, E.

1976   *The Sorrow of the Lonely and the Burning of the Dancers.* New York: St. Martin's.

Schildkrout, E., and C. A. Keim

1990   *African Reflections: Art from Northeastern Zaire.* Seattle, WA: University of Washington Press.

Schlee, G., ed.

2002   *Imagined Differences: Hatred and the Construction of Identity.* New York: Palgrave.

Scholte, J. A.

2000   *Globalization: A Critical Introduction.* New York: St. Martin's.

Scott, J.

2002   Prehistoric Human Footpaths Lure Archaeologists Back to Costa Rica. University of Colorado Press Release, May 20. http://www.eurekalert.org/pub_releases/2002-05/uoca-phf052002.php.

Scott, J. C.

1985   *Weapons of the Weak.* New Haven, CT: Yale University Press.

1990   *Domination and the Arts of Resistance.* New Haven, CT: Yale University Press.

1998   *Seeing Like a State: How Certain Schemes to Improve the Human Condition Have Failed.* New Haven, CT: Yale University Press.

Scudder, T.

1982   The Impact of Big Dam-building on the Zambezi River Basin. In *The Careless Technology: Ecology and International Development*, eds. M. T. Farvar and J. P. Milton, pp. 206–235. New York: Natural History Press.

Scudder, T., and E. Colson

1980   *Secondary Education and the Formation of an Elite: The Impact of Education on Gwembe District, Zambia.* London: Academic Press.

Scudder, T., and J. Habarad

1991   Local Responses to Involuntary Relocation and Development in the Zambian Portion of the Middle Zambezi Valley. In *Migrants in Agricultural Development*, ed. J. A. Mollett, pp. 178–205. New York: New York University Press.

Scupin, R.

2003   *Race and Ethnicity: An Anthropological Focus on the United States and the World.* Upper Saddle River, NJ: Prentice-Hall.

Sebeok, T. A., and J. Umiker-Sebeok, eds.

1980   *Speaking of Apes: A Critical Anthropology of Two-Way Communication with Man.* New York: Plenum.

Seligson, M. A.

1984   *The Gap between Rich and Poor: Contending Perspectives on the Political Economy of Development.* Boulder, CO: Westview.

Sered, S. S.

1996   *Priestess, Mother, Sacred Sister: Religions Dominated by Women.* New York: Oxford University Press.

Service, E. R.

1962   *Primitive Social Organization: An Evolutionary Perspective.* New York: McGraw-Hill.

1966   *The Hunters.* Englewood Cliffs, NJ: Prentice-Hall.

1975   *Origins of the State and Civilization: The Process of Cultural Evolution.* New York: W. W. Norton.

Shabecoff, P.

1989*a*   Ivory Imports Banned to Aid Elephant. *New York Times*, June 7, p. 15.

1989*b*   New Lobby Is Helping Wildlife of Africa. *New York Times*, June 9, p. 14.

Shanklin, E.

1995   *Anthropology and Race.* Belmont, CA: Wadsworth.

Shannon, T. R.

1989   *An Introduction to the World-System Perspective.* Boulder, CO: Westview.

1996   *An Introduction to the World-System Perspective*, 2nd ed. Boulder, CO: Westview Press.

Shepher, J.

1983   *Incest, a Biosocial View.* New York: Academic Press.

Shermer, M.

2002   *In Darwin's Shadow: The Life and Science of Alfred Russel Wallace.* New York: Oxford University Press.

Shigeru, K.

1994   *Our Land Was a Forest: An Ainu Memoir.* Boulder, CO: Westview.

Shivaram, C.

1996   Where Women Wore the Crown: Kerala's Dissolving Matriarchies Leave a Rich Legacy of Compassionate Family Culture. *Hinduism Today* 96(02). http://www.spiritweb.org/HinduismToday/96-02-Women_Wore_Crown.html.

Shore, B.

1996   *Culture in Mind: Meaning, Construction, and Cultural Cognition.* New York: Oxford University Press.

Shostak, M.

1981   *Nisa, the Life and Words of a !Kung Woman.* New York: Vintage Books.

2000   *Return to Nisa.* Cambridge, MA: Harvard University Press.

Shreeve, J.

1992   The Dating Game: How Old Is the Human Race? *Discover* 13(9): 76–83.

Shweder, R., and H. Levine, eds.

1984   *Culture Theory: Essays on Mind, Self, and Emotion.* Cambridge: Cambridge University Press.

Sibley, C. G., and J. E. Ahlquist

1984   The Phylogeny of the Hominoid Primates, as Indicated by DNA-DNA Hybridization. *Journal of Molecular Evolution* 20: 2–15.

Signo, A.

1994   *Economics of the Family.* New York: Oxford University Press.

Silberbauer, G.

1981   *Hunter and Habitat in the Central Kalahari Desert.* New York: Cambridge University Press.

Silverberg, J., and J. P. Gray, eds.
1992   *Aggression and Peacefulness in Humans and Other Primates.* New York: Oxford University Press.

Simons, A.
1995   *Networks of Dissolution: Somalia Undone.* Boulder, CO: Westview.

Simons, E. L., and P. C. Ettel
1970   *Gigantopithecus. Scientific American,* January, pp. 77–85.

Simpson, B.
1998   *Changing Families: An Ethnographic Approach to Divorce and Separation.* New York: Berg.

Slade, M. F.
1984   Displaying Affection in Public. *New York Times,* December 17, p. B14.

Small, M., ed.
1984   *Female Primates: Studies by Women Primatologists.* New York: Alan R. Liss.

Small, M. F.
1993   *Female Choices: Sexual Behavior of Female Primates.* Ithaca, NY: Cornell University Press.

Smith, B. D.
1995   *The Emergence of Agriculture.* New York: Scientific American Library, W. H. Freeman.

Smith, C. A.
1990   The Militarization of Civil Society in Guatemala: Economic Reorganization as a Continuation of War. *Latin American Perspectives* 17: 8–41.

Smith, M. E., and M. A. Masson, eds.
2000   *The Ancient Civilizations of Mesoamerica: A Reader.* Malpen, MA: Blackwell.

Smith, M. G.
1965   *The Plural Society in the British West Indies.* Berkeley: University of California Press.

Smitherman, G.
1986   *Talkin and Testifyin: The Language of Black America.* Detroit: Wayne State University Press.

Smuts, B. B.
1999   (orig. 1985) *Sex and Friendship in Baboons.* Cambridge, MA: Harvard University Press.

Solheim, W. G., II
1976   (orig. 1972). An Earlier Agricultural Revolution. In *Avenues to Antiquity: Readings from Scientific American,* ed. B. M. Fagan, pp. 160–168. San Francisco: W. H. Freeman.

Solway, J., and R. Lee
1990   Foragers, Genuine and Spurious: Situating the Kalahari San in History (with CA treatment). *Current Anthropology* 31(2): 109–146.

Sonneville-Bordes, D. de
1963   Upper Paleolithic Cultures in Western Europe. *Science* 142: 347–355.

Spindler, G. D., ed.
1978   *The Making of Psychological Anthropology.* Berkeley: University of California Press.

1982   *Doing the Ethnography of Schooling: Educational Anthropology in Action.* New York: Holt, Rinehart and Winston.

2000   *Fifty Years of Anthropology and Education, 1950–2000: A Spindler Anthology.* Mahwah, NJ: Erlbaum Associates.

Sponsel, L. E., and T. Gregor, eds.
1994   *The Anthropology of Peace and Nonviolence.* Boulder, CO: Lynne Reinner.

Spradley, J. P.
1979   *The Ethnographic Interview.* New York: Harcourt Brace Jovanovich.

Srivastava, J., N. J. H. Smith, and D. A. Forno
1998   *Integrating Biodiversity in Agricultural Intensification: Toward Sound Practices.* Washington, DC: World Bank.

Stacey, J.
1996   *In the Name of the Family: Rethinking Family Values in the Postmodern Age.* Boston: Beacon Press.

1998   *Brave New Families: Stories of Domestic Upheaval in Late Twentieth Century America.* Berkeley: University of California Press.

Stack, C. B.
1975   *All Our Kin: Strategies for Survival in a Black Community.* New York: Harper Torchbooks.

Staeck, J.
2002   *Back to the Earth: An Introduction to Archaeology.* Boston: McGraw-Hill.

Statistical Abstract of the United States
1991   111th ed. Washington, DC: U.S. Bureau of the Census, U.S. Government Printing Office.

1996   116th ed. Washington, DC: U.S. Bureau of the Census, U.S. Government Printing Office.

1999   *Statistical Abstract of the United States, 1999.* http://www.census.gov/statab/www/.

Statistics Canada

1998   1996 Census: Ethnic Origin, Visible Minorities. *The Daily*, February 17. http://www.statcan.ca/Daily/English/980217/d980217.htm.

2001   1996 Census. Nation Tables. http://www.statcan.ca/english/census96/nation.htm.

Staub, S.

1989   *Yemenis in New York City: The Folklore of Ethnicity.* Philadelphia: Balch Institute Press.

Steegman, A. T., Jr.

1975   Human Adaptation to Cold. *In Physiological Anthropology,* ed. A. Damon, pp. 130–166. New York: Oxford University Press.

Steinfels, P.

1997   Beliefs: Cloning, as Seen by Buddhists and Humanists. *New York Times,* July 12. http://www.nytimes.com.

Stephens, S., ed.

1996   *Children and the Politics of Culture.* Princeton, NJ: Princeton University Press.

Steponaitis, V.

1986   Prehistoric Archaeology in the Southeastern United States. *Annual Review of Anthropology* 15: 363–404.

Stern, A.

2000*a*   Experts Say 138 World Primate Species Endangered. Reuters. http://www.forests.org/archive/general/exsay138.htm.

2000*b*   More Than a Hundred Primate Species Endangered. http://www.foxnews.com/science/051200/primates.sml.

Stevens, W. K.

1992   Humanity Confronts Its Handiwork: An Altered Planet. *New York Times,* May 5, pp. B5–B7.

Stevenson, R. F.

1968   *Population and Political Systems in Tropical Africa.* New York: Columbia University Press.

Steward, J. H.

1955   *Theory of Culture Change.* Urbana: University of Illinois Press.

Stinson, S., ed.

2000   *Human Biology: An Evolutionary and Biocultural Perspective.* New York: Wiley.

Stocking, G. W., ed.

1986   *Malinowski, Rivers, Benedict and Others: Essays on Culture and Personality.* Madison, WI: University of Wisconsin Press.

Stoler, A.

1977   Class Structure and Female Autonomy in Rural Java. *Signs* 3: 74–89.

Stone, L.

2000   *Kinship and Gender: An Introduction,* 2nd ed. Boulder, CO: Westview.

2001   *New Directions in Anthropological Kinship.* Lanham, MD: Rowman and Littlefield.

Stoneman, B.

1997   Income Is Rising, So Is Poverty. *American Demographics,* Forecast, November 1997, http://www.demographics.com/publications/fc/97_fc/9711_fc/fc97111.htm.

Strathern, A., and P. J. Stewart

1999   *Curing and Healing: Medical Anthropology in Global Perspective.* Durham, NC: Carolina Academic Press.

Strathern, M.

1988   *The Gender of the Gift: Problems with Women and Problems with Society in Melanesia.* Berkeley: University of California Press.

Strum, S. C., and L. M. Fedigan, eds.

2000   *Primate Encounters: Models of Science, Gender, and Society.* Chicago: University of Chicago Press.

Suarez-Orozco, M. M., G. Spindler, and L. Spindler, eds.

1994   *The Making of Psychological Anthropology II.* Fort Worth: Harcourt Brace.

Susman, R. L.

1987   Pygmy Chimpanzees and Common Chimpanzees: Models for the Behavioral Ecology of the Earliest Hominids. In *The Evolution of Human Behavior: Primate Models,* ed. W. G. Kinzey, pp. 72–86. Albany: State University of New York Press.

Susser, I., and T. C. Patterson, eds.

2000   *Cultural Diversity in the United States: A Critical Reader.* Malden, MA: Blackwell.

Suttles, W.

1960   Affinal Ties, Subsistence, and Prestige among the Coast Salish. *American Anthropologist* 62: 296–395.

Swift, M.

1963   Men and Women in Malay Society. In *Women in the New Asia,* ed. B. Ward, pp. 268–286. Paris: UNESCO.

Swindler, D. R.
1998   *Introduction to the Primates.* Seattle: University of Washington Press.

Tague, R. G., and C. O. Lovejoy
1986   The Obstetric Pelvis of A. L. 288-1 (Lucy). *Journal of Human Evolution* 15: 237–255.

Tainter, J.
1987   *The Collapse of Complex Societies.* New York: Cambridge University Press.

Tanaka, J.
1980   *The San Hunter-Gatherers of the Kalahari.* Tokyo: University of Tokyo Press.

Tannen, D.
1990   *You Just Don't Understand: Women and Men in Conversation.* New York: Ballantine.

Tannen, D., ed.
1993   *Gender and Conversational Interaction.* New York: Oxford University Press.

Tanner, N.
1974   Matrifocality in Indonesia and Africa and among Black Americans. In *Women, Culture, and Society,* ed. M. Z. Rosaldo and L. Lamphere, pp. 127–156. Stanford, CA: Stanford University Press.

Tattersall, I.
1995a   *The Fossil Trail: How We Know What We Think We Know about Human Evolution.* New York: Oxford University Press.

1995b   *The Last Neanderthal: The Rise, Success, and Mysterious Extinction of Our Closest Human Relatives.* New York: Macmillan.

1998   *Becoming Human: Evolution and Human Uniqueness.* New York: Harcourt Brace.

Taylor, A.
1993   *Women Drug Users: An Ethnography of a Female Injecting Community.* New York: Oxford University Press.

Taylor, C.
1987   Anthropologist-in-Residence. In *Applied Anthropology in America,* 2nd ed., ed. E. M. Eddy and W. L. Partridge. New York: Columbia University Press.

1996   *The Black Churches of Brooklyn.* New York: Columbia University Press.

Teleki, G.
1973   *The Predatory Behavior of Wild Chimpanzees.* Lewisburg, PA: Bucknell University Press.

Terrace, H. S.
1979   *Nim.* New York: Knopf.

Terrell, J. E.
1998   The Prehistoric Pacific. *Archaeology,* vol. 51, no. 6. Archaeological Institute of America. http://www.archaeology.org/9811/abstracts/pacific.html.

Thomas, L., and S. Wareing, eds.
1999   *Language, Society and Power.* New York: Routledge.

Thomason, S. G., And T. Kaufman
1988   *Language Contact, Creolization and Genetic Linguistics.* Berkeley: University of California Press.

Thompson, W.
1983   Introduction: World System with and without the Hyphen. In *Contending Approaches to World System Analysis,* ed. W. Thompson, pp. 7–26. Thousand Oaks, CA: Sage.

Thomson, A., and L. H. D. Buxton
1923   Man's Nasal Index in Relation to Certain Climatic Conditions. *Journal of the Royal Anthropological Institute* 53: 92–112.

Tice, K.
1997   Reflections on Teaching Anthropology for Use in the Public and Private Sector. In *The Teaching of Anthropology: Problems, Issues, and Decisions,* ed. C. P. Kottak, J. J. White, R. H. Furlow, and P. C. Rice, pp. 273–284. Mountain View, CA: Mayfield.

Tobler, A. J.
1950   *Excavations at Tepe Gawra,* vol. 2. Philadelphia: University of Pennsylvania Museum.

Todt, R.
2000   Western Hemisphere Inhabited at Least 15,000 Years Ago. ABCNews.Go.com News Briefs, April 7. http://abcnews.go.com/sections/science/DailyNews/first_americans000407.html.

Toner, R.
1992   Los Angeles Riots Are a Warning, Americans Fear. *New York Times,* May 11, pp. A1, A11.

Toth, N., and Schick, K.
1986   The First Million Years: The Archaeology of Protohuman Culture. *Advances in Archaeological Method and Theory,* pp. 1–96.

Trask, L.
1996   FAQs about Basque and the Basques. http://www.cogs.susx.ac.uk/users/larryt/basque.faqs.html.

Trigger, B. G.
1993   *Early Civilizations: Ancient Egypt in Context.* New York: Columbia University Press.

Trudgill, P.
1983   *Sociolinguistics: An Introduction to Language and Society,* rev. ed. Baltimore: Penguin.

2000   *Sociolinguistics: An Introduction to Language and Society,* 4th ed. New York: Penguin.

Turnbull, C.
1965   *Wayward Servants: The Two Worlds of the African Pygmies.* Garden City, NY: Natural History Press.

Turner, B. S.
1998   *Readings in the Anthropology and Sociology of Family and Kinship.* London: Routledge/Thoemmes.

Turner, T.
1993   The Role of Indigenous Peoples in the Environmental Crisis: The Example of the Kayapo of the Brazilian Amazon. *Perspectives in Biology and Medicine* 36: 526–545.

Turner, V. W.
1969   *The Ritual Process.* Chicago: Aldine.

1974   *The Ritual Process.* Harmondsworth, England: Penguin.

1995   (orig. 1969). *The Ritual Process.* Hawthorne, NY: Aldine de Gruyter.

Tylor, E. B.
1889   On a Method of Investigating the Development of Institutions: Applied to Laws of Marriage and Descent. *Journal of the Royal Anthropological Institute* 18: 245–269.

1958   (orig. 1871). *Primitive Culture.* New York: Harper Torchbooks.

Ucko, P. J., and G. W. Dimbleby, eds.
1969   *The Domestication and Exploitation of Plants and Animals.* Chicago: Aldine.

Ucko, P., and A. Rosenfeld
1967   *Paleolithic Cave Art.* London: Weidenfeld and Nicolson.

U.S. Census Bureau
1998   Unpublished Tables—Marital Status and Living Arrangements, March 1998 (Update).

http://www.census.gov/prod/99pubs/p20-514u.pdf.

1999   *Statisical Abstract of the United States.* http://www.census.gov/prod/99pubs/99statab/sec01.pdf and http://www.census.gov/prod/99pubs/99statab/sec02.pdf.

Valentine, C.
1968   *Culture and Poverty.* Chicago: University of Chicago Press.

Valladas, H., J. L. Reyss, J. L. Joron, G. Valladas, O. Bar-Joseph, and B. Vandermeersch
1988   Thermoluminescence Dating of Mousterian "Proto-Cro-Magnon" Remains from Israel and the Origin of Modern Man. *Nature* 331: 614–616.

Van Bremen, J., and A. Shimizu, eds.
1999   *Anthropology and Colonialism in Asia and Oceania.* London: Curzon.

Van Cantfort, T. E., and J. B. Rimpau
1982   Sign Language Studies with Children and Chimpanzees. *Sign Language Studies* 34: 15–72.

Van der Elst, D., and P. Bohannan
1999   *Culture as Given, Culture as Choice.* Prospect Heights, IL: Waveland.

Van Schaik, C. P., and J. A. R. A. M. van Hooff
1983   On the Ultimate Causes of Primate Social Systems. *Behaviour* 85: 91–117.

Van Willingen, J.
1987   *Becoming a Practicing Anthropologist: A Guide to Careers and Training Programs in Applied Anthropology.* NAPA Bulletin 3. Washington, DC: American Anthropological Association/National Association for the Practice of Anthropology.

1993   *Applied Anthropology: An Introduction,* 2nd ed. South Hadley, MA: Bergin and Garvey.

2002   *Applied Anthropology: An Introduction,* 3rd ed. Westport CT: Bergin and Garvey.

Vayda, A. P.
1968   (orig. 1961). Economic Systems in Ecological Perspective: The Case of the Northwest Coast. In *Readings in Anthropology,* 2nd ed., vol. 2, ed. M. H. Fried, pp. 172–178. New York: Crowell.

Veblen, T.
1934   *The Theory of the Leisure Class: An Economic Study of Institutions.* New York, The Modern Library.

Vekua, A., D. Lordkipanidze, and G. P. Rightmire.
2002   A Skull of Early Homo from Dmanisi, Georgia. *Science,* July 5, pp. 85–89.

Verlinden, C.
1980   Colonialism. *Academic American Encyclopedia,* vol. 5, pp. 111–112. Princeton, NJ: Arete.

Viegas, J.
2000   Planet of the Dying Apes: Conference Reveals Steep Decline in Primate Populations. http://abcnews.go.com/sections/science/DailyNews/apeconference000512.html.

Vietnam Labor Watch
1997   Nike Labor Practices in Vietnam, March 20. http://www.saigon.com/~nike/reports/report1.html.

Vincent, J.
1990   *Anthropology and Politics: Visions, Traditions, and Trends.* Tucson: University of Arizona Press.

Vincent, J., ed.
2002   *The Anthropology of Politics: A Reader in Ethnography, Theory, and Critique.* Malden, MA: Blackwell.

Viola, H. J., and C. Margolis
1991   *Seeds of Change: Five Hundred Years Since Columbus, a Quincentennial Commemoration.* Washington, DC: Smithsonian Institution Press.

Von Daniken, E.
1971   *Chariots of the Gods: Unsolved Mysteries of the Past.* New York: Bantam.

Wade, N.
1997   Testing Genes to Save a Life without Costing You a Job. *New York Times.* September 14. www.nytimes.com.

2001   Gene Study Shows Ties Long Veiled in Europe. *New York Times,* April 10. http://www.angelfire.com/nt/dragon9/BASQUES2.html.

Wade, N., ed.
2001   *The New York Times Book of Fossils and Evolution,* rev. ed. New York: Lyons Press.

Wade, P.
2002   *Race, Nature, and Culture: An Anthropological Perspective.* Sterling, VA: Pluto Press.

Wagley, C. W.
1968   (orig. 1959). The Concept of Social Race in the Americas. In *The Latin American Tradition,* ed. C. Wagley, pp. 155–174. New York: Columbia University Press.

Wagner, R.
1981   *The Invention of Culture,* rev. ed. Chicago: University of Chicago Press.

Wallace, A. F. C.
1956   Revitalization Movements. *American Anthropologist* 58: 264–281.

1966   *Religion: An Anthropological View.* New York: McGraw-Hill.

1970   *The Death and Rebirth of the Seneca.* New York: Knopf.

Wallerstein, I. M.
1974   *The Modern World-System: Capitalist Agriculture and the Origins of the European World-Economy in the Sixteenth Century.* New York: Academic Press.

1980   *The Modern World System II: Mercantilism and the Consolidation of the European World-Economy, 1600–1750.* New York: Academic Press.

1982   The Rise and Future Demise of the World Capitalist System: Concepts for Comparative Analysis. In *Introduction to the Sociology of "Developing Societies,"* ed. H. Alavi and T. Shanin, pp. 29–53. New York: Monthly Review Press.

2000   *The Essential Wallerstein.* New York: New Press, W. W. Norton.

Wallman, S., ed.
1977   *Perceptions of Development.* New York: Cambridge University Press.

Ward, M. C.
2003   *A World Full of Women,* 3rd ed. Needham Heights, MA: Allyn & Bacon.

Ward, S., B. Brown, A. Hill, J. Kelley, and W. Downs
1999   Equatorius: A New Hominoid Genus from the Middle Miocene of Kenya. *Science EurekAlert!* August 27. http://www.eurekalert.org.

Warren, K. B.
1998   *Indigenous Movements and Their Critics: Pan-Maya Activism in Guatemala.* Princeton, NJ: Princeton University Press.

Washburn, S. L., and R. Moore
1980   *Ape into Human: A Study of Human Evolution,* 2nd ed. Boston: Little, Brown.

Watson, J. D.
1970   *Molecular Biology of the Gene.* New York: Benjamin.

Watson, P.
1972   *Can Racial Discrimination Affect IQ? In Race and Intelligence; The Fallacies behind the Race-IQ Controversy,* ed. K. Richardson and D. Spears, pp. 56–67. Baltimore: Penguin.

Watson, P. J.
1983   The Halafian Culture: A Review and Synthesis. In *The Hilly Flanks and Beyond: Essays on the Prehistory of Southwestern Asia,* ed. T. C. Young, Jr., P. E. L. Smith, and P. Mortensen. *Studies in Ancient Oriental Civilization* 36: 231–250. Oriental Institute, University of Chicago.

Weaver, T., gen. ed.
1973   *To See Ourselves: Anthropology and Modern Social Issues.* Glenview, IL: Scott, Foresman.

Weber, M.
1958   (orig. 1904). *The Protestant Ethic and the Spirit of Capitalism.* New York: Scribner's.

1968   (orig. 1922). *Economy and Society.* Translated by E. Fischoff et al. New York: Bedminster Press.

Webster's New World Encyclopedia
1993   College Edition. Englewood Cliffs, NJ: Prentice-Hall.

Weiner, J. S.
1954   Nose Shape and Climate. *American Journal of Physical Anthropology* 12: 1–4.

Weiner, J.
1994   *The Beak of the Finch: A Story of Evolution in Our Time.* New York: Alfred A. Knopf.

Weiss, K. M.
1993   *Genetic Variation and Human Disease: Principles and Evolutionary Approaches.* New York: Cambridge University Press.

Weiss, M. L., And A. E. Mann
1990   *Human Biology and Behavior: An Anthropological Perspective,* 5th ed. Glenview, IL: Scott, Foresman.

Wenke, R. J.
1996   *Patterns in Prehistory: Mankind's First Three Million Years,* 4th ed. New York: Oxford University Press.

Westermarck, E.
1894   *The History of Human Marriage.* London: Macmillan.

Weston, K.
1991   *Families We Choose: Lesbians, Gays, Kinship.* New York: Columbia University Press.

White, L. A.
1959   *The Evolution of Culture: The Development of Civilization to the Fall of Rome.* New York: McGraw-Hill.

White, T. D., and P. A. Folkens
2000   *Human Osteology,* 2nd ed. San Diego: Academic Press.

Whiting, B. E., ed.
1963   *Six Cultures: Studies of Child Rearing.* New York: Wiley.

Whiting, J. M.
1964   Effects of Climate on Certain Cultural Practices. In *Explorations in Cultural Anthropology: Essays in Honor of George Peter Murdock,* ed. W. H. Goodenough, pp. 511–544. New York: McGraw-Hill.

Whyte, M. F.
1978   Cross-Cultural Codes Dealing with the Relative Status of Women. *Ethnology* XII(2): 203–225.

Whorf, B. L.
1956   A Linguistic Consideration of Thinking in Primitive Communities. In *Language, Thought, and Reality: Selected Writings of Benjamin Lee Whorf,* ed. J. B. Carroll, pp. 65–86. Cambridge, MA: MIT Press.

Wilford, J. N.
1995   The Transforming Leap, from 4 Legs to 2. *New York Times,* September 5, pp. B5(N), C1(L).

2000   Ruins Alter Ideas of How Civilization Spread, May 23. www.nytimes.com.

2001a   Skull May Alter Experts' View of Human Descent's Branches. *New York Times,* March 22, late edition, final, section A, p. 1, column 1. www.nytimes.com.

2001b   African Artifacts Suggest an Earlier Modern Human. *New York Times,* December 2, late edition, final, section 1A, p. 1, column 5. www.nytimes.com.

2002a   Seeking Polynesia's Beginnings in an Archipelago of Shards. *New York Times,* January 8, Science Desk.

2002*b*   When Humans Became Human. *New York Times,* February 26, late edition, final, section F, p. 1, column 1. www.nytimes.com.

Wilk, R. R.

1996   *Economies and Cultures: An Introduction to Economic Anthropology.* Boulder, CO: Westview.

Williams, B.

1989   A Class Act: Anthropology and the Race to Nation across Ethnic Terrain. *Annual Review of Anthropology* 18: 401–444.

Willie, C. V.

2003   *A New Look at Black Families.* Walnut Creek, CA: Altamira.

Wilmsen, E. N.

1989   *Land Filled with Flies: A Political Economy of the Kalahari.* Chicago: University of Chicago Press.

Wilmsen, E. N., and P. McAllister, eds.

1996   *The Politics of Difference: Ethnic Premises in a World of Power.* Chicago: University of Chicago Press.

Wilson, C.

1995   *Hidden in the Blood: A Personal Investigation of AIDS in the Yucatan.* New York: Columbia University Press.

Wilson, D. S.

2002   *Darwin's Cathedral: Evolution, Religion, and the Nature of Society.* Chicago: University of Chicago Press.

Wilson, R., ed.

1996   *Human Rights: Culture and Context: Anthropological Perspectives.* Chicago: Pluto.

Winslow, J. H., and A. Meyer

1983   The Perpetrator at Piltdown. *Science* 83 (September): 33–43.

Winzeler, R. L.

1995   *Latah in Southeast Asia: The Ethnography and History of a Culture-Bound Syndrome.* New York: Cambridge University Press.

Wittfogel, K. A.

1957   *Oriental Despotism: A Comparative Study of Total Power.* New Haven, CT: Yale University Press.

Wolf, E. R.

1966   *Peasants.* Englewood Cliffs, NJ: Prentice-Hall.

1982   *Europe and the People without History.* Berkeley: University of California Press.

1999   *Envisioning Power: Ideologies of Dominance and Crisis.* Berkeley: University of California Press.

Wolf, E. R., with S. Silverman

2001   *Pathways of Power: Building an Anthropology of the Modern World.* Berkeley: University of California Press.

Wolpoff, M., B. Senut, M. Pickford, and J. Hawks

2002   Sahelanthropus or "Sahelpithecus"? *Nature* 419: 581–582.

Wolpoff, M. H.

1980*a*   *Paleoanthropology.* Boston: McGraw-Hill.

1980*b*   Cranial Remains of Middle Pleistocene Hominids. *Journal of Human Evolution* 9: 339–358.

1999   *Paleoanthropology,* 2nd ed. New York: McGraw-Hill.

Wolpoff, M. H., And R. Caspari

1997   *Race and Human Evolution.* New York: Simon & Schuster.

Woolard, K. A.

1989   *Double Talk: Bilingualism and the Politics of Ethnicity in Catalonia.* Stanford, CA: Stanford University Press.

World Almanac & Book of Facts

Published annually. New York: Newspaper Enterprise Association.

World Health Organization

1995   *World Health Report.* Geneva: World Health Organization.

Worsley, P.

1984   *The Three Worlds: Culture and World Development.* Chicago: University of Chicago Press.

1985   (orig. 1959). Cargo Cults. In *Readings in Anthropology* 85/86. Guilford, CT: Dushkin.

Wrangham, R. W.

1980   An Ecological Model of Female-Bonded Primate Groups. *Behavior* 75: 262–300.

1987   The Significance of African Apes for Reconstructing Human Social Evolution. In *The Evolution of Human Behavior: Primate Models,* ed. W. G. Kinzey, pp. 51–71. Albany: State University of New York Press.

Wrangham, R. W., ed.

1994   *Chimpanzee Cultures.* Cambridge, MA: Harvard University Press.

Wrangham, R., W. McGrew, F. de Waal, and P. Heltne, eds.

1994   *Chimpanzee Cultures.* Cambridge, MA: Harvard University Press.

Wrangham, R. W., and D. Peterson

1996   *Demonic Males: Apes and the Origins of Human Violence.* Boston: Houghton Mifflin.

Wright, H. T., and G. A. Johnson

1975   Population, Exchange, and Early State Formation in Southwestern Iran. *American Anthropologist* 77: 267–289.

1994   Prestate Political Formations. In *Chiefdoms and Early States in the Near East: The Organizational Dynamics of Complexity,* ed. G. Stein and M. S. Rothman, *Monographs in World Archaeology* 18: 67–84. Madison, WI: Prehistory Press.

Wright, S., ed.

1994   *Anthropology of Organizations.* London: Routledge.

Wulff, R. M., and S. J. Fiske, eds.

1987   *Anthropological Praxis: Translating Knowledge into Action.* Boulder, CO: Westview.

Yellen, J. E., A. S. Brooks, and E. Cornelissen.

1995   A Middle Stone Age Worked Bone Industry from Katanda, Upper Semliki Valley, Zaire. *Science* 268: 553–556.

Yetman, N., ed.

1991   *Majority and Minority: The Dynamics of Race and Ethnicity in American Life,* 5th ed. Boston: Allyn & Bacon.

1999   *Majority and Minority: The Dynamics of Race and Ethnicity in American Life,* 6th ed. Boston: Allyn & Bacon.

Young, W. C.

1996   *The Rashaayada Bedouin: Arab Pastoralists of Eastern Sudan.* Fort Worth: Harcourt Brace.

Zeder, Melinda A.

1997   The American Archaeologist: Results of the 1994 SAA Census. *SAA Bulletin* 15(2): 12–17.

Zulaika, J.

1988   *Basque Violence: Metaphor and Sacrament.* Reno: University of Nevada Press.

GLOSSARY

absolute dating   Dating techniques that establish dates in numbers or ranges of numbers; examples include the radiometric methods of ^{14}C, K/A, ^{238}U, TL, and ESR dating.

acculturation   The exchange of cultural features that results when groups come into continuous firsthand contact; the original cultural patterns of either or both groups may be altered, but the groups remain distinct.

Acheulian   Derived from the French village of St. Acheul, where these tools were first identified; Lower Paleolithic tool tradition associated with *H. erectus.*

achieved status   Social status that comes through talents, choices, actions, efforts, activities, and accomplishments, rather than ascription.

adapids   Early (Eocene) primate family ancestral to lemurs and lorises.

adaptation   The process by which organisms cope with environmental stresses.

adaptive   Favored by natural selection in a particular environment.

advocacy view   of applied anthropology; the belief that precisely because anthropologists are experts on human problems and social change, and because they study, understand, and respect cultural values, they should make policy affecting people.

aesthetics   Appreciation of the qualities perceived in works of art; the mind and emotions in relation to a sense of beauty.

affinals   Relatives by marriage, whether of lineals (e.g., son's wife) or collaterals (e.g., sister's husband).

age set   Group uniting all men or women born during a certain time span; this group controls property and often has political and military functions.

agnates   Members of the same patrilineal descent group.

agriculture   Nonindustrial systems of plant cultivation characterized by continuous and intensive use of land and labor.

ahimsa   Hindu doctrine that prohibits harming life, and thus cattle slaughter.

allele   A biochemical difference involving a particular gene.

Allen's rule   Rule stating that the relative size of protruding body parts (such as ears, tails, bills, fingers, toes, and limbs) tends to increase in warmer climates.

alluvial   Pertaining to rich, fertile soil deposited by rivers and streams.

ambilineal   Principle of descent that does not automatically exclude the children of either sons or daughters.

ambilocal   Postmarital residence pattern in which the couple may reside with either the husband's or the wife's group.

analogies   Similarities arising as a result of similar selective forces; traits produced by convergent evolution.

anatomically modern humans (AMHs)   Including the Cro-Magnons of Europe (31,000 B.P.) and the older fossils from Skhūl (100,000) and Qafzeh (92,000); continue through the present; also known as *H. sapiens sapiens.*

animism   Belief in souls or doubles.

Anthropoidea   One of two suborders of primates; includes monkeys, apes, and humans.

anthropoids   Members of Anthropoidea, one of the two suborders of primates; monkeys, apes, and humans are anthropoids.

anthropology   The study of the human species and its immediate ancestors.

anthropology and education
Anthropological research in classrooms, homes, and neighborhoods, viewing students as total cultural creatures whose enculturation and attitudes toward education belong to a larger context that includes family, peers, and society.

anthropometry   The measurement of human body parts and dimensions, including skeletal parts (*osteometry*).

antibody   A defending protein that reacts by attacking a foreign substance; see *antigen*.

antigen   A chemical substance that triggers the production of an antibody.

apartheid   Castelike system in South Africa; blacks, whites, and Asians have separate (and unequal) neighborhoods, schools, laws, and punishments.

apical ancestor   In a descent group, the individual who stands at the apex, or top, of the common genealogy.

applied anthropology   The application of anthropological data, perspectives, theory, and methods to identify, assess, and solve contemporary social problems.

arboreal   Tree-dwelling.

arboreal theory   Theory that the primates evolved by adapting to life high up in the trees, where visual abilities would have been favored over the sense of smell, and grasping hands and feet would have been used for movement along branches.

archaeological anthropology (prehistoric archaeology)   The study of human behavior and cultural patterns and processes through the culture's material remains.

archaic *Homo sapiens*   Early *H. sapiens*, consisting of the Neandertals of Europe and the Middle East, the Neandertal-like hominids of Africa and Asia, and the immediate ancestors of all these hominids; lived from about 300,000 to 30,000 B.P.

archaic state   Nonindustrial state.

art   An object or event that evokes an aesthetic reaction—a sense of beauty, appreciation, harmony, and/or pleasure; the quality, production, expression, or realm of what is beautiful or of more than ordinary significance; the class of objects subject to aesthetic criteria.

artifacts   Material items that humans have manufactured or modified.

arts   The arts include the visual arts, literature (written and oral), music, and theater arts.

ascribed status   Social status (e.g., race or gender) that people have little or no choice about occupying.

ASL   American Sign Language, a medium of communication for deaf and mute humans and apes.

assimilation   The process of change that a minority group may experience when it moves to a country where another culture dominates; the minority is incorporated into the dominant culture to the point that it no longer exists as a separate cultural unit.

attitudinal discrimination   Discrimination against members of a group because of prejudice toward that group.

Aurignacian   Upper Paleolithic tradition, 35,000 to 20,000 B.P.; tools usually found in narrow valleys or near cliff walls, and thick layers suggest long occupation; may have diffused into Europe from elsewhere.

australopithecines   Varied group of Pliocene–Pleistocene hominids. The term is derived from their former classification as members of a distinct subfamily, the Australopithecinae; now they are distinguished from *Homo* only at the genus level.

axis   Plant part that attaches the grains to the stalk; brittle in wild grains, tough in domesticated ones.

Aztec   Last independent state in the Valley of Mexico; capital was Tenochtitlan. Thrived between A.D. 1325 and the Spanish conquest in 1520.

balanced reciprocity   See *generalized reciprocity*.

band   Basic unit of social organization among foragers. A band includes fewer than 100 people; it often splits up seasonally.

berdaches   Among the Crow Indians, members of a third gender, for whom certain ritual duties were reserved.

Bergmann's rule   Rule stating that the smaller of two bodies similar in shape has more surface area per unit of weight and can therefore dissipate heat more efficiently; hence, large bodies tend to be found in colder areas and small bodies in warmer ones.

Beringia Area now under the Bering Sea; a dry land mass several hundred miles wide, exposed during the glacial advances.

bifurcate collateral kinship terminology Kinship terminology employing separate terms for M, F, MB, MZ, FB, and FZ.

bifurcate merging kinship terminology Kinship terminology in which M and MZ are called by the same term, F and FB are called by the same term, and MB and FZ are called by different terms.

big man Regional figure often found among tribal horticulturalists and pastoralists. The big man occupies no office but creates his reputation through entrepreneurship and generosity to others. Neither his wealth nor his position passes to his heirs.

bilateral kinship calculation A system in which kinship ties are calculated equally through both sexes: mother and father, sister and brother, daughter and son, and so on.

biochemical genetics Field that studies structure, function, and changes in genetic material.

biological anthropology The study of human biological variation in time and space; includes evolution, genetics, growth and development, and primatology.

biological determinists Those who argue that human behavior and social organization are biologically determined.

biological kin types Actual genealogical relationships, designated by letters and symbols (e.g., FB), as opposed to the kin terms (e.g., *uncle*) used in a particular society.

biomedicine Western medicine, which attributes illness to scientifically demonstrated agents: biological organisms (e.g., bacteria, viruses, fungi, or parasites) or toxic materials.

bipedal Two-footed.

Black English Vernacular (BEV) A rule-governed dialect of American English with roots in southern English. BEV is spoken by African-American youth and by many adults in their casual, intimate speech—sometimes called "ebonics."

blade tool The basic Upper Paleolithic tool type, hammered off a prepared core.

blended family Kin unit formed when parents remarry and bring their children into a new household.

blood feud Feud between families, usually in a nonstate society.

bone biology The study of bone as a biological tissue, including its genetics; cell structure; growth, development, and decay, and patterns of movement (*biomechanics*).

bourgeoisie One of Marx's opposed classes; owners of the means of production (factories, mines, large farms, and other sources of subsistence).

brachiation Under-the-branch swinging; characteristic of gibbons, siamangs, and some New World monkeys.

brideprice See *progeny price.*

bridewealth See *progeny price.*

broad-spectrum revolution Period beginning around 20,000 B.P. in the Middle East and 12,000 B.P. in Europe, during which a wider range, or broader spectrum, of plant and animal life was hunted, gathered, collected, caught, and fished; revolutionary because it led to food production.

bronze An alloy of arsenic and copper or of tin and copper.

bush school Held in a location remote from residential areas; young people go there when they reach puberty to be instructed in knowledge viewed as essential to adult status.

call systems Systems of communication among nonhuman primates, composed of a limited number of sounds that vary in intensity and duration. Tied to environmental stimuli.

caloric staple Major source of dietary carbohydrates—such as wheat, rice, or maize.

candomblé A syncretic "Afro-Brazilian" cult.

capital Wealth or resources invested in business, with the intent of producing a profit.

capitalist world economy The single world system, which emerged in the 16th century, committed to production for sale, with the object of maximizing profits rather than supplying domestic needs.

caprine From *capra,* Latin for "goat"; refers to goats and sheep.

Capsians Mesolithic North African foragers who based much of their subsistence on land snails.

cargo cults   Postcolonial, acculturative religious movements, common in Melanesia, that attempt to explain European domination and wealth and to achieve similar success magically by mimicking European behavior.

caste system   Closed, hereditary system of stratification, often dictated by religion; hierarchical social status is ascribed at birth, so that people are locked into their parents' social position.

catarrhine   Sharp-nosed; anthropoid infraorder that includes Old World monkeys, apes, and humans.

catastrophism   View that extinct species were destroyed by fires, floods, and other catastrophes. After each destructive event, God created again, leading to contemporary species.

catharsis   Intense emotional release.

Cenozoic   Era of recent life—birds and mammals.

ceremonial fund   Resources invested in ceremonial or ritual expenses or activity.

ceremonies of increase   Rituals held to promote the fertility and reproduction of plants and animals.

chiefdom   Form of sociopolitical organization intermediate between the tribe and the state; kin-based with differential access to resources and a permanent political structure. A rank society in which relations among villages as well as among individuals are unequal, with smaller villages under the authority of leaders in larger villages; has a two-level settlement hierarchy.

chromosomes   Basic genetic units, occurring in matching (homologous) pairs; lengths of DNA made up of multiple genes.

chronology   Time frame, sequence.

civilization   A complex society with a government and social classes; synonyms are *nation-state* and *state*.

clan   Unilineal descent group based on stipulated descent.

class   Zoological: Division of a kingdom; composed of related orders.

class consciousness   Recognition of collective interests and personal identification with one's economic group (particularly the proletariat); basic to Marx's view of class.

classic Neandertals   Stereotypical Neandertals of Western Europe, considered by some scholars to be too specialized to have evolved into *H. sapiens sapiens*.

cline   A gradual shift in gene frequencies between neighboring populations.

Clovis tradition   Stone technology based on a projectile point that was fastened to the end of a hunting spear; it flourished between 12,000 and 11,000 B.P. in North America.

collateral household   Type of expanded family household including siblings and their spouses and children.

collateral relative   A biological relative who is not a lineal; that is, is not in ego's direct line, such as B, Z, FB, or MZ.

colonialism   The political, social, economic, and cultural domination of a territory and its people by a foreign power for an extended time.

communal religions   In Wallace's typology, these religions have, in addition to shamanic cults, communal cults in which people organize community rituals such as harvest ceremonies and rites of passage.

communitas   Intense community spirit, a feeling of great social solidarity, equality, and togetherness; characteristic of people experiencing liminality together.

competence   What native speakers must (and do) know about their language in order to speak and understand it.

competitive exclusion   Ecological principle that if two similar species exploit the same ecological niche, any advantage on the part of one of them, even though minor, eventually will force the other from that niche.

complex societies   Nations; large and populous, with social stratification and central governments.

conspecifics   Individual members of the same species.

continental shelf   Offshore shallow-water zone over which the ocean gradually deepens until the abrupt fall to deep water, which is known as the continental slope.

continental slope   See *continental shelf*.

convergent evolution Independent operation of similar selective forces; process by which analogies are produced.

core Dominant structural position in the world system; consists of the strongest and most powerful states with advanced systems of production.

core values Key, basic, or central values that integrate a culture and help distinguish it from others.

correlation An association between two or more variables such that when one changes (varies), the other(s) also change(s) (covaries); for example, temperature and sweating.

cranium Skull.

creationism Explanation for the origin of species given in Genesis: God created the species during the original six days of Creation.

creative opposition Process in which people change their behavior as they consciously and actively avoid or spurn an external image or practice.

cross cousins Children of a brother and a sister.

cultivation continuum A continuum based on the comparative study of nonindustrial cultivating societies in which labor intensity increases and fallowing decreases.

cultural anthropology The study of human society and culture; describes, analyzes, interprets, and explains social and cultural similarities and differences.

cultural colonialism Internal domination—by one group and its culture/ideology over others; for example, Russian domination of the former Soviet Union.

cultural consultants Subjects in ethnographic research; people the ethnographer gets to know in the field, who teach him or her about their culture.

cultural convergence (or convergent cultural evolution) Development of similar traits, institutions, or behavior patterns as a result of adaptation to similar environments; parallel development without contact or mutual influence.

cultural determinists Those who relate behavior and social organization to cultural or environmental factors. This view focuses on variation rather than universals and stresses

learning and the role of culture in human adaptation.

cultural ecology The study of ecosystems that include people, focusing on how human use of nature influences and is influenced by social organization and cultural values.

cultural imperialism The rapid spread or advance of one culture at the expense of others, or its imposition on other cultures, which it modifies, replaces, or destroys—usually because of differential economic or political influence.

cultural learning Learning based on the human capacity to think symbolically.

cultural relativism The position that the values and standards of cultures differ and deserve respect. Extreme relativism argues that cultures should be judged solely by their own standards.

cultural resource management (CRM) The branch of applied archaeology aimed at preserving sites threatened by dams, highways, and other projects.

cultural rights Doctrine that certain rights are vested not in individuals but in identifiable groups, such as religious and ethnic minorities and indigenous societies. Cultural rights include a group's ability to preserve its culture, to raise its children in the ways of its forebears, to continue its language, and not to be deprived of its economic base by the nation-state in which it is located.

cultural transmission A basic feature of language; transmission through learning.

culturally compatible economic development projects Projects that harness traditional organizations and locally perceived needs for change and that have a culturally appropriate design and implementation strategy.

culture Distinctly human; transmitted through learning; traditions and customs that govern behavior and beliefs.

culture and personality A subfield of cultural anthropology; examines variation in psychological traits and personality characteristics among cultures.

cuneiform Early Mesopotamian writing that used a stylus (writing implement) to write wedge-shaped impressions on raw clay; from the Latin word for wedge.

curer   Specialized role acquired through a culturally appropriate process of selection, training, certification, and acquisition of a professional image; the curer is consulted by patients, who believe in his or her special powers, and receives some form of special consideration; a cultural universal.

cytoplasm   The outer area of the cell rather than the nucleus.

daughter languages   Languages developing out of the same parent language; for example, French and Spanish are daughter languages of Latin.

demonstrated descent   Basis of the lineage; descent-group members cite the names of their forebears in each generation from the apical ancestor through the present.

descent   Rule assigning social identity on the basis of some aspect of one's ancestry.

descent group   A permanent social unit whose members claim common ancestry; fundamental to tribal society.

development anthropology   The branch of applied anthropology that focuses on social issues in, and the cultural dimension of, economic development.

diaspora   The offspring of an area who have spread to many lands.

differential access   Unequal access to resources; basic attribute of chiefdoms and states. Superordinates have favored access to such resources, while the access of subordinates is limited by superordinates.

diffusion   Borrowing of cultural traits between societies, either directly or through intermediaries.

diglossia   The existence of "high" (formal) and "low" (informal, familial) dialects of a single language, such as German.

directional selection   Long-term selection of the same trait(s); may go on as long as environmental forces remain the same.

discourse   Talk, speeches, gestures, and actions.

discrimination   Policies and practices that harm a group and its members.

disease   A scientifically identified health threat caused by a bacterium, virus, fungus, parasite, or other pathogen.

displacement   A basic feature of language; the ability to speak of things and events that are not present.

domestic   Within or pertaining to the home.

domestic–public dichotomy   Contrast between women's role in the home and men's role in public life, with a corresponding social devaluation of women's work and worth.

domestic system   of manufacture, also known as "home handicraft production"; preindustrial manufacturing system in which organizer-entrepreneurs supplied raw materials to people who worked at home and collected finished products from them.

dominant   Allele that masks another allele in a heterozygote.

dowry   A marital exchange in which the wife's group provides substantial gifts to the husband's family.

dry farming   Cultivation that is rainfall-dependent, without irrigation.

dryopithecids   Zoological ape family living in Europe during the middle and late Miocene; probably includes the common ancestor of the lesser apes (gibbons and siamangs) and the great apes.

ecocide   Destruction of local ecosystems.

ecology   The study of interrelationships among living things in an environment.

economic typology   Classification of societies based on their adaptive strategies; for example, foraging, horticulture, pastoralism, agriculture.

economizing   The rational allocation of scarce means (or resources) to alternative ends (or uses); often considered the subject matter of economics.

economy   A population's system of production, distribution, and consumption of resources.

ecosystem   A patterned arrangement of energy flows and exchanges; includes organisms sharing a common environment and that environment.

egalitarian society   A type of society, most typically found among foragers, that lacks status distinctions except for those based on age, gender, and individual qualities, talents, and achievements.

ego   Latin for *I*. In kinship charts, the point from which one views an egocentric genealogy.

elite level   Archaeological term for evidence of differential access to strategic resources; found in chiefdoms and states.

emic   The research strategy that focuses on native explanations and criteria of significance.

emotionalistic disease theories   Theories that assume that illness is caused by intense emotional experiences.

empire   A mature, territorially large and expansive state; empires are typically multiethnic, multilinguistic, and more militaristic, with a better developed bureaucracy, than earlier states.

enculturation   The social process by which culture is learned and transmitted across the generations.

endogamy   Marriage between people of the same social group.

environmental racism   The systematic use of institutionally based power by a majority group to make policy decisions that create disproportionate environmental hazards in minority communities.

equity, increased   A reduction in absolute poverty and a fairer (more even) distribution of wealth.

estrus   Period of maximum sexual receptivity in female baboons, chimpanzees, and other primates, signaled by vaginal area swelling and coloration.

ethnic expulsion   A policy aimed at removing groups that are culturally different from a country.

ethnic group   Group distinguished by cultural similarities (shared among members of that group) and differences (between that group and others); ethnic group members share beliefs, values, habits, customs, and norms, and a common language, religion, history, geography, kinship, and/or race.

ethnicity   Identification with, and feeling part of, an ethnic group, and exclusion from certain other groups because of this affiliation.

ethnocentrism   The tendency to view one's own culture as best and to judge the behavior and beliefs of culturally different people by one's own standards.

ethnocide   Process in which ethnic groups survive but lose or severely modify their ancestral cultures.

ethnography   Field work in a particular culture.

ethnology   Cross-cultural comparison; the comparative study of ethnographic data, of society, and of culture.

ethnomusicology   The comparative study of the musics of the world and of music as an aspect of culture and society.

ethnoscience   See *ethnosemantics*.

ethnosemantics   The study of lexical (vocabulary) contrasts and classifications in various languages.

etic   The research strategy that emphasizes the observer's rather than the natives' explanations, categories, and criteria of significance.

Etoro   Papua New Guinea culture in which males are culturally trained to prefer homosexual behavior.

eugenics   Controversial movement aimed at genetic improvement by encouraging the reproduction of individuals with favored features and discouraging that of individuals with features deemed undesirable.

Eve theory   Theory that a small group of anatomically modern people arose recently, probably in Africa, from which they spread and replaced the native and more archaic populations of other inhabited areas.

evolution   Descent with modification; change in form over generations.

excavation   Digging through the layers of deposits that make up an archaeological site.

exogamy   Rule requiring people to marry outside their own group.

expanded family household   Coresident group that can include siblings and their spouses and children (a *collateral* household) or three generations of kin and their spouses (an *extended family* household).

expressive culture   The arts; people express themselves creatively in dance, music, song, painting, sculpture, pottery, cloth, storytelling, verse, prose, drama, and comedy.

extended family   Expanded household including three or more generations.

extradomestic   Outside the home; within or pertaining to the public domain.

extrasomatic   Nonbodily; pertaining to culture, including language, tools, and other cultural means of adaptation.

family, zoological Group of similar genera.

family of orientation Nuclear family in which one is born and grows up.

family of procreation Nuclear family established when one marries and has children.

fictive kinship Personal relationships modeled on kinship, such as that between godparents and godchildren.

First World The "democratic West"—traditionally conceived in opposition to a "Second World" ruled by "communism."

fiscal Pertaining to finances and taxation.

focal vocabulary A set of words and distinctions that are particularly important to certain groups (those with particular foci of experience or activity), such as types of snow to Eskimos or skiers.

folk Of the people; originally coined for European peasants; refers to the art, music, and lore of ordinary people, as contrasted with the "high" art or "classic" art of the European elites.

food production Cultivation of plants and domestication (stockbreeding) of animals; first developed in the Middle East 10,000 to 12,000 years ago.

foramen magnum "Big hole" through which the spinal cord joins the brain; located farther forward in *Australopithecus* and *Homo* than in apes.

forced assimilation Use of force by a dominant group to compel a minority to adopt the dominant culture—for example, penalizing or banning the language and customs of an ethnic group.

fossils Remains (e.g., bones), traces, or impressions (e.g., footprints) of ancient life.

fraternal polyandry Marriage of a group of brothers to the same woman or women.

functional explanation Explanation that establishes a correlation or interrelationship between social customs. When customs are functionally interrelated, if one changes, the others also change.

gametes The sex cells: eggs (ova) and sperms.

gender roles The tasks and activities that a culture assigns to each sex.

gender stereotypes Oversimplified but strongly held ideas about the characteristics of males and females.

gender stratification Unequal distribution of rewards (socially valued resources, power, prestige, and personal freedom) between men and women, reflecting their different positions in a social hierarchy.

gene Area in a chromosome pair that determines, wholly or partially, a particular biological trait, such as whether one's blood type is A, B, AB, or O.

gene flow Exchange of genetic material between populations of the same species through direct or indirect interbreeding.

gene pool All the alleles and genotypes within a breeding population—the "pool" of genetic material available.

genealogical method Procedures by which ethnographers discover and record connections of kinship, descent, and marriage, using diagrams and symbols.

general anthropology The field of anthropology as a whole, consisting of cultural, archaeological, biological, and linguistic anthropology.

generality Culture pattern or trait that exists in some but not all societies.

generalized reciprocity Principle that characterizes exchanges between closely related individuals. As social distance increases, reciprocity becomes balanced and finally negative.

generational kinship terminology Kinship terminology with only two terms for the parental generation, one designating M, MZ, and FZ and the other designating F, FB, and MB.

genetic evolution Change in gene frequency within a breeding population.

genitor Biological father of a child.

genocide Physical destruction of ethnic groups by murder, warfare, and introduced diseases.

genotype An organism's hereditary makeup.

genus (plural, *genera*) Group of similar species.

gibbons The smallest apes, natives of Asia; arboreal and territorial.

glacials The four or five major advances of continental ice sheets in northern Europe and North America.

globalization The accelerating interdependence of nations in a world system linked economically and through mass media and modern transportation systems.

gracile Opposite of robust.

grammar The formal organizing principles that link sound and meaning in a language; the set of abstract rules that make up a language.

green revolution Agricultural development based on chemical fertilizers, pesticides, 20th-century cultivation techniques, and new crop varieties such as IR-8 ("miracle rice").

Halafian An early (7500–6500 B.P.) and widespread pottery style, first found in northern Syria; refers to a delicate ceramic style and to the period when the first chiefdoms emerged.

head, village A local leader in a tribal society who has limited authority, leads by example and persuasion, and must be generous.

health-care systems Beliefs, customs, and specialists concerned with ensuring health and preventing and curing illness; a cultural universal.

hegemonic reading (of a "text") The reading or meaning that the creators intended, or the one the elites consider to be the intended or correct meaning.

hegemony As used by Antonio Gramsci, a stratified social order in which subordinates comply with domination by internalizing its values and accepting its "naturalness."

heterozygous Having dissimilar alleles of a given gene.

hidden transcript As used by James Scott, the critique of power by the oppressed that goes on offstage—in private—where the power holders can't see it.

Hilly Flanks Woodland zone that flanks the Tigris and Euphrates rivers to the north; zone of wild wheat and barley and of sedentism (settled, nonmigratory life) preceding food production.

historical explanation Demonstration that a social institution or practice exists among different populations because they share a period of common history or have been exposed to common sources of information; includes diffusion.

historical linguistics Subdivision of linguistics that studies languages over time.

Hogopans Nickname for the ancestral population of Miocene hominoids that eventually split three ways to give rise to humans, gorillas, and chimps; derived from the genus names *Homo*, *Gor*illa, and *Pan* (chimpanzee).

holistic Interested in the whole of the human condition: past, present, and future; biology, society, language, and culture.

Hominidae Zoological superfamily that includes fossil and living humans; according to some taxonomists, also includes the African apes.

hominids Members of the zoological family (Hominidae) that includes fossil and living humans.

Hominoidea Zoological superfamily that includes fossil and contemporary apes and humans.

hominoids Members of the superfamily including humans and all the apes.

Homo habilis Term coined by L. S. B. and Mary Leakey; immediate ancestor of *H. erectus;* lived from about 2 to 1.7 or 1.6 m.y.a.

Homo sapiens sapiens Anatomically modern humans.

homologies Traits that organisms have jointly inherited from their common ancestor.

homozygous Possessing identical alleles of a particular gene.

horticulture Nonindustrial system of plant cultivation in which plots lie fallow for varying lengths of time.

human rights Doctrine that invokes a realm of justice and morality beyond and superior to particular countries, cultures, and religions. Human rights, usually seen as vested in individuals, would include the right to speak freely, to hold religious beliefs without persecution, and to not be enslaved, or imprisoned without charge.

humanities Academic fields that study languages, texts, philosophies, arts, music, performances, and other forms of creative expression.

hybrid Mixed.

hydraulic systems Systems of water management, including irrigation, drainage, and flood control. Often associated with agricultural societies in arid and river environments.

hypervitaminosis D   Condition caused by an excess of vitamin D; calcium deposits build up on the body's soft tissues and the kidneys may fail; symptoms include gallstones and joint and circulation problems; may affect unprotected light-skinned individuals in the tropics.

hypodescent   Rule that automatically places the children of a union or mating between members of different socioeconomic groups in the less-privileged group.

hypoxia   A body's oxygen deprivation; the difficulty of extracting oxygen from the air increases with altitude because barometric pressure decreases and molecules of air are farther apart.

ideal types   Labels that make contrasts seem more extreme than they really are (e.g., big and little). Instead of discrete categories, there is actually a continuum from one type to the next.

identity politics   Sociopolitical identities based on the perception of sharing a common culture, language, religion, or "race," rather than citizenship in a nation-state, which may contain diverse social groups.

illness   A condition of poor health perceived or felt by an individual.

imperialism   A policy of extending the rule of a nation or empire over foreign nations or of taking and holding foreign colonies.

incest   Forbidden sexual relations with a close relative.

incest taboo   Universal prohibition against marrying or mating with a close relative.

inclusive fitness   Reproductive success measured by the representation of genes one shares with other, related individuals.

income   Earnings from wages and salaries.

independent assortment   Mendel's law of; chromosomes are inherited independently of one another.

independent invention   Development of the same cultural trait or pattern in separate cultures as a result of comparable needs and circumstances.

indigenized   Modified to fit the local culture.

indigenous peoples   The original inhabitants of particular territories; often descendants of tribespeople who live on as culturally distinct colonized peoples, many of whom aspire to autonomy.

individual fitness   Reproductive success measured by the number of direct descendants an individual has.

Industrial Revolution   The historical transformation (in Europe, after 1750) of "traditional" into "modern" societies through industrialization of the economy.

infanticide   Killing a baby; a form of population control in some societies.

institutional discrimination   Programs, policies, and arrangements that deny equal rights and opportunities to, or differentially harm, members of particular groups.

interglacials   Extended warm periods between such major glacials as Riss and Würm.

international culture   Cultural traditions that extend beyond national boundaries.

interstadials   Brief warm periods during a glacial; not to be confused with the longer interglacials.

intervention philosophy   Guiding principle of colonialism, conquest, missionization, or development; an ideological justification for outsiders to guide native peoples in specific directions.

interview schedule   Ethnographic tool for structuring a formal interview. A prepared form (usually printed or mimeographed) that guides interviews with households or individuals being compared systematically. Contrasts with a *questionnaire* because the researcher has personal contact with the local people and records their answers.

IPR   Intellectual property rights, consisting of each society's cultural base—its core beliefs and principles. IPR is claimed as a group right—a cultural right, allowing indigenous groups to control who may know and use their collective knowledge and its applications.

Iroquois   Confederation of tribes in aboriginal New York; matrilineal with communal long houses and a prominent political, religious, and economic role for women.

ischial callosities   Rough patches of skin of gibbons and Old World monkeys on the buttocks, adapted to sitting on hard rocky ground and rough branches.

ivory tower view of applied anthropology; the belief that anthropologists should avoid practical matters and concentrate on research, publication, and teaching.

Jomon Widespread (30,000 sites known) Japanese Mesolithic culture, dated to 6000 to 5000 B.P.; hunted deer, pigs, bear, and antelope, and also ate fish, shellfish, and plants.

Ju'hoansi Group of San (Bushmen) foragers of southern Africa.

key cultural consultant Person who is an expert on a particular aspect of native life.

kin-based Characteristic of many nonindustrial societies. People spend their lives almost exclusively with their relatives; principles of kinship, descent, and marriage organize social life.

kin terms The words used for different relatives in a particular language, as opposed to actual genealogical relationships (*biological kin types*).

kinesics The study of communication through body movements, stances, gestures, and facial expressions.

kingdom, zoological Group of related classes.

kinship calculation The system by which people in a particular society reckon kin relationships.

knuckle-walking A form of terrestrial locomotion in which long arms and callused knuckles support the trunk; the ape ambles around leaning forward.

Kwakiutl A potlatching society on the North Pacific Coast of North America.

lactase See *lactose.*

lactose A complex sugar in milk; its digestion requires an enzyme called *lactase* in the small intestine. Among most mammals, lactase production ceases after weaning, and the ability to digest milk is lost.

language Human beings' primary means of communication; may be spoken or written; features productivity and displacement and is culturally transmitted.

latent function A custom's underlying function, often unperceived by natives.

law A legal code, including trial and enforcement; characteristic of state-organized societies.

LDC A less-developed country; by contrast with an industrial nation.

leveling mechanisms Customs and social actions that operate to reduce differences in wealth and thus to bring standouts in line with community norms.

levirate Custom by which a widow marries the brother of her deceased husband.

lexicon Vocabulary; a dictionary containing all the morphemes in a language and their meanings.

life history Of a key consultant or narrator; provides a personal cultural portrait of existence or change in a culture.

liminality The critically important marginal or in-between phase of a rite of passage.

lineage Unilineal descent group based on demonstrated descent.

lineal kinship terminology Parental generation kin terminology with four terms: one for M, one for F, one for FB and MB, and one for MZ and FZ.

lineal relative Any of ego's ancestors or descendants (e.g., parents, grandparents, children, grandchildren); on the direct line of descent that leads to and from ego.

linguistic anthropology The descriptive, comparative, and historical study of language and of linguistic similarities and differences in time, space, and society.

linguistic relativity Notion that all languages and dialects are equally effective as systems of communication.

linguistic uniformitarianism Belief that explanations for long-term change in language should be sought in ordinary forces that continue to work today; thus, the forces that have produced linguistic changes over the centuries are observable in linguistic events (variation) taking place today.

linkages Interconnections between small-scale and large-scale units and systems; political, economic, informational, and other cultural links among village, region, nation, and world.

liturgical order A set sequence of words and actions invented prior to the current performance of the ritual in which it occurs.

liturgies Set formal sequences of words and actions; common in political events and rituals or ceremonies.

local descent group   All the members of a particular descent group who live in the same place, such as the same village.

longitudinal   Long-term; refers to a study carried out over many years.

longitudinal research   Long-term study of a community, region, society, culture, or other unit, usually based on repeated visits.

macroband   Assembly of foraging bands for intensive collecting or cooperative hunting.

magic   Use of supernatural techniques to accomplish specific aims.

maize   Corn; domesticated in highland Mexico.

majority groups   Superordinate, dominant, or controlling groups in a social-political hierarchy.

maladaptive   Harmful; selected against; conferring a disadvantage with respect to survival and reproduction.

mana   Sacred impersonal force in Melanesian and Polynesian religions.

manifest function   The reasons that natives offer for a custom.

manioc   Cassava; a tuber domesticated in the South American lowlands.

market principle   Profit-oriented principle of exchange that dominates in states, particularly industrial states. Goods and services are bought and sold, and values are determined by supply and demand.

marriage   Socially approved relationship between a socially recognized male (the husband) and a socially recognized female (the wife) such that the children born to the wife are accepted as the offspring of both husband and wife.

mater   Socially recognized mother of a child.

matriarchy   A society ruled by women; unknown to ethnography.

matrifocal   Mother-centered; often refers to a household with no resident husband-father.

matrilateral skewing   A preference for relatives on the mother's side.

matrilineal descent   Unilineal descent rule in which people join the mother's group automatically at birth and stay members throughout life.

matrilocality   Customary residence with the wife's relatives after marriage, so that children grow up in their mother's community.

matrons   Senior women, as among the Iroquois.

means (or factors) of production   Land, labor, technology, and capital—major productive resources.

medical anthropology   Field including biological and cultural, theoretical and applied, anthropologists concerned with the sociocultural context and implications of disease and illness.

meiosis   Special process by which sex cells are produced; four cells are produced from one, each with half the genetic material of the original cell.

melanin   Substance manufactured in specialized cells in the lower layers of the epidermis (outer skin layer); melanin cells in dark skin produce more melanin than do those in light skin.

Mendelian genetics   Studies ways in which chromosomes transmit genes across the generations.

Mesoamerica   Middle America, including Mexico, Guatemala, and Belize.

Mesolithic   Middle Stone Age, whose characteristic tool type was the microlith; broad-spectrum economy.

Mesopotamia   The area between the Tigris and Euphrates rivers in what is now southern Iraq and southwestern Iran; location of the first cities and states.

Mesozoic   Era of middle life—reptiles, including the dinosaurs.

metallurgy   Knowledge of the properties of metals, including their extraction and processing and the manufacture of metal tools.

microband   Small family group of foragers.

microlith   Greek for "small stone"; characteristic Mesolithic tool.

Middle Pleistocene   The period from the Mindel glacial through the Riss-Würm interglacial.

Mindel   The second major glacial advance in Europe.

minimal pairs   Words that resemble each other in all but one sound; used to discover phonemes.

minority groups   Subordinate groups in a social-political hierarchy, with inferior power and less secure access to resources than majority groups.

mitosis Ordinary cell division; DNA molecules copy themselves, creating two identical cells out of one.

mode of production Way of organizing production—a set of social relations through which labor is deployed to wrest energy from nature by means of tools, skills, and knowledge.

moiety One of two descent groups in a given population; usually moieties intermarry.

molecular anthropology Genetic analysis, involving comparison of DNA sequences, to determine evolutionary links and distances among species and among ancient and modern populations.

monocrop production System of production, often on plantations, based on the cultivation of a single cash crop.

monotheism Worship of an eternal, omniscient, omnipotent, and omnipresent supreme being.

morpheme Minimal linguistic form (usually a word) with meaning.

morphology The study of form; used in linguistics (the study of morphemes and word construction) and for form in general—for example, biomorphology relates to physical form.

Mousterian Middle Paleolithic tool-making tradition associated with Neandertals.

multiculturalism The view of cultural diversity in a country as something good and desirable; a multicultural society socializes individuals not only into the dominant (national) culture but also into an ethnic culture.

multiregional evolution Theory that *Homo erectus* gradually evolved into modern *H. sapiens* in all regions inhabited by humans (Africa, Europe, northern Asia, and Australasia). As the regional populations evolved, gene flow always connected them, and so they always belonged to the same species. This theory opposes replacement models such as the Eve theory.

multivariate Involving multiple factors, causes, or variables.

mutation Change in the DNA molecules of which genes and chromosomes are built.

m.y.a. Million years ago.

namesakes People who share the same name; a form of fictive kinship among the San, who have a limited number of personal names.

nation Once a synonym for "ethnic group," designating a single culture sharing a language, religion, history, territory, ancestry, and kinship; now usually a synonym for *state* or *nation-state.*

nation-state An autonomous political entity; a country like the United States or Canada.

national culture Cultural experiences, beliefs, learned behavior patterns, and values shared by citizens of the same nation.

nationalities Ethnic groups that once had, or wish to have or regain, autonomous political status (their own country).

native taxonomy Classification system invented and used by natives rather than anthropologists.

Natufians Widespread Middle Eastern culture, dated to between 12,500 and 10,500 B.P.; subsisted on intensive wild cereal collecting and gazelle hunting and had year-round villages.

natural selection Originally formulated by Charles Darwin and Alfred Russel Wallace; the process by which nature selects the forms most fit to survive and reproduce in a given environment, such as the tropics.

naturalistic disease theories Include scientific medicine; theories that explain illness in impersonal systemic terms.

naturists Those who argue that human behavior and social organization are biologically determined.

Neandertals *H. sapiens neanderthalensis,* representing an archaic *H. sapiens* subspecies, lived in Europe and the Middle East between 130,000 and 30,000 B.P.

negative reciprocity See *generalized reciprocity.*

négritude Black association and identity—an idea developed by dark-skinned intellectuals in Francophone (French-speaking) West Africa and the Caribbean.

neocolonialism A revival or new form of colonialism—the political, social, economic, and cultural domination of a territory and its people by a foreign power, often justified by the assertion that foreigners are more enlightened at governing than are natives of the colonial area.

Neolithic   "New Stone Age," coined to describe techniques of grinding and polishing stone tools; the first cultural period in a region in which the first signs of domestication are present.

neolocality   Postmarital residence pattern in which a couple establishes a new place of residence rather than living with or near either set of parents.

Nilotic populations   Populations, including the Nuer, that inhabit the Upper Nile region of eastern Africa.

nomadism, pastoral   Movement throughout the year by the whole pastoral group (men, women, and children) with their animals; more generally, such constant movement in pursuit of strategic resources.

nuclear family   Kinship group consisting of parents and children.

nurturists   Those who relate behavior and social organization to environmental factors. Nurturists focus on variation rather than universals and stress learning and the role of culture in human adaptation.

Oaxaca, Valley of   Southern Mexican valley that was an early area of food production and state formation.

office   Permanent political position.

Oldowan pebble tools   Earliest (2 to 2.5 m.y.a.) stone tools; first discovered in 1931 by L. S. B. and Mary Leakey at Olduvai Gorge.

Olmec   Elite-level society on Mexico's Gulf Coast, 3200 to 2500 B.P.

Olympian religions   In Wallace's typology, develop with state organization; have full-time religious specialists—professional priesthoods.

omomyids   Early (Eocene) primate family found in North America, Europe, and Asia; early omomyids may be ancestral to all anthropoids; later ones may be ancestral to tarsiers.

open class system   Stratification system that facilitates social mobility, with individual achievement and personal merit determining social rank.

opposable thumb   A thumb that can touch all the other fingers.

order, zoological   Division of a zoological class; a group of related suborders, such as the primates.

orthograde posture   Straight and upright; the posture among apes and humans.

osteology   The study of bones; useful to biological anthropologists studying the fossil record.

overinnovation   Characteristic of projects that require major changes in natives' daily lives, especially ones that interfere with customary subsistence pursuits.

paleoanthropology   The study of hominid evolution and human life as revealed by the fossil record.

paleoecology   The study, often by archaeologists, of ecosystems of the past.

Paleoindians   Early North American Indians who hunted horses, camels, bison, elephants, mammoths, and giant sloths.

Paleolithic   Old Stone Age (from Greek roots meaning "old" and "stone"); divided into Lower (early), Middle, and Upper (late).

paleontology   Study of ancient life through the fossil record.

paleopathology   Study of disease and injury in skeletons from archaeological sites.

Paleozoic   Era of ancient life—fishes, amphibians, and primitive reptiles.

palynology   Study of ancient plants through pollen samples from archaeological or fossil sites in order to determine a site's environment at the time of occupation.

pantheon   A collection of supernatural beings in a particular religion.

pantribal sodality   A non-kin-based group that exists throughout a tribe, spanning several villages.

parallel cousins   Children of two brothers or two sisters.

participant observation   A characteristic ethnographic technique; taking part in the events one is observing, describing, and analyzing.

particularity   Distinctive or unique culture trait, pattern, or integration.

pastoralists   People who use a food-producing strategy of adaptation based on care of herds of domesticated animals.

pater   Socially recognized father of a child; not necessarily the genitor.

patriarchy   Political system ruled by men in which women have inferior social and political status, including basic human rights.

patrilineal descent   Unilineal descent rule in which people join the father's group automatically at birth and stay members throughout life.

patrilineal-patrilocal complex   An interrelated constellation of patrilineality, patrilocality, warfare, and male supremacy.

patrilocality   Customary residence with the husband's relatives after marriage, so that children grow up in their father's community.

peasant   Small-scale agriculturalist living in a state with rent fund obligations.

performance   What people actually say; the use of speech in social situations.

Perigordian   Upper Paleolithic tradition that coexisted with the Aurignacian in Europe between 35,000 and 20,000 B.P. Perigordian tools usually are found in thin deposits and are scattered over large areas; evolved in Western Europe out of Mousterian antecedents.

periphery   Weakest structural position in the world system.

personalistic disease theories   Theories that attribute illness to sorcerers, witches, ghosts, or ancestral spirits.

phenotype   An organism's evident traits, its "manifest biology"—anatomy and physiology.

phenotypical adaptation   Adaptive biological changes that occur during the individual's lifetime, made possible by biological plasticity.

phone   Any speech sound.

phoneme   Significant sound contrast in a language that serves to distinguish meaning, as in minimal pairs.

phonemics   The study of the sound contrasts (phonemes) of a particular language.

phonetics   The study of speech sounds in general; what people actually say in various languages.

phonology   The study of sounds used in speech.

phylogeny   Genetic relatedness based on common ancestry.

physical anthropology   See *biological anthropology*.

pidgin   A mixed language that develops to ease communication between members of different cultures in contact, usually in situations of trade or colonial domination.

plasticity   The ability to change; notion that biology is affected by environmental forces, such as diet and altitude, experienced during growth.

platyrrhine   Flat-nosed; anthropoid infraorder that includes the New World monkeys.

Pleistocene   Epoch of *Homo*'s appearance and evolution; began two million years ago; divided into Lower, Middle, and Upper.

plural marriage   See *polygamy*.

plural society   A society that combines ethnic contrasts and economic interdependence of the ethnic groups.

polity   The political order.

polyandry   Variety of plural marriage in which a woman has more than one husband.

polygamy   Any marriage with more than two spouses.

polygyny   Variety of plural marriage in which a man has more than one wife.

Polynesia   Triangle of South Pacific islands formed by Hawaii to the north, Easter Island to the east, and New Zealand to the southwest.

polytheism   Belief in several deities who control aspects of nature.

polytypic species   Species with considerable phenotypic variation.

pongid   Zoological family that includes orangutans.

population genetics   Field that studies causes of genetic variation, maintenance, and change in breeding populations.

postcolonial   Referring to interactions between European nations and the societies they colonized (mainly after 1800); more generally, "postcolonial" may be used to signify a position against imperialism and Eurocentrism.

postcranium   The area behind or below the head; the skeleton.

posterior   Back; for example, posterior or back dentition—premolars and molars.

postmodern   In its most general sense, describes the blurring and breakdown of established canons (rules, standards), categories, distinctions, and boundaries.

postmodernism   A style and movement in architecture that succeeded modernism. Compared with modernism, postmodernism is less geometric, less functional, less austere, more playful, and more willing to include elements from diverse times and cultures; *postmodern* now describes comparable developments in music, literature, visual art, and anthropology.

postmodernity   Condition of a world in flux, with people on the move, in which established groups, boundaries, identities, contrasts, and standards are reaching out and breaking down.

pot irrigation   Simple irrigation technique used in Oaxaca; by means of pots, water close to the surface is dipped and poured on plants.

potlatch   Competitive feast among Indians on the North Pacific Coast of North America.

potsherds   Fragments of earthenware; pottery studied by archaeologists in interpreting prehistoric life styles.

power   The ability to exercise one's will over others—to do what one wants; the basis of political status.

practicing anthropologists   Used as a synonym for *applied anthropology;* anthropologists who practice their profession outside of academia.

prehensile   Grasping, as in the tail of the New World monkeys.

prehistory   The period before the invention of writing (less than 6,000 years ago).

prejudice   Devaluing (looking down on) a group because of its assumed behavior, values, capabilities, attitudes, or other attributes.

prestige   Esteem, respect, or approval for acts, deeds, or qualities considered exemplary.

primary groups   Primate groups composed of a permanently bonded male and female and their preadolescent offspring.

primary states   States that arise on their own (through competition among chiefdoms), and not through contact with other state societies.

primates   Monkeys, apes, and prosimians; members of the zoological order that includes humans.

primatology   The study of the biology, behavior, social life, and evolution of monkeys, apes, and other nonhuman primates.

primogeniture   Inheritance rule that makes the oldest child (usually the oldest son) the only heir.

Proconsul   Early Miocene genus of the pliopithecoid superfamily; the most abundant and successful anthropoids of the early Miocene; the last common ancestor shared by the Old World monkeys and the apes.

productivity   A basic feature of language; the ability to use the rules of one's language to create new expressions comprehensible to other speakers.

progeny price   A gift from the husband and his kin to the wife and her kin before, at, or after marriage; legitimizes children born to the woman as members of the husband's descent group.

proletarianization   Separation of workers from the means of production through industrialism.

prosimians   The primate suborder that includes lemurs, lorises, and tarsiers.

protolanguage   Language ancestral to several daughter languages.

psychological anthropology   The ethnographic and cross-cultural study of differences and similarities in human psychology.

public transcript   As used by James Scott, the open, public interactions between dominators and oppressed—the outer shell of power relations.

punctuated equilibrium   Model of evolution; long periods of equilibrium, during which species change little, are interrupted by sudden changes—evolutionary jumps.

questionnaire   Form (usually printed) used by sociologists to obtain comparable information from respondents. Often mailed to and filled in by research subjects rather than by the researcher.

race   An ethnic group assumed to have a biological basis.

racism   Discrimination against an ethnic group assumed to have a biological basis.

radiometric   Dating technique that measures radioactive decay.

random genetic drift   Change in gene frequency that results not from natural selection but from chance; most common in small populations.

random sample   A sample in which all members of the population have an equal statistical chance of being included.

ranked society A type of society with hereditary inequality but not social stratification; individuals are ranked in terms of their genealogical closeness to the chief, but there is a continuum of status, with many individuals and kin groups ranked about equally.

rapport A good, friendly working relationship between people, for example, ethnographers and their hosts and consultants.

recessive Genetic trait masked by a dominant trait.

reciprocity One of the three principles of exchange; governs exchange between social equals; major exchange mode in band and tribal societies.

recombination Following independent assortment of chromosomes, new arrangements of hereditary units produced through bisexual reproduction.

redistribution Major exchange mode of chiefdoms, many archaic states, and some states with managed economies.

refugees People who have been forced (involuntary refugees) or who have chosen (voluntary refugees) to flee a country, to escape persecution or war.

regulation Management of variables within a system of related and interacting variables. Regulation assures that variables stay within their normal ranges, corrects deviations from the norm, and thus maintains the system's integrity.

relative dating Dating technique, e.g., stratigraphy, that establishes a time frame in relation to other strata or materials, rather than absolute dates in numbers.

relativity Of evolution through natural selection; adaptation and fitness are in relation to specific environments, and traits are not adaptive or maladaptive for all times and places.

religion Belief and ritual concerned with supernatural beings, powers, and forces.

remote sensing Use of aerial photos and satellite images to locate sites on the ground.

rent fund Scarce resources that a social inferior is required to render to an individual or agency that is superior politically or economically.

replacement fund Scarce resources invested in technology and other items essential to production.

respondents Subjects in sociological research; the people who answer questions in questionnaires and other social surveys.

revitalization movements Movements that occur in times of change, in which religious leaders emerge and undertake to alter or revitalize a society.

rickets Nutritional disease caused by a shortage of vitamin D; interferes with the absorption of calcium and causes softening and deformation of the bones.

Riss The third major glacial advance in Europe.

rites of passage Culturally defined activities associated with the transition from one place or stage of life to another.

ritual Behavior that is formal, stylized, repetitive, and stereotyped, performed earnestly as a social act; rituals are held at set times and places and have liturgical orders.

robust Large, strong, sturdy; said of skull, skeleton, muscle, and teeth; opposite of gracile.

Romer's rule Evolutionary rule stating that an innovation that evolves to maintain an existing system can play a major role in changing that system.

sagittal crest Bony ridge atop the skull that forms as bone grows; develops from the pull of chewing muscles as they meet at the midline of the cranium.

sample A smaller study group chosen to represent a larger population.

San Foragers of southern Africa, also known as Bushmen; speakers of San languages.

Sapir-Whorf hypothesis Theory that different languages produce different ways of thinking.

schistosomiasis Disease caused by liver flukes transmitted by snails inhabiting ponds, lakes, and waterways, often created by irrigation projects.

schizoid view of applied anthropology; the belief that anthropologists should help carry out, but not make or criticize, policy, and that personal value judgments should be kept strictly separate from scientific investigation in applied anthropology.

science A systematic field of study or body of knowledge that aims, through experiment, observation, and deduction, to produce reliable explanations of phenomena, with reference to the material and physical world.

scientific medicine   As distinguished from Western medicine, a health-care system based on scientific knowledge and procedures, encompassing such fields as pathology, microbiology, biochemistry, surgery, diagnostic technology, and applications.

Second World   The Warsaw Pact nations, including the former Soviet Union, the Socialist and once-Socialist countries of Eastern Europe and Asia.

secret societies   Sodalities, usually all-male or all-female, with secret initiation ceremonies.

sectorial fallowing   Intensive horticulture; plots are cultivated for two to three years, then fallowed for three to five, with a longer rest after several of these shorter cycles.

sedentism   Settled (sedentary) life; preceded food production in the Old World and followed it in the New World.

segmentary lineage organization (SLO)   Political organization based on descent, usually patrilineal, with multiple descent segments that form at different genealogical levels and function in different contexts.

semantics   A language's meaning system.

semiperiphery   Structural position in the world system intermediate between core and periphery.

serial monogamy   Marriage of a given individual to several spouses, but not at the same time.

sertão   Arid interior of northeastern Brazil; backlands.

settlement hierarchy   A ranked series of communities differing in size, function, and type of building; a three-level settlement hierarchy indicates state organization.

sexual dimorphism   Marked differences in male and female biology, besides the contrasts in breasts and genitals, and temperament.

sexual selection   Based on differential success in mating, the process in which certain traits of one sex (e.g., color in male birds) are selected because of advantages they confer in winning mates.

sexual orientation   A person's habitual sexual attraction to, and activities with, persons of the opposite sex, *heterosexuality;* the same sex, *homosexuality;* or both sexes, *bisexuality.*

shaman   A part-time religious practitioner who mediates between ordinary people and supernatural beings and forces.

sickle-cell anemia   Usually fatal disease in which the red blood cells are shaped like crescents, or sickles, and increase the heart's burden by clogging the small blood vessels.

sisal   Plant adapted to arid areas; its fiber is used to make rope.

Sivapithecus   Widespread fossil group first found in Pakistan; includes specimens formerly called *"Ramapithecus"* and fossil apes from Turkey, China, and Kenya; early *Sivapithecus* may contain the common ancestor of the orangutan and the African apes; late *Sivapithecus* is now seen as ancestral to the modern orang.

slash and burn   Form of horticulture in which the forest cover of a plot is cut down and burned before planting to allow the ashes to fertilize the soil.

slavery   The most extreme, coercive, abusive, and inhumane form of legalized inequality; people are treated as property.

smelting   The high-temperature process by which pure metal is produced from an ore.

social fund   Scarce resources invested to assist friends, relatives, in-laws, and neighbors.

social race   A group assumed to have a biological basis but actually perceived and defined in a social context, by a particular culture rather than by scientific criteria.

society   Organized life in groups; typical of humans and other animals.

sociobiology   The study of the evolutionary basis of social behavior.

sociolinguistics   Study of relationships between social and linguistic variation; study of language (performance) in its social context.

sociopolitical typology   Classification scheme based on the scale and complexity of social organization and the effectiveness of political regulation; includes band, tribe, chiefdom, and state.

sodality   See *pantribal sodality.*

sororate   Custom by which a widower marries the sister of the deceased wife.

speciation   Formation of new species; occurs when subgroups of the same species are separated for a sufficient length of time.

species Population whose members can interbreed to produce offspring that can live and reproduce.

state (nation-state) Complex sociopolitical system that administers a territory and populace with substantial contrasts in occupation, wealth, prestige, and power. An independent, centrally organized political unit; a government. A form of social and political organization with a formal, central government and a division of society into classes.

status Any position that determines where someone fits in society; may be ascribed or achieved.

stereoscopic vision Ability to see in depth.

stereotypes Fixed ideas—often unfavorable—about what the members of a group are like.

stipulated descent Basis of the clan; members merely say they descend from their apical ancestor; they don't trace the actual genealogical links between themselves and that ancestor.

strategic resources Those necessary for life, such as food and space.

stratification Characteristic of a system with socioeconomic strata, sharp social divisions based on unequal access to wealth and power; see *stratum.*

stratified Class-structured; stratified societies have marked differences in wealth, prestige, and power between social classes.

stratigraphy Science that examines the ways in which earth sediments are deposited in demarcated layers known as *strata* (singular, *stratum*).

stratum One of two or more groups that contrast in regard to social status and access to strategic resources. Each stratum includes people of both sexes and all ages.

style shifts Variations in speech in different contexts.

subaltern Lower in rank, subordinate, traditionally lacking an influential role in decision making.

subcultures Different cultural traditions associated with subgroups in the same complex society.

subgroups Languages within a taxonomy of related languages that are most closely related.

suborder Group of closely related superfamilies.

subordinate The lower, or underprivileged, group in a stratified system.

subsistence fund Scarce resources invested to provide food in order to replace the calories expended in daily activity.

sumptuary goods Items whose consumption is limited to the elite.

superfamily Group of closely related zoological families.

superordinate The upper, or privileged, group in a stratified system.

supply and demand, law of Economic rule that things cost more the scarcer they are and the more people want them.

survey research Characteristic research procedure among social scientists other than anthropologists. Studies society through sampling, statistical analysis, and impersonal data collection.

symbiosis An obligatory interaction between groups that is beneficial to each.

symbol Something, verbal or nonverbal, that arbitrarily and by convention stands for something else, with which it has no necessary or natural connection.

syncretisms Cultural blends, or mixtures, including religious blends, that emerge from acculturation, particularly under colonialism, such as African, Native American, and Roman Catholic saints and deities in Caribbean vodun, or "voodoo," cults.

syntax The arrangement and order of words in phrases and sentences.

systematic survey Information gathered on patterns of settlement over a large area; provides a regional perspective on the archaeological record.

systemic perspective View that changes have multiple consequences, some unforeseen.

taboo Set apart as sacred and off-limits to ordinary people; prohibition backed by supernatural sanctions.

taphonomy The study of the processes—biological and geological—by which dead animals become fossils; from the Greek *taphos,* which means "tomb."

taxonomy Classification scheme; assignment to categories (*taxa;* singular, *taxon*).

teocentli Or *teosinte,* a wild grass; apparent ancestor of maize.

Teotihuacan A.D. 100 to 700, first state in the Valley of Mexico and earliest major Mesoamerican empire.

terrestrial Ground-dwelling.

text Something that is creatively "read," interpreted, and assigned meaning by each person who receives it; includes any media-borne image, such as *Carnaval.*

theory An explanatory framework, containing a series of statements, that helps us understand *why* (something exists); theories suggest patterns, connections, and relationships that may be confirmed by new research.

Third World The less-developed countries (LDCs).

Thomson's nose rule Rule stating that the average nose tends to be longer in areas with lower mean annual temperatures; based on the geographic distribution of nose length among human populations.

totem An animal or plant apical ancestor of a clan.

traditions, in tool making Coherent patterns of tool manufacture.

transecting groups Networks created through direct communication channels between groups that previously had, or otherwise have, trouble communicating—for example, physicians and patients.

transhumance One of two variants of pastoralism; part of the population moves seasonally with the herds while the other part remains in home villages.

tribe Form of sociopolitical organization usually based on horticulture or pastoralism. Socioeconomic stratification and centralized rule are absent in tribes, and there is no means of enforcing political decisions.

tropics Geographic belt extending about 23 degrees north and south of the equator, between the Tropic of Cancer (north) and the Tropic of Capricorn (south).

tundra Cold, treeless plains.

typology, economic See *economic typology.*

typology, sociopolitical See *sociopolitical typology.*

underdifferentiation Planning fallacy of viewing less-developed countries as an undifferentiated group; ignoring cultural diversity and adopting a uniform approach (often ethnocentric) for very different types of project beneficiaries.

uniformitarianism Belief that explanations for past events should be sought in ordinary forces that continue to work today.

unilineal descent Matrilineal or patrilineal descent.

unilocal Either patrilocal or matrilocal postmarital residence; requires that a married couple reside with the relatives of either the husband or the wife, depending on the society.

universal Something that exists in every culture.

Upper Paleolithic Blade-toolmaking traditions associated with early *H. sapiens sapiens;* named from their location in upper, or more recent, layers of sedimentary deposits.

urban anthropology The anthropological study of cities.

uterine Primate groups made up of mothers, sisters, daughters, and sons that have not emigrated.

variables Attributes (e.g., sex, age, height, weight) that differ from one person or case to the next.

vertical economy Economy based on environmental zones that, although close together in space, contrast in altitude, rainfall, overall climate, and vegetation.

vertical mobility Upward or downward change in a person's social status.

visual predation theory Theory that the primates evolved in lower branches and undergrowth by developing visual and tactile abilities to aid in hunting and snaring insects.

wealth All a person's material assets, including income, land, and other types of property; the basis of economic status.

westernization The acculturative influence of Western expansion on native cultures.

working class Or proletariat; those who must sell their labor to survive; the antithesis of the bourgeoisie in Marx's class analysis.

Würm The last glacial; began around 75,000 B.P. and ended between 17,000 and 12,000 B.P.

zygote Fertilized egg, created by the union of two sex cells, one from each parent.

GLOSARIO

absolute dating   fechado absoluto

acculturation   aculturación

Acheulian   achelense

achieved status   estatus adquirido

adapids   adápidos

adaptation   adaptación

adaptive   adaptativo

advocacy view (of applied anthropology)
visión defensora de la antropología aplicada

aesthetics   estética

affinals   parientes políticos (por matrimonio)

age set   grupo de edad

agnates   agnados o agnatos

agriculture   agricultura

ahimsa   ahimsa

allele   alelo

Allen's rule   Allen, Regla de

alluvial   aluvional

ambilineal   ambilineal

ambilocal   ambilocal

analogies   analogías

anatomically modern humans (AMHs)
humanos anatómicamente modernos

animism   animismo

Anthropoidea   Antropoidea

anthropoids   antropoides

anthropology   antropología

anthropology and education   antropología
y educación

anthropometry   antropometría

antibody   anticuerpo

antigen   antígeno

apartheid   apartheid

apical ancestor   ancestro primigenio

applied anthropology   antropología aplicada

arboreal   arbóreo-a

arboreal theory   teoría arbórea

archaeological anthropology (prehistoric
archaeology)   antropología arqueológica
(arqueología prehistórica)

archaic Homo sapiens   Homo sapiens arcaico

archaic state   estado arcaico

art   arte

artifacts   artefactos

arts   artes

ascribed status   estatus atribuido

ASL American Sign Language   Lenguaje
americano de señas

assimilation   asimilación

attitudinal discrimination   actitud
discriminatoria

Aurignacian   auriñacense

australopithecines   australopitecos

axis   eje

Aztec   azteca

balanced reciprocity   reciprocidad equilibrada

band   banda

berdaches   bardajes—catamitas

Bergmann's Rule   Bergman, Regla de

Beringia   Beringia

bifurcate collateral kinship terminology
terminología de parentesco colateral bifurcada

bifurcate merging kinship terminology
terminología de parentesco colateral fusionada

big man   caudillo

bilateral kinship calculation   deducción de
parentesco bilateral

biochemical genetics   genética bioquímica

biological anthropology   antropología
biológica

biological determinists   deterministas
biológicos

biological kin types   tipos de parentesco
biológico

biomedicine   biomedicina

bipedal   bípedo/a

Black English Vernacular (BEV)   Inglés
Negro Vernáculo

blade tool   utensilio de lasca

blended family   familia fusionada

blood feud   conflicto entre familias

bone biology   biología osteológica o de
los huesos

bourgeoisie   burguesía

brachiation   braquiación

brideprice   Ver progeny price

bridewealth   Ver progeny price

broad-spectrum revolution   revolución de
amplio espectro

bronze   bronce

bush school   escuela rural o escuela del arbusto

call systems   sistemas de comunicación

caloric staple   alimento de primera necesidad

caondomblé   candomblé

capital   capital

capitalist world economy   economía
capitalista mundial

caprine   caprino/a

Capsians   capsianos

cargo cults   culto post-colonial aculturador,
imitador de la cultura europea.

caste system   sistema de castas

catarrhine   catirrino

catastrophism   catastrofismo

catharsis   catarsis

Cenozoic   Cenozoico

ceremonial fund   fondo ceremonial

ceremonies of increase   ceremonias de
fertilidad

chiefdom   cacicazgo

chromosomes   cromosomas

chronology   cronología

civilization   civilización

clan   clan

class   clase

class consciousness   conciencia de clase

classic Neandertales   Neandertal clásicos

cline   clina

Clovis tradition   tradición Clovis

collateral household   hogar colateral

collateral relative   familiar colateral o lejano

colonialism   colonialismo

communal religions   religiones comunales

communitas   communitas—sentimiento grupal
o comunitario

competence   competencia

competitive exclusion   exclusión competitiva

complex societies   sociedades complejas

conspecifics   coespecífícos—de la misma
especie

continental shelf plataforma continental

continental slope vertiente continental, pendiente continental

convergent evolution evolución convergente

core centro

core values valores centrales

correlation correlación

cranium cráneo

creationism creacionismo

creative opposition oposición creativa

cross cousins primos cruzados

cultivation continuum continuum de cultivos

cultural anthropology antropología cultural

cultural colonialism colonialismo cultural

cultural consultants consejeros culturales

cultural convergence convergencia cultural

cultural determinists deterministas culturales

cultural ecology ecología cultural

cultural imperialism imperialismo cultural

cultural learning aprendizaje cultural

cultural relativism relativismo cultural

cultural resource management (CRM) administración de recursos culturales

cultural rights derechos culturales

cultural transmission transmisión cultural

culturally compatible economic development projects proyectos de desarrollo económico, culturalmente compatibles

culture cultura

culture and personality personalidad y cultura

cuneiform cuneiforme

curer curador/a

cytoplasm citoplasma

daughter languages idiomas derivados

demonstrated descent descendencia demostrada

descent descendencia

descent group grupo de descendencia

development anthropology antropología del desarrollo

diaspora diáspora

differential access acceso diferencial

diffusion difusión

diglossia diglosia

directional selection selección direccional

discourse discurso

discrimination discriminación

disease enfermedad

displacement alusión

domestic doméstico

domestic-public dichotomy dicotomía entre lo doméstico y lo público

domestic system sistema doméstico

dominant dominante

dowry dote

dry farming cultivo seco

dryopithecids driopitecos

ecocide ecocidio

ecology ecología

economic typology tipología económica

economizing economización

economy economía

ecosystem ecosistema

egalitarian society sociedad igualitaria

ego ego

elite level nivel de élite

emic émico

empires imperios

emotionalistic disease theories teorías emocionales de las enfermedades

enculturation culturización

endogamy endogamia

environmental racism racismo ambiental

equity increased incremento de la igualdad

estrus estro

ethnic expulsion expulsión étnica

ethnic group grupo étnico

ethnicity etnicismo

ethnocentrism etnocentrismo

ethnocide etnocidio

ethnography etnografía

ethnomusicology etnomusicología

ethnoscience etnociencia Ver ethnosemantics

ethnosemantics etnosemántica

etic punto de vista del investigador

Etoro Etoro

eugenics eugenesia

Eve Theory Theoría de Eva Mitocondrial

evolution evolución

excavation excavación

exogamy exogamia

expanded family household hogar familiar extendido

expressive culture cultura expresiva

extended family familia extendida

extradomestic extradoméstico/a

extrasomatic extrasomático

family, zoological familia zoológica

family of orientation familia de orientación

family of procreation familia de procreación

fictive kinship parentesco ficticio

First World Primer Mundo

fiscal fiscal

focal vocabulary vocabulario grupal

folk folk—folklórico

food production producción de alimentos

foramen magnum foramen magnum

forced assimilation asimilación forzada

fossils fósiles

fraternal polyandry poliandria fraternal

functional explanation explicación funcional

gametes gametos

gender roles roles de cada género o sexo

gender stereotypes estereotipos de cada género o sexo

gender stratification estratificación sexual

gene gen

gene flow flujo génico

gene pool conjunto de genes en una población

genealogical method método genealógico

general anthropology antropología general

generality generalidad

generalized reciprocity reciprocidad generalizada

generational kinship terminology terminología generacional de parentesco

genetic evolution evolución genética

genitor progenitor

genocide genocidio

genotype genotipo

genus (plural, genera) género (plural géneros)

gibbons gibones

glacials glaciales

globalization globalización

gracile grácil

grammar gramática

green revolution revolución verde o agrícola

Halafian Halafiense

head, village jefe de aldea

health-care system sistema de atención de la salud

hegemonic reading interpretación hegemónica

hegemony hegemonía

heterozygous heterocigótico

hidden transcript manifiesto oculto

Hilly Flanks Flancos Escarpados

historical explanation explicación histórica

historical linguistics   lingüística histórica

Hogopans   Hogopanes

holistic   holística

Hominidae   homínidae

hominids   homínidos

Hominoidea   Hominoidea

Hominoids   hominoides

Homo habilis   Homo habilis

Homo sapiens sapiens   Homo sapiens

homologies   homologías

homozygous   homocigótico

horticulture   horticultura

human rights   derechos humanos

humanities   humanidades

hybrid   híbrido

hydraulic systems   sistemas hidráulicos

hypervitaminosis D   hipervitaminosis D

hypodescent   hipodescendencia

hypoxia   hipoxia

ideal types   tiposó ideales clasificaciones

identity politics   identidad política

illness   enfermedad

imperialism   imperialismo

incest   incesto

incest taboo   tabú del incesto

inclusive fitness   eficacia biológica inclusiva

income   ingresos

independent assortment, Mendel's law of   ley Mendeliana de selección

independent invention   invención independiente

indigenized   indigenizado

indigenous peoples   pueblos indígenas

individual fitness   eficacia biológica individual

Industrial Revolution   Revolución Industrial

infanticide   infanticidio

institutional discrimination   discriminación institucional

interglacials   interglacial

international culture   cultura internacional

interstadials   interestadial

intervention philosophy   filosofía de la intervención

interview schedule   programa de entrevistas

IPR Intellectual property Rights   Derechos de la Propiedad Intelectual

Iroquois   iroqués

ischial callosities   callosidades isquiales

ivory tower view   visión de la torre de marfil

Jomon   Jomon

Ju'hoansi   Ju'hoansi

key cultural consultant   asesor cultural clave

kin-based   basado en el parentesco

kin terms   términos de parentesco

kinesics   comunicación corporal

kingdom, zoological   reino zoológico

kinship calculation   deducción de parentesco

knuckle-walking   locomoción sobre los nudillos

Kwakiutl   Kwakiutl

lactase   ver lactosa

lactose   lactosa

language   idioma

latent function   función latente

law   ley

LDC (less-developed country)   país subdesarrollado, en vías de desarrollo

leveling mechanisms   mecanismos de nivelación

levirate   levirato

lexicon   léxico

life history   historia de vida

liminality   liminar

lineage   linaje

lineal kinship terminology   terminología del parentesco lineal

lineal relative   pariente directo

linguistic anthropology   antropología lingüística

linguistic relativity   relatividad lingüística

linkages   vínculos

liturgical order   secuencia litúrgica

liturgies   liturgias

local descent group   grupo de descendencia local

longitudinal   longitudinal

longitudinal research   investigación longitudinal

macroband   macrobanda

magic   magia

maize   maíz

majority groups   grupos mayoritarios

maladaptive harmful   mal adaptado—dañino

mana   maná

manifest function   función manifiesta

manioc   mandioca

market principle   principio de mercado

marriage   matrimonio

mater   madre

matriarchy   matriarcado

matrifocal   matrifocal

matrilateral skewing   tendencia matrilateral

matrilateral descent   descendencia matrilateral

matrilocality   matrilocalización

matrons   matronas

means (or factors) of production   medios (o factores) de producción

medical anthropology   antropología médica

meiosis   meiosis

melanin   melanina

Mendelian genetics   genética mendeliana

Mesoamerica   América Central

Mesolithic   Mesolítico

Mesopotamia   Mesopotamia

Mesozoic   Mesozoico

metallurgy   metalurgia

microband   microbanda

microlith   microlito

Middle Pleistocene   Pleistoceno Medio

Mindel   Mindel

minimal pairs   pares mínimos

minority groups   grupos minoritarios

mitosis   mitosis

mode of production   modo de producción

moiety   partición social

molecular anthropology   antropología molecular

monocrop production   producción de monocultivo

monotheism   monoteismo

morpheme   morfema

morphology   morfología

Mousterian   Musteriense

multiculturalism   multiculturalismo

multivariate   multivariado

multiregional evolution   evolucion multiregional

mutation   mutación

m.y.a. Million years ago   m.a. millones de años atrás

namesakes   homónimos - tocayos

nation   nación

nation-state   estado-nación

national culture   cultura nacional

nationalities   nacionalidades

native taxonomy   taxonomía nativa

Natufians   Natufiense

natural selection   selección natural

naturalistic disease theories   teorías naturalistas de las enfermedades

naturists   naturistas

Neandertals   Neandertales

negative reciprocity   reciprocidad negativa

négritude   negritud

neocolonialism   neocolonialismo

Neolithic   Neolítico

neolocality   neolocalización

Nilotic populations   poblaciones nilóticas

nomadism, pastoral   nomadismo pastoral

nuclear family   familia nuclear

nurturists   nutricistas

Oaxaca, Valley of   Oaxaca, Valle de

office   puesto político

Oldowan pebble tools   herramientas de piedra de Olduvai

Olmec   Olmeca

Olympian religions   religiones olímpicas

omomyids   omómidas

open class system   sistema de clases abierto

opposable thumb   pulgar oponible

order, zoological   orden zoológico

orthograde posture   postura ortógrada

osteology   osteología

overinnovation   sobreinnovación

paleoanthropology   paleoantropología

paleoecology   paleoecología

paleopathology   paleopatología

Paleoindians   Paleoindios

Paleolithic   Paleolítico

paleontology   paleontología

Paleozoic   Paleozoico

Palynology   palinología

pantheon   panteón

pantribal sodality   hermandad pantribal

parallel cousins   primos paralelos

participant observation   observación participativa

particularity   particularidad

pastoralists   pastoralistas

pater   pater

patriarchy   patriarcado

patrilineal descent   descendencia patrilineal

patrilineal-patrilocal complex   complejo patrilineal-patrilocal

patrilocality   patrilocalización

peasant   campesino

perfomance   desempeño/actuación

Perigordian   Perigordiense

periphery   periferia

personalistic disease theories   teorías personalistas de las enfermedades

phenotype   fenotipo

phenotypical adaptation   adaptación fenotípica

phone   fon

phoneme   fonema

phonemics   fonémica

phonetics   fonética

phylogeny   filogenia

physical anthropology   antropología física

pidgin   lengua franca

plasticity   plasticidad

platyrrhine   platirrino

Pleistocene   Pleistoceno

plural marriage   Ver poligamia

plural society   sociedad plural

polity   orden político

polyandry   poliandria

polygamy   poligamia

progeny price   precio de la progenie

questionnaire   cuestionario

race   raza

racism   racismo

radiometric   radiométrica

random genetic drift   deriva génica aleatoria

ranked society   sociedad jerarquizada

rapport   relación amigable

recessive   recesivo

reciprocity   reciprocidad

recombination   recombinación

redistribution   redistribución

refugees   refugiados

regulation   regulación

relative dating   fechado relativo

relativity   relatividad

religion   religión

remote sensing   sensores remotos, percepción a distancia

rent fund   fondo de renta

replacement fund   fondo de reposición

respondents   entrevistados

revitalization movements   movimientos de revitalización

rickets   raquitismo

Riss   Riss

rites of passage   ritos de pasaje o iniciación

ritual   ritual

robust   robusto

Romer's rule   Romer, regla de

sagittal crest   cresta sagital

sample   muestra

San   San

Sapir-Whorf hypothesis   hipótesis de Sapir-Whorf

schistosomiasis   esquistosomiasis

schizoid view   visión esquizoide

science   ciencia

scientific medicine   medicina científica

Second World   Segundo Mundo o Mundo Socialista

secret societies   sociedades secretas

sectorial fallowing   barbecho sectorizado

sedentism   sedentarismo

segmentary lineage organization (SLO)   organización segmentaria de linaje

semantics   semántica

semiperiphery   semiperiferia

serial monogamy   monogamia serial

sertão   sertão

settlement hierarchy   jerarquía de los asentamientos

sexual dimorphism   dimorfismo sexual

sexual orientation   orientación sexual

sexual selection   selección sexual

shaman   shamán—chamán

sickle-cell anemia   anemia de las células falciformes

sisal   sisal

Sivapithecus   Sivapiteco

slash and burn   roza y quema o tala y quema

slavery   esclavitud

smelting   fundición

social fund   fondo social

social race   raza social

society   sociedad

sociobiology   sociobiología

sociolinguistics   sociolingüística

sociopolitical typology   tipología sociopolítica

sodality   Ver pantribal sodality

sororate   matrimonio de un hombre con la hermana de su esposa

speciation   especiación

species   especie

state (nation-state)   estado (estado-nación)

status estatus

stereoscopic vision visión estereoscópica

stereotypes estereotipo

stipulated descent descendencia estipulada

strategic resources recursos estratégicos

stratification estratificación

stratified estratificado/a

stratigraphy estratigrafía

stratum estrato

style shifts variaciones de estilo

subaltern subalterno

subcultures subculturas

subgroups subgrupos

suborder suborden

subordinate subordinado/a

subsistence fund fondo de subsistencia

sumptuary goods bienes suntuarios

superfamily superfamilia

superordinate de clase superior

supply and demand, law of ley de la oferta y la demanda

survey research investigación basada en encuestas

symbiosis simbiosis

symbol símbolo

syncretisms sincretismos

syntax sintaxis

systematic survey investigación sistemática

systemic perspective perspectiva sistémica

taboo tabú

taphonomy tafonomía

taxonomy taxonomía

teocentli teocentli o teocintle

Teotihuacan Teotihuacán

terrestrial terrestre

text texto

theory teoría

Third World Tercer Mundo

Thomson's nose rule regla de la nariz de Thomson

totem tótem

traditions, in tool making tradiciones en la fabricación de herramientas

transecting groups grupos transversales

transhumance transhumancia

tribe tribu

tropics trópico

tundra tundra

typology, economic tipología económica

typology, sociopolitical tipología sociopolítica

underdifferentiation subdiferenciación

uniformitarianism uniformismo

unilineal descent descendencia unilineal

unilocal unilocal

universal universal

Upper Paleolithic Paleolítico Superior

urban anthropology antropología urbana

uterine uterino/a

variables variables

vertical economy economía vertical

vertical mobility movilidad vertical

visual predation theory teoría de la predación visual

wealth riqueza

westernization occidentalización

working class clase trabajadora

Würm Würm

zygote cigoto

CREDITS

Photo Credits

Frontmatter

xxxii: (*Part 1*) Aleksander Nordahl/ dagfoto@online.no

Chapter 1

2: ©Joel Gordon; **4:** ©Spencer Grant/PhotoEdit; **7:** Smithsonian Institution; **8:** ©Barton Silverman/The New York Times; **9:** (*left*) ©Roberto Candia/AP/Wide World Photos; (*right*) ©David Cannon/Getty Images; **13:** Jerald T. Milanich; **14:** J. Kyle Keener; **15:** ©Christopher J. Morris/ Corbis; **17:** Courtesy Alicia Wilbur; **18:** ©Jorgen Schytte/Still Pictures/ Peter Arnold, Inc.; **21:** ©National Geographic Society; **23:** William Campbell/Corbis Sygma

Chapter 2

28: (*Part 2*) ©Wesley Boxce/Photo Researchers; **30:** ©Thomas Hoepker/ Magnum; **33:** ©Mike Yamashita/ Woodfin Camp & Associates; **34:** ©AP/Wide World Photos; **36:** ©Corbis-Bettmann; **38:** Charles Harbutt /Actuality; **39:** ©Mark Edwards/Still Pictures/Peter Arnold, Inc.; **42:** ©Jonathan Nourok/PhotoEdit; **43:** ©Erich Lessing/Magnum; **45:** ©UNEP/Peter Arnold, Inc.; **47:** Courtesy of Ann L. Bretnall; **48:** Professor Marietta Baba, Michigan State University

Chapter 3

56: ©Victor R. Boswell/National Geographic Society; **58:** ©Kenneth Garrett/National Geographic Society; **60:** ©Joe Brockert/AP/Wide World Photos; **62:** ©Michael K. Nichols/ National Geographic Society; **64:** Payson Sheets, University of Colorado, Boulder; **65:** ©Frank Lane Picture Agency/Corbis; **66:** ©Richard T. Nowitz/Corbis; **67:** ©Peter Turnley/ Corbis; **69:** Dr. Jerome Rose, University of Arkansas; **72:** ©Kenneth Garrett/ National Geographic; **73:** ©Jonathan Blair/Corbis; **74:** Leonardo L.T. Rhodes/Earth Scenes/Animals Animals; **75:** ©Y. Arthus/Peter Arnold, Inc.

Chapter 4

82: ©Catherine Karnow/Woodfin Camp & Associates; **84:** Jay Sand; **86:** *Noah's Ark* by Edward Hicks, 1846, $26^1/_2 \times 30^1/_2$, Oil on canvas, Philadelphia Museum of Art, Bequest of Lisa Norris Elkins; **91:** ©Dr. Gopal Mujrti/Phototake; **92:** ©Jean-Marc Giboux/Getty Images; **94:** ©Alfred Pasieka/Peter Arnold, Inc.; **95:** David Maxwell; **97:** ©Jean-Christian Bourcart/Newsmakers/Getty Images; **98:** ©Betty Press/Woodfin Camp & Associates; **101:** (*left*) ©Robert Caputo/Stock Boston; (*right*) ©Dennis Stock/Magnum

Chapter 5

108: ©Cyril Ruoso/Peter Arnold, Inc.; **110:** Christophe Boesch/Wild Chimpanzee Foundation; **111:** ©Mike K. Nichols/Magnum; **116:** (*left*) ©Kenneth Garrett/National Geographic Society; (*right*) ©O. Langrand/Peter Arnold, Inc.; **117:** Courtesy Jennifer Burns; **120:** ©Tom McHugh/Photo Researchers; **122:** ©Mack Henley/Visuals Unlimited; **124:** Orangutan Foundation International; **126:** ©Connie Bransilver/Photo Researchers, Inc.; **128:** ©M. Gunther/Peter Arnold, Inc.; **129:** ©Jane Goodall/National Geographic Society; **133:** ©C. Novellino/Peter Arnold, Inc.

Bringing It All Together

139: ©Mark Edwards/Still Pictures/ Peter Arnold, Inc.; **140:** ©Olivier Langrand/Peter Arnold, Inc.; **141:** ©Nigel Dickinson/Peter Arnold, Inc.

Chapter 6

142: ©Michael Nichols/National Geographic Society; **144:** ©A. Compost/Bios/Peter Arnold, Inc.; **148:** ©L. & D. Klein/Photo Researchers; **149:** (*left*) Denver Museum of Nature & Science; (*right*) ©Tom McHugh/ Photo Researchers; **151:** (*left*) ©Tom McHugh/Photo Researchers; (*right*) ©Roland Seitre/Peter Arnold, Inc.; **153:** (*left*) ©Science VU/Visuals Unlimited; (*right*) ©Manoj Shah/ Animals Animals; **154:** Russell Ciochon, U of Iowa; **156:** From *Rhetorica Christiana*, by Didacus Valades, 1579; **159:** ©AFP/Corbis; **158:** Courtesy Barbara Hewitt

Chapter 7

164: ©Thomas Ernsting/Bilderberg/ Aurora; **166:** Tim D. White/Brill Atlanta; **168:** ©Fred Mayer/Magnum; **171:** Kenneth Garrett; **175:** ©John Reader/Science Photo Library/Photo Researchers; **180:** ©Maurico Anton/ National Geographic Society; **182:** (*top a,b,c,d*) ©Luba Dmytryk/National Geographic Society; **182:** (*middle*) ©Des Bartlett/Photo Researchers; **183:** Alan Walker, Johns Hopkins University/ National Museums of Kenya, Kalakol Account; **184:** Kenneth Garrett; **187:** Courtesy Josh Trapani

Chapter 8

192: ©The Art Archive/Picture Desk; **194:** ©Gouram Tsibakhashvili/AP/ Wide World Photos; **196:** ©Richard Schlecht/National Geographic Society; **197:** ©Luba Dmytryk/National

Edwards/Still Pictures/Peter Arnold, Inc.; **492:** *(top)* ©James L. Stanfield/National Geographic Society; *(bottom)* ©Nita Winter/The Image Works; **494:** ©Najlah Feanny/Stock Boston; **495:** ©Photofest; **497:** ©Newsmakers/Getty Images; **500:** *(top)* ©D. H. Hessell/Stock Boston; *(bottom)* ©John Eastcott/Yva Momatiuk/Stock Boston; **502:** ©Richard Olenius/National Geographic Society

Chapter 19

512: ©Joanna B. Pinneo/Aurora; **514:** ©Bettmann/Corbis; **517:** ©Mark Edwards/Peter Arnold, Inc.; **519:** ©DPA/The Images Works; **521:** ©Pablo Bartholomew/Getty Images; **523:** Courtesy Kim Shah; **524:** ©Nina Ruecker/Getty Images; **526:** ©Betty Press/Woodfin Camp & Associates; **530:** ©Cary Wolinsky/Stock Boston; **533:** ©Mark Edwards/Still Pictures/Peter Arnold, Inc.; **535:** ©George Frey/AFP/Corbis; **537:** ©Thomas Kelly

Chapter 20

542: ©Jodi Cobb/National Geographic Society; **544:** ©Lindsay Hebberd/Corbis; **546:** ©Steve McCurry/Magnum; **549:** ©Mike Schroeder/Argus/Peter Arnold, Inc.; **552:** ©Steve McCutcheon/Visuals Unlimited; **553:** Wendy Stone; **554:** ©Stuart Franklin/Magnum; **556:** © David Alan Harvey/Magnum; **558:** ©George Holton/Photo Researchers; **563:** "Memories of Rio de Janeiro"; **564:** ©Martha Cooper/Peter Arnold. Inc.; **566:** Norman Rockwell Family Trust Copyright © 1943 the Norman Rockwell Family Trust

Bringing It All Together

574: ©John Bigelow Taylor/Art Resource; **576:** ©David Alan Harvey/Magnum; **577:** ©Galen/Odyssey/Chicago

Chapter 21

578: ©Peter Arnold, Inc.; **580:** ©M&E Bernheim/Woodfin Camp & Associates; **582:** ©Erich Lessing/Art Resource; **583:** ©Duane Burleson/AP/Wide World Photos; **585:** ©Peter Essick/Aurora; **587:** *(top)* ©Thierry Secretan/Cosmos/Woodfin Camp & Associates; *(middle)* ©Micheal Minardi/Peter Arnold, Inc.; **588:** Michele Burgess; **589:** ©Getty Images; **592:** ©Anthro-Photo; **598:** ©Kal Muller/Woodfin Camp & Associates; **602:** ©Disney Enterprises, Inc.

Chapter 22

608: ©Mohamed Torche/Explorer/Photo Researchers; **610:** Carolina Salguero; **612:** ©Gilles Peress/Magnum; **614:** ©Thomas Hoepker/Magnum; **619:** *(top)* ©James P. Blair/National Geographic Society; *(bottom)* ©Abbas/Magnum: **620:** ©Bruce Hunter/National Geographic Society; **621:** ©Robert Frerck/Corbis Stock Market; **623:** ©Yva Momatiuk & John Eastcott/Woodfin Camp & Associates; **627:** *(top)* ©Cary Wolinsky/Stock Boston; *(bottom)* ©Stephanie Maze/Woodfin Camp & Associates; **629:** Courtesy Anne Haggerson; **630:** *(top)* ©James P. Blair/National Geographic Society; *(bottom)* Joan Marcus

Chapter 23

636: *(Part 4)* ©Maria Stenzel/National Geographic Society; **638:** ©Fritz Hoffmann/The Image Works; **640:** Archives Charmet/Bridgeman Art Library; **642:** ©Hiroji Kubota/Magnum; **643:** *(top)* ©Bruce Dational Geographic Society; *(bottom)* David Reed; **646:** ©Mercury Archives/Image Bank/Getty Images; **647:** ©Hulton Archive/Getty Images; **648:** ©Culver; **650:** ©Dilip Mehta/Woodfin Camp & Associates; **651:** New York Public Library; **659:** ©Jean-Yves Rabeuf/The Image Works; **661:** ©V. Leloup/Gamma Presse

Chapter 24

666: ©Mark Edwards/Still Pictures/Peter Arnold, Inc.; **668:** ©Reuters/STR/Archive/Getty Images; **672:** ©Roger Viollet/Getty Images; **675:** ©Stuart Franklin/Magnum; **676:** ©Alexander Low/Woodfin Camp & Associates; **678:** Ricardo Funari; **680:** ©Jorgen Schytte/Still Pictures/Peter Arnold, Inc.; **682:** ©Lineair/Peter Arnold, Inc.; **683:** ©Marc & Evelyn Bernheim/Woodfin Camp & Associates; **685:** ©Reuters NewMedia Inc./Corbis; **686:** ©Noorani/Still Pictures/Peter Arnold, Inc.; **687:** Dr. Steven Lansing

Chapter 25

692: ©Bryan & Cherry Alexander/Photo Researchers, Inc.; **694:** Richard Strauss/Smithsonian Institution/National Museum of the American Indian; **696:** ©Corbis; **697:** ©Gueorgui Pinkhassov/Magnum; **699:** Steven Feld; **702:** ©Rob Crandall/Stock

Boston; **703:** ©Buu/Deville/Turpin/Gamma Presse; **706:** ©Andres Hernandez/Getty Images; **707:** *(top)* ©H. Schwarzbach/Argus/Peter Arnold, Inc.; *(bottom)* ©John Maier/Still Pictures/Peter Arnold, Inc.; **708:** ©Peter Marlow/Magnum; **711:** Ricardo Funari

Bringing It All Together

717: ©Martin Parr/Magnum; **718:** ©Mark Peterson/Corbis Saba; **719:** ©Mohamed Azakir/Reuters/Landov

Text and Illustration Credits

Front Matter

ii-iii: From *Student Atlas of World Geography*, Third Edition, by John L. Allen. Copyright © 2003 by The McGraw-Hill Companies, Inc. Reprinted by permission of McGraw-Hill/Dushkin, a division of The McGraw-Hill Companies, Guilford, CT 06437.

Chapter 1

4: Del Jones, "Hot Asset in Corporate: Anthropology Degrees," *USA TODAY*, February 18, 1999, p. B1. Copyright © 1999 USA TODAY. Reprinted with permission.

Chapter 2

30: Excerpts from Malcolm W. Browne, "Buried on a Hillside, Clues to Terror," *The New York Times*, February 23, 1999. Copyright © 1999 by The New York Times Co. Reprinted with permission. **36:** AAA Code of Ethics. Adapted from http://www.aaanet.org/committees/ethics/ethcode.htm. With permission of the American Anthropological Association.

Chapter 3

60: Excerpts from Stephen Kinzer, "Museums and Tribes: A Tricky Truce," *The New York Times*, December 24, 2000, section 2, p. 1. Copyright © 2000 by The New York Times Co. Reprinted with permission.

Chapter 4

84: Excerpts from Nicholas Wade, "DNA Backs a Tribe's Tradition of Early Descent from the Jews," *The New York Times*, May 9, 1999, section 1, p. 1. Copyright © 1999 by The New York Times Co. Reprinted with permission. **91:** Figure 4.5, Adapted from Joseph B.

Birdsell, *Human Evolution: An Introduction to the New Physical Anthropology.* Copyright © 1981 by Harper & Row, Publishers, Inc. Reprinted by permission of Pearson Education, Inc., Glenview, IL.

Chapter 5

110: "Chimp Tool Sites Show Evidence of Human-Like Behavior," CBC News Online, May 26, 2002. Reprinted with permission of the Canadian Broadcasting Corporation. **114:** Table 5.2, Adapted from Robert Martin, "Classification of Primates," in Steve Jones, Robert Martin, and David Pilbeam, eds., *The Cambridge Encyclopedia of Human Evolution* (Cambridge: Cambridge University Press, 1992), pp. 20-21. Reprinted with the permission of Cambridge University Press. **115:** Figure 5.2, From Roger Lewin, *Human Evolution: An Illustrated Introduction,* 3rd ed. (Boston: Blackwell Scientific Publications, 1993), p. 44. Reprinted by permission of Blackwell Publishing Ltd., Oxford, UK. **124:** Claudia Dreifus, "Saving the Orangutan," *The New York Times,* March 21, 2000. Copyright © 2000 by The New York Times Co. Reprinted with permission. **123:** Figure 5.6, From Clifford J. Jolly and Fred Plog, *Physical Anthropology and Archaeology,* 4th ed., p. 115. Copyright © 1986 by The McGraw-Hill Companies, Inc. Reprinted with permission. **127:** Figure 5.7, From Roger Lewin, *Human Evolution: An Illustrated Introduction,* 3rd ed. (Boston: Blackwell Scientific Publications, 1993), p. 45. Reprinted by permission of Blackwell Publishing Ltd., Oxford, UK.

Chapter 6

144: Guy Gugliotta, "Suddenly, Humans Age 3 Million Years," *The Washington Post,* April 18, 2002, p. A03. Copyright © 2002 The Washington Post. Reprinted with permission. **145:** Figure 6.1, Based on an original figure compiled by D. Quednau, N. Klaud, and R.D. Martin. By permission of Dr. Robert Dennis Martin, The Field Museum, Chicago, IL. **146:** Figure 6.4, From *Introduction to Physical Anthropology,* 6th edition, by Robert Jurmain and Harry Nelson, p. 210. Copyright © 1994 Wadsworth. Reprinted with permission of Wadsworth, a division of Thomson

Learning: www.thomsonrights.com. Fax 800 730-2215. **152:** Figure 6.5, From *Introduction to Physical Anthropology,* 6th edition, by Robert Jurmain and Harry Nelson, p. 302. Copyright © 1994 Wadsworth. Reprinted with permission of Wadsworth, a division of Thomson Learning: www.thomsonrights.com. Fax 800 730-2215. **157:** Figure 6.6, Tom Brown/2002. Copyright © The Christian Science Monitor. Reprinted with permission.

Chapter 7

166: Excerpts from John Noble Wilford, "Fossils May Be Earliest Human Link," *The New York Times,* July 12, 2001, p. A12. Copyright © 2001 by The New York Times Co. Reprinted with permission.

Chapter 8

194: Excerpts from John Noble Wilford, "Skulls in Caucasus Linked to Early Humans in Africa," *The New York Times,* May 12, 2000. Copyright © 2000 by The New York Times Co. Reprinted with permission. **200:** Figure 8.1, From Clifford J. Jolly and Randall White, *Physical Anthropology and Archaeology,* 5th ed., p. 271. Copyright © 1995 by The McGraw-Hill Companies, Inc. Reprinted with permission. **202:** Figure 8.2, From Clifford J. Jolly and Randall White, *Physical Anthropology and Archaeology,* 5th ed., p. 268. Copyright © 1995 by The McGraw-Hill Companies, Inc. Reprinted with permission. **209:** Figure 8.5, From Clifford J. Jolly and Randall White, *Physical Anthropology and Archaeology,* 5th ed., p. 277. Copyright © 1995 by The McGraw-Hill Companies, Inc. Reprinted with permission. **215:** Excerpts and Figure 8.9 from Marlise Simons, "Prehistoric Art Treasure Is Found in French Cave," *The New York Times,* January 19, 1995, pp. A1, A5. Copyright © 1995 by The New York Times Co. Reprinted with permission.

Chapter 9

228: Excerpts from Brent Staples, "A Hemings Family Turns from Black, to White, to Black," *The New York Times,* December 17, 2001, p. A20. Copyright © 2001 by The New York Times Co. Reprinted with permission. **232:** Excerpts from the American Anthropological Association

Statement on Race. From http://www.aaanet.org/stmts/racepp.htm. Reprinted with permission of the American Anthropological Association.

Chapter 10

254: Excerpts from Ben Harder, "Gene Study Traces Cattle Herding in Africa," http://news.nationalgeographic.com (April 11, 2002). Reprinted by permission of the National Geographic Society. **264:** Excerpts from Boyce Rensberger, "Iceman Yields Details of Stone Age Transition: Portrait of Life 5,300 Years Ago Emerges," *The Washington Post,* October 15, 1992. Copyright © 1992 The Washington Post. Reprinted with permission. **267:** Figure 10.4, From *The Emergence of Agriculture* by Bruce D. Smith, p. 12. Copyright © 1995 Scientific American Library. Reprinted by permission of Henry Holt and Company, LLC. Table 10.2, Data compiled from *The Emergence of Agriculture* by Bruce D. Smith. Copyright © 1995 Scientific American Library. Reprinted by permission of Henry Holt and Company, LLC.

Chapter 11

282: Excerpts from Ben Harder, "Ancient Peru Torture Deaths: Sacrifices or War Crimes?" http://news.nationalgeographic.com (April 29, 2002). Reprinted by permission of the National Geographic Society. **294:** Figure 11.2, Based on Map 1-1 from *Heritage of World Civilizations*: Vol. I, to 1650, 4th ed. by Craig/Graham/Kagan/Ozmant/Turner. Copyright © 1997 Prentice-Hall. Reprinted by permission of Pearson Education, Inc., Upper Saddle River, NJ. **296:** Figure 11.3, From Clifford J. Jolly and Fred Plog, *Physical Anthropology and Archaeology,* 4th ed., p. 115. Copyright © 1986 by The McGraw-Hill Companies, Inc. Reprinted with permission.

Chapter 12

320: Excerpts from David Glenn, "Anthropological Association's Report Criticizes Yanomami Researchers and Their Accuser," *Chronicle of Higher Education,* July 2, 2002. http://chronicle.com. Copyright © 2002 by The Chronicle of Higher Education. Reprinted with permission.

Chapter 13

344: Excerpts from Dean Schabner, "Culture Clash: Makah Say Whale Hunt Opponents Debase Indian Culture," http://abcnews.go.com (May 29, 2002). Courtesy of ABCNEWS.com.

Chapter 14

366: Excerpts from Bill Dedman, "Sosa vs. McGwire: It's a Race, but Is It Also about Race?" *The New York Times*, September 20, 1998. Copyright © 1998 by The New York Times Co. Reprinted with permission.

Chapter 15

392: Excerpts from Claudia Dreifus, "How Languages Came to Be, and Change: A Conversation with John McWhorter," *The New York Times*, October 30, 2001, p. F3. Copyright © 2001 by The New York Times Co. Reprinted with permission. **399:** Figure 15.1, From *Aspects of Language*, 3rd ed. by Dwight L. Bolinger and Donald A. Sears. Reprinted with permission of Heinle & Heinle, a division of Thomson Learning: www.thomsonrights.com. Fax 800 730-2215. **405:** Table 15.3, From *Sociolinguistics: An Introduction to Language and Society* by Peter Trudgill. Penguin Books 1974, Revised Edition 1983. Copyright © 1974, 1983 Peter Trudgill. Reproduced by permission of Penguin Books Ltd.

Chapter 16

424: Excerpts from Warren Hoge, "Kautokeino Journal: Reindeer Herders, at Home on a (Very Cold) Range," *The New York Times*, March 26, 2001, p. A4. Copyright © 2001 by The New York Times Co. Reprinted with permission. **427:** Figure 16.1, Key and adaptation of map by Ray Sim from *People of the Stone Age* (Encyclopedia of Humankind, Volume 2) by Gäran Burenhult, General Editor. Copyright © 1993 by Weldon Owen Pty Limited/Bra Bocker AB. Reprinted by permission of Weldon Owen Pty Limited, and HarperCollins Publishers Inc.

Chapter 17

456: Excerpts from Ilene R. Prusher, "Chat Rooms, Bedouin Style." This article first appeared in *The Christian Science Monitor* on April 28, 2000 and is reproduced with permission. Copyright © 2000 The Christian Science Monitor (www.csmonitor.com). All rights reserved.

Chapter 18

488: Excerpts from Patrick Wilson, "When Are Two Dads Better than One? When Women Are in Charge," http://alphagalileo.org (June 12, 2002). Reprinted by permission of the University of East London, UK.

Chapter 19

514: Excerpts from Denise Grady, "Few Risks Seen to the Children of 1st Cousins," *The New York Times*, April 4, 2002, p. A1. Copyright © 2002 by The New York Times Co. Reprinted with permission. **528:** Excerpts from Daniel Goleman, "Anthropology Goes Looking in All the Old Places," *The New York Times*, November 24, 1992, p. B1. Copyright © 1992 by The New York Times Co. Reprinted with permission.

Chapter 20

544: Excerpts from Pam Kosty, "Indonesia's Matriarchal Minangkabau Offer an Alternative Social System," http://www.eurekalert.org (May 9, 2002). Reprinted by permission of the University of Pennsylvania Museum of Archaeology and Anthropology.

Chapter 21

580: Excerpts from Norimitsu Onishi, "Rising Muslim Power in Africa Causes Unrest in Nigeria and Elsewhere," *The New York Times*, November 1, 2001, p. A14. Copyright © 2001 by The New York Times Co. Reprinted with permission. **586:** Table 21.1, Reprinted with permission from Victor Turner, *The Ritual Process: Structure and Anti-structure* (New York: Aldine de Gruyter), p. 106. Copyright © 1969 by Victor W. Turner. **595:** Table 21.3, From http://religioustolerance.org. Reprinted by permission of Ontario Consultants on Religious Tolerance. **596:** Table 21.4. Reprinted by permission of Preston Hunter. www.adherents.com.

Chapter 22

610: Excerpts from Matt Crenson, "Is There a Music Gene? Scholars Mull Music's Roots," http://abcnews.go.com (July 17, 2000). Reprinted with permission of The Associated Press. **611:** Definitions from *The Random House College Dictionary*. Copyright © 1982 by Random House, Inc. Reprinted by permission of the publisher.

Chapter 23

640: Excerpts from Jack Lucentini, "Bones Reveal Some Truth in 'Noble Savage Myth'," *The Washington Post*, April 15, 2002, p. A09. Reprinted by permission of Jack Lucentini. **656:** Table 23.1, From *An Introduction to the World-System Perspective*, 2nd ed. by Thomas Shannon. Copyright © 1989, 1996 by Westview Press. Reprinted by permission of Westview Press, a member of Perseus Books, L.L.C. **660:** Table 23.2, From John H. Bodley, *Anthropology and Contemporary Human Problems*, Mayfield Publishing. Copyright © 1985 by The McGraw-Hill Companies, Inc. Reprinted with permission.

Chapter 24

668: Excerpts from Alan Cowell, "Britain in Africa: Colonialism's Legacy Becomes a Burden," *The New York Times*, June 10, 2000. Copyright © 2000 by The New York Times Co. Reprinted with permission. **670:** Figure 24.1, From the *Academic American Encyclopedia*, Vol. 3, p. 496. 1998 Edition. Copyright © 1998 by Grolier Incorporated. Reprinted with permission. **673:** Figure 24.3, From the *Academic American Encyclopedia*, Vol. 8, p. 309. 1998 Edition. Copyright © 1998 by Grolier Incorporated. Reprinted with permission. **685:** Excerpts from Erik Eckholm, "Relocations for China Dam Are Found to Lag," *The New York Times*, March 12, 1998. Copyright © 1998 by The New York Times Co. Reprinted with permission.

Chapter 25

694: Excerpts from Ellen Herscher, "A Museum to Right Past Wrongs," http://www.archaeology.org (December 6, 1999). Reprinted with permission of *Archaeology Magazine*. Copyright © 1999 The Archaeological Institute of America.

Appendix

724: Adapted from *Prime-Time Society: An Anthropological Analysis of Television and Culture*, 1st edition, by Conrad Phillip Kottak. Copyright © 1990 Wadsworth, Inc. Reprinted with permission of Wadsworth, a division of Thomson Learning: www.thomsonrights.com. Fax 800 730-2215.

NAME INDEX

SUBJECT INDEX

Eugentics, definition of, 97, 103
Eulemur fulvus rufus, 117
European Economic Community. *See* EEC
Euthenasia, 462
Eve theory, 208–210, 219
Evolution
  analogies and, 112–113, 135
  biological anthropology and, 7–8, 57
  convergent evolution, 112, 135
  definition of, 103
  gene flow and, 95–96
  genetic evolution, 91–96
  homologies and, 112–113, 135
  human biological adaptation and, 96–102
  mutation and, 94
  natural selection and, 87, 91–94
  origin of species and, 85–87
  overview, 83, 85–87
  primates and, 57
  random genetic drift and, 94–95
Excavation, 70–72, 78
Exchange
  market principle and, 423, 441, 445, 479
  potlatching, 446–448, 450
  reciprocity, 423, 443–445
  redistribution, 423, 443, 445, 450
  "silent trade," 445
  types of, 423
  See also Trade
Exogamy, 132, 355, 513, 520, 538
Experimental archaeology, 72
Explaining, definition of, 22
Expressive culture, definition of, 611, 632
Extended families
  collateral households and, 492
  definition of, 492, 507
  as kinship group, 487
  overview of, 489–490
  patrilocal extended family, 490–491
  zadruga and, 490–491
  See also Families; Kinship groups; Nuclear families
Extradomestic, definition of, 561, 570
Extramarital sex, 551

Facial expressions, 391, 397–398
Falsification, 23
Families
  in Brazil, 495
  divorce and, 493, 494, 496
  of foragers, 496–497
  industrialism and, 491–492
  as kinship group, 487
  partible paternity and, 488–489
  See also Descent groups; Extended families;

Kinship groups; Nuclear families
Family enterprises, 381
Family of orientation, 369, 490, 507, 527
Family of procreation, 490, 507, 527
Family Ties, 494
Farming. *See* Food production
Fat Land: Supersizing America (Critser), 717
Father Knows Best, 493, 496
Fatherless households, 493
Fátima shrine, 600
Female avoidance, 556–558
Female genital mutilation, 353
Female infanticide, 461, 535
Feminine Mystique (Friedan), 566
Feminization of poverty, 543, 567–569
Fictive kinship, 430
Field Museum of Chicago, 144
Field notes, 325
Filariasis, 98
Finland, 97, 424
Fire, 201
"First World," 382
Fiscal systems, 479–480, 481
Fitness, 133
Flotation, 71–72
Fluorine absorption analysis, 74
Focal vocabulary, 402–403, 413
Folk, definition of, 617, 632
Folk music, 617
Folklore, 19, 357
Food production
  advantages of, 272–273, 275–276
  animal domestication and, 254–255, 268–270
  broad-spectrum revolution and, 255
  climate and, 257
  definition of, 25, 255, 277
  deforestation and, 271, 275, 276, 302, 303
  dental caries and, 275, 276
  diet and, 275, 276
  disadvantages of, 272–273, 275–276
  disease and, 275, 276
  economic development and, 259, 260, 261–263, 273
  environment and, 434
  farming communities, 262, 271–272
  farming development, 257–259, 270–271
  Hilly Flanks and, 257–259, 262, 277, 284
  irrigation and, 262, 272, 298
  maize and, 270, 271, 272, 277
  migration to Americas and, 266, 268
  Neolithic and, 256
  overview, 253, 255–257
  plant cultivation and, 254–255, 270, 271, 272
  pollution and, 275–276

population density and, 273, 275
  sedentism and, 257
  slavery and, 275, 276
  state societies, 262, 272, 281, 284, 287
  teocentli and, 271
  trade and, 262
  transition to, 256
  vegetation zones, 258
  vertical economy and, 259, 260
  world areas of inception of food production, 267
Football, 723–724
Foragers
  bands and, 428–429, 458–462, 477, 496
  correlates of, 428–429
  divorce and, 531–532
  economic structure of, 423, 426–431, 437
  as egalitarian, 432
  family and, 496–497
  gender and, 532, 551–553
  historically known foragers, 427
  kinship terminology and, 505–506
  land ownership and, 438
  nuclear families and, 461
  potlatching and, 445–448
  reciprocity and, 445
  religion and, 592
  risk reduction and, 434–435
  theft and, 462
  See also Political systems; specific people
Foraging
  birth rates and, 273
  broad-spectrum foraging and, 256
  diet of, 275
  egalitarian societies and, 286–287
  in Mexico, 304
  modern day foraging, 273
  problems with, 261
Foramen magnum, 175
Forced assimilation, 381, 695
Forensic anthropology
  application of, 30–32, 67
  as applied anthropology, 32
  definition of, 18
Fortresses, 293
48 Hours (CBS), 652
Fossils
  creationism and, 86
  dating fossils, 73–76
  definition of, 61, 78
  human link and, 166–167
  primate evolution fossil records, 144–145
  See also specific sites
Foster Parents Plan International, 50
Foundation for Forensic Anthropology of Guatemala, 30

Founder events, 314
France
  AIDS and, 99
  Basques and, 574–576
  colonialism and, 374, 670, 672, 673, 675, 686
  cuisine and, 628–629
  cultural imperialism and, 694, 701–702
  Dryopithecus family and, 155
  farming and, 263
  fossil sites in, 206, 207
  gender and, 562
  Industrial Revolution and, 645–646
  mission civilisatrice and, 675
  Neandertals and, 207
Fraternal polyandry, 515
Free Inquiry, 599
Fuegians, 427
Fulani people, 102
Functional explanation, definition of, 503, 507
Fund for Animals, 344

G. blacki, 154
G. giganteus, 154
Gabon, 122, 123
The Gambia, 123
Garbology, 12–13, 18
GATT (General Agreement on Trade and Tariffs), 359
Gender
  active-passive dichotomy, 562
  agriculture and, 561–564
  agriculturism and, 561–564
  Basque culture and, 577
  child care and, 550
  division of labor and, 432
  domestic work and, 549–550
  domestic-public dichotomy, 551–552, 570
  foragers and, 532, 551–553
  horticulturalists and, 553–558
  industrialism and, 565–569
  language and communication and, 401, 404–407
  overview of, 543
  patrilineal-patrilocal societies and, 556–557
  personality and, 546–547
  political systems and, 456–457
  recurrent gender patterns, 548–551
  reproductive period and, 550–551
  sexuality and, 551, 558–562
  See also Matriarchies; Matrilineal descent groups; Women
Gender identity, 240
Gender roles
  agriculture and, 561–564
  definition of, 543, 547, 570
  studies of, 546–547
Gender stereotypes, definition of, 547, 570

mode of production and, 436
overview of, 487
residence rules and, 492,
     499–500
in stratified nations, 492
See also Bands; Descent
     groups; Extended
     families; Families;
     Foragers; Marriage;
     Nuclear families
Kirghiz people, 436
!Kung people, 528
KNM. *See* Kenya National
     Museum
Knuckle-walking, 121
Koreans, 381, 381–382, 417
Kosovo Liberation Army, 372
Koss, 4
Kromdraai site, 174
Ksar Akil site, 224
Ku Klux Klan, 379
Kubu people, 427
Kuikuru people, 434
Kurds, 374
Kutse San, 460
Kuwait, 456–457
Kwakiutl people, 446–448
Kwashiorkor, 22–23

La Chapelle-aux-Saints site, 207
Labor
     gender and, 432, 565–567
     immigrants and, 644
     organization of, 647, 653
Lactase, 101–102
Lactose tolerance, 101–102
Laetoli site, 172, 174, 175
Lake Turkana site, 182, 198, 201
Lakher people, 518–519
Land ownership, 293–294, 438
Language and communication
     animal communication,
          394–396
     art and, 618, 620
     body language, 398
     bourgeoisie domination
          of, 647
     call systems, 394, 413
     colonialism and, 393
     color terminology and,
          402, 403
     creole languages,
          392–393, 408
     culture and, 395, 397–403
     daughter languages, 409, 413
     definition of, 393, 413
     development of, 392–393
     displacement and,
          395–396, 413
     endangered languages, 704
     focal vocabulary,
          402–403, 413
     gender and, 401, 404–407
     historical linguistics,
          409–410, 412, 413
     Internet and, 411
     isolated societies and, 393

kinesics and, 397, 413
language structure, 398–399
meaning and, 403
Nähñu language, 704
nonverbal communication,
     391, 396–398
overview, 391
personal space and, 397
pidgin languages, 358–359,
     392–393
power and, 404, 405
productivity and, 395, 413
protolanguages and,
     409–410, 412, 414
Quechua language, 704
Shwara language, 704
sign language, 394–395
slavery and, 393, 408, 702
sociolinguistics and, 391,
     403–409
in South Pacific, 313, 314
speech sounds, 398–399
stratification and, 406–407
subgroups in, 410, 414
thought and, 399–403
Laos, 670
Lapita people, 310–314
Laplanders, 424–425
Lascaux site, 214, 215, 222
Latent function, 522–523
Law, 478, 481
Law of supply and demand, 441
Learning, 129
Leave It to Beaver, 493, 496
Lebanan, ethnic conflicts in, 383
Lebanon, 383
Legal anthropology, 455
Lemba people, 84–85
Leveling mechanisms, 591, 604
Levirate, definition of, 531, 538
Lexicon, definition of, 398,
     402, 413
L'Hortus site, 207
Liberia, 110, 123
Life histories, 324, 328–329, 338
Liminality, definition of,
     585–586, 601, 604
Lineages, 487, 489, 498, 507
Lineal kinship terminology, 503,
     506, 508
Lineal relatives, definition
     of, 503
Linguistic anthropology
     definition of, 1, 15, 26
     education and, 19, 33
     fields of study of, 3, 391, 393
     language reconstruction
          and, 8
     overview, 15–16
Linguistic relativity, 404
Linguistic Society of America
     (LSA), 408
Liturgical orders, 584
Liver flukes, 43
Llongot people, 547
Local beliefs, 329–330
Local descent groups, 499

Locally based demand, 34
Longitudinal research, 325,
     331–332, 338
Long-term physiological
     adaptation, 6
Lophs, 151
Lourdes shrine, 600
Lower Pleistocene, 167–168
LSA. *See* Linguistic Society
     of America
Lucy skeleton, 171, 174, 175,
     195–196

m.y.a. (million years ago),
     146, 160
Maceration, 158
Madagascar, 64, 117, 149,
     322–323, 326–328. *See
     also* Betsileo people
     chiefdoms in, 476
     communication style in, 398
     foragers in, 426
     as French colony, 670,
          673, 686
     government organization
          of, 686
     indigenous intellectual
          property rights (IPR)
          and, 354
     Mikea people, 459
     ombiasa and, 697
     postmodernism and,
          710–711
     rice project in, 676–677
     sexuality and, 560
     slash-and-burn horticulture
          in, 431
     Tanosy people, 697
Magic, 579, 583–584, 585, 604
Maize, 270, 271, 272, 277
Majority groups, definition
     of, 369
Makah Tribe, 344
Malagasy, 703
Malagasy people, 117
Malaria, 93, 95, 98
Malaysia, 45, 121–122, 314, 426,
     445, 554, 648–651
Mali, 580, 611
Malnutrition, 678–679
Mammals, 112
Mana, 582–583, 604
Manifest function, 522–523
Manioc, 270, 271, 277, 434
Manual dexterity, 113–114,
     116, 118
Maori, 312, 427
Marind-anim tribe, 353
Market. *See* Exchange; Trade
Market exchange, 423, 479
Market principle, 441, 445, 450
Marriage
     as affinal relationship, 513
     age of women and, 529
     arranged marriages,
          528–529, 564
     Betsileo people and, 534–535

bridewealth and, 513,
     527–530, 531
civil marriages, 515
common-law domestic
     partnerships, 515
cousins and, 514–515
definition of, 515
descent groups and, 513
divorce and, 493, 494, 496,
     513, 531–533
endogamy and, 520–524
exogamy and, 516–519
as group alliance, 526–531
incest and, 516–519
Indian marriage customs,
     522–523
infertility and, 530
levirate and, 531
marital rights, 524–526
mating and, 132
overview of, 513
Pahari people and, 535–537
romantic love and, 528–529
same-sex marriage, 524–526
sororate and, 530–531
See also Plural marriage
Married with Children, 494
Masai tribe, 254, 468, 469, 477
Masturbation, 560, 561
Matai, 42
Match breakers, 532
Matchmakers, 532
Maters, definition of, 524, 538
Mating, 126, 132–133
Matriarchies
     anthropological studies of,
          544–545
     definition of, 544
     gender stratification
          and, 543
     patriarchies distinguished
          from, 545
     power and, 545
Matrifocal, definition of, 555, 571
Matrifocal societies, 555–556
Matrilineal descent groups
     definition of, 487, 491, 508
     divorce and, 531
     gender and, 553
     Iroquois Indians, 554–555
     kinship terminology,
          503–504
Matrilocality, 499–500, 508,
     531, 553
Matrons, definition of, 554–555
Maturation rate, 176, 200
Maximization, 439–440
Maya state, 272, 274, 299,
     302–305
Mayans, writing and, 640
Mbuti people, 426, 429–430,
     445, 549
McDonald's Corporation,
     717–720
Means, or factors, of production,
     438–439, 450
Measles vaccinations, 320

Naturalistic disease theories, definition of, 44, 52
Nature versus nurture, 8
Navaho Indians, 61, 435, 622, 628
Nayar people, 355, 491, 550
Nazis, 233, 245–246, 353, 696
Ndembu people, 585, 602
Neandertals
  cold-adapted Neandertals, 205–206
  definition of, 219
  discovery of, 205
  Eve theory, 208–209
  fossil site locations for, 204, 206
  as *H. Sapiens,* 112, 193
  H. Sapiens Sapiens and, 204
  mitochondrial DNA (mtDNA) testing and, 208–209
  modern people and, 206–209
  multiregional evolution, 210
  skull of, 197, 207
  tool use, 199
Negative reciprocity, definition of, 445, 450
Négritude, definition of, 374, 375, 385
Neolithic
  Çatal Hüyük and, 284–285
  definition of, 256–257, 377
  "Iceman" and, 264
  Mesopotamia and, 291
Neolithic Revolution, 256
Neolocality
  definition of, 492, 508
  residence rules and, 499
Nepal, 533, 535
Netherlands, 8, 670, 680
New age religions, 599–600
New Caledonia, 310
New Guinea, 236, 310
New World monkeys, 118–120
New York University, 225
New Zealand, 312, 313, 382
NGOs. *See* Nongovernmental organizations
Nickelodeon, 496
Niger, 580
Nigeria
  ethnic conflicts in, 383
  gender stratification and, 564
  gorillas and, 122
  Igbo people and, 526, 556
  international trade and, 644
  Islam and, 580–581
  Kalabari people, 614–615
  lactose tolerance and, 102
  music and, 619
  plural marriage and, 533–534
  television and, 706
  Tiv people, 615
  Yoruba people, 611, 622
Nightline (ABC), 381
Nike, 652–653
Nile Valley, 263, 281

Nilotes people, 100, 101, 231
Nittano site, 256
NMAI. *See* National Museum of the American Indian
"Noble savage myth," 640
Nok Nok Tha site, 266
Nomadic pastoralists, 423, 424–425, 435–436, 450
Nongovernmental organizations (NGOs), 32, 50, 332, 458, 569, 652–653, 676, 695
Nonsettler countries, 674
Nonverbal communication, 391, 396–398
North American Free Trade Agreement. *See* NAFTA
Norway, 345, 424–425
Notes and Queries on Anthropology (Royal Anthropological Society), 515
Novels, 371, 374
NOW (National Organization of Woman), 566, 569
NSF. *See* National Science Foundation
Nuclear families
  family of orientation and, 369, 490
  family of procreation and, 490
  foragers and, 461, 496–497
  as kinship group, 487, 489
  lineal kinship terminology and, 503, 506
  neolocality and, 492
  in North America, 491–493, 501–502
  overview of, 489–490
  universality of, 355
  See also Descent groups; Extended families; Families; Kinship groups
Nuer people, 402, 515–516, 524
Nutrition. *See* Diet

Oaxaca Valley, 271, 281, 296
Obesity, 717
Obsidian, 284
Occupational Safety and Health Administration (OSHA), 652
Odors, 398
Oedipus complex, 20, 44
Office, definition of, 474, 481
OH62 (Olduvai Hominid 62), 195
Ohio State University, 640
Oil exploration, 698–699
Okiek people, 427
Old World monkeys, 118–120, 151, 175
Oldowan pebble tools, 184
Olduvai Gorge site, 184, 202
Olduvai Hominid 62. *See* OH62
Olduvai site, 174
Oligocene epoch, 150

Olmec, 272, 287, 296–297
Olympian religions, 591, 592, 593, 604
Ombiasa, 697
Omomyids, 149, 160
On the Origin of Species (Darwin), 87, 205
Onas people, 428
Open class systems, 654–655, 662
Opera, 616
Opposable thumb, 113–114, 118, 135
Oral traditions, 478
Orangutans, 122, 124–125
Oreopithecus, 155
Oreopithecus bambolii, 155
Orthograde posture, 118
OSHA. *See* Occupational Safety and Health Administration
Osteology, definition of, 14, 67
Ouranopithecus, 157
Overfarming, 303
Overinnovation, 683–684, 688
Oxfam, 50
Oxford University, 84
Ozzie and Harriet. See Adventures of Ozzie and Harriet

P. major, 150
P. nyanzae, 150
Pacific Islanders, 239
Pahari people, 535–537
Painting, 611
Pakistan
  colonialism and, 382–383
  domestic violence and, 564–565
  food production and, 263, 281
  fossil discoveries in, 153
  Harappa and, 294
  Indus Valley and, 473
Paleoanthropology
  definition of, 14, 73, 78
  excavation and, 70–72
  hominid study and, 69–70
  research methods, 59, 63
  systematic surveys and, 70–71
Paleocene era, 144
Paleoecology, definition of, 11
Paleolithic, definition of, 199, 219
Paleolithic tools, 199
Paleontology, 14, 59, 73, 78
Paleopathology, 59, 67, 78
Paleozoic era, 146
Palestine, 382
Palmerston, Lord, 669
Paloindians, 266, 268
Palynology, definition of, 63, 78
PAN. *See* "Promoting Adequate Nutrition"
Pan troglodytes, 174, 176, 180
Panama, 473
Pantribal sodalities, 466–469, 481

Papua New Guinea
  big men and, 718
  cargo cults and, 597
  color terminology in, 403
  cultivation in, 434
  female avoidance and, 556–558
  gender studies in, 546–547
  homosexuality in, 353
  Kaluli people, 560, 698–699
  language and communication in, 310–311, 359, 400, 403
  oil exploration and, 698–699
  patrilineal-patrilocal societies and, 556
  religion and, 582–583
  state formation and, 302
  sugarcane and, 642
  tribal politics in, 463
Paraguay, 426, 459
Parallel cousins, definition of, 516, 538
PARC. *See* Xerox Palo Alto (California) Research Center
Partible paternity, 488–489
Participant observation, 324, 326
Particularity, definition of, 356, 360
Pastoral nomadism, 423, 424–425, 435–436, 450
Pastoralism
  definition of, 450
  diet and, 431
  economic basis of, 477
  as economic type, 423, 435–436, 437
  kinship groups and, 499
  nomadic pastoralists, 259, 423
  pastoral nomadism, 435–436
Patagonia, 426, 428
Pater, definition of, 516, 538
Patriarchies
  definition of, 543, 571
  dowry murders and, 528
  power and, 545
  sati and, 528
  violence and, 564–565
Patrikin, 518
Patrilineal descent groups, 487, 498, 503–504, 508
Patrilineal-patrilocal complex, definition of, 556, 571
Patrilineal-patrilocal societies, 556–557
Patriliny, 554, 555
Patrilocal extended families, 492
Patrilocality
  definition of, 499, 508
  gender stratification and, 564
  marriage and, 527, 554
Pawnee Indians, 549
Peasants, definition of, 441, 450
Pennsylvania State University, 194, 209, 236, 292